D0903376

Smashing the Liquor Machine

Smashing the Liquor Machine

A Global History of Prohibition

MARK LAWRENCE SCHRAD

OXFORD
UNIVERSITY PRESS

OXFORD
UNIVERSITY PRESS

Oxford University Press is a department of the University of Oxford. It furthers the University's objective of excellence in research, scholarship, and education by publishing worldwide. Oxford is a registered trade mark of Oxford University Press in the UK and certain other countries.

Published in the United States of America by Oxford University Press
198 Madison Avenue, New York, NY 10016, United States of America.

Library of Congress Cataloging-in-Publication Data
Names: Schrad, Mark Lawrence, author.
Title: Smashing the liquor machine : a global history of prohibition / Mark Schrad.
Description: New York, NY : Oxford University Press, [2021] |
Includes bibliographical references and index.
Identifiers: LCCN 2021000207 (print) | LCCN 2021000208 (ebook) |
ISBN 9780190841577 (hardback) | ISBN 9780190841591 (epub) |
ISBN 9780197523322
Subjects: LCSH: Prohibition—History. | Temperance—History.
Classification: LCC HV5088 .S37 2021 (print) |
LCC HV5088 (ebook) | DDC 364.1/332—dc23
LC record available at https://lccn.loc.gov/2021000207
LC ebook record available at https://lccn.loc.gov/2021000208

DOI: 10.1093/oso/9780190841577.001.0001

1 3 5 7 9 8 6 4 2

Printed by LSC Communications, United States of America

For my son, Alexander.
I wish you the joy of curiosity,
the curse of tenacity,
and the satisfaction of
crafting your desires into reality.

TABLE OF CONTENTS

PART III   THE UNITED STATES

NOTE ON TRANSLITERATION OF NAMES

In this book, Russian names generally follow the British standard (BGN/PCGN) transliteration, with some alterations to accommodate the widely accepted English equivalents of familiar historical figures (for example, Leo Tolstoy and Leon Trotsky, instead of Lev Tolstoi and Lev Trotskii). These alterations do not apply to the bibliographic references in the notes, which maintain the standard transliteration for those who wish to consult the original sources.

PREFACE

Windhaven Assisted Living Center, Cedar Falls, Iowa: July 8, 2018

"Prohibition?" my grandma Betty Nyberg replied, with a knowing smile and a dismissive wave of her hand.

"Oh, dear. Prohibition—that's when Peoria *really* started going downhill."

Grandma knew I'd long been fascinated with prohibition. We were very close. She knew I'd been researching this book on it for a decade already. Still, I never missed a chance to ask her to reminisce about prohibition. She lived it, after all. She was a teenager by the time prohibition was ultimately repealed. I'd heard all her stories before, but that didn't diminish my joy of hearing them, or her joy of recounting them.

She was born Betty Jane Dixon on July 10, 1918. Her father and uncle built Peoria's most successful fishing business: still running today on the east bank of the Illinois River. Grandma *hated* fish; the embarrassing stench clung to your hands, shoes, and clothes.

"Still, the fish were free, dear," she'd say. "You just had to go out and get them."

During the Great Depression, the Dixons hired scores of destitute men—many laid off from the nearby Caterpillar tractor factory—to pilot the boats and pull the carp from the river. Those fish put her through college, and bankrolled the Dixons' other moneymaking schemes: running a paddlewheel steamship line to St. Louis; a short-lived bus line overland to Quincy, Illinois; and—most notably—building their own plant for the rectification of whiskey. With plentiful grain, water, and coal, and easy access to transportation, Peoria was among the distilling capitals of the United States prior to prohibition. But unlike distilled whiskey that was aged in barrels to acquire its distinct taste, rectified whiskey was just industrial distillate with flavors and colors added. It was what Theodore Roosevelt would call "artificial whiskey," which was cheaper and easier to make, and thus far more profitable than the genuine article. Apparently that's what my great-grandparents were selling, when they weren't selling fish.

The men who ran the whiskey trucks were universally shifty and unscrupulous, Grandma remembered.

It's strange that the whiskey was what I remembered most about Grandma Betty. Every day at 5 p.m., she'd mix her evening Manhattan: two parts bottom-shelf blended whiskey, one part sweet vermouth, stirred. Some times she'd try to share it with me, but I always thought Manhattans tasted like gasoline.

In 2018, her entire extended family gathered over Fourth of July weekend to toast Manhattans to Betty's one hundredth birthday. But when it came time for our long drive back east, Grandma kept my wife and I rapt with prohibition and family stories, even as the last rays of a brilliant Iowa sunset passed through the blinds at her retirement-community apartment.

She bid us farewell with her trademark mischievous giggle, and the "See you later, alligator!" that was our send-off since I was a child.

"After a while, crocodile!" I smiled, closing the door behind us.

Grandma Betty passed away peacefully just a few hours later. We were the last to see her.

Something strange happened after Grandma's funeral, though. As we cleaned out her apartment, we found gallon after gallon of Grandma's whiskey and sweet vermouth. And after drinking one too many Manhattan tributes to her, I found myself actually enjoying that gasoline taste. In drinking habits at least, I've become my grandma, which is not at all a bad thing.

Grandma Betty was my personal link to the long-ago world of the Prohibition Era: that fascinating time between World War I and the Great Depression, which we sometimes glamorize, sometimes disparage, and frequently struggle to understand objectively. But just as we cannot bracket off my grandmother's upbringing in that era and relegate it to some distant past, neither can we quarantine prohibition history to some discrete timeframe, to be studied in isolation from ongoing social, political, and economic struggles. Indeed, many of the same dynamics of economic and political domination, exploitation, and resistance that I write about in this book still make headlines today: the Sioux Tribe of Standing Rock asserting their community's sovereignty against big-business backed by the coercive forces of the US government; the #MeToo movement truth-telling against an entrenched patriarchal system; and Black Lives Matter, reckoning with the deeply rooted political, social, and economic subordination of African American communities.

In each of these cases, the dynamics are crystal clear: historically marginalized groups—suffering—take it upon themselves to challenge the status quo of traditional power and privilege. In doing so, they force us into the discomfort of confronting the yawning chasm between who we are as a nation and who we imagine ourselves to be. On one side is soaring patriotic rhetoric about freedom and equality; on the other is a reality where women and minorities are neither free nor equal. On one side are allusions to the American promise of economic liberty, while on the other are those who suffer poverty and bear the real human costs of others' liberty. And—insofar as we're talking about allusions to the United States as a "Christian nation"—we have the image of Christ's love, forgiveness, and care for the marginalized and downtrodden, juxtaposed against the unscrupulous predations of those who wield political and economic power under the guise of being a good Christian.

Prohibitionism shared the same underlying ethos as all of these contemporary movements—not just in the United States, but around the globe. Prohibitionism wasn't moralizing "thou shalt nots," but a progressive shield for marginalized, suffering, and oppressed peoples to defend themselves from further exploitation. "All great reforms go together," as Frederick Douglass reminded us: abolitionism, women's suffrage, and liberation from the liquor traffic through temperance and prohibition.

For contemporary activists and those who study social movements, this book offers a cautionary tale as to what happens when the movement ends. If, like abolitionism or suffragism, the movement "wins" and everyone sees the natural rightness of their cause, its trailblazers and pioneers—like William Lloyd Garrison, Elizabeth Cady Stanton, Frederick Douglass, Susan B. Anthony, or Abraham Lincoln—are lionized as national heroes. Their statutes adorn government buildings, and their likenesses are coined on our currency.

But if the established economic and political powers-that-be win—as with the Twenty-First Amendment repealing the prohibitionist Eighteenth Amendment— woe be to the reformers' legacies. Many are simply ignored or written out of the textbooks. Those who were too well known to be ignored, like Carrie Nation or Wayne Wheeler, are recast as history's villains. Most interestingly, though, is what happens to the images of those leaders whose activism spans interrelated causes— not just the Garrisons, Stantons, Douglasses, Anthonys, and Lincolns, but the Leo Tolstoys, Mahatma Gandhis, Kemal Atatürks, Tomáš Masaryks, and Hjalmar Brantings of the world. Their biographers go auspiciously silent when it comes to their subjects' prohibitionism, as such a supposedly villainous trait doesn't jive with their otherwise heroic accomplishments. Best leave it out.

Writing this book was challenging and transformative for me too, especially as it meant branching out of my own comfort zone into areas where I admittedly have no lived experience. It was the question of prohibitionism that led me to write on Native American history, though I am not Native American. Similarly, I write on abolitionism without having experienced the everyday challenges of black life. I write about suffragism while not a woman; I write about Russia, India, and Africa, while not being Russian, Indian, or African. I wrote an entire book on temperance, often with one of my grandma's Manhattans in hand.

This disconnect troubled me deeply. It still does. But three things have helped me grapple with this issue. First is that the sources that I draw upon from generations and centuries ago are the same source materials that are available to every historical researcher, regardless of race, religion, ethnicity, gender, or sexual orientation. Second, I have actively sought out native-language primary source materials in every case, hoping to give a voice to subaltern experiences that have long been ignored. And finally, if research is limited to those who share the same lived experience as their subject matter, then who would be better positioned to chronicle political domination and oppression than a straight, white, middle-aged, middle-class American man? Even before my grandma told me that our family was once in the whiskey-selling business in Peoria, I've been aware of the privileges afforded to me based on my identity, and that power dynamic lies at the heart of this study.

This awareness extends to a deep scrutiny of the language we use to portray history. Many of the subjects in this book used vulgar, racist, misogynist, and degrading language—often because they were racists and misogynists, conveying vulgar and degrading ideas. Demeaning vulgarities and slurs—the "n-word" and beyond—are as tough to write as they are to read; but I purposely have not censored or sugarcoated the language, actions, or ideas of these historical figures. In fact, they underscore the central theme of this book, which is that norms change: things that were once commonly accepted (slavery, subordination of women, discrimination based on a racial hierarchy, etc.) are no longer considered appropriate. So when coming across the language of white supremacy that makes you feel uncomfortable, I ask that you reflect momentarily on what those words and actions represent in that historical moment, and why they were considered socially appropriate then, but are inappropriate today.

Ultimately, rights, justice, and progress are possible, though they often come in unexpected forms, and that's what we find here.

My list of personal debts is far shorter than my previous books: all the family members, friends, mentors, and inspirations for my earlier works helped me through this one, too. My loving wife, Jennifer, and our children, Alexander, Sophia, and Helena, have put up with more of my nonsense than anyone should ever have to. I thank my colleagues at Villanova University, and not merely for the subvention to assist with publication of this volume. Department chair Matt Kerbel provided tremendous guidance, and Jennifer Dixon, whose simple question of "If prohibitionism was really anticolonialism, why aren't you exploring Native Americans?" easily added three chapters to the manuscript. Dr. Dixon likewise helped me immensely in translating prereform Ottoman Turkish for inclusion into the book. J. D. Shindelar was most helpful in drafting the maps that appear throughout the book. Steven Schultz again agonized over every chapter, and put up with even my most petty semantic quibbles. Thank you all most deeply, in addition to the anonymous peer reviewers. Back in the pre-Covid beforetimes, I remember how, at every Schrad family gathering, my uncle Dick Schrad would not-so-subtly inquire when the next book was coming out. So I began sending him draft chapters, and he replied with insights that made the final manuscript that much better, even while enduring tremendous personal hardships. Much love to you, Dick and Pat, Cindy, Kevin and family; I'd hoped Doug would've loved this, the ever-curious world traveler he was.

Completing the manuscript in the spring of 2020—just as the Covid-19 pandemic hit—I had hoped quarantine might actually boost my productivity. I was wrong. Between learning new teaching modalities for my own courses, and helping our kids adapt to their new online educational reality, the final chapters were largely written between the hours of four and nine in the morning. Covid-19 also forced the closing of archives and special collections across the country and around the globe, causing further delays. But quarantine did allow me to get feedback on the first drafts from my son Alexander, to whom this book is dedicated, which was immensely gratifying.

Months in lockdown also gave me greater appreciation for the countries and archives that I was able to visit in person, as well as the global friends I'd made along the way. They include Dmitry Fedotov and Mikhail Teplyansky, hosts of the annual Alcohol in Russia conference in Ivanovo, Russia; Marie-Laure Djelic and Sigrid Quack, for their transnationalism conference in Cologne, Germany, Harald Fischer-Tiné, Jana Tschurenev, and their students at ETH-Zürich for organizing the Global Anti-Vice Activism conference in Monte Verità, Switzerland; Yanni Kotsonis for hosting The Great War and the Great Prohibitions workshop at NYU Abu Dhabi; Ernesto Savona and Francesco Calderoni of Università Cattolica in Milan, Italy; and Susannah Wilson at the University of Warwick for organizing the Prohibition: Perspectives from the Humanities and Social Sciences conference in conjunction with the British Academy in London, along with Cecilia Autrique Escobar for planning a follow-up colloquium at the Universidad Iberoamericana in Mexico City, which was ultimately cancelled due to Covid-19. All of this is on top of the countless librarians and archivists—many in far-flung corners of the globe—willing to help track down original documents and other archival materials that provide the granular substance of this book. You have my deepest gratitude and respect.

I save my most heartfelt appreciation, though, for the team at Oxford University Press: Emily Mackenzie, Angela Messina, Alison Block, Cheryl Merritt, and especially David McBride. For reasons that are still unclear to me, a decade ago, David took a chance on a young scholar (who'd already received more than a few politely worded rejections), and his weird obsession with the politics of alcohol. It was by his faith that *The Political Power of Bad Ideas* ever saw the light of day, only to be followed up by *Vodka Politics*, and now *Smashing the Liquor Machine* as the third installment in the trilogy. None of them would have been possible without him, and all three were enriched tremendously by his guidance.

ARCHIVAL SOURCES

Australia

State Library of New South Wales (Sydney)
Sir Joseph Banks Papers
University of Melbourne Archives (Melbourne)
Independent Order of Rechabites, Victorian District, 1861
Woman's Christian Temperance Union of Victoria, 1887– 1999

Belgium

Archives et Bibliothèque de l'Institut Emile Vandervelde (Archives and Library of the Emile Vandervelde Institute, Brussels)
Archives Emile Vandervelde
Parliamentary Papers

Canada

Library and Archives Canada (Ottawa, Ontario)
Department of External Affairs Fonds
Department of Justice Fonds
Records Relating to the House of Representatives
United Church of Canada Archives (Toronto, Ontario)
The Dominion Alliance for the Total Suppression of the Liquor Traffic Fonds

Czech Republic

Masarykův ústav a archiv Akademie věd ČR (Masaryk Institute and Archive, Academy of Sciences of the Czech Republic, Prague)
Tomáš Garrigue Masaryk Collection

Finland

Työväenliikkeen kirjasto (Library of the Labour Movement, Helsinki)

France

Bibliotheque Nationale de France (National Library of France, Paris)
Bulletin Consulaire Français

Germany

Geheimes Staatsarchiv Preußischer Kulturbesitz (Secret State Archives Prussian Cultural Heritage Foundation, Berlin)
Niedersächsische Staats- und Universitätsbibliothek, Göttingen (Göttingen State and University Library, Göttingen)
Staatsarchiv (State Archives, Hamburg)

Greece

The Service of Diplomatic and Historical Archives, Ministry of Foreign Affairs (Athens)

India

Maharashtra State Archives (Mumbai)
Home Department
Political Department

Ireland

Provincial Archives, Capuchin Friary of St. Mary of the Angels, Dublin
Fr. Theobald Mathew: Research and Commemorative Papers (CA/FM/RES)

New Zealand

Archives New Zealand (Auckland)
Department of Internal Affairs, Head Office
Legislative Department
Auckland Libraries Heritage Collections (Auckland)
Sir George Gray Special Collections

Russian Federation

Gosudarstvennyi Arkhiv Rossiiskoi Federatsii—GARF (State Archives of the Russian Federation), Moscow
f. 102—Departament politsii Ministerstva Vnutrennykh Del
f. 115—Soyuz 17-ogo Oktyabrya (Union of 17 October—Octobrist Party)
f. 374—Narodnyi komisseriat raboche-krest'yanskoi inspektsii SSSR (NK-RKI SSSR)
f. 579—Pavel Nikolaevich Milyukov (1856–1918)
f. 586—Vycheslav K. Plehve
f. 601—Imperator Nikolai II (1868–1918)
f. 660—Velikii Knyaz Konstantin Konstantinovich Romanov
f. 671—Velikii Knyaz Nikolai Nikolaevich Romanov, mladshee (1857–1916)
f. 1779—Kantselyariya vremennogo pravitel'stva—1917 (Chancellery of Provisional Government)
f. 5467—TsK profsoyuza derevoobdeloinikov
f. 5515—Narkomat truda
f. 6996—Ministerstvo finanasov vremennogo pravitel'stva—1917 (Ministry of Finance of Provisional Government)
Rossiiskii Gosudarstvennyi Arkhiv Ekonomiki—RGAE (Russian State Economics Archive), Moscow
f. 733—Tsentral'noe upravlenie i ob"edinenie spirtovoi promyshlennosti (Gosspirt)
f. 1562—Tsentral'noe statisticheskoe upravlenie (TsSU) pri Sovete Ministrov SSSR

South Africa

National Archives and Records Service of South Africa
Free State Archives Repository
National Archives Repository (Public Records of Former Transvaal Province), Pretoria
Pietermaritzburg Repository

Sweden

Riksarkivet (National Archives), Marieberg, Stockholm
Nykterhetskommitténs (17 november 1911) Kommitté N:o 85 arkiv
Finansdepartementets arkiv
Riksarkivet (National Archives), Arninge
International Order of Good Templars arkiv
Edvard Wavrinsky arkiv
Arbetarrörelsens arkiv och bibliotek (Labor Movement Archives and Library), Stockholm
Svenska Bryggeriindustriarbetareförbundets arkiv
General collections

Turkey

Türkiye Büyük Millet Meclisi Kütüphanesi (Library of the Grand National Assembly), Ankara

United Kingdom

British Library
India Office Records and Private Papers
Churchill College Archives Centre, University of Cambridge, Cambridge, England
John Michael De Robeck Papers, 1862–1928
Institute of Alcohol Studies, Alliance House Foundation, London
United Kingdom Alliance (UKA) Collection
National Archives, Kew
Cabinet Secretary's Notebooks
Foreign Office Papers, Public Records Office
Records of the British South Africa Company
Records of the Colonial Office
Records of the Dominions Office, High Commissioners to South Africa
Records of the Metropolitan Police Office
Parliamentary Papers, House of Commons
City of Westminster Archives Centre
Leeds Russian Archive, University of Leeds
Sir Peter Bark Papers
London School of Economics, London
Records of the League of Nations Union

Royal Anthropological Institute of Great Britain and Ireland (RAI), London
Aborigines Protection Society (A111)
School of Oriental and African Studies (SOAS), London University
Council for World Mission / London Missionary Society Archives
University of Glasgow Archive Services
Records of the Scottish Permissive Bill and Temperance Association (1885–1922)

United States

American Baptist Historical Society, Mercer University Archives (Atlanta, GA)
Walter Rauschenbusch Papers
Buffalo and Erie County Historical Society (Buffalo, NY)
Colgate Rochester Crozer Divinity School, American Baptist–Samuel Colgate Historical Library (Rochester, NY)
Rauschenbusch Family Manuscript Collection
Dickinson State University (Dickinson, ND)
Theodore Roosevelt Digital Library
Fenimore Art Museum Library (Cooperstown, NY)
William E. "Pussyfoot" Johnson Papers
Harvard University, Houghton Library (Cambridge, MA)
Harvard Theatre Collection
Theodore Roosevelt Collection
Historical Society of Pennsylvania (Philadelphia, PA)
Penn Family Papers, 1629–1834
Indiana University–Purdue University Indianapolis (Indianapolis, IN)
Frederick Douglass Papers Project
Kansas Historical Society (Topeka, KS)
Carrie Amelia Nation Papers, 1870–1919
Kansas WCTU / Mary Evelyn Dobbs Collection
Jotham Meeker Collection, 1825–1864
Isaac McCoy Papers
Library of Congress, Manuscript Division (Washington, DC)
Alexander Hamilton Papers, 1708–1917
Association Against the Prohibition Amendment Records, 1917–1933
Elizabeth Cady Stanton Papers, 1814–1946
Frederick Douglass Papers, 1841–1967
Henry Morgenthau Papers, 1856–1946
Law Library of Congress
Prints and Photographs Division
Richmond Pearson Hobson Papers, 1889–1966

Susan B. Anthony Papers, 1846–1934

Theodore Roosevelt Papers, 1858–1919

Thomas Jefferson Papers, 1606–1943

William McKinley Papers, 1847–1935

Woodrow Wilson Papers, 1786–1957

Lilly Research Library, Indiana University (Bloomington, IN)

Alice Masaryk Collection, 1879–1966

Miami University Archives (Oxford, OH)

Minnesota Historical Society (Minneapolis, MN)

Lawrence Taliaferro Papers, 1794–1871

National Archives (Washington, DC)

Letters Received by the Office of the Secretary of War Relating to Indian
Affairs

Records of the St. Louis Superintendency

Thomas Jefferson Papers

National Portrait Gallery (Washington, DC)

Nebraska State Historical Society (Lincoln, NE)

William Jennings Bryan Papers, 1860–1925

New-York Historical Society (New York, NY)

Isaiah Rynders Letters

New York Public Library (New York, NY)

George Kennan Papers, 1856–1987

Oberlin College Archives (Oberlin, OH)

James Monroe Papers, 1819–1898

Oberlin Temperance Alliance Records, 1870–1917

**Occidental College Special Collections and College Archives (Los
Angeles, CA)**

William Jennings Bryan Collection

Ohio Historical Society (Columbus, OH)

Warren G. Harding Papers, 1865–1923

**Ohio Historical Society, Temperance and Prohibition Papers
(Columbus, OH)**

American Issue Publishing Company Series, 1909–1934

Anti-Saloon League of America Series, 1894–1938

Ernest Hurst Cherrington Series, 1877–1950

Francis Scott McBride Series, 1872–1955

Howard Hyde Russell Series, 1855–1946

Intercollegiate Prohibition Association Series, 1892–1963

Office of General Counsel and Legislative Superintendent, ASLA Series,
1883–1933

Scientific Temperance Federation Series, 1881–1934

Standard Encyclopedia of the Alcohol Problem Series, 1904–1930
World League Against Alcoholism Series, 1900–1937
Pennsylvania Historical and Museum Commission (Harrisburg, PA)
Records of the Department of State
Presbyterian Historical Society (Philadelphia, PA)
American Sunday School Union Papers, 1817–1915
Princeton Theological Seminary Library (Princeton, NJ)
Robert Elliott Speer Manuscript Collection, 1867–1947
Rockefeller Archive Center (Sleepy Hollow, NY)
John D. Rockefeller Papers, 1855–1942
**Southern Historical Collection, Louis Round Wilson Special Collections
Library, University of North Carolina (Chapel Hill, NC)**
Edwin Yates Webb Papers, 1901–1955
Swarthmore College (Swarthmore, PA)
Friends Historical Library of Swarthmore College
Wichita State University Libraries (Wichita, KS)
Special Collections and University Archives
Wisconsin Historical Society (Madison, WI)
Draper Manuscript Collection: William Clark Papers
Draper Manuscript Collection: Thomas Forsyth Papers
**University of California at San Diego, Special Collections and Archives (San
Diego, CA)**
Joseph Gusfield Papers
University of Michigan, Bentley Historical Library (Ann Arbor, MI)
Prohibition Party Series, 1868–1933
University of Wisconsin–Madison Special Collections (Madison, WI)
Guy Hayler Temperance Tracts
University of Pittsburgh Archives (Pittsburgh, PA)
Thomas G. Masaryk Papers
University of Illinois at Urbana-Champaign (Urbana, IL)
Frederic Wines Collection on Social Problems
Woman's Christian Temperance Union Archive (Evanston, IL)
Woman's Christian Temperance Union Series, 1853–1939

Introduction—Everything You Know about Prohibition Is Wrong

Kiowa, Kansas: Thursday, June 7, 1900, 8:30 a.m.

For weeks before the vigilante rampage that would make her a household name, fifty-three-year-old Carrie Amelia Nation quietly walked the roadsides near the successful hotel she owned and operated in Medicine Lodge, Kansas. Deep in contemplation, she scoured the ground, picking up palm-sized rocks and brickbats. Purposeful and deliberative, she smuggled home those that had the right feel and heft, wrapping each one in old newsprint to look like innocent parcels.

"I did this until I got quite a pile," she recalled.[1]

Carrie (later "Carry") A. Nation was a God-fearing Christian of the purest sort—which brought her into frequent conflict with the organized church. For her, justice, love, and benevolence were not things to be talked about on Sunday and forgotten the rest of the week.[2] At her upscale hotel, she fed, clothed, and lodged the downtrodden and destitute—both white folks and black—in some cases for years at a time. Harboring and defending the undesirables and castoffs of the community irked her more "respectable" fellow parishioners. First, she was expelled from the local Methodist church; then the Episcopal church. When the preacher in the pulpit of the Medicine Lodge Christian Church denounced her neighbor as an "adultress" in the middle of services—based on nothing but the word of the woman's alcoholic husband—Carrie could not keep quiet. She shouted down the unjust allegation, and the preacher himself, in front of the entire congregation.

Imagine the scene as church elders tried—and failed!—to drag her bodily from the pews. And while they couldn't physically throw her out of the sanctuary that day, they did later expel her from the parish.[3]

No matter. Carrie still rode the width and breadth of Barber County, Kansas, collecting donations of food and clothing. She pressured storekeepers to donate additional groceries for the needy, lest she step onto the street and publicly denounce them as "thieving gougers of widows and orphans."[4] They usually complied.

As a volunteer jail evangelist, Carrie also served the penitent—bringing comfort, consolation, and the promise of heavenly salvation. To each inmate, she'd ask, what was the cause of your misery and woe? To a man, the answer came back: "Drink."

This was strange. "Dry" Kansas had been under statewide prohibition for twenty years. If there were no legal saloons anywhere in the state, where did they get their booze? A contrite inmate explained that anyone could get whiskey in the town of Kiowa, on the border with the Oklahoma Territory.

Moved, Carrie pled the remorseful man's case to the bailiff, but the bailiff wasn't listening. She then went to the county attorney to argue that the ones who *should* be behind bars are the unscrupulous men in Kiowa, running illegal saloons in open defiance of the law. The attorney "seemed very much annoyed because I asked him to do what he swore he would do," she recalled: he was oath-bound to arrest these illegal "jointers" and "dive-keepers." But he refused, even after Carrie filled his desktop with samples of the contraband whiskey she'd procured from Kiowa herself.

Determined, she took the train to Topeka and besought the state attorney general, also to no avail. The governor too "would not do his duty." Having exhausted every legal remedy, Nation rightly concluded that the government of "Kansas was in the power of the bitter foe to the constitution"—the liquor business—that paid bribes and kickbacks at all levels of local, state, and federal government to keep their illicit profits flowing.

As president of the county Woman's Christian Temperance Union (WCTU), Nation had already exhausted every nonviolent means of moral suasion against the liquor men: pleading with tavern-keepers, writing letters, signing petitions, organizing temperance marches, and praying in front of illegal saloons.[5] Nothing worked. And since women couldn't vote, she had no electoral recourse either. Women were legally powerless.

So, on the night of June 6, 1900, Carrie hitched up her buggy and rode the twenty miles south to Kiowa. Early the next morning, she visited the unlicensed, illegal bar of Mr. Dobson, whose own brother was the county sheriff.

"Mr. Dobson, I told you last spring to close this place, you did not do it, now I have come down with another remonstrance," Carrie said. "Get out of the way, I do not want to strike you, but I am going to break this place up."[6]

Hard and fast, she hurled bricks and stones at the whiskey bottles, glass mugs and tumblers, and the giant mirror behind the bar. The men—confused and terrified—huddled in the corner. When she ran out of her own projectiles, she grabbed pool balls and billiard cues to smash up the room.

Then she did the same to the saloon across the street.

And then a third.

Carrie was always clear that her attack was not against the booze in those bottles, nor the pitiable addicts getting drunk at 8:30 that Thursday morning, but against the predatory liquor traffic and the government that abetted it. "The smashing in Kansas was intended to strike the head of this nation the hardest blow, for every saloon I smashed in Kansas had a license from the head of this government which made the head of the government more responsible than the dive-keeper," she wrote. "I broke up three of these dives that day, broke the windows on the outside to prove that the man who rents his house is a partner also with *the man who sells*."[7]

The man who sells.

Carrie Nation's foe was not the drink or the drinker, but "the man who sells." This is important.

By the time she was done with the third saloon, a sizable crowd had grown in the streets, watching in bewilderment and amusement. The authorities did not know what to do. "I have destroyed three of your places of business," she declared to the onlookers, "and if I have broken a statute of Kansas, put me in jail; if I am not a law-breaker your mayor and your councilmen are. You must arrest one of us, for if I am not a criminal, they are."[8]

The town marshal, mayor, and city attorney huddled up, and ultimately decided *against* pressing charges. Carrie returned home triumphant. Papers across the nation carried the sensational news, making Carrie Nation an instant celebrity. Back home, the political community was stirred to action. One by one, the unlicensed dives of Barber County, Kansas, were shuttered, their proprietors convicted. Carrie didn't have to say a word.

Mrs. Nation then set her sights on the illegal saloons of Wichita. At 8:00 am sharp on the morning of Wednesday, December 28, she sauntered into the bar at the Carey Hotel, the most luxurious lodging in the city. "I decided to go to the Carey for several reasons," she said. "It was the most dangerous, being the finest. The low doggery will take the low and keep them low, but these so-called respectable ones will take the respectable, make them low, then kick them out."[9]

The drunks fled when Carrie started hurling rocks at the opulent glass mirror, and through a life-size oil painting of a buck-naked Cleopatra across from it. The shell-shocked bartender didn't even move as she brandished an iron rod and smashed all the bottles in the mahogany sideboards. She then set the barflies at the saloon across the street to flight in a similar fashion. By 8:30am, she was behind bars, having done some three thousand dollars in damage.[10]

Carrie was jailed for three weeks—forced to sleep without a pillow on the concrete floor, as the winter drafts poured in—without ever being charged for a crime. After springing her on a writ of habeas corpus, her cold and loveless second husband of twenty-five years, David Nation, joked that she could do far more damage with a hatchet than with a rock.

"That is the most sensible thing you have said since I married you," she laughed.[11] Within a year, David filed for divorce. Carrie donated her entire alimony to found a home for drunkards' wives in Kansas City—the first domestic violence shelter in the state.[12]

Carrie Nation had no need for wealth, luxury, and status, and no patience for those who pursued them. She lived "as harshly and simply and self-denyingly as Leo

Tolstoy," she said in admiration of the world-famous writer (Chapter 2), who was likewise excommunicated for decrying the man who sells liquor.[13]

Now armed with a hatchet that would become her iconic trademark, Nation made her way to Enterprise, Kansas, at the request of women's groups there. Enterprise saloon-keeper John Schilling knew that chivalry and decorum prevented a man from laying a finger on Mrs. Nation, even as she wrecked his illegal bar, loudly berated him, and shamed his trade from the street corner.

But that didn't stop his wife, Belle Schilling, from walking up and punching Carrie square in the face. Saying nothing, Carrie staggered to a nearby butcher. She emerged, holding a chunk of raw beef over her swollen black eye, and kept right on preaching. Four prostitutes paid by the Schillings then kicked Nation to the gutter, pulled out her hair and beat her bloody with sticks and whips.

Nevertheless, she persisted: over the next ten years until her death in 1911, Carrie Nation was arrested thirty-two separate times. Once she was apprehended under the dome of the US Capitol, after haranguing senators for "representing the interests of the brewers and distillers" over their own constituents.[14] At least her Capitol arrest was orderly.

In Kentucky, a barkeeper smashed the fifty-eight-year-old grandmother over the head with a chair. In London, she was pelted with rotten eggs. At Coney Island, a hail of peanuts and hotdogs preceded an angry New York lynch mob. It was hardly the only attempt to hang Carrie Nation from the nearest tree. Despite persistent

Figure 1.1 Study in contrasts: A stern Carrie Nation wielding a hatchet vs. a playful Carrie Nation wielding ice cream with an unidentified boy.

Source: Philipp Kester, *New York Times* photo archive. Kansas State Historical Society. DaRT ID: 209242.

death threats, she fought on—secure in her faith—fully embracing the dangers of her activism.[15] She was ready to die for the cause, and many men wished she would.

When a barkeeper—sweating red with rage—once pushed his pistol into her temple, she brushed him aside: "I am not afraid of your gun. Maybe it would be a good thing for a saloon-keeper to kill Carry Nation." Much like the abolitionist martyr John Brown, she was certain her murder would prompt the entire nation to rise up and "smash the dives."[16]

Explaining Carrie

Why Carrie Nation undertook her violent "hatchetations," as she called them, has been the subject of endless speculation by generations of historians and amateur psychiatrists. She was easy to mock as a Bible-thumping "crank," "a freak," "a lunatic," or a "puritanical killjoy," with all the baggage each of those terms carries.[17]

In his 1959 article "Crazy Carry the Party Pooper," David Shaw claimed (allegedly with the full weight of mid-century science to back him), that Nation's activism stemmed from the "glandular difficulties of the menopause that allowed suppressed forces to erupt violently."[18] Vaginas and hormones have long been men's favorite excuses for women who step out of line and defy patriarchal norms. It has the added effect of belittling women's actual motivations along the way.[19] But it wasn't just armchair Freuds dropping such misogynist and degrading accusations: the two most influential and widely read biographies blame menopause for Nation's supposedly "warped" focus on "the dangers of sexual irregularity."[20] Bestselling author Andrew Sinclair's *Prohibition: The Era of Excess* (1962) faulted Nation's "suppressed sexual desire," which was "perverted into an itching curiosity about vice, an aggressive prurience which found its outlet in violence, exhibitionism, and self-imposed martyrdom."[21]

Generations of writers and historians—almost all men—dismissed her as just plain insane: a "demented woman," "psychotic from an early age,"[22] suffering from a "personal history of disease and convulsion,"[23] and a "well-defined strain of madness."[24] Unsurprisingly, the chauvinist equation *outspoken woman = crazy woman* has a long history.[25]

Even Daniel Okrent's masterful *Last Call* (2011)—winner of the American Historical Association's prize for the best book on American history, and basis for the influential Ken Burns/Lynn Novick *Prohibition* documentary series—trivializes Nation as an ugly, incoherent lunatic. "Carry Amelia Moore Gloyd Nation was six feet tall, with the biceps of a stevedore, the face of a prison warden, and the persistence of a toothache. Her mother believed herself to be Queen Victoria," Okrent writes. "Her religious passions led her to sit on her organ bench and talk to Christ."[26]

By playing up her eccentricities, mocking her femininity, fundamentally misconstruing her religious beliefs, and laughing off her convictions, historians have made Carrie Nation a paper cutout of the temperance movement: easily crumpled up and thrown away, without ever needing to consider that her grievances actually had merit. Saloon-keepers *were* acting illegally. Politicians and law enforcement *were* corrupted by taking bribes to look the other way. Women *were* marginalized, disenfranchised, and powerless to stop it. A predatory liquor traffic *was* making money hand over fist by getting men addicted, and then bleeding them—and their families—to death.

Carrie had experienced all of this firsthand. Her first husband, Dr. Charles Gloyd, was a handsome and decorated Union Army physician. She idolized him. He adored her. They wrote romantic—even salacious—love letters to each other.[27] But it wasn't to last. Even as a newlywed, Gloyd locked himself up at the tavern or Masonic lodge, drinking till dawn, leaving his forlorn bride "hungry for his caresses and love."[28] In 1869, after just sixteen months of marriage, her beloved died from alcoholism, leaving Carrie with only her sorrow, a new baby, and a disapproving mother-in-law to care for. A widow at the age of twenty-two, she was penniless, hopeless, and powerless before the law. But from those depths of poverty and despair, she became self-reliant, strong, and willing to fight against unjust subjugation on behalf of the subjugated.

So when it came to her motivations, Carrie Nation always declared them clearly and consistently: "*You wouldn't give me the vote, so I had to use a rock!*"[29]

What's strange is that we still refuse to hear her, believe her, or take her seriously.

"She did not pick up her hatchet because she had suddenly gone off some psychological deep end," writes professor Fran Grace in her *Carry A. Nation: Retelling the Life* (2001)—the most thorough Nation biography, and notably the only one written by a woman. She was not a "cranky, insane woman traumatized by menopausal changes."[30] Rather than a rampaging fundamentalist, she gave everything of herself to those who had none, and worked tirelessly to defend those who could not defend themselves.

When Nation toured the United Kingdom in 1908–1909, many Brits were shocked that the woman they met "was not like any preconceived ideas of the violent and notorious saloon smasher" portrayed in the newspapers. They lauded her "remarkable wit," her "strenuous vigor," her "good sense of humor, a wise, general outlook upon life, a kindly, even modest, and unassuming manner," with "the light of a visionary in her eyes."[31]

Nor was she some uncompromising puritan, even when it came to booze. Once, when a contrarian physician tried to convince her that alcohol was harmless—maybe even healthful—the prohibitionist Nation took it as a challenge. She began chugging-down one bottle of Schlitz Malt after another. Horrified, the doctor begged her to stop, before this supposedly "healthful" drink gave her alcohol poisoning.[32] She made her point. She had no time for apologists and equivocators.

She did make time, however, for empathy and persuasion. Once, following a lecture in Chicago, she headed to the red-light district, itching for a fight. There she was surprised to find her own grandson, Riley White, tending bar.

"Go in and smash it if you want to," he sheepishly told her.

No. She would not.

Instead, she held a closed-door meeting inside: just Carrie, the saloon-keepers, and a few girls who'd been ensnared into a prostitution ring. "They treated me well and the women called me grandma. Poor women, they are dragged down by devils," she said. "It was the most remarkable meeting I ever had. Saloon-keepers and harlots have a much better chance of heaven than hypocrites who are in the church. I have no use for women who are afraid they will soil their skirts in trying to lift up their fallen sisters."[33]

Her fearlessness in leaving the privileged confines of the church to go slumming in the gutters, saloons, theaters, burlesque houses, and other bastions of misogyny certainly invited men's scorn.

"You poor, deluded, hysterical, half-crazed, religious maniac," one guy mansplained to her. "I do not believe you are so much to blame for your present state of raving imbecility as the unsexed men [and their] so-called temperance crusades, seem to have completely upset the molecules of your brains, that is of course, providing you have any."[34] This was hardly an isolated incident: hecklers and newsmen alike portrayed her as old, unattractive, mannish, and "unsexed." While in reality she stood just over five feet tall, even today, she's frequently depicted "as a hyperthyroid Amazon of nearly six feet, who required 'policemen seven feet high' to handle her."[35] Still, she took every withering slight with remarkable grace.

She was not some Bible-thumping, conservative "holy crone on a broomstick," seeking to legislate morality or "discipline" individual behavior.[36] If anything she was a populist progressive; rooted in communal consciousness and agrarian self-help, she fought tirelessly for good governance, women's rights, civil rights, and cleaning the corruption out of the body politic (Chapter 14). She matched her words with deeds time and again. In addition to her battered women's shelter in Kansas City, when she retired to Eureka Springs, Arkansas, she established "Hatchet Hall." Part rest home for the impoverished elderly, part safe haven for women fleeing abusive husbands, and part homeschool for their children, Nation built an intergenerational, self-reliant, sister-based commune that was ages ahead of its time.[37]

She did not view drinking as a sin, or the drinker as a sinner. Instead, like the prostitute, the prisoner, and the slave, the drinker was the victim, to be forgiven, loved and nurtured. The true sinner was the enslaver of men: the drink seller. And she would use all means at her disposal—from prayer and persuasion to hatchetation— to get *the man who sells* to change his ways.

Nor was her activism some crazy aberration: disenfranchised and disempowered women had been smashing saloons across the country for decades. In 1855, fifteen women were jailed for smashing a saloon in Illinois. The young lawyer who secured their acquittal went by the name of Abraham Lincoln (see Chapter 11).[38]

Carrie Nation was a devout, God-fearing Christian, but she was not inflexible or dogmatic. A strict sectarian would never be caught exploring the mysteries of rival faiths; Carrie however thoughtfully invited the sage counsels of Catholic priests. Around the dinner table, she and the Jewish guests who frequented her hotel grappled with ethical and theological questions late into the night. She came away from such encounters professing a deep admiration for Jewish self-sacrifice, which would have further horrified the evangelicals who'd already thrown her out of every Protestant church in town. From a young age, she scoffed at the self-righteous exclusivism of those claiming to be the one true church, and repeatedly expressed her "contempt for popular preaching."[39]

Nor was she some racist. As a child in antebellum Kentucky, Carrie's hardscrabble mother insisted that she live in the slaves' quarters, where she attended subversive slave meetings about white tyranny and worshipped with them in secret. She "imbibed some of their superstitions," Nation remembered, as well as their loud expressiveness in church, which further irritated her prairie white churchgoers. She did not discriminate in employing black people, housing them, or serving them through her charity work: often donating her lecture proceeds to the black African Methodist Episcopal (AME) Church. When she did speak at churches that denied blacks, she demanded that all be admitted entry. If that made racists uncomfortable, well, then *they* could leave. And they usually did . . . just before they'd return with more numbers to run Carrie and her African American acolytes out of town.[40]

And sure, Carrie Nation claimed that God spoke to her and told her to "Go to Kiowa" and make war on the saloons, though that in no way invalidates her activism. After all, two years prior, in 1898, President William McKinley claimed that God spoke to him, and commanded him to make war on Spain, take their colonial possessions "and civilize and Christianize them" (Chapter 15), but we don't teach that the Spanish-American War was due to McKinley's supposed insanity or menopausal hot flashes.[41]

Carrie Nation wasn't "crazy." She was a fierce and impassioned warrior-mother, who saw no inconsistency between those roles. She was Wonder Woman in a frock. A trailblazing social activist, she was the embodiment of the feminist empowerment mantra that "well-behaved women seldom make history."[42] Perhaps we should start recognizing her as such.

The World's Most Famous Prohibitionist

Quick: *Who's the world's most famous prohibitionist?*

I've asked this question for years to all manner of well-read people: scores of American academics, conference rooms full of professional historians, classrooms of bewildered students, or anyone unfortunate enough to casually ask what I research. The name Carrie Nation comes back *every single time*. This isn't surprising: Carrie's menacing, hatchet-wielding portrait is a prominent part of most prohibition histories and documentaries. When the National Constitution Center made an exhibit on *American Spirits: The Rise and Fall of Prohibition*, Carrie Nation was the first character you'd meet in your museum tour. Even though she died almost a decade *before* the Eighteenth Amendment ushered in the Prohibition Era in the United States, Carrie Nation is *vastly*—and quantifiably—more well known than the so-called father of prohibition Neal Dow, or even Andrew Volstead, whose name is on the prohibition enforcement law.[43]

This is not an idle question.

Who we see as the most famous prohibitionist highlights all sorts of our biases, misconceptions, and the limitations of our received wisdom on prohibition. Carrie Nation embodies everything *we think we know* about prohibitionists: angry, white, conservative, rural evangelicals—perhaps slightly unhinged and prone to violence—but seemingly intent on denying Americans' individual right to drink. In sum: she's become the perfect villain for American history, regardless of her actual motivations.

The same way we get Carrie Nation wrong, we get the entire movement for prohibition wrong. For generations, writers have described Nation as a "sinister bigot, a demented creature, the Hitler of morals and the Joe McCarthy of personal conduct."[44] Similarly, historians today vilify prohibitionists with the same language we use to describe Al Qaeda and international terrorists. They're "ruthless" "extremists," "cranks," "deeply antidemocratic" "fanatics and fools," who "stirred Americans' worst fears about race, class, and religion."[45] Prohibition was a "threat to individual freedoms" and a "wrongheaded social policy waged by puritanical zealots of a bygone Victorian era."[46]

This seems like rather flippant and casual dismissal of what was, in fact, the most popular, most influential, and longest-lived international social-reform movement in the history of the world.[47]

It is not just pop culture that gets temperance and prohibition wrong. The conventional wisdom among academic historians has reinforced that dastardly image. Historian Richard Hofstadter's Pulitzer Prize–winning *Age of Reform* (1955) and sociologist Joseph Gusfield's *Symbolic Crusade* (1963) both explained prohibition as a culture clash, pitting different social groups against one another. For them, prohibition was the last-gasp backlash of conservative, rural, native-born Protestants against the rising tide of urbanization, immigration, and multiculturalism in turn-of-the-century America. When—on election night 2016—CNN political analyst Van Jones labeled Donald Trump's victory a "whitelash against a changing country" by reactionary rural conservatives, he could have just as easily been describing the received wisdom on prohibition.[48]

Instead of challenging this image, generations of prohibition scholarship have doubled down on it. In recent years, James Morone's *Hellfire Nation* (2003), Daniel Okrent's *Last Call* (2010), and Lisa McGirr's *War on Alcohol* (2016) have expanded the culture-clash narrative to argue that prohibition was a weapon of the powerful white majority, used to subordinate and "discipline" already marginalized poor, urban, immigrant, and African American communities. As we'll see, just the opposite was true: temperance and prohibition were weapons of the weak and marginalized; defense against their systemic oppression.[49]

We're told that conservative, reactionary politics runs like a red thread of intolerance throughout all of American history: from sin-obsessed Puritans and nativist Know-Nothings on one end, through temperance advocates and prohibitionists, to McCarthyites, antiabortion evangelicals, and Trumpist "alt-right" white supremacists on the other. "Established by dint of repetition," portrayals of temperance and prohibition as reactionary intolerance have lamentably "achieved a kind of incantatory truth and ultimately have been enshrined as pieces of political folk wisdom," *despite* the historical reality rather than because of it.[50]

However, the dominant understanding of temperance and prohibition as a reactionary, authoritarian political aberration led by angry, white, midwestern evangelical women quickly runs into a bevy of uncomfortable questions: How does culture get translated into policy? How does culture clash explain dramatic policy shifts from one alcohol control regime to another, even as the cultural composition of the country remains largely the same?

How could women like Carrie Nation and the powerful Woman's Christian Temperance Union (Chapter 13) champion both ultraprogressive causes like suffragism *and* allegedly ultraconservative causes like prohibition at the exact same time?

How did "reactionary" temperance emerge from the ultraprogressive abolitionist, suffragist, and labor movements?

If prohibition was just the result of Bible thumpers, why was there no religious revivalism in America at the time (Chapter 14)?[51]

How are we to understand that the Eighteenth (prohibition) Amendment—the crowning achievement of this supposedly authoritarian movement—was passed with a 68 percent supermajority in the House of Representatives, 76 percent support in the Senate, and was ratified in record speed by forty-six of the forty-eight states all across North America, not *just* in the Midwest?

How are we to understand that this ultimate victory of "conservative" prohibition came smack dab in the middle of the Progressive Era (Chapter 16)?[52]

How can we blame women for the Eighteenth Amendment in 1919, if they were still legally disenfranchised until after the ratification of the Nineteenth Amendment in 1920 (Chapter 17)?[53]

And if the Eighteenth Amendment was really a war on the individual's right to drink, why doesn't it say so? If you read the brief text of the Amendment, it clearly

targets not the drinker, but those who traffic in alcohol. It seems odd that generations of dry activists would fight tooth and nail for something only to slip up and
omit it from their crowning achievement. Oops! Were they really that sneaky? Or
that stupid?

None of this adds up.

There's a Rest of the World?

Another misconception that stems from the conservative culture-clash narrative is
that prohibition was a uniquely American phenomenon. After all, how many other
countries have nativist evangelicals fearful of immigrants in the late nineteenth
century?

American exceptionalism is a lazy myth, and nowhere more so than in temperance history. From Russia and Norway to India and Turkey, the United States
was only one of between a dozen and two dozen countries to adopt prohibition,
depending on how (and what) you count. Moreover, representatives from almost
every nation and colony on earth were linked together by a robust, transnational
network to battle the liquor traffic.[54] Temperance was a truly global movement,
though this may be the first time you've heard of it, since most prohibition histories
stay comfortably within the geographic confines of the United States.[55]

The purpose of this book is to abandon our container-based understandings of
history—in which the only things that matter to a country are those things that
happen *within* the geographic confines of that country—in order to study this
movement both comparatively and transnationally.[56] That is not to say no one has
ever considered temperance and prohibition in non-American contexts. There are
good histories of temperance in Britain, Scandinavia, continental Europe, imperial Russia, India, and beyond,[57] as well as a few global histories of alcohol.[58] The
problem is, however, that the history of temperance and prohibition in any other
country is vastly overshadowed by the voluminous historical literature about the
United States. Since one would naturally assume that what causes prohibition in
one country likely causes it in another, dedicated researchers understandably tried
to cram their own country's temperance experiences into the conventional wisdom
culled exclusively from the United States, only to be disappointed that it doesn't fit at
all.[59] After all, there weren't a whole lot of conservative, Bible-thumping Protestant
evangelicals in imperial Russia, or secular Turkey, or communist Hungary, but each
experimented with prohibition, just like the United States.

It's easy to scoff, wave your hands, and *assume* that the reasons for temperance
and prohibition in Russia or Botswana or India or Turkey were fundamentally different from the reasons for temperance and prohibition in the United States. *But
what if they weren't?* Are you open to the possibility that these experiences may not

only be similar, but intimately and causally intertwined with each other? That's precisely what I'm asking you to consider in this book.

Beyond "container" prohibition histories—each country's history hermetically sealed off from any other—in more recent years, historians have begun considering temperance as a transnational movement. Unfortunately, these too fall victim to culture-clash logic derived from the single case study of the United States, exported to the rest of the world. Transnational historians claim that the global temperance movement was nothing more than a peculiar Anglo American missionary impulse—an early manifestation of American "cultural imperialism," or part of that "white man's burden" to civilize the globe.[60] In his *Reforming the World: The Creation of America's Moral Empire* (2010), historian Ian Tyrrell blames the moral perfectionism of Bible-thumping Protestant reformers and missionaries in disciplining peripheral peoples, linked "to the emergence of American imperialism and colonialism." In this colonial perspective, white, Christian missionaries are the true arbiters of morality and reform, not the indigenous people. For Tyrell and others, temperance was the weapon of the powerful over the powerless, rather than the other way around. "Cultural expansion in the form of missionaries and moral reform enlarged what could be termed the external 'footprint' of the United States in the 1880s and 1890s, creating conditions wherein a more vigorous economic and political expansion could be seriously considered," Tyrrell claims.[61]

Of course, the white-savior claim that only "civilized," Anglo American missionaries were capable of organizing temperance defense of indigenous communities against liquor exploitation only further marginalizes subaltern voices.[62] This is ironic. As locals in India were fond of saying, "To be under the influence of drink was sure proof that the man was a Christian or in danger of becoming one!"[63] They weren't alone. As it turns out, from Khama in Bechuanaland (Chapter 6) to Gandhi (Chapter 7) to Atatürk (Chapter 8), the most outspoken prohibitionists in the developing world were subaltern leaders taking matters into their own hands, in defense of their own communities *against* Western imperialism. And lest we think that the United States is somehow "exceptional," the first American prohibitionist was Little Turtle of the Miami tribe, struggling to save his own people against the "white man's wicked water" (Chapter 9). Even following the Civil War, some of the greatest advocates for prohibition were disenfranchised women and African-American communities. Global prohibition studies needs to be decolonized in more ways than one.

Still, the logic behind it is understandable: if you believe American prohibitionists are villains, hellbent on undermining individual liberty in the name of evangelical morality at home, it makes sense to assume that they'd have no qualms about imposing their conservative beliefs on the rest of the world too, right?

Again, as it turns out, just the opposite is true.

Figure 1.2 Russell Henderson, "Pick Up the Club," *American Issue*, January 4, 1919.
Source: The *American Issue* was the official periodical of the Anti-Saloon League of America, printed in Westerville, Ohio.

The Search for the Most Famous
Prohibitionist Continues

Friends and colleagues sometimes turn my world's-most-famous-prohibitionist question back on me. "Okay, if you're so smart: who could possibly have greater name recognition than Carrie Nation?"

Looking around the globe, I might suggest Tomáš Masaryk, the founding father of independent Czechoslovakia. Or maybe Nobel Peace Prize–winner Hjalmar Branting, the first Social Democrat prime minister of Sweden. What about Kemal Atatürk, secular revolutionary who saw prohibition as essential to combatting both British and Ottoman domination? Still not a big enough name? How about Vladimir Lenin: leader of the Bolshevik Revolution, who declared, "Death is preferable to selling vodka!"[64] Or the world's greatest writer, Leo Tolstoy? What about Mahatma Gandhi? These are some of the most important leaders of the twentieth century: prohibitionists every one, and not a conservative Bible thumper among them.

Okay, fine. But is there an *American* prohibitionist more well known than Carrie Nation? I'd suggest perhaps "the Great Commoner," Progressive champion William Jennings Bryan (Chapters 15–17) for starters. Or, sticking with three-named Willys: the great abolitionist reformer William Lloyd Garrison (Chapter 11). Or suffragist trailblazers like Elizabeth Cady Stanton or Susan B. Anthony (Chapter 12). Still not enough? How about Frederick Douglass? Or Abraham Lincoln (Chapter 11)? Or Thomas Jefferson (Chapter 9)? Stop me when you've heard of some of these prohibitionists.

These are the heroes of American history, not its villains.

Whether in the United States or around the world, each fought ceaselessly against the predations of the white man's liquor trade, which was backed by equally repressive, autocratic governments. The global temperance/prohibition movement was not "cultural imperialism"; if anything it was *anti*-imperialism.

It is no coincidence that the global movement against the predatory liquor traffic was the product of the Age of Empires. Imperialism scholars are the first to remind us that exploitation of the poor for the benefit of the rich was their entire purpose of empires: "modern empires were distinctively capitalist creations, founded, shaped, and driven by the profit motive."[65] We easily forget that addiction was a primary tool of conquest. Opium was Britain's preferred narcotic in China. And when the Ch'ing dynasty protested, and even prohibited the opium trade, Britain responded with not one but two Opium Wars (1839–42, 1856–60) to keep the opium profits rolling in.

The same thing was true of "the world's first 'narco-military' empire," the British East India Company—the primary revenues for which came from selling opium, ganja, and distilled spirits to natives unprepared for its addictiveness and potency. A nationwide rebellion against the company's excesses was only put down at the cost of nearly a million Indian lives (Chapter 7).[66] The same dynamics held with the British South Africa Company (Chapter 6), and the British occupations of Ottoman Turkey and Egypt (Chapter 8).

"We forget that wherever Western Civilization has gone, there has followed vice, social disease, and forty-horsepower gin. We forget that we flooded Africa with Bedford rum and strewed that whole continent of song with sorrow and newly made graves," wrote one of history's most fascinating figures: William E. "Pussyfoot" Johnson—who we'll meet time and again in this book. Pussyfoot was an American temperance activist and writer, who'd twice circumnavigated the globe to network with prohibitionist nationalists and revolutionaries across Asia, Africa, Europe, and North America. Of Muslim-majority countries, he reminisced,

> I am personally familiar with the streets and byways of Cairo, Alexandria, Port Said, Suez, Constantinople, and Jerusalem. And, to my own know-ledge, practically every liquor establishment and practically every other vile dump of the slums in these cities is conducted by someone who claims

to be a follower of Christ. . . . Wherever the flag of a Christian nation has gone, there, under its folds and under its protection, has followed the hated liquor traffic. That is the situation that has stared me in the face in every Oriental country on earth dominated by a Christian power.[67]

Temperance and prohibition were not instruments of the colonial "white man's burden," they were the means of fighting *against* it.

Lest we think that American history is "exceptional," consider the treatment of Native Americans. From the establishment of the first American colonies through to the twentieth century, there have been constant lamentations of the destruction the white man's liquor traffic wrought, and repeated efforts to prohibit the sale to Indians. But rather than some benevolent repression, we find that virtually every state or federal prohibition was "largely due to the efforts, the protests and the agitation of the Red Men themselves" (Chapter 9).[68]

This dynamic is most obvious to see when the exploiters are rich, educated, white Christians and the exploited are impoverished, illiterate, black or brown natives half a world away. But the same liquor exploitation is found in almost every empire of the nineteenth century, with temperance and prohibition being a defense against liquor subjugation by the imperial metropole. In the tsarist empire, temperance pitted the Finnish, Polish, and Baltic minorities against the Russian heartland (Chapter 2); the Czechs and Slovaks against the Austro-Hungarian Empire (Chapter 4); the Irish and Scots against London (Chapter 5); and even African Americans (Chapter 11), Native Americans (Chapters 9–10) and Filipinos against the US government (Chapter 15).

The exploitative nature of the liquor trade remains, even if we remove the ethnic, religious, or nationalist divisions. Profit doesn't discriminate. Both Tolstoy and Lenin were prohibitionists, because they both understood that the opulence and might of the great tsarist empire was built upon a vodka monopoly that was sucking the Russian peasantry dry (Chapter 2). The same thing happened in Sweden and Belgium (Chapter 3), and most notably the United States (Chapters 13–17).

Despite such vast religious and cultural differences, a broad, historical comparison uncovers a striking continuity: everywhere, the temperance-cum-prohibition movement harnessed the moral and material resources of organized religions into a broad-based, progressive movement to capture the instruments of legislation and statecraft against powerful, established political actors. In the United States as around the globe, temperance embodied a normative shift in which the exploitation of the weak, impoverished, and defenseless citizens for the benefit of predatory capitalists and a predatory state were no longer considered appropriate.

A one-paragraph article from July 1912 in the *American Issue*—the official organ of the prohibitionist Anti-Saloon League of America—titled "What Does It Profit?" most succinctly lays out the reality of prohibition, addressing the liquor industry's $50 million annual profits in Texas alone:

Where is the profit to Texas from the financial standpoint? Who furnishes the $50,000,000? Drinking men, their wives and children. Who gets the money? Saloon-keepers, brewers, wholesale dealers and distillers. What are they doing with it? Increasing their enormous fortunes and maintaining a state and national political machine to control state and national politics. . . . What can be done about it? Defeat saloon candidates, *smashing the liquor machine*, and adopt constitutional prohibition.

How and when can that be done? By electing [Texas Supreme Court Judge William] Ramsey, [Texas State congressman Morris] Sheppard, and other anti-liquor machine candidates this year, and the submission of a prohibition amendment in the near future.

This will turn $50,000,000 into constructive channels of trade and Texas will bloom as a rose.[69]

Democrat Morris Sheppard was duly elected US senator in February 1913 and represented Texas for the next twenty-eight years—championing women's suffrage, rural credit programs, child-labor laws, and antitrust initiatives. The following year, he introduced what would become the Eighteenth Amendment to the Senate floor. But even the "father of national prohibition" made clear he wasn't after booze, but after the corrupt liquor-political machine.[70] "I am not a prohibitionist in the strict sense of the word," he proclaimed. "I am fighting the liquor traffic. I am against the saloon. I am not in any sense aiming to prevent the personal use of alcoholic beverages." He would fight tooth and nail against the liquor trusts that made huge profits off the people's misery and poverty, but opposed measures that would "prevent a farmer from having a little hard cider" or a worker having a brew, so long as he wasn't being exploited for someone else's profit. When it came to prohibiting actual drinking, he was quite clear: "I don't think we care to go as far as that. That is too much of an invasion of personal liberty."[71] This wasn't double-talk or lawyer-ball: this was the purpose of prohibition, from the very mouth of its "father."

In this way, the temperance and prohibition movements have more in common with opposition to the British opium trade (and the wars they spawned), or contemporary efforts to reduce the social harms from cigarette smoke, or holding politically connected "Big Pharma" companies responsible for the opioid epidemic, in which predatory pharmaceutical companies reap obscene profits from the misery of their addicted customers. This is a far cry from traditional characterizations of Bible thumpers "legislating morality."[72]

By situating the American experience into a global context, rather than extrapolating assumptions about prohibition from the sole case study of the United States, we not only derive a more complete picture of temperance and prohibition as global movements, but we also get a better view of America's prohibition experience and the shortcomings in our conventional understanding of it. In particular, it helps us highlight the persistent problems associated with the US-centric paradigm—the seeming incongruity of a "reactionary" social movement in the Progressive Era, the disproportionate focus on nonsystematic, culturalist explanations, and the subsequent vilification of temperance advocates.

This is a history of prohibition the way you've never heard it. And you've likely never heard it because most writers on prohibition have been looking for the wrong things in the wrong places at the wrong times, using the wrong assumptions to ask the wrong questions and draw the wrong conclusions.

Why Prohibition?

This is a book about history, but it is not a history book, strictly speaking. It is not a chronological narrative of *this* thing that happened, followed by *that* thing that happened. Instead, this is a work of comparative politics. The chapters are arranged geographically and thematically to more effectively bring historical evidence to bear on the simple, two-word thesis question: *why prohibition?* What was that all about? What caused prohibition—not just in the United States, but in countries around the globe?

It sounds so simple, but surprisingly—for all of the books and articles written on temperance and prohibition—not one seems to have systematically investigated this most fundamental question. For all of their rich depth of archival-based knowledge of finely grained historical details, most professional historians are no longer interested in discerning causation: the "hows" and "whys" of history. Meanwhile, in political science and sociology—where causation is the coin of the realm—scholarly interest in temperance and prohibition is near zero.[73] So historians and social scientists largely work in complete isolation from one another, rather than engaging in constructive dialogue. Even academic publications and the scrutiny of peer review that comes with them tend to fall along well-entrenched disciplinary boundaries. This deserted wasteland between disciplines is where the weeds of misunderstanding grow and grow, until they become mighty and seemingly unassailable "truths."

As a work of comparative and transnational history, instead of beginning with *what we think we know* about prohibition as cultural "whitelash" based on the single case study (n = 1) of the United States, and then extrapolating that understanding to the rest of the world, let's see what temperance and prohibition look like in the rest of the world *first*, and then apply those insights to the United States.

The study of American politics is just as insular and devoid of international comparisons and context as the study of American history. Even David Mayhew—a leading scholar in that narrow world of American politics—noted that the question "Why did X happen in many places? can sometimes give better traction than: Why did X happen in the United States?"[74] As it turns out, when it comes to understanding the politics of prohibition, there's a lot to be learned by decolonizing and de-exceptionalizing American history by situating it in its proper global context.

Since temperance and prohibition were intimately tied to confronting political and economic subjugation in the age of imperialism, the chapters in this book are largely based around different empires: the Russian Empire, the German and Austro-Hungarian Empires, the British Empire, the Ottoman Empire, the American Empire, and so on. But rather than simply repeating the same one-thing-after-another template in this place or that, each chapter also draws out distinct political themes and "-isms" related to the so-called liquor question: temperance and anti-authoritarian communism (Chapter 2); temperance, social democracy, and the international labor movement (Chapter 3); temperance, war, and liberalism (Chapter 4); temperance and imperialism (Chapters 5–9, 15); temperance and abolitionism (Chapter 11); temperance and suffragism (Chapters 12–13); temperance and progressivism (Chapters 14, 16, 17). In this way—by building the argument in terms of an expansive variety of both international experiences *and* political perspectives—I hope to present a more satisfactory answer to "why prohibition" than we can get from the conventional culture-clash perspective derived from the single case study of the United States.

It hasn't been easy. This book contains primary and secondary source materials in fourteen different languages, drawn from 130 collections housed in 70 different archives in seventeen different countries across five continents. But hopefully the results will be worth it.

This approach has its benefits, but also limitations. In uncovering the causes of prohibition, this project is far less interested in its consequences. Fortunately, historians have that well covered. From the rise of Al Capone and organized crime, to the blossoming of jazz in underground speakeasies, to the Prohibition Era roots of the modern American surveillance and penal state, there are all manner of books that describe the experiences and legacies of prohibition and its repeal.[75] This will not be one of them.

This is a book about history, yes. But more fundamentally, it is also about how we misunderstand history, and the ramifications of that. It is about how norms and understandings evolve over time. It is about how our human brains struggle to make sense out of things that we don't quite understand, and what happens when we—consciously or unconsciously—rely on cognitive shortcuts to make sense of the world.

Getting as far away from the American experience as possible, Section I of the book takes us to visit the great empires of Europe. Chapter 2 begins with the world's first prohibition country—the Russian Empire. From Leo Tolstoy to Vladimir Lenin, critics and exiles railed against the tsar's exploitative vodka monopoly, which made the rich richer and the poor poorer. Chapter 3 pivots from Russian Bolshevism to European socialism, as Sweden's first Social Democrat prime minister and Nobel Peace Prize–winner Hjalmar Branting grappled with the liquor question in Scandinavia, while Emile Vandervelde did the same in Belgium and its Congo colony. In the continental empires of Germany it was liberals who rallied temperance against the conservative, liquor-producing *Junkers*, while Czechoslovak founding father Tomáš Masaryk made the case for abstinence, democratic liberation, and self-determination from the Austro-Hungarian Empire (Chapter 4).

Section II of the book looks at Britain's global empire. Chapter 5 examines the imperial dynamics of temperance in the British Isles, pitting the English core against the forces of temperance in Scotland and Ireland, as well as the white settler colonies of Canada, Australia, and New Zealand. Chapter 6 takes us to Africa, where prohibitionist natives like King Khama of Bechuanaland (Botswana) fought against the alcoholic incursions of Cecil Rhodes. From South Africa to India, Chapter 7 follows Mahatma Gandhi and his embrace of prohibition as a weapon against the exploitative British Raj. Chapter 8 examines prohibition as opposition to British colonialism within the Ottoman Empire, following the actions of Mustafa Kemal Atatürk in secular Turkey.

That is where the book was originally *supposed to* end: with a quick and tidy conclusion about what global experiences teach us about American prohibition.

But weird things happen when you start to understand American history in global context. You begin to appreciate history from a wider variety of perspectives. You start doubting the conventional wisdom and questioning long-held assumptions. You start looking at different topics, at different times and in different places. And in the end, your tidy one-chapter conclusion explodes into eight more chapters—making your tight studio record into a double album—rewriting vast swaths of American history. And it is at such times that you'll be especially fortunate to have both an editor and a spouse who understand why the book took two years longer to write than you originally thought it would.

So . . . Section III brings us full circle back to the United States, hopefully a little wiser for our journey. Chapters 9 and 10 directly apply the temperance-as-anti-imperialism framework to provide new perspectives on the liquor trade in the colonization of the United States, and native attempts to resist it. Chapter 11 looks at the origins of antebellum American temperance in the abolitionist movement, from William Lloyd Garrison to Frederick Douglass to Abraham Lincoln. To abolitionism and temperance we add the origins of the woman's rights movement in Chapter 12, with pioneers Elizabeth Cady Stanton and Susan B. Anthony taking on the corruption of the Tammany Hall liquor business. Chapter 13 looks at the marriage of prohibition, suffragism, and civil rights through the eyes of two Franceses: Frances Ellen Watkins Harper and Frances Willard. Chapter 14 turns to understanding the soul of progressivism, from the social gospel of Walter Rauschenbusch to the big-city anticorruption of Theodore Roosevelt. Chapter 15 then addresses William Jennings Bryan and temperance as opposition to America's imperial impulse in the Philippines and beyond. Chapter 16 examines prohibitionism as anti-saloon activism at the state level, before Chapter 17 brings all of these threads together to address the final push for federal prohibition amid the backdrop of World War I.

The conclusion—Chapter 18—steps back to answer the question: how have we gotten history so wrong, and for so long? And if prohibition ultimately wasn't a moralizing crusade against individual liberty at home, nor a cultural-imperial imposition abroad, then what was it?

My contention is that the global war on the liquor traffic was a transnational normative shift about the inappropriateness of benefitting from addiction and misery of the masses, precipitated in many countries undergoing the upheavals of industrialization and colonial domination. It was an attempt to put the welfare of society ahead of the needs of the state. Whether the beneficiary was the state monopoly, foreign colonists, or the so-called liquor trust of corrupt and conniving capitalist brewers and distillers,[76] temperance advocates fought to put the individual ahead of profit.

While moralizing evangelicals and organized religion were part of the prohibition story, they were only limited components of a broad political, social, economic, and cultural coalition, which was not antithetical to the ethos of progressive, democratic reforms, both in the United States and around the globe. For them, prohibition was an enabler of liberty, rather than a restraint upon it.[77] The transnational social movement which embodied and promoted this normative shift, championed prohibition and other alcohol control policies to harness the power of the state in order to constrain the worst excesses of the predatory liquor trade on behalf of the good of the people.[78]

Like other transnational progressive movements of the day—antislavery/abolitionism, socialism/labor rights, suffragism/women's rights, anticolonialism/indigenous rights—prohibitionism sought to remedy inequalities of wealth and power. Not surprisingly then, these movements reinforced each another, making common cause among "Marx, Jefferson and Jesus," even as they built upon the religious and missionary foundations for reform both in the United States and around the globe.[79] As William Jennings Bryan—the oratorical godfather of American progressivism and prohibitionism—argued, constraining the liquor trade "will bring the highest good to the greatest number, without any injustice for any, for it is not injustice to any man to refuse him permission to enrich himself by injuring his fellowmen."[80] In this sentiment—reminiscent of the quintessential Marxist struggle between exploiters and the exploited—he was echoing an argument made in dozens of different languages the world over.

One thing you've probably already noted in reading thus far is the sheer quantity of cross-references and callouts from one chapter to events, actors, and developments in another country in another chapter already passed or still yet to come. Think of them as hyperlinks. They're an intentional feature of the book, meant to highlight the transnational interconnectedness of the prohibitionist movement, linking together the developments across countries, even though each discrete chapter is presented as a more conventional, container-based national history.

Before turning to these empirical chapters, I should lay my cards on the table as to my own motivations for this research project. I undertook it not as some apologist for Bible-thumping Christians, or conservatives, or even abstainers from alcohol. Just the opposite: in fact I wrote much of this book with a Manhattan cocktail in hand.

My motivation is born of a fascination with the politics of the past—the contemporary politics of memory—who we're told to valorize and vilify, and why. It's the same desire to understand why one generation builds statues to historical figures, and the next tears them down.

My interest, then, is in history's villains. And if there's one thing Hollywood plot twists teach us—from *Captain Marvel* and *Godzilla* to *Terminator* and *Harry Potter*—it is that the villains portrayed at the beginning of the film are rarely the true bad guys at the end. They were just misunderstood. It always leads us to question those who propagate such misunderstandings and hateful images all along, and why.

PART I

THE CONTINENTAL EMPIRES

Two Tolstoys and a Lenin—Temperance and Prohibition in Russia

Spassk District, Tambov Province, Russian Empire: Wednesday, July 13, 1859

General Yegor Petrovich Tolstoy didn't hide his foul mood, even as the aging war hero hoisted himself atop his old war horse yet again.

The medals adorning his uniform testified to the military acumen and loyalty expected from Russia's most venerated aristocratic families. The distinctive epaulettes signified his valorous service in the 1827 war against Persia as aide-de-camp to the great Tsar Nicholas I himself. The white-cross medal on an orange-and-black ribbon signified the Order of St. George—the tsar's highest military honor—for his valiant siege of Varna during the Russo-Turkish War in 1829. In the attack, he sustained a head wound that nearly took his life, but cursed him with lifelong migraines that forced his early retirement from the military.[1]

Still, the tsar often entrusted General Tolstoy with special assignments: heading up civilian posts, military reforms, or containing the occasional cholera outbreak. This time, the emperor dispatched him to suppress one of those intermittent rebellions against the harsh injustices of serfdom, which occasionally proved more roisterous than the local authorities could handle. No matter. He'd ruthlessly crushed the nationalist aspirations of Polish rebels during the November Uprising in Warsaw in 1830–1831; he could do the same in tiny Spassk. The tsar, however, admonished General Tolstoy to handle his Russian subjects "with mildness."[2]

"Mildness," he scoffed.

Enserfed peasants throughout the region had been in open revolt for months— grumbling protests escalating to violence, inflammatory riots, and outright rebellion—and the emperor wanted it solved "with mildness"? The lickspittle mayors, governors, judges, and police had already proven themselves either too incompetent or too soft in disciplining their own people. That's why the tsar called in General Tolstoy, after all—along with the imperial army—to restore law and order.

By eleven o'clock on that July morning, the Kazan infantry regiment entered the town of Spassk. They occupied the entire town square beside the local prison. The townspeople curiously looked on as the soldiers saluted their adjutant general. From atop his horse, Tolstoy called the attention of all of the villagers there assembled. They gathered near, removing their hats. General Tolstoy then began lecturing them, reprimanding them, berating them for allowing such disorder to prevail among their community.

They had brought shame to the tsar. They had brought shame to Russia. And they had brought shame to him personally.

"On your knees!" Tolstoy commanded. There would be repentance—a mass cleansing by force—and it would begin now. The people sheepishly complied. All bowed down to the general, except one impudent boy—the well-to-do son of a local town official—who stood defiant with his hat still on. Tolstoy glared. He ordered the infantry regiment to beat him bloody where he stood, which they did. His horrified father dared say nothing.

This was only a preview of the punishments to come for the accused mutineers held in the prison. He ordered the soldiers to execute their duty "without pity." Thirteen accused peasants were laid on the ground, and beaten with rods for over an hour. General Tolstoy hovered above the scene, commanding the soldiers to beat ever harder, even as the guilty wailed in agony. Bloodied, the peasants "declared their obedience, and begged forgiveness for what they had done."[3] Onlookers who pleaded for their mercy were themselves roundly whipped by the police. The irate General Tolstoy stormed out of town the following day, after ordering that sixty-six more offenders be whipped, four imprisoned, and ten soldiers court-martialed. Elsewhere in the province, ninety protesters were sent to military courts, forced to run the gauntlet—beaten three hundred to eight hundred times—before being condemned to hard-labor prison colonies or punishment battalions, or exiled to Siberia.[4] Scenes like this were repeated time and again across Russia's heartland, as well as its Baltic and Polish provinces, where the disturbances originated.

But what did these peasants do that elicited such draconian punishment by the state? How did a protest become a crime requiring the tsar to send in his most trusted confidant to rectify it?

As it turns out, this was a temperance revolt.[5] The instigators—now broken and bloodied by the knout—had refused to drink vodka, and they had encouraged others to abstain. Their protest was against the predatory liquor traffic, and they were hardly alone.

In far-off London, famed liberal Russian emigre-dissident Aleksandr Herzen queried, "Is it true that the crime of sobriety has become so common in Tambov province that the governor has sent army units to suppress nondrinkers?" Crazy as that sounds, that's precisely what happened. "Meanwhile, in Penza and Saratov, temperance has had to be pacified with bayonets."

Herzen's article was titled *"Smert' ili kosushku!"*—literally, "Death or the Shot Glass."[6]

Stranger still is that this was not an isolated instance of the Kremlin "forcing the people to contribute to the revenue by their intemperance." The history of imperial Russia is peppered with temperance revolts and tax rebellions large and small, as the single greatest source of revenue for the mighty Romanov Empire came from their monopoly on the vodka trade. Without it, the empire would go bankrupt. Perhaps the instigators of the peasant protests didn't understand that if the Russian people ever sobered up, the Russian state would come crashing down—but the government knew. The imperial authorities weren't about to let that happen—not now or ever.[7]

"The teetotalers were flogged into drinking," observed one British journalist. "Some who doggedly held out had liquor poured into their mouths through funnels, and were afterward hauled off to prison as rebels; at the same time the clergy were ordered to preach in their churches against the new form of sedition, and the press-censorship thenceforth laid its veto upon all publications in which the immorality of the liquor traffic was denounced."

"These things sound incredible," he added, "but they are true."[8]

The Russian State and the Vodka Traffic

There is perhaps no stereotype more ubiquitous than that of the vodka-swilling drunk Russian. But it is not as though alcoholism is hardwired into the Russian DNA. As I argue in my previous book, *Vodka Politics: Alcohol, Autocracy, and the Secret History of the Russian State* (2014), the centrality of vodka in Russian society and culture is instead the result of hundreds of years of autocratic political and economic decisions, which built the financial might of the great Russian—and then Soviet—Empires on the drunken misery of the Russian people. If we understand temperance as a grassroots effort to defend society against the predations of an imperial state wielding the vodka trade as its cudgel, it should come as little surprise that virtually every effort at genuine temperance was actively subverted by the state, whether the conservative autocracy of the tsars or the communist autocracy of the Soviets.[9]

It was Ivan the Terrible who established Russia's system of profiting from the drunken misery of his own people. In besieging the rival Khanate of Kazan on the Volga River in 1552, he was impressed with the state-run taverns the tatars called *kabaks*, and decreed that Muscovy should have them too. Soon, the entire trade in alcoholic beverages was monopolized, with all profits funneled into the tsar's treasury. The same Law Code (*ulozheniye*) of 1649 that tied the Russian peasant to the land through serfdom also outlawed buying or selling vodka outside of the *kabak* system under penalty of torture.

Before the introduction of distillation, Russian peasants drank many of the same fermented alcoholic beverages as their European counterparts to the west: ales, beers, mead fermented from honey, kvas fermented from rye bread, or imported wines if they could afford it. The early *kabaks* offered a variety of fermented drinks, but by the sixteenth century, they began adding distilled *vodka*—the diminutive "little water"—to their menus. It quickly became clear that vodka was incredibly lucrative. According to Russian vodka historians, vodka is "the most primitive and the cheapest (in terms of production costs) drink in the world."[10] All a landlord needed was a simple still, water from the stream, and wheat or rye from the peasants working his lands, and he could turn around and sell them a concoction priced many times higher than its cost. In a peasant economy where cash was scarce, payments were more often in kind: owing ever-more harvested grains to the same landlord to whom he was already hopelessly indebted.

The quick-drunk potency of distilled vodka could not be rivaled by traditional fermented brews. Vodka would never rot like the grains made to distill it, nor would it ever spoil like fermented drinks. It was the perfect drug: highly potent, highly portable, and incredibly lucrative. No wonder that by the seventeenth century, vodka had elbowed out all of the bulkier, less profitable beers, ales, and meads in the *kabak*. Vodka became synonymous with Russian culture not because the Russian people demanded it, but because the Russian state supplied it.[11]

Vodka was a boon to the Muscovite state—filling Kremlin coffers, and financing Moscow's growth into the mighty Russian Empire that covered fully one-sixth of the earth's landmass. By the time of the temperance protests in the mid-nineteenth century, the vodka monopoly was the largest source of imperial finance, constituting over one-third of all state revenues. In a world before income taxes, fully 100 percent of the operating budget of the Russian army—the largest standing army in the world—came directly from the drunkenness of the Russian peasantry.[12]

A windfall for the state, the vodka monopoly was a disaster for Russian society—not only shackling the peasantry to the bottle, but spawning a system of entrenched corruption.

The village *kabak* became the primary interface between the peasant and a predatory state, and the tavern-keeper was its agent. Today, we romanticize the barkeep as a man with a gentle smile and a patient ear, who'd kindly serve you a drink and listen to your problems. But this wasn't *Cheers*, and the tavern-keeper wasn't your friend. In Russian, he was known as a "kisser" (*tselovalnik*), because he swore an oath to the tsar by kissing an Orthodox cross.

The tavern-keeper was a shyster. By his oath, he could never refuse even a habitual drunkard, lest the tsar's revenue be diminished. He'd take a bucket (*vedro*) of standard 40 percent vodka and water it down to four buckets of 10 percent strength, then sell it for the standard price, pocketing the rest. He'd undermeasure your shots and shortchange you, and while you argued, his pickpockets would quietly rob you from behind. The village tavern sucked every kopeck out of your tunic pocket.

And if you're still craving more, the tavern-keeper would take your tunic too, before callously throwing you, naked, out into the snowy night. Peasants pawned their clothes, their wagon wheels, and their livestock, or even drank on IOUs promising the tavern-keeper their crops come fall—including the grains they needed to feed their families for the next year. Whether the family starved was not the tavern-keeper's concern.[13]

Foreign visitors to the Russian Empire often remarked on the operation of this exploitative *kabak* system. Whether in the sixteenth century or the twentieth century, what is most striking is the continuity in the following descriptions.

"In every great towne of his Realme he hath a *Caback* or drinking house, where is sold *aquavitæ* (which they cal *Russewine*) *mead, beere, &c.*," wrote English ambassador Giles Fletcher the Elder, who was dispatched to Russia by Queen Elizabeth I in 1588:

> Out of these hee receiveth rent that amounteth to a great summe of money. Some yeeld 800, some 900, some a 1000 some 2000 or 3000. rubbels a yere. Wherein besides the base, and dishononourable means to encrease his treasurie, many foule faultes are committed. The poore labouring man, and artificer, manie times spendeth all from his wife and children. Some use to lay in twentie, thirtie, fourtie rubbels, or more into the *Caback*, and vowe themselves to the pot, till all that be spent. And this (as he will say) for the honour of *Hospodare*, or the Emperour. You shall have manie there that have drunk all away to the verie skinne, and so walk naked (whom they call *Naga*.) While they are in the *Caback*, none may call them foorth whatsoever cause there be, because he hindereth the Emperours revenue.[14]

A full half-century later, German ambassador Adam Olearius painted a strikingly similar picture of the taverns, which produced for the state "an extraordinary amount of money, since the Russians know no restraint in drinking vodka." Based upon his tours of the Russian Empire in the 1640s, Olearius wrote,

> The common people would bring all their earnings into the tavern and sit there until, having emptied their purses, they gave away their clothing, and even their nightshirts, to the keeper, and then went home as naked as they had come into the world. When, in 1643, I stopped at the Lübeck house in Novgorod, I saw such besotted and naked brethren come out of the nearby tavern, some bareheaded, some barefooted, and others only in their nightshirts. One of them had drunk away his cloak and emerged from the tavern in his nightshirt; when he met a friend who was on his way to the same tavern, he went in again. Several hours later he came out without his nightshirt, wearing only a pair of under-drawers. I had him called to

ask what had become of his nightshirt, who had stolen it? He answered with the customary "Fuck your mother," that it was the tavern keeper, and that the drawers might as well go where the cloak and nightshirt had gone. With that, he returned to the tavern, and later came out entirely naked. Taking a handful of dog fennel that grew near the tavern, he held it over his private parts, and went home singing gaily.[15]

While a night at the tavern could end happy and naked, cursing out a confused foreigner, far more often it ended tragically. When the Englishman Robert Ker Porter toured the Russian Empire in 1805, he described the tragic human toll of the exploitative liquor revenue machine:

> During the chilling blasts of winter, it is then that we see the intoxicated native stagger forth from some open door, reel from side to side, and meet that fate which in the course of one season freezes thousands to death. . . . After spending perhaps his last copeck in a dirty, hot *kaback* or public house, he is thrust out by the keeper as an object no longer worthy of his attention. Away the impetus carries him, till he is brought up by the opposite wall. Heedless of any injury he may have sustained by the shock, he rapidly pursues the weight of his head, by the assistance of his treacherous heels, howling discordant sounds from some incoherent Russian song; a religious fit will frequently interrupt his harmony, when crossing himself several times, and as often muttering his *gospodi pomilui*, "Lord have mercy upon us!," he reels forward . . . and then he tears at the air again with his loud and national ditties: staggering and stumbling till his foot slips, and that earth receives him, whence a thousand chances are, that he will never again arise. He lies just as he fell; and sings himself gradually to that sleep from which he awakes no more.[16]

For generations then, this was the harsh reality of Imperial Russia, where the *kabak* was the conduit through which the Russian state got Russian society addicted, profited handsomely from their misery, and then cast them off into the snowy darkness.

Corruption even infected the judicial system by way of the tavern. Small-claims litigants curried favor with the village judge by treating him to drinks. In fact, many taverns kept an open tab for the judge for just such a purpose: to be paid by the plaintiff or the defendant—sometimes both. At the *kabak*, you could find "witnesses" willing to testify to anything for vodka. "Bribing witnesses or getting them drunk takes place everywhere, and [peasants] are so used to this that it is considered natural," claimed one nineteenth-century account.[17]

"In the tavern, the tavern-keeper is dictator," Russian critics said at the time of the temperance revolt. "He knows only one authority—the authority of the tax farmer; one law, that of the tax farmer; one goal, to rob the people, to rob and rob again, using any method available."[18]

Indeed, the unscrupulous tavern-keeper only answered to the corrupt vodka tax farmer—or *otkupshchik*—who was, if anything, even more conniving. Every four years, these well-heeled parasites gathered in the capital of St. Petersburg to bid at auction for the exclusive right to administer the liquor trade in a given district for the next four-year term (*otkup*). Farming out tax collection was common practice in the Roman Empire and across medieval Europe: the state received a reliable stream of revenue without a burdensome government bureaucracy. However, the state also had to look the other way as the tax farmer lived with impunity in his new fiefdom of liquor.[19] "What is really sold at the tax farm auctions is an exemption from the rules," openly admitted Vasily Kokorev, Russia's most infamous *otkupshchik*.[20]

Even today, the roots of Russia's systemic corruption can be traced back to the liquor traffic administration, which blurred the distinction between public revenues and private profits. "Every person having any degree of influence receives regular cash payments from the tax farmers, according to their influence," explained one contemporary, "as well as a monthly gift of vodka."[21] Governors, mayors, police chiefs, commissioners, judges, lawyers, assessors, administrators—all were on the take, often in amounts that far exceeded their official salaries. Even the squeaky-clean governor of Kazan, Stepan Strekalov (like Tsar Nicholas I's trusted adjutant general Yegor Tolstoy) steadfastly and absolutely did not take bribes. "Though," as one contemporary explained, "he did receive an annual tribute from the tax farmers. For several tens of thousands of rubles, Strekalov allowed the tax farmers . . . to rob local households at their pleasure."[22] Once such agreements had been made with the unscrupulous tax farmers, the state was not only forbidden from prosecuting their abuses, it was actually obligated to protect these lawbreakers. As a scathing 1858 exposé in Aleksandr Herzen's liberal *Kolokol* magazine concluded, by "enabling the tax farmer, the government is consciously robbing the people—dividing up the spoils with the tax farmers and others who have participated in the crime."[23]

A royal commission in the 1850s exposed graft and bribery even at the highest levels of the imperial government, finding that forty-three of the tsar's forty-five governors were on the take. "To live in the middle of such conscious corruption was horrible, yet to remove it was impossible." Tsar Nicholas quietly lamented that he was the only honest man in Russia. "In despair, the czar threw the report of the commission into the fire."[24]

This, then, was the reality of the Russian liquor traffic on the eve of the great temperance rebellion.[25]

Importing Subversion

The roots of this temperance subversion can be traced half a world away to the antebellum United States and civic associations like the American Temperance Society (ATS—see Chapter 11), which features prominently in Alexis de Tocqueville's *Democracy in America* (1835).[26] Founded in 1826, the ATS was a self-help group: community members concerned about drunkenness banded together into local lodges and signed a "teetotal" pledge to abstain from overindulgence in spiritous liquors (fermented ales, ciders, beers, and wines were hardly seen as dangerous), leading to a rapid reduction in drunkenness. By the mid-1830s, one out of every five free Americans were ATS members.[27] But it wasn't just French intellectuals like Tocqueville who told of the successes of American grassroots organizations—seafaring merchants, abolitionists, and missionaries spread word of ATS triumphs across the British Isles, Scandinavia, and continental Europe (Chapters 3–5), leaving scores of temperance lodges in their wake.[28]

If vodka was the means of subjugation to the imperial autocracy, then it should not be surprising that temperance—as the means of political resistance—would enter Russia through its recently conquered European subjects. Catholic Poland and Lithuania were absorbed into Moscow's predominantly Orthodox empire in 1795, and Lutheran Finland soon thereafter. These populations—and their ecumenical and cultural links to Europe—were looked upon warily by the Orthodox tsars as dangerous conduits of enlightenment liberalism, and later socialism. Yet temperance was perhaps the more immediate threat to the empire.[29]

The first Russian article reporting on the successes of the American Temperance Society—as disseminated widely throughout Europe by American temperance emissary Robert Baird (Chapter 11)—appeared in Riga (now the capital of Latvia) in 1836. The imperial authorities were quickly flooded with petitions to establish ATS-inspired temperance lodges. Rather than encourage popular sobriety, the tsarist authorities roundly banned all temperance organizations, "lest they should be mistaken for separate religious sects."[30] Yet temperance activism persisted within the non-Russian Catholic and Lutheran communities.

By 1858, the Catholic clergy of Poland and Lithuania—with the blessing of Pope Pius IX—established their own Brotherhood of Sobriety, which took ATS lodges and temperance pledges against hard liquor, and mixed in Catholic teachings of the fraternal Independent Order of Rechabites and the Father Mathew temperance societies of Ireland. It was well known that the iconic Irish Catholic leader Father Mathew fought not only against drunkenness, but against imperial domination at the hands of the English and their Anglican Church (Chapter 5). The parallel with the struggles of Catholic Poles and Lithuanians against the Orthodox Russian Empire was clear.[31]

Within a year, fully three-quarters of the population of the imperial provinces of Grodno, Kaunas, and Vilnius (present-day Lithuania) had taken the pledge to boycott vodka. Liquor sales plummeted—down 33 percent in Grodno, 40 percent in Vilnius, and 70 percent in Kaunas—threatening ruin for the vodka tax farmers and the treasury. Reports from the region describe greater health, happiness, and prosperity. Taverns emptied. Crime went down. With less grain going to vodka distilleries, food prices became more affordable.[32]

This could not be allowed to continue. If the state were to encourage the health and sobriety of its citizens, it would face immediate bankruptcy. The lesson was clear.

Eventually, the state stepped in to deal with the temperance crisis, bailing out the tax farmers and administering the vodka trade directly. The finance ministry demanded that the Catholics renounce their temperance heresy and preach as the Orthodox did: that vodka was a "harmless" and even "necessary" indulgence. The ministry of internal affairs refused to go that far, but they did confiscate abstinence pledges and forbade the publishing of temperance materials.[33]

By 1859, temperance societies had spread not only throughout the Baltic and Polish provinces, but to thirty-two provinces of the Russian heartland around Moscow and the Volga. Undoubtedly this was fueled in part by the new tax-farm period beginning January 1, 1859, which resulted in sharp increases in the retail price of vodka for the peasants to pay.[34] Still, in migrating from the empire's Catholic and Protestant periphery to Russia's Orthodox core, the temperance movement lost much of its anticolonial character. Orthodox Christianity had long been the dominant religion in Russia, but since Peter the Great's ecclesiastical reforms in 1721, the Holy Synod was made answerable to tsarist authority—and even shared a building with the State Senate—effectively making the Church into the religious wing of the Russian government.[35] Its leaders and priests could hardly be expected to oppose the interests of the state. "If the Church would direct her maternal solicitude to the peasant's drinking," wrote D. MacKenzie Wallace, "she might exercise a beneficial influence on his material and moral welfare. Unfortunately she has a great deal too much inherent immobility to do anything of the kind."[36]

The boycott movement was largely peaceful, with local priests occasionally officiating the oath taking, though such outside support for the peasants against the state and its agents—the local vodka tax farmer and police—was erratic and unreliable.[37] Confronted with the outbreak of sobriety, tax farmers pressured the local police and prosecutors to investigate this "conspiracy not to drink tax farm vodka." According to one report, the tax farmer of Balashov district—backed by the police chief—directly confronted impudent serfs who refused to drink his vodka.

"This vodka is ruining us!" one peasant told the tax farmer. "It is a joke—8 rubles a bucket [*vedro*]! How many carts of grain would you need to buy a single bucket?"

"In any case, the vodka is terrible," replied another. "It's worse than river water."

"How dare you say that!" raged the tax farmer, who then roundly beat the peasant "in the customary manner," as they say. With help of the local police, the tax farmer

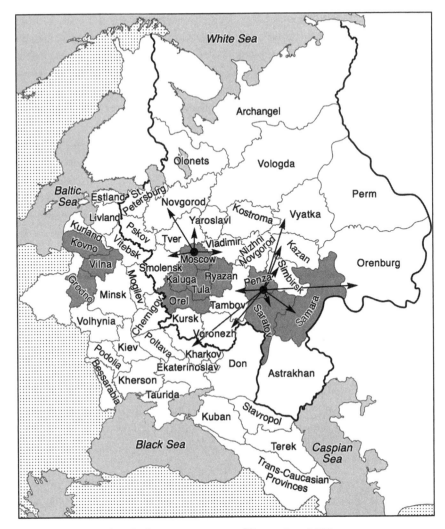

Figure 2.1 Geography of sobriety movement and liquor riots, 1859.
Source: Adapted from David Christian, *Living Water*, frontispiece.

unsuccessfully tried to hush-up the entire incident with offers of free vodka for the villagers. "But to their credit," the report notes, "not one of them would touch it."[38]

As the state hardened its resolve, confrontations became more frequent and more violent. Rioters smashed and looted taverns, wounding tavern-keepers, who were often saved only by the intervention of the police or troops stationed nearby. This is what ultimately prompted Tsar Nicholas I to call in the army and send General Yegor Tolstoy to bring order to the district and suppress the temperance revolt. In all, over 780 temperance "instigators" were tried before military tribunals, whipped, beaten, and exiled to Siberia.

In an autocratic empire where popular protest was the only political outlet for lower-class discontent, the temperance rebellion was a flashing-red warning light that the medieval tax-farm system was woefully outdated. The corruption and discontent it bred were becoming very real threats to the political stability of the empire itself.[39]

"The government cannot and must not lose sight of the effects of this system on the moral and economic welfare of the people," explained a report to the State Council in 1860. "Everyone knows that tax farming ruins and corrupts the people [nullifying] all efforts to introduce honesty and justice to the administration; and slowly leads the government into the painful situation of having not only to cover up the flagrant breaches of the law engendered by the system without which it cannot operate, but even to resist the people's own impulses to moral improvement through abstention. In this way, the government itself offers a model of disrespect for the law, support for abuse and the spreading of vice."[40]

Upon reading the report—and still smarting from Russia's embarrassing loss in the Crimean War—in 1861 Tsar Alexander II ("the Great") agreed to abolish the tax-farm system at the same time as his other great reform: the abolition of serfdom. From 1863 until the introduction of a state retail monopoly in 1895, the vodka trade would be regulated through a system of excise taxes. Still, the more things changed, the more they stayed the same. More often than not, the corrupt tax farmer didn't simply disappear, but instead moved upstream into the distilling business, fulfilling government liquor contracts. The tavern-keepers still happily took everything the peasant had to pawn in exchange for watered-down vodka. And—if anything—the state relied even *more* on selling vodka to its people, and would continue to scuttle any attempt at temperance and social well-being.[41]

Russian and Soviet historians have subsequently debated the "real" reasons behind these curious temperance rebellions. Were the peasants really protesting drunkenness and immorality? Or were they protesting high prices demanded by the tax farm administration? Or were they lashing out against the institution of serfdom itself? In reality, it is not an either/or situation: peasants had long been exploited by a corrupt liquor traffic, and by an entire state apparatus that profited handsomely from their misery. First in the imperial periphery, and later the Russian core, peasants found in temperance the means to oppose that alcoholic subjugation. Given the entrenched nature of the state's exploitative *kabak* system, perhaps we shouldn't be so surprised that peasant discontent boiled over into a temperance rebellion, and instead wonder what took so long for it to do so.

Finding the Real Tolstoy

This, then, was the political reality of Russian imperial domination and resistance for decades before the godmother of American temperance and suffragism—Frances

Willard of the Woman's Christian Temperance Union (WCTU, Chapter 13)—took up the issue of promoting sobriety in Russia. Admitting she knew little of empire of the tsars, in 1888 Willard reached out to famed journalist, explorer, and scholar of Russia, George Kennan, to inquire about temperance contacts there. Not to be confused with his twice-removed cousin of the same name (the writer, diplomat, and Cold War–era ambassador to Joseph Stalin's Soviet Union), George Kennan "the Elder" spent the 1860s through the 1880s traveling across Russia and Siberia, and had won international acclaim for his investigations into the inhumanity of the penal camps there.

His response was respectful to Willard, who was already recognized as among the foremost social reformers of her time. But he needed to explain that social activism in Russia would look much different than in the United States. "How are you going to get a temperance movement started in such a country?" Kennan replied,

> The Government derives a very large part of its revenue from an excise duty upon intoxicating liquor. If you attack its financial policy in this respect through the press, you are "warned" and if you continue your attacks your newspaper is suspended. The priests encourage drinking at marriages, christenings and all sorts of ecclesiastical ceremonies, and are often the first to set an example of drunkenness to their parishioners. If you call attention to this through the press, you are again warned because you are showing disrespect to the "Holy Orthodox Church" and are undermining the reverence of the peasants for the clergy. If you go into a peasant village and undertake to hold a temperance meeting, you are stopped by the police. If you talk with the peasants separately and try to get them to close or limit the dram shops by a communal decree, the liquor sellers bribe the police, trump up a charge of political "untrustworthiness" against you and declare that you are carrying on a secret revolutionary propaganda under the guise of temperance agitation. Eventually of course you prove your innocence, but you may lie six months or a year in prison while your case is being investigated, and your fate deters others from similar work. No matter in what direction you move, you are headed off by the Church or the State or both. All that remains for you to do is to write and circulate innocent temperance tracts among people who cannot read them, and to carefully avoid, even in doing this, everything likely to prejudice the interests of the horde of social parasites who live upon the peasants and derive profit in one way or another from the latter's weaknesses and vices.

Facing such overwhelming challenges, Kennan could only think of one temperance agitator across the vast expanse of Russia to suggest that Willard might contact: "Count Leo Nikolaievitch Tolstoy, Yasnaya Polyana, Government of Tula, Russia."[42]

Just the previous year, on the pages of *Century* magazine, Kennan had described his pilgrimage to meet the world-famous master of Russia's golden age of literature. Like his distant cousin Yegor (whom we've already met), Count Leo Tolstoy was born into a storied noble family in 1828. As a privileged aristocratic youth, he left the family estate at Yasnaya Polyana to cavort in nearby Tula, or party in the parlors of Moscow and St. Petersburg, where he began dabbling in writing.

After racking up heavy gambling debts, Leo joined the army in 1851, serving as an artillery officer in the disastrous Crimean War. The vivid military realism of his masterpiece *War and Peace* drew from his battlefield experiences in Crimea, and his "dissipated military life" of after-hours boozing, gambling, and frequenting prostitutes and brothels—as was expected among the officer class.[43] He was deeply moved by the inhumanity of war, since everyone was "too busy staggering about in smoke, squelching through wounded bodies, drunk with vodka, fear or courage."[44] He abandoned the military life soon thereafter.

With the emancipation of the serfs in 1861, Tolstoy returned to Yasnaya Polyana and founded schools for children of the peasants who still tilled the soil of the hereditary estate. Tolstoy lived and worked among the peasants rather than ruling over them. He married Sophia Andreevna Behrs and, with her unceasing editorial assistance, wrote scores of short stories, novellas, as well as the great novels *The Cossacks* (1863), *War and Peace* (1869), and *Anna Karenina* (1877), which won him international fame as perhaps the world's greatest writer. Russians joked that they had two tsars: Nicholas II and Leo Tolstoy.[45]

If anything, Tolstoy was the anti-tsar. He shunned his wealth, fame, aristocratic rank, and privilege for the simple but honest life of peasant farming. He wrote fewer works of fiction and more explorations into Christian ethics, pacifism, and brotherly love. These writings increasingly put Russia's "second tsar" at odds with its first one, to say nothing of confronting both the Russian imperial state and the Orthodox Church that supported it.

When George Kennan drew up to Count Tolstoy's provincial estate two hundred kilometers south of Moscow in 1888, he expected to find a well-kept gentleman, commensurate with his high birth and education. He was instead greeted by an imposing man in calfskin shoes and a coarse, homespun shirt. His iron gray hair parted, exposing a sun-weathered face, as though "molded with the fist and polished with a pickaxe." He was nevertheless eager to receive an American admirer who'd traveled so far.

"What books of mine have you read?" the count inquired quickly from his doorstep.

All of his great novels—Kennan stated—including *War and Peace, Anna Karenina,* and *The Cossacks.*

"Have you seen any of my later writings?"

No—unfortunately they'd only been released as the American had been off exploring Siberian prisons.

"Ah!" Count Tolstoy quickly replied, "then you don't know me at all. We will get acquainted."[46]

For much of the day, Kennan probed Tolstoy's pacifist gospel. Could violence ever be justified? Even as a matter of self-defense against evil? Kennan related the story of a woman—an accused revolutionary—he'd met during his investigations into the Siberian exile system, who'd been beaten bloody and forcibly stripped by a gang of police. What if it was his daughter? Would Tolstoy still refuse to fight to defend her honor against an officer acting unjustly?

Such vengeance, Tolstoy explained, would only make a bad situation worse by creating more victims. "In the hearts of perhaps a score of people you rouse the anti-Christian and anti-social emotions of hatred and revenge, and thus sow and broadcast the seeds of further strife. . . . It does not seem to me, Mr. Kennan, that this is way to bring about the reign of peace and good-will on earth."[47] The American was satisfied.

If violence begets evil, and the state is defined as having a monopoly on violence, then Tolstoy's philosophy required passive resistance to a state that demands people's subservience. "Patriotism is slavery," Tolstoy wrote—in a pamphlet banned

Figure 2.2 (Left to right) Varvara Feokritova, Leo Tolstoy dictates an article to his daughter, Alexandra Lvovna Tolstaya (right), and their typist Varvara Feokritova at their Yasnaya Polyana estate, September 1, 1909.
Source: Alamy Stock Photographs, Image ID: B9P824, This image was long used in advertisements for Remington's Standard Model 10 typewriter. See: *Typewriter Topics: The International Office Equipment Magazine* 31, no. 8 (August 1911): 233.

by imperial censors for obvious reasons—as it required "the abdication of human dignity, reason, and conscience; and a slavish enthrallment to those in power."[48] If violent resistance only spread misery, then passive resistance to government was the only answer.

"Mine is the true revolutionary method," Tolstoy told Kennan. "If the people of the empire refuse, as I believe they should refuse, to render military service,—if they decline to pay taxes to support that instrument of violence, an army,—the present system of government cannot stand. The proper way to resist evil is to absolutely refuse to do evil either for one's self or for others."[49] Such subversive teachings surely put him at odds with the tsarist authorities.

Still, it was Tolstoy's civic religion that most interested the American visitor.[50] "He rejects the whole doctrinal framework of the Christian scheme of redemption, including original sin, atonement, the triune personality of God, and the divinity of Christ, and has very little faith in the immortality of the soul," Kennan explained. "If he refers frequently to the teachings of Christ, and accepts Christ's precepts as the rules which should govern human conduct, it is not because he believes Christ was God, but because he regards those precepts as a formal embodiment of the highest and noblest philosophy of life, and as a revelation, in a certain sense, of the Divine will and character."[51] You certainly did not need an organized church to lead a noble, compassionate life.

"Of all the godless ideas and words there is none more godless than that of a Church," Tolstoy wrote in another essay that never made it past the censors. "There is no idea which has produced more evil none more inimical to Christ's teaching, than the idea of a Church."[52] Indeed, when examining the history of sanctimonious hatreds and centuries of religious wars, the "Church-fraud," as he often called it, did more bad than good.

But worst of all was when the state cloaked itself in the mantle of the church to legitimize its actions. "The sanctification of political power by Christianity is blasphemy; it is the negation of Christianity," Tolstoy explained. "In truth, the words a 'Christian State' resemble the words 'hot ice.' The thing is either not a State using violence, or it is not Christian."[53] Having long ago subsumed the Orthodox Church in service to the state, such incendiary criticisms were directed squarely against the tsarist autocracy itself.

Ironically, Kennan needn't have traveled halfway around the world to probe the origins of Tolstoy's philosophy. The roots of Tolstoyanism stretch back to the United States, with the temperate, pacifist, abolitionist Quakers (Chapter 9) and their equally temperate, pacifist, abolitionist fellow traveler, William Lloyd Garrison (Chapters 11–12). In 1884 Tolstoy published his treatise *What I Believe*, in which he suggests that Jesus's Sermon on the Mount—to turn the other cheek and love thy enemies—amounts to a clear, core commandment: "Never resist evil by force, never return violence for violence."[54]

In response, Tolstoy received letters and books from the Quakers of Philadelphia. As Tolstoy explained in his in-depth philosophical exploration, *The Kingdom of God Is within You* (1894), "Further acquaintance with the labours of the Quakers and their works showed me not only that the impossibility of reconciling Christianity with force and war had been recognized long, long ago, but that . . . nothing has contributed so much to the obscuring of Christian truth in the eyes of the heathen [Native Americans, Chapter 9], and has hindered so much the diffusion of Christianity throughout the world, as the disregard of this command by men calling themselves Christians."[55]

"In addition to what I learned from the Quakers," Tolstoy continued, "I received about the same time, also from America" (and also about the time of Kennan's visit), a letter from the son of American abolitionist William Lloyd Garrison (Chapters 11–12). The younger Garrison found in Tolstoy's pacifism and opposition to the state as an instrument of violence echoes of his father's conclusions from fifty years earlier—in Tolstoy's words: "that the establishment of universal peace can only be founded on the open profession of the doctrine of non-resistance to evil by violence (Matthew v. 39), in its full significance, as understood by the Quakers, with whom Garrison happened to be on friendly relations."[56]

From such foundations, Tolstoy lobbed rhetorical broadsides against the rank hypocrisy of a government based on the monopolization of violence, and the nominally "Christian" churches that support it: "In the same way they pretend to support temperance societies, while they are living principally on the drunkenness of the people, and pretend to encourage education when their whole strength is based on ignorance; and to support constitutional freedom, when their strength rests on the absence of freedom; and to be anxious for the improvement of the condition of the working classes, when their very existence depends on their oppression; and to support Christianity, when Christianity destroys all government."[57]

Tolstoy's revolutionary interest in temperance flowed quite naturally from this philosophical spring. "If men were to stop drinking, the government would lose its chief source of revenue," patriotic drinkers would say, as if to justify their own enslavement to the bottle and the system.[58] Not only did vodka impoverish and morally debauch the peasantry, the liquor traffic—whether by excise taxation or state monopoly—was the financial pillar of the state itself, which had to be resisted.

"Let us not deceive ourselves: all that [the impoverished worker] makes and devises, he makes and devises for the purposes of the government or of the capitalist and the rich people," wrote Tolstoy—in unabashedly Marxist terms—in his 1886 political treatise, *What Is to Be Done?* "The most cunning of his inventions are directly aimed either at injuring the people—as with cannon, torpedoes, solitary confinement cells, apparatus for the spirit monopoly, telegraphs, and so forth, or . . . for things by which people can be corrupted and induced to part with the last of their money—that is, their last labour—such as, first of all vodka, spirits, beer, opium, and tobacco."[59] For Tolstoy, the drunkenness he saw among the peasants of

Tula was clearly a consequence of the exploitative system of capitalist subjugation to the state.

It may be hard to believe, but visitors to Yasnaya Polyana report that Tolstoy actually had a jolly temperament and an infectious laugh beneath that gruff exterior. More surprising—given his conversion from a heavy-drinking aristocratic playboy in his youth to a temperate, vegetarian ascetic in his older years—Tolstoy maintained a playful toleration for even the worst drunks in his midst.[60] At Yasnaya Polyana, a light wine was always offered to his visiting guests, which he'd occasionally mix with water to chase his simple vegetarian meals. He'd drink watered-down rum for a cold or indigestion.[61] None of this relaxed attitude rendered Tolstoy a hypocrite: like most temperance advocates of the day, the focus of Tolstoy's enmity was not the drink or the drinker, but the system of trafficking liquor that enriched the state and subjugated society.

Though Tolstoy had long decried drunkenness in his writings, his temperance activism began in earnest around 1887—about the time of George Kennan's visit. It was at that time that his friend Dr. Piotr Alekseev returned from a tour of the United States and related to Tolstoy the great successes of temperance organizations there. Tolstoy soon took a teetotal pledge and enlisted local peasants into a sobriety society—the Union Against Drunkenness—on his Yasnaya Polyana estate.[62] The following year, his daughter reported the union claimed 350 members, plus an additional 500 hoping to join. "As far as I know nothing has been printed, because temperance societies are forbidden."[63] Were it not for Tolstoy's international acclaim, the authorities would have quickly scuttled such brazen temperance sedition.

Still, Tolstoy was an author rather than an organizer, so his greater contributions to temperance are to be found in his writings. His temperance essays—which circulated widely internationally, and underground within the empire—including "The First Distiller," "Serving God or Mammon," and "Why Do Men Stupefy Themselves?" are cloaked in the language of sin and redemption, suggesting that drunkenness was a private affair—not for pleasure, but the means by which a drunkard dulls the demands of conscience.[64] Indeed, in inaugurating his Union Against Drunkenness, Tolstoy argued that intoxication was the cardinal sin, since it enabled all sin: "the intoxicated person will not struggle with idleness, nor with lust, nor with fornication, nor with the love of power. And so in order to struggle with the other sins, a man must first of all free himself from the sin of intoxication."[65]

Some of his most passionate pleas for sobriety are to be found not in his public writings, but in his private letters to two of his sons—Andrei and Mikhail—who'd become violent alcoholics, destined for ruin. "God has given man an immortal soul and for the guidance of this soul—reason. And now man has thought up a means to stifle his reason so that his soul is left without guidance," Tolstoy wrote to one of his inebriate sons in 1895. To return to the path of happiness, he wrote Andrei, "the main thing necessary is for you to stop drinking vodka, and *in order to stop drinking it—to stop associating with people who drink it.*"[66]

Despite his polemical pleas to persuade his individual readers, Tolstoy argued resolutely that drinking was less an individual moral failing and more a social problem
of public concern.[67] "If a man is given to drink, and I tell him that he himself can
leave off drinking and that he must do so, there is a hope that he will listen to me,"
Tolstoy explained, "but if I tell him that his drunkenness is a complicated and difficult problem which we learned men are trying to solve at our meetings, then in all
probability he will, while awaiting the solution of this problem, continue to drink."[68]

For the remainder of his life, Tolstoy stepped up his ardent criticism of both the
Russian state and church. Ever since both serfdom and the vodka tax farm had been
abolished in the 1860s, Russia sold vodka through a free-market system. The excise
taxes still fattened the state's coffers. But in 1895 Tsar Nicholas II and his powerful
finance minister, Sergei Witte, inaugurated a new royal vodka monopoly "directed
first of all toward increasing popular sobriety, and only then can it concern itself
with the treasury."[69]

Perhaps the state was finally taking Tolstoy's message to heart.

What's more, with the blessing of the Orthodox Church, Witte established the
first officially sanctioned, nationwide temperance organization: the Guardianship
for Public Sobriety (*Popochitel'stvo o Narodnoi Trezvosti*). As a creature of the autocracy, the guardianship was the furthest thing from a grassroots civic organization.
Officially, it was run by the imperial Ministry of Finance. Perhaps not surprisingly,
it never promoted abstinence from drinking, only "moderation," lest the empire's
principal revenue stream should dry up.[70]

Thinking his temperance creation would please Russia's "second tsar," in 1896
Witte set off to Yasnaya Polyana to get Tolstoy's blessing. Count Tolstoy refused
even to meet with Witte, who was soon to become prime minister. "The chief evil
from which mankind suffers and the disorders of life come from the activities of
the government. One of the striking illustrations is that the government not only
permits but encourages the manufacture and distribution of the poisonous evil of
liquor, from the sale of which comes one-third of the budget," Tolstoy resolutely
wrote. "In my opinion, if the government really was making every effort for the good
of the people, then the first step should be the complete prohibition of the poison
which destroys both the physical and spiritual well-being of millions of people. . . .
Temperance societies established by a government that is not ashamed that it itself
sells the poison ruining the people through its own officials seem to me to be either hypocritical, silly, or misguided—or perhaps all three—something with which
I can no way sympathize."[71]

By the turn of the century, allusions to Russia's "drunken budget" became a commonplace critique of conservative, liberal, socialist, and radical critics of the tsarist
empire.[72] Time and again, Tolstoy explained that the tension between the people's
progress and well-being on the one hand, and the Russian church and state on the
other, could not continue. "That is why it is impossible to maintain this form of
government, and the orthodoxy that is attached to it, except by violence," as Tolstoy

wrote to Tsar Nicholas himself.[73] For such blasphemy, in 1901, the Holy Synod finally excommunicated Tolstoy.[74] His anarchist-temperance criticisms against the autocracy continued unabated until his death in 1910.[75]

Communism's Common Cause

Tolstoyanism was hardly the only revolutionary ideology in late tsarist Russia that preached both temperance and the demise of the state. Indeed, the same illegal printing presses that secretly circulated Tolstoy's banned works also printed the most incendiary agitation from Russia's restive Bolshevik movement, which sought the creation of a socialist revolution by any means necessary, including violence and bloodshed. Though they scoffed at his nonviolent pacifism and dedication to religion, underground communists actually found great inspiration in Tolstoy. "The criticism to which Tolstoy has submitted the existing order is radical; it knows no limits, no retrospective glances, no compromises," wrote Polish Marxist theorist Rosa Luxemburg. "The ultimate destruction of private property and the state, universal obligation to work, full economic and social equality, a complete abolition of militarism, brotherhood of nations, universal peace and equality of everything that bears the human image—this is the idea which Tolstoy has been tirelessly preaching with the stubbornness of a great and vehement prophet."[76] One Marxist revolutionary in particular read Tolstoy's works with great interest—Vladimir Lenin.[77]

Vladimir Ilyitch Ulyanov was only seventeen years old when his older brother, Aleksandr, was arrested in St. Petersburg in 1887 with a group of revolutionary socialists. The tsarist secret police had infiltrated their terrorist cell group and foiled their plot to assassinate Tsar Alexander III. The elder Ulyanov was the group's chief ideologue and bomb-maker. Aleksandr Ulyanov was just twenty-one when he was sentenced to hang at the gallows. When his stockpile of revolutionary literature—including writings by Leo Tolstoy, Nikolai Chernyshevsky, and Karl Marx—fell to his younger brother Vladimir, he read them voraciously, hardening his resolve to avenge his brother's martyrdom at the hands of a corrupt autocracy.[78]

Vladimir was particularly taken with the works of German philosophers Karl Marx and Friedrich Engels, and even translated their *Communist Manifesto* into Russian. Marxism was—and is—a critique of the industrial capitalist system, in which the wealthy ruling class lives at the expense of the impoverished workers (Chapter 3). When the downtrodden proletariat masses realize that the wealthy bourgeoisie is the source of their oppression, they will rise up against such injustice in a great proletarian revolution and institute a system of socialism, free of oppression at the hands of the rich. The state was just a "committee for managing the common affairs of the whole bourgeoisie" and would wither away following the revolution. Religion was "the opium of the people," meant to blind the proletariat to their own subjugation.[79]

Marx never wrote about Russia, which was a feudal, preindustrial backwater on the periphery of capitalist Europe. Still, his critiques resonated widely in a country where the gulf between the powerful aristocracy and the impoverished workers and peasants grew daily. Moderates sought to enlighten and raise up the underclass, while radicals like the brothers Ulyanov sought to make the revolution happen by any means necessary: bombs and bullets, assassination, subversion, and destabilization.

His fiery Marxist publications eventually landed Vladimir Ulyanov in prison—and then Siberia—on charges of sedition. By 1900 Ulyanov—now going by the *nom de guerre* Lenin—moved to the safer environs of Western Europe to continue his revolutionary agitation. In Europe or Russia, Lenin occasionally drank wine or beer, but never to excess. Drinking vodka was out of the question on philosophical grounds: vodka not only represented enslavement to the capitalist state, but clear-eyed sobriety would be necessary for the impending revolution.[80]

The Bolsheviks had an uneasy relationship with Tolstoy. On the one hand, they cheered as he laid bare the deep corruption of the bourgeois tsarist state and the moral bankruptcy of the Orthodox Church. On the other, they could not stomach his rejection of the state in any form, or his gospel of nonviolence. While in European exile, Lenin frequently lectured on Tolstoyanism.[81] Between 1908 and 1911 he wrote seven articles on Tolstoy, even going so far as to attribute the failure of the abortive Revolution of 1905—when labor strikes, peasant insurrection, and military mutinies amid the disastrous war with Japan only subsided with the promise of liberalization and constitutional reform—to the influence of Tolstoyan nonviolence.[82]

Still, when it came to pointing out how the capitalist tsarist autocracy leeched off the drunken society, Lenin picked up right where Tolstoy left off. An entire section of his *Development of Capitalism in Russia* espoused how distilling empowered the gentry vodka manufacturers at the expense of the peasantry. As a revolutionary prohibitionist, Lenin repeatedly hammered on the inappropriateness of the state liquor monopoly as the principal mechanism "of that organized robbery, that systematic, unconscionable plunder of national property by a handful of *pomeshchiki* (landowners), bureaucrats, and all sorts of parasites, plunder which is called the 'state economy of Russia.'"[83]

When the tsar's finance minister, Sergei Witte, resurrected the imperial vodka monopoly, Lenin predicted—correctly, as it turns out—that it would only enrich the aristocracy distillers and the state as the monopoly retailer, while "dooming millions of peasants and workers to permanent bondage."[84]

Lenin saw through Witte's hollow promise that government monopolization of the liquor traffic was the only way to rein in both corruption and drunkenness. "Instead of less drunkenness, we have more illicit trading in spirits, augmented police incomes from this trading, the opening of liquor shops over the protests of the population, which is petitioning against their being opened, and increased

Figure 2.3 Vladimir Lenin in his Kremlin apartment talking to the American journalist L. Ayre, February 21, 1920.
Source: Visual RIA-Novosti, Sputnik Images.

drunkenness in the streets," Lenin wrote in 1901. "But above all, what a new and gigantic field is opened for official arbitrariness, tyranny, favor-currying and embezzlement.... It is the invasion of a locust-swarm of officials, boot-licking, intriguing, plundering ... nothing but an attempt to cloak in legal forms the striving to grab the fattest possible slices of the state pie, a desire which is so prevalent in our provinces, and which, in view of the unrestrained power of the officials and the gagging of the people, threatens to intensify the reign of tyranny and plunder."[85]

It wasn't just Lenin who thought so. In the years before the revolution, Russian socialists of all stripes condemned the liquor trade, including firebrand theorist Leon Trotsky. "The propertied classes and the state bear responsibility for that culture which cannot exist without the constant lubricant of alcohol," the loquacious Trotsky argued. "But their historical guilt is still incomparably more terrible. Through fiscal means they turn alcohol, that physical, moral and social poison, into the main source of nourishment for the state. Vodka not only makes the people incompetent to manage their own destiny, it also covers the expenditures of the privileged. What a real devil's system!"[86]

Tsar Nicholas Dries Out

Marxist broadsides against autocratic corruption—and the vodka monopoly as the foremost specimen of the autocracy's "predatory economy"—endured to the end of the empire itself.[87] Indeed, by the 1910s, opposition to the tsar's drunken budget came not just from Tolstoyans and Bolsheviks, but critics from across the political spectrum, and from within the royal palace itself. "It is unbefitting for a Tsar to deal in vodka and make drunkards out of honest people," claimed none other than Grigory Rasputin—the hedonistic Siberian mystic who had won favor with the royal family. "The time has come to lock up the Tsar's saloons."[88]

But it wasn't Tolstoy, or Lenin, or even the mad monk Rasputin who effected a change of heart among the only decision-maker who truly mattered: Tsar Nicholas II. More likely, it was the influence of his uncles, cousins and military advisers.

Before ascending to the throne in 1894 at the age of twenty-six, Tsarevich Nicholas Aleksandrovich Romanov was a heavy drinker. As a teen, Nicholas would drink so much with the men in his elite Hussar regiment that the officers all "stripped naked and ran out into the streets of Tsarskoe Selo, which are usually deserted at night. They crouched on their hands and knees, raised their drunken heads to the sky and began to howl loudly." This was such a frequent occurrence that the commissariat waiter knew to bring a tub of vodka or champagne onto the porch in order to coax the drunken werewolves back into the barracks.[89] "No one could fail to notice," one contemporary noted, "that Nicholas Alexandrovich's body was being poisoned by alcohol, and his face was becoming yellow, his eyes glistened unhealthily, and bags were beginning to form beneath his eyes, as is customary with alcoholics."[90]

Upon ascending to the throne, the young tsar's favorite uncles—the grand dukes Sergei Aleksandrovich, Alexei Aleksandrovich, Nikolai Nikolaevich, and Konstantin Konstantinovich Romanov—all impressed upon him the need to put away the drunken debauchery and lead by sober example. Sergei Aleksandrovich Romanov was the powerful governor general of Moscow and held figurehead positions within the Guardianship for Public Sobriety, in addition to funding independent clinics to treat alcoholics.

The real turning point came with the disastrous war against Japan (1904–1905) and the resulting Revolution of 1905 that came close to toppling the empire itself. As part of its expanding designs in Asia, imperial Japan attacked the Russian outpost at Port Arthur on the Korean Peninsula, sinking Russia's small Pacific Fleet. After blockading the port, the Japanese battled some 250 miles inland against any reinforcements that were slow to arrive across the one-track Trans-Siberian Railroad. The decisive Battle of Mukden—one of the largest military conflicts in human history to that point, with over a million combatants—saw a numerically far superior Russian Army utterly decimated by a smaller, more disciplined Japanese

Army. War correspondents reported on the Russian retreat, as tottering, "beastly-drunk soldiers lost their rifles, shouted song, and fell down and rolled in the dust. The bushes were filled with motionless bodies."[91] St. Petersburg newspapers reported how "the Japanese found several thousand Russian soldiers so dead drunk that they were able to bayonet them like so many pigs."[92]

The alcohol problem wasn't limited to the front. The rallying points where young peasant men were conscripted into military service at bayonet point often degenerated into drunken riots, in which vodka-fueled mobs smashed into local taverns and murdered recruitment officers.[93]

Faced with such drunken chaos, the young tsar turned to his notoriously inebriate uncle, Grand Duke Alexei Aleksandrovich Romanov, who was commander of the Russian Navy, despite spending "less time on the fleet than he did on drinking bouts and various love affairs."[94] He devised the most harebrained military scheme ever. They would send forty-five coal-powered ships from the Baltic Fleet three-quarters of the way around the globe—eighteen thousand miles past the southern tip of Africa and India—to battle the Japanese in the Pacific. In the Dogger Banks between Britain and Denmark, the drunken and hallucinating fleet opened fire on what they thought was the Japanese Navy come to engage them, but was only a few British fishing trawlers, sinking one ship and killing three English fishermen.

"In the United States, in France, and even in Germany, unsparing reprobation of a deed so unjustifiable was freely uttered, and the belief was confidently expressed that the only possible explanation was to be found in the undiscipline and probable drunken frenzy of the Russian naval officers," wrote one reporter of the incident, which pushed Russia to the brink of war with Britain.[95] Instead of having its fleet summarily sunk by the mighty British Navy, the Russian government apologized, paid indemnities to the British fishermen, and sailed on to the Pacific—where the fleet was summarily sunk instead in the Tsushima Straits by the waiting Japanese.[96] The embarrassing military disaster further stoked the flames of revolutionary discontent at home, forcing Tsar Nicholas to accede to demands for a constitutional monarchy and elected parliament. The humiliated Tsar Nicholas was also forced to sue for peace with the Japanese, resulting in the Treaty of Portsmouth, mediated by US president Theodore Roosevelt (Chapter 16), for which he won the Nobel Peace Prize.

With the destruction of his fleet in 1905, Grand Duke Alexei Aleksandrovich resigned in disgrace, spending the rest of his days drinking and cavorting in Paris. Grand Duke Sergei Aleksandrovich would not be as fortunate: amid the chaos of the 1905 revolution, he was on the receiving end of a revolutionary's nitroglycerine bomb, which blew the governor of Moscow to bits. Days later, his fingers were found on the roof of a nearby building.[97] The instability was hitting frighteningly close to home.

Even after negotiating the Peace Treaty of Portsmouth, the Roosevelt administration kept a wary eye on the revolutionary instability that roiled the streets of

St. Petersburg and Moscow. After discussing the government's efforts to suppress the disorder, American diplomatic cables noted, "It would be still more to the point if they could compel the people to give up the consumption of vodka, which demoralizes them and at the same time furnishes an enormous indirect revenue to the Government."[98]

Eventually, the revolutionary fervor subsided, at which time it was up to another uncle of the tsar—the Grand Duke Nikolai Nikolaevich Romanov (often called by the diminutive "Nikolasha" to distinguish him from the tsar of the same name)—to make sure it didn't happen again. As a dedicated and able commander, he abolished military vodka rations and forbade alcohol sales in and around military encampments. But it wasn't just the Russian high command that learned the harsh lessons of 1905; it was military experts across Europe and around the world who understood that alcohol in the ranks was as much a foe as the enemy on the battlefield. Even the tsar's cousin—Kaiser Wilhelm II of Germany—summarized this emerging "cult of military sobriety" by announcing in 1910 that victory in the next European war would go to the army that is most sober (Chapter 4).[99]

By 1913 it seems that Tsar Nicholas himself had been won over to the cause of temperance. On an extensive tour of his domain, he was moved by "the painful pictures of public distress, the desolation of homes, the dissipation of economies, the inevitable consequences of drunkenness."[100] In January 1914 Nicholas appointed a new finance minister, Peter Bark, with the charge of making the treasury no longer "dependent on the ruination of the spiritual and economic forces of the majority of My faithful subjects."[101] But as it turns out, this decision only hastened the empire's demise ... and his own.

With the outbreak of the Great War in June 1914, Nicholas adopted a partial prohibition to aid in mobilizing the peasant conscripts for war—so as to prevent the riotous and drunken disorder that accompanied the call-ups for the war against Japan a decade earlier.[102] It didn't help. For one, the impoverished workers and peasants complained of discrimination: the cheap vodka that was their solace was now gone, but the wealthy aristocrats could still buy wine in well-to-do restaurants, or tap into their well-appointed wine cellars. For another, conscripts still rioted and ransacked the boarded-up liquor stores at the mobilization points. Still, despite the disorder, Tsar Nicholas only received glowing congratulations for a speedy and orderly war mobilization.[103]

Wartime prohibition was both temporary and partial, applying only in districts where the army was being mobilized or where there was active fighting. Enacting a permanent and total prohibition not only imperiled the empire's finances, it would mean infuriating the powerful aristocracy, since many noble families—including many within the Romanov family itself—owed much of their wealth to their private distilleries, which churned out alcohol for the tsarist retail vodka monopoly.[104]

But everything changed suddenly on September 27, 1914. On the Lithuanian front west of Vilnius, the rapidly mobilized Russian Army pushed forward against the undermanned Germans, who were retreating in disarray. At the forefront of the charge was a twenty-two-year-old platoon commander, Prince Oleg Konstantinovich Romanov: cousin to the tsar, and son of the tsar's favorite uncle, Grand Duke Konstantin Konstantinovich Romanov. Charging against the retreating Germans on horseback, Prince Oleg was shot through the right hip, a wound that quickly became infected.

Oleg's ailing father, the Grand Duke Konstantin, was at a health spa in Germany when the war broke out. His entire retinue had been arrested and was being held as political prisoners. Only news of the prince's plight—aided by entreaties of the Russian royal family to their cousins in Germany—secured their release. But with all borders closed, the aging grand duke and his entourage had to cross the Eastern Front on foot. By the time Konstantin Konstantinovich reached the military hospital in Vilnius, it was too late. From his deathbed, Prince Oleg had proclaimed that his death would only bolster the war effort, by showing that the Imperial House of Romanov was unafraid to shed its own blood for the good of the nation.[105]

The following day—September 28, 1914—Tsar Nicholas II sent a telegram to the grieving Grand Duke Konstantin in Vilnius, announcing he'd decided to "abolish forever the government sale of vodka in Russia." Reprinted far and wide, his telegram had the force of an imperial edict, making Russia the first prohibition nation on earth. The slain Prince Oleg would be the only Romanov to die in battle in World War I.[106]

The prohibition decision would be a fateful one. Forcing the country to quit cold turkey certainly didn't enamor drinkers to their tsar, especially as Russian forces were being decimated at the front. More importantly, closing all the legal vodka shops immediately produced a massive, unregulated, underground liquor trade across Russia. Already in the last half of 1914 alone, the Ministry of Agriculture uncovered 1,825 illegal distilleries. By 1915, it was 5,707.[107] When generals in militarized zones near the front smashed up the padlocked liquor stores so that the conscripts wouldn't be tempted by the booze, the Russian aristocrats sent the bill for their lost wares to the state: you break it, you bought it.[108] If that weren't enough, many gentry distillers who owed taxes to the state suddenly found themselves without a means of paying their debts, further starving the treasury.[109]

Indeed, the loss of fully one-third of state revenue while entering the greatest military conflagration in world history put the treasury in quite a bind.[110] "What if we do lose eight hundred million rubles in revenue?" asked Premier Ivan Goremykin. "We shall print that much paper money; it's all the same to the people."[111] The hyperinflationary consequences were a primary reason for the dethroning of the tsar in the February Revolution of 1917, and the deposing of the Provisional Government of liberal-socialist Aleksandr Kerensky by Lenin and the Bolsheviks in October of that year.[112]

When the Bolsheviks seized power, they inherited mass desertion at the front, increasingly drunken chaos in Petrograd, and royalist and foreign enemies on all sides. While Lenin declared his intention to pull out of the war and nationalize land in the name of the peasantry, the only tsarist policies he maintained were prohibition and grain requisitioning. "The proletariat as a rising class does not need drunkenness that would deafen or provoke them," Lenin proclaimed. "They need only clarity, clarity, and again clarity. The communist upbringing of the working class requires the rooting out of all vestiges of the capitalist past, especially such a dangerous vestige as drunkenness."[113]

When it came to wielding the state as an instrument of violence, Vladimir Lenin went far beyond anything Leo Tolstoy—or even the American saloon-smasher Carrie Nation—could have imagined. To root out the "counterrevolutionary" threat of alcohol, bootleggers were to be shot on sight. Alcohol warehouses were blown up with dynamite. Those found harboring alcohol would be "arrested and given a trial before a merciless court."[114] The organization Lenin charged with enforcing his draconian dry decree, the Extraordinary Commission, or *CheKa*, would later become known as the Committee for State Security, or KGB.[115] "The very nearest future will be a period of a heroic struggle with alcohol," Trotsky warned. "If we don't stamp out alcoholism, then we will drink up socialism and drink up the October Revolution."[116]

Only through such extreme measures did the new "red" government grow, expand, and ultimately defeat the royalist "white" forces—in addition to foreign interventions—in a bloody, multisided civil war, which left Russia devastated and starving through famine. Even despite such hardships, Soviet prohibition suffered the same fate as prohibitions anywhere: bootlegging, corruption, and disrespect for law. With starvation widespread, illegal distillation was still consuming 491 million kilograms of grain annually, according to the Soviets' own statistics.[117]

As corresponding reports of drunkenness flooded in, comrades questioned the wisdom of continuing an obviously failed policy. "We should not follow the example of the capitalist countries and put vodka and other intoxicants on the market," Lenin fired back, "because, profitable though they are, they will lead us back to capitalism and not forward to communism."[118]

In March 1922 Lenin was in failing health at the young age of fifty-two—perhaps from two bullets that had been slowly rusting in his neck since a failed 1918 assassination attempt. Still, Lenin rose one last time to address the Eleventh Congress of the Communist Party. "Whatever the peasant wants in the way of material things we will give him, as long as they do not imperil the health or morals of the nation," Lenin declared. "But if he asks for ikons or booze—these things we will not make for him. For that is definitely retreat; that is definitely degeneration that leads him backward. Concessions of this sort we will not make; we shall rather sacrifice any temporary advantage that might be gained from such concessions."[119] It was clear that prohibition would continue so long as Lenin had anything to say about it.

It wouldn't be long. The following month, Lenin had an operation to remove the bullets in his neck. In May 1922 he suffered the first in a series of strokes that initially forced his retirement from politics and, by January 1924, finally killed him. The fate of prohibition would fall to his successors.

Lenin's heir apparent, Leon Trotsky, had long been as dedicated to temperance principles as Lenin, declaring in *Pravda* in 1923 that prohibition was "one of the iron assets of the revolution," and that there could be "no concessions" to alcohol.[120] Yet behind the scenes, concessions were already being made, as Lenin was bedridden and Trotsky was slowly being leveraged out of power by his chief rival, Joseph Stalin. Beer and wine had already been made legal in 1923. With Trotsky effectively sidelined and soon to be exiled, in 1925 Stalin repealed prohibition. "Some members of the Central Committee objected to the introduction of vodka," he wrote, likely referring to Trotsky, "without, however, indicating alternate sources of revenues needed for industry."[121]

The reintroduction of the tsar's autocratic vodka monopoly—only now rebranded with a hammer and sickle—certainly helped fill the Soviet Union's empty coffers, but it did so by sacrificing public health and well-being. Even while Stalin was inaugurating a shock industrialization drive, the People's Commissariat of Labor (*Narkomtrud*) was flooded with reports of worker absences, employees showing up to work late or hung over, drunken fistfights, and assaults on factory and Communist Party members.[122]

When a visiting European labor delegation asked Stalin in 1927 how he could reconcile promoting the health and happiness of society with the needs of the Soviet autocracy, he replied, "The Party is aware of this contradiction, and deliberately created it, fully cognizant that this contradiction is itself the lesser evil." His justification was perhaps the most straightforward expression of autocratic statecraft:

> Of course, in general, it would be better to do without vodka, because vodka is evil. But that would mean temporarily going into bondage to the capitalists, which is an even greater evil. Therefore, we chose the lesser evil. Today, the state revenue from vodka is over 500 million rubles. Giving up vodka now would mean giving up that income, and there is no evidence to suggest that this would reduce drunkenness, since the peasants would produce their own vodka, and poison themselves with *samogon* (homebrew).[123]

Under Stalin's totalitarian domination—and right through the 1980s—any semblance of temperance activism on behalf of the health of the Soviet people was snuffed out, lest it interfere with the vodka revenues that constituted fully one-quarter of the income of the Soviet colossus during the Cold War. The traditional system had returned, in which people "were tempted to drink," if not actively "forced to do so"—as German baron August von Haxthausen succinctly described it back in 1843. "The Government could adopt no more salutary measure than to put it down, but there are great difficulties of effecting this: the farming of the trade in spirits yields an immense revenue, which cannot be relinquished, and could not be easily raised in any other way."[124] The revenue trap was as intractable under the Soviets as it had been under the tsars.

In many ways, Russia's seemingly eternal struggles with both societal alcoholism and autocracy even today can be traced to the missed opportunity of temperance. In other countries, temperance was a means of grassroots social organization to oppose the domination of the state through alcohol. And in that struggle, Russia boasted perhaps the most important voices of temperance in Tolstoy and Lenin. Still, the echoes of tradition and the temptation of state revenue proved too much for the Soviet autocracy, just as its tsarist predecessor.

"It must be remembered that the policy of the Russian Government has always been to keep the State wealthy at the expense of the population. Ever since Ivan the Terrible the Tzars [*sic*] have been fabulously rich princes of a very poor country," wrote Italian diplomat Luigi Viallari in 1905. "It enables the Government to undertake great schemes of territorial expansion while keeping the people in a state of economic subjugation and rendering them incapable of rising against their rulers. Of course the final object is to increase the wealth and the importance of the whole Empire, but everything is done from a narrow bureaucratic point of view, so that the end is apt to be forgotten in the elaboration of the means."[125]

3

The Temperance Internationale—Social Democrats against the Liquor Machine in Sweden and Belgium

Central Railway Station, Stockholm, Sweden: Friday, April 13, 1917

Their clothes were starting to stick to their bodies. They'd been in one cramped, humid train carriage after another for the last four days—no showers, no good night's rest. Vladimir Lenin and his weary entourage of revolutionaries struggled to return home to Russia amid the chaos of the European war.

Lenin could be found writing and agitating among the workers' beer halls in Zurich when the February Revolution of 1917 roiled Petrograd, as armed protesters, striking workers, and mutineers forced the abdication of Tsar Nicholas II.[1] If there was any hope for a communist revolution, Lenin needed to get back to Russia quickly. To further weaken their Russian foes, belligerent Germany agreed to deliver the would-be revolutionaries across their territory to the Baltic in a sealed train carriage. After a ferry ride to neutral Sweden came a slow train ride from Malmö to Stockholm, arriving just past dawn.

While his tired comrades alighted wearily from the train, Lenin was energized. With a spring in his step, he leaped onto the platform to greet the welcoming delegation of Swedish communists. The first to shake Lenin's hand was Ture Nerman: a radical Swedish teetotaller and prohibitionist, who'd recently split from the moderate Social Democrats to form the communist Left Party. (In the interwar years, the communist writer/poet/politician Nerman became known for delivering his speeches before parliament in the form of poems. He also would write *Arbetarrörelsens Nykterhetspolitik*, a detailed history of the temperance politics of the Swedish labor movement.)[2]

Handshakes and pleasantries aside, there was much for Lenin to do in Stockholm before their night train departed for Russia. It would be another slow, three-day journey along the Baltic coast: north through Lapland, then south through Finland to get to Petrograd. While their Russian comrades rested at the Hotel Regina, Nerman chaperoned Lenin through the streets of Stockholm: to the Russian consulate to obtain entry visas, to the telegraph office to message the Petrograd Soviet to dispatch men to meet him at the Finnish border, to the haberdashery for a less rumpled suit, and to the bookstore to grab some reading for another long train ride.[3]

Just as importantly, Lenin wanted to speak with Nerman and the other hardline Swedish communists about his planned Bolshevik Revolution in Russia, followed by the worldwide revolution that was sure to follow. Just as Sweden was crucial in getting the revolutionaries *into* Russia, it'd be even more central to exporting the revolution *out of* Russia. For a successful revolution to spread to Sweden and then the world, the Social Democrats would have to be united. Lenin worried about the schism that had developed between Nerman's leftists—who supported the Bolsheviks' militant revolutionism by any means necessary—and the "rightist" Social Democrats of Hjalmar Branting, who believed a Marxist revolution could be made by compromise and nonviolence: through ballots, not bullets and bayonets.

"Branting is smarter than you, but his politics are wrong," Lenin told Nerman and his communist leftists. History proves that the iron will of men of action overcomes mealy-mouthed moderates, "and history is a damn good teacher," Lenin said. Still, when it came to the formidable Branting, "He is petty bourgeois, a Menshevik, and believes in the Entente more than the peasantry, but he is still smarter than many of you."[4]

Lenin had developed such begrudging respect for Branting over the decades in the underground world of Marxist politics, and through the Second International: an ongoing alliance of labor parties from across the countries of Europe, coordinated by Belgian socialist Emile Vandervelde from International Socialist Bureau headquarters in Brussels. Lenin, Branting, and Vandervelde all agreed that capitalism was an unjust system in which the rich lived at the expense of the poor, and that the workers needed to organize to defend their interests. They all understood alcoholism as a social issue rather than an individual one: that drunkenness was not just the consequence of the workers' poverty and subjugation, but the way that the bourgeois state dominated and controlled them. Lenin, Branting, and Vandervelde all proselytized and practiced temperance accordingly. Branting and Vandervelde had helped spread Lenin's revolutionary literature across Europe. And when the original Russian Social Democratic Labor Party split into radical Bolshevik ("majority") and moderate Menshevik ("minority") factions in 1903, it was Hjalmar Branting who hosted a unity congress in Stockholm to get them working together again.[5]

Still, like many European Marxists, the Swedish Branting and the Belgian Vandervelde were put off by Lenin's ideological extremism, and his support for violence and terrorist tactics. When Lenin's revolution ultimately succeeded later in 1917, they both cheered it as a "world-historic breakthrough." But when both later visited Lenin's Russia, they were aghast at the Bolsheviks' "violent methods and in-discriminate terror," and bitterly disappointed by the suppression of dissent and the strengthening dictatorship of a small minority over the will of the majority.[6] There *had* to be a better way to build a more equitable society.

But that was still to come.

Hjalmar Branting did not meet with Lenin on that chilly spring day in Stockholm, but Branting certainly knew Lenin was passing through town. In his office, Branting received an urgent phone call from a breathless Swedish baron Erik Palmstierna:

"You know Kerensky"—the liberal-socialist leader of Russia's unstable 1917 Provisional Government, whom Lenin was fated to overthrow. "Telegraph him! Warn him that Lenin is leaving on the next train, and must be shot or thrown in prison when he reaches the border!"

Branting just laughed. "You are stupid. They don't do that."

"And you're nothing but an outdated liberal from the 1880s!" Palmstierna persisted. "Nowadays we need men of action!"

Branting laughed even harder at the intended insult, and then hung up the phone.

At 6:37 p.m., the engineer blew the whistle as the train containing Lenin and his comrades slowly chugged away from the Stockholm station. Ture Nerman waved from the platform. It arrived at the Finland Station in Petrograd three days later. The rest, they say, is history.

"What if . . . ," the Swedish baron was left to later wonder to his diary. "What if Branting had actually listened to my advice?"[7]

Drunk Sweden, Sober Sweden

Both politically and geographically, Scandinavia and the Low Countries are a half a world away from conventional American temperance and prohibition histories. But a closer examination of the evolutionary—rather than revolutionary—transformation of Sweden and Belgium from royal autocracies to prosperous and modern social-democratic welfare states can tell us a lot about temperance as a progressive labor issue. Social Democrats like Hjalmar Branting of Sweden and Emile Vandervelde of Belgium well understood how liquor capitalists profited handsomely from propagating drunkenness and misery, both among the working classes at home and of subjugated Africans in the far-off Belgian Congo. The fight for true political liberation, then, meant devising means of reining in the worst excesses of the liquor trade.

Nowadays, we think of Sweden as an economically prosperous, ultraprogressive, secular democracy, in which the king or queen is little more than a symbolic fig-urehead, like in Great Britain. But this certainly wasn't the case back in the nine-teenth century, when Sweden was an impoverished backwater on the fringes of industrialized Europe. Its once-formidable Baltic Empire had been reduced to just

Figure 3.1 Vladimir Lenin (at right, with umbrella) speaks with Swedish communist prohibitionist Ture Nerman as they leave the Stockholm Central Station, April 13, 1917. Stockholm mayor Carl Lindhagen follows immediately behind. Grigory Zinoviev holds a child's hand near the back of the pack.

Source: Photograph by Axel Malmström (1872–1945) (Stockholm-Stad i forvandling). This Swedish photograph is in the public domain as it is nonartistic (journalistic, etc.) and was created before 1969 (SFS 1960:729, § 49a). https://commons.wikimedia.org/wiki/File:Lenin_in_Stockholm_1917.jpg (accessed August 31, 2019).

the Scandinavian Peninsula of Norway and Sweden, and its heavy-handed royal autocracy had more in common with Russia's tsars than with the constitutional monarchy of today. What's more, its unwashed and largely illiterate peasantry were drowning in a sea of *brännvin*—brandy distilled from grain or potatoes—giving Sweden "the sad distinction of being the most drunken country in Europe."[8]

The parallels did not stop there. As in Russia, the widespread drunkenness was mainly attributed to the state-run liquor traffic, which not only subverted temperance activism, but—according to one 1904 account—also

> made the distilling and selling of spiritous liquors a State monopoly, and one of the principal sources of public revenue. The consumption of spirits was encouraged in every way in order to increase the receipts of the Treasury. Public servants knew they might count upon favour by inducing people to drink by every means in their power. Tea and coffee were prohibited to prevent undesirable competition; beer was unknown, wine rare; and the Government produce reigned supreme.

Perhaps they didn't need the army to crush sobriety by force as in Russia; still, according to nineteenth-century writers, "A stream of cheap liquor was made to flow over the country, and was poured down the throats of the people, making every Swede a drunkard, and of drunkenness a national blemish."[9]

Fast-forward to the mid-twentieth century: Sweden's corrupt royal autocracy had gradually been replaced by a modern, social-democratic welfare state with a vibrant civil society, without so much as a bloody putsch or a shot fired in anger. Its economy was thriving, its people's health soaring, and foreign observers hailed Sweden's halving of alcohol consumption as "one of the greatest victories of a nation over itself."[10] So, what happened?

Sweden, it turns out, is the land of evolution, not revolution; and temperance is the key to understanding its political development.

Swedish constitutionalism dates from Sweden's disastrous participation in the Napoleonic Wars, when the crown acceded to parliamentary government and laws protecting freedom of the press. Further reforms in the 1860s stipulated that all seats in the bicameral parliament, or *riksdag*, would be determined by election— although the upper chamber still represented the wealthy aristocracy. Government minsters still owed their positions to the king, rather than the parliament.[11]

What Sweden had that Russia lacked was freedom of political association, which channeled social-movement pressures into political activism. Liberal calls for freedom found expression in the suffragist and free-church movements. Liberals found common ground with early socialists fighting on behalf of Swedish workers, resulting in a political spirit of compromise, consensus, and pragmatism that became the hallmark of Swedish politics.[12]

Sweden's temperance development was likewise evolutionary. Decades before the news of American Temperance Society successes spurred a sobriety movement in Poland, Lithuania, and then the Russian heartland in the 1850s (Chapter 2), it had already prompted copycat self-help organizations, including the Swedish Temperance Society (*Svenska Nykterhetssällskapet*) in the 1830s and 1840s. Its members not only pledged abstinence from distilled spirits, they successfully lobbied the state for reform. The resulting Licensing Act of 1855 not only outlawed home distilling, it gave municipalities the ability to govern the liquor traffic in accordance with the wishes of the local population. At the behest of their residents, some rural governments even went "dry" by refusing to offer any alcohol licenses at all. Putting the liquor traffic in the hands of society rather than serving the interests of the state proved to be invaluable in the fight for sobriety, and led to dramatic decreases in drunkenness.[13]

From this came perhaps Sweden's greatest contribution to the battle against alco-tocracy: the so-called Gothenburg system, named after Sweden's second city, which adopted the arrangement in 1855. The system was neither aimed at drunks themselves nor the harms they caused. Instead it was squarely aimed at the liquor *traffic*: the eternal allure of tremendous profits that encouraged wealthy alcohol producers, saloon-keepers, and even the state to force ever-more liquor down people's throats.

It worked like this: municipal leaders organized a private company led by the town's most respected citizens and charged them with regulating the local liquor traffic and discouraging overconsumption in the name of the public good, not profits. Investors in the company received a maximum 5 percent yearly dividend, while the vast majority of the booze revenue was given to the community's agricultural, philanthropic, health, and welfare organizations that benefitted drinkers and nondrinkers alike. The results were immediate and dramatic. The inflow of money led to a boon in local grassroots activism, while temperance-minded citizens had a direct role in promoting sobriety.[14] The reductions in drunkenness and the sudden blossoming of civil society convinced many that the Swedes had solved the enigmatic "liquor question" by removing the profit motive that drove one man to exploit another. By the dawn of the twentieth century, Gothenburg systems of municipal dispensary had been adopted across Scandinavia and were making inroads into parts of the European continent and even the United States.

Still, there was more to be done.

Conservative Revolutionary

The planetarium may seem an unusual starting point for a future Nobel Peace Prize Laureate and man hailed as Sweden's greatest statesman, but from an early age, Karl Hjalmar Branting took a keen interest in science and astronomy.[15] By 1879, the young Branting was calculating advanced mathematical formulas for the nearby Stockholm Observatory, yet his analytic curiosity soon turned from the heavens to a more earthly realm. On his work breaks, he read the social critiques of Swedish novelist August Strindberg and Karl Marx's *Das Kapital*.[16] The only son of an upper-middle-class family—and schoolmate of the future king Gustav V—he was inspired by the exiled, nihilist Russian dissidents he'd met, who were ready to lay down their lives in the struggle for freedom.[17] Even in his youth, Branting cut a stern and imposing figure. But beneath the gruff veneer, friends remarked on his compassion, courage, tenderness, and motivation by a deep and abiding sense of justice.[18]

The year 1879 also saw the beginning of a new wave of temperance activism, with the founding of the first Swedish chapter of the nonreligious Independent (later, International) Order of Good Templars (IOGT). Within a few short years, IOGT membership in Sweden would outstrip even that in its native United States.[19] Through a growing network of lodges, libraries, and publications, the IOGT was a force for raising awareness of social issues.

So it should come as no surprise that it was in an IOGT lodge where, in February 1880, Hjalmar Branting attended a lecture by famed economist Knut Wicksell titled "What Are the Most Common Reasons for Drinking and How Can They Be

Eliminated?" The talk was anything but dry. Drunkenness and prostitution were borne of the workers' poverty—the Malthusian Wicksell argued—and poverty came from having more children than one could afford. According to Branting's letters and the newspapers the next day, when Wicksell concluded that the only logical solution was birth control, rather than the celibacy preached by the state Lutheran Church, a riotous confrontation erupted.[20] In 1884, Branting gave up astronomy and science to become a journalist and editor. He would later fill the pages of his influential *Social-Demokraten* newspaper with coverage of Wicksell's arguments on alcoholism and prostitution as symptoms of the people's oppression.[21] His interest in temperance as working-class liberation from exploitation continued throughout his long career as a journalist, labor activist, and politician.

"Drink is the curse of the working classes," Marxists often claimed.[22] Indeed, the "liquor question" and the "labor question" had been intertwined from the very beginning. Before coauthoring the *Communist Manifesto*, Friedrich Engels wrote of the disease-ridden degeneracy of the urban slums of industrialized Manchester and Liverpool, England (Chapter 5), and the rampant proliferation of distilled schnapps drunkenness in his native Germany (Chapter 4). Drunks face-down in the muddy gutter, addicts stepping over them to pawn their last possessions for more drink—that the workers "drink heavily is to be expected," Engels claimed.[23] For Marx and Engels—and generations of Marxists to follow—drunkenness and destitution were the product of an exploitative capitalist system that cared nothing for the worker. What's more, the monopolization of the means of production—including alcohol production—by the state or the ruling class was what made the rich richer and the poor poorer.[24] In brief: drunkenness was synonymous with the subjugation of the working class. This was as true in Sweden as it was in England or Germany. For Branting, then, temperance was integral to the socialist cause.

Hjalmar Branting was a master of pragmatism, promoting Marxist aims while holding fast to bedrock Swedish values of compromise, discussion, and consensus.[25] Unlike Lenin's unwavering dogmatism, Branting's struggle for the rights of the working class was undertaken with flexibility and empathy. Workers had to organize, Branting declared: both into trade unions to promote their interests on the shop floor, and into a political party to advance legislation on their behalf. But Marx's frequently offputting critiques of capitalism on moral grounds disappeared; the role of religion (Marx's famed "opiate of the masses") was depoliticized as a matter of private conscience.[26]

Before a meeting of the Gävle workers' club in 1886, the journalist Branting laid out the blueprint for Swedish social democracy in a speech titled "Why the Workers' Movement Must Become Socialistic." Drawing on conventional Marxist themes, he argued that the wealthy capitalist was an "unnecessary parasite on the social organism," and that capital should be the common property of society. Socialism was necessary because the alternatives didn't do enough.

Figure 3.2 Hjalmar Branting (1860–1925) and Swedish king Gustav V (1858–1950).
Source: Public domain.

"Liberalism's chief failing," Branting said, "is its belief that political reforms rectify everything when what is really required are social reforms."[27] But that shouldn't stop socialists from working with liberals and suffragists on the shared goals of promoting individual freedoms. The right of self-determination was crucial.

Well-to-do temperance sermonizers—who lecture the most impoverished drinkers to save their meager pennies spent in drink—engage in "nonsense" and "disgusting hypocrisy," he said, since they treat the symptom of drunkenness rather than the disease of subjugation. Branting was distrustful of religious fervor and those who peddled it. He sought the triumph of reason over superstition and mysticism, and sought certainty in socialism as both a political creed and philosophy of life. As such, Branting generally abstained from alcohol to lead with clarity of vision and purpose.[28] Still, he claimed socialists should work with their fellow travelers in temperance to promote the liberation of the workers from their bondage to the bottle.

Ultimately, these grand goals would be achieved through reform, not revolution. "Socialism is revolutionary in principle, but not in tactics," Branting told those workers in Gävle. The ends of a new and better world of brotherhood and solidarity are revolutionary. "But if by revolutionary you mean something to do with street riots, murder and plunder—then socialism is far from revolutionary, but instead must be described as conservative."[29]

The labor movement would be nonviolent, he proposed, but not to Tolstoyan extremes. The workers would certainly assert themselves, but only in defense. Socialism's coming was inevitable, Branting believed, but whether there would be a fight was up to the present leaders of the capitalist society. They controlled the police and army, after all. The means of socialist transition, then, would be the ballot box. "Universal suffrage is thus the price for which the bourgeoisie can buy its liquidation through administration rather than be declared bankrupt in the court of the revolution."[30]

Such radical positions did not sit well with the conservative monarchy, which repeatedly fined and arrested Branting for his libel.[31] Still, his predictions were incredibly prescient. Aware of the increasing power of Swedish liberalism and socialism, over the course of the next thirty years the monarchy—and the conservative aristocracy that supported it—gradually and begrudgingly acceded to universal male suffrage and political reform to shore up their own receding power. For Branting, the fight for universal suffrage was not an end unto itself, but the means for achieving social reforms for the workers.[32]

Back in 1889 the journalist-activist Branting cofounded the Swedish Social Democratic Worker's Party (*Sveriges socialdemokratiska arbetareparti*, or SAP), demanding universal suffrage, freedom of the press, an eight-hour workday, education, and social security. While maintaining its own focus on the workers, it would happily cooperate with liberals, suffragists, free-church proponents, temperance activists—anyone who would further the ends of improving the welfare of workers. But not *just* the urban workers: peasant farmers, fishermen, and "all who suffer under capitalism's yoke," he declared. Branting's ultimate goal was a broad-based, nationwide, popular movement.[33]

This nondogmatic social-democratic movement grew steadily. By the 1890s, organized unions were coordinating protests and strikes for improvement in labor conditions, while the SAP joined forces with the Liberal Party to demand further democratization. It was thanks to such liberal support that Branting became in 1896 the first socialist elected to the *riksdag*—Sweden's parliament—in a system in which the vote was still heavily restricted based on age, income, gender, and wealth.[34]

Nondogmatic pragmatism was as much a part of Branting's temperance as his social democracy. Though temperance and moderation were crucial in improving the conditions for the working class, he was put off by those pulpit sermonizers, who embody "a certain kind of absolutist fanaticism, which provokes resentment rather than sympathy for a movement."[35] As the IOGT grew into a truly mass social movement in Sweden around the turn of the century, however, it largely shed the odious dogmatism: instead of moralizing sermons, they increasingly relied on practical economic and public-health arguments. Branting not only approved of a mellower, moderate temperance, he saw it as necessary to his mission. In 1904—on the twenty-fifth anniversary of its founding in Sweden—Branting lauded the IOGT as having "time after time fought against an ever-deceptive enemy of our people, and has nurtured a cadre of stalwart fighters in the army of liberation." So long as Swedish temperance continued to be more "scientific and sociological, less sectarian and judgmental, and more widely understood," it would have the support of the labor movement. "Perhaps someday—when our human family has been liberated both spiritually and materially—such anti-alcoholism activism will no longer be necessary," Branting concluded. "But it is certain that—given our present realities and for a whole slate of reasons—Voltaire's famous slogan about God could be applied to the temperance movement: if it did not exist, it would be necessary to invent it."[36]

Branting's commitment to empowerment, liberation, and self-determination wasn't limited to workers in Sweden alone. Since empires are by nature mechanisms of capitalist exploitation—subjugating those in the imperial "periphery" for the wealth and benefit of those in the "metropole"—Branting stood with the oppressed, even when that metropole of exploitation was Stockholm itself. Following the Napoleonic Wars, in 1814 Sweden annexed Norway from Denmark, in compensation for ceding its Finnish possessions to the Russian Empire. While the united kingdoms of Norway and Sweden each had their own parliaments, currencies, and armed forces, Norwegians increasingly chafed that their foreign relations were controlled from Stockholm. In 1905, restive Norwegians overwhelmingly voted to dissolve their long-standing political union with Sweden: 368,208 in favor and only 184 (0.05 percent) against, making it one of the most lopsided democratic referenda in history.[37] Conservative and nationalist Swedes were ready to maintain the union by force, if necessary. The Norwegians prepared for war, too.

"*Norge ur dina händer, konung!*" (Hands off Norway, King!), Branting the great orator declared, thus coining the rallying cry of the peace movement.[38] The increasingly powerful Social Democrats backed up words with actions: organizing resistance to the call-up of military reserves and threatening a national strike in the event of an imperialist war. Branting's antimilitarism ultimately tipped the scales in favor of a peaceful divorce of Sweden and Norway, though such vocal opposition won him a three-year prison sentence, later commuted.[39] Still, he pondered the hypocrisy of a government that lauded the great Leo Tolstoy on the event of his eightieth birthday—whose pacifism was a beacon to all of humanity—while arresting and imprisoning those who spread his message.[40]

In any event, it is worth underscoring—when we consider temperance and prohibition as international phenomena—just how many temperance-minded leaders also were steadfast opponents of imperialism and colonialism (Chapters 5–10, 15). This makes sense, as empires are fundamentally capitalist political organizations, in which the rich and powerful profit from the subjugation of others, just as the capitalist liquor traffic profits from the subjugation of the impoverished drunkard. Temperance and anti-imperialism go hand in glove.

Red Rising

With its growing strength, Branting was increasingly willing to flex the muscle of the social-democratic labor movement to achieve political aims, such as opposing imperial militarism in Norway or securing the franchise at home. Amid a stagnant economy, rising unemployment, and ongoing frustration with Swedish employers, in 1909, Social Democrats called for a nationwide general strike, like the 1893 general strike in Belgium, when Belgian workers successfully forced the government to accede to universal male suffrage.

But even peaceful general strikes could quickly descend into bloody clashes. Anticipating potential unrest, Swedish trade unions petitioned the king ahead of the 1909 strike to close all of the liquor stores for the strike's duration. The crown willingly obliged, decreeing a temporary prohibition. Troops were mobilized to suppress the anticipated disorder, but happily found no disorder to suppress. Short on funds, the labor unions called off the unsuccessful strike after a month, without achieving universal suffrage, leading to disillusionment with the unions. However, the remarkable peacefulness of the protest emboldened the growing movement for complete prohibition in Sweden.[41]

By this time, Sweden boasted a robust civil society, with temperance firmly at its core. In addition to the nondenominational IOGT, there were the Lutheran-inspired National Order of Templars, the Swedish Blue Ribbon Society, the White Ribbon Society (linked to the World's Woman's Christian Temperance Union— Chapter 13) promoting temperance and suffragism, and the labor movement's own temperance order Verdandi, among dozens of others.[42] Irrespective of political leanings, fully two-thirds of the representatives in the *riksdag* were card-carrying members of temperance organizations.[43]

It would be crazy to expect uniformity among such a large and diverse movement. One question increasingly drove a wedge between moderates and absolutists: Which was better? A flexible liquor-control system, like the Gothenburg system that had been emulated across Scandinavia since its inauguration in 1855? Or complete prohibition of the liquor trade? Following the "dry" general strike of 1909, the prohibitionists conducted an informal nationwide plebiscite, with a stunning 99.1 percent of respondents in favor of making prohibition permanent.[44] The referendum was nonbinding, but it placed the question of total prohibition squarely on the political agenda. With such widespread temperance support, observers declared the coming of Swedish prohibition "as irresistible as fate."[45]

In the run-up to the elections of 1911—the first nationwide elections with universal male suffrage—the Social Democrats added a prohibition plank to their party platform. Eighty of the 142 party delegates were absolutists. Branting was an IOGT member, but he approached prohibition with caution and skepticism.[46] He had studied the question in some detail—indeed many of the studies of pre–World War I alcohol prohibition in various American states currently housed in the Swedish Labor Movement Archive are from Branting's personal collection.[47] He warned against drawing hasty conclusions from the monthlong prohibition of 1909, but when it was obvious that the prohibition position reflected the will of the majority of the delegates, he did not object.[48] With the expansion of the franchise, the Social Democrats nearly doubled their representation in the *riksdag* with 64 seats, placing them in a tie with the conservatives for the second most powerful party, behind only the liberals.

Once seated, 135 of the parliament's 230 representatives were prohibitionists. Accordingly, the lower chamber soon petitioned the new government of liberal prime minister Karl Staaff to take up the prohibition question. In 1911, he did so in an unusual way: by establishing an *ad hoc* Temperance Committee, charged by King Gustav V himself to study the alcohol issue—much like the Royal Commission on the Liquor Traffic had done in Canada in 1891–1892 (Chapter 5). Beyond just making recommendations, the committee was to draft actual legislation for "well-grounded and active arrangements to be made in order to limit the injurious effects of the liquor traffic, firstly by reforming the so-called Gothenburg system, and further by producing a satisfactory explanation in regard to a general prohibition of the sale of liquors."[49]

From 1911 through 1920, the Temperance Committee met, researched, debated, and periodically released specific, concrete legislative proposals. In fact, the operations of the Temperance Committee provided the blueprint for Sweden's emerging "corporatist" style of democracy, in which collective bargaining between peak organizations representing capital, labor, and other specific interest groups is done in conjunction with the government administration itself. It proved to be an effective method of resolving contentious political issues through compromise, consensus, and cooperation, insulated from the ebb and flow of daily politics and societal pressures.[50]

Prime Minister Staaff declared the committee be "composed of representatives from the different bodies which take an interest in increasing sobriety, and which should at the same time be a representative one so that its work would give evidence of a deep and candid feeling in favor of the great cause." By ensuring that proponents and opponents, drinkers and teetotalers, manufacturers and workers all had their say, "it is only in this manner that the work can be assured of attaining its aim."[51]

The committee consisted of eleven members from across the political spectrum, including the leaders of the top temperance organizations. Eight of the eleven were known prohibitionists, but the most noteworthy committee member was Stockholm physician Ivan Bratt. Dr. Bratt had made quite a stir in the local papers by arguing that prohibition could never be enforced so long as homebrewing traditions were so deeply entrenched, and law-abiding citizens saw no harm in an occasional drink. Prohibition, he argued, would lead to widespread unemployment and drive the liquor business underground, where it would breed corruption and disrespect for the rule of law.[52] Hjalmar Branting took particular interest in Bratt's work.[53]

In 1913, Dr. Bratt gave up his medical profession to develop an alternative "Stockholm system" of alcohol control, which augmented the existing Gothenburg dispensary in the capital with a system of individual liquor rationing. Equating liquor with dynamite—something that only responsible people should be allowed to use—Bratt's regulatory boards would determine who was permitted to buy alcohol and how much, with every purchase logged in the customer's ration book.[54] Branting attended the inauguration of Bratt's system in 1914, where they were confronted with the full wrath of the capital's drinkers, enraged in protest against the new ration books.[55] When the furor subsided, the *Brattsystem* was born, delivering a further 42 percent reduction in liquor consumption in Stockholm in its first five years, with corresponding drops in alcohol-related crimes, without the corruption and lawlessness of prohibition.[56]

Everything changed with the outbreak of the Great War in August 1914. Despite Sweden's official neutrality, Stockholm was teeming with conservative German sympathizers—and German spies. With war raging on the continent and the Baltic infested with hostile U-boats, Sweden was largely cut off from its trading partners. The longer the war dragged on, the deeper into crisis the economy sank. Still, Branting defended neutrality against conservative royalists and a military establishment itching to help their German friends fight the fearsome Russians.

As in other countries, Swedish prohibitionists marshaled calls for patriotic sacrifice and conservation of foodstuffs into demands for total prohibition. Yet such howls did not easily penetrate the corporatist Temperance Committee. Union representatives for glassblowers, brewers, distillers, restaurateurs, and hotel workers all argued that prohibition would decimate their industries, creating unemployment and pushing Sweden into the economic abyss.[57] The specter of mass unemployment led the *riksdag's* upper house to strike down prohibition legislation in 1914, 1915, and 1916, further enraging the prohibitionists.[58]

Against this backdrop, another schism threatened to fracture the Social Democrats. Like labor movements across Europe, the Great War already divided Swedish Social Democrats between national-patriots and internationalists, militants and pacifists, and radicals and moderates. In late 1915, a new, avowedly nonpartisan organization emerged—the Citizens' Freedom Association (*Förbundet för Medborgarfrihet*)—which petitioned not only against prohibition, but against the local veto and other instruments of local liquor control. The petition included the signatures of a handful of labor representatives. "It is impossible not to see in this call the party-political element, which they declare does not exist," Branting blasted. "The right completely dominates, drowning out the few liberal and social-democratic names." The association's call for a special antiprohibition vote in parliament "is completely outrageous," Branting railed from the pages of his *Social-Demokraten* newspaper. Amid the gloom and crisis of world war, the conservative antiprohibitionists "have ventured forth to put the dagger in the back of our movement."[59]

The bigger danger, however, came from the opposite direction. Within the Social Democratic Party, the radical prohibitionist Ture Nerman and his Leninist comrades rose and demanded the expulsion of those labor leaders who had signed the antiprohibition petition. Nerman's long-simmering dispute with the moderate Branting was now out in the open. He soon learned that Branting would fight Nerman's inflexible, antiprohibitionist dogmatism as vehemently as he fought prohibitionist dogmatism. "What makes us Social Democrats?" Branting wrote. "That we strive to transform society in a socialist and democratic direction. But obviously one can be both a socialist and a democrat without being a prohibitionist."

After acknowledging socialism's roots in temperance, Branting reasoned,

> Let us not behave as if our party were a Good Templar lodge, which casts out those who broke their sobriety pledge. We are a large political party, with masses of *both* absolutists and non-absolutists. They have to stick together to fight for the rights of the working people in society. It can happen, now as in the past, with goodwill and understanding of *both* sides. But through schisms and divisions, à la comrade Nerman, our party would go to ruin.[60]

Following a heated debate, the party narrowly voted to reprimand the antiprohibitionist socialists. Not long before hosting Lenin for his Stockholm stopover, Nerman and his small cadre of radical leftists officially seceded from the much larger Social Democratic Party, beginning their own communist Leftist Party. Still, Branting worked to reconcile divisions and cool tensions among the socialists, while recommitting to the ongoing pragmatism of the Temperance Committee.[61]

By the third year of the war, Sweden was in a full-blown economic crisis—the cost of living skyrocketed alongside unemployment. Food shortages raised talk of famine. Rationing was imposed. By the time Lenin met Nerman on his way to Russia in April 1917, street demonstrations and food riots were commonplace. The conservative government was terrified: just weeks earlier, they'd witnessed food riots stoking the flames of revolution across the Baltic in Petrograd, ultimately consuming the conservative tsarist regime, and now they watched as the radical Bolshevik Lenin was on his way there to finish the job. They pleaded with Branting to ensure that the annual May Day demonstrations would be peaceful, even as they were beset by foreign-policy scandals.[62] The coalition of liberals and Social Democrats stepped up their demands on the government, settling for nothing less than full democratization.

The election of 1917 was devastating for the conservatives. Branting's Social Democrats grabbed 31 percent of the seats, and the liberals another 28 percent. But ever the pragmatist, Branting recognized that the rise of a "socialist" government amid the tinderbox of global war would be unacceptable—both to the conservative king and all of Europe. Moderation was necessary, so instead of leading the cabinet as prime minister, Branting took the position of finance minister, allowing the liberals to head up the cabinet. Achieving democracy was his goal, after all, not winning specific government positions.[63]

The coalition government negotiated trade deals that eased the economic crisis and passed legislation that would allow for full democratization and universal suffrage. "In our politics we have always sought to promote what was attainable and to the advantage of the working class," Branting triumphantly declared to the *riksdag* in 1918. "Now, caught up in this great occasion, we are going to collect the Swedish workers' prize from this movement that they themselves have initiated; namely, that *democracy is brought into port*, that the old struggle for political equality between the previously suppressed classes and the others concludes with a complete victory for the idea of equality."[64] Universal suffrage was passed in 1919 and ratified in 1921, completing Sweden's successful transition to democracy.

Yet while the guns of European war finally fell silent, the war over prohibition still raged in Sweden. In 1920, the Temperance Committee issued its final recommendations for prohibition (over the unusually loud objections of Dr. Bratt) to the new prime minister—none other than Hjalmar Branting, whose Social Democrats had become the largest party in the *riksdag*. Though he disagreed with the prohibition proposal, Branting agreed that such a momentous policy decision must reflect the will of the people. Prohibition would be put to a vote in Sweden's first nationwide democratic referendum, scheduled for August 27, 1922. A two-thirds majority would compel the *riksdag* to pass legislation outlawing any liquors over 2.25 percent alcohol.[65]

As his critics were quick to point out, Branting was rarely seen in Stockholm. Instead, he was often in Geneva—working tirelessly to help construct a League of Nations for the self-determination of nations and the peaceful resolution of disputes, in hopes of preventing the horrors of world war from ever happening again (Chapter 17). Hailed as "the Great European," Branting was awarded the Nobel Peace Prize in 1921.[66] In September of that year, Branting's Social Democrats powered to a resounding victory in Sweden's first completely democratic elections, with Branting becoming the first socialist head of state to be elected through universal suffrage, and setting Sweden on a path to social-democratic equality and prosperity for the rest of the twentieth century.

Yet the thorny liquor question still had to be resolved. The run-up to the 1922 prohibition referendum was unlike anything Sweden had ever seen. Prohibitionists squared off against defenders of the liquor-control system, crisscrossing the country with speaking tours, leaflets, and newspaper editorials—each espousing economic, legal, medical, moral, and cultural reasons for voting one way or another. Antiprohibitionists in particular highlighted the failings of prohibition in the

United States, and in Sweden's immediate neighbors of Norway and Finland as well as Estonia and Russia.[67]

Ultimately, only 49 percent of Swedes voted in favor of a blanket prohibition, far short of the required two-thirds majority. It was the last gasp of absolutist prohibitionism in Sweden. Still, with Bratt's system of individual rationing wedded to Gothenburg dispensaries putting societal sobriety over private profit, Sweden could boast the best of both worlds: dramatic reductions in alcohol-related harms, but without the infringements on an individual's liberty to drink, or the bootlegging, corruption, and organized crime associated with prohibition.[68]

Ever the consummate Swede, Branting was too modest to boast.

In the end, the robustness of Swedish democracy owes much to the foundations laid by its first democratically elected socialist minister. "Faith in Branting has become so universal in our country that no counterpart to it is likely to be found . . . in this or any country," explained one Swedish writer in the 1920s.[69] Branting worked tirelessly, even as his deteriorating health forced him to cede the prime-ministership on January 24, 1925. He passed away exactly one month later.

Sweden's highly restrictive system of liquor control endured long after Branting's death. The individual liquor-ration books were only done away with in 1955, while the state's monopoly of the liquor trade proved to be one of the major sticking points of Sweden's accession to the European Union in 1995. Other EU members argued it was an impediment to free trade and market harmonization; Sweden argued that the restriction system was a public-health matter. In 1997, the European Court of Justice determined that, so long as the Swedish retail monopoly did not discriminate against selling products of non-Swedish origin, it was fully consistent with EU statutes and could continue limiting hours of sales and other restrictions in the interest of promoting sobriety and societal well-being.[70] Consequently, the liquor markets in Sweden and the other Nordic states continue to be among the most restrictive in Europe, along with Belgium's, whose route to alcohol restrictions in the interest of public health and well-being were likewise intimately intertwined with the country's liberalization, democratization, and socialist labor movement.

Temperance and Socialism in Belgium

Unlike agrarian Sweden or Russia, which early socialists largely ignored, historical developments in highly industrialized Belgium drew interest disproportionate to its small geographic size. Indeed, Karl Marx and Friedrich Engels moved to Brussels to write *The Communist Manifesto* in 1848. Belgium was "the paradise of capitalists," the German-born Marx proclaimed—but it was the Belgian socialist Emile Vandervelde who added the postscript, that "she must also be described as the hell, or at any rate the purgatory, of the working classes."[71]

The long and contentious political history of the Low Countries is marked by a division between the rural, Dutch-speaking north and the industrialized, French-speaking south. Amid the street battles of the Belgian Revolution of 1830, the southern provinces seceded from the Netherlands, though their independence wouldn't be formally recognized for nine more years. Even with independence, Belgium saw the cohabitation of two societies in one: Flemish farmers in the north versus Walloon workers in the south, with the capital of Brussels right in the middle. The coalfields of Wallonia were easy to access, just below the topsoil. Coal was exported to France and Germany, powering the rise of the iron, railroad, and textile industries, which transformed Belgium into the second-richest country in the world per capita, behind only the United Kingdom. Still, Belgian workers worked 20 percent longer and were paid only half as much as their British counterparts, making Belgian laborers "among the most miserable in western Europe."[72]

Unsurprisingly, they were often among the most drunken, too, with wine usage most prevalent among the French-speaking Walloons, while beer and gin flowed freely in the taverns in the Flemish north.[73] "To be always thirsty, everywhere, and under all circumstances, seems to be the national characteristic of the Belgian," declared one provincial governor, noting that the Belgian drinks in celebration and in sorrow, in good times and bad; to help him wake up in the morning, to help him work throughout the day, and to get him sleepy at night. "He drinks on Saturday because it is pay-day, on Sunday because it is rest-day, and on Monday because it is the 'morrow of yesterday.' He drinks when he is sad, and when he is gay he drinks more."[74]

Independent Belgium was a constitutional monarchy, in which the king controlled the military and foreign affairs but little else. The protections of civil liberties—guarantees of free speech, religion, and the press—were some of the most liberal in the world, though the right to vote for both the Chamber of Representatives and the Senate was reserved for wealthy men.[75] Over time, two main political camps formed: the Liberal Party—promoting personal liberties, free trade, and secularism—and the conservative Catholic Party that resisted such encroachments.

Alcoholism spread along with industrialization throughout late-nineteenth-century Belgium, largely unchecked by any domestic temperance organization. Restrictions on the alcohol trade were minimal to nonexistent: to run a bar in Belgium, one only had to get a standard business license, like any other shopkeeper. Consequently many families supplemented their meager incomes by running a small tavern out of the front room of their houses. Belgian beer "can be bought almost everywhere for a penny a glass," wrote a British study of the Belgian working class, "while the *petit verre* of gin (*genièvre*), the popular national spirit, costs a halfpenny."[76]

Liberals and Catholics both agreed that licensing and regulating alcohol for the public good was antithetical to free-trade principles. Still, many politicians worried about the rise of alcoholism associated with the flood of cheap gin.[77] To this end, in 1869, liberal finance minister (and future long-serving prime minister) Walthère Frère-Orban submitted to the Chamber of Representatives an exhaustive, comparative study of inebriety and alcohol-control legislation in the United States, Britain, and the other states of continental Europe.[78] Frère-Orban was skeptical of the "Maine Law" and state-level prohibitions in the United States (Chapter 11), but argued that gin and other potent distilled spirits absolutely needed some regulation.[79]

By then, however, the moneyed alcohol interests were both so widespread and politically well entrenched that any reform legislation was destined to fail. Brewers and distillers held influential positions within the government or lavished patronage upon important ministers—including Frère-Orban himself. So long as the duopoly of Liberals and Catholics held sway, there was little hope for effective temperance legislation in Belgium. Frère-Orban contented himself with "moral suasion" and subsidizing antialcohol education initiatives by the few temperance and sanitary organizations.[80]

But something remarkable happened in Belgium in 1885 that would have reverberations worldwide. Those same Belgian protections of free speech and assembly that fueled the international socialist movement—from Marx and Engels through the Brussels-based International Socialist Bureau—also brought together temperance organizers from across Europe and around the world. In September of that year, a small organization of doctors and professional hygienists interested in the study of alcoholism called together the *Meeting international d'Anvers contre l'abus des boissons alcooliques*: the Antwerp International Meeting Against Alcohol Abuse. Some 560 delegates from across Belgium, the Netherlands, France, Sweden, Switzerland, Britain, and even the United States met to debate different social and political approaches to alleviating the liquor question.[81]

So successful in networking like-minded activists and sharing information, the Antwerp meeting became a congress that rotated among the great capitals of Western Europe every two years—gradually expanding in both the quantity of attendees, official government delegates, and number of countries represented. (Though conventional temperance histories emphasize the centrality of the Anglo-American connection, Britain took twenty-five years to host this largest temperance convention, in 1909, and Washington, DC, first hosted only in 1920 [see Chapter 17].) Bringing together royal aristocrats, professional academics, official government ministers, and grassroots organizers, these biennial conventions acted "as an educational agency, as a centre of information, supplied by channels ramifying all over the globe," according to American attendee Gallus Thomann, "and in turn sending its radiating streams of enlightenment throughout the civilized world."[82] Indeed, the establishment of a formalized network of transnational temperance advocacy deepened ties and promoted knowledge of policy developments and strategies abroad, to be disseminated and debated back home.[83]

Just as Belgium provided fertile ground for the growth of the global Socialist International, it likewise begot a global Temperance International. The year 1885 would prove a turning point for antiliquor activism, both in Belgium and the world.

King Leopold's Spirits

The 1885 Antwerp temperance conference is rarely mentioned in history books, overshadowed by the 1885 Berlin Conference, which divvied up the continent of Africa between competing European empires. Belgium typically isn't considered among Europe's great empires—until we remember how King Leopold II seized a million square miles of Central Africa as a personal fiefdom, visiting upon it some of the greatest atrocities in world history. In a pattern repeated almost everywhere Europeans encountered indigenous peoples unfamiliar with Western liquor, and Western understandings of property rights, Europeans wielded the former to extract the latter.

While the mighty, seafaring empires of Europe had long before established refueling ports and then colonies all around the coasts of Africa, the vast interior remained largely unsettled by Europeans, save a handful of explorers and missionaries. As a relative latecomer to the Scramble for Africa, Leopold schemed how best to seize "a slice of this magnificent African cake," with its lucrative ivory and rubber resources.[84] To manufacture the veneer of a benevolent, humanitarian enterprise, Leopold supported the work of European cartographers, explorers, scientists, traders, and missionaries in the Congo basin. Still, the Belgian government was leery. "Belgium does not need a colony. Belgians are not drawn towards overseas enterprises," claimed Walthère Frère-Orban, now the prime minister. "Still, you can assure His Majesty of my whole-hearted sympathy for the generous plan he had conceived, as long as the Congo does not make any international difficulties for us."[85]

"The conquerors of Africa," wrote Adam Hochschild in his bestselling *King Leopold's Ghost*, "like those of the American West, were finding alcohol as effective as the machine gun." Bottles of highly potent, easily portable Belgian gin lubricated many native leaders into scrawling Xs onto land-cessation treaties that they had no hope of even understanding.[86] Leopold hired Sir Henry Morton Stanley—the British explorer who'd recently won fame for chronicling his journeys to find Dr. David Livingstone in East Africa (Chapter 6)—to establish trading posts and negotiate hundreds of these land-grab treaties. From the trading post at Vivi in 1880, he wrote, "I beg to assure that if it depended on me I would have no more to do with rum than with poison, but the traders have so supplied the people with rum that without it friendship or trade is impossible on the Lower Congo." In the absence of money, the colonizers paid local hirelings in booze; having become addicted, they would no longer work without it, making the provision of liquor "a constant topic of discord between us and them."[87]

Those trying to do honest commerce with African natives quickly found the market for their wares were crowded out by booze. Selling a native tribesman durable wares like a pot, plow, axe, or cloth was a one-off transaction: now the tribesman could return to his village with something his family could use for the next twenty years. What made booze the lifeblood of colonial exploitation is that— once you get the consumer addicted—demand becomes self-renewing. And if you become the sole dealer, feeding that insatiable demand, you'll find yourself in a very lucrative position, indeed.

The dynamics of alco-imperialism were well known. "The existence of the spirit trade destroys other trade," wrote the *Times* of London. "The native who buys spirits rarely buys anything else." From Westminster Abbey, even the Archbishop of Canterbury called the African liquor trade "a dread commerce, or rather it is an anti-commerce."[88]

"I regret it very much," claimed one European liquor trader of the demoralizing effects of his trade, though not troubled enough to stop. "I am myself a large dealer in spiritous liquors. I have on the road now thousands of gallons of rum and several thousand demijohns of gin, bound for the northern river countries, where I carry on the greater part of my business," Mr. Betts asserted. "Supposing you were to take a large shipload of goods into any part of them, the first business question that would be asked of you, is 'How much rum have you brought?' And, if you should say, 'I have neither rum nor gin,' it would be said of you that you have nothing, that you do not care for trade. If this traffic did not oppress business and hinder its growth as it does, merchants and traders would always get ten times as much produce to buy as they buy now. The liquor traffic is certainly ruinous to commerce proper."[89]

Little wonder that by 1885, "a river of rum, broad and deep almost as the Congo itself, has been pouring into Africa," amounting to some ten *million* gallons per year from the so-called civilized world. The lion's share—some eight million gallons annually—came from Germany and the Netherlands, in addition to 737,650 gallons of New England rum from the United States, and another 311,384 gallons from Great Britain. "The Christian's rum has blasted savage races all over the globe. They wither under its destructive contact," editorialized the *New York Tribune* about the morally bankrupt colonial endeavor. "At the rate it is now being poured into the Congo country only the usual results can be anticipated."[90]

So the question of the highly lucrative colonial liquor trade was hardly a trivial one when Africa's European colonists met at the Berlin Conference in 1885 to decide the status of the Congo. Indeed, it was front and center in determining the fate of this massive inland territory—the size of the United States east of the Mississippi—and its untold millions of potential addicts. Ultimately, at Berlin, Leopold struck a deal: in exchange for their recognition of his personal sovereign authority over the Congo, he'd allow the European empires to continue to trade liquor on the territory of his new Congo Free State. The halfhearted objections of the American, British, Italian, and even Belgian (!) representatives ultimately gave way to the French, German, and Dutch liquor interests. In the end, the European powers vowed to address the colonial liquor issue only "in such a manner as to conciliate the rights of humanity with the interests of commerce"—which is to say the commerce would not be impeded at all.[91]

Once recognized as the supreme, sovereign authority, Leopold prohibited natives from brewing their own traditional fermented beers and palm wine. Instead, Belgian traders added their cheap, low-quality, and often poisonous "trade gin"—spurned by even the most hard-up laborers back in Belgium—to the deluge of Western liquor flooding the Congo. This followed a pattern of liquor colonialism dating back to the region's original colonization by the Portuguese in the 1550s: here as in South Africa (Chapter 6), India (Chapter 7), the Middle East (Chapter 8), North America (Chapters 9–10), and beyond (Chapter 15), distilled liquor was the engine that fueled white colonial exploitation and domination.[92] Cheap gin was the means by which the Belgians enslaved and appropriated everything from the native Congolese. The Belgians used it to get native leaders drunk and steal their land out from under them, in lieu of actual wages for the backbreaking labor of laying mile after mile of railroad tracks, and as trade for the ivory and rubber they shipped back to Europe by the boatload, just as fur traders were doing with native tribes in North America (Chapter 10).[93]

In the Congo—as in all of these other colonized parts of the world—native leaders fought back against the trade that was decimating their populations. Subaltern voices rarely survived the colonizers' control over information, though horrified European travelers wrote of "the native chief whose clear sight and patriotic spirit led him to banish rum from his territory, and *whose protective measures were made futile by the manœuvres of a scoundrelly English trader who smuggled the liquor into the country.*" The report continued, "Think of the monstrous hypocrisy of so-called Christian nations, vaunting themselves on their enlightened civilization, pretending a desire that the Gospel should be carried to all peoples, and then *invading the Dark Continent armed with the rum bottle, and in cold blood debauching and ruining its people*" (emphasis in original).[94]

The cheaper the gin, the bigger the profit. And—as everywhere—the colonizers laid the blame for this horrid state of affairs not on themselves, but on the victims: pointing to the "insatiable" demand for this heretofore unknown liquor, usually wrapped in some self-serving justification about free markets and capitalist trade.[95]

This isn't some twenty-first-century revisionist history: in a withering critique of the 1885 Berlin Conference, the *New York Tribune* lambasted the American and British governments for capitulating to Leopold and "the German and Dutch makers and sellers of the vilest alcoholic poisons, literally dictated their own terms to the Great Powers, and secured solemn assent to the infamous principle that the right to sell rum on the Congo without restriction was of more importance than the right of the African people to protection against physical and mental ruin." But it wasn't just a matter of diplomacy, it was a matter of Western hypocrisy, blasting "the Christian merchants and traders, the smug pewholders, the supporters of foreign missions, the straight-laced professors [who] respond to the negro's demand with conscienceless alacrity. . . . This is what is called in the euphemism of state papers and conferences 'introducing civilization into Africa,' and the adoption of the means is termed 'protecting commerce.'"

The *Tribune* editorial concluded,

> Christendom, horrible as the mere statement must appear to conscientious men and women, is employing its power and its superior knowledge to make Africa drunk and to ruin and destroy the negro race. It is idle to mince the matter. That is what it comes to; that and nothing less. . . . To call that system Christian civilization which permits and even sanctions such infernal work as is being done on the Congo is a contradiction in terms. Not less obvious is it that if the spirit of Christianity among the so-called Christian nations is too feeble to put a stop to this infamous traffic, the practical nullity of the religion of Christendom must be conceded.[96]

Still, even with foreign assurances secured, the first years of Leopold's reign were not particularly profitable, given the German, Dutch, French, and British liquor competition. Indeed, in 1890 the king even required bailouts from the Belgian government, as he'd poured virtually all of his private royal fortune into building roads and outposts to better extract natural rubber, the demand for which expanded with the market for automobile tires. Most Belgians blithely ignored distant developments in the Congo. Rumors and reports of systemic human-rights violations were dismissively chalked up to foreign jealousies.[97]

Belgian rule visited some of the worst atrocities in the history of capitalism upon the natives of the Congo. To extract rubber for export, all "uninhabited" land was nationalized and doled out to private companies, which operated with complete impunity. Leopold's state demanded taxes, but since money was scarce, tributes were to be paid in labor, creating a veritable "slave society" under an all-powerful colonial administration. Those who refused to work were beaten or whipped, their children taken hostage and often killed.[98] Villages whose populations resisted were slaughtered en masse. Failure to meet rubber-production quotas was punishable by death. Belgian historian Jean Stengers called areas under company control "veritable hells on earth."[99]

"We were a party of thirty under Van Eycken, who sent us into a village to ascertain if the natives were collecting rubber, and, if not, to murder all, men, women, and children," explained one Belgian soldier. "We found the natives sitting peaceably.

We asked what they were doing. They were unable to reply, thereupon we fell upon them and killed them all without mercy."

Upon catching up with his soldiers, commander Van Eycken replied, "It is well, but you have not done enough." He then ordered his soldiers to "cut off the heads of the men and hang them on the village palisades," and after mutilating their bodies, "hang with women and children on the palisades in the form of a cross." So they did.

Van Eycken was himself killed shortly thereafter, as a mass uprising of Africans overwhelmed his rubber factory, after he and his men had slaughtered another village of sixty-two men, eighty-four women, and four children. Witnesses described his administrative district as "a vast charnel house."[100] And there were hundreds of Van Eyckens across the Congo.

"I made war against them," admitted the Belgian official Léon Fiévez. "One example was enough: a hundred heads cut off, and there have been plenty of supplies at the station ever since. My goal is ultimately humanitarian. I killed a hundred people, but that allowed five hundred others to live"—and to keep harvesting rubber for the company.[101]

When there weren't enough Belgian soldiers, Leopold's state outsourced the dirty work to the *Force Publique*, a native paramilitary organization that roamed the countryside, imposing brutal discipline. They chopped off hands of victims as proof to the colonial masters that they'd done their duty. Baskets of severed hands became the symbol of European capitalist exploitation of the Congo—a sort of currency. *Force Publique* soldiers were given bonuses for how many human hands they'd harvested.[102]

"Cut off hands—that's idiotic!" King Leopold reportedly scoffed upon seeing a newspaper cartoon of him slicing off hands with his sword. "I'd cut off all the rest of them, but not the hands. That's the one thing I need in the Congo!"

Since there were no reliable census data, estimates of the total loss of life range from five million to thirteen million Congolese killed under Belgian rule, with the Belgian government's own commission determining that fully half of the population of the Free State perished due to brutality, famine, and disease.[103]

"Rubber caused these torments," one Congolese man named Tswambe later recounted. "That's why we no longer want to hear its name spoken."[104]

Alcohol was a vital tool in this exploitation. In his 1892 travelogue, Belgian missionary Constant De Deken recorded how, as he rode slowly up the mighty Congo River, the steamship stopped at every port to unload alcohol. Indeed the hold held little else but "thousands of hectolitres of poison to kill the blacks, or to brutalize them." On the return trip, the same ship carried tons of rubber, ivory, and palm oil destined for Europe.[105]

"Is it not painful to think that we are to send the pioneers of 'civilization,'" wrote colonial physician Alphonse Moëller, "but they carry in their luggage barrels of 'eau de vie' and gin?" For a time, the alcoholization of the Congo drew greater international outrage than did the brutality and atrocities.[106] As the outspoken Emile

Figure 3.3 A dazed father, Nsala, brought to a missionary outpost the severed hand and foot of his five-year-old daughter, Boali, who was dismembered by the Anglo-Belgian Indian Rubber Company (ABIR) militia. Baringa, Congo State, May 15, 1904. The image was originally published in Mark Twain's *King Leopold's Soliloquy* (1905), a scathing indictment of Belgian colonial oppression.
Source: Mark Twain, King Leopold's Soliloquy: A Defense of His Congo Rule, 2nd ed. (Boston: P. R. Warren Co., 1905), 19.

Cauderlier wrote in his *Le Gin et le Congo*: "Of all the means the 'civilized' man of the Aryan race has imagined to tame, enslave, and if needed exterminate the primitive races, there is no means more direct and more infallible than to introduce among them the taste for alcohol."[107]

So, when Leopold again faced bankruptcy in 1898, he embraced levying duties on liquor imported into the colony. This not only helped alleviate his financial woes and quiet his critics, but also maintained the duplicitous image that he was somehow benevolently working to uplift the Congolese rather than decimate them. Although it violated his free-trade promises to other European traders, at the Brussels Anti-Slavery Convention (1889–1890), Leopold went even further: he declared a total prohibition on the sale of liquor *to the natives*—leaving the white man's liquor untouched—similar to the policies existing in the United States for the previous hundred years (Chapter 9). Other colonial powers agreed to extend the prohibition on the introduction of liquor to the natives of sub-Saharan Africa. North of the Sahara, they reasoned, the Muslim populations of North Africa had little trouble with alcohol (Chapter 8), while Southern Africa would be governed by British regulations (Chapter 6). Even Americans like Frances Willard of the Woman's Christian Temperance Union (Chapter 13) and future president

Theodore Roosevelt (Chapter 16) joined the international support for the Brussels prohibition as a benevolent measure to protect indigenous Africans. However, in reality, Belgian traders continued to smuggle gin into Congo "for their own use," with a wink and a nod from the government, while foreign competition—especially French absinthe—was barred completely.[108]

"It is true that the sale of alcohol to natives should be forbidden in all parts of Africa," wrote Sir Arthur Conan Doyle, an outspoken critic who'd called the Belgian genocide in the Congo the greatest crime ever known. "It is caused by the competition of trade. If a chief desires gin for his ivory, it is clear that the nation which supplied that gin will get the trade, and that which refuses will lose it." Prohibition, in other words, was not about benevolence, but further monopolizing the lucrative trade: "it is clear that the prohibition of alcohol springs from no high motive, but is purely dictated by self-interest."[109]

Indeed, after prohibition, Leopold's financial situation improved dramatically.

MAP BELOW SHOWS ON A SMALLER SCALE THE MUCH GREATER RANGE OF TREATY OF 1899, 20 DEG. N. LAT. TO 22 DEG. S. LAT.

Mohammedan prohibition protects native races in the parts of Africa north of portion covered by Treaty of 1899. and British prohibition protects most of the natives in the regions south of it.

Figure 3.4 "International Treaties for the Protection of Native Races": Map of prohibition zones in colonial Africa, from 20° north latitude to 22° south latitude. As the caption notes, "Mohammedan prohibition protects native races" north of the prohibition zone (Chapter 8), while British prohibition (Chapter 6) covers those areas to the south.
Source: Crafts et al., *Intoxicating Drinks & Drugs*, 30. See also: Wilbur F. Crafts and Sarah J. Crafts, *World Book of Temperance*, abridged ed. (Washington, DC: International Reform Bureau, 1909).

Emile Vandervelde: The Social Socialist

The year 1885 was significant not just for the international temperance convention in Antwerp and the Berlin *Kongokonferenz* formalizing King Leopold's personal empire, but it also saw the founding of the Belgian Labour Party in Brussels. That is where Emile Vandervelde—an energetic young botanist behind a pince-nez and goatee—got his first introduction to political activism. Eventually he would become one of the most influential socialists on the continent as chair of the Second International. As a student, Vandervelde focused on parasites in the insect world, but as he became more politically aware, he made parallels with parasites in the social world. These included alcoholics, "the lechery of the parasites who wear the cloak of religion," and the "predatory class of parasites": the bourgeoisie who profit from the workers' toil.[110]

Repeatedly elected and reelected to the Belgian parliament, the man described as a "cross between Vladimir Lenin and Santa Claus" became the first socialist government minister in world history—a radical development at the time—serving as justice minister, health minister, and minister of foreign affairs, even representing Belgium at Versailles and Locarno.[111] More than anyone, the humanitarian Vandervelde would unite the forces of temperance, democratic socialism, and anti-imperialism, with reverberations well beyond Belgium and its colony.

"Vandervelde is essentially a Socialist leader," as the prohibitionist Anti-Saloon League (ASL, Chapter 16) introduced him to their American readers: "not a revolutionary, but an evolutionist: he desires not only the economic liberation of the worker, but also his cultural and moral development." Indeed, even before their counterparts in Sweden, the Belgian socialists disavowed revolutionary violence, focusing instead on the democratic side of democratic socialism: coordinating workers' strikes and pressure politics to gain the right to vote and promote the interests of the working class. In addition to the promotion of universal suffrage and "the protection of the native races in Belgian Kongo," the ASL explained, "naturally his attention was early drawn to the alcohol question."[112]

When the International Congress Against Alcoholism held its seventh meeting in Paris in 1899, Vandervelde delivered a detailed report titled "Alcoholism and Labor Conditions in Belgium."[113] When the congress reconvened in Budapest six years later, he again was there, this time to deliver the socialists' antialcohol manifesto.

"I think that the Social Democrat can not be either disinterested in the alcohol question or confine himself to a more or less benevolent neutrality toward those who are working for temperance or abstinence in the labor organizations," Vandervelde proclaimed. Alcoholism is "a powerful, formidable factor in the revolutionary concerns of today."

Moving beyond the socialists' stale chicken-and-egg debates of whether the workers' drunkenness caused poverty or poverty caused drunkenness, Vandervelde argued that industrial capitalism had transformed traditional drinking habits, and not for the better. Industrialization allowed for the mass production of highly potent distilled spirits at cut-rate prices, while capitalist saloon-keepers and liquor producers reaped ever-greater profits by encouraging overindulgence in their addictive wares. It was industrial capitalism that profited from the workers' misery by prolonging their hours of work, and subjugating them to living in dangerous and unhealthy slums, making the worker turn to drink as a temporary respite from his misery.[114] Abstinence was necessary not only for revolutionary discipline, but to strike a blow against capitalism itself.

"Alcoholized laborers, in a moment of passing excitement, are good for riots, but they absolutely cannot be counted upon to lead well the painful and difficult work of freeing their class," Vandervelde explained. Socialism was not about drowning your misery, but fighting against it with open hearts, clear eyes, and unmuddied minds. Opposition to drunkenness was "not at all a matter of ignorant asceticism" or "depriving them of enjoyment," he said; instead "we want the world to show itself as it is, because the clear vision, the conscience responsive to wrongs, injustices, abuses which people suffer, are the preliminary conditions necessary to their suppression."

Since halfhearted measures give only halfhearted results, he urged all socialists to dedicate themselves fully to the cause of temperance as vital to combating capitalist exploitation as "the fundamental causes of moral and material pauperism."[115] Accordingly, as the socialist movement grew throughout Belgium, Vandervelde encouraged his comrades to make common cause with Good Templars, Blue Ribbon Societies, the World's WCTU (Chapter 13), and other temperance organizations, even though they were not avowedly in pursuit of strictly "socialist" goals.

Just as Hjalmar Branting's humanitarian defense of political rights wasn't limited to Swedish workers, so too did Emile Vandervelde's temperance and socialist dedication extend into anticolonialism. Indeed, his almost single-handed fight against the inhuman exploitations of King Leopold's colonial regime would be one of the loneliest of his political career.[116]

Belgians were largely indifferent to Leopold's personal project in the Congo—doubly so once his exploits stopped requiring bailouts from the Belgian government—dismissing horrific reports from British and American reporters as nationalist jealousy. Vandervelde was among the first Belgians to seize on the international alarm and adopt the Congolese cause as his own: linking the exploitation of Africans to the exploitation of the downtrodden Belgian proletariat, stacked in the city slums. "The cause of the blacks is your cause," Vandervelde declared to the Belgian workers in 1900, "not only because you are men, but because you are workers. In the end, this politics will threaten you as well."[117] But even among his fellow socialists, his pleas fell with a thud.

Despite being a lone voice in the woods, Vandervelde redoubled his efforts in 1903, arguing from the floor of parliament that colonialism "in the form that it takes under the capitalist regime" strengthens militarism and state power at the expense of popular sovereignty, while simultaneously enslaving indigenous peoples. He enumerated King Leopold's violations of the Berlin Convention: expropriating native lands, restricting free trade, and concentrating commercial profits in the hands of a small number of super-wealthy Europeans while condemning the Congolese to death camps and cannibalism. Since the Belgian government was a signatory to the Berlin agreement, they had both the moral and legal duty to act.

Not surprisingly, King Leopold took these attacks as a personal affront and waged a public-relations counterattack against the Belgian socialists and Vandervelde personally. Conservative Catholics and even Liberals rallied to the king's defense, leaving socialists alone to retell the "horrible stories of burned villages, of devastated plantations, of cut-off hands, and of innocent populations gunned down, all for having refused to cooperate with the rubber harvest."[118]

"My rights over the Congo cannot be shared," King Leopold proclaimed in 1906, "they are the fruits of my own labors and my own expenditure"—even though they most certainly were not. Popular opinion only turned against the king as he adopted such an omnipotent, authoritarian tone. Vandervelde charged that annexation of the Congo by the Belgian parliament was the only way to stop the king's atrocities and save the indigenous peoples.[119]

In a 1908 speech to the parliament, Vandervelde proclaimed he had come to a moment "in political life where one has a moral obligation to speak what one believes to be the truth," though his vehement condemnation of capitalist colonization was not widely shared. Still, he proposed a motion by the Belgian parliament to annex the Congo on behalf of the indigenous peoples and end Leopold's tyrannical, absolute rule. "I believe that the only way out of the indefensible system of oppression is parliamentary control over the Congo."[120]

Yet by the time the parliament took its historic vote the following year to finally wrest control over the Congo from the king himself, Vandervelde was gone, having embarked on his first of two tours of the Congo to chronicle the atrocities himself. "One thing is unfortunately very clear," he wrote in his resulting *La Belgique et le Congo* (1911), "under Leopold's regime, civilization itself, with its railroads, its steamboats, and its improved weapons has served for the most part only to intensify the pillage of natural wealth and exploitation of human material."[121] Unfortunately, Vandervelde realized, control by the Belgians would be only marginally better than control by Leopold, as the Belgian Congo remained a colony intended for exploitation by European capitalists. But by gaining increasing power within the government, Belgian socialists could change all of that.

The primary duty of the new government should be "to take energetic prophylactic and therapeutic measures to repair, at least in part, the evils which directly proceeded from the contact of blacks with 'civilized' Europeans." The high taxes and other prohibitions against introducing the white man's firewater to the natives "as an article of extraction," was a good start. He reported, "Cannibalism has been repressed and is no longer practiced openly; the scourge of alcoholism has receded in the Congo, and the Free State has applied—more strictly than in other colonies—the international prohibition against the liquor traffic. No one welcomes it more than us."

Still, the natives had already contracted both alcoholism and syphilis by means of European liquor and prostitution. Smuggling was rife through porous colonial borders, and rubber traders had begun to manufacture their own distilled "rudimentary schnapps," to equally devastating effect. What's more, the colonizer's science of distillation had been adopted by the colonized; colonial inspectors would find scores of native stills in virtually every village across the vast Central African terrain.[122] Alcoholization would remain an enduring legacy of colonial rule, even well after the Belgians had left.

Vandervelde's two tours in the Congo had made him one of the world's most respected indigenous rights activists, especially within European socialist circles, where even the Second International hadn't dared to touch the question.[123]

Figure 3.5 Belgian foreign minister Emile Vandervelde (1866–1938) (center with pince-nez, hat, and cane), commemorating the fiftieth anniversary of the covering of the River Senne and revitalization of the urban center, in front of the Bourse. Brussels, Belgium, 1923.
Source: Sueddeutsche Zeitung Photo / Alamy Stock Photo. Image ID: CPJ4DF.

Vandervelde and the Temperance International

In addition to his duties as writer, domestic parliamentarian, and international anticolonial crusader, Vandervelde also quickly assumed a leadership role within the transnational labor movement. In 1889, socialists from Germany, France, and Britain inaugurated the Second International: an ongoing collaboration of European socialist leaders to debate Marxist theory and discuss national strategies. A self-described "major bit player," Vandervelde was neither a beard-stroking theoretician nor a firebrand revolutionary. Instead, he was an accommodating moderator, who kept the unwieldy transnational organization together for a quarter century from the headquarters of the International Socialist Bureau in Brussels.[124]

Back in 1891, hundreds of socialists, revolutionaries, and trade unionists from across Europe convened in Brussels to join forces in the international class struggle. The young Vandervelde—still early in his career—presented an exhaustive study of labor conditions throughout Europe. It was built upon French anarchist Pierre-Joseph Proudhon's argument of a natural division of work between the sexes, which justified keeping women in the kitchen and out of the political sphere. Vandervelde recalled that after his presentation, the great German socialist Karl Liebknecht "loomed before me, very straight and very angry; he crushed me with his scornful reprimand."

"Very well: Courtesan or domestic slave," declared Liebknecht, "Is that how a socialist sees woman's role?"

Vandervelde was speechless in defense of the indefensible. "That was the crowning blow. On the question of socialist feminism, I had been converted." Consequently, Vandervelde would be a dedicated champion not only for temperance, indigenous rights, and workers' rights, but for women's equality, too. All these great reforms go together.[125]

The "woman's question" was just one of many that threatened to fracture the congregation of passionate socialists from across Europe. Then there was the "liquor question." And the "colonial question." And the "nationalism question." And the "ministerial question"—was it acceptable for a socialist to serve as a minister in a bourgeois government that oppressed the people? But the biggest question that divided radicals in the organization like Vladimir Lenin from moderates like Hjalmar Branting was whether socialists should condone violence in achieving political revolution. Despite heated disagreements between well-educated and headstrong delegates from across Europe, Vandervelde was praised by all sides for his ability to soothe egos and achieve political compromise, if not always consensus.[126]

Equally vital to the cause of international socialism was the temperance cause. While there was persistent disagreement as to the tactics of alcohol control—up to and including complete prohibition—radicals like Lenin, Trotsky, and Ture Nerman and moderates like Hjalmar Branting all agreed on the necessity of fighting alcohol, not only in the name of clear-headed revolutionary discipline, but to strike a blow against the financial foundations of the bourgeois state, whichever state that may be.

By unanimous assent, the issue of alcoholism had been placed on the agenda for the International Socialist Congress to be held in Vienna in 1914, with Emile Vandervelde himself in charge of drafting proposals on what to do about it. In addition to his speeches at the International Temperance Congresses, throughout the early 1900s he'd penned brochures for his fellow socialists arguing for total abstinence from distilled liquor. He also wrote on the nondogmatic International Order of Good Templars as the most flexible organizational structure for temperance activism, promoting the greatest degree of political freedom. He would know full well, as he also served on the Executive Committee of the Franco-Belgian Grand Lodge of the IOGT.[127]

Among his socialist comrades, there was little need to justify discussing the question. The German Social Democrats had repeatedly vowed over the previous decade to "fight against the abuse of alcohol among the working class." The Swedish delegation already had prohibition written into its party platform, while the Dutch embraced a local option. The Danish and English socialists wanted to restrict retail liquor sales. The Finns and Norwegians demanded total abstinence. The Swiss and Austrians had more specific plans for the uplift of the working class. But "what we have the right to ask of the Socialist and Labour International is to pronounce distinctly in favour of direct action against alcoholism, and to examine the best means of rendering such action effective."[128]

The discussion would be informed by an exhaustive report by Emanuel Wurm of Berlin on the effects of alcoholism, and a survey of the various means of combating it. "The social and intellectual uplift is the first condition for successfully fighting against the alcohol danger," including eight-hour workdays, increased wages, protection of women and children, and the establishment of institutions to promote education and public health. This was standard fare.

More controversial was the question of absolute prohibition. According to the Second International, prohibitory legislation would only be effective if the economic and social uplift of the workers had already been achieved; otherwise they would seek out ether, morphine, opium, hashish, or cocaine. Without doing the necessary legwork, calling for prohibition as a simple legislative solution to social ills "is nothing more than deliberate hypocrisy on the part of the propertied classes. They wish to make it appear as if they earnestly intend to uplift the proletariat. Meanwhile, they only want to remove the most unpleasant consequences of drunkenness from the public eye and at the same time are really opposing granting necessary funds for an earnest fight against alcoholism for the betterment of the people."

One need look no further for evidence of such hypocrisy, Wurm suggested, than the ten "dry" states in the United States, where liquor production and sale were nominally outlawed, but since federal law governs interstate commerce, dry states could do little to stop the traffic (Chapter 16). "Consequently, the secret sale of liquors was not restricted and the Prohibition Law does not hurt the alcohol capitalists, which was the real intention of the legislators all along."[129]

Restrictions on the number, hours, and operations of public houses were to be encouraged, so long as they reflected the democratic will of the population, as with the local option or the municipalization with the Gothenburg system. Ivan Bratt's system of individual rationing also showed great promise, but in 1914, it was too soon to judge the results. "It is absolutely useless to try to combat the abuse of alcohol by raising excise taxes or monopolization which increases the price of liquors," the report concluded. Not only did higher prices lower the workers' standard of living, it furthered the interests of the state and the powerful capitalists. "So long as countries obtain a large portion of their income from the taxes on spirits, they cannot have any interest in the reduction of the consumption of liquor, or in forbidding it; especially when the producers of spirits are the big landlords, who, as in Prussia and herewith in the German Empire, are in possession of the ruling power in politics" (Chapter 4). However, if such revenues were raised, it was the duty of Social Democrats to ensure that an ever-greater amount of those government receipts be dedicated to antialcoholism programs.

"Governments and Capitalists alike are interested in furthering the excessive use of alcohol," which was the primary impediment to true reform. Liquor sales enriched wealthy, politically connected capitalists, and liquor taxes filled government coffers—constituting 26 percent of all state income in tsarist Russia, 25 percent in the United States, 23 percent in Britain, 20 percent in the German Empire, 16 percent in Holland, 15 percent in Sweden and Belgium, 12 percent in Denmark, 11 percent in France and Norway, and 9 percent in Switzerland and the Austro-Hungarian Empire. "Any decrease in liquor consumption would compel the State to increase taxes on something else, the burden of which would probably not be borne by the poorer classes, as the drink duties are." The report concluded, "The emancipation of the working classes from the yoke of alcohol must therefore be the task of the working classes alone."[130]

It was up to Vandervelde to then offer political means of achieving that task. His suggestion was to ally socialists in every country with their local Good Templar temperance lodges. The IOGT "is founded upon the basis of absolute political, philosophical and religious neutrality. In the struggle against alcoholism, it can thus gather together men of all opinions and convictions." For example, the *Egalite №1* IOGT lodge he'd help form in Brussels held its meetings in the same *Maison du Peuple* or "People's Hall" that housed the International Socialist Bureau, was affiliated with the Belgian Labour Party, and disseminated socialist propaganda. All one had to do to be a member was pledge (1) to abstain from liquor and narcotics, and (2) "Neither to buy, manufacture, sell or offer alcoholic beverages, nor do anything to favor the industry or trade in intoxicating liquors," since the exploitative traffic was the target more so than the liquor itself.

"To speak frankly," Vandervelde said, there's "no real difference between the moderate use of fermented beer or wine and the complete abstinence from alcohol." It was the distilled liquors that were the primary problem. "If, therefore, we advocate total abstinence, it is less in the interest for those who abstain then of those who abuse—less about individual hygiene than social propaganda." Socialists should lead the workers by example. "Let us be tolerant, then for others, but let us be strict for ourselves," so that the working class as a whole will learn and "grow in dignity and power, and escape the tyranny of alcohol."[131]

In the end, Vandervelde encouraged the international workers' movement to raise awareness of the dangers of alcohol; lead through abstinent example; work to "suppress all traffic in strong drinks, or at least spirits"; and "through legislation, combat alcoholic capitalism in all its forms." The concrete policies—from limiting licenses to complete prohibition—would vary from one country to another. "But everywhere the labour and Socialist parties must put themselves in the front rank of those who wish the workers to be freed from the domination of the producers and retailers of alcohol."[132]

It was both a rousing and pragmatic call to confront the predatory liquor traffic to promote the health, happiness, productivity, and well-being of the people.

Or at least it would have been. The Vienna conference had been scheduled for August 23–29, 1914. On August 3, the German Empire invaded Belgium en route to France. This drew in the British as guarantors of Belgian neutrality, transforming an isolated confrontation in the Balkans into a full-blown European war. The convention in Vienna was cancelled. Despite Vandervelde's calls for international peace and socialist brotherhood against imperial militarism, one socialist party after another fell to patriotism and lined up to support their own national governments and armies.[133]

From World War to Vandervelde's Law

With the outbreak of war in August, civil authorities in Brussels and across the country outlawed the sale of distilled liquors: a well-meaning measure rendered utterly moot since the country was almost completely overrun by the Germans within a month's time. Still, King Albert formally instituted prohibition on liquors, wines, and beers in any zone occupied by Belgian or Allied troops—a wartime measure to be extended to all Belgian territory just as soon as it could be liberated. The German military authorities in the occupied territories oversaw the brewing of beer and distillation of gin, with draconian penalties for anyone caught peddling in alcoholic beverages outside the German trade.[134]

On August 4, the Belgian parliament held its final session before the nation was overrun by Germany. It was there that King Albert invited Vandervelde to serve as minister of state in an expanded cabinet of national unity, alongside Catholics and

Liberals. With the approval of other socialist delegates, he accepted—becoming the first socialist ever to serve as a high-ranking government minister, six years before Hjalmar Branting became prime minister of Sweden in 1920. Despite their previous antagonisms, Vandervelde ingratiated himself with his erstwhile Catholic and Liberal foes, and even kindled with King Albert himself an unlikely friendship that they would both greatly treasure. Indeed, by war's end, even the recalcitrant Catholics had warmed to Vandervelde and his onetime "radical" demands for universal suffrage (Belgian women, however, would not gain the vote until after the Second World War).[135]

During the war, Vandervelde pivoted from the cause of socialist internationalism to the cause of the victimized nation. In charge of wartime procurement, he traveled to the United States to lobby for American intervention and organize relief. Though President Woodrow Wilson was firm in his commitment to neutrality—at that time, at least—Vandervelde struck up an immediate rapport with former president Theodore Roosevelt (Chapters 16–17), who shared a longstanding interest in the defense and sobriety of the natives in the Belgian Congo.[136]

At the same time, Vandervelde tried not to let his ministerial duties hinder his continued efforts to reconcile the socialists of Europe under the banner of peace. In 1917, he brought nonaligned European socialists together in Stockholm for a peace conference. Working with Vandervelde for peace and reconciliation was Hjalmar Branting, whom Vandervelde praised among socialists as "the most influential and the one who shares most nearly our own point of view," including issues of suffrage, temperance, and anti-imperialism.[137]

When the February Revolution of 1917 toppled Tsar Nicholas II, Vandervelde congratulated the Russians and Alexander Kerensky's Provisional Government on the winning of their freedom from autocracy. Vandervelde traveled to Russia to see the revolution for himself, and "to greet the Russian Revolution in the name of the suffering Belgian workers and to ask from the Russian people assistance and support."[138] In May, he embarked on the same route around the Baltic from Stockholm to Petrograd that Lenin had taken only a month before. As fate would have it, the mild-mannered social-democratic "menshevik" would share a carriage compartment for the three-day train trip with the radical firebrand Bolshevik (and prohibitionist) Leon Trotsky, returning to Russia from his exile in the Bronx.[139]

In Petrograd, the old-world socialist Kerensky greeted Vandervelde warmly and was sympathetic to the Belgian's plea for Russia to stay in the war, so that the Germans couldn't shift their forces to the Western Front. The hardened workers in Petrograd he spoke to—and the war-weary Russian soldiers at the front he visited— were far less receptive to his pleas for moderation and international working-class cooperation.[140] Still, in his three months touring Russia—at a time when all government and police authority had collapsed amid "the most subversive revolution that the world has ever known"—he attributed the relative peace and calm to prohibition. "In Russia, the man of the people, when he is sober, is infinitely more peaceful, more docile, more sociable in a word, than the workman or peasant of our own countries," Vandervelde wrote, adding, "But he must be sober." Things might have turned out quite differently if vodka was more easily available; indeed, the fact that the tsar and his family were still alive testified to that fact, he suggested.[141]

The victory of Lenin's radical Bolsheviks in the October Revolution—and the country's quickening descent into terror and civil war—forced Vandervelde to re-think his overflowing optimism toward the workers' revolution in Russia. He scoffed at Lenin's false claim that the Bolsheviks were the only true heirs to Marxism. Even more worryingly, Lenin and the Bolshevik minority began undermining inde-pendent trade unions and arresting moderate leftists: the socialist revolutionaries who'd won two-thirds of the seats in the 1917 Constituent Assembly elections.[142] Still, as head of the Second International, in 1922 Vandervelde made for Moscow to act as the legal defense for his fellow socialists at the Bolshevik show trials. Guilty verdicts were a foregone conclusion, but he hoped that perhaps the solidarity of in-ternational socialist voices might save them from execution.

Upon arrival, his train was mobbed. "Down with the traitors to the working class!" shouted thousands of Muscovite workers. "It is a pity, friends, that we cannot hang him."[143] The Soviet prosecutors said they'd be happy if Vandervelde joined his compatriots in the dock, rather than being their defender. Ultimately, the Russian socialists were found guilty but allowed to flee to European exile. Still, his disillu-sionment with the Bolshevik regime was complete.

"For men schooled in the doctrine of Marx, it is a strange and painful thing to see realized," he lamented, "a sort of gigantic caricature of Marxism." Despite such promising beginnings, Vandervelde reaffirmed that it was impossible to have a so-cialist redistribution of wealth in which there was no wealth to redistribute in the first place. In its place, Lenin and then Stalin had built a "dictatorial, bureaucratic, hyperstatist socialism in a country where capitalism existed only in an embry-onic state," quite unlike the developed industrial capitalism Vandervelde had been battling in Belgium. Soviet society "has nothing in common with the democratic socialism that Marx and Engels had always conceived."[144]

Vandervelde may have pivoted away from socialist internationalism after the war, but he remained active in the international temperance cause. He was elected as a vice president of the World League Against Alcoholism (Chapter 17) and would maintain an active leadership role in the global prohibitionist struggle, especially in the Congo. On September 10, 1919, outside of Paris, the victorious powers of World War I and vanquished Austria signed the Treaty of Saint-Germain-en-Laye, formalizing the dissolution of the Austro-Hungarian Empire and affirming the cre-ation of a League of Nations. The same day and in the same place, the victorious powers signed a lesser-known Treaty of Saint-Germain-en-Laye, affirming the con-tinuation of the prohibition of the liquor traffic in the colonies and Mandate territo-ries of sub-Saharan Africa, including the Belgian Congo. Vandervelde served as the

Belgian delegate and was a motivating spirit in ensuring the continued protection of native communities from the exploitation of colonial liquor traders.[145]

Even more of Vandervelde's attention was focused back in Belgium. With King Albert's dedication to universal and equal manhood suffrage, Belgian socialism could shift from strikes and protests demanding political change from outside to parliamentary politics and change from within. One of the first orders of business on Armistice Day, 1918, was to reaffirm the wartime prohibition, but specifically on distilled spirits. "Vandervelde's Law," as it came to be known, made the alcohol market in Belgium one of the most heavily regulated in Europe. Taxes were increased on fermented wines and beer, but more importantly, Vandervelde's law prohibited the sale of gin and distilled liquors in quantities less than two liters—effectively banning their sale for on-site consumption in bars and cafés. The idea was to discourage consumption of these most powerful and addictive intoxicants by the working poor, and prevent their exploitation by capitalist distillers.

In many ways, it worked!

Today, Belgium is world famous for its high-quality beers, brewed in the traditions of Trappist monasteries—not the halfpenny gin that flooded the industrial slums a century earlier. Even though Vandervelde's antiliquor restrictions were repealed only in 1983, the average twelve and a half liters of gin and other distilled liquors that Belgians swilled in 1900 has since been *quartered*, down to around only three liters per capita annually: among the lowest rates of distilled-liquor consumption in Europe.[146] Perhaps we have Emile Vandervelde to thank for making Belgium a country known for high-quality beer, rather than cut-rate gin. And as Vandervelde himself noted with some pleasure back in the 1920s: drunkenness, alcohol-related medical disorders, and arrests for public drunkenness all declined dramatically, without the negative black-market-related effects of an American-style total prohibition.[147]

As justice minister, Vandervelde worked for reform within the system rather than revolution against it: instituting criminal-justice reforms, and pressing for an eight-hour workday, pensions and health services, and limitations on military service. He angrily chided his opponents—socialists and liberals—who opposed extending the vote to women. Socialism, it seems, would come more gradually than even he first thought.

Class struggle, he believed, was indeed the driving force of history, especially when it came to the question of the capitalist liquor traffic. But class struggle did not mean class warfare. Much more could be accomplished through progressive legislation and compromise.

4

Temperance, Liberalism, and Nationalism in the German and Austro-Hungarian Empires

University of Vienna, Austro-Hungarian Empire: Thursday, April 11, 1901

By the dawn of the twentieth century, temperance was already in full bloom in Europe's German-speaking heartland, taking root not just with socialists, but liberals and nationalists, too.

Those biennial temperance conventions—begun with the *Meeting international d'Anvers contre l'abus des boissons alcooliques* in Antwerp in 1885 (Chapter 3)—had grown steadily in importance as they rotated through Western Europe: Zurich, Switzerland (1887); Christiana (Oslo), Norway (1890); The Hague, Netherlands (1893); Basel, Switzerland (1895); Brussels, Belgium (1897); and Paris, France (1899). But now they were taking up an extended residency in the mighty continental empires of Germany and Austria-Hungary.

While the early conferences drew only two hundred to five hundred attendees, conventions in Vienna (1901), Bremen (1903), and Budapest (1905) welcomed one thousand to fifteen hundred guests each, including official government delegations representing countries across Europe and around the world.[1] The opening address was always given in the language of the host country, but the papers and discussions were usually conducted in French, German, or occasionally English, with participants switching languages even mid-sentence as the conversation warranted. The fast-paced, multinational, multilingual nature made the meetings "uncommonly interesting," according to attendees.[2]

The thirteen hundred representatives and government delegates who congregated at the University of Vienna in April 1901 were treated to a speech by one of the most controversial politicians of the day: Tomáš Garrigue Masaryk. After World War I, Masaryk would be hailed as a "champion of liberty" for the long-oppressed nations of Europe. As the founding father of independent Czechoslovakia, he would be popularly elected and reelected four times. But that was still twenty years in the future. Before the Great War, Masaryk was roundly considered "the best-hated man in the country."[3]

Perhaps the most outspoken liberal legislator in the Austro-Hungarian *Reichsrat*, in 1901 Professor Masaryk was already knee-deep in the anti-Semitic Hilsner Affair that was roiling the multiethnic empire. When the body of a young seamstress was found in the Bohemian woods, local authorities fingered Leopold Hilsner—an outcast Jewish cobbler's apprentice with special needs—and concocted an outlandish fantasy of Jewish blood-murder.[4] Hilsner's trial was based largely on hearsay and innuendo, since there was no hard evidence. The sensationalist portrayal, however, of a broad conspiracy of Jewish ritual sacrifice stoked anti-Semitism across Central Europe. In a series of well-researched articles, Masaryk—the articulate social scientist from Prague—not only defended Hilsner, but called his fellow Czechs "the laughing-stock of Europe" for believing such hate-filled hysterics.[5]

But anti-Semitism runs deep. Masaryk and his family were ostracized, threatened daily with violence and death. Distraught, Tomáš weighed packing up the entire family and fleeing to America, never to return. "I am in the homeland, and yet everything and everybody is quite alien to me," he wrote a friend. "That Hilsner affair, the conduct of university professors and of students—that has finished me off. At times it oppresses me like the desert does—on the other hand, I can contend with it and bear it only as one does in the desert—namely in isolation."[6]

Instead of abandoning Europe, the professor-legislator went to Vienna, where he'd been invited to speak on temperance to the International Conference on Alcoholism. He brought along his daughter Alice, who'd taken her father's courses in sociology and philosophy at Charles University. As an aspiring, politically engaged social scientist herself, she too took an interest in the temperance cause.[7]

As with the Hilsner Affair, Masaryk had no patience for the religious superstitions of evangelical sermonizers; instead he approached the recent phenomenon of mass alcoholism as befitting a professional sociologist. Drawing on evidence from doctors and social scientists and the logical arguments of philosophers and historians, he openly pondered: why do people even drink in the first place?

" '*In vino veritas*,' some people tell me. 'I can lose my inhibitions,' or 'cast off the trappings of civilization,' or 'I can relax and speak freely when I drink,'" he began. "From these explanations, you can see that alcoholism is, in fact, a romantic yearning for Rousseau's base and carnal 'natural state.'"

"Consider Tolstoy," Masaryk said. Masaryk openly admired the great Russian writer, having frequently debated with him at his Yasnaya Polyana estate, even becoming one of the first pledgees to Leo Tolstoy's Union Against Drunkenness in 1887 (Chapter 2).[8] "Tolstoy finds in the Russian *muzhik* (peasant) the embodiment of simplicity, as others have found this romantic ideal in the Indian savages of North America, each of which have their own associations with alcoholism"

(Chapters 9–10). Weaving together Schopenhauer's metaphysical voluntarism, Nietzsche's bacchanalian nihilism, and Comte's "fetishism" for justifying supernatural religious superstitions, Masaryk's temperance presentation concluded that modern alcoholism stemmed from a deep psychological need for the "artificial induction of a state of superstition."[9] And since superstitions were antithetical to modern rationalism, alcoholism impeded enlightenment and communal prosperity.

"The modern alcoholic simply does not want to see clearly; he feels the need, every now and then, to think less clearly," he declared to his audience, in German. "Alcoholism is therefore both culturally and politically unprogressive, conservative, and indeed," Masaryk paused, with a wink, "radical-reactionary." His political jab against his conservative opponents elicited a wave of approving laughter throughout the hall.

It was curious, he noted, that the "relaxation" and utopian feelings associated with alcohol existed alongside the greatest pessimism, depression, and suicide, which had been the focus of Masaryk's doctoral dissertation. His explanation—which was met with thunderous applause—was that "alcoholism is the self-delusion to the obvious defects of modern civilization."

Modern man is restless, Masaryk explained. He demands some pharmacological high. Modern man wants to swallow something that makes him content—if not for eternity, then at least for the moment. "Modern man is endlessly seeking everywhere for happiness—which is itself the source of his unhappiness."

After a brief pause, Professor Masaryk set aside his academic lecture and instead spoke from the heart. "I came here as a skeptic," he said, explaining to the audience he'd been an on-again, off-again drinker for his first fifty years. However, having subjected the political, social, and moral arguments on behalf of temperance to rigorous empirical and logical scrutiny, he could find no flaw. They had won his scientific mind to the cause: Masaryk would henceforth be a teetotaler! The thousand-plus attendees roared with approval.[10]

Masaryk's dry conversion applied only to his own habits. He bristled against prohibitionists' sweeping generalizations that alcohol is unnecessary everywhere and at all times. "There is much, apparently, that is unnecessary in the life of modern civilization, which nevertheless serve some purpose."

Still, the mounting medical, economic, sociological, and criminological evidence of the harms of alcoholism were unassailable, and the tactics of modern temperance were sound. It was a great benefit for the people of Vienna to hear the serious arguments and debates presented at the conference, Masaryk claimed, and even more important that the assembled reporters broadcast the findings throughout the German-speaking territories without condescending to stereotypes and drunk jokes.

"I conclude by confessing that the argument for abstinence has provided me with all the proof necessary that an alcohol-free life guarantees a higher conception of life, a happier and purer life, and ultimately a better life."[11]

As he descended the rostrum, he was greeted with thunderous approbation from the audience, a hug from his daughter Alice, and a vigorous handshake from Viennese optometrist Dr. Richard Fröhlich, a longtime admirer of Masaryk.

Over the course of the following days, those three struck up many conversations in the lecture halls and corridors, or strolling the nearby *Volksgarten*. Masaryk arranged for the young doctor to treat Alice's chronic vision problems. Alice was smitten with Fröhlich as a man of culture and conviction for leading efforts for temperance among the working class of Vienna. And though the two would never marry, Richard and Alice would later carry out a torrid love affair.[12]

At the end of the convention, however, the much-contented Masaryks boarded the train back to Prague. Rather than fleeing for America, they would stay in Europe, to continue the fight for freedom and self-determination.[13]

Blind Spots and Stereotypes

The vast Central European "beer belt"[14]—stretching from the shores of the North Sea southeast to the Danube basin—is largely an unexplored backwater of temperance history. After all, the German and Austro-Hungarian Empires did not experience a dramatic prohibition like the United States or Russia, nor did they experiment in alcohol-control policies, like Sweden or Belgium. Plus, anyone who's enjoyed a *Kölsch* along the Rhine, celebrated Oktoberfest in Munich, downed a Czech pilsner in Plzeň, or quaffed the lagers of Vojvodina can attest: alcohol is intimately intertwined with daily life across Central Europe. According to the World Health Organization, this region is among the hardest-drinking in the world, though largely imbibing beers and wines, rather than the more potent distilled spirits of Russia and Scandinavia.[15]

But this presents us with a puzzle: *why* do the peoples of the former German and Austro-Hungarian Empires largely prefer lighter fermented beers instead of the highly potent distilled vodkas, gins, rums, and whiskeys? The answer lies not in churches or pulpits (where historians are trained to look for temperance answers), but rather in the schools, shop floors, and parliamentary halls.

Since medieval times, Central Europe was ruled by dozens of quasi-independent kingdoms and principalities within the loose confederation of the Holy Roman Empire. As part of his conquest of Europe, Napoleon defeated and dissolved the empire in 1806, only to have a renewed German Confederation emerge from the Congress of Vienna in 1815. The main power rivalry within the Confederation was between the Hohenzollern Kingdom of Prussia in the north and the Austrian Empire of the Habsburgs in the southeast.

The brief but bloody Austro-Prussian War of 1866 finally spilt the two. The Austro-Hungarian Empire—a unique, multiethnic, constitutional monarchy— stretched from Bohemia south to the Adriatic and east to Transylvania. Amid a war of unification against France in 1870, the Kingdom of Bavaria and the other northern German principalities united into the German Empire, with Prussia at its core and Berlin its capital.

Yet for all of the violence, vitriol, and animosity between the north and south— *Kleindeutsch* and *Großdeutch*—there was more that united Germany and Austria than divided them. In 1879, the two entered into a Dual Alliance as a bulwark against Russia. And when Habsburg archduke Franz Ferdinand was slain by a Yugoslav nationalist in 1914, the Germans leaped to Austria's defense. Entangling alliances would ultimately draw all the great powers into World War I and lead to the complete destruction of both empires in due course. But within each empire was a remarkable movement of temperance activism that has gone almost completely unnoticed by historians. Let's consider each in turn.

Figure 4.1 Central Europe, 1815–1886, showing Prussia and the German states in the north, Austria and Hungary in the south, and the uneasy confederation between them.

Rise of the Conservative Prussian *Schnapsjunker*

Today, Germany is commonly associated with beer drinking—giving obligatory mention to Germany's famous 1516 *Reinheitsgebot*, or Beer Purity Law, which stipulated that only barley, hops, and water were acceptable ingredients in brewing. But the *Reinheitsgebot* wasn't just a recipe; it was government regulation of the alcohol traffic, which went far beyond specifying ingredients: it standardized measures and retail prices, under penalties of law, and specified that "WE, the Bavarian Duchy, shall have the right to order curtailments for the good of all concerned."[16] Viewed in this light, Germany's famous *Reinheitsgebot* was part of a very long, very deep tradition of regulating the alcohol market.

The Beer Purity Law corresponded to the arrival of distillation in the German-speaking world. The ancient Arabic science of distilling *al-kuhul* (Chapter 8)—heating a fermented mash until the alcohol evaporates, only to be captured, cooled, and condensed in a still—was rediscovered by thirteenth-century Italian alchemists seeking a medicinal elixir. They called it *aqua vitæ*: the water of life.

Knowledge of distillation migrated northward via Genoese trade routes to medieval monasteries and other centers of knowledge, where brewing was already a long-established practice. As this new technology spread, distilled spirits increasingly became used as a recreational beverage, rather than just a medicine.[17] By the time of the *Reinheitsgebot* in the sixteenth century, distilleries across Germany were cranking out so much distilled brandy (*Branntwein*) and schnapps that Hesse (1524) and Bavaria (1553) tried—unsuccessfully—to ban distilling, while other regions placed the trade in the hands of the church.[18]

It was the arrival of industrial distillates in Germany—rather than the traditional fermented beers and meads—that prompted Europe's first temperance movements. In 1600, Maurice, Landgrave of Hesse, established an "Order of Temperance" along with over two hundred German nobles who vowed to abstain from distilled spirits, though not fermented brews. "I wish the horrible stuff neither existed nor was drunk," replied Prussian king Frederick the Great (r. 1740–1786) to a proposed rum factory. Noting the upsurge in drunken disorder in Berlin, Frederick placed exorbitant taxes on distilled *Branntwein* to discourage its use.[19]

Following the French Revolution and Napoleonic Wars (1803–1815), only the South German states of Baden, Bavaria, and Württemberg established constitutional governments. Further east, Prussia remained a conservative monarchy, purging universities and forcing liberal activists underground.[20] This, then, was the political backdrop for Germany's rapid industrialization and economic transformation.

At the beginning of the nineteenth century, Germany was overwhelmingly rural and poor. Bleak economic prospects forced many young Germans to either emigrate to the New World or face pauperism and starvation. In 1848, this tinderbox of poverty, hopelessness, and popular discontent would explode into revolutionary upheavals across Central Europe.

It wasn't just the Industrial Revolution that set the stage for 1848; there was also the Schnapps Revolution of the 1830s and '40s. The Schnapps Revolution began in the east of Germany, with the conservative Prussian nobility known as the *Junkers*. East of the Elbe River (in present-day Poland), the *Junkers* controlled most of the arable farmland in Prussia. Lording over great estates tilled by armies of peasants, the *Junkers* monopolized German agriculture. This "ultra-conservative, privileged, haughty, and oppressive landed aristocracy of Prussia held a rod of iron over the industrial classes, and over the government itself," wrote Frederic Austin Ogg. *Junkers* populated virtually every high office of the German army, navy, and government administration. They sided with the government to put down the liberal 1848 revolution in Germany's southern and western kingdoms. "If Prussia ruled Germany, the *Junkers* ruled Prussia, and through it the Empire itself. They were a main prop of the Hohenzollern dynasty and of its autocratic, irresponsible system of government."[21]

The *Junker* class worked for the Prussian autocracy, but they also made the Prussian autocracy work for them, through political and economic concessions. So when agricultural prices plummeted in the 1830s, the *Junkers* extracted tax breaks from the Prussian government to build distilleries on their estates, turning surplus grains and potatoes into a flood of cheap *Branntwein*. By 1842, there were 2,327 urban and 7,994 rural distilleries across Prussia, annually pumping out some 265 million quarts of hard liquor, largely for domestic consumption. Beer sales plummeted as workers were awash in a sea of potent potato-based *Kartoffelschnaps* that even the poorest pauper could afford.[22] As part of the "truck system" (much like the *dop* system in British South Africa: see Chapter 6), this cheap liquor was used to pay workers in lieu of wages, and was an obligatory part of the room and board that peasants paid to their *Junker* landlords.[23]

The Schnapps Revolution fundamentally reordered both the German economy and German drinking practices in order to enrich the *Junker* aristocracy. Between 1806 and 1831, per-capita consumption of distilled spirits *tripled*.[24]

"The drunkenness that had once cost three or four times as much was now readily available every day, even to the very poor; a man could stay drunk all week for just 15 silver groschens," wrote Friedrich Engels of the low-quality and often poisonous schnapps. Known mostly for his collaborations with Karl Marx on *The Communist Manifesto* (1848), the Prussian-born Engels was an astute journalist and social critic. In chronicling how the rich got richer and the poor got poorer, the liquor trade was a consistent theme in his writing. Engels continued, "I still remember very well, how at the end of the 1820s, cheap schnapps flooded the Lower Rhine-Brandenburg industrial district. Namely in Bergisch, and especially in Elberfeld-Barmen, the working masses fell to drunkenness. From nine o'clock in the evening, besotted men—arm in arm, occupying the whole width of the street—swayed and howled disharmoniously from one tavern to the next, before finally staggering home."

Not surprisingly, the sudden spike in drunkenness produced a spike in crime. Traditional celebrations—once beer-soaked and jubilant—now devolved into furious brawls and knife fights under the influence of potent distillates. According to Engels, "The only industry that has produced more devastating effects" than the *Junkers'* schnapps trade "is the Anglo-Indian opium trade for the poisoning of China." He added, even that "was aimed against far-off strangers, not its own people."[25]

But in Germany as elsewhere the world over, the liquor traffic was incredibly lucrative. *Junker* profits and government tax revenues strengthened the conservative, east Prussian *Schnapsjunkers*, their government, and their military. What transformed this backward, half-literate, predominantly agricultural Prussian state—"on a soil that produces virtually nothing but potatoes and cabbage"—into a mighty, semifeudal, militant-reactionary empire? For Friedrich Engels, the answer was straightforward: "*Die Schnapsbrennerei*"—the distillery.[26]

Widespread drunkenness from the Schnapps Revolution set the stage for Germany's first sustained temperance movement. While visiting England in 1831, Prince (later King) Johann of the Kingdom of Saxony attended one of the first meetings of the British and Foreign Temperance Society (see Chapter 5) and learned of the early successes of Anglo-American abstinence societies. From Dresden, he sent word to his ambassador in Washington for more information about these organizations. In response to Johann's appeals, in 1835, the American Temperance Society (ATS; Chapter 11) dispatched Rev. Robert Baird as something of a roving temperance ambassador to Europe.[27]

No one was more important in advancing the European temperance cause than Baird. Upon arriving in Paris, both the French aristocracy and the American ambassador implored him to write a summary of American temperance progress in French—the literal lingua franca of educated European society. Thousands of copies of Baird's resulting *Histoire des sociétés de tempérence des États Unis d'Amérique* were printed in France; as he traveled across Europe, the work would be translated into German, Dutch, Swedish, Hungarian, Russian, and Finnish, too.[28] "The wide diffusion of information respecting one of the most remarkable moral enterprises which the world has ever witnessed," wrote Baird's son and biographer, "by means of a language which is read by almost every well-educated man in Europe was the motive which suggested the publication of this work."[29]

At the Tuileries Palace, Baird was granted an audience with French king Louis Philippe in 1841, before embarking on a tour of European royalty. In Stockholm, King Karl XIV Johan inaugurated the Swedish Temperance Society and vowed to mass produce a Swedish translation of Baird's *History* at his own expense.[30] A news report of Baird's ATS history in a Riga newspaper set off the wave of temperance petitions in Russia's Polish and Baltic provinces (Chapter 2).

One of history's first transnational social activists, Baird well understood that social organization depended entirely on a country's political institutions. An

American-style mutual assistance organization would not fare well in a powerful, church-tied autocracy in which freethinking temperance organizers were weeded out as schismatics. "Never was I more convinced of *the importance of going directly to the source of power*," Baird wrote of his audience with Tsar Nicholas I, who promised to translate his *History* into Russian and Finnish. "It will not be possible to form temperance societies here for years; but much may be done at once by diffusing information."[31]

The political challenges were just as daunting in Germany. Rather than a unified state, the nineteenth-century German Empire was an eclectic patchwork of semisovereign kingdoms. Some were predominantly Protestant, others Catholic, and all suspicious of one another. The western kingdoms on the Rhine to France tended to be liberal, constitutional monarchies, diametrically at odds with the reactionary Prussian *Junkers* east of the Elbe. Such a combination of regional jealousies, religious distrust, and partisan acrimony made building a political confederation well nigh impossible.

Consequently, the *Reichstag*—the parliament meant to represent all the kingdoms and interests of the German Empire—was both impotent and widely reviled. Germans put greater faith in the Kaiser and the bureaucracy, meaning true political reform on temperance would have to come "from above."[32] This helps explain why German temperance never morphed into familiar, American-style lobbying organizations: what's the point of lobbying the legislature if the legislature is powerless to enact reform?

Robert Baird's primary target, then, was the German royalty. He encouraged his host, Prince Johann of Saxony, to make his own temperance society based on the ATS lodge model. In Berlin, Baird was received "with honour and distinction" by the aging kaiser Friedrich Wilhelm III (r. 1797–1840), which "attracted the notice of the masses" as well as the German aristocracy. Much pleased, in 1835 the kaiser translated Baird's *History* and issued copies to every clergy member in his domain. His secretary of police established temperance societies in every province of Prussia. At a mass gathering in Berlin in 1837, Baird formally inaugurated the Temperance Society of Prussia. As across Europe, the hope was that the respectable aristocracy's patronage of temperance would inspire the lower classes. By 1841, there were over three hundred lodges with twenty thousand active members pledging abstinence solely from distilled liquors. Consumption and production of *Branntwein* plummeted accordingly, leaving the conservative *Junkers* to weigh their charge of leading by temperate example against their evaporating liquor profits.[33]

The first National Temperance Convention of Germany was held in Hamburg in 1843, bringing together independent lodges across the various German states. Together—in the presence of the Irish "apostle of temperance" Father Theobald Mathew (Chapter 5)—members pledged total abstinence from distilled spirits, and "caution against the abuse" of beers and wines. "The only means possible at that time for attaining any result at all was that of persuasion," wrote the organizer, J. H.

Böttcher, "as it was the only means legally admissible."[34] At rates on par with their British and American counterparts, by the Revolutions of 1848, some six hundred thousand German men—mostly artisans and smallholders at the bottom of the traditional economic hierarchy—had taken the temperance pledge.[35]

Some Prussian *Junkers* were torn between their own financial interests in the liquor trade and societal pressures to act as noble pillars of sobriety. "I wish I had never had any distillery at all!" exclaimed one such *Junker*, announcing the closing of the remaining stills on his vast estates in 1845. He wasn't alone. Thanks to the temperance wave, in that year alone, 18 Prussian distilleries had been permanently closed, 108 had ceased operation, *Branntwein* output plummeted by 45,000 hogsheads, and with it came a 254,489-thaler decrease in liquor excise revenues. When informed of these figures by the Prussian minister of home affairs, the young, progressive, reform-minded kaiser Friedrich Wilhelm IV (r. 1840–1861) replied, "I should consider it as the greatest blessing if, during my reign, the revenue for distillery tax would decrease so much as to come to naught."[36]

The Revolutions of 1848, however, would put a quick end to temperance's political inroads. As during great wars and other social upheavals, many social organizations disbanded, their members disappearing forever amid the tumult.

Bismarck Bolsters the Liquor Trust

The year 1848 marked the "Spring of Nations"—a wave of popular revolutions that roiled the conservative monarchies of Europe with demands for liberty and democracy. News that Parisian protesters had deposed King Louis-Philippe in February and established the Second French Republic prompted copycat uprisings, barricades, and street riots throughout economically depressed Germany. For a time, it looked as though sweeping political reform was inevitable. Mass street meetings of energized workers and liberals demanded constitutional changes, especially in the non-Prussian southern and western German lands. Frightened conservative monarchs—hoping to avoid deposition by violent mobs—invited emboldened liberals to hastily draw up new constitutions to pacify the protests.

In Frankfurt, liberals and nationalists created the first freely elected parliament of all of Germany, with hopes of establishing a constitutional monarchy. With his own power teetering, Prussian kaiser Friedrich Wilhelm IV at first played along. But as the winter of 1848–1849 approached and protests subsided, the kaiser called in the *Junker*-led army and crushed the street rebellions in Berlin. When the Frankfurt parliament offered him the throne of a constitutional monarchy, Friedrich Wilhelm scoffed, refusing such a "crown from the gutter." The parliament collapsed, as the Prussian army wiped up the last radical resistance from Saxony to Baden.[37]

Some diehard liberals doubled down on temperance as a political necessity, educating the masses to be responsible, democratic citizens. "Just as the temperance man repudiates *Branntwein*, he also rejects everything else which contradicts his Reason," claimed one such revolutionary broadsheet in 1848. "Just as he breaks the chains of sensual pleasure, he rebels against every other form of Bondage. Strengthened by the fight against *Branntwein*, he has learned to rise above prejudice, to endure scurrilous criticism for the sake of a lofty ideal, and to maintain courage and conviction amidst a struggle. All this he will carry over into every other aspect of his life; for freedom is a precious treasure, and he who has obtained even a portion of it will not rest until he possesses the whole."[38]

But those were the outliers. Smarting from the hardline crackdown, many liberals and socialists spurned temperance as having been captured by reactionaries in both the church and state. And with good reason: German conservatives howled that "spiritous beverages were the true, necessary and indispensable instigator" of the street protests, which often devolved into unruly, half-drunken mobs. For them, temperance offered a return to piety, order, and submissiveness.[39]

Still, for the next thirty years—from the 1850s through the 1870s, as Germany grew into an industrial powerhouse—temperance was a dead issue. Tensions between socialists, liberals, and conservatives compounded existing suspicions between Catholics and Protestants. Intermittent wars and crackdowns on leftist social organizations rendered a durable temperance movement almost impossible, especially as the Reich consolidated and turned further right.

The German Empire industrialized, urbanized, and modernized with astounding speed in the second half of the nineteenth century, thanks largely to the coal, iron, and steel of the Ruhr Valley, and an expanding railway network that bound together the far-flung states. As cities filled with thirsty industrial workers, urban breweries expanded to meet the demand, which further widened the beer/liquor divide.

Prussian schnapps was not some refined, upper-class drink, but rather a cheap, potent high that even the poorest German could afford—much like Russian vodka just across the frontier to the east. As in Russia, too, it was the means by which the conservative Prussian state and *Junker* aristocracy got rich off the peasants' misery. Germany even had its own version of the vodka-soaked tsarist *kabak*: the dank, dimly lit *Schnapshölle* (schnapps hall). German paupers often stumbled in alone and got thoroughly drunk as quickly as possible, before being cast out by an unscrupulous tavern-keeper.

Unlike distilled schnapps, fermented beer was too bulky and (prior to bottling technology) spoiled too easily to be transported far. Consequently, every German city of any size had one or more local breweries—often with their own unique brews—that catered mostly to local workers. The beer halls of Bavaria and the industrialized cities of western Germany were bright, airy, rambunctious places for industrial workers to unwind after a long day of work. Unlike the dank *Schnapshölle*, going to the beer hall was less about getting plastered and more about fraternization, bonding, and even political organization. In the wake of industrialization, beer became the symbol of the working class, while schnapps was scorned as a poor person's drink.[40]

In 1862 Kaiser Wilhelm I (r. 1861–1888) appointed Otto von Bismarck-Schönhausen as foreign minister and chancellor. A supremely able leader from the conservative *Junker* aristocracy, Bismarck would dominate European politics for the next thirty years. Bismarck's Machiavellian project was to unify Germany around Prussia at the exclusion of Austria and establish German hegemony over Europe. Bismarck famously declared, "The great questions of the time will not be resolved by speeches and majority decisions—that was the great mistake of 1848 and 1849—but by blood and iron."[41] Bismarck was true to his motto.

In 1864, he rallied the German states together with Austria for a quick, decisive war against Denmark to reclaim Schleswig-Holstein, before then turning around and making war on Austria two years later. Victory only solidified his authority and popularity. Fearing that Germany's rising status could alter the European balance of power, France invaded in 1870, which only forced the smaller western German states back into Bismarck's waiting arms. After trouncing France, the once-loose confederation of German states was recast into the German Empire, with Prussia at its core. The new 1871 Constitution was largely drafted by Bismarck himself.[42]

The imperial constitution was a jumbled mess of contradictions. It established a system of federal states, but foreign ambassadors still ran between Berlin, Dresden, Munich, and Stuttgart, too. On paper, the states were equal. In reality, Prussia dominated politically and militarily. Elected through universal manhood suffrage, the federal parliament, or *Reichstag*, was among the most democratic in Europe, but it was entirely subordinate to the kaiser and his administration, where the true power lay. In this dual system, the Prussian prime minister was also imperial chancellor, meaning he was responsible to not only the liberal, pan-German *Reichstag*, but also the Prussian *Landtag* of the conservative *Junker* aristocracy. At the epicenter of this unwieldy system stood Bismarck himself, orchestrating virtually all aspects of domestic and foreign policy, both within Prussia and the broader empire—with the begrudging assent of the all-powerful kaiser, of course.

"It is hard being emperor under Bismarck," Kaiser Wilhelm I once quipped.[43]

That temperance activism was virtually nonexistent during Bismarck's reign is no coincidence. Everywhere around the world, temperance was a progressive movement against predatory liquor sellers who capitalized on lower-class addiction to make money. In Germany, this pitted liberals and socialists as the champion of the everyman against the wealthy, *Junker* conservatives who were looking to exploit him. It is clear whose side Bismarck was on.

The 1870s and '80s witnessed the global Long Depression, prompted by the Vienna Stock Exchange collapse and the worldwide economic Panic of 1873. Coming so soon after the founding of the empire, this "founders' crash" hit the *Junker* aristocracy hard.[44] As governments everywhere were throwing up protectionist barriers to trade, Bismarck concocted a complex system of tax breaks, incentives, and kickbacks to keep his fellow *Junkers'* plantations afloat. The most notorious corruption was the *Liebesgabe*, or "gift of love": hundreds of millions of Reichsmarks in government subsidies to keep plantation distilleries churning out liquor. Lest they draw the wrath of liberals and socialists, the exact recipients of these "gifts of love" remained a state secret, but the lion's share flowed to the *Junkers* east of the Elbe.[45]

Bismarck's subsidies weren't *just* corrupt handouts to shore up his conservative base, though they were that, too. As with empires the world over, tariffs and alcohol taxes were the primary source of government revenue. By the twentieth century, 38.5 percent of all German tax revenues came from beer and liquor, representing some 11.5 percent of the total income of the German Reich. While tamping down alcohol abuse in the name of safer streets and increased labor productivity was always a popular government platitude, too much temperance would cut into the empire's finances and hamper its geopolitical ambitions. Indeed, German militarization in general—and its dreadnaught program in particular—relied largely on squeezing Germany's drinking class.[46]

Beyond propping up the Prussian liquor machine, Bismarck also sought to crush Germany's social-democratic opposition, which had been a bastion of temperance activism in other countries (Chapters 2–3). Ostensibly to curb the rise of left-wing radicalism, beginning in 1878—and extended throughout the 1880s—Bismarck's antisocialist laws banned all Social Democratic Party (SPD) associations, meetings, and newspapers, including harsh penalties for beer halls that harbored socialist meetings.[47] Bismarck's crackdown forced labor activists underground, just as the number of industrial workers across Germany was exploding.

Moritz Busch—Bismarck's inseparable confidant—relayed the following anecdote, as if to only underscore the chancellor's position on the liquor question. "At our table, we had cognac, red wine and Mainz champagne," wrote Busch of a typical dinner spread with Bismarck's aristocratic entourage. But someone pointed out that there was no beer.

"You're better off without it," Bismarck shot back. "The widespread use of beer is regrettable. It makes you dumb, lazy, and impotent. It is the fault of all those democracy-blatherers who drink it," adding, "A good corn brandy would be preferable."[48]

The so-called labor question would ultimately prompt Bismarck's downfall. In 1888, the ninety-year-old Wilhelm died; after a reign of only ninety-nine days, so too did his son, Friedrich III. The Hohenzollern throne then passed to Germany's last kaiser, Wilhelm II, who navigated his empire through to its final destruction in World War I. When a series of workers' strikes, street protests, and bloody police clashes spread from the industrial Ruhr Valley in 1889, the young emperor and his aging chancellor argued over what to do about it.[49]

Satisfying workers' grievances—wage increases, Sunday rest, protection for woman and child labor—would only embolden the Social Democrats, the reactionary Bismarck argued, just as the antisocialist laws were set either to expire or be renewed. Iron-fisted oppression was his proposed solution. Wilhelm II, on the other hand, argued that wealthy industrialists and mine owners bore part of the responsibility for the disturbances. Believing his role as sovereign was to mediate disputes, Wilhelm negotiated with both labor and capital, enacting a series of workers' protections that won him broad support of the German public. In 1890, the antisocialist laws were repealed, and the SPD won 19.75 percent of the votes in elections to the *Reichstag*. Days later—after flying into a violent rage at his king— Chancellor Bismarck was forced out, leaving Kaiser Wilhelm II to manage the unwieldy empire alone.[50]

German Temperance Reborn as Liberal Opposition

One striking commonality of temperance movements globally is that they become Trojan horses of social activism for otherwise politically disempowered and disenfranchised people: suffragists, abolitionists, and native rights advocates in the United States, nationalists in India; Bolsheviks under the tsars. So it is noteworthy that activists themselves dated the revival of the German temperance movement for social welfare to 1878: the beginning of Bismarck's antisocialist repression.[51]

For one, with the socialists sidelined, Bismarck embarked on an ambitious public welfare scheme, which catapulted Germany to the forefront of healthcare, social security, unemployment, old-age, and disability insurance—all with an eye toward winning greater public support.[52] The year 1878 also saw the tightening of the Reich's licensing laws, which limited the taverns and retail outlets that had proliferated under Bismarck. Local licensing bodies could regulate the retail outlets in the interest of the community, as long as the *Junkers'* prerogative of distilling was not inhibited.

Finally, 1878 brought the publication of *Der Alkoholismus*: Dr. Abraham Baer's exhaustive study of alcohol abuse, meant as a blueprint for government policy. Reflecting international academic consensus, Baer argued that the biggest challenge was not the aristocrats' wine or the workers' beer, but the epidemic of distilled schnapps that kept the lower classes in destitution. He argued that the state— including public schools and the military—had the duty to socialize Germans to abstinence, responsibility, and enlightenment. Patriotic elites should lead by temperate example.[53] Activists should focus on improving the housing and diet of the working class, developing recreational alternatives to drinking, and rehabilitating alcoholics rather than punishing them. Most importantly, they should pressure the government—not for blanket prohibitions that were doomed to fail—but for sensible liquor restrictions, including Swiss-style monopolization, or Swedish-style municipalization.[54]

These developments contributed to a second wave of German temperance activism in 1883, beginning with the *Deutscher Verein gegen den Missbrauch geistiger Getränke* (the "*Verein*")—or the German Association against the Abuse of Spiritous Liquors—the brainchild of liberal writer August Lammers. "It is not our intention to form a temperance society on the old plan, enforcing total abstinence from all spiritous liquor," claimed its president, Professor Werner Nasse.[55] It would focus not on "use" through traditional abstinence pledges, but curbing "abuse"—and not focus on fermented beer and wine, but only spiritous liquors, which made it a direct enemy of the conservative *Schnapsjunkers*. Among the 143 founding members were medical professionals (including Dr. Baer), professors, businessmen, clergy, civil servants, and five Reichstag members—all liberals. Only three signatories bore the titles of nobility, and none identified with the schnapps-producing Prussian agricultural estates.[56]

Enrollment in the *Verein* expanded dramatically in the 1890s, as liberalization and repeal of the antisocialist laws breathed new life into a working-class movement. Emancipated socialists didn't exactly flock to the new organization, nor were they met with open arms by the liberals. While there was a prohibitionist strain within German socialism, unlike with Lenin in Russia, Branting in Sweden, or Vandervelde in Belgium, the leading theorist of German socialism—the Prague-born, Vienna-educated Karl Kautsky—was only lukewarm on temperance.

In a series of articles on the "*Alkoholfrage*" in his influential *Die Neue Zeit*, Kautsky echoed Engels's argument that drinking habits—and especially the transition from traditional beers to potent distilled schnapps—were a product of industrial capitalism. "Like drink," he argued, "so has the drinker, so has the way to drink changed as a result of the revolution in the conditions of production."[57] The danger to the working classes came not from the respectable beer hall—where workers could congregate away from the prying eyes of the state—but from exploitation through schnapps. As one worker explained, the "cultivated and refined" beer-drinking worker sought "the highest treasures of humanity and equality with the ruling classes," whereas the lowly "*Lumpenproletariat*, depraved through *Schnaps*, ignorance, misery and want" had no such lofty ambitions.[58] Unlike other socialists who saw labor and temperance as natural allies, Kautsky concluded that temperance activism was futile without transforming the economic and political bases of the working class. What's more, he warned German socialists that buying into liberal idealizations of middle-class family life would "destroy the cohesion of the proletariat; it would be reduced to a mass of disconnected and therefore defenseless atoms."[59]

Abandoned by the socialists to battle alone against the conservative *Junker* establishment, "the temperance movement can thus be linked to a kind of liberal subculture—even counterculture—in imperial Germany," writes historian James S. Roberts. The mission of the *Verein* was to find a third way in German politics between the gridlock of class struggle and the stagnation of interest-group politics.[60]

The *Verein* didn't care to win hearts and minds through moral suasion; the recently arrived International Order of Good Templars and church-based temperance organizations had that covered. Nor did they bother lobbying a marginalized parliament for sweeping legislation, sure to be scuttled by entrenched conservatives. Instead they focused on administrative reform of the bureaucracy: stricter licensing laws, stepping up regulation of taverns, and building coffeehouses and recreational alternatives to drinking.[61] The *Verein* quickly found local allies: municipal authorities welcomed efforts to decrease crime, and even tavern owners were eager to weed out unscrupulous competitors who cut into their bottom line.

Most importantly, the *Verein* pushed for higher taxes on distilled *Branntwein* and schnapps to make them more expensive for the working poor, encouraging their migration to less potent (and more respectable) beer consumption.[62] This, of course, brought them into direct conflict with the most fundamental political reality of the German Empire: the privileged position of the East Prussian *Schnapsjunkers* and their ties to the imperial bureaucracy.

"We stand before the outrageous fact that the richest, most privileged people in Germany will not forgo their profits from the schnapps that poisons our people," wrote the *Verein's* general secretary Wilhelm Bode in 1898. He underscored that "they have even brought matters to such a point that our ministers speak of the interests of the alcohol-producing estate owners in a tone as though the most sacred interests of the nation were at stake."[63] Given the empire's financial reliance on alcohol revenues, there is truth to this.

The *Verein* proposed a Swiss- or Russian-style distribution monopoly, specifically on distilled spirits. The *Junkers* would still distill the liquor, which would then be sold to the state for rectification, packaging, distribution, and retail sales. The producers would still make a handsome profit, and the state would get a reliable stream of income without the Byzantine taxes and shadowy *Liebesgabe* to the distillers. But as in Sweden, with greater oversight would come greater quality control, and additional revenues could be directed to fighting alcoholism. The monopolization movement gained greater traction in the first decade of the new century—especially as politicians sympathetic to the *Verein* moved into positions of power within the bureaucracy—and just as debates over public finance heated up.[64]

Stumbling toward World War I, the German military vowed a massive buildup, especially of seapower. Naval commander Alfred von Tirpitz and Chancellor Bernhard von Bülow convinced the power-obsessed Kaiser Wilhelm that the British could only be negotiated with if Germany threatened their naval dominance. Germany dramatically expanded its battleship fleet, prompting fears of German militarism, arms buildups across the continent, and Germany's increasing diplomatic isolation.[65]

Rearmament and a massive fleet of new destroyers, battleships, and U-boats came close to bankrupting the Reich, with a national debt of 4.25 billion marks. Bülow tried to patch the budgetary hole in 1908 with 500 million marks in new revenue annually, three-fifths of which came from increasing alcohol and tobacco taxes. Flexing their political muscle, parliamentary conservatives hijacked the *Verein*'s plans for a state monopoly, and mutated it into a private one, in which the *Schnapsjunkers* would regulate themselves and set their own liquor prices, while pushing the revenue burden onto brewers—effectively doubling the tax rate on beer.[66]

As you can imagine, this did not sit well with workers and socialists. German militarism wasn't just being built by working-class muscle, but also being bankrolled by their livers. "It is alcohol which finances European militarism," wrote Ernest Barron Gordon on the eve of the Great War. "It has been said that the European nations poison themselves to pay for knives with which to cut each other's throats. More regrettable is it that the masses poison themselves to pay for their own chains."[67]

German politicians had been fearful of messing with the workers' beer ever since the Panic of 1873. Back then—at the beginning of the Long Depression—brewers in Frankfurt-am-Main raised the price of beer 12.5 percent, sparking one of the bloodiest urban riots in the Reich's history.[68] But by 1908, the riots were a distant memory, and the revenue seemed worth the risk.

The resulting *Bierkrieg*—or Beer War—of 1909 saw mass protests not only in Frankfurt, but in Dortmund, Essen, Leipzig, Breslau, and elsewhere. Angry workers vowed to drink no beer at increased prices. In some cities, labor leaders successfully negotiated to keep beer prices low.[69] Seizing the momentum, the SPD's annual party congress announced a nationwide schnapps boycott to widespread approval.

Socialists admitted that while the "favorable economic and hygienic byproducts of a spirits boycott are naturally very welcome," their main goal was to emphasize how the workers were bankrolling Germany's militarization while *Junker* aristocrats sacrificed nothing. "The boycott strikes at two enemies," announced the socialist daily *Vorwärts*, "the external and the internal: the exploitation and repression of the *Junkers* and the apathy and ignorance in our own ranks." By completely swearing off the *Junkers'* rotgut schnapps—but not the workers' beer—the socialists would strike at the heart of *Junker* power, undermine the government's militarization, and deliver "the proletariat's liberation from chains of its own making."[70]

In the first five months of the *Schnapsboykott*, consumption of distilled spirits dropped by 31 percent, though momentum was difficult to sustain.[71] The beer-drinking socialists had little pull over those among the impoverished masses who preferred cheap liquor. Plus the workers' voluntary boycott was only enforced half-heartedly (if at all) before quietly fading into obscurity in 1912.

Did it work, though? In the short term, from 1908 to 1913—the last full year for statistics before World War I—average per-capita consumption dipped from 110 to 100 liters of beer annually. More strikingly, over those same five years, consumption of distilled spirits was slashed by a quarter, from four to three liters of pure alcohol per person.

But the boycott was just the penultimate nail in the coffin of the once-mighty Prussian schnapps trade (World War I would provide the final one). The statistics were unmistakable: in the fifty years from the 1860s to the 1910s, German beer consumption more than doubled, while hard liquor—which dominated under Bismarck—was cut in half.[72]

Was it the moralizing admonishments of either temperance organizations or socialists that made the difference? Or the liberal *Deutsche Verein's* targeted licensing reforms and restrictions? Or was it rising wages, social protections, and an improved standard of living that pulled more Germans from the dregs of schnapps to the respectability of beer?

In the end, it was a combination of political, social, and economic factors that transformed Germany from a liquor country like Russia into a beer country like Belgium. So, the next time you find yourself celebrating Oktoberfest with friends and family in a festive Munich *biergarten*—rather than struggling to toss back a couple of shots in a dimly lit *Schnapshölle* alone—thank the German temperance movement.[73]

Temperance Weaponized

But there is a dark coda to the story. Like so much of German society in the lead-up to the Great War, temperance also got caught in the storm of militant nationalism, with implications that reverberated around the world.

There were nationalist undertones even within the liberal *Verein*, arguing— perhaps to win support among conservatives and capitalists—that Germany's international ambitions depended on its economic vitality. A drunken workforce would be a drag on productivity. "The more sober the German labor force, the more contented, the more capable they will be," argued physician Erich Flade, "and the more resilient Germany will be in the peaceful competition among nations."[74] But as the new century progressed, those overtures to peace disappeared. In an article titled "Alcohol and the Contest of Nations," physician Arthur Esche asked, "Will we maintain our prosperity in the economic competition among nations, with England, America, and East Asia? Can we emerge victorious from an armed conflict?" For Asche, the might of the Reich depended foremost on ensuring that the new generation of troops would be both healthy and sober.[75]

The German high command shared doctors' concerns about conscripts' health. The arch-conservative military watched in horror as the mighty tsarist empire was laid low in the Russo-Japanese War of 1904–1905—the first defeat of a European empire at the hands of an Asian foe in modern times—prompting mutinies, rebellions, and revolution that nearly toppled Tsar Nicholas II (Chapter 2).

Russian land forces in 1904 were trounced by the Japanese at Port Arthur, the eastern terminus of the Trans-Siberian Railway. International war correspondents described the lopsided result as a "scuffle between a drunken guardsman and a sober policeman."[76] Efforts to mobilize new conscripts were sabotaged and delayed by vodka-fueled mobs that ransacked taverns and murdered recruitment officers.[77] When Russia tried to send its Baltic Fleet from St. Petersburg around Africa and India to fight the Japanese in the Pacific, they only got as far as the Dogger Banks—the North Sea fishing areas between Denmark and England—before they drunkenly mistook a pair of unarmed British fishing trawlers for the Japanese navy, and opened a full-side barrage. Though the only ships the Russians succeeded in hitting were from their own fleet, international outrage spread, prompting threats of war from Britain.[78]

"In the United States, in France, and even in Germany, unsparing reprobation of a deed so unjustifiable was freely uttered," wrote one reporter, "and the belief was confidently expressed that the only possible explanation was to be found in the undiscipline and probable drunken frenzy of the Russian naval officers."[79] When the Baltic Fleet did get to the Far East, they were immediately sunk by the Japanese, forcing Russia to sue for peace. The Vienna-based *Neue freie Presse* wrote, "The Japanese did not conquer, but alcohol triumphed, alcohol, alcohol."[80]

European military minds—and especially German generals—drew three lessons from Japan's resounding victory that proved to be crucial to the outbreak of the Great War. First, Russia was weak, and would take forever to mobilize its drunken men for war. Second, the emerging military consensus suggested that the attacker held the strategic advantage over the defender (the "cult of the offensive").[81] Third, insobriety in the ranks could make the difference between winning and losing, and was a very real threat to a country's geopolitical ambitions (the "cult of military sobriety").[82] From 1905 to the outbreak of World War I in 1914, militaries across Europe and the United States busily reformed: slashing troops' traditional liquor rations, encouraging temperance in the ranks, and outlawing liquor sales in canteens and military stores, near military encampments and in war zones (Chapter 15).[83]

Leading this international military consensus was none other than Kaiser Wilhelm II himself. In the Baltic port town of Flensberg in 1910, Wilhelm addressed the cadets at the newly built Mürwik Naval Academy. "I know very well that the love of drink is an old heritage of the Germans. Henceforth, however, we must free ourselves in every direction from this evil by self-discipline," he said to the officers who would man the North Atlantic battleships and U-boats in the coming war.

"I have great pleasure in seeing that in the German Navy there are now Naval Lodges of the Good Templars instituted, of which some officers and a great many of those members of the crews are members. To join these Lodges cannot be too strongly recommended." Looking abroad, he pointed to the rival British, whose naval supremacy Germany sought to challenge: "Typical, in this direction, is Great Britain, where more than 20,000 officers and crew are abstainers," he noted.[84]

"The next war, the next naval encounter, will require of you sound nerves. These are undermined by alcohol, endangered, from youth up, by its use. . . . *The nation which drinks the least alcohol will be the winner! And that, gentlemen, should be you!*" This was not simply a matter of military necessity, he said, but of social leadership. "It is a question of the future for our navy and people. If you educate the people to give up alcohol I shall have sound and sensible subjects. It is a great coming question, for when the men pass out of the service they will bring these ideas to the country at large. If you stand for these principles my people will be raised morally."[85]

The great coming liquor question likely came quicker—and in different forms—than he'd imagined. The escalations and entanglements following the assassination of Austrian archduke Franz Ferdinand in 1914 brought Germany to war on the side of Austria-Hungary. Seizing the offensive, the German Schlieffen Plan sought to smash France by quickly attacking through Belgium, and then shipping off in full force to meet the slow-to-mobilize, drunken Russians.

Nothing went according to plan. The French put up a fight, bogging the Germans down in grisly trench warfare on the Western Front. Violating Belgian neutrality brought Britain into the fight in the west, too. Finally, having enacted prohibition, the Russians mobilized with astounding speed, catching Germany in a protracted two-front war that would bleed the country dry and lead to the downfall of the empire.[86]

The political and economic crises of the Great War reframed the liquor question as a patriotic/security issue, empowering the military. Popular willingness to endure economic sacrifices for the war cause, shortened time horizons, and new venues for policymaking produced a global wave of increased restrictions on alcohol, with eleven countries—including Russia and the United States—enacting wartime prohibitions on the trade (Chapter 17).[87]

Temperance against Empire in Austria-Hungary

In Germany, temperance was wielded largely by liberals and nationalists *in support of* the empire. Further south in Austria-Hungary, however, it was used by liberals and nationalists *against* the Habsburg monarchy. Given the two empires' radically differing demographic compositions, this makes sense. The kingdoms and principalities of the German Empire were overwhelmingly populated by ethnic Germans (aside from Slavic eastern Prussia, annexed through the 1795 partition of Poland).[88] The six hundred thousand Jews in the German Empire were counted among the sixty-five million German speakers.[89]

In the Austro-Hungarian "prison house of nations," by contrast, there was no dominant nationality. The Germans of Austria and the Sudetenland composed only 23 percent of the empire's population. Twenty percent were Hungarian, 12 percent Czech, 11 percent Serbo-Croatian, 10 percent Polish, 8 percent Ruthenian (Ukrainian), 6 percent Romanian, 4 percent Slovak, and 2 percent apiece Slovenes and Italians.[90]

Managing this roisterous amalgamation of peoples was left to Habsburg emperor Franz Joseph, who ruled for sixty-eight years—from the Revolutions of 1848 until his death during World War I. Franz Joseph ascended the throne after his uncle Ferdinand abdicated in hopes of placating the liberal revolutionaries in the Hungarian heartland. In the streets of Buda and Pest (now Budapest) in 1848, liberals including Lajos ("Louis") Kossuth clamored for freedom of the press, civil and religious equality, the abolition of feudal serfdom, the establishment of a Hungarian national guard, and a Hungarian parliament elected through manhood suffrage. Unable to subdue the revolution by force, the emperor reluctantly assented to a Hungary that was *de facto* independent, save for personal ties to the emperor himself.

As the revolution became a full-blown war for Hungarian independence and Austrian forces teetered on the verge of defeat, in 1849 Franz Joseph invited Russia to march into his empire "to prevent the Hungarian insurrection developing into a European calamity."[91] The conservative gendarme of Europe, Tsar Nicholas I, was more than happy to crush the liberal revolution and keep Franz Joseph on his throne. Russian forces invaded, subdued Hungary, and placed it under martial law. Kossuth joined the wave of liberal Hungarian and German "'48ers" who were welcomed as heroes in the United States, many of whom later fought for the Union in the American Civil War.[92]

Austria's uneasy confederation with Germany ended abruptly in 1866, following a disastrous defeat in the seven-week Austro-Prussian War. Teetering on the brink of bankruptcy, Austria was forced to reconcile politically with Hungary and reorganize the empire. The compromise of 1867 resurrected Hungarian sovereignty by establishing "the Dual Monarchy of the Austrian Empire and the Kingdom of Hungary." Foreign diplomacy, defense, and finance were governed by the monarch, Franz Joseph, while domestic politics were governed by separate parliaments in Vienna and Budapest, each with its own separate government and prime minister. Each conducted its own international trade relations within a shared customs union, though they maintained a common currency. As politicians and ministers quarreled among themselves, Emperor Franz Joseph "was respected by nearly all as the linchpin that held the empire together. Industrious and unimaginative, he seemed the bureaucrat supreme."[93]

Left out of this rickety two-state system, however, were the Czechs: the Kingdom of Bohemia was never elevated to sovereignty like Hungary, leaving nationalist frustrations to simmer. An even more dangerous tinderbox was located south in the Balkans. Since the 1870s, just over the southern border in Bosnia, nationalist rebellions were brutally suppressed by an Ottoman Empire, itself already weakened through repeated wars with Russia and other European empires (Chapter 8). In 1878, Austria-Hungary occupied Bosnia-Herzegovina, and in 1908 annexed into its empire this multiethnic patchwork of Bosniak Muslims, Orthodox Serbs, and Catholic Croats, prompting a series of Balkan Wars and ultimately the spark for World War I itself.

Drinking patterns within such an eclectic, multiethnic, multidenominational land were just as complicated as the empire's politics. However, just as the

German Empire had its divide between the beer-drinking west and the Prussian *Schnappsjunkers* in the east, a similar cultural and political divide existed in the Austro-Hungarian Empire. Most distilled liquor was produced and consumed among the Slovaks, Poles, and Ukrainians in the east, while beer was most prevalent among the Austrians, Czechs, and Sudetenland Germans in the west. Wine drinking was prevalent in Hungary and southward into the Balkans. In any case, consumption of all three skyrocketed throughout the Dual Empire in the second half of the nineteenth century. In 1865, beer consumption in Austria-Hungary was some twenty-four liters per person per year; by 1900 it was seventy-one liters. Over that same timeframe, per-capita consumption of distilled spirits rocketed from three and a half to ten liters, while wine jumped from ten to twenty-four liters.[94]

Emperor Franz II established a uniform system of excise taxes on alcoholic beverages in 1829, which was repeatedly amended by raising tax rates to pay for subsequent wars. Crucial to financing their joint military, liquor taxation was *not* devolved to each of the two kingdoms. Instead, a uniform system of spirits taxation was incorporated across the entire empire. Small-scale, private distillation was largely unregulated, but taxes were imposed on large-scale commercial distilleries, at rates that would be ratcheted up to meet the state's ever-increasing revenue needs.[95]

Temperance history in the Austro-Hungarian Empire likewise tracked closely with its German counterparts: an early wave in the 1830s and '40s associated with the arrival of Baird and the ATS model, only to be extinguished by revolution and war. Despite the "prison house of nations" sobriquet, the reorganized Dual Empire was surprisingly open to civic activism. From the capitals of Vienna and Budapest—and throughout the imperial periphery in the 1880s—arose dozens of cultural, political, and nationalist movements, including temperance.[96]

Just as Germany's liberal temperance *Verein* was inaugurated in 1883, the *Österreichischer Verein gegen Trunksucht*—the Austrian Association against Drunkenness—was established the following year, deploying identical political aims and tactics. Austria's *Verein* targeted the powerful, conservative distillers—overwhelmingly members of the aristocracy in the Slavic east—by reforming the liquor licensing system, while leaving alone the beers and wines of small farmers and vintners.

Also as in Germany, such "insider" legislation was increasingly supported by "outsider" temperance activists, led by the Social Democrats. It was the same Viennese optometrist Richard Fröhlich—with whom Alice Masarykova was so smitten—who helped found the *Verein der Abstinenten* (Society of Abstainers) in 1899, and was invited to host the biennial International Congress against Alcoholism in Vienna in 1901, where the two would meet and fall in love.[97]

Beyond its labor alliances, temperance activism merged with nationalist aspirations throughout the empire. Organizations like the Czechoslovak Abstainers' League (*Československý Abstinentní Svaz*) argued that abstinence was necessary for the education and uplift not just of the individual, but of the nation itself.

Incorporating liberalism, nationalism, and socialism gave temperance a mass appeal across central Europe that largely goes unappreciated by temperance historians.

To get some sense of the relative weight of temperance activism, from libraries and archives around the world, I obtained the minutes of every International Congress Against Alcoholism from 1885 to 1934 inclusive, and geo-located each of the 15,569 total participants listed. As Table 4.1 shows, the German and Austro-Hungarian Empires were far and away the largest providers of participants— outpacing both the British and Americans, who are most commonly associated with temperance activism.

This rising clamor for temperance was especially pronounced in the lead-up to the Great War. Beginning in 1881—and ratcheting ever upward thereafter— legislators tightened licensing regulations and expanded municipal surveillance of and control over liquor retailers. Consequently, consumption of harmful distilled spirits decreased throughout the empire, even as beer and wine production inched up, just as in Germany.[98]

In 1911, the Austrian half of the empire instituted an official government Temperance Commission to thoroughly study the liquor question and draft legis-lation, just as in corporatist Sweden. Completed in 1912, their suggestions—from increased taxation, minimum drinking ages, and restricting the hours and days of sales, to prohibiting retailers to sell to drunks on credit and encouraging temper-ance as part of health education in schools and the armed forces—were largely preempted by the outbreak of war in 1914, only to be dusted off and reinstituted by many of the empire's successor states.[99]

Of course, the Great War changed everything. Taxes on distilled spirits were quadrupled to squeeze every last heller out of the trade. Imperial commanders at the front declared, "It is forbidden to give spirits to any soldier, whether officer or private, in any shop, coffee-house, or other locality." As with most regulations, the wartime declarations against hard liquor were silent on fermented beer and wine, which were still consumed, even within the armed forces. Ultimately, the war reduced the consumption of all alcoholic beverages—partly due to patriotic, war-time conservation, but largely due to the complete destruction of the distilleries of Galicia and Bukovina—the spirits-producing heartland of the empire—which were decimated by fighting on the Eastern Front.[100]

Enter Masaryk

"*Pravda vitezi*," was Tomáš Garrigue Masaryk's guiding philosophy: "the truth al-ways prevails." He lived by those words first as a teacher, scholar, and philosopher, and later as prohibitionist, liberator, and the George Washington of independent Czechoslovakia.

Table 4.1 **Attendance at Biennial International Congresses Against Alcoholism, 1885–1934[1]**

Rank	Empire	Attendees
1	German Empire * Includes 61 from the territory of Prussian Poland, 45 from German Alsace-Lorraine, and 1 apiece from German Southwest Africa and Togoland.	2,214
2	Austro-Hungarian Empire † Includes 535 from the territory of Hungary, 295 from Czechoslovakia, 55 from Galicia/Austrian Poland, 61 from Hungarian Transylvania, 52 from Lombardy/Venetia, 49 from Vojvodina, 34 from Slovenia, 14 from Croatia, 3 from Bosnia.	2,114
3	British Empire ‡ This includes 1,760 from England, Scotland, Wales, Northern Ireland, and the Channel Islands; and 97 from overseas colonial possessions.	1,857
4	United States of America	1,435
5	Switzerland	1,419
6	Union of Sweden and Norway § 942 from Sweden, 203 from Norway.	1,145
7	Belgium ‖ Includes one delegate from the Congo.	1,131
8	The Netherlands ¶ Includes one delegate from Indonesia/Java.	1,063
9	France #Includes 4 from Algeria, and one each from Tunisia, Côte d'Ivoire, and French Indochina.	1,017
10	Denmark	687
	TOTAL OF ALL COUNTRIES	15,569

[1] Data available upon request, though sources and summary statistics can be found in the appendices to my PhD dissertation: Mark Lawrence Schrad, "The Prohibition Option: Transnational Temperance and National Decisionmaking in Russia, Sweden and the United States" (University of Wisconsin–Madison, 2007), 464–84.

Tomáš was born to a poor Moravian family in 1850. After false starts as a machinist's apprentice and smithy, he left for school, first in the Moravian city of Brno and then the imperial capital Vienna, where he initially developed his sense of Czech nationalism—even leading a Czech Students' Club.[101] He'd hoped to attend the prestigious Diplomatic Academy, but since such elite institutions were reserved for the Austrian aristocracy, he studied philosophy instead, defending his dissertation, *Suicide as a Social Mass Phenomenon of Modern Civilization*, at the University of Vienna.

While studying across the German border in Leipzig, Masaryk met Brooklyn-born art student Charlotte Garrigue. The two were soon wed in the United States, with Masaryk taking the unusual step of adopting her last name as his middle name to signify their coequal bond. "Like her husband, she had a passionate love for truth, and this characteristic impressed itself all the more strongly on Masaryk himself," wrote one biographer. "The young couple did everything together, worked and studied, read their favourite authors together. Until the War separated them their life was a long record of cooperation."[102] Tomáš was initially hesitant to take up an open position at Charles University in Prague in 1882, fearing that his command of the Czech language and literature was too rusty, but Charlotte supported him, and together they both mastered the language.

To better study Slavic literatures and cultures, Masaryk began making trips to Russia, meeting frequently with the great writer Leo Tolstoy himself (Chapter 2). "I am personally very fond of Tolstoy," he later wrote, "and my own ethical and religious persuasion have been shaped by frequent reflections on his life and teaching."[103] Undoubtedly one could chalk up his populist dedication to the common man, his antipathy toward an exploitative aristocracy, and even his prohibitionism to his relationship with Tolstoy, having taken the temperance pledge as one of the first members of Tolstoy's Union Against Drunkenness.[104]

One account even suggests that Masaryk's temperance is key to understanding his entire worldview: "People laugh and scoff at those who do not drink, because most people do drink. It is quite natural. When a small minority undertakes anything, the great majority stands by and watches them with ridicule," said biographer C. J. C. Street of Masaryk. He never feared being in the minority position, since progress rarely ever begins with the acclaim of the majority. "Over and over again, his most momentous decisions were hailed as the pronouncements of a fool, if not of a knave and traitor. But each time he held to them, maintaining them in the face of his opponents, until at last they were forced to admit the justice of his views."

Expanding beyond the classroom, in the 1880s and '90s, the public intellectual Masaryk refined his populist political philosophy, which he dubbed Realism. "Realism is an attempt to popularize the whole realm of science and philosophy," he declared. "Without distorting scientific exactitude, Realism strives to render science accessible to every class of people." For Masaryk, politics was part of that science, so he encouraged his students to become actively engaged in politics, as he did.[105]

He was elected to the *Reichsrat* in 1891 and the Bohemian regional parliament in 1892, but was disillusioned with the radicalism of the Young Czech Party and soon resigned. In 1900, amid the Hilsner Affair, he founded his own party on his own principles: the Czech Realist Party. The nationalist Realists sought liberty, democracy, and ultimately independence for the people of Czechoslovakia, the creation of a separate Yugoslav state of Serbs, Croats, and Slovenes, and workplace equality and universal suffrage for women.[106] He traveled frequently—to Russia to research, to America to speak, network, and receive honorary doctoral degrees—all while writing studies on humanity, ethics, and nationalism. In 1907, the Austrian half of the empire adopted universal manhood suffrage for legislative elections, and Masaryk was elected as the sole representative of his Realist Party. By 1911, he delivered his last university lecture in Prague, turning his attention to politics full time.

During this time Masaryk also fleshed out his liberal, nationalist political ideas, which were fully informed by the temperance he'd proclaimed to the International Convention back in Vienna. He penned not one but two political treatises on the liquor question—both of which would be reprinted in multiple editions in independent Czechoslovakia after the war: *O alkoholismu* (*On Alcoholism*) in 1905 and *O ethice a alkoholismu* (*On Ethics and Alcoholism*) in 1912. In them, Masaryk was less concerned about the traffic in alcoholic beverages and more about what sobriety and enlightenment meant for the exercise of democracy, as well as humane coexistence between neighbor nations.

"The strangest country I've found on my world travels is the one where strange people enjoy poison," Masaryk began his 1905 *On Alcoholism* speech to the workers in the East Moravian town of Vsetín. "I saw strange factories that produced the poison in bulk, and strange manufacturers where the poison was sold in small packages to be consumed on the spot." In this surreal place, the storefront advertisements read, "On sale—cheap! Impotence, mental illness and epilepsy." "Here you can buy poverty," and another: "Plague, cholera, and typhus for sale."

"These are truly weird inscriptions," he said. The signs at the local inn were stranger still: "Here you can get stupid." "This is where you can go mad, and become heartless, belligerent, and rude."

"And yet, all of these places do a thriving business," Masaryk said. In this strange country, the state, the aristocracy, and even church dignitaries reap incredible profits from this liquor machine. In Germany, over three billion Reichsmarks were annually spent on alcohol, and over fourteen million krones in Austria-Hungary, well in excess of the government budgets for each empire. "Both throne and altar are built on this poison!"[107]

Masaryk's conclusions were stirring, but they weren't exactly novel. In fact, he seems to have borrowed heavily from Austrian labor leader Victor Adler, who famously proclaimed, "Alcohol is a poison which differentiates itself from other poisons in this, that the state lives from it, and that not only is its obtaining not prevented, but a powerful machinery is constantly in operation to poison individuals and the masses."[108]

Masaryk looked at traditional Czech beer-drinking patterns and concluded that his people had always imbibed. "But it has only been since the beginning of the 19th century, in which industrial distillation became much easier, that hard liquor (*kořalka*) became our national drink," making widespread alcoholism the consequence of modern industrialization.[109] As a symptom of modernity, mass drunkenness had to be opposed, not simply for the health, happiness, and well-being of the drinker, but for the family, the community, and the nation itself.

Underscoring the importance of labor networks as conduits of transnational learning, Masaryk explained how "socialist leaders like Vandervelde in Belgium, Dr. Adler in Vienna and others understand this truth, and warn the workers against drinking." But just as Lenin called imperialism the highest stage of capitalism, and Vandervelde implored the Belgian workers to stand shoulder to shoulder with the brutalized Congolese against colonization, Masaryk also implored the assembled Czechs and Slovaks there in Vsetín to resist Austrian alco-imperialism. He told the tale of Lycurgus of ancient Sparta, who forced the tribes he conquered to get drunk, "because he knew: *a nation of drinkers is a nation of slaves!*"[110]

Drunkenness is poverty and slavery (*nesvoboda*); sobriety is freedom—but a freedom that only the people can attain for themselves by overcoming their own addictions. "Political freedom, religious freedom, every freedom is impossible where people drink," Masaryk proclaimed. "Alcoholism is antiquated, reactionary, and un-progressive: stymieing progress and development, entrenching old beliefs and superstitions. Today's politics are that of the pub—since the state itself profits from the taxes on liquor and distilled spirits."

Amid the ongoing Russo-Japanese War (1904–1905)—and five years before Kaiser Wilhelm famously proclaimed that sobriety produces military victory—Masaryk made the same nationalist argument in eerily similar words. While visiting the Baltic port city of Danzig (Gdansk), a priest told him of the struggle between Germans and Poles. "The future belongs to the nation that will drink less," said the priest. "And it is true! The nation that drinks more will inevitably succumb to the one that is more sober," Masaryk concluded. "The future of every nation—and especially the future of small nations—depends on their ability to stop drinking. . . . We must not be afraid to become sober!" he proclaimed, to wild applause.[111]

Though he long opposed the liquor traffic as the foundation of the imperial state, Masaryk never advocated for legislative prohibition, instead opting for reasoned persuasion to the benefits of abstinence, echoing the approach of continental and American temperance organizations. His *On Ethics and Alcoholism* (1912) is perhaps his most comprehensive and persuasive liberal, nationalist, temperance discourse.

The ethics of individualism—individual self-determination and individual self-control—were at the root of democratic self-government, freedom, and autonomy.

To attain such higher-order freedom and democracy meant casting off backward superstitions and slavish, drunken obedience in order to become clearheaded, critical-thinking, responsible citizens. "The ethics of progress require a higher mental state from the modern man; but alcoholism weakens and lessens the whole man: making him backward, reactionary, and hostile to progress," Masaryk claimed. "The drinker is the worst Philistine and reactionary" for buying into reactionary superstitions, his "gross materialism," and his own alcoholic self-deception.[112]

Progress, on the other hand, is both personal and social, for all individuals are rooted in history and society. We all contribute to history and society—and are influenced by them in turn. If the highest ethical duty is to love and serve one's neighbor, that means working to reduce the sources of physical and mental poverty, and leading by example. "It is therefore the duty of educational and political leaders to oppose outdated alcoholic superstitions, through logic, reason, and practical abstinence."[113]

Since alcoholism is the enemy of freedom, equality, and democracy, and the liquor machine everywhere entrenches absolutism, tyranny, and slavery, then according to the nationalist Masaryk, "It is the duty of every thinking man to actively help regenerate his nation, beginning by working vigorously on improving

Figure 4.2 Thomas G. Masaryk (center, with white hair and glasses, just to the left of the crack of the Liberty Bell), Philadelphia, PA, October 26, 1918.
Source: Corbis Images.

themselves, their families, and their children." Progressivism was not simply external activism, but conscious, internal improvement. Self-education, self-reform, self-renewal—"*that* is true patriotism today."

Masaryk concluded, "The future belongs to the sober: namely, those who have opted for a higher, more moral worldview and way of life."[114]

Into the Breach

Masaryk and his family were vacationing in Germany when news arrived of Archduke Franz Ferdinand's assassination. War mobilization meant no civilian trains, leaving the stranded Masaryks to observe war preparations—first in Germany, then in Austria. "During the whole mobilization I never saw a single drunken German," he noted, perhaps as a consequence of the kaiser's cult of military sobriety, "though whole trainloads of Austrian levies on their way back to report for duty were dead drunk. I know that they drank to drown despair, but that too reflects on the State."[115] He also noted that the Czech troops seemed immune from the rally-'round-the-flag patriotism that had whipped all of Europe into a frenzy. The sight of west Slavic Czechs and Slovaks marching under a Habsburg-German flag to fight and die against their east Slavic Russian brothers elicited fatalism rather than patriotism.

A quick sidebar: the foot-dragging Czech resistance to war is best captured in the iconic satire *The Good Soldier Švejk*, by anarchist Czech conscript Jaroslav Hašek. In a series of increasingly absurd encounters, the bumbling, pipe-smoking, beer-quaffing Czech soldier Joseph Švejk frustrates the Habsburg military authorities from within. In the end, it is never clear whether the simple, good-humored Švejk is genuinely incompetent or is faking incompetence as passive resistance to Austrian imperial authority. In either event, Švejk has become a national icon, his likeness beaming from every pub and souvenir stand in Prague.[116]

The Guns of August provided a transformational moment for the nationalist Masaryk, who had previously only pressed for greater Czech autonomy within the Austro-Hungarian Empire. Fellow Slavs fighting and dying on the wrong side convinced him that Czechoslovak independence was the only political course.[117] With his wife and children under surveillance and later house arrest, Masaryk fled Prague only to return triumphantly as president four years later.[118] From Geneva, Paris, and London, he coordinated resistance to the Habsburg monarchy. He networked with the leaders of the Western powers—agitating for Czechoslovak independence and planning for the postwar reorganization of Central Europe—while his Czech spies provided crucial intelligence for the Allied war effort.

After the February Revolution dethroned Tsar Nicholas II, in May 1917 Masaryk headed for Russia—following the exact same path through Stockholm to Petrograd that Lenin, Trotsky, Vandervelde, Branting, and countless others had

Figure 4.3 One of six hundred illustrations Josef Lada (1887–1957) created for *Osudy dobrého vojáka Švejka za světové války*, translated literally as *The Fateful Adventures of the Good Soldier Švejk during the World War*.

taken (Chapter 3). His intention was to organize legions of Czechoslovak prisoners of war—captured by the Russians—to fight alongside the Allies and against the Austrians and Germans. By the time he got to Moscow, however, he found nothing but Russians fighting each other. There, in the upscale Hotel Metropol, he slept on a mattress on the floor so as not to get hit by the ricocheting bullets and shrapnel from the Bolsheviks' urban warfare. "The worst thing of all," Masaryk said when the hotel finally fell to the Reds, "was when the guards got drunk on the wine they found in the cellar." Though unarmed and powerless, he demanded that the Bolshevik commander discipline the belligerent drunks, which he did. Despite almost getting shot on numerous occasions amid the chaos in Petrograd, Moscow, and Kyiv in 1917, "the only time I was really afraid was when the soldiers in Moscow got drunk; terrible things might have happened then."[119]

In Petrograd in June, he met diplomats from the United States, which had just entered the Great War to make the world "safe for democracy," according to President Woodrow Wilson's famous adage (Chapter 17). Wilson had personally dispatched delegates, including Senator Elihu Root, to ascertain how best to keep Alexander Kerensky's crumbling Provisional Government in the war. "I came here because there was an intrigue here," Masaryk told the American diplomats. Since Czechs preferred surrender to dying for the German cause, "there are said to be 350,000 Bohemian prisoners here." If he could secure permission from the Russian government—whichever Russian government could be found—he would organize them into an army to fight alongside the Americans in France.

The American diplomats were intrigued.

"America has brought in to the War this ideal element—to help others establish democracy. I hope this principle will prevail at the Peace Conference," Masaryk told the Root mission. Laying out his postwar vision, he continued, "At the Peace Conference the Bohemian people want a republic—an absolutely independent nation. It should include Bohemia and the Slovaks." This independent Czechoslovak state, along with a reconstituted Poland, "together will make a barrier against Germany." The Americans telegraphed Masaryk's proposal back to Washington, since it aligned with President Wilson's proclamation that America was fighting "for the rights of nations great and small and the privilege of men everywhere to choose their way of life."[120]

In the meantime, Masaryk got to work: negotiating diplomatically and tactfully with the Russian Provisional Government. Within months, he'd built a one-hundred-thousand-man army—an army without a state.

Getting Masaryk's new army of independence from the heartland of Russia to the Western Front in France was a daunting task. The Bolshevik Revolution and ensuing multisided civil war between communist "reds" and royalist "whites" made it impossible. With all other ports blocked, in 1918 Masaryk negotiated with the Bolsheviks for a months-long passage across the six-thousand-mile Trans-Siberian Railway to the Pacific port of Vladivostok, where they could then be evacuated to France. Suspicious that the Czechs might join the counterrevolutionary whites, Leon Trotsky's fledgling Red Army tried to disarm the Czechs in Siberia. The Czechs fought back. The Czech legion effectively seized control of much of the Trans-Siberian Railway until 1920—well after World War I had ended in 1919. The Czechs never ended up fighting along the Western Front in France, but instead would later return home to an independent Czechoslovakia, thanks largely to Masaryk.[121]

Across Siberia, Masaryk scurried ahead of the legion: to Vladivostok and Tokyo, and then sailing for the United States, where he received a hero's welcome. In Chicago—which Masaryk rightly claimed was "next to Prague, the largest Czech city in the world"—some two hundred thousand poured into the streets to greet him.[122] In Pittsburgh, he concluded an agreement with Czech and Slovak expatriates vowing to create a unified state. As the Austro-Hungarian Empire was in its death throes in mid-1918, Masaryk was busily negotiating with President Wilson and the French and British allies to recognize Czechoslovakia as an independent state. In October 1918 in Washington, DC, Masaryk drafted a formal Declaration of Independence, with his Czechoslovak National Council quickly recognized as the Provisional Government by Allied and American governments. For good measure, Masaryk met together with Polish, Yugoslavian, Ukrainian, Romanian, Baltic, and other representatives in Independence Hall in Philadelphia to proclaim a Mid-European Union of independent states, formed from the ruins of the once-mighty empires.[123]

The new, independent Czechoslovakia to which Masaryk would soon return would be a parliamentary republic, based on liberty, universal suffrage—both men's and women's—and protections for national minorities. Indeed, during Masaryk's four terms as president between the wars, Czechoslovakia was among the most stable and robust European democracies.[124]

Civil society flourished after World War I, as prewar temperance organizations like the Czechoslovak Abstainers' League were rebuilt. Led by Masaryk's temperate example, Czechoslovak legislation reined in the worst excesses of the liquor traffic: limiting the hours and locations of sales, instituting minimum drinking ages (sixteen for beer and wine, eighteen for more potent distilled liquors), and adopting the local option so that municipalities could inspect and restrict taverns. Most notably, the Czechoslovak Republic prohibited the sale of whiskey and other distilled spirits. Though this had little practical effect in the traditionally beer-drinking regions of Bohemia, it proved difficult to enforce in the spirits-drinking Slovak and Ukrainian-Carpathian regions. Still, rates of beer, wine, and spirits consumption in independent Czechoslovakia were far below their prewar levels as part of the Austro-Hungarian Empire.[125]

"I would like to have our whole country dry," Tomáš Garrigue Masaryk mused, after being voted the first president of an independent Czechoslovakia. Ever the realist, he recognized policy preference was in the minority in the newly democratic state. "As president I've tried to get my guests to give up wine and beer with their meals, but to no avail," Masaryk said. "Oh well, to each his own. I don't make a religion of abstinence, but from time to time I try to make my fellow citizens see that immoderate indulgence in alcohol is, to be blunt, stupid."[126]

Meanwhile, in Budapest and Vienna

The forces of liberalism and nationalism were not everywhere as triumphant as in Czechoslovakia following World War I. That many of the newly independent states were formed at the territorial expense of the once-mighty Kingdom of Hungary did not sit well with the Hungarians. Its Slovak and Carpathian lands were claimed by Masaryk and the Czechoslovaks, Romanian forces were battling to seize Transylvania, and Croatia was being cleaved off into the Kingdom of Yugoslavia. Hungary was in the process of losing 72 percent of its territory, half its major cities, and virtually all of its mineral resources.[127] Hungarian national humiliation rose in lockstep with hyperinflation, mass unemployment, and shortages of food, housing, and coal. Violent street protests became commonplace.

Finally, on October 31, 1918—in what would become known as the Aster Revolution—Social Democrats and Hungarian soldiers seized control of government offices throughout Budapest. Powerless, Franz Joseph's successor, King Charles IV, was forced to recognize the new Hungarian Democratic Republic of Mihály Károlyi. The interim prime minister's first order of business was to formally terminate the shaky Austro-Hungarian Compromise of 1867 and forever dissolve the Austro-Hungarian union.

Unnoticed amid the political tumult was the return of communist revolutionary Béla Kun. Kun was an Austro-Hungarian soldier who was captured by the Russians in battle in 1916 and shipped to a POW camp in the Ural Mountains. Radicalized by the revolutionary enthusiasm of 1917, he became an ardent communist, meeting Lenin and Bolshevik leaders in Moscow and Petrograd. He even volunteered to fight with the Red Army in the brutal Russian Civil War.

Lenin, Kun, and the Bolsheviks agreed that the political chaos in Budapest made Hungary ripe for proletarian revolution. When he returned in 1918, Kun was in constant radio-telegraph communication with Lenin. Ever the demagogue, he promised disaffected workers and soldiers that only the Communists—and not the milquetoast Social Democrats—could restore Hungary's greatness, and that Bolshevik Russia was ready to help fight to restore its former borders. (It wasn't.)

On March 21, 1919, Hungarian Communists seized control of the state. Kun proclaimed the new Hungarian Soviet Republic was not just allied with Bolshevik Russia, but was legally part of the soon-to-be Soviet Union, despite the thousand-mile separation between Moscow and Budapest. In lockstep with the Bolsheviks, Kun imposed the most brutal policies of Russian War Communism: nationalizing industry, forced collectivization, and gunpoint grain requisitions.

On the very first day of the revolution, the second order of the new Revolutionary Governing Council enacted prohibition to impose discipline and vigilance against counterrevolution, following the Petrograd example (Chapter 2). Drunks could find themselves in jail for a year. Drink sellers would face draconian penalties and the confiscation of all their property. Ignorance of any government decree was no defense—they were to be published on the front page of every newspaper.[128] State propaganda proclaimed that alcohol debased the working class, both morally and economically. The alcohol traffic—in Hungary meaning primarily the wine industry—was the most dangerous weapon of capitalist exploitation and had to be opposed by all means necessary.[129]

Prohibition met immediate pushback, undermining support for communism in the Hungarian countryside. Delegates complained that the military bureaucrats sent into the countryside to administer the prohibition often wound up stammering drunk. Moreover, there were the revenue considerations: by letting billions of krones worth of Hungarian wine spoil into vinegar, the communists were exacerbating the young state's financial crisis. The prohibition was ultimately relaxed on July 23, 1919, allowing each worker over eighteen years of age a half-liter of wine per day. This move was quickly overshadowed the following day, however, as military losses to the Romanians provoked an anticommunist coup and a brutal backlash known as the Red Terror. Within a week, the Soviet government collapsed. In the resulting White Terror, Hungarian communists, leftist intellectuals, Jews, and sympathizers were rounded up and executed, often without trial. Following the withdrawal of Romanian occupation forces, the conservative Kingdom of Hungary was reestablished in 1920. Prohibition was revoked along with all the other statutes of the previous regimes.[130]

Naval admiral Miklós Horthy would become regent of the now-landlocked kingdom, overseeing its rightward drift into becoming a Nazi German puppet state. Béla Kun fled to Moscow and agitated for European revolutions as part of the Comintern before falling victim to a Stalinist purge. In 1937 a secret court found him guilty of Trotskyism; he was shot later that day.[131]

As Budapest experimented with Lenin's revolutionary prohibitionism, next door in Red Vienna—so-called as, between 1918 and 1934, the city's democratically elected Social Democrats vowed to make Vienna a shining example of social democratic politics—liquor-control policy tracked more in line with Scandinavian socialism (Chapter 3).

All adult citizens—men and women—exercised voting rights in the new postwar republic. The new government quickly enacted an eight-hour workday, unemployment insurance, labor protections, healthcare, maternity and child-welfare services, rent freezes, and the building of public housing projects, financed through progressive taxation. "Here, in a purely capitalistic surrounding, a socialist municipality established a regime which was bitterly attacked by economic liberals," wrote political economist Karl Polanyi—who fled Béla Kun's Hungarian Soviet Republic for Vienna. In his touchstone *The Great Transformation* (1944), he wrote, "No doubt some of the interventionist policies practiced by the municipality were incompatible with the mechanism of a market economy. But purely economic arguments did not exhaust an issue which was primary social, not economic."[132]

As temperance and prohibitionism were diametrically opposed to economic exploitation, it makes sense that—as visiting American prohibitionist William Johnson noted—"the socialist movement in Austria is closely interwoven with the temperance movement." Johnson was a remarkable figure: a larger-than-life global emissary for the dry cause, with a nickname as colorful as his personality: "Pussyfoot." Johnson plays an outsized role in the following chapter on Great Britain, as well as virtually every chapter that follows it. But in this context, one of his European tours brought him to postwar Vienna, where he'd frequently pass the sprawling Hofburg Palace of the former Habsburg monarchy.

"That palace has 1,000 rooms, all for the use of one man," his Viennese host explained. "Ten minutes walk will bring us to a district where whole families are to be found in a single room. It was not right." Johnson reflected that this stark reality was "a stiffer argument for socialist doctrine than all the 'red' propaganda that a brigade of agitators could produce."[133]

On that ten-minute walk, the American visitor passed apothecary shops—windows "filled with an elaborate display of alcoholic beverages." Apparently the cash-strapped new government was selling off the former emperor's high-end luxury wines to help pay for their ambitious social programs. "They wanted to get rid of the stuff as quickly as possible so that the irreverent would not make sarcastic remarks about the government drink shop, especially at a time when the government is increasingly friendly to the temperance reform," Johnson wrote. Indeed, not just the mayor, but the new republic's parliamentary leaders and President Michael Hainisch were all temperance men.

But the best example of the power of socialist temperance, Johnson claimed, was the "success of one of the most extensive socialistic enterprises of modern times": the *Gemeindebau*, or community-constructed housing. To address the housing shortage for industrial workers, the state provided the land and building materials, the workers built the houses and apartment blocks where they would live. "This labor is expended in part on his own home and in part on somebody else's home and in part on enterprises of common use," Johnson explained. "By this method, the carpenter does only carpenter work, the bricklayer does only bricklaying work and so on." The *Gemeindebauten* blocks, such as Karl-Marx-Hof, became symbols of the socialist movement; later in the February Uprising of 1934, they became strongholds of organized socialist resistance against the eventual takeover of those Austrofascists who quickly snuffed out Austria's multiparty democracy.

"The unique part of the whole affair is that the entire establishment is prohibition territory," Pussyfoot said of the *Gemeindebauten*. "The common clubhouse or amusement concern consists of an elaborate building, with a restaurant, soft drink fountain, a hall for lectures and moving pictures and an illuminated beerless beer garden. No intoxicating liquors are either sold or allowed on the premises; even the name of the concern is '*Alkoholfreie Gaststätte des Arbeiter-Abstinentenbundes*' [Alcohol-free restaurant of the Workers' Abstinence Association], which proclaims it as a boozeless affair."[134]

Of course, the fascist takeover of Austria put an end to the Red Vienna period, and with it the achievements of the temperate socialist movement there. Still, in its experiment, "Vienna achieved one of the most spectacular cultural triumphs of Western history," the Christian socialist Polanyi wrote, "an unexampled moral and intellectual rise in the condition of a highly developed industrial working class which, protected by the Vienna system, withstood the degrading effects of grave economic dislocation and achieved a level never reached before by the masses of the people in any industrial society."[135]

In the end, Austria's interwar socialism differed dramatically from Hungary's Bolshevik experiment, as well as Czechoslovakia's multiparty liberalism—and yet the liquor question still permeated each.

PART II

THE BRITISH EMPIRE

5

Temperance and Self-Determination in the British Isles

Essex Street, London, United Kingdom: Thursday, November 13, 1919

Bill Johnson was uniformly loathed by drinkers across Britain. He didn't seem to mind. But even as the American prohibitionist took a quick afternoon nap—still addled with the flu that had followed him from mossy Glasgow—Johnson could hardly foresee the confrontation that awaited him in London that evening.[1]

Johnson was no stranger to confrontation. As a Wild West lawman, he smashed up illegal saloons throughout the dry Indian Territory of present-day Oklahoma (Chapter 16). After two of his deputies were gunned down in cold blood, he reverted to stealthy midnight raids, leading local reporters to call him "Pussyfoot." The nickname stuck.[2] After leaving the Indian Service, his celebrity only grew as a fixture of the Anti-Saloon League of America: muckraking the liquor traffic in Europe and stumping for statewide prohibition referenda across the United States ahead of the Eighteenth Amendment (Chapter 17).

With a similar local-option referendum scheduled for Scotland in 1920, the prohibitionist Scottish Permissive Bill Association wasted no time in inviting the famed American to make the dry case. So in 1918—with the Great War raging—Pussyfoot Johnson zigzagged across the submarine-infested North Atlantic for a speaking tour of the British Isles.

"Temperance lectures in Scotland and England were not exactly tea party affairs," he later wrote. "Breaking up public meetings was a national sport."[3] He'd been shouted down and pelted with rotten eggs, and mixed it up in brawls between "wet" paid goons and temperate ironworkers. But nothing prepared the American for his welcome to the imperial metropole of London.

Bill Johnson rose from his nap, donned his coat, and ambled down the Strand for Essex Hall, where he was to debate the merits of prohibition against a renowned London barrister.

"What's all the excitement about?" Johnson approached the leader of a roist-erous student crowd gathering outside the packed hall.

"We are laying in for Pussyfoot Johnson," came the response. "He thinks he is going to speak here this afternoon, but he isn't!"

"Do you know that bird when you see him?" Johnson asked the British student. He didn't.

"Well, I know him," Johnson said. "I see him every day." So Pussyfoot accurately described himself to the hoodwinked crowd before the constables admitted him through the gates into the hall.[4]

There was even greater disorder inside than out. The event was organized "to give the public an opportunity to hear both sides of the prohibition question," wrote *The Times*, but "the back of the hall was packed with students, who maintained a fire of lively interruptions, heedless of appeals for fair play to both sides." Over the din, a student leader stepped forward, declaring that it was only for Britishers to decide whether they should be wet or dry, not meddlesome Americans. Pussyfoot abso-lutely agreed. However, since he would not have been there without the invitation of his British hosts, he claimed the right to speak when so invited.[5]

And that's when all hell broke loose.

Like a wave, hundreds more students burst into the already-packed hall, tossing the more respectable audience members about like corks.

"It was 2,000 to one, but I began swinging and was doing pretty well in a hope-less cause when someone grabbed my ankles, gave a jerk, and down I went with practically the entire student population of London piled atop my flattened frame," Johnson later recalled.

As I struggled and squirmed under that mountain of flesh, hair and bone, I saw a hand poking down through the mass, reaching for my coat collar. I could move neither arms or legs, but I managed to surround the groping thumb with my teeth and gnawed away vigorously. Down came a piercing howl of pain. I recognized the voice; it was my bosom friend, Rev. Wilson Stuart, trying to pull me out of the mess. He was playing the good Samaritan and he got the usual Samaritan's reward to such an extent that he carried his wounded hand in a sling for days.[6]

With that, Johnson realized that this wasn't some life-and-death struggle, but the good-natured bad behavior of a student "rag." He submitted to the mob.[7] They hoisted Pussyfoot on their shoulders and out into the streets, occasionally pelting the American with bags of flour or christening him with bottles of beer.[8] For hours, he was paraded through West End thoroughfares as roisterous students waved anti-Pussyfoot banners. The front cover of Rome's *La Tribuna Illustrata* depicted students carrying a beleaguered man (not at all resembling the bald-headed Mr. Johnson) past the bronze lions of Trafalgar Square. "By this time, it seemed that all

Figure 5.1 Cover of *La Tribuna Illustrata* (Rome) depicting the Pussyfoot "rag" through London passing Trafalgar Square. A. Minardi, *La Tribuna Illustrata,* 30 Novembre–7 Dicembre 1919 (Vol. 27, n. 48).

London had turned out to join in the celebration," Pussyfoot reminisced. "Toughs and street corner loafers attached themselves to the procession at every step," diluting the students' numbers.[9]

"The boys never intended to harm me and I knew it," he recalled.

> I leaned over from my stretcher and joked with them. One handed me a cigaret (sic), which I smoked with considerable enjoyment. I had no hat, so I reached down and snatched the first that was handy. It was knocked off presently and I got another by the same method. Altogether, I had a

half dozen hats during the fray. There was nothing to worry about on that score; the supply was inexhaustible.[10]

As the procession passed Oxford Circus, the mob was met by six divisions of Metropolitan Police, amounting to two hundred bobbies.[11] A furious scrap ensued "in which blows flew like hailstones."[12] Police maneuvered a motor car close enough for Pussyfoot to jump for freedom.

"I made a desperate dive for it, tearing loose from a sea of hands which clutched at me and my rescuers so determinedly that they ripped the trousers off one policeman," Pussyfoot remembered. "So far as I know, those pants still are cherished as a souvenir by some London student."[13] Yet at that very moment of rescue, some rock or projectile whizzed through the air and caught Pussyfoot square in the right eye. The damage was so severe that his eye was unsalvageable and had to be removed.

The London Pussyfoot riot made headlines worldwide and established Johnson's credentials as a global celebrity. The American consulate demanded an investigation. So too did King George V and the British government, adding their sincerest public apologies to the mass outpouring of sympathy nationwide.[14] A delegation of penitent students visited Pussyfoot's hospital bedside, as reporters and photographers covered the encounter. From under a pile of head bandages, Pussyfoot's unmistakable smile beamed, telling the students, "You had a good time; I had a good time. I have no complaints. But if you want some real fun, get into the game against the greatest enemy of the human race—drink."[15]

Pussyfoot's good humor and fair play endeared him even to his detractors. In future speaking engagements, Johnson could always rely on battalions of rock-fisted sympathizers to stomp any mischief-makers to the curb. Britons nationwide took up a collection amounting to thousands of pounds for their wronged American guest, but Pussyfoot took not a shilling. Instead he donated everything to St. Dustan's Hospital for soldiers blinded in the Great War, which won him even greater respect. For years after the riot, Pussyfoot remained a feature at Madame Tussaud's wax museum in London, his bandaged, beaten likeness beaming with a smile between Voltaire and Horatio Bottomley.

In later years, Johnson reflected on the spirit of renewal and invigoration of the dry cause, which, he said, "made the loss of that eye seem a trivial matter. I would not care to have it back in exchange for the multitude of human things that grew up around its passing. Those things were worth a whole bushel basket full of eyes."[16]

English Core, Scottish Periphery

From Romans introducing brewing to the pagan Britons through wobbly Winston Churchill, British history is soaked in alcohol. Efforts to standardize, license, and control alcohol date back nearly as far: the same *Magna Carta* (1215) that constrained the power of the crown also standardized measures for selling wine and beer.[17] More modern efforts to confront drunkenness, however, were inexorably intertwined with the economic, social, and political differences among the English, Scottish, and Irish nations that constituted the United Kingdom.

Modern Britain dates from 1707, when, after centuries of acrimony, the Kingdom of England (including Wales) entered into a Treaty of Union with the Kingdom of Scotland. While the monarchy, government, and parliament were unified, the Scots retained their own distinct legal code, education system, and Presbyterian Church separate from the Anglicans. Similarly, the Acts of Union (1800) absorbed the crown of Ireland into a new "United Kingdom of Great Britain and Ireland," which would endure until the War of Irish Independence (1919–1921), when the largely Catholic Republic of Ireland won independence from protestant Northern Ireland and the rest of the United Kingdom.

Throughout the reign of Queen Victoria (1837–1901), Britain's economically stratified society underwent evolutionary (rather than revolutionary) political change. National politics were the purview of the monarch, her government ministers, and the two Houses of Parliament. The aristocratic House of Lords—the upper chamber, consisting of several hundred noblemen and high clergy whose hereditary station entitled them to serve—gradually waned in importance, retaining only a veto over legislation from the lower chamber. The House of Commons, by contrast, comprised nearly 700 elites elected from constituencies across England, Wales, Scotland, and Ireland. Parliamentary debates largely fell along partisan lines, between the constitutionalist Whigs (Liberal Party) and the royalist Tories of the Conservative and Unionist Party. The franchise—limited to just a half-million property-owning men at the beginning of the Victorian Era—was expanded to most middle-class men by the mid-nineteenth century; to most working-class men, too, by late century; and full adult suffrage for both men and women without a property requirement by 1928.[18]

If we're to understand prohibitionism as the political reform movement it was, three institutional challenges are worthy of note. First—built on wealth, rank, and title—the British political system had small-c conservatism baked in to its economic foundations in moneymaking. The aristocracy could be depended on to defend its wealth and status, using the power of the state to advance its capitalist interests if necessary. This was as true at home as it was in conquering new markets abroad as part of a globe-spanning empire on which the sun famously never set. Political reforms, like gradually expanding suffrage, resulted not from high-minded benevolence, but conservatives' begrudging calculations as how best to preserve their wealth and status.

Second—reflecting both population and wealth—political representation in London was overwhelmingly English. Of the 658 total members of the House of Commons during the mid-nineteenth century, only 105 (or 16 percent) represented Irish constituencies; Scotland had only 53 (8 percent). Such powerlessness fueled political frustrations, nationalism, and calls for greater autonomy through so-called Home Rule.

Third—regardless of nationality—the alcohol business was disproportionately represented both in Parliament and throughout the political aristocracy. For successful businessmen to ascend into the peerage—the British political and economic elite marked by hereditary titles and noble ranks—required wealth, a landed estate of one thousand acres or more, and usually the renunciation of ties to their business. Yet brewing easily reconciled with traditional gentry life, so unlike many industrial magnates, many British aristocrats never divorced from their brewing businesses. Toward the end of the Victorian Era, one in every five Members of Parliament (MPs) and one in four peers were alcohol manufacturers, stock owners, or trustees of the liquor industry. By the 1880s, famous brewers like Englishmen Sirs Michael A. Bass and Henry Allsopp joined Irish Sir Arthur Guinness (great-grandson of the namesake brewery's founder) and Scottish Sir Dudley Marjoribanks in Parliament; critics were led to dub the House of Lords "the beerage."[19] Even this entrenched liquor trade exhibited regional divisions, with London-based brewers being particularly disdainful of their provincial counterparts, especially in Scotland and Ireland.[20]

Any discussion of temperance—not only in the British Isles, but in Britain's global empire (Chapters 6–8)—must begin by acknowledging the disproportionate political might both of the English and of the alcohol business within this inherently conservative political-economic system. Indeed, that British history did not have the political "fireworks" of American prohibitionism may have less to do with any purported weakness of British temperance sentiment, and more with the overwhelming power of the conservative, English liquor establishment.

Standard British temperance histories that don't begin by laying out this institutional context struggle to explain why prohibitionism originated in the Scottish north and the Irish west of the country, where "the cause was to find much of its sustenance and vigour throughout the nineteenth century."[21] Understood within a global framework where temperance embodied opposition to imperial subjugation, however, this makes all the sense in the world.

That Pussyfoot Johnson should be welcomed so warmly in Scotland while being pilloried in London so clearly reflects this long-standing north-south divide. Ten years earlier, American prohibitionist Carrie Nation was hailed in Scotland before getting pelted with rotten eggs in England.[22] And sixty-three years before that, Frederick Douglass and William Lloyd Garrison experienced virtually the same thing (Chapter 11). Since they lacked sovereignty over their own policymaking, the frustrations of Scottish working-class and middle-class temperance activism were wedded to nationalist resistance against English aristocratic dominance.[23]

The father of British temperance was Scotsman John Dunlop, born near Glasgow in 1789.[24] Returning from France in 1828, he was troubled by the relatively low productivity of the Scottish working class, which he chalked up to their love of whiskey. Patterned after American Temperance Society (ATS) lodges and their pledges to abstain from distilled spirits (Chapter 11), Dunlop inaugurated the Glasgow and West of Scotland Temperance Society in 1829, soon renamed the Scottish Temperance Society.[25] The same year, his investigation into the ATS—*On the Extent and Remedy of National Intemperance*—sold an astounding 140,000 copies. As his study spread, so too did British temperance lodges.[26] Dunlop's society denounced not merely drunkenness but also the international slave trade and Britain's recently declared Opium War, which was forcing Chinese submission to the British East India Company's lucrative opium trade (Chapter 7).[27] These issues were all cut from the same cloth: standing up for the downtrodden against an oligarchic state that subjugated them.

From the beginning, then, it was predominantly Scots who spread temperance across Britain: most fruitfully across northern England, with progressively less fertile soil further south. Scotsman William Collins twice went to London to set up a temperance lodge, twice finding only hostility. Only in 1831 was a London Temperance Society inaugurated, but then quickly reorganized as an empire-spanning organization: the British and Foreign Temperance Society (BFTS). The following year, Joseph Livesey and "The Seven Men of Preston" signed the first teetotal pledge in England.[28] John Dunlop himself moved to London in 1839, hoping to broadcast his temperance message from the busy imperial metropole, but was ultimately frustrated by the lack of support.[29]

Undertaking systemic investigations, Dunlop asserted that drunkenness was no individual moral failing, but the result of a socioeconomic system that compels addiction. "The full triumph of slavery is where it has so blinded the mind, as to be unfelt as galling and debasing. The people of Great Britain and Ireland are slaves, as if in fetters, to drinking usage, and they know it not," Dunlop concluded. "The restoration of the Briton to that freedom," he said, will only arise from "the destruction of the compulsory system" of drinking customs and pursuit of social status that encourages inebriety. That push for liberation, he found, came far more often from the Scots rather than the English.[30]

The whole history of British prohibitionism turns on this divide: between north and south, Scots and English, Presbyterians and Anglicans. By the 1830s, fissures developed between temperance moderates—who opposed the traffic in just distilled spirits: whiskey and gin—and absolutists who vowed a "T-total pledge" to abstain from *all* alcohol, including fermented wine and beer. The English tended toward moderation, the Scottish (and Irish) toward total abstinence. Northerners called southerners halfhearted; the south viewed northerners as uncompromising "fanatics." Once the flagship National Temperance Society was finally established in London, suspicious northerners spurned it—setting up a teetotal rival: the British Association for the Prevention of Intemperance.[31] Even the later religious temperance organizations of the 1860s and 1870s—the Church of England Temperance Society, the fraternal International Order of Good Templars, friendly societies like the Rechabites, Band of Hope youth missions, the Salvation Army, and Blue Ribbon missionaries—all had their own north-south fissures.[32]

"Ireland Sober, Ireland Free"

To the north-south political, economic, and social divide between Scotland and England, we have to add the east-west divide between the Protestant English and the Catholic Irish. Though we commonly equate Irish culture with heavy drinking—from Guinness beer, Jameson's whiskey, and the drunken revelry of St. Patrick's Day—it may come as some shock that temperance was actually stronger in Ireland than anywhere else in the British Isles.

On its face, this claim of Irish temperance seems so contrary to our conventional perceptions as to be laughable. Nevertheless, it's true. In the nineteenth century, temperance claimed a far greater proportion of the Irish population than in England, Scotland, or even the United States. They had lower per-capita alcohol-consumption rates, too.[33] Standard histories that (falsely) proclaim American prohibitionism was a "symbolic crusade" to "discipline" the unwashed immigrant hordes (Chapter 18) have to grapple with this uncomfortable truth: the Irish Paddy fresh off the boat was statistically more likely to be a teetotaler than the heavy-drinking white, nativist evangelicals in the American heartland.[34]

Ireland is often called "Britain's first colony," and was the testing ground for many British colonial techniques used the world over: divide-and-conquer, settler colonialism (including liquor men), and requiring the Irish to pay for both their own defense *and* the British debt.[35] Perhaps the most enduring colonial legacy, however, was the colonizers' self-justifying alcohol narrative: painting a picture of "savage" inebriety among the subject population as a justification for continued colonial domination and exploitation under the guise of a "civilizing mission." The Americans used it in North America (Chapters 9–10, 15), and Europeans used it in Africa (Chapter 3), but the British used it *everywhere* they encountered native populations: Africa, South Asia, Australia, and the Middle East (Chapters 6–8). "So, in English eyes, the Irish became violent, cruel, and drunken to a degree that was scarcely human," noted temperance historian Elizabeth Malcolm. "While it is easy to detect and dismiss the excesses of this stereotype, it still remains remarkably persistent."[36]

Just as American temperance history stretches back long before the establishment of brick-and-mortar temperance lodges to the colonization of Native Americans (Chapters 9–10), Irish temperance was likewise deeply rooted in nationalist resistance to British colonization. By the eighteenth century, the Kingdom of Ireland—the largely Catholic island, including the Protestant north—was little more than an English client state, over which the British crown held sway in domestic politics.[37]

Inspired by the American and French Revolutions, in 1798, the Society of United Irishmen included temperance in its nationalist rebellion against British rule. The society argued—not without reason—that the English encouraged the consumption of whiskey to keep the Irish stupefied, submissive, and easier to control.[38] The nationalist leadership encouraged their followers "to promote a brotherhood of affection amongst Irishmen of every religious persuasion," and to "be sober, and promote sobriety in all your circles." More importantly, the United Irishmen targeted the liquor trade, which enriched the English at their expense: "abstain as much as possible from the consumption of exciseable articles, or those which pay high customary duties, such as *wine, spirits, sugar, tobacco, &c.*: you will thereby dry up the springs and sources of *corruption*, that powerful engine in the hands of your cruel and implacable enemies. A government which draws its resources from vice (such as GAMBLING and DRUNKENNESS), must fall so soon as the people become virtuous."[39]

The movement was ultimately infiltrated and crushed. The ensuing guerilla war forced Ireland's incorporation into an expanded "United Kingdom of Great Britain and Ireland" in 1800. Still, generations before traditional temperance lodges spread across the United States or Britain proper, Irish nationalists understood their subjugation through alco-imperialism. The financial foundations of English colonialism were built on the same booze that kept the Irish weak and pliable. From the beginning, then, Irish temperance was Irish patriotism.

As in Scotland, formal Irish temperance leagues dated from 1829—when Belfast Presbyterian John Edgar took up the cause and famously dumped all his family's liquor out the parlor window.[40] That year, Edgar founded the Ulster Temperance Society based upon the ATS model. Like ATS cofounder Lyman Beecher's *Six Sermons on Intemperance* (1826) in the United States (Chapter 11), Edgar's temperance aimed not at moral suasion among impoverished drunkards, but at the upper-class drink seller who made the profit. "Temperance Societies, all over the empire, could soon point to cases here and there in which individuals, from conscientious motives, had ceased to sell the drink of drunkards," Edgar wrote. "There were not wanting instances of distillers who, on the same grounds, abandoned the manufacture."[41]

Likewise as elsewhere, Irish temperance focused not on traditional beers, ales, and stouts, but the cheap, high-powered distilled whiskey, which was the scourge of the rural poor, especially in the Protestant north.[42] Before modern bottling techniques, beer was largely a town drink, especially among the workers of Dublin and Belfast. In the late 1700s, brewers like Arthur Guinness aligned with the anti-spirits movement, positioning beer as a "temperance drink." Irish brewers reasonably argued that drunkenness resulted from unlicensed hard-liquor dealers, who besmirched their otherwise respectable trade.[43]

With its nationalist overtones, temperance activism was wrapped up in Ireland's regional and sectarian divisions. In the predominantly Protestant, whiskey-drinking north, teetotalism was tied to the Orange Order: the unionist fraternal organization sworn to uphold the Ascendency of the landed Protestant minority over Catholic Ireland. They adhered to the colonizer's alcohol narrative: that the Rebellion of 1798 was evidence of the Catholics' bestial whiskey-driven incivility, for which abstinence would be Britain's civilizing reply.[44] Many dry loyalists feared ceding their temperance gospel to the Catholics, even when they preached the same message of abstinence.

Despite being falsely stereotyped in American histories as inherently hostile to temperance, Irish Catholics were at the forefront—with priests admonishing parishioners to "abandon as soon as they can the dangerous traffic" in intoxicants and to "embrace a more becoming way of making a living."[45] The Catholic Church in Ireland well understood the political and financial implications of promoting sobriety within an imperial state. In a letter of December 29, 1829, the Right Reverend Dr. James Doyle, bishop of Kildare, articulated:

> The great and insurmountable obstacle to the progress of Temperance Societies, and to [stopping] the torrent of drunkenness is found in the *revenue laws.* Could we but induce the Chancellor of the Exchequer to become a member of our society, and to square his budget by our rules, I have no doubt whatever but we should succeed in removing this pestilence of drunkenness out of the land. To eradicate the use of ardent spirits out of a country having such a climate as ours, and from among such a people as ours, is quite impossible; *but to diminish the use of ardent spirits to one-fiftieth part of its present amount, is in my opinion perfectly practicable.* But as it would be as easy to stop the mouth of the Euphrates as to stop the mouths of those who now drink whiskey in Ireland, they cannot be reclaimed until a better beverage than whiskey is provided for them, at even a lower expense. All of this could be done by the Chancellor of the Exchequer, if he found it more necessary to promote good morals than to secure a large revenue.... I have no hesitation in stating that if malting and brewing were exempted from tax, and the impost on whiskey raised, drunkenness in a little time would almost disappear from the country.[46]

While the clergy largely remained in the moderation camp, Catholic Ireland got its own apostle of teetotalism in Father Theobald Mathew, whose kindly features are chiseled on public statues throughout Ireland. Father Mathew labored for years among the poor of Cork. He saw the ravages of alcoholism on the faces of parishioners he laid in paupers' graves. His own brothers were heavy-drinking distillers.[47] Still, by 1838, Mathew overcame his own suspicions of temperance as some Protestant ruse and began administering a new pledge—not just of personal abstinence from drink, but also to dissuade others from its use. As his fame grew, he presented commemorative medals to anyone making the temperance pilgrimage to his Cork friary.[48]

When he made his first journey to Limerick in 1839, the temperance crowds were so massive that dozens were injured in the crush to see Father Mathew. Others fell into the nearby River Shannon and had to be dredged out. One woman was trampled to death. He described it as simultaneously "awful" and "glorious," as over three days, he'd administered the pledge to some 150,000 grateful Irish men and women.[49]

Father Mathew ceaselessly crisscrossed Ireland throughout the 1840s converting ever more pledges, both in rural districts and in towns. His celebrity grew along with his tours, expanding first to all of Britain, and then a whirlwind tour of the United States from 1849 to 1851 that "enfeebled" him.[50] "It has graciously pleased the Almighty to smite me with general Paralysis," the ailing priest wrote a friend in 1854. "My exertions in America, preaching temperance to the expatriated Irish, in that vast Republic, exhausted my strength." He would die of a stroke two years later.[51]

Still, on the eve of the Great Famine, as many as five and a half million of Ireland's eight million people—almost 70 percent—had taken Father Mathew's sobriety

Figure 5.2 "D. O'Connell, Esq., MP, Takes the Pledge. Dublin. Published by Michael Reilly," Cork Total Abstinence Society, Founded by the Very Revd. Theobald Mathew on the 10th of April, 1838.

Source: Library of Congress, Prints and Photographs Division, Washington, DC.

pledge.[52] From 1845 to 1849, the Irish potato famine claimed over a million victims from starvation and disease. Another million Irish sought refuge in the United States, where they were more likely than the old-stock Americans to patronize temperance.

Catholic temperance meetings were anything but dull, somber affairs. "Their music is loud and without taste," wrote German traveler Johann Georg Kohl, upon visiting one of Father Mathew's events in 1843, "the speeches declamatory and vaunting, the meetings often continue till the night is far advanced, and, by the temperance people, are concluded with dancing and noise." Even when Mathew collapsed in exhaustion around midnight, the jubilation and the temperance band would play on until dawn.[53]

Father Mathew's teetotal message was straightforward: sobriety brought prosperity. Money not wasted at the public house enriched the family. Avowedly nonpolitical and nonsectarian, he hoped to transcend class, religious, and political divisions. "Teetotalism and charity would heal the wounds which were inflicted by political and religious dissension and bigotry," he argued. "All creeds and classes will live together in unity and harmony, and, in a word, as Christians should live."[54]

Still, Anglicans and Presbyterians were hesitant to bow before a Catholic priest. Others suspected him as a cunning political operative: temperance starved the British treasury of liquor revenues, which would force the government to either disband the standing army or increase other taxes on the Irish, which would make British rule even less popular.[55]

Despite Mathew's desire to keep above politics, his temperance movement was increasingly co-opted to the nationalist cause: specifically, Daniel O'Connell's movement to repeal the Acts of Union with England. In 1839, in Bandon outside of Cork, the nationalist O'Connell spoke of Irish liberation "to all classes of my countrymen—Protestant, Catholic and Presbyterian." Of his audience, O'Connell inquired, "I hope many of you have been to Father Mathew," to which he was met with thunderous applause: fully half had taken the oath. After proclaiming three cheers for temperance, he concluded, "The blessings of God are poured upon the cause, and the moral glories of your country will be yet realized by the temperance societies of Ireland. I see great events in store for Ireland from the extension and spread of temperance; nor is there a national or political right—one based upon the principle of equality—that will not be conceded—and that not a little by reason of the temperance societies." His nationalist-temperance pronouncements were hailed by a frenzy of cheers.[56] Irish Ribbonmen—who proudly sported green ribbons in opposition to the Orange Order—took up the temperance cause.

Within a few years, temperance was recognized as synonymous with the independence movement, by its proponents, opponents, and foreign observers alike. "There can be no doubt," claimed the *Dublin Evening Mail* in 1842, "that the teetotal association is a branch of a political movement, the object of which is the dissolution . . . of the legislative union" between Ireland and Britain.[57] As the *Cork Examiner*

Figure 5.3 Total Abstinence Society Medal (1840). Cruciform text of pledge encircled by title of society, president (Fr. Theobald Mathew), and the date of foundation (10 April 1838). A large green ribbon is attached with the following embroidered text: + F[ather] M[athew], 1840, God Save Ireland.

Source: Total Abstinence Society Medal, 1840, CA/FM/RES/9/3/8, Fr. Theobald Mathew: Research and Commemorative Papers, Provincial Archives, Capuchin Friary of St. Mary of the Angels, Dublin, Ireland.

declared: "A nation of sober men, with clear heads, with firm and erect forms, with the proud strength of moral independence about them, shall and *must* have the full completion of their liberty."[58] Indeed, writing of his travels through Ireland in 1844, the German Kohl noted, "Temperance gives to the Irish greater domestic comfort, more order and moral strength, and stronger claims and hopes of 'National Independence.' Perhaps," he opined, "the temperance conspiracy and the independence conspiracy will yet merge into one."[59]

Temperance fueled nationalism, but in Ireland, nationalism weakened temperance. Mutual suspicion between Protestants in the north and Catholics in the south prevented a united front on Sunday pub-closing laws. The Great Famine of the late 1840s ravaged the country, but also smashed Irish alcohol producers—both licit and illicit—as dwindling stocks of potatoes and grains went to food, not booze.[60] The death of Father Mathew in 1856 left only a rump and disorganized Catholic temperance movement in Ireland, whereas Ulster Presbyterians in the north increasingly made common cause with the emerging prohibitionist organizations across Britain.[61]

Imperialist accusations and nationalist suspicions would continue to bedevil attempts at cooperation within the British temperance movement, which were further complicated by the news of prohibition in the American state of Maine in 1851. Now the movement was further fractured between preference for legislative means of reining in the liquor traffic versus "moral suasion" temperance, in addition to north versus south divisions, Protestants versus Catholics, moderation versus teetotalism, and imperial core versus periphery.

Still—before turning to the more general history of British temperance—it is worth emphasizing here the persistent anti-imperial, nationalist character of temperance in Ireland. When agitation for Irish Home Rule heated up in the 1870s, English MPs scoffed that Irish drunkenness was proof of their cultural unpreparedness for self-governance. "If drunkenness, with its train of vice, fighting, and murder—has become a national disgrace in Ireland, who inflicted it on us?" Dublin MP Sir Dominic Corrigan blasted back. "Not an Irish, but an English parliament."[62] Is it any wonder, then, that the leaders of the Easter Rising of 1916, Sinn Féin, and the Irish Republican Army who all fought against English imperial subjugation drew disproportionately from the ranks of Ireland's temperance organizations?[63]

British Prohibitionism and Backlash

News of Neal Dow's "Maine Law" victory in 1851—in which the northeasternmost American state refused to renew liquor licenses (Chapter 11)—spread quickly to Britain, especially among "progressives" intent on limiting the worst excesses of a debauching trade. In 1853, activists established the United Kingdom Alliance (UKA) to press the prohibitionist cause. Less concerned with the moral redemption of drunkards and more with the corrupt British liquor machine, the UKA was not a social organization but an avowedly political movement, formed to "agitate both inside and outside Parliament for the legal suppression of the liquor trade."[64]

The alliance was organized by Irish Quaker Nathaniel Card. The ailing Fr. Theobald Mathew from Cork was a member of the General Council. According to minutes of its first meeting, rising dry sentiment "in Glasgow, Edinburgh, and other parts of Scotland, was indicative of a deep and growing conviction in favor of some effective legislative measure," while the circulation of a supportive letter from Neal Dow himself (Chapter 11) convinced "several excellent friends who had previously manifested some hesitation" to convene the organization.[65]

As a political party, the United Kingdom Alliance was based not in London but in the northern city of Manchester. Its leaders were disproportionately Scotsmen. Of its top financial contributors, thirty-six were from the industrialized north or England (Lancashire, Yorkshire, and Durham), nineteen from Scotland, five from

Ireland, and only five from the metropolis of London itself.[66] While they took no issue with traditional moral-suasion temperance, they had no interest in legislating morality—as though there were some singular moral code that this motley collection of Presbyterians, Quakers, Catholics, Anglicans, and nonconformists could agree to anyway. The UKA included teetotalers and moderate drinkers: there were no abstinence pledges or purity tests, since the focus was not on personal habits, but on the political corruption and economic subjugation associated with profit seeking. "No consideration of Private Gain, or Public Revenue, can justify the upholding of a system so utterly wrong in principle, suicidal in policy, and disastrous in result, as the Traffic in intoxicating liquors," they proclaimed.[67]

The alliance's legislative task was daunting. The government was buoyed by significant liquor revenues, which it had a vested interest in maintaining. Wealth and property requirements for voting already disempowered many would-be reformers among the middle and working classes. Plus, restrictive legislation could be scuttled by hostile MPs in the Commons or the "beerage" in the House of Lords.[68] Then came the immense political clout of the conservative British brewers, distillers, vintners, and publicans, often known simply as "the trade," who used liquor to entice voters away from reformist candidates. Licensed pubs generated enough drink revenue for the propertied classes to sidestep their direct tax burdens, while creating a society that established "the wealth, luxuries, and pleasures of the few, upon the poverty, crime, and misery of the many."[69]

With the deck stacked against them, prohibitionists recognized that sweeping, Maine-style prohibition was unlikely. Instead, they focused on two incremental reforms: one was the local option—so-called Permissive Bill legislation permitting municipalities to revoke retail alcohol licenses. Indeed, the Scottish Permissive Bill and Temperance Association—which brought Pussyfoot Johnson to Britain sixty years later—was established in 1858, and quickly aligned with the UKA.[70] The other was legislation requiring pubs to stay closed on Sunday. While Sunday-closing laws would likely draw the support of devout sabbatarians, even the UKA was dubious that such a symbolic half-measure would siphon support away from more lasting reform.[71] Both local-option and Sunday-closing reforms would have to navigate not only political minefields but social, religious, and class challenges too.

Seemingly, Sunday closing was the lowest-hanging fruit and a way to bring the more conservative Anglican, Presbyterian, and even Catholic churches into the political fold. Recognizing the broader political and nationalist overtones, most churches punted on temperance, characterizing it as a private concern, rather than a church matter.

The Quakers were a noteworthy exception: in Britain and the United States, Quakers had banned their members from selling spirits since the 1780s (Chapters 9–10). Quakers' staunch opposition to slavery often took the form of rum boycotts, as part of a wide-ranging humanitarian movement not only against the slave trade and the liquor traffic, but also the opium traffic, the injustices of the East India

Company monopoly (Chapter 7), child labor, war, militarism, capital punishment, and the repressive Corn Laws, while supporting women's suffrage and working-class Chartism.[72] The transnational temperance movement—for which the Anglo-American linkage was central—was itself born of this constellation of empowering reforms (Chapters 11–12).[73]

Famously, the UKA was founded by Nathaniel Card, an Irish Quaker. More notable still was Quaker reformer Catherine Impey—active in the 1870s through the 1890s—whose highest values were temperance and antiracism. She was a member of the International Organization of Good Templars and had attended Woman's Christian Temperance Union meetings while visiting the United States, pushing both organizations to fight harder for racial inclusion. Failing that, she began her own temperance, antiracist newspaper, *Anti-Caste*, even hosting American temperance/antilynching activist Ida B. Wells during her confrontation with the WCTU's Frances Willard (Chapter 13).[74]

Quakers aside, that the establishment churches were suspicious of the largely secular, self-help temperance organizations makes sense when we see prohibition's roots in Chartist liberalism.[75] Originating with the industrial workers of Scotland and northern England, the "People's Charter" of 1838 called for liberal political reform. Over the following decades, millions of Chartists demanded male suffrage, secret ballot, and removing property qualifications to vote or hold office, while empowering their local communities. "And who," asked novelist Charles Kingsley in 1850, "my aristocratic readers, do you think, have been the great preachers and practisers of temperance, thrift, chastity, self-respect, and education? Who?—shriek not in your Belgravian saloons—the Chartists!"[76] Indeed, "teetotal Chartism" became a primary thrust of activism in the industrial north—improving the daily life of the impoverished worker while striking a blow against the aristocratic liquor machine.[77]

Radical Chartist founder William Lovett railed against the liquor trade that made the rich richer and the poor poorer. In addressing the "politically debasing, soul-subduing vice" of drunkenness, he lamented drunkards who "muddle their understandings and drown their intellect amid the drunken revelry of the pot-house—whose profligacy makes them the ready tools and victims of corruption or slaves of unprincipled governors, who connive at their folly and smile when they forge for themselves the fetters of liberty by their love of drink."

For Lovett and other Chartists, corrupt government teamed with a vicious aristocracy to keep the laboring masses uneducated, intoxicated, and unable to organize to claim their natural rights. Generations of British liberal, labor, and socialist reforms were rooted firmly in Chartism.

"Fellow-countrymen," Lovett declared, "*when we contend for an equality of political rights, it is not in order to lop off an unjust tax or useless pension, or to get a transfer of wealth, power or influence, for a party; but to be able to probe our social evils to their source, and to apply effective remedies to prevent, instead of unjust laws to punish.* . . . And if the teachers of temperance and preachers of morality would unite like us, and direct their attention to *the source* of the evil, instead of nibbling at the effects, and seldom speaking of the cause; then, indeed, instead of splendid palaces of intemperance daily erected, as if in mockery of their exertions—built on the ruins of happy home, despairing minds, and sickened hearts—we should soon have a sober, honest, and reflecting people."[78]

Reformers had reasons for optimism in making common cause between Chartist liberals and church conservatives for a Sunday tavern-closing bill. After all, a consensus Sunday-closing bill was implemented in temperate Scotland in 1854 without much ado.[79] Extending Sunday closing to wet England the following year, however, would provoke a violent backlash in London.[80]

Hyde Park—with its picturesque lake and magnificent gardens—is where London's high society paraded about in their resplendent carriages, especially on Sundays. So the descent of some *two hundred thousand* angry workers on June 24, 1855, would have been quite jarring indeed.

"Six days a week," proclaimed Chartist organizer James Finlen, "we are treated like slaves and now Parliament wants to rob us of the bit of freedom we still have on the seventh!" After three hours the protest erupted into chaos.[81]

"A babel of jeering, taunting, discordant ejaculations, in which no language is as rich as English, soon bore down upon [the aristocrats] from both sides," wrote German eyewitness Karl Marx for the *Neue Oder Zeitung*. After coauthoring *The Communist Manifesto* in 1848—and witnessing the revolutions that roiled continental Europe that year (Chapter 4)—Marx fled to London, where he would live the rest of his life, agitating and writing as a freelance journalist. Marx saw the riot as the inevitable backlash of the oppressed working class against the "dissipated, degenerating and pleasure-seeking aristocracy with a church propped up by the filthy profits calculated upon by the big brewers and monopolizing wholesalers." He claimed it was nothing less than the beginning of the English proletarian revolution.[82]

Once the dust settled, organizers vowed a repeat the following Sunday if Earl Grosvenor—the teetotaling Duke of Westminster and Whig MP—did not withdraw his signature Sunday-closing legislation. He quickly did so, before wisely leaving town for his safety.[83] On Sunday, July 1, some 150,000 workers returned to Hyde Park to celebrate the death of the Sunday-closing bill. The largely jubilant gathering was about to wind down peacefully, "but the police reckoned differently," observed Marx, as "the constabulary rushed from ambush, whipped their truncheons out of their pockets, began to beat up people's heads until the blood ran profusely."[84]

"Down with the police, down with the Sunday Bill!" chanted the crowd, as the disorder gradually subsided, leaving dozens hospitalized and at least one dead. The riotous backlash tarnished the image of Lord Grosvenor and the entire prohibition movement. Historians still debate who was to blame for the violence: Chartist agitators had planned a peaceful protest, while newspapers reported that the "attack appears to be stimulated by a set of men who do not belong to the working classes," who'd been paid by a wealthy publican from Fleet Street.[85] Such provocations were completely in character for the drink trade, as Pussyfoot could later attest. As British temperance historian Brian Harrison notes, "Barrels of beer were trundled up beside Anti-Corn Law, Complete Suffrage, Chartist and temperance open-air meetings of working people, and in the free distribution of their contents, all thought of political and moral reform vanished away."[86]

Either way, for the rest of the century, proponents of Sunday closing and other restrictions had to face the widely held fear that their legislation might produce large-scale public backlash on a potentially "revolutionary" scale.[87]

In the already lopsided battle between upstart British prohibitionists and the entrenched liquor trade, the violence in Hyde Park was a severe body blow to their efforts to pass even a local-option Permissive Bill. And this was all before heavy-weight political philosopher John Stuart Mill stepped into the fray to deliver a staggering haymaker to the prohibitionist cause by reframing it as an issue of individual liberty.

British Liberalism and Prohibitionism

Even as Karl Marx lived and wrote in London, the most influential English political philosopher of the day was John Stuart Mill. The child-prodigy son of Scottish (and temperate) philosopher James Mill, the nonconformist Mill worked for the British East India Company (Chapter 7) before penning his landmark *On Liberty*, with his wife Harriet Taylor Mill in 1859. Today, *On Liberty* is hailed as a monument to political liberalism: exploring the relationship between state authority and individual liberty, concluding that the individual could only progress morally if the state left him free to decide.[88]

But the context is important: *On Liberty* was written in the wake of the Maine Law and the championing of British prohibitionism by the United Kingdom Alliance. The empirical substance of *On Liberty* is actually about whether the state can prohibit the liquor traffic for the public good. Ultimately, Mill provided the libertarian ammunition used to attack prohibition for generations.

Mill laid down the futility of government legislating morality, warning of a backlash "among those whom it is attempted to coerce into prudence or temperance."[89] As a religious nonconformist, Mill dismissed any moral arguments for Sunday-closing laws, and discounted other political and economic arguments.

Then Mill summarily dispatched prohibitionists' insistence that they opposed not the individual's right to drink, but the profit-making from trafficking in addictive substances. "Prohibition of their sale is in fact, as it is intended to be, prohibition of their use," Mill claimed. Selling liquor may be a social act, but "the infringement complained of is not on the liberty of the seller, but on that of the buyer and consumer." Reorienting the debate toward individual rights effectively exonerated the liquor trafficker's predations; the man who sells simply disappears from the equation. In this way, Mill anticipated the blurring of political and economic rights of neoliberals a full century later (Chapter 18). Specifically taking the United Kingdom Alliance to task, he argued that whatever rights might be claimed by the society should never overshadow the freedom of the individual.[90]

In its fine print, *On Liberty* is more sympathetic to liquor-control arguments: as a trade that generates negative externalities for society, he saw it as a wholly appropriate target for government taxation, licensing, and regulation.[91] But the damage was done. Mill's broadsides not only reoriented debates over local-option Permissive Bills in Britain, but also recast prohibitionists not as defenders against predatory capitalism, but as enemies of individual liberty and the drinker's right to imbibe. What a person drinks is their own business, so long as no one else is harmed by it, right?[92] Virtually every modern history of prohibitionism has followed Mill's lead, and his paeans to the rights of the individual trumping the rights of the society remain popular with libertarians even today.

Rare among philosophers, in his later years Mill actually entered the political arena, serving as Liberal Party MP from 1865 to 1868. In the House of Commons, he championed social reform instead of repression in Ireland, denounced British colonial brutality in Jamaica, and famously became the first-ever British MP to call for women's suffrage.[93] Yet when it came to yet another Permissive Bill in 1868, he scoffed simply that the "use or non-use of alcoholic liquors is a subject on which every sane and grown-up person ought to judge for himself under his own responsibility."[94]

Amid the debate over the local-option Permissive Bill, Liberal back-bencher Sir Wilfrid Lawson shot back, "It is not the working men, it is the M.P.s in the House of Commons who wish to be considered practical and popular, who get up and say that for their part, although they hate drunkenness—though no man is as opposed to drunkenness as they are, they cannot do the wicked act of 'robbing the poor man of his beer.' What I do want to do is, not to rob the poor man of his beer, but to rob the rich man of his prey—of the plunder he makes out of the homes and happiness of the working men of this country."[95]

In the end, the 1868 Permissive Bill died. Yet, in a crowning irony even as Mill's masterwork *On Liberty* became the symbol of the Liberal Party, Lawson's local-veto prohibitionism increasingly became part of its political platform, as the Conservatives became the party of the liquor establishment.[96]

For his part, Lawson later became the long-serving president of the prohibitionist United Kingdom Alliance, coming into frequent conflict with Mill's antiprohibitionist acolytes, but not before raising what one MP called "one of the most serious questions ever presented to Parliament." In 1870, Lawson introduced a straightforward resolution: "That this House condemns the system by which a

Figure 5.4 John Stuart Mill, M.P. (circa 1865–1868)
Source: Library of Congress, Prints and Photographs Division, Washington, DC.

large portion of the Indian Revenue is raised from Opium," on the grounds that "this traffic in opium, fostered and promoted by our Government, is in itself immoral and injurious." It was well known that, after the Chinese emperor avowedly prohibited the enslaving narcotics trade, the British fought two wars (1839–1842 and 1856–1860) to keep it going, even as it undercut Britain's foreign policy: "You burned our palace; you killed our emperor," the Chinese protested, "you sell poison to the people; now you come professing to teach *us* virtue." It was similar to the accusations levied against the British alcohol trade in Ireland for years.

"I should have thought that with 1,000,000 of paupers at home caused by drink, we had quite enough to answer for without carrying all this misery to another nation," Lawson blasted. As a moral issue, there was widespread agreement that the British opium traffic should be roundly condemned. But as a practical matter, selling a highly addictive narcotic that perpetuated its own demand raised six million to eight million pounds annually for the British Raj that could not easily be replaced.

"I know very well that there is nothing which any man can say against opium that my hon. Friend is not ready to say against alcohol," Prime Minister William

Gladstone said of Lawson, a member of his own Liberal Party. "What do we do at home? How many millions do we raise upon the article gin? How many of our people drink gin, and make themselves beasts as much as the Chinese?" Gladstone asked the Commons. Explicitly equating the imperial opium traffic with the domestic liquor traffic, Gladstone suggested that if Lawson

> carried a Resolution that no more money should be raised from gin, and if people at home were ready to put their hands into their pockets for supplying the deficiency in the Revenue, then he thought we could go with clean hands to the black gentlemen 16,000 miles away and say—"You shall find money for your Revenue some other way." Then we should be acting honestly. But so long as we raised so many millions of Revenue from alcohol, and our people make beasts of themselves with it, he did not think the House could honestly assent to such a Motion as that before them. We were a white people, and we called ourselves a Christian people, and he thought we should pluck the beam out of our own eye before we sought to pick out the mote that was in our black brother's eye.

With that, the vote was taken. Lawson's condemnation was overwhelmingly defeated, 46 to 151. The exploitative British traffic would continue unimpeded, both at home and abroad. Nevertheless, Lawson would continue his opposition against British support of both the foreign opium trade and the domestic liquor trade as "a system of finance, clumsy, contemptible, and cruel."[97]

The political and economic power of the British liquor traffic continued to grow throughout the 1860s and '70s, even as the harms wrought by the trade were becoming increasingly evident. British public-house dynamics mirrored those in the German Empire, with its respectable beer halls—where workers went to socialize—versus the disreputable Prussian *Schnapshölle*, where the destitute got wasted on cheap, high-power spirits (Chapter 4). Britain's worst offenders were the dram shops, which peddled small shots (drams) of distilled gin, whiskey, rum, and brandy. As with the *Schnapshölle* and the Russian *kabak*, the dram shop was the most profitable, most predatory outlet, since its function was getting drunk as quickly as possible. High turnover and no food meant no waiters, no tables, no chairs, and no sociability—just drunken profits that extended the length of the bar. Industrialization and urbanization drew enterprising retailers, taking out liquor licenses and converting once-reputable taverns into "gin palaces" to push the more potent and more lucrative distilled spirits.

"Go inside," wrote one late-Victorian reporter of his experiences, "and you will find that the luxury is all a sham and the comfort all a delusion; there is often nowhere even to sit down—only infinite furniture of bottles, a sawdust floor, and a mahogany counter at which to stand and drink as much strong liquor as possible in the shortest time. The thing is so disgusting, so patently wrong, that it has bred violent and angry opposition." This—it should be noted—was written by an avowed *anti-prohibitionist*: the necessity of public-house reform was recognized far beyond temperance circles.[98]

After emerging victorious in the 1868 election, the Liberal government of Prime Minister William Gladstone committed to a major reform of Britain's licensing laws. Announced in Queen Victoria's speech in February 1870, the reform bill drawn up by Home Secretary H. A. Bruce (with little interest or input from Gladstone) was introduced in 1871, ultimately becoming law the following year. Pubs were to close at midnight in towns, and eleven o'clock in the countryside, and beer was not to be adulterated. It did give local magistrates some control over the issuance of licenses through a convoluted scheme, though it did not mandate even a reduction in the number of licenses. With nothing approaching a local-veto provision, the United Kingdom Alliance withdrew its support. Failing to satisfy even the drys, the Licensing Act of 1872 was a political disaster for Gladstone and the Liberals. It did nothing to curb pub abuses while simultaneously enraging the liquor machine, which threw its combined political muscle behind the rival Conservatives.[99]

From its proposal in 1871 until the election of 1874, "nearly every public-house in the United Kingdom was an active committee-room for the Conservative Party." Moreover, restive Irish nationalists split to form their own Home Rule League, taking 60 of the 101 parliamentary seats from Ireland, bringing Benjamin Disraeli's Conservatives to power. Ireland aside, "More immediately operative causes have determined the elections," read the defeated Gladstone's famous postmortem. "I have no doubt what is the principal. We have been borne down in a torrent of gin and beer."[100]

Home Rule Frustrations and Prohibitionist Failures

Whether it was the rising Home Rule movement—nationalists pressing for a devolution of policymaking authority over domestic affairs to an Irish legislature—or the Licensing Act that doomed Gladstone and the Liberals in 1874 is something of a false distinction. The temperance movement had long provided a Trojan horse for Irish nationalism, which only intensified by the 1870s.

Despite fears of another Hyde Park backlash, and separate from the licensing and pub-reform legislation, Irish MPs consistently pressed Gladstone's Liberal government for a Sunday pub-closing law. Their message was simple: "Give us what they have in Scotland."[101] Catholic, Liberal MP Major Myles O'Reilly first introduced an Irish Sunday-closing bill in 1867, only to have it voted down by the entrenched English liquor interests. He tried again in 1868 and 1869, succeeding only in driving Irish publicans further into the arms of the conservative English liquor dealers, who steadfastly opposed anything that would limit their sales and profits. Frustrated, O'Reilly pursued another path. In 1873, he cofounded the Irish Home Rule

League—the same third party that took 60 percent of the constituencies in Ireland in the 1874 elections, toppling Gladstone and the Liberals.[102]

Irish temperance forces weren't about to let the shocking rise of the Home Rule Association go to waste in the new Conservative parliament. Though in favor of continued union with Britain, Liberal MP and North-Irish Presbyterian minister Richard Smyth wielded the specter of Home Rule as a bulwark against English alco-imperialism. "I am quite willing that Ireland should be ruled by the Queen, Lords and Commons of the United Kingdom, and may that union never be shaken," Smyth proclaimed in reintroducing a Sunday-closing bill in 1874, "but I am not willing that the licensed victualers of Birmingham should constitute themselves a parliament for Ireland." The idea that the entrenched English liquor machine could scuttle temperance legislation for Ireland for their own profit shook his unionist faith. "Even to carry this resolution I do not want an Irish parliament, but I must add that if we had an Irish parliament, it is among the first that would be carried."[103]

Nevertheless, in the English-dominated "publicans' parliament," his Sunday-closing bill was defeated yet again. Only in 1878 did Irish drys succeed in getting an unsatisfying Sunday bill, which was watered down by liquor interests to exempt their biggest urban markets: Dublin, Belfast, Cork, Limerick, and Waterford. Moreover, it was a tentative, four-year measure, which only ensured that Irish temperance grievances would resurface for years to come.[104]

However, the Sunday bill debate did succeed in persuading the once and future prime minister, William Gladstone, now a minority-party MP. As the earlier debate over China, India, and the opium trade made clear, Gladstone was no temperance man. Rather, he worried that continued belittling of Ireland's reasonable pleas for equal legislation only fueled greater nationalism and played into the hands of the Home Rule Association. "If after giving [Sunday closing] to Scotland you withhold it from Ireland, you lay down the principle of inequality in your dealing between the three countries, the adoption of which principle, in my opinion, makes those who adopt it far more deadly enemies to the union."[105]

Nationalists pressed further, asking, "Will you serve the conspiracy of the vendors of drink in England, or will you obey the will and the eloquent voice of the whole people of Ireland?" More than anything, the temperance debate persuaded Gladstone that Home Rule was all but inevitable—that "Ireland ought to be governed by Irish ideas."[106] As he regained the premiership from 1880 to 1885, however, Gladstone demurred, recognizing that Home Rule would be difficult to get past the Commons, and impossible not to be vetoed by the conservative House of Lords. Too many Britishers still viewed Ireland through the colonizer's lens, in which constant news of Irish intemperance, protests, and violence provided evidence of their alleged incivility and unpreparedness for self-rule.[107]

In the nationalists' self-imagery, by contrast, noble Ireland had been shackled by the British and corrupted by drink—so the Home Rule Party and Catholic abstinence would be their redemption. "The great cause of intemperance in Ireland, as the great and fundamental cause of every other evil in Ireland, is the absence of self-government among the Irish people," wrote famed Home Rule MP T. P. O'Connor, "and until we have given to the Irish nation the dignity and self-respect of a self-governed people we shall not lay the real foundations of temperance principles."[108]

Temperance was a central tenet of the Home Rule movement, especially under Charles Stewart Parnell. First elected in 1875, Parnell assumed the leadership of the Home Rule Association in 1880, transforming it into the powerful Irish Parliamentary Party (IPP). In the election of 1885 (with expanded male suffrage), no party won an outright majority, while Parnell's IPP won 85 of the 103 Irish seats, and initially formed a coalition government with the Conservatives. Yet when the Liberal Gladstone announced his support for Irish Home Rule, Parnell and the IPP swung to his side. The 1886 Home Rule Bill—empowering an Irish assembly to decide its domestic affairs—split Gladstone's Liberal Party, with Liberal Unionists walking out to form their own faction. The bill was thrown out on the second reading, and Gladstone's government was thrown out shortly thereafter.

The issue of Home Rule lay dormant while the Conservatives held Parliament (1886–1892), yet Parnell held to Irish temperance as anti-imperialism. In speaking to Elizabeth Mathew—a collateral descendant of Fr. Theobald Mathew—in 1888, Parnell pined for a temperance revival against the English liquor traffic, claiming it "would put the government in a difficulty, besides being good for the people, by diminishing an enormous source of revenue."[109] Even as his health faltered and his leadership was challenged over an adultery scandal in which he fathered three children of an already-married woman, Parnell fought on. Shortly before his death in 1891, he rose before the Commons to argue *against* extending Sunday closing to Ireland's five biggest cities, precisely because it was an Irish, not English affair. "On what possible subject have Irish local claims and wishes a better right to be regarded than on the [Sunday-closing] question before the House?" Parnell blasted. "If honorable Members do not wish to prejudice this question beforehand by their meddlesome interference and bungling attempts to legislate in reference to the wants of people whom they cannot possibly understand, and in reference to a matter of which they are profoundly ignorant, they will [leave] the settlement of the question to the Parliament which we all hope to see soon established in Dublin."[110]

Following the election of 1892 in which no party won a majority of seats, the Liberals established a minority government in coalition with the Irish nationalists, returning the elderly Gladstone to the premiership for a fourth and final time. The following year, Gladstone himself drafted a Second Home Rule Bill to grant Ireland a bicameral parliament for domestic affairs. Unlike his first effort seven years earlier, the 1893 Government of Ireland Bill actually passed the Commons, only to be soundly vetoed by the conservative House of Lords. Frustrated, Gladstone resigned his premiership at the age of eighty-four. Queen Victoria filled his vacancy with Archibald Primrose, the fifth Earl of Rosebery, who was more interested in his Derby-winning racehorses than in politics. In the lead-up to 1895, the Liberals confronted a hostile electorate with no leadership and zero legislative accomplishments.[111] If that wasn't already a recipe for disaster, the Liberals added prohibition to the mix.

In 1893, Liberal prohibitionist and Gladstone's powerful chancellor of the exchequer, William Harcourt, introduced the Liquor Traffic (Local Control) Bill, which explicitly targeted the exploitative booze traffic. Based in Britain's deep traditions of local self-government, the local-option bill would allow voters to elect neighborhood boards that could reduce the liquor licenses in their district all the way down to zero if the community so chose through a two-thirds majority vote. Many MPs sided with the liquor-industry position that otherwise law-abiding tavern-keepers who lost their businesses to local prohibition deserved to be compensated for their livelihoods being taken away. The bill was never even brought up for a vote—another Liberal failure. Undeterred, Harcourt reintroduced the widely loathed bill in 1895—adding a referendum for reducing the number of pubs—even as a vote of no confidence in the unpopular Liberal Party prompted a new election.[112]

With the aid of hindsight, historians point to the 1895 election as the closest thing Britain ever got to a referendum on prohibition. The Liberals were assuredly hostile to the alarming degeneracy borne of the liquor traffic, and some three-quarters of Liberal election speeches mentioned Harcourt's local-veto proposal. Yet this wasn't some quixotic, one-off policy, but part of a broad, progressive platform to empower local communities through democracy at the expense of Westminster aristocrats, landlords, and the "beerage." Home Rule was all about the progressive devolution of policymaking to locally elected decision-makers; so too was education reform. So then why should the licensing of the liquor trade be dictated by the entrenched booze interests in London?[113]

The British liquor machine—allied with the rival Conservative and Unionist Party—fought back with a vengeance. While Liberals championed self-government, Conservatives emphasized personal liberties and property rights, as well as compensation for any publican whose business was unjustly closed through local veto. Good old-fashioned fear-mongering helped, too: workingman's pubs across the country posted misleading "this house will be closed if Liberals are elected" placards in their windows.[114]

Conservatives effectively turned the antiprohibitionist arguments of the Liberals' patron saint—John Stuart Mill—against them, by portraying local veto as an unreasonable infringement on individual liberty. By arguing that the workingman "has a perfect right to get his glass of beer," as Lord Arthur Balfour declared, the Conservatives and Unionists cast themselves as both the "true" defenders of liberty and the champions of the working-class drinkers, too.[115]

The result was a rout, for both Liberals and drys: 341 Conservatives and 70 Unionists returned to the House of Commons, but only 259 Liberals and their Irish allies. "Drink swept the country more thoroughly than it had ever done before," lamented the prohibitionist United Kingdom Alliance, which was destined for a long, slow decline. In their election postmortem, Liberals acknowledged that it wasn't Home Rule that was their undoing, but the local veto that was "the most difficult to defend from the standpoint of true Liberalism," and that their prohibitory measures were "a clumsy infringement on the doctrine of individual liberty."[116]

Even as much of the British prohibitionist movement learned the hard lessons of 1895 and (as we shall shortly see) turned toward pub reform, temperance remained central to Irish national identity. In 1898, temperate Jesuit priest, and author of the bestselling *Temperance Catechism*, James Cullen established the Pioneer Total Abstinence Association of the Sacred Heart as a devotional society, meant to free Irish Catholics from their subservience to the British liquor trade.[117] Unlike Fr. Mathew's mass temperance movement a half-century earlier, Cullen imagined the Pioneers as a small, elite, and principled vanguard of the abstinence army, vowing "to make Ireland permanently sober and Ireland permanently free." The Pioneers were explicitly nationalist: Cullen encouraged activism in Gaelic language revival and, echoing Sinn Féin, promoted Irish goods and economic self-sufficiency.[118]

"A drunken Ireland, England knew, could never be a free Ireland—then or now!" Cullen wrote in 1909. "And let us say it, during the last fifty years since Father Mathew's time, England could never have withheld self-government from Ireland if, by her shameful licensing opportunities and laws, she had not first stupefied, paralysed, degraded and disgraced the people she feared and hated." Laying bare the colonizer's alcohol narrative, he said, "Let the Irish drink and their slavery is secured—make Ireland and keep Ireland a nation of drunkards—then hold its people up to the scorn of the world and our object is gained!"[119] Cullen's lesson was clear: if drunkenness was political subjugation, Pioneer abstinence would be Ireland's salvation.

Organized in 1905, the nationalist Sinn Féin drew heavily from the temperance ranks, as did the Irish Volunteers (later, the Irish Republican Army), who took up arms for the cause of independence. Most notable was Irish revolutionary Patrick Pearse, leader of the 1916 armed Easter Rebellion in Dublin against British rule. Pearse and his brother William were both Pioneers and abhorred British pubs from an early age. They denounced the English drink traffic as a foremost mechanism of Ireland's oppression. They organized prohibitionist lectures and encouraged nationalist youth clubs to teach children the importance of Irish culture, language, and temperance.[120]

On Easter Monday, April 24, 1916, Pearse led an armed uprising in Dublin against British rule, proclaiming Ireland as an independent republic. Over the following week, nearly five hundred Irish rebels, British soldiers, and civilians were slain before the Easter Rising was ultimately put down. Thousands were wounded, mostly by British artillery and machine-gun fire. Patrick Pearse and his brother Willie were among the fifteen Irish leaders who were arrested, court-martialed, and executed by firing squad. They became martyrs for the nationalist cause, as Irish opinion galvanized against British rule.[121]

Only after World War I, and a bloody two-and-a-half-year guerilla war of Irish Independence (1919–1921), would Ireland be partitioned between the Protestant north—which would remain with Great Britain—and the Catholic Irish Free State to the south. Like nationalist movements throughout the British Empire, Irish independence was ultimately borne of temperance.

From Prohibition to Pub Reform

By the 1890s, the already powerful British liquor traffic was only growing stronger, more insatiable, and more cutthroat. As in the United States, they were consolidating into massive alcohol trusts that became known simply as "the trade." When three of London's main breweries merged into Watney, Combe, Reid & Company in 1899, it became the country's second-largest business, drawing parallels with John D. Rockefeller's Standard Oil Company (Chapter 16). By 1905, five of the fifteen biggest companies in Britain were breweries. "The power of the trade resembles more . . . the trusts in the United States than anything else that we have," claimed former prime minister Lord Rosebery.

The trade's political clout grew too, spreading from the "beerage" in the House of Lords to the Commons and even the government. During his time in power (1902–1905), Conservative prime minister Arthur Balfour—as well as half of his cabinet—drew dividends from breweries, while enacting legislation on the trade's behalf. Critics labeled such self-dealing as "the brewers' endowment bill." Lord Rosebery again raised the alarm: "Owing to the enormous influence wielded . . . by the drink traffic, we are," he said, "perilously near the corruption of our political system." Progressives simply lambasted it as "a kind of British Tammany" (Chapters 12, 16).[122]

The reason brewers were especially interested in undermining pub-licensing and Sunday-closing legislation was that the brewers now owned so many of the pubs. The so-called tied-house system saw rival brewers buying up once-independent public houses and leasing them out at a discount to publicans with the stipulation that they sell only the beers from the mother brewery, which was advertised predominantly on the facade. Such vertical integration of the British liquor trade was virtually identical to the saloon trade in the United States (Chapter 17).[123] The corruption and predations of tied-house pubs were similar to American saloons, too: adulterating alcohol or watering it down, aggressive sales tactics to hook their clientele. Once patrons had drunken up every shilling, pub owners would sell on credit, pushing the drinker further into debt—anything to make more money. With such cutthroat competition, brewers even engaged in so-called beer hawking: bypassing the middleman by employing delivery men to canvass working-class neighborhoods, selling beer door-to-door.[124]

While the social problem was the same in both the United States and the United Kingdom, the entrenched political power of the trade in Britain—plus the electoral massacre of prohibitionism in the 1895 election—forced progressive reformers to pursue other alternatives. Temperance activists—including Lady Henry Somerset, president of the British Woman's Temperance Union (BWTU), and her American colleague Frances Willard of the World's Woman's Christian Temperance Union (Chapter 13), who spent much of her final years in London—did not have far to go: just across the North Sea in Norway and Sweden, the Gothenburg system of municipal dispensary had been effectively reining in the worst excesses of the liquor trade for years (Chapter 3).[125]

Named for Sweden's second city, the Gothenburg system became the foremost alcohol-control rival to prohibition not just across Scandinavia, but in the United Kingdom, Canada, and the United States (Chapter 14). Gothenburg proponents took aim not at the booze itself, but at the profit motive that drove the liquor traffic. Remove the profit motive, and you minimize the problem. A private company, led by respected citizens would run the local trade in the interest of temperance taking only 5 percent dividends, returning all the rest of the profits to local civic organizations. This system of disinterested management not only led to sharp reductions in drunkenness and crime, but also to the blossoming of civil society across Scandinavia.

Post-1895 Britain was the Gothenburg era of British alcohol politics, uniting progressives of all stripes: temperance advocates, suffragettes, Free Church activists, and the burgeoning labor movement. "Politics will be purer when publicans are municipal employés, and parties no longer have any direct concern for them," wrote the Quaker Edward Pease, cofounder and secretary of the Fabian Society, Britain's foremost democratic-socialist organization. Intent on finding a workable solution to liquor trade predations, in 1898 Pease published *Liquor Licensing at Home and Abroad*, his investigation that looked favorably upon the municipal dispensary.[126]

Pease's short tract paled in comparison to the voluminous 784-page investigation the following year by the Quaker Joseph Rowntree and Liberal MP Arthur Sherwell in *The Temperance Problem and Social Reform* (1899). It became the British Gothenburger bible, using in-depth economic, crime, and social statistics to argue for disinterested management as the only way to curb the political power of the trade. Lady Somerset of the BWTU called it "the most valuable addition to the literature of the temperance cause that to my mind has yet to be given." Even Liberal MP Thomas Whittaker—vice president of the United Kingdom Alliance—broke ranks with the prohibitionists to side with Somerset, Rowntree, and Sherwell to found a separate Temperance Legislation League to promote disinterested management.[127]

Temperance activism was increasingly channeled through a new organization, the People's Refreshment House Association (PRHA), founded in 1896—a public company created to supervise and reform public houses along Gothenburg lines, and allocate excess profits to worthwhile organizations. As the name implied, the PRHA promoted food and nonalcoholic refreshments, to replace the get-drunk-quick atmosphere of public houses and gin palaces. Its promise of 5 percent returns made it a safe investment for reformers, since government bonds returned 3 percent and railroad bonds only 4 percent. And it paid social as well as monetary dividends: between 1870 and 1910, British per-capita beer consumption plummeted by 25 percent, while tea consumption rose by 70 percent.[128]

British temperance's municipal-control era worked wonders for remaking the pub as a respectable establishment—including affordable meals for middle- and working-class patrons—even though the profit margins on food were far less than for selling booze. Respectability was augmented by hiring salaried employees—men and women—from outside the trade to conduct the business, including civil servants and retired military officers who knew how to run a tight ship.

Before the outbreak of World War I, there was already an ongoing battle between the corrupt and disreputable tied-houses of old and local public-house trust companies—and the trust-houses were winning: both in customers and respectability. Increasingly, even progressive brewers began to understand that a well-regulated alcohol market preserved their privileged position against unscrupulous upstarts looking to undercut their product. By war's end, the grassroots Central Public House Administration, which was run on a county-by-county basis, alone was running 244 pubs and inns; the PRHA added another 150. All told, there were some 500 trust houses, with investments of £2 million.[129]

The man most responsible for this stunning turn was Sir Edgar Vincent, Lord D'Abernon: former president of the Ottoman Public Debt Administration (Chapter 8) and Conservative MP. By the 1890s, D'Abernon had become disillusioned with the political corruption and economic predations of the British liquor trade, converting him to Gothenburg progressivism.[130]

"The object of reform should be, not to hit the brewer and the distiller, but to get better results from them. And that is only possible if a broad view is taken of their position, if their difficulties are recognized, and if their cooperation is secured," D'Abernon explained in an interview to the *New York Times*. "Reformers have talked so much about the swollen profits of the brewing trade that many brewers do not realize how small their net profits are compared with the enormous turnover. If there was less extravagant competition and a little more intelligent adjustment and organization," profits could be maintained, even while drunkenness subsides. But it would be up to the state to provide that organization.[131]

With the outbreak of the Great War, D'Abernon was made head of the Liquor Traffic Central Control Board (CCB) to regulate the British liquor trade during the crisis of wartime. The CCB was granted sweeping powers according to the Defence of the Realm Act—passed four days after the British entry into Great War in August 1914—which empowered the state to requisition buildings and land for the war effort, imprison antiwar agitators, and impose censorship and other restrictions.

This included an immediate restriction in pub hours from noon to 3 p.m. and 6:30 to 9:30 p.m., to improve workplace discipline and curtail early-morning and late-night drinking. The CCB also increased taxes on beer and spirits to discourage their use and outlawed selling alcohol on credit, treating to drinks on the house, door-to-door beer hawking, and other traditional practices. Amid the crisis of war, such restrictions were accepted with little grumbling, either from customers or the trade itself.[132]

While resisting calls from some CCB members—including future prime minister Neville Chamberlain—to nationalize the British liquor trade outright, beginning in 1915, D'Abernon's board began taking direct control of the drink trade in areas of strategic importance to the war effort. From London and its environs, to the northeast coast of Scotland on the North Sea, and the industrial, munitions-producing areas around Carlisle and Gretna on the Scottish-English border, the CCB took control of some four hundred pubs, closing many others. "Fewer and better" was the reformist call.[133]

Carlisle was the scene of D'Abernon's greatest experiment in rehabilitating, rather than banishing, the liquor trade. Roughly half of the economically struggling, "old, evil-smelling, stuffy, ramshackle" tied-house pubs that served only alcohol were shuttered. Many of those that remained were transformed into "food taverns" that included sit-down and takeout meals, which became exceedingly popular with railway builders, factory workers, families, and working munitions girls alike. The CCB's new "reformed" pubs could promote moderation and respectability, while relieved of the siege mentality of the cutthroat profit-or-perish environment of old.[134]

In one telling instance of the sweeping changes, when the general manager of the CCB's Carlisle operation visited a reformed pub and saw a customer who'd drunken his fill, he instructed the barkeeper to cut him off. The puzzled bartender—formerly a tied-house licensee—assured him that the customer "could carry more liquor without getting into trouble with the police." The general manager explained that moderation and discipline were the new aim. "At the end of a long argument the ex-licensee exclaimed, 'Of course, I can easily work that way if the Board want it, if you tell me that I'm not to be dismissed for letting down the trade.' As soon as the managers realised that it was not a crime to 'let trade go by,' they readily accepted the Rule of the new régime, that sobriety, not turnover, was the first concern."[135]

During the war, the pervasive insobriety of Victorian England virtually disappeared—partly on account of the crisis, shortages, and sacrifices of wartime, and partly resulting from the reorganization of the British pub trade on more progressive foundations: replacing the profit-driven system with a well-regulated one in which moderation and sociability predominated. After the war, some of D'Abernon's wartime principles were continued and institutionalized in the 1921 Licensing Act, which folded the CCB into the Home Office. The act instituted shorter hours, eliminated sales on credit and door-to-door sales, and curtailed other unethical practices, while maintaining higher taxes on beer and spirits to discourage consumption.[136]

This, then, was the temperance situation that Pussyfoot Johnson found when he accepted the 1917 invitation by the Scottish Permissive Bill Association to help agitate for a referendum on prohibition for Scotland—and the ill-fated 1919 debate in London that devolved into a riot costing him an eye. Transformed by the war, many would-be temperance allies had pivoted from their failed frontal assault against the entrenched liquor traffic toward reforming it from within, through the same sort of municipal-control legislation that the United States would only adopt following prohibition's repeal in the 1930s. Pussyfoot and prohibition seemed an anachronism, and London's student body surely let him know.

With Ireland embroiled in strife amid its war for independence, the only region left agitating for prohibition was Scotland, for reasons having as much to do with nationalism as temperance. During the war, Lord D'Abernon and the CCB did impose additional restrictions—including the prohibition of distilled liquors—in strategically important Scottish counties, but left the local-veto question to the Scottish people to decide in their scheduled 1920 vote. Ultimately, the campaign between wets and drys was contentious, as Pussyfoot could certainly attest. In the end, only 23 of Scotland's 253 districts voted for no-license prohibition, 24 voted for increasing limitations on the trade, and 206 districts voted for no change. The vote ultimately signaled the death knell of prohibitionism in Scotland, and thus across the United Kingdom more generally.[137]

Britain's White Overseas Empire

The political dynamics of prohibitionism, nationalism, and progressivism were important not only to historical developments in the British Isles, but to the broader empire as well. Chapters 6 through 8 deal largely with British liquor imperialism—and prohibition as indigenous protection from it—in the colonies of South Africa, South Asia, and the Middle East. But it is also important to briefly note here developments in Britain's predominantly white settler colonies in Canada, Australia, and New Zealand, as they in many ways echo not just the political institutions of the mother country, but her temperance dynamics as well.

English and French colonization of present-day Canada was the same as the Janus-faced alco-imperialism in Britain's thirteen colonies to the south: Christian settlers professing the superior virtues of European civilization, while French and British traders swindled natives of their valuable furs with liquor enticements (Chapters 9–10). The Jesuits of New France claimed that drunkenness among Native Americans was unknown before the English captured Quebec in 1629, but when the French returned in 1632, they found the practice of swapping furs for booze widespread. Regardless of whether the French or English started the practice, brandy quickly became the chief source of profit for the Company of One Hundred Associates, the company entrusted by Cardinal Richelieu with a monopoly on the fur trade in New France. As in England's American colonies, church leaders and colonial governors tried to prohibit the trafficking of liquors to natives, to little avail: the profits were just too great. Canada's First Nations were subject to a patchwork of provincial protections akin to those in the United States, before a blanket prohibition was granted with the Indian Act of 1876.[138]

Given its proximity, Canada was long influenced by American temperance developments, with early societies dating to 1828 in Nova Scotia and Montreal, just two years after the American Temperance Society was founded in Boston (Chapter 11). Ancillaries of the International Order of Good Templars and the Woman's Christian Temperance Union also found fertile soil north of the border later on. And just as news of Maine Law prohibitionism prompted the United Kingdom Alliance in 1853, it also birthed the Canadian Prohibitory Liquor Law League the same year.[139]

Confederation with New Brunswick and Nova Scotia in 1867 established the Dominion of Canada as a self-governing constitutional monarchy under the British crown: a bicameral parliament in Ottawa legislated domestic policies, while foreign affairs were controlled by London until 1931. Canadian self-government was the blueprint for Home Rule advocates in Ireland. Even after confederation, Canadian liquor-control regulations—including local-option and prohibition questions—were often lost in disputes over whether such economic, welfare, and state-revenue concerns were more the purview of the Dominion Parliament or the provincial legislatures.

With its own newspaper, *The Pioneer*, and a constitution patterned after the United Kingdom Alliance, Canada's foremost prohibitionist organization—the Dominion Alliance for the Total Suppression of the Liquor Traffic—was organized in 1877. The alliance's major victory came the following year, when Secretary of State R. W. Scott introduced the Canada Temperance Act, which provided that a petition of one-fourth of the electors in any city or county could prompt a local referendum, in which the local liquor trade could be prohibited by a simple majority. Within a few years, Prince Edward Island, most of New Brunswick, Nova Scotia, and Ontario had voted themselves dry.[140]

At the same time as prohibition debates were sharpening between British Conservatives and Liberals in the 1890s, similar fissures were developing in Canada. Following a Conservative victory in 1891, the Canadian government punted on divisive liquor legislation, instead appointing a Royal Commission on the Liquor Traffic to conduct a wide-ranging study of the issue. The commission ultimately found in favor of increased taxation, reducing licenses, and other controls, while opposing outright prohibition.[141] When the Liberals won control of the government in the 1896 elections, they—in consultation with the Dominion Alliance—determined to settle the matter by putting the contentious question to the people: the world's first-ever advisory referendum on prohibition. Held in 1898, it found that only a 51 percent majority of Canadian voters favored prohibition. In Ottawa, the House of Commons decided this was too narrow a majority to constitute a mandate for nationwide prohibition, and instead simply expanded the scope of the 1878 Temperance Act.[142]

As in Britain, with the door effectively slammed on national prohibition, temperance advocates looked to reform the Canadian alcohol trade from within, drawing on the insights of Swedish and British Gothenburgers to develop effective municipal-dispensary liquor-control systems, especially among French-speaking Catholics of Quebec.[143]

Of course, everything changed when Britain declared war on Germany in August 1914, dragging the British Dominion of Canada into World War I. In the spirit of national conservation and sacrifice, between 1914 and 1917, every Canadian province except Quebec—including the separate British Dominion of Newfoundland— prohibited the liquor traffic, just as the wave of state-level prohibitions swept the United States to the south (Chapter 17).[144] Also like the United States, in 1918 Canada's federal government adopted an emergency prohibition on the production and trade in beverages over 2.5 percent alcohol by volume, which effectively dried up the wet bastion of Quebec for the duration of the war.

With demobilization and the ending of wartime prohibition in 1920, Quebec returned to its Gothenburg-type dispensary system. Bolstered by the examples of Quebec, the British Carlisle experiment, and the successes of the Scandinavian system, one by one, the other provinces and territories of Canada scrapped their prohibitions in favor of Gothenburg-type control boards. Prince Edward Island was the longest holdout, only re-legalizing the alcohol trade in 1948.[145]

In the end, the temperance history of Canada is what you might expect it to be: an amalgam of European alco-colonization of native peoples, the influence of nearby American temperance organizations and discourses against the growing might of the liquor trade, all filtered through British political institutions. It is hardly a footnote: developments in Canadian temperance and prohibition were instrumental in the adoption of similar liquor-control measures in the United States following the repeal of prohibition in the 1930s, and many of those state-level alcohol-control systems remain in place to this day.[146]

Also noteworthy are the striking similarities in Britain's alco-colonization of Australia and New Zealand. European explorers of various nations had sailed the coastlines of the Australian continent since the seventeenth century, but only after Captain James Cook's 1770 expedition—and the American Revolution soon thereafter—did the idea of establishing a permanent colony of New South Wales for British convicts gain traction. The introduction of alcohol to native aborigines, Torres Strait and Pacific Islanders, came from the very first contacts: in Tahiti, Tonga, and even Sydney Cove, European explorers including Captain Cook routinely invited tribal chiefs on board their ships, treating them to wine and rum.[147]

The so-called First Fleet of eleven ships arrived in 1787, establishing a permanent settlement at Sydney Cove the following year. Subsequent fleets brought ever more convicts, free settlers, and guard detachments.

In 1806, Vice-Admiral William Bligh—who'd famously been set adrift by mutineers on his HMS *Bounty* seventeen years earlier—was appointed governor of New South Wales by King George III. He was given a mandate to clean up the notoriously corrupt New South Wales Army. The colonial alcohol trade was supposed to be a crown monopoly with benefits accruing to the state. Instead, army officers smuggled in stills and began an incredibly lucrative illicit liquor trade, flooding Australia with so much rum that it was used as currency in barter transactions, both with aborigines and settlers. Drunkenness became widespread.

Previous attempts at reforming the army's illegal liquor trade proved unsuccessful. Ever the disciplinarian, Bligh clamped down on the import of alcohol to the Army Corps, banned bartering in rum, and outlawed all nongovernment stills.[148] In doing so, Bligh quickly made enemies not only with the army, but with the burgeoning aristocracy that profited from the trade. The resulting Rum Rebellion of 1808 was Australia's first and only military coup: four hundred soldiers arrested Governor Bligh and held him on a ship off Van Diemen's Land (Tasmania) for two years. The corrupt "Rum Corps" was ultimately recalled to England, replaced by the Seventy-Third Regiment and a new governor. While later historians have accentuated other grievances among the military and aristocracy leading to the Great Rebellion, Governor Bligh was quite clear what precipitated it. He named those particular civic leaders and military officers, "checked in the enormous practice of bartering Spirits, which had principally been almost the ruin of the Country, became privately discontented" at his checking of their trade, which led them to "Treason and Rebellion to the State."[149]

Distilling was the lynchpin of the entire colonial economy. Masters were allowed to pay servants and slaves part of their wages in distilled spirits, as in the Cape Colony of South Africa (Chapter 6). Aborigines bartered fish, seal skins, and whalebone for British liquor, which—following the standard European alco-colonization pattern—led to scenes of "terrible" drunken brutality: "Limbs are fractured, bones smashed, skulls laid open; no exclamation of pain escapes from these ferocious savages, the air resounds only with frightful vociferations." Based mostly on white-settler fears, a series of prohibitionary measures against selling to aborigines soon followed, to little effect. Following the federation of Australia, these native prohibitions were folded into state or territory laws, and only repealed in the 1950s through 1970s.[150]

Not surprisingly, in conducting a statistical survey of the Australasian colonies in the 1830s, Samuel Morewood found "a prodigious quantity" of alcohol consumption: "the quantity of spirits swallowed by each individual, yearly, comes to somewhat better than five gallons and three pints, which exceeds the consumption of the proportion for the population of Ireland by four gallons, and that of Scotland by more than three. If to this consumption of ardent spirits there be superadded the same quantity of wine and malt liquors, the amount will vastly exceed that used by the same number of inhabitants in any part of the world."[151]

Morewood noted that progress was being made, with the first temperance associations being established by English Quaker James Backhouse. Having pioneered temperance societies in Britain's Cape Colony in 1831–1832, Backhouse arrived in Van Dieman's Land (Tasmania), from whence his temperance message spread throughout Australia and New Zealand. Morewood lamented, "Few places, perhaps, on the face of the globe require the exertions of such institutions more."[152]

While temperance organizations like the International Order of Good Templars and the Independent Order of Rechabites were active through the 1860s and 1870s, the situation changed dramatically with the arrival of the Woman's Christian Temperance Union in the 1880s. The first WCTU chapters in the Australian and New Zealand colonies followed the visit of American temperance emissaries, including Mary Leavitt, in 1882 and 1884, but took off under Jessie Ackermann in the late 1880s and early 1890s. In accordance with Frances Willard's "Do Everything" policy, Ackermann expanded the scope of WCTU activism to everything from prison reform to kindergartens, childhood education, and women's welfare (Chapter 13). But the WCTU's core mission was temperance reform, which necessitated political empowerment and women earning the right to vote.[153]

The environment for political activism in the Australian and New Zealand colonies paralleled that in the American South at the time—one in which there was little history of women's independent political organization and few rival organizations for women, much less governed completely by women.[154] Consequently, the Australian WCTU exploded in activity, just at the same time as debates were heating up about the political future of the continent. The year 1883 saw the first of a series of conferences to unify the six self-governing British colonies—New South Wales, Queensland, Tasmania, Victoria, South Australia, and West Australia—into a federal commonwealth. Fiji and New Zealand opted out of the federation process, which continued in fits and starts throughout the 1890s. It culminated in 1901, with the establishment of the Commonwealth of Australia, with a federal system, a bicameral parliament, and a constitutional monarchy tied to the British crown, much as in Canada.

Temperance contributed to this widespread spirit of democratic self-determination by pushing for a local option, rather than outright prohibition. "What should stand in the way of the wishes of a free and reasoning people?" rhetorically asked temperance advocate Francis Bertie Boyce in 1893. "No people should have a semi-government institution, like an open bar, remain forced—ay, forced—upon them against their will. Free people, with the rights of citizens, will say, that the days of compulsion must go, and that local self-government on such a point must prevail."[155]

The WCTU extended such arguments about democracy to the question of women's suffrage in Australia and New Zealand. The WCTU of New Zealand was instrumental in compiling the so-called Monster Petition of some twenty-five thousand signatures demanding the right to vote, which was instrumental to 1893 legislation making New Zealand the first self-governing nation on earth to give women the ballot.[156] The WCTU was likewise in the vanguard in Australia, where in 1891 Ackermann unified the disparate colonial WCTU chapters into a federal WCTU of Australasia, in anticipation of federalization. Ackermann and the WCTU led South Australia to grant equal rights for women in 1894, and Western Australia in 1899. The remaining states followed suit only after the new federal parliament acted, granting Australian women the right to vote and hold office in 1902. There was one caveat: native women were still disenfranchised, as all aborigines—both men and women—were still denied citizenship rights. With suffragism largely secured, after World War I the WCTU turned to promoting "the cause of our native races, maintaining their rights to equal citizenship in this fair land of Australia, which is theirs by birth and love and tradition."[157]

Given prevailing "wet" sentiments and the politically powerful liquor trade, American-style prohibitionism was a pipe dream. Instead, the WCTU joined with other temperance activists to agitate for expanded local-option, liquor-control, and pub-reform legislation as in Britain and Canada.[158]

Even the selection of a national capital was influenced by the local-option question: temperance activists, progressives, and especially the Labor Party that swept to power in 1910 wanted to build a new capital, far distant from the entrenched big-city liquor machines in Sydney and Melbourne. Consequently, the new Australian Capital Territory of Canberra was established as a dry jurisdiction, with no licensed pubs or liquor outlets until 1928.[159]

Especially during World War I, the WCTU pushed state-level governments for Sunday closing, licensing restrictions, and limiting hours of pub operations. Though far from the European theaters of war, Australian and New Zealand Army Corps (ANZAC) forces fought valiantly against Atatürk at Gallipoli (Chapter 8), while the spirit of patriotic conservation and sacrifice permeated back home. The WCTU was successful in securing early-closing laws, which produced the infamous "six o'clock swill," as laborers who got off work at five o'clock had but one hour to drink before the six o'clock pub-closing time. And drink they did.[160]

The other thrust of temperance activism was in pursuit of Gothenburg-style municipalization reform. Just as Britain had its Carlisle experiment, Australia's version was the South Australian town of Renmark. As municipal-control debates permeated Australasian temperance circles, citizens of the Renmark Local Progress Committee in 1897 followed the Gothenburg playbook, collecting only 5 percent dividends in exchange for running the Renmark Community Hotel along temperance lines. It would be the only licensed liquor outlet in the rural district, funneling much-needed revenues toward local philanthropy. Renmark was largely a success, drying up the illicit "sly grog" trade and adding respectability to Australian drinking establishments. The system was replicated throughout South Australia and beyond.[161]

Against such a backdrop of gradual liquor-control successes, there was little appetite for prohibition in Australia. The main prohibitionist organization—the Australian Alliance Prohibition Council—was largely relegated to arguing against Gothenburg municipalization for making the state complicit in a troublesome trade. Their main goal may have been far-off prohibition, but they settled for simple local-option legislation wherever possible.

More action was found in New Zealand, which became a mostly independent, self-governing British dominion in 1907. The local New Zealand Alliance for Total Suppression of the Liquor Trade pushed to let the people decide the fate of prohibition through an advisory referendum—and they did! In a unique twist, the question of liquor licensing in New Zealand, up to and including prohibition, would be decided by national referendum—not just once, but *every three years*, coinciding with their general elections. Ostensibly, this was done to take this contentious question out of party politics. Consequently, Kiwis voted on prohibition twenty-six different times between 1911 and 1987. In the first referendum in 1911, 55.8 percent opted for prohibition, well below the necessary 60 percent majority threshold. During the

LINERS IN COLLISION IN THE ENGLISH CHANNEL: A VIEW OF THE DAMAGED PORTION OF THE NEW ZEALAND SHIPPING COMPANY'S STEAMER REMUERA, WHICH COLLIDED DURING A FOG WITH THE ELLERMAN LINER MARENGO, WHILE BOUND FROM LONDON TO AUCKLAND.

Figure 5.5 "Liners in Collision in the English Channel," *Auckland Weekly News*, September 14, 1922, 39.

Source: AWNS-19220914-39-5, Sir George Gray Special Collections, Auckland Libraries Heritage Collections, Auckland, NZ.

war, the New Zealand government rebuffed calls for prohibition, instead opting for six o'clock closing, as in Australia. After World War I, the threshold for the triennial prohibition referendum dropped to a simple majority of 50 percent, and in 1919, New Zealand came its closest to adopting prohibition, when 49.7 percent voted in favor.[162]

With victory so tantalizingly close, dry Kiwis hoped that a burst of energy might help put them over the top in the next referendum, scheduled for 1922. To that end, the prohibitionist alliances invited Pussyfoot Johnson—fresh off his wildly successful 1921 tour of British India (Chapter 7)—for a speaking tour of New Zealand and Australia. In July 1922—three short years after the London rag that made him a household name—the one-eyed Pussyfoot boarded the New Zealand steamship *Remuera*, headed for Auckland via the Panama Canal. Yet only one day out of London, in the fog of the English Channel, the *Remuera* was rammed by the British liner *Marengo*, its bow smashing directly into Pussyfoot's stateroom, "quite as if she had some personal grievance against me," as he noted.[163]

The ship limped back to port in London. Unfazed by the loss of his belongings as the ship took on water, within days Pussyfoot again headed down under to stump for prohibition—this time eastward through the Suez Canal.

When he arrived in Perth, Pussyfoot was met by Thomas Walker, the attorney general of West Australia. "Tom had once been the big stick of the wets in New South Wales," Pussyfoot explained, "but one night drank a little too much of the juice he was defending and, under this dubious inspiration, shot a man in the leg." In his embarrassment, Walker swore off booze, packed his bags, moved west, and started a new life as a prohibitionist, even making successful lecture tours of the United States. Johnson gave a series of lectures around Perth before continuing eastward.

At Adelaide, Johnson's train pulled in at eight o'clock, just as his lecture was scheduled to start. By the time he got to the hall, he found a packed, skeptical, and impatient audience. As he walked in, the host thrust a newspaper clipping into his hands and demanded that he answer for it. Not knowing what it said, a stunned Pussyfoot began reading aloud the article: one of the same London newsmen who'd so vilified Pussyfoot for trying to "put over" prohibition on England had written that now he was trying to do the same to Australia. The tabloid article even claimed he had a war chest of some ten million dollars with which to do it.

"Now that sort of thing is very hard to deny seriously and, at the same time, effectively," he later recalled. All eyes were on Pussyfoot.

"Yes," he said, "that is true. I have come to Australia with ten million dollars behind me."

Mouths agape, the audience was shocked.

"But it is so far behind me that I fear it will never catch up."

With that, a great roar of laughter went up, and the ridiculous accusation was cast by the wayside.[164] Ultimately, Pussyfoot never had such an endowment, and his stumping for local-veto initiatives failed to bring anything like prohibition to either Australia or New Zealand. After his visit, the December 1922 New Zealand referendum saw support for prohibition dip to 48.5 percent, a trend that would continue downward for the next six decades of polling.[165] Nevertheless, the experiences of temperance and alcohol control in Britain's white settler colonies remain an important—and consistent—part of the global history of prohibitionism as progressivism and anti-imperialism.

6

Black Man's Burden, White Man's Liquor in Southern Africa

Paddington Station, London, United Kingdom: Friday, September 6, 1895

They call September in London the "silly season," the annual autumnal lull in the life of the city. Following the electoral fireworks of the summer of 1895, which dealt the Liberals and their dry supporters a crushing defeat (Chapter 5), Parliament was late in wrapping up the summer term. Aristocratic MPs grumbled that the "Glorious Twelfth" of August—the start of the shooting season for red grouse—had already long passed. As London high society retreated to their country estates, the seaside, or the continent, the capital was unusually quiet.

All that changed about 4:30 p.m. on September 6, 1895, as the Great Western Railway's express train from the port of Plymouth chugged into Paddington Station. Weary from their two-week steamship voyage from Cape Town, a curious "trinity of dusky kings" stepped from their rail carriage into the British limelight. This marked the first time any leader of Britain's recently established Bechuanaland Protectorate—present-day Botswana—had made the arduous ocean voyage from South Africa to London: the metropole of Great Britain's world-spanning empire. English readers only knew of the Kalahari from the tales of explorer Dr. David Livingstone, we presume, or from journalist Henry Morton Stanley's adventures into the "dark interior" of the so-called Dark Continent.[1] Especially with so little else going on, the press was eager to verify Livingstone's portrayal of the Bechuana as friendly allies in expanding commerce and Christianity into the African interior.[2] Even in painting a sympathetic picture of their guests, however, reporters' descriptions belied the racial hierarchy—crowned by white Anglo-Saxons—that animated Britain's self-proclaimed "civilizing mission" of imperialism.

First stepped Bathoen, chief of the Ngwaketse kingdom, just beyond the northern border of Britain's Cape Colony. "He is a veritable Samson, and when he walks the earth seems to shake beneath him. He has a huge head—the flat spreading nose, the large open eyes, and the heavy lips of the true child of Ham." Then came the short, thick-set Chief Sebele of the BaKwena, whose kingdom lay farther north, and whose father had been baptized by Dr. Livingstone himself. "The cast of his face is almost European," wrote the *St. James Gazette*, "and if it were not for his dark copper hue he might very well pose as the double of an eminent barrister."

Finally stepped the most finely apportioned of the three: King Khama III. "A Cape tailor who knew how to use the shears had been at work upon his garb and had turned him out so that he should not disgrace the coloured population of Bloomsbury and Bayswater," wrote the *Gazette*, in language that was typical of the day. "The face beneath the hat was of a singular though negroid type." This Bamangwato ruler of the arid, Texas-sized kingdom in the heart of Africa, known simply as Khama's Land, was unquestionably the first among his equals. "Khama looks about five-and-forty. His woolly hair is sparse and faintly tinted with grey."

It took awhile for the porters to unload the luggage. Reporters seized the opportunity to interview the kings—through their irate translator, the missionary Rev. W. C. Willoughy—about their travels, experiences, and impressions.

"A pleasant voyage, I hope?" queried the reporter for the *Gazette*.

"Thanks! A very pleasant one. What astonished me," said Khama, "was that the vessel should find a straight road across the sea to England. On the sea there are no roads, yet the vessel came on a straight line. This was marvelous to us."

"And what do you think of the first sight of England, Khama?"

"I have never seen anything like it in any part of my own country," Khama replied, in reference to the arid, thistle lands of the Kalahari. "Everything is looking so marvelously fresh and green—such fine pastures, and trees so rich in foliage! I have never seen so beautiful a country as that we have passed through to-day."

The weary kings gazed upward at the latticework of the soaring iron arches of the Paddington station, as pleasantries turned to policies. "We are sorry in this country to learn that there are differences in Bechuanaland on the liquor question. Will you tell me what some of your people want?"

"I have for years tried to abolish the use of strong liquors in my country, and prevent the importation of European drinks," Khama replied, as the attendants unloaded bag after bag. "It is a matter of great surprise and sorrow to me that my efforts to prevent the consumption of intoxicants should be hampered by agitation in my country and outside it."

"And about your dispute with the Chartered Company," the journalist continued, referring to the British South Africa Company, run by Cecil Rhodes, whose brutality in the African diamond trade was matched only by the inhumanity of Belgian King Leopold II in the Congo (Chapter 3). "What is it you want the British Government to do now?"

"I would rather not talk about that until I have been to the Colonial Office. You see, the position—"

At that point, Willoughy, the road-weary missionary, stopped the interview. His "dusky charges" (as the reporters wrote) were to be escorted to the opulent London Missionary Society (LMS)—the same organization that had sent Dr. Livingstone to Africa in the first place.

The *Gazette* was left to conclude its brief interview, foreshadowing the showdown and the stakes in store:

> "Mr. Chamberlain," the Queen's new Secretary of State for the Colonies, "will be able to discuss matters with the Kings without the intervention of the missionaries, between whom and Mr. Rhodes a storm will shortly be brewing."[3]

To be sure, that singular tension between white missionaries on the one hand—who genuinely defended the interests of indigenous peoples—against the predatory imperialists like Cecil Rhodes, on the other, who sought only profits and power, was a defining aspect of the British imperial project . . . and, indeed, all modern empires.

Kalahari Crossroads

Colonialism was nothing new in South Africa. Centuries before the Berlin Conference of 1885 divvied up the entire continent between rival European empires, the people of southern Africa endured wave after wave of white settlement, enslavement, and subjugation to European companies, as well as to the states that backed those exploitative businesses with political legitimacy and military firepower.

First came the Dutch East India Company, which established a trading post at the Cape of Good Hope in 1652—a refueling post along its vital trade route to India and the Far East. In addition to trading in slaves, many Dutch settlers became independent farmers, or Boers, who moved ever farther inland, battling with black natives for prime farmland.

Then came the British, who seized control of the Cape Colony at the end of the Napoleonic Wars in 1814. The new British masters forced the Dutch settlers to adopt English language and culture, and forcibly emancipated their slaves. While the Cape of Good Hope became a British crown colony, the livid Dutch settlers undertook a "Great Trek" farther northeast, establishing the Boer republics of the Orange Free State and the Transvaal, later known as the South African Republic. Thus developed an uneasy, tripartite dynamic in southern Africa between British colonists; white, Dutch-speaking Boers (or Afrikaners); and the various native tribes.

The farther north from the coast—across the scrubland of the great Karoo plateau—the less hospitable and more arid the climate becomes. North of the Orange River (flowing west) and the Limpopo (flowing east), the savannah gives way to the great Kalahari Desert, where "the sheep have stones to eat, and thorns to pick their teeth with," as Mark Twain described it.[4] This is the rugged territory of the Tswana people, whose tribes had come together already in the 1850s to battle against the northward incursions of the Dutch Afrikaners. The 1860 peace agreement of Potchefstroom ended a decade of intermittent warfare and established the border between Bechuanaland and the Dutch Transvaal—present-day Botswana and South Africa—though Boer incursions into Bechuanaland continued, including the taking of slaves.[5]

The farmers, herders, and hunters of the Kalahari soon found themselves at the crossroads of competing European colonialisms. In the 1880s, Germans settled present-day Namibia, establishing the colony of German South West Africa. The British feared that the Germans would spread east across the Kalahari plains and link with the Boers in the Transvaal. Bechuanaland—and the strategically important "missionaries' road" linking the Cape Colony with British settlements in Zimbabwe and the Zambezi—became a vital north-south wedge against a potential east-west Boer-German alliance.[6]

Ever since Dr. Livingstone's famed explorations for the London Missionary Society, LMS missionaries had been active in the Kalahari, cultivating goodwill, including among the new Bamangwato chief, Khama, of northern Bechuanaland. In 1876, Khama composed the following letter:

> I, Kham[a], King of the Bagamangwato [*sic*], greet Victoria, the great Queen of the English people.
>
> I write to you, Sir Henry, in order that your Queen may preserve for me my country, it being in her hands. The Boers are coming into it. and I do not like them. Their actions are cruel among us black people. We are like money: they sell us and our children. I ask her Majesty to pity me and to hear that which I write quickly. I wish to hear upon what conditions her Majesty will receive me and my country and my people under her protection. . . .
>
> There are three things which distress me very much—war, selling people, and drink. All these I shall find in the Boers, and it is these things which destroy people to make an end of them in the country.[7]

In December 1884 a force of four thousand troops led by British major-general Charles Warren marched north from Cape Town to establish British sovereignty against German and Boer encroachments. The following spring, the land of the Tswana was carved into two parts: the smaller, southernmost portion became British Bechuanaland (and within a decade would be folded in to the Cape Colony, becoming part of South Africa). The vast, northern stretches became the Bechuanaland Protectorate—administered locally by Khama and other local chieftains while enjoying the protection of the British Empire.[8] "The native Chiefs fully recognise that the white population will extend over the country," Warren wrote back to London, "provided they in their turn are able to enjoy the protection of a powerful and just Government." As he concluded, "There is room for all."[9]

Still, all was not well, even among those southernmost areas that had become the Crown Colony of British Bechuanaland. When, in August 1895, the native chiefs there learned that the English and Dutch settlers had lobbied a receptive London for formal incorporation into the Cape Colony, Chief Montsioa—along with a petition from a hundred local chieftains—protested directly to Queen Victoria and her ministers, in terms that were virtually identical to Khama's pleas, and at the exact same time. "Help us again we pray you, do not let the Cape Government kill my people with their brandy," he wrote, fearful of what British alco-colonization would do to his tribe.

"We do not want it, it will destroy us, it will cause fighting and it will fill our land with sorrow and darkness. We are living nicely without the white man's brandy, please hold fast the hands of the Cape so that brandy may never be allowed in our country." But it was no use. While the annexation formally honored tribal prohibitions against the liquor trade, in reality, the loss of native sovereignty meant a flood of booze and white liquor peddlers.[10]

Even after annexation, Chief Montsioa continued his vocal protests against the inebriating of his people. But a chief without land and without sovereignty could be dispatched that much more easily.

Alcohol and Empire

Idali, tchwala, umshumyan, leting, boyaloa, ikwena . . . the indigenous tribes of southern Africa had many traditional varieties of "kafir beer" fermented from maize, grains, or honey. Native kafir was largely a light, sweet beverage of less than 3 percent alcohol fermented from malted corn and spring water, and only produced drunkenness when consumed in large quantities, as at weddings and religious ceremonies.[11] So, while alcohol was known before the white man arrived in Africa, widespread drunkenness and alcoholism were not much of a problem.

In his *Missionary Travels* (1858), explorer Dr. David Livingstone suggested as much when chronicling the day that one of his guides returned to camp drunk: "This was the first case of real babbling intoxication we had seen in this region." Suggesting its confinement to a particular class, he continued, "The boyaloa, or beer of the country, has more of a stupefying than exciting nature; hence the beer-bibbers are great sleepers, they may frequently be seen lying on their faces sound asleep."[12]

Of course, fermented beverages are a product of nature. The process by which yeasts interact with sugars to create alcohol was known to Stone Age people. Fermented wines and beers have been found in ancient Egyptian tombs, Armenian caves, and Chinese records going back thousands of years.[13] Yet nothing more vividly reflects the contrast between traditional and industrial societies than the difference

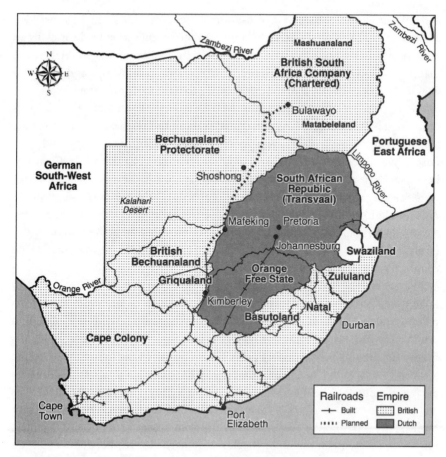

Figure 6.1 Map of South Africa, showing British and Boer territories, 1895.

between their drinks: fermented versus distilled alcohols. Hard liquor is not found in nature: it is a highly potent, man-made, industrial distillate, the product of a technological revolution that profoundly alters society.

Historians have long chronicled how industrialization and distillation upended traditional societies across Europe. Just as in precolonial Africa, alcoholism was rare in premodern Europe, because drinking was largely a communal affair. Fermented wines, meads, ales, and beers were imbibed, but opportunities to get drunk were few and far between: harvest time, saints' days, holidays, weddings, and other community celebrations. Traditional drinking was done in the open, for all to see: religious leaders and the entire village exercised a modicum of control by casting shame on villagers who overimbibed.[14]

But industrialization—and industrial alcohols—shattered traditional, rural society. The Industrial Revolution in Europe uprooted men, women, and even children from their villages, forcing them into ceaseless, backbreaking labor in the mines and mills. The pittance they were paid afforded them only squalor in disease-ridden and overcrowded urban slums. Distillation and commodification made drinking an individual rather than a communal affair. Unlike the holiday or harvest celebrations that punctuated the calendar of the rural village—when drinking was done in full view of the community and its elders—now dejected workingmen would slink daily to the tavern for distilled forgetfulness of their misery, often leaving their families destitute at home. Unlike milder, fermented beers and wines that allowed more time for socializing before inebriation, super-concentrated distilled liquors had one purpose: to get you as drunk as you can as quickly as you can. For example, in Germany, beer was the drink of the industrious workingman, while the dingy schnapps halls were dens of urban poverty and misery (Chapter 4). With capitalism's industrialization and imperialism—both across Europe and in far-flung colonies around the world—unscrupulous bar and saloon-keepers provided addictive escapism day or night, far from the prying eyes of the village community that had typically held drunkenness in check.

The individual became the subject of exploitation. Once hooked, an alcoholic would hand over his last penny, farthing, shilling, or kopeck to an unscrupulous tavern-keeper who rarely considered the drunkard's well-being enough to say, "You've had enough." Cutting off a drunkard made zero economic sense: less money for the saloon-keeper, less profit for his bosses in the liquor industry, and less tax revenue for his sovereign, as we saw in Russia (Chapter 2). Inebriates who ran out of money were either tossed to the gutter or they pawned away their clothes and possessions for drink, only then to be tossed to the gutter. A booming liquor business thrived from the ever-expanding drunken misery of the people. The state too had little interest in stemming the flow of liquor, since alcohol duties and taxes everywhere constituted the single most important source of state revenue in the era before income tax.[15] Resistance against predatory liquor capitalism backed by a predatory state took the form of temperance and democracy—which is why temperance worked hand-in-glove with efforts for liberalization, democratization, female suffrage, abolitionism, and protecting the rights of indigenous communities and impoverished workers.

Those are the dynamics of temperance and prohibitionism we find time and again in every corner of the globe.

But whereas European society had the luxury of gradually acclimating to such dramatic societal changes over generations and centuries, liquor's introduction into Africa could be measured in months—the impact was as immediate as it was devastating. As historian David Christian reminds us, "Distilled drinks were to fermented drinks what guns were to bows and arrows: instruments of a potency unimaginable in most traditional societies."[16] This was both more apt and more true in Africa than in the tsarist Russia that Christian was describing. Plus, the new, potent, distilled spirits never spoiled, so they could be easily bottled and shipped across great oceans, making them the perfect tool for overseas colonial domination. Just as the natives' arrows were no defense against the guns of the European imperialists, so too the native beers were no match for the white man's liquor. Indeed, colonialism in Africa, Asia, and North America was achieved with bottles as much as bullets.

So, we must pack away our twenty-first-century understandings of alcohol as a harmless, recreational beverage when we speak of the "white man's liquor." European colonists introduced drinks of a potency no African had ever encountered, and few could hope to handle, and the colonists did so deliberately. Take, for instance, so-called Cape Smoke—"a villainous concoction made by the grape farmers of the Cape, and fortified with tobacco juice and other worse flavourings," according to one contemporary author—which "had been freely imported and sold without let or hindrance. It was, of course, a source of considerable profit to the importers, and the results were obvious in the debauchery and degradation of the natives. This exploitation of other races by the whites has been a foul blot on our civilization, not only in South Africa, but throughout the world."[17]

Once the British outlawed slavery, alcohol became a ready means of payment both in the mines and on the farms. "In the Cape Colony it has been the custom on the wine-farms to pay part of the wages of the natives in wine or brandy, and so undeveloped was the Christian Conscience on the matter that one often heard the practice defended on the ground that it helped to kill off the natives and keep them down!"[18] Like the "truck system" in imperial Germany (see Chapter 4), the resulting *dop* (or *tot*) system—through which black labor was recruited, paid, and controlled with liquor—continued through apartheid rule and was only abolished by Nelson Mandela as part of the antiapartheid reforms of the 1990s.[19]

Indeed, gifting brandy to the natives and then chronicling their drunken fury was (as in Ireland, Chapter 5) used as justification for why British colonialism was necessary to tame the so-called Black Peril.[20] Brandy was an instrument of conquest and domination like the musket, and was often just as fatal. The colonizers knowingly used it as such.

The "gift" of booze was the key lubricant for the classic ruse: duping the tribal leader into agreeing to one document and then, through sleight of hand, signing another that stripped them of their sovereignty.[21] When that failed—as missionary John Mackenzie witnessed on the 1884 Warren expedition—white Europeans went "about at night with black bottles containing brandy, to excite the minds of the chief and people so that the natives might refuse the treaty, and thus be put in a false position from the outset, and be judged unworthy of any consideration. . . . This was my first opposition in Bechuanaland, and it was neither from natives nor from Boers, but from Englishmen,—or, at least, from my fellow-subjects under the Queen."[22]

Viewed in this light, African temperance and prohibitionism were not some eccentric preoccupations of naïve, native tribesmen who took to the teachings of Christian missionaries with a little too much zeal. Instead, they were inseparable components in the subaltern fight against European colonization itself.

As an editorial aside, let me be blunt: the willingness of generations of writers and historians—even today—to falsely ascribe any high-minded actions by native leaders instead to white Christian missionaries is appalling. European colonizers had no monopoly on morality or benevolence, especially as their actions showed the opposite. Such mis-portrayals only parrot and reinforce colonial stereotypes and racial hierarchies, while systematically denying African leaders' agency in addressing their own community's very valid concerns. Indeed, what greater test of a chief's sovereignty could there be than to prohibit the innocuous-looking but supremely potent European product that most threatened to subvert his traditional rule?

After all, what could colonizers reap and exploit? The land, for one, and the crops, game, and livestock that thrived on it; the mineral resources under it; and the sovereign people who controlled it. Shipping black families off into slavery at gunpoint was certainly bad enough, but making them slaves to liquor wasn't much better. The former expropriated their labor, the latter expropriated their wealth, while both took their dignity and often their lives.

Mirroring their divergent views on slavery, the Boers were even more ruthless than the British in their colonial alco-politics. In 1881, the Transvaal government granted a monopoly on distilled brandy to the Hatherley Distillery near Pretoria, making it the sole producer of cheap spirits, intended primarily for black consumption. The company that received the monopoly was called "*De Eerste Fabrieken in de Zuid Afrikaansche Republiek, Ltd.*" in Dutch: a proud boast that it was indeed "the first factory" of any kind in the Transvaal.[23] (South African Breweries—today a multibillion-dollar global conglomerate and the world's largest brewer—was founded shortly thereafter to provide British-style beer to a white clientele.) Like the *dop* system in agriculture, miners were often fed liquor while in the mines: if they ended up with larger booze debts to pay off, the longer they'd have to keep working for the white mine owners, rather than returning home to their villages.[24]

It is curious that—with the region's abundant mineral and agricultural resources—the first industrial factory of any kind in the region produced cheap booze intended for black laborers, rather than something more beneficial to the local economy and community. Of course, benefiting the locals was never the point of colonialism: exploiting them was. And as we see the world over, nothing turns subaltern labor into the colonizer's profit more effectively than does the liquor traffic.[25]

The liquor business boomed in 1886, when news of gold discovered on a sleepy Boer farm in the Witwatersrand unleashed a flood of prospectors and adventure-seekers even greater than in California a generation before. The boomtown of Johannesburg was hastily founded. Within a decade, it had become a bustling metropolis and one of the largest centers of commerce and finance on the African continent. The mines of the 'Rand contained a built-in customer base of some fourteen thousand black miners in 1890. By 1899 it was one hundred thousand. The flood of liquor that flowed down the gullets of the men in the mines yielded dividends of

Figure 6.2 Swiss photographer H. Ferdinand Gros's *Hatherley Distillery Near Pretoria*, circa 1888.
Source: Rod Kruger, "HF Gros and His Remarkable Collection of Early Transvaal Photographs," *Heritage Portal* (South Africa), May 13, 2016. HF Gros's Pictorial Description of the Transvaal, ZA TAB #_#_16344_#, National Archives Repository (Public Records of Former Transvaal Province), National Archives and Record Service of South Africa, Pretoria, South Africa.

some 12 to 20 percent annually for colonial investors and the new, white "Liquor Kings."

The mine owners grew increasingly worried. It wasn't the spike in alcohol poisonings, drunken disorder, burglaries, and murders among the mine workers that concerned them. Rather, they worried that the Liquor Kings' profits were cutting into *their* bottom line (even though many mine owners likewise turned handsome profits by operating liquor canteens).[26] Echoing the concerns of other capitalists, in 1896 the chairman of the Geldenhuis Deep Mine lamented that his operation "required 1,200 natives and so far had only 600, of whom about 100 were too drunk to work on the first two days of the week."[27] According to the white mine-owners, every day, between 15 and 25 percent of the black labor force was "disabled by drink."[28] Attempts to limit or prohibit black access to booze were only halfheartedly implemented, and were easy to circumvent.[29]

Liquor quickly became the scourge of the South African labor force: a parasite that drained their productivity, strength, and wallets, before often leaving them dead, too. Chemically analyzed liquor samples were often deemed unfit for human consumption, having been cut with creosote, turpentine, or other poisons. Liquor killed scores of black workers. "It was a common thing," noted one observer "to find 'boys' lying dead on the veld from exposure and the effects of the vile liquids sold them by unscrupulous dealers."[30] Alcohol poisoning was the primary cause of death among black miners. "Drink again," lamented the superintendent of the Johannesburg cemetery over yet another delivery from the morgue. "Several of these every week—the cursed stuff burns their insides, and they never recover after a drinking bout."[31]

The pattern of white alco-colonial dominance expanded into the twentieth century through the South African "beer hall system." Black workers described life in the massive, brick beer halls as "drinking in a cage," which it was. Beginning in Natal in 1908 and spreading quickly to the rest of the European dominions, the Native Beer Act created a Scandinavian-type municipal monopoly on the alcohol trade. The centuries-old traditions of indigenous brewing were outlawed; black workers could now only legally drink in the cramped squalor of the dank beer halls. All the profits, of course, went to the white municipal government, which used the money to build sprawling, prisonlike barracks for the black workers and pay the salaries of the white police force, while still turning a hefty profit. Little wonder that colonial rule in South Africa was rocked throughout the 1920s and '30s by beer hall boycotts, temperance pledges, and violent riots against the white-controlled liquor traffic, almost identical to those in imperial Russia in the 1850s (Chapter 2).[32] Even the violent 1976 Soweto Uprising saw the widespread burning of dozens of beer halls and bottle stores as mechanisms of apartheid oppression and black disempowerment.[33]

African leaders learned the necessity of confronting white alco-slavery early on. In southernmost Africa—where native tribes had a longer history of interaction with Dutch and British colonizers and their Cape Smoke—King Moshoeshoe tried to prohibit trafficking liquor as early as 1854 in what would later become Lesotho. "Whereas the spiritous liquors of the whites were unknown to former generations of our Tribe," his edict proclaimed, "and whereas spiritous liquors create quarrelling and strife, and pave the way to the destruction of society, (for surely the spiritous liquors of the white are nothing else than fire): It is therefore hereby made known to all that the introduction and sale of said spiritous liquor within Basutoland is henceforth prohibited." The law was never seriously enforced, and within a decade most of Moshoeshoe's people had become hooked on distilled liquor.[34]

To the north, Livingstone chronicled crossing the Orange River inland into the territory of Chief Waterboer. "Having witnessed the deleterious effects of the introduction of ardent spirits among his people, he, with characteristic energy, decreed that any Boer or Griqua [person of mixed African and European heritage] bringing brandy into the country should have his property in ardent spirits confiscated and poured out on the ground. The Griqua chiefs living farther east were unable to carry this law into effect as he did, hence the greater facility with which the Boers in that direction got the Griquas to part with their farms."[35]

The most comprehensive survey of native African attitudes toward the liquor trade was made by the Cape Parliament's Commission on the Liquor Traffic in 1884. Not surprisingly, tribal leaders were almost universally opposed to the debauching traffic. "I think the people ought not to be allowed to purchase brandy at all," claimed Tembu headman Mankai Renga. "*It is killing the people and destroying the whole country*" (emphasis in original).

"We do not wish to have canteens among us," claimed Make, heading a delegation of sixty Idutywa headmen. "A canteen ruins a man; brandy destroys our manhood. We are happy in this country because there are no canteens. . . . I say, do not let brandy come into the country."

One Transkeian chief agreed: "I am a brandy drinker myself, but I know that what has been said is right. *If brandy is introduced among us, we shall lose everything we have.*"

Such unanimity in testimonials by black tribal leaders led the Cape Colony's 1884 commission to conclude, "The use of spiritous liquors is an unmitigated evil; no other cause or influence is so completely destructive, not only of all progress and improvement [of native conditions], but even of the reasonable hope of any progress or improvement." Unfortunately, Sir Hercules Robinson—the governor of Cape Colony—was unmoved. Instead of strengthening native protections, in 1885 he rescinded them, opening new provinces and tribes to exploitation at the hands of white colonists. Native leaders continued to protest, to little avail.[36]

Likewise, in the British possessions directly bordering Khama's country, colonial administrators themselves admitted, "The greatest evil to contend against is the illicit brandy trade with natives." One magistrate in 1895 noted, "A considerable illicit sale of brandy to these Bastards [as the British colonists referred to the natives in these official documents] is carried on through the medium of low class Europeans"—of which there were many. The same reports show that the colonial magistrates' single largest source of government revenue came from the sale of liquor licenses.[37]

Historian Charles van Onselen concludes his "Randlords and Rotgut"—a landmark study of alcohol in colonial South Africa—with the following sentence: "*In all systems of capitalism—but perhaps especially in colonial regimes—alcohol has more to do with profits than with priests and is concerned with money rather than morality.*"[38] This is undeniable. Temperance and prohibitionism were everywhere a grassroots movement against predatory liquor traffic and the state that benefited from it. It is perhaps only more obviously so in colonial regimes as in British South Africa because the difference between the exploited and the exploiter was literally black and white.

"At the outskirts of civilisation things are not so complicated as at the centre," wrote J. D. Hepburn in his *Ten Years in Khama's Country* (1895), "and if that intricate piece of machinery called civilisation works everywhere else as it works here, then brandy selling means a heavy yearly loss to the merchants and manufacturers of the world."[39] It did.

Little wonder, then, that the greatest critics of the liquor traffic the world over also tended to be the most outspoken critics of imperialism: Leo Tolstoy and Vladimir Lenin against the tsarist empire (Chapter 2); Emile Vandervelde against Belgian imperialism in the Congo (Chapter 3); Tomáš Masaryk against the Austro-Hungarian Empire (Chapter 4); Daniel O'Connell (Chapter 5), Mahatma Gandhi (Chapter 7), and Kemal Atatürk (Chapter 8) all against the British; and William Jennings Bryan against American imperialism (Chapter 15). The dynamic of imperial subordination and capitalist exploitation to the liquor machine was everywhere the same.

What Some Men Would Do Here for Diamonds, What Some Men Would Do Here for Gold

Gold and diamonds are among the most-sought-after minerals on earth. Africa was blessed—or cursed—to have both in abundance. When gold was discovered in the Witwatersrand of the Transvaal in 1884 (producing the boomtown of Johannesburg), South Africa was already supplying 95 percent of the world's diamonds.

Following a tempestuous seventy-day sailing voyage from England, on September 1, 1870, a "tall, lanky, anæmic, fair-haired boy, shy and reserved in bearing" first entered the British colony of Natal on the southeastern tip of Africa.[40] It was an inauspicious beginning for a man destined to become one of the richest, most powerful men in the world. At only seventeen, his parents shipped the sickly, young Cecil Rhodes to join his brother Herbert on a cotton farm in Natal, hoping the drier climate would do him well.

The following year, the restless Rhodes boys left their plantation and joined the diamond rush. By 1873 the mining town of Kimberley was the second-largest town in southern Africa, with thirteen thousand whites and thirty thousand blacks mixing in a great tumult of construction, commerce, diamond digging, and diamond trading. Amid the temporary tents and huts were a smattering of saloons, brothels, rough hotels, and gambling dens. "Nothing is more common than to see the canteens adorned with a row of dead-drunk corpses at ten a.m.," complained John Merriman, future prime minister of the Cape Colony.[41] According to frontier physician Josiah Matthews, who set up a medical practice in Kimberley in 1872, at least two-thirds of his caseload came from "excessive indulgence in alcohol," usually the notorious Cape Smoke.[42]

The Rhodes brothers bought up a few small claims and got to picking and sifting for diamonds, using their profits to purchase neighboring plots. Together with his new business partner, Charles Durnell Rudd, Cecil acquired the old Boer farmstead of Johannes and Diederik de Beers, which soon began producing some of the world's most flawless diamonds. With financing from N. M. Rothschild & Sons, Ltd., in 1888 Rhodes and Rudd established De Beers Consolidated Mines, with Cecil as chairman and principal shareholder. The following year, De Beers struck a deal with the London-based Diamond Syndicate to purchase a fixed quantity of diamonds annually for a fixed price. This established De Beers as a near-monopoly supplier of the world's diamonds and catapulted Cecil Rhodes to unheard-of riches. In 1889 Rhodes also organized De Beers and the South African gold-mining interests into the British South Africa Company (BSAC, or the Chartered Company), with himself at the helm. With a Royal Charter patterned after the British East India Company (Chapter 7), Rhodes was intent on using De Beers's economic strength for "winning the north."[43] Indeed, just as the East India Company had subdued China with opium backed by tall ships and cannons, the South Africa Company would do the same with liquor bottles and bullets.

As prime minister of the Cape Colony (since 1890), Rhodes had the political levers of British colonialism; as chairman of De Beers, he wielded fantastic economic might; and as head of the Chartered Company—a state/company hybrid with its own army—Rhodes was able to carve out his own personal fiefdom in ruthless pursuit of ever more profit. Cecil Rhodes is often portrayed as the imperialist's imperialist: the embodiment of the European colonial spirit of white supremacy. He tells us as much himself, in his "Confession of Faith." Penned in 1877, before becoming the world's foremost diamond monopolist, Rhodes mused on how he could be most useful to Britain:

> I contend that we are the finest race in the world and that the more of the world we inhabit the better it is for the human race. Just fancy those parts that are at present inhabited by the most despicable specimens of human beings what an alteration there would be if they were brought under Anglo-Saxon influence. . . . Africa is still lying ready for us it is our duty to take it. It is our duty to seize every opportunity of acquiring more territory and we should keep this one idea steadily before our eyes that more territory simply means more of the Anglo-Saxon race more of the best, the most human, most honorable race the world possesses.[44]

His deeds matched his words. His policies in South Africa paved the way for modern-day apartheid—disenfranchising black Africans who'd previously met the property qualifications to vote, and kicking natives off of their traditional land to "stimulate them to labour." Rhodes claimed, "It must be brought home to them that in future nine-tenths of them will have to spend their lives in manual labour, and the sooner that is brought home to them the better."[45]

More brutal still were his northward imperial ambitions. Armed with the Royal Charter that gave Rhodes's British South Africa Company the right to administer the territory from the Limpopo north to the Zambezi River, he swindled the natives of Matabeleland (present-day southern Zimbabwe) into granting concessions to Rhodes. Agreements for mining gold and diamonds often included provisions for also conducting banking operations, building railways, governing land, and raising an army, while also charging Her Majesty's government for outsourcing such state-building enterprises to him.[46] Any remaining opposition by the native Matabele and their last king, Lobengula, was smashed in the First Matabele War (1893–1894), which brought the territory—Rhodesia—under company control. In the war, just 750 "police" of the Chartered Company, armed with early Maxim machine guns— along with 1,700 allied Tswana led by Khama—decimated over 10,000 Matabele spearmen.

On paper, Article 12 of the BSAC Charter expressly prohibited the sale of liquor to natives on territory controlled by the company.[47] In reality, since it wasn't a binding "law" in any sense, white colonists ignored it with impunity in their efforts to maximize their profits. Captain Charles Norris-Newman described the first or-ders of business following the Chartered Company's new conquest: "Licenses, both wholesale and retail, for trading and sale of liquors, were quickly granted and taken out, many stores and shops erected, and, in fact, the groundwork of future govern-ment was laid upon similar lines as those which had been adopted and proved so successful in Mashuanaland"—northern Zimbabwe, which the company had al-ready subdued.[48] Indeed, according to the company's shareholder reports, one of the first ordinances for this newly conquered territory farmed out taxation of the liquor trade. Within months, the Company had already licensed twenty-four liquor dealers.[49] The selling of the Rhodesian natives into alco-slavery continued apace.

With Rhodesia subdued and South Africa well in hand, Rhodes covetously eyed Bechuanaland in between. It was vital to his grandiose imperial ambitions to link Cape Town to Cairo by rail. Though British papers and the Colonial Office lauded Khama as a "loyal ally" for leading seventeen hundred troops in support of the company's colonization of Rhodesia, Rhodes busily "inquired how may men it would take to dispose of Khama and dispossess him of his country."[50]

Khama the King

Khama III, son of the Bamangwato rainmaker and "sorcerer chief" Sekgoma, was born about 1837. Along with five of his brothers, in 1862 Khama was among the first Tswana to be baptized into Lutheranism by members of David Livingstone's London Missionary Society.[51] His Christian faith brought him into ever-greater conflict with his polygamist father and tribal traditions. Still, Khama was well liked and respected both among Europeans and the loose confederation of Tswana tribes. Well educated, he spoke fluent Dutch—the language of European commerce at the time—and proved himself a brave warrior and leader in battle.[52]

Following those trailblazing explorers and missionaries were wave after wave of European hunters and traders. "At first we saw the white people pass, and we said, 'They are going to hunt for elephant-tusks and ostrich-feathers, and they will return where they came from,'" as Sebele later remarked to his London audience. "But now when we see the white men we say 'Jah! Jah!' ('Oh dear! Oh dear!'). And now we think of the white people like rain, for they come down as a flood, and we can do nothing to stop the flood."[53]

White hunters usually spent more time trading with native tribesmen for ivory rather than actually hunting elephants themselves. Instead of paying whatever competitive price the ivory markets of Natal or Cape Town would support, they'd bring wagon-loads of Cape Smoke to barter, since a drunken trading partner was that much easier to swindle.[54]

The allure of the colonial frontier drew all manner of criminals, frondeurs, reprobates, drunks, and malcontents, all emboldened by their presumed racial superiority. These Europeans were heavy drinkers: in Bulawayo, colonial doctors estimated that nine out of every ten European deaths were due directly or indirectly to drink. From the Cape northward, liquor would similarly decimate the native population.[55] The "perfect hell" of Shoshong—the chief settlement and trading post of the Bamangwato—was "essentially the place for a young man to go to, if he wished to be ruined in both body and soul. This was the trader's own talk, not the missionary's; and there was no exaggeration in that statement."[56] When the sun set, wolves, baboons, or hyenas sometimes snuck into town and made off with some goat or child, but more often the townspeople were threatened by the drunkenness and lawlessness of man. Pleas for action to the chieftain Macheng were pointless; he'd already become a slave to liquor and would die of alcohol poisoning shortly after being deposed by Khama in 1872. Missionary J. D. Hepburn, who lived in Shoshong, reflected in his memoirs,

> Brandy sellers will have many a death to account for among the chiefs and native headmen when the day of reckoning comes. "Civilise them off the face of the earth" is the sentiment expressed by some men, who call themselves Christians, and pride themselves on belonging to the good old Church of England. And brandy is their civilizing agent. Neither the good old Church nor the good old country has much to thank such for. War, waste of her wealth, and the blood-shedding of her brave, that is the debt she has paid to them already.
>
> And it is enough to make the heart of any man sad to recall how many an Interior white trader has also been civilised off the face of the earth by

it. Yes, it is indeed true, that many an Interior trader has paid the price of
his life to the propagation of this gospel. They were not all drunkards when
they became traders either. . . .

   Then it often happens that the brandy seller is brandy proof, and he sells
for the profit he gets, and holds himself blameless for the consequences.
Whether his profit is gain the future will reveal.[57]

None of this was secret; debauching and exploitation were part of the daily routine on the Kalahari plains, and when Khama deposed Macheng to become king in
1872, he vowed to stop it. The new Christian king instituted modernizing reforms
that often put him at odds with his people: he made peace with the Bushmen
and outlawed bride-buying, circumcision, traditional rainmaking rituals, and the
brewing of kafir beer. "I know of no other Interior chief who has even *attempted*
the half that Khama has *accomplished*," Hepburn wrote.[58] But more than anything,
he was opposed to the white man's liquor—a sterling conviction dating to a childhood encounter with a Boer trader who swindled his father by getting him drunk
on brandy.[59]

In 1873, three months after assuming the throne, he summoned together
twenty-one European traders and declared his intention to prohibit strong liquor.
"Ever since I saw the first white man," he declared, "we have been accustomed to see
them pull out a bottle and give one another something to drink. For a long time,
we thought it was a medicine, and it did not concern us for it was not given to black
men. I do not want to interfere with your personal habits, so long as they do not
become a nuisance to the town. If, when you give one another a drink, you turn
around and give it to my people also, I shall regard you as blameworthy."[60]

The white traders dickered as white traders do, and Khama conceded to allow
cases of brandy—allegedly for medicinal purposes—while forswearing the usual
larger casks. Yet the drunken revelry continued unabated. The king again called the
hungover traders together, browbeat them for breaking promises, and forbade even
cases of liquor, under threat of banishment.

A local white innkeeper—who'd done brisk business selling booze—then began
smuggling casks of liquor into Khama's dry territory, hidden among wagonloads of
grain. Shortly thereafter, a Zambezi-bound trader left Shoshong but didn't get far
before his driver fell drunk under the wagon wheel and was killed on the spot. "The
trader himself got away into the veldt," Hepburn recounted. "He began to rave, and
shot his oxen as they trekked in the yoke. He shot some of his people, and at last the
report came that he was killed by the Bushmen among who he had run wild—*mad
with bad brandy*."[61] The innkeeper who sold the liquor was banished that day.

Another European trader got drunk and barricaded himself in his home "naked,
and raving, and drinking as long as he had any drink left," Hepburn recalled. "Not one
of the Europeans dared go near. They feared he might blow his place up as another
had done."[62] Khama again warned the traders: *no liquor*. The following weekend,

Khama himself roused the feverish, disbelieving missionary J. D. Hepburn to come witness for himself the drunken destruction of his fellow countrymen—"their white shirts stained with blood. Their goods were strewn about the floor, a huge cask of water upset, and everything floating."[63]

Khama had had enough.

Hepburn described the scene, the following cold, dreary Monday morning, as Khama expelled the Europeans and their drink. He spoke plainly and sternly, like a friend betrayed, recounting the multitude of warnings, and yet they despised his laws because he was a black African.

"Well, I am black, but if I am black I am chief of my own country at present," Khama declared. "When you white men rule in the country then you will do as you like. At present *I* rule, and I shall maintain my laws which you insult and despise." He continued,

> You have insulted and despised me in my own town *because I am a black man*. You do so because you despise black men in your hearts. If you despise us, what do you want here in the country that God has given to us? Go back to your own country.

For each of the thunderstruck traders, banishment meant economic ruin. Still, Khama called out each by name, and listed their drunken transgressions.

> Take everything you have; strip the iron roofs off the houses. The wood of the country and the clay of which you made the bricks, you can leave to be thrown down. Take all that is yours, and go. More than that, if there is any other white man here who does not like my laws let him go too! . . . You know that some of my own brothers have learned to like the drink, and you know that I do not want them to see it even, that they may forget the habit; and yet you not only bring it in and offer it to them, but you try to tempt *me* with it. I make an end of it to-day. Go! Take your cattle, and leave my town, and never come back again![64]

From that point onward, Khama's sovereignty was his prohibition, and vice versa. After banishing the white man's liquor, he then forbade his people from brewing their traditional kafir beer, explaining, "You take the corn that God has given us in answer to prayer and destroy it. You not only destroy it, but you make stuff with it that causes mischief among you."[65]

Certainly, booze occasionally crept into Bechuanaland, but Khama was ever vigilant. In 1880, the young chief Moremi of the "Great Thirst Land" north of the Kalahari visited Shoshong and persuaded his men to brew some kafir. Khama dumped it on the ground, saying, "When I visit your town, I will respect your laws, Moremi." Undeterred, they brewed more. Khama returned, this time with a burning spear, which he thrust into the dry thatch of Moremi's hut, turning it to a smoldering heap. Moremi returned home to Ngami, where he later died of alcohol-related illness.[66]

For years, then, Khama's trusted agents kept watchful eyes over their kraals (hut villages), bringing before him anyone caught trading in liquor or brewing beer. "Leave my country!" was the usual reply, as their huts went up in smoke.[67]

Showdown for the Future of Bechuanaland

When Sir Charles Warren's British military expedition marched north from the Cape in 1885 establishing the Bechuanaland Protectorate, Khama consented to British rule, but not to their liquor. He wrote the deputy commissioner, "It is not the same thing to offer my country to Her Majesty to be occupied by English settlers, Her Majesty's subjects governed by Her Majesty's Ministers, and to allow men so worthless and unscrupulous in their characters as [liquor sellers] Messrs. Wood, Chapman and Francis to come outside of all Governments and occupy my country and put up their drink canteens and flood my country with their drink after all the long struggle I have made against it." He concluded more bluntly: "It were better for me that I should lose my country than that it should be flooded with drink."[68] He specifically called out William Curl Francis—the liquor trafficker he'd banished a decade before, who continued to defy Khama: "I pray Your Honour never to ask me even to open a little door to the drink; and Francis desires that, and has always desired it. That has been my constant battle with his firm."[69]

From that point, the Colonial Office largely assented to Khama's prohibition of the liquor traffic, which stood in stark contrast to the exploitative practices of both the Boers and Rhodes's Chartered Company. As John Smith Moffat, resident commissioner in northern Bechuanaland, wrote in 1892, "I find in the Protectorate that it is a regular grapple with the drink-selling interest. He has kept drink out of his country hitherto, and it will be a shame if, now that we in a measure take his affairs into our hands, we allow it to come in. I have refused all applications for licenses, and have made the grog-sellers my enemies in consequence."[70]

Yet despite British plaudits as a Christian king and a reliable ally in providing passage and troops to subdue Rhodesia, Cecil Rhodes—still envisioning a Cape Town–to–Cairo railway—continued to scheme how to depose Khama and take his land. In 1892 Rhodes proposed outsourcing the administration of the Bechuanaland Protectorate to his British South Africa Company, in return for a hefty subsidy. Khama raised the alarm, and London refused. In 1894 Rhodes tried to annex Khama's country through administrative trickery: filing paperwork to place Bechuanaland under the "Zambesian" rather than South African customs union, and then claiming the right of the BSAC to administer that. That ploy, too, was rebuffed. As colonial high commissioner Sir Henry Loch telegraphed London,

"Chief Khama has ever been a faithful friend and ally of Her Majesty's Government, and to hand over that Chief, his people and his territory, to be administered by a commercial company, dependent for their prosperity upon what they may get out of the country, would be a breach of faith such as I am sure the Government would not for a moment entertain."[71] In response, Rhodes undertook a smear campaign against Khama and the "ant's nest of negrophilists," as he called them, who supported him in London.[72]

It was against these persistent pressures that Khama gathered his fellow chiefs, Bathoen and Sebele, to voyage to London in 1895 to petition Queen Victoria and her government to keep Bechuanaland out of Rhodes's grasp. "The two points on which the natives seem to be apprehensive," forewarned the imperial secretary in Cape Town, "are the questions of land and liquor."[73]

But before departing, the three chiefs met with Rhodes in person at his massive Cape Town estate. Khama had met Rhodes before, and—wisely—insisted on their always being white witnesses to any meeting with Chartered Company representatives, so little did he trust them. Bluffing, Rhodes impressed upon the chiefs that the queen had already given the protectorate to him, and it was just a matter of timing to make it official. However, he'd make three promises to them: he did not want Khama's land, the chiefs would keep their judicial power in cases not involving white men, and he would respect prohibition: claiming to believe in "no liquor and no vote for the natives."[74] Of course, all of this was a lie, especially regarding prohibition, as white liquor dealers were already salivating at the thought of flooding dry Bechuanaland with booze.[75] Khama, Sebele, and Bathoen would not be provoked. Sitting stone-faced before the great colonizer, they said nothing, only hardening their resolve to take their case before the queen and her government.

In London, the Tswana chiefs had hoped to find a sympathetic ear in the new colonial secretary, Joseph Chamberlain. The wet Conservatives and Unionists had trounced the dry Liberals at the polls—largely about the liquor question—that very summer of 1895 (see Chapter 5), and the Bechuanaland question would be the new government's first political test.

Once a radical, anti-imperialist "little Englander," Chamberlain had come to believe that "the British race is the greatest of the governing races that the world has ever seen."[76] Yet while Rhodes's imperialism was exploitative, Chamberlain's was somewhat more benevolent, claiming, "It is the duty of a landlord to develop his estate."[77] And if the liquor traffic was hampering the advancement of the empire's wards while throwing a wrench in the machinery of global capitalism, then it had to be opposed. "Apart from the moral mischief, gin is the curse of trade," Chamberlain declared. "Cape smoke eats the life out of honest business. Trade rum paralyses all other trade. Therefore, if only that our working men may get employment at home, let us cease from poisoning our dark-skinned brethren abroad."[78]

While Chamberlain was away on holiday for the silly season, from September through November, Kings Khama, Bathoen, and Sebele embarked on a goodwill tour of Britain, from the southern seaside to the Scottish highlands. Beneath their unending gratitude for British hospitality, their starstruck impressions of British opulence, and kindhearted smiles that won them ever more admirers, the kings consistently pressed their case to preserve their sovereignty against both Rhodes's company and against the liquor traffic.[79]

It is important to recognize how this completely flips the script on traditional colonial history—written from the eye of the colonizer—in which subaltern populations are merely helpless objects of white imperial power. Rather than London imposing its will on Africa, Africa was taking the fight to London, fully cognizant of the power asymmetry. Khama and the kings long knew they stood little chance to oppose the British militarily. But they could press their peoples' interests through moral persuasion and soft-power diplomacy. What followed was a genius end-run around the traditional institutions of British imperial power: speaking directly to the people, with whom British sovereignty ultimately lay, at least according to Britain's own storied political traditions and philosophies. Such was necessary in confronting the inherent contradictions of an empire that professed liberty at home while pursuing subjugation abroad.[80]

In their first full-length interview in England, Khama laid out the two things he feared most: "Drink and the Devil. You send us your Bible, and you send us fire-water as well."

At this point, Bathoen chimed in: "I am an abstainer from drink, just like Khama. I have prohibited it in my land, and with my own hand destroyed five waterpots which I found had been filled with beer. . . . England is a country where all are Christians, and so you send your bad men away and they come to us. They drink and they go out shooting on Sundays, and when we see their evil ways we remind them that they would not dare to do that in England."[81]

An interview with the *Christian World* soon followed. Khama blamed alcohol for "the destruction of my people; they lose their good standing, and their food and speech because of it."

Chief Bathoen reiterated, "All kinds of evil come out of the beer-pot."

"I can say more about the habit of liquor than my younger brothers," interjected Sebele. "I know it in my own personal experience as the great destroyer. If a man should drink the fire-water of the traders, although he be a king, although he be a Christian, he will grow drowsy. Although he be a judge, he will no longer know how to speak amongst the people."

"Then you had no strong drink before the Europeans came?" inquired the *World*.

"Yes, we had it, there was no good in it; but the English [liquor] is worse, it is so strong, it is like fire," explained Sebele. "In the olden days we did not give liquor to the young men; now all have it. The white man's brandy is stronger than our *khadi* (honey beer). . . . I would that the English would help to keep it out instead of sending it into our lands."[82]

Throughout their tour, the kings pressed for an audience with the one person who could ultimately resolve their plight: Queen Victoria herself.

"We wish to see the Queen," declared Khama, explaining that his people "think the Queen is like God, and the Prince of Wales like Jesus Christ. If we return and say we have not seen her, they will say, 'See, it is as we said, all lies.' We believe it would be of great use, from a diplomatic point of view, for us to have audience of Her Majesty."[83]

Khama expounded further to a packed congregation in Leicester. "I heard while I was in my country in Bechuanaland that the Imperial Government was going to hand us over to the Chartered Company. You do not know the ways of the Chartered Company, because you are very far away and we are very near to them. We think that the Chartered Company will take our lands."

"Hear, hear!" replied the Leicester crowd.

"Besides, we are afraid they are not very careful about the liquor in the country, and this makes us very pained," said Khama. "This is why we come here in England, to let the people know what it is we ask. We say why should the home Government hand us over to the other people without asking us?"[84]

"Hear, hear!" the congregation again assented.

"We don't like to be governed by men whose one object is to take out metals from the earth," Bathoen interjected, "and whose business in life it is to hunt for precious stones, for they might take it into their heads to dig us in the same manner."[85]

The crowd laughed, however uneasily. Yet in Leicester as throughout their tour, ever more Britons championed the cause of the kings' sovereignty against colonization.

Following their visit, the *Newcastle Leader* wrote that the proposed rule of the BSAC over Bechuanaland would be a "cramping monopoly, supported by the harshest tyranny. . . . And as the chief interest of the white man is to make as much money as he can in the shortest possible time, it often happens that the 'nigger' experiences treatment which is sadly at variance with the high principles which the teachers sent out by the white men seek to inculcate."[86]

The *Review of Reviews* reprinted Khama's plea that "you, O British people, will not paralyse my efforts by compelling me to submit to the invasion of my country by the trader with his poisonous liquors." If Britain were to ignore Khama's calls for help, the papers editorialized, then the British people "should stand condemned as the most God-forsaken set of canting hypocrites on the whole round earth."

Even hardened, patriotic imperialists began to sympathize with the kings' plight: "It is all very well to say that if Khama's authority to enforce prohibition is taken away, the British Chartered Company—which at present is Mr. Rhodes—will promise not to allow the sale of drink in Khama's country. Mr. Rhodes, no doubt, will do his best to keep his promise; but Mr. Rhodes is naturally less keenly alive to the mischief of strong drink than the chief whose tribe perish like rotten sheep before the white man's fire-water."[87]

Following a visit by the chiefs, the people of Halifax, West Yorkshire, sent to Chamberlain in the Colonial Office in London a petition that would serve as a template for similar municipal entreaties from across England, opposing placing Bechuanaland under control of the BSAC contrary to the wishes of its inhabitants. "That the principle of handing over the administration of a remote territory to a company whose object is necessarily the acquisition of gain is open to strong objection . . . since it cannot be assumed that the motives of such a body or the spirit in which the affairs of the territory would be administered by it would always be beneficent."[88]

On November 4, 1895, the three chiefs received their most luxurious reception to date, hosted by Hugh Grosvenor, the first Duke of Westminster, at his splendorous Grosvenor House. Khama, Sebele, and Bathoen seemed little impressed by the original masterworks of Titian, Raphael, and Reubens on the walls. Still, beneath the gaze of Gainsborough's famed *Blue Boy* gathered a veritable who's who of British high society. The bishop of London himself rose to officially implore that "Her Majesty's Government will adhere to their decision not to allow the law of prohibition now in force in Khama's territory to be in any way altered," given that the degradation and demoralization were products of British commerce and colonialism.

"British commerce ought to be a blessing wherever it penetrated," the bishop explained, to grunts of "Hear, hear!" "But instead of this, all over the world where it came into contact with the native races it was inflicting on them the most dreadful curse that could be inflicted by human agency," which was to say: "this abominable trade in spiritous liquor among races quite unaccustomed to its use and unable to resist its temptation."[89]

The hospitable Duke of Westminster followed. With his noble rank and immense influence as the wealthiest Englishman of the Victorian Age, the Duke had been a Member of Parliament since the age of twenty-two, but he was more concerned with developing his estates and patronizing philanthropy than high politics. Among the humanitarian, agricultural, and sanitary organizations of which he was figurehead, Grosvenor presided over the United Committee for the Protection of the Native Races from the Liquor Traffic, on whose behalf he presented the chiefs with a framed copy of his address. Despite their political differences, he announced that the committee was "of one mind as to the prohibition of the liquor traffic" in Bechuanaland. "We take this opportunity," the Duke said to Khama, "of assuring you that we will use every opportunity of supporting your noble endeavors."

Khama reveled in the support. Not only had the chiefs won over British public opinion on their nationwide tour, now their cause was backed by the aristocracy. Such support was crucial, as Khama noted in his speech, because "To-day that power is more in the hands of white people, and they are working to bring liquor into the country, so that if I am not helped I shall be overcome by those who have power."[90] Khama well understood political power in the African context, and by appealing to both the masses and elites, he apparently understood political power in the British context as well.

As for the actual government, before embarking on his scheduled vacation, Secretary Chamberlain had met briefly with the kings on September 11. He requested that they spell out their position in writing, so that deliberations and policy decisions could be made upon his return. Their resulting plea cut straight to the point: "We fear the Company because we think they will take our land and sell it to others. We fear that they will fill our country with liquor shops, as they have Bulawayo and some parts of Mashonaland and Matabeleland. We see that they are not content with the concessions that we have given them, and that they want us also; we do not know what they wish to do with us." Even if BSAC rule was indeed inevitable, they offered a compromise—they'd willingly pay additional poll taxes, if only to delay annexation by ten years. And at whatever time Her Majesty should decide that they should be given to the company, "We pray that you will put strong words in the agreement to help us and protect us. Do not let them take away the land, which is the life of your children. Do not let them bring liquor into our country to kill our people speedily."[91]

When the Colonial Office suggested that the kings try to resolve their differences with Rhodes directly, they responded passionately, "The Company wants to impoverish us so that hunger may drive us to become the white man's servants who dig in his mines and gather his wealth. We do not wish to talk again with the Company; we wish to talk with you."[92]

As the British-based Aborigines Protection Society noted, "The ignorant Bechuana understood the situation better than Mr. Chamberlain."[93]

The chiefs' months-long tour culminated on November 6, 1895, in the Colonial Office (see Figure 6.3). Rather than a give-and-take negotiation, it was instead a dictation of terms by Secretary Chamberlain, albeit terms that were quite beneficial to Khama, Sebele, and Bathoen. The chiefs would pay an additional hut tax, allow a British officer in residence, and sacrifice a small strip of land for the construction of Rhodes's railway—all concessions they were prepared to give—in exchange for expanded territorial control elsewhere in the Kalahari. Most importantly, Bechuanaland would remain a protectorate under the authority of the queen, rather than Rhodes and the company.

"White man's strong drink shall not be brought for sale into the country now assigned to the Chiefs, and those who attempt to deal in it or give it away to black men will be punished. No new liquor license shall be issued, and no existing liquor license shall be renewed," declared Chamberlain. Adding—in words that would be echoed and hailed as the *Magna Carta* of Botswana—"Each of the chiefs, Khama, Sebele and Bathoen, shall have a country within which they shall live, as hitherto, under the protection of the Queen." Chamberlain continued, "The Chiefs will rule their own people much as at present," maintaining their sovereignty, rather than ceding it to Rhodes's Chartered Company.[94]

"BUNG" IN AFRICA.

Right Hon. J. Ch-mb-rl-n (to King Khama). "'LOCAL VETO' FOR BECHUANALAND? H'M!—A RATHER
TICKLISH BUSINESS! UPSET A GOVERNMENT HERE THE OTHER DAY!"

[*Khama, the Bechuana chief, arrived in England and was received by Mr. Chamberlain at the Colonial Office; . . . He desires to be assured
in the power of excluding intoxicants absolutely from his territories."—The Times.]

Figure 6.3 "'Bung' in Africa." Khama and Chamberlain as they appeared in the British satirical magazine *Punch* on September 21, 1895. "Bung" was a slang term for British brewers and the antitemperance liquor trade, which had helped topple the Liberal government in the election of 1895. Hence: "Right Hon. J. Ch-mb-rl-n (*to* King Khama). '*Local Veto* for Bechuanaland? H'm!—A rather ticklish business! Upset a government *here* the other day!'".

The three kings left the meeting understandably pleased.

A few short weeks later, it was Secretary Chamberlain who accompanied the three Tswana kings into the vaulted Green Drawing Room of Windsor Castle for their personal audience with Queen Victoria herself. "I am pleased that the chiefs have had this opportunity of coming to see me here," declared the Great White Queen. Pausing only for the translators, she continued, with the authority of her throne, "I confirm the settlement of their case which my Minister has made. I approve of the decision of my Ministers that the sale of strong drink shall be prohibited in your country and that those who attempt to deal in it or supply it to the natives shall be severely punished. . . . I feel strongly in this matter, and I am glad to see that the chiefs have determined to keep so great a curse from the people."[95]

Following the ceremonial exchange of gifts and pleasantries, the three kings returned to London, tremendously satisfied. When newsmen asked of their impressions, Sebele lauded, "Her Majesty is a very charming old lady. . . . But I had no idea that she was so short and stout." Some newspapers redacted the gaffe. "But I have seen her now, and shall go back home contented."[96]

Three days later, the chiefs boarded the steamship *Arundel Castle* for the voyage back to Africa. "We did not rejoice at the idea of having to live under the rule of the Company," Khama summarized. "We now rejoice because the British Government has separated us from that Company."[97]

One man who was not rejoicing was Cecil Rhodes. Even as the kings toured England, Rhodes was already brooding: "Is it not awful to think that the whole future of the British Empire out here may turn on a wretched Kaffer and a Secretary of State who listens to some fanatic in the House of Commons?"[98] Once it became clear that he would not be getting anything beyond a strip of land for his railroad, Rhodes fired off one angry telegram after another, like Donald Trump tweets. "I do object to being beaten by three canting natives especially on the score of temperance," one message fumed, suggesting the true scope of his ambitions. A telegraph in the Colonial Office back in London hammered out Rhodes's all-caps message: "IT IS HUMILIATING TO BE UTTERLY BEATEN BY THESE NIGGERS."[99]

Crafting a Nation

The silly-season visit of three African chiefs may have been an inconsequential footnote to history—perhaps were it not for what came next. Given Rhodes's conniving determination, it was assumed that Khama had achieved at best a temporary stay of execution for Bechuanaland. Indeed, once they disembarked from the ship in December 1895, the chiefs were told of a menacing military force of the BSAC under the leadership of Sir Leander Starr Jameson. When Khama caught up to him in the recently ceded railway strip, Jameson tried to reassure him of the company's benevolent intentions. The chiefs' mission to London, Jameson claimed, "hurt me very much, for the directors of the Chartered Company had on several occasions assured you that the interests of your country would be safe-guarded. You had no reason to distrust the Company and you had no right to go to England in the way you did."

"Dr. Jameson, you have got a smooth tongue," replied Khama, smiling. "But if, as you say, I should have relied on your friendship and peaceful intentions, can you tell me why these big guns are here? . . . My old friend, your ambition is to kill!"[100] With faith in the protection of Queen Victoria and her government, he left Jameson's expedition with the warning that it "will bring you nothing but shame and disgrace."[101]

He was right.

Jameson's actual military aim was to foment an insurrection across the border in the Dutch Transvaal. By secretly invading and whipping up British sympathizers to their cause, the uprising would serve as a pretext for an all-out British invasion to topple the rival Boers. The resulting Jameson Raid turned out to be a spectacular failure and marked the beginning of the end for Cecil Rhodes and the Chartered Company.

In a crowning irony, Jameson's attack was ultimately doomed by liquor. To take the Boers by surprise, the invaders planned to cut the telegraph lines so that the Dutch border outposts could not raise the alarm of invasion. However, while they succeeded in snipping the cables to Cape Town, a heavily drunken soldier failed to cut the telegraph line to Pretoria—cutting a Boer farmer's wire fence instead—so the Dutch were able to track and anticipate the entire invasion.[102] After being ambushed and decimated by Boer artillery, Jameson surrendered, was put on trial, and was imprisoned along with British coconspirators within Transvaal, including Cecil Rhodes's brother Frank.

Such reckless adventurism by the Chartered Company was denounced by the British government, which rolled back most of the company's concessions in Bechuanaland. After admitting that he authorized the raid, Rhodes stepped down from the BSAC in disgrace, thereby largely ending the threat to the chiefs' sovereignty over Bechuanaland and their prohibition there, despite repeated efforts by the white liquor interests "to repeal or break down all restrictions regarding the sale of intoxicating liquors, so that the wine and brandy farmers might have freer access to the native and coloured population."[103]

Figure 6.4 Botswana, 100-pula note: Detail.

Cecil Rhodes died in 1902; Kings Sebele and Bathoen both in 1910. The reign of King Khama lasted fifty years, until his death in 1923—allowing only fleeting exceptions to his prohibition of the liquor traffic during that time.[104] The enormous reservoir of public sympathy for the Tswana kings endured long after their 1895 tour of England. Subsequent British ministers readily understood that any attempt to undermine Khama's sovereignty or his prohibition would be met with tremendous and vocal opposition, not only from far-off Bechuanaland, but British voters in their home districts too.[105] When the Bechuanaland Protectorate gained its independence in 1966, the Republic of Botswana became an island of black African sovereignty between apartheid South Africa and white Rhodesia.

Today, Botswana is Africa's longest-running continuous multiparty democracy, largely free of corruption, with an excellent human-rights record.[106] Khama, Sebele, and Bathoen are lionized as the nation's founding fathers, with massive monuments in the capital Gaborone, and the portrait of the three kings' mission to London is even etched onto the Botswanan 100-Pula note. Were it not for their determination to keep the Great Thirstland dry, what we now know as Botswana would likely have become swallowed up as part of South Africa or Rhodesia, likely to the great detriment of the Tswana people living there.

|| 7 ||

Gandhi, Indian Nationalism, and Temperance Resistance against the Raj

Bombay (Mumbai), British India: Saturday, August 8, 1942

It truly was the darkest hour.

By 1942 most of Europe lay crushed under the Nazi jackboot, as British prime minister Winston Churchill so vividly described. The Americans were reeling from a surprise attack at Pearl Harbor. Not satisfied with controlling the Pacific and Southeast Asia, the Japanese set their sights on British India, too.

India was an alluring target for Japan: the British were already bogged down there, trying to suppress a nationalist protest movement based on noncooperation and nonviolence. If the Japanese war machine had so easily steamrolled active military resistance across East Asia, how much easier would passive resisters be?

Against this backdrop, on August 8, 1942, Mahatma Gandhi rose to address the All-India Congress Committee (AICC) at Bombay: the executive leadership of the Indian National Congress, which was spearheading India's independence movement. The seventy-three-year-old Gandhi had spent at least the last fifty years of his life struggling against unjust British colonial rule, earning him the enmity of imperialist "defenders of the realm," especially Churchill himself.

Doubts were already rising among nationalists over Gandhi's Quit India campaign, urging the British to simply walk away from the crown jewel in their empire. Indeed, with the Japanese threat looming on the horizon, many clamored for protection in allegiance with Churchill and the loathed British.

"Shall I ask the Japanese to tarry a while?" Gandhi asked rhetorically from the podium. The Japanese threat only added greater urgency to the push for independence, not dependence, the diminutive Gandhi claimed.

His speech concluded with his staunchest denunciation of British oppression yet. "Every one of you should, from this moment onwards, consider yourself a free man or woman, and act as if you are free and are no longer under the heel of this imperialism," Gandhi declared. "Here is a mantra, a short one, that I give you. You may imprint it on your hearts and let every breath of yours give expression to it. The mantra is: '*Do or Die.*' We shall either free India or die in the attempt."[1]

That night, the elderly Gandhi and the AICC leaders were all roused from their sleep and arrested, on the orders of Churchill himself, in hopes of crushing the Indian independence movement. When Kasturba—Gandhi's wife of sixty years—attempted to speak the following day, the British arrested her, too.

It was the thirteenth (and final) time that the British authorities arrested and imprisoned Gandhi. By then, the British had learned that punishing Gandhi with hard labor would backfire, producing nationwide street demonstrations that would have to be repressed themselves. What they needed was to mute his calls for independence, so London sought "no greater degree of detention than is necessary for that purpose." So they interned the Gandhis not in a standard colonial jail, but in the spacious Aga Khan Palace in Poona.[2]

Behind bars, the congress's leadership could not rally nationalist resistance or issue calls for peace and nonviolence. As news of Gandhi's arrest spread, millions of Hindus and Muslims across the subcontinent protested, chanting, "Do or die." British outposts and institutions were attacked. Train depots, police headquarters, telegraph and post offices, and most notably liquor stores were all set ablaze. The British responded with beatings and bullets; in some places, rebels were machine-gunned from the air. Thousands died; a hundred thousand nationalists were imprisoned, many subjected to public flogging and humiliation.[3] Gandhi spent the next two years cut off from his people.

It was a dark time not just outside the palace prison, but also within.

The old man's only remaining instrument of protest now would be yet another painful and draining hunger strike. Adding to his personal darkness was the sudden death of his much-adored secretary. Most devastating of all, though, was his beloved Kasturba's deteriorating health. Her heart, lungs, and kidneys were shutting down. Gandhi was at her bedside, night and day. Her only consolation was the visit of her children, including the Gandhis' long-estranged eldest son, Harilal.

Headstrong as his father, Harilal had rebelled against Gandhi's ascetic lifestyle and values. He severed ties with the family long ago, falling into alcoholism and lustful debauchery. Once—back in 1935—Harilal got clean, and Gandhi welcomed his prodigal son back home for a new beginning.[4] It didn't last. At this time, Gandhi learned that Harilal had even sexually molested his own daughter while drunk. "I wish that you better die than resort to alcohol in any manner. May God save you from lack of peace," he wrote Harilal with finality.[5] Turning to his extended family, Gandhi lamented, "Harilal is sanctifying his anatomy in the holy Ganges of liquor." To his nephew, Gandhi declared, "Forget Harilal completely now. I have almost forgotten him."[6]

But now in 1942, with his mother on death's door, Harilal had returned once more, bringing her great solace. With warm hearts, Mohandas and Kasturba watched as their three sons dined together for the first time in decades. But that too was fleeting. The next—and final—time Harilal came to visit his dying mother, he was stumbling down drunk. Kasturba wept and beat her own head in anguish. Days later, she passed away, her head cradled on Gandhi's lap.[7]

Even amid so much turmoil, pain, uncertainty, and loss, Gandhi spent his long, solitary hours of incarceration at Poona writing his *Key to Health*—a guide to happiness, longevity, and well-being. "My faith is brightest in the midst of impenetrable darkness," he once said.[8]

Among the greatest dangers to avoid, according to *Key to Health*, are intoxicants: alcohol and opium. While alcohol excites and opium numbs, they both enslave the addict for the benefit of the seller:

> Several years ago, what is known as the Opium War took place between China and Great Britain. China did not wish to buy opium from India. But the English wanted to impose it on China. India was also to blame, in that several Indians had taken opium contracts in India. The trade paid well and the treasury received crores of rupees as opium revenue. This was obviously an immoral trade and yet it went on flourishing. Finally, as a result of a mighty agitation in England, it was stopped. A thing of this type, which simply ruins people, should not be tolerated for a single minute.[9]

Yet with his experiences—both political and personal—it should come as little surprise that alcohol caught Gandhi's ire. "Alcohol makes a man forget himself and while its effects last, he becomes utterly incapable of doing anything useful. Those who take a drinking [*sic*], ruin themselves and ruin their people. They lose all sense of decency and propriety." Certainly the shadow of his alcoholic son Harilal loomed large here. Still, Gandhi contended that no one had "the same bitter experience of the evils of drinks as I have had." Living for twenty-one years in South Africa, he'd seen firsthand the struggles of Khama and the kings that brought them from Bechuanaland to London (Chapter 6). He'd seen indentured Indian laborers, once-respectable English gentlemen, and others fall into the gutter because of alcohol. But in British South Africa, the ones who suffered most were the natives:

> African Negroes were not given to drinking originally. Liquor may be said to have simply ruined them. Large numbers of Negro labourers are seen to waste all their earnings in drinking so that their lives become devoid of any grace. . . . That, as a result of such bitter experience, I have become a staunch opponent of alcohol, will not surprise the readers. In a nutshell, alcohol ruins one physically, morally, intellectually and economically.[10]

As with Khama in confronting Cecil Rhodes and British imperialism in South Africa, the question of prohibiting the white liquor trade would likewise play a pivotal role in India's push for independence. In India as in South Africa—and in empires around the world—the liquor trade was a colonial imposition that made the rich Europeans richer while making the poor Indians poorer. Opposing it through temperance, protest, and prohibition ultimately was less a reflection of Gandhi's personal abstemiousness, and far more a tool of nationalist resistance against an unjust European imperialism.

Neither Black nor White

Mohandas Karamchand Gandhi was born in 1869 to a middle-class, middle-rank, middle-caste Bania family in the West Indian coastal state of Gujarat. He was married at the age of thirteen, in a prearranged ceremony, as per custom. An unremarkable student, he graduated high school in 1887, then enrolled in college, only to quickly drop out. Friends encouraged Mohandas to study law in the far-off metropole of London. His devout and abstinent mother protested, as his wife, Kasturba, had just given birth to a son. Only when Mohandas took a solemn oath that he would not eat meat, drink alcohol, or be unfaithful to his wife did he receive their blessing.[11]

"In spite of the cold I have no need of meat or liquor," Gandhi wrote to his brother upon his arrival in London. "This fills my heart with joy and thankfulness."[12]

For three years, he studied law at the Inner Temple, before being called to the bar in 1891. In London, he patronized temperance and vegetarianism at a time when abstaining from both alcohol and meat was not only thought unhealthy for the damp climate, but politically radical, too. Even Gandhi's early writings from this time chastised the British for promoting the liquor trade as a foundation of their colonial empire.[13]

In 1893, he accepted a one-year legal position for a shipping company in Johannesburg, and sailed for Durban, Natal. Gandhi would spend the next twenty-one years in South Africa, honing his spiritual search for truth and justice, as well as his nonviolent political activism. On the ground in South Africa, the conditions for Indians were far different from what Gandhi could have envisioned.

For context: upon suppressing a bloody rebellion against the British East India Company, in 1858 Queen Victoria liquidated the company, and—in transferring control to the crown—proclaimed that she was "bound to the Natives of our Indian territories by the same obligation of duty which binds us to all our other subjects," and that Indians "of whatever race or creed, be freely and impartially admitted to offices in our service."[14] So when Gandhi moved to London, he held the rights of any Englishman—indeed two Indians had already won seats in the British Parliament.

When he arrived in South Africa, then, Gandhi naturally assumed he would maintain those same rights as a British citizen. His expectations were quickly and unceremoniously dashed as Mohandas was thrown off a train for having the audacity to be a "coloured" attorney in an all-white, first-class carriage. Gandhi soon found himself as a leading representative of the Indian immigrant population of Southern Africa, who saw themselves—as a matter of law—as citizens rather than subjects, with their barrister Gandhi pushing back against the colonizers' black-and-white racial hierarchy.

The legal status of the Indian immigrant population had long been debated in South Africa, partly against the backdrop of the liquor question. When, in 1889, the British administration of the colony of Natal on the southeastern tip of Africa proposed prohibiting the sale of liquor to blacks in the name of labor discipline, they debated extending the prohibition to Indians as well—a move Governor C. B. H. Mitchell ultimately opposed on legal grounds. "Their contract to come here as immigrant labourers places them under certain restrictions, but not under any restriction as to procuring liquor. It would be a manifest hardship to superimpose this condition on the immigrants already here, and, as regards the future, it would, I think, almost put a stop to the supply of Coolies from Madras, if this special condition were inserted in their agreements." Highlighting their intermediate status between the black Africans and the white Europeans, the governor concluded, "It would be unjust and impolitic to prevent Indians from obtaining liquor."[15]

Still, a narrative emerged: it couldn't be the good, law-abiding white liquor dealers who were to blame for the sudden epidemic in black drunkenness—it *must be* the Indians' fault. "I would beg to suggest as a means to put a stop to the drinking amongst Natives that a law be passed, that no Indian be allowed to buy spirits by the bottle or in any quantity," argued the colonial supervisor of Native Locations. "This would prevent them from selling it, and it is the Indians who permeate the country, diffusing the vile stuff among the Natives, trading with it for hides and fowls. This I have not seen but I have been told it, if they could not buy it they could not sell it, and why should one nation be more privileged than the other?"[16]

Angry whites in Natal Colony soon seized upon this narrative of the conniving "coolie" to push for the complete disenfranchisement of the Indian minority. In late 1895—shortly after Khama and the kings had returned from their temperance mission to London—Gandhi rebutted such allegations in a widely read pamphlet titled "The Indian Franchise." He wrote, "The latest argument advanced in favour of disfranchisement is that the Indian franchise would do harm to the Native population of the Colony. In what way this will happen is not stated at all. But, I presume, the objectors to the Indian franchise rely upon the stock objection to the Indian on the alleged ground that he supplies liquor to the Natives and this spoils them." Gandhi pointed out that of the 10,000 Natal residents who met the property requirements for voting, only 251 were Indian, and that "by far the largest number of them are traders who, it is well known, are not only teetotallers themselves, but would like to see liquor banished altogether from the land." Ever the lawyer: in calling out the stereotype Gandhi quoted the government's own Indian Immigration Commission, which found "that the people who make the loudest complaints against the Indian immigrants for selling or disposing of liquor to the Natives are the very persons who themselves sell liquor to the Native." In other words: the brown-skinned Indians make for convenient scapegoats, because they interfere in the white trade and reduce the white man's profit from black depravation. After all—Gandhi pointed out—of the thirty-one convictions for illegally peddling liquor, only three were Indian, and the rest were white Europeans.[17]

Gandhi's arguments did not sit well with the white colonists, nor did his decision to take up permanent residence in Natal. In 1896 Gandhi sailed for India to fetch his wife and children to come live in Africa with him. Upon their return, a mob of white nativists met the Gandhis' ship at the docks, shouting, "Black vermin!" and "We won't have the coolie here!" They accosted the Gandhis in the ill-lit streets of Durban, spitting on them. The mob beat Mohandas within an inch of his life before the police superintendent finally stepped in, perhaps preventing Gandhi from getting lynched. It was a scene eerily similar to a half-century earlier in Boston, Massachusetts, when the godfather of nonviolent resistance—temperate abolitionist William Lloyd Garrison—was likewise apprehended by the police to prevent his lynching at the hands of a riotous mob (Chapter 11). In an egregious example of victim blaming, the next day's *Natal Mercury* wrote that, for raising the passions of the people, "Mr. Gandhi has himself been very largely at fault" for getting beaten black and blue.[18]

Wartime provided a unique opportunity for reconciliation. In 1899 the long-simmering conflict between the Boers and Brits broke into the open when Britain invaded and subdued the Transvaal region. Throughout the Anglo-Boer War (1899–1902), Gandhi led five hundred Indian volunteers in providing medical support, winning high praise from the British command. In doing so—like Khama before him—Gandhi hoped to appeal to the nobler inclinations of the British. "If I demanded rights as a British citizen," Gandhi later wrote, "it was also my duty, as such, to participate in the defence of the British Empire. I held then that India could achieve her complete emancipation only within and through the British Empire."[19] He would again volunteer for British ambulance duty during the 1906 Zulu revolt and World War I.

Following the Anglo-Boer War, Gandhi moved to Johannesburg in the newly British crown colony of Transvaal. Once the Brits and the Boers had stopped fighting with each other, they turned their animus toward the nonwhite populations. One piece of colonial legislation stripped the predominantly Indian and Chinese populations of what few rights they had: refusing to legally recognize Hindu and Muslim weddings, limiting migration into southern Africa or across the borders between the British colonies, imposing ever higher taxes, and even rabid calls for the wholesale deportation of Asians from South Africa.

The crowning insult was the Asiatic Registration Act of 1906, which forced Indian and Chinese residents to register with the local authorities and to carry registration papers with them at all times. Over the following decade, Gandhi would be arrested and imprisoned six times by the British in Africa for refusing to comply with these unjust laws.

Increasingly inspired by the pacifism of Leo Tolstoy (Chapter 2), the civil disobedience of Henry David Thoreau, and the example of British and American suffragettes (Chapters 12–13), Gandhi first deployed his tactic of *satyagraha*—or passive resistance—which would become a hallmark of his later protests for Indian independence.[20] Rather than submitting to an unjust and forcible registration, he would defy the law and endure the harsh consequences. The tactic was effective at extracting concessions from the colonial government: jailing one prisoner of conscience was of little concern, but as the prison yards began overflowing with hundreds and then thousands of nonviolent Indian and Chinese protesters, the white authorities increasingly had a problem on their hands.[21] Between prison sentences, Gandhi continued the legal defense for Indians treated unjustly under the law—which often meant trumped-up accusations of violating the notoriously lax prohibition of liquor sales to natives.[22]

By this time, Gandhi was unquestionably the most famous "colored" man in Africa. While many followers endorsed his political platform and were willing to go to jail for Gandhi, only a handful of Indians and Europeans were willing to follow his spiritual guidance as well. Patterned after Leo Tolstoy's and John Ruskin's embrace of nature, homeopathy, and the simple peasant life—shunning meat, alcohol, and machinery—Gandhi and his motley band of Indian and European followers lived together in interfaith communities: first at the hundred-acre Phoenix settlement, and then at a thousand-acre Tolstoy Farm. Passive resisters and their families could help work the farm in exchange for living free of charge. Still, only a handful of political protesters would become spiritual seekers. Gandhi's community and movement actively included both men and women, Hindus of every caste, Sunni and Shi'ite Muslims, Jews, Catholics, Protestants, and even some African natives—all living and working in harmony.[23]

One of Gandhi's oldest and closest European followers—Hermann Kallenbach—donated the land and led the work at Tolstoy Farm. "I have given up meat-eating, smoking, and drinking, and practise asceticism," Kallenbach wrote. "What Tolstoy wants and what I too strive for, is to recognise the correct thing without disturbing my fellow man."[24]

Leo Tolstoy and Mahatma Gandhi had actually developed a mutual admiration through written correspondence. Indeed, the last letter Tolstoy wrote before he died in 1910 was to Gandhi. The two were united in leading nonviolent opposition to state tyranny, and Tolstoy saw Gandhi's struggles in the Transvaal as spiritually linked to the plight of Russian pacifists and conscientious objectors.[25] Though their brief correspondences do not include it, their position on the liquor traffic as a mechanism of the state debauching its own people was almost identical too.

Figure 7.1 Mohandas Gandhi (right) at Tolstoy Farm, South Africa, with his followers, the "sober, god-fearing, humane Englishman" Albert West, Hermann Kallenbach, and Moscow-born activist Sonja Schlesin. Robert Payne, *The Life and Death of Mahatma Gandhi* (New York: E. P. Dutton Co., 1969), 144.
Source: Age Fotostock.

In 1910 Gandhi published his *Hind Swaraj*, or *Indian Home Rule*—a statement of his political views and ambitions beyond South Africa. In addition to extolling freedom and passive resistance, Gandhi made a case for Indian nationalism against the incursions of British "civilization." The arrival of British railways and machinery prompted the switch to cash crops for export, which led to famine. British lawyers stoked divisions and consolidated European rule. British medicine hooked people on pills, unhealthy foods, and "spiritous liquors" in opposition to Hindu and Muslim spiritual traditions.[26] While such diagnoses were consonant with both moderate and extremist Indian nationalists, his prescription for peaceful, nonviolent resistance to rectify it most certainly was not.

Gandhi's focus had already turned to India, even as his final South African protest campaign picked up steam. In 1913 a renewed wave of nonviolent protests and arrests inspired nationwide strikes by the Asian community. The following year, the Union of South Africa passed the Indian Relief Act, which respected rites of marriage, repealed the unjust taxes, and allowed for free passage of those from South Asia. Content that his original goals in South Africa had been fulfilled after twenty-one years, Mahatma Gandhi returned home to India, with his family and a handful of faithful followers in tow.

To Make India Free, Make India Dry

As in South Africa, the British did not introduce alcohol to South Asia, but their colonial rule dramatically altered drinking practices there. Fermented beverages had been around since ancient times, and the Arabic science of distillation had likely spread to India even before arriving in Europe. Still, since intoxication is discouraged within Hinduism and Buddhism—and even more strongly prohibited in Islam, Jainism, and Sikhism—mass drunkenness wasn't much of a social problem before British colonization.[27]

Britain had ruled the Indian subcontinent since the mid-eighteenth century, largely through its East India Company: a private enterprise based in London, answerable to its shareholders. The primary aim, of course, was to maximize revenues from the territory under its control—less the cost of militarily subduing and governing half a continent—by collecting rents on land and taxes on economic activity. To this end, in 1790 the company began assessing an excise tax on distilled spirits, opium, and ganja, quickly becoming a primary source of company profit and state revenue.[28] This merging of political power and economic profit from liquor and opium made the East India Company "perhaps the world's first 'narco-military' empire," according to historian David Washbrook.[29]

Collection of the liquor tax was farmed out in much the same way as it was in the Russian Empire (see Chapter 2). British administrators auctioned off licenses to tax farmers for the right to manufacture and sell liquor in a given district without state interference. In India as in Russia, once the tax farmer paid his burden to the state, he invariably sought to maximize his revenue by selling as much liquor as possible. Also as in Russia, this led to a rapid growth in alcoholism and all its accompanying social ills, as well as the blossoming of corruption.[30]

By the mid-nineteenth century, Britain had become "the world's largest organized supplier of narcotics."[31] Fully 40 percent of the company's exports from India took the form of opium; that which was not consumed domestically—creating epidemics of addiction—was trafficked to China and sold for tea to be shipped back to Britain.[32] In terms strikingly similar to later generations of prohibitionists against the alcohol traffic, Ch'ing officials protested that the British were enslaving them to addiction, and getting rich in the process. When China declared prohibition against the opium trade, the British subdued them in two brutal Opium Wars (1839–1842 and 1856–1860), continuing their exploitative drug trade by force, and seizing the colony of Hong Kong along the way.[33]

When prohibitionist Liberal MP Sir Wilfrid Lawson rose before the House of Commons in 1870 to challenge British India's opium traffic (Chapter 5), he argued, "Surely a Christian country can understand the language of the Chinese Emperor when he said—'Nothing can induce me to derive a Revenue from the vices and misery of my people.'" What were Britishers to think "about a nation which becomes a wholesale druggist, administering poison to another nation, and calling this process the opening up of China?"

Opponents, including Prime Minister William Gladstone, agreed that if it were a simple question of morality, everyone would join in the condemnation of the exploitative trade. "But what would the Chancellor of the Exchequer say?" The opium traffic made between six million and eight million pounds annually for the British Raj, which could not be easily replaced without raising taxes elsewhere. The undersecretary for India blasted the prohibitionist Lawson as having "no compassion for the Indian taxpayer, none for the holders of our Government and railway stocks, whose property he was consciously or unconsciously threatening."

It was the same there's-no-other-way, revenue-trap justification for British narco-imperialism that would bedevil prohibition and liquor-traffic debates in India for generations. In the end, his resolution to condemn the Chinese opium trade was voted down by a three-to-one margin. Lawson lamented that "the people of England would be astonished [that] the argument from the Treasury Bench had been nothing but money, money, money, regardless of morality and Christian duty."[34]

Back in India, opposition to company rule had come to a head in 1857 in a bloody, nationwide rebellion that pushed the British crown to dissolve the loathsome and exploitative company. The administration, finances, and defense of the entire Indian subcontinent—from present-day Pakistan to Burma—would be reorganized and ruled directly by the crown through the colonial administration of the British Raj. The opium traffic and liquor traffic were both now the purview of the government.

But while the company was gone, the notorious liquor tax farm remained, producing alarming increases in alcoholism. "This system possessed the obvious advantage of bringing in revenue in lump sums without entailing expensive establishments. But its disadvantages were those inherent in all financial schemes for farming monopolies," wrote Sir William Wilson Hunter, the Scottish-born historian and long-serving member of the Indian Civil Service.

> From the revenue point of view it was unprofitable, for only capitalists could afford to purchase these farms, and their tendency was to combine to keep down the prices offered. From the moral point of view it was impolitic, because the farmers naturally tried to push their sales, and *neither* endeavored nor desired to put a check on consumption. From the consumers' point of view it was objectionable, as the farmers, having the monopoly of manufacture as well as of sale, made their liquor as cheaply as possible, since they had no inducement to turn out a good and therefore an expensive article. The only persons to whom the system was satisfactory were the farmers themselves, who made large fortunes.[35]

Thus, in 1878, the British passed the *Abkari* (Excise) Act, monopolizing for the colonial government the right to manufacture and sell intoxicating liquors and drugs in British India, ostensibly to "enhance the revenue, regulate consumption, and secure a good quality of liquor."[36] Predictably, the high-minded goals of controlling consumption and improving quality were sacrificed to revenue maximization. By the 1880s, the market was flooded with low-quality, adulterated drinks, and unscrupulous sellers trying "to make as much profit as possible."[37] Record profits and revenues came at the expense of record drunkenness. Newspapers in Bombay argued that what the British opium trade did to China, the British liquor traffic was doing to India.[38]

Backlash against British liquor excesses took the form of strikes, protests, and vows of sobriety eerily reminiscent of the temperance resistance against the Russian Empire's vodka domination three decades earlier (see Chapter 2). By 1885 the Bhandari caste—traditionally associated with the fermentation of "toddy," or palm wine—collectively refused to supply toddy to the state. The following year, an abstinence movement swept western India, as lower-class drinkers steadfastly refused to buy British liquor. "The poor openly complained of the government plundering the people with a view to replenish their treasury," contemporaries observed, accusing the British *abkari* system of "sucking the blood of the people."[39]

As with Russia's temperance boycotts, this placed the British imperial authorities in an unenviable situation. The strike was threatening to bankrupt the liquor sellers whom the Raj relied upon for revenue. Indeed, by 1886, newspapers reported that the movement had "so decidedly diminished the sale of liquor in some places as to alarm the liquor sellers [who] are actively engaged by intimidation and bribery in endeavouring to break up this combination against their iniquitous traffic."[40]

If the British were to advance the health and well-being of their Indian subjects by siding with the antiliquor movement, the entire system of imperial finance would collapse. London could hardly let its authority be challenged by a poor people's movement, so the Raj doubled down, casting its lot with the liquor trust. Indian drink-strikers were harassed, those preaching abstinence were jailed, their "dry" plans scuttled. Only by the 1890s—with gradual increases in quality and more affordable prices—did the antiliquor strikes subside, but the damage had been done. Even more so than before, the liquor traffic became synonymous with the worst excesses of British colonial occupation, while temperance activism against liquor— and the massive revenues generated by the British traffic—became a reliable tool of nationalist protest against British rule.[41]

Amid the raging antiliquor strikes and protests, in 1887–1888 British parliamentarian W. S. Caine toured India. Upon returning to London, he established the Anglo-Indian Temperance Association (AITA), with "a view to Parliamentary action regarding the excise policy and administration of the Indian Government, and which would also promote and guide an agitation throughout India for temperance reform."[42] The AITA allowed critics of the Raj's brutal imperial rule in India to network with like-minded temperance activists in the United Kingdom, lending greater respectability to the nationalist cause.

In India, activists' direct petitions to the Raj for *abkari* reform went nowhere, so the AITA did a boomerang around the autocratic British government in India by going directly to London, much as Khama did.[43] On April 30, 1889, AITA president and Member of Parliament Samuel Smith moved a resolution in the House of Commons that, "In the opinion of this House, the fiscal system of the Government of India leads to the establishment of spirit distilleries, liquor and opium shops, in large numbers of places where, till recently, they never existed, in defiance of native opinion and protests of the inhabitants, and that such increased facilities for drinking produce a steadily increasing consumption, and spread misery and ruin among the industrial classes of India, calling for immediate action on the part of the Government of India, with a view to their abatement."[44]

This was a direct affront to the image of the British imperialist as a benevolent purveyor of civilization. Undersecretary for India John Gorst was livid. But the motion passed, 113–100, compelling a thorough audit of the *abkari* administration and increased restrictions on the liquor traffic.[45] To be so scolded and disciplined by the mother country was utterly humiliating for the British Raj.

For decades, the AITA continued its lobbying in London and activism in India, becoming the primary temperance organization on the subcontinent, later to be joined by representatives of the United Kingdom Alliance (UKA; see Chapter 5), the International Order of Good Templars (IOGT), and the World's Woman's Christian Temperance Union (WWCTU; Chapter 13). Many of these other transnational temperance organizations were at a disadvantage by working primarily along denominational lines, especially in a primarily Hindu and Muslim country where Christians were a tiny minority. Still, it is particularly telling that the AITA's quarterly journal was titled *Abkari* and would act as an independent watchdog for the British *abkari* administration and the liquor trade more generally.[46]

Key to this oversight was the recently formed (1885) Indian National Congress (INC): the umbrella nationalist party that would later succeed in wresting India's independence from Britain. W. S. Caine boasted that half of AITA's members belonged to the INC, and that almost everyone involved in temperance were INC members, further evidence of the close ties between temperance and nationalism.[47] Still in London, completing his legal studies in 1891, Gandhi openly applauded Caine's "admirable crusade against the spread of the evil, but what can the energy of one man, however powerful, do against the inaction of an apathetic and dormant Government?" This was especially true of a government that "it seems, instead of stopping, [is] aiding and abetting the spread of alcohol."[48]

Indeed, some of the INC's nonviolent activism often associated with Gandhi actually originated in the Indian temperance movement years earlier. Take, for instance, the Poona Temperance Association, led by G. K. Gokhale, a mentor of Gandhi. Under his direction, in 1907, temperance volunteers began peacefully picketing outside of liquor shops, leading to dramatic drops in alcohol sales and government revenue. This caught the ire of F. G. H. Anderson, the assistant collector for Poona. When his efforts to shoo away the picketing temperance "politicals" (read: nationalists) failed, he called in the military to dispel them by force. Amid the temperance riot, peaceful picketers were beaten, arrested, and fined. Picketing the Raj's liquor stores was quickly outlawed, further souring attitudes toward the British authorities. From then on, as Gokhale himself noted in *Abkari*, "It was impossible to dissociate the temperance cause from politics," adding that temperance "would become more of a political question than it was a financial, moral, or a social question."[49]

Bal Gangadhar Tilak—the most famous independence activist before Gandhi— went even further, arguing that "the temperance movement will serve as a nice object-lesson in the present relations between the rulers and the ruled."[50] For promoting *swaraj*, or self-rule, Tilak would be arrested for sedition the following year. Indeed, as in autocratic societies elsewhere, temperance organizations were a Trojan horse for nationalist and anti-imperialist political activism. The burgeoning Indian National Congress provided a broad base of support for AITA activism, while links with the white, British AITA provided Indian nationalists at least some protection from persecution by colonial administrators, Tilak notwithstanding.[51] This was the political landscape of temperance and Indian nationalism that welcomed Mahatma Gandhi upon his return from South Africa in 1915.

Gandhi Arrives

From its incubator in temperance activism, India's nationalist movement only grew with Gandhi's return from South Africa in 1915. Now inexorably linked to the cause of independence, the liquor question became ever more politically charged under Gandhi. Gandhi's activism on behalf of the Indian minority in British South Africa won him the admiration of the Indian people and the scorn of the British colonial authorities, both of which intensified with the publication of his *Hind Swaraj* blueprint for Indian Home Rule. His nationalist bona fides already secure, Gandhi joined the INC upon his return to India and took a year to get acclimated to the political landscape, with Gokhale's assistance.

India was hardly immune from the global tumult of World War I. In exchange for British promises of self-rule following the war, Gandhi helped recruit Indian volunteers, millions of whom fought admirably for the empire. At the conclusion of the war, the British feared that the instability and wave of revolutions that had consumed the Russian, German, Ottoman, and Austro-Hungarian Empires might spread to India, wracked as it was by economic depression, unemployment, and food riots. British jitters increased as the INC and Muslim League joined forces to demand greater autonomy for the Indian subcontinent, even in defiance of draconian wartime laws that allowed the British to jail nationalists without due process. The confrontation ended in tragedy in the Jallianwala Bagh gardens of the northern city of Amritsar on April 13, 1919, when the troops of Brigadier-General Reginald Dyer opened fire on an unauthorized crowd of tens of thousands of unarmed Muslim, Hindu, and Sikh men, women, and children. Between three hundred and fifteen hundred were killed in Dyer's self-proclaimed effort "to punish the Indians for disobedience."[52] But instead of crushing the nationalist spirit, the massacre ignited nationwide disturbances, further emboldening the opposition.

In a halfhearted effort to placate rising nationalist tensions, the British passed the 1919 Government of India Act, which nominally created a "diarchy" in which the British viceroy would retain control over defense and foreign affairs, while devolving control over some domestic affairs—including agriculture, health, education, and the liquor trade—to regional administrators. This proved to be the death knell of the Anglo-Indian Temperance Association. With *abkari* administration now in the hands of (white) regional governors—who could still administer it with impunity, irrespective of local opinion—the AITA could no longer do its end around of the Raj by directly lobbying London. Its activism in India was largely taken over by nationalists within the INC.[53] Increasingly independent of white European influence, the cause of Indian temperance flourished under Gandhi's leadership.

In response to the Raj's draconian antisedition laws and emboldened by the brutal massacre at Amritsar in 1919, Gandhi and the INC launched their movement of *satyagraha*, or nonviolent noncooperation with the British authorities. While the colonizers had repeatedly proven themselves willing to use violence to maintain power, Gandhi urged passive resistance and civil disobedience. Gandhi's approach included *swadeshi*, or the boycotting of British goods that would undercut the empire's finances. Gandhi urged both rich and poor to follow his lead in spurning British institutions—courts, schools, administration buildings, government liquor, jobs, titles, and even textiles—instead spinning homespun cloth as both a symbolic and practical promotion of Indian independence. (The Indian flag, emblazoned with a traditional spinning wheel as a symbol of self-reliance, was first promoted by Gandhi at this time.)

Crucial to noncooperation, yet often overlooked, was picketing the liquor shops that were the bedrock of the Raj's finances. Not only would nationalists boycott liquor themselves, they would actively scare away would-be drinkers from the government stores. As customers evaporated, so too did government revenue. For its American audiences, the Anti-Saloon League's *American Issue* described the noncooperation movement as "led principally by an Indian lawyer and philosopher, Mahatma Kandhi [*sic*], whose ideas closely represent those of Count Tolstoi. The essence of this movement is a complete boycott of everything British. Gandhi and his followers, most of whom are drys as a matter of principle, have seized upon the drink situation as a form of attack upon British rule."[54]

The British chief excise inspector for Bombay, by contrast, portrayed the antiliquor protests in a decidedly different hue: "as to give one an idea that we are not at present living under the protection of the British Government, but in a place where vagabondage had full sway without the least fear of law and order." While not preventing entry by force, one of the (usually) seven or eight picketers would verbally harass would-be customers, sometimes hurling "very filthy language" as he entered. "It is when he comes out of the shop that the pickets surround him and greet him in such choice language such as whether he had been into the shop to drink his mother's or wife's urine or, if the customer is a Hindoo whether he had been there to drink cow's blood or in the case of a Mahomadan pig's blood. Naturally when such a scene is going on in front of the shop, a crowd collects," the embarrassing scuttlebutt further deterring the customer from ever returning.[55]

Picketing toddy shops and liquor stores was incredibly effective in striking at the empire's finances. In many locations, the yearly auctions for collecting the liquor-tax excise failed due to the noncooperation movement.[56] "Scores of liquor contractors were ruined and most of those remaining were on the brink of ruin," observed visiting American temperance advocates. "I visited dozens of liquor shops in many parts of the country where the dealers ruefully told me that they had had only one or two customers during the day. When I asked why, they invariably replied, 'Mr. Gandhi has told the people not to drink any more.'"[57]

The Raj, of course, cracked down as autocratic empires do: arresting scores of nonviolent protesters. At his court trial in February 1921, for picketing peacefully outside a liquor store, one Dr. L. V. Paranjpye defended his actions: "The loss of excise revenue to the government is absolutely necessary for I hold that the Indian government ought to forgo it when it is derived from the moral depravity of the vast masses of the people of India. It is a pity that the government should care more for its revenue than for the well-being of the people." Dr. Paranjpye was then sentenced to two months of hard labor.[58]

Yet despite Gandhi's steadfastness, some liquor protests turned violent. In November 1921, Bombay fell to riots against the Parsi minority, who were disproportionately represented among India's industrialists, landowners, moneylenders, and liquor-sellers.[59] "The main feature," wrote the local papers on the first day of rioting, "was the persistent attack on liquor shops," with hundreds of liquor shops falling to violent mobs.[60]

Gandhi bore witness to the violence himself and considered it to be among the movement's great failings. In "A Deep Stain," Gandhi wrote,

> As the day went up, the fury of the mob now intoxicated with its initial success rose also. They burnt tram-cars and a motor, smashed liquor shops and burnt two. . . . I found a liquor shop smashed, two policemen badly wounded and lying unconscious on cots without anybody caring for them.

As a fawning crowd of admirers gathered around Gandhi, he rebuked them for not coming to the aid of their fellow man. After tending to the wounded officers, Gandhi continued on, and "found to our horror a liquor shop on fire. Even the fire brigade was obstructed in its work" by the picketers. Only by the personal intervention of Gandhi were the terrified "inmates" of the burning liquor shop saved.[61] Others would not be so lucky. In one instance in Uttar Pradesh, twenty-three policemen were barricaded in their police station by an angry mob that then set it on fire, killing everyone inside.[62]

In a "humiliating confession of my incapacity," Gandhi lamented that his civil disobedience campaign was destined to fail without a popular spirit of nonviolence. Gandhi called off the *satyagraha* campaign, committing himself to prayer and fasting as penance. "If I can have nothing to do with the organized violence of the Government," he wrote, channeling Tolstoy, "I can have less to do with the unorganized violence of the people. I would prefer to be crushed between the two."[63] The British arrested Gandhi for sedition and in 1922 sentenced him to six years in prison, though he was released in 1924.

Mahatma Pussyfoot

The noncooperation riots and roiling "disturbances" delayed by a year the arrival in India of famed American prohibitionist William E. "Pussyfoot" Johnson, who'd been invited by AITA activists in 1920.[64] When last we tuned in to the dry misadventures of Pussyfoot Johnson in Chapter 5, he was the centerpiece of a student riot in the streets of London, which cost him the use of his right eye. His lighthearted response and affable personality made him a global celebrity: his wax likeness beamed from Madame Tussaud's, while in 1922 the *New York Times* listed Pussyfoot among its "Twelve Greatest American Men," alongside Henry Ford, Thomas Edison, Babe Ruth, Woodrow Wilson, Teddy Roosevelt, and the Wright Brothers.[65]

Hearing that the world's most famous prohibitionist had set his sights on India, the Raj was understandably nervous. "In those troublous days," Pussyfoot later reminisced, "it was necessary to have a special permit to enter India, particularly on a mission like mine which, frankly, was aimed at overthrowing one phase of the established order of things."[66]

Ultimately it was the British viceroy himself who telegrammed London: "Government of India have no objection to genuine temperance propaganda, but they think it likely that non-cooperation party, who have adopted prohibition as part of their propaganda, will endeavour to win him over for their own ends. . . . We do not suggest that passport should be refused, if persuasion fails we must of course face his visit."[67] In London and later in India, the AITA and British officials both impressed upon Johnson that he was on thin ice: his speeches and interactions should concentrate on temperance and relating his impressions of America, rather than getting involved in sensitive "political" issues.[68]

Upon his arrival in India, Pussyfoot was summoned by Sir George Lloyd (not to be confused with David Lloyd George, Liberal prime minister, 1916–1922), the infamous governor of Bombay, to inquire as to his intentions in India. "I have done everything I could to keep you out of India, but my wishes have been overruled in London," he told Pussyfoot. "However, now that you are here, I shall treat you right." Trading frankness for frankness, Pussyfoot was blunt about his mission, and did not sugarcoat the ways in which his fight against the liquor traffic might cause the governor trouble. "Every word you say against drink is true," Sir George Lloyd concluded as the two parted ways. "Liquor destroys thousands of people every year, but it is better that a thousand people be killed than that one Briton lose his liberty!"[69]

Thus began a whirlwind tour of the subcontinent, where the American visitor quickly became a celebrity of the noncooperation movement, giving prohibition lectures to rapt throngs of ten thousand to fifteen thousand Hindus and Muslims per event. This far exceeded the crowds of mere hundreds he'd been used to in the United States.[70]

So great was the demand for Pussyfoot that nationalists and well-wishers would routinely blockade the railroad tracks, compelling him to deliver impromptu temperance lectures from his train, even in the dead of night. On one such occasion between Ahmedabad and Delhi, Johnson's train was stopped at Jaipur at 2 a.m. by a crowd of fifteen hundred, demanding a speech. Johnson's secretary (and later, biographer), Tarani Prasad Sinha, insisted that his sleeping American guest not be disturbed.[71] The crowd persisted. Sinha devised a compromise. As Pussyfoot later told it, Sinha "pulled aside the little green curtain of my sleeping compartment, like some magician unveiling a sleeping beauty, and that whole crowd of 1500 people, in single file, went tip-toeing past, feasting their eyes on the delectable spectacle of Pussyfoot Johnson fairly wallowing in a sleep as sound as that of a drunken Sioux. And snoring melodiously."[72]

The lectures themselves could be politically uncomfortable—sometimes held in venues like the Town Hall at Delhi or Jallianwala Bagh in Amritsar, which had so recently been the site of British carnage. Often, the American orator was situated on stage—both physically and symbolically—between an Indian nationalist host and a white colonial official determined to keep a watchful eye on the event. "I didn't claim to be teaching India anything it didn't already know," Pussyfoot explained. "I admitted that India believed in and practiced total abstinence when my ancestors were living in caves and wearing the skins of animals. I insisted that America had only accepted the thought of the East and that I came as a convert."[73]

Johnson didn't stay apolitical for long, unflinchingly throwing his support behind the nationalists. "Mr. Gandhi has done a shrewd thing. Non-co-operation in the manufacture, sale, and use of alcoholic beverages is for India's unconditional good," Pussyfoot declared in an interview with the loyalist AITA's own *Abkari* journal. "Without respect of race, class, or creed, residents of India can wholeheartedly support any effort on the part of India's leaders to get rid of the drink traffic. No amount of financial embarrassment should stand in the way of this land freeing itself from the bondage of strong drink."[74]

Johnson had long professed an admiration for Gandhi, "the courageous and wise little passive rebel against British rule," and hoped to meet with him at his ashram at Ahmedabad. Though Gandhi was away when Pussyfoot came to call, Kasturba and the Gandhi family welcomed him warmly.[75]

The admiration, it seems, was mutual. Following Gandhi's release from prison in 1924, there was talk of reviving the *satyagraha* noncooperation campaign against the British. In demurring, Gandhi suggested they consider the example of Pussyfoot Johnson as a leader both in temperance and nonviolence. Harkening back to Johnson's London rag of 1919, Gandhi described how, while Pussyfoot

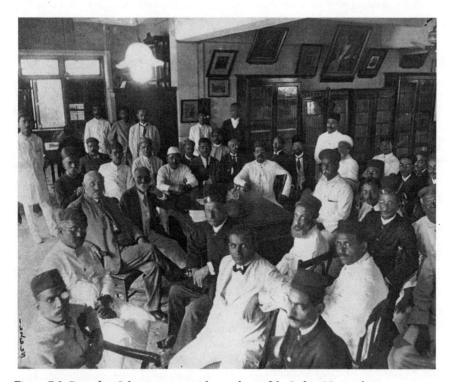

Figure 7.2 Pussyfoot Johnson meets with members of the Indian Nationalist Congress, 1922.

The caption on this original photograph erroneously claims that Gandhi is seated at the table, wearing a white hat. Despite a mutual admiration, Gandhi and Johnson never met in person. *Abkari* suggests that this photo was taken at the Bombay Club. "Mr. 'Pussyfoot' Johnson's Tour," *Abkari*, no. 127 (January 1922): 4, Box 4, Folder 37, Roll 22, World League Against Alcoholism Records, Temperance and Prohibition Papers, Ohio Historical Society. *Source*: Getty Images.

was trying to convert certain English students, he was stoned. The throw resulted ultimately in the loss of one eye. He pardoned the offenders, would not prosecute them and would not take compensation offered by the British Government. That was an instance of non-violence in thought, word and deed. If such non-violence can be insured here, I would not hesitate to revive the idea of picketing liquor shops again. But we stand discredited. In many places, our picketing in 1921 was far from non-violent. The political idea of embarrassing the Government was predominant with us, that of reforming the drunkard was a very secondary consideration. In the struggle of non-co-operation politics are made to subserve the moral end. If we can reform the drunkard, we reform also the administration and the administrators. Whereas, if we suppress the drunkard by force, we may deprive the Government of the liquor or the drug revenue for a time, but in the end the suppressed drinker or smoker will raise his head and the Government will raise an increased revenue. Not until we have men and women enough who would carry on picketing for the love of the drunkard even at the risk of their lives, can we dream of reviving picketing. I am afraid we ill deserve the praise given to us by Dr. Johnson.[76]

Gandhi personally abstained from alcohol but was famously tolerant of drinkers. Invited to gatherings where drinks were served, he would pass a liquor bottle to a fellow guest, even while preaching a lesson of abstinence, which some took to be a curious inconsistency. Gandhi argued that his teachings would resonate more through tolerance rather than intolerance. "I acquired the right to bring up courteously the subject of prohibition . . . by suffering the drinks being served there," he said, adding, "Love without tolerance is not worth the name."[77]

Still, while Gandhi was recognized as the moral father of the nation, it was not as though every protest or picket was coordinated from on high. Indeed, Indian social activism could develop with surprising spontaneity, as with the grassroots anti-drink movement that took root with Gandhi's release in 1924. "The depth and volume of the popular enthusiasm that was roused for ending the drink evil surprised even Mahatmaji," wrote C. Rajagopalachari in the *Hindu* in February 1924. Rajagopalachari—"CR" or "Rajaji"—was Gandhi's right-hand man, the engine of the prohibition movement, and future governor-general of India. "The potentialities of his own movement he knew full well; but the dynamic force spontaneity of the anti-Drink agitation and the swiftness with which it spread throughout the land was something which came on him unexpectedly. It was a wonderful justification of the plans and methods of national reform adopted by him, and strengthened in him his purpose as nothing else perhaps did."[78]

Akkarapatti and neighboring districts in the southeast of the Indian peninsula went dry through coordinated temperance protests. But the response of the British Raj was eerily similar to the tsar's response to the temperance boycotts in Imperial

Russia seven decades earlier (Chapter 2). With no more customers, and in deference to local sentiment, even the shop-renter—one Sellia Gownder—approached the white *abkari* administration for permission to close his shop. Instead, the Raj brought criminal proceedings against Gownder for not keeping his toddy shop open.

"I shall pay you your rent, what else do you claim?" asked the shop-renter.

The community had his back: "We shall pay you the whole year's stipulated Drink profit, what more can you want?" the villagers said, producing the forgone revenue.

Still, it wasn't enough. The revenue officer imposed a fine of fifty rupees against Gownder for unauthorized closure of a liquor store—and since it was a continuing offense, the fine could be repeated. "So civilisation can witness the Salem Collector fining the Akkarapatti renter a daily if not an hourly fine of Rs. 50 until the recalcitrant villagers come back to good sense and drink toddy!" wrote Rajagopalachari. Still, the villagers held firm. "They will plead guilty to the charge of combination against alcohol." The community would pay all penalties for not drinking, since among the villagers it was only the local revenue officials who seemed thirsty to drink.

"Think of a state of things where the Government of a country fines a village for not drinking!" CR wrote in the *Hindu*.[79] But as it turns out, this was part of the pattern of alco-imperialism not just in India, but the world over.

Nevertheless, Gandhi saw this groundswell of temperance as a golden opportunity to push forward with broad-based social reform. "He had every reason to expect the Christian missionaries to throw the weight of their great influence on the side of the people," CR wrote. "Their own professions as well as their general attitude towards him and his teachings justified this expectation." After all, was it not the same said Protestant sects (Chapter 14) who'd been credited with putting prohibition over in the United States just a few years earlier?

But it was not to be. Despite their historical portrayal as arbiters of morality and European "civilization," the white Christian missionaries largely sided with the *abkari* revenuers, the imperial drink traffic, and the British Raj. As the British government jailed hundreds of Indian protesters for abstaining from drink, and the police protected drunkards stumbling past picketers into the saloons, the missionaries remained deafeningly silent. The brazen hypocrisy of these evangelical forces, which Gandhi "had all his lifetime learnt to regard as friendly [but] were either severely opposed or criminally indifferent," was one of Gandhi's bitterest disappointments.[80]

All the same, the upswell of popular support for the anti-drink movement led Gandhi to shift from temperance suasion to legislative prohibition for India. "I have definitely come to the conclusion that merely preaching [abstinence] amongst the masses will not do, for they do not know what they are doing," Gandhi said in a 1925 prohibition speech in Madras. When critics pointed to the revenue benefits of the liquor trade, he remained resolute: "If we could persuade our legislators to give up this income from opium and drink, I would do so today. I would sacrifice the education of all our children, if we could not educate them without this revenue."[81]

On January 7, 1926, Rajaji wrote to Gandhi with a plan to explicitly harness the political energy of the anti-drink movement with the nationalist movement, proclaiming that "a prohibition campaign such as I intend can have no place for moderates who tremble at and retreat at the last moment from any form of strong action."[82] Within a few short months, Gandhi was pushing to add a prohibition plank to the official INC platform: linking the dirty money from a demoralizing traffic to the most amoral expenditure—maintenance of the army as the state's means of repression. "The only way to bring about total prohibition being to cut out from the military expenditure a part equivalent to the revenue derived from this immoral source."[83]

Meanwhile, under the auspices of the INC, Rajaji built a new organization: the Prohibition League of India (PLI). Meant to coordinate all temperance, abstinence, and prohibition organizations in India, the PLI aimed "to assist them to co-operate with each other in a common effort to free the country from the use of, and the traffic in, intoxicating drink and drugs." In correspondence with the British imperial authorities, he was always careful to add that, beyond prohibition, "It partakes in no other activities, political or social."

The league would network together the various indigenous temperance organizations, local lodges of the IOGT, the World's Woman's Christian Temperance Union, the Anglo-Indian Temperance Association, and the World League Against Alcoholism (Chapter 17). "Pussyfoot" Johnson was made an honorary lifetime member.[84]

CR himself was the fulcrum of the twin causes of prohibition and nationalism: not only was he the NLI's general secretary, he also headed the Indian National Congress's Prohibition Committee. Moreover, he published the organization's quarterly magazine, *Prohibition,* and lectured on temperance, nationalism, and prohibition throughout India.[85] According to CR, the threefold appeal of the INC henceforth would be, "Down with the drink traffic. Away with communal strife. Strengthen the Congress."[86]

Prohibition was nationalism, and vice versa.

Rajaji and Gandhi spoke with one voice as to the urgency of the drink question. Since the Muslim and Hindu communities in India both stood against British liquor as a vice and colonial imposition rather than a historically rooted local craft, there was no need to trifle with local-option votes or other halfway measures, as in Europe or the United States. "To talk therefore of a referendum in India is to trifle with the problem," Gandhi claimed.[87]

CR went even further: "Licensing boards and local options will only be incentives and opportunities for the vicious and powerful liquor interests to consolidate and strengthen themselves in our country as they have done in Western countries." While prohibition in the United States was hardly an unqualified success, Rajagopalachari argued, the main danger was the organized liquor interests in

Madras and other big cities waging an all-out wet propaganda war in opposition to "great world-wave against drink" (Chapter 17).

What white Americans, Europeans, and the British overlords didn't understand, CR claimed, was that John Stuart Mill's old right-to-drink argument (Chapter 5) was itself a colonial imposition, ill suited for the Indian subcontinent. "The whole mischief really arises out of the fact that our European rulers cannot realise the totally different place that liquor occupies in Indian life," in which drunkenness was considered indecent and wrong among even the lowest castes. "People do drink among us, and thanks to the Government policy, there is not a big village but has a licensed toddy shop where Government insists that a minimum quantity of spiritous drink must be kept for sale." CR concluded, "Any talk about the right to drink would raise tumultuous laughter in an Indian audience, whereas it would be gravely discussed by a European gathering."[88] In a series of weekly articles in the *Hindu* and *Young India*, Rajagopalachari took repeated aim at the right-to-drink argument as "not a plea for freedom of the individual," but rather "a cruel exhibition of selfish indifference to the welfare of the poor," for whom alcoholic addiction meant absolute ruin, rather than just an impediment to leisure.[89]

Having dispensed with the liberty objection, Rajaji then dealt with the revenue objection by arguing, what better use of the people's money could there be than keeping it in the pockets of the people? Instead of going to London, millions of rupees annually would stay in India, raising the living standards especially of those lowest castes most ravaged by the predatory liquor trade, where prohibitionist support was the highest.[90] The increased prosperity of districts where temperance boycotts had been most successful was evidence enough.[91] "Increase of excise revenue means increased drinking, nothing else," CR claimed in his lectures. "Every rupee of Abkari revenue is Satan's toll. It is not minted silver, but metallic counters of ruined homes, and hungry wives and children."[92]

In his public statements on prohibition, Gandhi echoed Rajaji. "I have not hesitated to give my opinion," Gandhi wrote in *Young India*, "that it was a wicked thing for the Imperial Government to have transferred this most immoral source of revenue to the provinces and to have thus made this tainted revenue the one source for defraying the cost of the education of Indian youth." While India could look to American and British temperance experiences for inspiration, Western comparisons would be of limited help, given the differences in traditional social attitudes toward drink, as well as the colonial nature of the liquor trade that was enriching them while impoverishing India. As for the revenue conundrum, Gandhi was clear: "I would rather have India reduced to a state of pauperism than have thousands of drunkards in our midst. I would rather have India without education if that is the price to be paid for making it dry."[93]

The INC's grassroots prohibitionism shone a light on the hypocrisy of a "civilizing" British Raj reliant on liquor revenues siphoned from the people. Hoping to undercut the prohibitionist movement, in 1928 the Raj undertook a halfhearted, face-saving public-relations campaign to highlight the dangers of alcoholism, without actually cutting into its own profit margins. And what was the result of such government-sponsored "temperance"? The following year, Indian beer consumption went *up* by 30 percent, and arrack consumption rose 11 percent. Toddy rose 5.7 percent, foreign liquor imports increased 26 percent, ganja sales increased 6.5 percent, and opium 1.5 percent. "Still," CR wryly noted, "we are asked to believe that the Government is pursuing the only correct policy in regard to the matter, as against the erroneous [prohibition] procedure adopted by America."[94]

The people needed to stay vigilant in their prohibitionism, CR argued, as the "drink interests are prepared to corrupt candidates and leaders with money, votes and power," just as the corrupt liquor machine operated in Western countries.[95] The prohibitionists had to act fast, before the colonial liquor interests became like their foreign counterparts: so politically, economically, and socially intertwined with the life of the country, they'd be nearly impossible to root out. Indeed, it was only by being protected by the British government that the liquor interests could operate so brazenly and openly against the public welfare.[96] For these reasons, "Prohibition is not a fad," CR proclaimed. "It is a people's programme, a prosperity programme, and a moral programme."[97]

With prohibitions repealed throughout Europe and on the ropes in the United States, by the late 1920s, India had become the global leader in antiliquor activism. In 1929—just weeks before the Black Tuesday stock market crash and ensuing Great Depression—Pussyfoot Johnson returned to India to bolster Gandhi's arguments for prohibition, sovereignty, and *swaraj*.

With another nationwide protest already in the works—including nonpayment of taxes and boycotting all British imports and institutions—Pussyfoot again undertook a whirlwind speaking tour, under the uneasy eye of the British Raj. Working hand-in-glove with C. Rajagopalachari, there was no longer any pretense of a boundary between prohibition and self-determination—an argument the American visitor was well poised to hammer home to nationalist crowds at every opportunity.[98]

Upon visiting the ancient city of Agra and its storied Taj Mahal, Pussyfoot penned an exclusive editorial titled "What Prohibition Means" that was splashed across the front page of Agra's *Mathur Patrika*. "The Prohibition movement is based on the ideal of human liberty and nothing else," he began. It is about the rights of families to prosper, rather than dwell "in a slum created by the liquor business." It is about "the right of taxpayers to have their money spent for public improvements, schools, parks, universities and things of that sort," rather than prisons and policing.

"That liberty that is claimed for the individual must also be claimed for a nation or a people," proclaimed Pussyfoot, a transparent allusion to defiance of the Raj's colonial liquor yoke. "God did not make any people to be slaves or serfs. It is men that enslaved each other and the time has come for better things, both for the individual and for the races of the world. This struggle will go on until each people will be not only free to run their own affairs, but will be free from the domination of the drink traffic that is and always has been a denial of every principle of human liberty."[99]

This theme of prohibition-as-human-liberty spoke directly to Indian nationalism, and differentiated liberationist temperance advocates in the United States from their colonial counterparts from England. Indeed, CR and Indian nationalists were far happier to work with impartial American temperance advocates over the British AITA, whose loyalty to the crown was always cause for suspicion.[100] In fact, when CR was later thrown into a British jail, he entrusted leadership of the INC's Prohibition League of India and its journal to American Ruth Robinson, the local representative of the World's Woman's Christian Temperance Union.[101]

Before sailing off from Karachi and into retirement in upstate New York (Chapter 18), Pussyfoot gave one final prohibition speech outside of the Municipal Building, which culminated in a flag raising. As he later recalled,

> The flag to be raised was the Hindu National Flag—the emblem of India's defiance of the might of the British Raj. It was a rebel flag—a signal for the opening of the National Picketing campaign. When that banner went aloft, the national Hindu movement, pregnant with strife and turmoil, would be officially launched. It was a delicate situation.
>
> I looked out at those expectant faces and quickly made my decision. Regardless of consequences, I would not fail them. Up went the flag.

His American prohibitionist colleagues—most notably Ernest Cherrington, leader of the World League Against Alcoholism—fretted over the potential political fallout, especially among the British. Pussyfoot simply answered, "That flag was not just the Hindu National Flag; it was a dry flag and I will raise the dry flag in any spot on earth where the people want it."[102]

Pussyfoot's flag raising coincided with a new wave of nationalist agitation. When the British let pass a 1929 deadline for awarding India "dominion status" and greater self-rule within the British Commonwealth, the INC responded with a renewed movement for civil disobedience. The campaign began by focusing on the unjust British salt tax, which comprised only 8.2 percent of the Raj's revenue, but whose burden fell disproportionately on the poor.[103] In 1930 Gandhi himself led 78 followers on a 240-mile march from his ashram at Sabarmati to the coastal village of Dandi to make their own salt in defiance of the laws. His symbolic action sparked a coordinated nationwide civil disobedience campaign that resulted in some 60,000 being jailed without trial, beginning with Gandhi himself.

Less well known than Gandhi's Salt March was the INC's redoubled attack on the financially vital liquor trade, coordinated by the soon-to-be-imprisoned Rajagopalachari. The noncooperation movement of the 1930s included standard tactics of old-school temperance activism: pledges of individual abstinence, developing temperance propaganda, plays, cinema, and other diversions.[104] More importantly, the picketing of state liquor stores returned with a vengeance. Teams of nationalist volunteers found that simply standing near a liquor shop "with the National Flag in hand is enough to stop all the business" conducted there.[105] But it wasn't just the liquor shops that the nationalists targeted: picketers also protested the government tax-farm auctions, where the wealthy liquor men annually gathered to bid on government tenders for the right to collect the *abkari* revenue, perhaps bringing them face to face with the people's protests for the first time.[106]

As in the noncooperation campaigns of the 1920s, the antiliquor protests often bordered on harassment, and occasionally even turned violent, which the British authorities gleefully highlighted to discredit the Gandhian nonviolence movement. Picketers were more often the recipients of violence, regularly beaten and imprisoned by the British authorities.[107]

The picketing activities were tightly controlled by Rajagopalachari himself, who developed very specific instructions about who could picket, when, where, and how. To avoid even the suggestion of physical intimidation against would-be drinkers, Rajaji preferred the youngest, least athletic, and most "frail-bodied volunteers" to picket the liquor stores. "The people that gather to drink or the men in the employ of the venders could easily give a thorough beating to them," CR wrote. "We have limited the lads to such small numbers that they could be attacked and badly assaulted by the liquor-shop men even if they had been big sturdy soldiers instead of being boys."[108]

For months, the anti-drink campaign was waged with heroic dedication against the financial foundations of the British Raj. "For the last six months, no area is dry by popular voluntary effort, not only unaided by legal enactment, but in spite of every effort on the part of *abkari* officials, interested licensees, policemen with the thirst of repression in their throats, a Government sitting above, biting its lips in anger at the growing loss of prestige and the threatened loss of revenue," CR proclaimed. "In spite of all this, the people have shown unmistakable proof that they do not want these public houses trafficking in poison and distributing ruin by a complete boycott through unofficial organisation."[109]

In the battle of state versus society, Indian civil society seemed to be winning, both through the Salt March and the anti-drink campaign. Gandhi, Rajaji, and the leaders of the INC had been through this enough times to know that the British would not—or could not—let this challenge go unanswered. Arrest and imprisonment were daily possibilities. What would happen to the movement if the leadership was again thrown in jail?

"The common people must now learn not to wait for instruction or instigation from so-called political leaders," Rajaji wrote in November 1931. With pro-independence protesters being arrested left and right—and just weeks from being again imprisoned himself—he urged, "The Government may force us to hold our tongues, or suppress or sap the power of the press. But it cannot ask people to drink against their will. I appeal, therefore, to all castes to go on organizing themselves against drink, whatever may happen to Congress workers." The more the British tightened the screws, the more India would harden its resolve—not just for independence, but prohibition as well—until the Raj saw its authoritarian hand produced only resentment, not revenue. "A lorry load of terrorism cannot sell an ounce of liquor if only the people are calm and intelligent."[110]

Soon, upward of sixty thousand nationalist picketers, protesters, and even INC leaders had been imprisoned for their temperance nationalism. The Indian National Congress even began breaking down traditional Indian gender barriers to political activism by allowing women to join in the liquor-store pickets. The optics of white authorities roughing up local women and children created more headaches for the British authorities, who often doubled down on their brutality by proposing publicly whipping antiliquor picketers, and separating picketing children from their families and placing them in reform schools.[111] "Hundreds and thousands of women have in the past picketed liquor shops, suffered insults and assaults," Gandhi wrote. "It was all peaceful persuasion, and it had succeeded so remarkably that in some provinces the excise revenue was almost reduced to zero."[112]

Still in jail, in 1931, Gandhi agreed with the British viceroy, Lord Irwin, to end the civil disobedience campaign in exchange for the release of the thousands of political prisoners, and promises of renewed independence negotiations. All hopes were quickly dashed the following year by Irwin's hardline successor as viceroy, Lord Willingdon. Hoping to crush the nationalist movement, Willingdon despotically outlawed the Indian National Congress, throwing Gandhi, Rajaji, Jawaharlal Nehru, and the entire INC leadership back in jail, along with some eighty thousand other activists.[113]

If temperance had previously been a Trojan horse for Indian nationalism, with its leaders in prison and its political activities outlawed, the INC retreated back into that horse. While nationalist political agitation was illegal, temperance activism aimed at "social reformation" remained legal. To the British authorities, CR went to great lengths to underscore that his Prohibition League of India was a non-Congress, nonparty organization, even though its members were almost exclusively Indian nationalists. Still, he confided to his international temperance colleagues that "the work of the League, however, it must be confessed, is largely merged in the general Congress work."[114] Even as the INC leadership remained in prison, antiliquor activism remained a vital outlet for congress volunteers.

Meanwhile in London, Parliament debated making concessions to pacify the Indian tumult, even over the vocal objections of hardline, anti-Indian Conservatives like Winston Churchill. The resulting Government of India Act of 1935 devolved significant authority from the Raj to the federal provinces, to be governed by elected Indian representatives. Overcoming initial skepticism, by 1937, the again-legalized Indian National Congress agreed to cooperate, forming ministries in those provinces—Madras, Bombay, Bihar, and the United and Central Provinces—where they had won majorities. Significantly, *abkari* administration had been transferred to Indian control, giving Gandhi, Rajaji, and the INC the opportunity to make good on their long-standing prohibition promises.[115]

Suddenly, the congress had to contend with the revenue trap at the core of imperial alcohol politics: the *abkari* provided 31 percent of all revenues in Madras province, and 33 percent in Bombay—significant funds that could not be easily replaced.[116] "The Central Government must get its drug income and the Local Government must get its liquor revenue and municipal bodies cannot be permitted to exercise their discretion," CR had claimed. "The Madras Government, and so many other provincial administrations, have entangled their finances and their affairs in the meshes of a liquor revenue which is a third of the entire Government receipts."[117]

Prohibition would mean forgoing that money, which was crucial to education, sanitation, and government administration. "Indeed one Minister told me that if I would help him to raise the revenue needed to make up for the loss caused by the drop in the drink revenue, he would introduce prohibition at once," Gandhi wrote. "It is an open secret that the reform has been delayed simply for the sake of the revenue. In other words, the people have been tempted to drink for the sake of raising the revenue. The black history of the opium trade bears out the truth of this statement."[118]

Hard decisions had to be made between Gandhi's prohibitionist ideals and political expediency, grappling with the same issues of state finance, economic productivity, and individual liberty that prohibitionists have faced the world over. Still, despite the wide range of political and economic challenges facing India, Gandhi's very first charge to the new congress ministries was to "enforce immediate prohibition by making education self-supporting instead of paying for it from the liquor revenue."[119]

"With me [prohibition] is a creed," Gandhi resolutely claimed, "and I would, if I could, fulfill it at any cost."[120] In a meeting with victuallers who had much to lose from prohibition, Gandhi explained that "it has been a passion ever since my close contact with the Indian immigrants in South Africa and also with the South Africans" (Chapter 6). Thinking of his own inebriate son, Harilal, he continued, "I have seen with my own eyes the terrible scourge drink can be. It has ruined people morally, physically, economically and it has destroyed the sanctity and happiness of the home. My heart bleeds as I think of the disaster that comes in its wake and I have really pined for the immediate introduction of prohibition."[121]

But prohibition in India would face heated opposition, perhaps most pointedly articulated by His Grace, the archbishop of Bombay. (This was hardly surprising, since Christian missionaries had long sided with the imperial drink trade.) "I would invite the Archbishop to study the history of the excise administration," Gandhi wrote, highlighting the indefensibility of building the Raj's finances on the misery of the people. If the archbishop was truly a man of Christ, "Let him and his assistants and disciples unconditionally become total abstainers and help the noble cause of temperance. They will lighten the task of the law-giver and help to make of the abolition of liquor traffic the success that it deserves to be in this land where the public conscience, i.e., the conscience of the dumb millions, is undoubtedly in favour of the abolition."[122]

While *abkari* policy was being debated, the usual counterpoints to prohibitionism were provided by Parsi businessmen and legislators who did not share Gandhi's dry leanings.

"Drunkenness is bad, not drink," began one delegate. "And for the sake of a few who drink, why penalize the whole community? I take two or three glasses of sherry every day and I know hundreds of others who talk of prohibition but who do drink and will do so in spite of prohibition."

"I do not drink, nor am I dealer in drinks. But this policy will ruin thousands, and I want you to realize your error," added a second delegate.

"But why should others regulate my life?" protested a third, echoing John Stuart Mill's rote liberty-to-drink argument (Chapter 5). "I tell you, although, I do not drink, if someone came and told me I might not drink, he would make my blood boil."

A final delegate—the influential Parsi businessman and legislator Sir Homi Mody—was even more blunt: "We do not believe in prohibition. Why do you tempt us to break the law? Drink has become part of our social habit, our daily life, and we want to drink."

Gandhi listened openly to their concerns and answered them thoughtfully. "Individual liberty is allowed to man only to a certain extent. He cannot forget that he is a social being, and his individual liberty has to be curtailed at every step," he argued. To become successful businessmen, Gandhi reminded them, each of these Parsi men had given up their traditional culture, manners, customs, and dress. But their drinking habits they couldn't change? "You may plead your weakness, but for heaven's sake don't advance the plea of individual liberty. There you have given away the whole case. You have sacrificed much for India, sacrifice this bad habit too."[123]

Sacrifice was what Gandhi asked, in order to achieve independence not only from the British, but from the bottle, too. But now that prohibition was at hand, Gandhi proposed a different sacrifice in exchange for the forgone *abkari* revenues: funding for the British military that subjugated the Indian people as much as the British liquor traffic.[124] Of course, though, military and defense policy strictly remained the purview of the British.

As for prohibition putting people out of work, Gandhi claimed, "What the Governments are in reality doing is not prohibiting drink but they are closing liquor shops which are absolutely under Government control. The shop-owners have no statutory protection save what they get from year to year. Every owner of a liquor shop knows that his license may not be renewed next year." And so the INC would simply not be renewing drink licenses in the interest of the public good.[125]

After much consideration and debate—though without any sort of popular referendum—the INC governments moved forward with *abkari* and finance reform that would have the practical effect of prohibition. The governments would use their legal discretion to gradually stop issuing liquor licenses. Ample accommodations and exceptions would be granted for religious or medicinal uses of alcohol. Excise ministers would be replaced by reliable, temperate nationalists, while Prohibition League volunteers would keep a watchful eye to ensure compliance by district police and magistrates. The budgetary shortfall would be made up with sales taxes and a 10 percent tax on property.[126]

"Well Done Bombay!" was the title of the article Gandhi wrote after the reform's adoption, ushering in prohibition on August 1, 1939. He recounted how especially the "labourers, who were the chief persons to benefit by the measure and who were at the same time the most affected by prohibition, attended in their thousands with their wives." Still, he acknowledged the policy did not meet with universal approval. Parsi liquor-sellers grumbled at the disappearance of their profits. Abstemious Muslims protested that they were now subject to new burdens of a property tax: since they didn't drink before, they didn't pay *abkari* taxes. Prohibition was not the end of the fight either: while closing the liquor shops removed the drinker's temptation, workers needed healthy alternatives for relaxation, support, and rehabilitation. Still, Gandhi claimed, "The glory of the effort in Bombay will be reflected not only throughout the province but it will be reflected all over India."[127]

India's glorious prohibition was not to last, thwarted by the British Empire's courts. In 1940, four Indians were arrested and tried for manufacturing and selling illicit liquor. The Bombay High Court acquitted them on the grounds that the amended *Abkari* Act deals only with the licensing and collection of revenue on an existing trade, rather than being a blanket prohibition of that trade. The liquor traffic could not legally be outlawed, the court surmised, because it would infringe upon the British government's retained legal right to regulate international trade and the trade between the various Indian federal states.[128] Upheld on appeal, the British ruling completely unmade the nationalists' prohibition.

By then, the Indian National Congress's experiment with responsible government in India had come to a close anyway. The year 1939 saw the outbreak of World War II, which drew in India as part of the British Empire, even over the protests of Indian nationalists. Now on a war footing, the British Raj reasserted its dominance over domestic as well as external affairs. In response, Gandhi initiated the Quit India movement that resulted in the arrest of the INC leadership and the imprisonment of Mohandas and Kasturba Gandhi at the Aga Khan Palace in Poona for the duration of the war.

Only in 1944, with the conclusion of the war in sight, was Gandhi released, along with one hundred thousand other nationalist political prisoners. Decolonization was finally at hand. Gandhi was flexible on many questions. He preferred that the subcontinent remain united in independence, rather than being divided into a Hindu-dominated India and a Muslim-dominated Pakistan, even as the massive bloodletting of partition confirmed his worst fears.

Gandhi, however, was less flexible when it came to the prohibition of the liquor trade. India won its independence in 1947, and Article 47 of its first constitution declared, "The state shall endeavour to bring about prohibition of the consumption except for medical purpose of intoxicating drinks and of drugs which are injurious to health." Still, this proved to be more symbolic rather than practical: enforcing prohibition was a low priority for India's first prime minister, Jawaharlal Nehru, who claimed that "a too rapid implementation of the Prohibition policy all over the country would lead to considerable difficulties."[129]

Administration of the liquor traffic was ceded to the federal states, with varying degrees of compliance. Some states continued the old British traditions of overreliance on the *abkari*, comprising up to a quarter of state revenues. Today, only Gandhi's home state of Gujarat retains prohibition, intended to limit liquor trafficking rather than drinking itself.[130]

By stigmatizing drinking as a foreign habit and a British imposition, abstinence became synonymous with patriotism, and a point of agreement between Hindus and Muslims. Uniting together to starve the powerful British Raj of liquor revenues was crucial to the noncooperation movement. Meanwhile, the idea of Indian high-minded abstinence and purity, superior to the corrupting influence of the British, became interwoven with India's postcolonial identity.[131] Temperance and prohibition were general features of resistance to European imperialism the world over, though perhaps nowhere was it as explicit as in Gandhi's movement for an India free from British alco-subjugation.

Pussyfoot's Postscript

Mahatma Gandhi lived long enough to see an India free, but not an India dry. On January 30, 1948—a year before independent India's new constitution was ratified—the great leader was gunned down by a right-wing nationalist assassin.

Gandhi's American admirer Pussyfoot Johnson preceded him in death by two years, passing in far more peaceful circumstances on his farmstead in upstate New York. Yet even as they both lived and struggled in their antiliquor agitation, and even as their victories seemed anything but assured, Johnson penned a loving prohibitionist eulogy to Gandhi, hidden for generations in the archives.

"Probably no man in history has caused so great a reduction in the consumption of liquor," began Pussyfoot. "It was all accomplished through his own personal influence, for probably no man in modern times has exercised such influence as has this humble Indian lawyer."[132]

Yet how could this diminutive, soft-spoken man succeed where so many others had failed? "His complete renunciation of all that is born of greed, his suffering in

Indian and South African jails, with no reproach for his enemies, his complete ab-
negation of self—these are the things that have made the Mahatma the most powerful man on earth today. Scourging, beatings, revilings, aches and pains, have only
added to his influence." By highlighting the inappropriateness of the imperial state
benefiting from the moral and economic subjugation of the people, by steadfast resistance to the state's exploitations, and by meeting the scorn and brutality of state
power with love and benevolence, the little man from Gujarat took on the greatest
empire on earth, and won.

Invoking the poetry of William Blake, Pussyfoot concluded,

"A tear is an intellectual thing,
And a sigh is the sword of an angel King.
And the bitter groan of a martyrs woe
Is an arrow from the Almightys bow.

"So Mohandas Kamarchand Gandhi challenged the greed of the world and laid it
low in the estimation of men."[133]

8

The Dry Man of Europe—Ottoman Prohibition against British Domination

Jerusalem, British Mandatory Palestine: Wednesday, October 6, 1926

Whether as conquerors or tourists, European Christians have long traveled to the Middle East to be transported back in time. They gaze upon the excavated wonders of the ancient world, visit sites described in Testaments both Old and New, and meet tradespeople doing the same work as their ancestors generations before. So it was with that nostalgia for antiquity that the globetrotting prohibitionist William E. "Pussyfoot" Johnson (Chapters 4, 5, 7, 14–18) arrived in Palestine in 1926.

"Of the carnival that stirs our hectic lives, the East knows nothing and cares nothing. It squats, cross-legged and serene, dreaming dreams, studying philosophy, milling peacefully over metaphysical problems, seeking the eternal meaning of things," he wrote, in terms most orientalizing. "That is the East where religions are cradled. All the great religions of this world have been conceived and born in Asia, and Jerusalem became the holy ground of Islam, the Wailing Place of the Jews and a whole bewildering treasure house of places and things sacred to the memory of Our Lord."

"So I went up to Jerusalem."[1]

Having twice circumnavigated the globe in promoting the temperance cause, Johnson was no stranger to the former Ottoman lands. He was a frequent visitor to the bustling bazaars of Cairo to the south and the winding streets of Istanbul in the north. This, however, was his first visit to the Holy Land, which became a British protectorate under a mandate of the League of Nations following World War I. Meant to prepare the protected peoples and territories for eventual independence, mandate rule amounted to little more than imperialism lite.[2]

Yet—as he dusted off his shoes and disembarked from his train at the terminus of the Jaffa-Jerusalem Railway—the very first thing Johnson saw of the Holy City and its ancient traditions was . . . a saloon. "The British Mandate authorities, diligently bent upon uplifting the people under their care," he sarcastically wrote, "had established a barroom in every important railway station in Palestine. So it was made convenient for a pilgrim to step from the train directly into a saloon in Jerusalem."[3]

Under the rule of the last effective Ottoman sultan, Abdul Hamid II—rightly denigrated as "Abdul the Damned" for his heavy-handed suppression of dissent and the massacre of Armenians and Assyrians—there were some twenty-five saloons operating in Jerusalem. "With his evil hand removed from control, however," Pussyfoot wrote, "the Mandate at once proceeded to remedy this condition and had done so well by October 6, 1926, when I arrived, that there were 300 saloons flourishing in Palestine!" Only one was run by a self-professed Muslim; the overwhelming majority were owned and operated by Christians and Jews—many newly arrived from Europe—though their drunken clientele did not comport so neatly along denominational lines.

Over the following weeks, in his usual way, Pussyfoot underscored the hypocrisy of "Christian" occupiers foisting drunkenness and debauchery on a native population that was both religiously and culturally opposed to it. He began by seeking out those he thought shared his antipathy for the colonial liquor traffic. In no time, he located the Jerusalem chapter of the World's Woman's Christian Temperance Union (Chapter 13)—a normally quiet group of some forty women, mostly American missionaries and teachers—who shared Pussyfoot's dismay about the sudden increase of both alcoholism and crime that arrived with the British and their saloons. After all, the British Mandate's own statistics provided to the League of Nations showed a near-doubling of crime: from 11,098 criminal cases handled by the police in 1921 to 19,701 cases in 1925, much of it in the vicinity of the European saloons.

That's when Lady Annie Plumer—wife of the viscount Herbert Plumer, Britain's High Commissioner for Palestine—stepped in. Unceremoniously declaring that "'Pussyfoot' Johnson has already made three speeches in Jerusalem, and that is enough," she forbade the WCTU from meeting at the local Young Women's Christian Association (YWCA). She was confident that was enough to quell any dry criticism of the colonial occupation.

Instead, such indignant, imperial heavy-handedness only energized women's activism in Palestine. The WCTU simply moved from the YWCA to the local YMCA, where Lady Plumer had no sway. "At the next regular meeting some sharp things were said about the Mandate authorities turning practically all of the railway stations into whisky holes and some remarks were made about the dismal fact that the first thing that a pilgrim sees on his arrival at Jerusalem was a barroom. And then some of the ladies felt that it was not just the right thing for the British Mandatory to increase the number of liquor shops by 1200 per cent."[4]

But it wasn't just foreign teachers who were incensed—nor the nonpartisan, transnational League of Nations Union, calling for the suppression of liquor and opium traders—but the local populations, too.[5] In the neither/nor world of Mandate imperialism, the Muslim population of Palestine and Transjordania had only limited political representation, in the form of the Grand Mufti: the famed Arab nationalist Haj Emin al-Husseini.[6] As it turns out, a number of Europeans had petitioned to open liquor shops in his semi-independent Transjordan province, so he summoned the great American prohibitionist Pussyfoot to discuss what to do about it. In turn, he sent Pussyfoot to Arif Bey al-Arif, effectively the secretary of state for Transjordania.[7]

With his letter of introduction from al-Husseini in hand, the American was welcomed by al-Arif with open arms. Together, the two decided to send messengers to Bedouin chieftains across the Arabian Peninsula for a council of war about the liquor question.

"From every direction those picturesque nomads came riding into Amman. They came on fine, desert-bred horses, their white robes fluttering as they galloped briskly along, rifles swinging beside their saddles," Pussyfoot recalled. "It was a momentous conference for them. Hatred for intoxicants is imbedded deeply within them by their religion, which proscribes liquor so stringently that, as the Grand Mufti explained to me, if a Moslem spilled, even accidentally, a single drop of alcohol on his clothing he is obligated to burn the desecrated cloth."

The Bedouin council was enthusiastic for a blanket prohibition law. Ever the realist, Johnson counseled them that the temptation for liquor profits was so powerful that British High Commissioner Plumer was sure to veto outright prohibition. Such a veto would effectively declare open season for the European liquor traffickers. Noting that Mandate law empowered municipal councils to issue liquor licenses in the cities, while the governor handled the outlying districts, Pussyfoot instead proposed a high-license law. By setting the cost of the liquor licenses so high that only Europeans could afford it, they could at least discourage their fellow Arabs from engaging in the deplorable trade, while all license revenues would remain in Transjordania to benefit the common good. Pussyfoot's compromise was ultimately agreeable to both the Bedouin war council and the British overlords. Still, it underscored how, in the Middle East as throughout the colonized world, temperance provided a bulwark against alco-imperialism.[8] "We in America . . . find it difficult to visualize what the Moslems see every day of their lives," Pussyfoot explained for his American readers. Throughout the Middle East, "every brothel, every gambling den and every rotten dump in the whole country has been and is being operated by someone who classes himself as a 'Christian' . . . and so these social cesspools have come to be pointed out as 'Christian Institutions.'"[9]

Pussyfoot asked his audience to set aside their religious stereotypes for a moment and consider what it would be like if the roles of exploiter and exploited were reversed. "Suppose that we found that practically every saloon, gambling joint, brothel and every rotten old dump in New York City was operated by a Moslem? What would we then say about the Moslem religion? Would we not rend the atmosphere with maledictions and ejaculations about the Mohammedan iniquity, and properly so." This was doubly the case for the well-chronicled abuses of the corrupt Ottoman tax-farm system, where the privilege of tax collection was sold at auction—primarily to Greeks and Armenians. "It was these so-called 'Christians' who did practically all of this dirty work. We forget that the chief sufferers of this miserable system were the Turkish people themselves."[10] The same was true of the liquor trade.

"In our smug satisfaction with ourselves, we do not or will not attempt to look at these things from the standpoint of the other fellow."[11]

A persistent inability to grasp the politics and the people of the Ottoman Empire has led generation after generation of Westerners to rely on crude stereotypes and cultural cutouts. Perhaps nowhere is that more true than regarding the history of the collapse and dismemberment of the sultan's empire following the First World War, and the rise of a modern, secular Republic of Turkey under Mustafa Kemal Atatürk. As it fundamentally regards the question of who should profit—us or them?— the liquor traffic accentuates the social, political, and economic complexities of an Ottoman Empire groaning under the weight of European colonization and capitulations. And as with oppressed communities in Asia, Africa, Europe, and North America, prohibitionism would be an important means of asserting national sovereignty and independence.

Myth and Reality in the Ottoman Empire

Wait . . . a chapter on the Ottoman Empire in a book on the global history of prohibition? Certainly this has to be the easiest, most straightforward chapter imaginable. The Ottoman Empire was a Muslim caliphate, and Islam strictly prohibits alcohol, so it has got to be an open-and-shut case. Right?

As it turns out, the Muslim position on alcohol and the politics of prohibition are both far more complicated and interesting than the conventional two-dimensional portrayals. For one, the Islamic world gave us both the word "alcohol"—al-kuhul in Arabic—and the science of distillation, pioneered by the ninth-century Arab chemist/philosopher/polymath al-Kindi.[12] For another, the Quran contains neither an explicit prohibition against drinking nor any mention of alcohol at all. Instead, it uses the term khamr—that which causes mental confusion—which is often translated in terms of wine or intoxication. The Quran's five most relevant ayas, or verses, dealing with khamr only suggest (albeit strongly) avoiding such befuddlement to focus on meditation and prayerfulness.

Far clearer condemnations against intoxication come from the teachings of the Hadith, which is attributed to the Prophet Muhammad, whereas the Quran itself is the word of God. Plus, since Islam is a diverse tradition with no hierarchy of religious authority, a wide variety of interpretations of the alcohol question across the Muslim world exist even today, from draconian prohibition in Saudi Arabia to drinking as a matter of personal choice in Turkey.[13]

Still, the norm among Muslim-majority countries has been abstinence from consuming alcohol. This makes for an interesting parallel with other non-European communities, from Africa (Chapters 3 and 6), India (Chapter 7), the Philippines (Chapter 15), and North America (Chapters 9–10), that likewise were forced to grapple with the liquor traffic as a tool of European imperial subjugation. So, when it came to British portrayals of Ottoman drinking, we should not be surprised find the same colonial depictions and narratives. "In the modern society of the Moslemic East," wrote famed traveler and Turkologist Ármin Vámbéry in 1906, "I have found that all consumers of spirituous drink are drunkards—i.e., that they go on drinking until they are quite intoxicated—also that *delirium tremens potatorum* was far more common amongst the Moslem Princes and grandees than with us in Europe."[14]

By the late nineteenth century, it was fashionable to refer to the Ottoman Empire simply as "the sick man of Europe." As a political entity, it was certainly a relic of a bygone world. Named for Osman—the thirteenth-century Turkish warrior-king whose descendants toppled Constantinople in 1453, and with it, the Byzantine Empire—the Ottoman Empire reached its peak in the sixteenth century: stretching from the Persian Gulf and the Arabian Peninsula westward to Egypt and the Mediterranean coast, northward through Palestine and Anatolia, stabbing north-westward through the Balkans toward Vienna.

But that was long ago.

The empire was an incoherent mess in every way. "The multinational, multi-lingual empire was a mosaic of peoples who did not mix," wrote historian David Fromkin. Beyond European stereotypes about "Turks" and "Arabs" lay a vast diversity of groups that had little in common with one another. In the capital of Istanbul—as in towns throughout the empire—Armenians, Jews, Greeks, and other minorities lived in cloistered, self-governing communities, speaking their own languages, largely isolated from the broader population. Nearly a quarter of the people of the Ottoman theocracy were non-Muslim.[15]

Administratively, the empire was run through a patchwork of autonomous confessional communities, known as *millets*, which mediated between the individual and the state: enforcing public order, regulating legal disputes, registering births and deaths. "All Ottoman subjects owed loyalty to the sultan, and Christians and Jews were required to pay special state taxes that Muslims were able to avoid," explains historian Charles King, "but in general people were born, wed, and died according to legal codes that were unique to their specific religious category."[16] This system of confessional self-rule extended to regulating alcohol: the Ottoman government required only a license and a tax paid on the manufacture of alcoholic beverages; aside from during the fast of Ramadan, there were no penalties for alcohol consumption.[17] For all of the nineteenth-century European handwringing and demands to "protect" various Christian communities, for centuries the Greek, Armenian, Turkish, and Jewish populations of the Ottoman Empire lived relatively peaceful (if self-contained) lives.[18]

Nominally, it was the sultan—both religious caliph and unquestioned autocrat—who gave coherence to this hodgepodge empire. But even this supreme authority was hardly consistent, especially regarding alcohol. On the one hand, Suleiman I ("The Magnificent," r. 1520–1566) prohibited wine-drinking among Muslims, and burned merchant ships laden with wine en route to Istanbul. Sultans Ahmed I (r. 1604–1617), Murad IV (r. 1623–1640), and Selim III (r. 1789–1807) all banned the sale of wine and liquor, often under harsh—but rarely followed—penalties.[19] On the other hand, Mahmud II (r. 1808–1839) reportedly died of *delirium tremens*, while the young leaders of the Tanzimat period of modernizing social reform (1839–1876)—Ali, Fuad, and Midhat Pasha—all drank copious amounts of booze.[20]

Other heavy drinkers included the (predominantly Turkish) soldiers stationed in the military garrisons scattered across the largely Arab territories from the Mediterranean coast to the Middle East and Arabian Peninsula, who were charged with maintaining tranquility throughout the empire.[21] Beyond those military outposts, most political power was diffused among local tribes, clans, sects, and cities, making centralized Ottoman authority more myth than reality. Even on the eve of World War I, the central government collected only 5 percent of taxes; the other 95 percent was farmed out to individual tax farmers—whose main interest was maximizing their own personal profits at the expense of the peasantry—like the corrupt liquor tax-farm systems in Imperial Russia (Chapter 2) and British India (Chapter 7).[22]

The Ottoman Empire was an empire that itself had been colonized by other empires. The British occupied and administered Cyprus beginning in 1878, and Egypt in 1882, to go along with many of the sheikdoms along the Persian Gulf. Since 1864, Lebanon was a separate province led by a Christian military governor, which could only act in consultation with six European powers. Imperial Russia claimed the right to protect the Orthodox communities within the Ottoman Empire; France claimed the same for Catholics. More importantly, since the Sublime Porte (the Ottoman government) defaulted on its debts in 1875, the administration of the empire's finances was taken over by the Ottoman Public Debt Administration (OPDA), consisting of British, French, German, Italian, Austrian, and Turkish representatives, led by Sir Edgar Vincent, the future Lord D'Abernon (Chapter 5). This foreign council controlled a quarter of Ottoman revenues, with exclusive authority over stamp duties, salt, and the liquor trade.[23] The tax on domestic alcoholic beverages was set at 15 percent, whereas duties on imported alcohol were only half that, putting the empire's storied winemakers at a competitive disadvantage, especially relative to the Europeans who imported significant amounts of alcohol for sale across the Ottoman territory.[24]

Most humiliating of all were the so-called capitulations: concessions that gave European traders a privileged economic position above Ottoman law. No Turkish policeman, for example, could enter the premises of a European-owned store or saloon without the permission of the latter's consulate, vastly complicating law enforcement. In all these ways, the liquor question in the Ottoman Empire was inexorably intertwined with questions of colonization and nationalism.

Stretching back to antiquity, Ottoman lands from Anatolia to Greece and the Balkans were famous for their bountiful vineyards and winemaking, traditions that continued even after subsequent generations adopted Islam. Indeed, when European vineyards were decimated by phylloxera, causing the Great French Wine Blight of the 1850s and '60s, it was Turkey that took up the slack, with vineyards in the Aydın region of southwestern Anatolia expanding tenfold—often planted by French and German settlers. In the late nineteenth and early twentieth centuries, grapes, wine, and raisins were Turkey's leading export items: Turkish vine-growers usually sold the grapes and raisins, Christian growers made the wine.[25]

Of course, the wine tax-farm was a vital source of both revenue for the state and profit for the tax farmer. As early as the seventeenth century, the superintendent of wine (*hamr emini*) was a rich and powerful man, with his own private army of a hundred armed men. The wine tax-farm in Istanbul was worth seventy thousand *kuruş* alone. As with the vodka tax-farm in Russia (Chapter 2), wine dealers in the Ottoman Empire paid off not only the superintendent, but also gave kickbacks to local governors, politicians, and police in order to keep plying their trade.[26] By blurring the distinction between public and private—mixing the collection of necessary government revenues with the personal profits of the tax farmer— such antiquated tax-farm schemes the world over have been breeding grounds for corruption.[27]

In February 1881 Edmond du Temple—the French vice-consul in the Turkish city of Bursa—reported on the Ottoman liquor trade, explaining that the pomace (or marc) left over after pressing grapes for wine is often used to distill a grappa-like liquor called *rakı*, "flavored with anise and resin, which is consumed on a wide scale. The inhabitants drink this liquor as an *apéritif*, and digestive aide. For them," du Temple reported back to Paris, "*rakı* takes the place of the various liquors used in France, for which will never be able to provide serious competition here."[28]

As far as government revenue was concerned, du Temple explained, "Each year, the government sells, at set prices, the vineyard tithe (*la dîme*). It would obviously have been desirable to give here the sale price for each locality; however, the grape tithe is generally sold together with the wheat tithe, so that it is almost impossible to determine the amount of tax levied by the government on grapes. Each year the government fixes a price for the *oke* (1.3 kg, 2.8 lbs) of grapes, which serves as a basis for levying taxes."

Such difficulty in estimating liquor revenues was compounded further at the next step of the process, where the winemakers and wine merchants of Bursa "had formed a corporation, composed mainly of Greeks." To hold the wine and bottle it for sale, as du Temple described it, they had transformed the ancient baths of the old city into massive vats, "which were well-suited for this industry."[29]

Non-Muslims also overwhelmingly controlled the retail alcohol trade: the saloons, beer halls, and cafés. The tavern-owners of Istanbul had their own trade association as far back as the seventeenth century, which the Ottoman authorities largely left alone, so long as they did not sell to Muslim customers and dutifully paid the requisite tavern licenses, which included a tax on prostitution.[30] A survey of the Sultan's capital of Istanbul in 1829 found that each and every one of the 554 taverns was owned and operated by Greeks, Armenians, or Jews—and all within the non-Muslim districts.[31] When American sociologist Clarence Johnson conducted a similar survey a century later in 1922, he found the same geography of drinking—with most of the "disreputable places" to be found in the non-Muslim Galata and Pera districts. Only now, there were far more of them. Of the 1,413 restaurants, cafés, beer halls, and wholesale liquor stores Johnson surveyed, 1,169 were Greek, 57 Armenian, 44 Russian, and 17 Jewish. Only 97 were Turkish-owned.[32]

The takeaway here is that while Ottoman attitudes toward alcohol were far more lax than what we might think based on crude stereotypes of Islam. Moreover, the liquor question was a potential wedge issue within the empire: a point of stark disagreement between Turks and Arabs, Muslims and Christians, and native inhabitants and outside colonizers. Not surprisingly, then, with the coming of the Great War and the eventual cleaving up of the empire, the question of prohibition became wrapped up in the broader geopolitics of war in Asia Minor.

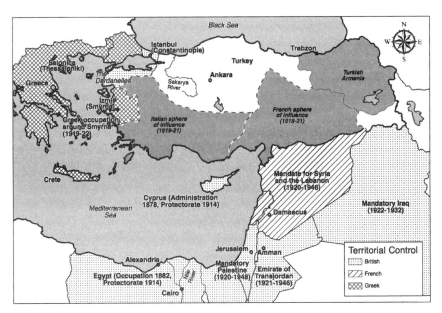

Figure 8.1 Map of the Dismemberment of the Ottoman Empire and Occupation of Turkey Following World War I.

Reform, War, and Collapse

Political liberalization in the Ottoman Empire—as with the European empires—proceeded in fits and starts, often in response to defeats in war. Following uprisings in Bulgaria in 1876—and their brutal suppression—the empire had nominally become a constitutional monarchy, but it lasted only fourteen months before Sultan Abdul "the Damned" Hamid II dissolved the parliament and restored his absolute rule. Fearful of infiltration by the sultan's secret police, reformist and radical political groups were forced underground.

A disastrous war with Russia in 1877–1878 led to further capitulations to the Europeans. Romania, Serbia, and Montenegro were cleaved out of the empire as sovereign states, while the Austro-Hungarians unilaterally occupied the Ottoman Empire's Balkan territories of Bosnia-Herzegovina and Novi Pazar. Such humiliations only increased nationalist opposition to the outdated sultanate.

Political dissent was effectively squashed in Istanbul, as throughout the empire, perhaps with the exception of Salonica: present-day Thessaloniki, the second-largest city in Greece. Back in the 1870s, it was a bustling Macedonian port town on the empire's unsettled Balkan frontier, and home to the Third Ottoman Army. One underground liberal opposition group had especially deep roots in Salonica: the Committee of Union and Progress (CUP), later known as the Young Turkey Party. Its supporters were known as "Young Turks." Comprising modernizing reformers, the CUP wanted to replace the absolute monarchy of the sultan with a representative, constitutional government.

In 1908, one junior army officer named Enver was summoned to Istanbul from his post in Salonica. Fearing that his CUP political activism had been discovered by the sultan's secret police, Enver instead fled into the hills. More spooked officers followed suit, taking their troops, guns, and ammunition with them. When the sultan sent the army in to quell the mutiny, the troops instead joined the growing Young Turk rebellion. Seizing control of Salonica, they telegraphed and coordinated with CUP cells across the empire. Having lost control of his army, in July 1908, Abdul "the Damned" abdicated his throne in favor of his brother and announced the restoration of the 1876 constitution. With it came multiparty politics and elections to the General Assembly.

The Young Turks sought to empower the elected lower house of parliament—the Chamber of Deputies—at the expense of the Senate, whose members were appointed by the sultan. The CUP promoted industrialization, modernization, and secularization of both the legal and education systems. In wriggling out from under the thumb of foreign domination, the Young Turks passed a prohibition on the importation of foreign alcoholic beverages, which was quickly scuttled by the OPDA as conflicting too much with European economic interests.[33]

But the empire's democratic experiment faced unbelievable external challenges. Capitalizing on the Ottoman disorder of 1908, the Austro-Hungarian Empire formally annexed Bosnia and Herzegovina. In 1910, Albania revolted. In 1911, the Italians invaded, defeated, and annexed Libya. In 1912–1913, the Balkan League of Bulgaria, Greece, Montenegro, and Serbia defeated the Ottomans in a series of Balkan Wars, seizing most of the Ottoman Empire's remaining European territories. Meanwhile, Istanbul was roiled by a series of coups, failed coups, and countercoups between rival parties and factions. In the 1913 coup, the CUP took control of the government, and Enver—now with the honorific title "Pasha" (akin to "Lord" in British English)—took over the war ministry. Cementing himself as the most important government official on the eve of World War I, he married the niece of the figurehead sultan, formally entering the royal family.

Fearful that the European predators would continue to carve up their empire until nothing was left, the CUP was desperate to find any ally willing to help protect and guarantee their rule. Enver Pasha ultimately found that ally in a very reluctant Germany.[34]

The assassination of Austrian archduke Franz Ferdinand in July 1914 and the escalations to war meant that the Germans and Austro-Hungarians were suddenly in the market for allies, too. Believing—as almost everyone did—that the war would be a quick and inconsequential one, Istanbul initially hoped to sit this one out. However, while the European powers were distracted, in September 1914 the Ottoman government unilaterally renounced all European capitulations and privileges, including those granted to Germany. In an extraordinary move, the German and Austrian ambassadors joined with their wartime enemies—the British, French, and Russians—in formal protest. Privately, however, the Germans and Austrians confided that they wouldn't press the issue. At the same time, the British, French, and Russian ambassadors likewise acquiesced, so long as Istanbul remained neutral. By October, all foreigners were made subject to Turkish laws and courts, and once-exempted foreign imports and trades were now taxed.[35]

In November 1914, to keep open the vital Mediterranean–Black Sea transit route with their allies in Russia, British warships bombarded the Turks' outer defenses of the Dardanelles. Believing the Turks were an inconsequential foe, this decision by First Lord of the Admiralty Winston Churchill very casually drew both sides into an expanded Middle Eastern theater of World War I.

As supreme commander of the armed forces, Enver Pasha styled himself as a national hero. His more astute German allies rightly saw him as an incompetent buffoon. Enver Pasha concocted a ridiculous military plan to cross the Caucasus Mountains, smash Russia's army, then pivot across the vast, harsh, and empty steppes of Central Asia, and scale the mountains into Afghanistan en route to conquering British India. It didn't seem to matter that his force would be outmanned and outgunned at every turn—and without any infrastructure, every bullet, shell, and ration would have to be transported those thousands of miles by camel.

Still, in December 1914, the disorganized Third Army embarked on this ambitious scheme by scaling the Caucasus—in the depth of winter—only to be immediately slaughtered by the Russians waiting on the other side. Of the one hundred thousand soldiers who attacked, eighty-six thousand never returned. A German military attaché described the decimation of their allies as "a disaster which for rapidity and completeness is without parallel in military history."[36]

Rather than take ownership of his disastrous military performance, Enver Pasha instead blamed defeat on the region's Christian Armenian population for supposedly siding with the Russians. Soon thereafter—in February 1915—Enver and the CUP ordered the mass deportation of Armenians from their eastern Anatolian homeland, fearing it would be the next province of the empire to secede. Within months, the deportations and ethnic cleansing gave way to the wholesale genocide of Armenians across the empire, planned and executed by nationalists within the CUP. By 1917, between eight hundred thousand and one and a half million Ottoman Armenians had been mercilessly killed.[37] And not just Armenians, but the ethnic cleansing of Christian Greeks and Assyrians, the internal deportation of Kurds, and the resettling of Muslim refugees from the Balkan Wars were all part of a nationalist effort to Islamize and homogenize the Turkish population and economy.[38]

The military situation was little better in the south, where the Ottoman Fourth Army was decimated in a failed attack on the Suez Canal. Even worse, having conscripted both the country's men and their pack animals, the bountiful harvests of 1914 and 1915 were left to rot in the fields, leading to widespread food shortages and famine. In a country with virtually no industry, agricultural exports dropped by three-quarters, and imports dropped 89 percent. With no trade to tax, the Porte did what the ill-fated tsarist empire did to pay its massive war debts (Chapter 2): it just printed more liras, which in turn put the economy in a hyperinflationary spiral. In short order, the war had smashed the Ottoman economy and society, and the clueless Young Turk government was powerless to fix it.[39]

The lone Ottoman bright spot (if one can call it that) came in 1915 when the British and French invaded the Gallipoli Peninsula, on the west bank of the strategically vital Dardanelles Strait. The swift victory the Allies had hoped for—which would clear the way for Allied invasion and occupation of the capital of Istanbul—instead bogged down into trench warfare as bloody as any seen in France. After nine months and hundreds of thousands of casualties on both sides, the British evacuated. The defensive, tactical genius of the Ottoman lieutenant colonel Mustafa Kemal raised him to the level of Turkish national hero. In Britain, Winston Churchill became the scapegoat for the piles of casualties for no discernible gain.

By the third year, the Great War had become less of a battle and more of a contest for political survival among all of the European empires. Somehow, the Ottoman Empire wasn't the first to collapse: in February 1917 Tsar Nicholas II was deposed by his mutinying armies. The Bolshevik seizure of power in October of that year—and the grueling, multisided civil war that followed—not only bought the Ottoman government some breathing space, but also flooded Istanbul with refugees.[40]

In 1918, with losses piling up on the Balkan front; an all-out Arab revolt in the south; British armies capturing Baghdad, Jerusalem, and Damascus; and an economic catastrophe on the home front, the Ottoman leadership conceded the war was unwinnable. On October 30, 1918, they inked the Armistice of Mudros, with a British Empire that was equally exhausted and desperate for peace. Little did they know that the British already had secret plans with the French to carve up the Ottoman Empire between them. By the terms of the secret Sykes-Picot Agreement, the French would get Lebanon, Syria, southeastern Turkey, and northern Iraq, and the British would take Mesopotamia, Jordan, and Palestine under mandate of the League of Nations.

The armistice was far less generous than the Turkish leadership told their beleaguered people. All Ottoman military forces were to be demobilized, surrendering to the Allies all forts and military garrisons, as well as all ports and railways. If that wasn't galling enough, the Ottoman leadership ceded to the Allies the right to occupy any Ottoman territory "in case of disorder," which the Europeans interpreted as carte blanche to do whatever they pleased. The British and Greeks occupied vast swaths of Anatolia itself, especially where they could project naval power along the Mediterranean, Bosporus, and Black Sea coastlines. In November 1918 the British occupied Istanbul, effectively holding both the sultan and his government hostage. And as elsewhere throughout the colonial world, where the British came, they brought the liquor traffic as part of their toolbox of imperial domination.

For Turkish nationalists—including the war hero Mustafa Kemal—it was too great a humiliation to bear.

The Strange Case of Kemal Atatürk

Today, Mustafa Kemal Atatürk is hailed both as one of the great leaders in modern world history and one of the drunkest. His greatness was a product of both his battlefield prowess and his nationalist political leadership in casting off the yoke of European imperialism and forging a modern, independent, secular Turkish state. While Atatürk's personal alcoholism is well documented, his patronage of prohibition as a tool of anti-imperialism is less well known. As is often the case with great leaders, their personal history becomes intimately intertwined with their country's history.

Well before he was given the honorific title *Atatürk*, or "Father of the Turkish People," he was simply known as Mustafa: a shy, well-loved, but proud boy, born to a middle-class Turkish family in Salonica (Thessaloniki) in 1881.[41] In school, his mathematics teacher gave him the additional name *Kemal*—"maturity" or "perfection" on account of his capabilities—to differentiate him from another Mustafa in the class.[42] Smitten by the regimentation and uniforms of the army officers of the Salonica garrison, Mustafa Kemal enrolled in military prep school. Upon matriculating from the prestigious Ottoman War Academy in Istanbul in 1902, he entered the Imperial Military Staff College to become an officer. By the time he was assigned to the Fifth Army in Damascus at the rank of staff captain in 1905, he already had thirteen years of military training under his belt.

According to Atatürk biographers—as well as friends and classmates who rose through the military ranks along with him—he learned two lessons particularly well, which were part of the unwritten curriculum: Turkish nationalism and a love of *rakı*. A dedicated student, he would not drink during the week, but on weekends he and his friends would escape to Beyoğlu (more commonly referred to as Pera)—the largely Christian district on the European side of the Bosporus—to drink and party at its multitudinous taverns.[43]

In an interview years later, Atatürk described his time at the War Academy: "During my first year, I fell into naive youthful revelries. I neglected my lessons. The year passed in a flash."[44] During his first two years, Atatürk drank mainly beer. It was only in his third year at the academy where he got his first taste of the more powerful, distilled, anise-flavored *rakı* that had already become virtually synonymous with Turkish national identity.[45] While on an excursion among the Prince Islands, where the ultra-wealthy of Istanbul had their summer homes, Mustafa Kemal took his first sip of *rakı*, having polished off his usual bottle of beer. "What a lovely drink this is," he told his friend. "It makes one want to be a poet."[46]

Such innocent beginnings gave way to a lifelong addiction to *rakı* that would eventually take his life: liver cirrhosis would claim Atatürk in 1938 at the age of fifty-seven.[47] In his final years, when his friends pleaded with him to cut back on his drinking, Atatürk made excuses in terms that might sound familiar to loved ones involved in an alcoholic's interventions:

> I've got to drink: my mind keeps on working hard and fast to the point of suffering. I have to slow it down and rest it at times. When I was at the War College and then at the Staff College, my mates in the dormitory usually had to wake me up in the morning. At night my mind would get fixed on a problem, and, as I thought about it, I was unable to sleep. I would spend the whole night tossing and turning in my bed, until finally I dozed off exhausted just before dawn. Then, naturally, I couldn't hear the sound of reveille. It's the same now. When I don't drink, I can't sleep, and the distress stupefies me.[48]

Atatürk's military education gave him a taste not only for *rakı* but for revolutionary nationalism. Intermittently arrested for his antimonarchist activities, he joined the CUP, in which military leaders openly aired their grievances against the sultan even while out drinking in the taverns.[49] When the Young Turks seized power from Sultan Abdul Hamid II in 1908, Mustafa Kemal was there.

Gaining a reputation as an effective military commander, he rose quickly through the ranks. He helped suppress a counterrevolution in Istanbul in 1909, and he was wounded in action in 1912, defending against the Italian invasion of Libya. Believing that a commander leads best from the front rather than the rear, he also saw action in both Balkan Wars. Yet his big breakthrough came in successfully repelling Winston Churchill's planned British invasion of Gallipoli during World War I.

Elevated to commander of the Second Army, he pushed back Russian incursions in 1917, but was less successful in slowing the British invasion and occupation of Palestine. Such military leadership required a keen eye and a sharp mind, so Mustafa Kemal never drank while on the job, but as soon as leisure time presented itself, he headed straight for the bottle.[50]

Following the Armistice of Mudros in October 1918—which ended World War I in the Middle Eastern theater—he returned to his office at the War Department in Istanbul. The conquering British fleet was moored in the bay, its big guns looming over the vanquished Ottoman capital. It was one thing for the Allies to cleave up the far-flung Ottoman lands between them, but for Turkish nationalists like Mustafa Kemal, far more humiliating was the occupation of Turkey itself. The French took Syria and the adjoining Turkish territories; Italy occupied southern Anatolia, including the Mediterranean port towns of Antalya and Konya. On the Aegean coastline, the Greeks landed at Turkey's second-largest city of Smyrna (İzmir), and carved out a chunk of Turkey that extended out some eighty miles in every direction. The British controlled the coastlines, the communication and transportation systems, Istanbul, and the strategically vital straits. The rump Ottoman authorities were only permitted to hold the rugged interior of Anatolia.[51]

British control of the capital meant that the last sultan, Mehmed VI, and his government were effectively held hostage even as they negotiated a final peace treaty. In May 1919 Mustafa Kemal left for the unoccupied interior, to raise an army of resistance, should the Allied peace terms prove to be as onerous as expected. When the Greeks landed at Smyrna (İzmir), Kemal was ordered to return to the capital. He refused. Instead, he organized both political and military resistance from Angora (Ankara) in the Turkish heartland. After Turkish nationalist parties swept the Ottoman parliamentary elections, in March 1920 Britain formalized its occupation of Istanbul: Allied troops replaced Ottoman police, martial law was declared, the parliament was dissolved, and hundreds of military and civilian officials—including legislators—were arrested and deported to prisons on Malta. In response, Atatürk called for nationwide elections to establish a new Turkish parliament—the Grand National Assembly (GNA)—to be seated in Ankara, far from British guns. In April, the GNA opened with Mustafa Kemal as presiding speaker. They declared the sultan to be a prisoner of the Allies, and his official acts invalid.[52]

In the suburbs of Paris, in August 1920 the Ottoman grand vizier signed the Treaty of Sèvres, which imposed more outlandishly severe terms than even the infamous Treaty of Versailles did for the vanquished German Empire.[53] All of the non-Turkish areas were divvied up among the Allies: the Middle East—from Libya and Arabia to Syria and Iraq—were all taken. The military occupation of Anatolia by the British, French, Greeks, and Italians would continue. Eastern Turkey would be carved off into an independent Armenian state. Even more galling, the shackles of European economic "capitulations" that the Ottomans cast off at the start of the Great War were reapplied. Back too was European control over rump Turkey's economy and finance. The Ottoman Public Debt Administration returned, with power over the national budget, the Ottoman Bank, and collection of tax revenues. Repayment of British, French, and Italian creditors were given top priority.[54] Turkey's subjugation and humiliation were complete.

Prohibition and the Turkish Resistance

This, then, was the political context for Turkish prohibition: a nationalist parliament struggling to claim its sovereignty from the European powers that both occupied its territory and controlled its finances. As Pussyfoot Johnson—a frequent visitor to Istanbul—explained, "Because of the historic Moslem attitude against intoxicating drink, and because practically the entire liquor business in Constantinople is in the hands of non-Moslems, or 'Christians' as they are officially classified, it is quite natural that drink should be the principal target against which Turkish reform activities are directed. And the drink is the paramount vulnerable thing that is open to attack by the Turk."[55]

It is certainly no coincidence that the first Muslim temperance organization in the whole history of the Ottoman Empire—the *Hilal-i Ahdar*, or Green Crescent Society—was only founded in Istanbul in March 1920: the exact time that the British were solidifying their military hold on the capital, shuttering the parliament and imposing martial law.[56] As everywhere else in their dominions, British occupation brought a flood of liquor traders who sought their fortunes in getting the locals addicted to alcohol. Under the British, the number of liquor outlets in the city ballooned to over fourteen hundred, only 7 percent of which were Turkish owned.[57] So, as in Ireland (Chapter 5), South Africa (Chapter 6), and India (Chapter 7), temperance was a means of resisting British alco-imperialism, with the Green Crescent Society imploring Muslims to starve the revenues of the European liquor dealers by abstaining from drink.

Given his routine travels through Turkey and the Middle East, the American prohibitionist Pussyfoot Johnson knew the men and women of *Hilal-i Ahdar* quite well. In fact, just like Rajagopolachari's nationalist Prohibition League of India (Chapter 7), the Green Crescent made Pussyfoot an honorary lifetime member.[58] That the members were all Turkish Muslims—as opposed to the Christian Greeks who overwhelmingly ran the liquor business—goes without saying. But *Quran*-thumping conservatives they were not. Prince (and later Caliph) Abdulmejid

II was the honorary president of the Green Crescent Society, but its main leader was Dr. Mazhar Osman Bey: pioneering neurosurgeon, head of medicine at three Turkish hospitals, and author and editor of books and medical journals on addiction and mental and emotional disorders.[59] Pussyfoot called him "one of the busiest and most brilliant men in Europe."[60] Professor Dr. Fahreddin Kerim served as general secretary, between time spent on his medical practice and his scientific research at Istanbul University. Led by "the foremost men in Turkey, chiefly medical and professional men," the society quickly grew to some twelve hundred members.[61]

"Wherever any movement for human betterment exists, there you will find women. The Green Crescent was no exception," claimed Pussyfoot. Foremost among them was Safyie Husseyin, known as the Florence Nightingale of Turkey for being the chief organizer of the Turkish Red Cross / Red Crescent organization. Her tireless medical work at Gallipoli—as Allied artillery crashed all around—saved countless lives, winning her widespread admiration and government decorations for valor.

"I want to organize a Woman's Christian Temperance Union in Turkey," Madame Husseyin proclaimed to a startled Pussyfoot.

Knowing she was a devout Muslim, he asked, "Do you know what the W.C.T.U. stands for?"

"I know all about it," she insisted. For her, the goals of liberation from the oppressive liquor traffic transcended religious differences. Pussyfoot put her in touch with the general secretary in London, and in no time at all, the World's Woman's Christian Temperance Union boasted an Istanbul chapter numbering over a hundred Muslim women (Chapter 13).[62]

Through Johnson, the World's WCTU, and other transnational activists, Turkey's temperance nationalists maintained links with the leading social-betterment organizations across Europe and the United States. Like those European and American counterparts, their activism was less driven by religious faith, but rather by faith in science and medicine to improve the human condition (Chapter 14). Their political agenda was one of liberation—not just from addiction, but from the predatory "Christian" liquor traffic that kept Turkey impoverished and subservient.

With twenty-five parliamentarians among their ranks, the clout of the Green Crescent Society extended to nationalist politics, especially following the opening of the Grand National Assembly in Ankara on April 23, 1920.[63] The ideologically diverse legislators quickly coalesced into two camps: Westernist modernists—led and epitomized by Mustafa Kemal—and the populist traditionalists known as the İkinci Grup, or "Second Group." And while they were unanimous in opposing Allied occupation and abolishing the sultanate, other issues like the status of religious schools and courts ignited more heated debates.[64]

Within the first week of the GNA's opening, a Green Crescent–backed prohibition bill was presented to the GNA by Ali Şükrü Bey, an outspoken former naval officer and Second Group parliamentarian from the Black Sea port town of

Trabzon. He had pushed for prohibition in the Ottoman parliament even before the British forced its closure.[65] "The evils and devastation that emerge from our people's increased consumption of alcohol, despite the Muslim religion's prohibition of drinking, are too destructive to count," said Ali Şükrü in presenting only the fourth piece of legislation before the GNA. "I proposed the acceptance of the following measures into a law in order to save our people whose deep ignorance and lack of restraint with alcohol always culminates with the destruction of homes by this great evil."[66]

His proposal outlawed the production, trade, and consumption of alcohol under penalty of flogging or fines, as well as confiscation and destruction of existing liquor stocks. With speaker Mustafa Kemal's assent, the proposal was submitted to relevant committees within each of the appropriate "provisional" ministries: religious affairs, justice, health, and finance.[67] In its early days, however, the Ankara government was careful not to delegitimize the *de jure* Ottoman state institutions in Istanbul. While the British had scuttled the Ottoman parliament, the rest of the ministries and institutions continued to function as before, with all of the preexisting colonized interests and political dynamics.

The durability of these interests was made readily apparent when the committees returned with their reports in May. Unsurprisingly, the religious affairs committee found prohibition to be consistent with the teachings of Islam. Reflecting scientific debates in Europe and the United States (Chapter 14), the health ministry touted the litany of public-welfare, crime-diminution, and health benefits of decreased drinking, while also decrying the transfer of Turkey's national wealth to foreigners through the liquor traffic. Deferring to these material and moral benefits, the justice ministry's only objection was that the prohibition issue could wait for better days, when the country wasn't in a battle for its very existence against foreign occupiers.[68]

It was the finance committee that objected most strenuously to the prohibition proposal. Prohibition would jeopardize the stream of liquor revenues—controlled by the European-run OPDA—which had already been "committed by the government to repay the outstanding debts to various states," most notably Great Britain. Instead, the finance committee proposed increasing the taxes on alcohol producers and consumers to both discourage consumption and maximize revenues—to be paid to the British and Allied powers that currently occupied their country. Besides, economic policies had always been best decided by the experts in the cabinet.[69]

The Grand National Assembly bristled, both at the executive's thinly veiled power grab, and the condescension that an elected parliament could not handle such a "complex" issue. "The executive cannot reap revenue at the expense of the nation's health, its very existence, and the happiness of its families," railed parliamentarian Hamdullah Subhi Bey, to thunderous applause. Whatever the outcome, it would be the GNA that decides, though Mustafa Kemal did request that the cabinet ministers put together a unified opinion on the matter.[70]

The prohibition issue would be intermittently debated over the subsequent months, especially in July 1920, when Atatürk's finance ministry did an abrupt about-face. Apparently having re-crunched the numbers, they presented a revised budgetary assessment without liquor taxes. While still underscoring prohibition's detrimental impacts on viniculture, they grumbled reluctantly, "There is no obstacle remaining from a financial standpoint to banning alcohol production, sales, and consumption."[71]

When the issue finally came for a final debate in September 1920, the finance ministry—backed by the OPDA—made a last-ditch push for a tax increase (from 15 percent to 20 percent) rather than prohibition, arguing that prohibition would not only make it impossible to pay back European creditors, but also undermine the government's ability to fund the army in its war of independence. What's more, a blanket prohibition would inflame tensions with the non-Muslim populations, the finance minister argued. Moreover, he asserted, the experiences of both the United States (Chapter 17) and Bolshevik Russia (Chapter 2) demonstrated the impossibility of enforcing prohibition.[72]

In response, as father of the prohibition legislation, Ali Şükrü Bey rose to refute each of the accusations. How could prohibition inflame tensions with non-Muslims, if Christian countries from the United States to Scandinavia and Russia were all implementing their own prohibitions? If the government could not enforce a prohibition law, how could it expect to enforce a tax law? And if the government can't enforce the law, isn't that an implicit critique of Mustafa Kemal's leadership? That's hardly patriotic, especially when the Turkish revenues that the finance ministry hoped to raise would go straight to enriching those European powers that Turkey was actively fighting against.[73]

As for enforcement, there was an entire country of patriotic Muslims ready to act as volunteer watchdogs. "This law also has genuine guardians," Ali Şükrü Bey claimed, "by which I mean the entire nation. If even I myself see those who are not complying with it, I would immediately call the police on them, whether they're citizens or government members; even if it was the Finance Minister himself!"

As the laughter rolled down at his expense, a frustrated finance minister Ferit Bey rose to respond, "If you are not able to see this, I will see to the opposite."[74]

The exchanges got even more heated as they turned to the financial aspects of prohibition. "In this country," Ali Şükrü Bey thundered, "120 million kilograms of alcoholic beverages are consumed, which means 120 million kilos' worth of money paid into the pockets of Greeks and Armenians!"

"They are building apartments!" interjected another representative.

Ali Şükrü then quoted reports from the areas that had recently been decimated by the genocide of Armenians, but found there to be twice as much drunkenness as before the war, even despite the massive population loss. It was a handful of Greek liquor traders who were turning the profit.

Such liquor exploitation "is how all of Greece has been developed," another parliamentarian noted.

"It is our money that is developing Greece," Ali Şükrü proclaimed. "Just so that the treasury can earn one million in tax revenue, at least ten million lira will go into the pockets of Christians, who display such explicit enmity against us."

And with that, he sat, amid thunderous applause of "*Aferin Şükrü Bey, aferin.*" Bravo, Şükrü Bey, well done.[75]

As if to underscore that the goal was not to legislate morality, parliamentarians asked whether other "intoxicants" like opium would also fall under the ban, since they likewise befuddle the mind and detract from prayer and meditation. "The British destroyed India with opium," it was pointed out (Chapter 7). Şükrü was quick to calm their fears, agreeing with those who argued that it was a major commercial crop, and so "it is not right to include opium in the prohibition and undermine the wealth of the country."[76] Ultimately it was not about morality or about the substance being used or abused; instead it was all about who benefitted from its sale: us or them.

Having framed prohibition as a tool to weaken the economic power of their non-Muslim, British, Greek, and Armenian foes—each actively carving out Turkish territory—the prohibition issue was finally put to a vote, which ended in a dead tie. Seventy-one legislators voted in favor, and seventy-one opposed, with three abstaining. The tiebreaker was left to the chairman of the session—scientist-turned-politician Konyalı Mehmet Vehbi Efendi—who voted in favor, with prohibition to take effect on February 28, 1921.[77]

The GNA records are notably silent on Kemal Atatürk's role in prohibition. Not a parliamentarian, he did not partake in the floor debates or voting; as chairman of the assembly, however, he had ample opportunity to table the motion instead of advancing it as he did. Had he been openly hostile to prohibition as contrary to his own alcoholic inclinations, the notoriously adroit and tactical Atatürk could have easily prevailed upon deputies—or his session chairman, Vehbi Efendi—to vote it down.[78] But he didn't, as it advanced their shared nationalist goal of undermining the finances of the colonial occupiers.

Of course, prohibition did not slow his personal alcohol consumption one bit: in fact, vast quantities of the best *rakı* were frequently smuggled into Kemal's residence and military encampments disguised as gas canisters. When dry parliamentarians pressed him on his drinking, Kemal replied, "You can't drink, but I can; you voted for the prohibition law, I didn't. I will respect the law publicly, but not privately."[79] After all, the *rakı* he was drinking was Turkish, and did not enrich the foreign liquor traffic.

So, for a time, Kemal's drinking was successfully kept out of the public eye. The international temperance press lauded him for making Turkey dry. Western news outlets even gave him the epithet "Pussyfoot Kemal" after the famed American prohibitionist, even before Turks honored him with the honorific title of "Atatürk" as father of the Turkish state (see Figure 8.2).[80]

History was not nearly as kind to Ali Şükrü Bey, the Second Group leader and true father of Turkish prohibition. Having written newspaper editorials ever-more-critical of Atatürk, Şükrü went missing in March 1923. Days later, his body was found, strangled to death. The culprit was Topal Osman Ağa—one of the most sadistic butchers in the genocide of the Armenians and Greeks, who had nevertheless risen to commander of Mustafa Kemal's personal bodyguard regiment. Apparently, he decided to take matters into his own hands. Atatürk ordered Osman to be taken into custody, but he would not go quietly. In the subsequent firefight with police, he was wounded, captured, and executed.[81]

Seeking an even greater measure of justice for their slain leader, Şükrü, the Second Group opposition dug up Osman's corpse, decapitated it, and placed the body on public display in Ulus Square in the heart of Ankara, strung up upside-down from the gallows.[82]

Figure 8.2 Mustafa Kemal Atatürk (right) in civilian clothes, October 19, 1923. The photo's original caption reads, "This photo, just arrived from Turkey, shows the famous Commander-in-Chief, Mustafa Kemal, in civilian clothes, with his wife and Ismet Pasha. Mustafa Kemal recently has become known as 'Pussyfoot' Kemal, as he has spoken in favor of a 'Dry' Turkey."

Turkey Resurgent, Turkey Dry

It was not just the Second Group in the GNA that did not see eye to eye with Mustafa Kemal. Many whispered that Kemal spent more time politicking in Ankara than commanding the army, even as the Turks were in near-constant entanglements with the British, the Greeks, the Armenians, and even the remnants of the sultan's old Ottoman Army.[83]

In June 1920 Kemal's nationalist troops attacked a British battalion outside Istanbul. In a panic, the British wired Greece for help. The Greeks were more than happy to provide reinforcements in exchange for a bigger slice of Anatolian territory to satisfy their pan-Hellenic dream. Then, something bizarre happened in Greece. The young Greek king, Alexander, died from a monkey bite. At nearly the same time, his pro-Allied government lost at the polls, bringing back the old pro-German government of King Constantine, who'd been forced from the Greek throne back in 1917. In response, both France and Italy cut their support from Greece and withdrew from the Treaty of Sèvres, leaving the British and Greeks to face the Turkish nationalists alone.

Like the Russians did to Napoleon a century before, Kemal sought to draw their foes ever farther into the Anatolian heartland, wearing them down. For a time, Greeks expanded their toehold in Turkey with a series of successful military campaigns. Summoning the bitter and divided GNA into secret session, Kemal proposed a Roman solution: the parliament should elect him dictator for three months. If his military leadership failed, he would assume all of the blame. This satisfied Atatürk's partisans, confident of victory, and his detractors, certain of his defeat.

With his new power, Kemal prepared for total war: requisitioning food, cloth, horses, and supplies from the population in order to make his last stand. Believing the Turks were all but finished, in August 1921 the overextended Greeks pushed to within fifty miles of Ankara before being ground down by Turkish defenses at the Sakarya River. The Greeks were exhausted and demoralized. Kemal was celebrated as a national hero.

The next twelve months were a veritable stalemate. Fearing that the war-weary British were considering an accommodation with Ankara, in the summer of 1922, Greek king Constantine made a bold gamble. He withdrew three regiments and two battalions from Anatolia to Thrace, the Turkish province on the European side of the Dardanelles. Hoping to prompt greater Allied involvement, Constantine announced that the Greeks would seize Istanbul and bring the war to an end.[84] Embracing the opportunity, Atatürk attacked the weak and overextended Greek forces that remained in Anatolia. It turned into a rout. From every direction, the Greeks fell back in disarray to the city of Smyrna (in Greek) or İzmir (in Turkish). The historic, multicultural, cosmopolitan city of some four hundred thousand was populated by equal number of Turks and Greeks, with sizable Jewish and Armenian quarters. The last Greek soldiers abandoned Smyrna on September 8, leaving the city utterly undefended when the fearful Turkish Army approached the following day.[85]

Upon arriving in the captured city, Mustafa Kemal first took up residence at Karşıyaka across the bay from İzmir. A Greek flag had been laid across the entrance of the house. Kemal refused to step on it, cultivating an image of magnanimity in victory.

Still, the stench from the slaughtered horses, livestock, and corpses of Greek soldiers, which had washed into the bay from battles upstream, was so overpowering, it forced Atatürk to relocate to a different residence in the İzmir city center. That evening, Atatürk and his small entourage dined at the upscale Kramer Palace Hotel. It was "full of Christians, both local and foreign," remembered his confidant, Falih Rıfkı Atay. The *maître d'* brusquely informed them that there were no tables available. Then, recognizing Kemal, a patron called out the name of the fearful Turkish commander, nearly setting off a panic in the restaurant.

Atatürk entered the salon and reassured the nervous diners that he wanted no one to be disturbed. They returned to their meals as the waiters quickly found a table for the conquering general.

"Tell me," Atatürk asked the hotel manager, who had come to personally take his order, "did King Constantine ever come here and drink a glass of *rakı*?"

"No, Your Excellency," the manager replied.

"In that case," he responded, "then why on earth did he want to capture İzmir?"[86]

The pleasantries were not to last long. Within days, discipline broke down in the Turkish ranks, leading to an orgy of looting, pillaging, and raping throughout the city, even as American, French, British, and Italian ships hurriedly evacuated refugees from the quay. To this day, it is unclear who started the fire that raged throughout city for a week, reducing the city's Greek and Armenian districts to rubble, while the predominantly Muslim and Jewish quarters escaped with far less damage. Conservative estimates suggest that at least ten thousand Greeks and Armenians perished in the ransacking and fire, with tens of thousands more rounded up and marched off to die inland. By the end of 1922, some one and a half million Greek refugees had fled Anatolia.[87]

Having taken İzmir, Kemal set his sights on Istanbul. "The frontiers we claim for Turkey exclude Syria and Mesopotamia but compose all the areas principally populated by the Turkish race," he told the *Daily Mail* in September 1922. "We must have our capital and I should in that case be obliged to march on Constantinople with my army, which will be an affair of only a few days. I must prefer to obtain possession by negotiation, though naturally I cannot wait indefinitely."[88]

Of course, all of the territory that Kemal's armies liberated became subject to the laws of the Ankara government, including prohibition. The predominantly Christian liquor traders of İzmir and environs (those who remained, at least) were forced to close up shop. As the Turks marched steadily north toward Istanbul—sopping "wet" thanks to the British occupation—they extended the geographic reach of prohibition, even as their commander continued to fill his off-duty hours getting drunk.[89]

The Turks met the British forces at Çanakkale, in the neutral zone on the coast of the Dardanelles. The overextended British had even less appetite for war than did their weary voters back home. With tensions high, Kemal's forces refused British orders to withdraw, instead approaching the British line with their rifles drawn butts forward—signaling they would not be the first to fire. In the end, the British relented, signing an armistice, which prompted the collapse of the Liberal government of David Lloyd George back in London.[90]

In November 1922, with the fighting effectively over, Kemal dispatched Mustafa İsmet İnönü—his hard-bargaining second in command (and future second president of Turkey)—to Lausanne, Switzerland, to negotiate a final peace settlement with the Allies. It would replace the outrageous and unjust Treaty of Sèvres and respect Turkish sovereignty. At the same time, the GNA deposed the feckless last sultan, Mehmed VI, whom the British bundled aboard a warship and sent into exile on the Italian Riviera. Though the sultanate had been abolished, the role of caliph—universal leader of Islam—remained. To fill it, the GNA elected Mehmed's cousin, the Grand Prince Abdülmejid II: president of the Green Crescent temperance society.[91]

The resulting Treaty of Lausanne was signed on July 24, 1923, recognizing the Kemalist GNA as the sovereign government of independent Turkey. In exchange for giving up any remaining claims to Egypt, Cyprus, and other former Ottoman territories, Turkey was established within its present borders: all of Anatolia, Istanbul and the vital straits region, and Thrace on the European side. Gone were the foreign "capitulations" as infringements on Turkish sovereignty. Gone too was the European-controlled Ottoman Public Debt Administration, putting Turkey in charge of its own financial decision-making. However, Turkey was saddled with paying the outstanding debt that the Ottoman Empire still owed to European creditors. Turkey made its last payment on the Ottoman debts only in 1954.[92]

Having established Turkey's independence, Atatürk set about modernizing Turkish politics and society, abolishing the caliphate in 1923 and establishing Turkey as a secular republic, with Ankara rather than Istanbul as the capital. Mustafa Kemal would serve as president until his death from liver cirrhosis in 1938.[93]

As for political reforms, the first GNA parliament was dissolved and reconstituted, with most of the Second Group opposition excluded. Atatürk's political party—the social democratic *Cumhuriyet Halk Partisi* (Republican People's Party)—would dominate every assembly through the 1950s. Turkey's modernization legislation was sweeping: secularizing the legal and educational systems; replacing the Arabic script with the Latin alphabet; abolishing the fez in favor of Western dress; mandating the adoption of surnames; building libraries, universities, roadways, and infrastructure; promoting gender equality and women's rights; and establishing universal suffrage earlier than many European countries.[94]

It is worth highlighting that, with Turkish sovereignty fully established, there was little need for prohibition as an anticolonial measure. The British, Greek, and Allied occupation forces were fully withdrawn from Turkish soil in October 1923, at the same time the GNA re-legalized winemaking. In April 1924—in a vote of 98 to 41, with five abstentions—prohibition was repealed, to be replaced by a government monopoly on alcohol, intended to maximize both oversight and state revenue from the liquor trade.[95] Ironically, that suggestion was the exact same as that made by the European-backed OPDA during the earlier debates on prohibition— back when the Europeans thought *they*, rather than the Turks, would profit from Turkish drinking. Prohibition was more about the politics of profit, and less about legislating morality.[96]

As for President Atatürk himself, he became an international icon and living legend. But his manic, work-hard-party-harder lifestyle would take its toll. While he largely did not drink during the daytime, his typical evening dinner with friends would begin with alcohol around eight o'clock and would last well into the night.[97] When his associates retired or went home, he would often drink *rakı* alone—contemplating, reading, or writing until the dawn.[98] His morning breakfast consisted of coffee and cigarettes.[99]

"Life is very short," he said, explaining that much time was lost to childhood, schooling, and sleep. "I wish that one day medical science will find a solution to sleep; that we'll be able to take a drug to replace it. I truly believe this," he said.[100]

Atatürk made no secret about his alcoholic excesses. He even joked about them. During the postindependence period of effective one-party rule, one French journalist famously quipped that Turkey was governed by one drunkard, one deaf man (İsmet İnönü), and three hundred deaf-mutes (the GNA).

"This man is mistaken," Atatürk interjected. "Turkey is governed by one drunkard."[101]

Many of the best Atatürk drinking stories come from Cemal Granda, who served as his personal butler for the last eleven years of his life. In one instance, he tells of Atatürk drinking aboard the presidential yacht off Moda Point one hot summer evening. An ever-growing crowd of admirers in rowboats gathered around the yacht. Atatürk ordered that all the wine on board be distributed to the crowd of seaborne well-wishers. Once all had a drink in hand, he raised a toast to them.

"Fellow countrymen," he proclaimed,

> The sultans of old used to drink, but always in secret. I, on the other hand, drink openly, and now you all are drinking with me. We drink together— we are all equal. There are rumors that I drink *rakı*, and it's true. I do. After all, remember that I'm just like you.

And with that, a great cheer went up in Moda Bay, as Atatürk drank his toast to (and with) his fellow citizens.[102]

After his first heart attack in 1923, his doctors and friends pleaded with Atatürk to cut back on his drinking, smoking, and coffee. He agreed, with a wink and a nod, and went right back to his old behavior. The same thing happened again after his second heart attack. After a night celebrating the third anniversary of the Turkish Republic, Atatürk was found passed out behind the wheel of his car.[103] He got drunk while hosting foreign dignitaries, including British king Edward VIII.[104] His personal physician claimed he drank between a half-liter to a full liter of *rakı* every night.[105]

In his later years, even political decisions were made at his dinner table. State documents were brought to him while he was at picnics or driving about. He ratified the 1936 Montreaux Convention regulating the Turkish Straits while drinking in an Ankara beer garden. "Atatürk's behaviour could be odd," biographer Andrew Mango claims, "but, as long as his health held up, his company was fun."[106]

But the fun gave out in 1937. His skin turned pale and waxy; there was blood in his urine. His doctors diagnosed him with liver disease, pleading again for him to stop drinking. But the late-night benders continued all the same.[107] Even on his deathbed in 1938, Atatürk summoned his right-hand man and soon-to-be successor as president, İsmet İnönü.

"İsmet," he said, "if my illness had been explained to me much earlier with all its severity, then I would have taken precautions from the start. I would not have allowed it to develop into such a serious state. It was not explained to me sufficiently, the truth was hidden."[108]

Pussyfoot of Istanbul

This, then, was the Turkey of the 1920s that American prohibitionist Pussyfoot Johnson visited time and again: ravaged by years of war, but rebuilding, modernizing, and optimistic, with a newfound independence and sense of destiny.

In one early visit, the heroic Madame Safyie Husseyin of the Green Crescent Society presented to Pussyfoot a pair of girls—two of the hundreds of thousands orphaned by years of internecine war. Touched, Johnson vowed to provide for their education. When local newspapers ran stories about "Pussyfoot and his daughters," every Turkish waif scurried to him for help. Never a man of great wealth, he funneled every spare penny from his global speaking engagements back to Istanbul to educate his "second family" of dozens of Turkish orphans, even as it bankrupted him (Chapter 18).[109]

At least once a year, he found time in his hectic itinerary to return to Turkey, establishing a base from which to explore the occupied lands of the Muslim Middle East. And on each of his visits, he found there the same dynamics of Western alco-imperialism as in South Africa, India, Australia, and other British domains. Recall that, upon visiting the British-administered Mandate of Palestine, the first thing that confronted any pilgrim to the Holy Land were the saloons, which the locals were virtually powerless to close.

He found the same situation in Egypt, occupied and administered by the British since they invaded in 1882. Even after Turkey renounced any claim to Egypt in the 1923 Treaty of Lausanne, the British still controlled the defense, administration, and finance of the Land of Pharaohs. When Pussyfoot arrived in Cairo in 1926, he was scorned by the local British aristocracy, while being welcomed with open arms by the Egyptians themselves.

The abstemious King Fuad invited him for a private audience. While strolling the royal gardens, Fuad pressed his American guest as to when England might go dry, as perhaps the only way to fight the British liquor establishment on his lands.

"Your Majesty, it will be a long time," Pussyfoot replied, "for England is not a progressive country like Egypt and America." The king rolled with laughter.

"In spite of the King's attitude," Pussyfoot later recalled, "Egypt could not take any drastic steps toward elimination of drink, because of the strangling capitulations with foreign powers. In 1926 there were 1,749 barrooms in Egypt. Of these, 726 were licensed. The rest were unlicensed and not subject to Egyptian control, because they were located in the European quarters of the four principal cities."[110] In Egypt as throughout the colonized world, prohibitionism was synonymous with opposition to exploitative European imperialism.

But nowhere was this temperance-as-national-self-determination dynamic as evident than in Johnson's second home of Istanbul: the capital of the Muslim world.

Johnson explained how, before the war, the American Mission Press in Istanbul once made the mistake of publishing some mild temperance pamphlets in Greek.[111] "The Greeks made such violent protests, denouncing it as 'Moslem propaganda,' that the leaflet had to be suppressed." Why? The Greeks had long been in charge of the city's liquor traffic. More worryingly—before prohibition—the Greek-Orthodox Holy Trinity Church in the Pera district "actually owned half a dozen drinking shops in its immediate vicinity and received the profits therefrom." With prohibition's repeal and replacement with a Turkish state monopoly, he wrote, "the licenses for these Holy Trinity places were not renewed, it being the policy of the authorities to eliminate so far as possible the Greek monopoly of saloons and dives. There thus appears to be a very acute reason for this Greek hostility to a little temperance teaching in Constantinople!"[112]

The other major foe of Turkish temperance reform was the sprawling Bomonti Brewery in Istanbul, which had long served as a center of the Ottoman alcohol traffic. It thrived during the years of British occupation, virtually monopolizing the beer trade in the sprawling metropolis. "And a horrible beer it makes," Pussyfoot wrote. "The frightful quality of this beer, a Turk told me, was the reason why dogs fled from the city some years ago."[113]

Jokes aside, the Bomonti brothers from Switzerland had come to Istanbul and set up shop back in 1894. Later, the brewery was run primarily by German immigrants.

Figure 8.3 Postcard showing the Bomonti Brewery in Istanbul.
Source: "Views of the Former Bomonti Brewery of Constantinople," Levantine Heritage Foundation.

Like liquor traffickers the world over, "Its managers understood the cohesive power of public plunder, and listen with a kindly ear when a Turkish politician is in need of campaign funds with which to advance his candidacy," Pussyfoot explained. "The allurements of 'backsheesh' [petty bribery] have not entirely been eliminated from Oriental life."[114]

With the final British evacuation of Istanbul in October 1923, the Kemalist prohibition became law there, too. It was then that Bomonti came calling to Ankara, with the promise of badly needed revenues from alcohol sales, if only the government would allow their business to continue. By early 1924, prohibition had been repealed in favor of a national alcohol monopoly. In its haste to nationalize the liquor traffic, the Turkish government gave a special exemption to the Bomonti brothers, who were permitted to continue their private brewing operation through 1938.[115] Of course, while the European-run ODPA was gone, Turkey's inherited debts remained, for which both nationalizing the liquor trade and taxing Bomonti would help. "There was a feeling that," as Pussyfoot recounted, "inasmuch as the Christians drank most of the liquor and we wanted to get rid of them, it was best to inaugurate a temporary license law and the Christians drink themselves to death while we made as much money as possible out of their undoing and pay the public debt."[116]

And so they did.

"My sorties into Turkey gave me a new understanding of the Turk," Pussyfoot reflected in his unpublished autobiography. "Until recent years, that word has been more an epithet than a name, He has been pictured as a monster with horns and flaming eyes, who ate hay and small children as a daily diet. His chief industry was the cutting of Christian throats." But especially amid Atatürk's modernizing reforms, Europeans were slowly coming to recognize Turks as good natured, "with the same vices, weaknesses and virtues that the rest of the world has inherited," if only liberated from the shackles of colonialism.[117]

Pussyfoot proclaimed that he found nothing in the *Quran* that contradicted his own Christian upbringing in the United States. The biggest difference between Islam and Christianity is that Muslims place the Prophet Muhammad above Christ, whereas Christians do not. He recounted how Muhammad provided asylum for the Jews when Jerusalem was sacked by the Romans, and that it was the Muslims who rescued Christian Egypt from the oppression of "Christian" Byzantium.

Even in the Great War of late, among the European belligerents, it was only the Ottoman Empire that refused to deploy chemical weapons. For all the finger-pointing about the polygamy and supposed brutality of Islam, Pussyfoot chronicled even worse atrocities committed in the Bible or in Christ's name. And when it came to his core concern about the liquor traffic, he reasonably pointed out that "Mohammed has created more total abstainers from alcohol than any other man in the history of the world. That is the simple truth and it is not dishonoring Christ or anybody else to frankly acknowledge it."[118]

This statement certainly does not fit our usual crude stereotypes of prohibitionists as close-minded Bible-thumpers, seeking to impose their Christian morality on everyone else. Similarly, understanding Turkish temperance as part of the Kemalist national project rather than *Quranic* conservatism challenges our preconceptions about temperance activism and the goals of prohibitionism.

"I know quite well that I am in for a drubbing at what I have here set down in English speech," Pussyfoot wrote, in anticipation of the backlash from Christian readers, long accustomed to tired stereotypes of bloodthirsty Muslims. "Ignorance and hate are very stubborn and don't like to be contradicted."[119]

But he was no apologist for the Turks. Atatürk showed they could take care of themselves. Nor was Johnson called to defend Islam: its three hundred million followers could—and did—speak for themselves. There was no shame in admitting that Muhammad had won millions more converts to the dry cause of self-determination than Christians ever had. Instead, "I plead for Christ," Pussyfoot said, "that should He come to Constantinople, He be not hit with a brick thrown by some 'Christian' at some other 'Christian.' I plead for common honesty in our dealings with other races and peoples whose religion does not agree with ours."

But if, as the Bible says, a tree shall be known by its fruits (Luke 6:43–45), then Western civilization had a lot of introspection to do. "A civilization that sends out the bloodhounds of drink, disease and vice into every corner of the world and then bawls, like Niobe weeping for her children, at the results, has abundant reason for changing its ways."[120]

Of course, it's one thing for an American to lob such anti-Western accusations from Istanbul or Cairo or Mumbai or Johannesburg, largely against the colonial exploitation of the British. But based on our received wisdom about the United States, we *know* that American temperance and prohibition *couldn't possibly* be a movement of self-determination and empowerment; it was all about reactionary Bible-thumpers, right? After all, Americans are fundamentally hostile to imperialism, since our country was founded as a rebellion against British colonial impositions, right?

As it turns out, no. American temperance and prohibitionism were cut from the exact same cloth as everywhere else in the world. Pussyfoot himself was primed to see that, as before he began his globetrotting escapades, he spent decades in the Indian Service (Chapter 16), protecting Native Americans against the exact same encroachments of white liquor traders that the Turks, Indians, and Africans all endured.

In fact, recasting temperance and prohibitionism—not as white people's history, but as a native struggle for sovereignty against a white, colonial liquor traffic—flips the script on our usual prohibition narratives. Even in the United States, temperance wasn't even primarily about Bible-thumping nineteenth-century Victorians, but about who profits from drunkenness and addiction. The history of American prohibitionism goes back hundreds of years earlier, not only to the foundation of the United States itself, but to the very first encounters between white settlers and Native Americans.

PART III

THE UNITED STATES

9

First Peoples, First Prohibitionists

Aisquith Street Meeting, Baltimore, Maryland: Saturday, December 26, 1801

The out-of-towners caught a few awkward stares as they hitched their horses outside the redbrick Quaker Meeting House in Baltimore. The man with the shock of blazing-red hair peering over the high collar of his army peacoat was Captain William Wells. His companion wore a thigh-length blue petticoat, European waistcoat—and moccasins. The cap that hung halfway down his back—festooned with some two hundred silver brooches—clinked with every step of his horse. He had tattoos, four earrings, and three silver nose piercings.[1] This was the fearsome Chief Mihšihkinaahkwa—known as "Little Turtle"—whose Miami tribe in present-day Ohio had only recently dealt the American military the worst defeat in its history.

Though as frontier warriors, both had partaken of unimaginable terror and bloodletting, the so-called redman and his redheaded accomplice had arrived on a mission of peace. Chief Mihšihkinaahkwa represented the Miami Confederacy: the united Native American tribes spanning from Ohio, around the Lake Michigan coast of *Shikaakwa* (Chicago), and into southern Wisconsin. "Friendly, liberal, docile, and fond of instruction," they were praised by early French explorers as "the most civilized of all the Indian nations."[2]

The two men had a complicated history. After killing William Wells's father in an ambush along the Ohio River, Little Turtle adopted the thirteen-year-old orphan, naming him *Apekonit*, or "Carrot Top." Gaining fluency in many Indian languages, Wells even fought in Miami war parties against incursions by white settlers. He married Little Turtle's daughter, Sweet Breeze. They had four children together before Wells returned to life among the white people, where his Indian knowledge became a tremendous military asset.[3]

The Treaty of Paris (1783) that ended the Revolutionary War legally ceded all British territorial claims west to the Mississippi to the United States, without regard to the people who had lived there for centuries. Still, the young American republic sought to subdue "their" new Northwestern Territory, which brought them face to face with Little Turtle. First came the overconfident (and often inebriated) General Josiah Harmar in 1790, whose militia was outmaneuvered and decimated by Little Turtle's men.[4] President George Washington then ordered General Arthur St. Clair to form a proper army and attack the Miami. In "the most decisive defeat in the history of the American military," of the thousand men St. Clair sent into the woods, only twenty-four returned. Little Turtle had destroyed one fourth of the entire US Army. Washington was livid.[5]

Over the next three years, Revolutionary War hero General "Mad" Anthony Wayne cobbled together a professional "Legion of the United States" to conquer this Northwest Frontier, with William Wells as an advance scout. Through a chance wilderness encounter, Wells told his adopted father Little Turtle of Wayne's approach, with an "overwhelming force" of some three thousand legionnaires.

"There are more long knives under the Great Snake [Wayne] than have ever come against us before," Little Turtle warned his tribesmen. They didn't listen.[6]

The two sides confronted each other in August 1794 along the Maumee River near present-day Toledo, Ohio, where the forest had recently been felled by a tornado. The Battle of Fallen Timbers lasted only an hour, at the cost of thirty to forty white soldiers killed. At least as many Miami, Shawnee, and Ottawa braves were killed before the tribesmen fled into the woods in retreat.[7]

What happened next would break the power of the Miami Confederacy forever.

"Burn everything," General Wayne then declared. "Cut down the crops of the Indians, destroy their villages. . . . I want to give this Little Turtle and his men a lesson which they will never cease to remember!"[8] His men complied.

Wayne's cavalry laid waste to the fertile Maumee Valley for fifty miles inland from Lake Erie—terrorizing and torturing men, women, and children to compel the Miami people "to bury the tomahawk and not to dare take it up again." Today, we'd call these war crimes: villages, fields, and orchards were burned to the ground. Those not murdered were left to die of exposure and starvation. "No imagination can probably exaggerate the woes which ensued," claimed John S. C. Abbott's *History of the State of Ohio* (1875), adding dismissively, "Such is war."

Slaughtered, starving, and thus "subdued," the natives "no longer cherished any hope of being able to check the advance of the white men. In this state of extreme suffering, they were so anxious for peace that they were ready to accept any such terms as the conqueror might dictate."[9] So, in 1795, Little Turtle led representatives of the Miami, Chippewa, Ottawa, Potowatomi, Wyandot, Delaware, Shawnee, Wea, Kickapoo, and Kaskaskia tribes to make peace at Fort Greene Ville (now Greenville, Ohio).[10] General Wayne welcomed the assembled chiefs with wampum and whiskey: "We will, on this happy occasion, be merry, without, however, passing the bounds of temperance and sobriety."[11]

He also read a letter from the Society of Friends—the pacifist Quakers—who had taken an interest in the peace and welfare of the Indians. "The Quakers are a people whom I much love and esteem for their goodness of heart and sincere love of peace with all nations," Wayne proclaimed, before disbursing agricultural implements and other Quaker gifts.[12]

Establishing the practice of exchanging land concessions for annual cash payments, the Treaty of Greenville ceded tribal rights to twenty-five thousand square miles of present-day Ohio to the United States in exchange for twenty thousand dollars in presents and a ninety-five-hundred-dollar annuity. The chiefs recognized the sovereignty of the US government, which in turn renounced all claims to Indian land beyond the treaty. After sealing the agreement by smoking the peace pipe, the confederated tribes never once violated the treaty. The same could not be said of their more "civilized" white counterparts.[13]

After making peace at Greene Ville, Little Turtle proclaimed himself "the true and faithful friend of the Americans." Undertaking multiple visits to the American capital with Wells as his interpreter, Little Turtle gained the trust and respect of Presidents Washington and John Adams, temperance founding-father Dr. Benjamin Rush, and the swashbuckling Polish American anti-imperialist Tadeusz Kościuszko.[14]

Figure 9.1 Howard Chandler Christy's painting *The Signing of the Treaty of Green Ville* (1945), which hangs in the State Capitol Building in Columbus, Ohio. Chief Little Turtle features prominently at left, and General Anthony Wayne at right. Midway between the two—beyond Little Turtle's outstretched hand—is William Wells. Meriwether Lewis, William Clark, and future president William Henry Harrison observe the treaty signing, at right.
Source: Ohio Statehouse, Capitol Square Review and Advisory Board.

Judging by the hotel and tavern bills on his diplomatic missions, Little Turtle was hardly an abstainer. Like most, he routinely drank the fermented ales and ciders that were safer even than bacteria-filled water. Still, by opposing the debauching traffic in whiskey—a European industrial distillate of a mind-bending potency never fathomed by traditional societies—he became America's first prohibitionist.[15]

The white man's liquor trade was the greatest impediment to the pacification and integration of the Native Americans. "These white traders strip the poor Indians of skins, gun, blanket, everything, while his squaw and the children dependent upon him be starving in his wig-wam," Little Turtle argued. "My people barter away their best treasures for the white man's miserable firewater."[16] Before President Adams, he pleaded that three thousand Indians had died from booze in one year alone. "More of us have died since the Treaty of Greene-Ville, than we lost by the years of war before, and it is all owing to the introduction of this liquor among us."[17] Adams wasn't listening.

But perhaps his presidential successor, Thomas Jefferson, would listen. This is what brought Little Turtle and Wells to meet the Quakers in Baltimore in 1801: to ask their help in lobbying the "Great Father" Jefferson and the American "Great Council" for prohibition.[18] "Most of the existing evils amongst your red brethren, have been caught from the white people," Little Turtle proclaimed, "not only that liquor which destroys us daily, but many diseases which our forefathers were ignorant of before they saw you." He continued,

> We plainly perceive, brothers, that you see every evil that destroys your Red Brethren. It is not an evil, brothers, of our own making; we have not placed it amongst ourselves; it is an evil placed amongst us by the white people. We look to them to remove it out of our country. If they have the friendship for us, which they tell us they have, they certainly will not let it continue amongst us any longer. Our repeated entreaties to those who brought this evil amongst us, we find, has not the desired effect. We tell them, brothers, to fetch us useful things—bring goods that will clothe us, our women and our children, but not this evil liquor which destroys our reason; that destroys our health; that destroys our lives. But all we can say on this subject is of no service, nor gives relief to your Red Brethren.[19]

As the Quakers listened in respectful silence, Little Turtle painted a picture of poverty and woe at the expense of the white liquor traders. "We shall lay these evils before our great and good Father; we hope he will remove them from amongst us. If he does not, there will not be many of his red children living long in our country," Little Turtle said of their mission to Jefferson. "We hope, brothers, and expect, that if you have any influence with the Great Council of the United States, that you will make us of it in behalf of your red brethren."[20]

Moved by the old warrior's passion that prohibition would bring both prosperity and interracial tranquility to the unsettled Northwest Territory, the Quakers threw their support behind Little Turtle's quest. The Society of Friends wrote to Congress, President Jefferson, and a sympathetic secretary of war, Henry Dearborn, claiming that the "introduction of ardent or distill'd spirits among them by the traders & others, is an evil of great magnitude."[21]

With the Quakers on his side, on January 2, 1802, Little Turtle respectfully informed President Jefferson that the American government was failing in its obligations under the Treaty of Greene Ville. Annuity payments were late or nonexistent; wares arrived spoiled, damaged, and useless; and white squatters were illegally settling beyond the treaty's line of demarcation. Even worse, they'd brought their whiskey with them. "Nothing can be done to advantage unless the Great Council of the sixteen fires [Congress] now assembled will prohibit any person from selling Spiritous Liquors among their Red Brothers," Little Turtle told Jefferson.

> Father, the introduction of this poison has been prohibited in our camps, but not the towns, where many of our hunters, for this poison, dispose of not only their furs, etc., but frequently of their guns and blankets and return to their families destitute.
>
> Father, your children are not wanting in industry, but it is the introduction of this fatal poison, which keeps them poor. Your children have not the command over themselves you have, therefore before anything can be done to advantage this evil must be remedied.
>
> Father, when our White Brethren came to this land, our forefathers were numerous, and happy, but since their intercourse with the white people, and owing to the introduction of this fatal poison, we have become less numerous and happy.[22]

Jefferson was just as moved as the Quakers. Since all men were "made by the same great Spirit," he replied with all apparent sincerity, "we consider ourselves as of the same family; we wish to live with [the Native Americans] as one people, and to cherish their interests as our own. The evils which of necessity encompass the life of man are sufficiently numerous—why should we add to them by voluntarily distressing & destroying one another?"[23] War Secretary Henry Dearborn affirmed Jefferson's vow to Little Turtle to rid "that poison introduced among his red children which has done them so much mischief." The administration would "consult with the great Council of the sixteen States, which is now sitting, on the subject of guarding you against this great evil."[24]

In an unprecedented step, Jefferson forwarded Little Turtle's plea to both houses of Congress, explaining, "These people are becoming very sensible of the baneful effects produced on their morals, their health & existence by the abuse of ardent spirits: and some of them earnestly desire a prohibition of that article from being carried among them. The legislature will consider whether the effectuating that de-sire would not be in the spirit of benevolence & liberality which they have hith-erto practised towards these our neighbors, and which has had so happy an effect towards conciliating their friendship. It has been found too in experience that the same abuse gives frequent rise to incidents tending much to commit our peace with the Indians."[25]

Congress agreed and in March 1802 passed America's first federal prohibition legislation as part of a sweeping "Act to Regulate Trade and Intercourse with the Indian Tribes, and to Preserve Peace on the Frontiers." The act authorized the pres-ident to take such measures "as to him may appear expedient to prevent or restrain the vending or distributing of spiritous liquors among all or any of the said Indian tribes." Taking Indians' livestock, crops, clothing, guns, or cooking utensils as barter for whiskey risked a fine of fifty dollars and thirty days in jail.[26] War Secretary Dearborn instructed territorial governors and the federal mediators living among the native tribes to strip the commercial licenses of any white trader found vending ardent spirits. As white expansion continued, virtually every new state and territory adopted its own Indian prohibitions—and always with the assent of tribal leaders.[27]

The federal government had little ability to enforce its prohibition, though. The legislation applied only to the vast expanses known as "Indian Country" beyond officially organized US states and territories. As white settlers encroached ever-farther westward, the blanket prohibition would become entangled in competing jurisdictions, and legally subverted by officials with dubious intentions. Once the government cleared title to ceded lands, distilleries popped up on former Indian territories like mushrooms after the rain, especially around critical river-trade and transportation junctures like St. Louis.[28]

Complaints by white European settlers trying to hold white whiskey traders accountable for violating the prohibition law normally fell on deaf ears.[29] But the settlers, at least, could exercise their political rights; Native Americans had none. Legally, native testimony before a court of law was not recognized as that of a human being until 1847; America's first peoples weren't granted citizenship until 1924, and their right to vote was not secured nationwide until 1962.[30] Often, natives' only nonviolent channel for political protest was to petition the Office of Indian Affairs, which was under the auspices of the War Department—evidence of the unequal and antagonistic relationship between colonizer and colonized.

Still, for the time, Little Turtle and Wells were pleased with the results of their mission. Little Turtle had won the first federal prohibition of the liquor traffic, and Jefferson had won a loyal intermediary in negotiating Indian affairs.[31] "We consider ourselves no longer as of the old nations beyond the great waters, but as united in one family with our red brethren here," President Jefferson wrote to "my friends and children" of the Indian tribes. He promised to protect the native tribes from the French, Spanish, and British, as well as those newly settled "bad men among your neighbors." Jefferson then proclaimed, "In establishing a trade with you, we desire to make no profit. We shall ask from you only what every thing costs us, and give you for your furs and pelts whatever we can get for them again."[32]

To say that white settlers and the US government failed to live up to Jefferson's lofty promises of fair trade and goodwill would be an understatement. For generations, US-Indian relations would suffer from exploitation, bloodshed, and tragedy, engulfing even those goodwill ambassadors, Wells and Little Turtle, themselves.

Both men died during the War of 1812. Little Turtle passed of natural causes at Wells's home at Fort Wayne on July 14. Wells died a month and a day later, though not nearly as peaceably. Wells volunteered to lead a group of Miami Indians on a rescue mission: to evacuate white settlers cowering in Fort Dearborn—in what is today downtown Chicago—from the siege of a belligerent Potowatomi tribe. Wells negotiated the surrender of the fort in exchange for safe passage to Fort Wayne. But, enraged upon finding all the abandoned fort's whiskey dumped on the ground, the Potowatomi massacred the retreating column along the dunes of Lake Michigan. Wells's frontier heroism is depicted on Chicago's famed Michigan Avenue drawbridges over the Chicago River, not far from where he was killed.[33]

White Man's Wicked Water

In the long, contentious history of alcohol in the United States, it may come as some surprise that America's "original prohibitionist" was Native American chief Mihšihkinaahkwa. "The fact that he wore feathers instead of a silk hat may, in part, account for his not having been given the place in the history of the temperance reform that his works justly entitle him to," at least according to former agent for the U.S. Indian Service, William E. "Pussyfoot" Johnson (Chapter 16).[34]

American prohibition is typically told as white people's history. If black, native, or immigrant communities are mentioned at all, they are usually depicted as mere objects, embodying white Americans' fears and incurring their political wrath. What we find, however, if we dig a little deeper, is that women, immigrants, African Americans, and Native Americans *all* had their own political interests, which often stood in direct opposition to the establishment. And each of these communities— disenfranchised, enslaved, or dismissed as subhuman—embraced prohibitionism as a political means to defend themselves against the addicting and debauching liquor traffic that brought such immense wealth to the white men who ran it. That even today Native Americans are widely portrayed as irredeemable drunks rather than the country's first prohibitionists tells us a great deal about the blind spots in our historical knowledge, and the durability of the colonizers' narratives.[35]

Fermented beverages were largely unknown in North America before European colonization—to say nothing of potent whiskeys and rums—which partly explains the devastating consequences of their sudden introduction to native populations in North America, as in colonial Africa (Chapters 3 and 6) and Asia (Chapters 5 and 7).[36] Native American communities were largely peaceful, hospitable, and spiritual, with no more understanding of the private ownership of land than of the air or water. The European colonists, on the other hand, "looked upon the natives as heathen to whom no consideration was due, and, often as mere beasts of prey which had no rights and which were to be exploited for the convenience and profit of the white race," according to subsequent historians. "From this point of view, the capturing of Indians as slaves and the traffic with them in whisky became logical enterprises on which to embark."[37]

The Mohegan tribes first encountered European distilled liquor on September 11, 1609, which is when English explorer Henry Hudson dropped anchor in New York Harbor. Striding ashore, Hudson offered the chiefs distilled spirits, which brought them an almost immediate stupor. Thereafter, they referred to the island as *Mahahachtanienk*, or "the place where we all became intoxicated." It was later shortened to "Manhattan."[38]

The *Mayflower* carried many hogsheads of beer, which was safer to drink than water. When Samoset—the first Native American to encounter the Pilgrims at Plymouth Colony—met them on March 16, 1621, he asked for beer along with biscuits, butter, pudding, and duck. But since the Pilgrims were running low, they offered him "strong water" of distilled spirits instead.[39] Within a week of contact, Captain Myles Standish negotiated a peace compact with the "Great King" Massasoit. Massasoit famously aided the Pilgrims through their first rough years, was celebrated at the first Thanksgiving, and maintained tranquility between the races for years thereafter. Still, at the conclusion of the agreement, Puritan governor William Bradford "called for some strong water, and drunke to him." Massasoit then "drunke a great draught that made him sweate all the while after" [sic].[40]

One of the most enduring stereotypes in American history is that of the drunken Indian. Certainly there is ample historical evidence to support it. It is curious, however, that European colonizers seem to follow the same playbook the world over:

Step 1: Introduce potent, industrial distillates to native populations that have no traditional experience with them.

Step 2: Sell or barter the addicting liquors to them for their furs, lands, human slaves, or any other objects of value.

Step 3: Feign alarm at the natives' resulting inebriation as evidence of *their* "savagery," rather than admit the culpability of the white colonizers who sell it.

Step 4: Use such "savagery" as justification for continuing the profit-making, colonial machinations under the guise of a "civilizing mission."

The British Empire ran this playbook in Ireland, India, Australia and the Middle East (Chapters 5–8), while virtually all the European imperial powers did the same in exploiting Africa (Chapters 3 and 6). Why should we expect the history of American colonization to be any different? By focusing solely on the drunk-enness of the Indian, the white man who sells the booze quietly slips away from our historical narratives. "The general prevalence of this vice among the Indians is in a great degree owing to unprincipled white traders, who persuade them to be-come intoxicated that they may cheat them the more easily, and obtain their lands or peltries for a mere trifle," wrote the Moravian John Heckewelder back in 1818. "Within the last fifty years, some instances have even come to my knowledge of white men having enticed Indians to drink, and when drunk, murdered them."[41]

But it wasn't just a few "unprincipled" bad apples who wreaked such havoc on Native American societies: the liquor trade was foundational to the entire system of colonial domination. The white man's "firewater" was the one European ware that had recurring demand: "Whereas a woolen blanket might last for many months and a metal knife or copper pot for years, liquor was quickly consumed, creating a demand that perpetuated itself."[42] Liquor, then, was an ideal mechanism for co-lonial trade and exploitation. As early as 1644, the investors of the Massachusetts Bay Company decreed "that it is not fit to deprive the Indians of any lawful comfort which God alloweth to all men by the use of wine, do order that it shall be lawful for such as are or shall be allowed license to retail wines to sell also to Indians so much as may be fit for their needful and refreshing."[43]

Almost immediately, the European colonists scrambled to contain the epi-demic of "swynish drunckennes [*sic*]" they themselves had unleashed. Blaming white traders who "too much affect and regard theire oune proffitt," in 1654, the Massachusetts Bay Colony limited the trade to ten licensed liquor sellers, who were "impowered and ordered to sell wine of any sort and strong licquors to the Indians as theire judgments shall seeme meete." It didn't help. Noting that Indian drunk-enness had gotten even worse, in 1657 the colony "doth heereby wholly prohibitt all persons, of what quallitje soeuer, henceforth to sell, trucke, barter, or give any strong licquors to any Indian, directly or indirectly."[44]

Still, colonization was fundamentally about profit, and taking advantage of Indians was incredibly lucrative. So much so that—prior proclamations notwithstanding—the Massachusetts Bay Colony farmed out a monopoly on the Indian fur trade to one Richard Way, who was given "all and euery benefit & advantages any ways accrewing to the country by virtue of the impose of wjne, brandy & rumme, with beavers, furrs & peltry, from hence to be traded with the Indians, together with the rates of drawing wine from the vintners." Any trader who defied the monopoly would be fined one hundred pounds.[45]

This was hardly a trivial footnote to America's bloody and drunken colonial his-tory. "Practically every Indian war," claimed Pussyfoot Johnson, "has been caused, directly or indirectly, by the traffic in intoxicating liquors. A drunken Indian commits an outrage, upon which infuriated whites retaliate with a similar outrage; Indians are robbed of their lands, ponies and blankets through being intoxicated with strong drink; in some variety of one of these transactions is found the germ of nearly every Indian slaughter that has disgraced the history of American colonization."[46]

For example: the bloodiest New England war was King Phillip's War (1675–1678), which began with raids on the tavern of settler John Woodcock, where the Indians had repeatedly been made drunk and swindled. "King Phillip"—the Wampanoag chief Metacomet, son of Massasoit—protested that when the white settlers got the Indians drunk, they were a threat not just to whites, but to sober Indians, too. His grievances were ignored. Having exhausted regular channels of diplomacy, the Wampanoag raided Woodcock's tavern, sparking waves of reprisals and counterattacks. When it was over, countless colonial towns had been destroyed; one out of every ten fighting-age white men had perished. King Phillip was ultimately killed and quartered; his limbs were hung from the trees, his hands were pickled in jars of rum and displayed in Boston, his head was placed on a pike and displayed publicly in Plymouth for a quarter century. His wife and children were sold into slavery, while the Protestant clergy called for their execution.[47]

Sadly, this was the bloody pattern of colonialism, not the exception.

Up and down the East Coast, colonies that strictly regulated the liquor trade were markedly more tranquil than those that were not. Consider Pennsylvania, which was chartered to the much-persecuted pacifist sect of English Quakers. In Boston, Quakers had been hung on the Commons for their beliefs; in New Amsterdam, they were imprisoned, tortured, and starved.[48] In Pennsylvania, the Quakers envisioned a haven that would—for the first time in either hemisphere—guarantee religious liberty for all inhabitants.

Immediately upon securing the grant from King Charles II in 1681, William Penn wrote a letter of peace and friendship to local Indian tribal leaders. "I am very Sensible of the unkindness and Injustice that hath been too much exersised towards you by the People of thes Parts of the world, who have sought themselves, and to make great Advantages by you," Penn wrote. Instead, he hoped they could "live Soberly and kindly together in the world . . . as Neighbors and friends."[49] Historians have labeled the Quakers' success in peaceful cohabitation as "one of the miracles of history."[50] But how did they do it? What was different about Pennsylvania? The Delaware and Lenape tribes weren't of exceptional temperament or culture. Instead it was the Quakers' respect, fair dealing, and refusal to profit from the natives' drunken misery that made all the difference.

Upon arriving in the New World and establishing his capital of Philadelphia— the "city of brotherly love"—Penn wrote back to England that the Native Americans were proper, elegant, and sagacious. "The worst is that they are ye wors for ye Christians who have propagated their views," Penn wrote in 1683. "Some of them are admirably sober, though ye Dutch & Sweed and English have by Brandy and Rum almost Debaucht y^m all and when Drunk ye most wretched of spectacles, often burning & sometimes murdering one another, at which times ye Christians are not without danger as well as fear."[51]

It was the Dutch West India Company that first explored and settled the present-day Mid-Atlantic and Delaware River Valley. Under the Dutch, the sale of liquor was a company monopoly.[52] From Fort Wilhelmus—an island in the Delaware River near present-day Burlington, New Jersey—the Dutch first sold liquor to the natives. After a falling out with the company, former director Peter Minuit (who famously founded New Amsterdam by swindling Manhattan from the natives for sixty guilders in trinkets) offered his services to the Swedish South Company, establishing fortifications for "New Sweden" near present-day Wilmington and New Castle, Delaware. The Swedes were then supplanted by the English, though they too found liquor to be the most profitable commodity to trade with the Indians. Together, the Dutch, Swedish, and English colonists were immensely suspicious of the newly arrived Quakers and resisted any Quaker efforts to curtail their lucrative liquor business.[53]

Yet in 1685, the Quakers met with the dwindling Ockanickon band of Delaware Indians, who'd happily traded corn, venison, fish, and fowl in the Pennsylvania counties of Chester and Delaware just west of Philadelphia. With the assembled Quakers listening intently, the *sachem* (chief) rose and explained that "seven Score of our People have been killed by reason of the drinking" of the liquor hawked first by the Dutch settlers, then the Swedes. He continued,

> Those People that sell it, they are blind, they have no Eyes, but now there is a People come to live amongst us, that have Eyes, they see it to be for our Hurt, and we know it to be for our Hurt; *They are willing to deny themselves of the Profit of it if for our good*; these People have Eyes; we are glad such a People are come amongst us. We must put it down by mutual consent; the Cask must be sealed up, it must be made fast, it must not leak by Day nor by Night, in the Light, nor in the Dark, and we give you these four Belts of Wampam, which we would have you lay up safe, and keep by you to be Witness of this Agreement that we make with you.[54]

It should come as little surprise, then, that fully four chapters of Penn's foundational "Great Laws" for the colony dealt with alcohol. Drunken and disorderly conduct was considered a minor legal offense. Strikingly, however, the Great Laws brought down the wrath of God—not against the drink or the drunkard—but against the man who sells: "Wheras divers Persons as English, Dutch, Sweeds &ct have been wont to Sell to the Indians Rum and Brandy and Such Like Distilled Spirrits," the Great Law declared, "whereby they make the poore Natives worse and not better . . . which is an heinous offence to God and a Reproach to the Blessed name of Christ and his Holy Religion It is therefore Enacted by the Authority aforesaid that no Person within this Province do from henseforth presume to Sell or Exchange any Rum or Brandy or any Other Strong Liquors at any time to any Indian within this Province."[55]

Frustrated white traders moved their liquor business either to the Dutch fort at Burlington or the Swedish forts of the "lower counties"—which became the Colony (and later state) of Delaware—and kept on selling. The Quaker prohibition wasn't perfect—both the Monthly Meetings and Yearly Meetings of the Society of Friends included admonishments of Quakers suspected of selling liquor to natives in violation of the law—but the relative tranquility between colonizer and colonized was striking in the Quaker settlements.[56]

Pennsylvania wasn't the only case where prohibition eased racial tensions. To the south, in Georgia, Governor James Edward Oglethorpe effected a prohibition and had likewise comparatively little strife with the natives.[57]

To the north, in the St. Lawrence River Valley of what would become Quebec, Algonquin leaders implored the French Jesuit settlers for protection against the liquor traders. The Jesuits agreed. From the 1640s to the 1660s, under Governors Vicomte d'Argenson and d'Avaugour, those white traders found guilty of selling liquor to natives were either whipped or shot. After French king Louis XIV personally interceded to reopen the liquor trade, Father Carheil described the utter human devastation: "Our missions are reduced to such extremity that we can no longer maintain them against the infinity of disorder, brutality, violence, injustice, impiety, insolence, scorn and insult, that the deplorable and infamous traffic in brandy has spread universally among the Indians of these parts. . . . In the despair in which we are plunged, nothing remains for us but to abandon them to the brandy-sellers as a domain of drunkenness and debauchery."[58]

As it turns out, in the long and contentious history of the colonization of native North America, "those who have been most successful in gaining the confidence of the Indians have been the Quaker and the Roman Catholic," according to McKenny and Hall's 1844 *History of the Indian Tribes of North America*. Those groups' successes had the same root. Rather than espousing the Protestants' complex schemes of heavenly salvation—debated and obsessed over by generations of European philosophers and theologians—Catholics and Quakers succeeded simply "by the observance of peace, humility, kindness, temperance, and justice."[59]

As we see time and again, when it comes to the long, bloody, and sorrowful history of American colonization, the question of war and peace more often than not turned on whether white settlers would respect native prohibitions or run roughshod over them.

Interestingly in that regard, the Philadelphia Campaign of the Revolutionary War saw the arrival of ragtag militias from across the colonies to defend the new capital of Philadelphia against the British. These militias were quick to violate the Quakers' prohibition agreements by trading liquor with the natives. So widespread was the practice even among the members of the Continental Army encamped at Valley Forge—and so great the backlash—that General George Washington had to enact his own prohibition on liquor trafficking. "All Persons whatever are forbid selling liquor to the Indians," Washington ordered. "If any sutler or soldier shall presume to act contrary to this prohibition, the former will be dismissed from camp, and the latter receive severe corporal punishment."

Washington found it necessary to enact prohibition not only to maintain peace with local Native American tribes, but to ensure sobriety and discipline among the soldiers themselves. Nine soldiers in each brigade of the Continental Army were charged "to seize the liquors they may find in the unlicensed tippling houses," and to "notify the inhabitants or persons living in the vicinity of camp that an unconditional seizure will be made of all liquors they shall presume to sell in the future."[60] Likewise, during their military campaigns, any unscrupulous sutler who "adulterated his Liquors or made use of Deficient Measures" in an attempt to get the soldiers drunk and make more money off of them would be court-martialed.[61]

For how often their names are invoked in latter-day debates over freedom and liberty, it is surprising how closely and frequently America's Founding Fathers regulated the exploitative liquor traffic, up to and including prohibition. It is also curious that—for all the historical talk of how the training at Valley Forge transformed a band of undisciplined militias into a regimented, disciplined, and unified army—the role of these liquor regulations and prohibitions never seem to get mentioned.

Revenue and Revolution

The immense revenue-generating power of selling alcohol—to whites as well as natives—meant that the liquor traffic was everywhere, even around military encampments. No wonder so many of the Founding Fathers were involved in the liquor trade: Samuel Adams and Patrick Henry were brewers, George Washington was both a vintner and distiller, while Thomas Jefferson, Andrew Jackson, John Calhoun, Henry Clay, and Aaron Burr were all winemakers. Moreover, much of the revolution was conceived in colonial taverns: sheltered spaces where pro-independence leaders could network and plot far from the prying eyes of British loyalists.[62]

From the earliest days of colonial settlement right through the advent of a modern income tax in the early twentieth century—some two hundred years of American history—taxes from the liquor trade were consistently among the largest sources of government revenue.[63]

In the absence of a sprawling government bureaucracy, liquor was relatively easy to tax. Tariffs on imported rum and whiskey could be easily assessed and collected dockside. Domestic manufacturers and retailers could be limited by issuing licenses, and then assessing taxes on the enterprises. While generating revenue was the primary focus, most colonial policies restricted the number of licenses, increased excises, or punished unscrupulous, unlicensed sellers—often justifying such restrictions in terms of their beneficial impacts on public health and morality.[64] That would continue even after the revolution.

Americans largely have not thought of themselves as colonizing people. After all, our country's very founding was a declaration of independence from European colonialism.[65] Still—from the indigenous perspective—the Revolutionary War was largely a war of white Europeans fighting other white Europeans on their land. Similar to the French and Indian War (1745–1763), the colonists and the British both enticed different native tribes to fight on their behalf. "Great Britain requested us to join with them in the conflict against the Americans, and promised the Indians land and liquor," claimed Seneca chief Cornplanter, who wished to stay out of the white men's quarrels.[66] As usual during wartime, the mask of humanity, decency, and European Christian virtue fell away, revealing base and carnal needs. For the British in particular, that meant "rum was dealt out without stint" to the natives, with predictable results.[67]

After the war, the new American government's biggest challenge was to repay the massive debts accrued in their revolutionary struggle. But under the Articles of Confederation (1781–1789), the central government was powerless. Each individual state was master of its own trade and commerce; with no power to tax, the central government could only go hat in hand and request contributions from the states. "It will be said there is no money in the treasury," wrote Thomas Jefferson from Paris to James Monroe in 1786. "There will never be money in the treasury till the confederacy shews its teeth."[68] Frustration over these chronic balance-of-payment issues led delegates to draft a new Constitution in Philadelphia with a stronger federal—rather than confederal—government.

Well before even approving the Bill of Rights, the very first item passed by the first Congress in 1789 was an affirmation of oaths to support the Constitution of the United States. The debate over the second order of business—righting the ship of public finance through the Tariff Act of 1789—was far more heated, as it had significant implications for states' rights, dramatically portrayed in the Broadway hit *Hamilton*. Given both its immense revenue-generating potential and perceived social benefits of higher prices and lower consumption, the first items listed on America's first tariff were Jamaican rum, all distilled spirits, molasses for making rum, Madeira wine, all other wine, cider, beer, ale, porter, and various other foodstuffs.[69]

This barely put a dent in the seventy-nine million dollars owed by both the federal government and the states to foreign lenders. Treasury Secretary Alexander Hamilton's plan to put the teetering government on firm financial footing required the federal government to assume the debts of all the states, and impose a domestic excise tax.[70] Tariffs on imports were one thing, but the revolution itself had been fought over the imposition of unjust domestic excises, so opposition was vehement. Hamilton argued forcefully that the country's first tax be on liquor production, which also might reduce the astronomical rates of liquor consumption in the so-called alcoholic republic: estimated at five gallons of distilled spirits consumed annually by every man, woman, and child, roughly three times current consumption rates, according to liquor historian W. J. Rorabaugh.[71] Even Hamilton's fiercest critics admitted that it was the least-worst option. According to James Madison—who preferred a weak central government—it would aid in reconstruction and would increase "sobriety and thereby prevent disease and untimely deaths."[72]

On a per-capita basis, the new tax was minimal, but its burden was not equally felt. The farmers of newly settled western Pennsylvania were hit especially hard. Rather than hauling their bulky crops up and over the Appalachian Mountains to markets in the east, they distilled their grains into whiskey, which was more compact, didn't spoil, and was far easier to transport. The locals bristled at the tax, as well as at the required registration of all stills. Tax collectors and US marshals who demanded payment from the distillers were whipped, tarred, and feathered. In 1794 President Washington called in the troops to subdue the Whiskey Rebellion and enforce the laws of the United States, by force if necessary.[73]

While the liquor tax was repealed after the war debts were repaid, as the least-worst option, such alcohol taxes would be ratcheted up time and again to fund every major war: the War of 1812, the Mexican-American War (1846–1848), the Civil War (1861–1865), the Spanish-American War (1898), and World War I—in addition to the never-ending series of Indian wars on the country's ever-expanding western frontier. Before the advent of a modern income tax at the beginning of the twentieth century, liquor taxes were the single largest contributor to the treasury of every major world power: 20 percent of all revenues for the German Empire (Chapter 4), 23 percent in the British Empire (Chapter 5), and 26 percent in the Russian Empire (Chapter 2). When it came to liquor revenues, the United States was hardly exceptional, clocking in at 25 percent of American government income.[74]

Just as with those European empires, it is no stretch to say that the political might of the United States was built upon liquor revenues. Weaning the government off of its addiction to alcohol taxes would be a tall order, but that is what later generations of temperance and prohibition activists ultimately sought to do: capture the institutions of the state in order to rein in the predations of the state-sponsored liquor traffic, in order to defend the health and well-being of society.

"You White People Make a Great Parade about Religion"

There's an ironic twist in many works that address the colonial nature of drinking: the implicit—and often explicit—assumption that if a native is won over to the cause of temperance, it must be on account of some Protestant missionary.[75] This assumption infers that white people have a monopoly on morality and common sense, and removes any agency from colonized, non-white, subaltern communities. As we've seen in Africa (Chapters 3 and 6), India (Chapter 7), and the Middle East (Chapter 8), none of that is true. While a smattering of white missionaries may be allies in supporting indigenous uplift, to attribute all political power to them belittles native concerns and activism. Perhaps nowhere is that better exemplified than in the United States, where Native Americans consistently pointed out the hypocrisy of the white man promoting religion, morality, and civilization in his right hand, while undermining all three with the liquor bottle in his left.[76] Native chiefs didn't need a white man to explain to them that liquor was killing off their people; they could see it with their own eyes.

Take, for instance, the founding of Cleveland, Ohio, longtime home of baseball's Cleveland Indians. In 1796, General Moses Cleaveland of the Connecticut Land Company arrived at the mouth of the Cuyahoga River and established the first white settlement in the so-called Western Reserve: western territory claimed by Connecticut. Negotiating with the Seneca chief Sagoyewatha—or Red Jacket— Cleaveland obtained everything east of the Cuyahoga for one hundred gallons of whiskey and a twenty-five-thousand-dollar annuity. During the negotiations, Red Jacket pressed Cleaveland: "You white people make a great parade about religion; you say you have a book of laws and rules which was given you by the Great Spirit, but is this true?" Red Jacket asked rhetorically. "No—it was written by your own people. They do it to deceive you. Their whole wishes center here," he said, pointing to Cleaveland's pocket. "All they want is the money."

He explained that white people came among them, promising to educate them in the ways of agriculture, only to swindle them and leave: "Our land is taken from us, and still we don't know how to farm it."[77]

Red Jacket's accusation was as scathing as it was obvious. Cleaveland was working for the Connecticut Land *Company*. Its original proprietors were a consortium of the fifty-seven wealthiest men in Connecticut, who authorized Cleaveland to make the most advantageous deals to maximize the profit for the company's shareholders.[78] This point is worth underscoring: colonialism has never been what colonizers say it is. The tale colonizers tell themselves is one of exploration, migration, and settlement: people used to live over there, and now we live over here. But empires, colonies, and imperialism weren't even primarily about migration, but rather subjugation and conquest for profit. Consider what we've already seen of the British South Africa *Company* and the British East India *Company* and—in North America—the Dutch West Indies *Company* and the Massachusetts Bay *Company* and the American Fur *Company* (Chapter 10). For native populations the world over, the disjuncture between what the white, Christian missionaries who lived among them were saying and what white colonists were doing constituted the most obvious hypocrisy. Natives knew it. Missionaries begrudgingly admitted it, too.

"Of the manner in which they have acquired this latter vice" of drunkenness, missionary John Heckewelder wrote in 1818, "I presume there can be no doubt. They charge us in the most positive manner with being the first who made them acquainted with ardent spirits, and what is worse, with having exerted all the means in our power to induce them to drink to excess."[79] In the United States as the world over, white missionaries were in the unenviable position as apologists for European colonialism—using the teachings of Christ to justify blatantly un-Christian behavior. It was everywhere an uphill battle.

Red Jacket was, if anything, an antimissionary. Born into the Wolf Clan of the Seneca Nation in the Finger Lakes region of upstate New York, he became a prominent advocate, orator, and negotiator between the US government and various Indian tribes. He often wore an embroidered scarlet jacket gifted him by the British for his services as a message runner during the Revolutionary War. Hanging around his neck was a giant medallion commemorating his 1792 meeting with George Washington, upon which he swore his fealty to the new United States. He even fought on the American side against the British in the War of 1812.[80]

Red Jacket was a negotiator at the Treaty of Big Tree, which ceded much of upstate New York to Founding Father and prominent land speculator Robert Morris: "*the great Eater with a big Belly* endeavoring to devour our lands," as Red Jacket called

Figure 9.2 Sagoyewatha, or Red Jacket, of the Wolf Clan of the Seneca Nation (1750–1830). Lithograph by C. B. King, circa 1836. Red Jacket shown wearing coat and large medallion depicting his 1792 meeting with George Washington.

Source: "Red Jacket. Seneca War Chief," Library of Congress, Prints and Photographs, LC-DIG-pga-07567.

him.[81] Red Jacket was the most steadfast among the assembled tribal chiefs—until the barrels of whiskey suddenly showed up. The negotiations devolved amid the "big drunk" that followed. At the end of the day, the assembled tribal leaders ceded much of upstate New York over Red Jacket's objections.[82] He had felt the sting of the white man's cunning hypocrisy.

So when in 1805 Boston missionary Jacob Cram requested permission to evangelize among the Seneca natives, Red Jacket sent him this most scathing reply: "We know that the great Spirit is better pleased with his red children than his Whites— When he bestows upon us a hundred fold blessing more than upon you," he wrote. "You say that you destroyed the son of the Great Spirit—perhaps this is the merited cause of all your troubles and misfortunes. But, brother, bear in mind that we had no participation in this murder."

Turning to evangelism, Red Jacket pitied the white man for their violence, divisions, and doublespeak. Not only would the natives not adopt Christianity, they were willing to send missionaries among the whites to teach *them* native habits and customs. "We cannot embrace your religion—it renders us divided and unhappy— but by your embracing ours we believe that you would be more happy & more acceptable to the great Spirit."

Instead of doting over the education and morality of the Seneca tribes, Red Jacket said,

> Go then and teach the whites. Improve *their* morals and refine *their* habits—Make *them* less disposed to cheat Indians—Make the whites generally less inclined to make indians drunk & to take from them their lands. Let us know the tree by the blossoms, and the blossoms by the fruit.— When this shall be made clear to our minds we may be more willing to listen to you. But until then we must be allowed to follow the religion of our ancestors.[83]

In later years, Red Jacket's rebuke has been listed among the greatest Native American orations.[84] Yet principled condemnations of white duplicity aside, Red Jacket had himself long ago succumbed to the addiction of alcoholism. "Often have I known him to make a great speech, rich in eloquence,—and in an hour afterward seen him drunk upon the ground," wrote one frontier captain.[85] He'd abstain before council meetings and other important affairs, only to get wasted afterward. His drunken belligerence with other native leaders and white delegates nearly scuttled the treaty negotiations at Big Tree. And even when he was wined and dined by George Washington himself, Red Jacket admitted, "Although I am fond of eating, I am more so of drinking."[86]

His later life was spent in an increasingly futile effort to defend his people against the encroachment of Christian missionaries, the white man's firewater, and American land companies. In 1810 he led a deputation of leaders of the Six Nations to Washington to complain that the Americans were acting in bad faith. While the tribesmen still held to the letter of the treaty, the government had stopped prosecuting the "bad men" who swindled and injured the natives with impunity. "We now call on your Government to fulfill this part of the Treaty, and make good the Damages done us by your bad people. Brother, Why should you hesitate to comply with a treaty you have made?" he asked rhetorically.[87]

In 1826 Red Jacket again traveled to Washington to complain about the corruption and underhandedness of David Ogden and the Holland Land Company in taking most of the Seneca reservation through bribery, intimidation, and liquor. His protests fell on deaf ears; Washington policymakers tittered that he'd been drinking again.[88] At the time he died of cholera in 1830, Red Jacket had been negotiating a reconciliation between those remaining Seneca Indians who had converted to Christianity and those who retained their tribal beliefs. Those non-Christianized Senecas were still sheltered and educated in Quaker schools.[89]

Ultimately, every one of Red Jacket's eleven children died of tuberculosis, which he interpreted as divine punishment for his intemperance. "Red Jacket was once a great man, and in favor with the Great Spirit. He was a lofty pine among the smaller trees of the forest," he self-eulogized on his deathbed. "But after years of glory he degraded himself by drinking the fire-water of the white man. The Great Spirit has looked upon him in anger, and his lightning has stripped the pine of its branches."[90]

Prophets versus Profits

Movements for temperance, abstinence, and prohibition by Native Americans were not limited to a handful of leaders like Little Turtle or Red Jacket. They were broad-based, indigenous movements for community protection against the predations of the white liquor traffic, generations before the same mantle—using the same logic and tactics against the same foe—was taken up by white Americans on their own behalf. That it is ritually excluded from every history of temperance and social activism only underscores how prohibition history, as we've previously been taught it, is largely white people's history.

Virtually everywhere white explorers and emissaries went, they found entire tribes of abstemious Indians: burned once by firewater, they'd sworn off "the Devil's blood" forever.[91] In the central Appalachians in 1806, explorers found tribes "strongly opposed to the use of spiritous liquors, and seldom held a council without some animadversions on their baneful effects—and nothing excited more wonder among the surrounding white people, than to find them entirely refuse liquor when offered to them. The Indians said, that when the white people urged them to drink whiskey, they would ask for bread or provisions in its stead."[92]

In 1807 agent John Sibley explored the Red River Valley, encountering the Heitan (Comanche) tribe, who "refused Spiritous liquor," explaining, "they Saw a Chief of the Panis Made Drunk by an American who had been in his Town & treated well by him & wished to return the Civility, as he would have a Civility Returned by being made Drunk, he was a Spectacle of Disgust, Pity Amongst them, not one of them would taste Anything that was Offered to them Afterwards." Other tribes he encountered farther inland were "*like all Other Indians*: fond of Tobacco, but will not taste Ardent Spirits."[93]

In the southern states, settlers encountered the Seminole (of central Florida), Cherokee (north Georgia), Creek (Alabama), and Choctaw and Chickasaw (Mississippi). For their adaptation to Western culture and constitutional forms of government (which included plantation slavery), they were dubbed the "Five Civilized Tribes." Each tribe resisted the encroachments of the white man's liquor, culminating in explicit prohibition legislation.

"We came here sober," declared the Choctaw chiefs upon their meeting with government representatives in 1801 (the same year Little Turtle met Jefferson), "we wish to go away so—We therefore request that the strong drink, which we understand our brothers have brought here, may not be distributed." Their 1820 Treaty of Doak's Stand authorized the US agent to destroy all liquor he found within the territory. The Choctaw Republic officially legislated its own prohibition law in 1827 and maintained a steadfast opposition to the white liquor trade throughout its political existence.[94]

In 1819 the National Committee and Council of the Cherokee Nation, at Newtown, Georgia, legislated that "No person or persons, not citizens of the Nation, shall bring into this Nation, or sell any spiritous liquors," under penalty of confiscation and a one-hundred-dollar fine. The Chickasaw followed in 1828.[95] Ultimately, the prohibitions by the Five Civilized Tribes would have important political ramifications both for their removal west to present-day Oklahoma (Chapter 10) and the advance of national prohibition in the early twentieth century (Chapter 16).

Back north in present-day Indiana and Ohio lived the temperate, generous, and humane chief Tecumseh—and his brother, the "Shawnee Prophet" Tenskwatawa—who built a vast multitribe confederacy to assiduously resist white encroachments and defend their native customs, by force if necessary. "We ought to consider ourselves as one man," Tenskwatawa proclaimed to governor (and future ninth US president) William Henry Harrison in 1808, "but we ought to live agreeably to our several customs, the red people after their mode, and the white people after theirs; particularly, that they should not drink whiskey; that it was not made for them, but the white people, who alone knew how to use it; and that it is the cause of all the mischiefs which the Indians suffer." He then pressed Governor Harrison: "You have promised to assist us; now I request you, in behalf of all the red people, to use your exertions to prevent the sale of liquor to us."[96]

The Shawnee initially had an ally in William Henry Harrison. Upon being appointed secretary of the Northwest Territory in 1801, he delivered to the War

Department a detailed cataloging of native complaints against white liquor sellers, concluding, "Of the truth of all those charges I am well convinced." In 1803 he wrote to Jefferson directly, pleading for stepped-up enforcement of the ban on giving or selling liquors to Native Americans in the Northwest Territory—a policy that dated back to 1790.[97] When the areas west of Ohio were reorganized as the Indiana Territory, Harrison was appointed governor. In his first message to the first Indiana legislature in 1805, Harrison browbeat the assemblymen: "You are witnesses to the abuses; you have seen our towns crowded with furious and drunken savages; our streets flowing with their blood; their arms and clothing bartered for the liquor that destroys them." In the interests of both the natives and their own white constituents—and their own conscience—Harrison implored the senators to prohibit the sale of liquor to Indians, which they then did; though only within a distance of forty miles around the capital.[98]

More important than Harrison's prohibition were the religious warnings of Tecumseh and the Shawnee Prophet that drunks would suffer eternal agony in the afterlife, which effectively dried up the whiskey business in the old Northwest. Tribesmen across the Shawnee Confederacy were "so thoroughly alarmed at the prospect of fiery punishment in the spirit world that, for a long time, intoxication became practically unknown among the western tribes."[99]

Neither the sobriety nor the peace were destined to last. For the better part of a decade, Tecumseh's confederacy fought against white encroachments upon their land, which brought them into repeated confrontations with Governor Harrison. In 1811, while Tecumseh was in the South recruiting allies among the Five Civilized Tribes, Harrison marched on Tenskwatawa at Tippecanoe (earning Harrison his famed nickname), fracturing the Confederacy and burning the Shawnee capital of Prophetstown to the ground. In hopes of founding an independent Indian state, Tecumseh cast his lot with the British in the War of 1812, during which he was ultimately killed by American forces.[100]

Indian temperance resistance didn't always end in war: if the white settlers actually respected tribal prohibitions, both sides could coexist quite harmoniously. Take, for instance, the Vermillion Kickapoos of Illinois, who were allied with Tecumseh and the Shawnees at Tippecanoe. The tribe had banished one of their own—Kennekuk—for murdering his uncle in a drunken rage. Left to work odd jobs among the white settlers, he developed his own syncretic religion that combined traditional mysticism with notions of a Christian afterlife in which drunks would face eternal damnation in the "burning pits of hell." Showing penance through self-flagellation, Kennekuk rejoined the tribe, which adopted the faith of the Kickapoo Prophet. Determined not to follow Tecumseh and the Shawnee Prophet in the ways of war, he preached temperance and nonviolence, not unlike Gandhi, Tolstoy, and the Quakers. He believed—correctly, as it turned out—that a sober, industrious, and good-neighborly tribe would deny the invaders the standard "drunken savage" pretext for demanding their removal, as white European settlers had used virtually everywhere else. The tribe ultimately prospered, and their removal westward was delayed for more than a decade.[101]

When the time did eventually come for the Kickapoo to be uprooted and moved west to Kansas, it wasn't entirely nonconsensual. The Kickapoo—like a surprising number of tribes—believed that relocation was the only way to escape the white man's poisons and predations.[102] Unfortunately, neither the destination nor the voyage would live up to the white man's promise. On the westward trail in Missouri, the Kickapoo tribe was beset by "a gang of whiskey merchants," who—when the tribe refused to buy their liquor—killed two Kickapoos and stole the tribe's horses.[103]

"We are afraid of the wicked water brought us by our white friends," the tribesmen told the agents as they approached their Kansas reservation. "We wish to get out of its reach by land or water."

Commissioner E. A. Ellsworth at Fort Leavenworth solemnly replied, "Your Great Father was very sorry when the wicked water was brought into the country; but he will stop it, and will punish the wicked men who brought it by Judges sent to try them."[104]

Unfortunately, few Native Americans—among the Kickapoo or elsewhere— understood the particular business dynamics of the liquor trade, which would conspire to ensure that the US government would never live up to those not-too-lofty promises of justice.

10

Liquor and the Ethnic Cleansing of North America

Butte des Morts, Michigan Territory (Wisconsin): Saturday, August 11, 1827

Surveying the shores of Lake Winnebago in the Northwoods of present-day Wisconsin, Thomas L. McKenney—the first US superintendent of Indian Affairs—ruminated upon his delegation's curious destination: Butte des Morts. "The French, having been the first to traverse these regions, have given names to almost everything that is distinguishable by a name," and this "Hill of the Dead" in French was the site of two vicious Indian battles nearly a century earlier. The bone-filled burial mounds were still visible.[1]

A lifelong Quaker and foremost architect of Indian policy in the early republic, in 1827 McKenney was tasked—along with governor of the expansive Michigan Territory, Lewis Cass—to hold a treaty council at Butte des Morts, among the Chippewa, Menominee, and Winnebago tribes. Formally delineating the borders between the tribes, they thought, might reduce intertribal tensions, especially amid growing rumors of removal westward. Over their respective political careers, McKenney and Cass sparred repeatedly over the trafficking of liquor among the Indians—McKenney steadfastly opposed and Cass reluctantly in favor—but on this day they worked together as government dignitaries. McKenney was doling out the requisite presents to an ever-growing crowd of Indians when a woman's terrified scream arose from the water's edge.

"A rush of a thousand Indians was made for the spot whence it proceeded," McKenney recalled. "I looked, and saw in the midst of the crowd a man's arm raised, with a knife in the hand. It fell—and then was heard another scream!"

A garrison soldier tackled the Indian before he could land a third, and likely fatal, blow. The perpetrator was held in the provision house, while McKenney bandaged the deep wounds on the old woman's arms. They then dispatched the native woman to army surgeons in Green Bay, fifty miles away.

Turns out, the attacker was the victim's son-in-law. The old woman and her daughter were packing their canoe with the received gifts when rumor spread of an approaching whiskey dealer. This caught the attention of the young brave. "The mother-in-law, well knowing that their calicoes, and blankets, and strouding, and pork, and beef, and flour, &c., would soon be parted from, in exchange for this fire-water, followed him, entreating him not to go, but to go home and enjoy what had been given them there," McKenney wrote. "She clung to him rather inconveniently, when he resolved on freeing himself by the use of his knife."[2]

All of this had transpired in the open, witnessed by hundreds of natives from competing tribes with differing conceptions of justice. Most braves—being of patriarchal tribes—likely sympathized with the attacker in dispatching his troublesome mother-in-law as he saw fit. So all were curious how the colonizers would handle the situation. When McKenney explained the situation to Governor Cass, his reply was swift:

"*Make a woman of him.*"

And so they did.

They gathered all of the Indians around—perhaps a thousand in total—to watch as sentries paraded the accused man from the storeroom and lashed him to a flag-staff atop one of the ancient mounds. "Every eye of chief, half-chief, brave, and squaw; aye, and of every child and it seemed to me of every dog also, was beaming with concentrated lustre, and every eye was upon us," McKenney wrote.[3]

Through the various tribal interpreters, Governor Cass summarized the case, emphasizing the mother's noble aim of defending her family from the poverty and hunger that follow the liquor man. "The whiskey trader cared for none of these things, but sought only to rob them of their blankets and calicoes, &c., and given them nothing in exchange for them but fire-water. The Great Spirit looked down and smiled on this act of the woman, and was angry at the bad conduct of the man, and with the whiskey trader."

In passing his judgment, Cass declared, "For this act, he shall be no longer a brave; he has forfeited his character as a man; *from henceforth, let him be a woman!*"

Growls of male disapproval and vengeance rippled through the crowd, but were drowned out by approving cheers from the native women, who—perhaps for the first time in their lives—had just seen their interests and status validated as just.

And so, McKenney scaled the mound and had the unquivering brave stripped naked. After removing his leggings, all that remained was his belt, holding a large butcher's knife. McKenney drew the knife from its scabbard and held it aloft to the rapt crowd.

With all of his force, McKenny then thrust the knife into the wooden flag staff above the brave's head, snapping it off at the handle. "No man who employs his knife as this man employs his, has a right to carry one," McKenney declared. He placed the handle into the culprit's hand, declaring that this would be the only knife he'd henceforth be allowed to carry.

The sentries then dressed him in an old granny's dirty petticoat, unshackled him, and sent him into the jeering Indian crowd. "I wish they had killed me. I went up the mound to be shot," he later told the interpreter, utterly humiliated. "I am no longer a brave; I'm a woman!"

McKenney later explained that this punishment was intended "to elevate the condition of women among the Indians. It was mild in its physical effects, but more terrible than death in its action and consequences upon the offender." For the duration of his dealings with the tribe as superintendent of Indian Affairs, this native never again caused trouble, and was condemned to the drudgery of women's work. Still, McKenney lamented that the infinitely more guilty party—the whiskey trader—had gotten off scot-free.

"These whiskey traders follow these poor fellows from river to river, and from wilderness to wilderness, and from lake to lake, entailing, from year to year, this unmitigated curse upon them," McKenney wrote. Upon these parasites, "these murderers of the Indian's health, and peace, and life—the law should have always, and ought now, to be armed with such frightful vengeance as to deter them," in essence, from ever profiting from the Indians' misery.

"Who can account for the apathy that pervades the councils of this great nation upon this subject?" the Quaker McKenney lamented. "And where shall be found a solution of the almost universal indifference with which a great portion of our race, *Christians*, as we profess to be, listen to the wail that reach them from the wilderness homes of these abused and cast-off people?"[4]

Just as that one whiskey trader escaped justice by disappearing from the scene at Butte des Morts, so too has the liquor traffic disappeared from our historical understanding of American westward expansion. We largely know about the Trail of Tears and the shameful legacy of how one solemn treaty after another was ripped up in order to uproot and ethnically cleanse the eastern half of the North American continent of its native inhabitants. But reducing Indian removal to just the two-faced dealings of Andrew Jackson obscures the larger role of the liquor traffic as a primary mechanism of American colonial subjugation and oppression. From the Midwest to the Deep South, unscrupulous white whiskey traders and monopolists used alcohol to decimate native tribes for their own profit. At the same time, those sympathetic to the Native Americans sought to defend their rights and interests through government protection from—and even isolation from—the predations of white settlers. So insatiable was the white man's greed, however, neither legislation nor distance could ultimately protect the Native Americans, even despite the promises of generations of American political leaders to do just that.

In brief: the tale of American ethnic cleansing can—and probably should—be told as a cautionary temperance tale. The fact that we don't generally consider Indian removal in terms of alcohol politics again underscores the degree to which prohibition history has largely been limited to white people's history.

Figure 10.1 Thomas Loraine McKenney (1856), oil on canvas, by Charles Loring Elliott. National Portrait Gallery, Smithsonian Institution, Washington, DC.
Source: National Portrait Gallery, East Gallery 136.

The Factory and the Monopolist

When President Jefferson vowed to Chief Little Turtle that the United States "desires to make no profit" in trading furs and pelts with the Indians (Chapter 9), he was referring to the so-called factory system of trade, begun under President Washington in 1796.[5] Fur hats and coats were all the rage in Europe and America, so the pelts of beavers, minks, and muskrats were the most valuable commodities native trappers had to offer. The government established trading posts—"factors" or "factories"—usually adjacent to frontier military forts. The idea was to forgo any profit in order to give the Indians top value for their furs by exchanging them for high-quality blankets, kettles, and other durables. Not simply a goodwill gesture, the system was also intended to draw the native tribes closer to the American government, by winning them over from the unscrupulous British, French, and Spanish traders who dominated the frontier trade from the Great Lakes to the mouth of the Mississippi. The factory system stimulated commerce by trading exclusively in

American-made goods, and sought to anchor natives to the land by dealing in agricultural implements: spades, scythes, plows, and seed.[6] The system flourished in its first years, but struggled against the encroachment of ever more white traders, who'd happily trade valuable Indian pelts for smuggled liquor, even in defiance of prohibition.[7]

When McKenney was made superintendent of Indian Trade in 1816, he doubled down on the factory system as a necessary stepping stone toward civilizing and integrating the Native Americans. He tirelessly stocked the factors with the highest-quality merchandise and expanded the system from a dozen outposts that dotted the vast western wilderness to over thirty. When supplies arrived at the trading posts in Green Bay, Prairie du Chien, and St. Peter's (now Minneapolis), Governor Cass described the goods as "the finest ever seen in his region."[8]

The eternal bugbear of benevolence was the white trader's single-minded quest for profits.[9] McKenney knew that the only way to save the factory system was to rein in unscrupulous small traders, for whom illicit whiskey was their most profitable commodity and most powerful weapon. "Its attraction for the Indian was irresistible, and by means of it he could be robbed of everything he possessed. No trader could do any business without it if his opponents were supplied with it. It was therefore the one indispensable article which the traders must have at any hazard."[10]

Any American citizen could post a one-thousand-dollar bond to the War Department to become a licensed trader among the Indians, who excelled at trapping the furs that were in such high demand on the East Coast and in Europe. However, a trader found violating government regulations on the trade—most importantly the prohibition on selling them liquor—would lose his license and his one thousand dollars. Unlicensed traders risked a one-hundred-dollar fine and thirty days in jail. The licenses were meant to bring a modicum of oversight and regulation, though McKenney admitted that over his fourteen years in charge of the Indian trade, "no one was successfully prosecuted for selling whiskey to Indians or for trading without a license."[11]

The only firewall between firewater and the Indians was the factory system. It was far from perfect, but it was economically self-sustaining, and abandoning it meant sacrificing the Indians to white greed.[12] For a time, McKenney hoped that the quality wares, wholesale prices, and favorable terms would squeeze out not only the British and French competition, but the petty traders too. But little did McKenney expect that the high-minded system—established under the immediate direction of President Washington—would be completely subverted by America's first business tycoon: John Jacob Astor.[13]

Historians lionize Astor as a self-made business titan who rose from poverty to become one of the wealthiest men in human history. By the 1840s, he had amassed some $20 million, or over $116 billion today. Much of that came from his American Fur Company, which consistently defied federal and state laws with impunity, in order to get Indian trappers drunk and take their valuable furs for pennies. "The

Astor fortune was based on alcohol and fraud," claims Howard Abadinsky's classic, *Organized Crime*, explaining, "Drunken Native Americans were systematically cheated by agents of Astor's American Fur Company. When the victims complained to the government, Astor's agents resorted to violence. When the Indians retaliated, troops were sent to quell the 'Indian disorder.'"[14]

Born Johann Jakob Astor in Germany in 1763, Astor immigrated first to London and then New York following the Revolutionary War, importing high-quality furs from (British) Montreal to export to markets in Europe. As his capital grew, so did his ambition. In 1800, he bought six ships to expand his fur-trade empire all the way to East Asia, within a decade becoming the "Prince of the China Trade."[15]

"King of the Drug Trade" would be a more accurate title: each of Astor's ships carried well in excess of five metric tons of Turkish opium destined for addicts in China, and they sailed constantly. As the Chinese narcotics trade was monopolized by the British East India Company (Chapter 7), Astor's low-grade Turkish opium— often cut with molasses or cow dung for even more profit—had to be smuggled ashore under cover of night. Astor made a fortune.[16] The Chinese people were decimated. By mid-century, the Qing dynasty would wage two quixotic Opium Wars to try to stem the onslaught of Anglo-American narcotics.

As the Napoleonic Wars raged in Europe, both the British and French regularly violated American maritime neutrality—molesting American merchant ships suspected of carrying war materiel, seizing their cargo, impressing their seamen into military service, and wreaking havoc on American commerce. In response, President Jefferson cut off trade relations with both countries through the Embargo Act of 1807, which largely swept away those pesky British and French small traders from the fur trade across the upper Midwest of the United States. The embargo also effectively shuttered Astor's lucrative import/export business.

Seizing the opportunity, Astor organized his holdings into the American Fur Company (AFC), which would soon monopolize the profitable northwestern fur trade. Writers today marvel over Astor's "cutthroat" competitiveness, but when it came to American Fur, that description was all too literal.

"The first step always taken in dealing with an 'opposition' was to crush it by sheer force if possible," wrote Hiram Chittenden's insightful history, *The American Fur Trade of the Far West* (1902). "When that did not succeed an attempt would be made to buy it out, admit it to an interest in the company, or divide the field with it."[17] That opposition took two forms: the patchwork of small traders and the US government's factory system.

Like an organized-crime syndicate, American Fur threatened and intimidated many small traders into taking up alternative lines of work. Others they co-opted as subcontractors. Those who became employees had to buy their provisions from AFC company stores at exorbitant prices, putting many traders in debt to Astor and the company. A surprising number of white traders who delivered their pelts to AFC in the 1820s and '30s disappeared mysteriously before they could cash their checks. American Fur just reported them as "killed by Indians." There would be no investigations. President Zachary Taylor called American Fur Company traders "the greatest scoundrels the world ever knew."[18]

One can only imagine what they had in store for the poor Indians.

The Indian trade "is too precarious for anybody to hazard anything in it until the factories were to be abolished," explained US Chief Army Engineer Charles Gratiot to Astor in 1814.[19] Not surprisingly, then, Astor focused all of his economic and political might at subverting McKenney and his beneficent system. The wolves were circling.

Officers in Green Bay wrote McKenney that American Fur Company agents "hold out an idea that they will, ere long, be able to break down the factories; and they menace the Indian agents and others who may interfere with them, with dismission from office through Mr. Astor." He received word from Arkansas that legal evidence against American Fur Company traders for violating the prohibition was almost impossible to obtain, and that "they are so numerous in this quarter and of such bad character I have been repeatedly told a witness would risk both life and property by giving evidence against them in a court of Justice." From Fort Mitchell in present-day Alabama came reports that "the contraband trade appears to pervade the whole Georgia frontier, [introducing] their merchandize into the very heart of the Creek nation."[20]

At stake was the entire future of the Native American tribes, and McKenney wasn't going down without a fight. At every session of Congress from 1816 until 1822, he recommended not only strengthening and expanding the factory system, but squeezing out the unscrupulous traders by making the Indian trade a government monopoly. If the private traders had the same noble intentions "of bettering the condition of our native Inhabitants," McKenney testified, then he had no problem with unregulated trade. But they had no such motives.[21] Legislators were sympathetic to expansion, but not monopolization—or, at least not *government* monopolization.

As for John Jacob Astor, he certainly wasn't without political power. First, he tried to go over McKenney's head to Secretary of War—and future vice president under John Quincy Adams and Andrew Jackson—John C. Calhoun. The tycoon pleaded that "we have been great sufferers" due to unfair competition from the factors. Calhoun knew better. Astor also dispatched the appropriately named Ramsay Crooks—AFC general manager—to lobby Congress. Within a month of his arrival, a bill was introduced to abolish the factory system completely.[22]

McKenney was open to compromise. He proposed to Congress licensing private traders to operate from fixed locations, with all revenue from the licenses to go to the betterment of the Native Americans. It was a tempting policy alternative, but was scuttled by his insistence that *"spiritous liquors should be excluded under the severest penalties."*[23]

The idea of a government monopoly was loathsome to Americans, argued Missouri's first senator (and Andrew Jackson's former aide-de-camp) Thomas Hart Benton, whose oratorical broadsides ultimately doomed the factory system in 1822. Senator Benton introduced stacks of evidence of alleged abuses and frauds perpetuated by the factory system, all based on testimonies of Crooks and other American Fur Company employees.

Did I mention that Senator Benton was also a lawyer for American Fur?[24]

Their argument benefited from the sudden circulation in Washington of an eight-page pamphlet lambasting the government factories. The anonymous "Backwoodsman" author, suspiciously, shared Crooks's writing style as well as his extensive knowledge of both the fur trade and the ins and outs about the operations of far-flung factories from the Canadian border south to the Gulf of Mexico that no humble "Backwoodsman" could have known.[25]

"You deserve the unqualified thanks of the community for destroying the pious monster," Crooks wrote to Benton after their legislation passed, abolishing the government factories. Crooks added, "the country is indebted for its deliverance from so gross and holy an imposition."[26]

Unregulated trade "was the true democratic policy," claimed Chittenden's *American Fur Trade*, but "it was a fatal error." Government monopolization would have been better for the Native Americans, better for conserving the fur-bearing animals, and "would have averted the long and bloody wars, the corruption and bad faith, which have gained for a hundred year of our dealings with the Indians the unenviable distinction of a 'Century of Dishonor.' "[27]

But that is not how fortunes are made.

As Chittenden further points out, "In opening the door to free competition in the Indian trade, it had nullified in advance any provision which it might enact for the exclusion of ardent spirits." And it is no coincidence that, with the demise of the government factory system in 1822, John Jacob Astor not only abandoned his Chinese opium-smuggling operation, but also made liquor the AFC's chief medium of exchange with the cash-strapped Indians.[28] There was more money to be made in getting the Indians drunk than getting the Chinese high. Plus, he could more effectively throw his political weight around in Washington than in far-off Peking.

While battling McKenney and the factories in Washington, Astor was careful to position the American Fur Company as an upstanding corporate citizen, which officially shunned trading in alcohol.[29] But with the factories gone—and with them any modicum of government oversight—Astor flooded the frontier with liquor and unscrupulous agents.

By 1825 the American Fur Company station at the strategic Great Lakes chokepoint of Mackinac Island, Michigan, had taken delivery of thirty-three hundred gallons of whiskey and twenty-five hundred gallons of fortified wines for use in acquiring Indian furs.[30] Yet as Chittenden explained—much like unscrupulous liquor men the world over—the scheming American Fur Company trader could make even a little alcohol go a long way:

> It was the policy of the shrewd trader first to get his victim so intoxicated that he could no longer drive a good bargain. The Indian, becoming more and more greedy for liquor, would yield all he possessed for an additional cup or two. The voracious trader, not satisfied with selling his alcohol at a profit of many thousand percent, would now begin to cheat in quantity. As he filled the little cup, which was the standard of measure, he would thrust in his big thumb and diminish its capacity by one-third. Sometimes he would substitute another cup with the bottom thickened by running tallow until it was a third full. He would also dilute the liquor until, as the Indian's senses became more and more befogged, he would treat him to water pure and simple. . . . The duplicity and crime for which this unallowable traffic is responsible in our relations with the Indians have been equaled but seldom, in even the most corrupt nations.[31]

Horrified, the US commander at Detroit wrote the War Department that "the neighborhood of the trading houses where whiskey is sold presents a disgusting scene of drunkenness, debauchery and misery; it is the fruitful source of all our difficulties, and of nearly all the murders committed in the Indian country."[32] This wasn't just an issue of commerce, but of national security on the northern frontier.

Crooks and Astor responded that—even though it was illegal according to federal, state, and territorial laws—selling liquor to natives was absolutely necessary, because their British-Canadian competitors were doing it, too. "If the Hudson's Bay Company did not employ ardent spirits against us, we would not," Astor wrote. "But without it, competition is hopeless; for the attraction is irresistible; and if the British traders alone possess the temptation, they will unquestionably not only maintain, but rivet their influence over all the Indians within their reach, to the detriment of the United States, in alienating their affections from us, and in the loss of trade to which we have an undoubted claim."[33]

In Michigan, Crooks and Astor found sympathy among Territorial Governor Cass and other like-minded politicians for breaking the law in order to "throttle" the competition—and the Native Americans in the process.[34] Astor claimed to be "in general utterly opposed to the introduction of spiritous liquors into the Indian Country," but believed not doing so risked abandoning the entire Great Lakes trade to the British. Claiming that the 1802 and 1822 laws only gave governors *discretion* to enforce prohibition, he decided to use that discretion to permit the AFC to unleash drunken havoc on the Indians.[35]

Governor Cass was a lifelong defender of Astor; some would allege—not without evidence—that this was attributable to bribes and kickbacks. Cass appointed Astor associates to political positions and ran interference for Astor and the American Fur

Company, downplaying their underhanded liquor practices to argue that the "monopoly is merely the influence of capital, skill & enterprise."[36]

History suggests otherwise.

As far back as 1817, Cass was doing Astor's bidding. When the Indian agent at
Green Bay prohibited the landing of whiskey, Cass agreed that the "total exclusion
of Spiritous liquors from the Indian Country is altogether proper." He then declared
that the Green Bay settlement was not technically "Indian Country," and gave the
liquor back to the fur traders.[37]

"If the sale of whiskey could be restricted to the vicinity of the British line," wrote
US colonel Josiah Snelling of Governor Cass's liquor loophole, "the mischief would
be comparatively trivial; but if permitted at all, no limits can be set to it." If the AFC
was granted the ultimate weapon in dominating the Indian trade, how could white
traders up and down the Mississippi not be expected to use it, too? "I will venture
to add," concluded the commander of American forces in the Upper Mississippi
Valley, "that an inquiry into the manner in which the Indian trade is conducted, and
especially by the North American Fur Company, is a matter of no small importance
to the tranquility of the borders."[38]

Astor bristled at the accusations. He flooded the War Department with
testimonials—from Governor Cass and others on his payroll—that AFC traders
were evenhanded in dealing with the Indians—angelic, even. The War Department
was more sympathetic to Colonel Snelling, even reminding him that the same 1822
law that scuttled the factory system actually empowered military officers and Indian
agents to search the traders' stores and their goods if liquor smuggling was even
suspected. If found, their wares would be seized, trading licenses revoked, and legal
proceedings begun. Snelling availed himself of this authority, and in 1826 deputized
troops to root out the smuggled liquor, even far from the British border. And they
found plenty.[39]

Government agents smashed AFC liquor stocks without compensation, and
confiscated and impounded so many ill-gotten pelts that it was starting to cut into
American Fur's bottom line. American Fur even appealed all the way to the US
Supreme Court on a writ of error, arguing that their alcohol was not intended for
trade with native tribes.[40] Astor bullied the new secretary of war James Barbour,
reminding him that his predecessor had ordered fort commanders "not to interfere
with the Indian traders," before threatening to sue the government if they didn't
cease and desist from enforcing the law.[41]

The government would not be cowed. In February 1827—shortly before the
two traveled together to Butte des Morts—McKenney informed Governor Cass,
"One single license to exercise *a discretion*, as to *quantity*, you must be aware is
equivalent to a universal grant. There is no controlling the evils of the practice short
of *an unqualified prohibition*." Cass reluctantly complied, even proclaiming publicly
that "every practicable method has been adopted by the government of the United

States, effectually to prevent this traffic," and that "these regulations are rigidly enforced."[42]

McKenney likewise instructed the outpost at St. Louis to close all loopholes, and enforce in toto the prohibition against the liquor traffic. There, the orders were received by the most influential figure on Indian affairs west of the Mississippi, General William Clark, world renowned for his wilderness expedition with Meriwether Lewis.[43]

From Lewis and Clark to the Trail of Tears

No consideration of American westward expansion would be complete without the famous Lewis and Clark expedition, though their legacies go far beyond mapping the uncharted western half of the North American continent.

In 1794, twenty-year-old Meriwether Lewis volunteered for the Virginia militia in putting down the Whiskey Rebellion, before then joining Anthony Wayne's Legion of the United States to subdue the Miami Indians of Little Turtle (Chapter 9). At Fallen Timbers, he was a rifleman under one commander William Clark. The two struck up an enduring friendship during the long, empty days preparing for the negotiations at Green Ville. Clark retired from military service at twenty-six for health reasons, while Lewis became private secretary to President Jefferson.

Following the Louisiana Purchase in 1803, Jefferson tapped Lewis to chart the vast western wilderness, find a northwest passage to the Pacific Ocean, and establish American claims to sovereignty. In short order, Lewis recruited Clark in 1804, and for the next two and a half years they led a thirty-man expedition over eight thousand miles—up the Missouri River, over the Rocky Mountains, down the Columbia River to the Pacific and then back again.[44]

Second in importance to only their firearms, Lewis and Clark initially set out with some 120 gallons of whiskey, both for consumption and trade. Meat and provisions could be found along the route; whiskey could not. At the very outset, two guardsmen were whipped and court-martialed for getting soused off the company's most precious commodity.[45] Lewis and Clark tried to make peace with the (numerically far superior) tribes along their route, many of whom were needful of "powder and ball, and a supply of their Great Father's milk," as they often referred to the white man's whiskey.[46] The most intense confrontation came as a Lakota Sioux chief—dissatisfied with the gifts and liquor—demanded ever more tribute in order to pass. Blunderbusses were loaded and bows were drawn in anger before cooler heads prevailed. The crew's celebration of July 4, 1805, at Great Falls used up the last of the expedition's whiskey. The final year and a half of the trip would be completely dry.[47]

More important than the wilderness voyage was what came after. Meriwether Lewis was appointed governor of the Louisiana Territory but died en route to Washington, DC, in 1809. Whether the indebted thirty-five-year-old had been robbed and murdered or committed suicide has never been determined definitively. Lewis's compatriot William Clark took up residence in St. Louis—first as US agent for Indian Affairs under McKenney, then governor of the Missouri Territory, and then superintendent of Indian Affairs within the War Department. Until his death in 1839, Clark was the most knowledgeable and influential voice on Indian relations west of the Mississippi.

In 1811—over twenty years before the Trail of Tears—Clark reported to the secretary of war that tribal chiefs had frequently broached the question of "the government's assigning to them a permanent tract of country to live on, where the white people might not encroach on them. Their people wish to be situated so as to prevent disputes which frequently take place between them and their nearest neighbors, and where the white people will not be permitted to sell them spiritous liquors." He had used every instrument in his power to enforce the prohibition against selling liquor to natives, but to no avail. Given the circumstances, physical removal of native tribes to protect them from the moral pollution of the white man's liquor wasn't an outlandish idea.[48]

This account suggests some uncomfortable truths about our understanding of American history. As much as we associate removal westward with Andrew Jackson and the Trail of Tears, the ethnic cleansing of Native Americans was hardly the work of one villain, and there were both benevolent and malevolent reasons to support the policy.

Before the late 1820s, piecemeal efforts to nudge native tribes westward—through the bribery of annuities, threats of force, and liquor-soaked peace treaties ultimately broken—continued as they had since Green Ville. "Removing Indians from the eastern United States, like running the postal service or paying pensions to war veterans, was part of the low-level background hum of operating the federal government."[49]

An outsider's view gives us greater perspective on attitudes toward the Native Americans in the wake of the destruction of the factory system. In 1831 Frenchman Alexis de Tocqueville—along with his colleague Gustave de Beaumont—traveled the length and breadth of the United States, immortalized in his classic study, *Democracy in America*.[50] The pair traveled to Buffalo, New York, to witness Indians gathering to receive their annuity payments for lands ceded to the government. Great drunkenness followed, which was the norm on payday.

"I don't believe I've ever experienced a more complete disappointment than at the sight of those Indians," Tocqueville wrote. These weren't the proud, "noble savages" of the European imagination, but small, malnourished, and depraved husks of men. "To the vices got from us was added something barbarous and uncivilized which made them still a hundred times more repulsive."

That evening, the pair happened upon the body of a young, half-dead drunken Indian brave lying in the road. Horrified, the two Frenchmen called out for help. Other tribesmen appeared, homeward bound from Buffalo. "They approached, brutally turned the body of their compatriot over so as to know who it was, and then resumed their march without even deigning to reply to our observations. Most of these men were themselves drunk."

Tocqueville and Beaumont even offered to pay for lodging him at an inn, but no one would help. "Some said to us: these men are used to drinking to excess and lying on the ground; they don't die from such accidents. Others admitted that the Indian would probably die, but one read on their lips this half-expressed thought: What is the life of an Indian?" In their travels across the country, they found white indifference to native suffering to be the general sentiment. More bitingly, Tocqueville wrote,

How many times, in the course of our travels, have we not encountered honest citizens who, in the evening tranquility seated by the fireside, said to us: Each day the number of the Indians grows less and less! It is not that we often make war on them, however; the brandy which we sell them cheap kills more of them every year than could our most deadly weapons. This world belongs to us, add they. God, in denying its first inhabitants the faculty of civilizing themselves, has predestined them to inevitable destruction. The true proprietors of this continent are those who know how to take advantage of its riches.[51]

In a letter home, Beaumont was even more cynical: "It would be too difficult to destroy them by war, that would cost men and money. A little time and much perfidy, there's something more certain and economical."[52] Such was the reality of Indian relations in the 1820s and '30s.

Whether Native Americans *should* be removed west of the Mississippi differed from whether they legally *could*. Looking at the human wreckage around them, many realists—among whites and natives alike—believed that isolation and physical distance from white Europeans and their liquor would be the only salvation. In the 1820s, for example, the Stockbridge tribe of Ohio voluntarily removed west to Wisconsin explicitly to get away from the white man's firewater, only to find American Fur Company liquor traders there, too. "It is an *evil* we wish to flee from, and we came into this distant clime with the hope of finding a resting place," they wrote in 1827. "But we are disappointed in this. We hope that some effectual measures will be adopted to stop it," adding, "believe us, on the success of this depends the interest and survival of thousands."[53] They were hardly alone.

When it came to relocating the Miami tribe from Indiana in 1830 (well after Chief Little Turtle's passing), McKenney and the Indian Office argued, "If you continue here where you now are . . . and let the white people feed you whiskey and bring among you bad habits, in a little while where will be the Miami Nation? They will all be swept off." With ever more white settlers—who didn't care whether the natives were moved or killed, but only that they were gone—McKenney and the Indian Office continued, "Situated as you are, your Great Father cannot prevent his white people from coming among you. He wants to place you in a land where he can take care of you and protect you against all your enemies, whether red men or white."[54] The Miami agreed to the treaty and removed west. McKenney reported that, based on his interactions, "the disposition of *the great body* of the Indians" were, like the Miami, actually *"anxious to remove,"* and for the same reason.[55]

Well before becoming president, Andrew Jackson argued that, legally, eminent domain empowered the government to seize private property for public use in exchange for just compensation, whether the citizen consented or not. So why should Indians be treated differently?[56]

Tensions were highest among the Five Civilized Tribes of the South, which were more populous, more geographically compact, and more politically organized than those in the North. "They were called 'Civilized' tribes," prohibitionist William "Pussyfoot" Johnson explained, "because they were in fact 'civilized,' more so in many respect than the white aggressors. For they lived in log houses, cultivated farms, wove cloth, had organized governments with Legislatures," and the Cherokee legislature first enacted a prohibition on the liquor trade over its tribal territories as early as 1819.[57]

Still, by 1828, the Georgia legislature declared that the Creek and Cherokee were not sovereign nations, but rather only Georgia's "tenants at will." Being subject to state law in Georgia—as in most states before the Civil War—meant powerlessness: they couldn't legally vote, sue, own property, testify in court, or obtain credit. Andrew Jackson privately admitted, "I was satisfied that the Indians could not possibly live under the laws of the state."[58]

The already-diminished Choctaw were willing to compromise. Tribal leaders wrote to Congress that there were indeed many "wretched and degraded" nomadic tribesmen who "it would give us great pleasure to see settled west of the Mississippi. It would be better for them, and better for those who remained. But you cannot persuade all to remove." The only just and humane alternative, the Choctaw suggested, was to grant those "civilized" tribesmen who had successfully taken up the plow and integrated with white society full rights as white citizens, especially if their lands were to be appropriated as that of American citizens. "Does it comport with an enlightened and liberal policy to continue the imposition of those degrading restrictions upon us?" they asked.[59] But as "Great Father," President Andrew Jackson had other ideas.

When gold was discovered on Cherokee lands in 1829, scores of white prospectors flooded into Cherokee territory. Violent confrontations erupted, turning Indian removal into a full-blown political and constitutional crisis. Upon his inauguration, Andrew Jackson's top priority was to pass and enforce the Indian Removal Act (1830), which allowed the government to negotiate the seizure of Indian lands in exchange for "just" compensation.[60]

At that time, the only unincorporated lands under federal control—those not organized as states or territories—lay west of Missouri (which became a state in 1821), Arkansas Territory (statehood, 1836), and Iowa (statehood, 1846). Everything beyond that was then called "permanent Indian territory," where tribes would be granted reservations and cash annuities in exchange for the seizing of their homelands east of the Mississippi.[61]

Andrew Jackson actually believed removal to be a benevolent gesture, and the only practical policy to save aboriginal civilizations from destruction.[62] "My children, listen," concluded Jackson in his address to the Creek Nation:

> My white children in Alabama have extended their law over your country. If you remain in it, you must be subject to that law. If you remove across the Mississippi, you will be subject to your own laws, and the care of your father the President.—You will be treated with kindness, and the lands will be yours for ever.[63]

Even Jackson's political opponents agreed. In one of his last reports before President Jackson fired him from his position of head of Indian Affairs in 1830, Thomas McKenney—who had spent a lifetime defending native tribes from the white man's debauchery and liquor—likewise implored Congress,

> *What are humanity and justice in reference to this unfortunate race?* Are these found to lie in a policy that would leave them to linger out a wretched and degraded existence, within districts of country already surrounded and pressed upon by a population whose anxiety and efforts to get rid of them are not less restless and persevering, than is the law of nature immutable, which has decreed, that, under such circumstances, if continued in, *they must perish?* Or does it not rather consist in withdrawing them from this certain destruction, and placing them, though even at this late hour, in a situation where, by the adoption of a suitable system for their security, preservation, and improvement, and at no matter what cost, they may be saved and blest?[64]

Reference to the Trail of Tears usually focuses on the rounding up and forced deportations of the Cherokee, Creek, Seminole, Choctaw, and Chickasaw Nations of the South—often by drunken and unsympathetic white militias—and their decimation through disease, malnutrition, and exposure over the thousand-mile trek. Yet the ethnic cleansing applied to virtually all tribes, north and south—who were preyed upon by unscrupulous liquor traders all along their sorrowful paths—only to find that distance would bring no relief. Unscrupulous white traders would be waiting to drain them west of Missouri, too.[65] And like white liquor traffickers throughout American history, their role in debauching subaltern populations largely gets passed over in silence by traditional histories.

William Clark and Black Hawk

As the US government's point man on Indian relations in the West, one of William Clark's more frequent interactions in St. Louis was with Ma-ka-tai-me-she-kia-kiak, or Black Hawk, from Saukenuk village, located on the Rock River as it empties into the Mississippi (present-day Rock Island, Illinois). "The origin of all our serious difficulties with the whites," as Black Hawk frequently complained to Clark, was the unjust 1804 Treaty of St. Louis, in which just four Sauk chiefs ceded all of eastern Illinois for a one-thousand-dollar yearly annuity. Their tribesmen were livid at the injustice, as the chiefs "had been drunk the greater part of the time while at St. Louis."[66]

Clark was sympathetic to Black Hawk, but claimed his hands were tied by the law. Meanwhile, ever more white settlers were making claims on Sauk land. As the encounters increased, so did the confrontations and violence. "Why did the Great Spirit ever send the whites to this island to drive us from our homes and introduce among us poisonous liquors, disease and death?" he asked in his bestselling autobiography, the first such by a Native American. "They should have remained in the land the Great Spirit allotted them."[67]

Not surprisingly, Black Hawk was an abstainer, who "touched not, tasted not, handled not, the accursed stuff," and encouraged his fellow tribesmen to do the same. During the War of 1812, his band raided both British and American vessels along the Mississippi, dumping their casks of whiskey in the river.[68] When a white settler started illegally selling whiskey in a nearby cornfield, Black Hawk went and dumped his whiskey on the ground, too.[69]

"I used all my influence to prevent drunkenness, but without effect. As the settlements progressed towards us, we became worse off and more unhappy," Black Hawk wrote about the 1820s. "Many of our people, instead of going to the old hunting grounds, when game was plenty, would go near the settlements to hunt, and, instead of saving their skins, to pay the trader for goods furnished them in the fall, would sell them to the settlers for whisky, and return in the spring with their families almost naked, and without the means of getting anything for them."[70] Again he complained to Clark—the great chief at St. Louis—and again to no avail.

Black Hawk was quickly exhausting legitimate means to protest his treatment at white hands, but that did not mean that war was the inevitable outcome.

Figure 10.2 Ma-Ka-Tai-Me-She-Kia-Kiah, or Black Hawk (1767–1838). Lithograph by John T. Bowen, circa 1838.
Source: *Ma-Ka-Tai-Me-She-Kia-Kiah, or Black Hawk, a Saukie brave*, Library of Congress, Prints and Photographs, LC-DIG-pga-11582.

In his exhaustive 1887 history, *The Sauks and the Black Hawk War*, Perry Armstrong's chapter heading cuts to the quick: "Whiskey the Ultimate as Well as the Primary Cause of the So-Called Black Hawk War of 1831."[71] In it, Armstrong describes the arrival of settler Joshua Vandruff to Saukenuk village in March 1829. When the Sauks returned from their downriver hunting expedition to Missouri, Black Hawk found that Vandruff—along with his entire family of fourteen—had taken up residence in Black Hawk's longhouse and fenced in his cornfield as theirs. In addition to being a breathtaking personal affront, all of Vandruff's actions were clearly illegal according to the terms of the 1804 treaty. Still, for a time, Black Hawk was determined to cohabitate peacefully with the white man who had quite literally invaded his home. The Sauks even granted Vandruff some of their improved farmlands to till while he built a cabin for his sprawling family. But like so many of the white squatters, Vandruff began illegally distilling and selling whiskey to the Sauk tribesmen.

"The white people brought whisky to our village, made our people drunk, and cheated them out of their horses, guns and traps," Black Hawk wrote. "This fraudulent system was carried to such an extent that I apprehended serious difficulties might occur, unless a stop was put to it." As the agent at nearby Fort Armstrong had admitted to Clark, that "almost every settler's house is a whiskey shop," Black Hawk then went to every settler and "begged them not to sell my people whisky," in the spirit of Jefferson's 1802 law. "I did this for fear some of the whites might get killed by my people when they were drunk."[72]

All of the white squatters complied except one: Joshua Vandruff, who relocated his operation to an island in the Rock River—which still bears his name—within shouting distance of the Sauk village on the overlooking bluff. He happily ferried tribesmen to his island and sold them whiskey there. "And there they remained from morn till night pouring down liquid poison, until their fiery eyes and seething brains were like burning, hissing volcanoes, and their tottering limbs refused to longer bear their weight." Upon returning from the hunting grounds in 1831, Black Hawk

> tried to persuade Mr. Vandruff to quit selling, bartering and giving whiskey to the Indians, or at least to certain Indians whose names he gave him, being habitual drunkards. He begged and coaxed, then endeavored to hire him to desist. This failing, he offered to purchase his entire stock, that he might turn the liquors into the river. To all of which Mr. Vandruff turned a deaf ear. He was obdurate, obstinate, saucy. This roused the just indignation of the old chief, who then told him that unless he quit selling ardent spirits to those Indians, whose names he had given him as confirmed drunkards, he would take forcible possession of his liquors and empty them on the ground or pour them in the river. Even this threat was disregarded by Mr. Vandruff, who kept steadily on in making worse than useless brutes of these unfortunate drunken Indians, by selling, bartering and giving them the villainous compound known as Ohio whiskey for the most trifling trinket, if he could do no better, converting them (for it has the same effect upon the Indian that it has upon the white man) from reasonable creatures into useless sots, worthless brutes, and howling devils.[73]

With no other recourse left, the old chief and a band of warriors canoed across the Rock River and—much like Carrie Nation decades later—smashed every single barrel and bottle of Vandruff's liquor with their tomahawks. Without ever saying a word, the Sauks silently returned to their village.

Enraged, Vandruff plotted his revenge. That a white man "should be driven from his God-given right of selling what he pleased, when he pleased, to whom he pleased, and for what he pleased, by an untutored old Indian, was too grievous to be borne."[74]

Vandruff drew up a list of grievances against the Sauk—including attempted murder—without ever mentioning the smashed whiskey that would have surely given away the game, especially to the abstemious Illinois governor, John Reynolds. Co-signed by his bartender, Benjamin Pike, the petition demanded the permanent removal of the Sauk tribe and Vandruff's right to personally appropriate all Sauk farmland in reparation for suffering such "injustice." On May 18, 1831, Vandruff took the petition, *not* to the US Army garrison at Fort Armstrong (now the Rock Island Arsenal) just five miles away, *nor* to William Clark in St. Louis—both of whom knew the reality of the situation and would have dismissed the conniving liquor seller out of hand—but overland through the downstate wilderness to Vandalia, and the newly elected governor of Illinois.

Based on Vandruff's baseless accusations, and believing the white squatters were in immediate peril, on May 26 the staunch Jacksonian Governor Reynolds mobilized the Illinois state militia for war, as he admitted, "without any requisition from the United States."[75]

To say that Black Hawk's account was different would be an incredible understatement. "We acquainted our agent daily with our situation, and through him the great chief at St. Louis [William Clark] and hoped that something would be done for us," he wrote. The white squatters had hoped to expedite the Sauk removal by burning their crops, livestock, and forty of their houses, whipping and terrorizing the Indian wives and children. "The whites were complaining at the same time that we were intruding upon their rights. They made it appear that they were the injured party, and we the intruders. They called loudly to the great war chief to protect their property," Black Hawk said.

"How smooth must be the language of the whites, when they can make right look like wrong, and wrong like right," he added.[76]

Unlike Keokuk and other Sauk tribesmen who acquiesced to the power of the white settlers, Black Hawk assembled allied tribal leaders to defend his homeland. "I told them that the white people had already entered our village, burned our lodges, destroyed our fences, ploughed up our corn and beat our people. They had brought whisky into our country, made our people drunk, and taken from them their horses, guns and traps, and that I had borne all this injury, without suffering any of my braves to raise a hand against the whites." All of this was true.

"I had appealed in vain, time after time to our agent, who regularly represented our situation to the chief at St. Louis, whose duty it was to call upon the Great Father to have justice done to us, but instead of this we are told that the white people wanted our country and we must leave it for them!" The great chief in St. Louis, William Clark, expressed sincere sorrow, but he had neither the ability nor authority to aid Black Hawk. The US government was again turning its back on the Native Americans it had vowed to defend and uplift. The lands of Saukenuk were ordered to be sold to Vandruff, newly arrived American Fur Company agent George Davenport (for whom my hometown of Davenport, Iowa, just across the

Mississippi is named), and other white settlers. If the Sauk dared return home, they would be removed by force.

That injustice was the last straw. There were no more avenues for the peaceful settlement of grievances, and the Sauk were not going to be cheated out of their land without a fight. They swore to capture, try, and execute Vandruff, Davenport, and squatters endeavoring to steal their land. "The trader stood foremost on this list," Black Hawk wrote. "He had purchased the land on which my lodge stood, and that of our graveyard also. We therefore proposed to kill him [Vandruff] and the agent [Davenport], the interpreter [Antoine LeClaire], the great chief at St. Louis [William Clark], the war chiefs at Forts Armstrong, Rock Island and Keokuk, these being the principal persons to blame for endeavoring to remove us."[77]

The first shots in the Black Hawk War were fired not by the US Army but by the nonfederalized Illinois militia, under the command of Governor Reynolds himself. At Stillman's Run, Black Hawk sent a delegation under the white flag of truce to negotiate a peace agreement. When the untrained, nervous, and perhaps even intoxicated militiamen noticed Sauk scouts watching from the woods, they panicked and shot the Sauk peace delegates. In response, Black Hawk attacked, routing the numerically far superior militia. A young militia volunteer named Abraham Lincoln helped clear the field and bury the dead. Among the mutilated bodies, dead horses, and ruined saddlebags, the militia's emptied whiskey kegs also littered the battlefield. Black Hawk himself smashed every liquor keg he came across.[78]

Now a full-scale Indian war, with mass atrocities on both sides, US Army regulars then took up the fight, hounding Black Hawk's band throughout northern Illinois and southwest Wisconsin throughout the summer of 1832. Finally, at Bad Axe on the Mississippi River, they brutally massacred the Sauk—warriors, women, and children alike—prompting the surrender and imprisonment of Black Hawk himself (guarded, incidentally, by a young Jefferson Davis).[79]

"You know the cause of our making war," Black Hawk proclaimed upon capture. "It is known to all white men. They ought to be ashamed of it." The Great Father in Washington and "his great council gave us fair words and big promises; but we got no satisfaction." The white men "smile in the face of the poor Indian to cheat him; they shake them by the hand to gain their confidence, to make them drunk, to deceive them, and ruin our wives. We told them to let us alone, but . . . they coiled themselves among us like the snake. They poisoned us by their touch."[80]

William Clark frequently visited Black Hawk while imprisoned at Jefferson Barracks near St. Louis. Distraught at seeing the proud old chief so humbled, Clark petitioned President Jackson for—and secured—his release.[81] Black Hawk relocated without incident west of the Mississippi, and died peaceably in southeast Iowa in 1838. Still, Clark's own Indian agent at Fort Armstrong confided that, had Clark taken action against the white squatters and whiskey traders as Black Hawk suggested, the entire war could have been avoided.[82]

American Government, American Fur, and American People

The Black Hawk War in the North and the Trail of Tears in the South ended the last resistance to white settlement east of the Mississippi. Those events also effectively removed outspoken native voices from the debate over their own future, which would be decided in the battle between the American government's halfhearted defense of the welfare of Native Americans and American Fur's insatiable quest for profits. Ultimately, profits would win, and the indigenous Americans would lose. From his headquarters in St. Louis, William Clark had a front-row seat to it all.

Throughout the 1830s, Clark's field agents reported almost constant violations of US laws prohibiting taking advantage of Native Americans by selling or bartering them liquor. From Fort Mitchell in Alabama came word that the liquor was being sold to the natives by members of the same military garrison who'd sworn to uphold the law.[83] From St. Peters (Minneapolis), agent Lawrence Taliaferro noted that "whiskey was really the most common article of traffic" among the American Fur Company traders, "and what is worse there appears to have been no exertion whatever used to put a stop to this greatest of all scourges among the Indians." When confronted, the AFC traders argued that under Governor Cass's interpretation, the company was legally allowed one gill (or teacup) of whiskey per employee per day. On paper, the ever-growing list of AFC employees contained many "dead souls" who didn't exist in real life. Taliaferro implored Clark to abolish this loophole and ensure "that no one drop be permitted to enter the country under any pretext whatever, for I do most solemnly assure you that this course is the only one that will be likely to put a stop to the trade in the article of whiskey with the Indians."[84]

But the worst fiascoes were not from the North or South, but among the newly resettled tribes west of the Missouri River. While federal law prohibited white traders from selling liquor to the natives on their new reservations in present-day Nebraska, Kansas, and Oklahoma, the allure of profits—getting natives drunk in order to swindle the government annuity payments they received in exchange for leaving their native homelands—was too much to resist.[85]

Liquor was lucrative. A St. Louis distiller could easily turn twenty-five cents worth of grain into whiskey, sell it at one dollar a gallon, and pocket the rest. In the 1830s, that same whiskey would fetch thirty-four dollars a gallon at Fort Leavenworth (Kansas), or sixty-four dollars at the mouth of the Yellowstone River—most likely being sold illegally to Native American customers in exchange for their federal annuity payments.[86] On top of that was the tried-and-true method of getting natives drunk in order to get them to pawn their furs, pelts, or anything else of value. And when the natives had nothing left to pawn, white traders would ply them with liquor on credit at predatory rates, claiming not only present Indian annuities and furs, but future ones, too.[87]

It is worth pointing out—as Clark did in 1830—that this "selfish policy of the traders whose interest it is to keep them in the hunter state [has] a tendency to counteract and totally defeat the best views which have as yet to be adopted by the Government."[88] Crops grown by hardworking, sedentary, and "civilized" tribes were of no value to the American Fur Company compared to the pelts obtained by the illiterate, nomadic trappers who were indebted to the company, and who'd become addicted to its liquor.

Consequently, the West was awash in illegal alcohol: distilleries (and, later, breweries) in St. Louis and Kansas City flooded the Great Plains, while distillers in Taos—then in Mexican territory—dominated the Mountain West and high-desert plains. History books often lament the unquenchable thirst of Great Plains Indians, but rarely do they mention the insatiable greed of white traders, acting in clear defiance of the law.[89]

The greatest parasite of all was John Jacob Astor and his American Fur monopoly, which doggedly pursued the source of their wealth—the Native Americans themselves—as they were pushed west. Only now, they were aided by industrial technology. Crooks persuaded Astor to construct a paddlewheel steamship— similar to the ones he used for smuggling opium overseas to Canton—but for smuggling whiskey up the Missouri River from St. Louis into Indian Country. One hundred twenty feet long, twenty feet abeam, with two eighteen-foot sidewheels, the *Yellow Stone* could make the round trip voyage faster and more frequently than even a flotilla of small, hand-paddled keelboats, and could smuggle thousands of gallons of whiskey at a time. "Wood provided the fuel for the boat, but whiskey was the fuel that made her voyage feasible and, indeed, made the American Fur Company thrive," claims a history of the *Yellow Stone*: "Whiskey made John Jacob Astor the richest man in America."[90] Following the spring thaw of 1831, the *Yellow Stone* began ferrying liquor from St. Louis to Indian Country, leading to an almost immediate spike in drunkenness and lawlessness up and down the frontier.

"Since the process of removal began, the evils of intemperance have greatly increased in every tribe as yet seriously affected by that process;—particularly the Choctaws, the Chickasaws, and the Cherokees of the Arkansas," Christian missionaries warned in a direct missive to Congress in 1831. "There were more deaths from drinking whiskey, in six months of the last year, than in six years previous. This enormous increase of the evil is accounted for simply by the fact, that dealers in whiskey were allured into the new Indian territory by the expectation, that, in accordance with the treaty of 1828, the United States would disburse considerable sums of money to the emigrants." This place that the government had made out to be a "sanctuary for Indians, to which their corrupters and tempters could never gain access," had been "immediately invaded and defiled by unprincipled men in the pursuit of gain."[91]

It wasn't just missionaries who were sounding the alarm. The government's own Indian agents were seeing the same thing. "Liquor flows as freely here as

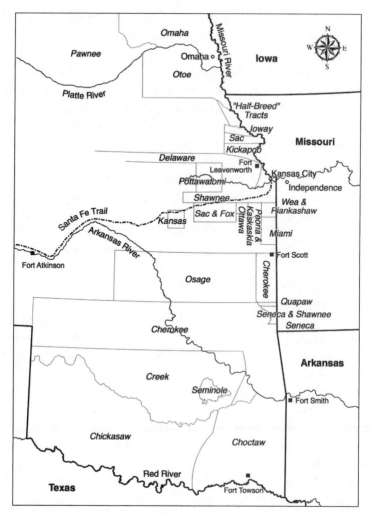

Figure 10.3 Map of the Indian Colonies west of Missouri and Arkansas, based on maps drawn by S. Eastman, Capt., US Army, 1853.

Source: Courtesy of Wichita State University Libraries, Special Collections and University Archives.

the Missouri," wrote agent John Dougherty from Fort Leavenworth (Kansas) in November 1831, noting that the AFC had not only been shipping liquor into Indian territory, they had even built an illegal distillery to manufacture it there, too. *"For God's sake, for the sake of humanity, exert yourself to have this article stopped in this country,"* he pleaded to Clark in St. Louis, otherwise, "the day is not far distant when they will all be reduced to the most abject misery ever inflicted by the Land of Civilized Man."[92]

Clark conveyed his alarm to the War Department in Washington, writing on November 20, 1831, that the loophole permitting liquor for use by white boatmen while in Indian Country had been utterly abused by the AFC and the *Yellow Stone*, which was now furnishing liquor "to the Indians by the gallon keg!"

"As those Traders have evinced so little good faith—such disrespect to the Government as to violate its most imperative laws, & so little humanity toward the Indians themselves, as to disregard the most sacred provision for their protection, I shall conceive it my bounded duty to recommend the total & entire prohibition of this article in the Indian Country, under any pretence, or for any purpose whatever," Clark wrote, suggesting that AFC traders ought to be brought to justice for their crimes.[93]

Unfortunately, the man in Washington who was on the receiving end of Clark's prohibition plea was none other than the AFC's longtime lapdog, Lewis Cass. Cass's double-dealing as governor—paying lip service to government prohibition while permitting Astor to violate it with impunity—was at least previously limited to the Michigan Territory. But in abandoning the governorship to become Andrew Jackson's secretary of war, charged with leading his Indian removal efforts, Cass's jurisdiction extended virtually everywhere.

Cass had long subscribed to the standard colonizer's view of natives and alcohol: blaming not the white man who illegally sold the potent industrial distillate, but the Indian's inherent "weakness" for liquor as grounds for their domination and expulsion. "Elsewhere habitual drunkards have paroxysms of intoxication followed by sobriety; but as long as the stimulus can be obtained, an Indian abandons himself to its indulgence, with the recklessness of desperation," Cass wrote. "We have seen many Indians, remote from the white settlements, who have never tasted of spiritous liquors, and we can testify, from personal knowledge, that the evil itself is almost unknown there." The only way to safeguard them from "further decline and eventual extinction" through liquor, according to the new secretary of war, was "the scheme for removing them to the country west of the Mississippi, and there establishing them in a permanent residence."[94]

Cass, of course, would never impede the profits of his patron, John Jacob Astor. Indeed, the very next day—while Clark's plea for greater prohibition enforcement was still in the mail—Cass delivered his annual report to Congress, in which he firmly laid the blame with the victims: the Native Americans themselves. "Indolent in his habits, the Indian is opposed to labor," Cass wrote, "devoted to the use of ardent spirits, he abandons himself to its indulgence without restraint. . . . He attributes all the misfortunes of his race to the white man and looks with suspicion upon the offers of assistance that are made to him," which seems like a tremendously self-serving portrayal of the dynamics on the ground. Still, Cass made it clear to Congress and his subordinates in the Indian service that Astor's liquor debauchery would continue unimpeded.[95]

From then on, even the most brazen ATC liquor sellers knew they had little to fear from government agents, and they often plied their trade in full view of the Indian agents themselves. "The white men told our young men to take some whiskey even to [Agent] Cummin's house and they would not let them be punished," Delaware and Shawnee chiefs told federal government representatives in 1834. "We are sorry my father that this is so—we have no laws and our great Father does not put into execution those he makes himself."[96]

In their new reservations farther south in Oklahoma, the Five Civilized Tribes did have their own laws, which were crystal clear on the matter, although the overwhelmed Indian Bureau would hardly enforce them either. Soon after their arrival, a council of the Choctaw "voted by acclamation that any citizen who should introduce intoxicating liquors into the Nation would be punished by one hundred lashes and the destruction of his stock," a prohibition consistently strengthened and enforced by leaders within the tribe.[97]

"It is as true as holy writ," their neighbors, the Cherokee, complained about the white settlers across the border in Arkansas, "that all who have whiskey will sell it to the Indians, and those who have not the article, will not attempt to prevent the sale of it." And when they sell to Indians and the Indians get belligerent, "the whites pretend to be awfully alarmed for their own safety."[98] Ultimately, the Choctaw, Cherokee, Chickasaw, Creek, and Seminole adopted a code of intertribal law among the Five Civilized Tribes, which notably included that "the five nations would coöperate in suppressing the sale of strong drink."[99]

Given the obscene profits to be made in bilking the newly settled Indians of their annuities, enforcing the prohibition was an uphill battle. In 1838 Montfort Stokes—the former governor of North Carolina who oversaw tribal settlements in Oklahoma—wrote, "There are no less than six dram shops at this time within two hundred yards of each other, where whiskey is openly and publickly sold." The consequences could be easily imagined: scenes of "drunkenness and riot among the Creeks, are such as have rarely been witnessed in any country," Stokes lamented.[100]

The biggest obstacle to tranquility on the frontier was the American Fur Company itself: its traders happily exploiting any legal loophole to get the Native Americans drunk for profit—as they had in claiming the whiskey onboard the *Yellow Stone* was for their own consumption, before turning around and plying it to the natives.[101] Others set up liquor shops right on the boundary of Indian Country. Indeed practically every road into Indian Country on a line from the western border of Arkansas, Missouri, and Iowa had its own liquor boom town to satiate the "dry" territories farther west.[102]

And then came the mixed-blood tracts. Hard-bargaining Chief White Plume of the Kansa tribe—who later died from alcohol consumption—insisted that the government grant one-mile-square individual reservations to each of the twenty-three half-bloods of the Kansa Nation. American Fur traders claimed (and their lawyers were inclined to agree) that these weren't tribal reservations, but fee-simple grants to individuals, who could do whatever they wanted. As a result, many mixed-blood Kansas and Osage tribesmen leased out these lands to whiskey traders: more wet islands in the dry sea of Indian Country.[103]

Military forts in the West, too, were technically not "Indian Country," so many soldiers jumped into the lucrative business of trading liquor to Native Americans, in defiance of the laws they were sworn to uphold. Even in close proximity to Fort Leavenworth on the Missouri River, Indians could obtain whiskey "with absolute impunity." On Missouri territory, directly opposite the river from the fort, "whiskey squatters" freely dealt liquor to Indians and the military alike.[104]

Then there were the Oregon and Santa Fe Trails westward across Indian territory, where whites set up "whiskey stations" and "traveling groceries," which exacerbated tensions with native tribesmen. Federal agents of the Indian Service calling on Cass's troops at Fort Leavenworth for help in enforcing the law were routinely "laughed at." Most Indian Service agents refused to call on the military at all, fearing they'd be "worsted in the end."[105] Clark reported that the likelihood of violent confrontation on the trails had less to do with the Indians but "more on the *temper & disposition* of the trading party": those with knowledge and respect for the Indians were likely to pass through unmolested, "but if on the contrary, the party is composed of raw young men, not only ignorant of Indians but destitute of a common knowledge of mankind," Clark wrote, "their destruction is certain."[106]

Frontier Injustice

"Should it be asked why those violating the Law are not prosecuted?" Clark wrote Cass. After all, the AFC traders were acting in clear defiance of both the letter and the spirit of the law. But trying to prosecute a white liquor trader "would be considered as a mere *farce*, as past experience shows."[107] Most obviously, Astor and the AFC had an army of lawyers to defend any erosion of their profitable trade all the way to the Supreme Court if necessary, while natives had no legal standing whatsoever before 1847. The meager resources of missionaries and other allies paled in comparison to the corporate juggernaut.[108]

A successful prosecution under the law would require the testimony of a witness to the entire process—the smuggling of the liquor into the trader's house, its reduction and packaging into casks, the delivery of those casks to Indian encampments, and its consumption by the natives—an impossibly high burden of proof, especially given the cutthroat reputations of AFC traders. The witness would also have to have tasted the liquor and found it to be spiritous. And of course, since Indians were not legally considered human beings, their own firsthand testimonials were inadmissible as evidence. Consequently, omnipotent liquor traders had very little to fear in appearing before white judges and all-white juries.[109]

In one 1842 case, a frontier Baptist missionary filed a formal complaint to the Indian Office at Fort Leavenworth against white liquor traders for violating the federal prohibition law. The litigants traveled miles to the nearest courthouse—on their own dime—only to find the case postponed to a later date, or reassigned to a jurisdiction even farther afield, all in an effort to inconvenience the witnesses and the prosecution's case. Ultimately, the missionaries did secure a rare guilty verdict— six years later, in 1848. The accused liquor seller was "found guilty, fined $1, and imprisoned one hour."[110]

Judicial rulings didn't help aid the natives' legal standing. The 1835 case *United States v. Cisna* found that "where the country adjacent to an Indian reservation had become so densely settled by non-Indians as to render it impracticable to execute the intercourse laws," such as those that governed Indian prohibition, "such laws were obsolete and federal jurisdiction ceased."[111] In other words, if too many white people settled nearby, the government threw its hands up, and native legal protections simply disappeared.

The US government finally waved the white flag of surrender against the liquor trade in 1854, abandoning all pretense to defending America's first inhabitants against the predations of white liquor traders. In negotiating another series of land-cessation treaties with the demoralized remnants of once-mighty tribes, the director of the Bureau of Indian Affairs, George Washington Manypenny, signed the Otoe-Missouria Treaty, which legalized the privileges of white settlers over native tribes in any unsurveyed territories. More importantly, the terms of the treaty charged not the government but the native tribes themselves with the duty of patrolling and preventing the introduction of white liquor sellers, under penalty of withholding future annuity payments.[112] This was a far cry from the benevolent promises of George Washington, Thomas Jefferson, and Thomas McKenney generations earlier.

In 1834 the aging John Jacob Astor largely divested from the liquor-for-furs business, selling much of his holdings in AFC and its subsidiaries to Crooks, so that Astor could focus on real-estate speculation in New York City.[113] But by then, the system of Indian exploitation on the prairies had already been established. The federal government was pumping out over a million dollars a year in annuities to the tribes west of the Missouri, while Missouri liquor traders were pumping in over a half-million gallons of whiskey. As cold political calculus, so long as the system of annuities flowed to the Indians, "it was the easiest thing in the world to keep them quiet," as Andrew Jackson's vice president John C. Calhoun bluntly put it, adding, "there were no people on earth so easy to deal with as our half civilized Indians."[114] Unsupported even by their own government, federal Indian agents were left to put occasional, half-hearted, and ultimately futile efforts to stop the exploitation.

"Since the day of payment [of Indian annuities], drunkards are seen and heard in all places," wrote Father Pierre-Jean DeSmet in 1839 from Bellevue, Nebraska: now a suburb of Omaha, but back then was the whiskey capital of Indian Country. "Liquor is rolled out to the Indians by whole barrels; sold by white men even in the presence of the agent. Wagon loads of the abominable stuff arrive daily from the settlements, and along with it the very dregs of our white neighbors."[115]

In 1841 Indian agent Isaac McCoy wrote the secretary of war that eight thousand gallons of whiskey were headed up the Missouri River for Indian Country in one shipment alone. By his estimate, more than thirty thousand gallons of unadulterated liquor were illegally brought into dry territory by the steamships each year. To interdict the traffic would require "all the dragoons in the United States Army."[116] But the dragoons weren't about to do anything.

Also in 1841, adventurer Rufus B. Sage—on the trails westward to explore the Rocky Mountains—befriended an encampment of white traders. As he chronicled in his *Rocky Mountain Life*, he was surprised to find that the traders' wagons were loaded down with twenty-four barrels of whiskey, by their own admission intended for Indians in defiance of the law. "Trading companies, however, find ways and means to smuggle it through, by the wagon-load, under the very noses of government officers, stationed along the frontiers to enforce the observance of laws." Stopping the flood would be an easy thing, Sage claimed, as the entire operation was conducted in open daylight, and the arrival of liquor shipments was the talk of the town for days and weeks beforehand. Government officials had knowledge of the white traders' predatory liquor trade, as well as both the manpower and legal authority to stop it. What they lacked was the will to do so.

"I am irresistibly led to the conclusion, that these gentry are willfully negligent of their duty; and, no doubt, there are often *weighty inducements* presented to them to shut their eyes, close their ears, and avert their faces, to let the guilty pass unmolested," Sage concluded. "Six or eight companies of Dragoons are stationed at Fort Leavenworth, ostensibly for the purpose of protecting Indians and suppressing this infamous traffic,—and yet it suffers no diminution from *their vigilance!* What *faithful* public officers!"[117]

The sorrowful testimonials of Native American carnage at the hands of white liquor traders would be difficult to believe, were it not for the sheer quantity of them. Whiskey was "as destructive and more constant than disease" in depopulating the Indians, wrote St. Louis superintendent David Mitchell of the over five hundred tribesmen he'd chronicled dying from the bottle, especially around annuity time. "Whenever money is around it soon finds its way into the hands of the whiskey dealers, who swarm like birds of evil omen around the place where annuities are paid."[118]

From their first encounters with the white man, Native Americans acquiesced to a subservient position of childlike wards of a patrimonial state that vowed to safeguard their best interests. The United States failed spectacularly in that goal, especially in confronting the predatory greed of monopolists, fur traders, and whiskey men. "Outraging every principle of morals, all law, and the dictates of humanity," wrote Indian commissioner Thomas Hartley Crawford of the white predators in 1842, "they deliberately place the instrument of destruction in his hand, and persuade him to use it, brutalizing him, and making victims of his wife and children, that they may fraudulently pick his pocket and strip his back of the blanket that covers it."[119]

From the front lines, Governor of Iowa Territory James Clark concurred: "They are the victims of fraud and intemperance, superinduced by the large sums paid them annually by the government, without proper guards to protect them against the superior cunning and avarice of unprincipled white men."[120] By the dawn of the Civil War, Indian Country was largely a fiction: a vast territory of enormous profit for bootleggers and early death for Native Americans.[121]

It is worth stepping back, perhaps, to see the forest for the trees. By the 1840s, the half-continent east of the Mississippi had been ethnically cleansed of its native inhabitants for white settlement. The remnants of once-prosperous tribes were dumped—broken—on the Great Plains, left to fend for themselves against the white man's predations, backed by the white man's state.

"Hovering like vultures," concluded an 1870 *Harper's* article, "the traffickers have caused wide-spread demoralization among all the tribes by the sale of intoxicating drinks, and are justly chargeable with much of the woe that our Barbarian Brethren have suffered," and neither church nor state seemingly did anything to stop them. Instead, the high-minded factory system intended to safeguard, educate, and elevate the Native Americans had been undermined by insatiable white greed into "a policy calculated to keep far from them all elevating and civilizing influences, and to perpetuate and intensify their degradation."

Those "just" annuity payments meant to uplift the natives became simply a net monetary transfer from the US government to a white business tycoon, filtered through the livers of thousands of dead Indians. And through it all, John Jacob Astor amassed the greatest private fortune in the history of the world.

"These are grave charges," as the *Harper's* article concluded, "but a thousand tongues can testify to their truth."[122]

The role of the liquor traffic in demoralizing and debauching the very native tribes that America's Founding Fathers had sworn to protect is a curious omission from conventional accounts of American history. This is an uncomfortable but necessary truth to grasp: that the history of American temperance and prohibition stretches back many generations before the nineteenth and early twentieth centuries, which is when most traditional prohibition histories begin. And rather than temperance being an effort by white evangelicals to "discipline" marginalized and minority communities, it was an effort led by those very communities to oppose their own political and economic subjugation.

11

"All Great Reforms Go Together"— Temperance and Abolitionism

Covent Garden Theatre, London, England: Friday, August 7, 1846

Only twenty-eight years old and half a world from home, Frederick Douglass was, legally, still a fugitive slave. The recent publication of his *Narrative of the Life of Frederick Douglass, American Slave* had set off a firestorm. The names, dates, places, and other specific details he divulged in it made the recapture of the world's most famous black man a very real danger. Friends urged him to flee abroad in case his owner attempted to reclaim his "property" by force—or worse. So, from 1845 to 1847, Douglass traveled the length and breadth of the British Isles, lecturing on the twin topics he deemed inseparable to the cause of freedom: abolition and temperance.

Douglass's deep and mutual affinity with the Irish was solidified in Cork, where his lecture was hosted by Ireland's apostle of temperance, Father Theobald Mathew (Chapter 5). "Seven years ago I was ranked among the beasts and creeping things; to-night I am here held as a man and a brother," Douglass told the two-hundred-strong congregation. "If I can but forget the position in which I once was, I can turn my attention to teetotalism, and shall be able to speak *as a man* for a few moments."

Turning to Father Mathew, he explained his steadfast opposition to intemperance in America. "I lectured against it, and talked against it, in the street, in the way-side, at the fire-side; wherever I went during the last seven years, my voice has been against intemperance. But notwithstanding my efforts, and those of others, intemperance stalks abroad among the colored people of my country."[1] In an argument that he would sharpen in repeated speeches across Britain, he proclaimed,

> If we could but make the world sober, we would have no slavery. *Mankind has been drunk.* I believe that if the slaveholder would be sober for a

moment . . . we could get a public opinion sufficiently strong to break the relation of master and slave. *All great reforms go together.*[2]

At a special ceremony in Dublin two days later, Father Mathew administered the teetotal pledge to Frederick Douglass, making him one of Mathew's six million Irish temperance vow-takers.[3] Dublin was also where Douglass, starstruck, met outspoken Irish nationalist Daniel O'Connell—"the distinguished advocate of universal emancipation, and the mightiest champion of prostrate but not conquered Ireland"—as Douglass's own *Narrative* described him.[4] The admiration was mutual, as was their shared dedication to liberation and temperance.[5] Together, the two addressed rallies of thousands in Ireland, with the Irishman taking to calling Douglass "the black O'Connell of the United States." Once back home, Douglass became a tireless champion for Irish Home Rule, and borrowed admiringly from O'Connell's speeches.[6]

"The cause of temperance alone would afford work enough to occupy every inch of my time," Douglass wrote to his abolitionist fellow traveler, William Lloyd Garrison. "In this country, I am welcomed to the temperance platform, side by side with white speakers, and am received as kindly and warmly as though my skin were white."[7] His scores of admirers across Ireland and Scotland went so far as to start a fund to buy Douglass's freedom from his American slave-master.[8] Still—as he wrote Garrison—"I shall be influenced by no prejudices in favor of America. . . . I have no end to serve, no creed to uphold, no government to defend; and as to nation, I belong to none."[9] Yet it was this very renunciation of patriotism that led to the biggest fireworks of Douglass's visit: a feisty confrontation at the first-ever World's Temperance Convention, held in London in August 1846.

The World's Temperance Convention brought together the foremost social activists of the day. John Dunlop, the Scottish father of British temperance, was there (Chapter 5). From the United States, William Lloyd Garrison made the trip, as did philanthrope Samuel Hanson Cox.[10] The convention was inaugurated by famed abolitionist and cofounder of the American Temperance Society Lyman Beecher (whose daughter, Harriet Beecher Stowe, would later write the antislavery polemic *Uncle Tom's Cabin*).[11] If that sounds like a lot of abolitionists at a temperance convention, that's because—as African American historians have pointed out—"by the 1840s, temperance and abolitionism had become virtually synonymous."[12] Indeed, the entire idea of a World Temperance Convention was a direct outgrowth of the same Quaker-inspired World's Anti-Slavery Convention of 1840 that also famously gave rise to the transnational woman's suffrage movement (see Chapters 12–13).[13] Abolitionism, suffragism, temperance: all great reforms did indeed go together, just like Frederick Douglass said.

On the first afternoon of the convention—as the abolitionist Garrison wrote home—"the Rev. Mr. Kirk, of Boston, incidentally defended the American slaveholders," causing a great commotion in the hall, less for the substance of his

Figure 11.1 "Portraits from the World Temperance Convention, at Covent Garden Theatre," *Illustrated London News*, August 15, 1846, 109.
The artist portrays Frederick Douglass (third row, third from right), with William Lloyd Garrison immediately behind him, and abolitionist Samuel H. Cox seated just in front and to the left of Douglass. Lyman Beecher is seated at center, immediately below the elbow of Mr. Alexander, chairman of the convention.
Source: British Newspaper Archive.

speech than for deviating from the narrow parameters of temperance.[14] Amid this rigid convention, Frederick Douglass was invited to rise and address the five thousand attendees in the cavernous Covent Garden Theatre. In his brief speech, he declared that he could not echo the "patriotic eulogies of America, and American Temperance Societies" because "there are, at this moment three millions of the American population, by slavery and prejudice, placed entirely beyond the pale of American Temperance Societies."

Cries of "Shame! Shame!" filled the hall.

"I do not say these things to wound the feelings of the American delegates," Douglass continued, only so that "they may be induced, on their return home, to enlarge the field of their Temperance operations, and embrace within the scope of their influence, my long neglected race." The conclusion of the sentence was drowned out by cheers of approbation.[15]

But that was hardly the end of it.

A letter from London written the following day soon appeared in the *New York Evangelist*. The rambling, venomous broadside against Douglass was penned by Rev. Samuel Hanson Cox, the Presbyterian cofounder of New York University.[16] "The moral scene was superb and glorious" at the temperance conference, as speakers from around the globe echoed Dr. Lyman Beecher's temperance optimism. That was—Cox claimed—until "Frederick Douglass, the colored abolition agitator and ultraist, came to the platform, and so spoke *a la mode*, as to ruin the influence, almost, of all that preceded! He lugged in anti-slavery or abolition, no doubt prompted to it by some of the politic ones, who can use him to do what they would not themselves adventure to do in person." Allegedly, Douglass "denounce[d] America and all its temperance societies together... as if not a Christian or true anti-slavery man lived in the whole of the United States."

"I came here his sympathizing friend—I am such no more, as I more know him," Cox concluded. "My own opinion is increasingly that this abominable spirit must be exorcised out of England and America, before any substantial good can be effected for the cause of the slave."[17]

Parroting colonists' standard disempowering tropes—that since a black man could have no free-thinking agency of his own, Douglass's actions must have been the handiwork of some white agitator—Cox's letter was reprinted in popular religious magazines across the United States. His fragile self-righteousness could hardly go unanswered. Frederick Douglass replied with perhaps the most glorious literary smackdown of the nineteenth century.

Putting quill to parchment, he wrote to Cox, "The obligations of courtesy, which I should be otherwise forward to discharge to persons of your age and standing, I am absolved from by your obviously bitter and malignant attack." Douglass's withering, sarcastic, five-thousand-word takedown would pull no punches.

"Sir, you claim to be a Christian, a philanthropist, and an abolitionist. Were you truly entitled to any one of these names, you would have delighted at seeing one of Africa's despised children cordially received, and warmly welcomed to a world's temperance platform, and in every way treated as a man and a brother," he laid in, with his tried-and-true tactic of pointing out the obvious hypocrisy of Christian prejudice. "I sincerely pity your littleness of soul."

As for the substance of his platform address, Douglass wrote, "The Temperance cause is dear to me. I love it for myself, and for the black man, as well as for the white man. I have labored, both in England and America, to promote the cause, and am ready still to labor; [but] it was not the poor bloated drunkard, who was 'ruined' by my speech, but your own bloated pride." He continued,

> You say I lugged in anti-slavery, or abolition. Of course, you meant by this to produce the impression, that I introduced the subject illegitimately.... or something foreign to the temperance platform—and especially a "world's Temperance platform." The meeting at Covent Garden was not a *white* temperance meeting, such as are held in the United States, but a "world's temperance meeting." ... All nations had a right to be represented there; and each speaker had a right to make known to that body, the peculiar difficulties which lay in the way of the temperance reformation, in his own

particular locality. In that Convention, and upon that platform, I was the recognized representative of the colored population of the United States; and to their cause I was bound to be faithful.

In concluding, Douglass took one last swipe at the self-professed abolitionist Cox's withdrawn friendship: "I do not deem it of sufficient value to purchase it at so high a price as that of the abandonment of the cause of my colored brethren, which appears to be the condition you impose upon its continuance.

"Very faithfully,

"Frederick Douglass."[18]

The Abolitionist Roots of American Temperance

Temperance and prohibition are so often vilified as reactionary, white people's movements that whenever historians come across temperance advocates equating the struggle against the liquor traffic with the struggle against slavery, they're met with open scorn and mockery.[19] That we honor abolitionists and suffragists while spitting upon prohibitionists—even though they are the exact same people—is one of the irrational, Jekyll-and-Hyde results of a deeply entrenched misreading of history. Temperance, anticolonialism, abolition, and suffragism were quadruplets: born of the same cloth, advocated by the same people, and often in the same language.

As elsewhere the world over, potent liquor was part and parcel of the colonization of North America. As in India and Africa, European settlers introduced mind-blasting distillates to Native American communities that had only known fermented beverages, and then—recoiling in horror—used the natives' inebriation as evidence of their savageness to justify their subjugation at white hands.[20] Moreover, the liquor traffic was central to the Atlantic "triangle trade." The galleons that brought African slaves to North America and the Caribbean were then loaded with sugar and molasses, bound for New England distilleries to be made into rum, which was then sent to West Africa to buy more slaves.[21]

In the colonies as back in Europe, distilled liquors like rum, gin, and brandy were thought of as energizing supplements and medications, even for children. Fermented beers, ales, and hard ciders were safer than water, as the alcohol killed off waterborne parasites and bacteria. Moreover, the liquor trade was an important source of state revenue and integral to the colonial domination of Native Americans (Chapters 9–10). Consequently, the American colonies and the early postindependence republic were awash in alcohol.[22]

Traditionally, American prohibitionists themselves traced their movement's genesis to this period. Specifically, they cite the 1784 publication of *An Inquiry into the Effects of Ardent Spirits upon the Human Body and Mind* by Philadelphia physician and Founding Father Dr. Benjamin Rush.[23] His inquiry into the addictiveness of hard liquors foreshadowed modern medical understandings of alcoholism as a disease rather than an individual moral failing. It also dovetailed with his pioneering addiction research that made Rush the "father of American psychiatry." If that wasn't enough, Rush signed the Declaration of Independence, served heroically as a battlefield medic for General Washington's Continental Army, and emerged from the Revolutionary War as "the nation's first great humanitarian." As a social activist, he fought not only for temperance, but also for the abolition of the slave trade, while helping found and fund two of the nation's first black churches. He promoted women's access to higher education, fought to end child labor and capital punishment, and was a vocal advocate for universal healthcare and public education that would be open to women, African Americans, and non-English-speaking immigrants.[24] All great reforms go together.

But the social organization of a genuine temperance movement begins in earnest in the 1820s in Boston, with the American Temperance Society (ATS) and its cofounder, the abolitionist Presbyterian minister Lyman Beecher. Beecher is perhaps best known as the paterfamilias of thirteen children, many of whom became influential social reformers in their own right: suffragist Isabella Beecher Hooker, women's education pioneer Catherine Beecher, suffragist minister Henry Ward Beecher (Chapter 13), and abolitionist author Harriet Beecher Stowe of *Uncle Tom's Cabin* fame. The apples didn't fall far from the reformist tree.

In 1826, after finding one of his dearest parishioners succumbing to alcohol addiction, Lyman Beecher delivered his famous *Six Sermons on Intemperance* from his pulpit at the Hanover Street Church in Boston.[25] Published the same year, this foundational document of the temperance movement is an especially fascinating read, as it completely upends historians' portrayals of temperance advocates as reactionary foes of liberty, supposedly browbeating drunkards about their moral failings.

"Intemperance is the sin of our land," Beecher proclaimed.[26]

Fair enough, but the crimes and social ills he catalogued were hardly new, and Beecher's opposition to them was hardly novel: indeed, a young printer named Benjamin Franklin had been reprinting denunciations of the "mischief" of rum as far back as 1736. With annual consumption rates of around five gallons of distilled spirits per person per year—some three times higher than consumption rates today—anyone with eyes could see the epidemic of drunkards stumbling through the streets of early America.[27]

But his *Six Sermons* were fundamentally different from the pleas for abstinence that usually arose from the pulpit, including Beecher's own previous sermonizing.[28] What made *Six Sermons* the cornerstone of an entire social movement was not, as is often assumed, its particular eloquence—rhetorically the sermons were pretty unremarkable—but rather *who* he blamed for intemperance and *what* he planned to do about it. Beecher did not speak of the evils of the alcoholic drink itself, or the fate of the drinker and his everlasting soul. Instead, Beecher's primary focus—which would also become the primary focus of generations of temperance advocates—was the drink *seller*. In the words of Carrie Nation decades later, the culprit was "the man who sells" (Chapter 1), and the entire system of profiting from one's neighbor's enslavement and misery. It was the same critique levied against the parasitic influence of liquor traders on the western frontier (Chapters 9–10), but it wasn't just the "savage" Native Americans the drink-sellers preyed upon, but their fellow God-fearing white men.

Like any Protestant sermon, Beecher drew from Holy Scripture. But he didn't describe woeful biblical tales of drunken sinners to underscore the moral shame of the individual. Instead, his favored Bible passage—which he quoted repeatedly—lambasts instead the liquor seller: "Woe unto him that giveth his neighbor drink, that puttest thy bottle to him, and makest him drunk also" (Habakkuk 2:15).[29]

Like a spider catching a fly in his web, the liquor dealer ensnared the hapless drunkard and then sucked him dry. "Those who vend ardent spirit will continue to supply their customers, in many instances, after they have ceased to be competent to take care of their property," Beecher proclaimed. Liquor dealers would sit by even as their victims' houses are foreclosed upon, their families tossed out in the street. Beecher's depiction of the predatory American drink seller could just as easily have described liquor dealers in Russia, Europe, South Africa, India, the Middle East, or any of the other global cases we've examined thus far.

If the problem was not the drink or the drinker, but ultimately the drink seller, Beecher's proposed solution (and the only thing he wrote in all caps) was "THE BANISHMENT OF ARDENT SPIRITS FROM THE LIST OF LAWFUL ARTICLES OF COMMERCE, BY A CORRECT AND EFFICIENT PUBLIC SENTIMENT; SUCH AS HAS TURNED SLAVERY OUT OF HALF OUR LAND, AND WILL YET EXPEL IT FROM THE WORLD." For reference—in the 1820s—state-level legislation had only recently outlawed slavery in the northern states, and abolitionists hoped that the same evolving normative pressures would, in time, produce similar results in the South. The Civil War was still a generation in the future, and hardly a predetermined outcome.

In the drink trade as with the slave trade, the "evil" was the traffic and the trafficker, not the thing being trafficked. Since the liquor sellers' livelihoods depended on peddling booze, one could hardly expect them to have some sudden, clear-eyed epiphany and voluntarily renounce their trade. "Let the consumer do his duty," Beecher said, proposing a temperance boycott, "and the capitalist, finding his employment unproductive, will quickly discover other channels of useful enterprise."

It was a matter of economics: simple supply and demand. "It is the buyers who have created the demand for ardent spirits, and made distillation and importation a gainful traffic," Beecher declared. "Let the temperate cease to buy, and the demand for ardent spirits will fall in the market three-fourths, and ultimately will fail wholly, as the generation of drunkards shall hasten out of time."

While forever the impassioned preacher, there was no vitriol in Beecher's vision—no vengeance for past sins in this world or the next—just a community dedicated to moving forward and pursing its welfare together, almost identical to American social-gospel activism at the end of the nineteenth century (Chapter 14). "This however cannot be done effectually so long as the traffic in ardent spirits is regarded as lawful, and is patronized by men of reputation and moral worth in every part of the land. Like slavery, it must be regarded as sinful, impolitic, and dishonorable."[30]

Like many abolitionist activists, Beecher reasoned that drunkenness was actually a greater threat than slavery: one-tenth of the American population were subjugated to the slave-master, while all of humanity was vulnerable to being enslaved to the liquor trader. The slave-master went home after sundown, they reasoned, while liquor's grasp knew no rest.[31] After recounting the inhumanity of slavery and the slaves' unthinkable suffering through the Middle Passage, Beecher made the case for rooting out the liquor seller. "It is only in the form of ardent spirits in the way of a lawful trade extended over the entire land," Beecher claimed, "that an armed host may land, to levy upon us enormous taxations, to undermine our liberties, bind our hands, and put our feet in fetters." His sermon concluded abruptly, but clearly: "The commerce therefore, in ardent spirits, which produces no good, and produces a certain and immense amount of evil, must be regarded as an unlawful commerce, and ought, upon every principle of humanity, and patriotism, and conscience, and religion, to be abandoned and proscribed."[32]

In the language of modern social science, Lyman Beecher might well be described as a norm entrepreneur: advocating grassroots citizen activism in the form of a consumer boycott against predatory capitalism. More often, he is simply caricatured as an excitable "Puritan," a "bumpkin and buffoon," and easily brushed aside.[33] Still, the rapidity with which his movement caught fire testifies to the changing normative landscape: it wasn't the booze that was suddenly deemed inappropriate, but the idea of making outlandish profits from the misery of one's fellow man.

Not content to simply lecture from the pulpit, Beecher took the fight to the men who sell, especially those who freely set up liquor booths on the Boston Common. "This preëmptive right of the people to the old Common for any purpose which they might choose had thus far been unquestioned till we of the Y.M.C.A., under Dr. Beecher as our captain, assaulted the stronghold of intemperance in these liquor booths," explained a fellow activist. "It was a mighty struggle—first, with the municipal authorities; second, with the judiciary; and lastly, with public sentiment. . . . Those ancient privileges of liquor-selling and of riotous revelry on Boston Common on public days, have never been restored in the least degree to this day."[34]

As the liquor dealers of Boston strategized how best to repulse this temperance threat to their business, Beecher lay in wait. Even into his later years, he would attend their meetings, listening quietly from the back before diving headlong into "a crowd of distillers, saloon-keepers, and topers," as one witness recalled.

"And then he poured forth a tremendous tempest of thunder and lightning, roaring, blazing, scorching, crackling and burning, hurling hot thunderbolts crashing through and through all the mighty breastworks which the liquor army had thrown up for the defence of their business." Thoroughly discouraged and defeated, the liquor traders left without a word in reply. "Reply! They might as well have replied to a tornado."[35]

Beecher's most enduring legacy, however, was the "association for the special purpose of superintending this great subject" that his *Sermons* foretold. Organized that same year of 1826, Beecher's highly successful American Temperance Society (ATS) not only helped members stay true to their "teetotal" pledges to abstain from purchasing distilled liquors, but also organized speaking tours and temperance auxiliaries, collected data on the liquor trade, and lobbied influential elites to lead by example through abstinence pledges.[36] Within a decade, the ATS claimed over one and a half million members in over eight thousand lodges—roughly one out of every five free adults in the United States.[37] The temperance boycott had a dramatic effect: liquor sales and consumption plummeted from around 7.1 gallons of pure alcohol per person per year in the 1820s–'30s to just 3.1 gallons by 1840.[38] While still higher than present-day consumption rates, such a rapid halving of liquor consumption—and similarly sharp declines in crime and other alcohol-related social ills—was almost miraculous.

Not surprisingly, temperance was taken up with unmatched zeal within the black community: freed African Americans in the North formed some of the first temperance lodges. The spiritual, moral, and economic uplift of both slave and freedmen became a central theme of the emerging black press and black convention movement.[39]

When French aristocrats Alexis de Tocqueville and Gustave de Beaumont conducted their tour of the antebellum United States in the 1830s to see what makes American democracy tick, they noted both the decimation of native tribes by the white man's liquor (Chapter 10) and the promise of civil society organizations, especially the ATS. Tocqueville's *Democracy in America*—hailed as "at once the best book ever written on democracy and the best book ever written on America"[40]—is worth quoting at length:

As soon as several of the inhabitants of the United States have taken up an opinion or a feeling which they wish to promote in the world, they look out for mutual assistance; and as soon as they have found each other out, they combine. From that moment, they are no longer isolated men, but a power seen from afar, whose actions serve for an example, and whose language is listened to. The first time I heard in the United States that a hundred thousand men had bound themselves publicly to abstain from spirituous liquors, it appeared to me to be more like a joke than a serious engagement; and I did not at once perceive why these temperate citizens could not content themselves with drinking water by their own firesides. I at last understood that these hundred thousand Americans, alarmed by the progress of drunkenness around them, had made up their minds to patronize temperance. They acted just in the same way as a man of high rank who should dress very plainly, in order to inspire the humbler orders with a contempt of luxury. It is probable that, if these hundred thousand men had lived in France, each of them would singly have memorialized the government to watch the public houses all over the kingdom. *Nothing, in my opinion, is more deserving of our attention than the intellectual and moral associations of America.*[41]

The world was indeed paying attention. Across Europe, eager reformers virtually mobbed seagoing abolitionists, missionaries, and even merchants—anyone who might have insight into the ATS as a template for their own activism.[42] That's how John Dunlop found out about the American Temperance Society and used it as a guide for the first temperance organizations in the British Isles (Chapter 5). It was an article simply describing the ATS published in Riga that initiated the liquor boycotts across the Russian Empire (Chapter 2). When ATS emissary Robert Baird arrived in France in the 1830s, his *Histoire des sociétés de tempérence des États Unis d'Amérique* became a bestseller across the continent (Chapter 4).[43] No wonder activists from around the globe reported back that the ATS "had its origin in the United States, but it must not have its end, till it has circumnavigated and blessed the *entire world*."[44]

Meanwhile, Back in Boston

Lyman Beecher was hardly a lone activist in Boston. In the early republic, the bustling port city was a true hotbed of "philanthropy," as the reformers called it: love of humanity. Even as the ATS message sailed from New England ports for audiences worldwide, in 1828 another reformist trailblazer was just getting his start.

At only twenty-five years old, William Lloyd Garrison was already a seasoned writer and printer when he moved from Newburyport, Massachusetts, to Boston, becoming the editor of the recently established *National Philanthropist:* the first publication to endorse both temperance and prohibitionist legislation.[45] The famed abolitionist, suffragist, and inspiration for the nonviolent resistance of Tolstoy (Chapter 2), Gandhi (Chapter 7), Martin Luther King Jr., and activists the world over got his start in temperance, which he espoused as his most foundational cause.

Inspired by Beecher's *Sermons*—perhaps buttressed by his own hardscrabble upbringing and his brother's alcoholic excesses[46]—Garrison took the ATS temperance pledge and set to the work of making the *National Philanthropist* the backbone of the temperance movement. Never a fan of minced words or halfway measures, Garrison joined Beecher's campaign for a ban of the liquor traffic that would be "Total with a capital Tee"—which is where we get "teetotal" temperance. "Moderate drinking is the down-hill road to intemperance" became the weekly's motto, under which appeared happy stories of barns raised in record time by sober hands, and the un-Christianness of debauching one's neighbor through selling him booze.[47]

Prior to Beecher's *Six Sermons*, Garrison said, "Intemperance was seldom a theme for the essayist; the newspapers scarcely acknowledged its existence except occasionally in connection with some catastrophe or crime, and it did not occur to any one that a paper devoted mainly to its suppression might be made a direct and successful engine in the great work of reform." It was only through persistence, work, and dedication that the *National Philanthropist* grew in circulation and clout, "till doubt and prejudice and ridicule have been swept away."[48]

There is an interesting—and often unquestioned—incongruity in histories of these early "philanthropists": proponents of temperance, abolition, and women's rights. The standard assumption is that this reformist spirit was borne of the Second Great Awakening in American Protestantism (1800–1835): a Christian revivalist movement in which the piety and perfectionism of the individual, combined with efforts to improve their earthly society, would hasten the coming of the millennium.[49] And while there were leaders like Lyman Beecher who had the title of "reverend" before their names, even more striking were those who were avowedly hostile to evangelism.

In addition to being an outspoken critic of slavery and intemperance, Garrison was an anti-Sabbatarian. At a time when the righteously devout were pressing for legislation to keep the Sabbath holy as per Scripture, Garrison pushed back fiercely. "To say that everything contained within the lids of the Bible is divinely inspired, and to insist upon the dogma as fundamentally important, is to give utterance to a bold fiction and to require the suspension of the reasoning faculties." Blind faith was equally absurd. "It is the province of reason to 'search the Scriptures' and determine what in them is true and what false—what is probable and what incredible—what is compatible with the happiness of mankind, and what ought to be rejected," Garrison wrote. Scripture and Christian teachings must be subjected to reason, scrutiny, and criticism, just as any claim. "Truth is older than any parchment and would still exist though a universal conflagration should consume all the books in the world," Garrison claimed. "To discard a portion of Scripture is not necessarily to reject the truth, but may be the highest evidence that one can give of his love of truth."[50]

While Garrison's morality undoubtedly inspired his temperance and abolitionist activism, they went far beyond the teachings of American Protestant churches, which more often than not condoned slavery based upon Holy Scripture rather than condemning it. He renounced organized churches as "cages of unclean birds and synagogues of Satan,"[51] as well as sanctimonious clergy, who "loved the fleece better than the flock, and were mighty hindrances to the march of human freedom and the souls of men."[52]

Like his acolyte Leo Tolstoy in Russia—half a century later and half a world away—Garrison would be pilloried as a "heretic" and "infidel" for opposing both church and state as the foremost foes of Christian equality and nonviolence. Garrison's example was "the spring of my awakening to true life," Tolstoy wrote in 1903, just after hosting American progressive prohibitionist William Jennings Bryan's visit to his Yasnaya Polyana estate (Chapter 15). "Garrison did not so much insist on the right of negroes to be free as he denied the right of any man whatsoever, or of any body of men, forcibly to coerce another man in any way."[53] Whether that power was wielded by the slaveholder with his whip, the saloon-keeper with bottle, or the state demanding conscription, the core principle was the same—and all must be steadfastly opposed. By showing the path to liberation, "Garrison will for ever remain one of the greatest reformers and promoters of true human progress," Tolstoy said, shortly before his death.[54]

In a letter to his hometown Newburyport *Herald* in 1830—a year before inaugurating his influential antislavery weekly, *The Liberator*—Garrison penned a principled defense against his would-be detractors:

> My "stubbornness" and "dogmaticalness" consist in ardently cherishing, and fearlessly avowing, the following *notions*:—That "all men are born equal, and endowed by their Creator with certain unalienable rights"— consequently, that a slave-holder or a slave-abettor is neither a true patriot, a good citizen, nor an honest man, in all his transactions and relations, and that slavery is a reproach and a curse upon our nation:
>
> —That intemperance is a filthy habit and an awful scourge, wholly produced by the moderate, occasional and fashionable use of alcoholic liquors—consequently, that it is sinful to distil, to import, to sell, to drink, or to offer such liquors to our friends or laborers, and that entire abstinence is the duty of every individual:—That war is fruitful in crime, misery, revenge, murder, and every thing abominable and bloody—and, whether offensive or defense, is contrary to the precepts and example of Jesus Christ, and to the heavenly spirit of the gospel—consequently, that no profession of christianity should march to the battle-field, or murder any of his brethren for the glory of his country. These are the first fruits of my *bigotry, fanaticism, rashness* and *folly*.[55]

In response to the philanthrope's urgent prose, Samuel J. May once pleaded with Garrison to "moderate your indignation, and keep more cool; why, you are all on fire." Garrison responded with a smile: "Brother May, I have a need to be *all on fire*, for I have mountains of ice about me to melt."[56]

These principles—nonviolent opposition to slavery, war, patriotism, and state violence—and a temperance focused more on the drink seller than the drinker were augmented by "another novelty which Garrison embraced": women's rights.

"Garrison as usual went to the extreme length of his opinion, and asserted not only the right of women to take the moral and social platform, but the political equality of the sexes—a doctrine for which the world was very far from being prepared then, even if it is prepared now," claims Goldwin Smith's 1892 Garrison biography.[57] Garrisonianism equated to peace, temperance, immediate emancipation, and women's rights.

All great reforms go together.

Of course we mustn't give way to hindsight's temptation to portray the obvious moral rectitude of Garrison's positions as being "obvious" at the time. Like Tolstoy, Gandhi, and Martin Luther King Jr., Garrison was loathed and even imprisoned by establishment powers and their conservative defenders.

In 1831 Garrison inaugurated his antislavery periodical, *The Liberator*, in Boston, which more than any other publication placed and kept slavery on the national agenda. It was also the year of Nat Turner's uprising in Virginia, in which rebellious slaves killed some sixty white slaveholders before Turner was finally apprehended, tried, and executed. Southern whites were terrified, blaming northern agitators like Garrison for fanning the flames of insurrection. The state of Georgia put out a five-thousand-dollar bounty for Garrison's capture; other states wanted him captured dead or alive.[58]

Undeterred, Garrison helped found the New-England (later, Massachusetts) Anti-Slavery Society in 1832: the leading megaphone of antislavery agitation before the Civil War. The Anti-Slavery Society was patterned "on the model of other benevolent organizations," like the American Temperance Society, to mobilize a network of local organizations.[59] Also like the ATS, their focus was more on the profiteer than the product: the white slave trader was the fundamental problem, not the slave. They hoped to "induce as many of our fellow-citizens as possible to become *anti-slaveholders*," and "endeavor by all means sanctioned by law, humanity, and religion, to effect the abolition of slavery in the United States."[60] As with the ATS, a network of antislavery societies multiplied across the country.

It was at a meeting of one such organization—the Boston Female Anti-Slavery Society—where conservative antiabolition forces confronted Garrison's ever-increasing agitation. His 1835 speech before these female abolitionists was drowned out by thousands of angry pro-slavery men. The mob ultimately tore Garrison's clothes, tied a rope around him, and dragged him toward Boston Common to lynch him, or at least tar and feather him. Ultimately Garrison was only saved when constables wrested him from the mob and threw him in jail on the orders of the mayor. Watching intently, the antiabolitionist mayor Theodore Lyman was no fan of Garrison's politics, but he would not tolerate bloodshed on his watch.[61]

There were scores of influential temperance-abolitionist reformers even beyond Garrison. Theodore Weld was considered "already the ablest temperance orator in the Northwest" (upstate New York) when he enjoined the abolitionist cause in the 1830s.[62] His influential and widely selling *American Slavery as It Is* (1839) galvanized the links between intemperance and slavery. "Arbitrary power is to the mind what alcohol is to the body; it intoxicates," Weld wrote, adding that man's thirst for power "is perhaps the strongest human passion."[63] Alcoholics and slave-masters alike were enslaved themselves to their own corporeal desires, as "the whole history of man is a record of real interests sacrificed to present gratification."[64]

Weld's *American Slavery as It Is* is considered second only to Harriet Beecher Stowe's *Uncle Tom's Cabin* in winning wider audiences to the antislavery cause. Not only was Stowe the daughter of ATS founder Lyman Beecher, but her fictitious account of the heartless, liquor-sipping master, Simon Legree, and the noble, suffering Christian slave, Tom ("he'll never get drunk"), all drew directly from Weld's writing.[65]

The Power of Black Temperance

It wasn't just fictional works like *Uncle Tom's Cabin* that nudged public sentiment more in the direction of abolition and temperance. Frederick Douglass's autobiographical *Narrative of the Life of Frederick Douglass* gave the American public a first-hand account of the alcoholic inhumanity of slavery. "It was deemed a disgrace not to get drunk at Christmastime," Douglass recounted of his slave upbringing on a Maryland plantation in the 1820s, as it "was the most effective means in the hands of the slaveholder in keeping down the spirit of insurrection." Highlighting the role of alcohol in white subordination of African Americans—just as with the alco-subjugation of Native Americans—Douglass continued,

> Their object seems to be, to disgust their slaves with freedom, by plunging them into the lowest depths of dissipation. For instance, the slaveholders not only like to see the slave drink of his own accord, but will adopt various plans to make him drunk. One plan is, to make bets on their slaves, as to who can drink the most whisky without getting drunk; and in this way they succeed in getting whole multitudes to drink to excess. Thus, when the slave asks for virtuous freedom, the cunning slaveholder, knowing his ignorance, cheats him with a dose of vicious dissipation, artfully labelled with the name of liberty. The most of us used to drink it down, and the result was just what might be supposed; many of us were led to think that there was little to choose between liberty and slavery. We felt, and very properly too, that we had almost as well be slaves to man as to rum. So, when the holidays ended, we staggered up from the filth of our wallowing, took a long breath, and marched to the field,—feeling, upon the whole, rather glad to go, from what our master had deceived us into a belief was freedom, back to the arms of slavery. I have said that this mode of treatment is a part of the whole system of fraud and inhumanity of slavery. It is so.[66]

Elsewhere, Douglass described the widespread southern custom of masters getting their slaves drunk on Saturday nights, because "if they had time to think, if left to reflection on the Sabbath day, they might devise means by which to obtain their liberty," adding, "In order to make a man a slave, it is necessary to silence or drown his mind. . . . To blind his affections, it is necessary to bedim and bedizzy his understanding. In no other way can this be so well accomplished as by using ardent spirits!"[67] These themes of insobriety, authoritarian subordination, and moral impoverishment would be central to Douglass's future writings, which included two more bestselling autobiographies.[68]

Little wonder, then, that by the 1830s and 1840s, the cause of abolition had become intimately intertwined with temperance—within both white and black abolitionist communities—and that Frederick Douglass had himself become an ardent champion of temperance. "I am a temperance man because I am an anti-slavery man," Douglass claimed on his British tour, "and I am an anti-slavery man because I love my fellow men."[69] But Douglass was hardly the only (or even the first) black apostle of temperance.

The Free African Society of Philadelphia refused membership to drinkers as early as 1788. When Lyman Beecher traveled to Philadelphia in 1830, his temperance lecture was attended by some two hundred black Philadelphians, including the fifty members of the influential African Methodist Episcopal (AME) Church. Free blacks established independent temperance organizations from Boston, Hartford, and New Haven to Brooklyn and Baltimore by the early 1830s, with the black clergy becoming influential voices of sobriety and uplift.[70] Douglass's coeditor of the abolitionist paper *North Star*, Martin Delany, organized a black temperance society in Pittsburgh in 1834; his resolution at the State Convention of the Colored Freemen of Pennsylvania called on blacks to pursue "total abstinence" in order to gain "the esteem of all wise and virtuous men."[71]

It wasn't just black leaders like Frederick Douglass and Martin Delany: temperance and abolitionism were virtually synonymous within the African American communities throughout the North. The Colored American Temperance Society— established in the 1830s with the expressed goal of "entire abstinence from the use of ardent spirits"—reported twenty-three auxiliaries in eighteen cities in its first year alone. More than one-quarter of the entire black population of Cincinnati during the 1840s were card-carrying temperance members. Such widespread temperance activism made it virtually impossible for African Americans to sell liquor within their own tightly knit communities. This actually reinforced the racial dynamic whereby the liquor traffic was part of the machinery of white oppression, and temperance the key to black liberation.[72]

As a young slave, south of the Mason-Dixon Line in Baltimore, Frederick Douglass taught himself to read and write before jumping a northbound train to freedom in 1838. He eventually settled in the New England crucible of social activism. He attended temperance and abolitionist meetings, and subscribed both to

William Lloyd Garrison's *The Liberator,* as well as Garrisonian nonviolent resistance against the injustice of slavery. Garrison first met the twenty-three-year-old fugitive slave in 1841. Impressed with his eloquence, Garrison struck up a friendship with Douglass and encouraged him to become an abolitionist orator. Under the auspices of the American Anti-Slavery Society, Douglass honed his oratorical skills on speaking engagements—often in temperance halls—across the Northeast and Midwest, where he occasionally confronted mobs of indignant whites.

Unlike Garrison and the American Temperance Society's focus on the liquor seller, Douglass's temperance activism centered on the moral uplift of the individual drinker—and collectively the uplift of the entire community—through a pledge of individual abstinence. In this way, Douglass's temperance aligned more with the Washingtonian movement than with the ATS. Begun in 1840 in Baltimore, the secular Washingtonian Total Abstinence Society eschewed all church affiliations and encouraged individuals to take a pledge of total abstinence from distilled liquors. A self-help forerunner of Alcoholics Anonymous that drew primarily from the lower classes, reformed drunkards worked together to keep each other true to their sobriety pledges and to serve as an example to others.[73] A loose network of independent Washingtonian societies flourished in the early 1840s, publishing testimonials of self-reformed drunkards, supporting lectures and speaking tours.[74]

Frederick Douglass's Washingtonian sentiments were on full display in his early speeches and writings: recounting first-person testimonials of alcohol's "slaves" who were able to self-emancipate. Drawing explicit parallels with the Founding Fathers, like Benjamin Franklin—who counseled temperate self-help to the colonists to highlight the immorality of "intemperate" British imperial power—Douglass saw the moral uplift of the black community as resistance of the colonized against imperial oppression.[75] During his British tour in 1846, when Douglass explained how whites enticed black Americans to drink, and then point to their inebriety "as a reason why their emancipation should not take place," his Irish audiences certainly understood, since that was how Irish nationalists saw their subjugation at English hands (Chapter 5).[76] This was the alcohol narrative of European colonizers in encountering native peoples everywhere they went.

Still, while Douglass embraced Washingtonian temperance, the feeling was seldom mutual. Most white temperance societies refused blacks, leaving African American communities to establish their own separate temperance organizations. Judging by abolitionist Samuel Cox's indignant reply to Douglass pointing this out at the World Temperance Convention in London, this issue was a sore spot within white temperance and abolitionist circles.[77]

The white abolitionist leaders were triggered when Douglass told the global convention in London, "About the year 1840, a few intelligent, sober and benevolent colored gentlemen in Philadelphia, being acquainted with the appalling ravages of intemperance among a numerous class of colored people in that city, and in finding themselves neglected and excluded from white societies, organized societies among themselves—appointed committees—sent out agents—built temperance halls, and were earnestly and successfully rescuing many from the fangs of intemperance."

That is, until August 1: the widely celebrated date of slave emancipation in the West Indies (Jamaica) and throughout the British Empire in 1834.[78] On August 1, 1842, some twelve hundred black members of the Moyamensing Temperance Society "selected this day to march in procession through the city, in the hope that such a demonstration would have the effect of bringing others into their ranks. They formed their procession, unfurled their teetotal banners, and proceeded to the accomplishment of their purpose. It was a delightful sight," Douglass explained.

"But, Sir, they had not proceeded down two streets, before they were brutally assailed by a ruthless mob—their banner was torn down, and trampled in the dust—their ranks broken up, their persons beaten, and pelted with stones and brickbats. One of their churches was burned to the ground, and their best temperance hall was utterly demolished," Douglass spoke, above mounting cries of "Shame! Shame!"[79]

Black churches and temperance halls were burned, "and the mob was backed up by the most respectable people in Philadelphia," Douglass hastened to add.[80]

What could possibly be the response to such vitriol and hatred? For the time, Douglass still adhered to Garrisonian nonviolence: by pledging oneself to total abstinence, one could not only undercut the liquor traffic, but also serve as a example of moral uplift for others to follow.[81]

Upon his return to the States in 1847, Douglass continued his temperance activism through the pages of his first abolitionist newspaper, *North Star*, in Rochester, New York. It was in Rochester where he collaborated with fellow black temperance/abolitionist Martin Delany, interspersing the paper with stories of Washingtonian self-help alongside news of slaves similarly freeing themselves from the slaveholder's bondage. People of color "must be temperance people, otherwise they may expect to remain in degradation," he proclaimed. *North Star* lambasted white temperance organizations like the Sons of Temperance for excluding blacks, and in one of its final issues in 1850, Douglass affirmed that "the home of a temperate, industrious, honest man will be his greatest joy."[82]

At the same time—with the potato famine raging in his native Ireland (Chapter 5)—Father Theobald Mathew made plans for a grand tour of the United States, which "will undoubtedly be attended by the best of consequences to the cause of temperance," Douglass wrote, "and will also prove highly gratifying to himself."[83] From 1849 to 1851, Father Mathew, an icon of abstinence, traveled some thirty-seven thousand miles across twenty-five states, administering the temperance pledge to more than half a million more converts—predominantly, but not exclusively, Irish Catholics—just as he had administered it to Frederick Douglass back in Dublin.

However, his visit created fissures within the temperance-cum-abolition movement.

One of Mathew's first stops was in Boston, where he was welcomed by the temperate William Lloyd Garrison. Well aware of Mathew's condemnations of American slavery while back in Ireland, Garrison was dumbfounded when Fr. Mathew refused to stand up for those principles while in the States. "I have as much as I can do to save men from the slavery of intemperance, without attempting the overthrow of any other kind of slavery," Fr. Mathew grumbled.

Even as he was fêted in Washington—dining with President Zachary Taylor and presented an honorary seat in the US House of Representatives—abolitionists blasted Mathew's hypocrisy. "In Ireland, you professed to be an uncompromising abolitionist," Garrison seethed in *The Liberator*. "Now that you are on American soil is there any reason why you should shun those whom you eulogized at home?"

If anything, Frederick Douglass's betrayal was more personal. "From our acquaintance with Father Mathew, we had fondly hoped," Douglass wrote, "that he would not change his morality by changing his locality; but that he would nobly avow, and stand hard by, the principles he professed to cherish in his own land. We are, however, grieved, humbled and mortified that he too, has fallen."[84]

Garrison's and Douglass's unified rebuke of Father Mathew turned out to be one of the last points of agreement between the two great abolitionists. The 1850s would provide a great schism to the twin causes of temperance and abolition.

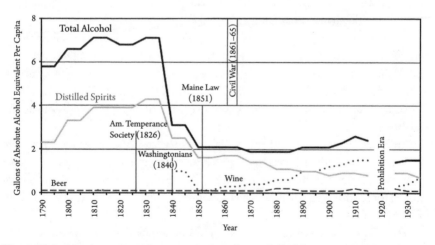

Figure 11.2 American per-capita consumption of pure alcohol, by source: 1790–1935.
Source: Harry G. Levine and Craig Reinarman, *Alcohol Prohibition and Drug Prohibition: Lessons from Alcohol Policy for Drug Policy* (Amsterdam: Centrum voor Drugsonderzoek, 2004); see also Merton Hyman et al., *Drinkers, Drinking, and Alcohol-Related Mortality and Hospitalizations: A Statistical Compendium* (New Brunswick, NJ: Rutgers Center for Alcohol Studies, 1980).

Schism

In 1851 Maine became the first state in the union to enact statewide prohibition of the liquor traffic through legislation. It was a game-changing event. According to traditional histories, this was the moment when activists pivoted from the innocent, noble focus on abstinence and moral suasion of temperance to the more nefarious "legislating morality" of prohibition.[85]

This is a gross oversimplification. The focus of prohibitionists after the 1851 Maine Law was the same as previous generations of temperance activists like Lyman Beecher and the ATS. They both targeted the predatory traffic in distilled spirits in which the profits of the liquor dealer came at the expense of his customers and community. Any difference between "temperance" and "prohibitionism" was one of means, not ends.

"There is and must continue to be an 'irrepressible conflict' between the liquor-traffic and the prosperity of the nation and the welfare of the people," wrote Neal Dow, the mayor of Portland, Maine, and the driving force behind the so-called Maine Law. "As that traffic flourishes, every legitimate industry languishes and dies."[86]

Later hailed as the "father of prohibition," Dow was a Quaker abolitionist and son of an even more famous Quaker abolitionist. As the story goes, the Washingtonian Dow was spurred to the cause of temperance on behalf of a female acquaintance. Her husband had been taken in by the rum sellers in Portland, where distilling from Caribbean molasses was still a major enterprise. When confronted, the saloon-keeper bristled with indignation at Dow's suggestion that perhaps he should not sell booze to the man, whose family was suffering.

"It is your business to sell rum, is it?" Dow fired back. "You have a license to sell rum, have you? Heaven helping me, I'll change all that!"[87] By 1842 Dow had convinced the aldermen of Portland not to renew the licenses of liquor sellers, though many traders continued to operate illegally. By 1851 his "Act for the Suppression of Drinking Houses and Tippling Shops" was overwhelmingly approved by the Maine legislature.[88]

Dow's critics were malicious. "A few years ago the jackdaw Mayor of Portland . . . was at the head of the nigger movement in that city," claimed Senator Cary from the floor of the Maine legislature, "but even Abolitionism was not strong enough for his diseased palate, and he has added temperanceism to his former stock of humbugs."[89]

While Dow's pioneering legislation would be struck down following a riot in Portland in 1855, the Maine Law became the template for similar dry legislation in states across the country, and inspired a new wave of temperance activism around the globe.

Perhaps the person most moved by Dow's prohibitionism was Frederick Douglass, who was working a similar transformation of the abolitionist cause from moral suasion to concrete action. In 1851 a long-simmering feud with his onetime mentor, William Lloyd Garrison, finally boiled over. In the pages of his newly formed *Frederick Douglass' Paper*, Douglass finally abandoned the passive rhetoric of Garrisonianism, embracing instead a more radical, activist political abolitionism, over opposition to a new Fugitive Slave Law, which demanded northern complicity with unjust slavery.[90] Both in abolitionism and prohibitionism, actions would speak louder than words.

In a column from November 1851, Douglass reported on the temperance sermon of reformer George Cheever, editorializing that Cheever "spoke first of the hopelessness of doing anything under present circumstances with moral suasion; secondly he showed the magnitude of the evils of the craft by which rumsellers have their wealth; and thirdly, the true remedy—a law like that of Maine."[91] For the du-ration of its existence, the pages of *Frederick Douglass' Paper* cheered the progress of prohibitory Maine Laws in states across the union, while back home in Rochester, he especially encouraged women to stand up and "demand of our Legislation the prohibition of the Liquor Traffic."[92]

Douglass's articles included the usual litany of alcohol's social ills, but was quick to underscore that progressive-minded prohibition was needed "for our protection against the liquor traffic." A serialized tale asked readers to reflect: "In your city, do you not, in the warm season when sickness prevails or threatens you, to prohibit the sale of certain vegetables? You do this for the protection of health and lives of the citizens. Such enactments you fully sustain as genuine law. How much more do we need the Maine Law! We need protection from the curse of the dram shops. To procure such laws, we must have the right kind of law-makers, and the people must obtain such by their VOTES."[93]

When the New York state legislature overwhelmingly enacted a prohibi-tory Maine Law in 1855, Doulgass devoted the entire front page of his paper to the triumph. Lambasting the ineffectiveness of simple moral-suasion tactics, he encouraged the state to stay true to the law and its enforcement. "The Temperance movement is a people's movement; by the people, and for the people. . . . It is the cause of the poor and the needy, and the friendless, who are not even friends to themselves." Such a progressive movement must be ever vigilant not to cede to the corrupting influence of the liquor business. Douglass concluded forcefully: "MORAL AND LEGAL SUASION UNITED, *by these we conquer!*"[94]

New York's statewide prohibition experiment lasted only a few short years be-fore being repealed, as the temperance cause faded with the outbreak of the Civil War in 1861. Yet even after the war—and the Thirteenth, Fourteenth, and Fifteenth Amendments abolishing slavery, and guaranteeing equal protection and the right to vote, respectively—Douglass remained steadfast in his prohibitionism as well as his advocacy of equal rights.[95] "For a long time I refused to commit myself to the doc-trine of absolute prohibition of intoxicating drinks, because I thought it interfered with the personal liberty of the citizen," he wrote in 1886. "But the sober contem-plation of the evils of intemperance not only upon the dram drinker, but upon his family, his friends, and upon society generally, has compelled me to go the whole length of prohibition."[96]

Amid a reinvigorated postwar temperance movement, Frederick Douglass encouraged black voters across the Reconstruction South to jump on the dry bandwagon. "You could not ask me to do a more consistent thing nor one more in harmony with my highest convictions of truth and duty," Douglass wrote in 1887, "than to ask the colored voters of that state to support by voice, vote, and co-operation, the grand Prohibition movement." With emancipation having been won with such sacrifice and bloodshed, it would be foolish for blacks to return to the slavery of the bottle. "Whisky arms the hand of violence. It stifles in the white race all ennobling sentiments of justice, kindness and good will," Douglass said. "Few things could do more for the elevation and happiness, or for the welfare of the colored people than the banishment of intoxicating liquors."[97]

The Great Emancipator

Of course no discussion of the abolition of slavery in the United States would be complete without the towering figure of Abraham Lincoln. The tales of Honest Abe's ascent from cabin-dwelling frontier boy to Civil War emancipator are well known. Yet his iconic legacy became a source of much myth-making over questions of liquor and temperance, with drys unabashedly proclaiming that "he was an ultimate prohibitionist, as he was an ultimate abolitionist."[98] Even wets conceded that Lincoln was an abstainer from a very young age, who encouraged others to likewise reject distilled spirits. Like Douglass, Lincoln was a temperance man. But was he a prohibitionist, too?

Lincoln's parents were pioneers on a dangerous frontier. As a child, Thomas Lincoln witnessed his father's murder in an Indian raid in Kentucky. After the family moved to south-central Illinois, his twenty-three-year-old son Abraham answered the call of Illinois governor John Reynolds to serve in the Illinois militia as it made war on Chief Black Hawk in 1831 (Chapter 10). Though he never saw military action, Abe was tasked with burying the battlefield dead. In frontier conditions where drinking was ubiquitous, it is noteworthy that Thomas and Abraham Lincoln were both abstainers.

Shortly after relocating to Springfield, Illinois, to practice law in 1836, Lincoln delivered what he often referred to as his "first temperance lecture." The construction of a new bridge was occasion for communal drinking, merry-making, and friendly sporting competition, including feats of strength. The strapping six-foot-four Lincoln was challenged to lift a full barrel of whiskey over his head, which he did with ease. When liquor started pouring from the bunghole, Abe took a mouthful of the whiskey before spitting it out over his right shoulder. To the crowd of onlookers, impressed with his physical prowess, he implored following his temperate example.

"My friends, you will do well and the best you can with it, to empty this barrel of liquor on the ground, as I threw the little part of it out of my mouth," Lincoln explained, arguing that booze would sap their health and vitality. "As a good friend, without counting the distress and wreckage of mind, let me advise that if you wish to remain healthy and strong, turn it away from your lips."[99]

Given the social context, it is unlikely anyone listened.

Still, Lincoln repeated this anecdote often enough that his political opponent Stephen Douglas later mocked him for it in the famed 1858 Lincoln-Douglas debates. "He could beat any of the boys wrestling, or running a foot race," Douglas said of Lincoln in their first debate, and "could ruin more liquor than all the boys of the town together": a jab that was immediately met with uproarious laughter from the crowd.[100] Douglas later accused Lincoln of once being a "grocery keeper"—a well-understood insinuation that he'd sold liquor on the sly—a charge that Honest Abe steadfastly denied, and for which generations of biographers and historians have found no evidence.[101]

As a member of the Illinois House of Representatives (1834–1842), Lincoln was a Whig in the mold of Henry Clay, espousing the merits of industrialization and a "free soil" antislavery approach that encouraged freed blacks to settle in the West African colony of Liberia. His temperance sentiment was more in line with the self-help abstinence pledges of the Washingtonians, rather than the ATS and their activism focused on the liquor seller. While entertaining political ambitions for the US House of Representatives, Lincoln articulated his temperance principles in a Washington's Birthday address to the Washingtonian Society of Springfield in 1842.

In his loquacious style, Lincoln chronicled the normative transformation temperance had wrought over the previous twenty years: from liquor's respectability to disdain; from indifference toward the drunkard's plight to empathy for him. Still, Lincoln argued against the direct tactics of the ATS: "too much denunciation against dram-sellers and dram-drinkers was indulged in. This is impolitic and unjust." Activists did not try to persuade liquor sellers, but instead lectured them "in the thundering tones of anathema and denunciation . . . that they were the authors of all the vice and misery and crime in the land." In the face of such self-righteous sermonizing, Lincoln argued that it was little wonder that drink sellers "were slow, very slow, to acknowledge the truth of such denunciations, and to join the ranks of their denouncers, in a hue and cry against themselves."[102]

The Washingtonian approach was kinder, more forgiving, and ultimately more persuasive, Lincoln thought. The most effective testimonials came not from paid speakers, self-serving lawyers, or firebrand pastors condemning the sinner to damnation, but from the reformed drunkard and his humble, soft-spoken tales. "By the Washingtonians this system of consigning the habitual drunkard to hopeless ruin is repudiated. They adopt a more enlarged philanthropy, they go for present as well as future good. They labor for all now living, as well as those hereafter to live." It was through these tactics of kind persuasion, Lincoln argued, that the cause "is now rolling gloriously on."

In this widely reprinted address, Lincoln foretold of a "temperance revolution. In it we shall find a stronger bondage broken, a viler slavery manumitted, a greater tyrant deposed—in it, more of want supplied, more disease healed, more sorrow assuaged." Through persuasion, reason, and humility, "even the dram-maker and dram-seller will have glided into other occupations so gradually as never to have felt the change, and will stand ready to join all others in the universal song of gladness." Again underscoring the links between temperance and abolitionism, Lincoln's speech concluded, "And when the victory shall be complete—when there shall be neither a slave nor a drunkard on the earth—how proud the title of that Land, which may truly claim to be the birth-place and the cradle of both those revolutions that shall have ended in that victory! How nobly distinguished that people, who shall have planted, and nurtured to maturity, both the political and moral freedom of their species."[103]

That Lincoln was a lifelong abstainer and champion of temperance is undeniable, but whether he was a prohibitionist is far less clear, and remains a matter of great historical contestation. Where documentation was sparse back on the frontier, historians cobbled together sworn affidavits attesting to the slain icon's unpublished speeches and actions. About 1900, Anti-Saloon League founder Howard Hyde Russell (Chapter 16) heard a remarkable tale from an elderly Illinois farmer, who told of an 1846 temperance rally in which this "young lawyer from Springfield" named Lincoln helped him and other schoolchildren affix their names to a Washingtonian pledge. Russell found three more eyewitnesses, giving sworn depositions as to their encounters with Lincoln fifty-four years earlier, some even having committed the pledge to memory.[104]

More contentious was the historical claim that Lincoln the prohibitionist advocated "moral suasion for the drunkard and legal suasion for the liquor seller."[105] With Neal Dow's prohibition passing in 1851, state legislatures nationwide debated their own Maine Laws, and the author of Illinois's prohibitory Maine Law was none other than Abraham Lincoln.

Though available evidence suggests that Lincoln certainly had a hand in the Illinois legislation,[106] much of the legend relies on the testimony of Rev. James B. Merwin—Lincoln's longtime prohibitionist colleague—who came to Illinois in 1854 to stump for the cause.[107] According to Merwin, Lincoln rose before a crowd at the Old State House to declare, "The law of self-protection is the first and primary law of civilized society. Law is for the protection, conservation and extension of right things, of right conduct, not for the protection of evil and wrongdoing," to say nothing of licensing and profiting from it. "This is the first and most important function in the legislation of the modern state. The prohibition of the liquor traffic, except for medicinal and mechanical purposes, thus becomes the new evangel for the safety and redemption of the people from the social, political and moral curse of the saloon."[108]

While other witnesses and records suggest that Lincoln—like most Illinois Whigs and Republicans—was supportive of Maine Lawism, only Merwin recounted this particular speech.[109] According to Merwin's accounts, Lincoln frequently condemned the "saloon," though his temperance addresses only ever referred to "dram shops" and "dram sellers." When pressed for more evidence of Lincoln's Illinois prohibitionism, Merwin claimed his copies of Lincoln's speeches were lost when Merwin's house was destroyed in the Great Chicago Fire of 1871.[110]

While statewide prohibition was inaugurated in Illinois in 1855—and endured the same difficulties of implementation (and ultimately repeal) as in Maine—Lincoln's attention turned almost exclusively to national politics and abolitionism. Before that, however, the Illinois lawyer offered an impassioned legal defense of fifteen temperate women who—perhaps foreshadowing the Kansas hatchetations of Carrie Nation years later (Chapter 1)—were accused of smashing up a saloon. Based on Lincoln's defense, the charges against the women were subsequently dropped.[111]

Upon winning the 1860 presidential election, Lincoln moved to Washington. And even though his victory prompted much jubilation and congratulatory back-slapping, he steadfastly refused to drink. In fact, the White House was effectively dry during Lincoln's four-plus years of residency there; even the signing of the Emancipation Proclamation itself was celebrated with nothing more alcoholic than spring water.[112]

The Civil War presented the president with scores of unprecedented challenges; from a temperance perspective, perhaps none was more difficult than the wildly unpopular Revenue Act of 1862. To pay the enormous costs of fielding the Union Army, Lincoln reluctantly acceded to imposing the first American tax on income, as well as a heavy tax on the liquor trade. For a purist like Lincoln, making the cash-strapped republic's finances reliant on a predatory liquor traffic was morally unconscionable, yet it was a practical necessity.[113]

If ever there was an opportunity to unequivocally state his prohibitionist principles as president, it was before a meeting with the Sons of Temperance in September 1863. Union victory at Gettysburg had turned the tide in the war, and Lincoln had recently been moved by his face-to-face meetings with Frederick Douglass. Against this backdrop, Lincoln's secretary, John Hay, chronicled that "an assembly of cold-water men & coldwater [sic] women" came to the East Room to make their case—following which, Lincoln humbly rose and proclaimed, "If I were better known than I am, you would not need to be told that in advocacy of the cause of temperance you have a friend and a sympathizer in me," before recounting his tales of personal abstinence on the Illinois frontier. On the question of preventing drunkenness in the army during the war—which was the purpose of the activists' visit—Lincoln calmly articulated how he'd rooted out drunk officers as consistent with the articles of war, and would be happy to pass along the activists' temperance wishes to the enlisted men. That "intemperance is one of the greatest, if not the very greatest of all evils amongst mankind . . . is not a matter of dispute," Lincoln claimed, but the "mode of cure is one about which there may be differences of opinion." While the prohibitionists blamed intemperance in the trenches for all Union defeats, the even-keeled Lincoln "could not see it," according to his secretary, since "the rebels drink more & worse whisky than we do."[114]

Perhaps the most curious legend of Lincoln's temperance temperament comes from the very final hours of his life—the afternoon of April 14, 1865—and is again reliant on the word of one sole witness: Reverend Merwin. To hear Merwin tell the tale, with the Civil War officially concluded, Lincoln turned to him and declared,

> Merwin, we have cleaned up, with the help of the people, a colossal job. Slavery is abolished. After reconstruction, the next great question will be the overthrow and abolition of the liquor traffic. . . . And you know, Merwin, that my head, and my heart, and my hand and my purse will go into that work. In 1842—less than a quarter of a century ago—I predicted, under the influence of God's spirit, that the time would come when there would be neither a slave nor a drunkard in the land. I have lived to see, thank God, one of those prophecies fulfilled. I hope to see the other realized.

Merwin thought it was an important and insightful statement, and asked whether he should publish it. "Yes, publish it as wide as the daylight shines," replied Mr. Lincoln—allegedly. And with that, the two friends parted: Merwin catching a northbound train to conduct business in New York, and the president to attend a play at Ford's Theatre. According to Merwin, it was only when he got to New York the following day that he heard news that the American president—his longtime compatriot in temperance—had been slain by John Wilkes Booth's bullet.[115]

The Empire Club Strikes Back

Sixth Ward, Manhattan, New York: Monday, November 4, 1844

"In the earlier years of my residence in New York," wrote Thomas Low Nichols of his experiences in the 1840s, "I had occasion to go one day into a porter-house, or grog shop, in one of the then up town, but not aristocratic wards of the city."

A pioneering dietician and quirky historical figure in his own right, Nichols wrote on trends in health and hydrotherapy for a British audience that was thirsty for stories of America. His descriptions of New York bars as tumbledown, exploitative flytraps for the working poor would have resonated in London, Dublin, Moscow, Johannesburg, or anywhere throughout the nineteenth-century world.

"Behind the bar was a strong, thick-lipped, muscular, determined-looking fellow, dealing out liquors to a set of very rough customers, in coarse trousers and red flannel shirts. They were not sparing in oaths, blackguardism, or tobacco juice." The floors were sticky with the tar from overflowing spittoons. The menacing thugs, petty criminals, and pickpockets sized up the intruder in their midst. Their trademark red shirts and stovepipe hats identified them as volunteer firefighters and members of the Bowery Boys: the most notorious of the early gangs of New York. At a time when an errant spark could burn down half of the city's wood-framed buildings, the city paid cash rewards to the volunteer fire companies that successfully doused the flames. Rival brigades often bare-knuckle brawled each other in the streets outside of burning buildings for the right to put out the fire and secure the lucre that came with it. In the process, they'd often loot the very buildings they were vowing to save.[1]

The brutish Paddy running the bar was their gang leader. Saloon-keepers the world over were the kingpins of the local community, and nowhere more so than New York's immigrant slums. He was the local pawnbroker, bail bondsman, and gatekeeper to job opportunities, both licit and illicit, making him a powerful political player.[2] And as Nichols described, like most barroom strongmen, this guy wasn't content with simply slinging whiskey. "His position as foreman of a company of perhaps a hundred rough and ready young men was not without its influence. They all had votes; they were able perhaps to vote more than once; and, what was still more important, they could shout, fight, vote and keep others from voting," turning the figurative economic muscle of the liquor traffic into literal political muscle. In big cities like New York, that meant throwing in with corrupt Tammany Hall Democrats and anti-immigrant, anti-Catholic "Know Nothings," so named for replying to specific questions about their xenophobic, nativist movement with a simple, "I know nothing."[3]

The man who "steered them to victory at the polls and fisticuffs at fires" was the notorious "Captain" Isaiah Rynders.[4] A former Hudson River boatman and knife-fighter, Captain Rynders built a thriving New York underworld of saloons and gambling dens, which he ran from his tavern at 11 Ann Street—Sweeney's House of Refreshment—a favorite firefighter hangout.[5] First from Sweeney's, and then later from his Empire Club on Park Row—which loomed menacingly over City Hall— Rynders "gathered a club of a hundred pugilists and assassins from the purlieus of the great city, and these he had trained for such scenes of violence as from time to time should further the domination of his party over the city." For years Rynders and his Empire Club thugs terrorized reform-minded Whigs and regular, law-abiding New Yorkers alike.

"'I am Isaiah Rynders! My club is here, scattered among you!" he'd declare on voting days in primarily Whig wards. "Damn you! If you don't leave these polls in five minutes, we will dirk every mother's son of you!" Everyone knew the Bowery Boys would love nothing less. Within minutes, hundreds of men fled without ever voting, "for fear of assassination."[6]

When the dietician Nichols finally met the fearsome Rynders face to face, he described him as "a lithe, dark, handsome man of medium size and sinewy form, with a prominent nose, and piercing black eyes—a knowing smile, and a sharp look altogether." Think of Daniel Day Lewis's character in the Martin Scorsese movie The Gangs of New York, for which Rynders and his men provided the inspiration.[7] Rynders "was cool and enterprising in his manners, and fluent and audacious in his speech. He had the reputation of being a member of the sporting fraternity, and one need not have been surprised to see him dealing at a faro table," serving liquor in his saloons, or regaling politicians at a black-tie affair.[8]

Captain Rynders was Gotham's first mob boss.

Yet as Nichols describes for his British readers, Rynders's crowning achieve-ment came in the presidential election of 1844. The imperialist Manifest Destiny of Democratic candidate James K. Polk meant annexing the Republic of Texas as a slave state and sending troops to occupy the Oregon territory, which was then disputed with British Canada. Whig reformer Henry Clay warned that annexation of Texas would mean war against Mexico on the southern border and with Britain in the north over Oregon. In a razor-tight contest, the presidency would go to whom-ever won the thirty-six electoral votes of the most populous state, New York, and its

'IM BOUND NOT TO RUN WID DER MACHINE ANY MORE
F.S.CHANFRAU IN THE CHARACTER OF "MOSE"

Figure 12.1 Bowery Boy Moses Humphrey, member of Fire Company 40, inspired the Broadway folk hero "Mose the Fireboy," popularly portrayed by actor Frank Chanfrau.
Source: "F. S. Chanfrau in the Character of 'Mose,'" 1848, Joseph Norton Ireland, *Records of the New York Stage from 1750 to 1860,* 33 vols. (New York: T. H. Morrell, 1867), Vol. II, Part XII, f. 44, TS 939.5.3, Harvard Theatre Collection, Houghton Library, Harvard University.

most populous region: Manhattan. Isaiah Rynders was the swing-state kingmaker of American electoral politics.

On November 4, 1844—the eve of the election—Rynders amassed a thousand skull-crackers outside of his Empire Club and led them on an ever-growing march through New York City: terrorizing any reformist Whigs into remaining at home, and herding all able-bodied men to the polls to vote for Polk and for Texas. Chanting their slogan "The Unterrified Democracy Is Coming!" the men marched through town, pelting Henry Clay supporters with hardened lumps of actual clay.[9] "A torchlight procession of twenty thousand men, pouring like a vast river of flame through the streets of a great city," Nichols described, "is a grand spectacle. The next day New York and the nation gave a majority for Polk, Dallas, Democracy, Texas, Oregon, war with Mexico, and war with England if necessary, which happily it was not."[10]

With Rynders tipping the scales, New York swung to Polk by just 5,100 of 486,000 votes cast. When the defeated Henry Clay himself met Rynders years later, he reportedly "inquired with a smile, 'Have I the honor of an acquaintance with the man who elected Mr. Polk? The Captain, being a modest hero, blushed and responded in the affirmative."

As acknowledgment of his service, Democratic president Polk rewarded Rynders with a lucrative no-show job in the New York customshouse, allowing Rynders to focus all his energy on his saloons, gambling dens, race horses, and other Tammany Hall machinations.[11]

For the next twenty years, Captain Rynders was the muscle behind the most corrupt political machine in American politics, making New York City his own flag-wrapped fiefdom, in which patriotic fealty to God, a pro-slavery Constitution, and an unbreakable union may—in his words—"be as true and unwavering, as un-changed and unchanging, as the great luminary of day in his course through the heavens."[12] Time and again, Rynders justified the use of mob violence as a demo-cratic means of enforcing the will of the people. No act was too extreme to protect the nation or its founding principles, as he interpreted them.[13]

The greatest threats he saw to conservative principles were the reformers: those "pests" with the audacity to believe that both women and blacks could be equal to the white man. "Shall we rashly endanger or destroy the liberty and happiness of a large portion of the family of man, and eventually, perhaps, of the whole civilized world, to gratify the morbid philanthropy of a few fanatical minds, who see no evil in anything but negro slavery, and no good in anything but abolitionism?" Rynders railed. "It is our duty, as friends of the Union, as friends of freedom, of liberty, of humanity, to defeat their schemes by every practicable effort," adding, "They strike a blow at human happiness that would be fatal, if not foiled by the strong arm of public patriotism and justice."[14]

Temperance advocates were doubly worse, Rynders claimed: not only did they threaten his livelihood in the liquor traffic, they offended his core principles just as much as the suffragists and abolitionists. Such "tyrannous fanatics, polit-ical hypocrites and public traitors" violated his "social rights," Rynders claimed. Speaking against a prohibitory Maine Law that reflected only "the voice of priests and old women," he again threatened that "we do not want mobs in our country; but it might be necessary to maintain our rights, that we should have a revolution on this subject." His speeches were met with wild applause in Tammany Hall.[15]

A curious thing happens when reading traditional prohibition histories: focusing solely on the Al Capones, Lucky Lucianos, and Bugs Morans of the 1920s under-world creates the false impression that it was the Eighteenth Amendment and fed-eral prohibition that created liquor corruption and organized crime, as if everything that came before it was perfectly innocent, clean, and legitimate. In reality, liquor-machine corruption was part and parcel of American urban politics for genera-tions before Al Capone; prohibition only forced it underground. In the nineteenth century, virtually every American city had its own Captain Rynders, embodying the bigotry, violence, and corruption of the white political establishment. Social activists knew this, and rightly viewed the liquor machine as the foremost impediment to democratizing reform. So one could only wonder what might happen when Captain Rynders and the fearsome New York liquor machine was confronted by the most marginalized, disenfranchised, and nonviolent social activists in American history.

Woman's Rights, Women's Roots

As Frederick Douglass said of the temperance, antislavery, and women's rights movements: all good reforms go together. Indeed, abolitionism and temperance were time-tested incubators for women's political activism in the antebellum United States. Unlike church or charity work, temperance and abolitionism involved social organization, fundraising, lobbying, petitioning, publishing pamphlets, and speaking tours.[16] From its founding in Boston in the 1820s, the American Temperance Society (ATS; Chapter 11) encouraged women as well as men to take the abstinence pledge and become active members in the organization. "Because, under the light of the gospel, which raises women in excellence of character and ability to do good to an equality with men, every association, composed of both, will more than double its influence over the public mind," claimed the ATS. To be successful, the movement needed "the influence of mothers as well as fathers; sisters as well as brothers."[17]

Certainly, most men were reluctant to welcome women into the politics of abolitionism and temperance on equal footing. But by the 1830s, it was becoming evident that women were not content with simply signing a pledge. In 1834, five hundred women from Elizabethtown, New Jersey, marched on the Court of Sessions, imploring the authorities not to license too many liquor shops. That same year, when a meeting of the Boston Temperance Society took up a resolution "to abolish the liquor traffic," the women who were consigned to simply watch from the gallery "manifested unanimously their approbation" through spontaneous applause, much to the chagrin of the men below.[18]

In temperance as in abolitionism, if men would not allow more than token participation in their political organizations, then women would start their own. In March 1835 the women of Montpelier, Vermont, organized their own Ladies' Temperance Convention. It was in October of that year, as you'll recall, that abolitionist William Lloyd Garrison was almost lynched on Boston Common by an angry mob, after addressing the Boston *Female* Anti-Slavery Society (Chapter 11). By the early 1840s, the trend was noticeable: wherever women were denied participation in abolitionist and temperance organizations, they actively formed their own. The self-help Washingtonian societies were soon matched by so-called Martha

Washingtonian societies. The Sons of Temperance fraternal organization was quickly mirrored by the Daughters of Temperance mutual benefit society, which claimed more than two hundred chapters and thirty thousand members by 1848.[19] From the Daughters of Samaria and United Sisters of Temperance to scores of other unaffiliated local organizations, temperance quickly became the core of American women's activism. "Rarely did women become involved in women's rights and then turn to temperance reform," historian Jed Dannenbaum said of the 1840s and 1850s. "Rather, women who had previously been active in the crusade against drink suddenly began to swell the ranks of the emerging women's rights movement."[20]

Rather than being the purview of Victorian prudes, women's temperance activism could be surprisingly radical. In New York City in 1846, Virginia Allen inaugurated *The Pearl: A Ladies' Weekly Literary Gazette, Devoted to the Advocacy of the Various Ladies' Total Abstinence Associations*. Just as Allen tore into the liquor interests who made "thousands of black and white in this city slaves of intemperance," she condemned "capitalists" and "rich monopolists" who exploited women's labor. From the pages of her temperance journal, she demanded full legal equality for women, including the right to vote. And while the struggle would be a long one, it would begin with temperance. "However woman may be oppressed—however deprived of political or social rights, her God-given influence of the destiny of the race may still be exerted," she claimed, by determining "whether the intoxicating bowl shall be dashed from the lips of mankind."[21]

So women had used temperance and abolitionism as platforms for political activism even well before the Seneca Falls Convention of 1848, which is usually hailed as the beginning of the women's rights movement in America.

To Seneca Falls and Beyond

What would one day become the movement for female suffrage began with a young Ms. Elizabeth Cady. In 1839 she had become smitten with the abolitionist and temperance ideals of writer and orator (and future cofounder of the Republican Party) Henry Brewster Stanton. "The thrilling oratory, and lucid arguments of the speakers, all conspired to make these days memorable as among the most charming of my life," she later recalled. "I had become interested in the anti-slavery and temperance questions, and was deeply impressed with the appeals and arguments. I felt a new inspiration in life and was enthused with new ideas of individual rights and the basic principles of government, for the anti-slavery platform was the best school the American people ever had on which to learn republican principles and ethics."[22]

The following year, the newlywed Stantons honeymooned in Britain, where they were to represent the American Anti-Slavery Society at the first-ever World's Anti-Slavery Convention in London: the same convention that spun off the first global temperance convention (Chapter 11). The fireworks at the conference started immediately, as Elizabeth Cady Stanton and other female delegates were refused their seats at this "gentlemen's" convention. Women would only be allowed to observe from the gallery, not participate.

Firebrand abolitionist and temperance man William Lloyd Garrison was one of only a handful of men who protested by sitting in solidarity with the women in the gallery. "After battling so many long years for the liberties of African slaves," Garrison blasted when finally allowed to speak, "I can take no part in a convention that strikes down the most sacred rights of all women." The chairman gaveled him to order for straying from the topic of abolitionism by speaking on women's rights, temperance, and universal suffrage.[23]

It was on the sidelines of the convention that Stanton struck up a friendship with fellow temperance/abolitionist reformer, the Philadelphia Quaker minister Lucretia Mott, who had been delivering temperance speeches across Ireland and England on her way to London.[24] Incensed at their unequal treatment, Mott and Stanton tried unsuccessfully to organize a separate women's abolitionist meeting, before vowing to "form a society to advocate the rights of women."[25] Eight years later, in 1848, Stanton, Mott, and the Quaker communities of upstate New York hosted the convention that would kick-start the women's rights movement.

In the intervening years, the Stantons moved first to Boston, hobnobbing with Garrison, Frederick Douglass, Louisa May Alcott, and Ralph Waldo Emerson, while Elizabeth honed her temperance oratory.[26] To escape Boston's damp climate on account of Henry's chronic lung congestion, the Stantons retreated inland to Seneca Falls, New York.

The Finger Lakes region was a bustling thoroughfare for America's westward expansion, and a fertile ground for philanthropy and social activism.[27] By the 1840s the twin villages of Seneca Falls and Waterloo boasted both Washingtonian and independent temperance societies, scores of teetotal businesses and hotels, temperance parades, and even its own temperance newspaper, the *Water Bucket*. By 1842 the town had voted itself dry, refusing to license any of the twelve liquor sellers in their midst.[28]

That same summer of 1842 in Seneca Falls, champagne glasses were raised in celebration of the wedding of twenty-two-year-old social reformer Amelia Jenks to Quaker printer Dexter Bloomer. "Will you not drink a glass of wine with me on this joyful occasion?" the groom asked his bride. "Surely it can do you no harm."

"No," she said with a loving, yet resolute smile. "I cannot,—I must not." The guests all admired her devotion to principles, as did her husband, Dexter, who went dry that day, too. "And ever after, to the end of her days," Amelia Bloomer's 1895 biography claims, "she was the firm and consistent advocate of Temperance and the unceasing enemy of strong drink in all its varied forms."[29] Bloomer would later become one of the most outspoken advocates for "woman's rights"—the rights of all women and womankind—which all began with temperance.

The arrival of her old friend Lucretia Mott for a yearly meeting of local Quakers in the summer of 1848 prompted Elizabeth Cady Stanton to convene a woman's rights convention in Seneca Falls—the first of its kind. From July 19 to 20, the local Wesleyan Chapel hosted some three hundred women factory workers, local towns-people like Amelia Bloomer, and activists including Frederick Douglass from nearby Rochester. The former slave "was the only man I ever saw who understood the degradation of the disenfranchisement of women," Stanton later said.[30] Douglass was a proud abolitionist and prohibitionist, but also a proud "woman's rights man." And while he frequently reminded white suffragist leaders of the double burdens borne by black women, he claimed that his greatest satisfaction in life was being the sole black representative at Seneca Falls: "the manger in which this organized suffrage movement was born."[31]

And while suffragism became synonymous with the early movement for woman's rights, women's disenfranchisement was only one wrong to be righted, albeit the most radical and least attainable by far. A full list of women's legal, political, economic, social, and cultural grievances was delivered that day by Elizabeth Cady Stanton. Her Declaration of Sentiments served as the bedrock for generations of women's rights activists to come.

"We hold these truths to be self-evident," Stanton nervously read aloud, deliberately invoking the Declaration of Independence, "that all men *and women* are created equal." But with increasing self-assurance, she listed the grievances of womankind. Not only could women not vote, but they were subject to both laws and taxes formed without their voice, which further their own subjugation. Women were barred from higher education and from all but a few occupations. Even if they could find a job, they were paid only a fraction of a man's wages, making it next to impossible to earn an independent living, making them ever more dependent on finding a husband. Women were barred from leadership positions not only in politics, but in the church as well. As an aside, Stanton spurned Christianity—and all religions—as superstitions that "perpetuate [women's] bondage more than all other adverse influences."[32]

But through marriage, women ceded what few rights they had to their husbands, making women, "in the eye of the law, civilly dead," according to Stanton. Women had neither property rights nor legal rights. Husbands could take their wives' income, beat them, or even imprison them with impunity. And lest she try to escape, both divorce and child-custody laws heavily favored men, tethering both a woman and her children to her husband. Of course, should that husband succumb to the temptations of the saloon-keeper, it was the woman who bore the brunt—from domestic violence to legal and financial ruin—through no fault of her own.[33]

The "history of mankind is a history of repeated injuries and usurpations on the part of man toward woman," Stanton concluded her Declaration of Sentiments, "having in direct object the establishment of an absolute tyranny over her."[34]

Resolutions addressing each and every grievance Stanton listed were endorsed unanimously—except for women's enfranchisement. Even Lucretia Mott denounced the proposal to give women the vote as too radical to be practical. The furor only subsided when Frederick Douglass rose and declared that "suffrage is the power to choose rulers and make laws, and the right by which all others are secured." In the end, even the suffrage resolution passed, though only with a bare majority.[35]

Local and national newspapers heaped scorn and derision on the women at Seneca Falls. Just who did they think they were, demanding their rights so audaciously? Some women wilted from the spotlight; others were emboldened by it, joining their male temperance counterparts "on the watch towers of politics and philanthropy," as Stanton put it. "The burning indignation of women, who had witnessed the protracted outrages on helpless wives and children in the drunkard's home," drove women to organize conferences, to speak out publicly, and to confront the liquor traffic directly as never before.[36] The movement gained even more momentum in 1851 with Neal Dow's prohibition of the liquor traffic in Maine, and the wave of state Maine Laws that then swept the country (Chapter 11).

Back in Seneca Falls, Amelia Bloomer noted that even the women who were skeptical of the radical call for suffragism nevertheless organized themselves into the Seneca Falls Ladies' Temperance Society, because for the first time they were awakened "that there was something wrong in the laws under which they lived."[37] The first issue of the society's newspaper, *The Lily*, was published on January 1, 1849, making it the first American periodical fully owned, edited, and written by women, for women.

"It is WOMAN that speaks through *The Lily*," declared editor Amelia Bloomer on page 1:

> It is upon an important subject, too, that she comes before the public to be heard. Intemperance is the great foe to her peace and happiness. It is that, above all, which has made her home desolate, and beggared her offspring. It is that above all, which has filled to the brim the cup of her sorrows, and sent her mourning to the grave. Surely she has a right to wield the pen for its suppression.[38]

Journalism in general—and *The Lily* in particular—become important avenues for social activism, beyond the male-dominated world of conferences and speech-making. *Lily* articles penned by Bloomer, Stanton, and other activists grew increasingly assertive not only on questions of temperance, but of property rights, education, labor rights, abolition, and women's dress. Amelia Bloomer most famously challenged men's expectations regarding traditional Victorian-era floor-length heavy dresses, which severely constricted women's freedom of movement. This presented a serious safety hazard around the home: imagine not being able to lift your legs while taking the children upstairs to bed, with a baby in one arm and a lit candle in the other. Instead, Bloomer promoted a knee-length dress worn as a belted tunic over bifurcated trousers, which would become synonymous with her name. Intended to give greater freedom to women—both literally and figuratively— the "bloomer" became the symbolic uniform of the woman's rights movement.[39]

The Lily nominally began as a temperance newspaper, calling for both women and men "to practice total abstinence and give their influence in all proper ways for the overthrow of the liquor traffic," which profited from men's addiction and led to the family's resulting poverty. But as with other suffragists, Bloomer recognized and articulated that the burden of insobriety that women disproportionately bore could not be effectively remedied until women were given a voice both in making and enforcing the laws. Annoyed, male temperance leaders frequently bemoaned that "she talks on temperance, but gives us a large supply of woman's rights, also." She was not about to back down from a fight. Bloomer wrote,

> Some of the papers accuse me of mixing Woman's Rights with our Temperance, as though it was possible for woman to speak on Temperance and Intemperance without also speaking of Woman's Rights and Wrongs in connection therewith. That woman has rights, we think that none will deny; that she has been cruelly wronged by the law-sanctioned liquor traffic, must be admitted by all. Then why should we not talk of woman's rights and temperance together? Ah, how steadily do they who are guilty shrink from reproof! How ready they are to avoid answering our arguments by turning their attention to our personal appearance, and raising a bug-bear about Woman's Rights and Woman's Wrongs! and a ready response to the truth we utter wells up from women's hearts, and breaks forth in blessings and a hearty God-speed in our mission.[40]

In April 1851 Bloomer and Stanton made the short trek to a woman's temperance convention in nearby Rochester, New York. "The circumstance of women coming together, not as idle spectators, but as real actors in the scenes of a grand public demonstration in behalf of Temperance, would have, of itself in the present instance, aroused a clamor," as Frederick Douglass described it. "But there was additional cause of excitement. It has been adroitly announced that the speakers on this occasion would appear in 'Bloomer Costume,' and, doubtless, this had its effect in three ways, to attract, to repel, and to make the Convention notorious."[41] The convention concluded by proclaiming that those who were indifferent to the cause of temperance were more guilty than the liquor traffickers themselves. Yet a far more significant development took place on the periphery of the meeting, where Amelia Bloomer introduced Elizabeth Cady Stanton to a young Susan B. Anthony, who'd been working for the Daughters of Temperance.[42] Stanton and Anthony would become lifelong friends and coworkers, and together did more than anyone to advance the twin causes of temperance and suffragism.[43]

Figure 12.2 When Anthony Met Stanton, bronze statue (1999), sculptor Ted Aub. Women's Rights National Historical Park, Seneca Falls, New York, depicting Amelia Bloomer (middle, in bloomers) introducing Susan B. Anthony (left) to Elizabeth Cady Stanton, with whom she would work for the causes of temperance and suffragism throughout the late nineteenth century.

Source: National Park Service.

Stanton and Anthony agreed that heavy drinking—and the liquor traffic that sustained it—was primarily a male problem, but one that had serious consequences for women. Abstinence pledges alone would not end the despotism of men over women: only fundamental changes in laws and attitudes toward women could do that.[44] Susan B. Anthony wrote, "Woman has so long been accustomed to 'nonintervention' with the business of law-making—so long considered it men's business to regulate the Liquor Traffic, that it is with much cautiousness that she receives the new doctrine which we preach; the doctrine that it is her right and her duty to speak out against the liquor traffic and all men and institutions that in any way sanction, sustain, or countenance it." Acquiescence to intemperance and its purveyors was the act of slaves and cowards. Even without the vote, it was up to women "to say to her husband, father, or brother, if you vote for any candidate for any office whatever, who is not pledged to total abstinence and the Maine law, we shall hold you alike guilty with the rum-seller. He who loves not humanity better than his whig or loco partyism, is not worthy the name of man nor the love and respect of woman."[45]

Yet even as women organized temperance associations and sent delegates to local, national, and even international temperance conventions expecting to be recognized as equals, they were met by entrenched opposition, especially by the clergy and religious establishment. In response to such a rebuke by the male delegates at a statewide temperance convention in 1852, these women formed the Woman's New York State Temperance Society. Elizabeth Cady Stanton served as president, with Amelia Bloomer and Susan B. Anthony as co-secretaries.[46] While Bloomer argued that only women should hold office in the organization, Stanton, Anthony, and the ever-present Frederick Douglass argued that such restrictions would be counter to the very principle of human equality that the organization and its members vowed to promote.

With the backing of some one hundred thousand signatures collected by the Daughters of Temperance, Susan B. Anthony read a letter drafted by Stanton that clearly fused temperance to the pursuit of woman's suffrage. "Inasmuch as Intemperance is in part protected by law, we who are the innocent victims of the license system, should [have] a voice in pulling it down."[47]

Frederick Douglass followed the activities of the Woman's Temperance Society with great interest. "The theme of these women, naturally enough, has been the peculiar and terrible sufferings of woman from the traffic in intoxicating liquors, and the necessity for the 'Maine Law' as a remedy," he wrote in *Frederick Douglass' Paper*. "The very moment woman rises in public to protest against the blighting traffic in rum, just so soon is raised the question of woman's rights."[48] Their temperance organization prompted Douglass to ruminate on the broader question of women's rights in the same issue. "A woman should have every honorable motive to exertion which is enjoyed by man, to the full capacities and endowments. The case is too plain for argument," Douglass wrote. "Nature has given woman the same powers, and subjected her to the same earth, breathes the same air, subsists on the same food, physical, moral, mental and spiritual. She has, therefore, an equal right with man, in all efforts to obtain and maintain a perfect existence."[49]

The first major temperance organization to actively encourage women's participation was the IOGT: the Independent (later International) Order of Good Templars. Founded in nearby Utica, New York, in 1851, and quickly spreading throughout the Northeast, Midwest, and Canada, the Templars encouraged men, women, and children to take a pledge of total abstinence, as well as used legislation to rein in the debauching liquor traffic by refusing retail licenses. That the IOGT was formed the same year as the Maine Law was no coincidence.[50]

Self-evident or not, women's temperance pioneers confronted constant reminders of white men's unwillingness to engage women as equals, just as much as men were unwilling to engage African Americans as equals. And perhaps nowhere was that more evident than in New York City in 1853.

Showdown in the Bloody Sixth

In the summer of 1851 Horace Greeley—self-made social activist and influential editor of the *New York Tribune*—steamed homeward across the North Atlantic from Europe. A lifelong teetotaler, philanthropist, and champion of universal freedoms, Greeley tirelessly patronized not just industrialism and workers' rights, but temperance, abolitionism, and women's rights, too.[51] On his travels, he'd hobnobbed with Queen Victoria, Alexis de Tocqueville, and Charles Dickens. He lambasted American slavery in speeches before the British and Foreign Anti-Slavery Society. But the highlight of his tour was visiting the first World's Fair at Hyde Park, in London, where the opulent glass-and-steel "Crystal Palace" showcased Britain's might to visitors from around the globe.

Sufficiently impressed, Greeley's London experiences solidified his belief that freedom and opportunity rested on the industry of a nation, and that his United States could compete and even surpass their old-world European counterparts in that regard. So, immediately upon landing stateside, Greeley conspired with his friend—the showman P. T. Barnum—to organize a World's Fair in Manhattan in 1853, replete with its own Crystal Palace.[52]

World's Fairs were gleaming showcases for both technological prowess and social progress, which made them lightning rods for social activism. Given the distances and difficulties of travel in the nineteenth century, the time horizons for organization, and the critical mass of important people, all manner of social movements piggybacked on World's Fairs. Temperance and suffragism led the way.[53]

The problem was that New York City during the Industrial Revolution was a seething, riot-prone cauldron of class, racial, ethnic, and immigrant-versus-nativist tensions, which Marx would have seen as ripe for a people's revolution. Gangs of murderous thugs ruled the boroughs on behalf of corrupt Democratic Tammany Hall politicians who gave them legal and political cover. It was no secret that the New York political machine was hostile—often violently so—to even the suggestion of abolishing slavery, recognizing women as equals, reining in their profitable liquor-trafficking operations, or closing the saloons that served as the dens for their political operations. Activists from upstate knew the dangers that awaited them.

The temperance/suffrage/abolitionist activists remembered their previous foray into New York City politics three years earlier, in 1850, when a meeting of the American Anti-Slavery Society was violently attacked by a xenophobic mob of Know-Nothing white nationalists. For days before the scheduled meeting, the conservative *New York Herald* stoked the flames of hatred against "these abolitionists, socialists, Sabbath-breakers, and anarchists," and their president—temperance-abolitionist William Lloyd Garrison—who, the *Herald* claimed, boldly urged the utter overthrow of the churches, the Sabbath, and the Bible. Nothing has been sacred with him but the ideal intellect of the negro race. To elevate this chimera, he has urged the necessity of an immediate overthrow of the Government, a total disrespect for the Constitution, actual disruption and annihilation of the Union, and a cessation of all order, legal or divine, which does not square with his narrow views of what constitutes human liberty.[54]

Garrison wrote to his wife that the "infamous *Herald*, for a week, has been publishing the most atrocious and inflammatory articles respecting us, avowedly to have us put down by mobocratic violence," putting himself and the participants in "imminent personal peril."[55] Garrison and his activists were going into the belly of the beast: the convention at the cavernous Broadway Tabernacle was in Lower Manhattan's "Bloody Sixth" Ward. Erected in 1836 and demolished in 1856, the Tabernacle at the corner of Broadway and Worth Street was just blocks from the notorious Five Points slum, which historians described as "a concentration of vice, disease, crowding and bloody conflict unparalleled in American history."[56]

The unquestioned king of the Bloody Sixth was none other than Captain Rynders: the corporeal embodiment of the liquor traffic and corrupt New York gang politics. As a "thorough-going sporting man"—devoted to gambling, fighting, horse-racing, politics, and bare-knuckle boxing—he financed his underworld operations through a constellation of saloons and green-grocery speakeasies across the Five Points. He co-opted local feuding gangs: the Plug Uglies, the Dead Rabbits, and the Roach Guards (named for a Five Points liquor dealer) to run protection rackets for saloons, brothels, and gambling dens.[57] Beyond the gangs, Rynders bankrolled thugs, maulers, and sluggers—including champion pugilist John Morrissey and knife-wielding eye-gouger Bill "the Butcher" Poole—who reveled in breaking up progressive Whig meetings.[58] To defend their lucrative trade, they even organized a Liquor Dealers' Protective Union, which Rynders used as a platform to attack temperance agitators.[59]

It is worth pausing here to point out that the conventional wisdom on temperance and prohibition is that it was a white, nativist backlash against modernization and immigration, intending to "discipline" the leisure of the newly arrived, lower-class Irish immigrants.[60] But in reality, the dynamic is completely backward. Many—if not most—of the impoverished, famine-fleeing Irish refugees who settled in American slums like New York's Five Points had taken Father Mathew's teetotal pledge (Chapter 5), while the saloons and liquor traffic—the true targets of temperance reform—were predominantly in the hands of established white nativists like Rynders, who built lives of luxury on the drunken misery of the poor.

Captain Rynders famously instigated the bloody Astor Place Opera House riots of 1849, which began with a petty argument over whether an American or Brit was the more talented Shakespearean actor. When the British actor William

C. Macready tried to take the opera-house stage, the American white nationalist Rynders amassed a rabid mob of more than ten thousand brick- and cobblestone-hurling men, attempting to burn the theater and hang Macready. With the police unable (and unwilling) to confront the Rynders mob, the disturbance was only put down by the muskets and artillery (!) of the New York Seventh Regiment. When the smoke cleared, hundreds of rioters and police lay injured; twenty-three were dead.[61]

These violent gangsters embodied everything the reformers fought against: proud white supremacists, who bristled at the idea of blacks or women being equals. And with their criminal empire built upon the corrupt liquor traffic, they snuffed out any whiff of temperance or Maine Law prohibitionism. "Enemies of our form of government are frequently found among us," Rynders once bellowed before a meeting of white nativists, "attacking with virulence the institution of African slavery." After speaking warmly of southern slavery as he'd seen it in his marauding days in the Mississippi Delta, and condemning abolitionists as "mad fanatics," he vowed to fight such progressivism by any means necessary.[62]

So then, not surprisingly, as Garrison opened the antislavery convention at the nearby Broadway Tabernacle, Rynders and his men hovered menacingly in the gallery. But when Garrison argued that belief in slavery was anathema to belief in

Figure 12.3 "Captain" Isaiah Rynders.
Source: From *Frank Leslie's Illustrated Paper*, January 24, 1885, 380, Library of Congress Collection.

Jesus, and that any Christianity that condoned slavery was a false religion, Rynders snapped. He rushed the stage with his thugs in tow.

All hell broke loose. Young abolitionists leaped to Garrison's defense. "If he touches Mr. Garrison I'll *kill* him!" one defender shouted, shaking his fist in the captain's face, while Rynders's spittle-filled vitriol landed on Garrison's bald pate. When someone shouted for the captain to watch his language on account of the ladies present, he growled, "I doubt very much whether white women who cohabit and mix with the woolly-headed negro are entitled to any respect from a white man."

"But," through it all, as the assembled journalists chronicled, "Mr. Garrison's composure was more than a coat of mail."

"You ought not to interrupt us," the pacifist Garrison calmly said. Following the Quaker tradition of hearing everybody, he told Rynders, "If you wish to speak, I will keep order, and you shall be heard."[63]

Rynders was taken aback: he was used to his fists doing the talking. Eventually he relented, but he stood uncomfortably onstage nearby, policing the speakers and their words. When Frederick Douglass rose, Rynders declared, "Now you can speak, but mind what I say: if you speak disrespectfully"—of the South, of slavery, or of the slavery-abetting Constitution—"I'll knock you off the stage."

"The gentleman who has just spoken has undertaken to prove that the blacks are not human beings," Douglass began. Challenging both the audience and Rynders simultaneously, he asked, "Am I a man?"

His boldness was met with thunderous applause, which Rynders tried to break by proclaiming, "*You* are not a black man; you are only half a nigger," apparently aware that Douglass's former white master was his father.

"Then," Douglass wryly smiled, "I am half-brother to Captain Rynders!" Years later Rynders admitted that the jab was "as good a shot as I ever had in my life."[64]

The eloquent Frederick Douglass ran rhetorical circles around Rynders, and any time one of the roughs tried to shout him down from the gallery, he'd proclaim, "It's of no use—*I've Captain Rynders here to back me*. We were born here," he said finally, "we are not dying out, and we mean to stay here."[65] The reformers rallied with applause.

Despite the Rynders mob's sporadic outbursts of "*the Constitution!*" and "*the Church!*"—both of which supported southern slavery—the rest of the day's proceedings went off without incident.[66] But the oratorically overmatched Captain Rynders would not be so humiliated a second time. The following day, Rynders and his horde broke up the meeting with overpowering shouts and raucous bellows rather than fisticuffs. Every single reformist speaker was sworn at, shouted down, and insulted. Rynders himself even put one speaker in a headlock and mockingly stroked the man's long beard. In the end, the captain proposed a sarcastic conference resolution that declared no "sufficient reasons for interfering with the domestic institutions of the South," in direct opposition to everything the reformers stood for. His rowdy mobsters carried the resolution by acclamation. Defeated—though miraculously not physically beaten—Garrison closed the convention.[67]

The 1853 World's Fair ensured that the two would meet again.

Horace Greeley—the philanthropist architect of the fair—was happy to hear that not only would a women's rights meeting be piggybacking on the festivities in Manhattan, but also a "World's Temperance Convention." Still, based on the women's prior disenfranchisement at the World's Anti-Slavery Convention in London, and Rynders's breaking of the 1850 meeting, the reformers harbored no illusions of a warm welcome in New York City.

As the World's Temperance Convention approached, both black and female temperance activists presented their credentials to attend. African American physician Dr. James McCune Smith was the first to be denied a seat at the conference, followed by the Reverend Antoinette Browne.[68] In the face of such racism and sexism, many activists walked out and established a parallel *Whole* World's Temperance Convention, which included delegates from Britain and Europe, but more importantly, included African Americans and female delegates, too.

As the women (and male women's rights activists like Garrison) walked out defiantly, evangelical church leaders shouted about biblical prohibitions against women speaking in church and scorned woman as "trampling the very Son of God under her blasphemous feet." Another reverend gloated that the women's departure "had thus gotten rid of the scum of the Convention."

One delegate remaining at the white men's convention explained how those activists had earlier disturbed "the Anti Slavery meetings in the same way, with their stuff and nonsense about 'Women's Rights.'" The convention's president blasted these "*women in breeches* as a disgrace to their sex." His scornful misogyny was met with approving cheers and laughter.[69]

Those activists were free to go form their own convention "where *both women and niggers had had their say*," another proclaimed. They should just "leave decent white men alone."[70]

Few sympathized with the walkout. The *New York Daily Times* ran an article titled, "The Female Pests," equating the activists' disruptions with those of Captain Rynders. "It is curious to see how naturally fanaticism on one subject begets equal fanaticism on every other," the *Times* opined on Garrison's dedication to abolitionism, women's rights, temperance, and "all his other insane vagaries." It was all just a publicity stunt, according to the *Times*. "The power of these she-males and their abettors is confined to the faculty of injuring every cause they espouse." From abolitionism to suffragism, they "have made every subject they have touched odious and contemptible in the public mind. They are now trying the same game on the Temperance cause."[71]

While both conventions debated similar issues—especially the sensation that was Maine Law prohibition—the Whole World's Temperance Convention at Metropolitan Hall was far more significant, and drew hundreds more attendees: "black and white, orthodox and heretic."[72] Horace Greeley himself chaired the Business Committee, and Susan B. Anthony was elected secretary. Conference Chairman Thomas Higginson's opening address claimed, "This is not a Woman's Rights Convention—it is simply a Convention in which Woman is not wronged—and that is enough," which was met with applause. This Whole World's Convention "knows no limitation of sect or sex—a spirit which knows no limitation of station or color—which knows no limitation except that between those who earnestly desire to prosecute the Temperance movement and that of those who would stand in its way."[73]

The first day of the proceedings was kicked off by none other than the "Greatest Showman" himself: Phineas T. Barnum. Well before entering the circus business, P. T. Barnum's American Museum at the nearby corner of Broadway and Ann Street was one of the city's most popular attractions. Not simply a freak show, zoo, and wax museum, the cavernous lecture hall at Barnum's museum also hosted matinees and theatrical performances, where liquor was banned as befitting a respectable establishment. Barnum's most successful show was *The Drunkard: or, the Fallen Saved* (1850), a temperance melodrama in which a conniving lawyer takes advantage of the hero by enticing him to drink himself into debt, but whose schemes are undone when, in the process of his dry epiphany, the hero discovers and reveals incriminating evidence of the villainous lawyer's predatory scheme. The temperance tale of *The Drunkard* ran for over one hundred performances at Barnum's without interruption, breaking all New York theatrical records.[74]

"I met a friend, who informed me that there were a great many 'isms' up here, and there were two classes of people present who had no right to be here," P. T. Barnum began his address. But, since "this was a World's Convention," he joked, "if there were any here who were not in the world they ought to be kicked out." The crowd of some two thousand attendees who filled the Metropolitan Hall tittered with laughter.[75] As for substance, the prohibitionist Barnum addressed the hot topic of the day: the prohibitory Maine Law:

> People say the Maine Liquor law is arbitrary and curtails men's privileges. It is not so. Have we not laws more arbitrary already? A man told me the other day he was going for no law which prevented him from eating and wearing what he pleased. I told him to go home then, and put on your wife's petticoats, and walk down Broadway, and see if there is not a law against your wearing what you please. Oh! I never thought of that. Talk of privileges, why you can't drive down Broadway without restrictions. You say you have a right to drive where you choose in the public street; but the law compels you to turn only to the right. Is not this arbitrary?[76]

Speaker after speaker—male and female, black and white—lauded the virtues of prohibition, though usually in less colorful terms than Barnum's. Suffragist pioneer

Lucretia Mott paraphrased Frederick Douglass's mantra about peace, temperance, abolition, liberty, and woman's rights: "all these great reformatory movements are in accordance with each other."[77]

Amelia Bloomer rose to the rostrum—in her trademark bloomers—and spoke for over an hour. "She sees that her prayers to rumsellers to desist from their murderous work have fallen upon hearts of stone," Greeley's *Tribune* summarized. "But though she is often weary, yet is she not hopeless."[78]

And while she spoke in favor of Maine Laws to combat the predatory liquor traffic, her primary focus was on empowering women to break their dependence on men, both in the political realm and in the home. Although inebriety was largely a male problem, women were complicit, too: from using alcohol as medicine and cooking with it, to refusing to stand up to drunken, abusive husbands. "No greater sin is committed than by woman consenting to remain the wife of the drunkard, rearing children in poverty and wretchedness"; she bluntly spoke on this very delicate topic:

> And yet public sentiment and law bid woman to submit to this degradation and to kiss the hand that smites her to the ground. Let things be reversed—let man be made subject to these various insults—and how long would he suffer anger, hunger, cold and nakedness! How many times would he allow himself to be thus trampled upon! (Applause.) Not long— not long—I think! With his right arm would he free himself from such degrading bondage. (Applause.) But thanks to a few brave hearts, the idea of relief to a woman has been broached to society. She has dared to stand forth and disown any earthly master. (Applause.) Woman must banish the drunkard from her society. Let her utterly refuse to be the companion of a drunkard, or the man who puts the intoxicating cup to his lips, and we shall see a new order of society. Woman must declare an unceasing war to this great foe, at all time and upon every occasion that presents itself. She must not wait for man to help her: this is her business as much as his. Let her show the world that she possesses somewhat of the spirit and the blood of the daughters of the Revolution! Such thoughts as these may be thought unladylike; but if they are so, they are not unwomanly.[79]

It was Emilia Bloomer's speech that brought down the house—not P. T. Barnum's—drawing thunderous applause from the diverse array of attendees.

Over the course of the convention, the delegates passed resolution after resolution as the official guidelines for organizational action going forward, which demanded confronting the predations of the liquor traffic, as well as celebrating woman's pivotal role in doing exactly that. Legislative restrictions on licensing liquor sellers— up to and including prohibitory Maine Laws—were overwhelmingly supported as effective means to curb the social harms associated with widespread drinking.

The one surprising dissenter was none other than William Lloyd Garrison. In the conference's waning minutes, Garrison rose to the podium to lodge a conscientious objection: not against the aims of prohibition, but the means. For Garrison, recognizing the validity of the Maine Law—as with *any* law—would mean recognizing the validity of the Constitution itself: an unjust document that not only enshrines and defends slavery, but also the right of the president to kill in the name of his people by waging war. "How could I, as a peace man, do this? How could I tell the poor slave that I am his friend and vote for this law?" Garrison asked. How could he square affirming the authority of the state to kill with his principled pacifism? "But I say to those voters who are not so sensitive on those points, that if you do vote at all, vote for the Maine Law. But, for one, I shall take that position which my conscience will sanction."[80]

After a rocky start, the convention was a resounding success—not just for the temperance cause, as Greeley himself editorialized in the *Tribune*, but for free speech and human equality.[81] But the activists couldn't rest on their laurels: after adjourning the Whole World's Temperance Convention, Mott, Bloomer, Stanton, Anthony, Garrison, Greeley, and scores of activists packed up and moved down the street to begin the Woman's Rights Convention—in the heart of the Sixth Ward. Held in the same Broadway Tabernacle where Captain Rynders had previously broken up Garrison's antislavery meeting three years earlier, Rynders again lay in wait for the social reformers—and this time, he would not even allow the delegates to get comfortable.

Almost from the moment that Lucretia Mott—now age sixty—was elected president of the convention and William Lloyd Garrison elected vice president, the rowdy Rynders mob gave the two-thousand-plus attendees all they could handle from their perch in the balcony. Speaker after speaker was loudly booed and heckled by these men who viewed the reformers as upstart anarchists—threats both to their financial interests and the moral fabric of the nation.[82]

Doing her best to rise above the din, Mott affirmed "the co-equality of woman with man" as their fundamental purpose, which drew jeers from the balcony. As the tumult ratcheted up, so did Mott, passing resolution after resolution over the jeers: respecting woman's equality before the law, woman's equality in the workplace, woman's equality in education, woman's role in religion and societal expectations, and equal pay for equal work. Mott saved her most scathing accusation for last: proclaiming that "the monopoly of the elective franchise, and thereby of all the powers of legislation and government, by men, solely on the ground of sex, is a monstrous usurpation—condemned alike by reason and common sense, subversive of all the principles of justice, oppressive and demoralizing in its operations, and insulting to the dignity of human nature."[83]

That didn't sit well with the Rynders mob.

The surviving minutes of the meeting record, as best they can, a riotous scene. Ellipses indicate where and when the words of one speaker after another were drowned out by jeers from the gallery. When Horace Greeley—the reformist organizer of the World's Fair himself—went to the balcony to reason with Rynders's rabble-rousers, he was greeted with a swift punch to the gut, which left him a crumpled heap on the floor.[84]

When William Lloyd Garrison's turn came to speak over the rabble, he explained that women "have enough of intellect; they have consciences and hearts pure and enlightened enough to enable them to give votes, when the vilest and most profligate and drunken men are permitted to do so," which was met with more animus from the balcony. After chronicling the sufferings wrought by women's inequality, Garrison declared,

> I have been called derisively, a *"Woman's Rights man."* I know no such distinction. I claim to be a Human Rights Man, and wherever there is a human being, I see God-given rights inherent in that being whatever may be the sex or the complexion. Our rights are equal, and whoever tramples on them is either a ruffian or a tyrant, unwilling that justice should reign in the world.[85]

One could only imagine how those words sat with Rynders and his nativist thugs: to hear their beloved Founding Fathers' principles as enshrined in the Declaration of Independence marshaled so effectively against their own bigotry. For the duration of the day, Rynders's men made a bellowing nuisance of themselves.

That evening, Antoinette Brown spoke, giving her account of being barred from the earlier World's Temperance Convention, where she said many white attendees came, "hoping not to be annoyed by women and negroes." After underscoring that "the Temperance movement, and that for Woman's Rights are, in some respects, one," she eyed the roughs in the balcony as being of the class "of genuine bigots, with hearts so ossified that no room can be found for one noble and expansive principle within those little stony cells."[86]

From that point until the close of business at 9:30 p.m., the session was repeatedly interrupted by disorder, disturbances, confusion, and "indecorous conduct" from the men in the balcony. Outnumbered and on the take, the smattering of policemen in attendance were powerless to confront the rambunctious mob.

The next morning, a rejuvenated Lucretia Mott opened the day's session by lambasting the "unreasonable and unreasoning disposition" of Rynders's men "to close their ears against the truth, or, rather, to drown its voice by vulgar clamor." Despite the taunts, chaos, and threats of violence, "not a scream was heard from any woman, nor did any of the 'weaker sex' exhibit the slightest terror, or even alarm, at the violent manifestation which invaded the peace of our assemblage."[87]

She may have spoken too soon. Rynders brought even more men this day: bellowing and laughing, whistling, stamping, and shouting, "Go it, Lucy!" With chants of "Shut up!" "Greeley!" and "Take a drink!" they made it impossible to hear.[88] The handful of police officers in the hall could only shrug. Confronting the angry mob of testosterone would provoke them only further.

They shouted down Garrison, Susan B. Anthony, Lucy Stone, and Wendell Phillips. Even the headstrong Quaker president Lucretia Mott had difficulty making herself heard. When the former slave from New York Sojourner Truth (an imposing figure in her own right) rose to speak, she was met with hisses from the balcony.

But Sojourner Truth wasn't having it. "I know that it feels a kind o' hissin' and ticklin' like to see a colored woman get up and tell you about things, and Woman's Rights. We have all been thrown down so low, that nobody thought we'd ever get up again; but we have been long enough trodden now; we will come up again, and now I am here."

The hissing and seething got even louder, as though a teakettle about to explode. That's what it was. But she didn't back down. "We'll have our rights; see if we don't: and you can't stop us from them; see if you can," Sojourner Truth proclaimed. "You may hiss as much as you like, but it is comin'. Women don't get half as much rights as they ought to; we want more, and we will have it."[89]

After that, all hell broke loose. The Rynders mob swept down the stairs beating the men, and even roughing up some of the women.[90] Chaos reigned on the floor of the Woman's Rights Convention, forcing Lucretia Mott to shut it down permanently. For safety's sake, Mott relied on the buddy system: having the male and female delegates exit two by two, assigning each black member a white companion to defend against the rabid, racist mob in their midst. Like the captain of a sinking ship, by the end Mott was the only reformer left, and without an escort. So, amid the chaos, she sought out Captain Rynders himself and demanded that he lead her to safety. Taken aback, Rynders reluctantly agreed: taking her by the arm, he led her through the riot and to safety outside.[91]

Days later, when the tumult subsided, Lucretia Mott and her party entered a restaurant where, as fate would have it, Captain Rynders was already dining. She boldly walked up to Rynders's table, sat down, ate, and conversed with the mob boss who was her political antithesis. By all accounts, it turned out to be a friendly and constructive encounter.

As Mott turned to leave, Rynders grabbed the arm of one of her companions, Miller McKim, and asked, "Is she your mother?"

"No," came the reply.

"Well," the puzzled gangster admitted as he scratched his head. "She's a good, sensible woman."[92]

The Maine Battle in New York

Following their World's Fair dustup, the reformers and the liquor interests retreated to their corners. The women returned to Seneca Falls to advocate for temperance reform, while Rynders went back to the Bloody Sixth. But that was hardly the end of their political confrontations, with the venue shifting to the New York statehouse in Albany. As we saw with Abraham Lincoln in Illinois (Chapter 11), the victory of Neal Dow's 1851 no-license law set off a wave of copycat Maine Laws across the antebellum United States. As the most populous state and the cradle of reformist activism, New York was again at the forefront.[93]

In 1854 the state assembly succeeded in passing a prohibitory Maine Law, which was quickly vetoed by Tammany-backed Democratic governor Horatio Seymour. But interfaction rivalries weakened the Democratic stronghold, allowing a Whig reformer, Myron Holley Clark, to narrowly capture the governor's office the following year. In 1855 Clark signed New York's Maine Law prohibition, which slapped huge fines and jail sentences on liquor dealers. Drunkards could avoid jail by simply disclosing who sold them the liquor in the first place.

The reformers upstate were overjoyed. Rynders and Tammany Hall were livid. Caught in between were the New York newspapers, endlessly pontificating over the issues that would mark the prohibition debate for the next eighty years: Its ends were noble, but were the means too extreme? Would it work? Could it be enforced? Was it constitutional? Would it impinge on individual liberty? And how would the entrenched liquor interests respond: the saloon-keepers, the businessmen, and the state that relied on liquor revenues?[94]

The reaction of Rynders and the liquor machine was as forceful as it was vitriolic.

"The Anti-Maine Law meeting last night was well worthy of Tammany,—a great jam, terribly hot, very noisy and enthusiastic beyond limit," claimed a *New York Daily Times* reporter fortunate (or unfortunate) enough to squeeze into the auditorium of Old Tammany, which was bursting at the seams with sweaty, beer-swilling "malcontents."[95]

"The platform was absolutely piled up with people, and the stairs, even, as well as every avenue of entrance, were choked up with belated participants," the *Times* wrote. "The speeches elicited tremendous bursts of applause, although it was quite obvious that none but those in the immediate vicinity of the platform could enjoy at first hand the eloquent efforts of the various speakers."

By approbation, the meeting resolved that prohibition was "the most flagrant and daring outrage upon every right of person," and that the temperance politicians behind it were "tyrannous fanatics, political hypocrites and public traitors." From that point forward, from within the sweaty walls of Old Tammany, Rynders himself would lead a political organization—the Liquor Dealers' Protective Union—to restore the "lost rights" of the city's liquor dealers and "sweep fanaticism and bigotry and hypocrisy from the land." Cheers erupted throughout Tammany Hall.

One Captain French, of French's Hotel on City Hall Park, clarified, "When I speak of the liquor dealers I want to be understood as comprising every man who deals in the remotest degree in liquor—importers, hotel keepers, brewers, distillers, merchants, jobbers, retailers and everybody, even the bottlers."

A shout came from the gallery: "*And the consumers, if you please!*" "No!" French emphatically declared. "With him it is a mere matter of personal gratification, but with us it is a matter of life and death."

It is hard to imagine a clearer articulation of the fundamental economic antagonism between the interests of the drinker and the liquor traffic that profited from his inebriety.

After repeated calls for him to speak, Rynders reluctantly rose to the rostrum to declare that he would "defend his social rights" against the fanatics in the statehouse, including wielding his tried-and-true threat of mob violence. Like a protection racket, Rynders portrayed his Liquor Dealers' Protective Union as a nonviolent means of resisting prohibition. Only if they failed would it "be necessary for them to appeal to the force of arms to protect their rights," he threatened.

Throughout 1855, the New York papers reported on how "the big guns of Tammany Hall, Messrs. Rynders & Co." organized liquor opposition in whiskey dens and beer saloons across the wards of South Manhattan, noting that "Tammany Hall had been faithful in all her nominations to the liquor principle." Rynders blamed their current Maine Law troubles on "the Temperance and the Reform, and last though not least, the niggers got together, and they had a party," which was met with laughter, and cheers of "Hurrah for Tammany Hall!" Hecklers who dared question the power of Tammany to promote the liquor sellers were kicked, collared, and thrown down the stairs. The meeting ended with a proclamation of defiance against tyranny, that "every man who leaves his gun goes over to the enemy," while others pined "for the chance to fire the first shot."[96]

In the waning days of campaign season, Rynders organized a massive pre-election protest in Central Park, drawing some fifteen thousand participants: "the washed and unwashed,—principally the latter," as the *Times* noted. Boss Tweed himself called the rally to order, denouncing prohibition as both tyrannical and unconstitutional. Speakers called for "a bold, open, manly resistance" to the Maine Law to challenge its validity. As in previous gatherings, voices called for Rynders to speak at this mass rally, one of the largest Gotham had ever seen.

He declared that they should obey the law while it is the law. But "if we cannot repeal it, why, we must either move to New Jersey or we must fight!" The crowd roared with laughter and cheers.

"My friends," Rynders concluded, "I don't advise a fight, because we can whip our opponents at the ballot-box. But if all remedies fail, it will be well enough to fight."[97]

In the end, the liquor dealers won, though only in part due to Rynders's political activism. In the summer of 1855, back in Portland, Maine, Mayor Neal Dow faced his own raucous mob protesting his statewide prohibition law. Questioning the ability of his own sheriff to control the riot, the former pacifist Quaker Dow himself led a band of militiamen and ordered them to fire into the crowd, wounding seven and killing one: the first bloodshed in the battle over Maine Law prohibition.[98] Dow was branded a murderer; his prohibition and heavy-handed tactics were disgraced accordingly. Shortly thereafter, the Maine Supreme Court hollowed out Dow's prohibition law, declaring that law enforcement had no legal standing to arrest and try liquor dealers.[99]

The New York Supreme Court followed suit in 1857, declaring New York's prohibition unconstitutional, and that selling liquor was not an indictable offense. In its place, the state passed a Liquor Excise Law, which limited licensed retailers and only forbid sales on Sundays (see Chapter 14) and—as a dig against Tammany Hall's corrupt tactics—on election days, too.

Undeterred, the New York Temperance Society made the first attempts at passing an amendment to the state constitution to legalize prohibition. "This is certainly a radical movement," wrote the *New York Times*, "and if it had any chance of success would be important. That it has none whatever, it is needless to say. The attempt to enforce an absolute prohibition in this State has had too recent a trial, and too signal a failure to afford encouragement of its renewal."[100]

The tale of Captain Isaiah Rynders and his Tammany Hall liquor machine should be a useful counterpoint for anyone falsely claiming that prohibition created political corruption with Al Capone in the 1920s, rather than a political movement that fought against it tooth and nail. Still, for the foreseeable future, Rynders and his Tammany-backed liquor traffic would rule New York politics—both the city and the state.

As one newsman quipped during the term of Tammany Democrat mayor A. Oakey Hall (1869–1872), "New York is now governed by Oakey Hall, Tammany Hall, and alcohol."[101]

A Tale of Two Franceses—Temperance and Suffragism in the United States

The Eleventh National Woman's Rights Convention, Union Square, New York: Thursday, May 10, 1866

Even in the years leading up to the siege of Fort Sumter in April 1861—and the bloody Civil War between North and South that followed—the abolitionist cause commanded far more urgency than its related reforms of temperance and suffragism. The ensuing four years of fratricide quieted social activism: there was little appetite for temperance or women's rights while awaiting grim news from Antietam, Shiloh, or Gettysburg. Still, in 1864, activists like Elizabeth Cady Stanton, Susan B. Anthony, and Lucretia Mott petitioned Congress—backed up with some four hundred thousand signatures—to forever abolish slavery by signing the Thirteenth Amendment.[1]

But following war's end and the assassination of the temperate emancipator Abraham Lincoln in 1865, debates over extending the rights and duties of citizenship—which had been won at such great sacrifice in the fields of battle—took on renewed urgency.

By the time the National Woman Suffrage Association—led by Stanton and Anthony—convened the first postwar woman's rights convention in New York City in May 1866, the Thirteenth Amendment abolishing slavery had already been ratified. What would become the Fourteenth Amendment—concerning citizenship rights and equal protection for all under the law—was still two years from ratification. The controversial Fifteenth Amendment, prohibiting discrimination based on race, color, or prior slave status, was still five years distant, and hardly a foregone conclusion.

With the ongoing debate over emancipation—not just liberation from slavery, but granting African American men equal citizenship rights with whites—whether women should also be granted legal equality seemed a very reasonable question indeed. As the representatives at the Woman's Rights Convention argued, what good reason for continued discrimination could there be? While the overwhelmingly white, northern, middle-class women were increasingly resolute, the convention spotlight was stolen by its foremost African American delegate: well-known social activist Frances Ellen Watkins Harper. Harper was the most prolific and bestselling black poet and author of the nineteenth century, who would later be hailed as the "mother of African American journalism."[2] Like most abolitionist suffragists, she was a vocal proponent of temperance.

"You white women speak of rights. I speak of wrongs," Harper thundered from the lectern alongside temperance and women's rights icons Susan B. Anthony and Elizabeth Cady Stanton. Underscoring the white women's privileged position, Harper told of her own attempts to desegregate public transit in the North,[3] some hundred years before Rosa Parks and the bus boycotts in the civil rights South: "Let me go to-morrow morning and take my seat in one of your street cars . . . and the conductor will put up his hand and stop the car rather than let me ride."

"They will not do that here!" one of the local New Yorkers interjected.

"They do in Philadelphia," Harper pushed back.[4] Black men were regularly thrown off the city's new horse-drawn streetcars and beaten in the streets, so it was up to black women's organizations to engage in civil disobedience.[5] She explained to the white suffragists that when a black woman got on Philadelphia's Eleventh Street Line, the conductor usually stopped the route, forced the white passengers off, and then returned back to the car barn rather than simply continue on. On a "good" day, Harper would not be kicked off, but forced to ride on the exposed front platform beside the driver, open to the elements and facing the ass of the horse that pulled the streetcar.

Cries of "Shame!" filled the hall.

Frances Harper continued: when the conductor tried to physically move her, she'd scream bloody murder. "The man said if I was black I ought to behave myself. I knew that if he was white he was not behaving himself. Are there not wrongs to be righted?" After she'd ridden as far as she needed and went to pay her fare, the racist conductor refused to take money from a black woman. Disgusted, she threw the money on the streetcar floor, leaving the uniformed white conductor to scurry after it, as she strutted past.[6]

"I felt the fight in me," Harper explained to the women's assembly, "but I don't want to have to fight all the time."

Even the heroic Harriet Tubman had been similarly humiliated. "The last time I saw that woman, her hands were swollen," Harper continued, "from a conflict with a brutal conductor, who undertook to eject her from her place. That woman, whose courage and bravery won a recognition from our army and from every black man in the land, is excluded from every thoroughfare of travel."

A shamed hush settled over the hall.

With the guns of the Civil War having only so recently been silenced, and the lessons of inequality and inhumanity having been so harshly learned, Harper passionately declared, "We are all bound up together in one great bundle of hu-manity, and society cannot trample on the weakest and feeblest of its members without receiving the curse in its own soul." And while her white suffragist sisters talked a good game about their own oppression, F. E. W. Harper underscored their complicity in oppressing others. As an activist, Harper embodied intersectionality long before that term was coined.

"Talk of giving women the ballot-box? Go on." If the white women of this country wanted to be taken seriously, they needed to first practice what they preached. "While there exists this brutal element in society which tramples upon the feeble and treads down the weak, I tell you that if there is any class of people who need to be lifted out of their airy nothings and selfishness, it is the white women of America."

And with that, she walked off stage.

Following such a withering J'accuse, one might imagine a chorus of indignant gasps, but no. Instead, convention secretary Susan B. Anthony immediately rose to the podium in agreement. "As women we can no longer seem to claim for ourselves what we do not for others—nor can we work in two separate movements to get the ballot for the two disenfranchised classes—the negro and woman," she explained. The only just form of government was one that was based upon the consent of the governed—all of the governed. "We, therefore, wish to broaden our Woman's Rights platform, and make it in name—what it ever has been in spirit—a Human Rights platform."

She followed with the resolution: "That the time has come for an organization that shall demand UNIVERSAL SUFFRAGE, and that hereafter we shall be known as the 'AMERICAN EQUAL RIGHTS ASSOCIATION.' "

The universal-suffrage resolution was carried unanimously.[7]

The conference proceedings leave no record of F. E. W. Harper's reaction to this vindication, but we might imagine at least a slight satisfaction from pushing the pre-dominantly white, middle-class ladies of the twin temperance-suffragist movement to become even more open, aware, and inclusive in their activism.

F. E. W. Harper and Temperance in the Reconstruction South

That the modern women's rights movement in the United States was firmly rooted in temperance has always been clear. But the temperance/suffragism tale we're ac-customed to hearing is overwhelmingly white people's history. From the big bang of women's activism in the Temperance Crusades of 1873–1874 to the establish-ment of the Woman's Christian Temperance Union (WCTU)—so vital to both the Eighteenth (prohibition) and Nineteenth (woman's suffrage) Amendments—the usual focus is on social organizations, temperance lodges, abstinence pledges, and

Figure 13.1 Frances Ellen Watkins Harper, 1825–1911, engraving circa 1872, from William Still, *The Underground Rail Road* (Philadelphia: Porter & Coates, 1872), 748.
Source: Library of Congress Prints and Photographs Division, Digital ID cph.3b23175.

political petitions orchestrated largely by white Protestant women in the northern states.[8]

But as our global perspective suggests, activism doesn't always come with lodges and pledges, especially among subaltern groups. King Khama led a prohibitionist revolt in Bechuanaland without lodges and pledges; India and Turkey only had a handful of organizations, and Native Americans had virtually none (Chapters 6–10). And yet each had significant episodes of temperance and prohibitionism as resistance to white colonial domination.

As it turns out, temperance sentiment was likewise widespread among newly freed African Americans in the Reconstruction South, especially among black women. Expanding our horizons beyond the usual lodges, pledges, and other formal trappings of social organization gives us a new understanding of temperance in America as part of a far broader, intersectional movement for liberation from traditional patriarchal authority: a common struggle that would even help reconcile the deep divisions between North and South left by the Civil War.

African Americans were lumped into the same racial hierarchy of so-called inferior races—and subjected to the same tired, colonial alcohol discourse—as subjugated populations the world over. Many white Americans, both North and

South, saw alcohol as a disinhibitor: unleashing bestial black brutality. Since the "selling of rum to Negroes" was thought "productive of disorder," the same colonial and early American prohibitions that covered Native Americans also applied to African Americans. In the South, prohibition was codified into the slave codes, which became ever more restrictive as fears of rebellions and insurrection mounted.[9] But with Union victory in the Civil War and the abolition of slave laws, southern freedmen were legally free to buy liquor, stoking racist fears "that the African's volatile disposition, combined with the exercise of a liberty to which he was unaccustomed," would lead to an orgy of alcoholic disorder.[10]

It wasn't true, of course. Throughout the Reconstruction South, drinking among African Americans was minimal. Even the holidays of Emancipation Day and the Fourth of July in the South were marred not by uninhibited freedmen but rather by drunken whites looking to disrupt black celebrations.[11] While there were no objective surveys of African American drinking, the first post–Civil War census in 1870 found that mortality from alcohol poisoning was significantly lower among black Americans than white, and that the rate of African American deaths from liver cirrhosis were only a quarter of that of the white population.[12] With even more finely grained demographic data, the 1880 census reported 0.7 deaths from alcoholism per 1,000 among blacks as opposed to 2.5 per 1,000 among whites, adding, "A large proportion of the deaths reported as due to alcoholism occur in connection with delirium tremens, and this form of disease is rare in the colored race."[13]

Still, the worry among activists—like those at the women's convention in New York—was that Reconstruction would simply pass the chains of black bondage from the white slaveowner to the white saloon-keeper. In the North, to be sure, the widespread temperance/abolitionist sentiment among close-knit black communities discouraged African Americans from entering a liquor trade dominated by whites (Chapter 11). The same racial dynamics took hold in the Reconstruction South, compounded by the inability of poorer blacks in the rural South to afford liquor-licensing fees. Moreover, among southern whites there was "a rooted objection to granting liquor licenses to Negroes, inasmuch as this would be equivalent to establishing colored centres of political activity."[14]

After the war, then, both in the North and South, the liquor traffic remained overwhelmingly in white hands, a fact well recognized by temperance activists. "If the Anglo-Saxons and the Hebrews would stop selling whiskey, I guarantee that the Ethiopians would stop drinking it," proclaimed one black delegate to the State Temperance Convention of Alabama in 1881.[15] Antiliquor measures were also a matter of safety and justice: a necessary prophylactic against vengeful, white lynch mobs, which were often fueled by whiskey.[16] Accordingly, activists like Frederick Douglass doubled down on prohibition as necessary to the substantive emancipation not just of black men, but of everyone. To be faithful to its promise of rights and liberties for all citizens—and especially its newly enfranchised ones—America had to confront the liquor machine.

"O save the black man from the curse of drink: he has become an integral part of our civilization. In saving him we shall save ourselves," Douglass thundered during his temperance addresses from the 1870s. He understood that uplift would be an uphill struggle—not only against temptation and addiction, but against white prejudice, too.

Douglass continued by proclaiming his hope for justice, sobriety, and equality. This movement, he said, was being led by "an earnest woman": none other than "Mrs. Frances Ellen Harper of Philadelphia," who had recently returned from a temperance tour of the southern states. "She reports that she saw and heard very little of drunkenness among the colored people," which defied the prevailing white stereotypes. Although "the taint of alcoholism is therefore not in the blood of the southern negro," Douglass claimed, "temperance work with him is still one of prevention and encouragement." Following Reconstruction, America's great task would be to remove the remaining barriers of inequality, oppression, and exploitation, so that *all* citizens could secure justice and contribute to the grand project of democracy. In this struggle, Frederick Douglass underscored that works of black temperance suffragists like Mrs. Harper were "of vital importance."[17]

So who *was* Frances Ellen Watkins Harper?

Born free in Baltimore in 1825, Frances Ellen was the only child of freed black parents, who both died when she was only three. She was raised by her maternal aunt and uncle, Henrietta Watkins and the civil rights activist Rev. William Watkins, minister at the African Methodist Episcopal (AME) Church on Sharp Street. In addition to adopting Watkins's name, she also drew inspiration from his teachings through the AME Church, which emphasized selfless philanthropy and service to the underserved black community.[18] As a teen, she labored as a seamstress and nursemaid for a white family that owned a bookshop and bindery, which permitted her to read extensively in her spare time. She began writing essays and poems for antislavery journals in 1839. Her first compendium of poetry, *Forest Leaves*, was published in 1845 by Baltimore printer and temperance leader James Young when she was just twenty years old.[19]

Even as she moved first to Columbus, Ohio, and then York, Pennsylvania, to teach at AME-affiliated schools for black youths, Harper continued to write. Her enormously popular second book, *Poems on Miscellaneous Subjects*, was first published in 1854, and reprinted multiple times. Foremost among those miscellaneous subjects was temperance. In her poem "The Drunkard's Child," she painted a sorrowful picture of the impacts of male drinking on the most vulnerable members of his family:

> He stood beside his dying child,
> With a dim and bloodshot eye;
> They'd won him from the haunts of vice
> To see his first-born die.
> He came with a slow and staggering tread,

A vague, unmeasuring stare,
And, reeling, clasped the clammy hand,
So deathly pale and fair.
. . .
And burning tears like rain
Poured down his bloated face;
Where guilt, remorse and shame
Had scathed, and left their trace.[20]

As a poet and author, Watkins joined the American Anti-Slavery Society as a traveling lecturer, delivering hundreds of speeches on social reform across the East and Midwest. In 1860 she married widower Fenton Harper, who died four years later, leaving her to raise their daughter, along with three other children from Harper's previous marriage. She would not remarry.[21]

Harper's outspokenness on the perils of intemperance—so central to both her poems and lectures—grew even sharper in articles in abolitionist papers, which made her a household name in reformist circles. This was the insightful young activist whom Susan B. Anthony and Elizabeth Cady Stanton invited to speak before the Eleventh National Woman's Rights Convention in 1866, reorienting the organization's focus toward universal suffrage and universal rights.

After the Civil War, Harper moved to the South, spending years as a teacher to newly liberated African American communities, while lecturing on integration, universal rights, and temperance, earning plaudits from Frederick Douglass. Drawing upon her experiences in the former Confederacy, in 1872 Harper published her widely read *Sketches of Southern Life*. Of course, it was full of temperance poems, including "Nothing and Something," on the familial and societal consequences of liquor-traffic predations:

It is nothing to me, the merchant said,
As over his ledger he bent his head;
I'm busy to-day with tare and tret,
And I have no time to fume and fret.
It was something to him when over the wire
A message came from a funeral pyre—
A drunken conductor had wrecked a train,
And his wife and child were among the slain.

It is nothing to me, the voter said
The party's loss is my greatest dread;
Then gave his vote for the liquor trade,
Though hearts were crushed and drunkards made.
It was something to him in after life,

When his daughter became a drunkard's wife
And her hungry children cried for bread,
And trembled to hear their father's tread.[22]

As if to offer a solution, the very next poem was "Signing the Pledge." It portrays
the drunkard's slavery to the bottle and the ruin it causes his family—before his
abstinence pledge rejuvenates the man and frees him from his bonds, making him
a virtuous man worthy of respect from his wife, child, aging mother, and the community beyond:

Do you see this pledge I've signed to-night?
My mother, wife, and boy
Shall read my purpose on that pledge
And smile through tears of joy.
To know this night, this very night,
I cast the wine-cup down,
And from the dust of a sinful life
Lift up my manhood's crown.
. . .
A captive bounding from my chain,
I've rent each hateful band,
And by the help of grace divine
A victor hope to stand.[23]

With her emphasis on "grace divine," Harper's writing—like her activism—never
strayed far from her Christian morality. Raised by an AME pastor and having taught
in AME-affiliated schools, Christian benevolence was never far from Harper's mind.
But like so many social activists, her Christianity was not fire-and-brimstone, but
rather of selflessness and service to building a more just community here on earth.
While social gospel public service helped motivate Progressive-Era reformism beginning in the 1890s (Chapter 14), F. E. W. Harper and scores of black activists
were doing the same thing a generation earlier. But unlike later Progressives, she did
not belittle or dismiss black agency. Instead, she focused on freedmen as not only
worthy of attention, but also capable of reforming themselves, embodying a black
progressivism devoid of patriarchal overtones.[24]

Perhaps nowhere are these dynamics as evident as in her *Sowing and Reaping*
(1876). Serialized for the AME's *Christian Recorder*, Harper was writing both from
and for the black community.[25] *Sowing and Reaping* was a temperance story, but
(like most temperance stories, actually) it was not about some drunkard redeemed,
but about doing what is right by your fellow man.

John Anderson, the story's protagonist, "made up his mind to be rich" by going
into the liquor business. For such wealth, "he is ready to sacrifice time, talent,

energy, and every faculty, which he possesses," Harper writes, "but oh how poverty stricken his soul will be."[26] It wasn't just white industrialists who exploited black communities for profit; African Americans could do it, too.[27]

"You cannot keep that saloon without sending a flood of demoralizing influence over the community," Anderson's friend pushes back:

> Your profit will be the loss of others. Young men will form in that saloon habits which will curse and overshadow all their lives. Husbands and fathers will waste their time and money, and confirm themselves in habits which will bring misery, crime, and degradation; and the fearful outcome of your business will be broken hearted wives, neglected children, outcast men, blighted characters and worse than wasted lives. No not for the wealth of the Indies, would I engage in such a ruinous business, and I am thankful today that I had a dear sainted mother who taught me that it was better to have my hands clear than to have them full.[28]

Harper is hardly subtle about the predations of the liquor traffic. When Anderson visits the opulent home of a retired whiskey dealer, she describes how "all the misery his liquor had caused . . . oozed in great drops from every marble ornament or beautiful piece of frescoe that adorned his home, for that home with its beautiful surroundings and costly furniture was the price of blood."

The noble heroine of *Sowing and Reaping* is Belle Gordon. She had been proposed to by the well-to-do Charles Romaine, which would set her up for a life of financial security. But when Charles refused to give up his drinking for her hand in marriage, Belle moved on.

"I don't think because Mr. Romaine drinks occasionally that I would have given him up," says her cousin. "Oh young men will sow their wild oats."

"And as we sow, so must we reap, and as to saying about young men sowing their wild oats, I think it is full of pernicious license," Belle pushes back. "A young man has no more right to sow his wild oats than a young woman. God never made one code of ethics for a man and another for a woman. And it is the duty of all true women to demand of men the same standard of morality that they do of women."

When it came to the central question of the liquor traffic, Belle blasted that "there are two classes of people with whom I never wish to associate, or number as my especial friends, and they are rum sellers and slave holders." Just because the liquor dealer "commits his crime against society within the pale of the law," it doesn't make him less of a criminal against humanity. In fact, that makes it even worse: "When crime is sanctioned by law, and upheld by custom and fashion, it assumes its most dangerous phase."[29]

For F. E. W. Harper, the answer to such social parasitism was empowering women with the vote. In the story's concluding pages, Harper's characters extol all of the usual reasons for why women shouldn't be given the vote: they could exercise their power at home by persuading their husbands to vote this way or that, or voting would sully women's dignity, since so many polling places were held in taverns anyway. To this, she replies,

> With all our influence we never could have the same sense of responsibility which flows from the possession of power. I want women to possess power as well as influence, I want every Christian as she passes by a grog-shop or liquor saloon, to feel that she has on her heart a burden of responsibility for its existence, I hold my dear that a nation as well as an individual should have a conscience, and on this liquor question there is room for woman's conscience not merely as a persuasive influence but as an enlightened and aggressive power.[30]

Published in its entirety in the mid-1870s, Harper's *Sowing and Reaping* was tremendously influential. By design, the characters were racially indeterminate: they could be white or black, since ultimately it wasn't race that was at issue, but economic inequalities and woman's disenfranchisement.[31] White readers could just as easily access the characters as could the intended readership of the black AME churches: the cornerstone of black social activism in the Reconstruction South. Yet F. E. W. Harper's poetry and serialized novels were only the tip of the iceberg of black women's activism, which often gets overlooked in the search for lodges, petitions, and other traditional signifiers of social organization.

Indeed, such activism paved the way for an explosion of women's social organization—black and white, North and South. As we shall see, the so-called Woman's Temperance Crusade of 1873–1874 empowered an entire generation of women's rights activists and forever changed the dynamics of social contention in America. But it would be foolish to think that such widespread organization emerged spontaneously out of nothing.

The Woman's Temperance Crusade

Dr. Diocletian "Dio" Lewis was a curious historical figure. Breaking from his studies at Harvard Medical School, he became interested in homeopathy, physical culture, and temperance. He helped pioneer the then radical, now commonplace notion that doctors should not just cure disease but work to prevent illness. He promoted exercise and gymnastics, even inventing the beanbag to help those with developmental disabilities safely engage in physical therapy.[32] Dr. Lewis declared, "Alcohol is a poison, and should not be taken into the stomach in any form, or under any circumstances," and encouraged total abstinence from all alcohol. He even advised "members of churches to shun the Lord's Supper, until unfermented wines are furnished."[33] In 1852 Dio Lewis and his wife, Helen, moved from New York to the

South, for fears of the tuberculosis that claimed three of her sisters. A homeopathic regimen brought her renewed health, and Dr. Lewis's "consumption cure" garnered nationwide attention.

Lewis's "fringe" homeopathy won him the suspicion of his southern neighbors; his condemnation of slavery and women's subordination won him their scorn. Nevertheless, in 1853 he joined the Sons of Temperance in Fredericksburg, Virginia, while bemoaning that the abstinence pledge did not include tobacco and that women were excluded. "In failing to enlist woman in the work, they were leaving out the element most essential and indispensable to success" of the temperance cause, and Lewis implored the organization to reconsider. Frustrated at their indifference, he wrote his first lecture: "The Influence of Christian Women in the Cause of Temperance." Along with additional talks on the importance of exercise and gymnastics, he began speaking to churches, women's schools, and universities across Virginia on the necessity of women's inclusion in temperance.[34]

In his temperance lecture, Lewis told of his own family: his father was a drinking man in Saratoga, New York, destined for the usual degeneracy. At the end of her rope, his mother and her friends went to the saloon to protest: they would occupy the saloon and pray until the saloon-keeper agreed to stop selling liquor. And he did. In this lecture—given hundreds of times across the South and the entire United States—he suggested that local women might use the same process to achieve the same results in their own communities. On at least twenty different occasions, local women rose to the challenge—most notably in 1858, when fifty women marched on the saloons of Dixon, Illinois—in prayerful, nonviolent protest for six days until all the grog shops had closed.[35]

The women's protests had been sporadic, local, and fleeting, until 1873, when Lewis's speeches ignited a grassroots movement of women's empowerment, which began in southwestern Ohio and soon swept across the nation.

On the evening of Sunday, December 22, 1873, Diocletian Lewis gave his temperance address in Hillsboro, Ohio. Though Lewis was her houseguest, fifty-seven-year-old matron Eliza Jane "Mother" Thompson was busy with housework and did not attend the lecture. Her children did, however. They returned with great excitement, telling of Lewis's blueprint: first imploring the local druggists, grocers, and physicians to pledge not to sell or prescribe alcoholic liquors, before moving up to the hoteliers and saloon-keepers. Some fifty women had agreed to try it in Hillsboro the next day, and sixty or seventy men vowed to back them. "You are on some committees to do work in the Presbyterian Church in the morning," her son told her, "and the ladies expect you to go with them to the saloons!"[36]

Mother Thompson was widely respected in Hillsboro. Her husband was a prominent attorney and judge; her father was the former governor, and her uncle a former US senator. She'd attended the Cincinnati school established by woman's education activist Catharine Beecher and her father, the temperance abolitionist Lyman Beecher (Chapter 11).[37] Still, as a respectable woman, she shared her husband's skepticism of all this activist "tomfoolery," before reluctantly agreeing. At the church the next morning, once the men adjourned to "leave this work with God and the women," the venerable Thompson was elected the women's leader.[38] After prayers, the ladies set about their work, getting three of the four druggists in town to willingly sign the pledge; the fourth postponed his decision. Then they set their sights on the saloons.

"It was a dark, cloudy, cold, and still December day, no sun shining from above, no wind playing around, a little snow leisurely dropping down," wrote Judge Thompson, Eliza's husband, as "the procession moved with solemn steps, as if each woman had been trained for that day's work from the cradle." There was no catcalling or harassment, only curiosity at the band of women. "Husbands saw their wives, sons and daughters their mothers, and neighbors their friends, moving along with the strange apparition, and knew not what it meant, until before some liquor saloon or hotel or drugstore, you could hear the singing of some familiar hymn warble through the air in tones of the most touching note; and then, solemn silence prevailing up and down street, the utterance of a soul-stirring prayer made by some lady, with all others kneeling around on curbstone or pavement or door-sill, could be heard ascending to the throne of God to avert the curse of intemperance."[39]

At first, the saloon-keepers were perplexed, and even a little amused by the women's activism. Some patrons continued to drink uncomfortably despite the women in their midst, their conversations drowned out by prayers and hymns. As the sit-ins continued in shifts for hours—and then days—patrons increasingly decided to stay home. The sight of the community's most respectable ladies kneeling in the filth of the worst dives in town shamed some saloon-keepers to capitulate. As one contemporary noted, when "the wives and mothers of the best citizens came, with tender words and earnest prayer, it was an enemy he hardly knew how to fight."[40]

Victory came even more swiftly at Diocletian Lewis's next stop: the town of Washington Court House, Ohio, where the protests began on Christmas Day. By the third day, the women were celebrating as the first saloon-keeper began pouring out his liquor. As one observer described it, "Axes were placed in the hands of the women who had suffered most"—presumably the wives of drunkards—as the barrels were rolled out. "Swinging through the air, they came down with ringing blows, bursting the heads of the casks, and flooding the gutters of the street. One good woman, putting her soul into every blow, struck but once for a barrel, splashing Holland gin and old Bourbon high into the air amid the shouts of the people. Four barrels and one cask were forced open, the proprietors giving a hearty consent."[41] By the eighth day, the women announced that all of the city's eleven saloons had surrendered, and the three druggists in town had agreed not to sell liquor except on prescription.[42]

"Not a dram of liquor can be had at Washington Court House," wrote famed abolitionist, teetotaler, and first president of the American Woman Suffrage Association

Figure 13.2 Two women temperance crusaders protesting outside of J. S. Mader's Saloon in Bucyrus, Ohio, 1874.
Source: John P. Hopley Family Audiovisual Collection, P 156, Box 2, Folder 9, P156_B02_F09.tif, Ohio History Connection.

(AWSA), Henry Ward Beecher. Yet another philanthropist offspring of Lyman Beecher (Chapter 11), in his *Christian Union* newspaper, Henry Ward Beecher chronicled how "the women expect to conquer the keeper of the saloon" who'd relocated outside the town border by "praying and singing from morning till night, and registering the name of every visitor to the saloon."

Stoked by Dio Lewis—who cancelled his usual lecture tour to focus on events in Ohio—the women's movement spread swiftly across the state.[43] Already by February 1874, Beecher described how women activists were everywhere producing similar results. "By alternations of two hours each, different groups of women keep up the siege upon a given point from six o'clock in the morning until a late hour at night. Women of the different religious denominations are heartily united in the work.... The sight of these women kneeling on the snow and ice and offering up their songs and supplications has melted many a stout heart."

As for the movement, like many, Beecher was skeptical that it could maintain momentum instead of "degrading into a mere exhibition of popular passion and frenzy." Acting in open defiance of traditional gender roles, the women certainly courted popular scorn. "And yet, when we think of the indescribable woes that follow the traffic in intoxicating liquors, there is something sublime in this moral uprising against it."[44]

Beecher wasn't the only skeptic. So were fellow suffragists Lucy Stone and her husband, Henry Brown Blackwell, with whom Beecher had formed the moderate, accommodationist AWSA—splitting from Elizabeth Cady Stanton and Susan B. Anthony's more "radical" National Woman Suffrage Association (NWSA), which demanded gender equality be included in both the Fourteenth and Fifteenth Amendments. Writing in their *Woman's Journal*, Stone and Blackwell applauded the temperance crusades for introducing thousands of women to political activism. But since protests alone were unlikely to unseat the liquor traffic, the AWSA hoped the crusaders would recognize the necessity of securing the vote in order to close the saloons.[45]

Despite their acrimonious division with the AWSA—the two would only reconcile in 1890—the NWSA shared their skepticism toward the crusades. Susan B. Anthony wrote that the image of proud women kneeling in saloon filth was a "desecration of womanhood." Although she participated in at least five crusades in Rochester, Anthony scoffed that—without the vote—women "will quickly learn the impossibility of accomplishing any substantial end."[46]

Even though she'd encouraged direct action just a few years before,[47] Elizabeth Cady Stanton denounced this "whisky war" as mob law: the only lawful means to bring liquor predations under control was by securing the vote.[48] In the absence of genuine women's empowerment, Stanton held that prohibitionists were nothing but "superficial reformers, mere surface workers."[49] Indeed, many single-issue suffragists feared prohibitionism would undercut the women's movement by drawing the fire of the politically influential liquor machine.[50]

Of course, crusade skepticism was well founded. It would be foolish to expect saloon-keepers to not defend their livelihood. "With ribaldry and sneers the liquor men had written and talked of the Woman's Crusade," wrote temperance pioneer Anna Gordon. "To them it was merely an absurd, ephemeral movement that would be quickly crushed by the age-long appetite and avarice of men. What could ballot-less and money-less women do against a business entrenched in politics and in partnership with the government of the United States?"[51]

Indeed, the longer the crusades went on, the stronger was liquor-industry blowback. In Adrian, Michigan, one saloon-keeper locked the picketing women inside, a move that backfired by raising the ire of the entire community and expanding sympathy for the women's cause. Plus, as the local newspaper reported, "During the progress of the siege it is safe to say that not much business was done at the bar of that saloon."[52] In some places, rowdy men doused the women in sour beer or physically accosted them. In Cleveland, Ohio, a quarter-mile-long nonviolent procession of some five hundred women was broken up by a half-drunk mob. Bankrolled by local brewers, they unleashed dogs on the women, kicked those who were praying on the ground, and beat others with brickbats.[53]

Still, they persisted. When saloon-keepers secured injunctions and restraining orders against them, the women responded in kind. Activists stationed outside saloons made careful records of what was being sold to whom and when, so if liquor was being sold illegally to minors or after hours, the women would take the saloon men to court also.[54]

The crusades even found their way into Frances Ellen Watkins Harper's novels. In *Sowing and Reaping*, the saloon-keeper grumbles that "this crusading has made quite a hole in my business."

"Now John Anderson," his wife replied, "tell that to somebody that don't know. I don't believe this crusading has laid a finger's weight upon your business."

"Yes it has," Anderson shot back, "and if you read the paper you would find that it has even affected the revenue of the state," underscoring the political influence of the liquor machine.[55]

The Woman's Crusade played an even bigger role in Harper's nonfiction work. "Lips that had been silent in the prayer meeting were loosened to take part in the wonderful uprising," she wrote in her history titled "The Woman's Christian Temperance Union and the Colored Woman."

> Saloons were visited, hardships encountered, insults, violence, and even imprisonment endured by women, brave to suffer and strong to endure. Thousands of saloon visits were made, many were closed. Grand enthusiasms were aroused, moral earnestness awakened, and a fire kindled whose beacon lights still stream over the gloomy track of our monster evil. Victor Hugo has spoken of the nineteenth century as being woman's era, and among the most noticeable epochs in this era is the uprising of women against the twin evils of slavery and intemperance, which had foisted themselves like leeches upon the civilization of the present age. In the great anti-slavery conflict women had borne a part, but after the storm cloud of battle had rolled away, it was found that an enemy, old and strong and deceptive, was warring against the best interests of society; not simply an enemy to one race, but an enemy to all races—an enemy that had entrenched itself in the strongholds of appetite and avarice, and was upheld by fashion, custom and legislation. To dislodge this enemy, to put prohibition not simply on the statute book, but in the heart and conscience of a nation, embracing within itself such heterogeneous masses, is no child's play, nor the work of a few short moons.[56]

For F. E. W. Harper and other activists, confronting the liquor traffic required the effort and goodwill of everyone, especially those victimized most. In that brief window before the coming of Jim Crow laws, this meant that the votes of recently liberated freedmen could tip the electoral balance in the South. In the cities of the East, the scads of arriving immigrants could likewise sway elections one way or another. On top of that, the Woman's Crusade of 1873–1874 demonstrated that women were equally capable as men of democratic self-government.[57]

Figure 13.3 Woman's Holy War: Grand Charge on the Enemy's Works (1874).
Source: Currier & Ives, New York, circa 1874, Library of Congress, Prints and Photographs Division,
Washington DC.

Frances Willard and the WCTU

What was it about Ohio in 1873–1874 that ignited—in the words of WCTU leader
Frances Willard—a movement like "a prairie on fire sweeping across the landscape"? After all, hadn't Diocletian Lewis been stoking that sentiment across the
country for the previous thirty years?[58]

Historians have speculated that a rise in public drunkenness in the 1870s sparked
such backlash—or that increased affluence and leisure time allowed middle-class
women to engage in greater social activism. More likely, however, the causes were
the Great Panic of 1873 and the ensuing depression, which only heightened uncertainty among women who were already economically vulnerable and politically
marginalized. Plus, Ohio was embroiled in a hotly contested convention to rewrite
the state constitution, where liquor men were pressing for decreased oversight
over their trade. Women were barred from these important political decisions that
would directly impact their welfare, which led to political activism by other means,
supported by church organizations, networks, and resources.[59]

Still, in the three months since Hillsboro, women had driven the liquor traffic out of 250 cities and villages. In Ohio, 130 towns had organized woman's crusades, plus 36 in Michigan, 34 in Indiana, 26 in Pennsylvania, and 17 in New Jersey. By the end of the year, some 912 communities across thirty-one states had organized their own crusades.[60] Led exclusively by women, the marches and protests included tens—if not hundreds—of thousands of women, most with no prior experience of political activism.[61]

One of those women would become the face of the American suffragist and temperance movement for the next twenty years: Frances E. Willard of Chicago. When the wave of women's protests crashed onto the shores of Lake Michigan in March 1874, Miss Willard was an accomplished teacher: comfortable and secure. Recently appointed first dean of women at Northwestern University, she was engaged to the university president, Charles Henry Fowler. She first took part in a peaceful women's petition to the Chicago City Council to simply enforce those Sunday-closing laws that were already on the books. As she later retold it, the petitioners "were treated with mocking slight and rudely jostled on the street by a band of rough men, half out for a lark, half ugly."

Willard railed against the men's cowardly behavior and publicly proclaimed that this wasn't just a women's fight, but it was "everybody's war." She soon called off her wedding to Fowler, resigned her position at Northwestern, and dedicated her full energy to fighting on the front lines of everybody's war.[62]

Frances Elizabeth Willard was born in 1839 in upstate New York, before her parents—abstainers, educators, and abolitionist conductors on the Underground Railroad[63]—relocated to the north Chicago suburb of Evanston, Illinois. She learned to read by way of *The Slave's Friend*: a children's antislavery magazine produced by the American Anti-Slavery Society. According to her friend in suffragism, Anna Gordon, this upbringing made her "more than any other modern reformer the friend of the negro race, and giving birth to a phrase in one of her prophetic mottoes: 'No sect in religion, no sex in citizenship, no sectionalism in politics.' "[64]

From a young age, the Willard children were encouraged to scribe a pledge of total abstinence in the family Bible. A "born organizer," even as a child she drew up charters for imaginary cities: "We will have no saloons or billiard halls, and then we will not need any jails."[65] Indeed, the reformist foundation of abolitionism and temperance predated Willard's suffragism. After graduating from North Western Female College, she spent two years from 1868 to 1870 touring and studying across Europe—learning French, German, and Italian. Willard visited Russia, Turkey, Egypt, and the Holy Land, too. She felt most at home in England, where she followed with great interest the early British suffragettes, who sought to fulfill John Stuart Mill's calls for female equality and voting rights for women (Chapter 5).[66]

The spirit of the temperance crusades of 1873–1874 brought about Willard's emancipation, professionally and personally. Willard had long chafed against traditional gender roles: from a young age, her friends called her Frank, and she wept when forced to abandon farm trousers for skirts, and to upbraid her hair as befitting a respectable girl.[67] Given prevailing societal and gender norms, Willard was troubled that her engagement to Northwestern president Fowler would mean abandoning her long-standing intimate friendship with Mary Bannister. In breaking off her engagement to Fowler, she explained that she could never provide him the adoration and submissiveness expected in a traditional Victorian marriage. She would never marry.

On the professional front, she argued that the university was not doing enough to prepare young women to become empowered and self-reliant—like her—rather than being dependent on a man. When Fowler denied Willard the necessary independence and self-government of the women's faculty, she resigned.

Without a husband, job, or livelihood—a frightening prospect for a legally disempowered woman in the 1870s—Willard dove headlong into the Woman's Crusade. She read everything she could find about the "armies of women" who "filled the streets of the cities and towns of Ohio, going in pathetic procession from the door of the home to that of the saloon, singing, praying, pleading with the rumsellers with all the eloquence of their mother-hearts."[68] She traveled east to study the liquor issue firsthand: visiting the tenement slums of New York (Chapters 12, 14), meeting with Dio Lewis in Boston, and learning of the Maine Law from Neal Dow himself (Chapter 11).[69]

In November 1874 Willard traveled to a national convention in Cleveland, Ohio, called by the various state-level women's organizations born of the temperance crusades. Ultimately, 135 female delegates (and an equal number of unofficial visitors) representing sixteen states elected officers and drew up a constitution for a permanent, nationwide Woman's Temperance Union. As an afterthought, they voted to add the word "Christian," as an homage to the church networks that facilitated their organization's growth. After only narrowly passing the "Christian" rebranding, the Woman's Christian Temperance Union (WCTU) was officially born.[70]

"We believe that God created both man and woman in His own image," began the WCTU's declaration of principles, "and, therefore, we believe in one standard for purity for both men and women, and in the equal right of all to hold opinions and to express the same with equal freedom." Drafted by Frances Willard herself, the organization's progressive principles went far beyond demanding the vote to include a living wage, an eight-hour workday, legal equality before the courts, and promotion of "justice as opposed to greed of gain." To that end, the WCTU encouraged its members to pledge to abstain from all fermented and distilled alcoholic beverages, "and to employ all proper means to discourage the use and traffic in the same."[71] Indeed, as temperance was concerned, Willard's constitution focused on diminishing "the number of liquor traders immediately," and a long-term goal of "the entire prohibition of the manufacture and sale of intoxicating liquors as a beverage."[72]

In a radical departure from any previous temperance or suffragist (or *any*) organization, men were barred both from voting and holding official positions. At the local, state, and federal levels, women alone would do the work and set the policies.[73] Nationally esteemed founder of the Methodist Home Missionary Society, editor of the *Christian Woman*, and pioneer of establishing orphans' homes, Annie Wittenmyer of Iowa was elected president.[74] Frances Willard was chosen corresponding secretary.

During the first, rough years in which the organization had little infrastructure and no financial support, the leadership consisted of the double-Ws: Wittenmyer and Willard. Wittenmyer represented traditional moral suasion—individual enlightenment and reformation—whereas Willard was for prohibition and suffrage. A woman of action, Willard traveled extensively, knitting together state and local branches. Since an organization was only as good as its outreach, she dove into publishing the *Woman's Temperance Union* newspaper, later consolidated as the *Union Signal*. As Willard's star rose, she pushed for a far broader political platform, writing to Wittenmyer in 1875 that "our object is not only to pull drowning men from the stream but to make our influence felt at the fountains of power."[75] Wittenmyer was unpersuaded.

The American centennial made the summer of 1876 one of great jubilation. In Philadelphia, the cradle of the American Revolution, Wittenmyer gaveled to order the WCTU's International Temperance Convention, proclaiming it as the "first international convention for women the world has ever known," consisting of delegates from Canada, England, Scotland, Japan, and twenty-one of the thirty-eight American states.[76] It was here that the idea of a permanent women's international temperance was first floated. Willard thought it would be the optimal platform to actively espouse "the woman's ballot as a weapon of protection to her home and tempted loved ones from the tyranny of drink."[77] Wittenmyer vetoed Willard using an international platform to speak on suffrage, and Willard complied, "but it's close at home," she wrote, "I don't know how long I can stand it."[78]

She wouldn't wait long. Just four months later, in WCTU organizational congresses, Willard began to refer to women's right to vote as the "home-protection ballot," which would advance all of the organization's stated goals.[79] In a masterstroke of public relations, "home protection" reframed traditional political debates in which men painted suffragists as uncompromising radicals seeking to overturn the male-dominated order. Instead of striking an offensive posture, emphasizing defense of women's traditional domicile made the WCTU more palatable to moderate men and women. "The home is the special care of women," Willard proclaimed. "Home protection shall be our watchword."[80]

At the sixth WCTU convention in Indianapolis in 1879, a massive banner with the one word—"prohibition"—hung from the balcony. It seemed the old temperance debate between Annie Wittenmyer's moral suasion and Frances

Willard's state and local prohibitionism had been won by the latter. Even more surprising was when Willard defeated Wittenmyer in the election for the organization's presidency. Wittenmyer conceded gracefully. Willard would be reelected president for the following nineteen years, until her death, providing unparalleled leadership as the WCTU grew into the largest women's organization in world history.[81]

In her second presidential address in 1881, Willard coined the phrase describing her entire approach to social reform: *Do Everything*.[82] "Every question of practical philanthropy or reform," Willard subsequently explained, "has its temperance aspect, and with that we are to deal."[83] Since temperance and women's rights overlapped with so many related social ills, she vowed that the organization should tackle them all.

This was a dramatic break with established patterns of women's activism. Suffragists Susan B. Anthony and Elizabeth Cady Stanton and the NWSA gave up on broader social and economic questions, believing that it would dilute activism and jeopardize the primary goal of securing the vote. They also believed that organized religion was a source of women's oppression, not a mechanism for their liberation.[84] Frances Willard did not share either of these worries.

It began with prison reform: establishing rehabilitative penitentiaries, police matrons, and halfway houses for female prisoners. Then came work with children: aiding homeless street urchins, supporting foster care, and promoting kindergartens. For ten cents a day, WCTU affiliates provided three daily meals for children of working parents, otherwise locked at home alone. Women—often abused and penniless—were routinely accepted along with their children. Add to that a peace movement, dress reform, sabbatarianism, vegetarianism, and homeopathy. And since intemperance in the United States—as throughout Europe—was interwoven with urban poverty, Willard forged strong links with the Knights of Labor and other trade unions to promote better working conditions and equal pay for equal work.[85] By 1889, in Chicago alone, the WCTU was running two nurseries, two Sunday schools, an industrial school, a domestic violence shelter, a free medical office, a restaurant, and lodging for itinerant men. The national convention that year passed resolutions opposing cigarettes and animal testing, petitioned state legislatures for free public kindergartens and police matrons at penal colonies, and implored Russian tsar Alexander III for more humane treatment of Siberian exiles.[86] Willard's goal was truly to do everything.

What allowed the WCTU to tackle so many issues and so rapidly become "the greatest women's organization of the century" was its flexible structure, allowing autonomous state and local chapters broad latitude to adapt the organization's goals to the their on-the-ground realities.[87] There was little to stop progressive chapters around the Great Lakes from pushing the envelope of reform, even as reluctant chapters in the South said little about dress reform, or even securing the vote.

Figure 13.4 "Let Go, but Stand By." Frances Willard learns to ride a bike at fifty-three (1895).
Source: Frances E. Willard, *A Wheel within a Wheel: How I Learned to Ride the Bicycle, with Some Reflections by the Way* (Chicago: Woman's Temperance Publishing Association, 1895), 56.

The Two Franceses: The WCTU and the Southern Question

Frances Willard was perpetually in motion, primarily across the northern states, where WCTU chapters were far more numerous. Yet in the 1880s, Willard began making repeated sorties to the South, on missions of integration and reconciliation. In the spring of 1881, she made a fourteen-week tour of the South, speaking in over fifty cities across every southern state, as well as establishing inroads with Native Americans in the Indian Territory (Chapter 16).[88] In doing so, she had to overcome lingering Civil War suspicions and enmity toward northerners, as well as a different political playing field: in the North, most social reformers were allied with the Republicans, whereas the South was solidly Democratic. Still, she found the common bonds of temperance made for warm receptions among southerners, both white and black.

"I had been told that to speak in public in the South was 'not to be thought of,' that all would be lost if I attempted anything beyond parlor meetings," Willard remembered. "But instead of this, their liberality of sentiment was abundantly equal to the strain; their largest churches were filled with the best, most influential and thoughtful people; their ministers were more united and earnest in the temperance cause than ours at the North; their editors, without the slightest subsidizing, were as kind and helpful as my own brother could have been." Noting how alcohol was less socially accepted in the South, that the liquor traffic was less institutionalized, and that earnestness and dedication were defining southern traits, Willard added that "temperance has an immense advantage at the South," even while lacking the traditional lodges and petitions.[89]

The admiration between Willard and the South was mutual. One Bishop Stevens of Charleston, South Carolina—previously Colonel Stevens of the Confederacy when he commanded the attack on Fort Sumter—introduced Willard to her Charleston audience: "This woman, this Northern woman, this Northern temperance woman, brings us the magic initials W.C.T.U. Shall we not interpret them in our case to mean, We come to unite the North and the South, and we come to upset the liquor traffic?"[90]

Willard likewise made headway among African Americans, speaking at black high schools and to black audiences at Atlanta and Clark Universities. Neither these visits, nor her unabashed Republican abolitionist background, seemed to dim the reception she had with white southerners.[91] In fact, ahead of a statewide prohibition referendum in 1881, Willard organized temperance in North Carolina, where she feared that a white northern woman might stir up racial antagonisms. She was shocked to find just the opposite: "Everywhere the Southern white people desired me to speak to the colored."[92] The North Carolina referendum ultimately failed, but the WCTU's legacy of grassroots organization across black and white communities endured.

She made another extensive southern tour in 1882—and again in 1883—every time dramatically expanding the WCTU's southern base. This was remarkable, as southern women had never taken part in any sort of nationwide grassroots reform movement, and the conservative resistance—that women should "know their place"—was especially strong there. Making the WCTU a truly national organization was no small feat, both for the organization and for national reconciliation: before the WCTU arrived, northerners and southerners had not worked arm in arm on anything in over two generations.[93]

Ultimately, Frances Willard was a hit in the South, among both white and black audiences. The WCTU offered white women a chance to look past skin color to see common bonds of humanity. At the same time, African American women valorized Frances Willard—a strong, smart heiress to the abolitionist legacies of William Lloyd Garrison and Frederick Douglass—as a working model of finer womanhood, dramatically at odds with the vacuousness of white southern belles.[94]

Creating a truly national organization meant promoting both geographic and racial representativeness. The WCTU found especially fertile grounds among the Five Civilized Tribes in Indian Territory (Chapter 16), since Native American tribes had been promoting prohibition of the predatory white man's liquor trade for generations before the WCTU came knocking (Chapters 9–10). Native Americans were hopeful that these women might pressure the federal government to actually enforce the protective liquor laws that were already on the books.

Willard actively fought against the nationalist tendencies within the predominantly white, Anglo-Saxon Protestant organization. She warmly welcomed Jewish and Catholic fellow travelers, and enthusiastically sent WCTU delegates to visit their organizations, forging bonds across faith communities. She adamantly condemned the persecution of Chinese migrants through the Chinese Exclusion Act (1882).[95] The WCTU deployed representatives to Ellis Island to greet boatfuls of European immigrants with temperance literature in sixteen different languages. By the mid-1880s the WCTU had official ancillaries working with German, Dutch, Scandinavian, Chinese, Spanish, and Polish immigrant communities, each in their own languages.[96]

Add to that the World's WCTU—founded by Willard in 1883—which we've already seen active in Sweden and Belgium (Chapter 3), and making forays into Imperial Russia (Chapter 2), India (Chapter 7), and Turkey (Chapter 8). The WCTU's global ambassador, Mary Clement Leavitt, organized chapters in the Sandwich Islands (Hawai'i) in 1885, before pushing westward across the Pacific to Asia, Australia, and New Zealand. Over the next six years, Leavitt traveled some one hundred thousand miles, organizing 130 temperance societies across forty-three countries and forty-seven languages, circulating prohibition petitions to virtually all "Governments of the World."[97] In many cases, Leavitt built upon the transnational temperance linkages already established by the International Order of Good Templars, as well as the biennial temperance conventions across Europe (Chapters 3–4), to which Frances Willard herself led delegations.[98]

The biggest challenge in making a cohesive movement came in integrating African Americans—both in the South and North—into a nationwide women's organization, which, like it or not, reflected many of the stereotypes and prejudices of its members. For help in this, Willard turned to Frances Ellen Watkins Harper.

Following her education work in the Reconstruction South, in 1871 F. E. W. Harper returned to Philadelphia. She purchased a redbrick rowhouse off South Street, just blocks from where an angry white nativist mob had torched black temperance halls and churches a generation before (Chapter 11).[99] She would live there until her death in 1911 at the age of eighty-five.

Of the WCTU, Harper wrote, "For years I knew very little of its proceedings, and was not sure that colored comradeship was very desirable, but having attended a local Union in Philadelphia [about 1875], I was asked to join and acceded to the request, and was made city and afterwards State Superintendent of work among colored people."[100]

Why did she accept the WCTU's request? Well, Frances Harper—much like Frances Willard—was an organizer and coalition builder. Through domestic violence and familial poverty, women bore the brunt of their husbands' insobriety regardless of whether they were black or white. Married women had no legal standing, could not own property apart from their husbands or sue for divorce, and were overwhelmingly reliant on their husbands for income.[101] As Harper had always pointed out, white women were privileged in not having to suffer racial discrimination on top of it all.

If Harper could persuade the predominantly white women in the largest, most powerful woman's organization to better understand the plight of African American women, then they could work together for improved conditions for all.[102] From her fiery address before the Woman's Rights Convention back in 1866, Harper believed such interracial alliances were crucial. Suffragism and temperance were a perfect medium, since the liquor traffic preyed on both white communities and black, North and South, and its influences were felt disproportionately by disempowered women, regardless of geography or skin color.[103]

As Harper told the convention back in 1866, she faced these issues firsthand when her husband of only four years died unexpectedly, leaving her alone to raise their child as well as three children from his previous marriage. That Harper's experiences were virtually identical to Carrie Nation's origin story (Chapter 1) only demonstrates how frequently this fate befell women of all races.

"My husband died in debt," Harper proclaimed, "and before he had been in his grave three months, the administrator had swept away the very milk-crocks and wash tubs from my hands. I was a farmer's wife and made butter for the Columbus market; what could I do when they had swept all away?" She had money from her book royalties and speaking engagements—from which she had purchased the farm—but since she had no legal standing, the mortgage was in her husband's name, allowing creditors to confiscate all of their material property upon his death.

"Had I died instead of my husband, how different would have been the result!" she said. No creditor would barge in, sell their beds, and take away their primary means of support. "I say, then, that justice is not fulfilled so long as woman is unequal before the law."[104] This was as true for white women as it was for black.

Though she had shared the stage with Susan B. Anthony and Elizabeth Cady Stanton, Frances Harper distanced herself from their radical demands that women's suffrage be included in the Fourteenth and Fifteenth Amendments. As political realists, Anthony and Stanton, along with the NWSA, were generally indifferent—if not outright hostile—to the work of freedwomen like Harper, actively laboring across racial lines.[105] Instead Harper—like Frances Willard—would align with the moderate AWSA of Lucy Stone and Henry Beecher, accepting black male suffrage first, before working for women's right to vote next.[106]

Harper was hardly alone among African American women turning to temperance activism. "Black women saw in the WCTU a chance to build a Christian community that could serve as a model of interracial cooperation on other fronts," claimed historian Glenda Gilmore.[107] Especially with their "do everything" focus, the WCTU could further cooperation on other fronts: antilynching laws, or support for education and anti-illiteracy programs that would equally benefit black and white communities.[108]

So in 1883 Harper accepted the WCTU's appointment as national superintendent for "Work among the Colored People of the North," though she ultimately worked across the entire United States.[109] Frances Willard announced the good news in the *Union Signal*, describing Harper (in the racially tinged language of the day) as "probably the most gifted and cultured woman of her race in the United States. She has a fervid and eloquent tongue and desires no better portion than to work among 'her very own.'" Recognizing the challenges of integrating the organization amid long-standing racial prejudices, Willard implored, "Write to her, dear sisters, and see if she can come and help influence your colored population for the right. And when she comes, remember as you have always done, so far as my experience goes, 'The laborer is worthy of his hire.'"[110]

It would be an uphill struggle against institutional discrimination to be sure. Harper described the on-the-ground challenge when—fed up with the discriminatory treatment of Georgia's white-dominated state WCTU—black women petitioned Harper to establish their own separate organization where African American activists could be free to organize themselves. Harper took their petition directly to Willard, who clarified that the national organization could not dictate laws to a state organization; however, "If the colored women of Georgia will meet and form a Woman's Christian Temperance Union for the State, it is my opinion that their officers and delegates will have the same representation in the National."

And so they did. In cases where black activism was stymied by racial bigotry in the southern states, African American women organized their own "colored" ancillaries, with rights equal to their white sisters. The president of the "Second Alabama" WCTU was warmly received by the national organization and made a member of the Executive Committee.[111] Black women in North Carolina followed suit. Tired of subordinate status within their state's WCTU, they formed their own "WCTU No. 2," which was recognized as equal by the national organization. They would not "exclude any white sisters who might wish to work with us," claimed the women of North Carolina No. 2, because "we believe all men are created equal" [*sic*].[112]

Still, such separate-but-equal segregation was a double-edged sword. On the one hand, it allowed African American women organizational space and independence born of their own activism. On the other, President Willard could not force the white ancillaries to cease their discriminatory practices, making her culpable in simultaneously empowering and disempowering southern black women.[113] Harper shared Willard's frustration, repeatedly applauding successful integration of unions in the North, while still defending the autonomy of black women to organize themselves, believing "as a general rule the colored women work better in unions of their own."[114] It was the best that could be made of a bad situation.

One can't read Harper's annual reports about her work among the "colored people" or her columns in the *Union Signal* without sensing her frustration with the WCTU's racial divisions. She repeatedly implored her white sisters to understand that generations of African Americans had suffered oppression, and that it was the *duty* of good Christian women to promote their equal rights.[115] In her 1885 report, she wrote that she'd sent about circulars offering her time and services to ancillaries, "but I did not find many Unions who seemed to desire either." She'd visited several states to help organize independent "colored" unions, but was hampered both by indifference and lack of resources.

"This race who had no option in its saddest wrong here are at your doors. What shall be your influence upon the future of this people?" Harper asked her WCTU sisters. "Shall it be the influence of an extended Christly sympathy which will look with anointed vision through the darkened skin and shaded countenance, and see their souls all written over with the handmarks of divinity, and the common claims of humanity which will try to draw them nearer to you in active co-operation, to work for a common cause, under the leadership of the ever blessed Christ? To some this work may not be congenial; it is pleasant to do easy things for Christ, but it takes moral and spiritual stamina to do the hard, dry and unpleasant tasks for the Master's sake."[116]

In her presidential address, Frances Willard echoed Harper's concerns. "Mrs. Harper is both faithful and capable, as we all know, but her department is crippled for lack of funds." Willard's solution was a mere ten-cent donation from every member of the organization. "This is all that is asked, and will yield a larger heavenly per cent than any other possible form of investment."[117]

Together, the two Franceses—Willard and Harper—continued the hard work of racially integrating the organization, confronting the deeply entrenched prejudices of rank-and-file members. In 1886 Harper wrote that she was "pained" by the indifference of her white colleagues toward racial injustices.[118] Such indifference was evident in WCTU discussions over the 1887 Blair Education Bill, which would have provided widespread support to disadvantaged southern black communities. During the WCTU's annual convention in Nashville, Tennessee, Harper pleaded with her "do everything" sisters: "I belong to a race having suffered ages of oppression, you belong to a race having ages of education, domination, civilization, and I simply ask this body to really indorse the aims of this educational bill for the people of my race." Receiving only lukewarm support from the delegates, President Willard threw her support behind Harper and persuaded a reluctant assembly to officially come out in favor of the bill.[119]

Despite her increasing frustrations, in 1888 F. E. W. Harper explained the stakes in stark terms: "Believing, as I do, in human solidarity, I hold that the Woman's Christian Temperance Union has in its hands one of the grandest opportunities that God ever pressed into the hands of the womanhood of any country. Its conflict is not the contest of a social club, but a moral warfare for an imperiled civilization. Whether or not the members of the farther South will subordinate the spirit of caste to the spirit of Christ time will show." To her black readers, she implored them to join with the WCTU, and "let your homes be the best places where you may plant your batteries against the rum traffic."[120]

But by the 1890s, the high hopes of the New South era were dimming. Interracial cooperation gave way to Jim Crow disenfranchisement and a spike in lynchings throughout the South. The creeping acrimony could also be found within the WCTU. In her final superintendent's report—delivered to the national convention in Atlanta in 1890—Harper reported a confrontation with a white delegate from Texas, who blamed black male voters for being gullible and having their votes easily bought off by the liquor interests (Chapter 16): "God knows you people need education along this line," claimed the white delegate, "not that they [black men] drink more, but their vote was bought by the liquor men, and defeated prohibition in Texas."

Harper shot back, pointing out that prohibition referenda had been defeated in the white North too, with no substantial black vote to blame it on. Furthermore, "if it was shabby for an ignorant black man to sell his vote, was it not a shabbier thing if an intelligent white man bought it?" If election corruption fueled by the overwhelmingly white liquor traffic was the issue, then such white delegates should begin by looking in the mirror, rather than blaming black Americans for being victims.[121]

Tensions were also rising between Harper and Willard. Willard's workaholic do-everything activism was spreading herself and her overextended WCTU too thin. By 1887 Willard refocused the organization's activism around its primary goal: securing woman's suffrage. Yet for F. E. W. Harper—and a growing cohort of black WCTU activists, including Sarah Jane Woodson Early, Mary Lynch, Emma Ray, Lucy Thurman, and others—the de-emphasis of the WCTU's educational and antilynching work looked like betrayal. At the very least, it felt like selling out to the bigoted white, southern ancillaries for the sake of political expediency.

This message was crystal clear when the WCTU was restructured in 1890, and the department for "Colored Work" was reorganized and demoted into a lesser division. With their organizational bases gone, black superintendents Harper and Early were effectively locked out of the Executive Committee, where key policy decisions were made, and denied access to their usual article space in the *Union Signal*.[122] Marginalized and frustrated, Harper nevertheless continued to work in a diminished capacity with the WCTU, believing it vital to the causes of suffrage and temperance.[123]

Iola's Struggle

Frances Harper's diminished role within the WCTU after 1890 allowed her to re-focus on her writing. In 1892 she published *Iola Leroy, or Shadows Uplifted*—the first major novel published by an African American woman—which spoke to all of her frustrations over race, women's rights, education, and temperance over the previous decade. The plot focuses on the beautiful heroine Iola—one-eighth black, who passes as white—and her struggles to come to terms with her ambiguous ra-cial identity, ultimately choosing to identify as black and encouraging her extended family to do so as well.

Threads of Harper's WCTU experiences are woven throughout the novel.[124] Iola is courted by a well-to-do New England suitor, Dr. Gresham, who insists—since her "eyes are as blue and complexion as white as mine"—that she identify as white as a condition of marriage.

"No, Doctor," Iola protests. "I am not willing to live under a shadow of conceal-ment which I thoroughly hate as if the blood in my veins were an undetected crime of my soul." Expanding her critique, she says, "You have created in this country an aristocracy of color wide enough to include the South with its treason and Utah with its abominations, but too narrow to include the best and bravest colored man who bared his breast to the bullets of the enemy during your fratricidal strife."

Dr. Gresham bristles, reminding Iola that he was a member of the Grand Army of the Republic—the fully integrated benevolent organization of Civil War veterans that pushed for black enfranchisement and literacy. In a thinly veiled dig against the women of the WCTU, Gresham argues, "I fear that one of the last strongholds of this racial prejudice will be found beneath the shadows of some of our churches. I think, on account of this social question, that large bodies of Christian temperance women and other reformers, in trying to reach the colored people even for their own good, will be quicker to form separate associations than our National Grand Army, whose ranks are open to black and white, liberals and conservatives, saints and agnostics."[125]

The scourge of the liquor traffic pops up time and again in *Iola Leroy*.[126] Yet from a temperance perspective, the most interesting character is Aunt Linda: patterned after freed slave turned abolitionist writer, Harriet Jacobs.[127] A former plantation slave, Aunt Linda is outspoken on the reformist triumvirate of abolitionism, suf-fragism, and temperance, beginning by highlighting how the cruelest slaveowners were the drunk ones.[128]

"Dem Yankees set me free, an' I thinks a powerful heap ob dem," says Aunt Linda, describing her life since emancipation. "But it does rile me ter see dese mean white men comin' down yere an' settin' up dere grog-shops, tryin' to fedder dere nests sellin' licker to pore culled people," underscoring how saloons are traps set up by white people to take away black people's money. "You jis' go down town 'fore sun up to-morrer mornin' an' you see ef dey don't hab dem bars open to sell dere drams to dem hard workin' culled people 'fore dey goes ter work. I thinks some niggers is mighty big fools."

"Oh, Aunt Linda, don't run down your race," responds Robert Johnson, a fellow former plantation slave turned Union lieutenant and temperance man. "Leave that for the white people."

"I ain't runnin' down my people," Aunt Linda shoots back. "But a fool's a fool, wether he's white or black. An' I think de nigger who will spen' his hard-earned money in dese yere new grog-shops is de biggest kine ob a fool, an' I sticks ter dat. You know we didn't hab all dese low places in slave times."

As if to replay Harper's confrontation with the Texas WCTU delegate, Aunt Linda points to the political corruption engendered by the saloons: "An' what is dey fer, but to get the people's money. An' it's a shame how dey do sling de licker 'bout 'lection times."

"But don't the temperance people want the colored people to vote the temperance ticket?" Robert asks.

"Yes, but some ob de culled people gits mighty skittish ef dey tries to git em to vote dare ticket 'lection time, an' keeps dem at a proper distance wen de 'lection's ober," Aunt Linda replies. "Some ob dem say dere's a trick behine it, an' don't want to tech it. Dese white folks could do a heap wid de culled folks if dey'd only treat em right."

"When our people say there is a trick behind it," says Robert, "I only wish they could see the trick before it—the trick of worse than wasting their money, and of keeping themselves and families poorer and more ignorant than there is any need for them to be."

In the end, Robert Johnson and his virtuous niece Iola Leroy convince even Aunt Linda to put away her homemade wine—not just for her sake, but for her family's well-being too.[129]

As the first major novel written by an African American woman, *Iola Leroy* was a success. Still it does beg the question of where such an unusual character name like "Iola" came from. As it turns out, it was an explicit reference to a young, headstrong, pro-temperance Memphis schoolteacher, Ida B. Wells. Iola was the pen name Wells used for writing anti–Jim Crow investigations in *The Living Way* weekly newspaper, making "Iola" a household name in black communities.[130] "She has become famous as one of the few of our women who handle a goose-quill, with diamond point, as easily as any man in the newspaper work," described one press activist in 1891. "If Iola were a man, she would be a humming independent in politics. She has plenty of nerve, and is sharp as a steel trap."[131]

Before she rose to national prominence as an antilynching activist, in 1889 Ida Wells had hosted Frances Harper in Memphis on one of her WCTU missions. The two formed a fast friendship, with Harper inviting Wells to stay at her home in Philadelphia during the AME national conference.[132]

Figure 13.5 Ida B. Wells, circa 1891.
Source: Penn, *The Afro-American Press, and Its Editors*, 49, Library of Congress Prints and Photographs Division, PN4888.N4P4.

Antilynching and temperance were interwoven, and not simply as liberation from injustice. The boilerplate excuse for any particular lynching was that the black man had been caught allegedly raping a white woman, often with a supplemental allegation of "while drunk" peppered in for flavor. As Ida Wells's research uncovered, however, in less than a third of such lynchings was there any prior sexual relationship at all, and even in many of those cases, the relationship was consensual.[133] The rape allegation was just a cover. Still, this white-supremacist framework dovetailed nicely with the colonizer's narrative that alcohol fueled the disinhibition of subaltern populations, which in turn justified their repression by white "civilization." So it makes sense that the rise of Jim Crow in the 1890s was accompanied not only by more frequent lynchings, but also the growth of white fears over drunken black rapists, even though blacks drank far less than their white counterparts.[134]

For Ida Wells, one episode hit especially close to home. In 1892 a white mob lynched two black men in Memphis, including one of Ida Wells's close friends. Horrified and outraged, Wells took to the papers not only to decry the injustice but to chronicle lynching across the South. In her weekly *Free Speech* column of May 21, 1892, she listed the eight lynchings across the South in the preceding week. "The same programme of hanging, then shooting bullets into the lifeless bodies was carried out to the letter," she wrote. "Nobody in this section of the country believes the old threadbare lie that Negro men rape white women." Perhaps if white men were to look a little closer, they might reach conclusions "which will be very damaging to the moral reputation of their women."[135]

Her editorial elicited a firestorm. Literally.

The *Free Speech* office was burned to the ground by a white mob. Wells's coeditor was run out of town under threat of hanging and castration. The paper's former owner was pistol-whipped and forced to denounce her. Friends telegrammed her that whites were posted at the railway stations, ready to lynch her the moment she stepped foot back in Memphis.[136] Ida Wells never returned, opting instead to continue chronicling southern horrors as a traveling antilynching activist. She even stopped in Philadelphia to visit Frances Harper before embarking for London, where she was invited by Quaker temperance activist and *Anti-Caste* publisher Catherine Impey (Chapter 5) to speak with British temperance and antilynching leagues.[137]

When in London in 1893, Wells met with Frances Willard, whom she'd known from Willard's WCTU forays into the South in the 1880s.[138] "Miss Frances E. Willard, our great temperance leader, had been the guest of Lady Henry Somerset and the British Women's Temperance Association for nearly two years," Wells wrote in her biography. In her bid to expand the global reach of the World's WCTU, "She too had travelled all over the kingdom, and made wonderful addresses in the interest of temperance."

British antilynching audiences naturally asked Wells's opinion, as a black woman, of the venerable Willard. Wells claimed that Willard's "only public expression about which I knew had seemed to condone lynching."[139] British temperance activists scoffed indignantly. So, on her second trip to Britain in 1894, she brought a clipping of the offending interview Willard had given on "The Race Problem" to the pro-temperance *New York Voice* in 1890. Taking place in the lead-up to the WCTU's national convention in Atlanta, Willard's *New York Voice* interview largely parroted the white colonial alcohol discourse.

The published interview began with Willard touting her abolitionist roots, her extensive WCTU work among black communities in the South, and claiming "so far as I know, I have not an atom of race prejudice. With me the color of the heart and not of the skin is what settles a human being's status."[140] Turning to suffrage, she promoted educational tests for the franchise, so that only educated citizens— be they white or black—could vote, while incentivizing all citizens to uplift and educate themselves. Though they sound inherently discriminatory and contentious today, education tests were considered a reasonable and practical means of promoting an enlightened and engaged electorate. Even F. E. W. Harper supported them as an incentive for the downtrodden black community.

But the biggest racial bombshell in Willard's published interview came next, in applying the white colonial alcohol discourse to the race question:

> The Anglo-Saxon race will never submit to be dominated by the Negro so long as his altitude reaches no higher than the personal liberty of the saloon and the power of appreciating the amount of liquor that a dollar will buy. New England would no more submit to this than South Carolina. "Better whiskey and more of it" has been the rallying cry of great dark-faced mobs in the Southern localities where Local Option was snowed under by the colored vote. Temperance has no enemy like that, for it is unreasoning and unreachable. To-night it promises in a great congregation, a vote for temperance at the polls to-morrow; but to-morrow twenty five cents changes that vote in favor of the liquor seller.... The colored race multiplies like the locusts of Egypt. The grog shop is its centre of power. The safety of woman, of childhood, of the home, is menaced in a thousand localities at this moment, so that men dare not go beyond the sight of their own roof-tree.[141]

While this interview caused an immediate uproar among the black press back when it was originally published in 1890, mainstream outlets virtually ignored it. "Marked copies of their journals were sent to her, my own among the number," Wells wrote in her autobiography. "But so far as anyone knew, Miss Willard had never retracted or explained that interview."[142]

A year before her Memphis offices were burned to the ground, in 1891 Wells penned a rebuttal to Willard—and the broader alcohol discourse—in the same *AME Church Review* frequented by F. E. W. Harper. "The belief is widespread that our people will patronize the saloon as they do no other enterprise," Wells wrote. "Desiring to secure some of the enormous profits flowing into Anglo-Saxon coffers, many of our young men are entering the nefarious traffic for the money it brings, and thus every year sacrificing to the Moloch of intemperance hundreds of our young men," arguing that the greatest challenge to the African American community came from within.

Then she turned to black economic subjugation: "At the close of the year, when farmers receive pay for the year's work, thousands of dollars, which might flow into honorable channels of trade and build up race enterprises, are spent for liquor to inflame the blood and incite to evil deeds," Wells wrote. "That which is not directly spent for liquor is lost or wasted; and thus, year in and out, one of the most useful factors in race progress—the farmer—is kept at a dead level, without money, without ambition, and consequently at the mercy of the landholder."

The solution, Wells argued, was "harmonious and consistent combination of agitation and effort" toward temperance from the entire black community: the AME Church, preachers, organizers, and citizens. "An organized combination of all these agencies for humanity's good will sweep the country with a wave of public sentiment which shall make the liquor traffic unprofitable and dishonorable, and remove one of the principal stumbling blocks to race progress," Wells concluded.[143]

But it wasn't her temperance position that concerned those British activists already attuned to the racial fissures within American temperance, but rather Wells's accusation that WCTU president Frances Willard actually condoned lynching. It was to back up these allegations that Wells brought a hard copy of Willard's explosive *New York Voice* interview with her when she returned to Britain in 1894.

It is unclear exactly what happened next. However, in the May 6, 1894, issue of the British antilynching newspaper *Fraternity*, Wells reported that she had met face to face with Willard on the sidelines of the British Woman's Temperance Association meeting and had amicably hashed out their differences. "I have seen Miss Willard and talked with her, and she sees the subject of lynching as she never saw it before, because she, like others, made the mistake of judging the negro by what his accusers say of him and without hearing his side of the story."[144]

By all accounts, that should have been the end of it.

Nevertheless, the editors at *Fraternity* went ahead and reprinted Willard's inflammatory interview from 1890 anyway, igniting a media firestorm that would impact both women forever. In London, what followed was a back-and-forth series of letters in the *Westminster Gazette*. Willard was adamant that "neither by voice nor pen have I ever condoned, much less defended, any injustice toward the colored people," and couldn't be held responsible for American racists who did. Wells shot back that "Miss Willard is no better or worse than the great bulk of white Americans on the Negro question. They are all afraid to speak out, and it is only British public opinion which will move them, as I am thankful to see it has already begun to move Miss Willard."[145]

Back in the United States, the feud fractured reformers between those who defended Willard and those who attacked her for not doing more. In Philadelphia, Harper remained notably silent on the dispute.[146]

At the 1894 WCTU national convention in Cleveland, Willard used her presidential address to again denounce racism and lynching, folding in condemnations of British colonial oppression against black South African populations (Chapter 6) and the Turkish slaughter of its Armenian minority (Chapter 8), though the colonizing stereotype about black men's predilection for drunkenness remained.[147] She urged the national organization to adopt an even more strongly worded antilynching resolution, highlight the organization's long-standing activism within African American communities, and reinstate the Department of Colored Work. At the same time, she took the opportunity to call out Miss Wells—who was in attendance at the convention—suggesting that the "laudable efforts she is making are greatly handicapped" by statements impugning her white allies as inviting rape at the hands of black men.[148] Wells replied, "I wish it were possible not to make such allusions, but the Negro race is becoming as careful as to its honor as the white race."[149]

The dust-up raised the visibility of Ida Wells as a foremost civil rights activist, while the accusations of racism followed Frances Willard for the rest of her life. By association, the Wells-Willard debacle tainted both the WCTU and the temperance movement more generally as a fundamentally racist, white nationalist undertaking, even as Willard strengthened her commitment to temperance organization among black women.[150]

Just weeks before his death in 1895, the great abolitionist-suffragist-prohibitionist Frederick Douglass typed out one of his last letters—co-signed by ten prominent civil rights leaders and abolitionists, including the children of William Lloyd Garrison—defending Frances Willard as a champion not just of temperance and women's rights but civil rights, too. After a detailed recounting of her service to the cause of equality, Frederick Douglass concluded, "In view of these facts we feel that for any person or persons to give currency to the statement harmful to Miss Willard as a reformer is most misleading and unjust. Through her influence many of the State Unions have adopted resolutions against lynching, and the National Union has put itself squarely on record in the same way, while the Annual Addresses of the President have plainly indicated her disapproval of such lawless and barbarous proceedings."[151]

No matter. The damage was done.

Frances Ellen Watkins Harper never weighed in on the Willard-Wells dispute, though one can't help but read her "An Appeal to My Countrywomen" (1896) in the context of the day. While chronicling white women's seemingly endless sympathy for Armenian orphans, Russian exiles, and drunkards, she wrote,

> Weep not, oh my well-sheltered sisters,
> Weep not for the Negro alone,
> But weep for your sons who must gather
> The crops which their fathers have sown.[152]

Harper would remain a lifelong WCTU member until her death in 1911. Moreover, both Harper and Ida Wells would become founding members of the National Association of Colored Women's Clubs: influential in the emerging women's club movement for the promotion of progressive and inclusive public policies.

Willard the Christian Socialist

Much of this history of intersectional progress has understandably been overshadowed—first by the Wells-Willard clash, then by the creeping implementation of repressive Jim Crow laws across the South.. But the legacy of women's activism—black and white—in the post-Reconstruction South was not so easily snuffed out. The WCTU helped lay the groundwork for statewide prohibitions that would sweep the South between 1907 and 1910 (Chapter 16). But it went far beyond that: as historian Edward L. Ayers argues in his *Promise of the New South* (2007), "Women of both races found an elevated role in the prohibition movement," and the WCTU in particular gave women, regardless of race, their first opportunity at political activism. In the words of one Mississippi activist, the WCTU was "the generous liberator, the joyous iconoclast, the discoverer, the developer of Southern women."[153]

In the 1880s, even as violence and lynchings ended Reconstruction, prohibitionist rallies made the point of announcing that all were welcome to attend, regardless of color. Black and white speakers shared the same stage and applauded each other's accomplishments, even as black voters were courted by both wet and dry politicians. Such interracial bridges were reinforced by religious and class sympathies. Those who took all of Christ's teachings seriously recognized both the fundamental precepts of human equality and the need to uplift downtrodden communities. "In all these ways," Ayers concludes, "the prohibitionists forged relatively open and democratic—if temporary—racial coalitions."[154]

The conflict between Willard and Wells subsided, in part due to Willard's failing health: pernicious anemia exacerbated by her tireless work schedule. She spent ever more time in London with her friend Lady Somerset, before dying in 1898 at age fifty-eight.[155]

The WCTU was Willard's legacy: under her leadership, the organization became by far the biggest, most influential women's organization in history, with nearly two hundred thousand members, as compared to just thirteen thousand in the National American Woman Suffrage Association.[156] In the years before her death, Willard wielded the political power of the "do everything" WCTU, throwing its endorsement behind reformers of all persuasions to promote women's rights and curb the excesses of the liquor traffic. For a time, she flirted with the idea of merging with the similarly minded Prohibition Party, established in 1869 as the first political party in American history to admit women as full and equal members. But the Prohibition Party's influence peaked in 1884, when its meager 1.5 percent of the nationwide vote likely spoiled the presidential election for the reformist Republicans.[157] It soon became clear that no single-issue political party could break the two-party duopoly. By 1889 Willard was looking elsewhere for political influence, most notably with the farmers of the Populist Party, as well as the growing American labor movement.[158]

Though rank-and-file WCTU members did not follow—and her successor as WCTU president, Lillian Stevens, would roll back her "do everything" platform to focus primarily on temperance[159]—Willard found a new spiritual home with the growing social gospel movement (Chapter 14). Gospel socialism was not a doctrine of eternal salvation in the afterlife, but using Christ's example as a blueprint for doing right by one's fellow man here on earth: giving aid to the poor, marginalized, and downtrodden, and certainly not exploiting one's fellow man through the exploitative sale of liquor.

Willard became a member of the Society of Christian Socialists in 1889, adding contributor to and coeditor of *The Dawn* newspaper to her endless list of occupations. She joined the Knights of Labor, and—spending more time in London—the British Fabian Society, forerunner to the Labour Party. Even while embroiled in the Ida Wells controversy, Willard dedicated much of her 1893 presidential address to gospel socialism, urging the women of the WCTU to patronize "that blessed trinity of movements: Prohibition, Woman's Liberation and Labor's uplift."[160]

Showcasing the old oratorical flare that had inspired a generation of American women to action, Willard proclaimed to her rapt audience in Chicago, "In every Christian there exists a socialist; and in every socialist a Christian; for as someone has wisely said, you cannot organize a brotherhood without brothers." She continued,

> It is only too apparent that there are two kinds of socialism; one gives and the other takes. One says "all thine is mine"; the other says "all mine is thine." One says "I," the other "we." One says "my," the other "our." One says "down with all that's up," the other "up with all that's down." It will take several generations to change the set of brain and trend of thought, so that in place of an individual we shall have corporate conscience. But the outcome of the Gospel and the golden rule will at last make it intuitive with us to say "*our* duty" rather than always "*my* duty." That is, we shall conceive of society as a unity which has such relations to every fraction thereof, that there could be no rest while any lacked food, clothing or shelter, or while any were so shackled by the grim circumstances of life that they were unable to develop the best that was in them both in body and mind.[161]

From there, she extolled the necessity of enlisting all allies together in the struggle for temperance, women's rights, and labor rights. She lauded Pope Leo XIII—the "working man's Pontiff"—for bringing the resources of the Catholic Church into the liberation struggle.

"I charge upon the drink traffic that it keeps the people down, and capitalists and politicians know it. Nothing else could hold wage-workers where they are to-day except the blight that strong drink puts on all their faculties and powers," Willard proclaimed. "But for drink the slums would rise to the level of organization Trades Unions, and through political machinery would dethrone those who reap the fruits but have not sown the seeds of industry."

The WCTU had often acted as good-faith mediator in disputes between capital and labor, and had long called for an eight-hour workday and other labor protections. Now she called for women to go further: to use women's growing social and political influence to shine a light on the injustices heaped upon labor.

In her speech, she asked her listeners to imagine the tropical forests of Africa, in which a few, high-canopy trees cut off light to the forest floor, and the life desperately trying to grow there. So too with the human jungles of American capitalism, she said, where sprawling monopolistic trusts, political machines, and the liquor traffic suffocated all those who toil beneath. "The wholesome influence of nature—sunbeam and sky, air, earth, and water—must be more intelligently and equally provided for each and all," Willard explained. "Then will come the tall, well-developed and harmonious growths, and not till then. But this means that sort of socialism, which is best defined as 'Christianity applied.' "[162]

Indeed, very little about women's temperance and suffragism was reactionary. Frances Willard embodied this spirit of "do everything" revolution throughout her entire life, but especially so near the end with her explicit embrace of gospel socialism.

The 1890s saw the changing of the guard in terms of progressive activism. The old-guard reformers—William Lloyd Garrison, Frederick Douglass, Lucretia Mott, Elizabeth Cady Stanton, Susan B. Anthony—were all dead or soon to be.[163] In joining them, from her deathbed Frances Willard implored her well-wishers and WCTU compatriots to follow this social gospel. "Oh, how I want our women to have a new concept of religion; the religion of the world is a religion of love; it is a home religion; it is a religion of peace," she said.

"Only the Golden Rule of Christ can bring the Golden Age of Man."[164]

The Progressive Soul of American Prohibition

Johns Hopkins Hospital Cancer Ward, Baltimore, Maryland: Sunday, May 19, 1918

There is nothing more sanguine than a eulogy for a faithful man.

Walter Rauschenbusch was a faithful man.

What Martin Luther King Jr. was to the civil rights movement, Walter Rauschenbusch (1861–1918) was to the social justice movement of the Progressive Era: a transformative figure hailed as "the foremost interpreter of contemporary Christianity," and one who died well before his time. Indeed, the Baptist Reverend Dr. Martin Luther King Jr. always listed the Baptist Reverend Dr. Walter Rauschenbusch among his most significant spiritual and political influences, for articulating how racism, sexism, imperialism, and oppression were fundamentally hostile to Christian love and justice.[1]

Born in Rochester, New York, to German immigrants, Rauschenbusch eschewed old-world Lutheranism to become a Baptist minister, social reformer, and one of the most influential progressive thinkers of the 1890s through the 1910s. Republican president Theodore Roosevelt sought out his wise counsels, as did Democrats William Jennings Bryan and Woodrow Wilson. So too did British prime minister David Lloyd George, and countless governors, senators, politicians, labor leaders, and social activists.[2]

"But he was not an evangelist of the Billy Sunday type"—the famously brash Presbyterian temperance orator. "He did not speak or cry aloud in the streets; there was no cheap sentimentalism about his evangelism," claimed Rauschenbusch's longtime secretary and friend Dores Robinson Sharpe. His manner was humble, direct, factual, and compassionate.[3]

His was the Christianity of the age, and it was progressive to its core. "Social Christianity is not traditional Christianity *plus something else tacked on*," explained Sharpe. "Social Christianity is the progressive, and ultimately complete, renovation of the world (individuals, society, churches, institutions) by the spiritual power of Jesus Christ and the dynamic ideal of the Kingdom of God."[4] This Kingdom of

God—which formed the core of Rauschenbusch's social gospel—was not some pillowy paradise in the clouds. It is right here on earth and could be built with human hands, compassionate hearts, and clear minds—by following Jesus's example.

"Christianity is in its nature revolutionary," Rauschenbusch proclaimed. Jesus always sided with the poor against the rich, the powerless against the powerful, presenting a radical challenge to the political order. It was only the individual's single-minded obsession with getting into heaven that switched Christianity's focus from this world to the next, and "substituted asceticism for a revolutionary movement."[5]

But individual salvation could not be won in isolation, claimed Rauschenbusch. It was the entire society—rich and poor together—who would stand in judgment before the Lord.[6] If good Christians are to follow Christ's example by championing justice and aiding the poor, he reasoned, they should damn well concern themselves with the exploitative capitalist system that produces such injustice and poverty in the first place. And since the predatory liquor traffic was everywhere the generator of poverty, injustice, and corruption, it goes without saying that he was in favor of its prohibition.[7]

In the end, the "ultimate and logical outcome" of Christianity's confrontation with the crisis of industrial capitalism was to embrace socialism. It was not the radical Bolshevism of Lenin (Chapter 2), but the nonviolent, egalitarian democratic socialist principles of Hjalmar Branting in Sweden and Emile Vandervelde in Belgium (Chapter 3), and Karl Kautsky in Germany (Chapter 4) that were most in tune with the modern Protestant ethos of the day. "Approximate equality is the only enduring foundation of political democracy," Rauschenbusch wrote, adding, "The sense of equality is the only basis for Christian morality."[8] That European socialists more often scoffed at religion as organized superstition was their loss, because evangelical Christianity was well equipped to provide socialism with a moral compass.

When his magnum opus, *Christianity and the Social Crisis*, was published in 1907, Rauschenbusch fled to Germany on sabbatical to duck the anticipated ecclesiastical backlash. Instead, it met with rave reviews—selling some fifty thousand copies—and ensconced Rauschenbusch as one of the foremost public intellectuals in America.[9]

Sharpe reminisced fondly over these years, when his boss was everywhere in demand as a public speaker. One sunny Chicago afternoon in the summer of 1912, after finishing yet another invited lecture, Rauschenbusch bounded into a corner grocery for strawberries, crackers, and milk. Together the two friends made their way to Lake Michigan, kicked off their shoes, and let the water lap at their feet as they ate.

As the evening sun set over the city, the pastor suddenly turned to his close confidant and asked, "How do you think of me and my work?"

"I think of you as an evangelist," Sharpe replied earnestly, "and of your work as evangelism of the truest sort."

Rauschenbusch brightened. "I have always wanted to be thought of in that way." As the two men joyously embraced, ankle deep in the lake's baptismal waters, he added, "Your testimony gives me new fighting power."[10]

But the warm sun was soon to set. In 1914 the Great War drenched Europe in blood and "set great doors swinging heavily on weary hinges, closing within the darkness of despair the hopes of a once bright-hearted world." Humanity, dignity, and fellowship were sacrificed upon the altars of nationalism, militarism, and hatred.[11] War was the ultimate negation of both Christian love and social progress. Soon thereafter, Rauschenbusch's health deteriorated, with no discernible cause.

"I may go to Johns Hopkins," he wrote Sharpe. Twenty years of unrelenting work had worn him down, though even from his hospital bed, he pleaded for peace, sober self-restraint, open-mindedness, and love.[12]

"Since 1914 the world is full of hate, and I cannot expect to be happy again in my lifetime," he wrote in one of his last letters.[13] He'd previously exposed how, in militaristic societies, "war is idealized by monuments and paintings, poetry and song. The stench of the hospitals and the maggots of the battle-field are passed in silence." Wars are largely fought not for high ideals—social justice or human rights—but for personal spite, military ambition, and the protection of exploitative colonial and capitalist ventures. Once we awaken to this reality, Rauschenbusch proclaimed, "the mythology of war will no longer bring us to our knees, and we shall fail to get drunk with the rest when martial intoxication sweeps the people off their feet."[14]

Even as one medical test after another proved inconclusive, Rauschenbusch wrote from his hospital bed, lauding those anti-imperial, antiwar champions from William Jennings Bryan (Chapters 15–17) to the pacifist Quakers.[15] In his final published letter, Rauschenbusch hoped the Allies would topple the militaristic, reactionary Russian, Austro-Hungarian, and German Empires and finally "free the world from imperialism."[16]

Making peace with his own mortality—and not wanting to burden his family—in May 1918 Rauschenbusch left Johns Hopkins and returned home to await his fate. "I dread nothing more than a dreary old age," he wrote Sharpe:

> I have often prayed to God to grant me an honorable discharge when my work is done. Is this what He now offers me? . . .
>
> I should find it hard to part from my family and a few friends like you. But otherwise I keep wondering if God is not intending to be very kind to one of his servants who, for reasons known to Him, has carried a heavy load for 30 years and yet has done the day's work as well as the next man.
>
> With love and a smile. Walter.[17]

On July 25, 1918, Sharpe received a Western Union telegram from newly widowed Pauline Rauschenbusch that read simply, "Walter fell asleep quietly today his warfare is ended."

It was inoperable colon cancer that ultimately took him. He was only fifty-six.[18]

Dores Robinson Sharpe wept.

"In beautiful Rochester," he later eulogized, "I found an infinitely lovely soul—serene, simple, courageous, honest and friendly—a *great good man*."

But who is a great man? "It is he who inspires others to think for themselves," he said, but it goes well beyond that. "He is great whom many love and others hate, but whom all men respect and none ever forget. The great man *does what we dare not do and says what we would say* if we had the mind and the courage. He is great to whom go writers, reformers, teachers, statesmen, theologians, preachers, scholars,—each to draw more and more knowledge."

By these, and all other standards, Walter Rauschenbusch was a great good man, which is the most sublime tribute I can imagine.[19]

Figure 14.1 Walter Rauschenbusch, 1892.
Source: Courtesy of the American Baptist Historical Society, Atlanta, GA. Photo from RG 1003, box 74, folder 2.

But it is not as though his great goodness perished with his passing. Rauschenbusch's social justice values were shared by millions of evangelical Christians across the country, and provided the soul not just of American progressivism but American prohibitionism, too.

Can I Speak with You for a Moment about Jesus?

Standard histories of American prohibition make a big to-do about religion. Many chalk the entire temperance movement up to evangelical Christianity, vilifying its proponents as rural, white, nativist, Bible-thumping killjoys (see Chapter 18). But drawing a straight line from culture or religion as "cause" to a particular policy "effect" isn't so easy. A whole host of economic, political, social, and institutional factors complicate such blanket cultural explanations, even in the simplest of scenarios.

But prohibition is not a simple scenario for religious explanations of political outcomes. The decades leading up to prohibition saw no great religious revival, no third Great Awakening of American Protestantism like in the 1730s or 1820s. There was no mass stampede of converts to evangelical Christianity. People weren't teeming into overpacked churches to slake their insatiable thirst for Jesus. Just the opposite, in fact.[20]

What *did* change as the new century approached was, first, the content of the religious message—the gospel of social justice was in the ascendency—and, second, the willingness of religiously inspired leaders to move out of the pulpits and into the streets, organizing for both social and political activism. Walter Rauschenbusch was an outspoken proponent of this shift from me-focused to other-focused Christianity, but he was hardly alone. Similar sentiments were espoused by a whole army of clergy: Washington Gladden, Josiah Strong, Charles Stelzle, Charles F. Aked, as well as Purley Baker and Howard Hyde Russell of the Anti-Saloon League of America (Chapter 16), which proclaimed itself as "the church in action against the saloon."[21] But it wasn't even just the pastors: politicians like William Jennings Bryan drew from such moral founts to promote similar political ends.

Venerated historian Richard Hofstadter once claimed that the best test of the mood of society "is whether its comfortable people tend to identify, psychologically, with the power and achievements of the very successful or with the needs and sufferings of the underprivileged." During the rapid industrialization of the Gilded Age of the 1870s through the 1890s, the middle class marveled at the riches and conquests of the Astors, Rockefellers, Carnegies, Morgans, Vanderbilts, and other tycoons. But such unbridled capitalism left a yawning gap between the ultrarich and the masses of urban and rural poor.

The Progressive Era (1896–1920) was a reverse wave of public sentiment, largely supportive of remedying the vast inequalities in wealth and power. Activists and politicians looked to democratic mechanisms to capture the power of government and rein in the predations of unbridled capitalism in defense of the common man. Antitrust and bank regulation diluted the power of the Gilded Age oligarchy; an income tax shifted the financial burdens from the impoverished masses to the elites; expanding suffrage, democratic referenda, and directly electing senators and other politicians would break up Tammany Hall and the corrupt political machines (Chapter 12), which the rich bankrolled to protect their interests. The liquor traffic was the center of all of this. "With its vast financial resources and its alliance with commercialized vice, government-favored business, and machine politicians," historian James Timberlake writes, "the liquor industry stood out as one of *the most corrupt and predatory of all economic interests*, a major obstacle to political reform, and a prime factor in the breakdown of honest government in the cities."[22] Prohibition wasn't some aberration from progressivism; prohibition *was* progressivism.

Of course, an increased religious concern for the downtrodden didn't *cause* prohibition any more than it caused the Pure Food and Drug Act, the Clayton Anti-Trust Act, or other Progressive Era policies. However, it is difficult to understand the shifting focus toward the well-being of industrial workers, urban slums, hardworking farmers, and colonized peoples without a deeper understanding of the social gospel.[23]

Like so many on the Christian left rather than the religious right, Walter Rauschenbusch upsets all of our two-dimensional stereotypes of evangelical Christianity. He was compassionate, not commanding; cosmopolitan, not conservative; socialist, not reactionary. He wasn't anti-immigrant; he was the son of immigrants. He didn't loathe the big city; he lived there. But because he doesn't fit our stereotypes of evangelicals and prohibitionists, the most influential evangelical of his day almost never appears in traditional prohibition histories.[24]

For ages, evangelical leaders implied that drinking was wrong, though "they refrained from actually stating it. They did not hesitate, however, to condemn participation in the liquor traffic as a sin," writes James Timberlake in his *Prohibition and the Progressive Movement*.[25] Calling out the profiteer and drink-seller rather than the drinker was a consistent theme of the traditional temperance movement, going back to its origins in Lyman Beecher's *Six Sermons on Intemperance* (1827). As noted back in Chapter 11, rather than fire-and-brimstone admonitions of eternal damnation for the drunkard, the only Scripture Beecher quoted in his temperance sermons instead took aim at the drink-seller: "Woe unto him that giveth his neighbor drink, that puttest thy bottle to him, and makest him drunk also" (Habakkuk 2:15).[26] So the temperance message had not changed: it had always been progressive.

What had changed in America in the single generation from the Civil War's end in 1865 until 1900 was an economic shift from the farms to big-city factories, and the more than doubling of the population from thirty-one million to seventy-six million Americans. New York City was the main port of entry for the five hundred thousand European immigrants arriving annually by 1886—the year Rauschenbusch took up his pastorate in the dirty, dilapidated slums of New York's Hell's Kitchen. The year

1886 was also when the Haymarket Riot took place in Chicago—where six policemen were bombed while breaking up a peaceful workers' rights demonstration—which stoked a national hysteria about the "dangers" of immigrants, urban poverty, and simmering discontent among the lower classes.[27]

That it exacerbated poverty and attracted and encouraged corruption were the two main reasons for the church to get into the political fight against the saloon. Rauschenbusch addressed each one in turn.

Hell's Kitchen is where he developed his social gospel. "I saw how men toiled all their life," Rauschenbusch said, "and at the end had almost nothing to show for it; how strong men begged for work, and could not get it in the hard times." As pastor, his job was to conduct funerals for the poor, whether they died of starvation, alcoholism, or the typhoid and cholera that decimated the tenements.

"Oh, the children's funerals! They gripped my heart," he agonized. "That was one of the things I always went away thinking about—why did the children have to die?"[28]

He didn't have to go far to find an answer for what to do. In fact, the answer came to him, in the form of socialist economist Henry George. George was one of the most famous Americans of the day—behind only Mark Twain and Thomas Edison—for his popular writings on economic inequality. Just as Rauschenbusch arrived in Hell's Kitchen in 1886, George was waging an ultimately unsuccessful third-party campaign for mayor of New York City. Rauschenbusch became one of his most enthusiastic supporters.[29]

Henry George's bestselling *Progress and Poverty* (1879) asked why poverty seemed to be so much worse in well-established cities like New York rather than newly settled California. The culprit, he concluded, was the big-city aristocracy, who profited not from their own labor, but from exorbitant rents on the tenement houses of the poor, exacerbating the chasm between rich and poor. To protect their outlandish wealth, the super-rich "carry wards in their pockets, make up the slates for nominating conventions, distribute offices as they bargain together." This ruling class didn't comprise wise men of noble character, but rather "gamblers, saloon-keepers, pugilists, or worse, who have made a trade of controlling votes and of buying and selling offices and official acts."[30] As we saw of Tammany Hall in Chapter 12, this was an exceedingly apt description. For George and his followers, economic inequality was inseparable from political corruption, and both had to be tackled together. And right at that intersection of economic inequality and political corruption stood the saloon.

George repeated the standard socialist line that remedying intemperance was impossible without first improving the social conditions of the working class. But even more important, he said, was driving liquor out of politics: "For the 'rum power' is certainly a fact of the first importance. It is an active, energetic, tireless factor in our practical politics, a corrupt and debauching element, standing in the way of all reform and progress, a potent agency by which unscrupulous men may lift themselves to power, and an influence which operates to lower public morality and official character."[31]

Henry George's proposed solution was a so-called "single tax" on unearned income from things that the ultrarich *owned*—like rents from tenement slums—rather than things they *made*. "We would tax but three things," George proclaimed: the value of land, the estates of the wealthy, and "such business as it is deemed good policy to restrain and regulate, such as liquor saloons, gaming houses, etc."[32] Shifting the burden away from tariffs and taxes on consumer goods would help the lower classes, while government revenues could be used for poverty-alleviation measures, similar to the successful Swedish Gothenburg system (Chapter 3). George's single tax was one of the most hotly debated policy ideas of the day.

Though George lost the 1886 election for mayor—largely on account of the entrenched rum power[33]—his campaign reinforced Rauschenbusch's conviction that unearned wealth was inherently parasitic and needed to be reined in by the state, not just for the benefit of the impoverished, but for the soul of the country. "I owe my own first awakening to the world of social problems to the agitation of Henry George in 1886," Rauschenbusch wrote, "and wish here to record my lifelong debt to this single-minded apostle of a great truth."

Rauschenbusch's contribution to American progressivism was to take George's great Marxist truth, baptize it, Christianize it, and inject it into the mainstream of evangelical teaching. "The fact is that socialism is the necessary spiritual product of capitalism. It has been formulated by that class which has borne the sins of capitalism in its own body and knows them by heart," he wrote. "There is no way of taking the wind out of the sails of the socialist ship except to sail alongside of it and in the same direction."[34]

In Christianizing socialism, he relied heavily on the sectarianism—and even the temperance—of Leo Tolstoy (Chapter 2). According to his biographers, it is difficult to find any of Rauschenbusch's essays that are *not* overly gushing with praise for the great Russian writer. He agreed with Tolstoy that Jesus's core commandments to love thy neighbor and never raise a hand in violence "were the obligatory and feasible laws of Christian conduct."[35] Furthermore, Tolstoy's call to selfless Christian service dovetailed perfectly with Henry George's ethics: that wealth siphoned from the labor of others was a clear violation of Jesus's core commandment.[36]

The church needed socialism. But socialism also needed the church, Rauschenbusch claimed. Political philosophers from Karl Marx to Henry George were to be applauded for pointing out the exploitation of the poor by the rich, but what evangelical Christianity offered was a grassroots organization that replaced selfish, material motivations with unselfish, moral ones. "True Christianity emphasizes to the utmost the value of the individual," Rauschenbusch wrote in the *American Journal of Sociology* in 1896, but "it also contains the principle of association, and implants the trustworthiness, love and unselfishness which cement men together and make association a workable idea."[37] And if the church stood aside as the chasm between haves and have-nots grew ever wider, it would lose whatever moral authority and community reputation it had left, as even the morale of good churchgoers eroded. "I have seen church members take positions in the liquor trade against the protest of their conscience and their social pride," he lamented in this regard.[38]

Rauschenbusch burst into the evangelical mainstream in 1907 with the publication of his *Christianity and the Social Crisis*. Hailed as "the first definitive narrative of a Christian political social vision for twentieth-century society," it was fundamentally a temperance tract, fingering the liquor traffic as the foremost culprit of capitalism's degeneracy.[39]

"I can conceive of nothing so crushing to all proper pride as for a workingman to be out of work for weeks, offering his work and his body and soul at one place after the other, and to be told again and again that nobody has any use for such a man as he," Rauschenbusch writes, invoking his Hell's Kitchen past. "It is no wonder that men take to drink when they are out of work; for drink, at least for a while, creates illusions of contentment and worth. The Recessional of Alcohol has the refrain, 'Let us forget.'"

Drunkenness compounds the hopelessness and burdens of unemployment and poverty, leading to domestic violence, divorce, and suicide, even as whole families descend into pauperism, where they die prematurely from disease. "Tuberculosis and alcoholism are social diseases, degenerating the stock of the people, fostered by the commercial interests of landowners and liquor dealers, thriving on the weak and creating the weak." There is nothing in the natural order that produces unemployment, poverty, alcoholism, and social disease: they are only inevitable in capitalism.[40]

The social gospel was the soul not only of prohibition but of all progressive reform, especially consumer protection. Industriousness and commerce are productive and inherently good, Rauschenbusch claimed. But these core virtues turn to vice when unscrupulous men without a social conscience put profits over people. Producers cut corners, adulterated foods with coal-tar and benzoic acid, and sold meats well after they'd spoiled in order to make a buck—which was why Progressives had pressed for the Pure Food and Drug Act, which had passed just the previous year, 1906 (Chapter 17). This, in turn, led Rauschenbusch straight back to alcohol:

> The liquor traffic presents a striking case of a huge industry inducing people to buy what harms them. It is militant capitalism rotting human lives and characters to distill dividends. In the atrocities on the Congo [Chapter 3] we have the same capitalism doing its pitiless work in a safe and distant corner of the world, on an inferior race, and under the full support of the government. The rapacity of commerce has been the secret spring of most recent wars. Speculative finance is the axis on which international politics revolve. The points in the indictment against our

marvelous civilization could be multiplied at pleasure. It is a splendid sinner, "magnificent in sin."[41]

Indeed, American alco-imperialism in the Caribbean and the Philippines would differ little from the Belgians in the Congo, or the British everywhere else (Chapter 15).

Consistent with temperance teaching going back to Beecher's *Six Sermons*, Rauschenbusch explained that it wasn't drinking that was the sin; it was the insatiable greed that defrauds the consumer, denigrates the worker, and "corrupts all it touches": politics, education, even the church itself. As Jesus proclaimed in his Sermon on the Mount (Matthew 6:19–24)—and Tolstoy reminded—one cannot serve both God and Mammon (money).

The core moral dilemma, as the theologian Rauschenbusch argued, is that every human institution creates its own self-justifying narratives and philosophies. Consider, for instance, the "white man's burden" and the colonial alcohol narratives that justified the European imperial project; the hero worship of exploitative business tycoons; the prosperity theology of today, in which ostentatious wealth is touted as proof of God's blessing; or the German Empire's glorification of war while belittling the human sacrifice. Like capitalism and militarism, Rauschenbusch claimed "where alcoholism dominates the customs of a people, it weaves a halo around itself in the songs and social observances of the people, till joy and friendship seem to be inseparable from mild narcotic paralysis of the nerve centres."

To confront each of these overlapping "isms"—alcoholism, militarism, and capitalism—requires first recognizing and then dispelling their self-justifying mythologies. "We are assured that the poor are poor through their own fault; that rent and profits are the just dues of foresight and ability; that the immigrants are the cause of corruption in our city politics; that we cannot compete with foreign countries unless our working class will descend to the wages paid abroad. These are all very plausible assertions, but they are lies dressed up in truth." But the worst lie is the persistent self-deception of profiteers denying—even in the face of contrary evidence—that their livelihoods come at the expense of someone else. So many self-serving cognitive biases operate to prevent a man from condemning the means by which he makes a living, "we must simply make allowance for the warping influence of self-interest when he justifies himself and not believe him entirely."[42]

Ultimately, then, when these opposing forces of capitalism and morality clash, only one can emerge victorious: "If the Church cannot Christianize commerce, commerce will commercialize the Church." And "to be 'commercialized' means to be demoralized," hollowed out, and corrupted by greed.[43]

What, then, is the church to do to alleviate this social crisis, born of capitalism? For one, it can hold a mirror up to those businessmen in the pews and awaken them to the human consequences of their self-interest. Indeed, Rauschenbusch was a longtime friend and beneficiary of temperate Ohio tycoon John D. Rockefeller

(Chapter 16), on whom his entreaties about the necessity of active philanthropy and recognizing the exploitative roots of such immense wealth were not wasted.[44]

Such realizations, though, could never be imposed by outside force: it was up to the individual to awaken themselves.[45] Beyond that, men so awakened "would be compelled to consider how industry and commerce could be reorganized so that there would be a maximum of service to humanity and a minimum of antagonism between those who desire to serve it," by eliminating those profit-making professions that harm instead of help, with the liquor traffic foremost among them.

For another, the church can sanctify the works of social activists reaching out to the poor: the YMCA, YWCA, the Salvation Army, the labor and temperance activists. Religion gives selfless toil purpose, dignity, and joy, and a stubborn courage when confronting politicians and entrenched interests. Scattered throughout all classes of democratic society are "a large number of men and women whose eyes have had a vision of a true human society and who have faith in it and courage to stand against anything that contradicts it, and public opinion will have a new swiftness and tenacity in judging on right and wrong. The murder of the Armenians, the horrors of the Congo Free State, the ravages of the liquor traffic in Africa, the peace movement, the protest against child labor in America, the movement for early closing of retail stores—all these things arouse only a limited number of persons to active sympathy; the rest are lethargic." Indeed, creating a more just society and hastening the Kingdom of God here on earth can best be achieved through an army of benevolent social activists, schooled in the political and economic challenges of capitalism, and motivated by faith to remedy them.

Regarding temperance activism in particular, Rauschenbusch's social gospel seems to have been motivated as much by developments and discourses on alcohol in Europe as in the United States. In fact, on his occasional sabbaticals to Germany, Rauschenbusch would extensively research the politics of the liquor trade in Central Europe. His lectures—both in German and in English—reflected on the progress of temperance against alcoholic capitalism on both continents.[46] The plight of economic migrants leaving Europe for the promise of America—and the exploitative reality when they got to the tenement slums of Hell's Kitchen—were of particular concern. Consistent with European liberal and socialist arguments, Rauschenbusch argued that the church had a greater role in promoting individual abstinence, especially from among the aristocratic classes, that the common man would emulate. Moreover, combining faith in religion with faith in scientific achievement, "the Church should undertake a new temperance crusade with all the resources of advanced physiological and sociological science." When promoted by the church, temperance could make America less calloused to the plight of others, more kind, open-minded, and more prepared to meet the challenge of enlightened, democratic self-governance.[47]

This, then, was the core of the social gospel and the heart of progressive social reform. It wasn't focused on otherworldly salvation, but was deeply and consciously involved with remedying the inherent shortcomings in predatory capitalism, of which the liquor traffic was the most insidious example.

Faith in Science

It wasn't just Rauschenbusch and social gospelers who saw faith in God as consistent with faith in scientific knowledge to build a better life here on earth. After all, the Progressive Era was the golden age of science. Iconic names like Thomas Edison, Nikola Tesla, Alexander Graham Bell, and the Wright Brothers all jump to mind. Less heralded, but just as important, the foundations of modern medical science, as well as social science (political economy and sociology), were being laid at this time, which dramatically impacted the prohibition movement. For the first time, scientific data about the physiological impacts of alcohol could be produced and scrutinized. Sociologists and political scientists could collect criminal, financial, and social data to measure the effects of specific social policies. "To a generation of Americans that was coming to place more and more of its faith in science," historian James Timberlake suggests, "the scientific argument was probably more important than the religious one in promoting temperance reform."[48]

While the physiological effects of chronic heavy drinking had been obvious for centuries, only in the late nineteenth century did medical science explode long-standing myths about purported benefits of moderate alcohol consumption. Long considered a warming stimulant, British researchers in 1866 demonstrated that alcohol consumption actually *lowers* body temperature. Only in 1892 did German scientists conclude that—rather than stimulating the brain—alcohol acts as an anesthetic or narcotic, with depressing effects on the nervous system, even in moderate quantities. A whole battery of medical studies demonstrated the damage even occasional drinking had on the brain, nervous system, heart, liver, stomach, kidneys, and immune system. Others highlighted the physiological and mental "degeneracy" of children of alcoholics.[49]

Today, even casual drinkers have likely made their peace with these well-known health risks, substantiated by volumes of peer-reviewed research. But a century ago, this was contentious, headline-grabbing stuff. And like any public debate, there was breathless hyperbole on all sides. Some bristled at the outlandish claims of social hygienists that alcohol was everywhere a poison even in the smallest quantities. Others—like Carrie Nation in Chapter 1—scoffed at doctors who insisted that drinking (like smoking tobacco) was harmless; healthful, even. Yet beyond all the bluster, for the first time in history, there was an emerging global *scientific* consensus about the dangers of alcohol. Consequently, it wasn't exclusively—or even primarily—religious "zealots" who had reason to patronize temperance: cutting-edge scientific discoveries won a great many progressive adherents to the cause as well.

Medical science and alcohol studies invigorated the prohibitionist movement, in the form of so-called scientific temperance. The Woman's Christian Temperance Union even developed a Department of Scientific Temperance Instruction, under the leadership of Mary H. Hunt, to not only publicize new scientific investigations into the harms of alcohol, but encourage their teaching as part of public-school physiology courses. With the growing power of the WCTU in the publishing world, Hunt established a *de facto* veto over any textbook that didn't include scientific temperance instruction. In 1906 Hunt even developed her own Scientific Temperance Federation in Boston, publishing books, pamphlets, and a quarterly *Scientific Temperance Journal*, replete with the latest peer-reviewed research on alcohol. While often debated and challenged—as befitting the scientific method—such mandatory instruction in scientific temperance laid the groundwork not only for prohibition but also for modern drug-education programs.[50]

The scientific approach to temperance was hardly some niche concern. Instead, it influenced many aspects of American political and economic life. With evidence of alcohol's harmful health effects mounting, universities from Wisconsin and Michigan to Princeton and California forbade their student-athletes from drinking during the competitive season. Many professional sports teams followed suit.[51]

If liquor was bad for collegiate football, baseball, and basketball players, it was also bad for college-age boys who enlisted in the military. Physicians in the British, American, and European armed forces were increasingly awakened to the toll alcohol was taking on military preparedness, and thereby national security as well. Military doctors charted dramatically higher levels of mortality from cholera, influenza, typhoid, and other communicable diseases among heavy-drinking soldiers rather than abstinent ones.[52] Such findings only strengthened the "cult of military sobriety"—that drink was a significant impediment to military victory—by armed forces around the globe (Chapters 4, 15, 17).

Still, many of the most detailed studies of alcohol-related mortality came from insurance underwriters and the actuarial sciences. A joint investigation of the Actuarial Society of America and the Medical Directors' Association pooled data on over two million policyholders from 1885 to 1908. Heavy drinkers—those who imbibed more than two ounces of alcohol per day—had a mortality rate 86 percent higher than the average policyholder and were twice as likely to die from liver cirrhosis, diabetes, tuberculosis, pneumonia, or suicide.

Those who reported only occasionally drinking to excess had a mortality rate 46 to 74 percent higher than average, while even abstinent, reformed alcoholics had a 32 percent higher mortality rate. Most surprising was that moderate drinkers— those who had fewer than two beers daily—had an 18 percent higher mortality rate. The scientific temperance folks pounced on such studies as further confirmation that moderate drinking wasn't as healthful as some of its most vocal proponents suggested.[53]

Since heavy drinkers cost insurers more and die earlier, they are riskier investments. Consequently insurance companies began incentivizing temperance by offering lower premiums to nondrinkers, just as they do today in discriminating in favor of nonsmokers over smokers.

And just as modern airlines have strict "bottle to throttle" rules against pilots drinking between eight and twelve hours before operating an aircraft—since one drunken pilot would imperil all of the passengers onboard and one crash could bankrupt an airline—the same was true for railroad employees, and bus and trolley drivers a hundred years ago. This industrial safety movement was supercharged by another progressive reform: the passing of the first workmen's compensation laws in 1908. These laws saddled employers and their insurers with the costs of compensating workers for accidents and injuries on the job. Accordingly, many businesses immediately sought to reduce those risks and costs by improving workplace safety, which meant promoting temperance and giving preference to sober workers over chronic inebriates. This is all to say nothing of the increased economic efficiency of temperate workers over their drunken counterparts. Sobriety was good for business.[54]

Scientific temperance wasn't some connivance of Victorian Bible-thumpers looking to legislate morality. Instead, it was part and parcel of the modern industrial economy, and the progressive politics that sought to rein in its excesses.

Social science also was on the march. Newly minted economists, sociologists, and political scientists applied scientific methodology, logic, and rules of evidence to confront pressing social and political problems. In the words of Supreme Court Justice Louis Brandeis, the American states were "laboratories for social experimentation,"[55] and nowhere was that more true than in policies confronting the liquor traffic. For example, policy researchers could examine the whole bevy of economic data, crime rates, personal savings figures, and so forth to determine whether, for example, the purported benefits of prohibition were being realized in dry Tennessee, as compared to wet Kentucky, just across the border.

And there were far more policy options than just the "prohibition" or "no prohibition" alternatives implicit in most history books.[56] There was the Gothenburg system—in which the municipal liquor trade was entrusted to a corporation of esteemed citizens, who'd restrict the local traffic in the interest of temperance, not profits—which had so effectively minimized the worst excesses of the liquor traffic that the system had been emulated across Scandinavia (Chapter 3), the United Kingdom, Australia and Canada, too (Chapter 5). Then there were state-level dispensaries—most notably in South Carolina—in which the state regulated the retail trade in the interest of public sobriety. There were local-option states—like Massachusetts, Illinois, Ohio, and Indiana—in which local communities could vote themselves dry in accordance with local wishes. Then came "high license" states— Pennsylvania, New York, Utah, and Washington—that followed the Danish model of restricting the number of retail outlets by limiting the number of licenses, or making those licenses extremely expensive to obtain. Added to that were all sorts of government monopolization schemes, like those used in the Russian Empire (Chapter 2), Belgium (Chapter 3), Germany (Chapter 4), France, and Switzerland.[57] What the United States offered political scientists—both American and visiting researchers from around the world—was the opportunity to see all of these different policy systems operating simultaneously in the same country, so as to more objectively measure and compare their effects and effectiveness.

Given such a wide competition of policies and ideas, the prohibition option was hardly the inevitable, insatiable force most prohibition histories make it out to be. For instance, Swedish researcher H. J. Boström spent all of 1906 and 1907 studying the American states. His voluminous study began by noting that while seventeen states had experimented with prohibition at one time or another, all those statutes had all been repealed, except in Maine, Kansas, and North Dakota.[58] His colleague Gerhard Halfred von Koch wanted to study American prohibition but could only find it in Maine and Kansas.[59] Fellow Swede Eyvind Andersen's 1909 book simply lambasted the American *förbudskomedien,* or "prohibition comedy."[60] This hardly sounds like the inevitable march to the Eighteenth Amendment that most prohibition histories portray.

Indeed, in the early Progressive Era, it was *not* prohibition that was on the rise, but rather the Swedish Gothenburg system of disinterested management.[61] In 1891 Athens, Georgia, dumped its ineffective local prohibition for a Gothenburg-type dispensary, which was quickly emulated in cities across the Deep South.[62] By 1893 South Carolina adopted its own statewide dispensary system.[63] In the 1890s, both the Commonwealth of Massachusetts and the US Department of Labor commissioned exhaustive studies of the Gothenburg system in Sweden and Norway, with Massachusetts calling for its immediate adoption statewide.[64]

From the social-scientific perspective, the Gothenburg alternative received perhaps its greatest support from a group known as the Committee of Fifty for the Investigation of the Drink Problem. Founded in 1893 by prominent businessmen, professionals, and academics—including progressive economist Richard T. Ely—the committee sought to move beyond subjective opinions on the liquor question by establishing a body of objective, scientific "facts, which may serve as a basis for intelligent public and private action."[65] Between 1893 and 1905 the committee published thorough, dispassionate investigations into the legislative, economic, social, political, and physiological aspects of the liquor trade. Demonstrating further fissures within the movement, the committee explicitly called out the WCTU's Department of Scientific Temperance Instruction: both for misrepresenting the science by calling alcohol a "poison" in every form and even the smallest doses. Plus the pedagogy of scaring elementary-school kids straight with unsound temperance propaganda was sure to backfire when students got older and found that the science didn't universally support those conclusions.[66]

As for prohibition, the committee concluded it was unworkable: pushing the admittedly corrupt liquor trade underground, where it breeds graft, fraud, and malfeasance.[67]

The objectively superior "substitute for the saloon," according to their research, was a less rigid framework, allowing communities to vote themselves dry through a local option if they so wished, but also removing the private profit motive from the liquor trade. In the end, the committee endorsed the Gothenburg-type dispensary system as used in Sweden, Norway, and South Carolina.[68] Indeed, a detailed consideration of all the articles on the liquor question published in the American popular press shows that articles about the Gothenburg or dispensary systems greatly outstripped articles on prohibition from the 1890s through about 1905.[69]

Still, proponents of government license and dispensary options had to confront temperance advocates who reasonably argued that government regulation—and its subsequent dependence on liquor revenues—made the state itself complicit in a predatory trade. "By legalizing this traffic we agree to share with the liquor seller the responsibilities and the evils of his business," claimed President William McKinley. "Every man who votes for license becomes of necessity a partner to the liquor traffic and all its consequences—the most degrading and ruinous of all human pursuits."[70]

As a tactical concern, if national prohibition were ever to become a reality, prohibitionists would have to debunk these liquor-control alternatives. Much of the untold history of American prohibition revolves around just that, beginning with a figure we've already encountered time and again: William E. Johnson. In London, his speeches prompted street riots (Chapter 5); in India, he was welcomed as a liberator among Gandhi's nationalists (Chapter 7); and he worked with Turkish nationalists in the Green Crescent Society (Chapter 8). But even a decade before earning the "Pussyfoot" sobriquet that followed him his whole life for making stealthy raids on illegal saloons in the Indian Country of Oklahoma, Johnson started out as a muckraking journalist for the New York Voice. His editors—Dr. Isaac K. Funk and Adam W. Wagnalls—smiled pleasantly as circulation rose with Johnson's salacious investigations into the proliferation of saloons around elite East Coast universities, including Yale and Princeton.[71]

When an ailing Frances Willard (Chapter 13) visited New York shortly before her death in 1897, Johnson ghost-wrote speeches for her. He frequented some of the seediest dives in New York City and penned scathing exposés. And when the Spanish-American War broke out the following year, Johnson toured the camps of army regulars and volunteer regiments—most famously Teddy Roosevelt's Rough Riders—chronicling the drunkenness associated with the army canteens (Chapter 15). But more importantly, while touring the South, he dug up evidence of a corrupt tax-avoidance scheme within South Carolina's vaunted dispensary system: blasting the whole "rotten" enterprise as a material witness in court cases. "My testimony was printed in pamphlet form and widely distributed," Johnson wrote. For casting shade over the foremost alternative to prohibition, "I felt rather good over the outcome."[72]

In 1899 Johnson boarded a steamship for Sweden to muckrake the vaunted Gothenburg system in its native habitat. Though he found the Swedish system to be undertaken "with remarkable purity of purpose," he was quick to convey to his American readers that it could not be expected to work similarly in the United States.[73] Rather than making the state a partner in liquor-control and temperance, such broadsides reframed the state as a coconspirator in the debauching and deplorable liquor trade. In doing so, Johnson was happy to describe his research as "ammunition" for the cause of total prohibition.[74]

"The Gothenburg yarns caught on in America," Johnson wrote. "The drys, both in Scandinavia and America, were elated."[75]

Paired with *ad-hominem* attacks against the "pro-alcohol pedants on the Committee of Fifty" for touting the objective benefits of liquor control, the persistent salvos against "the Gothenburg–South Carolina matter" by Johnson and other journalists were widely credited with halting the dispensary legislation in both Massachusetts and California, and burying the foremost alcohol-control alternative to prohibition.[76]

Debates over Gothenburg dispensaries and other liquor-control alternatives are not just some footnote to prohibition history. Not only do they highlight the rising importance of social-scientific evidence and rationality in policy debates regarding the liquor question, but more importantly, they highlight a central concern of the Progressive Era: corruption and "liquor machine" politics. Specifically, they articulated the widespread concern that the state should not be in bed with big business, especially when that business thrives on addicting and debauching customers, families, and entire communities.

The Rough Rider against the Liquor Machine

The Progressive Era of American politics came in with a bang, quite literally. On September 6, 1901, the recently reelected president William McKinley was hobnobbing with the public at the Pan-American Exposition in Buffalo, New York, when unemployed anarchist Leon Czolgosz approached and shot the president twice in the abdomen at point-blank range. A week later, McKinley's vice president, Theodore "TR" Roosevelt, was sworn in as the twenty-sixth president. At only forty-two years of age, he was by far the youngest. As president, Roosevelt would push a progressive "Square Deal" agenda of trust-busting, corporate regulation, and consumer protection. And while the "Rough Rider" cultivated an image of plainspoken frontier machismo, his progressive roots were firmly planted in New York City, while his attitude toward alcohol was downright temperate.[77]

Born into Manhattan high society, the Harvard-educated Roosevelt could have lived in opulence and comfort from his father's sumptuous inheritance. Instead— following the death of both his wife and mother on Valentine's Day 1884—he dove headlong into the corrupt world of New York City politics, where even the best-intentioned elected officials were undercut by unelected political machines.[78]

In his autobiography, Roosevelt claimed his fellow socialites "laughed at me, and told me that politics were 'low'; that the organizations were not controlled by 'gentlemen'; that I would find them run by saloon-keepers, horse-car conductors, and the like," adding that they "would be rough and brutal and unpleasant to deal with." Nevertheless, he sought out the local Republican Association, which "held its meetings in Morton Hall, a large, barn-like room over a saloon."[79]

There he befriended Joe Murray: an Irish-immigrant Civil War veteran who had "long performed the usual gang work for the local Democratic leader." Once spurned by Tammany Hall, Murray flipped to the Republicans out of spite. The trustworthy Murray, along with his good-humored associate Jake Hess, helped Roosevelt campaign as state alderman in New York's Twenty-First District against the political machines.

"At first they thought they would take me on a personal canvass through the saloons along Sixth Avenue." Roosevelt later explained:

> The canvass, however, did not last beyond the first saloon. I was introduced with proper solemnity to the saloon-keeper—a very important personage, for this was before the days when saloon-keepers became merely the mortgaged chattels of the brewers—and he began to cross-examine me, a little too much in the tone of one who was dealing with a suppliant for his favor. He said he expected that I would of course treat the liquor business fairly; to which I answered, none too cordially, that I hoped I should treat all interests fairly. He then said that he regarded the licenses as too high; to which I responded that I believed they were really not high enough, and that I should try to have them made higher. The conversation threatened to become stormy. Messrs. Murray and Hess, on some hastily improvised plea, took me out into the street, and then Joe explained to me that it was not worth my while staying in Sixth Avenue any longer, that I had better go right back to Fifth Avenue and attend to my friends there, and that he would look after my interests on Sixth Avenue. I was triumphantly elected.[80]

This, then, was how Theodore Roosevelt described his baptism into politics. He could battle for economic justice and clean governance publicly, while Murray and Hess finessed the traditional big-city liquor machine. He was reelected to the State Assembly in Albany by landslide margins from 1882 through 1884, gaining a reputation as a power player in the most populous and important state in the union.

When socialist Henry George chose to mount a third-party campaign for mayor of New York City in 1886, his big-ticket opponent was none other than the Republican Teddy Roosevelt. When a delegation of liquor men asked his position on enforcing the liquor regulations, George replied he, like Roosevelt, "would enforce the law without fear and without favor." With both the socialist and Republican candidates taking steadfast, principled positions, the liquor machine then threw the enormous clout of the distillers, saloons, their gangs, and even policemen on the take behind the Democrat, Abram Hewett.[81] In the end, the city's populist, progressive vote was split between George (68,110) and Roosevelt (60,435). With 90,552 votes, the mayorship of the sprawling, immigrant metropolis went to Tammany Hall's handpicked anti-immigrant, nativist candidate, Abram Hewitt.[82]

The machine wins again.

Smarting from his third-place finish, Roosevelt retired to his ranch in North Dakota. He penned articles on frontier life and big-game hunting, as well as a scathing exposé titled "Machine Politics in New York City" (1886), which echoed almost verbatim Henry George's indictments of the roots of political corruption in the liquor trade. Going back at least to the days of Captain Rynders (Chapter 12), "the liquor-saloons [had] become the social headquarters of the little knots or cliques of men who take most interest in local political affairs; and by an easy transition they become the political headquarters when the time for preparing for the elections arrives; and, of course, the good-will of the owners of the places is thereby propitiated,—an important point with men striving to control every vote possible."[83] Little wonder that 633 of the 1,007 nominating conventions and primaries for candidates of all parties took place in New York saloons.

It wasn't that these ward bosses were universally bad men, but the qualities that made for a successful machine politician or boss were the opposite of those that made for an honest public servant. The only way to beat the machine, Roosevelt said, was through a populist "uprising" of decent people—from houses of worship, colleges, and factory floors—willing to organize and defy the machine bosses. This was progressivism.

In 1894, New York Republicans finally wrested political control from the Tammany Democrats and coaxed Roosevelt to take the position of commissioner of the city's notoriously corrupt police force. Conversations with muckraking journalists Lincoln Steffens and Jacob Riis convinced TR to take on "the tap-root" of corruption in the police force: the liquor men, who comprised more than half of the Tammany Hall leaders.[84] "The saloon-keepers are always hand-in-glove with the professional politicians, and occupy towards them a position such as is not held by any other class of men," Roosevelt wrote in 1895. "The influence they wield in local politics has always been very great; and until we took office no man ever dared seriously to threaten them for their flagrant violation of the laws. Their power was a terror to all parties."[85]

The biggest fireworks, however, came over enforcing New York's so-called "blue laws." Conventional prohibition histories point to such laws banning liquor sales on Sundays as evidence of Bible-thumping prohibitionists' puritanical quest to keep the Sabbath holy. But—as Commissioner Roosevelt pointed out in *McClure's Magazine*—New York State's Sunday-closing law was passed in 1892, when both the statehouse and governor's mansion were stacked with *pro*-liquor-machine Tammany Democrats.[86]

Wait. What's going on here?

Temperance evangelism wasn't to blame, TR explained, but underworld corruption. Powerful saloon-keepers who had the politicians and the police both on the bankroll sold liquor on Sundays in open defiance of the law. Those struggling, small-time barkeeps who couldn't afford the protection racket would be harassed, fined, and prosecuted mercilessly until they either played ball or went bankrupt. This corruption was so brazen, pro-liquor periodicals even bragged about swapping blackmail for political support. Everything was out in the open.[87]

"Incredible though it seems," Police Commissioner Roosevelt claimed,

> it is a fact within my own knowledge, that when a saloon-keeper respected the law, the police department as well as the police magistrates deliberately strove to persuade him to violate it; they wished to have him in their power. Of course the result was that the officers of the law and the saloon-keepers became inextricably tangled in a network of crime and connivance at crime. The most powerful saloon-keepers controlled the politicians and the police, while the latter in turn terrorized and blackmailed all the other saloon-keepers. The decent and honest men among the saloon-keepers were those who suffered most. . . . The whole system thus put a premium on blackmail and corruption among the police, and a premium on law-breaking among the saloon-keepers.[88]

What drew the liquor men's ire was not that Roosevelt vowed to enforce the Sunday-closing laws, but that he vowed to enforce them *impartially* and universally. "As honorable men, faithful to our oaths of office, we could take no other action," Roosevelt explained. The law was clear; their duty as law enforcers was clear. And so they did—arresting first "the owner of the big corner saloon, the man whose political influence had heretofore allowed him to disregard the law, before we turned our attention to his smaller brother."

Of course, the politicians howled. So did the press, tarring Roosevelt a prude for enforcing obsolete blue laws. Roosevelt responded, "I was only enforcing honestly a law that had hitherto been enforced dishonestly." And that was the crux of the matter.

During his tenure as police chief, arrests on Sunday were halved, and tranquility settled over the tenements. Even the Liquor Dealers' Association admitted that some nine-tenths of their members had been bankrupted by simply enforcing the existing laws. "The police force became an army of heroes," the muckraking Danish American journalist Jacob Riis wrote, at least "for a season."[89]

"The other day there was a great parade of the liquor men here," Theodore wrote to his sister Anna in 1895. "They asked me to review it, in a spirit of irony; but I accepted and rather non-plussed them by doing so."[90] The saloon-keepers' parade drew some 150,000 attendees, and as more than 30,000 marchers paraded by with

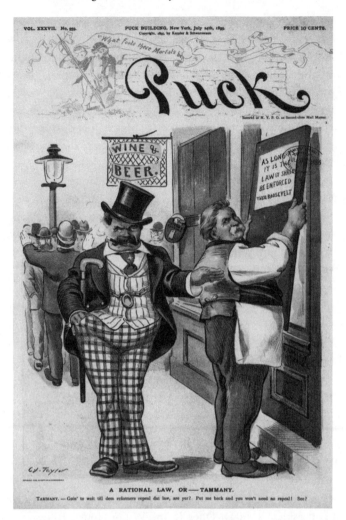

Figure 14.2 A saloon-keeper boards up his shop in accordance with Sunday-closing laws. The board reads, "As long as it is the law it shall be enforced, Theo. Roosevelt." The Tammany Hall politician implies a corrupt alternative with the caption: "Tammany— Goin' to wait till dem reformers repeal dat law, are yer? Put me back and you won't need to repeal! See?" Charles Jay Taylor, "A Rational Law, Or—Tammany," *Puck,* magazine cover, vol. XXXVII, no. 959, July 24, 1895.
Source: Library of Congress Prints and Photographs Division.

anti-Roosevelt banners, their object of derision smiled, waved, and "laughed louder than any one else" from atop the reviewing stand.[91]

But when TR left New York to become assistant secretary of the navy in 1897, the city's liquor situation snapped back to corrupt normalcy. "This was partly because public sentiment was not really with us," Roosevelt later wrote. "The people who had demanded honesty, but who did not like to pay for it by the loss of illegal pleasure, joined the openly dishonest in attacking us."

Plus, they'd found loopholes in the law. One corrupt magistrate noted the law permitted taking alcohol with meals and declared that seventeen beers and one pretzel constituted a meal. Machine politics wins again: saloons reopened in defiance of the law, "and the yellow press gleefully announced that my 'tyranny' had been curbed," Roosevelt wrote. "But my prime object, that of stopping blackmail, was largely attained."[92] And that—not enforcing arbitrary moral codes—was the entire point.

Of course, corrupt liquor-machine politics wasn't limited to New York City. Virtually every city across the country had its own Tammany equivalent. As progressive journalist Lincoln Steffens pointed out, the quickest way to disrupt any municipal government meeting was to do what some huckster in St. Louis did: tip a kid to rush into a closed government session and call out, "Hey mister! Your saloon is on fire!" Within moments, a quorum of the House of Delegates had grabbed their jackets and run for the doors.[93]

Still, it was in New York City where Roosevelt's progressivism was born. Though he identified as a Republican, his politics drew heavily from the socialism of Henry George and Walter Rauschenbusch. "It is ignoble to go on heaping up money," claimed Police Commissioner Roosevelt. "I would preach the doctrine of work to all, and to the men of wealth the doctrine of unremunerative work" in service to the community. So struck by Roosevelt's commitment, Rauschenbusch would frequently quote him as an example of the duty of Christian public service, worthy of emulation.[94]

Despite their partisan differences, the Republican Roosevelt and the Christian socialist Rauschenbusch long maintained a mutual admiration, even through Roosevelt's meteoric rise from secretary of the navy (1897) and Rough Rider in Cuba (1898) to the vice presidency (1900), and ultimately succeeding the slain McKinley as president (1901). Once in the White House, Roosevelt consulted Rauschenbusch over his progressive policy proposals, which largely met with the great evangelical's approval.

In one such meeting, Rauschenbusch told Roosevelt that the coming of American socialism was well nigh inevitable.

"Not so long as I am President," thundered Roosevelt. "For I will sail the ship of state alongside the ship of socialism and I will take over everything that is good in socialism and leave the bad. What will socialism do then?"

"I suppose the ship of socialism will sink," Rauschenbusch replied with his trademark humility, "but that is no matter if you really save her valuable cargo." Both men smiled.[95]

As for the liquor question, both likewise agreed on the urgency of reining in the political power and the economic predations of the liquor traffic. "When the liquor men are allowed to do as they wish, they are sure to debauch, not only the body social, but the body politic also," Roosevelt wrote during his tenure as police commissioner. He concluded, ominously, "If the American people do not control it, it will control them."[96]

15

Prohibition against American Imperialism

Yasnaya Polyana, Government of Tula, Russian Empire: Thursday, December 3, 1903

The southbound mail train from Moscow crept slowly along the tracks. A blizzard in the heart of Russia was not something to be trifled with. It was 1 a.m. before the engine wearily pulled into the sleepy provincial town of Tula.

Collars upturned against the wind, four travelers tumbled out. With no porters around, they dragged their steamer trunks to the only hotel still open, their tracks quickly drifting over behind them. The proprietor likely didn't recognize the clean-shaven foreigner in the fur *ushanka* hat as one of the most influential global politicians of the era. The American signed the hotel registry not in Russian, but in English: William Jennings Bryan.[1]

He went by many other names as well: "The Boy Orator of the Platte," for the loquaciousness that made the Nebraska Democrat—at thirty-six years old in 1896—the youngest-ever big-party nominee for president; "The Silver Knight of the West," for championing silver coinage to alleviate the financial suffering of hard-working western farmers; and "The Great Commoner," for standing up for the rights and dignity of the downtrodden everyman against big-business oppression. His passion, eloquence, and populism remade the Democratic Party from the party of moneyed privilege into defenders of America's working class, reshaping the American political landscape in the process.

But in 1903 Bryan was still smarting from electoral defeat to Republican William McKinley, not once but twice: both in 1896 and 1900. Understandably, he took a step away from American politics and embarked upon a series of overseas explorations and speaking tours. In Germany, he studied progressive policies such as the public ownership of utilities. In Sweden, he scrutinized the Gothenburg system of liquor control (Chapter 3), which the temperate Bryan admitted had led to a "large decrease" in alcoholism.[2] He met with British prime minister Arthur Balfour in London, Pope Pius X in Rome, and Tsar Nicholas II in St. Petersburg. But the meeting he'd treasured most—that had sent him halfway around the globe from the snowy, windswept flatlands of Nebraska to the snowy, windswept flatlands of Tula—was with Russia's great writer, philosopher, pacifist, and apostle of temperance, Leo Tolstoy.[3]

Despite differences of language and distance, the two men had already developed a mutual admiration. For Bryan—a Presbyterian who wore the progressive social gospel of Walter Rauschenbusch (Chapter 14) on his sleeve—Tolstoy was second only to the Bible in inspiring his condemnations of capitalist exploitation and militarism.[4] As early as 1899 Tolstoy had praised Bryan's denunciation of America's "imperialist maniacism" in both Cuba and the Philippines following the Spanish-American War.[5] Bryan reciprocated by publishing Tolstoy's broadsides in the very first issue of his popular weekly newspaper *The Commoner*: "You Americans . . . preach liberty and peace, and yet you go out to conquer through war."[6] If Tolstoy—in far-off Russia—could see that exploitative commercialism was the heart of imperialism, surely so too could Bryan's American readers.

So, even despite the lousy weather, lousy transportation, lousy amenities, and lousy rest, Bryan was downright giddy to complete the pilgrimage to Tolstoy—just as George Kennan (Chapter 2), Tomáš Masaryk (Chapter 4), and many others had done before him. At daybreak, Bryan, his fourteen-year-old son William Jr., their interpreter, and a secretary clamored aboard a rickety landau for the precarious fifteen-verst ride through drift-covered roads "not fit for wheel nor sleigh" to the great writer's Yasnaya Polyana estate.[7]

Tolstoy was used to hosting guests enraptured more by his fame than his philosophy. But Bryan was no celebrity seeker. Rather than a tepid, routine interview, together the two quickly delved deeply into their shared beliefs about universal Christian love, temperance, the corrupting influence of liquor money and profits, the dignity of labor, and simple agrarian farmwork as the cradle of virtue. As if to cement their bond as kindred spirits, much of their discussion took place outside on the farm: over chores, riding horseback, even decorating Christmas trees for the peasant children on the estate. The Nebraskan was happy to lend a hand, though Tolstoy's daughters giggled at the awkward American's expensive, city-cut, double-breasted fur coat, held back with a humble peasant's plain leather belt.[8]

Instead of some narrow politician, Tolstoy found Bryan to be "a thoughtful, deeply religious man . . . animated by very lofty aspirations." Tolstoy later recounted his discussions about nonviolent resistance with "the remarkably intelligent and progressive American, W.J. Bryan" in a preface he was writing about Tolstoy's own spiritual influence, pacifist abolitionist William Lloyd Garrison (Chapter 11).[9]

Still, Tolstoy thought it odd for a man of such spiritual caliber to "give his heart to political activity," since the state itself was the primary instrument of violence and oppression. Bryan replied that Tolstoy had only ever lived under the tsar's autocratic rule. Perhaps if he lived in a democracy—where nonaristocrats could capture state power to make policies on behalf of the commonwealth—he might relax his anti-statism.[10]

Figure 15.1 William Jennings Bryan (right) visits Leo Tolstoy at his Yasnaya Polyana estate, December 5, 1903 (Left to right: Russian translator T. Suslov, William Jennings Bryan Jr., Leo Tolstoy, and William Jennings Bryan).
Source: Photo by A. L. Tolstoy. Published in: William Jennings Bryan, Under Other Flags: Travels, Lectures, Speeches (Lincoln, NE: Woodruff-Collins Printing Co., 1904).

Perhaps.

However, time was of the essence. Thanks to a scheduling snafu, if Bryan hoped to make it back to St. Petersburg for his planned second audience with Tsar Nicholas, they would have to leave at noon.

No matter. The Great Commoner cancelled on the all-powerful emperor in order to more deeply explore spiritual and political questions with his most humble inspiration.

After lunch, they rode horses, though the seventy-six-year-old Tolstoy promised to keep it short, so as not to fatigue his American guest. When Bryan's horse slipped on the ice, they thought it best to just walk them through the snow-filled forests as they talked. The Boy Orator's anecdotes elicited chuckles and belly laughs from Tolstoy. They joked, debated, and pontificated nearly uninterrupted for twelve straight hours.

It was "the most wonderful day of my life," Bryan proclaimed.

Around 10 p.m., Bryan and his son finally left Yasnaya Polyana to catch a midnight train back to Moscow. Bryan joyously vowed to return one day along with his wife, "even if our path is twice as long."[11] But he never did.

"I wish with all my heart success in your endeavor to destroy the trusts and to help the working people to enjoy the whole fruits of their toil," Tolstoy bid Bryan farewell from Russia, "but I think that this is not the most important thing of your life. The most important thing is to know the will of God, concerning one's life, i.e. to know what He wishes us to do and to fulfill it. I think that you are doing it and this is the thing in which I wish to you the greatest success."[12]

The visit was an epiphany for Bryan. "Until then, he had esteemed Tolstoy, now he became a disciple," claimed one historian. He didn't share Tolstoy's anti-statist anarchism or his absolute pacifism (Bryan subsequently supported American involvement in World War I and armed interventions in the Caribbean), but he'd become a dyed-in-the-wool Tolstoyan: "He revered Tolstoy as the living incarnation of the doctrine of love and the purest example of man's potential to achieve universal brotherhood, next only to Jesus."[13] Antitrust, antimilitarism, anti-saloon: Bryan biographer Michael Kazin even quipped that Tolstoy could have drafted the Democratic Party's progressive platform.[14]

Bryan used his unique position to spread Tolstoy's message to an entire generation of Americans: he filled the pages of *The Commoner* with Tolstoy's teachings. His famed lectures dripped with Tolstoyanism peans to love, peace, and nonresistance to evil.[15] Bryan kept his treasured photograph with Tolstoy in his living room; Tolstoy kept the same photo in his library.[16]

When Bryan made his triumphant return to electoral politics by winning the Democratic nomination for the 1908 presidential election, he had Tolstoy in his corner. "I can sincerely say that I wish Mr. Bryan success in his candidature to the Presidency of the United States," Tolstoy wrote.

> From my own standpoint, repudiating as it does all coercive Government, I naturally cannot acquiesce with the position of President of the Republic; but since such functions still exist, it is obviously best that they should be occupied by individuals worthy of confidence.
>
> Mr. Bryan I greatly respect and sympathise with, and know that the basis of his activity is kindred to mine in his sympathy with the interests of the working masses, his antimilitarism and his recognition of the fallacies produced by capitalism.
>
> I do not know, but hope Mr. Bryan will stand for land reform according to the Single Tax system of Henry George [Chapter 14], which I regard as being at the present time, of most insistent necessity, and which every progressive reformer should place to the fore.[17]

But 1908 wasn't 1900 or 1896. Incumbent Republican president Theodore Roosevelt had become wildly popular by embracing many of Bryan's progressive reforms: trust-busting, workman's compensation, and shorter working hours.[18]

Bryan and the Democrats painted the Republicans—Roosevelt and his anointed successor, Secretary of War and former colonial governor of the Philippines, William Howard Taft—as the party of militarism and imperialism, opposed to Bryan's Jeffersonian self-determination and Tolstoyan pacifism. On issues of labor, trusts, corruption, electoral reform and campaign finance, Republicans were at best halfhearted in their dedication to populist reform. "I'm not advocating anything revolutionary," Roosevelt once explained. "I am advocating action to prevent anything revolutionary."[19]

Still, it wasn't enough. Bryan fell to the Republicans for a third time.

While remaining a stalwart within the Democratic Party, after his 1908 defeat, Bryan felt unencumbered by the necessity for political compromise, instead championing a full-throated Tolstoyan progressivism. No more compromises with the saloons that were multiplying across the land, and the corrupt machine politics that came with them. When brewers and liquor men moved to take over Nebraska's Democratic Party in 1909, Bryan finally had had enough—he completely endorsed full prohibition. "If I have any apologies to offer, I shall not offer them to the liquor interests for speaking now," Bryan proclaimed to disgruntled Nebraska Democrats. "I shall offer them to the fathers and mothers of this state for not speaking sooner."[20] The following year, he came out for women's right to vote, one of the first men in his party to do so.

The entire range of reforms: "taxation, trust regulation, labor, the monetary system, peace and disarmament, temperance, anti-imperialism, woman's suffrage," Bryan listed, "these questions are before us." True to his social gospel roots, he added, "they must be settled, and church members must take their part in the settlement."[21]

Yet it was this progressive morality that most starkly differentiated Bryan's progressivism from that of his Republican rivals, perhaps most vividly illustrated by Roosevelt's 1909 attack against the ailing Tolstoy in his final year of life.

From his postelection African hunting safari (where he sided with socialist Emile Vandervelde against Belgium's colonial brutality in the Congo, while still defending American colonial atrocities in the Philippines), Roosevelt blasted Tolstoy's abstemious asceticism as "foolish," "immoral," and "revolting" evidence of the "wickedness" of a "mystical zealot," who "has in him certain dreadful qualities of the moral pervert." Imagine calling Jesus Christ a moral pervert.

"This attack upon the dying Tolstoy is truly Rooseveltian, both in ego and object," *The Commoner* replied. "Over the shoulder of this blameless and consecrated saint, whose sands of life are running fast, the ex-president strikes as one mightily miffed, at the candidate of the democracy in the last national election." Certainly, no one should be taking moral cues from America's "big stick" militarist. Unlike "the killer and the jingoist" Roosevelt, who at that moment was gleefully having African big game herded in front of his blunderbuss for slaughter, Bryan wrote, "Tolstoy never had the blood-thirst and was not a man glorifying in more Dreadnaughts, for he did not like the man-killing business."[22]

When death finally claimed Tolstoy in 1910, Bryan eulogized Russia's great pacifist and great prohibitionist: "He has been called the apostle of love, and no one since the Apostle Paul has preached it more persistently or practiced it more consistently." He concluded, "The night is darker because his light has gone out."[23]

America's Imperial Impulse

The chapter on American imperialism is "the worst chapter in almost any book," declared James A. Field Jr. in the flagship *American Historical Review* in 1978. But not for the conquest, occupation, and suppression of foreign lands; the blood-thirsty "jingoist" ultranationalism and white supremacy; the litany of torture and war crimes; or the intellectual contortions necessary to justify such subordination with America's liberal founding traditions. Field was more dismayed with the tendency of historians to chalk up American militarism and imperialism to insatiable capitalists, a supercharged military, and homegrown racism.

But such sweeping, hindsight-driven narratives discount change and historically contingent events.[24] If airport security had stopped the terrorists with their box-cutters on September 11, 2001, would the United States have invaded Afghanistan? Doubtful. Similarly: had the gunpowder not detonated a massive explosion on board the USS *Maine*, moored in Havana harbor in 1898, would the United States have waged war on Spain? Sometimes contingent events lead to consequences and changes in popular attitudes that could hardly have been foreseen.[25]

Still, the United States has always had a Jekyll-and-Hyde relationship to empires and imperialism. On the one hand, the United States began as thirteen colonies rebelling against British imperial domination. On the other, the entire territory of the United States was seized from the original Native American inhabitants, and US wealth built in part on the unpaid labor of generations of African slaves.[26] So perhaps America's imperial impulse in the 1890s—embracing territorial conquest from Cuba and the Caribbean to the Philippines in the Pacific—is only an aberration to our national self-image and the narratives we like to tell ourselves, rather than to our national history *per se*.

At first blush, imperialism may seem like a strange detour for a book about alcohol prohibitionism. But a curious commonality is just how frequently the most outspoken prohibitionists were also the most vocal opponents of colonial empires and militarism. Our global journey began with temperance protests in Russia, against a militarized autocracy that quite literally was forcing vodka down peasants' throats. Prohibitionist Leo Tolstoy rebelled against such exploitation. So did prohibitionist Vladimir Lenin, who most clearly articulated that imperialism was the "highest stage of capitalism," in which lust for profit drives capitalist states to seek out new resources, markets—and indeed people—to exploit (Chapter 2).[27]

Hjalmar Branting won his Nobel Peace Prize for fighting for Norwegian self-determination against his own, native Sweden, and Emile Vandervelde probably should have won one for standing up for the native Congolese against the atrocities of his own Belgian king, Leopold II (Chapter 3). Temperate Tomáš Masaryk fought for Czechoslovak independence from the Austro-Hungarian Empire (Chapter 4). Daniel O'Connell fought British alco-imperialism for national self-determination in Ireland, just as King Khama did in Bechuanaland, Mahatma Gandhi did in India, and Kemal Atatürk did in Turkey (Chapters 5–8). Even in the United States, temperance-minded Quakers, abolitionists, and suffragists all fought the same fundamental foe: man's exploitation by man.

The pursuit of justice, human dignity, and communal self-determination against predatory capitalism was what wove together the progressive ethos of not only prohibitionism, abolitionism, and suffragism, but anti-imperialism and antimilitarism as well. "We are all bound up together in one great bundle of humanity," as Francis Ellen Watkins Harper said (Chapter 13), "and society cannot trample on the weakest and feeblest of its members without receiving the curse in its own soul."[28]

The reformers trained their fire on the American Army canteens, where the predations of militarism and capitalism met. With a wink and a nod from the state, the US Army ran a bustling liquor trade, as corrupt and exploitative as any civilian saloon. Lured by the siren's song of profits, commanding officers would exploit the young (largely underage) soldiers in their charge to drink their fill, even at the expense of military readiness. Not only would the rapid wartime expansion of the military indoctrinate an entire generation of young men into the army drinking culture, American overseas imperialism brought canteen debauchery everywhere with them. Little wonder, then, that America's age of empire was marked by a strident grassroots anti-canteen movement to protect both soldiers and civilians alike from liquor-machine predations.

America's "worst chapter" of imperialism usually begins with the explosion on board the USS *Maine* in Havana harbor in 1898. Our thumbnail sketch of the resulting Spanish-American War is then of a relatively quick and painless encounter ending with Teddy Roosevelt leading his volunteer Rough Riders up San Juan Hill to defeat the Spanish Empire. In reality, it was only quick and painless because the United States did what it would do in World Wars I and II: ride in like the cavalry at the very end to tip the scales in someone else's war. The once-mighty Spanish Empire had been fighting insurgencies and nationalist rebellions in Cuba, the Philippines, and Puerto Rico for decades, sapping their economic and military resources. The Philippine Revolution against Spain had been raging since 1896; Cuba's War of Independence was already in its third year when the United States finally joined in.

Both in Cuba and the Philippines, nationalist fighters cheered the arrival of the Americans—even coordinated their military activities with them—believing that independence was finally at hand. But elation turned to betrayal as peace was brokered between Spain and the United States alone, with no Cuban, Puerto Rican, or Filipino representatives present. Ultimately, the United States occupied Cuba and purchased the Philippines from Spain for twenty million dollars. Guam and Puerto Rico were thrown in for free. For these islands and their millions of inhabitants, all that happened in 1898 was the replacement of their Spanish imperial overlords for American imperial overlords. Their struggles for independence would continue, but now against the United States.[29]

The United States suddenly had an overseas empire dropped in its lap, with very little idea of what to do with it. The nation was already contorting itself—trying to square its commitment to lofty, republican principles of freedom and equality against institutionalized structures of white supremacy, in which African Americans were disenfranchised by Jim Crow laws and Native Americans were herded onto ever-smaller reservations. Add to that now the formal trappings of empire overseas.[30]

The dilemma is succinctly summarized by two huge coffee-table books of that time handed down to me from my great-grandparents: *Our Islands and Their People* (1899). It was clear that the islands were "ours," but not necessarily the people who lived on them. Would they be citizens or subjects?[31] In 1901—five years after upholding "separate but equal" Jim Crow institutions—the Supreme Court's "Insular Cases" decision delineated that constitutional rights and protections accrued to citizens of the states, whereas unincorporated territories (like the ever-shrinking Indian Country) were the remit of the federal government. Congress, of course, could "incorporate" territories and make them states, as they would later with Alaska and Hawai'i. Statehood would be the only means of making America's imperial subjects into rights-bearing citizens.[32]

Even as the Rough Riders were charging up San Juan Hill in 1898, anti-imperialists in Congress preemptively forbade the annexation of Cuba. But what about the eight million people in the Philippines, Puerto Rico, and Guam? That roughly equaled the entire African American population of the United States. As Republican Speaker of the House of Representatives Thomas Brackett Reed quipped, "I s'posed we had niggers enough in this country without buyin' any more of 'em; and here we are buyin' ten million of 'em at two dollars a head, and yaller-bellyed niggers at that."[33]

Certainly there were white supremacist reasons for isolationism, too.

President William McKinley was similarly troubled, until one night his prayers to "Almighty God for light and guidance" were answered: returning them to Spain or other European empires would be "cowardly and dishonorable"; independence was off the table as "they were unfit for self-government." Ultimately, "there was nothing left for us to do but take them all and to educate the Filipinos, and uplift and Christianize them, and by God's grace do the very best we could by them," in

a old-world, colonial, white-man's-burden process he called "benevolent assimilation."[34] It was anything but.

In the spring of 1898, US naval commander George Dewey gave full assurances
to Filipino rebel leader Emilio Aguinaldo that the United States would recognize the independence of the Philippines... *if* Aguinaldo's revolutionaries helped
America defeat the Spanish.[35] Aguinaldo agreed, and in August besieged the capital of Manila alongside the US Army, forcing Spain's surrender. However, President
McKinley declared there would be "no joint occupation with the insurgents," and
that the Filipinos "must recognize the military occupation and authority of the
United States."[36] What followed was an uneasy standoff in which the United States
ruled the waves and occupied Manila, but Aguinaldo's forces effectively controlled
the rest of the archipelago.

The American forces took all too quickly to the role of imperial occupiers, reflecting the worst colonial prejudices and practices found from the Belgians
(Chapter 3) to the Brits (Chapters 5–9), and much of it revolved around the liquor
trade. Rumors of American scandals and atrocities attracted the future "Pussyfoot,"
William E. Johnson. Having exposed the corruption of the South Carolina dispensary and muckraked the dives of the Northeast (Chapter 14), in 1899 Johnson
sensed a story and headed for the Philippines.

"When Manila was taken, there was one small brewery and two saloons in the
Philippine Islands. Yet even before Manila was actually occupied, a shipload of
American liquor came into the harbor, with a man wearing an American uniform
directing operations as a 'volunteer aide,'" wrote Johnson. "When the shipload
safely landed, he took off the uniform and proceeded to open saloons everywhere.
Bedlam resulted. The Filipinos were being 'civilized' with a vengeance."[37]

This wasn't just some "dry" journalist's assessment: the former American consul
in Manila—and frequent presidential adviser—the Honorable Ogden E. Edwards,
testified that "drunkenness was practically unknown among the natives or Spaniards"
during his thirty-six years in the Philippines. Both the alcohol and tobacco trades
had been monopolized and controlled by the Spanish state.[38] "The Spanish cafés
sold mostly Spanish wines, and men would sit an hour chatting over a glass or two
of wine, and smoking in front or in them, with never a sign of intoxication. Nothing
like the American saloon was ever known in Manila while I lived there."[39]

The juxtaposition between Spanish and American military occupation was stark.
"The immense amount of drunkenness and rough horse-play were a surprise to the
Filipinos after what they had seen of Spanish soldiers, who, although poor and badly
clad, were never addicted to drunkenness and always bore themselves with characteristic Castilian dignity and good breeding," reported one journalist. The haughty
and racist attitudes toward the locals bred contempt. Furthermore, the "indiscrimi-
nate opening of 'saloons' contributed vastly to increase this drunkenness and crime,
especially as they were generally kept by adventurers and unscrupulous rascals. In
fact, so given over was Manila to the 'grab-as-can' element, that in a very short time

all the scum of the earth infesting every port in the East between Port Said and Shanghai hurried off to Manila to ply their nefarious trades,—people who would never have dared to approach within sight of Manila under Spanish rule, which kept all these pimps, bawds, Bagdad Jews and nauseating scum at a respectable distance."[40]

Such orientalizing anti-Semitism aside, so many reports of the drunken scandals arose that the military intimidated journalists, censoring and impounding their reports, lest they undercut the jingoistic patriotism and support for war back home. They were only partly successful. In a widely reprinted letter home from his travels in the Philippines, John J. Valentine—the first president of Wells Fargo & Co.—described Manila's main drag, the Escolta: "facetiously referred to as the 'Yankee beer chute,' [it] resembles somewhat a midway, and is all but literally lined with saloons. I counted four hundred in a little over a mile. These are mostly kept by Americans. The largest cafe, known as the Alhambra, has frequently closed its bar at four in the afternoon because its stock of liquor was exhausted."[41]

Drunken American soldiers roamed the streets with absolute impunity, con-temptuously calling the locals "yuyu," "nigger," or worse. They looted homes and

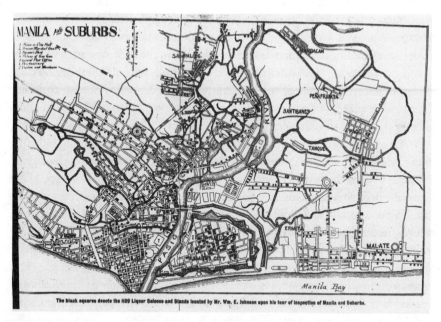

Figure 15.2 Manila and suburbs map. "The black squares denote the 1109 Liquor Sellers and Stands located by Mr. Wm. E. Johnson upon his tour of Inspection of Manila and Suburbs." The Escolta, or "Yankee Beer Chute," is visible as the dense concentration of saloons to the left of the Pasig River, just above the bridge.

Source: Endpiece map in: Henry Hooker Van Meter, *The Truth about the Philippines: From Official Records and Authentic Sources* (Chicago: Liberty League, 1900).

raped Filipino women on the streets in broad daylight. Any man who tried to stop them would be beaten or shot. The impression was even made on Filipino children, who would play "American" by staggering around the neighborhood as if drunk, before "passing out" face down on the ground.[42]

"Six drunken American soldiers entered the home of a respectable native on Calle Cervantes. They proceeded to terrorize the occupants, broke open trunks and helped themselves to whatever was wanted," began one published report from July 29, 1899. Even more horrific than the details is the fact that it was representative of American occupation, rather than an outlier. The drunken Americans then entered the house of one Rufino Sanches, "forcing their way at the point of a revolver. After helping themselves to whatever they wished, two of the reformers held the struggling husband by force while the others ravished the screaming wife before his eyes. When the aged mother of the woman began to plead for mercy, her pleadings were silenced by one of the soldiers who knocked her down with the butt of his revolver." The children fled the house in terror. When the police arrived, they arrested the one soldier who was passed out drunk on the floor, apprehending a few other suspects nearby in a similar state. "It is one of the most realistic lessons of 'benevolent assimilation' that the natives of this neighborhood have yet had."[43]

Bearing witness to drunken looting, gang-rapes, and the "orgies of the newcomers, the incessant street brawls" resulting from the twenty-fold increase in saloons, renowned authority of the Philippines John Foreman noted they "were hardly calculated to arouse in the natives admiration for their new masters." Even among avowed non-prohibitionists, experts universally agreed that the excesses of the liquor traffic—unbridled, unregulated, and untaxed—were not only exploiting the native Filipinos, but undercutting the entire imperial presence.[44] "If old Glory must fly over these drinking dens," one observer noted, "let her fly at half mast."[45]

The most galling thing for progressives worried about the corrupting influence of big business on the government was that the entire liquor operation was given political cover by the American authorities, including the military governor, Major General Elwell Stephen Otis (1898–1900), and then governor-general—and future US president—William Howard Taft (1901–1903). According to Otis's own records, in the first ten months of the occupation, he had licensed 158 saloons, 77 wholesale liquor dealers, 613 wine rooms, 15 distilleries, and 1 brewery.[46] Jingoistic imperialists defended the liquor flood as necessary to pay the enormous costs of military occupation. However, since the Philippines were neither an American state nor territory, "American liquors exported, even to our own Philippine Islands, escape all taxation," according to the Internal Revenue Bureau, severing any links between alcohol revenues and military expenditures. American imperialism was an absolute boon to the liquor trade: a massive new market of millions of customers to addict and debauch, virtually untaxed and unregulated, with the might of the American military to provide support and cover. It was almost too good to be true.[47]

Added to the 1,109 drink outlets that the future Pussyfoot Johnson mapped out in Manila alone, there were five hundred to six hundred opium dens. Each one had gambling rooms in the rear, and "slave girls upstairs whom they rent for immoral purposes," often with dozens of spectators looking on, as Johnson wrote. "These dens of infamy, where girls are held as slaves for legalized rape, are licensed by the American military tyranny as saloons along with the brothels."[48]

Ah yes, the brothels: previously outlawed by the Spanish, prostitution (and the accompanying venereal diseases) was happily introduced by the American occupiers. Based on police reports and interviews with locals, Johnson estimated some two hundred licensed brothels in Manila, including "about 600 prostitutes who are under the direct control of the military authorities, who represent American Christian civilization here."[49] Although far more American lives would be lost to tropical and venereal diseases in the Philippines than to combat, the US military reasoned that regulating saloons and brothels would ensure greater quality control, prevent servicemen from falling prey to unscrupulous natives, or going AWOL if their drinking and cavorting entertainments led them off the military post.[50]

"Not a prostitute can land in Manila without the express permission of the United States military authorities," wrote Johnson. He added, "Women of this class who pay a 'tip' of $50 to the custom house officers find no difficulty in getting ashore." The military corruption didn't stop at the shoreline. The military's Department of Municipal Inspection (or "Department of Prostitution," as it was locally known) required every call girl to pay four pesos every week for the pleasure of medical examinations at the hands of military physicians. "Moreover, she is obliged to take out a wine and beer license at a cost of one hundred pesos every six months."[51]

It wasn't just that the American military tolerated the liquor interests, they *actively supported* them, in the form of the army canteen. Beyond the saloons, brothels, and opium dens, Johnson chronicled some 200 military canteens in the Philippines, "about 150 of these places were saloons run by the American Commercial Company, whose manager has a 'pull' with the army officers and is given special privileges," in exchange for giving the military captains 5 percent of the take. "The Commercial Company has the advantage of shipping its goods upon United States boats and transporting them on land with United States hospital supplies by the mules and wagons of the government. At places where provisions have been scarce beer has been plenty, and the means of transportation monopolized for bringing beer."[52]

Conscientious servicemen who dared challenge this American military liquor machine faced their own uphill battles. Confronting widespread reports that "the proprietors of a number of shops and drinking places were selling to our soldiers liquors that were causing great demoralization, disease, more or less permanent mental aberrations, and in some cases death," in 1900 the army appointed Dr. Ira C. Brown—a major in the Medical Corps—as health inspector for liquor.[53] Unsurprisingly, what was being peddled as genuine bourbon or scotch whiskey often turned out to be poisonous methylated alcohol with a "mixture of candy," sugar, and artificial colors and flavors to mask the taste. A raid on one manufacturer found no distilling apparatus, but merely "a few tubs and barrels in which to mix the ingredients and from which the finished product was in a few minutes turned out for bottling."

After a series of warnings, Dr. Brown smashed the (licensed!) manufacturer's wares—which later prompted an international legal arbitration, as the proprietor was a British citizen. "Many of the native and Chinese dealers were prosecuted, convicted, and punished," recalled the commanding officer. "The only reason [the British liquor dealer] was not prosecuted and punished was that, he being a white man and a foreigner, the authorities were averse to sending him to the old Spanish jail, which was the only prison available at the time."[54]

At the end of his investigations, Dr. Brown compiled an objective and withering report that "condemned the whisky sold by a monopolistic syndicate operating with the connivance of American military authorities." Such a scathing indictment would never see the light of day, so the military buried it and bundled Dr. Brown on the next ship out of Manila. However, for three days his ship was held in harbor as typhoons ravaged the island. In that time, William Johnson blew the whole case wide open with a blistering editorial on the front page of the Manila Freedom, demanding Dr. Brown's return and the report's publication.

Not surprisingly, officials from the military censor's office swooped in and confiscated an entire print run of the Manila Freedom. According to Pussyfoot, the censors later admitted, "We just wanted to punish you for running the story on Brown's investigation. In the future, you just let this whisky business alone and we'll get along all right."[55] Business is business, to be sure; and in this case—as with colonial domination everywhere during the Age of Empire—the business of military domination went hand-in-glove with the liquor business.

If that weren't enough, by this time, the combustible tinderbox of drunkenness, debauchery, and American racist impunity in the Philippines had exploded into all-out war.

Tensions came to a head on the night of February 4, 1899, when American sentries were ordered to occupy a defensive outpost that had been disputed between US and Filipino forces. Around eight o'clock that evening, four Filipino soldiers approached, staggering drunk and unarmed.[56] Private William Walter Grayson of the First Nebraska twice called at the men to halt. One "impudently shouted 'halto' at me," Grayson recalled. "Well, I thought the best thing to do was to shoot him." Grayson killed two of the Filipinos, and Private Orville Miller shot a third. The two retreated to the American bunkhouse, where—in his words—Grayson announced, "Line up fellows, the 'niggers' are in here all through these yards."[57]

For the next six hours, the Americans unleashed a constant barrage of artillery and small-arms fire at the Filipino positions, even though it was too dark to see what they were shooting at.[58] The ensuing Battle of Manila would not only be the opening salvo in the Philippine-American War, it would also be its bloodiest. The ragtag, untrained colonials were decimated by superior American firepower. Aguinaldo re-peatedly tried to broker a ceasefire, but the Americans weren't interested. "Fighting having begun, must go on to the grim end," declared Military Governor Otis.[59]

As long-colonized subjects without their own army or experienced leadership, the Filipinos stood little chance of besting the American occupiers in conventional warfare. Aguinaldo instead ordered his men to become *insurrectos*: guerilla fighters who could ambush American positions, and then melt back into the populace. Traditionally occupying and subduing all of the Philippines' seven thousand jungle islands would prove an impossible task. Despite repeated claims of American vic-tory, the fighting and atrocities continued in the southernmost Moro Province until 1913, making the Philippine War the second-longest American war.[60] And it all began with an encounter between drunken soldiers.

"By truckling to the liquor traffic in the Philippines, our government was guilty of shedding the first blood of our Philippine war," wrote H. H. Van Meter in his *Truth about the Philippines* (1900). His explicit condemnation of American alco-imperialism continued:

> By the debauchery resultant therefrom the Filipinos were disgusted, and by the accompanying insults and injuries were rightfully indignant.
>
> The American saloon as the advance guard of American civilization, was justification for resisting American encroachments, entire.
>
> Our government has betrayed the best interests of our soldiers, the sa-cred trust of the welfare of the Filipinos, and the noblest sentiments of our country, to murderous greed, the motive power of "criminal aggression."[61]

At the time of Van Meter's writing, the worst of the insults, injuries, atrocities, and aggression had only just begun.

Guerilla warfare is a terrible thing, as it blurs the line between the military and civilian realms. The Americans tried to win hearts and minds by building roads and schools, even though Congress appropriated zero funds for anything other than military occupation.[62] So rather than the carrot, the United States used the stick, wreaking military vengeance on communities even vaguely suspected of harboring Filipino partisans. The army adopted a practice called "reconcentration": herding the "pacified" populations into camps where they could be monitored. Anything outside the camps was open season: crops and entire villages were torched, exacerbating famine; civilians were waterboarded, tortured, and killed—sometimes gleefully.[63] Ironically, it was Spain's use of reconcentration in Cuba that provoked the United States to "liberate" its colonies in the first place. It "sounds awful," confessed future governor-general William Cameron Forbes: "It works, however, admirably."[64]

The worst bloodletting came during the Balangiga Massacre, where the atrocities differed only in degree. On September 28, 1901, some five hundred disgruntled townspeople of Balangiga on the eastern island of Samar rose up and staged a coordinated machete attack on the US Ninth Infantry, hacking fifty-four American servicemen to death.[65] A horrified American public—and the newly inaugurated president Theodore Roosevelt—demanded vengeance, which was left to General Jacob Smith. As a veteran of the Wounded Knee Massacre, "Hell-Roaring Jake" was no stranger to atrocities; when it came to pacifying Samar Island, he proclaimed, "I want no prisoners. I wish you to kill and burn, the more you kill and burn the better it will please me. I want all persons killed who are capable of bearing arms in actual hostilities against the United States."

When his subordinates twice asked for clarification, they were told "to kill everyone over ten years old." And so they did: patrolmen "gunned down every native in the vicinity regardless of age or sex."[66] Smith and his officers would ultimately be court-martialed for their war crimes, but not before thousands—if not tens of thousands—of Filipino civilians had been massacred on their orders.[67] All told, between two hundred thousand and one million civilians—as many as one out of eight Filipinos—died from the war, starvation, and disease under the United States' "benevolent assimilation."[68]

"KILL EVERY ONE OVER TEN."
Criminals because they were born ten years before we took the Philippines.
—*The New York Evening Journal.*

Figure 15.3 Jacob Smith's order "Kill Every One Over Ten" became the title for this illustration on the front page of the *New York Evening Journal*, May 5, 1902, 1. The subtitle states "Criminals because they were born ten years before we took the Philippines."
Source: *New York Journal*, May 5, 1902.

War over the Canteen

The Philippine War is one of the darkest chapters in American history, which is perhaps why it is so infrequently discussed. However, the war supercharged two of the great movements of the Progressive Era—antimilitarism and prohibitionism— which coalesced around the US Army canteen: essentially military saloons run with government capital for (corrupt) private profit.[69]

Drinking has been a staple of war-fighting around the globe for centuries, but attempts to reduce military drunkenness are usually cast aside once the bullets start flying.[70] However, with the Spanish-American War, the excesses of the military post "exchange"—or the "canteen" in British colonial parlance—came under greater scrutiny. According to War Department regulations from 1885, "The post exchange will combine the features of reading and recreation rooms, a cooperative store, and a restaurant. Its primary purpose is to supply the troops at reasonable prices with the articles of ordinary use, wear, and consumption not supplied by the Government, and to afford them means of rational recreations and amusement. Its secondary purpose is, through exchange profits, to provide the means for improving the messes."[71] The sale of distilled liquors—rum, gin, brandy, and whiskey—in the armed forces was outlawed by teetotal president Rutherford B. Hayes in 1881, but beer was still freely sold in army canteens, even when those canteens were located in dry prohibition states.[72]

This set up the first confrontation over the canteen. In 1890 the Woman's Christian Temperance Union (WCTU) started a petition- and letter-writing campaign to Congress to prohibit beer in the canteens too, based on scientific and actuarial findings about its deleterious effects (Chapter 14). "At military posts and garrisons the jurisdiction of the United States is complete," proclaimed Republican senator Eugene Hale from dry Maine, who would later become an outspoken opponent of America's imperialist endeavors. "It would be a scandal if the Government should directly or indirectly engage in this traffic, especially in states where the statutes prohibit it."[73] This was not simply a moral issue or a military-discipline issue; it was also a states-rights issue.

Ultimately, Congress passed compromise legislation: that all liquors, wine, and beer would be banned from sale in those US Army canteens located in prohibition states. Still, in the cloistered world of the US military, even acts of Congress such as this were routinely ignored.[74]

The problem was that, throughout the 1890s, the army canteen looked more like a saloon than a country store, since alcohol was the most highly demanded and most profitable commodity. Since the post exchange was overseen by the post commander, brewers and distillers would prevail upon army officers to sell their booze. Their bribes and kickbacks could be quite persuasive. And since the excess profits of the post exchange were to be kept completely within the regiment—ostensibly to improve mess halls, hospitals, and other facilities—the post commander operated with minimal oversight or scrutiny.

Whether motivated by personal temperance, the need for military discipline, or just following the law, some commanders operated dry posts. Most army colonels, however, played ball with the liquor men. Some were won over by the dirty money, others by a genuine desire to improve the military post's facilities, or even to prevent soldiers from going AWOL to solicit nearby civilian saloons. Regardless of the reason, the canteen liquor traffic made US Army colonels into *de facto* saloon-keepers, with a financial stake in selling addictive and potentially poisonous liquors to their own subordinates.

Before the war, such corruption was necessarily small scale: in 1897 the United States had only 27,865 active-duty personnel, mostly lifelong soldiers in isolated encampments dotting the American West. With the outbreak of the Spanish-American War, that number increased almost tenfold to 209,714: mostly school-age recruits and volunteers in their teens and twenties.[75] Suddenly, an entire generation of young volunteers—many of whom were leaving home for the first time, and even more who'd never before had a drink—were marching off to war in far-off, tropical climes under commanders who profited in getting them drunk in the army canteens.

There wasn't just the temptation for a young private to drink, but a command to both drink alcohol *and sell it*. Since the canteen was a huge logistical operation, "our young men, who had enlisted to fight for the safety and honor of their country, were compelled, in some instances under penalty of arrest and punishment, to become saloon-keepers and bartenders, and the boys of our homes and Sunday-schools and churches were tempted, by the sanction of the United States Government, to do violence to their home training and become drunkards."[76]

It was not crazy for concerned citizens to raise alarms at the brazen hypocrisy and conflict of interest.

At the outbreak of the Spanish-American War in 1898—even before making for Manila—William "Pussyfoot" Johnson toured the dozens of army bases that ringed the Gulf Coast from Louisiana to Florida, in preparation for action in Cuba and the Caribbean.

Camp Thomas at Chickamauga, Georgia, hosted some fifty thousand troops along with fifty regimental canteens, turning some five thousand dollars per day in beer profits. The canteen for the Twelfth New York Volunteers alone had a bar seventy-five feet long and employed three bartenders, serving three hundred soldiers at a time on paydays. Post commanders at Tampa outsourced the canteen trade to a local liquor man, with half the gross receipts going to the regimental treasury. "A soldier was usually detailed to see that the rum-seller properly divided the spoils," according to reports. "Sometimes another soldier was detailed to watch the first soldier." Still, a regimental audit found no trace of the purported benefits. Oftentimes it was just the opposite: "The 7th Infantry managed to get about $200 in profits out of their canteen, but they spent over $10,000 at the canteen in order to harvest this amount."[77]

When Johnson got to Camp Coppinger, near Mobile, Alabama, the seven-thousand-odd troops hadn't been paid in two months. Soldiers protesting to headquarters were offered up to three-quarters of their pay in "beer checks" to be redeemed at the local canteen. Many of the soldiers had already bartered their army-issued hats, coats, and shoes for booze. The canteen of the Eleventh Infantry alone was two hundred feet long, employing ten bartenders, selling between 98 and 125 kegs of beer every day. The residents of Mobile—a dry town by law—were understandably incensed as drunken and disorderly soldiers spilled out of their encampments, started street brawls, accosted women, and filled the city jails.

Ten thousand troops were stationed at Lakeland, Florida—a prohibition city of only fifteen hundred residents, who protested (to no avail) that the camp's three canteens violated state law. Drunken fistfights were a daily occurrence. "Some of the troops were colored and when under the influence of canteen beer they got extremely insolent toward the whites both in the camp and in the town," noted one reporter of the racial tensions at Lakeland. "The white soldiers under similar

BEER CANTEEN OF THE ELEVENTH INFANTRY.

Run contrary to law at Mobile, Alabama. The bar was 200 feet long. Ten bartenders were employed, and receipts were as high as $600.00 per day. The photograph was made just after they had closed in order to move to another part of the Camp.

Figure 15.4 Beer canteen of the Eleventh Infantry at Camp Coppinger, Mobile, Alabama.
Source: Dunn, *Anarchism, or, Shall Law Be Nullified?*, 7.

influences exhibited great spite toward the colored troops. The result was an almost endless series of fights, with bloodshed and murder, wholly innocent citizens in no way connected with the camp or the sale of liquor there being among the victims."[78]

In one instance, a racial slur quickly erupted into an all-out street riot of three hundred stone-drunk soldiers. Shots were fired, killing a local resident bystander. One African American soldier was thrown in the dock, and all the canteens were ordered closed by the commanding officer. Similar reports came from Camp Cuba Libre in Jacksonville, where a mob of drunken soldiers from the Eleventh New Jersey Volunteers threatened to burn down the whole camp upon discovering that the bartender had cheated them by watering down their drinks. Order was only secured by treating the mutinous soldiers with free booze until they passed out.[79] This was hardly the picture of military discipline promoted by the army and its defenders.

Teddy Roosevelt's famed Rough Riders encamped in Tampa, where the canteen bartender "was a beardless Texas boy who said that before taking that position he had never tasted liquor." The availability of canteen beer didn't keep the men in camp: instead they'd frequent the "two saloons and one brothel ran under military supervision."[80]

The culmination of the brief Spanish-American War came in July 1898, when the US Navy decimated the Spanish fleet, allowing the army to then capture the strategic port city of Santiago—often remembered for the Rough Riders' charge up San Juan Hill. With the war all but over, Major General William "Pecos Bill" Shafter "resolutely refused to allow the opening of saloons at Santiago and would not permit the unloading of cargoes of liquor that were hurried to the scene by American dealers." Yet, just as on the mainland, saloons still popped up despite—and often because of—the military authorities. The scope of such military corruption will likely never be known, as generals who engaged in such illegal activities were unlikely to keep strict account of their bribes and kickbacks.

Victory in Cuba was relatively swift and bloodless, with fewer than four hundred American deaths in under a month of fighting. But for every one battlefield fatality, there were ten American deaths from disease, especially a withering epidemic of yellow fever. Initial press dispatches from July 1898 attributed the outbreak of disease to "the foul conditions in a saloon" that military governor Leonard Wood "had ordered closed three or four times," which certainly speaks to the tenacity and staying power of the liquor men.[81]

Military doctors implored that "the slow and continuous use of alcohol causes a marked deterioration in the constitution," and that "no intoxicating liquor of any kind should be drunk" to minimize susceptibility to the outbreak.[82] It was of little use: the yellow fever was already rampant. By August, a group of military officers including both Roosevelt and Shafter wired Washington requesting that their "army of convalescents" be withdrawn from Cuba, since after only forty days in the field "not twenty per cent are fit for active work."[83]

The US military retreated just as quickly as it came, leaving behind only a small occupation force, its canteens, and saloons—all of which failed to impress the Cubans. For instance, to celebrate the Fourth of July, the Americans set up a field day of sports and entertainment in Havana, which turned ugly.

"Before two o'clock in the afternoon, when the field exercises were at their best, many of the soldiers were too drunk to know their own names," reported the *Havana Post*. "And when the game of baseball was in progress, fights were too numerous to count and nearly everybody who had gathered expecting to see a higher class of outdoor sports left in disgust." An editorial two days later pulled no punches: "The permitting of the army canteen on the grounds to the right and in front of the grand stand, gave the visitors, American and Cuban, an enforced opportunity of witnessing the disgraceful spectacle of perhaps a hundred drunken soldiers, many of whom were violently disorderly, even to engaging in fist-fights and general brawls in the presence and ostensibly under the supervision of the officers of the batteries. It is doubtful if such a disgusting and disgraceful spectacle has even before been offered the people of Cuba upon the occasion of a public celebration."[84]

The situation got so bad that the military commanders in Havana and across Cuba were forced to declare total prohibition. "When saloons or the like sell or give intoxicating liquors to soldiers they will be summarily closed and the proprietors and their employees arrested," declared circular #7 from military headquarters in Havana. Soldiers found possessing intoxicating liquor would be arrested and court-martialed for insubordination. Amid the looming threat of disease, "the health and welfare of the troops is the first consideration" for the prohibition decree, "as well as to the discipline of the command and the good repute of American soldiers."[85]

But while the occupation and scandals were winding down in Cuba, they were only beginning in America's other new colonial possession: the Philippines. Back in the States, newspaper readers were mortified by stories of pitiable American soldiers going blind or dying from poisonous homebrew, sold by "conniving" Filipinos in tumbledown roadside shacks. "The rottenest American whiskey ever brewed is 'angel food' compared with that vile stuff," claimed one soldier.[86]

But the tables turned as it became increasingly clear that it wasn't unscrupulous Filipinos getting the Americans drunk, but more often unscrupulous Americans getting both natives and American soldiers drunk. The Filipinos weren't the primary customers at the Yankee Beer Chute in Manila that John J. Valentine described, but "our own boys are their customers, and many of them boys, who prior to their arrival at Manila, had not, I venture to say, ever touched a glass of intoxicating liquor." He claimed that "Moral suicide awaits nine out of every ten young men" who ventured to the Philippines, and "Had I a son, I would feel somewhat as though I was consigning him to almost certain destruction."[87]

The tenfold expansion in the size of the army with the war was a tenfold expansion in potential booze customers. And just as liquor sellers weren't about to pass up that opportunity to turn enormous profits, neither were temperance activists about

Figure 15.5 "The Moral of the Canteen Question," by Louis Dalrymple, *Puck*, June 20, 1900. In this decidedly pro-canteen cartoon, the cherub Puck examines "the result of abolishing the canteen" on the left, with soldiers drunk on whiskey at the "off limit saloon," versus good-natured soldiers drinking beer and seltzer at the US Army "canteen as it is" on the right. Unfortunately, this often proved to be an artificial distinction.
Source: AP101.P7 1900, Prints and Photographs Division, Library of Congress, Washington DC.

to let them do so without a fight, especially when the honor of the United States and its military were at stake.

So, in 1899, another WCTU pressure campaign led to legislation, thought to settle the canteen controversy once and for all. Section 17 of the Army Reorganization Bill read quite clearly: "That no officer or private soldier shall be detailed to sell intoxicating drinks as a bartender or otherwise, in any post exchange or canteen, nor shall any other person be required or allowed to sell such liquor in any encampment or fort, or on any premises used for military purposes by the United States."[88]

But before the bill could be enacted, McKinley's attorney general, John W. Griggs, effectively nullified it. "Employment is a matter of contract, and not of requirement or permission," Griggs claimed, so although soldiers couldn't act as bartenders, it would still "be lawful and appropriate for the managers of the post exchanges to employ civilians for that purpose."[89] Since the bill quite explicitly stated the opposite, this raised a constitutional question: does the attorney general have the authority to override laws passed by Congress?

All of a sudden, the canteen was an issue of high politics. The disenfranchised ladies of the WCTU were taking on the entire US military establishment, backed by the patriotic public sentiments of wartime. Incredibly, in the face of such long odds, the ladies won.

News outlets, like the satirical *Puck* magazine (Figure 15.5), reflected the military's "patriotic" position: essentially that soldiers are going to get drunk one way or another, so why not keep it in house by selling them "healthful" beer, rather than going off-post to the unscrupulous liquor dealer? Ironically, such juxtapositions against the private saloons were themselves implicit condemnations of the debauching liquor traffic.

Others, like the *New York Evening Post*, published condescending and misogynist editorials, painting the WCTU as meddlesome busybodies, unable to understand their own best interests amid the new American alco-imperialism:

> We observe that the returned chaplains, with their tales of the ravages of the American saloons in Manila, are stirring up the temperance women and the religious press to demand that the President interfere. He could undoubtedly suppress the traffic by a stroke of his pen. It is not a question of the law about army canteens. It is a part of the military administration of the city of Manila. There lies before us a copy of "General Orders, No. 2," issued in Manila on January 4, 1900, fixing a regular system of saloon licenses. The rates run from $200 to $1,200 a year—the money to be paid, of course, to the United States. Clearly the power that can tax or regulate the liquor traffic by military order could suppress it. Having absolute authority, it might be supposed that our Methodist President would at least go as far as Colonial Secretary Chamberlain [Chapter 5] in trying to stamp out the rum trade in distant dependencies. But the good Mr. McKinley will explain to the anxious temperance workers that he is not a free agent in this matter. In the first place, he needs the license money. The Philippine venture is costing a pretty penny, and there must be something to show on the right side of the ledger. Then the dear ladies must not forget that the brewers are our most ardent expansionists. Beer is now our leading export to Manila. To do anything to cut off that trade would enrage the brewers and seriously injure the Republican party in the presidential campaign. Would not the Woman's Christian Temperance Union and the churches rather have beer and whisky flowing like water in Manila than do anything to imperil President McKinley's re-election?[90]

The idea that saloon licenses would help fund the war was patently ridiculous, of course, since neither the huge volume of liquor sold in those saloons nor the enormous profits made from it could be taxed. Moreover, claiming that greater beer exports beget expanded military power belied a breathtaking ignorance of government budgeting and finance.

The showdown before Congress was just as colorful and hyperbolic as the public debates in the newspapers. In his testimony, Secretary of War Elihu Root made no qualms that he saw canteen opposition as a farce. "The post exchange is a club, and the men get together there and they play dominos and checkers and billiards, and they read and talk and smoke and they drink their glass of beer, and it is an agreeable place and the men do not go away," Root said. If they were to prohibit "the sale of beer and light wines in the canteen, you break that up, and the result is going to be as soon as it gets around it will stop our enlistments. This is a matter of serious practical consequence. The men are not going to enlist when they understand that they are going to be confined to reform school."[91]

Other military leaders followed. Colonel Francis L. Guenther of the Fourth Artillery called the canteen "one of the best things that has ever been done for the enlisted men," reducing dissatisfaction, desertions, and court-martialing for insubordination. To stop selling beer would be "almost criminal." Army Inspector-General Joseph C. Breckinridge claimed "all the tendencies of the canteen are reformatory, all beneficial," *especially* for college-age boys away from home for the first time. "I do not know of anything myself that would so soon destroy the Army as doing away with the canteen," declared Henry C. Corbin, adjutant general of the army.[92]

Based on such testimony by the military's heavy hitters, you'd think the saloon foes stood little chance. But the temperance forces—including a dozen women of the WCTU and representatives of the newly incorporated Anti-Saloon League (ASL)—fought such jingoism, militarism, and imperialism with science, data, and facts.

Mary Hunt of the WCTU and Scientific Temperance Federation (Chapter 14) wasted no time in throwing down the gauntlet. Speaking as a mother: "You ask much of us when you ask us to put a sword into the hands of our sons for the defense of liberty." Her own son, she noted, had only recently been killed in action during the Spanish-American War. "It is a great deal that we know they must go to face the cannon, that they must face the musket and the sword," but in reference to state-sanctioned liquor: "if in addition to that the Government itself puts in their way that which is more deadly than the sword or the musket, we as mothers must utter our urgent plea that this thing must stop."

From there, Mrs. Hunt launched into a litany of scientific temperance studies demonstrating the addictive nature of even light alcohol, many studies undertaken by the military itself. The debate should not be one of differing opinions, Hunt suggested, but of science, statistics, and facts.

The senators agreed.

Immediately, committee chairman Senator Joseph Roswell Hawley—himself a major general in the Civil War—replied with one of the army's most popular arguments: that the canteen made for happier soldiers: "In the seven years after the canteen was established the desertions were 4.53 per cent; in the seven years prior thereto, before the canteen was established, they were 9.18 per cent."

"Mr. Chairman," Mrs. Hunt fired back, "am I to infer from that that a drunken soldier is more loyal to the flag and more patriotic?" Her accusation knocked Senator Hawley back on his heels. "As a mother of a soldier, I would resent such an imputation."[93]

The senators didn't get much further with the next witness, Mrs. Margaret Dye Ellis of the WCTU, who entered into the record testimonials of American, British, and French military leaders about the benefits of temperance in the ranks. "An examination of the records in the Government Bureau of Statistics, in this city, shows that the liquor traffic is literally following the flag into our new colonial possessions with strides that are appalling," quantifying the deluge of liquor flowing into Cuba, Puerto Rico, and the Philippines.

Then Vermont Republican senator—and former secretary of war under Benjamin Harrison—Redfield Proctor scoffed that this was all just the spoils of war, simply replacing Spanish alcohol with American products. Ellis fired back with objective statistics from the US, Philippine, and Spanish governments showing that the amount of all wines and liquors imported into the Philippines from all countries during the first ten months of American occupation (1898–1899) had already quadrupled annual imports under Spanish rule. The amount of beer had increased *eighteen-fold* since the Americans arrived.[94]

If the statistics weren't damning enough, Mrs. Ellis drove home the point by holding up a copy of the *Manila Times* and reading out the twenty-two different advertisements for American-made liquor in the city's foremost daily newspaper. "'Old Government blackberry brandy,' 'Scotch whiskies the most healthful for this climate,' etc. *Twenty-two* advertisements!" she railed. Like the other senators, the old war secretary Proctor had no response to the evidence of American alco-imperialism.[95]

"We consider the canteen question as a part of this great world movement for protection of 'child races' against the vices of civilization," then testified global temperance activist Wilbur Crafts. How was it anything but hypocrisy that the Senate encourage drunkenness in America's new overseas colonies, while the Senate's own Committee on Foreign Affairs was issuing scathing condemnations of the European empires for doing the exact same thing in Africa?[96]

Crafts then exploded the army's image of the innocent and innocuous canteen by reading into the record a letter from William Johnson, summarizing his visits to a hundred-odd army canteens from Maine to the Philippines. "With one or two exceptions, I have never been able to find anything of the nature of a reading room in connection with the beer saloon," Johnson claimed. Most canteens were still operating in violation of congressional legislation, with soldiers still being detailed to act as bartenders. "For the most part, these beer canteens were located on prohibition territory, in defiance both of the State laws and of an express law of Congress. In every case the beer canteen was merely a common groggery. In many cases whisky was sold as well as beer [and in] one case the canteen was operated in connection with a brothel."[97]

The dry activists were particularly adept at turning the military's own arguments against them. After all, Secretary Root and the military generals all agreed that drinking was bad for the recruit, even if they reluctantly viewed it as a necessary evil.

But even if the canteen system worked perfectly—with no corruption and all drink proceeds going to improve mess and hospital facilities—what sense did it make to punish those soldiers who did the healthful, responsible thing and abstain from drink? The pro-canteen crowd had no reply. "The Government is amply able to provide for all the needs of the officers and enlisted men," claimed Edwin Dinwiddie of the Anti-Saloon League, "and it should not permit the resort to the menacing inducement to drink by such a system, for few men are liable to share with comfort regularly the profits of a fund they do not help to create."

In the end, the anti-canteen activists arrived well prepared with reams of data and scientific studies, and came across as eminently reasonable.

"Our position is rational and common sense," claimed Dinwiddie. Instead of the utopian idealists they'd been portrayed as in the press, "We do not claim this bill will reform or revolutionize the Army. We believe the trend is in the right direction." The prohibitionists were in harmony with emerging best military practices among the British and French armies, and with the US Army's own physicians, citing the military's own arguments and data.[98]

Ultimately, Congress agreed that the cons of the canteen system outweighed the pros, and passed sweeping anti-canteen legislation in January 1901.

The anti-canteen victory emboldened the larger prohibition movement. In particular, it marked the arrival of a new organization on the national stage: the Anti-Saloon League of America. To this point, the Anti-Saloon League was a pressure group focused primarily on lobbying for state-level prohibitions, and throwing their support behind dry candidates of either party to get them elected to Congress (Chapter 16). But only in 1898 did the ASL establish a Washington headquarters—headed by Rev. Edwin C. Dinwiddie—to lobby directly for temperance legislation. The ASL's coordination with the WCTU and other temperance organizations to testify directly before Congress was critical to ultimately securing the Anti-Canteen Law of 1901. It also showcased to progressives the ability to harness the power of government to rein in big-business exploitation and corruption, even when those interests were as entrenched and powerful as the liquor industry and the US Army.[99]

It also fused the cause of prohibitionism and anti-imperialism. And perhaps no single American embodies those twin causes more than the Boy Orator of the Platte, William Jennings Bryan.

Anti-Imperialism, Prohibitionism, and William Jennings Bryan

Of the two main political parties, the Republicans were long the standard-bearers of the great reforms: abolitionism, suffragism, temperance, and anti-militarism. The Democrats, by contrast, were the party of Wall Street capitalism; Tammany Hall; corrupt, big-city machine politics; and repression of racial minorities in the

Solid South. Its philosophical transformation into its modern form as an inclusive, liberal-progressive party happens during the Progressive Era, due largely to William Jennings Bryan.[100] Here too, prohibition is integral to the story.

Born in 1860 and raised in Illinois, young Bill Bryan developed a zeal for oratory. This was at a time when public speaking was part art, part sport—when great speeches were reprinted in newspapers, discussed, and dissected like baseball box scores. Wordsmithery and elocution were key to both politics and religion, and Bryan developed a knack for all of them from a very young age. His parents were Democrats and abstainers, and he remained faithful to both party and principle throughout his life. "Even before I had any clear understanding of the temperance question, I began signing the pledge" of abstinence, he wrote in his autobiography. A temperance orator found one of his signed pledges from 1872, when he was twelve.[101] His nondogmatic parents nurtured young Will's independent spirit: rather than demand he become a Baptist like his father or a Methodist like his mother, they encouraged him to explore all churches and faiths. At thirteen, he became a Cumberland Presbyterian: a small, inclusive, community-oriented sect that was among the first denominations to ordain both women and African Americans as clergy. And while his faith was of defining importance to his reformist zeal, he was equally nondogmatic about it: perfectly content to attend congregations of other denominations wherever he went, and unwilling to foist his own moral beliefs upon others.[102]

After passing the bar in Illinois, Bryan was hard up for work as a lawyer. One of his first clients was a family friend, John Sheehan, who'd become a saloon-keeper. "He said he knew that I was not in sympathy with his business, but that he thought I might be willing to collect some small bills that men owed him for the liquor they had bought," Bryan remembered. "I told him that I did not drink myself nor advise drinking, but that I thought those who bought liquor ought to pay for it."[103] He was pleasant, sympathetic, and also quite persistent when collecting debts. He later recalled the entire episode as a lesson in flexibility and compromise.

In 1887 William and his new bride, Mary Elizabeth Baird Bryan, moved to the prairie boomtown of Lincoln, Nebraska, to set up a legal practice with his Republican law-school friend, Dolph Talbot. "Bill was chairman of the Democratic city committee and Talbot was chairman of the Republican city committee. Both committees used the Bryan-Talbot offices for meetings," remembered none other than Pussyfoot Johnson, who—as fate would have it—had an office on the same block while attending the University of Nebraska. Indeed, Pussyfoot's first wife, Lillie M. Trevitt Johnson, was for a time Bryan's secretary.

"We used to argue over prohibition, and some of the discussions were pretty hot," Pussyfoot recalled. Showcasing Bryan's agreeability, Johnson said, "He was as much in sympathy with temperance as I was, but he was firmly opposed to any sumptuary legislation and for that reason he strung along with the opposition." That is, until Bryan backed a local-option bill, and his erstwhile "wet" colleagues heaped scorn on him, driving him "into the dry camp where his heart belonged. Thus, in their stupidity, they gave the drys one of the most eloquent tongues that ever pleaded the cause of prohibition," Pussyfoot remembered.[104]

Bryan soon found himself leading the faction of insurgent Democrats: accusing the more conservative, Wall Street Democrats of having too little sympathy for fellow citizens in economic trouble. These reformists increasingly questioned the party's long-standing opposition to federal intervention to help. After all, it wasn't just the urban poor in Walter Rauschenbusch's Hell's Kitchen tenements (Chapter 14), or blacks in the Jim Crow South (Chapter 13) who were suffering the excesses of capitalism. One bad harvest could likewise throw farmers—the rural proletariat—into the abyss of poverty. Getting urban factory workers, black sharecroppers, and midwestern farmers to join forces against their common class-based exploitation would create the largest democratic political insurgency in American history: the populist movement.[105]

In Bryan's Nebraska and up and down the Great Plains, working-class citizens increasingly railed against "the money power." These were the greedy East Coast capitalists who profited from the farmers' toil: banks charging outlandish interest, railroads hiking rates on freight during harvest time—all aided by a corrupt political establishment that put the interests of the wealthy above the common good. The last straw was not some natural disaster, but a manmade, capitalist one. The harvest of 1889 was unusually bountiful, but with so much corn on the market, prices plummeted, forcing foreclosures and bankruptcies among America's small farmers.

The political backlash became known as the Agrarian Rebellion. Across the South and Great Plains, agrarian and labor activists demanded reform: reining in the East Coast "trusts," protecting union organizers, providing public-sector jobs for the unemployed, reducing tariff rates, and letting farmers bypass financial exploitation by the banks by allowing commercial crops to be used as collateral. In 1890 Bryan successfully ran for Congress by championing these populist, working-class concerns, most notably expanding the coinage of silver at a fixed sixteen-to-one ratio with the gold standard that was the basis of the northeastern capitalist establishment. "Free silver" became a progressive rallying cry across the Midwest and Deep South, as it would loosen the money supply, leading to higher prices for the farmers' crops and easing their credit burdens.[106]

While his speechmaking eloquence and agrarian populism won Bryan many fans among the farmers of rural Nebraska, he also had to contend with Omaha city politics, where the liquor question was a far greater political concern.[107] Ironically, Bryan's grappling with the corrupt liquor machine in Omaha mirrored almost exactly his rival, Theodore Roosevelt's confrontations with Manhattan's Sixth Avenue saloon-keepers as the gatekeepers to the world of New York politics (Chapter 14).

On the eve of Bryan's baptism into politics, journalists described the "disgraceful" 1887 primary in Omaha, where "Every ward heeler was liberally supplied with money, whiskey and street car tickets" for men staggering from one precinct to another, voting up to ten separate times regardless of residence. As the biggest city in the state, electoral victory would be impossible without Omaha, which meant playing ball with the saloon-keepers and ward heelers, who—as with Captain Rynders in New York (Chapter 12)—were usually one and the same.[108]

The organized liquor interests ruled Omaha almost from the very beginning. Distillers and brewers set up shop along the banks of the Missouri River from Bellevue to Omaha, with many of their wares destined for Indian reservations up and down the Great Plains, from North Dakota to Oklahoma (Chapter 10), in exchange for tribal annuities. By the time Bryan showed up, Omaha boasted scores of breweries and distilleries, crowned by Willow Springs, the third-largest distiller in the entire country. It would be political suicide for any upstart politician to antagonize this well-organized force that had already spent millions of dollars undermining dry attempts to add a prohibition amendment to the state constitution.[109]

Little wonder, then, that candidate Bryan, in Lincoln, "would dismiss his Sabbath-school class a little early so as to run over to Omaha and meet the boys in the bar of the Paxton Hotel to keep track of how things were going."[110]

The hypocrisy of a temperance sermonizer slumming about in saloons would be a salacious scandal. It was none other than the young Pussyfoot Johnson who was tasked with tailing "Bryan's excursions into Omaha's underworld." Johnson could have spared his time. "Beyond learning that Bryan did in fact visit the back room of Ed Lathrop's saloon and like resorts where frailer sisters 'sat for company' and political workers of humbler rank frequently drank more than was good for them, there was nothing to report on William Jennings Bryan. He never drank anything stronger than sarsaparilla." For his part, Johnson denied keeping tabs on Bryan. However, as a newsie, he did keep Bryan abreast of the liquor establishment's vote-swapping plans to ensure that the governor (and thus the state) remained wet.[111]

Though his personal abstinence was well known, Bryan was careful not to openly antagonize the Omaha liquor establishment, even vocally speaking out *against* prohibition. "The prohibitionists and anti-prohibitions are in two classes," Bryan claimed. "The people who, in exercising their personal rights, use liquor, do not interfere with those who do not. The other side should be as honorable. It is unjust for one man to say that another must 'like like I.' "[112] Some historians even argue that it was Bryan's finessing of the liquor question even more than his agrarian populism that broke Nebraska's Republican stronghold, electing the Democrat Bryan for the first time in 1890, and reelecting him in 1892.[113]

The young Democrat's penchant for speechmaking and forceful denunciation of the big-business fiscal conservatism of his own party's president, Grover Cleveland, fueled Bryan's meteoric rise in Congress. His progressivism gained an added urgency when Wall Street speculation led to the Great Panic of 1893, plunging the country into a severe economic depression that the Cleveland administration seemed both unable and unwilling to solve. In a time before social-welfare safety nets, some 20 percent of the workforce lost their jobs. Almost overnight, some three million workers were suddenly destitute and hungry, forced to forage for themselves and their families. Those spared the crushing unemployment faced demoralizing wage reductions.[114] In terms starkly similar to the social gospel of Walter Rauschenbusch and others (Chapter 14), Bryan championed progressive policies—free silver, federal insurance for bank deposits, a graduated income tax—as a morality-infused crusade for the soul of the nation.[115]

Bryan's progressivist takeover of the Democratic Party culminated at the 1896 Democratic National Convention at the newly constructed Chicago Coliseum, where—in response to his famous "Cross of Gold" speech—the delegates abandoned incumbent president Grover Cleveland's big-business conservatism and embraced Bryan as champion of the common man.

"We are fighting in the defense of our homes, our families, and posterity," Bryan railed from the rostrum. "We have begged, and they have mocked when our calamity came. We beg no longer; we entreat no more; we petition no more." When it comes to the moneyed elites, "We defy them!" Finally, when it came to the people's silver versus Wall Street gold, Bryan left his most righteous, Jesus-inspired takedown for last: "We will answer their demand for a gold standard by saying to them: You shall not press down upon the brow of labor this crown of thorns, you shall not crucify mankind upon a cross of gold!"[116]

The Coliseum exploded. "Everyone seemed to go mad at once," marveled the *New York World*. Bryan was paraded through "hills and valleys of shrieking men and women."[117] Bryan won the nomination for not just the Democratic Party but for the upstart Populist Party too. And although anti-Democrat antagonism was too much to beat Republican William McKinley in the general election, the Democratic Party had a new standard-bearer, and an entirely new working- and middle-class orientation that persists through the present day.

Everything changed with the outbreak of the Spanish-American War in 1898, adding anti-imperialism to the list of progressive grievances. Bryan personally responded to President McKinley's call for 125,000 volunteers by organizing the Third Nebraska Volunteers, becoming colonel of the regiment. "Humanity demands that we shall act," he proclaimed. "Cuba lies within sight of our shores and the sufferings of her people can not be ignored unless we, as a nation, have become so engrossed in money-making as to be indifferent to distress."[118]

Bryan's military service was uneventful. America's "splendid little war" in Cuba was over before the Third Nebraska could ever fire a shot. The regiment spent most of its time at the infamous Camp Cuba Libre near Jacksonville. As colonel, the decision to establish a canteen for the men of the Third Nebraska was ultimately his. Unsurprisingly, when the brewers pressed Bryan, he steadfastly refused.[119] While the canteens of other regiments caused drunken discord with the locals—including mobs and murders—the Third Nebraska was dry. Colonel Bryan spared no expense to provide alternative amusements: books, sporting goods, and church services.

While other encampments were decimated by illness and venereal disease, the Third Nebraska reported virtually none.[120]

After months of encampment in Florida, Bryan resigned command of the Third Nebraska following the Treaty of Paris in December 1898, though as a volunteer he could have left at any time. His successor was a decorated Civil War veteran, Lieutenant Colonel Victor Vifquain, who quickly reversed course and opened a canteen for the Third Nebraska. As the debates over the canteen were heating up in Congress, Vifquain wrote an open letter to Secretary of War Elihu Root, juxtaposing the near-miraculous conditions in his "scrupulously clean" canteen against the supposed dry tyranny under Bryan. "It is a pity that people, altogether strangers to military discipline, efficiency, comfort and health, should be allowed to interfere in the interior management of our military establishment," wrote Vifquain, following the military line. "I hope they will not succeed."[121] Ultimately, the anti-canteen forces won.

"I had five months of peace in the army," Bryan quipped, "and resigned to take part in a fight": the fight against American imperialism in the Philippines. Bryan easily won the Democratic nomination for the 1900 presidential election, setting up a rematch with the incumbent William McKinley. But rather than gold or silver, the 1900 election would be "a contest between democracy and plutocracy": whether the United States would be a republic or an empire.[122] Imperialism—Bryan argued— violated the core American principle that sovereignty comes from the consent of the governed. The atrocities in the Philippines violated Jesus's invocation from the Sermon on the Mount to do unto others as you would have them do unto you.

Imperialism brings militarism and war, which always and everywhere harm the poor, not the rich. "It means an increase in government of the power of aristocratic and privileged classes. Militarism means the profusion of the taxpayer's money everywhere except in the taxpayer's own home," Bryan argued. "Imperialism has been described as 'the White Man's Burden,' but since it crushes the wealth-producer beneath an increasing weight of taxes, it might with more propriety be called The Poor Man's Load."[123]

Politically, antimilitarism was fraught with difficulties. On one side, the outspoken American Anti-Imperialist League—boasting heavy hitters from industrialist Andrew Carnegie and former president Grover Cleveland to Mark Twain and labor leader Samuel Gompers—only reluctantly endorsed Bryan, largely due to divisions over the Democrats' other progressive positions.[124] Meanwhile, Democrats had to also contend with racists in their own ranks—especially in the Solid South—who opposed imperialism not based on high-minded ideals, but rather as a potential challenge to the established racial hierarchy. Such political calculus surely underlay Bryan's outspokenness on the question of Filipino oppression, as well as his conspicuous silence on the question of African American oppression in the Jim Crow South.[125]

Echoing the anti-canteen crowd, Bryan argued that imperialism wasn't just bad for the Filipinos, but for Americans, too. As he now could attest from firsthand experience in the military: "The hospital records show the extent to which our soldiers yield to the temptations which surround the post, and the saloons that follow our army speak forcibly of the dangers which attend foreign service," Bryan wrote. "Can we afford to subject the morals of our young men to such severe tests unless there is some national gain commensurate with the loss?"[126]

Ultimately, anti-imperialism wasn't enough. Bryan lost to McKinley—45.5 percent to 51.6 percent and 155 electoral college votes to McKinley's 292—even worse than in 1896. Yet with McKinley's assassination the following year, his foremost Republican opponent became Theodore Roosevelt. Despite partisan differences, Roosevelt shared both Bryan's larger-than-life persona and his trust-busting progressivism.

At this point—twice defeated—Bryan retreated from electoral politics. He founded *The Commoner* newspaper back in Nebraska, delivered his trademark eloquent speeches on the Chautauqua lecture circuit, and embarked on those global tours that took him halfway around the world to meet his idol, Leo Tolstoy.

Bryan's commitment to the progressivism of the social gospel was unquestionable. After his Tolstoyan pilgrimage, however, he returned to the political fray with unquenchable vigor, further inspired by "the Count's ideas on work, poverty, wealth, social classes, and religion."[127] And while most histories focus on Bryan's relentless trust-busting as the embodiment of his progressivism, arguably his turn from milquetoast temperance to outright prohibitionism more so showcased the political implications of his Tolstoyan, social gospel principles.

In the pages of the nationwide *Independent* magazine, Bryan defended his embrace of prohibition after so many years of vacillating. His logic was thoroughly progressive: beginning not with entreaties to the Bible, but with science. Drawing from the scientific temperance literature, he pointed to one medical study after another showing the deleterious effects of even moderate alcohol consumption. Moreover, "social statistics show that the number of accidents is greater among those who use alcohol and the life tables prove that the average expectancy of those who use alcohol is much less than the expectancy of those who do not use it," Bryan wrote. Noting that temperate workers were more employable and less risky to insurers, he added, "The business world confirms the testimony of the scientists and the students of sociology."[128] The long history of liquor control was itself testimony to the fact that the saloons—unlike most other businesses—were peddling addictive and injurious products.

Much of the political debate over prohibition turned on the question: who decides? Local option was the most granular alternative: a town or county could vote itself dry. But what about an entire state? Or the country as a whole? It seemed as though the movement was toward expanding the size of the decision-making unit from local to national. Still, for Bryan, debates over units of analysis were tangential to the core argument: "whether the prohibition is applied to a large area or a small one, namely, that *the man who opposes the sale of liquor is asking nothing for himself except relief from injury at the hands of the others, while the man who insists upon the sale of liquor is asking something for himself which cannot be granted without injury to others.*"[129]

The logic of prohibitionism was the same logic as anti-imperialism: protection of a community against an unwanted and predatory outside force seeking to exploit them for financial gain. Though the Philippines would not gain independence until 1946, American debates over colonialism gradually subsided as Aguinaldo's resistance was bled dry, just as debates over prohibition were picking up steam.

Accordingly, if we want to understand the coming of the Eighteenth Amendment and the final triumph of prohibition in the United States, we need not look to federal-level politicians in Washington, DC. Instead, we need to begin by examining those communities and states most clamoring for protection from liquor predations and subordination. After all, prohibition was never something that was imposed by a powerful establishment from on high, but rather was the result of democratic, grassroots people power across the United States. The liquor machine's greatest victims may have been the nation's most dispossessed and disenfranchised—women, African Americans, and Native Americans—but as liquor predations spread, so too would the social activism to oppose it.

16

A People's History of American Prohibition

Department of the Interior, Office of Indian Affairs, Washington, DC: Monday, August 6, 1906

"The biggest turning points of my life have always come about in oddly casual ways," wrote William E. "Pussyfoot" Johnson in his unpublished memoirs. "On a pleasant day in June, 1906, I was sitting at my typewriter desk in Washington, pounding out some bread-winning effusion, when Rev. E. M. Sweet, Jr., Secretary of the Indian Territory Church Federation, walked in and sat down."

"Do you want a job?" Sweet asked, without so much as an introduction.

"No, thanks. I have too many already," Johnson replied without ever looking up from his machine. As a "dry" investigative journalist, he'd already won some notoriety for exposing the corruption of the state liquor dispensary in South Carolina (Chapter 14), the alcoholic abuses of the US Army canteens in the Deep South during the Spanish-American War, and American alco-imperialism in the Philippines (both Chapter 15).

"But look here, I have a job that you *must* accept." Sweet had come on direct orders from President Theodore Roosevelt at the White House.

Johnson stopped typing.

Sweet explained that white settlers in the territories of Arizona, New Mexico, and especially Oklahoma were clamoring for statehood, while politicos in Washington hoped that new states and representatives would alter the partisan balance of power in DC.[1] Unlike previous administrations that had run roughshod over treaties with Native American tribes, Roosevelt, his progressive commissioner of Indian Affairs Francis E. Leupp, and Rev. Sweet together vowed that the rights of the so-called Five Civilized Tribes—the Cherokee, Choctaw, Creek, Seminole, and Chickasaw Nations—should be preserved, *especially* their prohibition against the white man's liquor traffic (Chapter 10). They needed an "untouchable" antiliquor man to clean up the notoriously wet, notoriously corrupt Indian Service, just as Roosevelt had cleaned up the corrupt New York police force a decade earlier (Chapter 14).[2] Johnson was their man. Sweet offered a generous salary of two thousand dollars per year, plus control of his own budget for hiring deputies.

"I knew, generally, the conditions prevailing in the Territory and considered it a place where there was little likelihood of living to enjoy the mellowness of old age," Johnson remembered. "As a convenient way of turning down the proposition, I told him I would not take the job for less than twenty-five hundred dollars and prerequisites. Then I went back to rattling my typewriter, well pleased with my diplomacy."

Fine. Sweet agreed. Twenty-five hundred dollars it was. Bill Johnson reluctantly accepted.

"I had the idea in the back of my head that I would use part of this additional pay in 'accident insurance,'" he recalled, "but after I had started in on the job and went to apply for the insurance, I found that I would have to pay three premiums instead of one because of my hazardous job."[3]

So, on August 6, 1906, Johnson was promptly commissioned as Chief Special Officer to Suppress the Liquor Traffic in the Indian Territory of what is today eastern Oklahoma. Given special disbursing rights, neither his funding nor operations were subject to Washington infighting, red tape, or corruption.[4]

"Clean up the Indian Territory," instructed Roosevelt, the eternal good-government crusader. "I don't care how you do it, but *do* it! If you don't we will send someone else down there who will." Secretary of the Interior James R. Garfield (son of the former president) added only, "get as many [of the liquor men] in jail as you can. Keep them in jail as long as you can and when they get out, put them right back in again!"

"Those were the only instructions I ever received during the Roosevelt administration," Johnson wrote, "and I followed them right down to the last exclamation mark."[5]

Notwithstanding the lack of federal courts and jails—to say nothing of streets or highways—over the next five years, Johnson secured over forty-four hundred criminal convictions of predatory liquor men selling booze in defiance of tribal and territorial laws. Johnson's jurisdiction began in Oklahoma, but soon expanded to defending Native American reservations across the vast American West from liquor exploitation, winning him the universal scorn of white whiskey traders and the adoration of native tribes.[6]

Only when the political winds shifted in Washington in 1911 was Johnson elbowed out of the Indian Service. Cognizant of his service and sacrifices on their behalf, the Santa Clara tribe of New Mexico—upon hearing of his dismissal— invited Johnson to settle with them and manage their tribal affairs. "All we have is yours, now and always," wrote the Santa Clara council. "This is but a small pay for the manhood you have restored to this village by stopping the liquor traffic here. You may go down in apparent defeat before the whisky ring in Washington, but in the hearts of a quarter of a million American Indians, you are a hero." The council concluded, "Come and be a good Indian with us."[7]

The respect was mutual. Freshly unemployed, Johnson made for New Mexico to be among friends. After many days of celebration and negotiation with the tribal elders, Johnson convinced them that he could best continue his fight—their fight—against the debauching liquor trade far beyond the limits of the Santa Clara pueblo.

Though bittersweet, Johnson's send-off from the Indian Service was far more pleasant than his introduction to it five years earlier. His first liquor raid came in Tulsa in 1906, but the offenders simply posted bond and went right back to peddling booze. Their cases were added to the years-long backlog in the courts. In the end, they usually got tossed out anyway.

"This bloke from the east is going to 'clean us up,' " they openly joked.[8]

Johnson doubled down, deputizing a motley band of—as he described them—"hardy, two-fisted, unperfumed fellows, who enjoyed the 'sport' " of frontier justice. Reformed moonshiners, Native American scouts, convicted murderers, gunslingers, and former US marshals, they were all united in taking the fight to the liquor men who'd wronged them and wronged their families, their communities, or their sense of justice.[9]

When they raided the "king of the bootleggers"—Alex Sellers in Eufaula—Sellers simply stashed his wares in a three-thousand-pound Hall safe and laughed in the lawmen's faces. That is, until Johnson climbed up on the safe and smashed the lock with a sixteen-pound sledgehammer, revealing eighty-one bottles of contraband. Sellers was marched off to jail, and Johnson's tough-guy reputation began.[10]

Just south of Caney, Kansas, liquor men seized upon a surveying error that left a twelve-foot gap between dry Kansas and Indian Territory to build a bizarre two-story building—sixty feet long and twelve feet wide—with a saloon on the first floor and gambling den upstairs. The proprietors of this "Monte Carlo" sold liquor freely and argued their location was outside the jurisdiction of both Kansas and the Indian Territory. Johnson reasoned that, if there was no law to constrain them, there was no law to restrain him either. So with his Indian deputies disarming the proprietors, Johnson proceeded to wreck the saloon more thoroughly than Carrie Nation had done six years earlier due west on the border in Kiowa (Chapter 1).

"I ripped and tore and smashed with an axe to my heart's content and when I got through there was little left," he recalled. "I even smashed the cash register and confiscated thirty dollars. Illegal? Well, I suppose so, but it was effective."[11]

For a time, he'd earned the nickname "Smiling Bill" Johnson, since he took a bit too much pleasure in the fisticuffs, barroom brawls, and saloon smashings.[12] One day, though, liquor men put a three-thousand-dollar bounty on his head, and an assassin shot down two of his deputies in cold blood. Undeterred, Johnson switched from brazen daylight assaults on illegal liquor operations to stealthy nighttime ones, prompting journalists in the Indian Territory to bestow upon him the nickname "Pussyfoot." The moniker stuck, becoming a household word as Johnson traversed the globe (Chapters 4, 5, 7, and 8).[13]

Still, with the combined Indian and Oklahoman Territories set to enter the union in 1907 as the single state of Oklahoma, Republicans worried that—as Roosevelt's political appointee—Pussyfoot's actions against the liquor traffic might undermine their electoral support and throw the new state into the Democrats' ranks. When even close Rough Rider friends pressured Roosevelt to fire Pussyfoot, TR refused.

"I know of nothing that more clearly illustrates the character of Theodore Roosevelt," Pussyfoot later wrote. "This was no big issue before him; it involved only a $2,500 enforcement officer, yet he refused to make any compromise with what he believed right."[14]

Pussyfoot stayed on, expanding and intensifying his defense of Native American rights against the white man's wicked water. Meanwhile, Oklahoma would enter the Union as a Democratic state, but also a prohibition state: the first in a wave of state-level prohibitions that swept the South, paving the way for national prohibition.

Progressivism against the Liquor Machine

The Republican administration of Theodore Roosevelt was unique in embracing many of the progressive political reforms also pushed by William Jennings Bryan and the Democratic opposition. As Roosevelt's social gospel confidant, Walter Rauschenbusch, suggested in Chapter 14, the only move that could defeat socialism was to pull the rug out from under it: adopt similar, progressive policies that would blunt the worst excesses of unbridled capitalism and state power, while promoting the wellbeing of the masses.[15]

Battling the insular, plutocratic cabal of wealthy economic and political elites, progressives sought to capture the state in order to restrain itself. Through democratizing reforms, progressives took politics out of the hands of special interests and gave the power to the people. Their ultimate goal was containing the excesses of big business and alleviating the suffering of the working poor.

Sure, despite such progressive consensus, partisan differences persisted. Bryan was a silver man, Roosevelt was for the gold standard; Roosevelt was the almost-cartoonish avatar of American imperialism, while Bryan was anti-imperial to his core. But those issues faded after William McKinley was assassinated in 1901, making Roosevelt president, and even more so in Roosevelt's second term (1905–1909).

Even as he seethed against "Bryanism," and labor unions as "a genuine and dangerous fanaticism" and "a semi-socialistic, agrarian movement," Roosevelt wielded the progressive Sherman Antitrust Act to rein in John D. Rockefeller's Standard Oil Trust and break up J. P. Morgan's railroad monopoly.[16] When Walter Rauschenbusch claimed that socialism was the wave of the future, Roosevelt replied, "Not so long as I am president"—before admitting to adopting socialist ideas "so far as those theories are wise and practicable."[17]

Figure 16.1 William E. Johnson as a chief special officer in the Bureau of Indian Affairs, ca. 1906.

Source: "Johnson, William E. 'Pussyfoot,'" in: Ernest H. Cherrington, ed., *Standard Encyclopedia of the Alcohol Problem*, 6 vols., vol. 3 (Westerville, OH: American Issue Press, 1926), 1410.

One thrust of progressive policy was confronting the oligopoly of big business. Less a "trust-buster" and more a trust-regulator—blaming only "bad" bankers rather than all corporate power—Roosevelt's rhetoric against Wall Street as "malefactors of great wealth" was progressive through and through. Such vast economic power had to be accountable to the people. Roosevelt's war against corporate greed bolstered his popularity, even among workers.[18]

"I find it very difficult to be partisan now," Bryan joked in his famed *Let the People Rule* address, "for if I make a straight-out Democratic speech, the first thing I know the president makes one of the same kind and then the subject immediately becomes nonpartisan."[19]

Roosevelt wasn't about to cede anything to Bryan and the progressives, not even temperance. Though he opposed federal prohibition, he believed in local-option referenda to let the people themselves decide whether to be wet or dry, while stringently and evenly enforcing the saloon regulations already on the books—just as he had done as police commissioner in New York City (Chapter 14).[20] "The regulation of the liquor traffic, so as to expose it to strict supervision, and to minimize its attendant evils would do immense good," Roosevelt wrote. "But even if the power of the saloons was broken and public office no longer a reward for partisan service, many and great evils would remain to be battled with."[21]

With the teetotaler Bryan likewise advocating for saloon regulation, the bipartisan progressive consensus extended to confronting "the most predatory and dangerous of all big businesses": the liquor industry.[22]

Whether valorized as "titans of industry" or denigrated as "robber barons," when we talk about the corrosive concentration of wealth in the Gilded Era, our minds usually go to John Jacob Astor's American Fur Company (Chapter 10), the railroads of Cornelius Vanderbilt, the steelworks of Andrew Carnegie and J. P. Morgan, John D. Rockefeller's Standard Oil Company, and the like.[23] Today, we don't think of Adolph Coors, Jack Daniel, Eberhard Anheuser, or Adolphus Busch in the same light, but the progressives at the time sure did: with some $916 million in invested capital in 1915, liquor was the fifth-largest industry in the United States, and its predations were manifest.[24]

The world over, alcohol has been one of the most profitable commodities, either for private entrepreneurs or state monopolies: transforming pennies worth of grain, yeast, and water into dollars' worth of product. As one American saloon-keeper put it, "You take a glass of the stuff and throw it on the ceilin'. What sticks there is beer; the rest is profit." With increasing rates of alcohol consumption, by the turn of the century the American liquor industry was netting some $1.5 billion in revenues annually, even accounting for the ever-larger share siphoned off by state and federal governments for tax revenue.[25]

Moreover—while many brewers and distillers had humble origin stories—by the twentieth century, the liquor industry became increasingly industrialized, consolidated, and politically powerful. Between 1899 and 1914, alcohol consumption in the United States increased from 17.7 to 22.8 gallons per capita. Meanwhile, the number of breweries dropped from 1,509 to 1,250, and the number of distilleries was halved from 967 to 434, due to consolidation into larger, more profitable conglomerates.[26] The United States was still overwhelmingly a spirits-drinking country, with 85 percent of American whiskey produced by the Distilling Company of America trust.[27]

Since—before the advent of mass bottling and canning—beer was bulkier, spoiled more easily, and was more difficult to transport than spirits, breweries were concentrated in cities, such as Anheuser-Busch and Lemp in St. Louis, Moerlein in Cincinnati, and Pabst, Schlitz, and Blatz in Milwaukee.[28] Those cities that didn't already have a near-monopoly brewer soon had combinations of smaller producers to control the price and production for the local market. United Breweries of Chicago became a cartel of the top thirteen beer-makers there; sixteen of the twenty brewers in Baltimore combined into the Maryland Brewing Company, whereas the ten largest brewers in Boston came together as the Massachusetts Brewery Company, controlling half of the total beer output there. Meanwhile, the American Malting Company—organized in 1897—bought up malt houses across the country, soon selling 60 percent of all the malt used by brewers nationwide.[29]

While the liquor interests in the Midwest and Great Plains sold both to thirsty local workers and shipped to more distant native tribes, the brewers of New York and Brooklyn had a captive and ever-growing immigrant clientele. There was no need to hunt for distant customers; the human harvest came to them. In New York, the secretive "Associated Brewers"—more colloquially known as just "The Pool"—controlled 85 percent of the beer market through coordination of seventy-four of the city's breweries, almost all with links back to Tammany Hall (Chapter 12). Associated Brewers included the famed Liebman's Sons in Bushwick—brewers of Rheingold— F. & M. Schaefer, Nassau Brewers, and dozens of others. "The brewers deal carelessly in a commodity whose accompaniments are about as innocuous as dynamite," wrote Arthur Huntington Gleason in his investigation into New York brewing for *Collier's*. "As individuals, and as a body, they have flooded the community with beer, have honeycombed the city with saloons, and have created a class of liquor dealers always in debt and therefore always forced to make profits in vile ways."[30]

Like the big oil, steel, and financial trusts, alcohol manufacturers were also integrating vertically: acquiring ever more saloons and retail liquor outlets—through so-called chattel mortgages—to maximize their own revenue and squeeze out the competition. "High license" policies intended to reduce the number of retail outlets (and raise government revenue), by increasing the cost of a license to operate a saloon to five hundred to fifteen hundred dollars annually, only threw independent saloon-keepers into the arms of the big brewers. As with Roosevelt and the Sunday-closing laws, the biggest supporters of such alcohol regulations were the corrupt brewers themselves (Chapter 14). The doubling of the beer tax to fund the Spanish-American War (Chapter 15) squeezed the saloons even further. Oftentimes, the brewer would buy the saloon from the distressed saloon-keeper and then lease it back to him, requiring that he sell *only* their brand of beer. By 1909, fully *70 percent* of the saloons in the United States were owned or controlled by the brewers. In New York City alone, The Pool of big brewers owned hundreds of saloons outright, and held the chattel mortgages of nearly four thousand indebted saloon-keepers, plus another four thousand more "corners" and "block stands" through which liquor was peddled.[31]

"With a business of this kind there is only one limit to competition," wrote economic journalist George Kibbe Turner in 1909: "the consumer. There are natural and fixed centers of thirst in cities ... corners on busy avenues, locations opposite great factories, places in the tenement sections can be counted upon to sell about so much beer. And if these places are held under control by a brewery, it can hope to dispose of its product regularly, and with less cut in prices than in a furious competition to sell to a middleman."[32] These were the business dynamics fueling the race to expand and consolidate the liquor trade—and as with any race, victory went to the strong.

Of course, we should not be misled by historical romanticism or falsely equate the saloons of yesteryear with the well-regulated taverns and restaurants of today. Nowadays, the bartender is your cheery neighborhood friend who'll sell you a beer, listen to your troubles, and pack you into a cab if you've had too much. That's not what the saloon was.

The saloon-keeper was there to make money off you, period. A drunkard sent home was profit lost. Better to keep the addict in the saloon all night until his last penny is spent, and then sell him some more on credit, barter, or pawn. It is again worth pointing out that when Carrie A. Nation made national headlines for smashing saloons back in Kansas (Chapter 1), not only were those saloons operating illegally in a dry state with the connivance of local officials, she was also usually smashing them—and sending the barflys to flight—*at eight o'clock in the morning.* During the Woman's Temperance Crusade of 1873–1874, picketers arrived even earlier, routinely beginning their anti-saloon protests at 6 a.m. (Chapter 13).

If that weren't enough, the saloon-keeper had other enticements to bilk money out of your pocket. Many illegally set up gambling rooms or entered into partnerships with prostitutes to work the upstairs bedrooms, while pickpockets and grifters fleeced the customers at the rail: all to the good, so long as the saloon-keeper got his cut. Many of these were expected terms of the chattel mortgage.

Indeed, one of the curious commonalities from this global history of prohibitionism is just how similar the exploitations of the unregulated liquor trade were around the world. The American saloon-keeper ran the exact same playbook as the Russian *tselovalnik* (Chapter 2), or the Prussian *schnapsjunker* (Chapter 4), or the mine operators of the Witwatersrand gold rush in South Africa (Chapter 6). Anything was okay, so long as it turned a profit: selling cheap whiskey from expensive bottles, watering down or adulterating drinks, and selling to anyone willing to buy, including women, children, and known drunkards.[33] If this unmasking of the predations of the liquor traffic comes as a shock to you today, it was hardly shocking to folks back then. This was the reality that temperance forces had long been fighting, and it didn't take a "fanatic" to see it.

Though saloon-keepers tried to maintain a facade of respectability, it is not as though they kept their intentions secret. "We must create the appetite for liquor in the growing boys," remarked one liquor man before the Retail Liquor Dealers' Association of Ohio. "Men who drink . . . will die, and if there is no new appetite created, our counters will be empty as well as our coffers. Nickels expended in [booze] treats to boys now will return in dollars to your tills after the appetite has been formed."[34]

It was also not as though one had to go spelunking into temperance periodicals to find such details. Exposés of saloon excesses were a regular feature of progressive magazines like *The Outlook* and *The Independent*, as well as those mainstream molders of middle-class opinion like *Collier's Weekly* and *McClure's Magazine*. In

1908, *Collier's* ran a "Saloon-in-Our-Town" editorial contest, asking readers of all political persuasions about their own experiences with the saloons. Instead of a few dozen submissions, they received over three thousand. "The mining camp of Nevada, the Vermont no-license town, the Tennessee village, the Maine prohibition city, the Middle West country town, the Texas settlement—all have sent their brief and clean-cut statement," the editors explained. The awarding of the winner would have to be delayed, as they'd only read through two thousand of the three thousand submissions, adding, "We are grateful, though overworked."[35]

With such a wealth of material, *Collier's* ran editorials of saloon conditions nationwide for weeks. First prize, though, was awarded to one Emma Brush of an upstate "southern tier New York town" that had just completed its first dry year under local no-license laws:

> We had good saloons, if one may so use the words. The keepers and their families were our friends and neighbors. But they were too many, they grew insidiously upon us. They took the best corners; they inter-penetrated and clutched the town. Their hold was increasing upon all the forces of our lives. But, worst of all, they stood open there day and night to our youth— easy schools of habit, with no entrance requirement and minimum fees— sanctioned by us, apparently.

And what of the effect of the anti-saloon law? Mrs. Brush candidly wrote, "We know that drink is being sold, as in rear rooms at the lower hotel, by one druggist, strangely at the harness-shop, and at a farm a mile out. We know that the drinkers will drink, our old liars will go on lying, our consumptives are bound to cough. But youth! youth remains to us!" Overall, the effects seemed positive: modest increases in prosperity and "increased town pride and athletic success and right marrying, that for these alone we are ready, with the farmer's wife, to go down in the dirt to keep the saloon from reestablishment in our town."[36]

Indeed, by the middle of the 1900s decade, anti-saloon sentiment was decidedly mainstream nationwide. Such widespread recognition of the very real economic concerns are usually downplayed in traditional prohibition histories, intent on instead concocting culture-clash imagery of some rural cabal foisting their evangelical zealotry on an unwitting country. Instead, there was a very real and widespread concern over the saloon—especially in the big cities—that had nothing to do with some deeply harbored xenophobic hatred for the largely immigrant clientele. Instead, the focus was on protecting those immigrants from the economic predations of the white, nativist saloon-keeper, and bringing to heel his corrupt political machine.

"Capital—the great unmoral force of invested money—will be served in modern life," continued Turner in *McClure's*. "It will bend every possible effort, and override every possible obstacle, moral or physical. This is a law no more applicable to brewing than to the making of nails." Without practical or legal restraint, the brewing industry fought—as all capitalist entrepreneurs fight—for the greatest possible profit, which "has entangled itself with the worst elements of the city saloon, the greatest single corrupting force of the past fifty years." For Turner and other economic commentators, the difference between the liquor traffic and other capitalist entrepreneurship was that it worked against the public good rather than in support of it. "Every normal commercial incentive drives it to sell the greatest possible amount of its wares; and any agency that tries to flood the community with any alcoholic drink certainly does not add to the public welfare."[37]

The city saloon business, then, was the embodiment of pure predatory capitalism, feasting upon a growing urban population home to a quarter of the American people, rightly making it a primary target for progressive reformers. "The first step— not only here but through all European civilization as well," Turner concluded, "is to remove the terrible and undisciplined commercial forces which, in America, are fighting to saturate the populations of cities with alcoholic liquor."[38]

If the saloon's abuses weren't enough, we need to also address the corruption spawned by big-city liquor-machine politics: political corruption that dwarfed the more well-known oil, steel, railroad, and financial trusts. As President William McKinley warned back before the turn of the century—in exchange for an ever-increasing share of liquor-taxation revenues—the liquor dealers "have taken the government into partnership, because they can use government for the purpose of protecting their business."[39]

Undoubtedly the worst liquor machine was Tammany Hall, which had for generations ruled New York politics through the liquor trade (Chapter 12). By the 1890s, eleven of New York City's twenty-four aldermen were saloon owners, and Tammany Hall kingpins from "Boss" Tweed and "Captain" Rynders before the Civil War through Timothy "Dry Dollar" Sullivan, "Big Tom" Foley, and Charles Francis Murphy in the Progressive Era all launched their political careers through the saloons and liquor trade.[40]

Such political corruption was a staple of city politics. To keep the saloon profits rolling even in violation of local, state, and federal laws required all manner of kickbacks to politicians and bribes to local officials and policemen to look the other way. This corruption was the focus of Carrie Nation's saloon smashings in "dry" Kansas (Chapter 1), and police commissioner Theodore Roosevelt's even-handed enforcement of New York's Sunday-closing laws in 1895 (Chapter 14). Once Roosevelt had moved on to national politics, the graft schedule for New York saloons was roughly $5 per month to sell illegally on Sundays, $25 per month to harbor prostitutes, and another $25 to run a gambling den. These "fees" would be collected by Tammany Hall gangsters and ward heelers, who would then disperse it among the politicians. Each saloon contributed roughly $6.50 per month to the local Retail Liquor Dealers' Association to buy off the local police patrolmen.[41] The state excise bureau was in on the grift, too: when local drys would raise a stink about an unruly saloon, they'd step in and revoke its license. Once the furor had blown over, the saloons would have to buy new licenses from the state, often being allowed to operate freely until they recouped their losses, whereupon the entire process would be repeated.[42]

"The chiefest evils of the New York saloon to-day are (1) the corruption of the police force, (2) the hospitality to crime and criminals, (3) the alliance with politics, (4) the concentration of the social evil, and (5) doctored drinks," wrote Arthur Gleason in his *Collier's* investigative series. "The principal reason for the existence of these evils is that the average saloon, if run straight and in accordance with the law, wouldn't pay expenses. So the dealer supports his wife and children on the profits of the illegitimate side-lines. Pressure from the brewer, from the Tammany local organization, from the police, and from an oversupply of competitors, had driven the liquor dealer into an alliance with evil."[43]

When a 1904 New York grand jury investigation found that the state Liquor Dealers' Association had amassed a sizable slush fund for the sole purpose of bribing state legislators, it surprised no one. "For many years the liquor interests, like the railway interests, have followed the policy of keeping the Legislature in good humor," wrote *The Nation*:

> Through affiliations, now with Tammany, now with the rural Democracy, and now with the Republican machine, the liquor dealers have managed to secure at each election the control of a considerable number of Senators and Assemblymen. To this nucleus of defenders they have from time to time, as occasion has required, added recruits either by direct bribery or by forming log-rolling combinations on bills of all kinds. In this dirty business, partisan lines have largely been obliterated; for when the pinch has come, Republicans have vied with Democrats in subserviency to the traffic in drink.[44]

Liquor-machine politics was not just a New York problem. Virtually every city of any size had its own mini-Tammany machines, operating hand in glove with the local liquor interests. Perhaps the most brazen was in Louisville, Kentucky, where the incumbent city machine went to great lengths to defeat a progressive, good-governance outsider in the 1905 elections. On election day, a hundred Louisville bar-keepers were deputized as election officials. At the end of the day, some forty-five hundred fraudulent votes were cast, of which four thousand had their residences listed as the upper rooms of various saloons. "Voting places in ten precincts were moved, nine of them to the rear of some saloon, and in each of these ten precincts the voters were found to have cast their ballots in alphabetical order," recounts historian James Timberlake. "With the help of the police, dozens of reformers serving as election watchers were thrown out of the polling places, and some were knocked down, clubbed and beaten."[45]

Even Pussyfoot Johnson's saloon smashings across nominally dry Indian Territory brought him into conflict not just with the petty hucksters, bootleggers, and frontier saloon owners, but also the big corporate trusts that backed them. For Pussyfoot, that meant confronting the Oklahoma Brewery: a subsidiary of the Anheuser-Busch Brewing Association of St. Louis, which specialized in flooding its product into dry Indian Territory against tribal will.[46]

"The brewers began to work on me," Pussyfoot wrote in 1907. "Every few days I was arrested" for disrupting their illegal traffic. "Damage suit after damage suit was filed against me until they reached the flattering total of $157,000"—a lifetime's income, had he lost.

"Instead of defending, I attacked," wrote Pussyfoot. For illegally peddling their wares, he secured eight indictments against the Oklahoma Brewery and their local agents, and another four indictments against August Busch, Sr. himself for violating federal law and the rights of the Native Americans. Only then did the Anheuser-Busch Company relent on their own legal challenges against that singular prohibition officer.[47]

But—as one of the foremost brewing trusts—it was not as though Anheuser-Busch stopped there. Between 1900 and 1911 the Anheuser-Busch and Lemp Breweries of St. Louis formed a trust with brewers in San Antonio, Galveston, Dallas, and Houston to bankroll antiprohibitionist politicians in Texas. The brewers agreed to contribute twenty cents from every barrel sold to a special political fund, both to sway politicians and buy votes in blatant violation of state laws. In a leaked letter, the local agent of the San Antonio Brewing Association in the town of Goliad, Texas, wrote, "I have paid a few anti [prohibition] Negro and Mexicans, but can't hold up the whole business, for as soon as this gets out among them, the whole damned business will expect some help from me." When the state of Texas finally brought suit against them, the brewers pleaded *nolo contendere*—no contest—to the staggering fine of $289,000 plus court costs.[48]

The liquor interests were not content with buying votes and state politicians: their influence crept into the halls of power in Washington, too. In 1900 Fred Dubois— the opportunistic former senator from Idaho, who'd been estranged from his Republican Party for championing the silver cause—waged a campaign to get his old Senate seat back. One of brewer Gustave Pabst's agents wrote, "Dubois will surely be the next senator from Idaho. I think it could be for the interest of the brewers to have his cooperation—he is aggressive and able—if you think well of it—send me $1000–$5000. I think it will be the best investment you ever made."[49] It was. After switching party affiliation from Republican to Democrat—something unheard of in those days—Dubois was among the most reliably wet votes, even relentlessly hounding Utah senator Reed Smoot to resign on account of his (dry) Mormon beliefs.[50]

Yet perhaps the most damning examples of liquor-machine corruption came from Adolphus Busch himself, who wrote to The Pool of Associated Brewers in New York in 1906:

> We must pay over to the United States Brewers' Association whatever it may require to represent us properly before Congress, where we have most important bills to defend. We must defeat the Hepburn-Dolliver Bill [enthusiastically supported by President Roosevelt, it empowered the Interstate Commerce Commission and regulated railroad shipping rates], which is the most dangerous and antagonistic to our industry and which makes Prohibition possible. Then we want to defeat any bill which may be brought up to increase the revenue tax on beer, with which we are now threatened; we want to re-establish the military canteen at all army posts and on our Men of War; and in all Reciprocity Treaties, we want our government to see that American beer enters foreign countries with a moderate and reasonable duty and not one which is prohibitive. . . . We want further to see that no Prohibition is enforced in the District of Columbia or embodied in the Constitution of Oklahoma when the latter is admitted to statehood.
>
> All this will cost lots of money; we do not want to spend one cent bribing people, but we will have to be liberal with the Press of many states and with friends to gain the ear of Senators or members of Congress.[51]

There was no need to hide the intent to lobby, bribe, or outright buy legislators: such liquor-machine corruption had been standard fare in the halls of Congress and statehouses across the country for decades. It didn't take some puritanical zealot to want to clean it up. Indeed, the actual battle lines of prohibition weren't between religion and drink, but capitalist profits versus the common good.

Saloon versus Anti-Saloon

An unvarnished consideration of the economic and political challenges posed by the liquor industry necessarily precedes any meaningful discussion of efforts to remedy them. Unfortunately, this is rarely the case for conventional histories, which rush to stereotype American prohibitionists as conservative "thou-shalt-nots" hellbent on taking away Americans' freedom to get soused (Chapter 18). In that genre, no one organization is as maligned as the Anti-Saloon League (ASL), roundly credited (or blamed) for the Eighteenth Amendment and national prohibition.

"The two ideas that drove the ASL were focus and intimidation," claims Daniel Okrent in his award-winning *Last Call*. " 'Intimidation' might seem too tough a word for the forthright application of democratic techniques, but as practices by the ASL, democracy was a form of coercion."[52]

Figure 16.2 The Liquor Dealer: His Supports and His Burdens (1908). In this *Collier's* editorial cartoon, the liquor dealer is upholding the ward heelers, brewers, politicians, and police, while being supported by the gamblers, thieves, and prostitutes below. The dumbfounded drunkard and the impoverished urchin exist only at the margins.

Source: Boardman Robinson, "The Liquor Dealer: His Supports and His Burdens," Collier's, May 2, 1908, 13.

Sounds dastardly. Of course, this ignores and excuses the actual physical coercion, intimidation, and outright bribery of the city liquor machines that they were fighting (Chapter 12)—but never mind.

Okrent then lays out the threats, "tacit collaboration," and "legislative parlor tricks" the Anti-Saloon League used to put prohibition over on an unwilling population, as devised by "the brilliant, monomaniacal ASL leader, Wayne Wheeler," as historian James Morone dubbed him.[53] Of course, the actual history of the ASL was not nearly as one-sided or desultory.

Indeed, if we go back to the first *History of the Anti-Saloon League*—written in 1913, well before national prohibition—the tone is dramatically different. Written by ASL stalwart Ernest Cherrington, one might expect it to be somewhat self-serving, but in it he makes it clear from the beginning that the ASL was developed for the singular reason of opposing the economic and political abuses of the liquor trusts:

The annual tribute paid by the American people to the Moloch of rum had grown to the vast sum of almost $1,500,000,000. The hands of the officers of the law in the cities and towns of the nation were tied, all too often, by the cords of graft woven into the saloon. State legislatures were submissive to the supreme authority of this monster liquor machine, with its undisputed ability to make or unmake politicians. And the federal government itself, hushed by the cold bribe of a one hundred and eighty million dollar annual federal tax, had grown deaf and dumb on all questions affecting this institution, which, by a presumed divine right, held the throne in the world of finance and trade. . . . In short, the saloon controlled politics. It dictated political appointments. It selected the officers who were to regulate and control its operations. It had its hand on the throat of legitimate business. It defiantly vaunted itself in the face of the church. It ridiculed morality and temperance. It reigned supreme.[54]

In terms of the organization's practical genesis, we can trace it back to the same Woman's Temperance Crusades that began in Ohio and swept through the Midwest in 1873–1874, ultimately producing the Woman's Christian Temperance Union (Chapter 13). In the college town of Oberlin, Ohio, the local Temperance Alliance was founded on March 20, 1874. With the president of Oberlin College as its head, the alliance worked "by all lawful measures to suppress the traffic" of alcoholic liquors within the town.[55]

The alliance was already a decade old when Howard Hyde Russell came to town in 1884. Russell was a successful attorney and Republican politician in Corning, Iowa, who'd enrolled in the theological seminary at Oberlin College to begin a second career in ministry. He quickly became a force in local temperance politics. He was lukewarm on the WCTU's "do everything" policy, and scoffed that the threadbare Prohibition Party could ever break the two-party duopoly. Prohibitionist reformers in the North tended to be Republican and promoted civil rights for African Americans, whereas the growing prohibitionist sentiment both among whites and blacks in the Jim Crow South had to contend with single-party Democrat rule. Getting such widely differing constituencies to agree on any policy platforms beyond prohibition was a fool's errand. Thus, to achieve prohibition, only an explicitly "*all*-partisan approach" seemed appropriate. After all, that's how the liquor industry operated: they didn't tie themselves to any one party, but rather played the field, throwing their money behind any politician who might support them, regardless of political affiliation.[56]

If prohibition—which in 1888 meant merely state-level prohibition for Ohio— were ever to become a reality, the organization would have to be grassroots to its core. Russell envisioned a statewide network of temperance activists, knowledgeable of local political dynamics and personalities, tied together by a full-time, salaried organizer and a newspaper to publicize their efforts to would-be voters.[57] After five years of mission work in the urban slums of Chicago and Kansas City—akin to Walter Rauschenbusch's New York mission (Chapter 14)—in 1893 Russell returned to Oberlin and reorganized the Oberlin Temperance Alliance into the Ohio Anti-Saloon League to push for local-option legislation.[58]

Of course, the selection of the name wasn't some coy misdirection: "It was the Anti-Saloon League, not the Anti-Liquor or Anti-Beer League," notes ASL historian K. Austin Kerr. Despite vilification by historians, the ASL never opposed alcohol itself, nor the individual's right to drink: even actively *opposing* so-called bone-dry laws that would have made actual consumption of alcohol a crime.[59]

Russell emulated the modern, corporate structure of the very liquor traffic he opposed. The league was led by a ten-member board of trustees—with representatives from all political parties and all supporting church denominations—which hired the state superintendent and supported the four specialized departments: agitation, legislation, law enforcement, and finance. To confront the vertically integrated "liquor trust," he proposed a "temperance trust": encouraging existing temperance organizations to formalize ties with the league and accept its leadership. Local auxiliaries of volunteers—financially self-supporting, as they were formed among existing church congregations—raised funds, organized speaking tours, distributed literature, and served at the polls on election day. As the organization grew, high-profile annual Anti-Saloon Congresses were held, emulating shareholders' meetings in the corporate world.[60]

With the Panic of 1893 and the ensuing years of deep economic depression, it was an awful time to start a new social organization reliant on donations. So the ASL's early years were lean ones. The only bright spot was the patronage of Ohio's wealthiest prohibitionist: Standard Oil magnate and philanthropist John D. Rockefeller of Cleveland. Rockefeller had heard Russell preach in Cleveland and invited him to speak to his Sunday school class on temperance. From there, the two developed a lifelong friendship, with Russell describing Rockefeller as a "sincere Christian" and friend of the temperance cause.[61]

Rockefeller first donated two thousand dollars to the Ohio ASL in 1894 and would bankroll both state and national prohibitionist organizations well into the 1920s.[62] Rockefeller's seed money allowed Russell to hire a skeleton crew of activists who would lead the organization to dry victory—first in Ohio, and eventually nationwide. First came Good Templar counselor Edwin Dinwiddie as chief organizer; Prohibition Party orator John G. Woolley as traveling speaker; Ernest Cherrington to head the *American Issue* magazine and the publications division in the Columbus suburb of Westerville, Ohio; and a young Oberlin graduate, Wayne B. Wheeler, as an "agitator and organizer."[63] With just a bootstrap budget insufficient to contesting statewide elections—much less going toe-to-toe with the liquor juggernauts—the ASL did notch their first small victory. In 1895 the ASL took on the outspoken wet Republican state senator John Locke from rural Madison County. Russell and the league canvassed Locke's district west of Columbus and persuaded the local delegates to the Republican nominating convention to select a more sympathetic, dry representative instead. They did.

It was a minor victory, but it proved to the ASL that their grassroots strategy could work.[64]

Soon the Ohio ASL was being deluged with queries from temperance fellow travelers in other states, seeking both to network with the organization and to learn from their success. Ancillaries from the National Temperance Society and the WCTU floated the idea of a national convention to inaugurate a new political movement to suppress the saloon—not only at the local and state levels, but the national level, too—based upon Ohio's nonpartisan methods. Accordingly, with an executive committee including WCTU stalwarts Ellen Foster and Annie Wittenmyer (Chapter 13), and Russell as national superintendent, the Anti-Saloon League of America was born in 1895 at a national convention in Washington, DC.[65]

Still, most of the league's grassroots activity was concentrated at the state and local levels, with Ohio leading the way. By 1900 the Ohio league boasted one hundred thousand temperance voters on its mailing lists, whom they could inform as to where their local representatives stood on saloon issues. However, effective temperance legislation in Columbus was consistently undermined by the brewers and distillers—with their bottomless campaign donations and bribery slush-funds—that kept progressive legislative proposals from ever seeing the light of day. So, the ASL declared the necessity of confronting Ohio's liquor-machine and political bosses "before the people can have a chance to express their will regarding the saloon at the polls," wrote Purley Baker in the *American Issue*. "Unless we succeed in smashing party bossism, we might as well be Russian serfs."[66]

The league didn't wait long to flex its muscle. In 1904 a local-option bill sailed through both chambers of the state legislature, only to be vetoed by Republican governor Myron T. Herrick. This was a shock. Herrick had previously been in the league's good graces and he shared the Republican Party affiliation of President Roosevelt and many temperance sympathizers. As governor, he was the most powerful Republican in a state where Democrats had been in the minority for a generation. In a word: Herrick *was* the political establishment.[67]

Dismayed, the ASL looked for an alternative within the Republican Party, settling on Warren G. Harding. As a state senator, Harding had voted in favor of local option, and his unsuccessful run at the governorship in 1903 landed him as Ohio's lieutenant governor. Though he ultimately rebuffed the ASL's encouragement to run for governor again in 1905, his friendship with Wayne Wheeler, Purley Baker, and the Ohio ASL would come in handy a decade later in Washington, DC (Chapter 17).[68]

True to its omnipartisan approach, the league then prevailed upon the Democrats—with whom they also maintained cordial relations—to nominate former US congressman John M. Pattison as their gubernatorial candidate in 1905.

The election would be a clear-cut showdown between the wet Republican incumbent and a dry Democrat challenger.

The campaign was as unusual as it was bitter. Stumping across the state, the Democrat Pattison was welcomed by sympathetic communities, including prominent Republicans. The *American Issue* denounced those saloons that remained open due to the governor's veto as "Herrick saloons." Both the league and the WCTU pounded the pavement to turn out dry voters. Herrick's Republican campaign lambasted ASL leaders like Russell and Wheeler as shysters, fleecing their churchgoing followers to live in luxury in Columbus. Aggravated, Governor Herrick's close friend John D. Rockefeller slashed his annual donation to the league from five thousand to three thousand dollars. It didn't matter: the Ohio league had raised and spent seventy-three thousand dollars on their campaign for "home rule" and "the people" against "party bossism." And it worked. While every other Republican for state office won handily, Governor Herrick was trounced by a forty-five-thousand-vote margin.[69]

Pattison's victory was a national bombshell. Not only did it prove that the league's nonpartisan, grassroots campaign could be scaled up to defeat entrenched political elites, it also warned politicians that they ignore the dry vote at their peril. More immediately, as the perceived kingmakers of Ohio politics, the ASL was deluged with requests for patronage appointments by carpetbaggers and political opportunists. But the league made it clear that they were above the usual *quid pro quo* of party bossism. "The League, in all its efforts is not actuated by any desire for the spoils of office for its members or its friends," the *American Issue* proclaimed, noting that it had no requests to make of Governor-Elect Pattison. "We propose to remain entirely aloof from all political alliances, and to operate with an eye alone single to the advantage of the temperance cause."

Both through word and through deed, the ASL fashioned itself as the antithesis of machine politics.

For his part, Pattison attended his inauguration in January 1906 but returned home that day feeling ill. He died of Bright's disease (kidney nephritis) in June at the age of fifty-nine, having never returned to the executive office. The governorship passed to Lieutenant Governor Andrew Harris: a Republican and a dry. When the Ohio legislature passed an increase in the saloon tax in 1906, the ailing Pattison did not veto it. Nor did his successor veto the legislature's county-option bill two years later. In the 1906 elections, all major-party candidates for statewide office had openly supported local-option legislation, except one wet Democrat, who was soundly defeated. "No sane man in Ohio any longer doubts that the liquor support is a blight rather than a blessing at the polls," wrote the *American Issue*.[70]

Even well before their breakout victory in Ohio in 1905–1906, the ASL had dedicated itself to a state-by state, grassroots political strategy, with a firm organizational basis in existing churches and faith communities. The idea of national prohibition wasn't even on their radar until perhaps 1913, given the entrenched nature of the liquor machine in Washington.

But this clashes with the popular historical imagery of the ASL as a bunch of quasi-authoritarian evangelicals, looking to foist their morality on an unwitting population. In actuality, the Anti-Saloon League was pragmatic, not dogmatic— democratic, not autocratic. Their interest was not in imposing prohibition on those who didn't want it, but in helping those who did want liberation from the saloons to organize, using their democratic people-power to promote good governance.

"The truth is, a strong public sentiment against the drink habit and traffic is the main thing," Howard Hyde Russell explained. "Without public demand no law can be passed, and it is worthless when it is passed."[71]

Instead of quixotic moral crusades, the ASL focused its limited resources in those states and localities where it would most effectively curb liquor predations. This meant gauging community sentiment and local organizational resources. If the people didn't want statewide prohibition, but rather county option or local option, then go for that. If county option wasn't palatable, but a community favored reduction in the number of saloon licenses or restricting hours of operation, then work for that. "Do not strive after the impossible," the Ohio state body told its local ancillaries. "Study local conditions and reach after the attainable."[72] Flexibility and compromise were the calling cards of the Anti-Saloon League in their state-to-state battles against the entrenched wet political machines.

Indeed, it is striking—for an organization now roundly vilified for its alleged dogmatism—just how frequently Anti-Saloon League forces were called upon as honest brokers of political compromises both in Washington and in the states. We'll see that repeatedly when considering the Oklahoma question.

Unlike the entrenched liquor machine, the Anti-Saloon League sought neither financial gain nor the personal or political advancement of its members. Also unlike the liquor industry, the ASL had neither the financial resources nor the moral bankruptcy to bribe politicians, buy votes, or employ ward heelers to intimidate its opponents. Though it meant fighting with one hand tied behind its back, the ASL would have only public support as a political weapon: using democratic means to hold leaders, legislators, and liquor sellers accountable.

Such nondogmatic realism extended to the candidates that they did support. There was no purity test for ASL backing beyond the expectation that elected politicians honestly fulfill their promises. The Anti-Saloon League never made a candidate's personal drinking habits a condition for political support. "It frankly preferred a wet legislator who would vote dry to a teetotaler who would vote wrong," as historian James Timberlake noted, adding that if such practicality seemed familiar, it was the same realistic methods that the liquor interests had used for years. The ASL just "deodorized and disinfected them, and turned them back on the liquor traffic."[73]

Most crucial to the movement was agitation and publicity. If a candidate was elected on a platform of voting for some dry policy—local option or state prohibition—and then ended up going to the capital and voting with the liquor interests, the ASL would publicize that hypocrisy, not just to the representative's constituency, but to everybody. The Anti-Saloon League made no attempt to co-erce its followers, but instead showcased the difference between a legislator's public statements and his voting records, and let the votes fall where they may. It's the same "accountability politics"—highlighting the difference between political ac-tors' words and deeds—that Helsinki Watch Committees used to shame the Soviet Union's oppressive human rights record, or that domestic pressure groups ranging from the NRA to the ACLU use in compiling "scorecards" for legislators' voting records. It is in the same progressive spirit of opening up the government to public scrutiny, and that "an informed electorate is vital to the proper operation of a de-mocracy" that undergirds the 1965 Freedom of Information Act. Such transparency and accountability tactics were pioneered by the Anti-Saloon League.[74]

Normally, historians trace such transparency initiatives back to early investiga-tive journalists, whose inquiries often swayed public opinion and voting behavior. Such "muckrakers"—as President Roosevelt coined the unflattering term, for those willing to go down into the filth of corruption and expose it—were a mainstay of the Progressive Era, shining a light into the largely unseen world of unrestrained capitalism and political cronyism.[75]

Upton Sinclair's *The Jungle* (1906) is always the classic example. Hoping to draw attention to the hopelessness and poverty of urban immigrant communities as a broad indictment of corporate greed and corruption, the socialist Sinclair worked undercover in the meatpacking plants in the stockyards of Chicago. Against that dismal backdrop, his novel portrays a newly arrived Lithuanian couple who be-come ensnared in the cycle of poverty, disease, and desperation. Yet what caused the greatest public outcry were the graphic descriptions of unsanitary working conditions, which prompted the Roosevelt administration to sign into law both the Federal Meat Inspection Act and the Pure Food and Drug Act (1906). These reforms became hallmarks of progressive legislation and the dramatic extension of federal oversight and power in the name of the common good.[76]

All of this is perfectly true, of course. But what seems to be missing from almost every historical and literary consideration is that *The Jungle* was a scathing tem-perance tale to its core. If you go back and read it, Sinclair mentions drunkenness twenty-eight times, various forms of alcohol sixty-two times, saloons sixty-five times, plus an additional twenty mentions of saloon-keepers. His condemnations of the liquor traffic were as damning and as influential as if he were a member of the Anti-Saloon League himself. Chapter 1, page 1 begins with a Lithuanian wedding reception in "the rear room of a saloon in that part of Chicago known as 'back of the yards'"; and it all goes downhill from there.

Immediately after that brief moment of community celebration came the reck-oning with the predatory saloon-keeper:

> By him you were sure to be cheated unmercifully, and that even though you thought yourself the dearest of the hundreds of friends he had. He would begin to serve your guests out of a keg that was half full, and finish with one that was half empty, and then you would be charged for two kegs of beer. He would agree to serve a certain quality at a certain price, and when the time came you and your friends would be drinking some hor-rible poison that could not be described. You might complain, but you would get nothing for your pains but a ruined evening; while, as for going to law about it, you might as well go to heaven at once. The saloon-keeper stood in with all the big politics men in the district; and when you had once found out what it meant to get into trouble with such people, you would know enough to pay what you were told to pay and shut up.[77]

The Jungle returns to the saloon time and again, as both the poor immigrant's portal to the world of unregulated slaughterhouse labor, and his temporary res-pite from it—just as Anti-Saloon League activists had long portrayed. Between the slaughterhouses and tenement homes was Whiskey Row, where you could warm yourself next to the stove with friends and drift off into intoxication. "And then his wife might set out to look for him, and she too would feel the cold; and perhaps she would have some of the children with her—and so a whole family would drift into drinking, as the current of a river drifts downstream," Sinclair wrote. "As if to com-plete the chain, the packers all paid their men in checks, refusing all requests to pay in coin; and where in Packingtown could a man go to have his check cashed but to a saloon, where he could pay for the favor by spending a part of the money?"[78]

The Jungle doesn't stop with the economic exploitations by the saloons, but depicts the political corruption as well. The main character, Jurgis Rudkus, encounters a ward heeler, who registered him and his Lithuanian coworkers, before taking them "into the back room of a saloon, and showed each of them where and how to mark a ballot, and then gave each two dollars, and took them to the polling place, where there was a policeman on duty especially to see that they got through all right. Jurgis felt quite proud of this good luck till he got home and met Jonas, who had taken the leader aside and whispered to him, offering to vote three times for four dollars, which offer had been accepted."

Only then did the immigrant Jurgis get an explanation for this unusual ritual. Unlike back in the autocratic tsarist empire, America was a democracy. "The officials who ruled it, and got all the graft, had to be elected first; and so there were two rival sets of grafters, known as political parties, and the one that got the office which bought the most votes. Now and then, the election was very close, and that was the time the poor man came in." But that was only for state or national elections, since the Democratic machine ruled local Chicago politics, from the stockyards to the tenements. On election day, hundreds of these ward heelers would go out from the saloons to deliver the required votes, "all with big wads of money in their pockets and free drinks at every saloon in the district. That was another thing, the men said—all the saloon-keepers had to ... put up on demand, otherwise they could not do business on Sundays, nor have any gambling at all."[79]

The Jungle was all a damning indictment of liquor-machine politics.

While Sinclair's gritty realism may have been shocking to many readers, it certainly wasn't to Anti-Saloon League founder Howard Hyde Russell, who'd done mission work in those very Chicago slums. Certainly, the ASL and organized temperance were happy to promote the works of Sinclair and fellow travelers in progressivism.[80] But that misses the point: any line that we draw between "progressive muckrakers" on the one side and "prohibitionists" on the other would be completely artificial. Back in the 1890s, it was Danish American investigative journalist Jacob Riis who led Police Commissioner Theodore Roosevelt through the seedy slums and saloons of New York that were corrupting his police force. Roosevelt called him "the best American I ever knew."[81] It was muckraker Lincoln Steffens—who likewise enjoyed President Roosevelt's good graces—who blew the lid off the liquor-machine control of St. Louis and Louisville, just as Sinclair had done for Chicago.[82]

But there's a whole other realm of investigative journalists and muckrakers who have long disappeared from public memory, because we've segregated them behind the even more desultory "prohibitionist" label. Perhaps there was none more influential a publicist in muckraking the liquor traffic than Pussyfoot Johnson himself. We've already encountered him muckraking East Coast college dives and investigating Gothenburg systems of liquor control (Chapter 14), as well as his exposés of the army canteens in the South during the Spanish-American War and the American colonial saloons in the Philippines (Chapter 15). But even well before he made his way to the Indian Territory to enforce prohibition, he was casting light on the corruption of the liquor industry.

Amid a highly contentious prohibition campaign in Nebraska back in the 1890s, young journalist William E. Johnson made up some official-looking letterhead for Johnson's Pale Ale. ("My ale was *very* pale," he later joked.) On it, he wrote to politicians, businessmen, and fixers asking for advice "to manage the newspapers and the politicians; and how to get around the preachers."[83] When the wets wrote back, describing how they would rig elections and buy off politicians, Johnson turned around and published their responses, with devastating effect.

Decades later, when West Virginia placed prohibition before the voters in a 1912 statewide referendum, Pussyfoot used the same tactic. He wrote to every newspaper editor in the state, claiming to have thousands of dollars to spend not on advertisements but to run antiprohibition news articles and editorials. Amazingly, seventy editors took the bait, going so far as to list price schedules for selling out their readership to wet interests by the column-inch. Fewer than a dozen editors maintained their journalistic integrity. When Pussyfoot published their communiques in *Collier's*—with its nationwide middle-class readership—it ignited a political firestorm.[84]

"The practice of selling space to whisky interests was pretty generally wiped out," Pussyfoot later wrote with some satisfaction. "Editors hesitated to print even honest expression of wet opinion, for fear they would be accused of taking money to cram propaganda down their readers' throats in the sugar-coated guise of news or editorials." Those newspapers that had proven their ethics above reproach were rewarded with more subscribers. Ultimately, West Virginia voted itself dry by some ninety thousand votes.[85]

Such muckraking exposure of backroom corruption was wholly in line with Anti-Saloon League progressivism; in fact, after the West Virginia escapade, the ASL hired Pussyfoot to run its publishing wing (Chapter 17).[86] Since the ASL could not buy votes or politicians, accountability politics were its most effective weapon: expose liquor-machine corruption to the people, and let the voters have their say. As Anti-Saloon League influence grew, elected politicians too were forced into an uncomfortable reckoning: did their loyalties lie with the increasingly dry sentiment of their constituents, or with the corrupting liquor interests that were paying them under the table?

As for those who protested against his leaking confidential correspondence as being unethical, Pussyfoot only replied, "It is not the first time that I have set a trap for skunks."[87] That much was true.

The Sequoyan Roots of American Prohibition

The Achilles heel of most history books (including this one) is that we read history backward. We start with the outcome that we want to explain—in this case, a national prohibition amendment—and dig backward through history to see what caused it. With a heavy dose of hindsight bias, we concoct engrossing narratives—revolving around important events, actors, and organizations like the ASL or WCTU—in which every development builds to that inevitable climax.[88]

But nothing about American prohibition was inevitable. When Howard Hyde Russell established the Ohio Anti-Saloon League in 1893 to push back against the saloons of Oberlin, he did it without the historian's knowledge of how the next twenty-five years would unfold: the elections, depressions, wars, and every twist and turn of American history. Indeed, even a decade before the Eighteenth Amendment, American prohibitionism seemed dead in the water. By the turn of the twentieth century, those Maine Laws that had been a fixture of New England and midwestern politics had been repealed even in Maine, replaced by high-license, restrictive taxation schemes, and state dispensaries (Chapter 14). When Swedish policy researchers came to the United States to study alcohol-control policies, the only two prohibition states left were far-off North Dakota and Kansas, where Carrie Nation's saloon-smashings showed how ineffective (and corrupting) those state dry laws were in practice.[89]

Indeed, prohibition barely seemed like a thing worth talking about, much less adding to the Constitution. One effective trick that public policy scholars have long used to determine what political issues are on the public agenda—before the advent of modern public-opinion polling—is to scrutinize the *Reader's Guide to Periodical Literature*, an annual digest of the articles in the most widely read magazines in America.[90] It's an imperfect proxy to be sure, but as Figure 16.3 demonstrates, before about 1907, prohibition just wasn't a big deal in American politics.[91]

So, what happened in 1907?

For that, we need to turn to the American state that never was: Sequoyah.

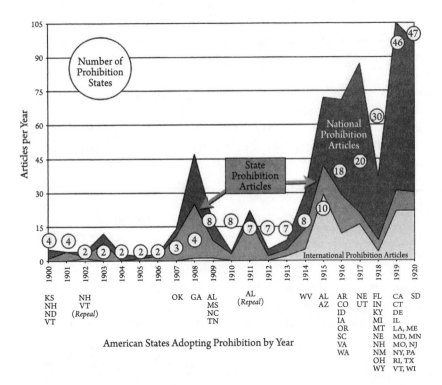

Figure 16.3 Cumulative number of articles per year in the *Reader's Guide to Periodical Literature* dedicated to prohibition at the state, national, and international levels, overlaid with the number of "dry" prohibition states per year, 1900–1920.

Source: Adapted from: Mark Lawrence Schrad, *The Political Power of Bad Ideas: Networks, Institutions, and the Global Prohibition Wave* (New York: Oxford University Press, 2010), 73. State-level data compiled from: Ernest H. Cherrington, ed., *Standard Encyclopedia of the Alcohol Problem*, Vols. 1–6 (Westerville, OH: American Issue Press, 1924–1930); "Union Signal Honor Roll," Union Signal, October 18, 1917, 3. Cherrington, *The Evolution of Prohibition in the United States*, 8–9.

From the American founding, the vast and politically unorganized Indian Country beyond state and territorial boundaries was administered by the federal government. Thanks to Thomas Jefferson, Chief Little Turtle, and generations of Native American leaders, one of the central pillars of Indian Affairs was the steadfast prohibition against the white man's debauching liquor trade (Chapter 9). But such prohibition laws and solemn treaties were ignored with impunity by colonizers pushing westward, driving Native Americans from their ancestral lands onto eversmaller reservations west of the Mississippi, where they and their federal annuities were easy prey for unscrupulous white liquor men (Chapter 10).[92] Following the Land Run of 1889—in which white homesteaders famously rushed to claim for themselves "unassigned" Cherokee, Creek, and Seminole lands—the Indian territory that had once spanned half a continent was reduced to a few counties of what is today eastern Oklahoma.

The land rush ensured that the region had sufficient population to be organized as a territory and eventually a state. But would it enter as one state or two? White or native? Wet or dry? Democrat or Republican? Each of these questions had political reverberations far beyond Oklahoma.

Following their ethnic cleansing and forced removal over the Trail of Tears to reservations west of Arkansas, each of the Five Civilized Tribes (Chapter 10) signed treaties in which the United States vowed that their lands would never be incorporated into any state or territory without the tribes' consent.[93] Each tribe also wasted no time in legislating prohibition laws "for protection from the white man's liquor," according to Indian agent Pussyfoot Johnson.[94] By the terms of the Curtis Act of 1898, the tribes acceded to give up their tribal sovereignty effective March 4, 1906, with the stipulations not only that "the lands now occupied by the Five Civilized Tribes shall, in the opinion of Congress, be prepared for admission as a State to the Union," but also that "the United States agrees to maintain strict laws in the Territory against the introduction, sale, barter or giving away of liquor or intoxicants of any kind or quality."[95]

Thus, not only did the native tribes fully expect that their territories would gain admission as an American state, but a dry state as well, just as tribal sovereignty and Indian prohibition had been interlinked for ages. The assembly of the Five Civilized Tribes made it crystal clear that their two-state expectation was a direct result of the saloon question, writing in an official petition to both houses of the US Congress in 1903,

> The Indians desire a state formed out of the Indian Territory at the expiration of their several tribal governments, in order that they may incorporate in the constitution a provision prohibiting the sale of intoxicating liquors. A prohibition clause could not be embodied in a constitution for a state formed by the union of Indian Territory and Oklahoma, because Oklahoma is now a saloon territory.

It is well known that the political, civil, and religious conditions of the Indians in the Territory of Oklahoma are seriously affected by the liquor traffic, which is nowhere more arrogant than in Oklahoma. The extension of the liquor business over the Indian Territory is earnestly desired by the wholesale liquor dealers of the United States.

The communique to Washington underscored that both the railroad trusts and "the wholesale liquor dealers have already pooled their interests and arranged to maintain a strong lobby in Washington until the Indian Territory is made a part of Oklahoma," making the native reservations ripe for harvest and exploitation.[96]

On the same day they appealed to DC politicians, the tribes likewise put out a call to temperance organizations and dry voters nationwide to impress upon their elected representatives the urgency of the situation. "Ours is a just cause," they claimed, in calling for temperance defense of native rights:

Therefore, Be it resolved by the General Council of the Choctaw Nation in regular session assembled:

That we earnestly request the various religious and temperance organizations of the United States to assist the Indians of the Five Civilized Tribes in their efforts to prevent the annexation of Indian Territory to Oklahoma, either in part or in whole, and to secure an independent state for Indian Territory on March 4, 1906, under a constitution that will prohibit the sale of intoxicants within the boundaries of such state, thereby protecting the Indians from the baleful influence of intoxicating liquors.[97]

The response from the temperance community was overwhelming. Representatives in DC were flooded with thousands of letters and petitions from temperance organizations and churches across the country—estimated to speak on behalf of some thirty-six million Americans—in defense of Indian statehood and prohibition.[98]

The response was heard not just in Washington, but locally too. The WCTU had already become a political mainstay across both the Oklahoma and Indian Territories. Growing steadily since Frances Willard's foundational visits in 1888, by the time of statehood it had chapters in virtually every city and town.[99] Its influence was overshadowed only by the Oklahoma Anti-Saloon League, inaugurated by Howard Hyde Russell in 1898 at the invitation of local civic leaders in Oklahoma City. True to form, the ASL professed absolute neutrality on the two-state question, though "we nevertheless record a firm conviction that the people of Oklahoma . . . are not warranted in asking statehood with Indian Territory at a disregard of their solemn treaty contracts with the Indians."[100]

Still, the dry movement was enlisting additional allies. There was Rev. E. W. Sweet—who'd drafted Pussyfoot Johnson into the Indian Service—and

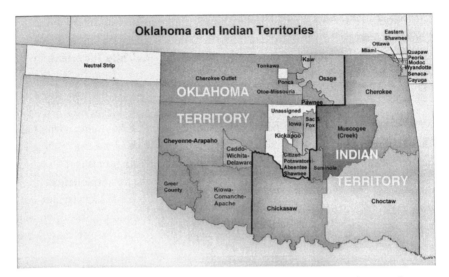

Figure 16.4 Tribal lands of Oklahoma and Indian territories, 1900. Based on Rand McNally and Company, Map of the Indian and Oklahoma Territories, 1892, Library of Congress Geography and Maps Division, adapted by Alexander Schrad.

his appropriately named Indian Territory Church Federation for Prohibition Statehood, stumping locally for a dry constitution.[101] Then, unexpectedly, famed saloon-smasher Carrie Nation moved to Oklahoma in the spring of 1905. "I know my work and mission is world wide," she proclaimed, "but at present Oklahoma is the storm center." Though she left her saloon-smashing ways back in Kansas, she set up her own prohibitionist newspaper, *The Hatchet*, in Guthrie, and organized her Prohibition Federation to push for statehood and constitutional prohibition.[102]

In June 1905 a single-statehood convention was held in Oklahoma City, with the intent of convincing Congress that public sentiment was solidly unified around a one-state solution.[103] In response, that fall the Five Civilized Tribes gathered in Muskogee to hold a constitutional convention for a separate state to be called Sequoyah, named for the Native American polymath who standardized the Cherokee language. Though an equal-suffrage provision was narrowly voted down by the delegates, the Sequoyah constitution included many progressive provisions: strong workers' rights protections and the inclusion of direct-democracy referenda and re-call of elected officials, which progressives had long seen as crucial to accountability and allowing "the people to break the shackles of political corruption and to enable their governments to destroy the liquor traffic."[104] While making allowances for a state-run alcohol dispensary in every county for medicinal, mechanical, and scientific purposes, section ten of the Sequoyah Constitution was quite explicit: "the manufacture, sale, barter or giving away of intoxicating liquors or spirits of any kind within this State is forever prohibited."[105]

The most influential delegate to the Sequoyah convention was the floor leader, Charles N. Haskell. Though not native himself, the plainspoken dry Democrat moved to Muskogee some years before to develop the town's business and railroad infrastructure, and became so sympathetic to the local Creek tribe, they made him their representative.[106] "Neither territory really desires joint statehood," he explained. "Indian Territory earnestly desires prohibition; Oklahoma Territory does not." And since the US government was duty bound to maintain prohibition for the native tribes, separate statehood seemed like the only true solution.[107]

Haskell was understandably skeptical of their prospects in Washington, where tribal sentiment was often taken into consideration on policy matters but was rarely the deciding factor. Still, Haskell brokered a deal with the tribal leaders: "I'll go down the line with you fighting for separate statehood. Furthermore, I'll pay all the incidental expenses of the convention and the election *if* you will agree to approve joint statehood if Congress denies us separate statehood." The chiefs agreed, signing their impromptu agreement on the back of Turner Hotel letterhead.[108]

While the Sequoyah Constitution had been drafted by the convention, it still had to be ratified by the people. When the results of the vote came in—the first organized, democratic election ever held in Indian Territory and the whole history of Indian Country—the results shocked even the cynics: of the 65,352 votes cast (both white and Native Americans), 56,279 favored separate, dry statehood; only 9,073 opposed.[109]

This, then, was the political challenge that faced lawmakers in Washington. Yet in the hearings on Capitol Hill, the Anti-Saloon League's national representative, Edwin Dinwiddie, offered a practical compromise: admit Oklahoma as a single state, but a dry one. The ASL proposed that Congress stipulate—as a condition of statehood—that Oklahoma's state constitution include an explicit prohibition for twenty-one years, after which time the issue could be revisited, thus maintaining the federal government's moral (and legal) obligations to the native tribes.[110] It was an intriguing idea, especially for one-state proponents, including President Roosevelt.[111] When Roosevelt signed into law the final Enabling Act of 1906, the anti-saloon compromise was diluted even further, necessitating a constitutional prohibition that applied only to those Indian territories that would have been Sequoyah.[112] It was a start.

Suddenly—with the form and composition of its government up for grabs—in the fall of 1906, Oklahoma became the epicenter of national politics: Democrats versus Republicans, wets versus drys. Anti-Saloon League stalwart Edwin Dinwiddie moved to Oklahoma to organize the local ASL and WCTU chapters in a push for "Prohibition Statehood": extending the Sequoyah prohibition to the entire state.[113]

An even more influential dry outsider arrived in the form of William Jennings Bryan, fresh from his global tours, rejuvenated and eager to reenter the political fray. Embarking on a grueling whistle-stop tour across the twin territories—usually introduced by the chiefs of the Five Civilized Tribes—the Great Commoner gave rousing progressive speeches to adoring crowds of thousands, then tens of thousands. The famously temperate Bryan urged voters to elect Democratic delegates whose sympathies most closely aligned with their own agrarian-populist interests.[114] The size of the electoral landslide shocked everyone, including Bryan: the 112 delegates to the constitutional convention would be composed of 99 Democrats, 1 independent, and 12 Republicans. Delivering such an impressive win solidified Bryan's return as the standard-bearer for the Democratic Party nationwide.

The overwhelming Democratic majority meant that most of the convention delegates from the eastern part of the state were largely the same men who'd drafted the dry Sequoyah constitution the previous year, led by dry Democrat Charles Haskell. Unsurprisingly, then, the Oklahoma state constitution mirrored the Sequoyah constitution, in some cases almost verbatim. "It was progressive," in the words of one historian, "progressive to the point where it appeared dangerously radical to many people."[115] Women were granted a limited right to vote: only in school elections, but it was far more than most other states allowed. The direct primary, ballot initiative, referendum, and recall powers were there from the Sequoyah draft, as were the beefed-up protections for labor, extensive controls on corporate power, and provisions that "the right of the state to engage in any occupation or business for public purposes shall not be denied or prohibited." Add to that the progressive stipulation that "monopolies are contrary to the genius of a free government, and shall never be allowed."[116]

The most contentious debates raged over prohibition, with Haskell leading the charge against the liquor traffic. "The liquor interests had no political convictions," Haskell explained. "The forces behind it gathered around them the worst elements in society and used them as the balance of power to defeat any party that would not favor the liquor traffic. This condition had a tendency to put men in office who were influenced and even corrupted by the liquor interests."[117]

Despite Haskell's firm convictions, the liquor interests certainly were not about to go down without a fight. And even as the Anti-Saloon League and WCTU watched on from the sidelines of the convention, the delegates were busy hammering out a compromise.

As Haskell later recalled, Edwin Dinwiddie of the Anti-Saloon League and Reverend Sweet from the Indian Territory Church Federation for Prohibition Statehood came to him with the committee report, stipulating prohibition for Indian Territory and local option for the rest of Oklahoma. "We don't want you to be disappointed," they told Haskell. "We have swallowed our ambitions to some extent and we want you to do the same, and support this report."

"Now look here, Sweet," Haskell thundered, "let's not waste any time. I won't support your report. I am here for statewide prohibition when we reach that question and you know it. I am not asking you what you think you can get from this convention. I know what you can get. Just tell me right quick what you would like to have."

"Statewide prohibition," Dinwiddie equivocated, worried of losing fully their hard-fought practical compromise. Ultimately, it was Haskell who passionately persuaded both the prohibition committee—and then the entire convention—of the corrupting influence of the liquor machine, and the enforcement nightmare that would come of having a state that was legally half wet and half dry.[118]

In the end, the delegates agreed to let the people decide: prohibition statehood would be presented as a separate proposition, to be voted on at the same time as the state constitution. If the majority so willed it, prohibition would become part of the constitution.[119]

If that weren't enough—assuming the constitution would be ratified— Oklahoma voters would also be voting on a new slate of politicians to fill the roles vacated by the old, Washington-appointed territorial administration. For his deft handling of the constitutional conventions, the Democrats ran Charles Haskell at the top of the ticket; he'd be squaring off in the contest for governor with the boyish Republican incumbent governor of Oklahoma Territory, Frank Frantz. As a fellow Rough Rider captain who'd charged up San Juan Hill alongside Teddy Roosevelt, he enjoyed the president's good graces and was only thirty-four when Roosevelt elevated him from obscure postmaster of Enid, Oklahoma, to Osage Indian Agent to governor of Oklahoma Territory in 1906.[120]

With so much to be decided, the yearlong lead-up to the elections of September 1907 was one of nonstop campaigning, politicking, and mudslinging. William Jennings Bryan returned to stump for Haskell, prohibition, and adoption of "the best constitution in the United States today," before then parlaying his Oklahoma mojo into reclaiming the Democratic nomination for president for a third time. With Roosevelt having (perhaps foolishly) vowed not to seek reelection in 1908, the Republican case was presented by Secretary of War William Howard Taft, making the battle for Oklahoma a dress rehearsal for the 1908 election between Taft and Bryan. Taft's convoluted position was a hard sell: Oklahomans should "vote down" the constitution, because it was too long and too progressive; but if they *did* vote for it, they should then elect Republicans to fill the new offices.[121]

Incumbent Republican governor Frank Frantz was so worried about his party's prospects, he even pressed President Roosevelt to fire Chief Special Officer Pussyfoot Johnson. Johnson had been making headlines, smashing up illegal saloons across the Indian Territory, and since he was appointed by the Republican Roosevelt, Frantz fretted that he was imperiling the support of the Oklahoma liquor interests and the votes that came with it.

"Let Johnson alone; more power to his elbow," came the blunt, Rooseveltian reply.

"I stayed in the Territory," Pussyfoot later recalled. "The Democrats won—as they probably would have won, anyway—the constitution and the prohibition clause were adopted."[122]

Oklahoma was a milestone victory for the dry cause: not only was a new state admitted with a "clean" constitution, but it was the first time in two decades that any state of any kind had voted itself dry.[123]

But of course the fight didn't end there. With the new state legislature engaged in its first raucous session in the temporary capital of Guthrie, the new governor Charles Haskell tapped Pussyfoot for help in crafting legislation to enforce the prohibition. "He asked me to hop right back on the train, go to Oklahoma City and bring to Guthrie with me the entire staff of the Anti-Saloon League—stenographers and all." So he did.

Given his expertise as a federal prohibition-enforcement agent, Pussyfoot contributed insights into effective search-and-seizure and other legal provisions. But most important would be to define what constituted the contraband in the first place. Pussyfoot's pet definition stemmed from the standards brewers themselves had written into previous tax laws: "intoxicating liquor" was any liquid "which is capable of being used as a beverage and which contains as much as one half of one percent of alcohol, measured by volume."

After some hemming and hawing, Governor Haskell persuaded the legislature to pass the bill, with the 0.5 percent definition included. As one state after another enacted their own prohibitions over the next decade, many copied Oklahoma's model. When nationwide prohibition finally became a reality with the ratification of the Eighteenth Amendment in 1919, it likewise required an enforcement provision: the Volstead Act. At that point, Pussyfoot wired Anti-Saloon League leader Wayne Wheeler—who drafted the federal legislation along with Minnesota representative Andrew Volstead—suggesting the 0.5 percent provision.

"He caught the point like a flash," Pussyfoot remembered. "'That's got to go in!' he said emphatically.

"And in it went."[124]

The Southern Dry Wave

Dry Oklahoma wasn't some trivial sideshow: both wet and dry political interests understood it as a major confrontation, one in which the organized liquor interests went down in defeat. Still, Oklahoma in 1907 could be dismissed as a one-off aberration, were it not for what happened next. Over the next two years, one state after another built on Oklahoma's momentum and voted to join the prohibition ranks: Georgia, Alabama, Mississippi, North Carolina, and Tennessee constituted a veritable "dry wave" that swept the Deep South. Prohibition legislation was passed by both houses of the Arkansas statehouse too, but the bills failed to be reconciled.[125] Of course, these southern states did not have significant Native American minorities, but significant—and largely disenfranchised—African American populations. In each case, statewide prohibition was not some imposition from above, but the result of generations of grassroots organizing against the liquor traffic—from dry communities, to dry counties, to dry states.

Southern prohibitionism is something of an enigma for historians. After all, isn't prohibition supposed to succeed in places where temperance organizations were the *strongest*? But these were the very states of the Deep South that the Anti-Saloon League themselves admitted that—much like Frances Willard and the WCTU before them—they had their most difficulty in establishing an organizational foothold.[126] The usual answer, then, is to rely on crude stereotypes and tired colonial alcohol discourses to chalk up southern prohibition to the Ku Klux Klan (KKK) and racists trying to "discipline" African Americans in the Jim Crow South.[127]

There are quite a few problems with that explanation. First, the modern KKK was organized in 1915, which makes it an unlikely cause for prohibition in 1908. Second, the object of the reform movement—the saloons and liquor traffic that built their economic and political power at the expense of the poor—was overwhelmingly in white hands, not black. Third, the argument that liquor was subjugation to white power, and prohibition meant community uplift and freedom from that political and economic oppression was clearly and consistently articulated by the black churches, which had been the most vocal proponents of prohibition going back to the Reconstruction Era (Chapter 13). Fourth, the wet forces were far weaker, more dispersed geographically, and far less organized to defend their predatory practices than the vast brewing and liquor trusts of the North. Finally, in the Democrats' one-party South, liquor interests had fewer opportunities to flex their political muscle by throwing their weight behind rival parties or candidates more disposed to do their bidding. At the very least, expanding the view to political and economic factors—rather than just cultural ones—gives us a much broader understanding of the actual dynamics of the prohibition movement in the South: all of which was clear to the activists and political players of the day.

"While the Anti-Saloon League was born in the North," wrote ASL chronicler Ernest Cherrington in 1913, "the temperance sentiment in the South generally was far in advance of that in the North, and the application of the Anti-Saloon League method of crystallizing sentiment for tangible results naturally operated more quickly and more effectively in the states of the Southland than elsewhere where sentiment was not so strong."[128] In explaining this "tidal wave of temperance reform," Cherrington went on to applaud the able leadership of southern anti-saloon activists: Bishop Charles Betts Galloway of Mississippi, Reverend George Young of Kentucky, and Bishop James Cannon of Virginia, who helped to close eleven thousand saloons in 1908 alone.[129]

Cherrington then emphasized that the thing they were fighting against—the liquor traffic—was in utter disarray, both locally and nationally. Perhaps with the exception of the Distilling Company of America and the whiskey distillers of Kentucky, most of the big brewing interests were in the North: St. Louis, Milwaukee, and Cincinnati. Corrupt liquor-machine politics likewise was a more of a feature of

New York, Chicago, Omaha, and the cities of the North—where organized liquor could more easily tip the scales in favor of one party over another—rather than in the Solid South.

To the extent that the wet side had a countervailing strategy, it was not to defend the South, but to counterattack in the North. In particular, they focused their efforts on taking-down Governor Andrew Harris in the Anti-Saloon heartland of Ohio, as well as local-option Republican gubernatorial candidate James Watson next-door in Indiana. In the 1908 elections, the organized liquor forces succeeded in unseating both drys at the top of their tickets, only to find to their horror that the vast majority of down-ticket representatives to the legislatures of both states were prohibitionists. The resulting state legislatures in both states were thus overwhelmingly dry, and weren't about to repeal local-option laws as the saloon forces wanted. Instead, they piled additional restrictions on the liquor trade.[130]

To their credit—and partly as a consequence of their electoral drubbings— the organized liquor interests themselves recognized the merits of the anti-saloon outcry. Saloons could be objectively awful places. As a public-relations gesture to clean up their tarnished popular image, brewers' trusts in Ohio and elsewhere hopped on the dry bandwagon—establishing "vigilance bureaus" to self-police, en- sure compliance with state liquor laws, and shut down some of the most vile and disreputable saloons that were giving the whole industry a bad name. To look the part of a good corporate citizen, the United States Brewers' Association condemned saloons that sold to minors and that encouraged prostitution and gambling, and ac- tually urged the passage of stricter laws to regulate their trade.

But in many ways, it was too little, too late.

"We dislike to acknowledge it, but we really believe the entire business all over has overstayed the opportunity to protect itself against the onward march of pro- hibition," admitted J. E. Nolan, editor of *Beverages*—the official publication of the National Liquor League—in response to Georgia's prohibition. "Five years ago a united industry might have kept back the situation that now confronts it, but to-day it is too late. . . . Might as well try to keep out the Hudson River with a whisk-broom."[131]

Weakness of the organized liquor forces aside, even contemporaries grappled with the causes of southern prohibition. "The obvious cause, and the one most often given in explanation, is the presence of the negro," wrote journalist Frank Foxcroft in the *Atlantic Monthly*. "It is said that the vote for prohibition in the South represents exactly the same reasoning which excludes liquor from Indian reservations, shuts it out by international agreement from the islands of the Pacific, and excludes it from great areas in Africa under the British flag."

But Foxcroft reminded his primarily northern readership that "the presence of the negro furnishes only a partial explanation of the prohibition movement of the south. It is a noticeable fact that, during the debate in the Georgia legislature upon the pending prohibitory bill, the negro was not once mentioned as a reason for the enactment of prohibition." Instead, he noted that liquor-industry predations were suffered both by white communities and black, and were opposed by white communities and black, and were being roused by "the ablest and most far-sighted leaders of Southern opinion," both white and black.[132]

In southern African American communities, the black churches were at the forefront of temperance and prohibitionism.[133] And in terms of its leaders, one need look no further than Booker T. Washington: the activist first president of the Tuskegee Institute in Alabama, dedicated to African American higher education. Washington famously networked with many of the most influential figures of the day, including those with antiliquor sentiments: Theodore Roosevelt and William Jennings Bryan, John D. Rockefeller, William Howard Taft, Susan B. Anthony, and even Leo Tolstoy.[134] Lost among the usual considerations of his civil rights leadership is that Washington had a long-standing interest in the liquor question in the South.

Even in the 1890s Washington won plaudits for his dry activism. The Mount Vernon Military Barracks north of Mobile had been repurposed as an internment camp for "Apache Captives"—including the famed Geronimo—who actively resisted the white colonial encroachments into their native lands in New Mexico and Arizona. In 1891 Washington lobbied for the abolition of the debauching liquor traffic around the camp. "If the Bill should pass, you will have done much to save the tribe," wrote the Massachusetts Indian Association.[135]

More immediately in Tuskegee, the Woman's Club—of which Washington's wife Margaret was president—protested that the selling of liquor in the Negro Building was "an insult to at least the womanhood of the Negro race."[136] In his personal correspondence, Washington often spoke out against the liquor traffic as an impediment to the uplift of the African American community, even going so far as to oppose Gothenburg-style municipal dispensary alternatives. "It is bad for an individual to be engaged in the sale of liquor, and it is much worse for an entire community to be engaged in the traffic of liquor, through the agency of a dispensary," he claimed, with the revenue benefits outweighed by the social harms.[137] Yet with the coming of statewide prohibition across the South, his interest in the dry cause kicked into high gear.

In 1907 Booker T. Washington published a detailed study of Mound Bayou, Mississippi (population four thousand): the only all-black town in the South. Poring through the town's court records, Washington found it "a remarkably quiet and sober place," save perhaps for the occasional outsider swooping in to sell liquor illegally on the weekends. Interviewing Isaiah Montgomery—the town's founder and head of the business league—as to the reason for the lack of crime and high moral standards of the community, Montgomery pointed to the importance of public support: "The people recognize that the laws, when they are enforced, represent the sentiment of the community and are imposed for their own good. It is not so easy for them to realize that where the government is entirely in the hands of white men."

Perhaps the most notable example of that community sentiment was Mound Bayou's longstanding prohibition against the liquor traffic. The white liquor interests at the state and county level had repeatedly tried to legalize the booze traffic. In their all-black town, "a colored man might run the saloon here," Montgomery explained, "but in the rest of the county they would be in the hands of white men. We would pay for maintaining them, however, and we would be the ones to suffer. We voted the law down and there has been no attempt to open the county to the liquor traffic since."[138]

Interracial mistrust and mutual suspicions had long plagued the southern dry movement. White prohibitionists often viewed their black counterparts as unreliable partners, even pointing to exposés of the liquor traffic stealing elections by getting black voters drunk, or by exploiting their poverty by buying their votes. But as civil rights activist and professor W. E. B. DuBois argued—like Frances Ellen Watkins Harper did before him (Chapter 13)—these developments were as much of an indictment of the white liquor traffickers' amorality and willingness to bribe, as it was of African American poverty. Furthermore, he condemned the opportunism of white "'reformers,' who for eleven months in the year take every opportunity to show their contempt for a black face, suddenly a few weeks before election order the Negro voters to vote for their measures on pain of further disfranchisement. When some Negroes refuse to do this, we are told in triumphant tones that Negroes are not worthy of the ballot!"[139]

While W. E. B. DuBois and Booker T. Washington had their differences, they were united in opposing white misperceptions of African American temperance. "I have read much in the Northern papers about the prohibition movement in the South being based wholly upon a determination or desire to keep liquor away from the negroes and at the same time provide a way for the white people to get it," wrote Washington in 1908. "I have watched the prohibition movement carefully from its inception to the present time, and I have seen nothing in the agitation in favor of the movement, nothing in the law itself, and nothing in the execution of the law that warrants any such conclusion. The prohibition movement is based upon a deep-seated desire to get rid of whiskey in the interest of both races because of its hurtful economic and moral results. The prohibition sentiment is as strong in counties where there are practically no colored people as in the Black Belt counties."[140]

In this, his most detailed study of southern prohibitionism, Washington traced the strength of black temperance from the Reconstruction Era, bolstered by the strength of local churches—both white and black—across the South. That temperance sentiment was strong enough to rebuff even the suspicions of Anti-Saloon League activists from the North as being lowly carpetbaggers, looking to foist northern politics and morality on an unwilling South. Frances Willard's "we come to unify" goodwill forays and WCTU activism fostered ever greater cooperation across the North-South divide (Chapter 13). Washington's studies tracked statistical improvements in crime and socioeconomic indicators in the urban centers of Atlanta and Birmingham under prohibition—which Washington expanded upon in his subsequent criminological study on "Negro Crime and Strong Drink"[141]—but always with an eye toward the racial disparities in every case.

> Directly and indirectly, the members of my own race have suffered, perhaps more than any other portion of the population, from the effects of the liquor traffic. But the educated men and the leaders of the race have been quick to see the advantages that would come from the total suppression of the saloon. Everywhere in the South this class have given their votes to the support of prohibition even where it brought them in opposition to the men whom they have been disposed to regard as their friends, in the support of those whom they have been accustomed to regard as their enemies. In Birmingham the negroes formed an organization, and cast nearly all of the registered colored vote for prohibition.

After giving a nod to temperance as empowering otherwise disenfranchised women as political actors across the South, Washington concluded: "No one who is at all acquainted with the conditions in the South can doubt the depth and the genuineness of the feelings that are behind prohibition in the South, which is in no way a political maneuver, but an inspired movement of the masses of the people [as] an intellectual awakening and a moral revolution."[142]

Of course, as an outspoken leader, Booker T. Washington's insights into the complicated relationship of African Americans to the liquor trade weren't limited to either black or southern audiences. His powerful statements on the practical benefits of prohibition caught the attention of the European transnational temperance community, which was eager to learn from the South's early experiments with prohibition. In 1909 Washington responded to Russian count Lyudvik "Louis" Skarzynski—official representative of the imperial Russian Ministry of Foreign Affairs, bankroller of the biennial European temperance congresses (Chapters 3 & 4)—on his investigations into the American experience.[143]

"The masses of the Negro people in the South are, as you perhaps know, a class corresponding in a way to the peasant classes of Europe." Speaking on their behalf, he argued that "the prohibition laws as enacted in the South will not only be a great help to the Negro people themselves, but to the whites as well," as had been borne out by social statistics. Arrests had decreased, economic well-being had increased, and even the money filtered through state dispensaries "is now more satisfactorily used," he claimed. As for European suspicions that the black lower classes would turn to moonshining and bootlegging, Washington did "not believe that, taken as a whole, the Negro people will be found secretly promoting traffic in liquor. I believe in the Southern State, as a whole, that the prohibition laws are being honestly enforced," and that "Negroes quite sincerely deprecate the use of liquor among the masses of our people, as we have some knowledge of the demoralizing degradation which its use has wrought among us."[144] One can only infer what insights the tsar's government ministries may have taken from this report in dealing with the vodka monopoly and the impoverished Russian peasantry (Chapter 2).

Ultimately, then, cultural and racial questions were only part of the broader economic and political dynamics of prohibition, not just among Native Americans in Oklahoma, but also among African Americans in the South. Though understanding prohibition as the empowerment of oppressed and disenfranchised communities may run against our present-day conventional wisdom on prohibitionism as a reactionary white people's movement, contemporary observers understood this quite clearly as a liberation movement from economic exploitation, which transcended racial, religious, gender, and geographical divides.

"The South needs for its development capital, and intelligent and diversified labor. It cannot attract either if industry is made irregular and life and property insecure through the multiplication of doggeries and dives," concluded Foxcroft's 1908 consideration of southern prohibition:

> In the South, moreover, as elsewhere in the United States, the saloon interests themselves are largely responsible for the revolt against them, which leads up to these drastic laws. Rapacious, lawless, and cruel, unmindful of the public welfare and of private rights, defiant of restraint and impudently insistent upon their right to do as they please, they have worn out the patience of the public. They have elected and have controlled sheriffs, mayors, aldermen, and legislators, until the people have awakened to the fact that the short and simple, not to say the only way, to get rid of the saloon in politics is to get rid of the saloon. No explanation of the southern situation is complete that does not recognize this fact.[145]

The Battle for a Dry America

Republican National Convention, Chicago Coliseum; Chicago, Illinois: Tuesday, July 28, 1908

"Vote for Taft this time. You can vote for Bryan anytime!" read a popular campaign button from the 1908 Republican National Convention at the Chicago Coliseum.[1] It was a solid burn. The Democrat William Jennings Bryan had just secured his party's nomination for president for the third time, up against William Howard Taft: Theodore Roosevelt's handpicked successor, secretary of war, and former governor-general of the Philippines.

With both parties claiming the mantle of progressivism, the Republican National Convention tried to sharpen the partisan distinction by riding on Roosevelt's record and never even mentioning the uninspiring Taft. "Mr. Roosevelt's policies have been progressive and regulative; Mr. Bryan's destructive. Mr. Roosevelt has favored regulation of the business in which evils have grown up so as to stamp out the evils and permit the business to continue." The legacy of the vigorous and popular Roosevelt administration was far more inspiring than the visage of his portly successor.

When it came to banking trusts, industrial trusts, or the liquor trust, the Republicans claimed the pattern was the same: "The tendency of Mr. Bryan's proposals has generally been destructive of the business with respect to which he is demanding reform. Mr. Roosevelt would compel the trusts to conduct their business in a lawful manner and secure the benefits of their operation and the maintenance of the prosperity of the country of which they are an important part; while Mr. Bryan would extirpate and destroy the entire business in order to stamp out the evils which they have practiced."[2]

Ironically, despite his well-known teetotalism, Bryan tiptoed around the prohibition question on yet another nationwide whistle-stop campaign in 1908, so as not to alienate potential "wet" voters. Policy—including alcohol-control policy, local option, and statewide prohibition—should follow the expressed will of the people, which Bryan was intent on empowering. "Shall the people control their own

Government and use that Government for the protection of their rights and for the promotion of their welfare? or shall the representatives of predatory wealth prey upon a defenseless public, while the offenders secure immunity from subservient officials whom they raise to power by unscrupulous methods?" This was the very core of his 1908 "Shall the People Rule?" platform.[3]

But another demoralizing electoral defeat—52 percent to to Bryan's 43 percent, equating to a 321 to 162 loss in the electoral college—prompted a reassessment. With good reason, Bryan suspected that the organized liquor machines helped engineer his defeat in the crucial swing states of Missouri, Illinois, Indiana, and Ohio, and thwarted his efforts to get empowering initiative and referendum measures through the Nebraska statehouse. This only confirmed what Bryan had always known: saloon power was the enemy of progressive reform. Only after 1908—with no more elections to contest and no wet voters to appease—did America's most popular orator come out for nationwide prohibition as the only way to liberate the people and smash the political corruption of the liquor machine.[4]

William Jennings Bryan also came out vocally in favor of women's suffrage in 1910, years before most men in his party. Juxtaposed against Roosevelt's machismo militarism, Bryanism stood for women's empowerment, peace, and prohibition. It was social gospel progressivism dressed in Christian morality (Chapter 14).[5] Since universal, Tolstoyan "love was the law of life, and forgiveness the test of love, and service the measure of greatness," then only men who served altruistically to empower women were truly doing God's work.[6] Of course, suffrage was an end in and of itself, but only the electoral empowerment of women could rightly honor and reward their political activism, Bryan argued. While the leadership of organizations like the Anti-Saloon League was largely populated by men, it was women who shouldered the brunt of the grassroots activism, the campaigning and letter writing, and that was vital to the cause of all humanity.[7]

"God never made alcohol necessary to the human body, mind, or soul," Bryan wrote in explaining his support of prohibition.[8] Nor was the peddling of liquor some wholesome, Christly activity—just the opposite in fact. So it was fully in accordance with the teachings of Christ to liberate one's fellow man from their chains of slavery—not just the subjugation of alcoholism, but to those who make money by selling it to them. While Bryan had always promoted the rights of communities and states to vote themselves dry, now it was time to come together as a nationwide community to achieve this great aim.

"The national triumph of prohibition will be, therefore, the final result of the lesser triumphs," he proclaimed, "and those who labor to secure it will have the satisfaction of knowing that, in protecting themselves from the economic burdens, the social demoralization and the moral menace of the saloon, they are not only not injuring others—even those who most strenuously oppose the movement—but are helping to create conditions which will bring the highest good to the greatest number, without any injustice to any, for it is not injustice to any man to refuse him permission to enrich himself by injuring his fellowmen."[9]

For his part, Bryan would help lead this movement from outside the usual political channels. Following his third, stinging defeat in 1908, he would no longer run in elections, but he was still the most admired orator of his generation. His words commanded attention. Plus, with its nationwide circulation, Bryan's influential *The Commoner* would ratchet up its scathing indictments of the predatory saloon business. Finally, he was still a Democrat through and through. Bryan still vowed to lead his party in an ever-more progressive direction, declaring his overarching political goal to be "protection of the people from exploitation at the hands of predatory corporations."[10]

And that's exactly what he would do.

Shifting to a National Strategy

Bryan was hardly alone in speaking in favor of prohibition. Buoyed by the victory of statewide prohibitions across the South in 1907–1908 and local-option advances in the North, progressive prohibition sentiment was on the rise nationally, and with it rose the temperance organizations. State-level Anti-Saloon Leagues continued to expand and thrive, exposing wet political deceit, while throwing their ever-growing political clout behind dry candidates. Meanwhile—having brokered the compromise over Oklahoma—the league's national headquarters in Washington continued to monitor Congress.

As always, the ASL's approach was a practical one, meant to augment their grassroots advances. Whatever gains were being made with prohibition at the state level were consistently undermined by neighboring wet jurisdictions. Long-standing "original package" laws presented a massive loophole: individuals in dry territory could import liquor across state lines—and even sell it to others—so long as it stayed in its original package.[11] According to the Constitution, the only body that could regulate such interstate commerce was the federal government.

This wasn't just dry excuse-making for why prohibition's touted benefits weren't being realized, or some nefarious attempt to erode individual liberty to drink; this was a big deal, and both sides knew it. Wet lawyers encouraged brewers, distillers, and wholesalers large and small to "avail themselves of the privilege" of selling by express companies willing to ship cash-on-delivery (COD) to customers in prohibition states. Anheuser-Busch established an entire mail-order department to ship beer by the crate directly to consumers.

"Drummers" toured prohibition states to drum up the liquor business, sharing "samples" of their wares and taking orders. Technically, it was the shipping companies—many set up by the liquor trust themselves—that did the trafficking and selling. As everywhere in the liquor industry, a few bribes here and there were enough to get corrupt law enforcement to look the other way. Shipping companies knowingly trafficked in liquor addressed to fictitious consignees, which would be stored in warehouses, available to anyone wishing to "claim" them. Express offices in dry states effectively became clandestine liquor stores, and everybody knew it. To avoid detection by law enforcement, liquor crates would be labeled as coffee, groceries, or other goods. "Dear Sir—we are holding at your risk a package of books," said the notifications from the express agency in dry Bainbridge, Ohio, "and you should get them at once as they are leaking badly."[12]

As drys were fixated on Oklahoma in 1906–1907, a consortium of brewers— Pabst, Blatz, Schlitz, and Anheuser-Busch—organized a self-described "invasion" of Carrie Nation's dry Kansas just over the border. Hoping to capitalize on prohibition frustrations, they bankrolled over a hundred barkeepers and opened illegal saloons across the state with all their beer shipped in across state lines, prompting a legal showdown. Some four and a half million gallons of liquor flooded dry Kansas annually.[13]

To stem these corrupt abuses, both the Anti-Saloon League and WCTU pressed for interstate commerce laws at both the state and federal level to increase transparency. The 1909 COD Act—a compromise largely drafted with the input of Wayne Wheeler of the ASL—was incredibly modest: only requiring shippers to clearly and honestly label their contents (liquor or not), as well as requiring the consignee to be an actual person. It wasn't much, but it was progress. In addition, the law was fully consistent with the new progressivism in utilizing the powers of the federal government under Taft to regulate interstate commerce.[14]

The next logical step—a federal measure to ban the interstate traffic in booze— was delayed by a schism within the temperance movement in 1910. The ASL's chief lobbyist in Washington, Edwin Dinwiddie, was hired away by an upstart rival temperance organization: the Inter-Church Temperance Federation. The schism was patched up only when the organizations put aside their differences and traveled together as the American delegation to the thirteenth biennial International Congress Against Alcoholism in The Hague in 1911. Upon their return, they agreed to redouble their efforts to achieve an interstate commerce bill.[15]

Thanks in part to grassroots temperance activism delivering ever-more dry representatives to Congress in the 1910 midterm elections, the legislative field was more fertile still. President Taft even invited ASL representatives to the White House to assure them that he would not veto an interstate regulation bill, if Congress were to pass one. In December 1911 the drys got together to draft what would eventually become the Webb-Kenyon Act to prohibit the shipment or transportation of liquor into territory where they were "intended by any person interested therein, to be received, possessed, sold, or in any manner used, either in the original package or otherwise in violation of any law" of the receiving state. The language was largely drafted by Fred Caldwell, a longtime member of the Oklahoma Anti-Saloon League. Caldwell had been appointed by Governor Charles Haskell (Chapter 16) as

Oklahoma's state prohibition-enforcement attorney, where he dealt with organized liquor's constant attempts to flood his state, and from where he developed an expertise in interstate commerce law. To defend against wet attempts to dilute the bill, in 1912 the ASL persuaded Iowa Republican senator William S. Kenyon and Texas Democratic representative Morris Sheppard to introduce the Caldwell-drafted bill simultaneously in both houses—although its ultimate passage and adoption would get sucked into the infamous multiparty political melee that was the 1912 election.[16]

Sidebar: The Liquor Question in Party Politics, 1912

Without question, the Republican Party dominated national politics from the Civil War through World War I. However by the twentieth century, the GOP had become two parties in one body: a progressive faction led by Teddy Roosevelt and a more conservative, moneyed aristocracy, championed by Roosevelt's successor, William Howard Taft. It didn't take Karl Marx to point out that the interests of both the wealthy capitalists and the working masses didn't often align. Still, during his presidency, Roosevelt held the party together through his overwhelming popularity and iconic charisma. The conservative faction grumbled quietly as he pulled the party further leftward. But after effectively passing the baton to President Taft in 1908, Roosevelt left the scene, embarking on a yearlong African safari to hunt big game during 1909 and 1910.

Of course, politics followed Roosevelt to Africa. While touring the Belgian Congo, Roosevelt made common cause with Belgian socialist Emile Vandervelde in support of prohibiting the trade in liquor to enslave and debauch Africans in the colonies (Chapter 3).[17] Meanwhile, African message runners brought Roosevelt's camp news from home, including Taft's dismissal of numerous Roosevelt appointees and abandonment of Roosevelt's conservationist and antitrust policies in deference to big-business interests.[18]

The rift deepened after Roosevelt's return stateside. Ahead of the 1910 midterms, he stumped for a new nationalism that would place "human welfare" over the corporate interests championed by Republican conservatives.[19] There were policy differences big and small, but—as Roosevelt told the *Saturday Evening Post*—one that infuriated him most was Taft's coziness with the liquor trust to undermine his crowning achievement: the Pure Food and Drug Act.[20]

Before regulation, food producers were under no obligation to acknowledge the myriad of cheap, harmful, and potentially even poisonous preservatives and fillers they were putting into their food products in an effort to lower costs and boost profits. As a truth-in-labeling law to protect public health against corporate malfeasance, the Pure Food and Drug Act imposed harsh penalties for the adulteration or misbranding of "any article of food, drug, *or liquor*."

That liquor fell under the purview of Roosevelt's signature legislation was a nightmare for the industry. No one wanted to be seen as defending poison over purity, but every step of the way, the National Wholesale Liquor Dealers' Association fought to weaken and undermine the law. They chafed that only grain alcohol, aged for years in barrels to remove impurities, could be labeled "whiskey." In reality, most alcohol failed to meet that purity standard. Even before being watered down or cut with additives by unscrupulous saloon-keepers, most modern liquor was rectified: industrially distilled ethyl alcohol, with caramel coloring and flavors added to make it taste like genuine barrel-aged whiskey.[21] (Today, a similar distinction is made between "straight" and "blended" whiskeys.) Rectifiers, which made up the lion's share of spirits producers, obviously did not want to list all of the additives and impurities on their labels and howled at Roosevelt's decision—supported by his scientists, health experts, and attorney general—that such rectified spirits be clearly branded as "imitation whiskey." They lobbied and pleaded with the administration that (rightly) no one would buy something called "imitation whiskey." Roosevelt stuck by his guns.[22]

But with Roosevelt out of the way, the liquor machine found a much more pliable figure in Taft. In 1909 he reversed Roosevelt's decision, declaring that all grain alcohol could be labeled as "whiskey."[23] The liquor trust was elated. Roosevelt was livid.

In early 1912 Roosevelt decided to take his party back, challenging Taft for the Republican nomination for president. He won a series of these newfangled state primary elections, including Taft's home state of Ohio. In a May interview titled "Why Roosevelt Opposes Taft," Roosevelt explained,

> I regard the pure-food law, with the meat-inspection act, as one of the great achievements of my Administration. It was my earnest endeavor to enforce that law with fairness to food manufacturers, but without favor to those engaged in mis-branding or adulterating food and drugs. Soon after its passage the National Wholesale Liquor Dealers' Association, venders [sic] of imitation whisky, who had defeated the pure-food bill in the Senate on more than one occasion, sought to break down the administration of the law and secure unwarranted license to perpetrate their misrepresentations on the public.

By reversing course, Taft "gave the imitation-whisky interests all that they had ever demanded," Roosevelt claimed. Not only was it a victory for liquor-machine chicanery over transparency and public knowledge, but it also undermined the entire point of the bill. If you could call industrial distillates with added flavors and colors "whiskey," then you could call pure coffee cut with chicory "coffee" or tea mixed with willow leaves "tea"; and at that point, the whole notion of purity standards in the public interest goes out the window.[24]

The schism between Roosevelt and Taft broke out into an all-out war the following month at the Chicago Coliseum, site of the Republican National Convention. Though the progressive Roosevelt had won the primaries, the party establishment was dominated by the conservatives, who fell in line to nominate Taft as the Republican presidential candidate. Roosevelt and his delegates stormed out of the convention. They returned to the Chicago Coliseum that August to nominate Roosevelt as their candidate for the newly established Progressive Party, which aimed "to dissolve the unholy alliance between corrupt business and corrupt politics."[25] Having agreed to cover the convention as a political commentator for *The World*, the prohibitionist Democrat William Jennings Bryan smiled with satisfaction from the balcony.[26]

The Progressive "Bull Moose" convention at Chicago—so-called as Roosevelt claimed to have the strength of a bull moose—was unlike any major party convention before. There was "not a saloon-keeper in the crowd," one newsie wrote. It was a "plain folks' convention," lacking in the usual politicos, convention "rounders," and "protégés of plutocracy," instead populated by businessmen, "clean cut and successful looking,—assuredly not the type of individual who accepts a gold brick either in business or in politics,—the farmer, the manufacturer, the minister, the doctor, and, of course, the lawyer."[27]

Most notable of all were the women. "Instead of forcing your way through a crowd of tobacco-stained political veterans," the *New York Times* wrote, "you raise your hat politely and say, 'Pardon me, Madam.'"[28] Since the Progressives championed equal suffrage, the floor was populated by scores of suffragettes, social workers, and advocates for working girls' rights. "Nor could these people be classed as cranks or impractical idealists, riding impossible hobbies," journalist William Menkel reported. "They were men and women who had labored long and ardently for social and industrial betterment, and their opinions were the result of knowledge and experience."[29]

Unlike the Republican convention, there was no doubt who the nominee would be, and the party platform was a difference of night and day. The Progressives promoted a sweeping platform of equal suffrage, transparency in campaign finance, workers' rights and industrial protections, minimum-wage standards for women, "a living wage in all industrial occupations," an eight-hour workday, development of highway infrastructure, organization of a department of labor, public health, a national health service, and an assertion "that the people shall have the ultimate authority to determine fundamental questions of social welfare and public policy," rather than capitalist trusts and their political machines.[30] Consistent with his progressivism, Roosevelt favored nationwide prohibition in 1912, though it was not explicitly made part of the party platform.[31]

The Republican split all but assured victory for the Democrats. Still leading his party without running, William Jennings Bryan's goals were just as progressive as the Progressives' and Roosevelt's: "protection of the people from exploitation at the hands of predatory corporations."[32] The frontrunners for the Democratic nomination were Speaker of the House Champ Clark from Missouri and former Princeton University president and governor of New Jersey, Woodrow Wilson. Both were able leaders whom Bryan knew well.

With Taft's star already in eclipse as the defender of big business, the organized liquor traffic threw its weight behind the Democratic campaign of Champ Clark. Anheuser-Busch and the liquor machine delivered the delegates of his home state of Missouri, while in the Illinois primaries, it was the brewers and distillers that organized anti-Wilson protests. The Dallas *News* proclaimed that in the Texas campaign, "the opposition to Dr. Wilson is compounded chiefly of these three elements: spoils, whisky and privilege." Ahead of the Democratic National Convention in Baltimore, the Clark campaign suddenly launched an advertising boom. On its front page, the *New York Times* explained, "The principal source of the Clark campaign fund is said to be the liquor interests of the country. They are much concerned about the bill providing against inter-State shipment of liquor": the ASL-supported legislation that was still languishing in the House, where Speaker Clark held tremendous sway.[33]

For his part, Wilson was a pragmatist. Though only an occasional drinker, Wilson preferred to stay aloof from the divisive prohibition fight. Much like Bryan previously had, Wilson supported the ability for communities to vote themselves dry through local option or statewide prohibition as the expressed will of the people, but he was mum on national prohibition. He feared that making what he thought was a private issue into a political one would exacerbate party rifts and complicate other reforms.[34]

When the Democratic National Convention opened in Baltimore, Clark had a majority of delegates but was short of the two-thirds necessary to secure the nomination. Only on the thirteenth round of balloting did the Democratic delegates from New York State—influenced by the wet Tammany Hall machine—throw their support as a bloc behind Clark. But party stalwart William Jennings Bryan hadn't yet played his hand.

Bryan—who had recently lamented to friends that the liquor interests had a grip on the Democratic Party that must be broken—announced he was switching his vote from Clark to Wilson, but only so long as Wilson got no support from the corrupt New York machine. At that point, fisticuffs erupted on the floor between rival delegates. But when the smoke ultimately cleared, on the forty-sixth ballot, Wilson received the two-thirds majority to secure the nomination, with Bryan retaining his role as Democratic kingmaker.[35]

The political fireworks continued into the fall, as the three candidates were joined by a fourth contender: Socialist Eugene Debs, who argued for working-class empowerment as the route to genuine democracy. With Debs, Wilson, and Roosevelt all promoting different flavors of progressivism—trust busting, empowerment of women, and workers against the corporate oligarchy—Taft effectively gave up. He delivered the occasional anti-Roosevelt speech between rounds of golf, waiting to return to civilian life.[36]

Roosevelt recognized winning would be a long shot. Still, he conducted a vigorous national campaign. Little did Roosevelt know he was being stalked on his tour by a disgruntled New York saloon-keeper. Thirty-six-year-old John Flammang Schrank owned a saloon and neighboring tenement building at 370 East Tenth Street in the East Village of New York City, and had become agitated by newspaper reports about Roosevelt seeking an unprecedented third term. Buying a Colt .38, he was intent on stopping that when he finally caught up to Roosevelt in Milwaukee.

According to trial testimony, Schrank had spent most of the day of October 14, 1912, in the Milwaukee saloon of Herman Rollfink. He "drank five or six beers" that afternoon. Around seven o'clock, he bought the bar a round of drinks and asked the musicians to strike up "The Star Spangled Banner." He laughed and danced and drank, before heading down the street to kill Roosevelt, who was en route to deliver a campaign speech. Outside the Hotel Gilpatrick, Schrank pushed through a crowd of admirers and shot Roosevelt in the chest from a distance of six feet. Ironically, it was the Milwaukee saloon owner Rollfink who immediately subdued the shooter.[37]

"He pinked me, Harry," Roosevelt told his aide, as a scuffle ensued.

Blunted by fifty pages of his typewritten campaign speech in his breast pocket, the bullet lodged between the fourth and fifth rib on his right side. As a hunter and Rough Rider, Roosevelt was no stranger to gunshot wounds. He correctly determined that since he wasn't coughing up blood, the bullet hadn't penetrated his lungs. It would stay lodged in his chest for the rest of his life.

"Don't hurt him; bring him to me here!" commanded Roosevelt to the crowd, which was intent on tearing the assassin limb from limb. They obeyed. For a moment, he looked Schrank straight in the eyes, saying nothing, before turning to his scheduled speech at the Milwaukee Auditorium. "This may be my last talk in this cause to our people, and while I am good I am going to drive to the hall and deliver my speech."

Within five minutes, Roosevelt was on stage. "Friends, I shall ask you to be as quiet as possible," he began. "I don't know whether you fully understand that I have just been shot, but it takes more than that to kill a bull moose." The crowd gasped, then cheered.

Some shouted it was a fake, to which Roosevelt opened his suit coat to show his bloody undershirt, before pointing to the holes in his speech manuscript. "The bullet is in me now, so that I cannot make a very long speech," he said, "but I will try my best."

He spoke for an hour and a half, with aides and doctors hovering nearby, waiting to catch him if he collapsed.

"I am in this cause with my whole heart and soul; I believe in the Progressive movement—a movement for the betterment of mankind, a movement for making life a little easier for all our people, a movement to try to take the burdens off the man and especially the woman in this country who is most oppressed. I am absorbed in the success of that movement. I feel uncommonly proud in belonging to that movement."

With unrivaled sincerity, he extolled the necessity of labor organization, women's empowerment, trust-busting, and the importance of the interstate commerce bill in "helping solve some of our industrial problems with the anti-trust law." Only after lambasting both the Democrats and Republicans as reactionaries compared to his progressivism did Roosevelt finally relent and go to the hospital.[38]

Out of respect and fairness, Wilson and Taft suspended their campaigning while Roosevelt convalesced—not a big stretch for Taft. In the end, it didn't matter. Wilson won in a landslide: his 42 percent of the nationwide vote translated into 82 percent of the Electoral College. Roosevelt and the Progressives came in second with 27 percent, Taft and the Republicans third at 23 percent, and the Socialist Debs with 6 percent. Riding Wilson's coattails, Democrats secured a two-thirds majority in the House and held the Senate. For his indispensable leadership, Bryan was awarded the top cabinet post as Wilson's secretary of state. True to his temperance roots, diplomatic receptions under Bryan would be dry, with grape juice replacing the usual wine and champagne.[39]

After the election, President-Elect Wilson let it be known that he wanted the stalled Webb-Kenyon Bill on interstate commerce decided one way or another, "so that it might not hang over" his incoming administration. The impasse was finally broken in February 1913. Ernest Cherrington hurriedly telegrammed his Anti-Saloon League colleagues: "Party lines were cut to pieces. Speaker Clark gave a square deal straight through." But lame-duck President Taft had one last trick up his sleeve. In exchange for the significant campaign contributions by the liquor machine, Taft vowed to scuttle any further liquor trade regulations. Going back on his earlier promise to the ASL, he vetoed the Webb-Kenyon Bill. But Taft had grievously miscalculated the growing power of the dry forces in Congress. Just two hours after Taft's veto, the Senate overrode it, 63 to 21. The next day, the House enacted the bill, 244 to 95, strengthening the powers of the federal government and energizing dry hopes for a nationwide prohibition.[40]

Toward National Prohibition

"The Time Has Come," announced the *American Issue* in March 1913. The Anti-Saloon League would pivot from its piecemeal, state-by-state approach to begin pressing for nationwide prohibition and what would eventually become the Eighteenth Amendment to the Constitution. The ASL was a latecomer to the party: the WCTU had issued a similar proclamation back in 1911.[41]

From a legal standpoint, there had long been debate as to whether federal prohibition could be achieved with just a law, or whether a constitutional

Figure 17.1 Wayne B. Wheeler, general counsel for the Anti-Saloon League, ca. 1920.
Source: Prints and Photographs Division, Library of Congress, Washington, DC.

amendment and a law were needed. The saloon traffic had long argued—repeatedly and unsuccessfully—that the Fourteenth Amendment's provision stating, "No State shall make or enforce any law which shall abridge the privileges or immunities of citizens of the United States," extended to their "right" to sell intoxicating liquors. This *could* render any prohibition bill unconstitutional unless the Constitution was so amended. The Supreme Court had repeatedly swatted down that interpretation in the past, but they could reverse course in the future, undoing all the prohibitionists' efforts.[42] Another potential legal pitfall was that the Constitution only gave the federal government authority over interstate commerce; everything else devolved to the states. Without an amendment giving the federal government at least some jurisdiction over the liquor traffic, any federal prohibition law risked being deemed unconstitutional on these grounds, too. Finally, as a purely practical matter, drys thought etching prohibition into the Constitution would ensure its permanence, as no previous constitutional amendment had ever been repealed.

Longtime ASL executive director Wayne Wheeler joined Edwin Dinwiddie in Washington, heading the League's lobbying efforts as general counsel and legislative superintendent. By decade's end, the ASL would be recognized both by friend and foe alike as "the most powerful and successful reform lobby in Washington."[43] Wayne Wheeler became the public face of prohibitionism, first for better, then worse. To be sure, behind the *pince-nez* and Ned Flanders mustache was an accomplished lawyer, principled organizer, and skilled lobbyist who channeled popular sentiment into a constitutional amendment. However, the notion that Wheeler was an unelected and power-hungry political boss—"the most masterful and powerful single individual in the United States [who] controlled six Congresses, dictated to two Presidents," directed legislation and handpicked the elected representatives of both parties—is largely the product of wet fantasies and propaganda: reframing and delegitimizing prohibition as an antidemocratic policy imposed by an all-powerful tyrant.[44] As with the vilification of prohibitionism more generally, this false image is the one that has stuck in the popular imagination even today.

Back in 1913, both popular sentiment and the political landscape overwhelmingly favored Wheeler and the ASL's push for national prohibition. Big-business Taft was gone, replaced by the progressive Woodrow Wilson, with the prohibitionist Bryan at his side. The newly seated Congress was more sympathetic to the dry wishes of its constituents than its predecessors, thanks in part to ASL agitation and exposing of liquor-machine corruption. "Every defense the liquor traffic has erected has been battered down except the defenseless appeal to greed and appetite," wrote ASL general superintendent Purley Baker. "It no longer has advocates; it must depend for its existence upon partisans."[45]

With Democratic majorities in both houses, Wilson's progressive domestic agenda—establishing the Federal Trade Commission to enforce antitrust violations, and the Federal Reserve to create a central banking system—steamed ahead. Also in the spring of 1913 was the ratification of the Sixteenth Amendment, levying a federal income tax, primarily on the rich for the benefit of the poor. The Wilson administration used it to shift the country's finances forever away from tariffs on foreign trade and liquor toward a more reliable stream of income taxes. As prohibitionists pointed out, the progressive income tax divorced the government from its financial need to rely on regressive liquor revenues drawn mostly from the poor, which—as in virtually every country around the globe—had been a primary pillar of government revenue since America's founding.[46]

Wilson himself was largely mum on liquor questions, lest they distract from his other progressive goals. "He was not a prohibitionist nor was he a champion of the saloon," recalled ASL leader Wayne Wheeler. "During his term as President I do not recall any utterances by which he gave any help whatever to the dry cause. Yet while he was in the White House more dry legislation was enacted than during any other comparable period." Though Wilson didn't take up the banner of prohibition, he didn't actively oppose it either, which came as an immense frustration to the organized liquor forces, who'd hoped to curry favor with him.[47]

Still, Anti-Saloon League leaders expected the fight for nationwide prohibition would take a generation—or twenty years at the very least. They keenly understood the hurdles in front of them. First, getting the required two-thirds majority in both houses of Congress would be a formidable task. The 1913 ratification of the progressive Seventeenth Amendment—allowing for the direct election of senators by the voters rather than state legislatures, to awaken "a more acute sense of representation to the people," in Bryan's words—would help the ASL's publicity strategy, though not before the 1918 midterm elections. The bigger challenge would be getting thirty-six states to then ratify the prohibition amendment.[48]

Finally, as a political issue, the liquor question had always been a battle of drys versus wets. And since it had been politically entrenched within corrupt machine politics for generations, the organized wet interests had always held the upper hand. But after a series of stinging defeats culminating in the veto override of the Webb-Kenyon Bill, the organized liquor trust was hopelessly divided. Distillers and the National Wholesale Liquor Dealers' Association blamed brewers for not joining them in a united front. The United States Brewers' Association downplayed the threat and focused on cleaning up the image of saloons. Used to simply buying off politicians, neither the brewers nor distillers had the kind of grassroots voter-mobilization capacity that the Woman's Christian Temperance Union and the Anti-Saloon League possessed.[49] American prohibition is as much a story of liquor-machine collapse as it is of one-sided temperance crusades.

Prohibition and the Great War

On June 28, 1914, presumptive heir to the Austro-Hungarian throne, Archduke Franz Ferdinand and his wife, the Duchess Sophie, were gunned down in their motorcade as they rode through the streets of Sarajevo. By initiating the entanglement of military alliances that drew all the great European empires—and eventually the United States—into World War I, those two bullets fired by Yugoslav nationalist assassin Gavrilo Princip ultimately killed some fifteen million soldiers and civilians worldwide.[50]

The war accelerated the coming of prohibition in the United States, though *how* it did so is not nearly as straightforward as conventional histories often suggest. Perhaps the most persistent prohibition myth is that—in the words of Groucho Marx in *Animal Crackers* (1930)—"it was put over on the American people while our boys were '*over there*'!" Even the more nuanced version amounts to little more than a conspiracy theory: that prohibition was "put over" on the American public against their will by those upstart suffragist women. What's more, if they weren't fighting valorously overseas, our sensible American men surely would have put a stop to it.[51]

Nonsense. As Bryan wrote, such conspiracy theories "only prove that some people are so absorbed in their own affairs that they do not know their country."[52]

For one, aside from a few sparsely populated states of the Mountain West, American women didn't have the right to vote. The Nineteenth Amendment guaranteeing female suffrage came *after* the Eighteenth Amendment and prohibition. In fact, the only woman to vote for the Eighteenth Amendment was the first (and at that time, only) American congresswoman: Jeannette Rankin of Montana. The other 281 congress members who made up the supermajority in the House for prohibition were all men, as was the supermajority of senators who affirmed it, 65–20.[53]

Second, it is not as though there was some national referendum on prohibition that the two million men of the American Expeditionary Force (AEF) missed while fighting in France in 1917–1918. There wasn't. The election that brought overwhelmingly dry majorities to Congress was in 1916, a year before the AEF even existed. And third, there's no data anywhere suggesting that the two million doughboys in Europe were any more wet (or dry, for that matter) in their sentiments than the other thirty million eligible voters who remained stateside.[54] In sum, the remarkably persistent—and highly misogynist—conspiracy theory that prohibition was "put over" on the freedom-loving American drinking man is bunk, and always has been.[55]

That's not to say that the war had no effect on prohibition. It most certainly accelerated the process. But context matters. It makes about as much sense to speak of the coming of American prohibition in isolation from global context as it does to talk about American involvement in World War I without international context: it doesn't make any sense at all. But that's how national histories are written.

We've already seen how wartime mobilization led Tsar Nicholas II to impose the world's first nationwide prohibition in 1914 in the Russian Empire (Chapter 2), followed by similar prohibitions in Belgium (Chapter 3), and increased restrictions against the liquor trade in the German and Austro-Hungarian Empires (Chapter 4), the British Empire (Chapter 5), and the Ottoman Empire (Chapter 8). Even though the United States did not join the war until 1917, this international avalanche of anti-saloon sentiment was incredibly important to the advance of American prohibition. In 1922 Sir Arthur Newsholme—Britain's top public-health expert—wrote of prohibition, "No doubt in bringing about the final step, events in Europe had a great influence on America."[56]

The question, of course, is how.

When the war broke out in the summer of 1914, few Americans were concerned. It looked like just another of those lamentably bloody Balkan Wars that seemed to erupt annually. Besides, Europe was far away. "Within a few months, however, the issues of the war began to clarify; the rumors as to the German outrages in Belgium and France were proved to be based on terrible truth; the whispering of Germany's world ambitions grew into the rumble of war as Germany's Mexican and Japanese plots were dragged to light," wrote one military observer. "When American citizens were murdered on the high seas by German sub-marines, and American ships were sunk, the war clouds grew darker and more menacing."[57]

From the summer of 1914 to the US declaration of war in April 1917—almost three full years—American politics was conducted not under wartime conditions but under the ever-encroaching shadow of war. It was under this war shadow that the crucial elections of 1916 took place.

While American foreign policy may have remained isolationist, public interest certainly wasn't. Americans demanded, devoured, and debated news of the latest developments in the European war. This was a boon to the temperance movement, as the war had unleashed a veritable wave of prohibitionism and suffragism across Europe.[58] Both the Central Powers—the German, Austro-Hungarian, and Ottoman Empires—and their Allied rivals in Britain, France, and Russia all seemed to agree that the liquor traffic was their common foe (Chapters 2–8).

"There is no social movement in our day more amazing than the world-wide rebellion against rum domination," wrote A. C. Archibald in the WCTU organ, the *Union Signal* in 1915:

> Who would have dreamed that autocratic Russia would so soon become a prohibition nation? Whiskey-ridden England, . . . France, and even Germany, have taken steps to check the liquor traffic. Canada has outlawed the saloon from a number of her provinces. Newfoundland voted dry at an election last month. In our own country eighty per cent of the territory is dry and sixty-five per cent of the people are living in districts where the saloon is no longer tolerated. What is the basis of this world-wide phenomena? Such world movements were never built on sand foundations.[59]

For all the effort traditional prohibition histories spend framing American temperance advocates as irredeemable xenophobes embracing anti-beer—and therefore anti-German—sentiment, it is remarkable that America's new celebrity poster child of global temperance was German kaiser Wilhelm II himself. After all, it was Wilhelm who most vividly encapsulated the global "cult of military sobriety" by proclaiming that victory in the next European war would go the nation that drank the least (Chapter 4).[60] Now that war was upon us, and all belligerents agreed with the Kaiser, including the American military.[61]

Writing in 1915, the colonel of the US Army Medical Corps, L. Mervin Maus, even argued that destruction of the liquor machine might provide a silver lining for such a terrible war. "Even if the war in Europe costs ten billion dollars, if it destroys five million human lives and devastates the fairest countries of the world, it will be a small price to pay compared with the value of total abstinence among those nations for succeeding generations," Maus claimed. "This is not only a war of men against

THE LATEST RECRUIT.

Figure 17.2 Kaiser Wilhelm II as "the latest recruit" to the temperance water wagon, joining Teddy Roosevelt, William Jennings Bryan, and Woodrow Wilson. Robert Carter for the New York *Sun* (1913).
Source: Reprinted in: "Topics in Brief," *Literary Digest,* September 13, 1913, 412.

men, but a war against the greatest evil the world has ever known . . . the effects of alcohol upon the human mind."[62]

The other new hero was Wilhelm's third cousin in Russia, Tsar Nicholas II. Rightly, the American temperance press had long echoed Tolstoy, Lenin, and anti-tsarist critics everywhere who fingered the imperial Russian vodka monopoly as the means by which the rich got rich off the drunken misery of the impoverished peasants.[63] But in embracing the cult of military sobriety, Nicholas proclaimed prohibition in Russia in August 1914 as a military-mobilization measure, making Russia the world's first prohibition country. To commemorate the sacrifice of Prince Oleg Konstantinovich Romanov on the Lithuanian front in October 1914, Nicholas made Russian prohibition permanent (Chapter 2). In some ways, it worked. While not flawless, Russia's mobilization was far more orderly than the disastrous Russo-Japanese War a decade earlier, and allowed Russia to put armies in the field more quickly than their German and Austro-Hungarian foes. British wartime prime minister David Lloyd George even hailed prohibition of their Russian allies as "the single greatest act of national heroism."[64]

Consequently, the American temperance press celebrated every early Russian victory in East Prussia and Galicia as a victory for the prohibition cause.[65] Almost overnight, Europe's most reactionary monarch was congratulated for his high-minded progressivism in abolishing Russia's "drunken budget."[66] Breathless reports extolled the virtues of "the miracle-working law of Russia," in freeing the Russian peasantry from the shackles of the state's vodka monopoly. Russians were suddenly far happier, far healthier, far wealthier, and far more productive than ever before.[67] It all sounded too good to be true, but Red Cross volunteers, foreign diplomats, war reporters, government ministers, academics, and even public-opinion surveys all came to the same—though in hindsight obviously overstated—conclusions about prohibition's beneficial effects.[68]

Even as Russia's first, pyrrhic victories turned to years of carnage and loss in 1915–1917, pulling the empire apart at the seams, Russia's besieged finance minister Peter Bark time and again maintained that everything was fine: the groundswell of economic productivity would more than make up for any loss of the state's vodka revenues. "Russia's finances rest upon the most solid foundation in the world," Bark quite falsely claimed in 1916, alleging a 50 percent increase in economic productivity thanks to prohibition. "The economic prosperity of the Russian people is now greater than was ever conceived possible before the beginning of the war," and that this condition was "accounted for principally by the growing thrift and economy of the peasants since the enforcement of prohibition."[69]

In 1916 the international lesson seemed to be clear. "Russia has demonstrated that we need no graded course—regulation, Gothenburg System, local option, education of sentiment up to prohibition," argued American prohibitionists. "The more radical and general the prohibition, the more successful. Prohibition 'fails,' not because there is too much of it, but too little."[70]

Within a year, the empire collapsed, Tsar Nicholas abdicated, and Bark fled to London, never to return to Russia.[71] Stateside, however, temperance forces could even frame the downfall of the tsarist regime in the 1917 February Revolution as a victory for prohibition. Not only was it "an alcohol-less, and therefore, a bloodless revolution," but also replacing the haze of alcoholism with clear-minded sobriety allowed Russian citizens to cast off the yoke of repression in favor of a "provisional democratic government," whose very first act was to affirm the prohibition measure.[72]

There would be no such spinning the October Revolution of 1917, though. It was well known that Vladimir Lenin and the Bolsheviks were prohibitionists, but their communist ideology was political kryptonite in the United States. Quietly, then, American prohibitionists' favorite foreign argument—Russia—disappeared forever from the temperance press.[73]

"Russia was doing fine till some nut took their vodka away from them," poked satirist Will Rogers in 1919, "and they went back to look for it and nobody has ever heard of them since." America's cowboy philosopher wasn't about to let prohibitionists forget, adding, "Any time a dry is up talking just mention one word and he is through—Russia."[74]

Of course, none of those subsequent revolutionary developments on the other side of the globe could have possibly been foreseen by American prohibitionists years earlier. In fact, just as the European war was ramping up back in the summer of 1914, so was the war against the liquor machine in the United States. In pivoting from the state to the federal level, the Anti-Saloon League—through progressive Alabama Democrat Richmond P. Hobson—made its first attempt to submit a federal prohibition amendment.

This so-called Hobson Resolution read simply, "The sale, manufacture for sale, transportation for sale, importation for sale, and exportation for sale of intoxicating liquors for beverage purposes in the United States and all territory subject to the jurisdiction thereof, and exportation, are forever prohibited."[75]

On December 22, 1914, the House of Representatives debated the prohibition amendment for ten straight hours. Since the purpose of this book is to better understand prohibitionists' motivations, it is worth quoting at length its introduction to the floor by Congressman Philip Campbell, Democrat of Kansas. In many ways, Campbell encapsulates the diverse themes of this book: the focus on the liquor traffic as an exploitative trade rather than the morality of drinking, democratic self-determination, America's long history of Native American prohibitions, the anti-canteen movement, the cult of military sobriety, as well as learning from global experiences to inform the American policy process.

"Mr. Speaker," Campbell began,

> this rule makes in order a discussion and vote on an amendment to the Constitution of the United States to prohibit traffic in intoxicating liquors. The resolution is submitted to the States in the usual way for their consideration. It raises this great question for the first time in the House of Representatives.
>
> Already the people have voted for the suppression of the traffic in intoxicating liquors covering 76 per cent of the area of the United States, and 57 per cent of the population.
>
> The Government at Washington has for years prohibited the traffic in intoxicating liquors on Indian reservations and at military reservations and posts, and recently at naval stations and in the Navy and all United States soldiers' homes.
>
> Twelve years ago the Congress prohibited the sale of intoxicating liquors in the Capitol Building.
>
> Why should any commodity be under the ban of the law to the extent that this already is in the United States? Evidently because the traffic in intoxicating liquors is a bad thing. These are times of great events. Europe has staged, let us hope, the last act in the tragedy of war. [Applause.] Incident

to that great tragedy some important things have been done. The Czar of Russia, at the beginning of the war, deemed it important to his Empire and to his people that he should have under his control the best physical and mental fiber that his people possessed, and he issued a ukase prohibiting during the continuance of the war traffic in alcoholic liquors. The Czar of Russia took this important action in the face of the fact that the ukase denied to the treasury of the Russian Empire almost a half billion of dollars in revenue on the very threshold of an expensive war. Evidently the Czar deemed it more important to his Empire and his people that he should prosecute the war with men free from the influence of alcoholic liquors than that his treasury should have a half billion dollars a year for the payment of the expenses of the war.

After then describing how France had prohibited the sale of absinthe and the kaiser had famously proclaimed to his sailors that victory in the next war would go to the most sober, Campbell was interrupted by German-born Republican Richard Bartholdt, representing the wet bastion of St. Louis, Missouri: "Does my friend regard this as an argument for prohibition?"

"I submit it as such," Campbell replied.

"The Emperor speaks of self-discipline, so that it is an argument for temperance and not prohibition," replied Bartholdt. "We agree with him."

"The Emperor evidently believed that it was essential to his people that they abstain from the use of intoxicating liquors so that they could serve their country well in war," Campbell replied. "If mental and physical fiber of the highest order are important in war, they are alike important in peace, for the duties of peace are no less important than those of war. If the Emperor of Germany deems it detrimental to the naval cadets in the service of his navy to use intoxicating liquors, the American people who look well to the peace of their country may likewise take steps to provide for a sober people to engage in the pursuits of peace."[76]

The debate continued from 10 a.m. to 10 p.m., with even the pro-liquor wets like Bartholdt arguing in favor of temperance, but against prohibition on technical and practical grounds. When the final votes were tallied, the prohibitionists secured a majority—197 to 189 opposed—but well below the two-thirds required to submit the amendment to the states.[77]

While the prohibition amendment failed in 1914, the prohibitionists themselves were energized. With ever more American states voting themselves dry, and the crisis of wartime prompting a global clampdown against the corrupting liquor traffic, prohibitionists felt they were on the right side of history, even as the clouds of war grew increasingly dark. The elections of 1916 would prove to be critical.

Strangely, Woodrow Wilson and the incumbent Democrats were actually the underdogs going into the 1916 presidential election. The progressive/conservative split that had divided the Republican Party in 1912 was all patched up, and the

GOP challenger—Supreme Court Justice Charles Evans Hughes—was the odds-on favorite.

Now it was the Democrats' turn to try to hold together a fracturing party. With rising German militarism, submarine warfare in the North Atlantic, and a roiling revolution south of the border in Mexico, the Wilson administration's policy of neutrality was squeezed from all sides. Even as secretary of state, William Jennings Bryan's Tolstoyan appeals to nonviolence were increasingly marginalized by those calling for American "preparedness" for war. When German U-boats sank the RMS *Lusitania* in May 1915—killing 1,200 civilians including 128 Americans—Bryan saw the lurch to war as all but inevitable and resigned his post as America's chief diplomat. He returned once again to the lecture circuit as America's most respected orator.[78]

Freed from officeholder inhibitions and decorum, Bryan's impassioned speeches of 1915–1916 were some of the most influential of his career. On the one hand, he was still at heart a Democratic partisan, passionately pleading that Wilson's reelection was America's best chance to keep out of a disastrous war.

On the other hand, Bryan was intent on reaching across partisan divides to make common cause in pursuit of the interest nearest to his heart: prohibition. Indeed, in the lead-up to the 1916 election, his widely read *The Commoner* seemed to have as many prohibition articles as the WCTU's *Union Signal* or the ASL's *American Issue*. Though the Democrats already commanded majorities in the legislature, no single party could push through a constitutional amendment securing two-thirds of Congress and three-fourths of the states to ratify it. After all, as Bryan said, the liquor interest "owes allegiance to no party and is interested in no principles of government. It is solely concerned with the money to be derived from the sale of liquor." Ultimately, he argued, it was in the interests of both parties to work together to give the corrupting element no safe harbor.

When speaking in Ohio, for instance, Bryan encouraged the state's Republicans to clean house and the Democrats would do the same—not out of morality but political necessity. "If we drive the liquor interests out of the Democratic Party and the Republican Party receives them, then the Republican Party will get all of our bad men," Bryan proclaimed, adding wryly, "and Heaven knows it has enough bad men already."

"If, on the other hand, the Republican Party drives out the liquor interests and we welcome them, we will get the bad men of the Republican Party, and we haven't room for any more bad men than we now have!"

Since the liquor traffic had no allegiance other than its own profit, the obvious solution was to join forces against it. Prohibition could reform both political parties from within. "Let us for one day lay aside the tariff question, the trust question, the money question, and other national questions upon which we differ, and unite to free the State from the manufacture and sale of alcoholic liquor."[79]

And, ultimately, that's what they did: both sides, together.

When the final votes were tallied in November 1916, Wilson narrowly won reelection, thanks largely due to Bryan's campaigning in swing states.[80] Having mended their party split, the united Republicans cut into the Democrats' commanding majorities in the House and Senate.

But it was neither the Republicans nor Democrats who were the biggest winners in 1916; it was the drys. "We didn't try to convert the Presidential candidates," explained Wheeler. "We knew Wilson was not in favor of national prohibition. We also felt that Hughes wasn't openly for it. So we concentrated on Congress."[81]

Dry sentiment was not "manufactured," Wheeler pointed out, but directed by the ASL to where it would do the most good. Riding the crest of the global prohibition wave, the Anti-Saloon League was suddenly flush with eager volunteers, voters, and financial contributions, which made their "hearing from home" strategy all the more effective. It worked like this: the ASL's Washington bureau monitored representatives' voting records and kept close tabs on their rival pro-liquor lobbyists. If a representative started wavering on his commitments, they'd wire the home districts, and the local organizations would do the rest. "Within twenty-four hours a storm of telegrams would break over that member's head and he would realize that a revolution had broken loose back home."[82]

The grassroots efforts kicked into overdrive in 1916. "We laid down such a barrage as candidates for Congress had never seen before and such as they will, in all likelihood, not see again for years to come," Wheeler explained.[83] Billed as "the church in action," the Anti-Saloon League networked with church denominations to turn out the dry vote. But they needed persuasive arguments and materials, which is where Pussyfoot Johnson reentered the picture.

In a fortuitous turn—in a railway dining car back in 1912—the talkative Johnson struck up a conversation with a fellow traveler, who turned out to be Ernest Hurst Cherrington: general manager of the ASL's American Issue Publishing Company in Westerville, Ohio.

"Cherrington was a big, handsome, 250-pound amphibian, as full of peculiarities as a dog is of fleas," Johnson later recalled the encounter. "I have been closely associated with him ever since that day, and I know just as much about him now as I did then."

Over plates of bluefish and peanuts, Cherrington offered Johnson the post of managing editor of the league's publishing operations. Out of a job since being elbowed out of the Indian Service (Chapter 16), Pussyfoot agreed.

"We choked the mails with thirty-five periodicals, mostly state editions of the *American Issue*, plus the *American Patriot*, an alleged monthly magazine," Johnson said. By the 1916 elections, "we were tossing ten tons of printed matter into the post office every twenty-four hours, and 125 employees were struggling in a delirium of activity. Westerville became the smallest town in the nation to have a second class post office. Four more houses were bought to increase mailing capacity. We had a bear by the tail with a downhill pull and we were setting up a terrific din throughout the United States."[84]

As the prohibition drive gained steam, Pussyfoot was pulling double duty: managing the information arm of the Anti-Saloon League while simultaneously on the road as a national and international emissary for prohibition. In 1913 he traveled to Russia to muckrake the economic exploitation and political corruption of the tsarist vodka monopoly, publishing articles and even the first English-language study of Russian alcohol history (Chapter 2). His firsthand experiences and temperance contacts fleshed out reports of Russia's "miraculous" transformation once the vodka monopoly was banned.[85] From there, he traveled across the German and Austro-Hungarian Empires to attend the fourteenth International Congress on Alcoholism in Milan, Italy (Chapter 4). Once there, he delivered a report to his international audience not about the progress of temperance *per se*, but about the United States Brewers' Association, the National Wholesale Liquor Dealers' Association, and the political clout that these corrupt liquor-machine trusts exercised in undermining the prohibitionist cause. As part of the official American delegation, they were charged by Secretary of State William Jennings Bryan to lobby the Europeans to bring their temperance convention to the United States. Ultimately, they succeeded: Washington, DC, would host the fifteenth International Congress on Alcoholism, which would be delayed five long years by the war.[86]

Back stateside, Johnson split time between the publishing house in Westerville, Ohio, and organizing for statewide prohibitions in his old Indian Service stomping grounds in the West from Arizona and Colorado to Idaho, Oregon, and Washington. All of these states would vote themselves dry in 1915–1916.[87]

But it wasn't just Pussyfoot and the Anti-Saloon League that kicked into high gear. The Woman's Christian Temperance Union likewise saw an opportunity for progressive change. Pushing for women's empowerment through suffrage both as an end in itself and as a means of defending the home against the saloon, the WCTU organized grassroots political activists nationwide for the twin causes of suffrage and temperance. Among the scads of leaflets and pamphlets the WCTU churned out for its activists in the lead-up to the 1916 elections, its most popular and persuasive was "Regenerated Russia," which detailed the dramatic economic, political, moral, and mobilizational benefits prohibition had wrought there.[88] Since the war broke out two years earlier, mainstream magazines and newspapers likewise ran glowing coverage of "the marvelous change [that] has swept over Russia like a cyclone with the noise left out."[89]

After generations of anti-saloon activism, election night—Tuesday, November 7, 1916—was when America overwhelmingly voted for prohibition. Wheeler recalled that "the lights burned late at our Washington office." Volunteers and ASL agents were tabulating and telegraphing the congressional races, even as returns from California delayed the results of the tight presidential election. "We knew late election night that we had won," Wheeler said. "Many hours before the country knew whether Hughes or Wilson had triumphed, the dry workers throughout the nation were celebrating our victory. We knew that the prohibition amendment would be submitted to the States by the Congress just elected."[90]

The Sixty-Fifth Congress (1917–1919) was an unusual one. The Republicans won 216 seats to the Democrats' 214, but in forming a coalition with the three elected Progressives and one Socialist, the Democrats narrowly held the House. On strictly partisan questions, it was a nail-biter; but on prohibition, it was a landslide. To the absolute majority the dry camp had in 1914, the Republicans brought

Figure 17.3 "Campaign Edition" of the *Union Signal,* September 28, 1916. In the caption, Uncle Sam pleads, "Mr. Ballot Box, we depend on you to clean up some of the black territory of the United States at the November 7 election. We cannot afford to lag behind the Dominion of Canada, Russia, and Roumania in abolishing the liquor traffic" (although Romania never formally enacted prohibition).

Source: *Union Signal,* September 28, 1916.

sixty-five *more* drys to the cause, and the Democrats another twenty. Additionally, eight more states had voted themselves dry in 1916 alone, with even more territory voting dry through local option. No wonder Wheeler and the Anti-Saloon League were jubilant.[91]

America Enters the War

With such overwhelming majorities, a prohibition amendment could easily have been drafted, passed, and submitted to the states on day one of the new Congress. But President Wilson himself requested a delay. In the spring of 1917 Germany announced a policy of unrestricted submarine warfare and stepped up its attacks against American shipping. Wilson—who had just won reelection on the platform of keeping America out of the war—asked Congress for a declaration of war against the German Empire, in order to "make the world safe for democracy." Dry leaders agreed to delay the prohibition resolution until after Wilson got his declaration and all the supplemental legislation necessary for war mobilization. Key to that preparedness was the Lever Food and Fuel Control Act to preserve vital foodstuffs for the war effort. Since in countries the world over, liquor was deemed nonessential—and even deleterious—to the war effort, the Anti-Saloon League pressed for a prohibition addendum. When minority wets threatened a filibuster on behalf of the brewing interests, Wilson again asked the prohibitionist ASL to back down in order to pass a clean bill. Again, they did. "For nine months the Legislative Committee of the Anti-Saloon League stood by, in accordance with its promise to the President," Wheeler recalled. "During this period the entire nation was called upon to conserve food. It seemed to us an anachronism that the President, after calling on 100,000,000 people to save food, should permit its waste in the manufacture of beverage intoxicants."[92]

But while the drys were in a holding pattern, their wet opponents weren't. Democrat James Reed from the wet bastion of Missouri—well known for his Senate speeches advocating for an American racial hierarchy with the "white race" on top—had long wanted to stick it to the prohibitionist reformers.[93] Hoping to humiliate the drys in any way possible, Senator Reed proposed a "bone dry" amendment to an interstate-mail bill that would criminalize not just the sale of intoxicants, but their individual *purchase* as well. Not expecting any legislative fireworks that day, ASL leaders Wayne Wheeler and James Cannon looked on with astonishment from the Senate gallery. They were even more stunned when the commerce bill and amendment passed 45 to 11, without any meaningful debate.

The difference between legally *selling* alcohol and *buying* (or using) it seems utterly insignificant today, but it made all the difference. Indeed, the source of our enduring popular misunderstandings of prohibition are to be found precisely here. The entire temperance-cum-prohibition movement was about defending the individual consumer and the community against the underhanded and predatory sellers of an addictive substance. As its very name suggests, the Anti-Saloon League opposed the saloon, not the drinker.

So when Reed pressed the ASL's hand with his "bone dry" move, they hesitated. The measure had passed the Senate but could still be blocked in the House of Representatives. Dry congressmen looked for leadership from Wheeler and the league. They demurred. The ASL would take no official position on the Reed amendment, and encouraged each representative to vote his conscience. The next day, the House overwhelmingly passed the measure, 321 to 72. President Wilson refused to veto it in order to keep the mails moving during mobilization.

Consequently, with Reed's "bone dry" amendment on the books, prohibitionists and state governments were given the legal ability to criminalize the individual purchase and consumption of alcoholic beverages, though, notably, no state ever did so. Prohibition, after all, was directed against the seller, not the buyer. Still, Reed's maneuver allowed wets to lambaste prohibitionists as enemies of individual freedom in the spirit of John Stuart Mill's critiques (Chapter 5)—an image of reactionary, "purityrannical" killjoys that endures even today, a century after prohibition.[94]

The war declaration impacted the politically adroit liquor industry, too, but not in the way you might expect. One standard trope of modern prohibition histories is that wartime patriotism begot a wave of anti-German hysteria that unfairly victimized the largely German brewing industry.[95] "The worst of all our German enemies," went one oft-quoted jingoist trope, "the most treacherous, the most menacing are Pabst, Schlitz, Blatz, and Miller."[96]

Yet primary sources—even from prohibitionists themselves—suggest nativist xenophobia wasn't much of a factor, when contrasted with the economic and political dimensions. When discussing the war, William Jennings Bryan eschewed any talk of the Germans as "butchers" or "autocrats," instead denouncing those who stood to profit from the carnage, including the liquor traffic.[97]

Historians' allegations usually revolve not around the liquor industry itself but the National German-American Alliance (NGAA). Supported by big brewing trusts to promote German cultural heritage and greater German-United States political understanding, the NGAA also opposed prohibition. When the NGAA refused to support the war declaration, it was Theodore Roosevelt himself who led the scathing rebukes that culminated in congressional investigations. Yet by then, the NGAA had already "[begun] to raise money for the American Red Cross and stopped agitation against prohibition."[98]

At best, the NGAA dust-up and anti-Germanism were sideshows in the prohibition drama. The big breweries—Pabst, Schlitz, Blatz, Miller, and Anheuser-Busch— were certainly established by German immigrants, but that was in the 1850s, before the Civil War. By the time World War I rolled around, they were already on their second or third generation of American ownership.

More important than cultural arguments were the brewers' political maneuvers: throwing their erstwhile allies—the distillers—overboard to save themselves. Ironically, it was strikingly similar to the alcohol dynamics in the German and Austro-Hungarian Empires, where beer was glorified as a respectable, temperate, working-man's drink, while distilled schnapps was cast as the exploiter of the poor (Chapter 4). The brewers made their break with the establishment of the US Food Administration in 1917.

Diving headlong into the biggest war in human history meant more than just mobilizing the military, but asking all of society to sacrifice for the war effort: donating weapons, ammunition, and even horses and livestock for their country. With its "meatless Mondays" and "wheatless Wednesdays," the US Food Administration spearheaded the patriotic conservation efforts, and the "nonessential" liquor trade was squarely in their crosshairs. In debates over the Food Administration Bill, brewers joined with labor unions to save beer as necessary for industrial workers. They also joined in the chorus, claiming that hard-liquor distillers were parasitic to the war cause, and the grains used in distillation could better be put toward the patriotic conservation effort.

The distillers felt betrayed, because they were. As a wartime measure, the resulting Lever Food and Fuel Control Act effectively prohibited the manufacture and sale of whiskey and distilled spirits effective September 10, 1917. It also authorized the president—as commander in chief of the military—to limit, regulate, or prohibit the use of grains and foodstuffs for wine and beer, and limit their alcoholic content.[99]

Beer was spared, for the moment.

In 1917 the United States Brewers' Association (USBA) took out full-page pronouncements titled "The Brewers to the Public" in major newspapers nationwide to announce both their divorce from liquor and their self-flagellating repentance. Their marriage to distillers was not voluntary, the USBA claimed, but since the saloon was the only retail outlet where both beer and whiskey could be sold, it soiled beer's good name. "Thus our product has been unjustly and improperly linked with those influences, over which we have no control, that have actually promoted intemperance. For years we have hoped, with the wine-growers, that some factor might intervene which would enable us to sever, once and for all, the shackles that bound our wholesome products—light wine and beer, the handmaidens to true temperance, to ardent spirits in popular mental association and actual business practice." The Brewers' Association concluded that the Lever Food Bill "prohibiting the distillation of spiritous liquors has broken those chains at last."[100]

"I am very much afraid," wrote the prohibitionist William Jennings Bryan to North Carolina Democratic congressman Edwin Webb in July 1917, "that the separation of beer from whiskey will give to beer a prestige that will reopen the liquor question in all the prohibition states." To forestall the brewers' comeback, Bryan urged that Webb—as head of the Judiciary Committee—submit the constitutional amendment "*at once.*"[101]

But amid all the tumult of war, the drys were unsure whether they still had the votes. With Bryan helping corral the drys on the Democratic side, Wayne Wheeler called up Teddy Roosevelt "to use the big stick in our behalf" with the Republicans, should the need arise. (It didn't.)[102]

Instead, at that crucial point, in stepped Republican senator—and future Prohibition Era president—Warren G. Harding. "Harding was an organization Republican, not a total abstainer and, at that time, not what one would call a genuine dry," recalled Wheeler, citing Harding's token stock in a startup brewery back in Ohio, where the two had long known each other (Chapter 16).

Senate wets believed it would take years or even decades to get a prohibition amendment ratified if it was submitted to the states, during which time the unresolved liquor question would hang over American politics. But Harding had a compromise idea that might allay fears of senators on the fence. From the Senate floor, Harding summoned Wheeler to talk about it.

"You fellows ought to agree to have some limitation put on the time for ratification," Harding told Wheeler. Five years, perhaps.

"He said if we would agree to it he felt sure there were three or four Senators who would vote for submission who otherwise probably would not do so," Wheeler recalled. He was skeptical, in that no proposed amendment had ever come with a time limit. Nevertheless, the Anti-Saloon League again compromised. In August 1917 Harding introduced a measure to add a five-year ratification clock—extended to six years in the ensuing debate—and suddenly he and seven other senators who were not usually among the drys voted in favor of submitting the prohibition amendment: 65 to 20 (36 to 12 among Democrats, 29 to 8 among Republicans).[103]

The measure bounced back to the evenly divided House of Representatives, where Democrat Champ Clark was still Speaker. There, pro-wet congressmen argued that state-level prohibitions always gave the saloon business a grace period of six to twelve months to wrap up their affairs and move into other lines of work. Shouldn't the same be done at the national level?

"There was no very good answer to this argument," Wheeler noted, "so we traded jackknives with them." They'd give the liquor traffic one year from ratification before prohibition would become effective, in exchange for adding another year to the ratification clock. They also relented to giving both the federal government and the states concurrent jurisdiction to enforce it. Ultimately, on December 17, 1917, this compromise measure that passed House, 282 to 128. The next day, the Senate affirmed the House's changes, 47 to 8, submitting the prohibition amendment to ratification by the required three-fourths of the states.[104] The final version read,

Section 1. After one year from the ratification of this article the manufacture, sale, or transportation of intoxicating liquors within, the importation thereof into, or the exportation thereof from the United States and all territory subject to the jurisdiction thereof for beverage purposes is hereby prohibited.

Section 2. The Congress and the several States shall have concurrent power to enforce this article by appropriate legislation.

Section 3. This article shall be inoperative unless it shall have been ratified as an amendment to the Constitution by the legislatures of the several States, as provided in the Constitution, within seven years from the date of the submission hereof to the States by the Congress.[105]

Most significantly, it was not a "bone dry" measure meant to outlaw possession or individual consumption of alcohol. Indeed, when it was debated in the Senate, Georgia Democrat Thomas Hardwick proposed outlawing purchase and personal use of alcohol too, but it was quickly rejected.[106] The onus of prohibition was where it had always been since Lyman Beecher's *Six Sermons on Intemperance* a century before, or Carrie Nation two decades before: protecting the community from the man who sells.

This difference between outlawing the selling of liquor versus the buying of liquor seems trivial today. After all, don't they both stop the same transaction and thus impinge upon the rights of the drinker to consume whatever he or she pleases? Doesn't this, then, make prohibition and prohibitionists the enemies of freedom?

Such allegations are the bugbear of prohibition histories. I unpack this question more fully in the conclusion, but the important point is that it is *our* common conceptions of freedom that have changed over time. *Economic* "right to buy" liberties became intertwined with American definitions of *political* rights only after the Second World War (Chapter 18). As much as we like to think that "freedom" is a universal value—eternal and unchanging—our popular conceptions of freedom have always evolved. So if prohibitionists a century ago run afoul of our definitions of freedom today, that's more on us than it is on them: we are the ones who have moved the goalposts.

The Ratification Cascade

Having passed with supermajorities in Congress, the process then moved to securing the necessary three-quarters of state legislatures to ratify the prohibition amendment. Wets and drys alike anticipated a battle that would take many years. "To the surprise of the whole country," Wayne Wheeler recalled, "it took only twelve months and twenty-nine days," making it the speediest ratification in American history.[107]

Once both houses of the Mississippi state legislature were assembled on January 8, 1918, it took them only fifteen minutes to make it the first state to ratify the prohibition amendment. "The attitude of modern Mississippians toward alcohol had, of course, been reflected in the state-wide prohibition act," reported the *Chicago Herald*. "But it was not imagined that the anti-saloon fight was so dull an issue that the legislature would consume only fifteen minutes in ratifying the Federal amendment." With only eight dissenting votes, prohibition cleared its first hurdle. Dry Virginia followed two days later.[108]

The first real challenge, then, was Kentucky: the heart of the bourbon belt. Wayne Wheeler himself went to Frankfort, only to find that the state's legislators were largely for prohibition, making Kentucky the third state to ratify. By August 1918, fourteen states across the South and West had ratified, while most states were slated to take up the issue when they reconvened in January of the new year.[109]

But most of these were low-hanging fruit: states with long-standing state prohibitions. The challenge would be in going into liquor-machine strongholds like Illinois—where the brewers of Chicago and distillers of Peoria dominated the state legislature—and New York and the Tammany machine.

As if the suffering of the biggest and deadliest war in human history (to that point) wasn't enough, 1918 saw the arrival of the deadliest pandemic in modern history. The so-called Spanish Flu likely did not originate in neutral Spain, but the lack of wartime press censorship meant it was more widely reported on there than elsewhere. In the end, it killed more than fifty million people worldwide, and some 675,000 in the United States: six times as many Americans as who were killed in the European war.

Those saloons still operating in wet enclaves in 1918 were forcibly closed—along with schools and churches—to slow the spread of the virus.[110] Frightened, some individuals turned to guzzling whiskey as an untested folk cure, with predictable and oftentimes tragic results. Scientific temperance advocates explained that liquor had "no value" in combating the flu, which was true. Nevertheless, hard-up drinkers who thought they knew better than the experts smuggled booze into hospitals and influenza wards, or sought out doctors who were willing to write them a prescription for medicinal liquor.[111]

"In only one instance would I use whiskey for an influenza case," claimed Dr. Harvey Wiley—chief chemist at the US Department of Agriculture and driving force behind Roosevelt's Pure Food and Drug Act—"and that would be where I wished to hasten the departure to Heaven of the patient."[112] Indeed, just as saloons were deemed nonessential to the war effort, the Spanish Flu pandemic reinforced scientific arguments that liquor was nonessential to public health, too.

While drys were gearing up to do battle in the remaining undecided states, in the fall of 1918 they were also working in Washington to end the brewers' stay of execution. Tied to an agricultural appropriation bill was a provision to bring brewing under the same prohibitory restrictions that befell distilling in the wartime

Food Administration Bill. In private correspondence with the drys on Capitol Hill, President Wilson bristled that such a wartime prohibition of both distilled and fermented drinks was an overreach. Constitutional prohibition was already well on its way, so why did they need to flex their muscle by pushing through an additional wartime measure?[113]

To that, the drys had an overwhelming battery of economic, patriotic-sacrifice, domestic-tranquility, public-health, and safety arguments for why, under war-time conditions, "the liquor traffic is a liability instead of an asset," and therefore why beermakers should not be exempt from the wartime prohibition on distilled liquors.[114] As William Jennings Bryan argued, to ask citizens to conserve foodstuffs and plant war gardens "and yet be indifferent to the conversion of the products of our prairies into alcohol would be saving at the spigot and wasting at the bunghole." He added, "Alcohol impairs efficiency, and we cannot, at a crisis like this, permit an impairment of efficiency either in our soldiers or in our producers." Former pres-ident Teddy Roosevelt agreed: "Now that the war is on, let us forbid any grain or corn being used in the manufacture of intoxicating liquors."[115]

It was a hard argument to rebut, amid the backdrop of war. So, on November 21, 1918—ten days *after* the fighting in Europe had ceased—Congress passed wartime prohibition. Of course, the armistice did not end the war or wartime conditions; it just stopped the shooting. For the United States, the war wouldn't officially be over until President Wilson could go to Paris to help negotiate the final Peace of Versailles in 1919. Remaining publicly aloof from the prohibition issue, Wilson didn't veto the wartime prohibition measure, especially since any veto was likely to be overridden anyway. According to the bill's provisions, after June 30—amendment or not—prohibition would be the law of the land until the troops were home and fully demobilized. Indeed, July 1, 1919, would be the day the United States went dry.[116] "War prohibition will brighten into constitutional prohibition as the morning opens into day," William Jennings Bryan wrote.[117]

Christmas 1918 and New Year's 1919 were especially festive holidays. The War to End All Wars had ended, and President Wilson and diplomats from around the globe went scurrying for Versailles to begin building the postwar political order. On the home front, state legislatures were being called into session, with the prohibi-tion amendment the first thing on their docket. On January 2, the industrial state of Michigan became the sixteenth state to ratify prohibition, though it had already voted itself dry through statewide prohibition the year before. On Tuesday, January 7, Ohio and Oklahoma—both dry—ratified too. Wednesday it was Idaho and Maine. Thursday, West Virginia joined the ranks, bringing the number of ratifying states to twenty-one. But that was nothing compared with the avalanche of states the following week.

On Monday, January 13, California, Tennessee, and Washington all voted for prohibition. On Tuesday, Arkansas, Indiana, dry Kansas, and the wet bastion of Illinois joined them. On Wednesday, the state legislatures of Alabama, Colorado,

Iowa, Oregon, and New Hampshire voted dry. But it was Thursday, January 16, 1919, that the prohibition amendment was ratified by the requisite three-quarters of the states when Nebraska became the thirty-sixth state to ratify. North Carolina, Utah, Missouri, and Wyoming all voted for prohibition along with Nebraska that day, too, with Minnesota and Wisconsin joining the next day for good measure.

With prohibition already set to become the law of the land one year later—January 17, 1920—there still remained that great wet bastion of New York. As the country's quintessential political liquor machine, the Tammany Hall Democrats were as vehemently opposed to prohibition as they had been for the past seventy years (Chapters 12, 14, and 16), speaking out against the amendment in no uncertain terms. So, the Anti-Saloon League approached the state's Republicans with a practical argument: with the issue already settled, why on earth would they want to be seen as being in bed with the Democrats in opposing prohibition? As supermajorities in Washington and ratification across the country showed, dry sentiment was the wave of the future—and if Republicans hoped to capitalize on it, the politically savvy move would be to vote in favor of ratification, as a rebuke to Tammany Hall. Reluctantly, the Republican caucus—including many with wet sympathies—threw its weight behind prohibition. On January 29, 1919, New York State voted for ratification: 27 to 24 in the Senate, and 81 to 66 in the House.[118]

By February, the dry victory was complete: forty-five of the forty-eight states voted in favor of the prohibition amendment. "We needed for ratification three to one," William Jennings Bryan said of the state vote. "We secured for ratification fifteen to one!" For every one state that rejected prohibition, fifteen voted in favor.[119] In just over a year's time, the sweep was nearly universal: only Connecticut and Rhode Island voted to reject the amendment. In the end, 80.5 percent of state legislators voted for prohibition. In fourteen states, the vote was unanimous. By 1920 the United States would join eleven other countries in outlawing the booze traffic.[120]

Still, there remained the question of wartime prohibition without war. On May 9, 1919, Woodrow Wilson's secretary, Joseph Tumulty, telegraphed the president in Paris—where he was negotiating the postwar political order—about lifting the wartime prohibition. Since the bullets weren't flying and nationwide prohibition was already penciled in to begin on January 17, 1920, what harm could there be in opening the saloons in the meantime for one last hurrah? "We are being blamed for all this restrictive legislation because you insist upon closing down all breweries and thus making prohibition effective July first. The country would be more ready to accept prohibition brought about by Constitutional amendment than have it made effective by Presidential ukase."

Sympathetic, Wilson consulted with his attorney general, who clarified that the president has no legal authority to overrule an act of Congress. That legislation stated clearly that the prohibition on the manufacture and sale of alcoholic beverages would end not with the cessation of hostilities but with the demobilization and return of the American Expeditionary Forces from Europe. The most the president could legally do was urge Congress to enact a temporary reprieve for the saloon. On May 20 Wilson wrote Congress: "The demobilization of the military forces of the country has progressed to such a point that it seems to me entirely safe now to remove the ban upon the manufacture and sale of wines and beers, but I am advised that without further legislation I have not the legal authority to remove the present restrictions."[121] The overwhelmingly dry congressional leadership was un-persuaded. War prohibition would remain.

Of course, the Eighteenth Amendment wasn't a law *per se*. It didn't define what "alcohol" or the "liquor traffic" was, what exemptions there might be for industrial-manufacturing or religious uses, or even what criminal penalties there would be for violating prohibition. For all those details, you would need a law. The amendment only meant that such legislation could not be struck down as unconstitutional.

The writing of the actual prohibition bill was largely done in the spring of 1919 by the head of the House Judiciary Committee, Andrew Volstead of Minnesota, in con-sultation with the Anti-Saloon League's Wayne Wheeler. Volstead "was the logical man to sponsor the measure," Wheeler said. "He had been a member of the House for about sixteen years, had been prosecuting attorney of his county in Minnesota, which had voted dry, and had had practical experience in prosecuting bootleggers," all of which would come in handy in crafting legislation to give both the federal gov-ernment and states concurrent jurisdiction over prohibition enforcement.[122]

Wheeler provided prohibition-enforcement provisions culled from state-level legislation, most notably Oklahoma and Pussyfoot Johnson's one-half-of-one-percent definition of intoxicating beverages (Chapter 16).[123] The challenge for Volstead was not in simply copying state prohibitions, but fitting them into existing federal law and federal statutes to make them air tight against the legal challenges they were sure would arise. Volstead crafted it for months. "As hard work as I ever did," he recalled. The Volstead Act was introduced into Congress on May 19, 1919.[124]

When the final version of Volstead's National Prohibition Bill was passed by both houses and landed on President Wilson's desk for signature that fall, he vetoed it on procedural grounds, as it did not repeal the wartime prohibition measure. "In all matters having to do with the personal habits and customs of large num-bers of people," he admonished Congress, "we must be certain that the established processes of legal change are followed."[125]

Just three hours later, the House of Representatives voted to override Wilson's veto, 176 to 5. The next day, the Senate concurred, 65 to 20. As of January 17, 1920, prohibition would become the law of the land.[126]

For his part, Woodrow Wilson—ailing from the overwhelming strains of both managing domestic politics and engineering the postwar international political architecture—still harbored dreams of running for a third term in 1920. Recognizing the futility of working with a dry Congress, Wilson focused instead on adding an explicit wet plank to the Democratic Party platform at their nominating conven-tion. "We recognize that the American saloon is opposed to all social, moral, and economic order, and we pledge ourselves to its absolute elimination by the passage of such laws as will finally and effectually exterminate it," read Wilson's proposed plank. "But we favor the repeal of the Volstead Act and the substitution for it of a law permitting the manufacture and sale of light wines and beer." Yet the public sentiment of both the Democratic convention and the nation at large was so overwhelmingly dry, the president's proposed plank never even got a hearing. Worries over Wilson's failing health pushed the Democrats to instead choose—on the forty-fourth ballot—Ohio governor James Cox as their nominee in 1920. Cox would ultimately lose to the Republican Warren G. Harding, who had brokered the Senate compromise on the Eighteenth Amendment.[127]

The World League

With American prohibition permanently ensconced in the US Constitution—from which no amendment had ever been repealed—prohibitionists confronted an existential crisis. Believing the battle had been forever won, many simply moved on from temperance to follow different pursuits. Others warned against passivity, channeling grassroots activism into vigilant oversight and enforcement of prohibition. Still others directed their temperance activism outward toward the rest of the world. It was in this later capacity that, on June 7, 1919, the Anti-Saloon League launched the World League Against Alcoholism (WLAA): the longtime pet project of Ernest Cherrington and Pussyfoot Johnson.[128]

As Johnson recalled, the WLAA began two years earlier, in 1917, over an extra slice of pie at Williams' Eating Emporium in Westerville, Ohio. It was there that Johnson told Cherrington he'd been invited by the Scottish Permissive Bill Association in Glasgow to help them organize for a Scottish prohibition referendum (Chapter 5).

"What did you do about it?" Cherrington asked.

"I turned it down, of course," Pussyfoot replied.

"Why did you do that?"

"Great Scott!" Pussyfoot turned. "How many jobs do you want me to have?"

"Suppose," Cherrington replied, "that you write these Scottish folks that you will go for nothing if they pay your expenses. We will take care of your salary"—which is ultimately what happened.

"And then he unfolded to me his dream of an international organization, tying together all the existing temperance bodies in a great, world-wide network," Pussyfoot recalled. "I could kill two birds with one stone while abroad by sounding out European dry leaders."[129]

So in 1917—two years before the formal establishment of the WLAA—Pussyfoot Johnson zigzagged his way across the U-boat-infested waters of the North Atlantic to champion the Scottish cause. "I lived for months in bereaved Scottish homes and knew the tragedy of them," Pussyfoot wrote, as scores of Scottish sons and husbands were dying at the front daily. "Except in Glasgow, Edinburgh and Inverness, I seldom entered a hotel. I was quartered in homes with people who were enduring their grief silently and patiently. I heard not a murmur of discontent, although scarcely a home in the Highlands had not offered up its human sacrifice." And when peace was proclaimed in November 1918, Pussyfoot joined in the joyous celebrations in the streets of Aberdeen.[130]

That evening, Pussyfoot hopped the night train for London. Once there, he opened the office of what would become the World League Against Alcoholism, at 69 Fleet Street in the heart of London. It was from London that Pussyfoot launched his famous sorties across Europe, Asia, Africa, and the Middle East (Chapters 4–8), ultimately giving thousands of speeches across twenty-three foreign countries, while building a list of some three thousand fellow activists and leaders in the global dry cause.[131] Still, one of his lower-profile assignments may have been even more important.

In the spring of 1919, Pussyfoot Johnson headed to Paris, where President Woodrow Wilson and diplomats from thirty-two countries were hammering out the details for the Versailles Treaty, the League of Nations, and the new institutions of the postwar world order. Two proposals were especially worrying to drys, both in the United States and around the world. First was a free-trade provision that would oblige state parties to open their markets to foreign trade in all goods, including alcoholic beverages. For the United States, this could have meant allowing imports of French brandies, German beers, and Italian wines in violation of the national prohibition law. The second was a treaty provision to loosen the prohibitions on the sale of beer and wine to what they called the "child races": Africans under European colonial domination, and Native Americans in the United States. Given his years in a prohibition officer in the Indian Service, Pussyfoot understood alco-colonization only too well; it was not the first time that profit-minded liquor interests worked to undermine colonial prohibitions that indigenous populations had fought so hard for (Chapters 3, 6, 7, 9–10), and it certainly would not be the last.[132]

Paris was already roiling with agitators for a myriad of causes, further complicating the treaty negotiations, so the prohibitionists were urged to work quietly and without publicity. As the American representatives, Pussyfoot and the ASL's Bishop James Cannon linked up with other like-minded world leaders. "Lord D'Abernon, chairman of the British Control Board [Chapter 5] was a leading spirit," Johnson wrote, "as was T. G. Masaryk, who later became first president of Czecho-Slovakia [Chapter 4]. Dr. Ivan Bratt, of Sweden, was on hand with his peculiar liquor rationing proposal [Chapter 3], as well as other Swedish delegates who didn't agree with his ideas at all."

Pussyfoot was charged with soliciting moderate, persuasive delegates for the delicate matter, over "notoriously hot prohibitionists" like the British pacifist Guy Halyer, whose International Prohibition Confederation had been a decade-long forerunner of the World League Against Alcoholism. "We did plenty of spade work without much noise," Johnson said. The international coalition convened daily before ultimately persuading the "Big Four"—the United States, Britain, France, and Italy—to abandon the contentious pro-liquor planks in favor of national, sovereign policymaking regarding the liquor question.[133]

It was with such diplomatic compromise and tact that the World League Against Alcoholism undertook its international mission. Occasionally derided in the historical literature as some American cultural-imperialist impulse to foist American prohibitionism and Anti-Saloon League tactics on an unwilling world (Chapter 18), the WLAA simply acted as a clearinghouse of information and facilitator of transnational networking, just as the International Prohibition Confederation, the World's WCTU, and the International Order of Good Templars had been doing for decades.[134] After all, the biennial Congresses on Alcoholism began in Europe in 1885, thirty-five years before the WLAA. Moreover, Frederick Douglass and William Lloyd Garrison attended the first World's Temperance Convention way back in London in 1846 (Chapter 11).[135]

Johnson, Cherrington, and the WLAA knew full well that Anti-Saloon League tactics were sure to backfire in foreign contexts. "The plan of the movement does not contemplate that the temperance folk of America are going to foreign lands and force Prohibition on them," claimed the Anti-Saloon League in 1918, "there is no such thought. . . . The idea is to help the people that are facing this problem and are asking us to help."[136] Certainly, throwing whatever weight they might have behind this dry candidate over that wet one would come across as American meddling, discredit host-country temperance forces as American pawns, and thus weaken the international movement.

When Dr. Karl von Langi, president of the Czechoslovak Abstainer's League in Bratislava, wrote to the WLAA soliciting financial assistance, Pussyfoot replied, "It has not been our policy to directly subsidize foreign organizations for two reasons. One is that it would raise the outcry of 'American interference' and the other"— since by 1928 American support for prohibition was waning amid calls for repeal— "is that the liquor interests of the world are making such a terrific fight on American prohibition that we have real difficulty in financing our own work."[137]

This hardly sounds like American cultural imperialism. Just the opposite, in fact. With American prohibition up against the ropes beginning with the elections of 1928, Johnson and the WLAA tried to get well-known international drys— Mahatma Gandhi and Lord and Lady Astor of Britain—to tour the United States in hopes that their celebrity would shore up the American prohibitionist cause. Gandhi never visited the United States, and the impact of Lady Nancy Astor— American-born suffragette and prohibitionist who became Britain's first seated woman Member of Parliament—ultimately did little to stem the repeal tide.[138]

Still, the WLAA never went anywhere they weren't invited—something Pussyfoot Johnson made clear from his first forays into Scotland in 1918 at the behest of the Permissive Bill Association (Chapter 5). If the rough-and-tumble reception he received in Scotland wasn't enough, the Pussyfoot riot through the streets of London that cost him his eye in the fall of 1919 surely hammered home the dangers of being perceived as a meddlesome foreign agent. Nevertheless, Pussyfoot returned to Anti-Saloon League headquarters in Westerville, Ohio, as a national hero.[139]

In many ways, the WLAA was just an institutionalization of the global networking that Pussyfoot Johnson had been doing all along.[140] Cherrington was the organization's general secretary, and Harry B. Sowers—treasurer of the Anti-Saloon League—took on the additional role of treasurer of the World League; but otherwise its organization reflected the diversity of its global aims. The WCTU's Anna Gordon was elected one of the WLAA presidents, along with Howard Hyde Russell, Dr. Robert Hercod of Switzerland, and the Right Honorable Leif Jones of London. Its vice presidents—including Emile Vandervelde of Belgium (Chapter 3)—hailed from nineteen different countries on six continents. At its pinnacle of activism in the mid-1920s, the WLAA boasted sixty-one affiliated temperance organizations; two hundred temperance publications; a separate students' organ—the Intercollegiate Prohibition Association; and a continued close working relationship with the League of Nations in Geneva. All of this was in a fraternal effort to defend communities the world over from the predatory capitalism—and indeed imperialism—of the liquor traffic.[141]

Reporting on the organization's activities to the WLAA council in 1927, General Secretary Cherrington listed the dozens of countries and thousands of activists networked, estimating some 1.3 million individuals having heard WLAA-affiliated speeches, and that the publicity in newspapers around the globe was worth millions of dollars. Much of this was due to Pussyfoot Johnson, who "surpass[es] anything in the way of a great world educational tour in the interest of the cause of human welfare ever undertaken by any organization or individual in the history of the world," Cherrington claimed.

"That is a strong statement," he went on, "but the details of his remarkable journeyings will bear out the truth of the statement. The record of his journeys reads like a series of romances." His adventures spanned not just Oklahoma and the Indian Territories of the American West (Chapter 14), but Russia (Chapter 2), Scandinavia (Chapter 3), Continental Europe (Chapter 4), the British Isles (Chapter 5), sub-Saharan Africa (Chapters 3 and 6), India and Ceylon (Chapter 7), Egypt, Turkey, and the Middle East (Chapter 8), China and the Philippines (Chapter 15), as well as Australia and New Zealand (Chapter 5). "When the true history of the world's temperance reform has been written," Cherrington concluded, "the services rendered by our distinguished representative, William E. Johnson, will stand out in a peculiar light as one of the greatest achievements in that particular line in the record of temperance activities."[142]

So it is especially curious that Johnson is seldom even mentioned in standard prohibition histories, which focus solely on the American experience.

Returning our focus from the transnational dimensions of prohibitionism to the chronology of developments in the United States, the World League was established in that yearlong window between the ratification of the Eighteenth Amendment in January 1919, and its taking effect in January 1920. Ostensibly, that grace period was to allow for the liquor interests—the brewers, distillers, saloon-keepers, and those in their employ—the time to wind up their operations and retool into different lines of work. Some remained above board: switching to the manufacturing of soft drinks, malted milk, fruit juices, cheeses, and ice cream.[143] Others would take their business underground.

The final triumph of American prohibition was remarkably anticlimactic. There were no riots as with Pussyfoot in London, nor great jubilation in the streets. Contrary to popular imagery, there was no mad dash for booze on Prohibition Eve, January 16, 1920: there were no going-out-of-business-forever fire sales at liquor stores. The country had already been dry for the last half-year, thanks to the Wartime Prohibition Act, and before that thirty-two states had already gone dry through statewide prohibition votes. In Norfolk, evangelist Billy Sunday held a mock funeral for his old enemy John Barleycorn. So too did a handful of restaurants and hotels, but "the spontaneous orgies of drink that were predicted failed in large part to occur," wrote the *New York Times*. "With little that differed from normal wartime prohibition drinking habits, New York City entered at 12:01 o'clock this morning into the long dry spell." Behind debates over ratifying the Peace of Versailles and a war scare with Bolshevik Russia, the dawn of a dry America was barely page-one news.[144]

Epilogue: Washington and the World

On Tuesday, September 21, 1920—just a few short months after prohibition became the law of the land—the Fifteenth International Congress on Alcoholism opened in Washington, DC. It had been seven years since the previous conference was held in Milan, Italy, in 1913. The Great War had not only delayed the biennial conference by five years, it had fundamentally changed the global temperance movement.

For the activists who gathered at the Pan American Union Building—just across the street from the West Wing of the White House—it was a chance to reconnect with old friends, and mourn those friends lost to time, to the war, or to the global Spanish flu pandemic. There were no representatives from the vanquished and collapsed empires of Germany, Austria, or Russia.

But it was also a time of great optimism. Perhaps a new and better international order could be built atop the wreckage of the past. As Secretary of the Navy Josephus Daniels noted in his welcoming address, the newly formed League of Nations on which the hope of global peace rested included prohibitions against trafficking in slaves, arms, and liquor in the colonies and mandates under its tutelage. More immediately, for the first time in its thirty-five-year history, the congress was being held in the United States, and for the very first time ever, it was being held in a prohibition country. The congress chairman was none other than the ASL's Edwin Dinwiddie, with Ernest Cherrington as secretary.

Following Daniels's welcome came a parade of greetings from delegates from around the world, most sharing the same message: their countries will be looking on with keen interest as the United States embarks upon its so-called noble experiment with prohibition.

"What is the pleasure of the congress?" Chairman Dinwiddie then asked the hall. "We have a few moments left."

The thirteen hundred attendees suddenly erupted with cries of "Bryan! Bryan!"

As head of the temperance committee of the Federal Council of Churches and the progressive Interchurch World Movement, the former secretary of state was especially keen on international temperance developments. He had even attended the WLAA's conference on global prohibitionism in November 1918, just a week after the armistice.[145] So the great orator, prohibitionist, and pacifist rose from his chair to prolonged applause. The normally loquacious Bryan would keep his remarks brief, as he was scheduled to speak at greater length at the close of the convention.

"Two causes have been on my heart for many years," Bryan quietly noted:

> One is world peace, and the other is Prohibition. To me the signs of the time point to a victory for our fight against the two enemies of the human race, the two greatest enemies; and I am made more hopeful because woman, who has suffered more than man from both, has entered the arena of politics. Her mighty influence will be felt in the settlement of these questions, the question of alcoholism, and the question of war, and her influence will be felt in the settlement of every other question that involves a moral principle, and there are no great questions that do not involve a moral principle. War has sacrificed the husbands and the sons upon the altar of Mars, and alcoholism has dragged husbands and sons down to premature graves.

After Bryan's brief remarks, Chairman Dinwiddie let the congress attendees in on a little secret: none of this would have been possible without Bryan's leadership. Before the Great War tore Europe apart, and before the global wave of prohibition rendered both the United States and countries and territories around the world dry, it was Secretary of State William Jennings Bryan who commissioned the American delegation to the 1913 Congress in Milan. He'd instructed Dinwiddie, Cherrington, and Pussyfoot Johnson to invite the organization to meet in Washington next. And in 1914, it was Bryan who secured federal funds to help defray the costs of hosting such a meeting. Though it was ultimately delayed five years, Bryan delighted in seeing it through to fulfillment.[146]

At the close of the convention on Friday—after four days of speeches and discussions about the progress of the antiliquor cause around the world—Bryan would have the last word.

"Mr. President, Ladies, and Gentlemen," Bryan began with a laugh, "I do feel at home in this neighborhood!" situated, as they were, just a block from the White House. "And I feel at home in this gathering, and I think it's very fortunate that this meeting, that is, this Congress provided for several years ago, when we could not foresee the situation as it exists to-day . . . during the first year of this Nation's existence as a saloonless nation."

> And, my friends, I do not know that this nation can better render a service to this cause than to furnish inspiration and facts to those who can use them in their lands better than they could be used by people from this country going into these lands. They will speak to their own people, and their sympathy can not be questioned, and those who oppose them there can not appeal to any prejudice or excite any feeling against a foreigner who would interfere in their affairs. We can furnish them with the facts, we can fill them with enthusiasm, and send them back with unanswerable arguments against the traffic in their own lands.[147]

For over an hour Bryan spoke of the history of the American temperance movement, stretching back to Lyman Beecher (Chapter 11), who "delivered six powerful sermons against drink; and if you will read them, you will find in them almost every argument that we've made since in favor of total abstinence and legislation against the liquor traffic." Those speeches energized a movement against the saloon that would become national in scope. The churches were important in instilling a basic sense of right and wrong, and that exploiting thy neighbor by selling him drink is wrong. In that moral capacity he told of the Good Templars, the Woman's Christian Temperance Union (Chapter 13), and the Anti-Saloon League (Chapter 16).

"But the conscience has only been one part," Bryan emphasized. "Science has contributed." Medical science allowed us to better understand addiction and pinpoint the harms of alcoholism on the body, while economic and social sciences have allowed us to understand its harms on society, the economy, and the polity (Chapter 14). Business had contributed, too, as employers always prefer a sober employee to a drunken one.

"But, my friends, these are some of the things that have contributed to the victory of our cause," Bryan continued. Underscoring the normative shift behind prohibitionism, he claimed,

> The respectability argument finally came over to our side. It used to be respectable for people to defend the saloon. It's not now. The saloon has

been tried; the saloon has been convicted; the saloon has been sentenced; and the saloon has been executed.... It's no longer respectable to be on the side of the liquor traffic. It's an outlawed traffic; it's a fugitive from justice. And, my friends, respectability is now on our side, and respectability is tremendous argument in support of any cause.

When it came to the task of a constitutional amendment, Bryan explained how the two great parties, the Republicans and the Democrats, "laid aside their differences on other subjects, and stood together for the home against the home's greatest enemies," invoking the WCTU's "home protection" slogan. As much as one party or the other might claim all the glory—or later shoulder all of the blame—"when the nation has arrived at the point where it's to go forward, the two parties join together, and they carry their standards side by side as the nation moves forward to higher ground. That's true of all our great reforms, and it's true in a very special degree of this."

Having emancipated itself from liquor-machine predations, Bryan proclaimed America's readiness to help other willing countries to do the same. When Americans found remedies for the typhoid fever that had so devastated Bryan's regiment in the Spanish-American War (Chapter 15), they shared it with the world. When they found remedies for the yellow fever that killed thousands of Americans building the Panama Canal, they shared it with the world. When Woodrow Wilson devised his Fourteen Points and a League of Nations to inoculate against the scourge of war, he shared it with the world. Why should alcohol be any different? "We found that the saloon was the breeding-place of the germ of alcoholism, and so we adopted Prohibition." Now that we have a vaccine, "we want to give it to the world."

It was his concluding optimism that enraptured Bryan's global audience. "I have faith that it's going to triumph throughout the world. We've traveled so fast, we've gone so far, that I believe now that I shall yet live to see the day when there will not be an open saloon under the flag of any civilized nation in all this world!"

America, he was confident, could lead the world against the twin scourges of war and liquor subjugation, and he was honored that so many had come from so far to learn from America's experiences—good and bad—in shared pursuit of this noble aim. "And if by coming here tonight and by recalling what has been done in this country, I can contribute even a small part toward helping them in their fight in other lands, I shall be happy for the opportunity thus afforded," Bryan concluded. "I thank you for your attention."[148]

Conclusion—Where Did We Go Wrong?

Smithville Flats, New York: Monday, June 3, 1935

"Say. Mr. Man.

"Will you and your brood be voyaging up this way on your usual summer outing?" wrote retired prohibitionist William E. "Pussyfoot" Johnson from his modest farmstead in upstate New York. The typewritten letter was addressed to Harry B. Sowers, his longtime friend and treasurer of the Anti-Saloon League (ASL) in Westerville, Ohio. "If so, we will be disappointed if you don't place our old dump on your calling stations. Come along. We have chickens and garden produce to ease your gnawing hunger pains, so come along."

The once-mighty Anti-Saloon League—which, more than any organization, had secured the triumph of American prohibition—had fallen on hard times amid the Great Depression. So too had their world-famous ambassador, Pussyfoot. But even in his mid-seventies, he kept his same old self-deprecating sense of humor. "I have a doctor making some repairs on my cadaver, but he reports that I will live for some time to come," he wrote Sowers. "Anyhow, I will not die before autumn and that is encouraging."[1]

The handwritten letters to League Treasurer Sowers from *Mrs.* Johnson on the same letterhead—often marked strictly confidential, with instructions to destroy after reading—were far less encouraging.

In its heyday, the Anti-Saloon League was one of the biggest, most successful political organizations in America. But after the Eighteenth Amendment was ratified, "a large number of temperance people threw up their hats, cheered and said, 'Hallelujah, it's done,'" as ASL chief Wayne Wheeler reflected. "It is nearly always that way after every great forward movement. Nerves and muscles must relax and that is what happened in our case."[2]

Enthusiasm waned. Subscriptions, dues, and donations—the financial lifeblood of the organization—all dried up. In Westerville, the once-thriving ASL publication hub was reduced to a skeleton crew. Then in 1929 came the stock-market crash and a decade-long Great Depression. In 1933 the Twenty-First Amendment was proposed, passed, and ratified with breakneck speed, erasing the Eighteenth Amendment from the Constitution. It was the final nail in the coffin of American prohibition.

Discredited and bankrupt, the ASL could no longer fund Pussyfoot's insurance or his meager pension.[3] After his first wife died, Pussyfoot married May Stanley: the young widow of one of Johnson's Wild West Indian Service deputies who was murdered in the line of duty (Chapter 16).[4] Though he vowed to care for May, more often she cared for him. But her investments in US Steel and General Motors were wiped out in the Black Tuesday stock market crash. The twenty-five hundred dollars she'd invested with Swedish "Match King" Ivar Kreuger turned out to be a Ponzi scheme.

The Johnsons were destitute.

With no money for the mortgage or back taxes, the bank was threatening to foreclose on their farm. Brushfires claimed their fields in summer; their well had frozen solid in winter. With no money for coal, the elderly Pussyfoot scavenged the forest for wood for the furnace. She once discovered her threadbare husband slumped over on top of his typewriter, convulsing in a seizure.[5] The hardships and strains had broken Pussyfoot, both physically and mentally, but he was too proud to admit it.

Every month, she'd plead with Sowers to send fifty dollars, twenty dollars, *anything*. "Mr. Sowers," she wrote, "I don't know what the situation is for the League, but at the same time I know you and other officials are at least eating food. . . . I don't even get food money from my husband because he gets no money with which to buy it."[6] Sowers usually was able to send at least something.

But—a silver lining, perhaps! May explained to Sowers that a Syracuse newspaperman—with connections at the *Saturday Evening Post*—thought he could sell the story of Pussyfoot's adventures, either as a book or a series of articles. After all, this was an American who'd gone into the anti-tsarist underground in Russia, chronicled American atrocities in the Philippines, and aided Gandhi's nonviolent independence movement in India. He'd survived assassination attempts, bar fights, bombings, and shipwrecks at sea. He crossed the Mojave Desert on foot and gazed upon the majesty of Mount Everest with the one eye he hadn't lost in that London riot (Chapter 5). The *Los Angeles Evening Herald* said he'd "been abused in more different languages than any man on earth."[7] Certainly there should be some popular interest in his life story, right?

"Mr. Johnson is working about 12 hours a day on his memoirs," Mrs. Johnson wrote. "The man from Syracuse comes every few days to work with him. Mr. Johnson has written over 150 [pages] already. The Syracuse man furnishes *all the paper* since we don't have the money for paper. I do hope it sells so that Mr. Johnson can clear up some of the debt and get on his feet a little bit."[8]

But no publisher wanted it. No one cared. Thoroughly discredited, prohibitionism had left such a bad taste in people's mouths that not even its most flamboyant advocate could find an audience. When Pussyfoot finally died in 1945, fewer than fifty

Figure 18.1 "William E. (Pussyfoot) Johnson's Last Photograph," ca. 1939.
Source: Box 1, Folder 1, William E. "Pussyfoot" Johnson Collection, 180–1, Fenimore Art Museum Library, Cooperstown, NY.

mourners braved the blizzard to lay to rest a man the *New York Times* once listed among its "Greatest American Men."[9]

Though it likely made little difference to postwar critics, writers, and scholars— eager to paint an entire generation of now-deceased activists as foes of freedom— Johnson's unpublished *Confessions* provided a final defense of prohibitionism.

"I think the label 'prohibitionist' should be properly defined," Pussyfoot wrote:

> I am not a prohibitionist at all, in the full sense of the word. I am for pro-
> hibition of the liquor traffic, for reasons which I consider good and un-
> answerable, but beyond that I am, in every instinct and inclination, an
> ardent anti-prohibitionist. Every law in the American penal code is a pro-
> hibition statute; each prohibits someone from doing something. I am so
> completely anti-prohibitionist that I firmly believe one-half of the existing
> prohibitions should be wiped from our statute books and their enforcers
> amputated from the public payrolls.

So, the great Pussyfoot Johnson was actually a *libertarian* prohibitionist? How are we to square that with the well-entrenched historical narrative that prohibitionists were this country's greatest foes of liberty?

The answer lies in that subtle difference in the target of prohibitionists' activism: battling against the drink seller, not the drinker. Just as the ASL demurred
on Senator James Reed's 1917 "Bone Dry" amendment outlawing the purchase or
consumption of alcohol (Chapter 17), Pussyfoot—like most prohibitionists—was
steadfastly against such sumptuary legislation.

"I am definitely and irrevocably against any law prohibiting a man from taking a
drink; or getting soused, for that matter. I believe that everyone has a personal and
natural right to drink all the liquor his skin will hold," Pussyfoot wrote on. "There
should be no laws to prohibit a man from making a fool of himself—either from
eating or drinking—if he wishes to do so. . . . When a law says otherwise, I find myself bellowing in the ranks of the anti-prohibitionists. I have no more use for legal
meddling than I have for lumbago."[10]

Pussyfoot continued his *Confessions* with the same rebuke he used against
Winston Churchill, when in 1929 Churchill lampooned the "arrogance and impotence" of American prohibitionists.[11] To wit:

> I never have proposed or supported a law forbidding a man to take a drink,
> or to eat spoiled meat. But I think it urgently necessary to have laws which
> will prohibit a butcher from selling spoiled meat. And I think it equally as
> important to have laws which prohibit the sale of liquor.
>
> This is entirely a different matter. The question of individual rights and
> good or bad taste no longer is involved. When a man opens an establish-
> ment for the sale of liquor or rotten meat for human consumption, he
> performs a social act. Society is then directly concerned and is charged
> with the duty of protecting itself.
>
> I would place the traffic in intoxicating liquors on exactly the same basis
> as the sale of spoiled meat, impure drugs or adulterated foods.[12]

As a reminder, both the Pure Food and Drug Act and the Federal Meat Inspection
Act were passed in 1906 during the Roosevelt administration (Chapter 17), and are
hailed as monuments of Progressive consumer- and community-protection law. The
same Progressive Era that witnessed prohibition also saw the Harrison Narcotics
Act (1914), the Federal Trade Commission Act (1914), the Clayton Anti-Trust
Act (1914), the creation of the Federal Reserve (1913), and a myriad of other
reforms giving power to the people at the expense of the Gilded Age aristocracy.
Add to that the other Progressive Era constitutional amendments: the Sixteenth
(1913), levying an income tax on the ultra-wealthy; the democratizing Seventeenth
(1913), allowing the citizens of a state to directly elect their own senators; and the
Nineteenth (1920), which finally gave women the right to vote.

Though it was cut from the exact same cloth of community protection, democratization, and empowerment as all these reforms, somehow the Eighteenth

Amendment is singled out by historians and often vilified as—allegedly—the only amendment that curtails individual freedom.[13]

Why?

There's a curious tell in—of all places—Wikipedia. For all its breadth and depth of coverage, Wikipedia never claims to reflect the unquestionable, big-t "Truth"—rather, just the verifiable consensus on any given topic.[14] So it is interesting that Wikipedia notes that "*at the time*" the Eighteenth Amendment "was generally considered a progressive amendment"—before then parroting the received wisdom that it was the handiwork of Bible-thumping temperance reactionaries.[15] So, what changed? Certainly, the events of history never changed. Nor did the motivations of the activists generations ago.

So if *they* didn't change, it must be *us* who did: *our* consensus understandings of history have changed. Since this book is also about the politics of memory—who we honor and who we vilify in our collective past—I want to find out why, when, and how that happened.

Where Did We Go So Wrong?

Certainly, prohibitionists were scorned even when they were alive, as were suffragists, abolitionists, nationalists, and others who challenged existing power structures. But once the last prohibitionists were dead and gone, no one was left to correct the record, even as a new generation of postwar historians ran roughshod over their legacies. If I had to narrow down precisely when prohibition history got switched down the wrong track, I'd say it was 1955.

In that year, venerated Columbia University professor Richard Hofstadter published his Pulitzer Prize–winning history of progressivism: *The Age of Reform: From Bryan to F.D.R.* Even critics hail it as "the most influential book ever published on the history of twentieth-century America," which has "shaped virtually every discussion of modern American reform" for generations.[16] Hofstadter's flair was in moving beyond simple historical description to proffering causal explanations for events and outcomes. Based on his reading of Sigmund Freud, Max Weber, and a wide swath of influential sociologists and psychologists, Hofstadter's historical explanations for American politics rely on behavioral concepts like "status anxiety," "anti-intellectualism," and the "paranoid style."[17]

Hoftstadter's persuasive writing and satisfying narratives—and the public celebrity that came with them—irked traditional historians. They pointed out that Hofstadter didn't actually do any original research himself, solely relying on the secondary works of earlier historians, and largely reflective of their shortcomings.

He scoffed that the "archive rats" (as Hofstadter called them) were just jealous.[18]

Hoftstadter's *Age of Reform* is built around his so-called agrarian myth: the American valorization of the small, independent farmer. To conform with his sweeping narrative, Hofstadter decouples prohibitionism from its progressive moorings, and reframes it as emblematic of American urban-rural, anti-immigrant, anti-minority cultural conflict—chalking it up to the same "rural Protestant enthusiasm" that begot the Ku Klux Klan.

This is the Hofstadter line that would be parroted by generations of prohibition scholars:

> Prohibition was a pseudo-reform, a pinched, parochial substitute for reform which had a widespread appeal to a certain type of crusading mind. It was linked not merely to an aversion to drunkenness and to the evils that accompanied it, but to the immigrant drinking masses, to the pleasures and amenities of city life, and to the well-to-do classes and cultivated men. It was carried about America by the rural-evangelical virus: the country Protestant frequently brought it with him to the city when the contraction of agriculture sent him there to seek his livelihood.[19]

No nuance. No archival sources. No consideration of the prohibitionists' stated motivations. Most notably: no mention of the *man who sells*. By sleight of hand, Hofstadter repositions generations of temperance activists as being enemies not of predatory capitalism but of the drinkers themselves. The long American temperance struggle from Little Turtle and Frederick Douglass to Elizabeth Cady Stanton, F. E. W. Harper, and Walter Rauschenbusch gets folded into a simple blanket condemnation of some rural-evangelical crusade against "evil."

"To hold the Progressives responsible for Prohibition would be to do them an injustice," Hofstadter claimed. The Progressive argument that capitalism was "one of the means by which the interests, in this case the 'whisky ring,' fattened on the toil of the people," he dismissed as empty propaganda. Instead—setting in place the conventional wisdom of generations of future historians—Hofstadter argued it was evangelicals' moral zealotry combined with the World War I calls to patriotic sacrifice that whipped the nation into a frenzy of irrationalism. "While it was at its pitch the dry lobbyists struck, and when they were finished the Prohibition mania was fixed in the Constitution; and there it remained for almost fifteen years, a symbol of the moral overstrain of the preceding era, the butt of jokes, a perennial source of irritation, a memento of the strange power of crusades for absolute morality to intensify the evils they mean to destroy."[20] Instead of scrutinizing this claim, generations of academics—myself included—acquiesced to it.

The year 1955 also marked the debut of influential prohibition scholar Joseph Gusfield, longtime chair of sociology at the University of California, San Diego. His first publication, "Social Structure and Moral Reform: A Study of the Woman's Christian Temperance Union," in the *American Journal of Sociology* (1955), built upon similar assumptions as Hofstadter, namely that temperance was a "moral reform": a cultural issue, rather than a social or economic one.[21] But his full broadside against prohibitionism only came with the 1963 publication of his *Symbolic Crusade: Status Politics and the American Temperance Movement*.

Gusfield's scorn for temperance advocates drips from page one, arguing that their "moralism and utopianism bring smiles to the cynical and fear to the sinners. Such a movement seems at once naive, intolerant, saintly, and silly."

Rather than acknowledging temperance's complex economic and political dimensions, Gusfield flattens them into being simply a symbolic cudgel in battles between competing cultural groups. He writes, "Temperance has usually been the attempt of the moral people, in this case the abstainers, to correct the behavior of the immoral people, in this case the drinkers. The issue has appeared as a moral one, divorced from any direct economic interests in abstinence or indulgence."[22] Having chronicled how—over the previous seventeen chapters—temperance activists in the United States and around the world argued just the opposite in their own words, it's hard to come to any conclusion other than Gusfield's sweeping assumptions are just plain wrong.

But Gusfield digs his hole deeper. Explicitly citing Hofstadter, he argues that the use (not selling) of alcohol differs between rival cultural groups: "Protestants, Catholics, and Jews, native and immigrant, Negro and white," as they battle each other for dominance, status, prestige, and political power.[23] As "each status group operates with an image of correct behavior which it prizes and with a contrast conception in the behavior of despised groups whose status is beneath theirs," Gusfield recasts temperance as a cultural cudgel in maintaining a clear racial hierarchy to maintain the American white Anglo-Saxon Protestants on top, and everyone else subordinate.[24]

Never mind that these were not homogenous groups. For a supposed bunch of "drys," rural evangelicals sure drank *a lot*.[25] So did Catholics and Jews, immigrants and old-stock nativists, blacks, whites, and Native Americans. But there was also strong temperance sentiment within Protestant, Catholic, Jewish, immigrant, white-nativist, black, and Native American communities, too. And never mind that the temperance activists themselves seldom self-identified as part of Gusfield's reified cultural groupings, and even more seldom acted on their behalf.[26] Acknowledging those realities only muddies Gusfield's supposedly clear-cut cultural divisions over temperance.

But this misses the point entirely: temperance wasn't about drinking culture—the who, what, how, and how much different communities drank—but about opposing exploitation and profit. In this regard, it is worth noting that, even beyond the general anti-Semitism, Jewish communities occasionally drew prohibitionists' ire: based less on drinking customs within close-knit Jewish quarters, and more on "Jews' longstanding commercial relationship with alcohol" and the broader liquor traffic. Still, in charting their fraught and indeterminate relationship with temperance, in her *Jews and Booze: Becoming American in the Age of Prohibition* (2012), Marni Davis describes Jewish suspicions and hesitancy toward "Christian temperance" organizations, while acknowledging "groups like the WCTU sometimes served as models for Jewish organizations," and that "American Jews sympathized with concerns that alcohol exacerbated poverty and other societal problems."[27]

More to the point: both in the United States and around the world, the true target of prohibitionism—the liquor traffic—was overwhelmingly the purview of powerful, white, self-identified Christians. By falsely portraying prohibitionism as the sword of powerful groups in maintaining their privileged position, rather than the shield of marginalized communities against their subordination, Gusfield turned prohibition history completely on its head.

According to Gusfield, if minorities don't bow down to the morals of the dominant cultural group, they would have to be coerced or disciplined. In this culture-clash worldview, temperance reflected

> the cultural struggle of the traditional rural Protestant society against the developing urban and industrial social system. Coercive reform became the dominating theme of Temperance. It culminated in the drive for national Prohibition. The Eighteenth Amendment was the high point of the struggle to assert the public dominance of old middle-class values. It established the victory of Protestant over Catholic, rural over urban, tradition over modernity, the middle class over both the lower and the upper strata.[28]

Gusfield's new orthodoxy became the intellectual blinders for generations of prohibition scholars. This meant (1) focusing on culture and religion at the expense of politics and economics, (2) falsely recasting temperance activism as being against the individual drinker rather than the predations of big business, (3) equating temperance with evangelical Protestantism and reactionary conservatism, and (4) casting the conflict as between cultural groups rather than between society and the state.

In subsequent decades, Gusfield and others built a wide-reaching narrative of prohibitionism as social control against immigrants, minorities, and the poor: a quasi-totalitarian "benevolent repression," dictating how marginalized groups used their leisure time and private lives.[29] It all *felt* sufficiently plausible that generations of astute scholars adopted this framework, donning the blinders of culturalism.[30]

Recently, for instance, Brown University political scientist James Morone claimed that prohibition was an attempt "to tame the urban Gomorrahs." Harvard historian Lisa McGirr's *The War on Alcohol: Prohibition and the Rise of the American State* (2016) focuses on "moral crusaders" and even the KKK in foisting prohibition on immigrant, black, and poor communities, claiming "it was, after all, enacted to discipline their leisure in the first place."[31] Of course, this would come as quite a shock to Frederick Douglass, Frances Ellen Watkins Harper, Booker T. Washington, Walter Rauschenbusch, the Quakers, the Five Civilized Tribes, and scores of activists who fought to uplift black, immigrant, native, and disadvantaged communities against the "white man's wicked water."

Measured by its duration, membership, and scope, the temperance-cum-prohibition movement was the longest-lasting, most widely supported, and most expansive social movement in both American and global history.[32] But rather than accounting for such a durable, broad base of support, it more often than not gets dismissed as an incoherent hodgepodge, "a political crazy quilt," which—thanks only to a fortuitous constellation of dastardly forces—put prohibition over on the freedom-loving American people.[33] The movement had its own political party, dozens of organizations, thousands of chapters, and millions of adherents the world over—hardly something that can be laughed off as lunacy or the result of unexpected constellations of tangentially related political forces.

Sometimes a Saloon Is Just a Saloon

If prohibitionism was just the "symbolic crusade" that Gusfield suggests, then the focus of the activists' ire—the saloon—could be refashioned into a symbol of *anything* to fit those preconceptions. Carrie Nation smashed saloons. So did Black Hawk. The Woman's Crusaders picketed them. Theodore Roosevelt made sure they were closed. The Anti-Saloon League put the object of their opposition right there in their name. But subsequent histories desperately want to portray the saloon as anything but the predatory business it actually was.

To justify their culture-clash narratives, historians have labeled the saloon as "the public symbol of alcohol" or "the ultimate symbol of public vice."[34] Saloons were "bastions of male privilege" and "symbolized the rise of male leisure and a growing commercialism that tapped into it." According to this take, women's anti-saloon activism had nothing to do with their economic vulnerability and political subordination, but rather because they "lagg[ed] behind men in 'leisure' consumption," and "women were angry at the saloons for further cordoning off spaces of male privilege."[35]

If drinking was an individual's right, and prohibitionist crusaders were just chasing around made-up symbols, then historians could portray the saloon as a virtuous, working-class institution, completely at odds with the gritty, exploitative, and corrupt reality. "The barroom served many functions—meeting place, reading room, music hall, ethnic preserve, and male bastion," claimed historian Michael McGerr. "The saloon was also the place where workers dropped the discipline of the workplace and loosened self-control."[36]

Such sanitized portrayals of men blowing off steam embody what I call "the Ted Danson Effect," in which we falsely project our bar experiences of today backward to the saloons of yesteryear. Neighborhood taverns nowadays are cozy, respectable places "where everybody knows your name," like on the '80s sitcom *Cheers*. There,

Danson's character—bartender Sam Malone—always greeted you with a joke and cold brewski. It was your home away from home. Like a therapist or best friend, the bartender would listen to your troubles and help you forget them. And if you had one too many at closing time, he'd make sure you got home safely. He cared.

But as we've seen time and again throughout this book—both in the United States and around the world—saloons weren't cozy, happy places. They were dark and smoky, with overflowing spittoons and sticky floors. Saloons were "a noxious institution, in fact inextricably bound up with prostitution, gambling, police corruption and crime."[37] Unlike *Cheers*, the saloon-keeper wasn't your friend: his aim was to get as much of your money as possible, through undermeasuring or watering down your drinks, running up your tab, or enticing you with his gaming tables and prostitutes. He'd use his clout—and his fists—to intimidate those who disagreed with him, and use his ill-gotten profits to corrupt politicians and keep the machine churning. The popular image of the saloon-keeper shouldn't be Ted Danson from *Cheers*, but Daniel Day Lewis's character in *Gangs of New York*, patterned after Captain Rynders (Chapter 12).

Sending a drunkard home meant sending his profit home. Pointing out this reality isn't "revisionist history" on my part. Just the opposite, in fact. As we saw in Chapter 16, by the Progressive Era, saloon-keepers themselves were openly admitting to such predations, and in some cases atoning for them.

Saloons were an actual, real blight on the local community, whether they were operating legally or illegally. To oppose them wasn't some act of madness, menopause, or messianism. Some might argue that prohibition was actually victorious in fundamentally altering, strenuously regulating, and making respectable retail alcohol outlets in the post-prohibition era. But the point is: *the saloon was not a symbol* of something else. It was the *actual thing* temperance advocates had opposed since the very start. They've told us so, time and again. It is amazing that we go to such lengths in developing narratives and symbolism so that we don't have to believe them.

Why Vilify?

A bland historiography of prohibition studies doesn't necessarily explain why we look back on temperance activists with the same seething, "they hate our freedoms" vitriol normally reserved for Al-Qaeda, ISIS, and international terrorists.

In her famous "Do Everything" speech of 1893 (Chapter 13), WCTU president Frances Willard proclaimed, "The history of the reformer, whether man or woman, in any line of action is but this: when he sees it all alone, he is a fanatic; when a good many see it with him, they are enthusiasts; when all see it, he is a hero. The radiations are as clearly marked by which he ascends from zero to hero as are the lines of latitude from the North Star to the Equator."[38]

The descent from "hero" back down to "fanatic"—think of Carrie Nation—or to be forgotten as a "zero" like Pussyfoot Johnson seems to follow the same gradations.

Even back in 1908, social reformer George Hammell noted how the leaders we valorize in hindsight were usually dismissed as fanatics, dreamers, and cranks in their day:

> But in religion and in politics the reformer is always pronounced a heretic—at first. Martin Luther, John Wesley, George Fox, were heretics. Paul was a heretic. Jesus of Nazareth was a heretic. Wendell Phillips, Lloyd Garrison, Abraham Lincoln were political heretics. The great Republican party was, in its beginning wholly heterodox according to the prevailing political standards of that period, and was as bitterly denounced and hated by the "vested interests" of that time as are the radical parties of the present by the "predatory wealth" of today. Whoever and whatever disturbs the Established Order in any time or place is always heretical.[39]

We've already laid bare the temperance and prohibitionism of those once-heretical American icons Abraham Lincoln and William Lloyd Garrison whom Hammell mentions. As for famed abolitionist orator Wendell Phillips, he too proclaimed, "We don't care what a man does in his own parlor. He may drink his champagne or whiskey, and we don't care." However, "the moment he undertakes to sell liquor, the State has an absolute and unlimited right to step in." It is not the liquor, but those who profit from the booze trade "that make the masses tools in the hands of designing men to undermine and cripple law."[40]

So, we should probably add Phillips's name to the list of America's dry "fanatics," along with Garrison and Lincoln. They're in good company with William Penn, Thomas Jefferson, Little Turtle, Red Jacket, Black Hawk, Frederick Douglass, Elizabeth Cady Stanton, Susan B. Anthony, Frances Willard, Frances Ellen Watkins Harper, Ida B. Wells, Booker T. Washington, Walter Rauschenbusch, William Jennings Bryan, and Theodore Roosevelt (Chapters 9–16). This is to say nothing of "reactionaries" such as Leo Tolstoy, Vladimir Lenin, Hjalmar Branting, Emile Vandervelde, Tomáš Masaryk, Daniel O'Connell, King Khama, Mahatma Gandhi, or Kemal Atatürk (Chapters 2–8).

Still, this doesn't explain *why* we vilify prohibitionists; or why—for most of the valorous figures listed above—we conveniently forget their prohibitionism. For that, we have to dig a little deeper.

The most doggedly enduring critique of prohibitionists—from John Stuart Mill (Chapter 5) through the present—is that they were enemies of freedom and individual liberty, and steadfastly opposed to the drinker's right to imbibe. In the Ken Burns and Lynn Novick documentary *Prohibition* (2011), essayist Pete Hamill appears on screen to explain to us that "virtually every part of the Constitution is about expanding human freedom. Except prohibition, in which human freedom was being limited."[41]

Well, no. The Constitution condoned slavery and the disenfranchisement of women, African Americans, and Native Americans. And of course, in "expanding human freedom" for blacks, the Thirteenth Amendment explicitly took away white Americans' perverse freedom to own slaves. In the same way, the Eighteenth Amendment took away (disproportionately white) Americans' perverse freedom to profit from selling booze. The underlying political logic of prohibitionism was in concert with America's loftiest ideals: namely that no American has the right to subjugate another for their own benefit.

Indeed, that is how prohibitionists themselves understood their activism. They wrote books like *Prohibition: An Adventure in Freedom* (1928) or *The Second Declaration of Independence, or a Suggested Emancipation Proclamation from the Liquor Traffic* (1913) without so much as a hint of irony.[42] They were enablers of democracy and self-determination, and defenders of the community and the right to exercise sovereignty over their own affairs without the disproportionate influence of autocratic interests.

Even their opponents viewed prohibitionists this way. When Pussyfoot Johnson stumped for prohibition in London in 1919—sparking the street riot that cost him his right eye—the usually unsympathetic *Daily Mail* tried to size up the American visitor. "Pussyfoot is no moral fanatic, no anemic prince of virtue, no puri-tyrannical old woman, no suburban Torquemada," they wrote. "He is an organizer behind the scenes, quiet, patient, tactful, energetic. . . . *It just so happens to be his business job of work in life is to make the world soft for democracy.*"[43]

Nor—like prohibitionists the world over—was it the case that Pussyfoot was some ascetic, who wanted to force others to abstain like he did. "I like the taste of liquor," he admitted. The prohibitionist Lenin drank beer while in European exile; Tolstoy drank rum for a cold (Chapter 2). Little Turtle drank beer and cider as they were safer than water (Chapter 9). Carrie Nation slammed beers until doctors admitted it wasn't harmless (Chapter 1). Atatürk drank gallons of *rakı* just because he wanted to (Chapter 8). Leaders of the United Kingdom Alliance occasionally imbibed, too (Chapter 5). And yet these were all prohibitionists who opposed the exploitative selling of addictive substances. Likewise, Pussyfoot drank "plenty of the stuff" to gather information and build criminal cases while in the Indian Service. "I have not had a drink of liquor in a dozen years," he said in a 1926 interview, "and yet I would take a drink of liquor right now if I thought it would advance the prohibition cause."[44]

The temptation to just dismiss them all as hypocrites is strong, I know. But that's just the tenacious power of the old Hofstadter/Gusfield culture-clash framework, telling you that what "really" motivated prohibitionists was their religion or culture, rather than political or economic justice. It's also the hubris of claiming that you, reading this—a hundred years later—know better what "truly" motivated prohibitionists than they themselves knew.

Of course, it is one thing to tear down a popular historical interpretation, and another thing entirely to offer up a new one in its place. But what I'm going to suggest—and this is the benefit of studying prohibitionism in a broad, international context rather than an overly narrow US-centric one—is that the reason we have such a hard time wrapping our minds around prohibitionism is *not* because of what *they* did a century ago, but rather because *our* understandings of liberty have changed. Americans especially love to cite the Founding Fathers in defense of universal freedoms, without thinking twice about how our basic understanding of freedom has changed dramatically over time.

The Constitution, of course, was founded on Enlightenment principles of (small-r) republicanism and (small-l) liberalism: stressing consent of the governed and liberty from government limits on *political* rights. "Congress shall make no law," begins the First Amendment, preventing the free expression of religion, or "abridging the freedom of speech, or of the press; or the right of the people peaceably to assemble, and to petition the Government for a redress of grievances." These are political rights.

Political rights are separate from economic liberties. *Economic* liberalism stretches back to Adam Smith and his *Wealth of Nations* (1776), arguing for minimal government interference in the free market and the defense of private property as the basis for a capitalist economic system. For much of American (and European) history, political liberties and economic liberties were widely understood as two separate, distinct entities. Search as we might, there is no capitalist "right to buy" enumerated anywhere in the Constitution.

But something changed in the immediate post–World War II decades, about the same time Hofstadter and Gusfield were developing their cultural explanations for prohibition. The distinction between political and economic liberties began to blur, to the point where any impingement of one's economic rights was roundly construed to be a violation of their political rights as well. Examples of this abound, but some of the most egregious were during the Covid-19 pandemic, when antimask protesters demanded that stores, bars, and barber shops reopen, because—they claimed—that they had a *right* to go shopping, go drinking, or get a haircut. Again, since the document deals with political rights, not economic ones, there is no right to shop in the Constitution.

The philosophical foundations for this blurring of economic and political rights arose with the postwar "Austrian school" or "Chicago school" of economics in the 1950s and '60s. Never mind that "New Deal" Keynesianism—an activist state remedying market failures by putting people to work and regulating the worst excesses of capitalism—had not only overcome the Great Depression and won World War II, but also powered the postwar economic boom. Influential Austrian economists Ludwig von Mises and Friedrich von Hayek—as well as their

University of Chicago acolyte Milton Friedman—pushed for a return to the *laissez-faire* economic liberalism of Adam Smith.[45] As their defense of unregulated capitalism moved from the sidelines to the intellectual mainstream—providing the foundations for Thatcherism in Britain and Reaganomics in the United States—any state infringement upon economic rights was increasingly construed as an infringement upon political rights, too.

But while this neoliberalism became so universal in the English-speaking world (where the vast majority of prohibition studies are produced) that we do not even think to question it, this changing understanding of rights and freedoms was not exported to other liberal democracies, such as in Scandinavia, continental Europe, and Japan.

So it fell to Finnish sociologists and public-health researchers Anu-Hanna Anttiila and Pekka Sulkunen to point out that "political liberalism, especially in the Nordic countries, has long been divorced from market liberalism," whereas "in the Anglo-Saxon world the connection between the two was made only in the mid-20th century, notably by Ludwig von Mises and later by his student Friedrich Hayek, who argued that interference with the market necessarily implies interference with citizenship rights."[46]

We falsely vilify prohibitionists as enemies of freedom because our *understandings of freedom have changed.*

You needn't take my word for it. Go back and read Supreme Court decisions on prohibition and the "right to drink" question. Throughout the late nineteenth century, the Supreme Court repeatedly affirmed that any right to consume liquor "does not inhere in citizenship. Nor can it be said that government interferes with or impairs any one's constitutional rights of liberty or of property when it determines that the manufacture and sale of intoxicating drinks, for general or individual use, as a beverage, are, or may become, hurtful to society and constitute, therefore, a business in which no one may lawfully engage." The Court added, "No one may rightfully do that which the law-making power, upon reasonable grounds, declares to be prejudicial to the general welfare."[47]

Not only is there no "right to buy" or "right to drink" in the Constitution, the Supreme Court said there's no capitalist "right to sell" either, especially goods that are injurious to the community. In the 1890 case of *Crowley v. Christensen*—which challenged the constitutionality of California's statewide liquor regulations—the Supreme Court concluded, "There is no inherent right in a citizen to sell intoxicating liquors by retail. It is not a privilege of a citizen of the State or of a citizen of the United States. As it is a business attended with danger to the community, it may, as already said, be entirely prohibited, or be permitted under such conditions as will limit to the utmost its evils."[48]

This distinction between economic "rights" and political liberties is a crucial one. In much of the rest of the world—and also for most of American history, save the last sixty years—economic freedom and political freedom were completely separate concepts, and people understood them as such. We don't now. Part of the reason we vilify prohibitionists and misstate their intentions is not so much because of what they did, but our inability to understand it within the neoliberal, Anglo-Saxon understandings of liberty and freedom that we've all grown up with and never questioned.

Ultimately then, journalists could rightly describe prohibitionists like Pussyfoot as making the world "soft for democracy," because he was. Americans could champion prohibition as an "experiment in Social Democracy," and declare it "an attempt to gain relief from a social, rather than a political or legal form of oppression—to gain a new form of freedom" without hypocrisy, because they were doing just that.[49] But the more we are socialized into thinking that our current conceptions of rights and liberties are now and forever have been universal, the harder it becomes to understand history on the other side of that distortion.

If narrow, misguided, culturalist frameworks and changing understandings of freedom aren't enough to explain why we've historically vilified prohibitionists, we need to account for our own narcissism, too. A trio of cognitive biases: hindsight bias, confirmation bias, and the so-called bias blind-spot go far in explaining the persistence of flawed perception over reality in historical studies.

As human beings, each of us is confident (and often overconfident) in the rightness of our own perceptions. Social psychology tells us that when we encounter people who don't see the world as we do, our brains assume that—since *we* must be right and virtuous—*they* must be wrong, and that their wrongness stems from either their ignorance or evil intent. For historians (myself included), this logical fallacy is compounded by hindsight bias. Since it is the historian, not the object of the study (the prohibitionist), who ultimately knows how subsequent history unfolds, there is an even stronger temptation to view ourselves as all-knowing, impartial, and omniscient, while chalking up any of our misunderstandings to the supposed stupidity or duplicity of the prohibitionists. Psychologists call this pointing out of other people's cognitive flaws without acknowledging your own the "bias blind-spot."[50]

This, in turn, fuels a third source of error, confirmation bias: searching out evidence that confirms our preexisting worldviews while downplaying disconfirming evidence. If you wanted to find out why Carrie Nation smashed saloons, for example, you could ask her. She was very clear: "You wouldn't give me the vote, so I had to use a rock!"[51] But since that doesn't conform to historians' own prohibitionists-as-reactionaries, culture-clash worldview, later writers instead sought out evidence of her supposed wrongness, duplicity, or nefarious intent. They highlight her menopause, her faith, her failed marriage, and her *mother's* history of mental illness as motivation for attacking saloons as "symbols of masculinity," rather than accept Carrie's own word as to what she herself was thinking (Chapter 1).

Even in the pages of their own books, we can see prohibition historians grappling with their own biases, as they try to get historical evidence to conform to

Hofstadter's and Gusfield's misguided culture-clash narrative. Take, for instance, *The War on Alcohol* (2016) by Harvard historian Lisa McGirr, whose work I greatly respect and admire. In it, she depicts how Texas senator Morris Sheppard introduced the ultimately failed 1914 prohibition amendment. She writes, "*Without any apparent sense of contradiction*, he backed the constitutional amendment, declaring 'I am not a prohibitionist in the strict sense of the word. . . . I am fighting the liquor traffic. I am against the saloon, I am not in any sense aiming to prevent the personal use of drink.'"[52]

More than anything, this passage hits at the core of our problem. For Morris Sheppard in 1914, there was no contradiction in opposing the exploitative saloon business but not opposing drink. For historians a hundred years later, though, this seems to be a huge contradiction, fundamentally because *our* understandings have changed, not theirs.

Yet rather than take the prohibitionist senator at his word, Sheppard gets portrayed as either being too stupid to recognize what to *us* seems to be *his* obvious inconsistency, or being an evil, two-faced politician willing to say anything in order to achieve his nefarious aims. Such cynical portrayals resonate even more today in the post-Watergate era, when popular trust in government and politicians is abysmally low. Nowadays, it can be hard to imagine a past in which legislators were largely trusted rather than viewed with suspicion, which is just another contemporary bias that we project backward in time at our own peril.[53]

At the very least, it is worth acknowledging how much our understandings of the past are neither completely omniscient, perfectly objective, nor unbiased, but rather influenced by the widely held worldviews, biases, and assumptions of the present. In that regard, this book is no exception. Yet in confronting the history of prohibition, it seems we've been far more willing to concoct elaborate narratives that are more soothing and satisfying to our modern understandings, even as they become further divorced from the prohibitionists' reality in confronting the liquor traffic.

The Traffic Disappears

That our basic historical understandings of temperance and prohibition have changed significantly over time is not some radical, "revisionist" hypothesis, but something that empirical data can demonstrate.

Google Books has digitized some fifteen million books going back to the early 1800s, comprising some five hundred billion words.[54] Their Ngram Viewer allows users to search for particular words and multiword phrases (n-grams), and see how their usage has changed over time. How frequently a word or phrase is used is presented on the y-axis as a percentage of all of the billions of words in the digitized corpus every year. Recently, scholars have used this big data to track changes in language usage, notoriety, and popular understandings over time. If we limit our search to prohibition-related terms from the corpus of books published in the United States from 1870 through 2000, we get the result in Figure 18.2.

Perhaps the most striking feature is that the phrase we use almost exclusively nowadays to describe our subject—alcohol prohibition—was rarely if ever used, even during the height of the Prohibition Era. In fact, we only start to speak consistently about "alcohol prohibition" in the 1970s, with usage of the term consistently increasing after that.

Instead—if you go back and read original publications from that time—both prohibitionists and their opponents spoke in terms of *traffic*: most often the "drink traffic" or the "liquor traffic." Influential books carried titles such as: *An Argument for the Legislative Prohibition of the Liquor Traffic* (1857), *Alcohol and the State: A Discussion of the Problem of Law as Applied to the Liquor Traffic* (1878), *Popular Control of the Liquor Traffic* (1895), Pussyfoot's own *The Federal Government and the Liquor Traffic* (1911), and even *A Defense of the Liquor Traffic* (1887).[55] Indeed, just to fit "liquor traffic" onto this graph, I had to deflate the numbers by a power of ten: otherwise it would have been literally off the charts, so frequently was the term used. But nowadays, it is not: both "drink traffic" and "liquor traffic" have been buried by "alcohol prohibition" since the mid-1980s. (Interestingly, liberal arguments about the individual's "right to drink" remain remarkably consistent over time, with a yearly frequency around 2.0×10^{-9}.)

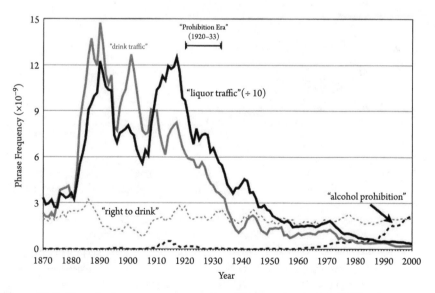

Figure 18.2 Changing language usage over time: Phrases related to prohibition in American books, 1870–2000.

Source: Google Books Ngram Viewer, https://books.google.com/ngrams/.

The data on the disappearing "traffic" checks out with other indicators of evolving popular understandings. Policy process scholars have long coded articles listed in the extensive *Reader's Guide to Periodical Literature* (1890–1982) as a measure of the salience of a policy or problem. When we graph published articles with "liquor traffic" in either the title or subject in the *Reader's Guide*—grouped into five-year bins—it tracks quite closely with the Ngram data. We can do the same thing with the hundreds of "liquor traffic" books and printed materials in the holdings of the Library of Congress, and get a similar outcome. All of this data, presented together in Figure 18.3, tells a compelling story: whereas the predominant focus of prohibition was understood to be against the "liquor traffic," it isn't anymore. The "traffic" has all but disappeared.

This is not semantic hair-splitting; this is a crucial distinction.

"Liquor" is a fundamentally different thing from the "liquor traffic." Liquor is the stuff in the bottle; the traffic is a system of exploitation based on the pursuit of profits. From the very beginning of the global temperance movement—with the

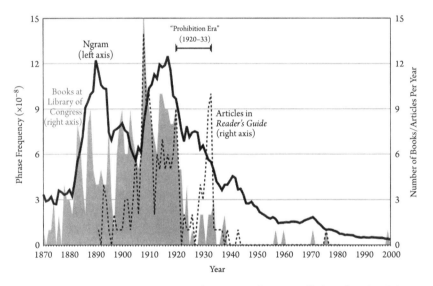

Figure 18.3 The disappearing "liquor traffic": Ngram frequency (left axis) vs. book/printed materials in the Library of Congress, and articles in the *Reader's Guide to Periodical Literature*, 1870–2000.

Source: Datasets available upon request. Data from the Library of Congress were compiled from a search of the 162 million titles and subjects in the Library of Congress Catalog (https://catalog.loc.gov/vwebv/searchBrowse) on May 26, 2019, resulting in a dataset of 341 books and printed materials incorporating the phrase "liquor traffic." The *Reader's Guide to Periodical Literature* is an index of some three million articles from 550 leading American magazines and journals from 1890 to 1982 and was chosen to include periodicals rather than simply the books that make up both the Library of Congress and Ngram series. Limiting the search to those articles with titles or subject matter dealing with the "liquor traffic" leads to a dataset of 191 articles. For legibility and ease of presentation, the articles in both the *Reader's Guide* and Library of Congress series were grouped into five-year bins.

publication of Lyman Beecher's *Six Sermons on Intemperance* (1826)—it wasn't the alcohol that was considered evil, but the act of making money by selling it to others (Chapter 11).

To be against the liquor traffic and not the alcohol in the bottle is not hypocrisy. Think of the traffic in "blood diamonds." Is the stone the problem, or the people using unscrupulous means to make money from it? Or human trafficking: one can denounce the modern-day slave traffickers while fighting for the rights of the people being trafficked. Consider drug trafficking: taking painkillers for a migraine while denouncing big pharma for fueling the opioid epidemic doesn't make you a hypocrite. You can take medical marijuana and still decry the fourteen billion dollars El Chapo and the brutal Sinaloa Cartel has made trafficking narcotics into the United States. Indeed, one of the most powerful arguments for state regulation of marijuana—both medical and recreational—is that it removes the private profit motive that fuels the corruption and brutality of the international drug *traffic.*[56]

Likewise, it was entirely consistent for prohibitionists to oppose the predatory liquor traffic as a cause of poverty, disenfranchisement, and depredation, while having empathy for the drunkard who consumed it.[57] It's the traffic that makes all the difference.

When the traffic disappears from the literature and from our minds, our focus shifts from the drink seller to the drinker and the drink itself. In other words, while writers vilify prohibitionists based on the assumption that they were against alcohol, history's real villains—the corrupt and unscrupulous traffickers—get off scot-free. Take the hard case of Carrie Nation, where our investigation began. For generations, Nation has been held up as the avatar of menacing, Bible-thumping prohibitionism by those wedded to the culturalist narrative. But if you read what she wrote, she never claimed that the drunkard was doomed to eternal damnation. That was reserved for *the man who sells.* "By licensing rum, we are fostering a power that is increasing the weakness, and preventing the self-control of its citizens. This is conspiracy, treason, black as night," she wrote. "Hell is made for those who take license to sin."[58]

The rise of e-books and digitized literature gives us a handy new tool to see whether contemporary writers faithfully represent or misrepresent temperance advocates: do a keyword search for the word "traffic." You'll be shocked at how seldom the term—again, the thing that was the *central focus of temperance and prohibition*—is actually used in temperance and prohibition studies.

For instance, Daniel Okrent's award-winning history *Last Call: The Rise and Fall of Prohibition* (2010) mentions "traffic" in relation to the alcohol trade only thirteen times over 468 pages. W. J. Rorabaugh's *Prohibition: A Concise History* (2018) mentions it eight times in 133 pages—but only once when not in a quote from one of his prohibitionist subjects. Over the 575 pages of James Morone's *Hellfire Nation* (2003), the liquor traffic is mentioned only five times, which is less than its seven mentions of prostitution as the "startling traffic in white girls." Reid Mitenbuler's

Bourbon Empire mentions the traffic only once—in a Wayne Wheeler quote—and never in the author's own words.[59] But this is not to fault these authors and their works: they all draw from the flawed culture-clash narrative laid down by Hofstadter and Gusfield. Hofstadter's *Age of Reform* (1955) mentions the traffic only once, and Gusfield's *Symbolic Crusade* (1963) twice—both in a direct quote from WCTU president Anna Gordon.[60]

Little wonder we've gotten history so wrong.

Correcting the Rewrite of American History

It is bad enough that we get temperance wrong, but when we generalize from our misunderstandings, we get American and global history wrong, too.

The greatest divide among historians—as *New Yorker* critic Adam Gopnik explains—is between academics who study the broad ocean-tides of history and the biographers who tag the mighty whales that make the ocean of history worth watching in the first place.[61] This is a useful distinction, but when we get history wrong, it impacts both the oceanographers and the whalers in different ways.

Many of the prohibitionists profiled in this book are some of the biggest "whales" of the nineteenth and twentieth centuries: from Abraham Lincoln to Vladimir Lenin. But biographers rarely mention their prohibitionism, deemed unimportant or unflattering to their portrayals. For instance, David W. Blight's masterful biography *Frederick Douglass: Prophet of Freedom*—winner of the 2019 Pulitzer Prize in history—highlights his tireless activism on behalf of abolition and women's suffrage, but is completely silent on his foundational prohibitionism, making only occasional reference to Douglass's speeches given at temperance halls and meetings.[62]

Nicholas Buccola's *Political Thought of Frederick Douglass* (2012) does grapple with Douglass's prohibitionism, but is still entangled in our present-day fusion of political and economic liberties, as well as our popular misconceptions of temperance. "Douglass was in most instances a liberty man, but he had his limits," Buccola claims. "His embrace of the cause of prohibition, whatever its merits, was illiberal" and antithetical to individual rights. Of course, this was certainly not how Douglass understood his own prohibitionism; such portrayals reflect our errors, not his.[63]

Looking abroad, Andrew Mango's 666-page *Atatürk* (1999) biography makes frequent mention of his subject's *rakı* addiction, but not his support for secular prohibition.[64] Victor Sebestyen's *Lenin: The Man, the Dictator, and the Master* (2017) includes a footnote about the reactionary tsar's "foolish prohibition which left a giant black hole in the budget," but never mentions Lenin's steadfast continuation of that policy. Robert Service's *Lenin: A Biography* (2000) doesn't address his temperance or prohibition at all.[65] In each of these cases and many more—as we've seen—temperance and prohibition were not somehow peripheral to their motivations and political ideologies. They were core to them. The people themselves each said so, explicitly and repeatedly. However, since temperance and prohibition have been erroneously considered to be conservative/reactionary policies, they don't square with the image of these leaders as progressives and revolutionaries. Perhaps it is due to confirmation bias among biographers that, despite their exhaustive personal investigations and intellectual portraits, such a large part of their subjects' stories are so conspicuously—and consistently—absent.

When the particulars of history don't make sense to the historian, they disappear from our histories. This is why history then needs to be rediscovered. Perhaps the politics of the liquor trade is not of particular interest to the present-day biographer, but that doesn't mean the subjects thought so.

Chapter 16 of this book, dealing with prohibition and progressivism, is titled "A People's History of American Prohibition." I chose it as an explicit homage to one of the history profession's most influential "oceanographers" of history, Howard Zinn. Instead of a top-down retelling of the great leaders and events of American history, his *People's History of the United States* (1980) chronicles grassroots American history from the bottom up. And despite entire chapters on abolitionism, women's suffrage, labor rights, progressivism, and anti-imperialism, Zinn's *People's History* never mentions prohibition at all. Temperance is mentioned only once, as a passing reference to "other movements of reform," rather than as the linchpin that held all these progressive movements together.[66] Even this touchstone work on the systemic exploitation of the poor by a powerful elite—and the movements to rein in those abuses—completely whiffs on the largest, most significant people's movement, likely because prohibitionism has been falsely portrayed for so long as a reactionary, rather than revolutionary, movement.[67]

But things get even worse when we use these false foundations of prohibition to build broader generalizations and conceptual frameworks.[68] Take, for instance, Michael McGerr's history of the Progressive movement: *A Fierce Discontent* (2001). "Progressives wanted not only to use the state to regulate the economy," McGerr writes, "strikingly, they intended nothing less than to transform other Americans, to remake the nation's feuding, polyglot population in their own middle-class image."[69] To be sure, civic associations winning control of the state to curb the excesses of industrial capitalism was consistent with prohibitionism, but the idea of a totalitarian remaking of human nature à la *Homo sovieticus* is a bit of a stretch.[70] Still, McGerr uses temperance as his primary example of progressives attempting to legislate morality and discipline other socioeconomic groups, rather than the liquor traffic itself.

"An odd figure, Carry A. Nation was nevertheless quite representative," McGerr assures us. "Her 'smashings' laid bare much of the logic and passion that spurred the progressive crusades to reshape adult behavior." Like Nation, "progressives were inspired by an emotional, evangelical Protestantism," even though Nation had been thrown out of every evangelical church in town. And rather than take Nation at her word that the focus of her scorn was "the man who sells," McGerr refashions the saloon into symbols of masculine behavior and pleasure that she intended to regulate.[71]

"To reshape adult behavior," McGerr concludes, progressive "middle-class reformers fought to ban liquor, eradicate prostitution, and limit divorce."[72] This paints a distorted picture of reformers. Temperance activists, again, did not ban the liquor in the bottle or harbor machinations of remaking adult behavior, but rather regulating capitalist excesses. To the extent that Nation and the WCTU opposed prostitution, it was not because sex was a vice, but because women were forced into subordination—the culmination of poverty, lack of economic opportunities, and the absence of legal and political rights. And indeed, fighting for women's empowerment—including the right to divorce abusive, drunken husbands—was a centerpiece of suffragist and temperance reform from the very beginning.[73] In sum, building from faulty understandings of temperance leads us to falsely cast progressive reformers in the United States as being *for* many of the things they fought for generations *against*.

It's not just the history of the left that suffers from our misunderstanding of temperance, but the history of the right, too. Morone's *Hellfire Nation: The Politics of Sin in American History* falsely positions temperance as one case study in moralizing crusades against "sin" and "vice." "The holy warriors," Morone claims, "scoff at politics as usual, they will not compromise. After all, they see a nation teetering between right and wrong, salvation and perdition."[74] That American prohibitionists embraced the usual mechanisms of politics to curb capitalism's excesses, and delayed, negotiated, and compromised to a fault seems not to matter, so long as the *image* of religious-based intolerance persists.

In his prohibition case study, Morone doubles down hard on the flawed Hofstadter/Gusfield culture-clash narrative: "The dreams of sobriety kept evolving—from improving people to controlling them, from pulpits into politics. The fear of others—Irish, German, African American—pushed the moralists toward Prohibition laws," Morone wrote. "Something had to be done about these hard-drinking swarms of un-Americans."[75] His claims that white nativists and Know-Nothings "latched onto" prohibition "to control the urban mobs" again gets prohibitionism completely upside-down and backward. Temperance was a weapon of the marginalized and disenfranchised—Native Americans, African Americans, women, and immigrant communities—against exploitation by corrupt, nativist, Know Nothing saloon-keepers like Captain Rynders (Chapter 12), and against the predatory liquor *traffic*, which had always been in the hands of the white powers that be.

Turning to Frances Willard and the progressive WCTU, Morone scoffed that they were "intoxicated by analogies to the abolitionists" and "constructed fantastic parallels with the battle against slavery."[76] Never mind that, as abolitionist, suffragist, and prohibitionist Frederick Douglass himself said, all these great reforms go together. Ultimately, the works of Morone, McGerr, McGirr, Okrent, and others vilifying prohibitionism all trace back to a fundamentally flawed, overly narrow, culturalist paradigm, built on shifting conceptions of liberty and reinforced by logical fallacies and cognitive biases. Those are all sins of the present, not the past.

The sum result of these distortions and misperceptions is that American prohibition history—as it has traditionally been told—is white people's history. Take a look at Ken Burns and Lynn Novick's *Prohibition* documentary series. Of the twenty-two historical figures they profile—from Neal Dow to Carrie Nation to Al Capone—all of them are white. Of the seventy-seven photos on the project's online gallery, only one contains a person of color: a drunkard passed out on the streets of New York.[77] There is no mention of black prohibitionism from Frederick Douglass and F. E. W. Harper to Ida Wells and Booker T. Washington, no mention of Native American prohibitionists from Little Turtle to Black Hawk. These seem like glaring omissions from America's prohibition history.

This is not meant to browbeat Burns and Novick; their job as documentarians is to report on the conventional wisdom, not unlike Wikipedia in that way. But that conventional wisdom has failed. Informed by Hofstadter's and Gusfield's erroneous culture-clash narrative—white, nativist, Anglo-Saxon Protestants using temperance to "discipline the leisure" of African Americans, Native Americans, and others to keep these rival "status groups" down in order to maintain their own place atop the racial hierarchy—we don't even bother to look into black temperance activism, Native prohibitionism, or subaltern activism more generally, because it is assumed they have no agency in a white people's history. American prohibition history desperately needs to be decolonized, and a broader, comparative perspective can help with that.

Unfortunately, the handful of previous attempts to broaden the history of prohibition beyond the United States seem just as allergic to subaltern perspectives, largely because they're premised on the same faulty, culturalist assumptions. Ian Tyrrell's *Reforming the World: The Creation of America's Moral Empire* (2010) begins by positioning transnational temperance as a cultural-imperial impulse of American Protestant "moral reformers" to convert a largely non-white colonial world against "vice"—while rarely mentioning that it was the colonizing Christians who were the source of that vice.[78] Tyrrell parrots the Gusfeldian characterization of temperance activists motivated by a perfectionist, evangelical "social purity" impulse to slay the drink "evil," rather than protecting indigenous communities against the predations of capitalism and colonialism itself.[79]

Just as the culturalist approach downplays black and Native activism in American history, it similarly disempowers indigenous populations around the globe. Mirroring the imperialism-justifying "white man's burden" worldview, in which European colonialists' activism mattered and subaltern populations were assumed to have no agency, Tyrrell barely mentions the widespread prohibitionism that was instrumental to Indian anticolonial nationalism (Chapter 7). Instead, he focuses largely on white, Christian missionaries and temperance activists, presumably motivated by a supposed "outward push of domestic preoccupations."[80] He goes so far as to claim that Pussyfoot Johnson went to India because he "saw an opportunity for asserting American influence" there. Pussyfoot would've been the first to object that he was some symbol of "American moral hegemony." Whether in India or elsewhere, his professed policy was never to go anywhere he wasn't invited to help local populations free themselves from the predatory, imperial liquor traffic (Chapter 17).[81]

India "seeks freedom from the liquor traffic foisted upon her by an alien power," Pussyfoot stated quite clearly. "She wants the West to send her the best that she has and not the worst."[82]

Gandhi was clear, too, in declaring that the white colonizer's liquor trade was an "enemy of mankind," a "curse of civilization," and "one of the most greatly-felt evils of the British rule."[83] That Tyrrell makes only one passing remark about Gandhi's boycott of liquor shops—and completely omits the temperance and prohibitionism that were core to both Gandhi's political worldview and his anticolonial liberation—only makes sense within an upside-down, culture-clash framework where temperance is understood as cultural-imperial imposition, rather than a key weapon in the fight against it.[84]

If we listen to subaltern voices the world over, rather than ignore them, they tell us this repeatedly, consistently, and clearly. In addressing a congregation in Chicago in 1896, Narasimha Charya—a Brahman from Madras—tried to dispel Westerners' picture of "Christianity standing with a Bible in one hand and the wizard's wand of civilization in the other," by pointing out the other side: "That is the goddess of civilization with a bottle of rum in her hand. . . . Oh, that the English had never set foot in India!" he proclaimed at the height of British colonialism. "Oh, that we had never tasted the bitter sweets of your civilization, rather than it should make us a nation of drunkards and brutes!"[85]

The same lament was shared over European alco-colonization of the Congo, even before King Leopold took it for his own (Chapter 3). "On the one hand are the missionaries. On the other hand is the rum of Christendom. Free rum against a free Gospel!" wrote the *New York Tribune*. "What is being done out there in the name of commerce is a world-crime of a character so colossal, of an immorality so shameless and profound, that if it could be regarded as a type and illustration of nineteenth century civilization, it would be necessary to denounce that civilization as a horrible sham and a conspicuous failure."[86]

"Is it consistent to go forth with the Bible in one hand and this poisonous drug in the other?" asked parliamentarian Sir Robert Nicholas Fowler in debates over British opium and liquor trafficking that was the cornerstone of imperial finance. "I believe the conduct of the Government with regard to this question is one of the greatest blots to be found in the history of England, reflecting dishonour upon us as a moral, a civilized, and a Christian people."[87]

The United States was hardly immune to the anti-imperial criticism it heaped on European empires. It found the same thing with their civilizing mission of "benevolent assimilation" in the Philippines (Chapter 15). It was said of the Filipinos that "as a rule the grade of their morality rises with the square of the distance from churches and other civilizing influences," wrote David Starr Jordan, founding president of Stanford University. In other words, "This means that the churches are not keeping up with our saloons and gaming houses."[88]

King Khama of Bechuanaland put it even more bluntly: "If a white man wants to concoct any wickedness, he uses beer for his purpose" (Chapter 6).[89] Or the Native Americans of the Miami tribe who urged Little Turtle, "We had better be at war with the white people. This liquor they introduce into our country is more to be feared than the gun and tomahawk" (Chapters 9–10).[90]

In this context we note again how—from Hjalmar Branting, Emile Vandervelde, and Wilfrid Lawson of the United Kingdom Alliance, to William Jennings Bryan and Pussyfoot Johnson—the most influential prohibitionists tended to be the most outspoken foes of imperialism, rather than defenders of it. As Pussyfoot himself explained,

> We forget that wherever western civilization has gone, there has followed vice, social disease and forty horse power gin. We forget that we flooded Africa with Bedford rum and strewed that whole continent of song with sorrow and newly made graves. We forget that Colonial America habitually offered rewards for the scalps of men, women and children, by act of the colonial authorities. We forget that, in our own land, we nearly annihilated the finest aboriginal race that ever came into the world. We forget that we sent Hell Roaring Jake Smith into the Philippine islands to spread our "Christian" civilization. I was there and saw it. When I protested to a high American Army officer against certain indiscriminate killing, he blurted back, "what of it? We have left 50,000 bastard children to take their places."[91]

As if only to underscore how distinctly prohibitionism wasn't cultural imperialism, but rather anti-imperialism, in his 1927 report to the World League Against Alcoholism, Johnson noted that he was enthusiastically greeted throughout the colonized world—from sub-Saharan Africa to India and the Middle East and Turkey—*precisely because* his message resonated not only with long-standing dry religious and cultural traditions, but also with subaltern political resistance.

"Under the pressure of this oriental opinion," Pussyfoot wrote, "the ruling authorities of these Eastern countries, mostly British, and mostly friends of the liquor traffic, have accepted the situation and have not only not actively opposed my visits, but have extended to me most generous British hospitality, even though my preachments were not at all in harmony with their personal and official views."

The anti-imperial message flowed that much easier following the Eighteenth Amendment in the United States, because it was evidence, in Pussyfoot's words, that "America has adopted the attitude of the oriental peoples as to intoxicants."[92]

So What Was It?

So if temperance and prohibition weren't American "cultural imperialism" abroad, and weren't borne of the insatiable desire of rural, evangelical Bible-thumpers to "discipline" and subordinate already-subordinate immigrants and minorities at home, then what was this whole book about anyway? As we've seen, there are no self-justifying "exceptionalisms" here: if temperance and prohibition were the same all over the globe and at the same time, it is unlikely that causes are unique in every single case.

In summary, my hypothesis (which, of course, can and should be subjected to scrutiny) is that prohibitionism was part of a long-term people's movement to strengthen international norms in defense of human rights, human dignity, and human equality, against traditional autocratic exploitation.[93] More precisely, temperance activists held that building the wealth of the state or of moneyed elites upon the misery and addiction of society was no longer appropriate.

"When the drink traffic is reinforced and backed up with Government control," claimed C. Rajagopalachari in India in 1931, "and Government finance is mixed up with it, and licenses are sold by Government to the highest bidder, it is not easy to attack the drink evil without attacking the Government."[94] And that is precisely why prohibitionists the world over sought political power to rein in liquor predations.

Norms, of course, are just guidelines of socially acceptable behavior, and these norms change over time. One hundred years ago, women were considered inferior to men, so it was widely seen as appropriate to deny them rights of political equality. Today, not so much. Two hundred years ago, it was seen as acceptable to own other human beings as slaves. Today, that's abhorrent. It used to be seen as normal and appropriate to wage offensive wars of colonial domination. Now that is strictly prohibited by scores of treaties and the UN Charter.[95]

As international relations scholar Martha Finnemore points out, for ages, if a foreign government owed your private bankers money, it was seen as perfectly acceptable to blockade, bomb, and invade their country until they paid up. France invaded Vera Cruz, Mexico, in 1838 to collect debts. The French, Spanish, and British did the same in 1862. In 1902 Germany and Britain blockaded Venezuela's ports and bombarded its installations until they paid up. Then, in 1907, the practice suddenly stopped—not because the material conditions had changed, but because our normative understandings about the use of force changed. To us nowadays, even the suggestion of using the military to collect private bankers' debts sounds obviously ludicrous.[96]

Indeed, it is the apparent "obviousness" of these positions that alerts us that the underlying norms have changed—which makes this an extremely handy tool for analyzing history *as well as* our evolving interpretations of history. As Finnemore notes, we have an overwhelming tendency "to treat motivations or interests as obvious and to take for granted the context that gives rise to them," and not always consciously. "Most of us are products, and captives, of our own normative context, and, like the decision makers we analyze, we take a whole range of ideas, beliefs, and contexts for granted."[97] Like our shifting understanding of political and economic liberty, or trust in government, we are products of a normative context that changes over time.

Perhaps the most significant normative evolution of the last three hundred years (and counting) is the movement of human rights and human equality.[98] This is the broad umbrella normative change that unites together all of these modern people's movements: the spread of enlightenment liberalism and democracy, abolitionism and transnational opposition to the slave trade, the international movement for women's equality and suffrage, socialism and the modern labor-rights movement, decolonization and the expansion of universal human rights. Each of these movements stands together in chipping away traditional, absolutist understandings of who are (and who are not) rights-deserving human beings, and what the state can (or cannot) do to them. In each case, these changing norms are given voice by civic activists and popular social movements, within a country and networked transnationally.[99]

Temperance and prohibitionism fit seamlessly underneath this broad umbrella. Like the transnational abolitionist, suffragist, socialist, indigenous rights, and human rights movements, the transnational temperance network stitched together like-minded social reformers into a global network based on the common goal of curbing the predatory profits of the liquor traffic.[100]

As it turns out, this is how prohibitionists themselves understood what they were doing. In his *Passing of the Saloon* (1908), activist George Hammell wrote that "the New must always find its expression outside of the old. Moral sentiments, which develop according to their own laws, force new alignments. Fundamental reforms of this era"—by which he meant democracy, liberty, abolitionism, suffragism, temperance, and human rights—"originally declared unpopular, are based upon eternal principle, inspired by high ideals. They are indices of the better day that is to come." Even before the storm clouds of World War I were forming, Hammell noted that the most prominent international political feature has been this sweeping normative change.

> In republican countries like our own, in limited monarchies like England and Germany, in retrogressive, despotic countries like China, Russia, Persia and Turkey, is witnessed the growth of the spirit of democracy. In our own country more and more the tendency is to get the government

back into the hands of the people. Everywhere there is an outcry against the political machine, bossism, graft, centralization and so on. . . . In other words, one of the most promising signs of the times is the tendency every-where among all nations and peoples toward realizing the idea of govern-ment of the people by the people for the people. When responsibility for the liquor traffic in any particular community is thrown directly upon the people of that community themselves, they abolish it. . . . This principle is well illustrated in the success of the local option contests everywhere. Politicians will deal and dicker with and pander to an evil, but the people, when made responsible, abolish it.[101]

In the United States as around the world, temperance and prohibition were un-derstood as part of this great progressive change, not antithetical to it. Temperance and prohibition placed the welfare of society over aristocratic profits and state revenues, which required harnessing the powers of the state to do it. Whether the addictive traffic enriched a state-run monopoly, or foreign colonists, or a "liquor trust" of corrupt and unregulated capitalists, activists fought to put people over profit.[102]

The movement looked different in different countries, given the widely varying institutional, economic, political, and (yes) cultural contexts. But temperance wasn't about culture clash or "disciplining" the underclass, but a broad-based, pop-ulist coalition of "Marx, Jefferson and Jesus."[103] Rather than a simple culture-clash narrative, this broader framework underscores the mutually reinforcing economic, political, and sociocultural dimensions of prohibitionism.

"Marx" represents opposition to the economic subjugation of the poor by the rich, whether in Russia (Chapter 2), Europe (Chapters 3–5), the colonized world (Chapters 6–10), or the United States (Chapters 11–17). In 1920—the same year as the triumph of American prohibition—one account claimed, "Liquor is a very harmful substance . . . but throughout the world, capitalists produce alcohol with all their might. Why? Because to ply the people with drink is extremely profitable." The authors were not Anti-Saloon League members, but rather Nikolai Bukharin and Evgenii Preobrazkenskii in their *ABC of Communism*.[104] That it was said by Bolshevik revolutionaries doesn't make it any less true. Indeed, the critiques of the exploitations inherent in global capitalism and imperialism—both by radical Bolsheviks and traditional Marxist social democrats—is perhaps their most en-during intellectual legacy. That many of history's most venerated capitalists—from Cecil Rhodes (Chapter 6) and King Leopold II (Chapter 3) to John Jacob Astor (Chapter 10) and even Adolphus Busch (Chapter 16)—built their great wealth upon addiction, drunkenness, misery, and poverty by trafficking in liquor only vindicates socialists' damning accusations, beginning with the writings of Karl Marx and Friedrich Engels themselves (Chapters 3–5).

"Jefferson" embodies the fight for political liberty, democracy, and both individual and communal self-determination. Temperance's common cause with Jeffersonian liberalism was a defining feature of Tomáš Masaryk's push for Czechoslovak independence (Chapter 4), Hjalmar Branting's drive for Swedish democratization (Chapter 3), to say nothing of American movements for emancipation, women's suffrage, anti-imperialism, and progressivism (Chapters 11–17). That Thomas Jefferson himself was instrumental in bringing about the first American federal prohibition—covering the Indian Country beginning in 1802—is just the cherry on top.

"Jesus," of course, represents the religious institutions, resources, and moral arguments that fed the temperance movement, whether they were Protestant, Catholic, Orthodox, Jewish, Muslim, Hindu, Buddhist, Native-American spiritualist, or pacifist Quaker. The Quakers—it should here be noted—are the only religious organization in the world ever to be awarded a Nobel Peace Prize—not only for their pacifism, but for their enduring promotion of equality, abolition of slavery, social justice, and community uplift.[105] Relatedly, from William Penn and Thomas McKenney to Neal Dow and Lucretia Mott; from the Yearly Meeting of the Society of Friends, to the foundation of the World Anti-Slavery and World Temperance Conventions; and even to the Society for the Suppression of the Opium Trade in China and India, Quakers have arguably made far more significant and lasting contributions to the course of temperance than evangelical Protestants, whom Hofstadter, Gusfield, and their acolytes have long typecast as Bible-thumping "thou-shalt-not"ers, and the villains of prohibition.[106]

But again, the overly narrow Gusfeldian focus on culture without the economic and political context—Jesus without Marx and Jefferson—leads to some pretty distorted conclusions. It would be like claiming that the struggle for civil rights was exclusively a religious movement, since its leaders—from the Reverend Martin Luther King Jr. and the Reverend Fred Shuttlesworth to the Reverend Ralph Abernathy and the Reverend Jesse Jackson—were all Protestant pastors.[107] While it is hard to deny the moral dimensions of the civil rights movement, it is impossible to deny the historic economic, social, and political subjugation as well. But thanks to Gusfield, Hofstadter, and others, we've had no problem using this unduly narrow lens to interpret and misconstrue temperance history.

The Dog That Didn't Bark: Latin America

One way to test this norm-change hypothesis would be to examine the "dogs that didn't bark": those regions of the globe that are conspicuously absent from global temperance histories, including this one. Take Latin America, for instance. From Mexico in the north to Argentina in the south, temperance activists seems to have had a tougher slog in Latin America than in other areas of the globe. Why?

The usual—and unsatisfying—explanation has been to blame "culture": Latin Americans have more moderate drinking patterns, it is more culturally acceptable, or it has something to do with the Catholic Church's deep ties to the drink traffic.[108] Yet perhaps it might have more to do with broader economic and political trends, too. The vast majority of Latin American countries gained their independence in the 1810s and 1820s, well before industrialization and the wave of normative change and activism. There was no need to make common cause between temperance and nationalism—as with O'Connell, Khama, Gandhi, or Atatürk (Chapters 5– 8)—because these countries were already free of European imperialism. Perhaps the timing of independence is worth examining more systematically as a potential causal variable.

For instance, we know that the sale of *mezcal* distilled from Mexican agave plants was a primary source of colonial revenue for the Spanish crown going back to the seventeenth century. In 1785 Spanish king Carlos III even tried to ban native alcoholic beverages in order to sell even more Spanish-made wines and spirits into New Spain.[109] But by the 1820s, Mexico and most all of Latin America were independent, so the temperance movement could not assume the mantle of nationalism or community protection against the far-off metropole, as in Ireland, India, South Africa, or the Middle East. Moreover, the production and sale of alcohol in Mexico were not centralized: the farming of agave to be fermented into *pulque* or distilled into *mezcal* or tequila was largely done by small, independent farmers, which made it hard to rally against an organized "liquor trust."[110]

During the Mexican Revolution and Civil War (1910–1920) that toppled the dictatorship of Porfirio Díaz, revolutionary leaders discouraged drunkenness as anathema to military discipline. As part of the global cult of military sobriety (Chapters 4 and 17), revolutionaries imposed wartime prohibition on the districts under their control, sometimes for years.[111] When the victorious revolutionaries ratified the world's most progressive constitution in 1917—the first in the world to defend social as well as political rights: redistributing land, protecting labor rights, and nationalizing key industries in the name of the people—Article 117 explicitly required both federal and state governments to actively combat alcoholism, which they did by shuttering, regulating, and taxing the liquor trade.

"In fact, all revolutionary presidents expressed concern with the problem of alcoholism," claims historian Gretchen Pierce. It created health and familial problems and prevented uplift from engaging in democratic society. Also, "The anti-alcohol campaign was the height of revolutionary reform because it directly helped the poor and women in general," just as socialists, suffragists, and progressives in the United States and the world over had argued.[112] Plus, as they pointed out, "When an *hacendado* (hacienda owner) wanted to prevent his workers from organizing and demanding a higher salary, he would give them *pulque* or other alcoholic beverages to pacify them. It was also common practice for *hacendados* to pay their workers in drink, rather than in cash, which established a system of debt servitude."[113] If this sounds exactly like plantation owners in the American South (Chapter 11) or the *dop* system in colonial South Africa (Chapter 6), that's because it was. "Pulque is opposed to the principal idea of the Revolution, which is to raise up the spirit of the masses," revolutionary legislator Dr. José Siurob y Ramírez claimed. One could easily find similar statements at the same time in Russian, Hungarian, Czech, Polish, and scores of other languages.

And when, at "the high point of activism, zeal, and idealism of the social revolution," Mexico in 1929 inaugurated its nationwide temperance organization, the *Comité Nacional de Lucha contra el Alcoholismo* (National Committee for the Struggle against Alcoholism), it was led not by a smattering of American missionaries and the twenty-odd temperance lodges they'd established across the country, but by President Emilio Portes Gil himself.[114] And rather than being supported only by evangelical Protestants who composed less than 2 percent of the largely Catholic population, the temperance cause was supported by governors, mayors, policemen, teachers, labor unions, and community organizations. Leading scholars concluded that Mexican temperance "was not merely a project imposed from above but, rather, one that had support that cut across various levels of society."[115]

Even without undertaking a full, in-depth case study, it seems that understanding national experiences with temperance within the broad movement of anticolonialism, progressivism, and opposition to predatory capitalism travels much further—and explains far more—than narrow explanations based solely on religion, culture, or the influence of white missionaries.

To Be Less Wrong

In the end—beyond simply chronicling the development of temperance and prohibitionism around the world—there are three big-picture takeaways from this comparative history.

First is the benefit of wide perspectives. The modern academic enterprise is largely premised on narrow fields of specialization. In history or the social sciences, graduate students are driven to become experts on a single country (n = 1)—or even a single institution, phenomenon, or historical era within it—in complete isolation from everything else. This system wouldn't exist if it didn't have merit, and excellent scholarship abounds owing to such narrow specialization. But as students of comparative politics have long known—and as the emerging fields of comparative history and transnational history are coming to realize—much can be gained by exploring beyond our narrow fields of vision and national "containers" of politics and history. Broader perspectives not only present a more complete view of international and transnational development, but can challenge the very foundations of our narrow conceptions themselves. We need more integration, more synthesis, more exploration beyond the bounds of nationality and discipline. And that means encouraging academics to read and speak in multiple languages, to experience many cultures, to swim in many seas, to study the ocean tides as well as the whales, and to see the forest for the trees.

Second is to recognize the awesome power that historians—and historical narratives—have in shaping our understandings of both the past and present. When African American novelist, playwright, and civil rights icon James Baldwin debated conservative pundit William F. Buckley in 1965, Baldwin described how narrow, stilted, dominant narratives ingrained his subordination as a young black man in the Jim Crow era. "When I was growing up, I was taught in American history books that Africa had no history, and neither did I. That I was a 'savage'—about whom the less said, the better," Baldwin explained to a rapt Cambridge audience. "And of course I believed it. I didn't have much choice: those were the only books there were. Everyone else seemed to agree."[116]

Our understandings of the past have a powerful influence on how we view the present, too. "Temperance" today is wrongly used as a cudgel to lambaste austere killjoys and right-wing antiabortionists encroaching on human rights. Instead, if there's a modern-day equivalent to temperance, it comes in confronting the opioid epidemic. Think about it: a highly addictive narcotic, leaving a nationwide mess of death, disease, addiction, and poverty in its wake. Sound familiar? The unfortunate addicts aren't the villains; they're the victims. And those most active in confronting the epidemic are taking on corporations like McKesson or Purdue Pharmaceuticals—which skirted government oversight and aggressively pushed doctors to prescribe their highly addictive OxyContin, all in order to reap massive profits from the misery of their customers—both in the United States and around the globe.[117] To apply this framework to the 2020s rather than the 1920s, just reread the book, but every time you see the phrase "liquor traffic," replace it with "big pharma." You get the picture.

Still, the weight of both popular and scholarly consensus can be mighty tough to resist. When everyone else seemed to agree that prohibitionists were vile, liberty-hating conservatives, it could be hard to square that image with that of Frederick Douglass or Leo Tolstoy or Mahatma Gandhi: some of the least vile, least conservative world leaders in history.

I must admit that it took me many years to challenge these images, interpretations, and stereotypes. I succumbed to academic groupthink.[118] My first book—*The Political Power of Bad Ideas: Networks, Institutions, and the Global Prohibition Wave* (2010)—based on years of dissertation fieldwork, explored some of these preconceptions. I traced what I thought to be "bad" (or in economic speak, "suboptimal") alcohol-policy ideas through different national political institutions in Sweden, Russia, and the United States to explain prohibition, Gothenburg dispensaries, or other alcohol-control policy outcomes.

"The prohibition of alcohol was a mistake—a historic policy gaffe and a political fiasco" were the very first words of my introduction.[119] While researching prohibition history, I did my due diligence. I read Hofstadter and Gusfield, and of course I believed them. To paraphrase James Baldwin: I didn't question it, everyone else seemed to agree. I parroted the widely held scornful assumptions that prohibitionism was a "crusading debauch" carried about America and the world "by the rural-evangelical virus."[120] While my analysis of political institutions was largely separate, I was wrong in my basic historical understandings of temperance activists and their motivations.

It can be hard to admit when you're dead wrong about something.

But the final takeaway is that correcting our errors is how we learn, grow, and progress. The entire scientific exercise is the relentless pursuit of being less and less wrong. We used to believe that the Earth was the center of the universe, until Copernicus and Galileo came along. Newtonian mechanics held sway for some two hundred years before Einstein's theory of relativity. The entire progress of humankind is premised on coming to terms with wrong explanations, and coming up with better ones.[121] It is a process. And while this book offers only but a modest rethinking of a particular era in human history, perhaps one day it too will be proven wrong.

NOTES

Chapter 1

1. Carry A. Nation, *The Use and Need of the Life of Carry A. Nation* (Topeka, KS: F. M. Steves & Sons, 1908), 130.
2. This harkens back to an original, pre–eighteenth century, Christian-Platonic notion of justice: not as eye-for-an-eye Kantian legal justice under sovereign law, but as positive love, benevolence, universal charity, and generosity toward all, as found in the works of St. Augustine, Shakespeare, and Leibniz. See: "Justice as Love and Benevolence" in: Patrick Riley, *Leibniz' Universal Jurisprudence: Justice as the Charity of the Wise* (Cambridge, MA: Harvard University Press, 1996), 141–98.
3. Fran Grace, *Carry A. Nation: Retelling the Life* (Bloomington: Indiana University Press, 2001), 83, 99–100. See also: Letter, Edward Andrew Braniff to Carrie Nation, February 28, 1901, Carrie Amelia Nation (1870–1919) Papers, MC 744, Box 1, Series 3, Folder 3, Kansas Historical Society, Topeka. See similar interruptions in New York City. "Carrie Nation Halts Abuse from 'Elijah,'" *New York Times*, October 21, 1903, 1.
4. Robert Lewis Taylor, *Vessel of Wrath: The Life and Times of Carry Nation* (New York: New American Library, 1966), 79. Grace, *Carry A. Nation*, 101.
5. Ibid., 140–41. Nation, *Use and Need of the Life*, 126–27.
6. Ibid., 133–34. Also: Grace, *Carry A. Nation*, 147.
7. Nation, *Use and Need of the Life*, 134 (emphasis mine).
8. Ibid., 135.
9. Ibid., 144.
10. Grace, *Carry A. Nation*, 151. "Nation, Carry A(melia)," in: Ernest H. Cherrington, ed., *Standard Encyclopedia of the Alcohol Problem*, 6 vols., vol. 4 (Westerville, OH: American Issue Press, 1928), 1850.
11. *Hearst's International Combined with Cosmopolitan*, Vol. 124 (1948), 130. Also: Letter, Carrie Nation to David Nation, February 5, 1901, Carrie Amelia Nation (1870–1919) Papers, MC 744, Box 1, Series 2, Folder 2, Kansas Historical Society, Topeka.
12. Nation, *Use and Need of the Life*, 187–88. On the Carrie Nation Home, see also: Kansas WCTU/Mary Evelyn Dobbs Collection, MC 170, Box 1, Folders 5–10, Kansas Historical Society, Topeka.
13. Grace, *Carry A. Nation*, 246.
14. Nation, *Use and Need of the Life*, 247.
15. "Mrs. Nation's Campaign," *The Times* (London), January 26, 1909, 6. Grace, *Carry A. Nation*, 168, 86, 226.
16. Nation, *Use and Need of the Life*, 160–64. Grace, *Carry A. Nation*, 155–59.

17. Robert Smith Bader, *Prohibition in Kansas: A History* (Lawrence: University Press of Kansas, 1986), 140.

18. Dale Shaw, "Crazy Carry the Party Pooper," *Argosy: The Largest-Selling Fact-Fiction Magazine for Men*, October 1959, 2.

19. Carroll Smith-Rosenberg, *Disorderly Women: Visions of Gender in Victorian America* (New York: Alfred A. Knopf, 1985), 185–92. On rationalizing away others' behavior, see: Kathryn Schulz, *Being Wrong: Adventures in the Margin of Error* (New York: HarperCollins, 2010), 108–10.

20. Taylor, *Vessel of Wrath*, 79. Herbert Asbury, *Carry Nation* (New York: Alfred A. Knopf, 1929), 55.

21. Andrew Sinclair, *Prohibition: The Era of Excess* (Boston: Little, Brown & Co., 1962), 57.

22. Quoted in: Grace, *Carry A. Nation*, 6. Inez Haynes Gillmore, *Angels and Amazons: A Hundred Years of American Women* (Garden City, NY: Doubleday, Doran & Company, 1933), 204–206.

23. Norman H. Clark, *Deliver Us from Evil: An Interpretation of American Prohibition* (New York: W. W. Norton & Co., 1976), 83.

24. Herbert Asbury, "The Background of a Crusader: The Story of Carry Nation," *The Outlook and Independent*, July 17, 1929, 443.

25. Mary K. Haman, "Wild Women of the Progressive Era: Rhetoric, Gender, and Agitation in the Age of Reform" (Pennsylvania State University, 2009), 195.

26. Daniel Okrent, *Last Call: The Rise and Fall of Prohibition* (New York: Scribner, 2010), 24. *Prohibition: A Film by Ken Burns and Lynn Novick*, PBS, http://www.pbs.org/kenburns/ prohibition/people/ (accessed November 3, 2018). Other historians similarly dote on her "pug-faced" appearance and Amazonian claims of being six feet tall. Eric Burns, *The Spirits of America: A Social History of Alcohol* (Philadelphia: Temple University Press, 2004), 134.

27. Instead of burning the passionate love notes as Gloyd instructed, Carrie kept them and reread them throughout her life, leaving them among her papers when she died. Charles Gloyd– Carrie Moore correspondence, November–December 1865; Carrie Amelia Nation, *Diary and Scrapbook*, May 25, 1873, 223; n/d 1874, 236. Carrie Amelia Nation Papers (1870–1919), MC 744, Box 1, Series 1, Kansas Historical Society, Topeka, https://www.kansasmemory. org/item/219778 (accessed January 19, 2021). Grace, *Carry A. Nation*, 41.

28. Nation, *Use and Need of the Life*, 62.

29. *Topeka Daily Capital*, February 8, 1901. *Chicago Tribune*, February 8, 1901. Haman, "Wild Women of the Progressive Era," 89.

30. Grace, *Carry A. Nation*, 6.

31. Quoted in: Ibid., 256. When she was being tossed into a paddy-wagon in Denver, one policeman threatened, "One of these days you'll get into jail and never get out." "Ha!" she snapped back at the cop without missing a beat: "One of these days you'll get into hell and never get out!" Ibid., 247.

32. Nation, *Use and Need of the Life*, 131. Of course, the Puritans drank more than their fair share of beer and distilled liquor, too. See Chapter 9.

33. Grace, *Carry A. Nation*, 185.

34. Ibid., 225.

35. "I am fishing," she wrote. "I go where the fish are, for they do not come to me." Ibid., 215–16, 23.

36. James P. Moore Jr., *Prayer in America: A Spiritual History of Our Nation* (New York: Doubleday, 2005), 207. Gaines M. Foster, *Moral Reconstruction: Christian Lobbyists and the Federal Legislation of Morality, 1865–1920* (Chapel Hill: University of North Carolina Press, 2002), 1, 224. On "disciplining" leisure, see: Lisa McGirr, *The War on Alcohol: Prohibition and the Rise of the American State* (New York: W. W. Norton & Company, 2016), xviii, 13, 41–42.

37. Grace, *Carry A. Nation*, 107, 15–18, 267.

38. "Lincoln, Abraham," in: Cherrington, ed., *Standard Encyclopedia of the Alcohol Problem*, vol. 4, 1555. Ervin Chapman, *Latest Light on Abraham Lincoln and War-Time Memories* (New York: Fleming H. Revell Company, 1917), 162–63.

39. Grace, *Carry A. Nation* , 94. Also: 8, 54, 79, 98.

40. Ibid., 24–25, 95, 244.

41. Ibid., 142–44. On McKinley's prayerful visions, see: Nell Irvin Painter, *Standing at Armageddon: The United States, 1877–1919* (New York: W. W. Norton & Company, 1987), 147. Niall Ferguson, *Colossus: The Rise and Fall of the American Empire* (New York: Penguin, 2004), 49.

42. Laurel Thatcher Ulrich, *Well-Behaved Women Seldom Make History* (New York: Alfred A. Knopf, 2008), xiii. Grace, *Carry A. Nation*, 257.

43. "American Spirits: The Rise and Fall of Prohibition," *National Constitution Center*, Philadelphia, PA, https://prohibition.constitutioncenter.org/exhibition.html (accessed November 3, 2018). Statistics on Dow/Volstead comparison, see: Mark Lawrence Schrad, "Why Do We Blame Women for Prohibition?," *Politico Magazine*, January 13, 2019. https://www.politico.com/magazine/story/2019/01/13/prohibition-women-blame-history-223972 (accessed January 20, 2019).

44. Bader, *Prohibition in Kansas*, 140. On Nation as warrior-mother, see: Grace, *Carry A. Nation*, 257.

45. Reid Mitenbuler, *Bourbon Empire: The Past and Future of America's Whiskey* (New York: Viking Press, 2015), 170. Okrent, *Last Call*, 99, 171, 269. McGirr, *War on Alcohol*, 17. Lilian Lewis Shiman, *Crusade against Drink in Victorian England* (New York: St. Martin's Press, 1988), 90.

46. McGirr, *War on Alcohol*, 120, 248.

47. Jed Dannenbaum, "The Origins of Temperance Activism and Militancy among American Women," *Journal of Social History* 15, no. 2 (1981): 3. James S. Roberts, *Drink, Temperance, and the Working Class in Nineteenth-Century Germany* (Boston: George Allen & Unwin, 1984), 7.

48. Richard Hofstadter, *The Age of Reform: From Bryan to F.D.R.* (New York: Random House, 1955). Joseph Gusfield, *Symbolic Crusade: Status Politics and the American Temperance Movement* (Urbana: University of Illinois Press, 1963). Joseph R. Gusfield, "Social Structure and Moral Reform: A Study of the Woman's Christian Temperance Union," *American Journal of Sociology* 61, no. 3 (1955). Josiah Ryan, "'This Was a Whitelash': Van Jones' Take on the Election Results," *CNN.com*, November 9, 2016, https://www.cnn.com/2016/11/09/politics/van-jones-results-disappointment-cnntv/index.html (accessed May 15, 2019).

49. James A. Morone, *Hellfire Nation: The Politics of Sin in American History* (New Haven, CT: Yale University Press, 2003). McGirr, *War on Alcohol*. Okrent, *Last Call*. See also: Clark, *Deliver Us from Evil*. Sinclair, *Prohibition*. Joseph Gusfield, "Benevolent Repression: Popular Culture, Social Structure and the Control of Drinking," in *Drinking: Behavior and Belief in Modern History*, ed. Susanna Barrows and Robin Room (Berkeley: University of California Press, 1991).

50. Paul Aaron and David Musto, "Temperance and Prohibition in America: A Historical Overview," in *Alcohol and Public Policy: Beyond the Shadow of Prohibition—Panel on Alternative Policies Affecting the Prevention of Alcohol Abuse and Alcoholism*, ed. Mark Moore and Dean Gerstein (Washington, DC: National Academy Press, 1981), 127–28.

51. James Timberlake, *Prohibition and the Progressive Movement, 1900–1920* (Cambridge, MA: Harvard University Press, 1963), 18.

52. See: Mark Lawrence Schrad, "Constitutional Blemishes: Understanding American Alcohol Prohibition and Repeal as Policy Punctuation," *Policy Studies Journal* 35, no. 3 (2007): 438, 47.

53. Schrad, "Why Do We Blame Women for Prohibition?"

54. Mark Lawrence Schrad, "Myth: Prohibition Was Uniquely American," in *Ten Shots of Knowledge: The Distilled Truth about Prohibition's Greatest Myths*, ed. Michael Lewis and Richard Hamm (Baton Rouge: Louisiana State University Press, 2019). Mark Lawrence Schrad, "The Transnational Temperance Community and the Regulation of the Alcohol Traffic," in *Transnational Communities: Shaping Global Economic Governance*, ed. Marie-Laure Djelic and Sigrid Quack (Cambridge: Cambridge University Press, 2010).

55. W. J. Rorabaugh, *Prohibition: A Very Short Introduction* (New York: Oxford University Press, 2017).

56. On global, transnational, and comparative challenges to traditional "container" approaches to national history, see: Sebastian Conrad, *What Is Global History?* (Princeton, NJ: Princeton University Press, 2016), 4–5, 37–41. Julian Go and George Lawson, "Introduction: For a Global Historical Sociology," in *Global Historical Sociology*, ed. Julian Go and George Lawson (Cambridge: Cambridge University Press, 2017), 2–15.

57. See: Brian Harrison, *Drink and the Victorians: The Temperance Question in England, 1815–1872* (London: Faber and Faber, 1971). Shiman, *Crusade against Drink*. Elizabeth Malcolm, *"Ireland Sober, Ireland Free": Drink and Temperance in Nineteenth-Century Ireland* (Syracuse, NY: Syracuse University Press, 1986). Greg Marquis, "'Brewers and Distillers Paradise': American Views of Canadian Alcohol Policies, 1919 to 1935," *Canadian Review of American Studies* 34, no. 2 (2004). Lennart Johansson, *Systemet lagom: Rusdrycker, interesseorganisationer och politisk kultur under förbudsdebattens tidevarv 1900–1922* (Lund: Lund University Press, 1995). Bror Lyckow, *En fråga för väljarna? Kampen om det lokala vetot 1893–1917* (Stockholm: Stockholms Universitetet, 2001). Walter Thompson, *The Control of Liquor in Sweden* (New York: Columbia University Press, 1935). An Vleugels, *Narratives of Drunkenness: Belgium, 1830–1914* (London: Pickering & Chatto, 2013). Roberts, *Drink, Temperance, and the Working Class in Nineteenth-Century Germany*. Patricia Herlihy, *The Alcoholic Empire: Vodka and Politics in Late Imperial Russia* (New York: Oxford University Press, 2002). Mark Lawrence Schrad, *Vodka Politics: Alcohol, Autocracy, and the Secret History of the Russian State* (New York: Oxford University Press, 2014). Kate Transchel, *Under the Influence: Working-Class Drinking, Temperance, and Cultural Revolution in Russia, 1895–1932* (Pittsburgh, PA: University of Pittsburgh Press, 2006). John Wuorinen, *The Prohibition Experiment in Finland* (New York: Columbia University Press, 1931). Max Henius, *Modern Liquor Legislation and Systems in Finland, Norway, Denmark and Sweden* (Copenhagen: L. Levison Junr. Akts., 1931). Robert Eric Colvard, "A World without Drink: Temperance in Modern India, 1880–1940" (University of Iowa, 2013). Harald Fischer-Tiné and Jana Tschurenev, eds., *A History of Alcohol and Drugs in Modern South Asia: Intoxicating Affairs* (New York: Routledge, 2014).

58. See, for instance: David T. Courtwright, *Forces of Habit: Drugs and the Making of the Modern World* (Cambridge, MA: Harvard University Press, 2002). Rod Phillips, *Alcohol: A History* (Chapel Hill: University of North Carolina Press, 2014). Susannah Wilson, ed., *Prohibitions and Psychoactive Substances in History, Culture and Theory* (New York: Routledge, 2019).

59. Cecilia Autrique Escobar, "'To Save the Mexican Race from Degeneration': The Influence of American Protestant Groups on Temperance and Prohibition in Mexico, 1916–1933," in *Prohibitions and Psychoactive Substances in History, Culture and Theory*, ed. Susannah Wilson (New York: Routledge, 2019).

60. See, for instance: Ian Tyrrell, "Prohibition, American Cultural Expansion, and the New Hegemony in the 1920s: An Interpretation," *Histoire sociale/Social History* 27, no. 54 (1994), Ian Tyrrell, "Women and Temperance in International Perspective: The World's W.C.T.U., 1880s–1920s," in *Drinking: Behavior and Belief in Modern History*, ed. Susanna Barrows and Robin Room (Berkeley: University of California Press, 1991). Ian Tyrrell, *Woman's World, Woman's Empire: The Woman's Christian Temperance Union in International Perspective, 1880–1930* (Chapel Hill: University of North Carolina Press, 1991). Ruth Dupré, "The Prohibition of Alcohol Revisited: The U.S. Case in International Perspective," *Cahier de recherche* 4, no. 11 (2004). Marquis, "'Brewers and Distillers Paradise.'" Jessica R. Pliley, Robert Kramm, and Harald Fischer-Tiné, eds., *Global Anti-Vice Activism, 1890–1950: Fighting Drinks, Drugs and "Immorality"* (New York: Cambridge University Press, 2016).

61. Ian Tyrrell, *Reforming the World: The Creation of America's Moral Empire* (Princeton, NJ: Princeton University Press, 2010), 4. Also problematic is the subject and time frame in question. *Formal* transnational temperance organizations, like the World's WCTU and the

World League Against Alcoholism—the focus of these transnational histories—were relative latecomers to the transnational temperance scene, lagging far behind their European-based counterparts. Dorothy Staunton, *Our Goodly Heritage: A Historical Review of the World's Woman's Christian Temperance Union, 1883–1956* (London: Walthamstow Press, 1956). Susan Mary Brook, "The World League against Alcoholism: The Attempt to Export an American Experience" (MA thesis, University of Western Ontario, 1972). Ian Tyrrell, "World League against Alcoholism (W.L.A.A.)," in *Alcohol and Temperance in Modern History: An International Encyclopedia*, ed. Jack Blocker Jr., David Fahey, and Ian Tyrrell (Santa Barbara, CA: ABC-CLIO, 2003). On the deeper history of European transnational temperance organizations, see: Mark Lawrence Schrad, *The Political Power of Bad Ideas: Networks, Institutions, and the Global Prohibition Wave* (New York: Oxford University Press, 2010).

62. See, for instance: Colvard, "World without Drink," 33.

63. "India," in: Ernest H. Cherrington, ed., *Standard Encyclopedia of the Alcohol Problem*, 6 vols., vol. 3 (Westerville, OH: American Issue Press, 1926), 1298.

64. Vladimir I. Lenin, "Casual Notes," in *Collected Works, Volume 4: 1898–April 1901* (Moscow: Progress Publishers, 1972), 404–405. Original in: *Zarya*, No. 1 (April 1901).

65. Stephen Howe, *Empire: A Very Short Introduction* (New York: Oxford University Press, 2002), 77. On alcoholism as a colonial imposition, see: Courtwright, *Forces of Habit*, 11–14. Phillips, *Alcohol*, 4–5.

66. David A. Washbrook, "India 1818–1860: The Two Faces of Colonialism," in *The Oxford History of the British Empire, Volume 3: The Nineteenth Century*, ed. Andrew Porter (New York: Oxford University Press, 2001), 404. Erica Wald, "Governing the Bottle: Alcohol, Race and Class in Nineteenth-Century India," *Journal of Imperial and Commonwealth History* 46, no. 3 (2018): 401.

67. William E. Johnson, "Babylon and Way Stations" (Cooperstown, NY: Fenimore Art Museum Library, 1930), 2:19 and 3:7–8.

68. William E. Johnson, *The Federal Government and the Liquor Traffic*, 2nd ed. (Westerville, OH: American Issue Publishing Company, 1917), 196.

69. "What Does It Profit?," *American Issue* 20, no. 7 (1912): 15 (emphasis mine).

70. George B. Tindall, *The Emergence of the New South: 1913–1945* (Baton Rouge: Louisiana State University Press, 1967), 19.

71. "Extension of Remarks of Hon. Martin A. Morrison, of Indiana, in the House of Representatives, Wednesday, January 24, 1917," in: *Congressional Record, Appendix and Index to Parts 1–5*, 64th Congress, 2nd Session, Vol. 54 (Washington, DC: Government Printing Office, 1917), 223, 738. Clark, *Deliver Us from Evil*, 95.

72. Mark Lawrence Schrad, "Why Americans Supported Prohibition 100 Years Ago," *New York Times*, January 17, 2020, https://www.nytimes.com/2020/01/17/opinion/prohibition-anniversary-100.html (accessed January 20, 2020).

73. Beyond my own previous work, one notable exception is Ann-Marie Szymanski's *Pathways to Prohibition*. Yet Szymanski's focus is not on what caused prohibition, but rather using American temperance and prohibition as a setting to study whether divergent (radical or moderate) tactics among social movement organizations cause different policy outcomes. Ann-Marie Szymanski, *Pathways to Prohibition: Radicals, Moderates, and Social Movement Outcomes* (Durham, NC: Duke University Press, 2003). Schrad, *Political Power of Bad Ideas*.

74. David R. Mayhew, "U.S. Policy Waves in Comparative Context," in *New Perspectives on American Politics*, ed. Lawrence C. Dodd and Calvin Jillson (Washington, DC: CQ Press, 1994), 335–36.

75. McGirr, *War on Alcohol*. Okrent, *Last Call*. Clark, *Deliver Us from Evil*. Larry Engelmann, *Intemperance: The Lost War against Liquor* (New York: Free Press, 1979). David E. Kyvig, *Repealing National Prohibition*, 2nd ed. (Kent, OH: Kent State University Press, 2000). Hugh Ambrose and John Schuttler, *Liberated Spirits: Two Women Who Battled over Prohibition* (New York: Berkley, 2018).

76. See, for instance: Richmond P. Hobson, *The Truth about Alcohol* (Washington, DC: Government Publishing Office, 1914), 22.

77. Consider both the following prohibitionist books *and* their titles: Harry S. Warner, *Prohibition: An Adventure in Freedom* (Westerville, OH: American Issue Press, 1928). Emmett D. Nichols, *The Second Declaration of Independence, or a Suggested Emancipation Proclamation from the Liquor Traffic* (Boise, ID: Emmett D. Nichols, 1913).

78. This normative shift has been little studied, even among experts. Vice historian David Courtwright alludes to it, claiming that in "one of history's great about-faces," by the late nineteenth century, the same stratum of Western political and economic elites that had long driven the unregulated global trade in alcohol and drugs acceded to restrictions and prohibitions, often at significant financial loss. Courtwright focuses on the material interest of elites: that industrialization created powerful entrepreneurs whose business interests were harmed by drunkenness, who balanced out those elites for whom the liquor trade was still profitable. While this logic holds merit, it is incomplete: it overlooks the broad-based, transnational prohibition movement that drove the normative shift about the inappropriateness of the state profiting from the misery of society. Courtwright, *Forces of Habit*, 167–78.

79. Here I borrow from Jim Bissett, *Agrarian Socialism in America: Marx, Jefferson, and Jesus in the Oklahoma Countryside, 1904–1920* (Norman: University of Oklahoma Press, 1999).

80. Quoted in: McGirr, *War on Alcohol*, 29.

Chapter 2

1. Evgenii Dolgov, "Kazanskii Voennyi Gubernator E. P. Tolstoi," *Gasyrlar avazy—Ekho vekov* 1, no. 1 (2004), http://www.archive.gov.tatarstan.ru/magazine/go/anonymous/main/?path=mg:/numbers/2004_01/04/04_1/ (accessed January 9, 2018).

2. David Christian, *Living Water: Vodka and Russian Society on the Eve of Emancipation* (Oxford: Clarendon Press, 1990), 345–50, which in turn draws from *Pod sud*, April 1, 1860, x, 50–53.

3. Ibid., 347.

4. Ibid., 336.

5. In the *Great Soviet Encyclopedia*, this event is referred to alternatively as the "Liquor Tax Rebellion" and *trezvennoe dvizhenie*, or "temperance movement." V. A. Fedorov, "Liquor Tax Rebellion (*Trezvennoe dvizhenie*)," in *Bol'shaia sovetskaia entsiklopediia*, ed. A. M. Prokhorov (New York: Macmillan, 1981), 101.

6. "Smert' ili kosushku! *Kolokol* List 8, 15 Sentabrya 1859g.," in *Kolokol: Gazeta A. I. Gertsena i N. P. Ogareva* (Moscow: Izdatel'stvo akademii nauk SSSR, 1962), 430.

7. Eustace Clare Grenville Murray, *The Russians of To-Day* (London: Smith, Elder & Co., 1878), 30. David Christian, "A Neglected Great Reform: The Abolition of Tax Farming in Russia," in *Russia's Great Reforms, 1855–1881*, ed. Ben Eklof, John Bushnell, and Larissa Zakharova (Bloomington: Indiana University Press, 1994), 105. Christian, *Living Water*, 295.

8. Murray, *The Russians of To-Day*, 29–30. Similarly: Fedorov, "Liquor Tax Rebellion (*Trezvennoe Dvizhenie*)," 101.

9. Mark Lawrence Schrad, *Vodka Politics: Alcohol, Autocracy, and the Secret History of the Russian State* (New York: Oxford University Press, 2014), xiii.

10. Boris V. Rodionov, *Bol'shoi obman: Pravda i lozh' o russkoi vodke* (Moscow: Izdatel'stvo AST, 2011), 413. William Blackwell, *The Beginnings of Russian Industrialization: 1800–1860* (Princeton, NJ: Princeton University Press, 1968), 26.

11. Schrad, *Vodka Politics*, 79–80.

12. Arcadius Kahan, *The Plow, the Hammer, and the Knout* (Chicago: University of Chicago Press, 1985), 329, 37. Schrad, *Vodka Politics*, 114.

13. Aleksei Tolstoi, *Petr Pervyi* (Kishinev: Kartya Moldovenyaske, 1970), 22. Nikolai I. Turgenev, *Rossiya i russkie* (Moscow: Knigoizdatel'stvo K. F. Hekrasova, 1915), 212.

14. All *sic*. Giles Fletcher, *Of the Russe Commonwealth: 1591* (Cambridge, MA: Harvard University Press, 1966; reprint, 1966), 43–44.

15. Samuel H. Baron, ed., *The Travels of Olearius in Seventeenth-Century Russia* (Stanford, CA: Stanford University Press, 1967), 142–44, 198.

16. Robert Ker Porter, "Excerpts from 'Travelling Sketches in Russia and Sweden,'" in *Seven Britons in Imperial Russia: 1698–1812*, ed. Peter Putnam (Princeton, NJ: Princeton University Press, 1952), 312–13.

17. GARF f. 586 (Vycheslav K. Plehve), op. 1, d. 117, l.41; and f. 586, op. 1, d. 120, l.62, Gosudarstvennyi Arkhiv Rossiskoi Federatsii (GARF) (State archive of the Russian Federation), Moscow. V. Polivanov, "Zapiski zemskogo nachal'nika," *Russkaya mysl'* 9–10 (1917): 32; cited in Stephen P. Frank, *Crime, Cultural Conflict, and Justice in Rural Russia, 1856–1914* (Berkeley: University of California Press, 1999), 213.

18. V. Fedorovskii, "Podolsko-Vitebskii otkup," *Sovremennik* (1859), Mar. "Sovremennoe obozrenie," 1; cited in Christian, *Living Water*, 110. See also: Ivan Pryzhov, *Istoriya kabakov v Rossii* (Moscow: Molodiya sily, 1914), 59–74.

19. Christian, *Living Water*, 200. Linda T. Darling, *Revenue-Raising and Legitimacy* (Leiden: E. J. Brill, 1996), 119–20.

20. V. A. Kokorev, "Ob otkupakh na prodazhu vina," *Russkii vestnik* Book 2, Sovremennaya letopis' (1858): 42; cited in: David Christian, "Vodka and Corruption in Russia on the Eve of Emancipation," *Slavic Review* 46, no. 3/4 (1987): 481.

21. *Ekonomicheskii ukazatel'* 41 (October 1858); cited in Christian, "Vodka and Corruption in Russia on the Eve of Emancipation," 473. See also: Mikhail E. Saltykov, *Tchinovnicks: Sketches of Provincial Life, from the Memoirs of the Retired Conseiller De Cour Stchedrin (Saltikow)*, trans. Frederic Aston (London: L. Booth, 1861), 98.

22. Petr A. Zaionchkovskii, *Pravitel'stvennyi apparat samoderzhavnoi Rossii v XIX v.* (Moscow: Mysl', 1978), 155; cited in Christian, *Living Water*, 148–49. Sergei V. Volkov, *Generalitet Rossiiskoi imperii: Entsiklopedicheskii slovar' generalov i admeralov ot Petra I do Nikolaya II*, 2 vols., vol. 2 (Moscow: Tsentrpoligraf, 2009), 587–88.

23. "Koe chto ob otkupakh, *Kolokol* list 10, 1 marta 1858 g.," in *Kolokol: Gazeta A. I. Gertsena i N. P. Ogareva* (Moscow: Izdatel'stvo akademii nauk SSSR, 1962), 79.

24. Samuel M. Smucker, *The Life and Reign of Nicholas the First, Emperor of Russia* (Philadelphia: J. W. Bradley, 1856). Zaionchkovskii, *Pravitel'stvennyi apparat*, 156.

25. A later (1860) report to the State Council admitted as much: "Everyone knows that tax farming ruins and corrupts the people; keeps the local administration itself under a sort of 'farm,' which nullifies all efforts to introduce honesty and justice to the administration; and slowly leads the government into the painful situation of having not only to cover up the fla-grant breaches of the law engendered by the system, and without which it cannot operate, but even to resist the people's own impulses to moral improvement through abstention. In this way, the government itself offers a model of disrespect for the law, support for abuse and the spreading of vice." Translated in: Christian, *Living Water*, 357.

26. Alexis de Tocqueville, *Democracy in America*, ed. Richard D. Heffner, abridged ed. (New York: Mentor Books, 1956), 201. On the history of the transnational temperance move-ment, see: Mark Lawrence Schrad, *The Political Power of Bad Ideas: Networks, Institutions, and the Global Prohibition Wave* (New York: Oxford University Press, 2010), 31–61.

27. Jack Blocker Jr., *American Temperance Movements: Cycles of Reform* (Boston: Twayne Publishers, 1989), 11–14.

28. American Temperance Society, *Permanent Temperance Documents of the American Temperance Society*, vol. 1 (Boston: Seth Bliss, 1835), 52–53, 492. Also: Ian Tyrrell, *Woman's World, Woman's Empire: The Woman's Christian Temperance Union in International Perspective, 1880–1930* (Chapel Hill: University of North Carolina Press, 1991), 12. Douglas Charles Strange, *British Unitarians against American Slavery, 1833–65* (Rutherford, NJ: Fairleigh Dickinson University Press, 1984), 61.

29. Audronė Janužyte, "*Historians as Nation State-Builders: The Formation of Lithuanian University, 1904–1922*" (University of Tampere, 2005), 22. Likewise: Piotr S. Alekseev, *O p'yanstve s predisloviem gr. L. N. Tolstago* (Moscow: 1891), 93.

30. Dawson Burns, *Temperance History: A Consecutive Narrative of the Rise, Development, and Extension of the Temperance Reform*, 2 vols. (London: National Temperance Publication Depot, 1889), 120, 255. Murray, *The Russians of To-Day*, 19. See also: Robert Baird correspondence to the American Sunday School Union from St. Petersburg, October 20, 1840, Presbyterian Historical Society, American Sunday School Union Papers, 1817–1915, Reel 45, Series I, C:1840B, no. 200–202. J. M. Crawford, "Russia," in: John Stearns, *Temperance in All Nations: History of the Cause in All Countries of the Globe* (New York: National Temperance Society and Publication House, 1893), 1:331–32.

31. Egidijus Aleksandravičius, *Lietuvių atgimimo istorijos studijos, tom 2: Blaivybė Lietuvoje XIX amžiuje* (Vilnius: Sietynas, 1991), 61. On Bishop Motiejus Valančius and temperance in Kovno guberniia: Janužyte, "Historians as Nation State-Builders," 21. In Poland and western Ukraine, see: Boris Savchuk, *Korchma: Alkogol'na politika i rukh tverezosti v Zakhidnii Ukraini u XIX — 30-kh rokakh XX st.* (Ivano-Frankivs'k: Lileya-NV, 2001), 138–230. See also: Barbara J. Falk, *The Dilemma of Dissidence in East-Central Europe* (Budapest: CEU Press, 2003), 18. Patrick Rogers, *Father Theobald Mathew: Apostle of Temperance* (Dublin: Browne and Nolan Limited, 1943).

32. Aleksandravičius, *Blaivybė Lietuvoje XIX amžiuje*, 72. Christian, *Living Water*, 295. Christian, "A Neglected Great Reform," 105.

33. Christian, *Living Water*, 325–26. Deriving from reports in: *Svedeniya*, ii, 235–37.

34. Ibid., 299.

35. Andrei P. Tsygankov, *The Strong State in Russia: Development and Crisis* (New York: Oxford University Press, 2014), 41. Pryzhov, *Istoriya kabakov v Rossii*.

36. D. MacKenzie Wallace, *Russia* (New York: Henry Holt and Company, 1877), 99. See also: R. E. F. Smith and David Christian, *Bread and Salt: A Social and Economic History of Food and Drink in Russia* (New York: Cambridge University Press, 1984), 93.

37. Christian, *Living Water*, 300, 06, 11.

38. *Moskovskie vedomosti*, no. 62, March 13, 1859. Translated in: Ibid., 314. Also: "Smert' ili kosushku!"

39. Christian, *Living Water*, 349–50.

40. Ibid., 350. Schrad, *Vodka Politics*, 121–22.

41. P. V. Berezin, *Na sluzhbe zlomu delu* (Moscow: I. N. Kyshnerev i Ko., 1900). Mikhail Fridman, *Vinnaya monopoliya, tom II: Vinnaya monopoliya v Rossii*, 2 vols., vol. 2 (Petrograd: Pravda, 1916), 70–74. Schrad, *Vodka Politics*, 108. On emancipation and protest, see: Evgeny Finkel and Scott Gehlbach, *Reform and Rebellion in Weak States* (New York: Cambridge University Press, 2020), 17–33.

42. Letter, George Kennan to Frances Willard, August 29, 1888, Woman's Christian Temperance Union Series (1853–1939), Folder 47, Roll 15: Temperance and Prohibition Papers, Evanston, IL. Similar appraisals: Murray, *The Russians of To-Day*, 30–33.

43. Leo Tolstoy, *A Confession and Other Religious Writings* (New York: Penguin Classics, 1987), 23.

44. A. N. Wilson, *Tolstoy* (New York: W. W. Norton & Company, 1988), 117.

45. Anna A. Tavis, "Authority and Its Discontents in Tolstoy and Joyce," in *Leo Tolstoy*, ed. Harold Bloom (Broomall, PA: Chelsea House Publishers, 2003), 66.

46. George Kennan, "A Visit to Count Tolstoi," *Century Illustrated Magazine* 34, no. 2 (1887): 255.

47. Ibid.: 257.

48. Leo Tolstoi, "Patriotism and Christianity," in *The Complete Works of Lyof N. Tolstoï: Patriotism, Slavery of Our Times, General Articles* (New York: Thomas Y. Crowell Co., 1928), 45–46.

49. Kennan, "A Visit to Count Tolstoi," 259. He expands his prescription of peaceful noncompliance with state authority more fully in: Leo Tolstoi, "Slavery of Our Times," in *The Complete*

Works of Lyof N. Tolstoï: Patriotism, Slavery of Our Times, General Articles (New York: Thomas Y. Crowell Co., 1928), 375–76.

50. Martin Green, *Tolstoy and Gandhi, Men of Peace* (New York: Basic Books, 1983), 86. Přemysl Pitter, *Chelčický, Tolstoi, Masaryk* (Prag: Verlag der Deutschen Gesellschaft für Sittliche Erziehung, 1931), 10.

51. Kennan, "A Visit to Count Tolstoi," 260–61.

52. Leo Tolstoi, "Church and State," in *The Complete Works of Lyof N. Tolstoï: Patriotism, Slavery of Our Times, General Articles* (New York: Thomas Y. Crowell Co., 1928), 146.

53. Ibid., 150.

54. Title sometimes translated as *My Religion*. Leo Tolstoi, *My Religion*, trans. Huntington Smith (New York: Thomas Y. Crowell & Co., 1885), 94. Even here, Tolstoy includes passages on the oppressed, wretched, masses "of unhappy people who sleep in hovels, and subsist upon strong drink and wretched food," who are unable to achieve their higher calling to enlightenment (183–84).

55. Leo Tolstoy, *The Kingdom of God Is within You: Christianity Not as a Mystic Religion but as a New Theory of Life*, trans. Constance Garnett, 2 vols., vol. 1 (London: William Heinemann, 1894), 2–3.

56. Ibid., 4. More generally, Tolstoy acknowledged a debt of gratitude to American writers William Lloyd Garrison, Theodore Parker, Ralph Waldo Emerson, Adin Ballou, Henry David Thoreau, William Ellery Channing, John Greenleaf Whittier, James Russell Lowell, and Walt Whitman: "a bright constellation, such as is rarely to be found in the literatures of the world." He continued, "And I should like to ask the American people, why they do not pay more attention to these voices (hardly to be replaced by those of Gould, Rockefeller and Carnegie), and continue the good work in which they made such hopeful progress." Leo Tolstoi, "Pis'mo Eduardu Garnetu, 21 iyunya, 1900 g.," in *Polnoe sobranie sochinenii, tom 72: Pis'ma, 1899–1900*, ed. Vladimir G. Chertkov (Moscow: Gosudarstvennoe izdatel'stvo khudozhestvennoi literatury, 1933), 396–97.

57. Tolstoy, *The Kingdom of God Is within You*, 211.

58. Leo Tolstoy, *Serving God or Mammon*, trans. Leo Pasvolsky (Westerville, OH: American Issue Publishing Company, 1910[?]), 4. See also: R. F. Christian, *Tolstoy's Diaries*, 2 vols., vol. 1 (New York: Charles Scribner's Sons, 1985), 249.

59. Leo Tolstoy, *What Then Must We Do?*, trans. Aylmer Maude (London: Oxford University Press, 1925), 295–96. In recent decades, *What Is to Be Done?* has become the more conventional and widely accepted translation.

60. Nikolai N. Gusev, "Lev Tolstoi's Daily Regime," in *Reminiscences of Lev Tolstoi by His Contemporaries* (Moscow: Foreign Languages Publishing House, 1961), 234. Sophia A. Tolstaya, *The Diaries of Sophia Tolstoy*, trans. Cathy Porter (New York: Random House, 1985), 383. "I cannot recall those years without horror, loathing, and heartache. I killed people in war, summoned others to duels in order to kill them, gambled at cards; I devoured the fruits of the peasant's labour and punished them; I fornicated and practised deceit. Lying, thieving, promiscuity of all kinds, drunkenness, violence, murder . . . there was no crime I did not commit, and yet I was praised for it all and my contemporaries considered, and still consider me, a relatively moral man." Tolstoy, *A Confession and Other Religious Writings*, 22–23, 30. Also: R. F. Christian, ed., *Tolstoy's Letters*, 2 vols., vol. 1 (New York: Charles Scribner's Sons, 1978), 15.

61. Ilya I. Mechnikov, "A Day with Tolstoi in Yasnaya Polyana," in *Reminiscences of Lev Tolstoi by His Contemporaries* (Moscow: Foreign Languages Publishing House, 1961), 235. Tolstaya, *The Diaries of Sophia Tolstoy*, 80. Henri Troyat, *Tolstoy* (New York: Doubleday and Company, 1967), 578. Thomas Stevens, "With Count Tolstoy (1891)," in *Americans in Conversation with Tolstoy: Selected Accounts, 1887–1923*, ed. Peter Skirin (London: McFarland & Company, 2006), 47, 50.

62. Evgeniya P. Gritsenko, "Deyatel'nost' L. N. Tolstogo i ego sem'i protiv p'yanstva," *Istoriya. Istoriki. Istochniki*, no. 1 (2015): 39–44. Alekseev, *O p'yanstve s predisloviem gr. L. N. Tolstago*,

93. Aylmer Maude, *The Life of Tolstoy: Later Years* (New York: Dodd, Mead and Company, 1911), 339.

63. "Tolstoy, Leo Nikolaiëvitch, Count," in *Standard Encyclopedia of the Alcohol Problem*, ed. Ernest H. Cherrington (Westerville, OH: American Issue Press, 1930), 2655. Maude, *Life of Tolstoy*, 339.

64. Tolstoi, *Serving God or Mammon*, 6–7. Gritsenko, "Deyatel'nost' L. N. Tolstogo," 44. Charlotte Alston, *Tolstoy and His Disciples: The History of a Radical International Movement* (London: I. B. Tauris, 2014), 18.

65. Quoted in: Patricia Herlihy, *The Alcoholic Empire: Vodka and Politics in Late Imperial Russia* (New York: Oxford University Press, 2002), 111–12.

66. R. F. Christian, ed., *Tolstoy's Letters*, 2 vols., vol. 2 (New York: Charles Scribner's Sons, 1978), 525; also 527–32, 602–603.

67. See: Tolstoi, *Serving God or Mammon*, 5.

68. Leo Tolstoy, "Carthago Delenda Est," in *The Complete Works of Lyof N. Tolstoï: Patriotism, Slavery of Our Times, General Articles* (New York: Thomas Y. Crowell Co., 1928), 83.

69. Quoted in Kate Transchel, *Under the Influence: Working-Class Drinking, Temperance, and Cultural Revolution in Russia, 1895–1932* (Pittsburgh, PA: University of Pittsburgh Press, 2006), 31. Irina R. Takala, *Veselie Rusi: Istoriia alkogol'noi problemy v Rossii* (St. Petersburg: Zhurnal Neva, 2002), 100–103.

70. D. G. Bulgakovskii, *Ocherk deyatel'nosti popechitel'stv o narodnoi trezvosti za vse vremya ikh sushchestvovaniya, 1895–1909 g.*, 2 vols. (St. Petersburg: Otechestvennaya tipografiya, 1910). V. A. Hagen, *Bor'ba s narodnym p'yanstvom: Popechitel'stva o narodnoi trezvosti, ikh sovremennoe polozhenie i nedostatki* (St. Petersburg: Gosudarstvennaya Tipgrafiya, 1907). David Lewin, "Das Branntweinmonopol in Russland," *Zeitschrift für die gesamte Staatswissenschaft* XXV (1908).

71. Leo Tolstoy, "Letter to A. M. Kuzminskii, November 13–15, 1896," in *Polnoe sobranie sochenenii, tom 69* (Moscow: Gosudarstvennoe izdatel'stvo khudozhestvennoi literatury, 1954), 205–206. Quoted in: Herlihy, *The Alcoholic Empire*, 15.

72. Vladimir I. Gurko, *Features and Figures of the Past: Government and Opinion in the Reign of Nicholas II*, trans. Laura Matveev (Stanford, CA: Stanford University Press, 1939), 530. Marc Lee Schulkin, "The Politics of Temperance: Nicholas II's Campaign against Alcohol Abuse," (PhD dissertation, Harvard University, 1985), 151–95. See also: f. 115 (Soyuz 17-ogo Oktyabrya), op. 1, d. 111, l. 3; GARF, f. 115, op. 1, d. 19, l. 1–317; GARF, f. 115, op. 2, d. 16, l. 1, 16; GARF, f. 115, op. 2, d. 18, l. 1–63; GARF, f. 1779 (Kantselyariya vremennogo pravitel'stva, 1917), op. 1, d. 709, l. 1.

73. Troyat, *Tolstoy*, 567.

74. Fedor Stepun, "The Religious Tragedy of Tolstoy," *Russian Review* 19, no. 2 (1960): 164. Tavis, "Authority and Its Discontents in Tolstoy and Joyce," 67.

75. Gritsenko, "Deyatel'nost' L. N. Tolstogo," 39.

76. Roza Lyuksemburg, "Lev Tolstoi," in *O Tolstom: Literaturno-kriticheskii sbornik*, ed. Vladimir M. Friche (Moscow: Gosudarstvennoe izdatel'stvo, 1928), 125. Rosamund Bartlett, *Tolstoy: A Russian Life* (New York: Houghton Mifflin Harcourt, 2011), 345–46.

77. Nadezhda Krupskaya, *Reminiscences of Lenin*, trans. Bernard Isaacs (New York: International Publishers, 1970), 40.

78. Philip Pomer, *Lenin's Brother: The Origins of the October Revolution* (New York: W. W. Norton & Co., 2010), 127–28. Michael Burleigh, *Earthly Powers: The Clash of Religion and Politics in Europe, from the French Revolution to the Great War* (New York: HarperCollins, 2007), 280.

79. On the state: Karl Marx and Friedrich Engels, *The Communist Manifesto* (New York: International Publishers, 1948), 11. On religion: Karl Marx, *Critique of Hegel's "Philosophy of Right"* (New York: Cambridge University Press, 1970), 131.

80. Helen Rappaport, *Conspirator: Lenin in Exile* (New York: Basic Books, 2010), 175–76. Robert Hatch McNeal, *Bride of the Revolution: Krupskaya and Lenin* (Ann Arbor: University of Michigan Press, 1972), 76.

81. See: Letter to his mother from Paris, January 6, 1911, in: Vladimir I. Lenin, *Letters of Lenin*, trans. Elizabeth Hill and Doris Mudie (New York: Harcourt, Brace, 1937), 294–95.

82. Bartlett, *Tolstoy*, 434–35. Vladimir I. Lenin, "Leo Tolstoy as the Mirror of the Russian Revolution (1908)," in *Collected Works, Volume 15: 1908–1909* (Moscow: Progress Publishers, 1973).

83. Vladimir I. Lenin, "The Development of Capitalism in Russia," in *Collected Works, Volume 3: The Development of Capitalism in Russia* (Moscow: Progress Publishers, 1960), 290–91. Vladimir I. Lenin, "Duma i utverzhdenie byudzheta," in *Polnoe sobranie sochinenii tom 15: fevral'-iyun' 1907* (Moscow: Gosudarstvennoe izdatel'stvo politicheskoi literatury, 1961).

84. Vladimir I. Lenin, "The Serf-Owners at Work," in *Collected Works* (London: Lawrence & Wishart, 1961), 95. Original in: *Iskra*, no. 8, September 10, 1901.

85. Vladimir I. Lenin, "Casual Notes," in *Collected Works, Volume 4: 1898–April 1901* (Moscow: Progress Publishers, 1972), 407–408. Original in: *Zarya*, no. 1, April 1901.

86. Ian D. Thatcher, "Trotsky and *Bor'ba*," *Historical Journal* 37, no. 1 (1994): 116–17. Original in: Anon, "Gosudarstvo i narodnoe khozyaistvo," *Bor'ba*, no. 2, pp. 3–8. Reprinted in: Leon Trotsky, *Sochineniya, tom IV: Politicheskaya khronika* (Moscow: Gosudarstvennoe izdatel'stvo, 1926), 525–33.

87. *Pravda*, March 15, 1913. Vladimir I. Lenin, "Spare Cash," in *Collected Works, Volume 18: April 1912–March 1913* (Moscow: Gosudarstvennoe izdatel'stvo politicheskoi literatury, 1963), 601–602.

88. Vladislav B. Aksenov, *Veselie Rusi, XX vek: Gradus noveishei rossiiskoi istorii ot "p'yanogo byudzheta" do "sukhogo zakona"* (Moscow: Probel-2000, 2007), 152–54.

89. Viktor P. Obninskii, *Poslednii samoderzhets, ocherk zhizni i tsarstvovaniia imperatora Rossii Nikolaia II-go* (Moscow: Respublika, 1992), 21–22. Nicholas often got so drunk, he needed to be carried back home. Robert K. Massie, *Nicholas and Alexandra* (New York: Athenium, 1967), 19–20.

90. Petr A. Zaionchkovskii, *Rossiiskoe samoderzhavie v kontse XIX stoletiya* (Moscow: Mysl', 1970), 47–48.

91. Vinkentii V. Veresaev, *In the War: Memoirs of V. Veresaev*, trans. Leo Winter (New York: Mitchell Kennerley, 1917), 259–60.

92. Reported in the *Vil'no voenno-listok*; cited in George Snow, "Alcoholism in the Russian Military: The Public Sphere and the Temperance Discourse, 1883–1917," *Jahrbücher für Geschichte Osteuropas* 45, no. 3 (1997): 427.

93. Joshua A. Sanborn, *Drafting the Russian Nation: Military Conscription, Total War, and Mass Politics, 1905–1925* (DeKalb, IL: Northern Illinois University Press, 2003), 13. Veresaev, *In the War*, 23.

94. Petr A. Zaionchkovskii, *The Russian Autocracy under Alexander III*, trans. David R. Jones (Gulf Breeze, FL: Academic International Press, 1976), 22.

95. Contstantine Pleshakov, *The Tsar's Last Armada: The Epic Voyage to the Battle of Tsushima* (New York: Basic Books, 2003), 98–99. Sydney Tyler, *The Japan-Russia War* (Philadelphia: P. W. Ziegler Co., 1905), 364.

96. Michael Graham Fry, Erik Goldstein, and Richard Langhorne, *Guide to International Relations and Diplomacy* (London: Continuum, 2002), 162. Frederick McCormick, *Tragedy of Russia in Pacific Asia*, 2 vols., vol. 2 (New York: Outing Publishing Company, 1907), 280. Pleshakov, *Tsar's Last Armada*, 324–25.

97. W. Bruce Lincoln, *The Romanovs: Autocrats of All the Russias* (New York: Dial Press, 1981), 651. Edith Martha Almedingen, *An Unbroken Unity: A Memoir of Grand-Duchess Serge of Russia, 1864–1918* (London: Bodley Head, 1964), 52.

98. Letter from Assistant Secretary of State Robert Bacon to Ambassador to Russia George von Lengerke Meyer, July 28, 1906, Theodore Roosevelt Papers, Library of Congress Manuscript Division, https://www.theodorerooseveltcenter.org/Research/Digital-Library/Record?libID=o53643, Theodore Roosevelt Digital Library, Dickinson State University, Dickinson, North Dakota (accessed April 20, 2020).

99. Schrad, *Vodka Politics*, 175–76. On the cult of military sobriety, see: Schrad, *Political Power of Bad Ideas*, 141, 173–74. On the kaiser's proclamation: "Kaiser Wilhelm Seeks to Curb Drink Evil," *Union Signal*, September 25, 1913. James S. Roberts, *Drink, Temperance, and the Working Class in Nineteenth-Century Germany* (Boston: George Allen & Unwin, 1984), 68–69.

100. Boris V. Ananich and Rafail S. Ganelin, "Emperor Nicholas II, 1894–1917," ed. Donald J. Raleigh and Akhmed A. Iskenderov (Armonk, NY: M. E. Sharpe, 1996), 390. W. Arthur McKee, "*Taming the Green Serpent: Alcoholism, Autocracy, and Russian Society, 1881–1914*" (PhD dissertation, University of California–Berkeley, 1997), 522.

101. William Johnson, *The Liquor Problem in Russia* (Westerville, OH: American Issue Publishing House, 1915), 191. Peter L. Bark, "Memoirs" (n/d), in Special Collections, Leeds University Library, Sir Peter Bark Papers, Leeds Russian Archive, University of Leeds.

102. John Newton, *Alcohol and the War: The Example of Russia* (London: Richard J. James, 1915), 5. Guy Hayler—Temperance Tracts, University of Wisconsin–Madison, Vol. XXVIII, No. 13. Bark, "Memoirs," Ch. IX, 21.

103. GARF, f. 102 (Departament politsii, 4-oe deloproizvodstvo), op. 1914, d. 138 "Obezporyadkakh zapisnykh nishnikh chinov prizvannykh na voinu," ll. 24–120. Alfred Knox, *With the Russian Army, 1914–1917*, 2 vols., vol. 1 (London: Hutchinson & Co., 1921), 39.

104. GARF, f. 671 (v. kn. Nikolai Nikolaevich Romanov—mladschii), op. 1, d. 47, l. 1. See also: D. N. Borodin, "Vinnaya monopoliya," *Trudy Kommissii po Voprosu ob Alkogolizm: Zhurnaly zasedanii i doklady* III (1899): 173. Mikhail N. Nizhegorodtsev, "Alkogolizm i bor'ba s nim," *Zhurnal russkago obshchestva okhraneniya narodnago zdraviya* 8 (1909).

105. See Konstantin's letters to the tsar: GARF, f. 601 (Imperator Nikolai II), op. 1, d. 1268, ll. 179–80, 184. See also GARF, f. 579 (Pavel N. Milyukov), op. 1, d. 2571, ll. 1–4; GARF, f. 660 (V. Kn. Konstantin Konstantinovich Romanov), op. 2, d. 195, l. 1. John Curtis Perry and Konstantin Pleshakov, *The Flight of the Romanovs: A Family Saga* (New York: Basic Books, 2001), 124.

106. *Russkoe slovo* (Moscow), October 7, 1914. Reprinted in Johnson, *The Liquor Problem in Russia*, 200.

107. GARF, f. 6996, op. 1, d. 346, l. 5–397, esp. 51–52.

108. GARF, f. 1779, op. 1, d. 705, l. 5; GARF, f. 1779, op. 2, d. 299, ll. 1–7; GARF, f. 6996 (Ministerstvo Finansov Vremennogo Pravitelistva, 1917), op. 1, d. 293, ll. 5, 6, 17, 28, 33–38; GARF, f. 6996, op. 1, d. 296, ll. 17; GARF, f. 6996, op. 1, d. 299, ll. 2–376; GARF, f. 6996, op. 1, d. 300, ll. 1–245; GARF f. 6996, op. 1, d. 340, ll. 1–4; GARF, f. 6996, op. 1, d. 342, ll. 1–8.

109. GARF, f. 6996, op. 1, d. 345, ll. 8, 28. See also: GARF, f. 6996, op. 1, d. 345, ll. 9–21 and 39–46.

110. M. Bogolepoff, "Public Finance," in *Russia: Its Trade and Commerce*, ed. Arthur Raffalovich (London: P. S. King & Son, Ltd., 1918), 27, 346. Alexander M. Michelson, *Russian Public Finance during the War* (New Haven, CT: Yale University Press, 1928), 45.

111. Quoted in: Vladimir N. Kokovtsov, *Out of My Past: The Memoirs of Count Kokovtsov*, trans. Laura Matveev (Stanford, CA: Stanford University Press, 1935), 473.

112. Aleksandr P. Pogrebinskii, *Ocherki istorii finanasov dorevolyutsionnoi Rossii (XIX–XX vv.)* (Moscow: Gosfinizdat, 1954), 126–28. John Hodgson, *With Denikin's Armies* (London: Temple Bar Publishing Co., 1932), 79.

113. Ivan V. Strel'chuk, *Alkogolizm i bor'ba s nim* (Moscow: Molodaya gvardiya, 1954), 13.

114. John Reed, *Ten Days That Shook the World* (New York: Random House, 1935), 309. Anatolii I. Razgon, *VTsIK Sovetov v pervye mesyatsy diktatury proletariata* (Moscow: Nauka, 1977), 215–38. See also: f. 733 Tsentral'noe upravlenie i ob'edinenie spirtovoi promyshlennosti, Gosspirt, op. 1, d. 4433, Rossiiskii Gosudarstvenni Arkhiv Ekonomiki (RGAE), Moscow, Russia.

115. Yuri S. Tokarev, "Dokumenty narodnykh sudov (1917–1922)," in *Voprosy istoriografii i istochnikovedeniia istorii SSSR: Sbornik statei*, ed. Sigismund N. Valk (Leningrad: Izdatel'stvo Akademii nauk SSSR, 1963), 153.

116. Speech reprinted in *Rabochaya gazeta*, January 13, 1926. Quoted in: Transchel, *Under the Influence*, 75.

117. GARF, f. 374 (Narodnyi komissariat raboche-krest'yanskoi inspektsii SSSR), op. 15, d. 1291, ll. 18–22.

118. Vladimir I. Lenin, "X vserossiiskaya konferentsiya RKP(b)," in *Sochineniya tom 32: fekabr' 1920–avgust 1921* (Moscow: Gosudarstvennoe izdatel'stvo politicheskoi literatury, 1951), 403. See also: "Even Russia Is Better under Vodka Prohibition," *American Issue*, November 12, 1919, World League Against Alcoholism Series, Box 5, Folder 51, Roll 25, Temperance and Prohibition Papers, Ohio Historical Society.

119. Translated version in: Anna Louise Strong, *The First Time in History: Two Years of Russia's New Life (August 1921 to December 1923)* (New York: Boni and Liveright, 1924), 168.

120. Leon Trotsky, "Vodka, tserkov', i kinematograf," *Pravda*, July 12, 1923.

121. Joseph Stalin, "Pis'mo Shinkevichu (20 marta 1927 g.)," in *Sochineniya tom 9: dekabr' 1926–iyul' 1927* (Moscow: Gosudarstvennoe izdatel'stvo politicheskoi literatury, 1948), 191. See also: "Soviet Russia Re-Introduces Vodka," Monthly Notes, October 1924, World League Against Alcoholism Series, Box 5, Folder 51, Roll 25, Temperance and Prohibition Papers, Ohio Historical Society.

122. GARF, f. 5515 (Narodnyi komissariat truda), op. 20, d. 7, ll. 29, 32, 43, 46, 48, 50, 52–53, 117. See also GARF, f. 5467 (TsK Profsoyuza derevoobdeloinikov), op. 11, d. 179, ll. 1–14; GARF, f. 5467, op. 14, d. 108, ll. 17–20. On alcoholism statistics, see RGAE, f. 1562 (TsSU pri Sovete Ministrov SSSR), op. 1, d. 490, ll. 9–10.

123. Joseph Stalin, "Beseda s inostrannymi rabochimi delegatsiyami: 5 noyabrya 1927 g.," in *Sochineniya tom 10: 1927 avgust–dekabr'* (Moscow: Gosudarstvennoe izdatel'stvo politicheskoi literatury, 1952), 232–33. Also: Stalin, "Pis'mo Shinkevichu (20 marta 1927 g.)," 192. Letter from A. Korovine, "Instructions to the Delegates of the Moscow and the Regional Soviets for Combating Alcoholism," January 28, 1929, 1–5, World League Against Alcoholism Records, Box 5, Folder 51, Roll 25, Temperance and Prohibition Papers, Ohio Historical Society.

124. Baron August Freiherr Haxthausen, *The Russian Empire: Its People, Institutions, and Resources*, trans. Robert Faire, 2 vols., vol. 2 (London: Chapman and Hall, 1856), 174–75, 408–409. See also: John P. LeDonne, "Indirect Taxes in Catherine's Russia: II. The Liquor Monopoly," *Jahrbücher für Geschichte Osteuropas* 24, no. 2 (1976): 203.

125. Luigi Villari, *Russia under the Great Shadow* (New York: James Pott and Company, 1905), 250.

Chapter 3

1. Helen Rappaport, *Conspirator: Lenin in Exile* (New York: Basic Books, 2010), 175–76. Robert Hatch McNeal, *Bride of the Revolution: Krupskaya and Lenin* (Ann Arbor: University of Michigan Press, 1972), 76.

2. Ture Nerman, *Arbetarrörelsens nykterhetspolitik* (Stockholm: Wilhelmssons Böktryckeri, 1966), 49–53.

3. Catherine Merridale, *Lenin on the Train* (New York: Metropolitan Books, 2017), 192–96. Jan Bolander, "Branting och de ryska revolutionärna," in *Bilden av Branting*, ed. Jan Lindhagen (Stockholm: Tidens Förlag, 1975), 317. Vandervelde called wartime Stockholm a "halfway house" between East and West. Emile Vandervelde, *Three Aspects of the Russian Revolution* (London: George Allen & Unwin, 1918), 206–207.

4. Pavel V. Moskovskii and Viktor G. Semenov, *Lenin v Shvetsii* (Moscow: Politizdat, 1972), 164.

5. Ibid., 13. Nils-Olof Franzén, *Hjalmar Branting och hans tid* (Stockholm: Bonniers, 1985), 220. See: Vladimir I. Lenin, *Polnoe sobranie sochinenii*, tom 4 (Moscow: Political Literature Publishers, 1967), 559. Vladimir I. Lenin, *Letters of Lenin*, trans. Elizabeth Hill and Doris

Mudie (New York: Harcourt, Brace, 1937), 137. Carl-Göran Andrae, "The Swedish Labor Movement and the 1917–1918 Revolution," in *Sweden's Development from Poverty to Affluence, 1750–1970,* ed. Steven Koblik (Minneapolis: University of Minnesota Press, 1975), 239.

6. "K. Hjalmar Branting," in *Svensk biografiskt lexikon,* ed. Bertil Boëthius, vol. 6 (Stockholm: A. Bonnier, 1926), 14, https://sok.riksarkivet.se/sbl/artikel/16868 Riksarkivet, Stockholm (accessed January 31, 2018). Bolander, "Branting och de ryska revolutionärna." See also: Howard B. Christensen, "The Question of Swedish Intervention into the Revolution and Civil War in Finland, January–February 1918" (MA thesis, University of Wisconsin– Madison, 1978), 90. Hjalmar Branting, "Lenin (1924)," in *Hjalmar Branting: Tal och skrifter, Vol. XI: Litteraturkritik och varia* (Stockholm: Tidens Förlag, 1930), 231–32.

7. Franzén, *Hjalmar Branting och hans tid,* 308–09. Also: "Kak Lenin vozvrashchalsya v revolyutsionnuyu Rossiyu. 13 aprelya," *KPRF Sevastopol,* April 13 2017. http://sevkprf.ru/как-ленин-возвращался-в-революционну/ (Accessed January 31, 2018).

8. O. G. von Heidenstam, *Swedish Life in Town and Country* (New York: G. P. Putnam's Sons, 1904), 193. Swedish consumption statistics: Statens folkhälsoinstitut (Swedish National Institute of Public Health), *Försäljning av spritdrycker, vin och öl i Sverige under åren 1861–1999* (Stockholm: Statens folkhälsoinstitut), 12–16. Switzerland Bureau fédéral de statistique, *Question de l'alcoolisme. Exposé comparatif des lois et des expériences de quelques états étrangers, par le bureau fédéral de statistique* (Berne: Imprimerie K.-J. Wyss, 1884), 672.

9. Von Heidenstam, *Swedish Life in Town and Country,* 193–94.

10. Ibid., 187, 93. See also: Victor Nilsson, *Sweden* (New York: Co-Operative Publication Society, 1899), 387.

11. Rune Premfors, "Sveriges demokratisering: Ett historiskt-institutionalistiskt perspektiv," *SCORE Rapportserie* 3 (1999): 30–33. Hugh Heclo, *Modern Social Politics in Britain and Sweden: From Relief to Income Maintenance* (New Haven, CT: Yale University Press, 1974), 35.

12. Dankwart A. Rustow, *Politics of Compromise: A Study of Parties and Cabinet Government in Sweden* (Princeton, NJ: Princeton University Press, 1955), 53.

13. Johan Pontén, *Historia kring alkoholen: Från syndafloden till dagens Sverige* (Stockholm: Natur och kultur, 1967), 72–88. Hanna Hodacs, "Det civiliserade, protestantiska och nyktra Europa: Om nykterhetstankens spridning i det tidiga 1800-talets Sverige," *Spiritus,* no. 4 (2002): 14–16. Nykterhetskommittén, *Betänkande VI, 1: Redogörelse för lagstiftningen i Sverige om rusdryckers försäljning, 1800–1911* (Stockholm: 1914), 14–22. Arbetarrörelsens arkiv och bibliotek, General Collections, 9341: Stockholm, Sweden. Karl Höjer, *Svensk nykterhetspolitik och nykterhetsvård* (Stockholm: P. A. Norstedt & Söners Förlag, 1955), 23–24.

14. John Bergvall, *Restriktionssystemet: Hur det kommit till, hur det arbetar, vad det uträttat* (Norrtelje: Nortelje Tidnings Boktryckeri AB, 1929), 9. Nykterhetskommittén, *Betänkande VI, 1,* 41–42. Olov Kinberg, "Temperance Legislation in Sweden," *Annals of the American Academy of Political and Social Science* 163 (1932). Per Frånberg, "Den Svenska supen," in *Den Svenska supen,* ed. Kettil Bruun and Per Frånberg (Stockholm: Prisma, 1985), 34. Even muck-raking American prohibitionist William E. "Pussyfoot" Johnson studied the Gothenburg system, finding it conducted "with remarkable purity of purpose." Fred A. McKenzie, *"Pussyfoot" Johnson: Crusader, Reformer, a Man among Men* (London: Hodder and Stoughton, 1920), 39.

15. Edwin Björkman, "What Is the Matter with Sweden?," *Everybody's Magazine,* April 1918, 94.

16. Nils Beyer, *Den unge Hjalmar Branting* (Stockholm: P. A. Norstedt & Söners Förlag, 1985), 76–82. Franzén, *Hjalmar Branting och hans tid,* 23–24. Per Meurling, "Det revolutionära 80-talet," in *Bilden av Branting,* ed. Jan Lindhagen (Stockholm: Tidens Förlag, 1975), 50–51.

17. Ibid., 51–57. Beyer, *Den unge Hjalmar Branting,* 68. Zeth Höglund, "Till Hjalmar Brantings karakteristik," in *Hjalmar Branting: Tal och skrifter, Vol. I: Socialistisk samhällssyn I* (Stockholm: Tidens Förlag, 1929), 12–15.

18. "K. Hjalmar Branting," vol. 6, 14, https://sok.riksarkivet.se/sbl/artikel/16868 Riksarkivet, Stockholm (accessed February 6, 2018).

19. Michele Micheletti, *Det civila samhället och staten: Medborgarsammanslutningarnas roll i svensk politik* (Stockholm: C. E. Fritzes AB, 1994), 231. Also: Oskar Petersson, *Goodtemplarordens i Sverige historia* (Stockholm: Svenska Nykterhetsförlaget, 1903).

20. Beyer, *Den unge Hjalmar Branting*, 80–81. See also: Herbert Granliden, *En frihetskamp genom seklerna: Den svenska nykterhetsrörelsens historia i ord och bild* (Stockholm: Förlagsaktiebolaget svenska folkrörelser, 1953), 346. On the Lutheran Church and Swedish temperance, see: Sidsel Eriksen, "Drunken Danes and Sober Swedes? Religious Revivalism and the Temperance Movements as Keys to Danish and Swedish Folk Cultures," in *Language and the Construction of Class Identities: The Struggle for Discursive Power in Social Organisation—Scandinavia and Germany after 1800*, ed. Bo Stråth (Gothenburg: Göteborgs Universitet, Historiska Institutionen, 1990), 66–69.

21. Hjalmar Branting, "Knut Wicksell och socialismen (1886)," in *Hjalmar Branting: Tal och skrifter, Vol. I: Socialistisk samhällssyn I* (Stockholm: Tidens Förlag, 1929), 179. Hjalmar Branting, "Om prostitutionen (1886)," in *Hjalmar Branting: Tal och skrifter, Vol. I: Socialistisk samhällssyn I* (Stockholm: Tidens Förlag, 1929), 184–88. Hjalmar Branting, "De Wicksellska föreläsningarna (1886)," in *Hjalmar Branting: Tal och skrifter, Vol. I: Socialistisk samhällssyn I* (Stockholm: Tidens Förlag, 1929), 189–94. Hjalmar Branting, "Knut Wicksell om socialiststaten (1886)," in *Hjalmar Branting: Tal och skrifter, Vol. I: Socialistisk samhällssyn I* (Stockholm: Tidens Förlag, 1929), 195–98.

22. Joseph R. Gusfield, "Social Structure and Moral Reform: A Study of the Woman's Christian Temperance Union," *American Journal of Sociology* 61, no. 3 (1955): 225. I have found no evidence that the statement originated with Karl Marx himself.

23. Friedrich Engels, *The Condition of the Working Class in England in 1844* (London: Swan Sonnenschein & Co., 1892), 127–29. Friedrich Engels, "Preußischer Schnaps im deutschen Reichstag (1876)," in *Marx-Engels-Werke* (East Berlin: Dietz Verlag, 1962), 40.

24. David Christian, "Accumulation and Accumulators: The Metaphor Marx Muffled," *Science and Society* 54, no. 2 (1990). Karl Marx, *Capital: Volume 3* (New York: Penguin Classics, 1991), 927.

25. Sheri Berman, *The Social Democratic Moment: Ideas and Politics in the Making of Interwar Europe* (Cambridge, MA: Harvard University Press, 1998), 48–58.

26. Tim Tilton, *The Political Theory of Swedish Social Democracy: Through the Welfare State to Socialism* (Oxford: Clarendon Press, 1990), 16–21.

27. Ibid., 20. Hjalmar Branting, "Vaför arbetarrörelsen måste bli socialistisk (1886)," in *Hjalmar Branting: Tal och skrifter, Vol. I: Socialistisk samhällssyn I* (Stockholm: Tidens Förlag, 1929), 116.

28. Tilton, *Political Theory of Swedish Social Democracy*, 33. Lennart Johansson, *Systemet lagom: Rusdrycker, interesseorganisationer och politisk kultur under förbudsdebattens tidevarv 1900–1922* (Lund: Lund University Press, 1995), 64, 121. Nerman, *Arbetarrörelsens nykterhetspolitik*, 12.

29. Branting, "Vaför arbetarrörelsen måste bli socialistisk," 115–18.

30. Ibid., 115. Tilton, *Political Theory of Swedish Social Democracy*, 20.

31. Robert J. Goldstein, *Political Repression in 19th-Century Europe* (London: Croom Helm, 1983), 43.

32. Hjalmar Branting, "Rösträtt och arbetarrörelse (1896)," in *Hjalmar Branting: Tal och skrifter, Vol. III: Kampen för demokratin I* (Stockholm: Tidens Förlag, 1927), 128–30. Tilton, *Political Theory of Swedish Social Democracy*, 25.

33. Tilton, *Political Theory of Swedish Social Democracy*, 26. Hjalmar Branting, "Socialdemokratiska vänsterföreningen (1912)," in *Hjalmar Branting: Tal och skrifter, Vol. VIII: Stridsfrågor inom arbetarrörelsen* (Stockholm: Tidens Förlag, 1929), 238–39. Also: Samuel Edquist, *Nyktra svenskar: Godtemplarrörelsen och den nationella identiteten: 1879–1918* (Uppsala: Studia Historica Upsaliensia, 2001), 163.

34. Sheri Berman, *The Primacy of Politics: Social Democracy and the Making of Europe's Twentieth Century* (New York: Cambridge University Press, 2006), 155. Sigvard Nyström, "Branting, fackföreningsrörelsen och socialismen," in *Bilden av Branting*, ed. Jan Lindhagen (Stockholm: Tidens Förlag, 1975), 191.

35. Hjalmar Branting, "Antiförbudsrörelsen (1915)," in *Hjalmar Branting: Tal och skrifter, Vol. VIII: Stridsfrågor inom arbetarrörelsen* (Stockholm: Tidens Förlag, 1929), 305. On moderation more generally: Per Frånberg, "The Social and Political Significance of Two Swedish Restrictive Systems," *Contemporary Drug Problems* 12, no. 1 (1985): 58.

36. Hjalmar Branting, "Nykterhetsfrågan (1904)," in *Hjalmar Branting: Tal och skrifter, Vol. VII: Ekonomisk och social arbetarpolitik* (Stockholm: Tidens Förlag, 1928), 93–94. Nerman, *Arbetarrörelsens Nykterhetspolitik*, 29. On the split between absolutists and moderates within the IOGT, see: Frånberg, "Social and Political Significance," 54.

37. Tor Bjørklund, *Hundre år med folkeavstemninger Norge og norden 1905–2005* (Oslo: Universitetsforlaget, 2005). Statistisk årbok 2000, Tabell 4: Folkeavstemninger, Stemmeberettigede, deltakelse og avstemningsresultat, etter fylke, 1905–1994, Norwegian statistical bureau (Statistisk sentralbyrå), https://www.ssb.no/a/histstat/aarbok/ht-000130-004.html (accessed July 11, 2019). On prohibition and temperance in Norway, see: Per Ole Johansen, *Brennevinskrigen: En krønike om forbudstidens Norge* (Oslo: Gyldendal Norsk Forlag, 1985). Edwin A. Pratt, *Disinterested Management in Norway* (London: P. S. King & Son, 1907). Edwin A. Pratt, *Licensing and Temperance in Sweden, Norway, and Denmark* (London: John Murray, 1907).

38. Hjalmar Branting, "Norge ur dina händer, konung! (1905)," in *Hjalmar Branting: Tal och skrifter, Vol. V: Svensk försvars- och fredspolitik* (Stockholm: Tidens Förlag, 1927), 144–45.

39. "Hjalmar Branting," *The Living Age*, October 26, 1918, 215. "K. Hjalmar Branting," vol. 6, 14. Irwin Abrams, *The Nobel Peace Price and the Laureates* (Nantucket, MA: Watson Publishing International, 2001), 97–98.

40. Gerhard Magnusson, *Socialdemokratien i Sverige*, 3 vols., vol. 2, kamptider (Stockholm: P. A. Norstedt, 1921), 155–56. See also: Hjalmar Branting, "Systemet Petersson (1909)," in *Hjalmar Branting: Tal och skrifter, Vol. IV: Kampen för demokratin II* (Stockholm: Tidens Förlag, 1929), 25–26.

41. "Hjalmar Branting," 216. Moritz Marcus, *Aktiebolaget stockholmssystemet 1913–1938* (Stockholm: I. Marcus Boktryckeriaktiebolag, 1938), 13. Nyström, "Branting, fackföreningsrörelsen och socialismen," 195–96.

42. International Order of Good Templars arkiv (EIIaa: Övervalintendentens rapporter till Sveriges storloge) Förenings- och organizations arkiv (73), Riksarkivet, Arninge. Letter, Hjalmar Branting to Edvard Wavrinsky, July 8, 1911, Edvard Wavrinsky arkiv, 1883–1889, 1911: Förenings- och organizations arkiv (73), Riksarkivet, Arninge. Nykterhetskommittén, *Betänkande IX: Underdånigt betänkande med förslag till lag om alkoholvaror m. m.* (Stockholm: 1920), 176–78. Rapport, 15 Juli, 1902, 3–4. See also: Nerman, *Arbetarrörelsens nykterhetspolitik*, 19–22. Johan Bergman, *Den svenska nykterhetsrörelsens historia, från forna tider till våra dagar* (Stockholm: Svenska Nykterhetsförlaget, 1898), 218–22. Hilding Johansson, *Folkrörelserna och det demokratiska i Sverige* (Karlstad: Gleerups, 1952). Pehr Johnsson, *Sveriges blåbandsförenings historia, utgiven med anledning av tjugufem-åriga tillvaro* (Örebro: Örebro Nya Tryckeri-Aktiebolag, 1911), 6–13. Bengt Michanek, *Nykterhetsrörelsen: Den heliga kon* (Stockholm: Jacob Boëthius AB, 1972), 12.

43. Gunnar Huss, "Social Movements and Institutions," in *Sweden of To-Day*, ed. Magnus Blomstedt and Fredrik Böök (Stockholm: A. B. Hasse W. Tullbergs Förlag, 1930), 232. Sven Lundkvist, *Politik, nykterhet och reformer: En studie i folkrörelsernas politiska verksamhet, 1900–1920* (Uppsala: Uppsala University Press, 1974), 135.

44. This with 55 percent voter turnout. Sven Lundkvist, "Nykterhetsrörelsen," in *Den svenska historien 9: Industri och folkrörelser, 1866–1920* (Stockholm: Albert Bonniers Förlag, 1968), 166.

45. Walter Thompson, *The Control of Liquor in Sweden* (New York: Columbia University Press, 1935), 23.
46. Johansson, *Systemet lagom*, 62–65. Edquist, *Nyktra svenskar*, 51, 291. Nerman, *Arbetarrörelsens nykterhetspolitik*, 35–38. See also Branting's correspondence with International Chief Templar, Edvard Wavrinsky: Hjalmar Branting to Edvard Wavrinsky, July 8, 1911, Edvard Wavrinsky arkiv, Riksarkivet (National archives)—Arninge, 1883–1889, 1911.
47. Björn Schauman and Allan Zilliacus, *En blick på rusdryckslagstiftningen i Amerika* (Helsingfors: Hufvudsbladets nya tryckeri, 1908). Gerard Halfred von Koch, *Rusdrycksförbud: Studier av amerikansk nykterhetsrörelse och rusdryckslagstiftning* (Stockholm: A. B. Svenska nykterhetsförlaget, 1910). Arbetarrörelsens Arkiv och Bibliotek (ARAB), Stockholm, placering 16304, 3817.
48. Johansson, *Systemet lagom*, 64–65.
49. Nykterhetskommittén, *Betänkande V: Underdånigt betänkande med förslag till förordning angående försäljning av rusdrycker m. m.* (Stockholm: 1914), xi–xiii. ARAB, placering 9340. On Staaff more generally: Guy Hayler, *Prohibition Advance in All Lands: A Study of the World-Wide Character of the Drink Question*, 2nd ed. (London: International Prohibition Confederation, 1914), 69–72.
50. Hans Meijer, *Kommittépolitik och kommittéarbete. Det statliga kommittéväsendets utvecklingslinjer 1905–1954 samt nuvarande function och arbetsformer* (Lund: C. W. K. Gleerup, 1956), 349.
51. Hayler, *Prohibition Advance in All Lands*, 70–71. "Premier of Sweden on National Temperance," *Union Signal*, October 2, 1913, 4.
52. Ivan Bratt, *Kan nykterhetsfrågan lösas utan totalförbud? Ett reformprogram* (Stockholm: Albert Bonniers Förlag, 1909). Ivan Bratt, *Nykterhetspolitiska utvecklingslinjer* (Stockholm: Bonnier, 1909; reprint, 1911). Kettil Bruun, "Bratts genombrott," in *Den svenska supen: En historia om brännvin, Bratt och byråkrati*, ed. Kettil Bruun and Per Frånberg (Stockholm: Prisma, 1985), 53–55. Håkan Westling, *Ivan Bratt: Legendarisk läkare systemets grundare* (Stockholm: Atlantis, 1997).
53. Johansson, *Systemet lagom*, 64–65.
54. Marcus, *Aktiebolaget stockholmssystemet 1913–1938*, 58. Bruun, "Bratts genombrott," 62–65. Bratt, *Kan nykterhetsfrågan lösas utan totalförbud?* Svante Nycander, "Ivan Bratt: The Man Who Saved Sweden from Prohibition," *Addiction* 93, no. 1 (1998): 19. Ivan Bratt, "How Sweden Does It," *Forum* 85 (April 1931), Box 2, Bratt File, Association Against the Prohibition Amendment Records, Manuscripts Division, Library of Congress, Washington, DC.
55. Johansson, *Systemet lagom*, 82.
56. Nykterhetskommittén, *Betänkande V*, 193–231, 346–63. ARAB, placering 9340. Marquis W. Childs, *Sweden: The Middle Way* (New Haven, CT: Yale University Press, 1936), 107. John Bergvall, *The Liquor Legislation in Sweden* (Stockholm: Systembolagsföreningarnas Förtroendenämnd, 1931), 7–8, 41.
57. *Protokoll over Sv. Bryggeriarbetareförbundets 4:de congress. Stockholm den 7, 8 och 9 juli 1911* (Stockholm: A.-B. Arbetarnes Tryckeri, 1911), 24–25. Svenska Bryggeriarbetareförbundets Arkiv, 1B 22/17, ARAB. *Svenska Bryggeriindustriarbetareförbundet historia, 1899–1948*, (Stockholm: n/d), 112–15. Also: Nykterhetskommittén, *Betänkande VI, 2: Protokoll vid kommitténs sammanträden med särskilt tillkallade sakkunnige* (Stockholm: 1914), 1–70. ARAB, placering 9342. Ragnar Casparsson, *Svenska Bryggeriindustriarbetareförbundet, 1899-1929: En kort historik, utarbetad på uppdrag av förbundsstyrelsen* (Stockholm: Aktiebolaget Arbetarnes Tryckeri, 1929), 131–46.
58. Nykterhetskommittén, *Betänkande III: Kungl. Maj:ts nådiga proposition nr. 81, Bihang till riksdagens protokoll, 1915* (Stockholm: 1914), 23–25. Bilaga till nr. 22 Handlingar som legat till grund för Nykterhetskommitténs betänkande V, den 5 jan. 1914, vol. II. Finansdepartementets arkiv, Nr. 24, juli 1914. Riksarkivet (E Ia: 2307–2309). Nerman, *Arbetarrörelsens Nykterhetspolitik*, 38–41.
59. From *Social-Demokraten*, November 24, 1915. Branting, "Antiförbudsrörelsen," 303–9.

60. Branting, "Antiförbudsrörelsen," 308.
61. From *Social-Demokraten*, November 29, 1915. Branting, "Antiförbudsrörelsen," 310–12.
62. Steven Koblik, "Wartime Diplomacy and the Democratization of Sweden in September-October 1917," *Journal of Modern History* 41, no. 1 (1969): 29–32.
63. Ibid., 41–42.
64. Hjalmar Branting, "Demokratins genombrott (1918)," in *Hjalmar Branting: Tal och skrifter, Vol. IV: Kampen för Demokratin II* (Stockholm: Tidens Förlag, 1929), 313–14. Tilton, *Political Theory of Swedish Social Democracy*, 28.
65. Nykterhetskommittén, *Betänkande IX*, 302–8. "Förslag till lag om allmänt rusdrycksförbud," Nykterhetskommitténs (17 Nov. 1911) protokoll, 9 Dec. 1916: Bih. A (s. 1-5). Riksarkivet (YK85: AI: 1). Johansson, *Systemet lagom*, 203.
66. *Seventh Session of the International Labour Conference* (Geneva: International Labour Office, 1925), 6.
67. Protokoll vid Sverges Storloges 40:de årsmöte, 10 juli 1922, 87–88. International Order of Good Templars arkiv (AI—Storlogens årsmötesprotokoll med bilagor: 14), Förenings- och organizations arkiv (73), Riksarkivet, Arninge. Westling, *Ivan Bratt*, 148. Premfors, "Sveriges Demokratisering," 42. On Estonia, see: "The Strategic Importance of Esthonia in the European Prohibition Contest," *The American Issue*, August 23, 1919; and David Ostlund, "Esthonia's Bratt System and Its Results," July 23, 1921, 1–3, Box 4, Folder 5, Roll 20, World League Against Alcoholism Records, Temperance and Prohibition Papers, Ohio Historical Society. On Finland: David Ostlund, "Prohibition Conditions in Finland," November 1920, 1–3, Box 4, Folder 10, Roll 21, World League Against Alcoholism Records, Temperance and Prohibition Papers, Ohio Historical Society.
68. Nerman, *Arbetarrörelsens nykterhetspolitik*. Mark Lawrence Schrad, *The Political Power of Bad Ideas: Networks, Institutions, and the Global Prohibition Wave* (New York: Oxford University Press, 2010), 102.
69. Berman, *Social Democratic Moment*, 45. Quoting: Gustaf Möller, "Hjalmar Branting," in *Hjalmar Branting: Festschrift* (Stockholm: Tiden, 1920), 9.
70. See: Mark Lawrence Schrad, "Dodging the Bullet: Alcohol-Control Policy in Sweden," in *Dual Markets: Comparative Approaches to Regulation*, ed. Ernesto U. Savona, Mark A. R. Kleiman, and Francesco Calderoni (New York: Springer, 2017), 228–32.
71. Emile Vandervelde, "The Future of Belgium," *National Review* XLVII, no. 280 (1906): 595.
72. E. J. Hobsbawm, *The Age of Empire: 1875–1914* (New York: Vintage Books, 1989), 99. Marc Reynebeau, *Een geschiedenis van België* (Tielt: Lannoo, 2009), 149.
73. An Vleugels, *Narratives of Drunkenness: Belgium, 1830–1914* (London: Pickering & Chatto, 2013), 16–33. "Belgium," in: Ernest H. Cherrington, ed., *Standard Encyclopedia of the Alcohol Problem*, 6 vols., vol. 1 (Westerville, OH: American Issue Press, 1925), 306.
74. From an address of Hainaut governor, Baron R. du Sart de Bouland, July 7, 1903. In: Benjamin Seebohm Rowntree, *Land & Labour: Lessons from Belgium* (London: Macmillan and Co., 1911), 412.
75. Franz Hayt and Denise Galloy, *La Belgique: Des tribus gauloises à l'État fédéral*, 5th ed. (Bruxelles: De Boeck Education, 2006), 96.
76. Rowntree, *Land & Labour*, 413. Vleugels, *Narratives of Drunkenness*, 45, 108.
77. "One cannot dream of legally restricting the number of public houses," wrote Catholic prime minister Paul Joseph de Smet de Naeyer in 1907. "Any legislation for such a purpose would be contrary to the spirit of professional and commercial liberty." Rowntree, *Land & Labour*, 413–16.
78. Hubert Joseph Walthère Frère-Orban, *De l'abus des boissons enivrantes: Renseignements déposés à la chambre des représentants* (Bruxelles: M. Hayez, 1868), 13–105.
79. Ibid., 105–53.
80. Ibid., 153. Vleugels, *Narratives of Drunkenness*, 108–10. *Annales parlementaires. Sénat.* Séance du 4 August, 1887, p. 516. *Annales Sénat.* Séance du 15 July, 1887, pp. 1645–49. On support

for Frère-Orban: Els Witte, Jan Craeybeckx, and Alain Meynen, *Politieke geschiedenis van België: Van 1830 tot heden* (Antwerp: Standaard Uitgeverij, 2010), 57.

81. *Meeting international d'Anvers contre l'abus des boissons alcooliques 11, 12 et 13 septembre 1885: Compte rendu publié au nom du comité organisateur* (Brussels: A. Manceaux, 1886). More generally, see: "International Temperance Congresses," in: Ernest H. Cherrington, ed., *Standard Encyclopedia of the Alcohol Problem*, 6 vols., vol. 3 (Westerville, OH: American Issue Press, 1926), 1343–45.

82. Gallus Thomann, *The Second International Temperance Congress, Held at Zürich, Switzerland, in the Year 1887* (New York: United States Brewers' Association, 1889), 5. Specifically on the Antwerp meeting: Gallus Thomann, *Some Thoughts on the International Temperance Meeting, Held at Antwerp in September, 1885* (New York: United States Brewers' Association, 1886). On the biennial meetings and attendees, see: Schrad, *Political Power of Bad Ideas*, 48–52.

83. See, for instance, in Sweden: Riksarkivet-Arninge (RA-A), "Scandinavian Grand Lodge of Connecticut IOGT to Grand Lodge, 20 June 1922," IOGT arkiv, AI:14, ss. 87–88; Riksarkivet-Arninge, Sweden. "Skand. Storlogen af Minnesota to Edvard Wavrinsky, n/d 1891," IOGT arkiv, AI:14, "Equity to Wavrinsky, Feb. 1, 1919," RA-A. Edvard Wavrinsky arkiv, Korresp. 1883–1889, RA-A. "Lewis to Wavrinsky, Feb. 16 1892," Edvard Wavrinsky arkiv, Korresp. Bih. V, vol. V, RA-A. In Russia, see: GARF, f. 115 (Soyuz 17-ogo Oktyabrya), op. 1, d. 19, l. 1; GARF, f. 115, op. 2, d. 16, ll. 1–3, 32; GARF, f. 115, op. 2, d. 18, l. 2; GARF f. 586 (Vycheslav K. Plehve), op. 1, d. 276, l. 6; GARF f. 586, op. 1, d. 375, ll. 1–3; GARF, f. 6996, op. 1, d. 483, ll. 1–6; GARF f. 6996, op. 1, d. 484, ll. 1–11; GARF, f. 579 (Pavel N. Milyukov, 1856–1918), op. 1, d. 2545, l. 1. Linkages with American activists are discussed in greater detail in Chapters 14–17.

84. As written to an aide in London. Adam Hochschild, *King Leopold's Ghost: A Story of Greed, Terror, and Heroism in Colonial Africa* (Boston: Houghton Mifflin Harcourt, 1999), 58. See also: Francesco Spöring, *Mission und Sozialhygiene: Schweizer Anti-Alkohol-Aktivismus im Kontext von Internationalismus und Kolonialismus, 1886–1939* (Göttingen: Wallstein Verlag, 2018), 138.

85. Neal Ascherson, *The King Incorporated: Leopold the Second and the Congo* (London: Granta Books, 1999), 136.

86. Hochschild, *King Leopold's Ghost*, 71–72. "In exchange for that cross the chieftains received from their new white friends bales of cloth, crates of gin, military coats, caps, knives, a livery uniform, or a coral necklace." David Van Reybrouck, *Congo: The Epic History of a People*, trans. Sam Garrett (New York: Ecco, 2015), 51.

87. Henry Morton Stanley, *The Congo and the Founding of Its Free State: A Study of Work and Exploration* (New York: Harper & Brothers, 1885), 158–59. Committee of the Aborigines Protection Society, "'Devil's Work' on the Congo," *Poisoning of Africa Papers* 11, 1895, 2–3: Reel 8, Aborigines Protection Society (A111), Royal Anthropological Institute of Great Britain and Ireland, London, England.

88. Committee of the Aborigines Protection Society, "A Ruinous Trade," *Poisoning of Africa Papers* 4, 1895, 1: Reel 8, Aborigines Protection Society (A111), Royal Anthropological Institute of Great Britain and Ireland, London, England. Also: "Opening-up Africa: Rum-Bottle against Bible," *New York Tribune*, December 3, 1887, 6.

89. Committee of the Aborigines Protection Society, "What Traders Say," *Poisoning of Africa Papers* 6, 1895, 2: Reel 8, Aborigines Protection Society (A111), Royal Anthropological Institute of Great Britain and Ireland, London, England.

90. I Committee of the Aborigines Protection Society, "'Devil's Work' on the Congo," 2; "Opening-Up Africa," 6.

91. "Belgian Kongo," in: Cherrington, ed., *Standard Encyclopedia of the Alcohol Problem*, 303. Hochschild, *King Leopold's Ghost*, 72.

92. Richard Harding Davis, *The Congo and Coasts of Africa* (London: T. Fisher Unwin, 1908), 13. Committee of the Aborigines Protection Society, "Poison for Africans," *Poisoning of Africa*

Papers 1, 1895, 1–2, and Committee of the Aborigines Protection Society, "'Devil's Work' on the Congo," 1.

93. Emile Cauderlier, *Le Gin et le Congo* (Bruxelles: Imp. Lefèvre, 1895), 5. Octave Louwers and Iwan Grenade, *Codes et lois du Congo belge: Textes annotés d'après les rapports du conseil colonial, les instructions officielles et la jurisprudence des tribunaux* (Bruxelles: Weissenbruch, 1923), 519. Giovanni Trolli, *Exposé de la législation sanitaire du Congo belge et du Ruanda-Urundi* (Bruxelles: Ferd. Larcier, 1938), 603.

94. Archdeacon F. W. Farrar, "Africa and the Drink Trade," *Contemporary Review* 52 (July 1887): 45. In: Robert Elliott Speer (1867–1947) Manuscript Collection; Series VII: Clippings and Mimeographed Material. Subject File; Box 122, File 122:4, Princeton Theological Seminary Library, Princeton, NJ.

95. Vleugels, *Narratives of Drunkenness*, 89–90.

96. "Opening-up Africa," 6.

97. Janet L. Polasky, *The Democratic Socialism of Emile Vandervelde: Between Reform and Revolution* (Oxford: Berg Publishers, 1995), 57. On the colonial liquor question from a German perspective, see: Gustav Müller, "Der Branntwein in Kamerun und Togo," *Afrika* 5 (1896): 87–101.

98. David Renton, David Seddon, and Leo Zeilig, *The Congo: Plunder and Resistance* (New York: Zed Books, 2007), 28–31.

99. Jean Stengers, "The Congo Free State and the Belgian Congo before 1914," in *Colonialism in Africa, 1870–1914*, ed. L. H. Gann and Peter Duignan (New York: Cambridge University Press, 1969), 270.

100. H. R. Fox Bourne, *Civilisation in Congoland: A Story of International Wrong-Doing* (London: P. S. King & Son, 1903), 253.

101. Quoted in: Hochschild, *King Leopold's Ghost*, 166.

102. Peter Forbath, *The River Congo: The Discovery, Exploration, and Exploitation of the World's Most Dramatic River* (New York: Houghton Mifflin, 1991), 374.

103. Hochschild, *King Leopold's Ghost* , 224–33.

104. Quoted in: Ibid., 166.

105. Constant De Deken, *Deux Ans au Congo* (Anvers: Clément Thibaut, 1900), 36. Similar reports: Davis, *Congo and Coasts*, 157–58.

106. Vleugels, *Narratives of Drunkenness*, 90. Quoting from: L. Nys, "'De Ruiters van de Apocalyps: 'Alcoholisme, tuberculose, syphilis' en degeneratie in medisch België. 1870–1940," *Tijdschift voor Geschiedenis* 115, no. 1 (2002): 29.

107. Cauderlier, *Le Gin et le Congo*, 5.

108. Vleugels, *Narratives of Drunkenness*, 90. On the Brussels prohibition more generally, see: "Correspondence, 1891: Petitions," 1 in: Woman's Christian Temperance Union Series, Roll 17, Folder 57, WCTU Archive, Evanston, Illinois. John Newton, *Alcohol and Native Races: The Case of Our West African Colonies* (Westminster: The Native Races and the Liquor Traffic United Committee, 1915). Guy Hayler Temperance Tracts, Vol. XXVIII, No. 11, Special Collections, University of Wisconsin–Madison. J. Grant Mills, *The Brussels African Conference, 1890–1891. A Paper Read at the World's Temperance Congress, Chicago, June, 1893, and at the International Congress against the Abuse of Alcoholic Drinks Held at the Hague, August 1893* (London: Native Races and Liquor Traffic United Committee, 1893). Guy Hayler Temperance Tracts, Vol. II, No. 27; *Report of the Special Temperance Conference: Held in the Chamber of Commerce, Manchester, on Nov. 23, 1895* (Manchester: Salford and District Temperance Union, 1895). Guy Hayler Temperance Tracts, Vol. II, No. 6. On Roosevelt: Wilbur F. Crafts et al., *Intoxicating Drinks & Drugs in All Lands and Times* (Washington, DC: International Reform Bureau, 1909), 50–51, 222–25. J. Grant Mills, "Revision of the Brussels General Act, 1890–1891," in: *Bericht über den V. Internationalen Kongress zur Bekämpfung des Missbrauchs geistiger Getränke zu Basel, 20–22 August 1895* (Basel: Schriftstelle des Alkoholgegnerbundes, 1896), 146–51. "Petition to the Senate of the United States," 1891, Folder 57, Reel 17, Woman's Christian Temperance Union Series, Temperance and Prohibition Papers.

109. Arthur Conan Doyle, *The Crime of the Congo* (New York: Doubleday, Page & Company, 1909), 121. See also: Van Reybrouck, *Congo*, 103. When the biennial Congress Against Alcoholism returned to Brussels in 1897, King Leopold II was celebrated with the honorific of "Haut Protecteur." *VIe Congrès international contre l'abus des boissons alcooliques, tenu à Bruxelles du 30 aout au 3 Septembre 1897, Compte-rendu* (Antwerp: L. Braeckmans, 1898), ix. See also: D. Zacher, "Zur Afrikanischen Branntweinfrage," in: *Compte-rendu du XIV Congrès international contre l'alcoolisme, Milan, 22–28 septembre 1913* (Milan: A. Bari, 1921), 219–24.

110. Jean Massart and Émile Vandervelde, *Parasitism: Organic and Social*, trans. William MacDonald (London: Swan Sonnenschein & Co., 1895), 95. Citing: Armand Corre, *Les criminels* (Paris: O. Doin, 1889), 163–70.

111. Pagan Kennedy, *Black Livingstone: A True Tale of Adventure in Nineteenth-Century Congo* (New York: Viking, 2002), 189.

112. "Vandervelde, Émile," in: Ernest H. Cherrington, ed., *Standard Encyclopedia of the Alcohol Problem*, 6 vols., vol. 6 (Westerville, OH: American Issue Press, 1930), 2740–41. On disavowal of violence being more consistent with Marxism than violent means: Terry Eagleton, *Why Marx Was Right* (New Haven, CT: Yale University Press, 2011), 1–29.

113. Emile Vandervelde, *L'alcoolisme et les conditions du travail en Belgique: Rapport presente au VIIe Congres contre l'abus des boissons alcooliques, session de Paris 1899* (Paris: 1900). *VIIe Congrès international contre l'abus des boissons alcooliques, session de Paris, 1899*, 2 vols. (Paris: Au siège social de l'Union française antialcoolique, 1900).

114. Emile Vandervelde, *The Attitude of the Socialist Party toward the Alcohol Question: A Paper Read at the Tenth International Congress against Alcoholism* (Westerville, OH: American Issue Publishing Company, 1907), 12, 16. Original: Emile Vandervelde, "L'attitude des partis socialistes dans la lutte contre l'alcoolisme," in: *Xème Congrès international Contre l'alcoolisme, tenu à Budapest du 11 au 16 septembre 1905, rapports et compte-rendu des sénaces et des réunions,* (Budapest: F. Kilián successeur, 1905), 218–44. Spöring, *Mission und Sozialhygiene*, 103.

115. Vandervelde, *Attitude of the Socialist Party toward the Alcohol Question*, 23.

116. Polasky, *Democratic Socialism of Emile Vandervelde*, 54–55.

117. Emile Vandervelde, *Annales parlementaires, Chambre des députés, Compte rendu analytique*, April 24, 1900, 1129. Cited in: Polasky, *Democratic Socialism of Emile Vandervelde*, 59.

118. Polasky, *Democratic Socialism of Emile Vandervelde*, 62–63. Citing: Emile Vandervelde, "Les Belges et l'etat indépendant du Congo," *Vie Socialiste* (1905).

119. "Letter of King Leopold to the Secretary General," June 3, 1906, in: *Parliamentary Papers, Correspondence Respecting the Independent State of the Congo* (London: Harrison and Sons, 1907), Cd. 3450, 11.

120. Polasky, *Democratic Socialism of Emile Vandervelde*, 74. Also: "Une enquête de M. Todoroff: la vérité sur la Russie (1925)," EV/I/54 in: Articles de presse d'Emile Vandervelde: Salle 3, 321–22, Archives Emile Vandervelde, Archives et Bibliothèque de l'Institut Emile Vandervelde, Brussels, Belgium.

121. Emile Vandervelde, *La Belgique et le Congo: Le passé, le présent, l'avenir* (Paris: Félix Alcan, 1911), 98.

122. Ibid., 95–96, 228–30. See also: Bourne, *Civilisation in Congoland*, 202.

123. Polasky, *Democratic Socialism of Emile Vandervelde*, 79–82.

124. Émile Vandervelde, *Souvenirs d'un militant socialiste* (Paris: Denoël, 1939), 147.

125. Ibid., 143. Polasky, *Democratic Socialism of Emile Vandervelde*, 88. "Suffrage des femmes, 1931," EV/III/120, Dossiers: Salle 3, 324–26, Archives Emile Vandervelde, Archives et Bibliothèque de l'Institut Emile Vandervelde, Brussels, Belgium. Frederick Douglass alluded to this same slate of great reforms a generation earlier. (See Chapter 11.)

126. Polasky, *Democratic Socialism of Emile Vandervelde*, 103–12. On Branting in the Socialist International, see: Per Meurling, "Hjalmar Branting och arbetarinternationalen," in *Bilden av Branting*, ed. Jan Lindhagen (Stockholm: Tidens Förlag, 1975), 322–47.

127. Émile Vandervelde, *Essais socialistes: l'alcoolisme, la religion, l'art* (Paris: Félix Alcan, 1906), 41–101. Émile Vandervelde, *Les socialistes et les bons templiers*, 3rd ed. (Collonges-sous-Salève: Grande Loge franco-belge, 1910), 1–16.

128. Emile Vandervelde, "4e Commission: l'alcoolisme," *Congrès Socialiste International de Vienne (23–29 août 1914): dokuments*, no. 4 (1914): 3–4. Työväenliikkeen kirjasto (Library of the Labour Movement, Helsinki, Finland), 327.322. HELDA 2821715. On different national responses, see: Emanuel Wurm, "4e Commission: l'alcoolisme. La lutte contre les dangers de l'alcool," *Congrès Socialiste International de Vienne (23–29 août 1914): dokuments*, no. 4 (1914): 22–26. Työväenliikkeen kirjasto (Library of the Labour Movement, Helsinki, Finland), 327.322. HELDA 2821715.

129. Wurm, "4e Commission: l'alcoolisme," 9–11.

130. Ibid., 13–16, 27–28.

131. Vandervelde, "4e Commission: l'alcoolisme," 5–7.

132. "En combattant sur le terrain legislatif, le capitalisme alcoolique sous toutes ses formes." Ibid., 7–8.

133. Vandervelde, *Three Aspects of the Russian Revolution*, 206–207.

134. "Belgium," in: Cherrington, ed., *Standard Encyclopedia of the Alcohol Problem*, 315.

135. Polasky, *Democratic Socialism of Emile Vandervelde*, 134–35.

136. Ibid., 113–18. Crafts et al., *Intoxicating Drinks & Drugs*, 220–25.

137. Vandervelde, *Three Aspects of the Russian Revolution*, 226. On Hjalmar Branting's support for Vandervelde, especially in the Congo, see: Hjalmar Branting, "Socialdemokratin, dess uppkomst och utveckling," in *Hjalmar Branting: Tal och skrifter, Vol. II: Socialistisk samhällssyn II* (Stockholm: Tidens Förlag, 1929), 178–79.

138. A. J. Sack, *The Birth of the Russian Democracy* (New York: Russian Information Bureau, 1918), 358–60.

139. The two had differing impressions of their train ride. "Souvenirs de 1917: pourquoi je suis allé en Russie et pas à Stockholm," EV/I/187 in: Articles de presse d'Emile Vandervelde: Salle 3, 321–22, Archives Emile Vandervelde, Archives et Bibliothèque de l'Institut Emile Vandervelde, Brussels, Belgium. On Trotsky's run-ins with the Anti-Saloon League in New York: Kenneth D. Ackerman, *Trotsky in New York, 1917: A Radical on the Eve of Revolution* (Berkeley, CA: Counterpoint Press, 2016), 81. On his revolutionary prohibitionism, see: Mark Lawrence Schrad, *Vodka Politics: Alcohol, Autocracy, and the Secret History of the Russian State* (New York: Oxford University Press, 2014), 211–26. Leon Trotsky, "Vodka, tserkov', i kinematograf," *Pravda*, July 12, 1923. "Gosudarstvo i narodnoe khozyaistvo," *Bor'ba*, no. 2, pp. 3–8, reprinted in: Leon Trotsky, *Sochineniya, tom IV: Politicheskaya khronika* (Moscow: Gosudarstvennoe izdatel'stvo, 1926), 525–33.

140. Sack, *The Birth of the Russian Democracy*, 361. William Henry Chamberlin, *The Russian Revolution, Volume I: 1917–1918* (Princeton, NJ: Princeton University Press, 1987), 155. Vandervelde, *Three Aspects of the Russian Revolution*, 130–31.

141. Vandervelde, *Three Aspects of the Russian Revolution*, 27–28.

142. See: "Le bonhomme Lénine," EV/I/185 in: Articles de presse d'Emile Vandervelde: Salle 3, 321–22, Archives Emile Vandervelde, Archives et Bibliothèque de l'Institut Emile Vandervelde, Brussels, Belgium.

143. Polasky, *Democratic Socialism of Emile Vandervelde*, 148–51. Marc Jansen, *A Show Trial under Lenin: The Trial of the Socialist Revolutionaries* (The Hague: Martinus Nijhoff Publishers, 1982), 38.

144. Emile Vandervelde, "Le chaos Russe," in *Journalisme socialiste* (Brussels: l'Eglantine, 1930), 52. Emile Vandervelde, *L'alternative capitalisme d'état ou socialisme démocratique* (Brussels: L'Eglantine, 1933), 206. Polasky, *Democratic Socialism of Emile Vandervelde*, 156–58.

145. "Convention Relating to the Liquor Traffic in Africa and Protocol. Signed at Saint-Germain-en-Laye, September 10, 1919," Treaty Series No. 19 (London: His Majesty's Stationery Office, 1919), 115–19, in: Box 3, Folder 4, Roll 14, World League Against Alcoholism Papers,

Temperance and Prohibition Papers. See also: Robert Hercod, "Alcoholism as an International Problem," *British Journal of Inebriety* 23, no. 3 (1926): 118.

146. Thomas Karlsson and Esa Österberg, "Belgium," in *Alcohol and Temperance in Modern History, an International Encyclopedia*, ed. Jack Blocker Jr., David Fahey, and Ian Tyrrell (Oxford: ABC-CLIO, 2003), 103–105. Rates of 4.7 liters of pure alcohol in 1900 and 1.2 liters in 2000 were divided by 37.5 percent ABV, the minimum standard for gin.

147. "La loi sur l'alcool et ses résultats," EV/I/35 in: Articles de presse d'Emile Vandervelde. Salle 3, 321–22. Also: "Alcool, 1935–1938," EV/III/6, and "Taxe sur les bieres fortes, 1935," EV/III.121, in: Dossiers. Salle 3, 324–26, Archives Emile Vandervelde, Archives et Bibliothèque de l'Institut Emile Vandervelde, Brussels, Belgium. See also: Rod Phillips, *Alcohol: A History* (Chapel Hill: University of North Carolina Press, 2014), 277. "Belgium," in: Cherrington, ed., *Standard Encyclopedia of the Alcohol Problem*, 316–17.

Chapter 4

1. Mark Lawrence Schrad, *The Political Power of Bad Ideas: Networks, Institutions, and the Global Prohibition Wave* (New York: Oxford University Press, 2010).

2. Gallus Thomann, *The Second International Temperance Congress, Held at Zürich, Switzerland, in the Year 1887* (New York: United States Brewers' Association, 1889), 7. See also: Mark Lawrence Schrad, "Policy Effectiveness in Historical Context: Pre-Prohibition Liquor-Control Studies Revisited," *World Medical and Health Policy* 6, no. 3 (2014): 194.

3. C. J. C. Street, *Thomas Masaryk of Czechoslovakia* (New York: Dodd, Mead & Company, 1930), 135. Vladimir S. Walzel, Frantisek Polak, and Jiri Solar, *T. G. Masaryk: Champion of Liberty* (New York: Research and Studies Center of CFTUF, 1960).

4. Hilsner was frequently described as "mentally inferior" or "mentally deficient" (*schwachsinnig*). See: Daniel M. Vyleta, *Crime, Jews and News: Vienna 1895–1914* (New York: Berghahn Books, 2007), 193.

5. Street, *Thomas Masaryk*, 132–33.

6. Walzel, Polak, and Solar, *T. G. Masaryk*, 15. Street, *Thomas Masaryk*, 135.

7. Seznam přednášek, Alice Masaryk Collection (1879–1966), Box 1, Folder 1, Lilly Research Library, Indiana University, Bloomington. Also: Roman Szporluk, *The Political Thought of Thomas G. Masaryk* (Boulder, CO: East European Monographs, 1981), 122.

8. Patricia Herlihy, *The Alcoholic Empire: Vodka and Politics in Late Imperial Russia* (New York: Oxford University Press, 2002), 112. Citing, in turn: *Izvestiya Tolstovskogo Muzeiya* (St. Petersburg), nos. 3–5 (1911), 11. Herlihy notes: He was the 221st to sign. Antonín Měšťan, "Masaryk on Tolstoy and Gorky," in *T. G. Masaryk (1850–1937), Volume 3: Statesman and Cultural Force*, ed. Harry Hanak (New York: St. Martin's Press, 1990), 150–51. Karel Čapek, *President Masaryk Tells His Story* (London: George Allen & Unwin, Ltd., 1936), 161–66.

9. *Bericht über den VIII. internationalen Congress gegen den Alkoholismus, abgehalten in Wien, 9–14 April 1901* (Leipzig: F. Deuticke, 1902), 232–33.

10. Ibid., 234. Karel Čapek, *Talks with T. G. Masaryk*, trans. Michael Henry Heim (New Haven, CT: Catbird Press, 1995), 238.

11. *Bericht über den VIII. internationalen Congress gegen den Alkoholismus*, 234–35. Masaryk made a similar conclusion in penning a brief foreword to the Czech edition of an antialcohol lecture by Dr. Gustav von Bunge, translated by his daughter, Dr. Alice Masarykova. Gustav von Bunge, *K otázce alkoholu: slovo k dlníkum* (Prague: Nákladem Bratří Suschitzkých ve Vídni, 1906), 4.

12. See: Bruce R. Berglund, *Castle and Cathedral in Modern Prague: Looking for the Sacred in a Skeptical Age* (Budapest: Central European University Press, 2017), 115–25. H. Gordon Skilling, *Mother and Daughter: Charlotte and Alice Masaryk* (Prague: Gender Studies, 2001), 78–79. See also: Josette Baer, *Seven Czech Women: Portraits of Courage, Humanism, and Enlightenment* (Stuttgart: Ibidem-Verlag, 2015), 84, 224. On Fröhlich's temperance socialism,

see: Julius Deutsch, in *Antifascism, Sports, Sobriety: Forging a Militant Working-Class Culture*, ed. Gabriel Kuhn (Oakland, CA: PM Press, 2017), n/p.

13. Letter, Alice Garrigue Masaryková to Charlotte Garrigue Masaryková, October 13, 1906, Thomáš Garrigue Masaryk Collection, Korrespondence III, Box 60, Folder 34, Masarykův ústav a archiv Akademie věd ČR (Masaryk Institute and Archive, Academy of Sciences, Czech Republic).

14. Frank Jacobs, "Distilled Geography: Europe's Alcohol Belts," *Big Think*, July 23, 2010, https:// bigthink.com/strange-maps/442-distilled-geography-europes-alcohol-belts (accessed August 2, 2019).

15. World Health Organization, *Global Status Report on Alcohol and Health* (Geneva: World Health Organization, 2018), 40–45.

16. Mikuláš Teich, *Bier, Wissenschaft und Wirtschaft in Deutschland, 1800–1914* (Vienna: Böhlau Verlag, 2000), 22–24. Also: Birgit Speckle, "'Reinheitsgebot' und 'Chemiebier': Die Auseinandersetzung um das deutsche Reinheitsgebot für Bier aus kulturwissenschaftlicher Sicht," in *Kommunikation und Konflikt: Fallbeispiele aus der Chemie*, ed. Ortwin Renn and Jürgen Hampel (Würzburg: Königshausen und Neumann, 1998), 117.

17. Dr. Seidel, "Der Alkoholismus in Deutschland," *Zeitschrift für die gesamte Staatswissenschaft/ Journal of Institutional and Theoretical Economics* 63, no. 3 (1907): 456–57. I discuss this migration at length in: Mark Lawrence Schrad, *Vodka Politics: Alcohol, Autocracy, and the Secret History of the Russian State* (New York: Oxford University Press, 2014), 70–74.

18. "Germany," in: Ernest H. Cherrington, ed., *Standard Encyclopedia of the Alcohol Problem*, 6 vols., vol. 3 (Westerville, OH: American Issue Press, 1926), 1090–91.

19. Peter T. Winskill, *The Temperance Movement and Its Workers: A Record of Social, Moral, Religious, and Political Progress*, 4 vols., vol. 1 (London: Blackie & Son, Ltd., 1892), 22–23. Also: Mark Lawrence Schrad, "The First Social Policy: Alcohol Control and Modernity in Policy Studies," *Journal of Policy History* 19, no. 4 (2007): 438. Charlemagne himself (742–814) was notoriously strict in rooting out drunkenness among his soldiers, clergy, monks and traders. Frederick III organized an Order of Temperance in 1439, and other, lesser attempts at temperance organization among the higher ranks punctuated the 1500s. "Germany," in: Cherrington, ed., *Standard Encyclopedia of the Alcohol Problem*, 1090–92.

20. James J. Sheehan, *German Liberalism in the Nineteenth Century* (Chicago: University of Chicago Press, 1978), 7–50.

21. Frederic Austin Ogg, *The Governments of Europe* (New York: Macmillan, 1923), 681. See also: Frederic Austin Ogg, *Economic Development of Modern Europe* (New York: Macmillan, 1918), 208.

22. C. F. W. Dieterici, *Statistische Uebersicht der wichtigsten Gegenstände des Verkhers under Verbrauchs im preußischen Staate und im deutschen Zollverbande*, 5 vols., vol. 3 (Berlin: Mittler, 1844), 331–34. Ernst Engel, *Die Branntweinbrennerei in ihren Beziehungen zur Landwirtschaft, zur Steuer und zum öffentlichen Leben* (Dresden: Kuntze, 1853). Friedrich Engels, "Preußischer Schnaps in deutschen Reichstag (1876)," in *Marx-Engels-Werke* (East Berlin: Dietz Verlag, 1962), 39–40.

23. James S. Roberts, "Drink and Industrial Work Discipline in 19th-Century Germany," *Journal of Social History* 15, no. 1 (1981): 27. Lynn Abrams, *Workers' Culture in Imperial Germany: Leisure and Recreation in the Rhineland and Westphalia* (New York: Routledge, 1992), 74. Ogg, *Economic Development*, 63.

24. James S. Roberts, *Drink, Temperance, and the Working Class in Nineteenth-Century Germany* (Boston: George Allen & Unwin, 1984), 16. Also: Engel, *Die Branntweinbrennerei*, 129. Jonathan Sperber, *Rhineland Radicals: The Democratic Movement and the Revolution of 1848– 1849* (Princeton, NJ: Princeton University Press, 1991), 18.

25. Engels, "Preußischer Schnaps," 40–42.

26. Ibid., 46. See also: Lawrence Wilde, "Engels and the Contradictions of Revolutionary Strategy," in *Engels after Marx*, ed. Manfred B. Steger and Terrell Carver (Manchester: Manchester University Press, 1999), 207.

27. Alfred Grotjahn, "Der Alkoholismus nach Wesen, Wirkung und Verbreitung," *Bibliothek für Socialwissenschaft mit besonderer Rücksicht auf sociale Anthropologie und Pathologie* 13 (1898): 327–28. J. H. Böttcher, "Notes on the History of the Temperance Reform in Germany, &C.," in *Proceedings of the International Temperance and Prohibition Convention, Held in London, September 2nd, 3rd, and 4th, 1862*, ed. James C. Street, Frederic Richard Lees, and Dawson Burns (London: Job Caudwell, 1862), 35. Baird was a member not only of the ATS, but also the French Evangelical Association and the Presbyterian missionary American Sunday School Union. Barbara A. Sokolsky, *American Sunday School Union Papers, 1817–1915: A Guide to the Microfilm Edition* (Sanford, NC: Microfilming Corporation of America, 1980), 1.

28. John Allen Krout, *Origins of Prohibition* (New York: Alfred A. Knopf, 1925), 178.

29. Henry M. Baird, *The Life of the Rev. Robert Baird, D.D.* (New York: A.D.F. Randolph, 1866), 106–107.

30. Ibid., 111, 113, 122–24, 135, 156. Robert Baird, *Visit to Northern Europe*, 2 vols., vol. II (New York: John S. Taylor & Co., 1841), 196, 347. David Carnegie, *The Licensing Laws of Sweden: And Some Account of the Great Reduction of Drunkenness in Gothenburg* (Glasgow: Glasgow Philosophical Society, 1872), 2. Robert Baird, *Historisk teckning af nykterhets-föreningarna i Nord-Amerikas Förenta Stater: jemte några upplysningar angående dessa föreningar i andra länder: öfversättning* (Stockholm: S. Rumstedt, 1843).

31. Emphasis in original. Baird, *The Life of the Rev. Robert Baird, D.D.*, 195. "Robert Baird to American Sunday School Union, October 20, 1840, St. Petersburg," in: Presbyterian Historical Society, American Sunday School Union Papers, 1817–1915, Reel 45, Series I, C:1840B, no. 200–202. That social organization in general—and temperance organization in specific—is dependent on domestic political institutions is one of the key theoretic takeaways of my first book: Schrad, *Political Power of Bad Ideas*.

32. As J. H. Böttcher notes, "This want of interest and good example in the nobility, and in those of distinguished position, is felt the more, as the principle of loyalty towards sovereigns is so deeply rooted in the German character that we are accustomed to expect everything from the higher regions." Böttcher, "History of the Temperance Reform," 56. Likewise, see: James J. Sheehan, *The Career of Lujo Brentano: A Study of Liberalism and Social Reform in Imperial Germany* (Chicago: University of Chicago Press, 1966). Roberts, *Drink, Temperance, and the Working Class*, 56.

33. Böttcher, "History of the Temperance Reform," 38. Robert Baird, *Geschichte der Mäßigkeits-Gesellschaft in den Vereinigten Staaten Nord Amerikas* (Berlin: Eichler, 1837). On lodges and numbers: Wilhelm Bode, *Kurze Geschichte der Trinksitten und Mässigkeitsbestrebungen in Deutschland* (Munich: J. F. Lehmann, 1896), 36–37. Grotjahn, "Der Alkoholismus," 328.

34. Böttcher, "History of the Temperance Reform," 42–43.

35. Roberts, *Drink, Temperance, and the Working Class*, 25–27. See also: Krout, *Origins of Prohibition*, 178. "Bekämpfung der Trunksucht, Bd. 1 (1834–1845)," Nr. 9382 in: I. HA Rep. 151 Finanzministerium 06.05.01.11 Alkoholmißbrauch. Geheimes Staatsarchiv Preußischer Kulturbesitz, Berlin.

36. Böttcher, "History of the Temperance Reform," 44.

37. Sperber, *Rhineland Radicals*, 350. Hugh LeCaine Agnew, *The Czechs and the Lands of the Bohemian Crown* (Stanford, CA: Hoover Institution Press, 2004), 117.

38. "Der Mäßigkeitsverein inmitten der politischen Bewegung," *Mäßigkeits-Zeitung* 9, no. 5 (May 1, 1848): 34. Cited in: Roberts, *Drink, Temperance, and the Working Class*, 35–36.

39. "Vorwort," *Der Volksfreund. Monatsblatt des Breslauer Vereines gegen das Branntweintrinken* 3, no. 1 (January 1849): 1. Translated in: Roberts, *Drink, Temperance, and the Working Class*, 34.

40. Roberts, *Drink, Temperance, and the Working Class*, 87. Also: "Bekämpfung der Trunksucht, Bd. 2 (1845–1878)," Nr. 9383 in: I. HA Rep. 151 Finanzministerium 06.05.01.11 Alkoholmißbrauch. Geheimes Staatsarchiv Preußischer Kulturbesitz, Berlin.

41. Otto von Bismarck, "Blut Und Eisen, 30 Sept. 1862," in *Die gesammelten Werke. Bd. 10. Reden: 1847–1869*, ed. Wilhelm Schüßler (Berlin: Verlag für Politik und Wirtschaft, 1928), 139–40.

42. Giles MacDonagh, *The Last Kaiser: The Life of Wilhelm II* (New York: St. Martin's Press, 2000), 42–44.

43. Lothar Gall, *Otto Von Bismarck und die Parteien* (Paderborn: F. Schöningh, 2001), 146. Christopher Clark, *Kaiser Wilhelm II: A Life in Power* (New York: Penguin Books, 2009), 40–47.

44. Hannah Catherine Davies, *Transatlantic Speculations: Globalization and the Panics of 1873* (New York: Columbia University Press, 2018), 110–11. Gerhard Masur, *Imperial Berlin* (New York: Basic Books, 1971), 64–65. Steinberg, *Bismarck: A Life*, 330–32.

45. Peter-Christian Witt, *Die Finanzpolitik des deutschen Reichs von 1903 bis 1913* (Lübeck: Matthiesen, 1970), 44–54. Hans-Ulrich Wehler, *Das deutsche Kaiserreich, 1871–1918*, 2nd ed. (Göttingen: Vandenhoek & Ruprecht, 1975), 142–46. Hans Rosenberg, *Große Depression und Bismarckzeit: Wirtschaftsablauf, Gesellschaft und Politik in Mitteleuropa* (Berlin: de Gruyter, 1967), 69–91. James S. Roberts, "Drink and the Labour Movement: The Schnaps Boycott of 1909," in *The German Working Class, 1888–1933: The Politics of Everyday Life*, ed. Richard J. Evans (London: Croom Helm, 1982), 80–107.

46. Roberts, *Drink, Temperance, and the Working Class*, 77–79.

47. Vernon L. Lidtke, *The Outlawed Party: Social Democracy in Germany, 1878–1890* (Princeton, NJ: Princeton University Press, 1966), 70–81. James S. Roberts, "Wirtshaus und Politik in der deutschen Arbeiterbewegung," in *Socialgeschichte der Freizeit*, ed. Gerhard Huck (Wuppertal: Hammar, 1980), 130.

48. "Das schadet nichts. Die weite Verbreitung des Bieres ist zu beklagen. Es macht dumm, faul und impotent. Es ist Schuld an der demokratischen Kannegießerei, zu der sie sich dabei zusammensetzen. Ein guter Kornbranntwein wäre vorzuziehen." Moritz Busch, *Graf Bismarck und seine Leute während des Kriegs mit Frankreich*, 4th ed., 2 vols., vol. 1 (Leipzig: Wilhelm Grunow, 1878), 17. See also: Gallus Thomann, *Some Thoughts on the International Temperance Meeting, Held at Antwerp in September, 1885* (New York: United States Brewers' Association, 1886), 35.

49. MacDonagh, *Last Kaiser*, 114–24.

50. Clark, *Kaiser Wilhelm II*, 50-65.

51. Wilhelm Bode, "August Lammers." *Nordwest* 16, no. 1, cited in: Arved Emminghaus, *August Lammers: Lebensbild eines deutschen Publizisten und Pioner der Gemeinnützigkeit aus der zweiten Hälfte des Vorigen Jahrhunderts* (Dresden: Böhmert, 1908), 158–59. Bode, *Kurze Geschichte*, 111–13.

52. Gøsta Esping-Anderson, *Three Worlds of Welfare Capitalism* (Princeton, NJ: Princeton University Press, 1990), 59–60. Theda Skocpol, *Protecting Soldiers and Mothers: The Political Origins of Social Policy in the United States* (Cambridge, MA: Belknap Press of Harvard University Press, 1992), 160. Seidel, "Alkoholismus in Deutschland," 467–71.

53. Abraham Baer, *Der Alkoholismus: Seine Verbreitung und seine Wirkung auf den Individuellen und socialen Organismus sowie die Mittel, Ihn zu Bekämpfen* (Berlin: Hirschwald, 1878), 528–45 Roberts, *Drink, Temperance, and the Working Class*, 48–52.

54. Baer, *Der Alkoholismus*, 425–80.

55. Or: the D.V.g.d.M.g.G., as it was abbreviated. Here, we'll just refer to it as the *Verein*, or association. Grotjahn, "Der Alkoholismus," 344. Christian Stubbe, *Der Deutsche Verein gegen den Mißbrauch geistiger Getränke, 1883–1908* (Berlin: Mäßigkeitsverlag, 1908), 11–15. Wilhelm Martius, *Die zweite deutsche Mäßigkeitsbewegung, oder der deutsche Verein gegen Mißbrauch geistiger Getränke und die Enthaltsamkeitsvereine* (Heilbronn: Henninger, 1886), 1–16. "Germany" in: Cherrington, ed., *Standard Encyclopedia of the Alcohol Problem*, 1095.

56. Grotjahn, "Der Alkoholismus," 339–40. The main archives of the Deutscher Verein gegen den Mißbrauch geistiger Getränke—later Deutscher Verein gegen den Alkoholismus—were destroyed by fire during World War II in either 1944 or 1945. Robert N. Proctor, *The Nazi War on Cancer* (Princeton, NJ: Princeton University Press, 1999), 318, n. 64.

57. Karl Kautsky, "Der Alkoholismus und seine Bekämpfung," *Die Neue Zeit 9*, pt. 1, no. 27–30 (1890/1): 40.

58. Moritz Theodor Wilhelm Bromme, *Lebensgeschichte eines modernen Fabrikarbeiters* (Jena: Diedrichs, 1905), 267.

59. Kautsky, "Der Alkoholismus," 107–108. Also: Karl Kautsky, "Noch einmal die Alkoholfrage," *Die Neue Zeit 9*, pt. 2, no. 37 (1890/1). On the taverns as necessary to the socialist movement, see James S. Roberts, "The Tavern and Politics in the German Labor Movement, c. 1870–1914," in *Drinking: Behavior and Belief in Modern History*, ed. Susanna Barrows and Robin Room (Berkeley: University of California Press, 1991), 101–108.

60. Roberts, *Drink, Temperance, and the Working Class*, 64. Also: Ulrich Linse, "Die Lebensreformbewegungen," *Archiv für Sozialgeschichte* 17 (1977): 538–43.

61. See: "Handakten von Senator C. H. Schemmann mit Tagesordnungen der Sitzungen der Behörde für das Schankkonzessionswesen und Materialien für Entscheidungen in Schankkonzessionssachen," and "Gast- und Schankwirtschaften sowie Kleinhandlungen mit Spirituosen in Geesthacht (1898–1926)," 5, in: Schankkonzessionswesen (1898–1926) 376-4, Staatsarchiv Hamburg.

62. Roberts, *Drink, Temperance, and the Working Class*, 69–70.

63. Wilhelm Bode, *An die Politiker* (Hildesheim: Selbstverlag des Verfassers, 1898), 4, 12. Stubbe, *Der deutsche Verein*, 64.

64. See: "Liebesgaben: Sammlung von Geldspenden und Liebesgaben für Feldtruppen und Lazarette," CI x 5a, in: Senat-Kriegsakten (1888–1940) 111-2, Staatsarchiv Hamburg.

65. Margaret MacMillan, *The War That Ended Peace: The Road to 1914* (New York: Random House, 2014), 83–141. MacDonagh, *Last Kaiser*, 2.

66. Roberts, *Drink, Temperance, and the Working Class*, 79–81. Wilhelm Gerloff, *Die Finanz- und Zollpolitik des Deutschen Reichs* (Jena: Fischer, 1913), 521. See also: "Deutscher Verein gegen den Mißbrauch geistiger Getränke. Bekämpfung der Animierkneipen (1908–1909)," 2, in: Schankkonzessionswesen (1898–1926) 376-4, Staatsarchiv Hamburg.

67. Ernest Gordon, *The Anti-Alcohol Movement in Europe* (New York: Fleming H. Revel Company, 1913), 160.

68. Sandra Halperin, *War and Social Change in Modern Europe: The Great Transformation Revisited* (New York: Cambridge University Press, 2004), 376. Charles Tilly, Louise Tilly, and Richard H. Tilly, *The Rebellious Century, 1830–1930* (Cambridge, MA: Harvard University Press, 1975), 311.

69. "Vom Bierkrieg," *Vorwärts*, August 27 and September 8, 1909. See: Roberts, "Drink and the Labour Movement."

70. "Zwei Kulturaufgaben," *Vorwärts*, September 15, 1909. Roberts, *Drink, Temperance, and the Working Class*, 99, 105.

71. Consumption totaled 16.2 million gallons from October 1909 to February 1910; 23.6 million gallons were consumed during the same time frame the previous year. Guy Hayler, *Prohibition Advance in All Lands; a Study of the World-Wide Character of the Drink Question*, 2nd ed. (London: International Prohibition Confederation, 1914), 87.

72. Walther G. Hoffman, Franz Grumbach, and Helmut Hesse, *Das Wachstum der Deutschen Wirtschaft seit der Mitte des 19. Jahrhunderts* (Berlin: Springer, 1965), 172–74, 650–54. Switzerland Bureau fédéral de statistique, *Question de l'alcoolisme. Exposé comparatif des lois et des expériences de quelques états étrangers, par le bureau fédéral de statistique* (Berne: Imprimerie K.-J. Wyss, 1884), 672. Roberts, *Drink, Temperance, and the Working Class*, 44, 109. Spirits consumption dropped from six liters of pure alcohol per person annually to around three.

73. Roberts, *Drink, Temperance, and the Working Class*, 117–24. Birgit Speckle, *Streit ums Bier in Bayern: Wertvorstellungen um Reinheit, Gemeinschaft und Tradition* (Münster: Waxman Verlag, 2001). Hayler presents dueling perspectives on the German beer hall: Hayler, *Prohibition Advance in All Lands*, 87.

74. Erich Flade, *Der Kampf gegen den Alkoholismus—Ein Kampf für unser deutsches Volkstum* (Berlin: Mäßigkeitsverlag, 1905), 20.

75. Arthur Esche, "Der Alkohol im Wettkampf der Völker," *Mäßigkeits-Blätter* 29, no. 12 (1912): 181. Roberts, *Drink, Temperance, and the Working Class*, 68.

76. Frederick McCormick, *Tragedy of Russia in Pacific Asia*, 2 vols. (New York: Outing, 1907), 1:27, 2:278–82. Ernest Barron Gordon, *Russian Prohibition* (Westerville, OH: American Issue Publishing Company, 1916), 8.

77. Vinkentii V. Veresaev, *In the War: Memoirs of V. Veresaev*, trans. Leo Winter (New York: Mitchell Kennerley, 1917), 23. Joshua A. Sanborn, *Drafting the Russian Nation: Military Conscription, Total War, and Mass Politics, 1905–1925* (DeKalb: Northern Illinois University Press, 2003), 13.

78. Richard Michael Connaughton, *The War of the Rising Sun and Tumbling Bear: A Military History of the Russo-Japanese War, 1904–5* (New York: Routledge, 1991), 246. Contstantine Pleshakov, *The Tsar's Last Armada: The Epic Voyage to the Battle of Tsushima* (New York: Basic Books, 2003), 98.

79. Pleshakov, *Tsar's Last Armada*, 98–99. Sydney Tyler, *The Japan-Russia War* (Philadelphia: P. W. Ziegler Co., 1905), 364. On the incident more generally, see: Schrad, *Vodka Politics*, 160–68.

80. Ernest Poole, "Two Russian Soldiers," *The Outlook*, September 2, 1905, 21–22. Herlihy, *The Alcoholic Empire*, 52.

81. Jack Snyder, *The Ideology of the Offensive: Military Decision Making and the Disasters of 1914* (Ithaca, NY: Cornell University Press, 1984), 79–81. Stephen Van Evera, "The Cult of the Offensive and the Origins of the First World War," *International Security* 9, no. 1 (1984).

82. Schrad, *Political Power of Bad Ideas*.

83. Marr Murray, *Drink and the War from the Patriotic Point of View* (London: Chapman and Hall, 1915). A. W. Harris, "A Compensation of the War," *Union Signal*, June 8, 1916, 5. George Snow, "Alcoholism in the Russian Military: The Public Sphere and the Temperance Discourse, 1883–1917," *Jahrbücher für Geschichte Osteuropas* 45, no. 3 (1997): 428–29. Vladimir P. Nuzhnyi, *Vino v zhizni i zhizn' v vine* (Moscow: Sinteg, 2001), 234. On the history of the German military liquor rations, see: Bode, *Kurze Geschichte*, 68. In the Austro-Hungarian military, see: "Austria-Hungary," in: Ernest H. Cherrington, ed., *Standard Encyclopedia of the Alcohol Problem*, 6 vols., vol. 1 (Westerville, OH: American Issue Press, 1925), 238. Hayler, *Prohibition Advance in All Lands*, 96.

84. Hayler, *Prohibition Advance in All Lands*, 84.

85. "Kaiser Wilhelm Seeks to Curb Drink Evil," *Union Signal*, September 25, 1913. Gordon, *The Anti-Alcohol Movement in Europe*, 325–26.

86. Peter L. Bark, "Memoirs," Sir Peter Bark Papers, Leeds Russian Archive, Special Collections, Leeds University Library (n/d), chap. 9, p. 21. Alfred Knox, *With the Russian Army, 1914–1917*, 2 vols., vol. 1 (London: Hutchinson & Co., 1921), 39. As it turns out, while faster than in 1905, the Russian mobilization was rocked with just as much drunken violence as before. State Archives of the Russian Federation (GARF), f. 102 (Departament politsii, 4-oe deloproizvodstvo), op. 1914, d. 138, "Obezporyadkakh zapisnykh nishnikh chinov prizvannykh na voinu," ll. 24–120. GARF, f. 102, op. 1914, d. 138, ll. 100–105. Russian State Historical Archives (RGIA), f. 1292, op. 1, d. 1729. Joshua A. Sanborn, "The Mobilization of 1914 and the Question of the Russian Nation: A Reexamination," *Slavic Review* 59, no. 2 (2000): 277.

87. Schrad, *Political Power of Bad Ideas*, 195–97. Mark Lawrence Schrad, "Myth: Prohibition Was Uniquely American," in *Prohibition's Greatest Myths: The Distilled Truth about America's*

Anti-Alcohol Crusade, ed. Michael Lewis and Richard F. Hamm (Baton Rouge: Louisiana State University Press, 2020), 106–30.

88. Jens Boysen, "How the Great War Changed the Mental Map of the Prussian Poles," in *Nations, Identities and the First World War: Shifting Loyalties to the Fatherland*, ed. Nico Wouters and Laurence van Ypersele (London: Bloomsbury Academic, 2018), 86.

89. Here using the 1910 census as a baseline. Volker R. Berghahn, *Imperial Germany, 1871– 1914: Economy, Society, Culture and Politics* (Providence, RI: Berghahn Books, 1994), 102–103.

90. A. J. P. Taylor, *The Habsburg Monarchy, 1809–1918* (Chicago: University of Chicago Press, 1976), 263–71. "Volkszählung vom 31. Dezember 1910," in *Geographischer Atlas zur Vaterlandskunde an der österreichischen Mittelschulen* (Vienna: Kartographische Anstalt G. Freytag & Berndt, 1911). See also: Solomon Wank, "The Habsburg Empire," in *After Empire: Multiethnic Societies and Nation-Building*, ed. Karen Barkey and Mark von Hagen (Boulder, CO: Westview Press, 1997), 45–49.

91. Gunther E. Rothenberg, *The Army of Francis Joseph* (West Lafayette, IN: Purdue University Press, 1998), 35.

92. Lajos Kossuth, *Authentic Life of His Excellency Louis Kossuth, Governor of Hungary* (London: Bradbury and Evans, 1851), 17–32, 126–27. *Louis Kossuth and the Lost Revolutions in Hungary and Transylvania* (London: John Rodwell, 1850), 276–91.

93. William M. Johnston, *The Austrian Mind: An Intellectual and Social History, 1848–1938* (Berkeley: University of California Press, 1983), 38.

94. "Austria," in: Cherrington, ed., *Standard Encyclopedia of the Alcohol Problem*, 230. On the nineteenth-century expansion of lager beer into traditionally wine-producing regions of the Kingdom of Hungary and Vojvodina, see: Anica Tufegdžić and Mirjana Roter Blagojević, "Golden Era of Lager Breweries in the Southern Austro-Hungarian Empire," *Industrial Archaeology Review* 37, no. 1 (2015): 34–38. On the spirits-producing regions, see: Sophie Daszinska-Golinska, "Die industrielle Spiritusverwendung als Mittel zur Bekämpfung des Alkoholismus," in: *Xème Congrès international contre l'alcoolisme, tenu à Budapest du 11 au 16 septembre 1905, rapports et compte-rendu des sénaces et des réunions*, (Budapest: F. Kilián successeur, 1905), 178–81.

95. "Austria," in: Cherrington, ed., *Standard Encyclopedia of the Alcohol Problem*, 234–35.

96. Stephen Howe, *Empire: A Very Short Introduction* (New York: Oxford University Press, 2002), 56.

97. Deutsch, "Antifascism, Sports, Sobriety," n/p. Also: "Oesterreichischer Verein Gegen Trunksucht," in: Ernest H. Cherrington, ed., *Standard Encyclopedia of the Alcohol Problem*, 6 vols., vol. 5 (Westerville, OH: American Issue Press, 1929), 2042. Hayler, *Prohibition Advance in All Lands*, 95.

98. Otto von Komorzynski, *Die Gewerbe-Ordnung samt den sie ergänzenden und erläuternden Gesetzen* (Vienna: Manzsche k.u.k. hof-verlags- und universitätsbuchhandlung, 1908), 2:205– 32. "Austria," in: Cherrington, ed., *Standard Encyclopedia of the Alcohol Problem*, 230–34.

99. "Austria," in: Cherrington, ed., *Standard Encyclopedia of the Alcohol Problem*, 235.

100. Hayler, *Prohibition Advance in All Lands*, 96. "Austria-Hungary," in: Cherrington, ed., *Standard Encyclopedia of the Alcohol Problem*, 238.

101. Street, *Thomas Masaryk*, 91–92. "Pravda vitezi," at 281. Walzel, Polak, and Solar, *T. G. Masaryk*, 9–10.

102. Street, *Thomas Masaryk*, 79.

103. Měšťan, "Masaryk on Tolstoy and Gorky," 150–51. Quoting from the third, unfinished volume: Tomáš Garrigue Masaryk, in *The Spirit of Russia, Volume 3*, ed. George Gibian (London: George Allen & Unwin, 1967), 196. More generally: Tomáš Garrigue Masaryk, *Russland und Europa: Studien über die geistigen Strömungen in Russland*, 2 vols., vol. 1 (Jena: Diederichs, 1913), 5. Přemysl Pitter, *Chelčický, Tolstoi, Masaryk* (Prag: Verlag der Deutschen Gesellschaft für Sittliche Erziehung, 1931), 11–14.

104. Herlihy, *The Alcoholic Empire*, 112. Citing, in turn: *Izvestiya Tolstovskogo Muzeiya* (St. Petersburg), nos. 3–5 (1911), 11. Walzel, Polak, and Solar, *T. G. Masaryk*, 14. Masaryk's magisterial two-volume investigation, *Russia and Europe*, understandably has some rather in-depth consideration of Tolstoy's politics, especially as they regard Marxism and anarchism. Masaryk, *Russland und Europa*, 1:129; 2:210, 68–69, 380–82.

105. Street, *Thomas Masaryk*, 104–16.

106. Eva Schmidt-Hartmann, *Thomas G. Masaryk's Realism: Origins of a Czech Political Concept* (Oldenbourg: R. Oldenbourg Verlag, 1984), 150.

107. Tomáš Garrigue Masaryk, *O alkoholismu: Předneseno v dělnickém domě na vsetíně dne 11. září 1905*, 2nd ed. (V Praze: Pokrok, 1908), 3.

108. Adding, "I hold the fight against alcoholism to be one of the most important parts of my personal work." Gordon, *The Anti-Alcohol Movement in Europe*, 157. Similarly, see: Böttcher, "History of the Temperance Reform," 52.

109. Masaryk, *O alkoholismu*, 4–5.

110. Emphasis in original: "*národ pijanův je národem otroků!*" (ibid., 13).

111. Ibid., 14–16.

112. Tomáš Garrigue Masaryk, *O ethice a alkoholismu* (Praha: Tiskem A. Reise, 1912), 8–10. See also: Gordon, *The Anti-Alcohol Movement in Europe*, 315-16.

113. Masaryk, *O ethice a alkoholismu*, 12. Similarly, see Masaryk's foreword in: Bunge, *K otázce alkoholu: Slovo k dlníkum*, 4.

114. Masaryk, *O ethice a alkoholismu*, 16–17, 24.

115. Čapek, *Masaryk Tells His Story*, 229–30.

116. Jaroslav Hašek, *The Good Soldier Švejk*, trans. Cecil Parrott (New York: Everyman's Library, 1993), xii–xxiii.

117. Street, *Thomas Masaryk*, 166–78.

118. "Dr. Masaryk, Who Awaits Military Trial for Treason in Austria, a Pioneer Prohibition Worker," *Union Signal*, May 18, 1916, 8.

119. "Telegram to the Czechoslovak Army in Russia, 1918," in: Thomas G. Masaryk Papers, Box 1, Folder 3, University of Pittsburgh Archives. Čapek, *Masaryk Tells His Story*, 256–65.

120. Kevin J. McNamara, *Dreams of a Great Small Nation: The Mutinous Army That Threatened a Revolution, Destroyed an Empire, Founded a Republic, and Remade the Map of Europe* (New York: PublicAffairs, 2016), 100, 127–28.

121. Ibid. Also: Joan McGuire Mohr, *The Czech and Slovak Legion in Siberia, 1917–1922* (Jefferson, NC: McFarland & Company, 2012). "Telegram to the Czechoslovak Army in Russia, 1918," in: Thomas G. Masaryk Papers, Box 1, Folder 3, University of Pittsburgh Archives.

122. Street, *Thomas Masaryk*, 223.

123. Letter to President Wilson on the Mid-European Union, November 1, 1918, Box 1, Folder 8, Thomas G. Masaryk Papers, University of Pittsburgh Archives. Walzel, Polak, and Solar, *T. G. Masaryk*, 22–25.

124. Herbert Francis Sherwood, "A New Declaration of Independence," *The Outlook* 120 (1918): 406–407. Mark Mazower, *Dark Continent: Europe's Twentieth Century* (New York: Vintage Books, 1998), 6, 26. "Interview with an Unidentified English Journalist, 1918," Box 1, Folder 11, pp. 1, 4, 8, Thomas G. Masaryk Papers, University of Pittsburgh Archives.

125. Elizabeth Putnam Gordon, *Women Torch-Bearers: The Story of the Woman's Christian Temperance Union* (Evanston, IL: National Woman's Christian Temperance Union Publishing House, 1924), 78. "Czechoslovakia," in: Ernest H. Cherrington, ed., *Standard Encyclopedia of the Alcohol Problem*, 6 vols., vol. 2 (Westerville, OH: American Issue Press, 1924), 751. Jaroslav J. Zmrhal, "Temperance Education in Czecho-Slovakia," 1920, 1: Box 3a, Folder 31, Reel 18, World League Against Alcoholism Records, Temperance and Prohibition Papers, Ohio Historical Society.

126. Čapek, *Talks with T. G. Masaryk*, 238. Elizabeth P. Gordon, "Co-Operation with Czecho-Slovakia," *Union Signal*, March 18, 1920, 4.

127. Miklós Molnár, *A Concise History of Hungary* (New York: Cambridge University Press, 2001), 262. István Deák, "The Habsburg Empire," in *After Empire: Multiethnic Societies and Nation-Building*, ed. Karen Barkey and Mark von Hagen (Boulder, CO: Westview Press, 1997), 133.

128. Jenö Pongrácz, ed., *A Forradalmi Kormányzótanács és a népbiztosságok rendeletei*, vol. 1: 1919. március 21.–április 9. (Budapest: Proletárjog, 1919), 13.

129. Piroska Munkácsi, *A Magyar Tanácsköztarsaság plakátjai az Országos Szechényi Könyvtárban* (Budapest: Országos Széchényi Könyvtár, 1959), 194. Cited in: Frank Eckelt, "*The Rise and Fall of the Béla Kun Regime in 1919*" (PhD dissertation, New York University, 1966), 221. See also: "Budapest's Bolshevist Posters: 'Alcohol Is Dead, Don't Let It Come to Life,'" *Union Signal*, February 19, 1920, 12.

130. K. Pándy, "Report of General Secretary of the Hungarian League Against Alcoholism," 1924: Box 4, Folder 33, Roll 22, World League Against Alcoholism Records, Temperance and Prohibition Papers, Ohio Historical Society.

131. L. S. Eremina and Arsenii B. Rogniskii, eds., *Rasstrel'nye spiski: Moskva, 1937–1941* (Moskva: Obshchestvo "Memorial": Zven'ya, 2000), 229. "Kun, Bela Morisovich," in: *Otkrytyi spisok*, Memorial. https://ru.openlist.wiki/Кун_Бела_Морисович_(1886) (accessed August 21, 2019).

132. Karl Polanyi, *The Great Transformation: The Political and Economic Origins of Our Time* (Boston: Beacon, 1944), 298. Gareth Dale, "Karl Polanyi in Vienna," *Historical Materialism* 22, no. 1 (2014): 38.

133. William E. Johnson, "That House with One Thousand Rooms" (undated manuscript), 1–4, Box 3, Folder 27, Roll 15, World League Against Alcoholism Papers, Temperance and Prohibition Papers, Ohio Historical Society, Columbus.

134. Ibid. On temperance *Gemeindebauen*, see: Christoph Mandl, *Wiener Wohn-Sinn: Gemeindebauten in Wien von Anbeginn bis Heute* (Hamburg: Tradition GmbH, 2016). "Matteottihof," *Wien Geschichte Wiki*, https://www.geschichtewiki.wien.gv.at/Matteottihof (accessed June 12, 2020).

135. Polanyi, *Great Transformation*, 299. See also: Santhi Hejeebu and Deirdre McCloskey, "The Reproving of Karl Polanyi," *Critical Review* 13, no. 3–4 (1999): 304.

Chapter 5

1. "London Daily Mail Imagined It Saw an 'American Invasion Plot' and Set All England into Furor of Excitement over Prohibition," *American Issue*, November 17, 1919, Box 3a, Folder 39, Roll 19, and "Additional Facts Relating to Attack on Johnson by London Medical Students," *American Issue*, January 3, 1920, Box 3a, Folder 40, Roll 19, World League Against Alcoholism Series, Temperance and Prohibition Papers, Ohio Historical Society, Columbus.

2. "The Tiger Claws of 'Pussyfoot' Johnson," *Literary Digest*, May 1, 1926, 38. Fred Lockley, "'Pussyfoot' Johnson," *Overland Monthly and Out West Magazine* 90, no. 2 (1932): 49. "Agent Cheerful over Plot to Kill Him. Government Agent Reports in an Unconcerned Way of Plans to Remove Him," *Philadelphia Inquirer*, 1907, 9. "Keeping Rum from Indians. Outlaws Put Price on Head of United States Special Officer," *Philadelphia Inquirer*, 1907, 2.

3. William E. Johnson, "*Confessions of 'Pussyfoot' Johnson*," (Cooperstown, NY: Fenimore Art Museum Library, n/d), XIII, 4–5.

4. Ibid., XIII, 21.

5. "Mr. 'Pussyfoot' Captured and Paraded," *The Times*, November 14, 1919, 12.

6. Johnson, "Confessions," XIII, 21. Also: "Mob 'Pussyfoot' in London Streets," *New York Times*, November 14, 1919. http://query.nytimes.com/mem/archive-free/pdf?res=9D0CE5DB1F 3BEE3ABC4C52DFB7678382609EDE (accessed October 3, 2014).

7. Gillian Orr, "Bad Behaviour That's All in a Good Cause: Students Are Carrying On the Rag Tradition," *Independent*, February 2, 2012. https://www.independent.co.uk/news/education/higher/bad-behaviour-thats-all-in-a-good-cause-students-are-carrying-on-the-rag-tradition-6298083.html (accessed June 1, 2018).

8. Johnson, "Confessions," XIII, 21. "Mr. 'Pussyfoot' Captured and Paraded," 12.

9. Johnson, "Confessions," XIII, 23.

10. Ibid.

11. MEPO 2/1961, 21A, Records of the Metropolitan Police Office, National Archives (UK), Kew.

12. Johnson, "Confessions," XIII, 24.

13. Ibid., XIII, 24. National Archives (UK), Kew, Records of the Metropolitan Police Office, MEPO 2/1961. "Mr. 'Pussyfoot' Captured and Paraded," 12.

14. "Mr. 'Pussyfoot's' Injured Eye," *The Times*, November 15, 1919, 9. Records of the Metropolitan Police Office, MEPO 2/1961, National Archives (UK), Kew. Circular Letter from the chairman of Barclay, Perkins and Co. Ltd. to Its Shareholders, December 31, 1919. Reference 789/617, City of Westminster Archives Centre. Also: "Mr. 'Pussyfoot' Captured and Paraded," 12. Johnson, "Confessions," XIV, 1.

15. Johnson, "Confessions," XIII, 25. See also: Tarini Prasad Sinha, *"Pussyfoot" Johnson and His Campaign in Hindustan* (Madras: Ganesh & Co., 1922), 69.

16. Johnson, "Confessions," XIII, 27.

17. "England," in: Ernest H. Cherrington, ed., *Standard Encyclopedia of the Alcohol Problem*, 6 vols., vol. 3 (Westerville, OH: American Issue Press, 1926), 910–39. Of particular interest was the Leadhills Association, a Scottish community's opposition to distillation in 1760. See: Ernest H. Cherrington, ed., *Standard Encyclopedia of the Alcohol Problem*, 6 vols., vol. 5 (Westerville, OH: American Issue Press, 1929), 2386.

18. T. A. Jenkins, *Parliament, Party and Politics in Victorian Britain* (Manchester: Manchester University Press, 1996), 32.

19. David W. Gutzke, "The Social Status of Landed Brewers in Britain since 1840," *Histoire sociale/Social History* 17, no. 33 (1984): 104–107. David W. Gutzke, *Protecting the Pub: Brewers and Publicans against Temperance* (Woodbridge, Suffolk: The Royal Historical Society/Boydell Press, 1989), 25. David W. Gutzke, *Pubs & Progressives: Reinventing the Public House in England* (DeKalb: Northern Illinois University Press, 2006), 26–27.

20. Jenkins, *Parliament, Party and Politics*, 73. Elizabeth Malcolm, *"Ireland Sober, Ireland Free": Drink and Temperance in Nineteenth-Century Ireland* (Syracuse, NY: Syracuse University Press, 1986), 169.

21. Lilian Lewis Shiman, *Crusade against Drink in Victorian England* (New York: St. Martin's Press, 1988), 9. Brian Harrison suggests this is because Scotland and Northern Ireland were not affected by the 1830 Beer Act, which lowered duties in an effort to promote beer production at the expense of distilled spirits. Brian Harrison, *Drink and the Victorians: The Temperance Question in England, 1815–1872* (London: Faber and Faber, 1971), 87. This approach turns on its head conventional British temperance histories, which seek to explain Scotland as anomalous, rather than the English metropole. See, for example: David W. Gutzke, "Progressivism in Britain and Abroad," in *Britain and Transnational Progressivism*, ed. David W. Gutzke (New York: Palgrave Macmillan, 2008), 49.

22. "Mrs. Nation's Campaign," *The Times* (London), January 26, 1909, 6. Fran Grace, *Carry A. Nation: Retelling the Life* (Bloomington: Indiana University Press, 2001), 255–56.

23. Bernard Aspinwall, "Democracy and Drink," in *Britain and Transnational Progressivism*, ed. David W. Gutzke (New York: Palgrave Macmillan, 2008), 102.

24. Dawson Burns, *Temperance History: A Consecutive Narrative of the Rise, Development and Extension of the Temperance Reform*, 2 vols., vol. 2 (London: National Temperance Publication Depot, 1889), 106. Total Abstinence Society, "Temperance Reformation in Scotland: With Special Reference to John Dunlop and Greenock: A Century of Work and

Progress, 1829–1929" (paper presented at the Scottish Temperance Movement: Centenary Celebrations, Greenock, Scotland, October 20–21, 1929).

25. "Scotland," in: Cherrington, ed., *Standard Encyclopedia of the Alcohol Problem*, 2388.

26. John Dunlop, *On the Extent and Remedy of National Intemperance* (Glasgow: William Collins, 1829), 28–29. Samuel Couling, *History of the Temperance Movement in Great Britain and Ireland; from the Earliest Date to the Present Time* (London: William Tweedie, 1862), 34–35. See also: Harrison, *Drink and the Victorians*, 101.

27. Aspinwall, "Democracy and Drink," 107.

28. Scotsman Henry Forbes established the first English society in Bradford. Shiman, *Crusade against Drink*, 12. James Weston, *Joseph Livesey: The Story of His Life, 1794–1884* (London: S. W. Partridge & Co., 1884), 50–51. Ruth Elizabeth Spence, *Prohibition in Canada* (Toronto: Ontario Branch of the Dominion Alliance, 1919), 516.

29. Irene Maver, "Dunlop, John (1789–1868)," in *Alcohol and Temperance in Modern History: An International Encyclopedia*, ed. Jack Blocker Jr., David Fahey, and Ian Tyrrell (Santa Barbara, CA: ABC-CLIO, 2003), 214.

30. John Dunlop, *The Philosophy and System of Artificial and Compulsory Drinking Usage in Great Britain and Ireland* (London: Houlston and Stoneman, 1939), 256–57.

31. Shiman, *Crusade against Drink*, 22. In Ireland, the Irish Temperance Union coordinated teetotal organizations. Kohl claims that " 'Teetotal' is, however, an old Irish word in general use, which signifies *entirely*, as 'he is teetotally ruined.' " J. G. Kohl, *Travels in Ireland* (London: Bruce and Wyld, 1844), 108.

32. Shiman, *Crusade against Drink*, 109, 174-201. I.O.G.T., *The Leading Temperance Organisation in the World* (Birmingham: I.O.G.T. Grand Lodge of England, 1890[?]). Guy Hayler— Temperance Tracts (University of Wisconsin), Vol. XI, No. 78.

33. Malcolm, "*Ireland Sober, Ireland Free*," 331–33.

34. One 1848 account boasts that the Irish "temperance movement is the most remarkable example exhibited by any modern nation." Aubrey De Vere, *English Misrule and Irish Misdeeds. Four Letters from Ireland, Addressed to an English Member of Parliament*, 2nd ed. (London: John Murray, 1848), 216. On identity politics in American temperance, see: Joseph Gusfield, *Symbolic Crusade: Status Politics and the American Temperance Movement* (Urbana: University of Illinois Press, 1963). Lisa McGirr, *The War on Alcohol: Prohibition and the Rise of the American State* (New York: W. W. Norton & Company, 2016).

35. Terrence McDonough, *Was Ireland a Colony? Economics, Politics and Culture in Nineteenth-Century Ireland* (Dublin: Irish Academic Press, 2005). Mary Gilmartin and Lawrence D. Berg, "Locating Postcolonialism," *Area* 39, no. 1 (2007): 122. On revenues drained from Ireland: De Vere, *English Misrule and Irish Misdeeds*, 120–23. On settler brewers: Jane H. Ohlmeyer, "A Laboratory for Empire? Early Modern Ireland and English Imperialism," in *Ireland and the British Empire*, ed. Kevin Kenny (New York: Oxford University Press, 2004), 40. On paying defense and debt: Kevin Kenny, "Ireland and the British Empire: An Introduction," in *Ireland and the British Empire*, ed. Kevin Kenny (New York: Oxford University Press, 2004), 12.

36. Malcolm, "*Ireland Sober, Ireland Free*," 332.

37. Patrick Kelly, "William Molyneux and the Spirit of Liberty in Eighteenth-Century Ireland," *Eighteenth-Century Ireland/Iris an dá chultúr* 3 (1988): 136–37.

38. Elizabeth Malcolm, "Temperance and Irish Nationalism," in *Ireland under the Union: Varieties of Tension*, ed. F. S. L. Lyons and R. A. J. Hawkins (Oxford: Clarendon Press, 1980), 110–11. Also: "Dr. William Drennan to Mrs. M. McTier. August 12, 1796," in: D. A. Chart, ed., *The Drennan Letters* (Belfast: H.M.S.O., 1931), 237–38. Nancy J. Curtin, *The United Irishmen: Popular Politics in Ulster and Dublin, 1791–1798* (Oxford: Clarendon Press, 1994), 35.

39. *Report from the Committee of Secrecy, of the House of Lords in Ireland, as Reported by the Right Honourable John Earl of Clare, Lord High Chancellor* (London: J. Debrett, 1798), appendix XXIV, p. 8 (italics and capitalization in original).

40. William Dool Killen, *Memoir of John Edgar, D.D., LL.D.* (Belfast: C. Aitchison, 1867), 28–29.

41. Ibid., 64. Also 32.

42. Malcolm, "*Ireland Sober, Ireland Free*," 72.

43. Ibid., 26. See also: John Bickerdyke, *The Curiosities of Ale & Beer* (London: Swan Sonnenschein & Co., 1889), 15–16.

44. Malcolm, "*Ireland Sober, Ireland Free*," 74–82.

45. Quoted in: John F. Quinn, *Father Mathew's Crusade: Temperance in Nineteenth-Century Ireland and Irish America* (Amherst, MA: University of Massachusetts Press, 2002), 183.

46. William John Fitzpatrick, *The Life, Times, and Correspondence of the Right Rev. Dr. Doyle, Bishop of Kildare and Leighlin*, 2 vols., vol. II (Boston: Patrick Donahoe, 1862), 167–68 (emphasis in original).

47. Malcolm, "*Ireland Sober, Ireland Free*," 109–10. "He was asked once what first turned his thoughts toward total abstinence. 'My dear,' he answered, 'I thought how terrible it would be if I myself ever became a drunkard.'" John F. Maguire, *Father Mathew: A Biography* (London: Longmans, Green, 1865), 58–61. Colm Kerrigan, *Father Mathew and the Irish Temperance Movement, 1838–1849* (Cork: Cork University Press, 1992), 49.

48. *Journal of the American Temperance Union* IV, no. 1 (1840): 48. Patrick Rogers, *Father Theobald Mathew: Apostle of Temperance* (Dublin: Browne and Nolan Limited, 1943), 45. Many such Irish temperance medals—including those predating Fr. Mathew—are held at the Provincial Archives of the Capuchin Friary of St. Mary of the Angels. CA/FM/RES/9/3/1-11, Fr. Theobald Mathew: Research and Commemorative Papers, Provincial Archives, Capuchin Friary of St. Mary of the Angels, Dublin, Ireland.

49. Malcolm, "*Ireland Sober, Ireland Free*," 116. Quinn, *Father Mathew's Crusade*, 68–70.

50. Letter, Fr. Theobald Mathew, Nashville, TN, to Sr. Magdalen, Cork, April 28, 1851, CA/FM/RES/1/2, Fr. Theobald Mathew: Research and Commemorative Papers, Provincial Archives, Capuchin Friary of St. Mary of the Angels, Dublin, Ireland.

51. Letter, Fr. Theobald Mathew to Richard Foley, May 31, 1854, CA/FM/RES/1/2, Fr. Theobald Mathew: Research and Commemorative Papers, Provincial Archives, Capuchin Friary of St. Mary of the Angels, Dublin, Ireland.

52. Susan Campbell Bartoletti, *Black Potatoes: The Story of the Great Irish Famine, 1845–1850* (New York: Houghton Mifflin, 2001), 17. Estimates range from 4.3 million to 5.5 million. Malcolm, "*Ireland Sober, Ireland Free*," 125. German traveler Kohl heard "no less than five millions" from Mathew's "own mouth." Kohl, *Travels in Ireland*, 94.

53. Elizabeth Malcolm, "Popular Recreation in Nineteenth-Century Ireland," in *Irish Culture and Nationalism, 1750–1950*, ed. Oliver MacDonagh, W. F. Mandle, and Pauric Travers (New York: Palgrave Macmillan, 1983), 47–48.

54. Malcolm, "*Ireland Sober, Ireland Free*," 120.

55. Ibid., 118. Of course, others in foreign lands—such as revolutionary socialist Nikolai Chernyshevsky in the Russian Empire—were able to draw their own conclusions as to the anti-imperial nature of Fr. Mathew's temperance crusade. Nikolai G. Chernyshevskii, "Otkupnaya sistema (*Sovremennik*, 1858)," in *Izbrannye ekonomichesie proizvedeniya, tom 1* (Moscow: Gosudarstvennoe izdatel'stvo politicheskoi literatury, 1948), 685–87.

56. "Mr. O'Connell's Speech in Bandon," *Journal of the American Temperance Union* IV, no. 1 (1840): 47.

57. Malcolm, "*Ireland Sober, Ireland Free*," 132. M. R. Beames, "The Ribbon Societies: Lower-Class Nationalism in Pre-Famine Ireland," *Past & Present*, no. 97 (1982): 138.

58. Malcolm, "Temperance and Irish Nationalism," 80–83. Joseph Valente, *The Myth of Manliness in Irish National Culture, 1880–1922* (Urbana: University of Illinois Press, 2011), 214–15.

59. Kohl, *Travels in Ireland*, 95.

60. Malcolm, "*Ireland Sober, Ireland Free*," 202–203.

61. Ibid., 181.

62. Sir Dominic Corrigan, "Sale of Liquors on Sunday (Ireland) Bill," House of Commons, Wednesday, 9th July 1873, "Hansard's Parliamentary Debates, Third Series," (London: Cornelius Buck, 1873), vol. 4, 98.

63. See, for instance: Richard P. Davis, *Arthur Griffith and Non-Violent Sinn Fein* (Dublin: Anvil Books, 1974), 25. Eric Taplin, "Liverpool: The Apprenticeship of a Revolutionary," in *James Larkin: Lion of the Fold*, ed. Donal Nevin (Dublin: Gill & Macmillan, 2006).

64. Frederic Richard Lees, *One Hundred Objections to a Maine Law; Being a Sequel to the "Argument" of the United Kingdom Alliance for the Legislative Prohibition of the Liquor Traffic* (Manchester: United Kingdom Alliance, 1857). Shiman, *Crusade against Drink*, 75. See also: Switzerland Bureau fédéral de statistique, *Question de l'alcoolisme. Exposé comparatif des lois et des expériences de quelques états étrangers, par le bureau fédéral de statistique* (Berne: Imprimerie K.-J. Wyss, 1884), 621–35.

65. "Minutes of First Meeting of Members of General Council of the United Kingdom Alliance, held in Manchester, June 1st, 1853, Nathaniel Card, Esq., in the Chair," in: *United Kingdom Alliance (Formed June 1st, 1853) to Procure the Total and Immediate Legislative Suppression of the Traffic in All Intoxicating Liquors* (Manchester: Smith, Barnes, and Blackley, 1853), 2–6. UKA Documents, Vol. 1, United Kingdom Alliance (UKA) Collection, Institute of Alcohol Studies, Alliance House Foundation, London. See also: "Maine Law and Temperance: Item Written by Nathaniel Card's Daughter Marry Hannah Card," 1851, Alliance House Foundation, London.

66. Brian Harrison, "The British Prohibitionists 1853–1872: A Biographical Analysis," *International Review of Social History* 15, no. 3 (1970): 379–80.

67. Frederic Richard Lees, *An Argument for the Legislative Prohibition of the Liquor Traffic* (Manchester: United Kingdom Alliance, 1857), 113. "Minutes of First Meeting of Members of General Council" in: *United Kingdom Alliance*, 8, United Kingdom Alliance (UKA) Collection, Institute of Alcohol Studies, Alliance House Foundation, London. Aspinwall, "Democracy and Drink," 108.

68. Nicholas Baldwin, "The Membership and Work of the House of Lords," in *The House of Lords: Its Parliamentary and Judicial Roles*, ed. Paul Carmichael and Brice Dickson (1999), 40–43. Lees, *Argument for Legislative Prohibition*, 128–30.

69. Harrison, *Drink and the Victorians*, 389. Jenkins, *Parliament, Party and Politics*, 73. Malcolm, *"Ireland Sober, Ireland Free,"* 169.

70. Malcolm, *"Ireland Sober, Ireland Free,"* 169. Citing: A. E. Dingle, *The Campaign for Prohibition in Victorian England: The United Kingdom Alliance* (London: Croom Helm Ltd., 1980), 17–18. "Scottish Permissive Bill and Temperance Association," in: Cherrington, ed., *Standard Encyclopedia of the Alcohol Problem*, 2402.

71. See: Timothy Watchful, *Sunday Closing: Three Dialogues between Farmer Goodall and Neighbour Thoughtful* (London: William Freeman, 1867), 6–8.

72. Ian Tyrrell, *Sobering Up: From Temperance to Prohibition in Antebellum America, 1800–1860* (Westport, CT: Greenwood Press, 1979), 18. Harrison, *Drink and the Victorians*, 93. Shiman, *Crusade against Drink*, 47, 52–53. Malcolm, *"Ireland Sober, Ireland Free,"* 66, 99. The Unitarians were similarly opposed. Douglas Charles Strange, *British Unitarians against American Slavery, 1833–65* (Rutherford, NJ: Fairleigh Dickinson University Press, 1984), 61.

73. Mark Lawrence Schrad, *The Political Power of Bad Ideas: Networks, Institutions, and the Global Prohibition Wave* (New York: Oxford University Press, 2010), 43. *The Proceedings of the World's Temperance Convention, Held in London, August 4th and Four Following Days* (London: Charles Gilpin, 1846), 4, 32, 41–43. More generally: Bette Fladeland, *Men and Brothers: Anglo-American Antislavery Cooperation* (Urbana: University of Illinois Press, 1972).

74. Caroline Bressey, *Empire, Race, and the Politics of Anti-Caste* (London: Bloomsbury Academic, 2015). David M. Fahey, "Catherine Impey," in *Oxford Dictionary of National Biography*, ed. H. C. G. Matthew and Brian Harrison (New York: Oxford University Press, 2004), 213. David M. Fahey, *Temperance and Racism: John Bull, Johnny Reb, and the Good Templars* (Lexington: University Press of Kentucky, 1996), 139–46.

75. Andrew T. N. Muirhead, *Reformation, Dissent, and Diversity: The Story of Scotland's Churches, 1560–1960* (London: Bloomsbury T&T Clark, 2015), 100.

76. Charles Kingsley, *Alton Locke* (London: Chapman and Hall, 1856), 19.

77. Edward Royle, *Chartism*, 3rd ed. (London: Routledge, 1996), 33–34. Brian Harrison, "Teetotal Chartism," *History (London)* 58, no. 193 (1973): 198–99, 203.

78. William Lovett, *The Life and Struggles of William Lovett, in His Pursuit of Bread, Knowledge, and Freedom* (London: Trübner & Co., 1876), 95, 97.

79. This was the so-called Forbes MacKenzie Act. *Report on the Workings of the Forbes Mackenzie Act (Public Houses "Scotland" Act)* (Glasgow: Scottish Licensed Victuallers' Association, 1858).

80. This being the 1855 Wilson Patton Act. Lees, *Argument for Legislative Prohibition*, 103–104. Brian Harrison, "The Sunday Trading Riots of 1855," *Historical Journal* 8, no. 2 (1965): 223.

81. Karl Marx, "Agitation over the Tightening-Up of Sunday Observance (July 2, 1855)," in *Karl Marx, Frederick Engels: Collected Works* (New York: International Publishers, 1980), 323.

82. Karl Marx, "Anti-Church Movement—Demonstration in Hyde Park (June 25, 1855)," in *Karl Marx, Frederick Engels: Collected Works* (New York: International Publishers, 1980), 302–303. Temperance sneaks in to quite a few Marxist writings. Frederick Engels laid the blame for drunkenness among the industrial poor in Manchester and Liverpool on an exploitative capitalist system that cares nothing for the worker. "On Saturday evenings, especially when wages are paid and work stops somewhat earlier than usual, when the whole working-class pours from its own poor quarters into the main thoroughfares, intemperance may be seen in all its brutality. I have rarely come out of Manchester on such an evening without meeting numbers of people staggering and seeing others lying in the gutter. . . . And when their money is spent, the drunkards go to the nearest pawnshop [to] pawn whatever they possess. . . . When one has seen the extent of intemperance among the workers in England, one readily believes Lord Ashley's statement that this class annually expends something like twenty-five million pounds sterling upon intoxicating liquor." Friedrich Engels, *The Condition of the Working Class in England in 1844* (London: Swan Sonnenschein & Co., 1892), 127–29. David Christian, "Accumulation and Accumulators: The Metaphor Marx Muffled," *Science and Society* 54, no. 2 (1990). In their *Communist Manifesto*, Marx and Engels describe "conservative or bourgeois socialism" thus: "A part of the bourgeoisie is desirous of redressing social grievances in order to secure the continued existence of bourgeois society. To this section belong economists, philanthropists, humanitarians, improvers of the condition of the working class, organisers of charity, members of societies for the prevention of cruelty to animals, temperance fanatics, hole-and-corner reformers of every imaginable kind." Karl Marx and Friedrich Engels, *The Communist Manifesto* (New York: International Publishers, 1948), 57.

83. Marx, "Agitation over Sunday Observance," 323.

84. Ibid., 326–27. MPs and witnesses all agreed that the disturbance in Hyde Park was a direct result of the liquor laws. See: "First Report from the Select Committee on Sale of Beer, &c. Act," HC407 (London), July 20, 1855, 14–18, 34, 42, British Parliamentary Papers, House of Commons. See also: "Report of the Commissioners Appointed to Inquire into the Alleged Disturbance of the Public Peace in Hyde Park on Sunday, July 1st, 1855; and the Conduct of the Metropolitan Police," London: Houses of Parliament, 1856. British Parliamentary Papers, House of Commons.

85. Harrison, "The Sunday Trading Riots of 1855," 227. *The Examiner*, July 7, 1855, 428.

86. Harrison, *Drink and the Victorians*, 389.

87. Malcolm, "*Ireland Sober, Ireland Free*," 192.

88. John Stuart Mill, *Autobiography* (New York: Henry Holt and Company, 1873), 47–48, 250. "Mill, John Stuart," in: Ernest H. Cherrington, ed., *Standard Encyclopedia of the Alcohol Problem*, 6 vols., vol. 4 (Westerville, OH: American Issue Press, 1928), 1771. Harrison, *Drink and the Victorians*, 108.

89. John Stuart Mill, *On Liberty* (Boston: Ticknor and Fields, 1863), 160–61.

90. Ibid., 171–75.

91. Ibid., 193–97. See also: Samuel Fothergill, *Liberty, License, and Prohibition: An Examination of the Arguments of John Stuart Mill, in His Work on Liberty, in Relation to the Liquor Traffic* (Manchester: Tubbs & Brook, 1871[?]).

92. "No person ought to be punished simply for being drunk," Mill argues, but whenever "there is a definite damage, or a definite risk of damage, either to an individual or to the public, the case is taken out of the province of liberty, and placed in that of morality or law." Mill, *On Liberty*, 155–59. "Drunkenness, for example, in ordinary cases, is not a fit subject for legislative interference," Mill later claims. However, someone who is liable to commit crimes while drunk thus commits a crime by putting themselves into that state: "The making himself drunk, in a person whom drunkenness excites to do harm to others, is a crime against others." Mill, *On Liberty*, 188–90. Harrison, *Drink and the Victorians*, 209.

93. Duncan Brack and Membery York, "The Search for the Greatest Liberal," *Journal of Liberal History* 56 (2007): 7.

94. Quoted in: Jessica Warner, *All or Nothing: A Short History of Abstinence in America* (Toronto: McClelland & Stewart, 2008), 148.

95. "The Poor Man's Beer and the Rich Man's Prey," September 5, 1868, in: Wilfrid Lawson, *Wit and Wisdom of Sir Wilfrid Lawson: Being Selections from His Speeches, 1865–1885* (London: Simpkin, Marshall, 1886), 17.

96. Brack and York, "The Search for the Greatest Liberal," 7. Duncan Brack, "The Greatest Liberal: John Stuart Mill," *Journal of Liberal History* 57 (2007–2008): 9. Shiman, *Crusade against Drink*, 189, 219. David M. Fahey, "The Politics of Drink: Pressure Groups and the British Liberal Party, 1883–1908," *Social Science* 54, no. 2 (1979): 77.

97. Wilfrid Lawson, *The Opium Traffic between India and China. The Debate in the House of Commons on Sir Wilfrid Lawson's Motion, Tuesday, May 10, 1870* (London: Aborigines' Protection Society, 1870), 3–4, 6–7, 24–25. Wilfrid Lawson, *Sir Wilfrid Lawson: A Memoir* (London: Smith, Elder & Co., 1909), 334.

98. Filson Young, "The Unpublic House," *Saturday Review of Politics, Literature, Science and Art*, June 1, 1912, 681–82. Gutzke, *Pubs & Progressives*, 5–8.

99. John Morley, *The Life of William Ewart Gladstone*, 3 vols., vol. II (New York: Macmillan, 1903), 388–90. Malcolm, "*Ireland Sober, Ireland Free*," 217–18. In particular, see Sir Wilfrid Lawson's arguments in the House of Commons: "Permissive Prohibitory Liquor Bill—Bill 3," May 8, 1872, *Hansard Parliamentary Debates*, 3d ser., vol. 211 (1872).

100. Morley, *The Life of William Ewart Gladstone*, II:495. R. C. K. Ensor, *England, 1870–1914* (Oxford: Clarendon Press, 1936), 21.

101. Sir Dominic Corrigan, "Sale of Liquors on Sunday (Ireland) Bill," House of Commons, July 9, 1873, *Hansard Parliamentary Debates*, 3d ser., vol. 4, 98 (1873).

102. Malcolm, "*Ireland Sober, Ireland Free*," 201. *Proceedings of the Home Rule Conference Held at the Rotunda, Dublin, on the 18th, 19th, 20th and 21st November, 1873* (Dublin: Irish Home Rule League, 1874), 92–93. Liberals' Irish Sunday-closing bills were defeated in 1872 and 1873 also.

103. Richard Smyth, "Sale of Intoxicating Liquors in Ireland on Sunday," May 8, 1874, House of Commons, *Hansard Parliamentary Debates*, 3d ser., vol. 218, 2002 (1874).

104. William Lecky, "Sale of Intoxicating Liquors (Ireland) Bill," May 12, 1897, House of Commons, *Hansard Parliamentary Debates*, 3d ser., vol. 49, 266 (1897).

105. D. A. Hamer, *Liberal Politics in the Age of Gladstone and Rosebery: A Study in Leadership and Policy* (Oxford: Clarendon Press, 1972), 88–89. Michael Barker, *Gladstone and Radicalism: The Reconstruction of Liberal Policy in Britain, 1885–1894* (New York: Barnes & Noble Books, 1975), 208–11.

106. John Bright, "Public-Houses (Ireland)—Resolution," May 12, 1876, House of Commons, *Hansard Parliamentary Debates*, 3d ser., vol. 229, 562 (1876). George Barnett Smith, *The Life and Speeches of the Right Honourable John Bright, M.P.* (London: Hodder and Stoughton, 1882), 311.

107. Roy Jenkins, *Gladstone: A Biography* (New York: Random House, 2002), 553.

108. Malcolm, *"Ireland Sober, Ireland Free,"* 263, 296. John Ireland, *How Fare the Irish People? An Address* (Dublin: Irish Association for the Prevention of Intemperance, 1882), 7–8.

109. F. S. L. Lyons, *Charles Stewart Parnell, a Biography* (Toronto: Gill & Macmillan, 2005), 385–86. See also: Alan O'Day, *The English Face of Irish Nationalism: Parnellite Involvement in British Politics, 1880–86* (Toronto: Gill and Macmillan, 1977), 24.

110. Charles Stewart Parnell, "Intoxicating Liquors (Ireland) Bill," April 15, 1891, House of Commons, *Hansard Parliamentary Debates*, 3d ser., vol. 352, 634–35 (1891).

111. Paul A. Readman, "The 1895 General Election and Political Change in Late Victorian Britain," *Historical Journal* 42, no. 2 (1999): 468.

112. Fahey, "Politics of Drink," 78. Axel Gustafson, *The Foundation of Death: A Study of the Drink-Question*, 3rd ed. (Boston: Ginn, Heath, & Company, 1885), 485. Shiman, *Crusade against Drink*, 220–24.

113. Shiman, *Crusade against Drink*, 227–29. Gutzke, "Progressivism in Britain and Abroad," 47. As Liberal candidate D. M. Watson explained, "I desire to see local self-government carried out to its fullest extent and therefore advocate local control of the Drink Traffic by the people themselves." Readman, "The 1895 General Election": 472. David Brooks, ed., *The Destruction of Lord Rosebery: From the Diary of Sir Edward Hamilton, 1894–1895* (London: Historians' Press, 1986), 106.

114. Shiman, *Crusade against Drink*, 226. Readman, "The 1895 General Election ," 474.

115. Readman, "The 1895 General Election," 479.

116. Thomas Scanlon, "Wanted: A New Liberal Programme," in *The Westminster Review. July to December (Inclusive) 1895* (London: Frederick Warne and Co., 1895), 358–59. Shiman, *Crusade against Drink*, 228. Fahey, "Politics of Drink," 79.

117. Lambert McKenna, *Life and Work of Rev. James Aloysius Cullen, S.J.* (London: Longmans, Green and Co., 1924), 101–104.

118. Elizabeth Malcolm, "The Catholic Church and the Irish Temperance Movement, 1838–1901," *Irish Historical Studies* 23, no. 89 (1982): 15–16.

119. Quinn, *Father Mathew's Crusade*, 178. Malcolm, *"Ireland Sober, Ireland Free,"* 319.

120. Joost Augusteijn, *Patrick Pearse: The Making of a Revolutionary* (New York: Palgrave Macmillan, 2010), 51, 93. Ruán O'Donnell, *Patrick Pearse: 16 Lives* (Dublin: O'Brien Press, 2016). Padraic Pearse, "The Murder Machine (1912)," in *Collected Works of Padraic H. Pearse: Political Writings and Speeches* (Dublin: Phoenix, 1916), 30.

121. Much of the fighting in Dublin occurred near Marrowbone Lane Distillery, which had its own volunteer corps. Fearghal McGarry, *The Rising: Ireland: Easter 1916* (New York: Oxford University Press, 2016), 190, also: 248, 51.

122. Gutzke, *Pubs & Progressives*, 26–27. Gutzke, "Progressivism in Britain and Abroad," 57.

123. Kevin H. Hawkins and C. L. Pass, *The Brewing Industry: A Study in Industrial Organisation and Public Policy* (London: Heinemann, 1979), 35.

124. Timothy Davies, "Beer Hawking in London," July 31, 1907, House of Commons, *Hansard Parliamentary Debates*, 3d ser., vol. 179, 953–54 (1907). "Beer Hawking," *The Brewers' Journal*, April 15, 1908, 275. David W. Gutzke, *Women Drinking Out in Britain since the Early Twentieth Century* (Manchester: Manchester University Press, 2016), 272.

125. Scanlon, "Wanted: A New Liberal Programme," 365.

126. Edward R. Pease, *The Case for Municipal Drink Trade* (London: P. S. King and Son, 1904), 126. Edward R. Pease, *Liquor Licensing at Home and Abroad* (London: Fabian Society, 1898), 4–14.

127. Joseph Rowntree and Arthur Sherwell, *The Temperance Problem and Social Reform* (London: Hodder and Stoughton, 1899), 783. Gutzke, "Progressivism in Britain and Abroad," 48.

128. Gutzke, *Pubs & Progressives*, 29–30.

129. Gutzke, "Progressivism in Britain and Abroad," 48.

130. Paul Auchterlonie, "A Turk of the West: Sir Edgar Vincent's Career in Egypt and the Ottoman Empire," *British Journal of Middle Eastern Studies* 27, no. 1 (2000): 55.

131. "Efficiency Results from Drink Reform: Lord D'Abernon Believes Rules Should Be Maintained after the War," *New York Times*, June 4, 1916, 18.

132. Ibid. Central Control Board, *Defence of the Realm (Liquor Control) Regulations* (London: H. M. Stationery Office, 1915). Duncan Millar, "Central Control Board (Liquor Traffic)," October 26, 1916, House of Commons, *Hansard Parliamentary Debates*, 3d ser., vol. 86, 1430 (1916). "Central Control Board (Liquor Traffic)," in: Ernest H. Cherrington, ed., *Standard Encyclopedia of the Alcohol Problem*, 6 vols., vol. 2 (Westerville, OH: American Issue Press, 1924), 537–38.

133. Gutzke, *Pubs & Progressives*, 54.

134. Ibid., 59. John Greenaway, *Drink and British Politics since 1830: A Study in Policy Making* (New York: Palgrave Macmillan, 2003), 105.

135. Henry Carter, *The Control of the Drink Trade: A Contribution to National Efficiency, 1915–1917* (London: Longmans, Green and Co., 1918), 215.

136. Gutzke, *Pubs & Progressives*, 108–109. "England," in: Cherrington, ed., *Standard Encyclopedia of the Alcohol Problem*, 936.

137. Shiman, *Crusade against Drink*, 238–44. Aspinwall, "Democracy and Drink," 116. "Scotland," in: Cherrington, ed., *Standard Encyclopedia of the Alcohol Problem*, 2397. See: *Scottish Reformer* 35 (April 1920). GB 248, DC 019/2/2/4. Records of the Scottish Permissive Bill and Temperance Association (1885–1922), University of Glasgow Archive Services, Glasgow, UK.

138. Père Camille de la Rochemontaix, *Les Jésuites et la Nouvelle France au XVIIe siècle* (Paris: Letouzey et Ané, 1895), I:40; I:314–19. Spence, *Prohibition in Canada*, 19–20. Thomas H. Johnson, "On the Subject of Suppressing the Liquor Traffic among Indians," March 1861, 1, RG13-A-2, Box 5, No. 1861-313, Department of Justice Fonds, Library and Archives Canada, Ottawa. See also: "Act to Regulate the Liquor Traffic of the Island of St. John," 1785, 1–5, MG9-C1, Container 2, Records Relating to the House of Representatives, Library and Archives Canada, Ottawa. Robert A. Campbell, "Making Sober Citizens: The Legacy of Indigenous Alcohol Regulation in Canada, 1777–1985," *Journal of Canadian Studies/Revue d'études canadiennes* 42, no. 1 (2008): 108.

139. "Canada," in: Cherrington, ed., *Standard Encyclopedia of the Alcohol Problem*, 489–91.

140. Spence, *Prohibition in Canada*, 122. See also: Scott Act Addresses, 1880, Box 6, File 14, Fond F4048, the Dominion Alliance for the Total Suppression of the Liquor Traffic Fonds, United Church of Canada Archives, Toronto, Ontario. Reginald G. Smart and Alan C. Ogborne, *Northern Spirits: A Social History of Alcohol in Canada*, 2nd ed. (Toronto: Ontario Addiction Research Foundation, 1996), 44.

141. F. S. Spence, *The Facts of the Case: A Summary of the Most Important Evidence and Argument Presented in the Report of the Royal Commission on the Liquor Traffic Compiled under the Direction of the Dominion Alliance for the Total Suppression of the Liquor Traffic (1896)* (Toronto: Coles Publishing Company Limited, 1973). Colonial Office (United Kingdom), "Information for the Royal Commission on Liquor Traffic," May 20, 1892, RG25-B-1-a, Box 53, no. 1861-313, Department of External Affairs Fonds, Library and Archives Canada, Ottawa.

142. Benoit Dostie and Ruth Dupré, "'The People's Will': Canadians and the 1898 Referendum on Alcohol Prohibition," *Explorations in Economic History* 49, no. 4 (2012): 498.

143. Spence, *Prohibition in Canada*, 540–42.

144. The Premier, "Criminal Code Amendment Regarding Interference by Liquor Traffic in Dry Provinces," April 1915, RG13-A-2, Box 193, No. 1915-764, Department of Justice Fonds, Library and Archives Canada, Ottawa.

145. See also: Minutes, Board of Control, Ontario, 1923, Box 6, File 4, Fond F4048, the Dominion Alliance for the Total Suppression of the Liquor Traffic Fonds, United Church of Canada Archives, Toronto, Ontario.

146. Schrad, *Political Power of Bad Ideas*, 80, 151. William P. Eno, *A Definite Plan for a Proposed Reasonable Regulation as a Suggested Substitute for Attempted Prohibition, with a Study of State Control System in Quebec and Sweden and Regulation in England and France, with Particular Respect to Their Effect on Sobriety and Maintenance of Respect for Law and Order* (Washington, DC: 1924). F. G. R. Gordon, *How Sweden and Quebec Control the Liquor Traffic* (Haverhill, MA: Record Publishing Co., 1926). Association Against the Prohibition Amendment, *The Quebec System: A Study of Liquor Control* (Washington, DC: AAPA, 1928). Association Against the Prohibition Amendment, *Government Liquor Control in Canada* (Washington, DC: AAPA, 1930). Henry Anderson, "Liquor Control: A Substitute for Prohibition," *Forum*, April 1931, Box 2, Anderson File, Association Against the Prohibition Amendment Records, Manuscripts Division, Library of Congress, Washington, DC.

147. Maggie Brady, *Teaching "Proper" Drinking? Clubs and Pubs in Indigenous Australia* (Acton: Australian National University Press, 2018), 8–12.

148. See: Copy of Proceedings Concerning Importation of Two Stills by John MacArthur and Captain John Abbott, October 24, 1807, 1–12, Series 40.077, Sir Joseph Banks Papers, State Library of New South Wales, Sydney.

149. William Bligh, "An Account of the Rebellion," June 30, 1808, 2, Series 40.091, Sir Joseph Banks Papers, State Library of New South Wales, Sydney. More generally: Stephen Dando-Collins, *Captain Bligh's Other Mutiny: The True Story of the Military Coup That Turned Australia into a Two-Year Rebel Republic* (Sydney: Random House Australia, 2010).

150. Samuel Morewood, *A Philosophical and Statistical History of the Inventions and Customs of Ancient and Modern Nations in the Manufacture and Use of Inebriating Liquors* (Dublin: William Curry, Jun. and Company, 1838), 264. Brady, *Teaching "Proper" Drinking?*, xvii–xviii, 14.

151. Morewood, *Philosophical and Statistical History*, 262.

152. Ibid., 266. "Backhouse, James," in: Ernest H. Cherrington, ed., *Standard Encyclopedia of the Alcohol Problem*, 6 vols., vol. 1 (Westerville, OH: American Issue Press, 1925), 252.

153. Ian Tyrrell, "International Aspects of the Woman's Temperance Movement in Australia: The Influence of the American WCTU, 1882–1914," *Journal of Religious History* 12, no. 3 (1983): 286–89. On Rechabites, see: Minute Book, District Officers, 1861, Box 1, 1979.0091, Independent Order of Rechabites, Victorian District, 1861, University of Melbourne Archives, Melbourne.

154. Raewyn Dalziel, "New Zealand Women's Christian Temperance Union, 1885–," in *Women Together: A History of Women's Organisations in New Zealand/Ngā Rōpū Wāhine o te Motu*, ed. Anne Else (Wellington: Historical Branch, Department of Internal Affairs, 1993), 72–74, W4313, Department of Internal Affairs, Head Office, Archives New Zealand, Auckland.

155. Franci Bertie Boyce, *The Drink Problem in Australia, or: The Plagues of Alcohol and the Remedies* (Sydney: Edwards, Dunlop & Co., Ltd., 1893), 143–44.

156. Women's Suffrage Petition 1892/Petihana Whakamana Pota Wahine 1892, 27184, Legislative Department, Archives New Zealand, Auckland. Ministry for Culture and Heritage, "Women's Suffrage Petition," *New Zealand History*, March 13, 2018, https://nzhistory.govt.nz/politics/womens-suffrage/petition (accessed August 12, 2020).

157. *Minutes of the First Intercolonial Woman's Christian Temperance Union Held in Victoria for the Purpose of Forming a Woman's Christian Temperance Union of Australasia*, 1891, Box 18, Series 245, Control 1. Also: Equal Status and Aboriginal Welfare Departments, Box 83, Series 186, 2001.0085, Woman's Christian Temperance Union of Victoria, 1887–1999, University of Melbourne Archives, Melbourne. Patricia Grimshaw, "Gender, Citizenship and Race in the Woman's Christian Temperance Union of Australia, 1890 to the 1930s," *Australian Feminist Studies* 13, no. 28 (1998): 199–204. Tyrrell, "International Aspects of the Woman's Temperance Movement," 288–89.

158. Boyce, *Drink Problem in Australia*, 142.

159. "Australia," in: Cherrington, ed., *Standard Encyclopedia of the Alcohol Problem*, 227–28. Ian Warden, "Ditty Details End of Drink Drought," *Canberra Times*, August 6, 2012, https://

www.canberratimes.com.au/story/6167149/ditty-details-end-of-drink-drought/ (accessed August 6, 2020).

160. Walter Phillips, "'Six O'Clock Swill': The Introduction of Early Closing of Hotel Bars in Australia," *Historical Studies* 19, no. 75 (1980): 250. Maggie Brady, "Radical Actions: Aboriginal and Non-Aboriginal Women's Temperance Activism in Nineteenth- and Twentieth-Century Australia," *Social History of Alcohol and Drugs* 33, no. 2 (2019): 299–300.

161. Brady, *Teaching "Proper" Drinking?*, 44–53.

162. There were two prohibition referendums in 1919, and none in 1931 or 1951. Benoit Dostie and Ruth Dupré, "Serial Referendums on Alcohol Prohibition," *Social Science History* 40, no. 3 (2016): 497–98. See also: James Coker and J. Malton Murray, *Temperance and Prohibition in New Zealand* (London: Epworth Press, 1930).

163. Johnson, "Confessions," XVII, 1. "Collision Imperils 562. Liner Beached after Crash in Channel—Pussyfoot Johnson Aboard," *New York Times*, July 22, 1922. "Liners in Collision in the English Channel," *Auckland Weekly News*, September 14, 1922, 39, AWNS-19220914-39-5, Sir George Gray Special Collections, Auckland Libraries Heritage Collections, Auckland, NZ.

164. Johnson, "Confessions," XVII, 3–5.

165. Dostie and Dupré, "Serial Referendums," 299.

Chapter 6

1. Martin Dugard, *Into Africa: The Epic Adventures of Stanley & Livingstone* (New York: Broadway Books, 2003), 34.

2. David Livingstone, *Missionary Travels and Researches in South Africa* (New York: Harper & Brothers, 1858), 124–29. "Chief or Charter? The Future of Bechuanaland," *St. James Gazette*, September 9, 1895, 3–4. "An African Chief: Khama of Bechuanaland," *Woman's Signal*, September 12, 1895, 169.

3. "A Trinity of Dusky Kings: A Station Platform Interview with Khama," *St. James Gazette*, September 7, 1895, 3–4.

4. John Charles Harris, *Khama: The Great African Chief* (London: Livingstone Press, 1922), 10.

5. Jeff Ramsay, "The Batswana-Boer War of 1852–53: How the Batswana Achieved Victory," *Botswana Notes and Records* 23, no. 1 (1991).

6. "Thomas Upington, Colonial Secretary, to Governor and High Commissioner, September 17, 1884," in: Colonial Office, *Further Correspondence Respecting the Affairs of the Transvaal and Adjacent Territories* (London: Eyre and Spottiswoode, 1884), C-4252, 6–7.

7. John Nixon, *The Complete Story of the Transvaal* (London: Sampson Low, Marston, Searle, and Rivington, 1885), 73–74.

8. John Mackenzie, *Austral Africa: Losing It or Ruling It* (London: Sampson Low, Marston, Searle & Rivington, 1887), 192. Anthony Sillery, *The Bechuanaland Protectorate* (New York: Oxford University Press, 1952), 55.

9. Colonial Office, *Commission and Instructions to Major-General Sir Charles Warren, K.C.M.G., as Special Commissioner to Bechuanaland; with a Memorandum by Sir C. Warren* (London: Eyre and Spottiswoode, 1884), C-4227, 5–6.

10. "Letter from Montsioa to Queen Victoria, August 16, 1895," in: Colonial Office, *Correspondence Relative to the Transfer of the British Bechuanaland to the Cape Colony* (London: Eyre and Spottiswoode, 1896), C-7932, 24–25. "We have been loyal, contented and happy under Her Majesty's Imperial government. We have prospered because our interests have been guarded. We have felt the benefit of a just law against the sale of liquor to our people and ourselves. We know we should have been ruined to day if that law had not been in force. We have always had our grievances justly and fairly settled and we know that if this country is annexed to the Cape Colony, instead of being prosperous we shall become ruined." "Petition of All the Chiefs and Headmen of the Batlapin Nation, May 14, 1895," in: Colonial Office, *Correspondence Relative to the Transfer of the British Bechuanaland to the Cape Colony*, C-7932, 6–7. Formal

continuation of prohibition through the annexation act: "Act No. 41 of 1895," in: Colonial
Office, *Correspondence Relative to the Transfer of the British Bechuanaland to the Cape Colony*,
C-7932, 17–22.

11. See: "Kafir beer" in: Ernest H. Cherrington, ed., *Standard Encyclopedia of the Alcohol Problem*,
6 vols., vol. 3 (Westerville, OH: American Issue Press, 1926), 1422–23. "Union of South
Africa," Ernest H. Cherrington, ed., *Standard Encyclopedia of the Alcohol Problem*, 6 vols., vol. 6
(Westerville, OH: American Issue Press, 1930), 2699.

12. Livingstone, *Missionary Travels*, 323.

13. Brian Hayden, Neil Canuel, and Jennifer Shanse, "What Was Brewing in the Natufian?
An Archaeological Assessment of Brewing Technology in the Epipaleolithic," *Journal
of Archaeological Method and Theory* 20, no. 1 (2013): 102–104. Patrick E. McGovern,
Ancient Wine: The Search for the Origins of Viniculture (Princeton, NJ: Princeton University
Press, 2003).

14. David Christian, "Traditional and Modern Drinking Cultures in Russia on the Eve of
Emancipation," *Australian Slavonic and East European Studies* 1, no. 1 (1987). Mark
Lawrence Schrad, *Vodka Politics: Alcohol, Autocracy, and the Secret History of the Russian State*
(New York: Oxford University Press, 2014), 83–91.

15. Charles van Onselen, "Randlords and Rotgut, 1886–1903: An Essay on the Role of Alcohol
in the Development of European Imperialism and Southern African Capitalism, with Special
Reference to Black Mineworkers in the Transvaal Republic," *History Workshop* 1, no. 2 (1976).
Alexander Etkind, *Internal Colonization: Russia's Imperial Experience* (Malden, MA: Polity
Press, 2011), 145–46.

16. David Christian, *Living Water: Vodka and Russian Society on the Eve of Emancipation*
(Oxford: Clarendon Press, 1990), 25.

17. Harris, *Khama*, 52–53. Also: John H. Bovill, *Natives under the Transvaal Flag* (London: Simpkin,
Marshall, Hamilton, Kent, and Co., 1900), 37. Committee of the Aborigines Protection
Society, "Poison for Africans," *Poisoning of Africa Papers* 1, 1895, 1–2, Reel 8, Aborigines
Protection Society (A111), Royal Anthropological Institute of Great Britain and Ireland,
London, England. Similarly, see also: Ladysmith Magistrate and Commissioner, "Colonial
Office Re-Punishment of Drunkenness among Workers at the Ladysmith Dam" (1852), NAB
1/LDS_3/3/1_H41/1852_1, Pietermaritzburg Archives Repository, National Archives and
Records Service of South Africa.

18. Harris, *Khama*, 53.

19. L. London, "The 'Dop' System, Alcohol Abuse and Social Control in South Africa: A Public
Health Challenge," *Social Science & Medicine* 48, no. 10 (1999). Scully aptly describes this
system as one in which laborers were "both the instruments and the victims of their own op-
pression." Pamela Scully, "Liquor and Labor in the Western Cape, 1870–1900," in *Liquor and
Labor in Southern Africa*, ed. Jonathan Crush and Charles Ambler (Athens: Ohio University
Press, 1992), 59.

20. Guy Hayler, *Prohibition Advance in All Lands; a Study of the World-Wide Character of the
Drink Question*, 2nd ed. (London: International Prohibition Confederation, 1914), 242. See
also: Charles Ambler and Jonathan Crush, "Alcohol in Southern African Labor History," in
Liquor and Labor in Southern Africa, ed. Jonathan Crush and Charles Ambler (Athens: Ohio
University Press, 1992), 6.

21. Neil Parsons, *King Khama, Emperor Joe, and the Great White Queen: Victorian Britain through
African Eyes* (Chicago: University of Chicago Press, 1998), 188. Neil Parsons, *The Word of
Khama* (Lusaka, Zambia: NECZAM, 1972), 5.

22. Mackenzie, *Austral Africa*, 192–93.

23. Transvaal Concessions Commission, "Hatherley Distillery Concession," October 16, 1900,
in: *Report of the Transvaal Concessions Commission, Dated 19th April 1901, Part II: Minutes of
Evidence* (London: House of Commons, 1901), 71–72. Charles van Onselen, *New Babylon*,

New Nineveh: The Witwatersrand, 1886–1914 (Johannesburg: Jonathan Ball Publishers, 2012), 7–17.

24. Charles H. Ambler, "Africa, Southern," in *Alcohol and Temperance in Modern History: An International Encyclopedia*, ed. Jack Blocker Jr., David Fahey, and Ian Tyrrell (Santa Barbara, CA: ABC-CLIO, 2003), 12. Paul la Hausse, *Brewers, Beerhalls, and Boycotts: A History of Liquor in South Africa* (Johannesburg: Ravan Press, 1988), 16. Michael Fridjhon and Andy Murray, *Conspiracy of Giants: The South African Liquor Industry* (Johannesburg: Divaris Stein, 1986), 28–30, 38–40.

25. See: Hatherley Distillery, "Draft Letter from Colonial Secretary to Hatherley Distillery," ZA TAB CT_288_CONF JL21/03_1; Hatherley Distillery Company, "For the Purchase of the Company's Stock, by the Government," ZA TAB CT_288_CONF JL21/03_1; and Hatherley Distillery Company, "Re: Terms and Conditions under Which Above Company Was Allowed to Dispose of Its Stock of Spirits and Other Liquors," ZA TAB CT_41_1879/ 04_1—all at National Archives Repository (Public Records of Former Transvaal Province), National Archives and Record Service of South Africa, Pretoria, South Africa.

26. La Hausse, *Brewers, Beerhalls, and Boycotts*, 14–15. Van Onselen, "Randlords and Rotgut," 40–42, 50, 53, 67.

27. G. Blainey, "Lost Causes of the Jameson Raid," *Economic History Review* 18, no. 2 (1965): 358.

28. Van Onselen, "Randlords and Rotgut," 53. La Hausse, *Brewers, Beerhalls, and Boycotts*, 13.

29. See: "Report of the Committee of the Executive Council, September 14, 1889," in: Colonial Office, *Despatch from Governor Sir C. B. H. Mitchell, K.C.M.G., on the Subject of the Liquor Traffic among the Natives of Natal* (London: Eyre and Spottiswoode, 1890), Cd. 3094, 4–6.

30. Rod Phillips, *Alcohol: A History* (Chapel Hill: University of North Carolina Press, 2014), 227–28. Fridjhon and Murray, *Conspiracy of Giants*, 29.

31. Bovill, *Natives under the Transvaal Flag*, 36–37. La Hausse, *Brewers, Beerhalls, and Boycotts*, 17. On the liquor situation more generally, see also: "Liquor Traffic Certain Native Territories in S.A." (1890), VAB AMPT PUBS_29_C6102_1, Free State Archives Repository, National Archives and Records Service of South Africa.

32. Ibid., 22–38. Paul la Hausse, "Drinking and Cultural Innovation in Durban: The Origins of the Beerhall in South Africa, 1902–1916," in *Liquor and Labor in Southern Africa*, ed. Jonathan Crush and Charles Ambler (Athens: Ohio University Press, 1992), 96–98.

33. Charles D. H. Parry and Anna L. Bennetts, *Alcohol Policy and Public Health in South Africa* (New York: Oxford University Press, 1998), 6. Ambler and Crush, "Alcohol in Southern African Labor History," 1. More generally: Anne Kelk Mager, "Apartheid and Business: Competition, Monopoly, and the Growth of the Malted Beer Industry in South Africa," *Business History* 50, no. 3 (2008): 272–90.

34. Peter Sanders, *Moshoeshoe: Chief of the Sotho* (New York: Holmes & Meier Publishers, 1975), 281. Leonard Monteath Thompson, *Survival in Two Worlds: Moshoeshoe of Lesotho, 1786–1870* (Oxford: Clarendon Press, 1975), 199. See also: Records of the Dominions Office, High Commissioners to South Africa, DO 119/32, "Basutoland: Liquor Traffic and Measures to Control; Refutal of Sir Baden Powell's Remarks on the Traffic," folio no. 85, National Archives (U.K.), Kew. By 1890, investigations into drunkenness in Basutoland provided a mixed outlook: Colonial Office, *Correspondence Relating to the Liquor Traffic in Certain Native Territories in South Africa* (London: Eyre and Spottiswoode, 1890), C-6102, 8–11. King Sekhome likewise attempted prohibition: Harris, *Khama*, 93–94.

35. Livingstone, *Missionary Travels*, 119.

36. Committee of the Aborigines Protection Society, "What Natives Say," *Poisoning of Africa Papers* 8, 1895, 1–3, Reel 8, Aborigines Protection Society (A111), Royal Anthropological Institute of Great Britain and Ireland, London, England. See also: H. R. Fox Bourne, *The Bechuana Troubles: A Story of Pledge-Breaking, Rebel-Making and Slave-Making in a British Colony* (London: P. S. King & Son, 1898), 6, Reel 8, Aborigines Protection Society (A111), Royal Anthropological Institute of Great Britain and Ireland, London, England.

37. "Report of the Civil Commissioner and Resident Magistrate, Gordonia, for the Year 1894–95," in: Colonial Office, *British Bechuanaland: Annual Reports for 1894–5* (London: Eyre and Spottiswoode, 1896), C-7944-15, 44–46. See also: "Annual Report of Civil Commissioner, Mafeking, 1894-5," in: Colonial Office, *British Bechuanaland*, C-7944-15, 14. Revenue: Colonial Office, *British Bechuanaland*, C-7944-15, 54.

38. Van Onselen, "Randlords and Rotgut," 85 (emphasis mine).

39. James Davidson Hepburn, *Twenty Years in Khama's Country* (London: Hodder and Stoughton, 1895), 119.

40. Basil Williams, *Cecil Rhodes* (New York: Henry Holt & Company, 1921), 11.

41. Martin Meredith, *Diamonds, Gold, and War: The British, the Boers, and the Making of South Africa* (New York: PublicAffairs, 2007), 35. Robert I. Rotberg, *The Founder: Cecil Rhodes and the Pursuit of Power* (New York: Oxford University Press, 1988), 63.

42. Meredith, *Diamonds, Gold, and War*, 35.

43. Arthur Keppel-Jones, *Rhodes and Rhodesia: The White Conquest of Zimbabwe, 1884–1902* (Montreal: McGill-Queen's University Press, 1983), 58–59.

44. John E. Flint, *Cecil Rhodes* (Boston: Little, Brown & Co., 1974), 248–52.

45. Rotberg, *The Founder*, 471. Similarly: "Letter of C. J. Rhodes to Colonial Office, April 19, 1892," in: Colonial Office, *Correspondence Respecting Proposed Railway Extension in the Bechuanaland Protectorate* (London: Eyre and Spottiswoode, 1893), C-7154, 13.

46. "Mr. C. J. Rhodes to Colonial Office, January 17, 1899," in: British South Africa Company, *Correspondence with Mr. C. J. Rhodes Relating to the Proposed Extension of the Bechuanaland Railway* (London: Darling & Son, 1899), C-9323, 8–17. See also: Keppel-Jones, *Rhodes and Rhodesia*, 59, 64.

47. "Rhodesia," in: Ernest H. Cherrington, ed., *Standard Encyclopedia of the Alcohol Problem*, 6 vols., vol. 5 (Westerville, OH: American Issue Press, 1929), 2281.

48. Charles L. Norris-Newman, *Matabeleland and How We Got It* (London: T. Fisher Unwin, 1895), 150.

49. British South Africa Company, "Report on the Company's Proceedings and the Condition of the Territories within the Sphere of Its Operations, 1889–1892" (paper presented at the Second Shareholders Meeting, London, November 29, 1892), 9, 30–31.

50. Parsons, *King Khama*, 49. Also: "Letter of Imperial Secretary to Mr. A. Beit, February 16, 1892," in: Colonial Office, *Correspondence Respecting Proposed Railway Extension*, C-7154, 8–10. Harris, *Khama*, 87. Bourne, *Bechuana Troubles*, 7. Reel 8, Aborigines Protection Society (A111), Royal Anthropological Institute of Great Britain and Ireland, London, England.

51. Harris, *Khama*, 15. "Khama, Chief of the Bamangwato," *Review of Reviews* 12 (1895): 304.

52. Julian Mockford, *Khama: King of the Bamangwato* (London: Jonathan Cape, 1931), 48–50.

53. Parsons, *King Khama*, 103.

54. Hepburn, *Twenty Years in Khama's Country*, 119. Neil Parsons, "The Economic History of Khama's Country in Botswana, 1844–1930," in *The Roots of Rural Poverty in Central and Southern Africa*, ed. Robin Palmer and Neil Parsons (Berkeley: University of California Press, 1977), 117–99.

55. Keppel-Jones, *Rhodes and Rhodesia*, 55.

56. Sic. Hepburn, *Twenty Years in Khama's Country*, 116.

57. Ibid., 116–18. Also: Harris, *Khama*, 28. Mockford, *Khama*, 65–66.

58. Hepburn, *Twenty Years in Khama's Country*, 121–22; also 140.

59. Parsons, *Word of Khama*, 5.

60. William E. Johnson, "Babylon and Way Stations" (Cooperstown, NY: Fenimore Art Museum Library, 1930), VI, 3. See also: Harris, *Khama*, 52–54. "Khama, Chief of the Bamangwato," 310.

61. Hepburn, *Twenty Years in Khama's Country*, 141–43.

62. Ibid., 143–44.

63. Ibid., 144–45. Harris, *Khama*, 52–54.

64. Hepburn, *Twenty Years in Khama's Country*, 146–48. "Khama, Chief of the Bamangwato," 310. See also: Johnson, "Babylon and Way Stations," VI, 4. Parsons, *King Khama*, 84. Committee of the Aborigines Protection Society, "Khama and the Drink Traffic," *Poisoning of Africa Papers* 12, 1895, 1–2, Reel 8, Aborigines Protection Society (A111), Royal Anthropological Institute of Great Britain and Ireland, London, England.

65. Hepburn, *Twenty Years in Khama's Country*, 151.

66. Harris, *Khama*, 71–72.

67. Mockford, *Khama*, 77.

68. "Khama, Chief of the Bamangwato," 311. Hugh Marshall Hole, *Passing of the Black Kings* (London: Philip Allan, 1932), 313–14. Colonial Office, "Further Correspondence Respecting the Affairs of the Transvaal and Adjacent Territories," British Parliamentary Paper C4252 (London: Houses of Parliament, 1884), 1–37. In the same letter, Khama declares that he is "not baffled" by the mutual affinity with Britain, as "there are certain laws of my country which the Queen of England finds in operations, and which are advantageous for my people. . . . I refer to our law concerning intoxicating drinks, whether among black people or among white people." Parsons, *Word of Khama*, 6–7.

69. Parsons, *Word of Khama*, 8. "An African Chief," 167.

70. Harris, *Khama*, 87. Sillery, *The Bechuanaland Protectorate*, 66. Committee of the Aborigines Protection Society, "Khama and the Drink Traffic," *Poisoning of Africa Papers* 12, 1895, 3, Reel 8, Aborigines Protection Society (A111), Royal Anthropological Institute of Great Britain and Ireland, London, England.

71. Christopher M. Paulin, *White Men's Dreams, Black Men's Blood: African Labor and British Expansionism in Southern Africa, 1877–1895* (Trenton, NJ: Africa World Press, 2001), 211.

72. Parsons, *King Khama*, 50.

73. "Imperial Secretary Graham Bower to the Secretary, BSAC, August 7, 1895," in: Colonial Office, *Correspondence Relative to the Visit to This Country of the Chiefs Khama, Sebele, and Bathoen, and the Future of Bachuanaland Protectorate* (London: Eyre and Spottiswoode, 1896), C-7962, 4–5.

74. Parsons, *King Khama*, 64, 69–70.

75. "Question of Authorising the Sale of Liquor in the Territories of the Chief Khama. Letter from Mr. H. Bridgman, etc." (1894), NAB CSO_1418_1895/166_1, Pietermaritzburg Archives Repository, National Archives and Records Service of South Africa.

76. Joseph Chamberlain, *Foreign & Colonial Speeches* (London: George Routledge & Sons, Limited, 1897), viii, 89. See also: Peter T. Marsh, *Joseph Chamberlain: Entrepreneur in Politics* (New Haven, CT: Yale University Press, 1994), 546–47.

77. "The Right Hon. Joseph Chamberlain. A Character Sketch," *Review of Reviews* 13 (1896): 193.

78. "Khama, Chief of the Bamangwato," 312.

79. "London Missionary Society's Centenary: Another Speech by Khama," *St. James Gazette*, September 24, 1895, 7. "Khama on His Mission," *St. James Gazette*, September 25, 1895, 7.

80. Bourne, *Bechuana Troubles*, 3–4, Reel 8, Aborigines Protection Society (A111), Royal Anthropological Institute of Great Britain and Ireland, London, England.

81. Quoted in: Parsons, *King Khama*, 79.

82. *Christian World*, September 12, 1895. Quoted in: Parsons, *King Khama*, 84–85.

83. "An African Chief: Khama of Bechuanaland," *Woman's Signal* 89 (1895): 167.

84. Quoted in: Parsons, *King Khama*, 129–31.

85. Ibid., 144.

86. Ibid., 92. Similarly, see: Committee of the Aborigines Protection Society, "Khama and the Drink Traffic," *Poisoning of Africa Papers* 12, 1895, 4, Reel 8, Aborigines Protection Society (A111), Royal Anthropological Institute of Great Britain and Ireland, London, England.

87. "Khama, Chief of the Bamangwato," 312.

88. *Bradford Observer*, October 15, 1895. Reproduced in: Parsons, *King Khama*, 170–71.

89. "Khama at Grosvenor House," *South Africa*, November 9, 1895, 334. Niedersächsische Staats- und Universitätsbibliothek Göttingen.

90. Ibid., 335.

91. "Chiefs to Sir Robert Meade," September 24, 1895, in: "Papers Concerning Visit of Chiefs Khama, Sebele, and Bathoen of Bechuanaland Protectorate to England, 1895, includes letters from Joseph Chamberlain," Africa Odds Box 29, Council for World Mission/London Missionary Society Archives, School of Oriental and African Studies (SOAS), London University. Also: "Letter of Chiefs Khama, Sebele, and Bathoen to the Colonial Office, September 24, 1895," in: Colonial Office, *Correspondence Relative to the Visit of the Chiefs*, C-7962, 13–14.

92. "Letter of Chiefs Khama, Sebele, and Bathoen to the Colonial Office, November 4, 1895," in: Colonial Office, *Correspondence Relative to the Visit of the Chiefs*, C-7962, 20.

93. Bourne, *Bechuana Troubles*, 8. Reel 8, Aborigines Protection Society (A111), Royal Anthropological Institute of Great Britain and Ireland, London, England.

94. "Colonial Office to the Reverend W. C. Willoughby, November 7, 1895," in: Colonial Office, *Correspondence Relative to the Visit of the Chiefs*, C-7962, 21–22. Sillery, *The Bechuanaland Protectorate*, 72–73. "Magna Carta": Parsons, *King Khama*, 254. These positions, including prohibition, were then solidified in an October 18, 1895, proclamation by Hercules Robinson, imperial governor of the South African colonies. "Bechuanaland Protectorate," in: Colonial Office, *Correspondence Relative to the Visit of the Chiefs*, C-7962, 26–27.

95. There are multiple authoritative accounts of the queen's exact words, while conveying the same sentiment. Here, I draw from both Mockford, *Khama*, 178, and Parsons, *King Khama*, 227.

96. Quoted in: Parsons, *King Khama*, 229.

97. Quoted in: Ibid., 235.

98. Ibid., 66.

99. Parsons, *Word of Khama*, 13. Also: Parsons, *King Khama*, 222–23.

100. Mockford, *Khama*, 183–84.

101. Quoted in: Parsons, *King Khama*, 244. See also: War and Colonial Department and Colonial Office, Africa, "Disturbances in the South African Republic (Dr. L. S. Jameson's Raid), 1896," CO 879/44/4, National Archives (UK), Kew.

102. W. Douglas MacKenzie, *South Africa: Its History, Heroes and Wars* (Chicago: Co-Operative Publishing Company, 1899), 248. K. C. Tessendorf, *Along the Road to Soweto: A Racial History of South Africa* (New York: Atheneum, 1989).

103. Hayler, *Prohibition Advance in All Lands*, 236.

104. Colonial Office, *Reports by the High Commissioner on His Visits to Basutoland and the Bechuanaland Protectorate in 1906* (London: Darling & Son, 1906), Cd. 3094, 4–6. J. Mutero Chirenje, *Chief Kgama and His Times c. 1835–1923: The Story of a South African Ruler* (London: Rex Collings, 1978), 103. Specifically, the development of a domestic cottage industry in home-brewing sorghum beer in Botswana deserves mention. Steven Haggblade, "The Shebeen Queen and the Evolution of Botswana's Sorghum Beer Industry," in *Liquor and Labor in Southern Africa*, ed. Jonathan Crush and Charles Ambler (Athens: Ohio University Press, 1992), 396–97.

105. Parsons, *King Khama*, 34. A pattern reminiscent of the "boomerang model" of transnational activism. Margaret Keck and Kathryn Sikkink, *Activists beyond Borders: Advocacy Networks in International Politics* (Ithaca, NY: Cornell University Press, 1998).

106. Rorisang Lekalake, "Botswana's Democratic Consolidation: What Will It Take?," *Afrobarometer Policy Paper* 30 (2016).

Chapter 7

1. Louis Fischer, *The Life of Mahatma Gandhi* (New York: Collier Books, 1950), 386. Rajmohan Gandhi, *Gandhi: The Man, His People, and the Empire* (Berkeley: University of California Press, 2008), 467.

2. Ironically, debates in the British Cabinet as to what to do with Gandhi, and whether "it would be a mistake to let him die in detention"—as per Lord Halifax—were only taken up following a discussion of monopolizing the liquor traffic in the West African colonies. National Archives (UK), Kew, Cabinet Secretary's Notebooks, August 10, 1942, CAB 195/1/27, 104–106.

3. Gandhi, *Gandhi*, 472.

4. "Letter to Harilal Gandhi, February 14, 1935," in: Mahatma Gandhi, *Collected Works of Mahatma Gandhi*, 98 vols. (New Delhi: Publications Division Government of India, 1999), vol. 66, 223–24. Also, "Letter to Harilal Gandhi, April 12, 1935," in: Gandhi, *Collected Works of Mahatma Gandhi*, vol. 66, 414.

5. This letter of June 19, 1935, is not included in the exhaustive *Collected Works*. Shyam Bhatia, "Gandhi's Letters to Son May Trigger Storm," *The Tribune*, May 12, 2014, https://www.tribuneindia.com/2014/20140512/main8.htm (accessed October 13, 2018).

6. "Letter to Manilal and Sushila Gandhi, September 30, 1895," in: Gandhi, *Collected Works of Mahatma Gandhi*, vol. 68, 27. "Harlial spends the whole day immersed in a tub of liquor." Letter of August 15, 1935 (Gandhi, *Collected Works of Mahatma Gandhi*, vol. 67, 330). Ramachandra Guha, *Gandhi: The Years That Changed the World, 1914–1948* (New York: Alfred A. Knopf, 2018), 480. See also: letters of June 6 (Gandhi, *Collected Works of Mahatma Gandhi*, vol. 67, 234–35); July 11 (vol. 67, 244); July 15 (vol. 67, 256); August 9 (vol. 67, 315); August 17 (vol. 67, 338); and October (n/d) 1935 (vol. 68, 112–13).

7. Gandhi, *Gandhi*, 490. See also: Arun Gandhi, *Kasturba: A Life* (New York: Penguin, 2000). Fischer, *Life of Mahatma Gandhi*, 394–95.

8. Mahatma Gandhi, *The Moral and Political Writings of Mahatma Gandhi: Truth and Nonviolence* (New York: Oxford University Press, 1986), 427.

9. Mohandas K. Gandhi, *Key to Health*, ed. Jitendra T. Desai, trans. Sushila Nayar (Ahmedabad: Navajivan Publishing House, 1948). *Key to Health*, in: Gandhi, *Collected Works of Mahatma Gandhi*, vol. 83, 241–42. In the Indian numbering system, a crore is equal to 10,000,000 rupees.

10. Gandhi, *Key to Health*, 27. Gandhi, *Collected Works of Mahatma Gandhi*, vol. 83, 240–41.

11. Ramachandra Guha, *Gandhi before India* (New York: Random House, 2014), 23–24, 33. See also: Mohandas Gandhi, "Speech on Prohibition, Madras, March 24, 1925," *The Hindu*, March 24, 1925, in: Gandhi, *Collected Works of Mahatma Gandhi*, vol. 31, 35.

12. Mohandas Gandhi, "Letter to Lakshmidas Gandhi, November 9, 1888," in: Gandhi, *Collected Works of Mahatma Gandhi*, vol. 1, 2.

13. Political Department, *Compilations*, no. 140, vol. 108 (1892), Maharashtra State Archives, Mumbai. See also: Guha, *Gandhi before India*, 49.

14. Robert A. Huttenback, *Gandhi in South Africa: British Imperialism and the Indian Question, 1860–1914* (Ithaca, NY: Cornell University Press, 1971), viii.

15. "Letter of Sir C. B. H. Mitchell to Lord Knutsford, December 17, 1889," in: Colonial Office, *Despatch from Governor Sir C. B. H. Mitchell, K.C.M.G., on the Subject of the Liquor Traffic among the Natives of Natal* (London: Eyre and Spottiswoode, 1890), C-5897-13, no. 83, 4.

16. "Report by Supervisor of Native Locations, Ralph Clarence, June 24, 1889," in: Colonial Office, *Despatch from Governor Sir C. B. H. Mitchell*, C-5897-13, no. 83, 14–15. Indeed, in response to a Native Affairs query, nine of the twenty-two British magistrates polled blamed Indians, Coolies, and Creoles for the increase in drunkenness, while only two blamed licensed and unlicensed retailers. "Circular, Secretary for Native Affairs," in: Colonial Office, *Despatch from Governor Sir C. B. H. Mitchell*, C-5897-13, no. 83, 9–11.

17. Mohandas Gandhi, "The Indian Franchise, December 16, 1895," in: Gandhi, *Collected Works of Mahatma Gandhi*, 288–90. See also: Huttenback, *Gandhi in South Africa*, 50.

18. Guha, *Gandhi before India*, 118–23.

19. Simone Panter-Brick, *Gandhi and Nationalism: The Path to Indian Independence* (London: I. B. Tauris & Co., 2015), 76.

20. Ajay Skaria, *Unconditional Equality: Gandhi's Religion of Resistance* (Minneapolis: University of Minnesota Press, 2016), 3–6.

21. Guha, *Gandhi before India*, 268–73.

22. A representative case from 1907 involved one Mr. Suleman Wadi, who was falsely accused of illegally selling liquor to a native. Gandhi pleaded before the court that the sale of liquor was against their religion, that the defendant was a man of good standing, and no evidence of wrongdoing existed. Still the authorities were not persuaded. "Every Indian has to be cautious," Gandhi wrote of the case in his new circular for civic activism, the *Indian Opinion*. "The whites as well as the Natives will not be afraid of trapping other people to serve their own interest. As Mr. Wadi is innocent, he has nothing to be ashamed of. Shame lies not in being gaoled, but in committing a crime." Mohandas Gandhi, "Need for Caution," *Indian Opinion*, August 17, 1907, in: Gandhi, *Collected Works of Mahatma Gandhi*, vol. 7, 142. Similarly, see: vol. 7, 171, 180–81, 315–17, 348, 378, 453.

23. David Fahey and Padma Manian, "Poverty and Purification: The Politics of Gandhi's Campaign for Prohibition," *The Historian* 67, no. 3 (2005): 494. Guha, *Gandhi before India*, 288–89, 394, 533. Huttenback, *Gandhi in South Africa*, 281–83.

24. Quoted in: Guha, *Gandhi before India*, 396. See also: Sankar Ghose, *Mahatma Gandhi* (New Delhi: Allied Publishers Limited, 1991), 60. James D. Hunt, "Gandhian Experiments in Communal Living—The Phoenix Community and the Tolstoy Farm in South Africa," *Peace Research* 30, no. 1 (1998): 83.

25. Martin Green, *Tolstoy and Gandhi, Men of Peace* (New York: Basic Books, 1983), 95–97. Surendra Bhana, "The Tolstoy Farm: Gandhi's Experiment in 'Co-Operative Commonwealth,'" *South African Historical Journal* 7, no. 1 (1975), 88-100.

26. Mohandas K. Gandhi, *"Hind Swaraj" and Other Writings: Centenary Edition*, ed. Anthony J. Parel (New York: Cambridge University Press, 2009), 62.

27. "Arrack" in: Ernest H. Cherrington, ed., *Standard Encyclopedia of the Alcohol Problem*, 6 vols., vol. 1 (Westerville, OH: American Issue Press, 1925), 208–209. James McHugh, "Alcohol in Pre-Modern South Asia," in *A History of Alcohol and Drugs in Modern South Asia: Intoxicating Affairs*, ed. Harald Fischer-Tiné and Jana Tschurenev (New York: Routledge, 2014), 29–44. Gina Hames, *Alcohol in World History* (London: Routledge, 2012), 91–92.

28. Erica Wald, "Governing the Bottle: Alcohol, Race and Class in Nineteenth-Century India," *Journal of Imperial and Commonwealth History* 46, no. 3 (2018): 401. "India," in: Ernest H. Cherrington, ed., *Standard Encyclopedia of the Alcohol Problem*, 6 vols., vol. 3 (Westerville, OH: American Issue Press, 1926), 1298.

29. David A. Washbrook, "India, 1818–1860: The Two Faces of Colonialism," in *The Oxford History of the British Empire, Volume III: The Nineteenth Century*, ed. Andrew Porter (New York: Oxford University Press, 2001), 404. See also: Amar Farooqui, "Opium, the East India Company and the 'Native' States," in *A History of Alcohol and Drugs in Modern South Asia: Intoxicating Affairs*, ed. Harald Fischer-Tiné and Jana Tschurenev (New York: Routledge, 2014), 45–46.

30. Robert Eric Colvard, "A World without Drink: Temperance in Modern India, 1880–1940" (PhD dissertation, University of Iowa, 2013), 42–43.

31. James H. Mills, *Cannabis Britannica: Empire, Trade and Prohibition, 1800–1928* (New York: Oxford University Press, 2005), 4. See also: Farooqui, "Opium, the East India Company."

32. Washbrook, "India, 1818–1860," 403. On the ties between China and colonial India in the international tea and opium trades, see: Andrew B. Liu, *Tea War: A History of Capitalism in China and India,* (New Haven: Yale University Press, 2020), 9–10, 33–38.

33. Wilbur F. Crafts, "Brief Chronology of Opium Wars and Anti-Crusades," March 12, 1913, 1–3, Box 3a, Folder 23, Reel 18, World League Against Alcoholism Records, Temperance and Prohibition Papers, Ohio Historical Society. David T. Courtwright, *Forces of Habit: Drugs and the Making of the Modern World* (Cambridge, MA: Harvard University Press, 2002), 34–35.

34. Wilfrid Lawson, *The Opium Traffic between India and China. The Debate in the House of Commons on Sir Wilfrid Lawson's Motion, Tuesday, May 10, 1870* (London: Aborigines Protection Society, 1870), 4, 12, 19, 25.

35. William Wilson Hunter, *Bombay, 1885 to 1890: A Study in Indian Administration* (Bombay: Indian Spectator Office, 1900), 379.

36. Ibid. See also: *The Bombay Abkari Act, No. V of 1878* (Bombay: Government Central Press, 1878). "Abkari," in: Cherrington, ed., *Standard Encyclopedia of the Alcohol Problem*, vol. 1, 3.

37. G. W. Kurkaray, "Report on Native Newspapers, Bombay," 8. Bombay: Government of Bombay, 1879, 11. Quoted in: Colvard, "World without Drink," 65. See also: John Newton, *W. S. Caine, M.P. A Biography* (London: James Nisbet & Co., 1907), 235.

38. D. R. Tarkhadkar, "Native Newspaper Report, Bombay," 20. Bombay: Government of Bombay, 1880. Quoted in: Colvard, "World without Drink," 59.

39. G. M. Sathe, "Native Newspaper Reports, Bombay," 12–13. Bombay: Government of Bombay, 1886. Quoted in: Colvard, "World without Drink," 80–81. See also: "Memorandum on the Alleged Increase in Intemperance in India," in: India Office (Abkari Administration), *Copy of a Despatch Received from the Government of India, Dated 25th June 1887, Relating to the System of Licenses for the Distillation and Sale of Spiritous Liquors in Force in the Various Provinces of India* (London: Eyre and Spottiswoode, 1887), no. 269, 16.

40. G. M. Sathe, "Native Newspaper Reports, Bombay," 16. Bombay: Government of Bombay, 1886. Quoted in: Colvard, "World without Drink," 85.

41. On resistance against British drunkenness, disease, prostitution, and other transgressions, see also: Harald Fischer-Tiné, *Low and Licentious Europeans: Race, Caste and "White Subalternity" in Colonial India* (Hyderabad: Orient BlackSwan, 2009), 90–230.

42. "Anglo-Indian Temperance Association," in: Cherrington, ed., *Standard Encyclopedia of the Alcohol Problem*, vol. 1, 168.

43. Explicitly invoking here again the "boomerang pattern" of transnational advocacy networks. Margaret Keck and Kathryn Sikkink, *Activists beyond Borders: Advocacy Networks in International Politics* (Ithaca, NY: Cornell University Press, 1998). Margaret Keck and Kathryn Sikkink, "Historical Precursors to Modern Transnational Social Movements and Networks," in *Globalization and Social Movements: Culture, Power, and the Transnational Public Sphere*, ed. John Guidry, Michael Kennedy, and Mayer Zald (Ann Arbor: University of Michigan Press, 2000).

44. Newton, *M. S. Caine, M.P.*, 237.

45. See: John E. Gorst's report in: India Office (Abkari Administration), *Copy of a Despatch on the Sale of Spiritous Liquors*, no. 269, 3–4.

46. Colvard, "World without Drink," 107–108.

47. Lucy Carroll, "Origins of the Kayastha Temperance Movement," *Indian Economic & Social History Review* 11, no. 4 (1974): 434.

48. Mohandas Gandhi, "Indian Vegetarians," *The Vegetarian*, February 21, 1891, in: Gandhi, *Collected Works of Mahatma Gandhi*, vol. 1, 22.

49. C. K. Gokhale, "Mr. R. C. Dutt, C.I.E., and the Hon. G. K. Gokhale, C.I.E., on Temperance Reform," *Abkari: The Quarterly Organ of the Anglo-Indian Temperance Association* I, no. 73 (1908): 91. Quoted in: Colvard, "World without Drink," 145.

50. Syed Shamsuddin Kadri, "Native Newspaper Reports, Bombay" (Bombay: Government of Bombay, 1908). Quoted in: Colvard, "World without Drink," 145. Also: C. Rajagopalachari, "Statement on Abkari Revenue and Local Bodies, *Hindu*, April 9, 1918," in *Selected Works of C. Rajagopalachari: Vol. I, 1907–21*, ed. Mahesh Rangarajan, N. Balakrishnan, and Deepa Bhatnagar (New Delhi: Orient BlackSwan, 2014), 71–72.

51. Colvard, "World without Drink," 121.

52. Alfred Draper, *Amritsar: The Massacre That Ended the Raj* (London: Cassell, 1981), 157.

53. Colvard, "World without Drink," 163–66. Albert Porter, "Anglo-Indian Temperance Association of England Urges Prohibition in India," *American Issue*, November 1, 1919, Box 4,

NOTES

Folder 35, Roll 22, and Frederick Grubb, "British Parliament Confers on India Full Control of the Liquor Traffic," *American Issue*, August 21, 1920, Box 4, Folder 36, Roll 22, World League Against Alcoholism Records, Temperance and Prohibition Papers, Ohio Historical Society.

54. "British Government Gives India Entire Control of Liquor and Education," *American Issue*, May 28, 1921, Box 4, Folder 36, Roll 22, World League Against Alcoholism Records, Temperance and Prohibition Papers, Ohio Historical Society.

55. This according to Bombay's chief excise inspector of Bombay. J. Talyarkhan, "Letter to Superintendent of Salt and Excise, Bombay, 1921," in: Judicial Department, *Home (Special) Department, 1908–1949*. Maharashtra State Archive, Mumbai. See: Colvard, "World without Drink," 170. See also letter of Inspector of Salt and Excise, V. E. Xavier, "Letter, 1921," in: Judicial Department, *Home Department (Special) Department, 1908–1949*. Maharashtra State Archives, Mumbai.

56. Colvard, "World without Drink," 180. C. Rajagopalachari, "Editor's Notes, *Young India*, July 13, 1922," in *Selected Works of C. Rajagopalachari: Vol. II, 1921–22*, ed. Mahesh Rangarajan, N. Balakrishnan, and Deepa Bhatnagar (New Delhi: Orient BlackSwan, 2014), 195–96.

57. William E. Johnson, "Babylon and Way Stations" (Cooperstown, NY: Fenimore Art Museum Library, 1930), III, 5.

58. "Participant in Gandhi Movement Sentenced," *American Issue*, June 18, 1921, Box 4, Folder 36, Roll 22, World League Against Alcoholism Records, Temperance and Prohibition Papers, Ohio Historical Society.

59. David Hardiman, *The Coming of the Devi: Adivasi Assertion in Western India* (New York: Oxford University Press, 1987), 99–128. Fahey and Manian, "Poverty and Purification," 497–98. See also: "The Meaning of Prohibition, June 11, 1939," in: Gandhi, *Collected Works of Mahatma Gandhi*, vol. 76, 25.

60. Government of Bombay, "The Bombay Disturbances. Govt. Press Note, Effect of Immoderate Propaganda, Govt.'s Determination," *The Leader*, 17 December 1921, Quoted in: Colvard, "World without Drink," 175.

61. Mohandas Gandhi, "A Deep Stain," November 13, 1921, in: Gandhi, *Collected Works of Mahatma Gandhi*, vol. 25, 126–27.

62. Shahid Amin, *Event, Metaphor, Memory: Chauri Chaura 1922–1992* (Berkeley: University of California Press, 1995), 15. Guha, *Gandhi*, 145–46.

63. Gandhi, "A Deep Stain," 128–29. See also: Guha, *Gandhi*, 146–47, 334.

64. "William E. Johnson to Ernest Cherrington," October 2, 1920: Box 4, Folder 36, Roll 22, World League Against Alcoholism Records, Temperance and Prohibition Papers, Ohio Historical Society.

65. "Twelve Greatest American Men," *New York Times*, July 23, 1922, http://query.nytimes.com/mem/archive-free/pdf?res=9D01E5D61E30E633A25750C2A9619C946395D6CF (accessed May 20, 2013).

66. William E. Johnson, "Confessions of 'Pussyfoot' Johnson" (Cooperstown, NY: Fenimore Art Museum Library, n/d), XV, 4.

67. "Proposed Tour of India and Ceylon of Mr ('Pussyfoot') W E Johnson, on Behalf of the World League Against Alcoholism, May 1921," in: India Office Records and Private Papers, British Library, IOR/L/PJ/6/1750, File 3190, p. 10. William E. Johnson to Ernest Cherrington," June 28, 1925, 11–13, Box 1, Folder 5, William E. "Pussyfoot" Johnson Papers, Fenimore Art Museum Library, Cooperstown, NY.

68. Ibid., p. 3. Tarini Prasad Sinha, *"Pussyfoot" Johnson and His Campaign in Hindustan* (Madras: Ganesh & Co., 1922), 87, 171. See also: Ian Tyrrell, *Reforming the World: The Creation of America's Moral Empire* (Princeton, NJ: Princeton University Press, 2010), 216.

69. Johnson, "Confessions," XV, 5. " 'Pussyfoot's' Tales of India," December 8, 1921, Box 1, Folder 3, William E. "Pussyfoot" Johnson Papers, Fenimore Art Museum Library, Cooperstown, NY. Also: Sinha, *"Pussyfoot" Johnson and His Campaign in Hindustan*, 173.

70. "'Pussyfoot' (William E.) Johnson in India," 1928, 1–13, Box 1, Folder 7, William E. "Pussyfoot" Johnson Papers, Fenimore Art Museum Library, Cooperstown, NY. "Mr. 'Pussyfoot' Johnson's Tour," *Abkari*, no. 127, January 1922, 3–12: Box 4, Folder 37, Roll 22, World League Against Alcoholism Records, Temperance and Prohibition Papers, Ohio Historical Society. Harry Malcolm Chalfant, *These Agitators and Their Idea* (Nashville: Cokesbury Press, 1931), 354–55. William E. Johnson, "What I Found in India," *The Continent*, January 19, 1922, 59.

71. Sinha, *"Pussyfoot" Johnson and His Campaign in Hindustan*.

72. Johnson, "Confessions," XV, 10. Johnson, "What I Found in India," 59.

73. Johnson, "Confessions," XV, 15. Pussyfoot's solemn impressions of Jallainwalla Bagh: Sinha, *"Pussyfoot" Johnson and His Campaign in Hindustan*, 242. "William E. Johnson to Ernest Cherrington," September 15, 1921, Box 1, Folder 3; and "William E. Johnson to Ernest Cherrington," June 28, 1925, 12–13, Box 1, Folder 5, William E. "Pussyfoot" Johnson Papers, Fenimore Art Museum Library, Cooperstown, NY.

74. Brenton Badley, T., "Pussyfoot," *Abkari: The Quarterly Organ of the Anglo-Indian Temperance Association* I, no. 125 (1921). Cited in: Colvard, "World without Drink," 196.

75. Johnson, "Confessions," XV, 8, 17. Sinha, *"Pussyfoot" Johnson and His Campaign in Hindustan*, 205–206. Mohandas Gandhi, "Notes," *Young India*, December 1, 1921, in: Gandhi, *Collected Works of Mahatma Gandhi*, vol. 25, 175.

76. Mohandas Gandhi, "Notes," *Young India*, April 17, 1924, in: Gandhi, *Collected Works of Mahatma Gandhi*, vol. 27, 264.

77. Mohandas Gandhi, "What Should Be Done Where Liquor Is Being Served?" *Navajivan*, March 22, 1925, in: Gandhi, *Collected Works of Mahatma Gandhi*, vol. 31, 2.

78. C. Rajagopalachari, "A Great Crime: Editorial, *Hindu*, February 1, 1924," in *Selected Works of C. Rajagopalachari: Vol. III, 1923–25*, ed. Mahesh Rangarajan, N. Balakrishnan, and Deepa Bhatnagar (Hyderabad: Orient BlackSwan, 2015), 358.

79. C. Rajagopalachari, "Views on Government's Attitude towards Anti-Drink Campaign, *New India*, May 7, 1924," in *Selected Works of C. Rajagopalachari: Vol. III, 1923–25*, ed. Mahesh Rangarajan, N. Balakrishnan, and Deepa Bhatnagar (Hyderabad: Orient BlackSwan, 2015), 398–99.

80. Rajagopalachari, "A Great Crime," 358–59. Also: C. Rajagopalachari, "Appeal to Support Anti-Drink Campaign, *Hindu*, May 20, 1924," in *Selected Works of C. Rajagopalachari: Vol. III*, 402. It is worth juxtaposing this reality against colonial, prenationalist temperance claims about India, that "The drinking customs have done much to hinder the progress of Christianity in India, so much so that it is a prevailing idea among the heathen that they are taught by the tenets of the Christian religion!" "Temperance in India," in: *Centennial Temperance Volume: A Memorial of the International Temperance Conference, Held in Philadelphia, June, 1876* (New York: National Temperance Society and Publication House, 1877), 896.

81. Mohandas Gandhi, "Speech on Prohibition, Madras, March 24, 1925," *The Hindu*, March 24, 1925, in: Gandhi, *Collected Works of Mahatma Gandhi*, vol. 31, 37. Similarly, see: Johnson, "Babylon and Way Stations," VIII, 13. These sentiments were echoed in: C. Rajagopalachari, "Letter to Mahadev Desai, March 7, 1924," in *Selected Works of C. Rajagopalachari: Vol. III*, 368.

82. C. Rajagopalachari, "Letter to Mahatma Gandhi, January 7, 1926," in *Selected Works of C. Rajagopalachari, Vol. IV, 1926–30*, ed. Mukesh Kumar and Shilpa Menon (Hyderabad: Orient BlackSwan, 2017), 1–2.

83. Mohandas Gandhi, "Drugs, Drink and Devil," *Young India*, March 22, 1926, in: Gandhi, *Collected Works of Mahatma Gandhi*, vol. 35, 117.

84. C. Rajagopalachari, "Letter to the Secretary to the Government of Madras, Health Department, May 14, 1929," in *Selected Works of C. Rajagopalachari, Vol. IV*, 258–63. See also: "Constitution of the Prohibition League of India, 1926," in *Selected Works of C. Rajagopalachari: Vol. IV*, 490–91. Also: "The Prohibition Convention in India," (undated manuscript), 1–6, Box 4, Folder 39, Roll 22, World League Against Alcoholism Records, Temperance and Prohibition Papers, Ohio Historical Society.

85. Shakti Sinha, "Preface," in *Selected Works of C. Rajagopalachari: Vol. IV*, xix.

86. C. Rajagopalachari, "Appeal to Strengthen the Congress, *Hindu*, January 29, 1926," in *Selected Works of C. Rajagopalachari: Vol. IV*, 16.

87. Mohandas Gandhi, "Drugs, Drink and Devil, *Young India*, April 22, 1926," in: Gandhi, *Collected Works of Mahatma Gandhi*, vol. 35, 117. Fahey and Manian, "Poverty and Purification," 500–501. Similarly: C. Rajagopalachari, "Demand for Total Prohibition, *Hindu*, February 10, 1926," in *Selected Works of C. Rajagopalachari: Vol. IV*, 22.

88. C. Rajagopalachari, "The Right to Drink? *Young India*, December 16, 1926," in *Selected Works of C. Rajagopalachari: Vol. IV*, 86–87. Similarly, see: C. Rajagopalachari, "The Truth about Prohibition, *Hindu*, July 2, 1926," in *Selected Works of C. Rajagopalachari: Vol. IV*, 59–63. C. Rajagopalachari, "Prohibition Notes, *Young India*, January 27, 1927," in *Selected Works of C. Rajagopalachari: Vol. IV*, 97–99. Reporting on the progress on prohibition in Ontario, Canada, and the United States: C. Rajagopalachari, "Look on That Picture and This! *Young India*, January 13, 1927," in *Selected Works of C. Rajagopalachari: Vol. IV*, 93.

89. C. Rajagopalachari, "Prohibition Notes, *Young India*, March 3, 1927," in *Selected Works of C. Rajagopalachari: Vol. IV*, 107. More generally: C. Rajagopalachari, "Indian Prohibition Manual, *Tamil Nadu State Archives*, November 1931," in *Selected Works of C. Rajagopalachari: Vol. V, 1931–35*, ed. Shakti Sinha, Ravi K. Mishra, and Narendra Shukla (Hyderabad: Orient BlackSwan, 2019), 242.

90. C. Rajagopalachari, "A Prohibition Bill, *Young India*, April 7, 1927," in *Selected Works of C. Rajagopalachari: Vol. IV*, 115. C. Rajagopalachari, "The War against Drink, *Young India*, November 12, 1931," in *Selected Works of C. Rajagopalachari: Vol. V*, 206–207.

91. C. Rajagopalachari, "Ministers and Prohibition, *Hindu*, August 25, 1927," in *Selected Works of C. Rajagopalachari: Vol. IV*, 140.

92. C. Rajagopalachari, "Speech on Prohibition Campaign, *Hindu*, May 11, 1929," in *Selected Works of C. Rajagopalachari: Vol. IV*, 251.

93. Mahatma Gandhi, "Total Prohibition," *Young India*, September 8, 1927, 296: Box 4, Folder 38, Roll 22, World League Against Alcoholism Records, Temperance and Prohibition Papers, Ohio Historical Society. Mahatma Gandhi, "Weekly Letter, *Young India*, September 15, 1927," in *Social Service, Work and Reform, Vol. 1*, ed. V. B. Kher (Ahmedabad: Navajivan Publishing House, 1976), 306.

94. C. Rajagopalachari, "Statement on Madras Ministers and Prohibition Measures: A Story of Betrayal, *Hindu*, September 24, 1928," in *Selected Works of C. Rajagopalachari: Vol. IV*, 203. C. Rajagopalachari, "Views on the Drink Evil, *Hindu*, November 9, 1929," in *Selected Works of C. Rajagopalachari: Vol. IV*, 329.

95. Rajagopalachari, "Statement on Madras Ministers and Prohibition Measures," 203.

96. C. Rajagopalachari, "Critics Answered, *Sunday Times*, August 9, 1931," in *Selected Works of C. Rajagopalachari: Vol. V*, 79. More generally on the "illicit" question: Rajagopalachari, "Indian Prohibition Manual," 248.

97. C. Rajagopalachari, "Views on the Elections and Prohibition, *Hindu*, March 23, 1929," in *Selected Works of C. Rajagopalachari: Vol. IV*, 234–35.

98. Stanley Wolpert, *Gandhi's Passion: The Life and Legacy of Mahatma Gandhi* (New York: Oxford University Press, 2001), 133. C. Rajagopalachari, "Views on Excise Minister's Apologia, *Hindu*, March 5, 1929," in *Selected Works of C. Rajagopalachari: Vol. IV*, 225–26. Gopalkrishna Gandhi, ed., *My Dear Bapu: Letters from C. Rajagopalachari to Mohandas Karamchand Gandhi, to Debdas Gandhi and to Gopalkrishna Gandhi* (New York: Penguin, 2012). "The character of my harangues did serve to pour oil on the flames. I intended that they should." Letter, William E. Johnson to Ernest Cherrington, April 1, 1929, 1–3, Box 14, Folder 8, Roll 41, Ernest H. Cherrington Series, Temperance and Prohibition Papers, Ohio Historical Society.

99. William E. Johnson, "What Prohibition Means," *Mathur Patrika*, V, March 1929, 1–2, Box 4, Folder 39, Roll 22, World League Against Alcoholism Records, Temperance and Prohibition Papers, Ohio Historical Society.

100. See: C. Rajagopalachari, "Letter to Mary J. Cambell, June 22, 1931," in *Selected Works of C. Rajagopalachari: Vol. V,* 36. Mary J. Campbell of Waterloo, Iowa, was a WCTU member, and one of the vice presidents of the Prohibition League of India. See: Margaret B. Denning, "Signs of Prohibition Progress in India," *Union Signal,* February 17, 1916, 15. Mary J. Campbell, "Organizing for Temperance in India," *Union Signal,* February 19, 1920, 13. C. Rajagopalachari, "The Drink Evil, *Hindu,* August 5, 1929," in *Selected Works of C. Rajagopalachari: Vol. IV,* 291.

101. C. Rajagopalachari, "Letter to Ruth Evelyn Robinson, January 6, 1932," in *Selected Works of C. Rajagopalachari: Vol. V,* 291–92. See also: Ian Tyrrell, *Woman's World, Woman's Empire: The Woman's Christian Temperance Union in International Perspective, 1880–1930* (Chapel Hill: University of North Carolina Press, 1991), 109–11. On World's WCTU work in India, see: Frances E. Willard, *The "Do-Everything Policy": Address before the Second Biennial Convention of the World's Woman's Christian Temperance Union, and the Twentieth Annual Convention of the National Women's Christian Temperance Union. World's Columbian Exposition, Chicago, Illinois, USA, October 16th to 21st, 1893* (London: White Ribbon Publishing Co., 1893), 18–24, HV5015 .Z9, Box 2, No. 9, National American Woman Suffrage Association (NAWSA) Collection, Library of Congress, Washington, DC, https://www.loc.gov/resource/rbnawsa.n8352/ (accessed January 20, 2021). Also: Letter, William E. Johnson to Ernest Cherrington, August 17, 1930, Box 14, Folder 10, Roll 41, Ernest Cherrington Series, Temperance and Prohibition Papers.

102. Johnson mused further on this point: "Some of my fastidious American friends shuddered over the incident, but my British friends never complained. They never do. A Briton is always ready to give and receive hard knocks. He is the best sportsman in the world. He goes into the most remote corners of the universe to organize governments, collect taxes, build roads, scatter Bibles, and peddle whisky. If anyone objects, he calmly takes another whisky and soda and pursues his way, untroubled. There is no malice about it: he is simply anointing the earth with great gobs of civilization." Johnson, "Confessions," XIX, 17. "Ernest Cherrington to William E. Johnson," June 14, 1929, Box 14, Folder 8, Roll 41; and "William E. Johnson to Ernest H. Cherrington," June 22, 1930, Box 14, Folder 10, Roll 41, Ernest Hurst Cherrington Series, Ohio Historical Society. See also: Letter, C. Rajagopalachari to William Johnson, December 16, 1935, Box 1, Folder 12, William E. "Pussyfoot" Johnson Papers, Fenimore Art Museum Library, Cooperstown, NY.

103. Wolpert, *Gandhi's Passion,* 142–43. Dennis Dalton, ed., *Mahatma Gandhi: Selected Political Writings* (Cambridge: Hackett, 1996), 72.

104. Rajagopalachari, "Indian Prohibition Manual," 222. See also: Robert Eric Colvard, "'Drunkards Beware!': Prohibition and Nationalist Politics in the 1930s," in *A History of Alcohol and Drugs in Modern South Asia: Intoxicating Affairs,* ed. Harald Fischer-Tiné and Jana Tschurenev (New York: Routledge, 2014), 179–85.

105. Government of India, "Report of Native Newspapers, Bombay" (Bombay: Bombay Presidency, 1878). Quoted in: Colvard, "World without Drink," 228.

106. C. Rajagopalachari, "Statement on Picketing of Liquor Shop Auctions, *Hindu,* August 1, 1931," in *Selected Works of C. Rajagopalachari: Vol. V,* 74–75.

107. See: Colvard, "'Drunkards Beware'!," 176.

108. C. Rajagopalachari, "Views on Alexander Ranken Cox's Statement, *Hindu,* July 20, 1931," in *Selected Works of C. Rajagopalachari: Vol. V,* 67. Also: C. Rajagopalachari, "Is It Coercion? *Young India,* October 29, 1931," in *Selected Works of C. Rajagopalachari: Vol. V,* 188.

109. C. Rajagopalachari, "Statement on Prohibition in Pollachi, *Hindu,* July 19, 1931," in *Selected Works of C. Rajagopalachari: Vol. V,* 60–61.

110. Rajagopalachari, "The War against Drink, *Young India,* November 12, 1931," 208.

111. A.S., "Secret Memo to Home Department (Political), 1929," in: *Judicial Department, Home (Special) Department, 1908–1949.* Maharashtra State Archive, Mumbai. Originally cited in: Colvard, "World without Drink," 259. See also: A. O. Koreishi, "Letter to Commissioner

J. H. Garrett, 1930," in: Judicial Department, *Home (Special) Department, 1908–1949,* Maharashtra State Archive, Mumbai.

112. "Interview to Deputation of Victuallers' Association, June 2, 1939," in: Gandhi, *Collected Works of Mahatma Gandhi,* vol. 76, 7–8. See also: Guha, *Gandhi,* 348–49.

113. Wolpert, *Gandhi's Passion,* 163–66.

114. C. Rajagopalachari, "Letter to Grace D. Easterbrook, December 15, 1931," in *Selected Works of C. Rajagopalachari: Vol. V,* 272. Rajagopalachari, "Letter to Madras Health Secretary," 258–63.

115. Colvard, "World without Drink," 261–62.

116. David Hardiman, "From Custom to Crime: The Politics of Drinking in Colonial South Gujarat," *Subaltern Studies* 4 (1985): 165. Fahey and Manian, "Poverty and Purification," 498.

117. Rajagopalachari, "Statement on Prohibition in Pollachi, *Hindu,* July 19, 1931," 60.

118. Mohandas Gandhi, "The Meaning of Prohibition, June 11, 1939," in: Gandhi, *Collected Works of Mahatma Gandhi,* vol. 76, 25.

119. Guha, *Gandhi,* 506, 13–14.

120. Mohandas Gandhi, "Interview to Deputation of Victuallers' Association, June 2, 1939," in: Gandhi, *Collected Works of Mahatma Gandhi,* vol. 76, 7.

121. Ibid., vol. 76, 7–8. Gandhi explicitly mentions Harilal in the same context in a separate interview the same day. Mohandas Gandhi, "Interview to Parsi Deputation, June 2, 1939," in: Ibid., vol. 76, 9.

122. Gandhi, "Meaning of Prohibition," 24–28.

123. Gandhi, "Interview to Parsi Deputation," in: Gandhi, *Collected Works of Mahatma Gandhi,* vol. 76, 10.

124. Mohandas Gandhi, "Statement by Subhas Chandra Bose, July 11, 1939," in: Ibid., vol. 76, 417–18. Also: Gandhi, "Meaning of Prohibition," 25. Rajaji suggested the same thing a decade earlier in a letter to AITA delegate Frederick Grubb. C. Rajagopalachari, "Letter to Frederick Grubb, *C. Rajagopalachari Papers* (NMML), December 15, 1931," in *Selected Works of C. Rajagopalachari: Vol. V,* 274.

125. Gandhi, "The Meaning of Prohibition," 24.

126. Colvard, "World without Drink," 265. Gandhi, "Statement by Subhas Chandra Bose," in: Gandhi, *Collected Works of Mahatma Gandhi,* vol. 76, 417–18.

127. Mohandas Gandhi, "Well Done Bombay!" *Harijan,* August 12, 1939, in: *Collected Works of Mahatma Gandhi,* vol. 76, 200–201. On Parsi and Muslim opposition, see: Mohandas Gandhi, "Statement to the Press, July 13, 1939," in: Ibid., vol. 76, 122.

128. *Sheth Chinubhai Lalbhai,* Bombay High Court, April 11, 1940, https://www.casemine.com/judgement/in/56b49357607dba348f0066e6 (accessed November 8, 2018). This is largely the opposite of debates over federal versus state prohibition politics in the lead-up to the Eighteenth Amendment in the United States.

129. Fahey and Manian, "Poverty and Purification," 504.

130. Carolyn Heitmeyer and Edward Simpson, "The Culture of Prohibition in Gujarat, India," in *A History of Alcohol and Drugs in Modern South Asia: Intoxicating Affairs,* ed. Harald Fischer-Tiné and Jana Tschurenev (New York: Routledge, 2014), 210. Fahey and Manian, "Poverty and Purification."

131. Fahey and Manian, "Poverty and Purification," 490–91. Heitmeyer and Simpson, "Culture of Prohibition in Gujarat," 210.

132. Johnson, "Babylon and Way Stations," III, 3.

133. Ibid., III, 13.

Chapter 8

1. William E. Johnson, "Confessions of 'Pussyfoot' Johnson" (Cooperstown, NY: Fenimore Art Museum Library, n/d), XVII, 19.

2. Daniel Gorman, "Liberal Internationalism, the League of Nations Union, and the Mandates System," *Canadian Journal of History* 40, no. 3 (2005): 451–52.

3. William Johnson, "So I Went up to Jerusalem," *Home and State* 28, no. 3 (1927): 7. Johnson, "Confessions," XVII, 19. *The Home and State*, Anti-Saloon League of Texas Files, -Q- 178.05 H752, Briscoe Center for American History, University of Texas at Austin. See also: Oscar S. Heizer (American Consul), "Report on Alcohol Situation in Jerusalem," March 18, 1924, 1–6, Box 5, Folder 38, Roll 24, World League Against Alcoholism Records, Temperance and Prohibition Papers, Ohio Historical Society.

4. Johnson, "So I Went up to Jerusalem," 7.

5. Minutes, Executive Committee, 1920–21, April 7, 1921, and May 5, 1921, Resolutions 433 and 493, Records of the League of Nations Union, F 2/3, pp. 64, 88, London School of Economics, London. On demands for the revenues gained from such exploitative trades to be kept in the Mandate for benefit of the local population, see: Minutes, Executive Committee, 1920–21, January 13, 1921, Resolution 347, Records of the League of Nations Union, F 2/3, pp. 29–30, London School of Economics, London.

6. Weldon C. Matthews, *Confronting an Empire, Constructing a Nation: Arab Nationalists and Popular Politics in Mandate Palestine* (London: I. B. Tauris, 2006), 31–32.

7. Idir Ouahes, *Syria and Lebanon under the French Mandate: Cultural Imperialism and the Workings of Empire* (London: I. B. Tauris, 2018), 236, n. 110.

8. Johnson, "Confessions," XVII, 20–22.

9. William E. Johnson, "Babylon and Way Stations" (Cooperstown, NY: Fenimore Art Museum Library, 1930), III, 2, 7–8. Pussyfoot was hardly alone in his condemnations. In a tour of Palestine and Syria, the WCTU's Mary Campbell interviewed a liquor seller who admitted, "Moslems now drink much but they do not sell. The Christians are the reservoir from which the Moslems get the drink." Campbell editorialized, "Alas, this is true all through Palestine." Mary Campbell, "Conditions in Palestine," *Union Signal*, October 22, 1932, in: Box 5, Folder 38, Roll 24, World League Against Alcoholism Records, Temperance and Prohibition Papers, Ohio Historical Society.

10. Johnson, "Confessions," XVII, 22.

11. Johnson, "Babylon and Way Stations," III, 7–8.

12. Ahmad Y. al-Hassan, "Alchemy, Chemistry, and Chemical Technology," in *The Different Aspects of Islamic Culture, Volume 4: Science and Technology in Islam, Part II: Technology and Applied Sciences*, ed. Ahmad Y. al-Hassan (Beirut: UNESCO Publishing, 2001), 69. Laurence Michalak and Karen Trocki, "Alcohol and Islam: An Overview," *Contemporary Drug Problems* 33, no. 4 (2006): 525.

13. Michalak and Trocki, "Alcohol and Islam," 527–34, 547–48. The most significant *Quranic* verses are 4:43, 5:93–94, 16:67, and 2:219: "They ask thee concerning wine and gambling. Say: 'In them is great sin, and some profit, for men; but the sin is greater than the profit.'" See also: Nile Green, "Breaking the Begging Bowl: Morals, Drugs, and Madness in the Fate of the Muslim Faqīr," *South Asian History and Culture* 5, no. 2 (2014): 228.

14. Arminius Vámbéry, *Western Culture in Eastern Lands: A Comparison of the Methods Adopted by England and Russia in the Middle East* (New York: E. P. Dutton and Company, 1906), 218–19.

15. David Fromkin, *A Peace to End All Peace: The Fall of the Ottoman Empire and the Creation of the Modern Middle East* (New York: Henry Holt & Company, 1989), 34–35.

16. Charles King, *Midnight at the Pera Palace: The Birth of Modern Istanbul* (New York: W. W. Norton & Company, 2014), 58.

17. Ibid., 143. "Turkey," in: Ernest H. Cherrington, ed., *Standard Encyclopedia of the Alcohol Problem*, 6 vols., vol. 6 (Westerville, OH: American Issue Press, 1930), 2683–87.

18. Johnson, "Babylon and Way Stations," II, 13–14.

19. François Georgeon, "Ottomans and Drinkers: The Consumption of Alcohol in Istanbul in the Nineteenth Century," in *Outside In: On the Margins of the Modern Middle East*, ed. Eugene L. Rogan (London: I. B. Tauris, 2002), 9–10. Horatio Southgate, *Narrative of a Tour through*

Armenia, Kurdistan, Persia, and Mesopotamia, 2 vols., vol. 2 (London: Tilt and Bogue, 1840), 315–30. Ami Boué, *La Turquie d'Europe*, 4 vols., vol. 2 (Paris: Arthus Bertrand, 1840), 250. Despite his draconian antialcohol policies, Murad IV was reportedly a notorious drunkard, who died young due to overindulgence in drink. J. V. C. Smith, *Turkey and the Turks* (Boston: James French and Company, 1854), 25.

20. Smith, *Turkey and the Turks*, 25–26. Tuncer Baykara, "Değişme ve Medeniyet Anlayışı Açısından XIX. Asırda Osmanlı Yöneticilerinin Aile Yapısı," in *Sosyo-Kültürel Değişme Sürecinde Türk Ailesi* (Ankara: T. C. Başbakanlık Aile Araştırma Kurumu, 1992), 203–11.

21. Georgeon, "Ottomans and Drinkers," 11.

22. Charles Issawi, *The Economic History of Turkey, 1800–1914* (Chicago: University of Chicago Press, 1980), 353. More generally, see: İlkay Sunar, "State and Economy in the Ottoman Empire," in *The Ottoman Empire and the World-Economy*, ed. Huri İslamoğlu-İnan (New York: Cambridge University Press, 1987), 65–73. Reşat Kasaba, *The Ottoman Empire and the World Economy: The Nineteenth Century* (Albany: State University of New York Press, 1988), 13–15.

23. Issawi, *Economic History of Turkey*, 361–62. Harry N. Howard, *The Partition of Turkey: A Diplomatic History, 1913–1923* (New York: Howard Fertig, 1966), 47. Paul Auchterlonie, "A Turk of the West: Sir Edgar Vincent's Career in Egypt and the Ottoman Empire," *British Journal of Middle Eastern Studies* 27, no. 1 (2000): 55.

24. Donald C. Blaisdell, *European Financial Control in the Ottoman Empire: A Study of the Establishment, Activities, and Significance of the Administration of the Ottoman Public Debt* (New York: Columbia University Press, 1929), 112–13. Kemal H. Karpat, *Studies on Ottoman Social and Political History: Selected Articles and Essays* (Leiden: Brill, 2002), 279. See also: Giampaolo Conte and Gaetano Sabatini, "The Ottoman External Debt and Its Features under European Financial Control (1881–1914)," *Journal of European Economic History* 3 (2014): 71–75.

25. M. Cillière, "Situation commerciale, industrielle et agricole de la Turquie," in *Bulletin Consulaire Français*, ed. Ministère du Commerce de l'Industrie et des Colonies (Paris: Imprimerie Nationale, 1891), 487, Bulletin Consulaire Français: Bibliotheque Nationale de France, Paris. Donald Quataert, "Ottoman Reform and Agriculture in Anatolia, 1876–1908" (PhD dissertation, UCLA, 1973), 217. Similarly: E. L. Cutts, *Christians under the Crescent in Asia* (New York: Pott, Young & Co., 1877), 262. Note similarities with the French wine-colonization of Algeria. Owen White, *The Blood of the Colony: Wine and the Rise and Fall of French Algeria* (Cambridge: Harvard University Press, 2021), 31–37.

26. Fariba Zarinebaf, *Crime and Punishment in Istanbul, 1700–1800* (Berkeley: University of California Press, 2010), 100.

27. Mark Lawrence Schrad, *Vodka Politics: Alcohol, Autocracy, and the Secret History of the Russian State* (New York: Oxford University Press, 2014), 94–95. More generally, see: Linda T. Darling, *Revenue-Raising and Legitimacy* (Leiden: E. J. Brill, 1996), 119–20. George Tennyson Matthews, *The Royal General Farms in Eighteenth-Century France* (New York: Columbia University Press, 1958), 11.

28. Edmond du Temple, "État de la viticulture, de la récolte des raisins et de la fabrication des vins et spiritueux dans le vilayet de hudavendighiar et spécialement dans le sandjak de brousse en 1880," in *Bulletin consulaire français*, ed. Ministère du commerce de l'industrie et des colonies (Paris: Imprimerie Nationale, 1881), 484, Bulletin consulaire français: Bibliotheque Nationale de France, Paris. The grape marc is left to ferment in open barrels for twenty to twenty-five days, when it is then distilled, with anise added. See also: Cutts, *Christians under the Crescent in Asia*, 253–57.

29. Du Temple, "État de la viticulture," 484. The confusion had not cleared up even a decade later, as the French vice-consul to Rhodes reported in 1891 almost an identical account: M. Cirilli, "Production, commerce et navigation de l'île de Rhodes en 1889–1890," in *Bulletin*

consulaire français, ed. Ministère du commerce de l'industrie et des colonies (Paris: Imprimerie Nationale, 1891), 527, Bulletin consulaire français: Bibliotheque Nationale de France, Paris.

30. Zarinebaf, *Crime and Punishment in Istanbul*, 100.

31. Georgeon, "Ottomans and Drinkers," 12.

32. Clarence Richard Johnson, *Constantinople To-Day, or: The Pathfinder Survey of Constantinople; a Study in Oriental Social Life* (New York: Macmillan, 1922), 263.

33. Emine Ö. Evered and Kyle T. Evered, "A Geopolitics of Drinking: Debating the Place of Alcohol in Early Republican Turkey," *Political Geography* 50 (2016): 55.

34. Fromkin, *A Peace to End All Peace*, 40–50.

35. Ibid., 69.

36. "Turkey," in *Encyclopædia Britannica* (London: Encyclopædia Britannica Company, 1922), vol. XXXII, 802.

37. Peter Balakian, *The Burning Tigris: The Armenian Genocide and America's Response* (New York: HarperCollins, 2003), 200–201. Likewise, see: correspondence between US ambassador to Istanbul Henry Morgenthau Sr. and President Woodrow Wilson. Letter, Henry Morgenthau to Wilson, January 11, 1915, Box 7, Reel 7, Henry Morgenthau Papers, Manuscript Division, Library of Congress.

38. Jennifer M. Dixon, *Dark Pasts: Changing the State's Story in Turkey and Japan* (Ithaca, NY: Cornell University Press, 2018), 32–33.

39. Issawi, *Economic History of Turkey*, 366.

40. Fromkin, *A Peace to End All Peace*, 155–67.

41. Andrew Mango, *Atatürk* (London: John Murray, 1999), 29–33. Surnames were not widely in Turkey used before the Surname Law of 1934.

42. Ali Fuat Cebesoy, *Sınıf Arkadaşım Atatürk: Okul ve Genç Subaylık Hatıraları* (İstanbul: İnkılap Publishing House, 1967), 6. Ayşe Afet İnan, *Atatürk hakkında hâtıralar ve belgeler* (Ankara: Türk Tarih Kurumu Basımevi, 1959), 8.

43. Cebesoy, *Sınıf arkadaşım Atatürk*. Falih Rıfkı Atay, *Çankaya: Atatürk'ün doumundan ölümüne kadar* (İstanbul: Doğan Kardeş Basımevi, 1969), 31.

44. Mango, *Atatürk*, 45–46.

45. Georgeon, "Ottomans and Drinkers," 8, 26.

46. Atay, *Çankaya*, 31. Cebesoy, *Sınıf arkadaşım Atatürk*, 32. Mango, *Atatürk*, 47. Patrick Kinross, *Atatürk: The Rebirth of a Nation* (London: Weidenfeld & Nicholson, 1964), 16–17.

47. E. Elif Vatanoglu-Lutz, İnci Hot, and Mustafa Çoban, "What Do We Know about the Medical Biography of Kemal Atatürk (1881–1938)? A Summary of the State of Knowledge and Outlook on Relevant Issues for Further Research," *Journal of Medical Biography* 21, no. 3 (2013): 140–42.

48. Mango, *Atatürk*, 46. Quoting: Celâl Bayar, *Atatürk'ten hatıralar* (İstanbul: Sel Yayinlari, 1955), 19.

49. Mango, *Atatürk*, 74.

50. Hasan Rıza Soyak, *Yakınlarından hatıralar* (İstanbul: Sel Yayınları, 1955), 26, 93.

51. On anticipating Turkish backlash to Greek occupation: "Smyrna, Diomedis to the Greek Legation, Paris," February 1, 1919, A/5/VI 6, in: The Service of Diplomatic and Historical Archives (Y.D.I.A.) of the Ministry of Foreign Affairs, Athens, Greece. Nikolaos Petsalēs-Diomēdēs, *Greece at the Paris Peace Conference (1919)* (Thessaloniki: Institute for Balkan Studies, 1978), 194.

52. Fromkin, *A Peace to End All Peace*, 405–408, 428.

53. Isaiah Friedman, *British Miscalculations: The Rise of Muslim Nationalism, 1918–1925* (New Brunswick, NJ: Transaction Publishers, 2012), 96, 217. Michael Mandelbaum, *The Fate of Nations: The Search for National Security in the Nineteenth and Twentieth Centuries* (New York: Cambridge University Press, 1988), 61.

54. Blaisdell, *European Financial Control in the Ottoman Empire*, vii, 213–20. See also: Murat Birdal, *The Political Economy of Ottoman Public Debt: Insolvency and European Financial Control in the Late Nineteenth Century* (London: Bloomsbury Academic, 2010).

55. Johnson, "Babylon and Way Stations," II, 7.

56. "Turkey," in: Cherrington, ed., *Standard Encyclopedia of the Alcohol Problem*, 2687. Also: "Green Crescent Society," http://www.nargilegercekleri.com/en/?page_id=313 (accessed August 13, 2016). Johnson, "Babylon and Way Stations," II, 10.

57. Johnson, *Constantinople To-Day*, 263.

58. Johnson, "Confessions," XVIII, 7. William E. Johnson to Ernest Cherrington, June 28, 1925, 9, Box 1, Folder 5, William E. "Pussyfoot" Johnson Papers, Fenimore Art Museum Library, Cooperstown, NY. On India: "Constitution of the Prohibition League of India, 1926," in *Selected Works of C. Rajagopalachari: Vol. IV, 1926–30*, ed. Mukesh Kumar and Shilpa Menon (Hyderabad: Orient BlackSwan, 2017), 490–91.

59. See: Sait Naderi, *Mazhar Osman ve Türkiye'de nöroşirürjinin doğuşu* (İzmir: Dokuz Eylül Yayınları, 2004).

60. Johnson, "Confessions," XVIII, 7.

61. Johnson, "Babylon and Way Stations," II, 11.

62. Johnson, "Confessions," XVIII, 7. Johnson to Cherrington, June 28, 1925.

63. Johnson to Cherrington, June 28, 1925.

64. Evered and Evered, "Geopolitics of Drinking," 52–53. Karpat, *Studies on Ottoman Social and Political History*, 217–23.

65. On Şükrü's opposition to the liquor traffic, see: Kadir Mısıroğlu, *Şehid-i muazzez Ali Şükrü Bey* (İstanbul: Sebil Yayinevi, 1978), 33–34.

66. Onur Karahanoğulları, *Birinci Meclisin İçki Yasağı: Men-i Müskirat Kanunu* (Ankara: Phoenix Yayınevi, 2007), 11. Evered and Evered, "Geopolitics of Drinking," 53.

67. Minutes of the Grand National Assembly, TBMM Zabıt Ceridesi, c.1, İ:6, April 28 1336/1920, c:1, s. 114, Türkiye Büyük Millet Meclisi Kütüphanesi (Library of the Grand National Assembly), Ankara, Turkey, https://www.tbmm.gov.tr/kutuphane/tutanak_sorgu.html (accessed February 2, 2020).

68. TBMM Zabıt Ceridesi, c.1, İ:17, May 5, 1336/1920, c:3, 329–31.

69. TBMM Zabıt Ceridesi, c.1, İ:17, May 5, 1336/1920, c:3, 330. Karahanoğulları, *Birinci Meclisin İçki Yasağı*, 18. The finance ministry's proposal was later to only increase the tax from 15 percent to 20 percent. TBMM Zabıt Ceridesi, c.1, İ:64, September 13, 1336/1920, c:2, 102–104.

70. TBMM Zabıt Ceridesi, c.1, İ:17, May 5, 1336/1920, c:3, 333, and c.l, İ:32, July 12, 1336/1920, c: 2, 247.

71. Evered and Evered, "Geopolitics of Drinking," 54.

72. Karahanoğulları, *Birinci Meclisin İçki Yasağı*, 32–34.

73. Ibid., 34–38.

74. Ibid., 35–36. Many thanks to Jennifer Dixon and Şener Aktürk for assistance with these translations from Ottoman Turkish.

75. Ibid., 38. TBMM Zabıt Ceridesi, c.1, İ:64, September 13, 1336/1920, c:2, 107–108.

76. TBMM Zabıt Ceridesi, c.1, İ:65, September 14, 1336/1920, c:1, 122–23. Karahanoğulları, *Birinci Meclisin İçki Yasağı*, 54–55.

77. TBMM Zabıt Ceridesi, c.1, İ:65, September 14, 1336/1920, c:1, 126.

78. See: Dankwart A. Rustow, "Atatürk as Founder of a State," *Dædalus* 97, no. 3 (1968): 802–805.

79. Oğuz Akay, *Atatürk'ün sofrası* (İstanbul: Truva Yayınları, 2007), 44. Karahanoğulları, *Birinci Meclisin İçki Yasağı*, 122.

80. Kinross, *Atatürk*, 261–62. Mango, *Atatürk*, 292.

81. George W. Gawrych, *The Young Atatürk: From Ottoman Soldier to Statesman of Turkey* (London: I. B. Tauris, 2013), 180. Bruce Clark, *Twice a Stranger: The Mass Expulsions That Forged Modern Greece and Turkey* (Cambridge, MA: Harvard University Press, 2009), 113.

82. Uğur Mumcu, *Kürt-İslam ayaklanması, 1919–1925* (İstanbul: Tekin Yayınevi, 1991), 194.

83. Mango, *Atatürk*, 292.

84. Archival sources suggest that the British were not just skeptical, but outright hostile to the Greek plan. See: "Simopoulos to Ministry of Foreign Affairs," July 21, 1922, 3.1, no. 7632; and "Baltazzis to Rangabe," July 14, 1922, 4.1, no. 7185, in: The Service of Diplomatic and Historical Archives (Y.D.I.A.) of the Ministry of Foreign Affairs, Athens, Greece. Also: "War Office to Foreign Office, Copy Report of Harrington, July 17, 1922," July 17, 1922, FO 371/ 7884-E7444/27/44, Foreign Office Papers, Public Record Office, Kew, London. "Notes on Constantinople and the Near East," August 15, 1921, Papers on British Policy, De Robeck Papers, DRBK 6/13, 1919–1921, Churchill College Archives Centre, University of Cambridge, Cambridge, England.

85. George Horton, *The Blight of Asia: An Account of the Systematic Extermination of Christian Populations by Mohammedans and of the Culpability of Certain Great Powers; with the True Story of the Burning of Smyrna* (Indianapolis: Bobbs-Merrill, 1926), 78–82.

86. Falih Rıfkı Atay, *The Atatürk I Knew: An Abridged Translation of F. R. Atay's Çankaya*, trans. Geoffrey Lewis, 2nd ed. (İstanbul: Yapive Kredi Bankasi, 1982), 175–76. Mango, *Atatürk*, 349.

87. Norman M. Naimark, *Fires of Hatred: Ethnic Cleansing in Twentieth-Century Europe* (Cambridge, MA: Harvard University Press, 2002), 52. Mark Biondich, *The Balkans: Revolution, War, and Political Violence since 1878* (New York: Oxford University Press, 2011), 92. Fromkin, *A Peace to End All Peace*, 546. On the burning more generally: Vasilēs I. Tzanakarēs, *Smyrnē, 1919– 1922: Aristeids Stergiadēs enantion Chrysostomou* (Athēna: Metaichmio, 2019). Marjorie Dobkin Housepian, *Smyrna 1922: The Destruction of a City* (New York: Newmark Press, 1988).

88. Interview with Ward Price, *Daily Mail*, September 15, 1922. David Walder, *The Chanak Affair* (London: Hutchinson and Co., 1969), 182. Eleftheria Daleziou, "Britain and the Greek- Turkish War and Settlement of 1919–1923: The Pursuit of Security by 'Proxy' in Western Asia Minor" (PhD dissertation, University of Glasgow, 2002), 257.

89. "Turkey" in: Cherrington, ed., *Standard Encyclopedia of the Alcohol Problem*, 2685. Canan Balkan, "The Anti-Alcohol Movement in the Early Republican Period in Turkey" (MA thesis, Bogaziçi University, 2012). "The Anti-Alcohol Movement in Many Lands: Turkey," *Union Signal*, June 14, 1923, 13. On Atatürk's drinking in the military: Hüsrev Gerede and Sami Önal, *Hüsrev Gerede'nin anilari: Kurtulus Savasi, Atatürk ve devrimler: 19 Mayis 1919–10 Kasim 1938* (İstanbul: Literatür Yayincilik, 2002), 239.

90. Fromkin, *A Peace to End All Peace*, 551–52.

91. Johnson, "Babylon and Way Stations," II, 11. King, *Midnight at the Pera Palace*, 87. On Turkish positions going into the negotiation, see: Mustafa Kemal Atatürk, "Sulh Şartlari, İç ve diş siyasî meseleler (Sept. 2, 1922)," in *Atatürk'ün Söylev ve Demeçleri III (1918–1937)* (Ankara: Türk Tarih Kurumu Basimevi, 1954), 48–52.

92. Gürkan Beriş, "Osmanli Borçlanma tarihi—Ottoman Debt History" (2010). Archived at https://web.archive.org/web/20101125180142/http://gberis.e-monsite.com/ categorie%2Cosmanli-borclanma-tarihi-ottoman-debt-history%2C3219214.html (accessed January 20, 2021).

93. Vatanoglu-Lutz, Hot, and Çoban, "What Do We Know about Atatürk?," 139–41.

94. Austin Bay, *Ataturk: Lessons in Leadership from the Greatest General of the Ottoman Empire* (New York: Palgrave Macmillan, 2011), 161.

95. TBMM Zabıt Ceridesi, c.8, İ:32, April 8, 1340/1924, c:2, 448–49. Also: Atay, *Çankaya*, 399.

96. Karahanoğulları, *Birinci Meclisin İçki Yasağı*, 36, 49.

97. Ruşen Eşref Ünaydın, "Anafartalar kumandani Mustafa Kemal'le mülakat ikinci gün," *Türk Dili* 1956, 607. Vatanoglu-Lutz, Hot, and Çoban, "What Do We Know about Atatürk?," 139–40.

98. Bedi Şehsuvaroğlu, *Atatürk'ün sağlik hayati'* (Istanbul: Hürriyet Yayınları, 1981), 19–20. Şükrü Tezer, *Atatürk'ün hatira defteri* (Ankara: Türk Tarih Kurumu Basimevi, 1972), 68, 208. Falih Rıfkı Atay, *Babanız Atatürk* (İstanbul: Doğan Kardeş Basımevi, 1966), 99.

99. Cemal Granda, *Atatürk'ün uşaği idim* (İstanbul: Hürriyet Yayınları, 1973).

100. Tahsin Öztin, *Mustafa Kemal'den Atatürk'e: Anilar* (İstanbul: Hür Yayin, 1981), 34–36. See also: 112, 144.

101. Kinross, *Atatürk*, 261.

102. Granda, *Atatürk'ün uşaği idim*, 242–44.

103. Mango, *Atatürk*, 439–40, 460.

104. Though it seems on that occasion they drank whiskey rather than rakı. Cebesoy, *Sınıf Arkadaşım Atatürk*, 51.

105. Şehsuvaroğlu, *Atatürk'ün sağlik hayati'*, 19–20. Security guards reported Atatürk drank less than 250 mL per night. "Atatürk'ün gecede 250 gramdan çok rakı içtiğini görmedim." Özdemir Hazar, *Yeni Asır*, 16 Eylül 1981, 2. Cited in: Vatanoglu-Lutz, Hot, and Çoban, "What Do We Know about Atatürk?," 139–40. See also: Hikmet Bil, *Atatürk'ün sofrasi* (Istanbul: Basildigi yer, 1955), 18.

106. Mango, *Atatürk*, 513.

107. Ibid., 518–19.

108. Yekta Güngör Özden, "Atatürk gerçeğine küçük bir katkı," *Anıtkabir Dergisi* 2 (2000): 21. Quoted in: Vatanoglu-Lutz, Hot, and Çoban, "What Do We Know about Atatürk?," 141.

109. Johnson, "Confessions," XVIII, 3–9.

110. Ibid., XVII, 25–26. See also: Johnson to Cherrington, June 28, 1925. J. H. Larimore, "World League Office in Cairo Is Plan; Pussyfoot Says Orient Leans to Drouth," *American Issue*, May 10, 1924, and "Pussyfoot Received with Open Arms by the Egyptians," *American Issue*, January 19, 1924, both in: Box 3a, Folder 37, Reel 18, World League Against Alcoholism Records, Temperance and Prohibition Papers, Ohio Historical Society.

111. On the American Mission Press, see: David G. Malick, *The American Mission Press: A Preliminary Bibliography* (Chicago: Atour Publications, 2008).

112. Johnson, "Babylon and Way Stations," II, 7.

113. Ibid., II, 7–8.

114. Ibid., II, 8. Also: Pierre Hecker, "Heavy Metal in the Middle East: New Urban Spaces in a Translocal Underground," in *Being Young and Muslim: New Cultural Politics in the Global South and North*, ed. Linda Herrera and Asef Bayat (New York: Oxford University Press, 2010), 330.

115. The government subsequently reversed itself, nationalizing Bomonti in 1934. "Views of the Former Bomonti Brewery of Constantinople," Levantine Heritage Foundation, http://www.levantineheritage.com/bomonti.htm (accessed January 20, 2021). See also: "Bomonti ihalesi iptal oluyor," *Hürriyet*, August 25, 2006, https://www.hurriyet.com.tr/ekonomi/bomonti-ihalesi-iptal-oluyor-4978394 (accessed February 10, 2020).

116. Quoted in: "Turkey" in: Cherrington, ed., *Standard Encyclopedia of the Alcohol Problem*, 2685–86.

117. Johnson, "Confessions," XVIII, 7.

118. Johnson, "Babylon and Way Stations," III, 5–7.

119. Johnson, "Confessions," XVII, 23. On anti-Muslim attitudes, see: Kamil Aydin, *Western Images of Turkey* (Ankara: British Council, 1999).

120. Johnson, "Confessions," XVII, 17–18.

Chapter 9

1. These descriptions cobbled together from: Calvin M. Young, *Little Turtle (Me-She-Kin-No-Quah), the Great Chief of the Miami Indian Nation* (Indianapolis: Sentinel Ptg. Co., 1917), 141–42. Harvey L. Carter, *The Life and Times of Little Turtle: First Sagamore of the Wabash* (Urbana: University of Illinois Press, 1987), 84.

2. Young, *Little Turtle*, 22, 88. Bert Anson, *The Miami Indians* (Norman: University of Oklahoma Press, 1970), 7–15. The Miami tribe, Confederation, and river in Ohio had nothing to do with the city in south Florida, established more than a century later.

3. John McDonald, *Biographical Sketches of General Nathaniel Massie, General Duncan McArthur, Captain William Wells, and General Simon Kenton: Who Were Early Settlers in the Western Country* (Dayton, OH: D. Osborn & Son, 1838), 184. Carter, *Life and Times of Little Turtle*, 82–84.

4. James M. Perry, *Arrogant Armies: Great Military Disasters and the Generals behind Them* (Hoboken, NJ: John Wiley & Sons, 1996), 40–45. Emilius O. Randall, *History of Ohio: The Rise and Progress of an American State* (New York: Century History Company, 1912), vol. II, 518. Carter, *Life and Times of Little Turtle*, 108. Soon thereafter, it was prohibited to sell intoxicating liquors to soldiers within ten miles of any military fort in the Northwest Territory. See: "An Act Prohibiting the Sale of Spiritous and Other Intoxicating Liquors to Soldiers in the Service of the United States Being within Ten Miles of Any Military Post within the Territory of the United States Northwest of the River Ohio, 1790," in: William Clark Papers, Series M, Vol. 1, Reel 39, Draper Manuscript Collection, Wisconsin Historical Society, Madison.

5. Charles H. L. Johnston, *Famous Indian Chiefs: Their Battles, Treaties, Sieges, and Struggles with the Whites for Possession of America* (Boston: L. C. Page & Company, 1909), 295–99. Also: Young, *Little Turtle*, 58–59.

6. McDonald, *Biographical Sketches*, 190–91. Johnston, *Famous Indian Chiefs*, 300. Biographer Harvey Lewis Carter suggests that Wells and Little Turtle had together hatched a plan to bring peace between the races. Carter, *Life and Times of Little Turtle*, 112–15.

7. Alan D. Gaff, *Bayonets in the Wilderness: Anthony Wayne's Legion in the Old Northwest* (Norman: University of Oklahoma Press, 2004), 327.

8. Johnston, *Famous Indian Chiefs*, 305.

9. John S. C. Abbott, *The History of the State of Ohio: From the Discovery of the Great Valley, to the Present Time* (Detroit: Northwestern Publishing Company, 1875), 374–75. Young, *Little Turtle*, 87–88.

10. Young, *Little Turtle*, 90–92.

11. "Treaty of Greenville Minutes," 1795, Miami University Archives, CIS-NO: ASP07 Ind.aff/ 67/1 Serial Set, https://ohiomemory.org/digital/collection/p267401coll36/id/22026/ rec/3 (accessed June 11, 2019). On Greene Ville more generally: Mary Stockwell, *Unlikely General: "Mad" Anthony Wayne and the Battle for America* (New Haven, CT: Yale University Press, 2018), 284.

12. Young, *Little Turtle*, 92, 106. See also: "Baltimore Yearly Meeting Indian Committee Minutes," 1795–1815, 48, RG2/By/6, Friends Historical Library of Swarthmore College.

13. Carter, *Life and Times of Little Turtle*, 149, 57–58. Young, *Little Turtle*, 113–14.

14. Little Turtle renounced scalping, torturing prisoners, burning at the stake, and other inhumane military practices. Johnston, *Famous Indian Chiefs*, 307. George W. Corner, *The Autobiography of Benjamin Rush: His "Travels through Life" Together with His Commonplace Book for 1789– 1813* (Westport, CT: Greenwood Press, 1970), 240–41. See also: Benjamin Rush, *An Inquiry into the Effects of Ardent Spirits upon the Human Body and Mind* (Springfield, MA: Thomas Dickman, 1817). Anthony F. C. Wallace, *Jefferson and the Indians: The Tragic Fate of the First Americans* (Cambridge, MA: Belknap Press, 1999), 117–19. Kościuszko gave Little Turtle a pair of guns with instructions to "shoot dead the first man who ever comes to subjugate you or to despoil you of your country." Young, *Little Turtle*, 145.

15. On Little Turtle and Wells's hotel and tavern tabs, see: Carter, *Life and Times of Little Turtle*, 7, 161.

16. Johnston, *Famous Indian Chiefs*, 307. Similarly, at Baltimore: "After his reason comes back to him, he gets up and finds where he is. He asks for his peltry. The answer is, 'You have drunk them.' 'Where is my gun?' 'It is gone.' 'Where is my blanket?' 'It is gone.' 'Where is my shirt?' 'You have sold it for whisky!!' Now, Brothers, figure to yourself what a condition this man must be in—he has a family at home, a wife and children that stand in need of the profits of his hunting. What must their wants be, when he is even without a shirt!" "A Brief Account of the Proceedings of the Committee Appointed by the Yearly Meeting of Friends Held in Baltimore," 1806, 20, BX7747.3.A1B1 c.2, Friends Historical Library of Swarthmore College.

17. Young, *Little Turtle*, 149. William E. Johnson, *The Federal Government and the Liquor Traffic*, 2nd ed. (Westerville, OH: American Issue Publishing Company, 1917), 197, 200.

18. "Baltimore Yearly Meeting Indian Committee Minutes," 1795–1815, 51, RG2/By/6, Friends Historical Library of Swarthmore College. As an aside: given the inequalities in technology and advancement, Native Americans were infantilized and subordinated to white Europeans, referring to the president as the "Great Father," responsible for raising and protecting his children. American presidents referred to natives as their "children." By contrast, the Quakers referred to everyone as brothers and sisters.

19. "A Brief Account of the Proceedings of the Committee Appointed by the Yearly Meeting of Friends Held in Baltimore," 1806, 17–19. See also: "Baltimore Yearly Meeting Indian Committee Minutes," 1795–1815, 50. Johnson, *Federal Government and the Liquor Traffic*, 199–200.

20. Johnson, *Federal Government and the Liquor Traffic*, 201.

21. "Quaker Dispatch to the Secretary of War, Henry Dearborn," December 31, 1801, RG75 (M 271), Letters Received by the Office of the Secretary of War Relating to Indian Affairs, 1800–1823, Reel 1, 1800–1816, National Archives, Washington, DC.

22. "Address of Little Turtle, [4 January 1802]," Thomas Jefferson Papers, National Archives, https://founders.archives.gov/documents/Jefferson/01-36-02-0168-0002 (accessed June 12, 2019). Barbara B. Oberg, ed., *The Papers of Thomas Jefferson, Vol. 36: 1 December 1801–3 March 1802* (Princeton, NJ: Princeton University Press, 2009), 280–86. Reproduced in: Leonard U. Hill, *John Johnston and the Indians in the Land of the Three Miamis* (Columbus, OH: Stoneman Press, 1957), 17.

23. "Jefferson's Reply, 7 January 1802," Thomas Jefferson Papers, National Archives, https://founders.archives.gov/documents/Jefferson/01-36-02-0168-0003 (accessed June 12, 2019). Oberg, ed., *Jefferson Papers, Vol. 36*, 286–87.

24. "Henry Dearborn's Reply, 7 January 1802," Thomas Jefferson Papers, National Archives, https://founders.archives.gov/documents/Jefferson/01-36-02-0168-0004 (accessed June 12, 2019). See also: Oberg, ed., *Jefferson Papers, Vol. 36*, 287–89.

25. "From Thomas Jefferson to the Senate and the House of Representatives, 27 January 1802," Thomas Jefferson Papers, National Archives, https://founders.archives.gov/documents/Jefferson/01-36-02-0289 (accessed June 12, 2019). Oberg, ed., *Jefferson Papers, Vol. 36*, 440–43. Thomas L. McKenney and James Hall, *History of the Indian Tribes of North America, with Biographical Sketches and Anecdotes of the Principal Chiefs*, Vol. III (Philadelphia: Daniel Rice and James G. Clark, 1844), 114.

26. Excludes skins and furs key to the Indian fur trade. Sections 9 & 21, Chapter 13, "An Act to Regulate Trade and Intercourse with the Indian Tribes, and to Preserve Peace on the Frontiers," March 30, 1802, Seventh Congress, Session 1, Statutes at Large, Law Library of Congress, Washington, DC, https://www.loc.gov/law/help/statutes-at-large/7th-congress.php (accessed January 20, 2021). Richard Peters, ed., *The Public Statutes at Large of the United States of America, from the Organization of the Government in 1789, to March 3, 1845*, 8 vols., vol. 2 (Boston: Charles C. Little and James Brown, 1850), 142–46. Wallace, *Jefferson and the Indians*, 206–12.

27. Francis Paul Prucha, *American Indian Policy in the Formative Years: The Indian Trade and Intercourse Acts, 1790–1834* (Cambridge, MA: Harvard University Press, 1962), 104, 107. In the colonial era, New Jersey's statute dates only from 1751, as compared to 1674 in New Haven Colony, 1642 in New Netherland, and 1633 in Massachusetts Bay. See: Gallus Thomann, *Colonial Liquor Laws* (New York: United States Brewers' Association, 1887), 10, 87, 143–45, 166, 177. Johnson, *Federal Government and the Liquor Traffic*, 160–73. E. Benjamin Andrews, *History of the United States: From the Earliest Discoveries of America to the Present Time*, 6 vols., vol. 1 (New York: Charles Scribner's Sons, 1925), 195. John G. Woolley and William E. Johnson, *Temperance Progress of the Century* (Philadelphia: Linscott Publishing Company, 1905), 35. Some early Indian agents were reluctant to reside among

the tribes, citing the near-constant harassment for "food, tobacco and liquor." "Jean Pierre Chouteau to Osage Agency," December 8, 1816, Records of the Central Superintendency of Indian Affairs: 1813–1878, RG75 (M 856), Records of the St. Louis Superintendency, Reel 2, National Archives, Washington, DC. See also: "A Talk between General Wilkinson and a Deputation from the Cherokee Nation," June 10, 1802, RG75 (M 271), Letters Received by the Office of the Secretary of War Relating to Indian Affairs, 1800–1823, Reel 1, 1800–1816, National Archives, Washington, DC. "Unsigned Letter from Rocky [Rock] Island," May 11, 1829, Records of the Central Superintendency of Indian Affairs: 1813–1878, RG75 (M 856), Records of the St. Louis Superintendency, Reel 2, National Archives, Washington, DC.

28. William E. Unrau, *White Man's Wicked Water: The Alcohol Trade and Prohibition in Indian Country, 1802–1892* (Lawrence: University Press of Kansas, 1996), 18, 31.

29. For example, the Humane Abolition Society of Fort Wayne was established in 1822 to hold white traders accountable for violations of the prohibition law. But when their evidence of wrongdoing was consistently ignored by "the proper civil officials," this nascent temperance society disbanded. Ibid., 23.

30. Ibid., 57. See also: Laughlin McDonald, *American Indians and the Fight for Equal Voting Rights* (Norman: University of Oklahoma Press, 2010).

31. See: "Thomas Jefferson to Chief Little Turtle," December 21, 1808, in: Thomas Jefferson Papers, Series 1: General Correspondence, 1651–1827, Reel 042, Library of Congress, Manuscripts Division, https://www.loc.gov/resource/mtj1.042_1362_1364/?st=gallery (accessed June 24, 2019).

32. "President's Talks to the Picara and Mandan Nations," 1806, RG75 (M 271), Letters Received by the Office of the Secretary of War Relating to Indian Affairs, 1800–1823, Reel 1, 1800–1816, National Archives, Washington, DC.

33. Nathan Heald, "Captain Heald, Massacre at Chicago: Letter of October 3, 1812," in *Official Letters of the Military and Naval Officers of the United States, During the War with Great Britain in the Years 1812, 13, 14, & 15*, ed. Jon Brannan (Washington, DC: Way & Gideon, 1823), 84–85. Thomas Forsyth Papers, 1804–1833, Series 1T, Vol. 1, Draper Manuscripts, Wisconsin Historical Society, Madison. William Heath, *William Wells and the Struggle for the Old Northwest* (Norman: University of Oklahoma Press, 2015), 375–88. Ann Durkin Keating, *Rising Up from Indian Country: The Battle of Fort Dearborn and the Birth of Chicago* (Chicago: University of Chicago Press, 2012).

34. Johnson, *Federal Government and the Liquor Traffic*, 204.

35. Young, *Little Turtle*, 149.

36. Perhaps with the exception of the Pueblos of the American Southwest, Mexico, and Central America, which had some domestic traditions of fermenting alcohol. "Aborigines of North America," in: Ernest H. Cherrington, ed., *Standard Encyclopedia of the Alcohol Problem*, 6 vols., vol. 1 (Westerville, OH: American Issue Press, 1925), 3. McKenney and Hall, *History of the Indian Tribes of North America*, 9–10. Gina Hames, *Alcohol in World History* (London: Routledge, 2012), 50–56.

37. "Aborigines of North America," in: Cherrington, ed., *Standard Encyclopedia of the Alcohol Problem*, vol. 1, 13. McKenney and Hall, *History of the Indian Tribes of North America*, 9–10.

38. John Heckewelder, *History, Manners, and Customs of the Indian Nations Who Once Inhabited Pennsylvania and the Neighbouring States [1818]* (Philadelphia: Historical Society of Pennsylvania, 1876), 73–75, 262. Evan T. Pritchard, *Native New Yorkers: The Legacy of the Algonquin People of New York* (San Francisco: Council Oak Books, 2002), 35.

39. Nathaniel Philbrick, *Mayflower: A Story of Courage, Community, and War* (New York: Viking, 2006), 93.

40. Edward Winslow, *Mourt's Relation, or Journal of the Plantation at Plymouth [1622]* (Boston: John Kimball Wiggin, 1865), 93.

41. Heckewelder, *History, Manners, and Customs*, 263. Similarly: Lewis Cass, "Remarks on the Policy and Practices of the United States and Great Britain in Their Treatment of the Indian,"

North American Review 24 (1827): 404. See also: Claudio Saunt, *Unworthy Republic: The Dispossession of Native Americans and the Road to Indian Territory* (New York: W.W. Norton & Co., 2020), 5, 11.

42. Randall Craig Davis, *"Firewater Myths: Alcohol and Portrayals of Native Americans in American Literature"* (PhD dissertation, Ohio State University, 1991), 33. Also: Yasuhide Kawashima, *Puritan Justice and the Indian: White Man's Law in Massachusetts, 1630–1763* (Middletown, CT: Wesleyan University Press, 1986), 82–88.

43. Woolley and Johnson, *Temperance Progress*, 35. See also: Alice C. Fletcher, "Indian Education and Civilization: A Report Prepared in Answer to Senate Resolution of February 23, 1885," in *The Executive Documents of the Senate of the United States, for the Second Session of the Forty-Eighth Congress and the Special Session of the Senate Convened March 4, 1885* (Washington, DC: Government Printing Office, 1888), 43.

44. Nathaniel B. Shurtleff, ed., *Records of the Governor and Company of the Massachusetts Bay in New England, Vol. IV, Part I* (Boston: William White, 1854), 201, 89.

45. In 1668, for the amount of six hundred pounds sterling. James Alton James, *English Institutions and the American Indian*, Johns Hopkins University Studies in Historical and Political Science (Baltimore: Johns Hopkins University Press, 1894), 27.

46. Johnson, *Federal Government and the Liquor Traffic*, 183–84.

47. "Aborigines of North America," in: Cherrington, ed., *Standard Encyclopedia of the Alcohol Problem*, vol. 1, 13–14. Johnson, *Federal Government and the Liquor Traffic*, 192.

48. John Fiske, *The Dutch and Quaker Colonies in America*, 2 vols. (Boston: Houghton Mifflin, 1899), vol. 1, 232–37.

49. All *sic*. "Letter from William Penn to the Kings of the Indians in Pennsylvania: London, August 18, 1681," Penn Family Papers, 0485A, Historical Society of Pennsylvania, Philadelphia, https://hsp.org/education/primary-sources/letter-from-william-penn-to-the-king-of-the-indians (accessed June 13, 2019).

50. Frederick B. Tolles, "Nonviolent Contact: The Quakers and the Indians," *Proceedings of the American Philosophical Society* 107, no. 2 (1963): 95.

51. "Wm. Penn to Henry Savell, 30 May, 1683," in: Samuel Hazard, ed., *Pennsylvania Archives. Selected and Arranged from Original Document in the Office of the Secretary of the Commonwealth, Vol. I: 1664–1747* (Philadelphia: Joseph Severns & Co., 1852), 68–69.

52. Thomann, *Colonial Liquor Laws*, 131.

53. Thomas J. Sugrue, "The Peopling and Depeopling of Early Pennsylvania: Indians and Colonists, 1680–1720," *Pennsylvania Magazine of History and Biography* 116, no. 1 (1992): 24. Fletcher, "Indian Education and Civilization," 62.

54. Thomas Budd, *Good Order Established in Pennsylvania and New Jersey [1685]* (Cleveland: Burrows Brothers Company, 1902), 65–66. Emphasis mine. Seven score equates to 140 tribesmen lost to liquor.

55. "The 'Great Law'—December 7, 1682." Record Group 26: Records of the Department of State, Pennsylvania Historical & Museum Commission, http://www.phmc.state.pa.us/portal/communities/documents/1681-1776/great-law.html (accessed June 14, 2019). See also: Fiske, *Dutch and Quaker Colonies*, vol. 2, 153–59.

56. Sugrue, "Peopling and Depeopling," 25.

57. Thomann, *Colonial Liquor Laws*. Also: Henry A. Scomp, *King Alcohol in the Realm of King Cotton, or, a History of the Liquor Traffic and of the Temperance Movement in Georgia from 1733 to 1887* (Chicago: Blakey Print Co., 1888). Ernest H. Cherrington, *The Evolution of Prohibition in the United States of America: A Chronological History of the Liquor Problem and the Temperance Reform in the United States from the Earliest Settlements to the Consummation of National Prohibition* (Westerville, OH: American Issue Press, 1920), 34.

58. "Aborigines of North America," in: Cherrington, ed., *Standard Encyclopedia of the Alcohol Problem*, vol. 1, 15. Johnson, *Federal Government and the Liquor Traffic*, 193–96.

59. McKenney and Hall, *History of the Indian Tribes of North America*, 141. One could similarly include the Shakers in this regard. James Mooney, "The Ghost-Dance Religion and the Sioux Outbreak of 1890," in *Fourteenth Annual Report of the Bureau of Ethnology, Part 2* (Washington, DC: Government Printing Office, 1896), 760.

60. *Orderly Book of General George Washington, Commander in Chief of the American Armies, Kept at Valley Forge, 18 May–11 June, 1778* (Boston: Lamson, Wolffe and Company, 1898), 13, 35.

61. *Valley Forge Orderly Book of General George Weedon of the Continental Army under Command of General George Washington, in the Campaign of 1777–8* (New York: Dodd, Mead & Company, 1902), 210, 290.

62. W. J. Rorabaugh, *The Alcoholic Republic: An American Tradition* (New York: Oxford University Press, 1979), 5, 30, 49, 63, 73, 102–104. James C. Scott, *Domination and the Arts of Resistance: Hidden Transcripts* (New Haven, CT: Yale University Press, 1990), 121. Ted Smith, "Eight Founding Fathers' Insane Drinking Habits," *Thrillist*, January 9, 2015, https://www.thrillist.com/drink/nation/presidential-drinking-habits-washington-jefferson (accessed January 8, 2019).

63. See: Tun Yuan Hu, *The Liquor Tax in the United States* (New York: Columbia University Graduate School of Business, 1950).

64. Thomann, *Colonial Liquor Laws*, 6–7, 145–48. Rorabaugh, *The Alcoholic Republic*, 28. Such laws date from 1683 in Pennsylvania, 1648 in New York, 1647 in Rhode Island, 1640 in Connecticut, 1633 in the Massachusetts Bay Colony, and as early as 1619 in Jamestown Colony, Virginia. For an extended discussion, see: Mark Lawrence Schrad, "The First Social Policy: Alcohol Control and Modernity in Policy Studies," *Journal of Policy History* 19, no. 4 (2007), 432–37.

65. See: Ian Tyrrell and Jay Sexton, "Introduction," in *Empire's Twin: U.S. Anti-Imperialism from the Founding Era to the Age of Terrorism*, ed. Ian Tyrrell and Jay Sexton (Ithaca, NY: Cornell University Press, 2015), 7–9. Ian Tyrrell, *Reforming the World: The Creation of America's Moral Empire* (Princeton, NJ: Princeton University Press, 2010), 2.

66. "Cornplanter to Pennsylvania Governor " February 2, 1822, in: William L. Stone, *The Life and Times of Red-Jacket, or Sa-Go-Ye-Wat-Ha; Being the Sequel to the History of the Six Nations* (New York: Wiley and Putnam, 1841), 452.

67. McKenney and Hall, *History of the Indian Tribes of North America*, 85. See also: Wilbur R. Jacobs, *Diplomacy and Indian Gifts: Anglo-French Rivalry along the Ohio and Northwestern Frontiers, 1743–1763* (Palo Alto, CA: Stanford University Press, 1950), 53.

68. "Letter XXVI. To Colonel Monroe. Paris, August 11, 1786," in: Thomas Jefferson Randolph, ed., *Memoir, Correspondence, and Miscellanies, from the Papers of Thomas Jefferson*, vol. 1 (Charlottesville, VA: F. Carr, and Co., 1829), 43. Also: "Editorial Note: Jefferson's Proposed Concert of Powers against the Barbary States," Thomas Jefferson Papers, National Archives, https://founders.archives.gov/documents/Jefferson/01-10-02-0424-0001 (accessed June 16, 2019). Jefferson expressed his envy of the polite and temperate nature of the French while negotiating in Paris. "In the pleasures of the table they are far before us, because, with good taste they united temperance. They do not terminate the most sociable meals by transforming themselves into brutes. I have never yet seen a man drunk in France, even among the lowest of the people." "Letter CXVII. To Mr. Bellini. Paris, September 30, 1785," in: Randolph, ed., *Memoir, Correspondence, and Miscellanies*, vol. 1, 328.

69. "Chapter II—An Act for Laying Duty on Goods, Wares, and Merchandises Imported into the United States," July 4, 1789, First Congress, Session 1, Statutes at Large. Law Library of Congress, Washington, DC, https://www.loc.gov/law/help/statutes-at-large/1st-congress.php (accessed January 20, 2021). Peters, ed., *Public Statutes at Large*, Vol. I, 24–25. More generally, see: William Hill, "First Stages of the Tariff Policy of the United States," *Publications of the American Economic Association* 8, no. 6 (1893): 34.

70. Eric Lomazoff, *Reconstructing the National Bank Controversy: Politics and Law in the Early American Republic* (Chicago: University of Chicago Press, 2018), 16–17. In 1789 Thomas

Jefferson clarified, "*Impost* is a duty paid on any imported article, in the *moment of its importation*, and of course, it is collected in the seaports only. *Excise* is a duty on any article, whether imported or raised at home, and paid in the *hands of the consumer or retailer*; consequently, it is collected through the whole country. These are the true definitions of these words as used in England, and in the greater part of the United States. But in Massachusetts, they have perverted the word excise to mean a tax on all liquors, whether paid in the moment of importation or at a later moment, and on nothing else." "Letter CVCV. To J. Sarsfield. Paris, April 3, 1789," in: Randolph, ed., *Memoir, Correspondence, and Miscellanies*, vol. II, 453–54.

71. Alexander Hamilton, *Report of the Secretary of the Treasury to the House of Representatives, Relative to a Provision for the Support of the Public Credit of the United States* (New York: Francis Childs and John Swaine, 1790), 17, Library of Congress, Manuscripts Division, Alexander Hamilton Papers, Reel 21, Speeches and Writings file. Alexander Hamilton, *Act Imposing Certain Inland Duties on Foreign Wines [1790, Jan. 9]* (1790), Alexander Hamilton Papers, Reel 21. Alexander Hamilton, "Federalist No. 12," in *The Federalist: A Commentary on the Constitution of the United States, Being a Collection of Essays Written in Support of the Constitution Agreed Upon September 17, 1787, by the Federal Convention*, ed. Alexander Hamilton, John Jay, and James Madison (New York: Modern Library, 1937). On consumption rates, see: W. J. Rorabaugh, "Estimated U.S. Alcoholic Beverage Consumption, 1790–1860," *Journal of Studies on Alcohol* 37 (1976), 357–64..

72. James Madison, *Papers*, ed. William T. Hutchinson and William M. Rachal, 17 vols., vol. 13 (Chicago: University of Chicago Press, 1962), 366. Ron Chernow, *Alexander Hamilton* (New York: Penguin Press, 2004), 342. For critics beyond Madison, see: Gallus Thomann, *Liquor Laws of the United States; Their Spirit and Effect*, 2 vols., vol. 1 (New York: United States Brewers' Association, 1885), 4, 13–15. Rorabaugh, *The Alcoholic Republic*, 50–51.

73. Young, *Little Turtle*, 71. See also: Alexander Hamilton, "Second Report on Public Credit, Dec. 13, 1790," in *Select Documents Illustrative of the History of the United States, 1776–1861*, ed. William MacDonald (New York: Macmillan Co., 1898), 62–63.

74. Emanuel Wurm, "4e Commission: l'alcoolisme. La lutte contre les dangers de l'alcool," *Congrès Socialiste International de Vienne (23–29 août 1914): dokuments*, no. 4 (1914): 13–16, 27–28.. Työväenliikkeen kirjasto (Library of the Labour Movement, Helsinki, Finland), 327.322. HELDA 2821715. See also: Hu, *The Liquor Tax in the United States*, 50 (Figure 1). Brenda Yevlington, "Excise Taxes in Historical Perspective," in *Taxing Choice: The Predatory Politics of Fiscal Discrimination*, ed. William Shughart (New Brunswick, NJ: Transaction Publishers, 1997), 47. Increasing liquor taxes to fund war and increase state capacity nicely illustrates Tilly's so-called ratchet effect. "How War Made States, and Vice Versa," in: Charles Tilly, *Coercion, Capital and European States, AD 990–1990* (Cambridge, MA: Blackwell Press, 1990), 67–95.

75. Tyrrell, *Reforming the World*, 3–5.

76. "But the Indians, it seems, had little confidence in what the missionaries told them, as the so-called Christian trades who dealt commonly with them with the design of gain through nothing but cheating and lying to become rich in a short time. They used all manner of stratagems to get the furs of the savages cheap; they made use of lies and deceptions to gain double if they could. . . . Such practices, without doubt, caused an aversion against a religion which was falsely professed by men of so base a type." Young, *Little Turtle*, 21. See also: Heckewelder, *History, Manners, and Customs*, 265.

77. Randall, *History of Ohio*, vol. II, 581–82.

78. Amy DeRogatis, *Moral Geography: Maps, Missionaries, and the American Frontier* (New York: Columbia University Press, 2003), 22.

79. Heckewelder, *History, Manners, and Customs*, 262, 65.

80. Sagoyewatha, "Red Jacket on the Religion of the White Man and the Red (1805)," in *The World's Famous Orations*, ed. William Jennings Bryan (New York: Funk and Wagnalls Company, 1906), 9. Granville Ganter, ed., *The Collected Speeches of Sagoyewatha, or Red Jacket*

(Syracuse, NY: Syracuse University Press, 2006), xxvi–xxvii. See also: Samuel G. Drake, *Biography and History of the Indians of North America. From Its First Discovery to the Present Time*, 7th ed. (Boston: Antiquarian Institute, 1837), 101.

81. See: "Receipt of the Seneca Nation, Buffalo Creek Village," May 13, 1803, May 16, 1805, April 24, 1809, and May 11, 1801, RG75 (M 271), Letters Received by the Office of the Secretary of War Relating to Indian Affairs, 1800–1823, Reel 1, 1800–1816, National Archives, Washington, DC. Norman B. Wilkinson, "Robert Morris and the Treaty of Big Tree," *Mississippi Valley Historical Review* 40, no. 2 (1953): 257.

82. Wilkinson, "Robert Morris and the Treaty of Big Tree," 268–71. Livingston County Historical Society, *History of the Treaty of Big Tree* (Geneseo, NY: Livingston County Historical Society, 1897), 28, 40. Ryan K. Smith, *Robert Morris's Folly: The Architectural and Financial Failures of an American Founder* (New Haven, CT: Yale University Press, 2014), 160–61.

83. Emphasis mine. See: "Indian Collection," Box 1, Folder 1, BECHS B00-2, Buffalo and Erie County Historical Society, Buffalo, New York, https://docs.google.com/document/d/1YLGiNs7xor0rtqYHpqCPPtrASGby9zS3Mn-lkKGBv_E/pub (accessed June 19, 2019). "Variant Text of the Reply to Rev. Jacob Cram, November 1805," in: Ganter, ed., *Collected Speeches of Sagoyewatha*, 147–48. See also: Stone, *Life and Times of Red-Jacket*, 208–209.

84. This thanks in part to inclusion in William Jennings Bryan's ten-volume *World's Famous Orations* compilation. Sagoyewatha, "Red Jacket on the Religion of the White Man and the Red (1805)." Red Jacket's reply is often mischaracterized as his "Speech to the U.S. Senate," though he never addressed Congress in his lifetime, according to his biographies. Some of his speeches were read into the *Congressional Record* in 1903 by Jim Crow segregationist Alabama senator John Tyler Morgan. See: *Congressional Record: Containing the Proceedings and Debates of the Fifty-Seventh Congress, Second Session*, vol. XXXVI, part II (Washington, DC: Government Printing Office, 1903), 1999–2000.

85. Remark of Colonel Worth. Stone, *Life and Times of Red-Jacket*, 279.

86. Ibid., 156, 365.

87. "Red Jacket, in Behalf of Himself, and the Other Deputies of the Six Nations to the Secretary of War," February 19, 1810, Letters Received by the Office of the Secretary of War Relating to Indian Affairs, 1800–1823, Reel 1, 1800–1816, National Archives, Washington, DC.

88. Stone, *Life and Times of Red-Jacket*, 314–16. Ganter, ed., *Collected Speeches of Sagoyewatha*, xxviii.

89. Ganter, ed., *Collected Speeches of Sagoyewatha*, xxix. Stone, *Life and Times of Red-Jacket*, 392–94. See also: "To Quakers at Buffalo Creek on Alcohol," October 2, 1803, in: Ganter, ed., *Collected Speeches of Sagoyewatha*, 134.

90. "Our Barbarian Brethren," *Harper's New Monthly Magazine* XL, no. CCXL (1870): 801.

91. Heckewelder, *History, Manners, and Customs*, 264.

92. Halliday Jackson, *Civilization of the Indian Natives; or, a Brief View of the Friendly Conduct of William Penn towards Them in the Early Settlement of Pennsylvania* (Philadelphia: Marcus T. C. Gould, 1830), 51, also: 14, 44.

93. "The Agent for Indian Affairs in the Territory of Orleans (John Sibley) to the Secretary of War," entries of January 5, 1807 and November 8, 1807, 61–62, RG75 (M 271), Letters Received by the Office of the Secretary of War Relating to Indian Affairs, 1800–1823, Reel 1, 1800–1816, National Archives, Washington, DC. Emphasis mine.

94. Angie Debo, *The Rise and Fall of the Choctaw Republic* (Norman: University of Oklahoma Press, 1934), 48.

95. Johnson, *Federal Government and the Liquor Traffic*, 216–18. William G. McLoughlin, *After the Trail of Tears: The Cherokees' Struggle for National Sovereignty, 1839–1880* (Chapel Hill: University of North Carolina Press, 1993), 127.

96. Benjamin Drake, *Life of Tecumseh, and of His Brother the Prophet; with a Historical Sketch of the Shawanoe Indians* (Cincinnati, OH: Queen City Publishing House, 1856), 107–108. Johnson, *Federal Government and the Liquor Traffic*, 208.

97. See: "An Act to Prohibit the Giving or Selling Intoxicating Liquors to Indians Residing in or Coming into the Territory of the United States Northwest of the River Ohio, 1790," in: William Clark Papers, Series M, vol. 1, Reel 39, Draper Manuscript Collection, Wisconsin Historical Society, Madison.

98. Johnson, *Federal Government and the Liquor Traffic*, 205–206. Prucha, *American Indian Policy*, 104–105.

99. Mooney, "Ghost-Dance Religion," 673. See also: Thomas Forsyth, "An Account of the Manners and Customs of the Sauk and Fox Nations of Indian Tradition," in *The Indian Tribes of the Upper Mississippi Valley and Region of the Great Lakes*, ed. Emma Helen Blair (Cleveland: Arthur H. Clark Company, 1912). In: Thomas Forsyth Papers, 1804–1833, Series 9T, Vol. 9, No. 51, Draper Manuscripts, Wisconsin Historical Society, Madison.

100. McKenney and Hall, *History of the Indian Tribes of North America*, 100–102.

101. "E. A. Ellsworth to Office of Indian Affairs," September 2, 1833, Letters Received Office of Indian Affairs 1824–1881, RG75 (M234), Western Superintendency, Roll 921, National Archives. Joseph B. Herring, *Kenekuk, the Kickapoo Prophet* (Lawrence: University Press of Kansas, 1988), 31–32.

102. "General William Clark to the War Department," January 13, 1829, Letters Received Office of Indian Affairs 1824–1881, RG75 (M234), St. Louis Superintendency, Roll 749, National Archives.

103. Perry McCandless, *A History of Missouri, Volume II: 1820–1860* (Columbia: University of Missouri Press, 1972), 55–56. Unrau, *White Man's Wicked Water*, 41. Similarly, see: Claudio Saunt, *Unworthy Republic*, 159.

104. "E. A. Ellsworth to Office of Indian Affairs," September 2, 1833. See also: William E. Unrau, *The Rise and Fall of Indian Country, 1825–1855* (Lawrence: University Press of Kansas, 2007), 102.

Chapter 10

1. Thomas L. McKenney, *Memoirs, Official and Personal; with Sketches of Travels among the Northern and Southern Indians*, 2nd ed. (New York: Paine and Burgess, 1846), 84–85.

2. Ibid., 88–89. Also: Willard Carl Klunder, *Lewis Cass and the Politics of Moderation* (Kent, OH: Kent State University Press, 1996), 54. "Thomas McKenney to Thomas Forsyth, August 9, 1827," in: Thomas Forsyth Papers, 1804–1833, Series 2T, vol. 2, no. 34, Draper Manuscripts, Wisconsin Historical Society, Madison.

3. McKenney, *Memoirs, Official and Personal*, 89. See also: William T. Young, *Sketch of the Life and Public Services of General Lewis Cass* (Detroit: Markham & Elwood, 1852), 95.

4. McKenney, Memoirs, Official and Personal, 92–93.

5. "President's Talks to the Picara and Mandan Nations," 1806, RG75 (M 271), Letters Received by the Office of the Secretary of War Relating to Indian Affairs, 1800–1823, Reel 1, 1800–1816, National Archives, Washington, DC. Also: Anthony F. C. Wallace, *Jefferson and the Indians: The Tragic Fate of the First Americans* (Cambridge, MA: Belknap Press, 1999), 206–12.

6. Wayne Morris, "Traders and Factories on the Arkansas Frontier, 1805–1822," *Arkansas Historical Quarterly* 28, no. 1 (1969): 30.

7. Royal B. Way, "The United States Factory System for Trading with the Indians, 1796–1822," *Mississippi Valley Historical Review* 6, no. 2 (1919): 224. Hiram Martin Chittenden, *The American Fur Trade of the Far West* (New York: Francis P. Harper, 1902), 13.

8. Herman J. Viola, *Thomas L. McKenney: Architect of America's Early Indian Policy: 1816–1830* (Chicago: Swallow Press, 1974), 12–13, 54. On the number and operation of outposts: Morris, "Traders and Factories," 29–32.

9. Prucha begins his consideration by calling whiskey "the greatest source of difficulty in the Indian trade." Francis Paul Prucha, *American Indian Policy in the Formative Years: The Indian Trade and Intercourse Acts, 1790–1834* (Cambridge, MA: Harvard University Press, 1962), 102.

10. Chittenden, *American Fur Trade*, 23.
11. Viola, *Thomas McKenney*, 55–56. Also: "The destroying effects of ardent spirits among them, *is horrid in the extreme*. Whiskey, they find all over their country, but find it more plentifully as they are situated nearer to the white settlements. In these latter cases, our Government is not at all blameable, only as it has rendered the Indians radically ignominious. It has made laws forbidding the introduction of ardent spirits into their country; but it has not power, in the present posture of affairs, to enforce their observance. The evils of intemperance have not been perceivably lessened by all the laws made to repress it." Isaac M'Coy, *Remarks on the Practicability of Indian Reform, Embracing Their Colonization*, 2nd ed. (New York: Gray and Bunce, 1829), 13.
12. Chittenden, *American Fur Trade*, 16.
13. Prucha, *American Indian Policy*, 110. On Washington: Way, "United States Factory System," 223. With apologies to T. J. Stiles, Astor made his millions a full generation before Vanderbilt. T. J. Stiles, *The First Tycoon: The Epic Life of Cornelius Vanderbilt* (New York: Alfred A. Knopf, 2009).
14. Howard Abadinsky, *Organized Crime* (Boston: Allyn and Bacon, 1981), 60. On wealth: "The Wealthiest Americans Ever," *New York Times*, July 15, 2007, http://archive.nytimes.com/www.nytimes.com/ref/business/20070715_GILDED_GRAPHIC.html (accessed July 15, 2019). Malcolm Gladwell, *Outliers: The Story of Success* (New York: Little, Brown and Company, 2008), 57. Alexander Emmerich, *John Jacob Astor and the First Great American Fortune* (London: McFarland & Company, 2013), 62.
15. Eric Jay Dolin, *When America First Met China: An Exotic History of Tea, Drugs, and Money in the Age of Sail* (New York: W. W. Norton & Co., 2012), 93. More generally: James R. Fitcher, *So Great a Proffit: How the East Indies Trade Transformed Anglo-American Capitalism* (Cambridge, MA: Harvard University Press, 2010), 217.
16. Axel Madsen, *John Jacob Astor: America's First Multimillionaire* (New York: John Wiley & Sons, 2001), 167. John R. Haddad, *America's First Adventure in China: Trade, Treaties, Opium, and Salvation* (Philadelphia: Temple University Press, 2013), 74–77. Kendall Johnson, *The New Middle Kingdom: China and the Early American Romance of Free Trade* (Baltimore: Johns Hopkins University Press, 2017), 57–59. David Sinclair, *Dynasty: The Astors and Their Times* (New York: Beaufort Books, 1984), 114.
17. Chittenden, *American Fur Trade*, 345.
18. Madsen, *John Jacob Astor*, 195. Chittenden, *American Fur Trade*, 345. Abadinsky, *Organized Crime*, 123. Anna Youngman, "The Fortune of John Jacob Astor," *Journal of Political Economy* 16, no. 6 (1908): 365–66. "Cutthroat": see, for instance: John D. Haeger, *John Jacob Astor: Business and Finance in the Early Republic* (Detroit: Wayne State University Press, 1991).
19. Chittenden, *American Fur Trade*, 16.
20. "John Fowler to Thomas McKenney, June 14, 1819," Secretary of War, Letters Received, RG 107, M-74 (13), National Archives; "William Bowen to Thomas McKenney, April 27, 1817," Secretary of War, Letters Received, RG 107, M-234(10). Viola, *Thomas McKenney*, 56.
21. Viola, *Thomas McKenney*, 57.
22. Ibid., 58. See also: Landon Y. Jones, *William Clark and the Shaping of the West* (New York: Hill and Wang, 2004), 263–64. It should be noted that John Quincy Adams claimed, "I regard the temperance movement of the present day as one of the most remarkable phenomena of the human race." "The Presidents of the United States and the Alcohol Question," *Union Signal*, February 10, 1921, 7.
23. Viola, *Thomas McKenney*, 67.
24. Way, "United States Factory System," 232. Madsen, *John Jacob Astor*, 198.
25. Viola, *Thomas McKenney*, 61–63.
26. There is some discussion as to whether Crooks meant "unholy" in writing "holy," which is telling. Chittenden, *American Fur Trade*, 15. Prucha, *American Indian Policy*, 92. Elbert B. Smith,

Magnificent Missourian: The Life of Thomas Hart Benton (Santa Barbara, CA: Greenwood Press, 1973), 82. Sinclair, *Dynasty*, 107.

27. Chittenden, *American Fur Trade*, 16.
28. Ibid., 24. Also: Madsen, *John Jacob Astor*, 196.
29. Emmerich, *John Jacob Astor*, 114.
30. Madsen, *John Jacob Astor*, 198. Prucha, *American Indian Policy*, 113.
31. Chittenden, *American Fur Trade*, 24. Also: George Frederick Ruxton, *Life in the Far West*, 2nd ed. (London: William Blackwood and Sons, 1851), 93.
32. Madsen, *John Jacob Astor*, 198.
33. Ibid., 200. Emmerich, *John Jacob Astor*, 115.
34. Donald Jackson, "The Short, Dramatic Life of the Steamboat Yellow Stone," *American Heritage* 38, no. 4 (1987): 123. Viola, *Thomas McKenney*, 60. Chittenden, *American Fur Trade*, 27. "Under the adroit management of this same Crooks, the American Fur Company, after throttling the official factors, then proceeded to push its private rivals to the wall, destroying all but the shrewdest and most unscrupulous." Way, "United States Factory System," 234.
35. Prucha, *American Indian Policy*, 112.
36. Klunder, *Lewis Cass*, 33. William Conkey Phillips, "*The American Fur Company, 1817–1827*" (MA thesis, University of Wisconsin–Madison, 1931), 32. Abadinsky, *Organized Crime*, 123.
37. "John Bowyer to Cass, July 22, 1817," in *Wisconsin Historical Collections*, XIX, 466–67; "Bowyer to Cass, Dec. 15, 1817," XIX, 487–88; "Cass to Bowyer, January 22, 1818," XX, 16–17, https://www.wisconsinhistory.org/Records/Article/CS15286 (accessed January 20, 2021). See also: Lawrence Taliaferro, "Journal, Volume 8, May 1827–May 1829," in: Lawrence Taliaferro Papers, 1813–1868, M35, Reel 3, Manuscripts Collection, Minnesota Historical Society. Prucha, *American Indian Policy*, 117.
38. "Colonel Josiah Snelling to Secretary of War John C. Calhoun, Jan. 10, 1825," in Secretary of War, Letters Received, S-163 (19), 1825; "Colonel Josiah Snelling to Secretary of War James Barbour, Aug. 23, 1825," in *American State Papers: Indian Affairs*, II, 661; "Secretary of War James Barbour to Colonel Josiah Snelling, Sept. 17, 1825," in Indian Affairs, Letters Sent (hereafter IA, LS), vol. 2, p. 156. Cited in: Prucha, *American Indian Policy*, 113.
39. "William Clark to Secretary of War James Barbour, October 19, 1825," in: Records of the Central Superintendency of Indian Affairs: 1813–1878, RG75 (M 856), Records of the St. Louis Superintendency, Reel 2, National Archives, Washington, DC.
40. Prucha, *American Indian Policy*, 120.
41. Emmerich, *John Jacob Astor*, 116. "John Jacob Astor to Secretary of War James Barbour, May 26, 1826," in: Indian Affairs, Letters Received (hereafter IA, LR), Miscellaneous; "Thomas McKenney to William Clark, May 29, 1826," in IA LS, vol. 3, p. 107; "Thomas McKenney to John Jacob Astor," May 29, 1826, in IA LS, vol. 3, p. 108. Prucha, *American Indian Policy*, 113–14.
42. Lewis Cass, *Remarks on the Policy and Practices of the United States and Great Britain in Their Treatment of the Indian* (Boston: Frederick T. Gray, 1827), 43–44.
43. "Thomas McKenney to Lewis Cass, February 20, 1827," in IA, LS, vol. 3, p. 390; "Lewis Cass to Thomas McKenney, March 25, 1827," in IA, LR, Michigan Superintendency; "Thomas McKenney to Lewis Cass, April 19, 1827," in: IA, LS, vol. 4, 24; "Thomas McKenney to William Clark, April 13, 1827," in IA, LS, vol. 4, 24; "Thomas McKenney to James Barbour, February 15, 1828," in IA, LS, 4, 294. See also: Prucha, *American Indian Policy*.
44. Wallace, *Jefferson and the Indians*, 96–97.
45. See: William Clark Diary in: William Clark Papers, Series M, Vol. 6, Reel 39, Draper Manuscript Collection, Wisconsin Historical Society, Madison. Also: Elin Woodger and Brandon Toropov, "Alcohol," in *Encyclopedia of the Lewis and Clark Expedition* (New York: Facts on File, 2004), 27. See also: Robert R. Hunt, "Gills and Drams of Consolation: Ardent Spirits on the Lewis & Clark Expedition," *We Proceeded On* 17, no. 3 (1991).

46. G. Mercer Adam, *Makers of American History: The Lewis & Clark Exploring Expedition, 1804–'06* (New York: The University Society, 1905), 25.

47. Woodger and Toropov, "Alcohol," 27. See also: "July 4, 1805 [Lewis]," *Journals of the Lewis and Clark Expedition*, https://lewisandclarkjournals.unl.edu/item/lc.jrn.1805-07-04 (accessed July 11, 2019). On the Lakota Sioux incident, see:Kira Gale, *Meriwether Lewis: The Assassination of an American Hero and the Silver Mines of Mexico* (Omaha, NE: River Junction Press, 2015), 216. Stephen A. Ambrose, *Undaunted Courage: Meriwether Lewis, Thomas Jefferson, and the Opening of the American West* (New York: Touchstone, 1996), 169–70.

48. "William Clark to the Secretary of War," April 10, 1811, RG75 (M 271), Letters Received by the Office of the Secretary of War Relating to Indian Affairs, 1800–1823, Roll 1, 1800–1816, National Archives, Washington, DC.

49. Stuart Banner, *How the Indians Lost Their Land: Law and Power on the Frontier* (Cambridge, MA: Belknap Press, 2005), 198.

50. Alexis de Tocqueville, *Democracy in America*, ed. Richard D. Heffner, abridged ed. (New York: Mentor Books, 1956).

51. George Wilson Pierson, *Tocqueville in America (1938)* (Baltimore: Johns Hopkins University Press, 1996), 233–35.

52. "Beaumont to Chabrol, July 24, 1831," in: Ibid., 235.

53. William E. Unrau, *White Man's Wicked Water: The Alcohol Trade and Prohibition in Indian Country, 1802–1892* (Lawrence: University Press of Kansas, 1996), 25–26.

54. "John Tipton to Col. Thomas McKenney," January 31, 1830, and "Journal of the Proceedings of the Council Held with the Miami Nation of Indians at the Fork of the Wabash, in the State of Indiana, by Governor George B. Porter of Michigan, General William Marshall of Indiana, and the Reverend J. F. Schermehorn, Commissioner Appointed by the President of the United States to Negotiate with Said Nation for the Purpose of Their Lands," n/d, 1830, Letters Received, Office of Indian Affairs, 1824–1881, RG75 (M234), Miami Agency, Roll 416, National Archives, Washington, DC. See also: Leonard U. Hill, *John Johnston and the Indians in the Land of the Three Miamis* (Columbus, OH: Stoneman Press, 1957), 17.

55. McKenney, *Memoirs, Official and Personal*, 244.

56. Banner, *How the Indians Lost Their Land*, 202.

57. William E. Johnson, *Ten Years of Prohibition in Oklahoma* (Westerville, OH: American Issue Publishing Company, n/d), 4.

58. Daniel Walker Howe, *What Hath God Wrought: The Transformation of America, 1815–1848* (New York: Oxford University Press, 2007), 348.

59. "Choctaw Nation to the Congress of the United States, February 18, 1825," reproduced in: McKenney, *Memoirs, Official and Personal*, 120–22.

60. Howe, *What Hath God Wrought*, 347–49. William E. Foley, *Wilderness Journey: The Life of William Clark* (Columbia: University of Missouri Press, 2004), 209. Unsurprisingly, drunkenness played an outsized role in the confrontations. John Ehle, *Trail of Tears: The Rise and Fall of the Cherokee Nation* (New York: Anchor Books, 1988), 86–88.

61. U.S. Statutes at Large, 4:564. Unrau, *White Man's Wicked Water*, 37.

62. Andrew Jackson, "Indian Removal and the General Good (December 6, 1830)," in *The Removal of the Cherokee Nation: Manifest Destiny or National Dishonor?*, ed. Louis Filler and Allen Guttman (Boston: D.C. Heath and Company, 1962), 49–51.

63. "Indian Talk. From the President of the United States to the Creek Indians, through Colonel Crowell, March 23, 1829," in: Thomas Brothers, *The United States of North America as They Are; Not as They Are Generally Described: Being a Cure for Radicalism* (London: Longman, Orme, Brown, Green, & Longmans, 1840), 178.

64. Banner, *How the Indians Lost Their Land*, 208. On McKenney's dismissal: McKenney, *Memoirs, Official and Personal*, 206.

65. Foley, *Wilderness Journey*, 209. On the drunkenness of white military authorities, see Claudio Saunt, *Unworthy Republic: The Dispossession of Native Americans and the Road to Indian Territory* (New York: W.W. Norton & Co., 2020), 159, 276, 295–98.

66. Black Hawk, *Autobiography of Ma-Ka-Tai-Me-She-Kia-Kiak, or Black Hawk, Embracing the Traditions of His Nation, Various Wars in Which He Has Been Engaged, and His Account of the Cause and General History of the Black Hawk War of 1832, His Surrender, and Travels through the United States*, trans. Antoine LeClaire (St. Louis: Continental Publishing Co., 1833), 23–24. Armstrong gives more vivid details of the negotiation revelry: Perry A. Armstrong, *The Sauks and the Black Hawk War, with Biographical Sketches, Etc.* (Springfield, IL: H. W. Rokker, 1887), 59. Wilkie disputes that there were five, rather than four chiefs. Franc B. Wilkie, *Davenport Past and Present: Including the Early History, and Personal and Anecdotal Reminiscences of Davenport* (Davenport, IA: Publishing House of Luse, Lane & Co., 1858), 17. See also: "Extract of a Letter from Gen. William Clark to the Secretary of War, January 8, 1822," in: William Clark Papers, Series M, Vol. 2, Reel 39, Draper Manuscript Collection, Wisconsin Historical Society, Madison.

67. Black Hawk, *Autobiography of Ma-Ka-Tai-Me-She-Kia-Kiak*, 29.

68. Armstrong, *Sauks and the Black Hawk War*, 151. Black Hawk, *Autobiography of Ma-Ka-Tai-Me-She-Kia-Kiak*, 48.

69. Thomas Forsyth, "An Account of the Manners and Customs of the Sauk and Fox Nations of Indian Tradition," in *The Indian Tribes of the Upper Mississippi Valley and Region of the Great Lakes*, ed. Emma Helen Blair (Cleveland: Arthur H. Clark Company, 1912). in: Thomas Forsyth Papers, 1804–1833, Series 9T, Vol. 9, No. 56, Draper Manuscripts, Wisconsin Historical Society, Madison.

70. Black Hawk, *Autobiography of Ma-Ka-Tai-Me-She-Kia-Kiak*, 66–67.

71. Armstrong, *Sauks and the Black Hawk War*, 148. Forsyth, "Manners and Customs of the Sauk and Fox."

72. Black Hawk, *Autobiography of Ma-Ka-Tai-Me-She-Kia-Kiak*, 72–73. Corroboration in: Wilkie, *Davenport Past and Present*, 21, 159. "Thomas Forsyth to William Clark, April 9, 1824" in: Thomas Forsyth Papers, 1804–1833, Series 4T, Vol. 4, No. 186, Draper Manuscripts, Wisconsin Historical Society, Madison. See also: Jones, *William Clark*, 288.

73. Armstrong, *Sauks and the Black Hawk War*, 150–52.

74. "Unfortunately, the morals of the white pioneers of that locality and time were not up to the present standards," Armstrong wrote of the situation. Ibid., 152–53.

75. Ibid., 154–56. Wilkie, *Davenport Past and Present*, 24. Vandruff's petition: Frank E. Stevens, *The Black Hawk War: Including a Review of Black Hawk's Life* (Chicago: Frank E. Stevens, 1903), 82. Vandruff repeatedly sued the government over his loss of property, but the US House of Representatives Committee on Indian Affairs found his claims were "not within the beneficial provisions of the non-intercourse act" and were summarily dismissed. See: "Joshua Vandruff," *Committee on Indian Affairs*, House Report 196, June 13, 1854, 33rd Congress, 1st Session, Vol. 743, no. 2. The archives of Thomas Forsyth—the long-serving Indian agent at Fort Armstrong—are especially illuminating. Thomas Forsyth Papers, 1804–1833, Series 4T-6T, Draper Manuscripts, Wisconsin Historical Society, Madison.

76. Black Hawk, *Autobiography of Ma-Ka-Tai-Me-She-Kia-Kiak*, 74. Forsyth, "Manners and Customs of the Sauk and Fox." On the pillaging of Saukenuk, see: Wilkie, *Davenport Past and Present*, 21–22. Wilkie also describes the great settler sport of using a glass of whiskey to entice an Indian to come close, and then punch him in the face, placing bets on who "could *knock* a drunken Indian the farthest." When one Indian protested against such treatment, he was beaten to death with a rail (49–50).

77. Black Hawk, *Autobiography of Ma-Ka-Tai-Me-She-Kia-Kiak*, 75–76.

78. Stevens, *Black Hawk War*, 141. Jung seems to infer that the whiskey kegs strewn about the battlefield were empty on account of being consumed by the militiamen. Patrick J. Jung, *The Black Hawk War of 1832* (Norman: University of Oklahoma Press, 2007), 89.

79. William James Cooper, *Jefferson Davis, American* (New York: Alfred A. Knopf, 2000), 53–55. The US Department of War by that time was led by Lewis Cass. Young, *General Lewis Cass*, 124–25.

80. Samuel G. Drake, *Biography and History of the Indians of North America. From Its First Discovery to the Present Time*, 7th ed. (Boston: Antiquarian Institute, 1837), 161. Stevens, *Black Hawk War*, 239.

81. Jay H. Buckley, *William Clark: Indian Diplomat* (Norman: University of Oklahoma Press, 2008), 210–11. Jung, *Black Hawk War*, 96.

82. Buckley, *William Clark*, 268, n. 64. Forsyth, "Manners and Customs of the Sauk and Fox," 221. Foley, *Wilderness Journey*, 247.

83. Prucha, *American Indian Policy*, 109.

84. "Major Lawrence Taliaferro to William Clark," May 18, 1830, Letters Received Office of Indian Affairs, 1824–1881, RG75 (M234), St. Louis Superintendency, Roll 749, National Archives, Washington, DC. See also: "Superintendent of Indian Affairs William Clark to Lewis Cass, Secretary of War," November 20, 1831, 3, Letters Received Office of Indian Affairs, 1824–1881, RG75 (M234), St. Louis Superintendency, Roll 749, National Archives, Washington, DC. Also: Lawrence Taliaferro, "Journal, Volume 10, December 1830–June 1831," in: Lawrence Taliaferro Papers, 1813–1868, M35, Reel 3, Manuscripts Collection, Minnesota Historical Society, http://www2.mnhs.org/library/findaids/01236.xml (accessed July 31, 2019).

85. Under penalty of fines of three hundred to five hundred dollars and confiscation of the alcohol. *U.S. Statutes at Large*, 4:564. Unrau, *White Man's Wicked Water*, 37.

86. "John Bean to E.A. Ellsworth," November 6, 1833, Letters Received Office of Indian Affairs, 1824–1881, RG75 (M234), Western Superintendency, Roll 921, National Archives, Washington, DC. William E. Unrau, *The Rise and Fall of Indian Country, 1825–1855* (Lawrence: University Press of Kansas, 2007), 107.

87. For example, an Indian could get one dollar in trade for a six-pound buckskin, and trade it for gunpowder at twenty cents per pound. But on credit in the fall, the trader would charge four dollars per pound for the same gunpowder—a 1,900 percent markup. Youngman, "Fortune of John Jacob Astor," 362.

88. "William Clark to Secretary of War John Eaton," August 30, 1830; "Major Lawrence Taliaferro to William Clark," May 18, 1830: both in Letters Received Office of Indian Affairs, 1824–1881, RG75 (M234), St. Louis Superintendency, Roll 749, National Archives, Washington, DC.

89. "Private interest and desire for gain tempted many to surreptitiously furnish the Indian with fire-water in spite of the statute book." Alice C. Fletcher, "Indian Education and Civilization: A Report Prepared in Answer to Senate Resolution of February 23, 1885," in *The Executive Documents of the Senate of the United States, for the Second Session of the Forty-Eighth Congress and the Special Session of the Senate Convened March 4, 1885* (Washington, DC: Government Printing Office, 1888), 63. Also: Ruxton, *Life in the Far West*, 228. William E. Unrau, *Indians, Alcohol, and the Roads to Taos and Santa Fe* (Lawrence: University Press of Kansas, 2013), 86–87.

90. Jackson, "Short, Dramatic Life," 123. See also: Prucha, *American Indian Policy*, 136.

91. Jeremiah Evarts, "Memorial of the American Board of Commissioners for Foreign Missions (1831)," in *Cherokee Removal, the "William Penn" Essays and Other Writings*, ed. Francis Paul Prucha (Knoxville: University of Tennessee Press, 1981), 304.

92. "I am every day more and more concerned of the ruining effect that Spiritous Liquors have on the Indians of this Country; and firmly believe that unless the introduction of it into the Indian Country is entirely Prohibited; the day is not far distant when they will all be reduced to the most abject misery ever inflicted by the Land of Civilized Man." He then quotes an extract. Given "the bad effects of Spiritous liquor among the Indians gave as his opinion, that it ought to be prohibited in the Indian Country, and in it expressed a wish that the Government would take measures to do so." "John Dougherty to William Clark," November 10, 1831, Letters Received Office of Indian Affairs, 1824–1881, RG75 (M234), St. Louis Superintendency,

Roll 749, National Archives, Washington, DC. On the AFC distillery, see: Buckley, *William Clark*, 163.

93. "Superintendent of Indian Affairs William Clark to Lewis Cass, Secretary of War," November 20, 1831, 3, Letters Received Office of Indian Affairs, 1824–1881, RG75 (M234), St. Louis Superintendency, Roll 749, National Archives, Washington, DC. See also: Foley, *Wilderness Journey*, 254.

94. Cass, *Remarks on the Policy and Practices*, 42–47.

95. Lewis Cass, "Report of the Secretary of War," November 21, 1831, *House Document* 2/2, 22nd Congress, 1st Session, Serial 216, pp. 31–32. Quoted in: Benjamin F. Comfort, *Lewis Cass and the Indian Treaties: A Monograph on the Indian Relations of the Northwest Territory from 1813 to 1831* (Detroit: Cass Tech. Printery, 1923), 43. Abadinsky, *Organized Crime*, 123. As secretary of war, Cass signed off on other questionable activities on Astor's behalf. In 1832 Crooks and the AFC began striking medals similar to those given as a source of status to tribal leaders by the US government, only instead of the president's image, it was adorned with the likeness of John Jacob Astor. Competitors complained to Cass that the AFC was usurping the functions and symbolism of the US government. Cass consented to the Astor medals. Chittenden, *American Fur Trade*, 342–43. Despite their differences, Clark did subsequently work with Cass to overhaul federal statutes on Indian trade in 1834 to the benefit of the AFC, perhaps bolstered by Clark's shared anti-British sentiment. Foley, *Wilderness Journey*, 248–49.

96. E. A. Ellsworth, "Private Council with the Delaware and Shawnee Chiefs," n/d, 1834, Letters Received Office of Indian Affairs, 1824–1881, RG75 (M234), Western Superintendency, Roll 921, National Archives, Washington, DC. For his part, Ellsworth encouraged the chiefs to abstain from alcohol, and for good measure also suggested, "If you become a happy nation, you must restrain your women from intercourse with bad men," who often carried venereal diseases.

97. Angie Debo, *The Rise and Fall of the Choctaw Republic* (Norman: University of Oklahoma Press, 1934), 55.

98. "Captain John Stuart to General R. Jones, June 9, 1838," Letters Received Office of Indian Affairs, 1824–1881, RG75 (M234), Western Superintendency, Roll 922, National Archives, Washington, DC. Unrau, *White Man's Wicked Water*, 42.

99. Debo, *Rise and Fall of the Choctaw Republic*, 66.

100. "Montfort Stokes to Joel Roberts Poinsett, Secretary of War, June 5, 1838," Letters Received Office of Indian Affairs, 1824–1881, RG75 (M234), Western Superintendency, Roll 922, National Archives, Washington, DC.

101. "William Clark to Lewis Cass, November 20, 1831," Letters Received Office of Indian Affairs, 1824–1881, RG75 (M234), St. Louis Superintendency, Roll 749, National Archives, Washington, DC.

102. Unrau, *White Man's Wicked Water*, 27, 41.

103. *U.S. Statutes at Large* 12:628; *John Brown and Jane Brown v. Adel (Clement) Blemarde*, 3 Kan. 35. Also: Robert Joseph Keckeisen, "The Kansa 'Half-Breed' Lands: Contravention and Transformation of United States Indian Policy in Kansas" (MA thesis, Wichita State University, 1982). Cited in: Unrau, *White Man's Wicked Water*, 28, 50–51.

104. Unrau, *White Man's Wicked Water*, 44. Taliaferro notes that, at St. Peter's, the first Indian murder "was caused by the giving of a bottle of whiskey to the old 'White Buzzard,' by Colonel Leavenworth at Cold Water Camp, which was productive of some very sharp correspondence between the commanding officer and the Indian agent." Lawrence Taliaferro, *Auto-Biography of Maj. Lawrence Taliaferro (1864)*, vol. 6, *Collections of the Minnesota Historical Society* (Minneapolis: Minnesota Historical Society, 1894), 234. In: Lawrence Taliaferro Papers, 1813–1868, M35, Reel 4, Manuscripts Collection, Minnesota Historical Society, http://www2.mnhs.org/library/findaids/01236.xml (accessed July 31, 2019).

105. Unrau, *White Man's Wicked Water*, 46–47.

106. "Superintendent of Indian Affairs William Clark to Lewis Cass, Secretary of War," November 20, 1831, 3, Letters Received Office of Indian Affairs, 1824–1881, RG75 (M234), St. Louis Superintendency, Roll 749, National Archives, Washington, DC. More generally: Unrau, *Indians, Alcohol and the Roads*, 86–87, 136–37.

107. "Superintendent of Indian Affairs William Clark to Lewis Cass, Secretary of War," November 20, 1831, 3. See also: Foley, *Wilderness Journey*, 254.

108. Prucha, *American Indian Policy*, 120–26. Likewise, see the lawsuit with AFC trader Alexis Bailly. Lawrence Taliaferro, "Journal, Volume 8, May 1827–May 1829," in: Lawrence Taliaferro Papers, 1813–1868, M35, Reel 3, Manuscripts Collection, Minnesota Historical Society, http://www2.mnhs.org/library/findaids/01236.xml (accessed July 31, 2019). Taliaferro, *Auto-Biography*, 203.

109. "Superintendent of Indian Affairs William Clark to Lewis Cass, Secretary of War," November 20, 1831, 3. Also: E. A. Ellsworth, "Private Council with the Delaware and Shawnee Chiefs." See also: Unrau, *White Man's Wicked Water*, 57. Rufus B. Sage, *Rocky Mountain Life; or Startling Scenes and Perilous Adventures in the Far West* (Boston: Wentworth & Company, 1858), 52.

110. Jotham Meeker, "Journal Entry: September 5, 1848," Jotham Meeker Papers, 1825–1864, Microfilm Roll MS 618, Kansas Historical Society, Topeka.

111. Unrau, *White Man's Wicked Water*, 78.

112. Ibid., 89–90.

113. Youngman, "Fortune of John Jacob Astor," 364–65. Chittenden, *American Fur Trade*, 364.

114. "Indian Appropriation Bill," *Congressional Globe*, 24th Congress, 1st Session, May 18, 1836, 468–69.

115. Unrau, *White Man's Wicked Water*, 42–43. William E. Johnson, *The Federal Government and the Liquor Traffic*, 2nd ed. (Westerville, OH: American Issue Publishing Company, 1917), 222.

116. "Isaac McCoy to John C. Spencer, Secretary of War," October 25, 1841, Box 12, Folder 9, Roll MS 613, Isaac McCoy Papers, Kansas Historical Society, Topeka. See also: "Isaac McCoy to John C. Spencer," May 17, 1842, Box 13, Folder 1, Roll MS 613, Isaac McCoy Papers, Kansas Historical Society, Topeka.

117. Sage, *Rocky Mountain Life*, 52 (emphasis in original). Similar conclusions in: Buckley, *William Clark*, 191.

118. "St. Louis Superintendent David Mitchell to T. Hartley Crawford, Commissioner of Indian Affairs," September 12, 1842, in: United States Office of Indian Affairs, *Annual Report of the Commissioner of Indian Affairs for the Year 1842* (Washington, DC: Government Printing Office, 1843), 425.

119. "T. Hartley Crawford to William Wilkins, Secretary of War," November 25, 1844, in: United States Office of Indian Affairs, *Annual Report of the Commissioner of Indian Affairs, Transmitted with the Message of the President at the Opening of the Second Session of the Twenty-Eighth Congress, 1844–1845* (Washington, DC: C. Alexander, Printer, 1844), 9.

120. "Administration of Indian Affairs," *The United States Magazine, and Democratic Review* XVIII (1846): 334–35.

121. Unrau, *White Man's Wicked Water*, 52, 91.

122. "Our Barbarian Brethren," *Harper's New Monthly Magazine* XL, no. CCXL (1870): 810. Similarly: John Heckewelder, *History, Manners, and Customs of the Indian Nations Who Once Inhabited Pennsylvania and the Neighbouring States [1818]* (Philadelphia: Historical Society of Pennsylvania, 1876), 262. Fletcher, "Indian Education and Civilization," 63.

Chapter 11

1. Frederick Douglass, "Intemperance and Slavery: An Address Delivered in Cork, Ireland, on 20 October 1845," in *The Frederick Douglass Papers. Series One: Speeches, Debates and Interviews. Volume 1: 1841–1846,* ed. John W. Blassingame (New Haven, CT: Yale University Press, 1979), 56.

2. Ibid., 58. Tom Chaffin, *Giant's Causeway: Frederick Douglass's Irish Odyssey and the Making of an American Visionary* (Charlottesville: University of Virginia Press, 2014), 80–81.

3. Robert S. Levine, *Martin Delany, Frederick Douglass, and the Politics of Representative Identity* (Chapel Hill: University of North Carolina Press, 1997), 104.

4. Frederick Douglass, *Narrative of the Life of Frederick Douglass, an American Slave* (Boston: Anti-Slavery Office, 1849), vii.

5. Bruce Nelson, "'Come out of Such a Land, You Irishmen': Daniel O'Connell, American Slavery, and the Making of the 'Irish Race,'" *Éire-Ireland* 42, nos. 1&2 (2007): 69. Chaffin, *Giant's Causeway*, 60–61.

6. Indeed, even the words Martin Luther King Jr. borrowed from Frederick Douglass in the 1960s to describe the black American experience were originally from O'Connell. Lee Jenkins, "Beyond the Pale: Frederick Douglass in Cork," *Irish Review*, no. 24 (1999): 83. Tom Chaffin, "Frederick Douglass's Irish Liberty," *New York Times*, February 25, 2011,

7. Quoted in: Chaffin, *Giant's Causeway*, 38.

8. David W. Blight, *Frederick Douglass: Prophet of Freedom* (New York: Simon & Schuster, 2018), 145. See also: "Buying Frederick Douglass's Freedom, 1846: A Spotlight on a Primary Source by Hugh Auld," *Gilder Lehrman Institute of American History*, https://www.gilderlehrman.org/content/buying-frederick-douglass%E2%80%99s-freedom-1846 (accessed January 3, 2019).

9. Jenkins, "Beyond the Pale," 82.

10. Garrison had previously written, "As the temperance cause is somewhat unpopular in England, and the great mass of abolitionists there are in the daily habit of using wine, porter, and other intoxicating liquors, I said much privately and publicly in favor of total abstinence, and rebuked them faithfully for their criminal indulgence. In short, I did what I could for the redemption of the human race." William Lloyd Garrison, "To Henry C. Wright, August 23, 1840," in: Louis Ruchames, ed., *The Letters of William Lloyd Garrison, Volume II (1836–1840)* (Cambridge, MA: Belknap Press, 1971), 681. Wendell Phillips Garrison and Francis Jackson Garrison, *William Lloyd Garrison, 1805–1879: The Story of His Life Told by His Children*, 4 vols., vol. III: *1841–1860* (Boston: Houghton, Mifflin and Company, 1894), 158. The only two surviving attendees of the 1846 conference reminisced about temperance and abolitionism fifty-four years later at the 1900 World Temperance Congress. Dawson Burns, "The World's Convention of 1846: Two Veterans' Personal Experiences," in *The World's Temperance Congress of 1900: Journal of the Proceedings*, ed. John Turner Rae (London: Ideal Publishing Union, 1900), 11–12.

11. Harriet Beecher Stowe, *Uncle Tom's Cabin* (London: Adam and Charles Black, 1904).

12. Donald Yacovone, "The Transformation of the Black Temperance Movement, 1827–1854: An Interpretation," *Journal of the Early Republic* 8, no. 3 (1988): 290.

13. Douglas H. Maynard, "The World's Anti-Slavery Convention of 1840," *Mississippi Valley Historical Review* 47, no. 3 (1960): 452. *The Proceedings of the World's Temperance Convention, Held in London, August 4th and Four Following Days* (London: Charles Gilpin, 1846), 4.

14. William Lloyd Garrison, "To Helen E. Garrison, August 4, 1846," in: Walter M. Merrill, ed., *The Letters of William Lloyd Garrison, Volume III (1841–1849)* (Cambridge, MA: Belknap Press, 1973), 362.

15. Frederick Douglass, *Selected Speeches and Writings* (Chicago: Lawrence Hill Books, 1999), 40, 46.

16. Cox's abolitionist credentials included having his Five-Points home in Manhattan ransacked during the Anti-Abolitionist Riots of 1834.

17. Frederick Douglass, *Correspondence between the Rev. Samuel H. Cox, D.D., of Brooklyn, L.I. and Frederick Douglass, a Fugitive Slave* (New York: American Anti-Slavery Society, 1846), 5–6.

18. Ibid., 7–16.

19. See, for instance: James A. Morone, *Hellfire Nation: The Politics of Sin in American History* (New Haven, CT: Yale University Press, 2003), 289.

20. Gallus Thomann, *Colonial Liquor Laws* (New York: United States Brewers' Association, 1887), 143–45, 166–87. William Johnson, *The Federal Government and the Liquor Traffic* (Westerville, OH: American Issue Publishing Co., 1911), 160–73.

21. Clifford Lindsey Alderman, *Rum, Slaves, and Molasses: The Story of New England's Triangular Trade* (New York: Crowell-Collier Press, 1972).

22. W. J. Rorabaugh, *The Alcoholic Republic: An American Tradition* (New York: Oxford University Press, 1979), 233. W. J. Rorabaugh, "Estimated U.S. Alcoholic Beverage Consumption, 1790–1860," *Journal of Studies on Alcohol* 37 (1976). Morone, *Hellfire Nation*, 283–84.

23. Benjamin Rush, *An Inquiry into the Effects of Ardent Spirits upon the Human Body and Mind* (Springfield, MA: Thomas Dickman, 1817). Rush's *Inquiry* went through many subsequent editions.

24. Harlow Giles Unger, *Dr. Benjamin Rush: The Founding Father Who Healed a Wounded Nation* (New York: Da Capo Press, 2018), 1–2. Stephen Fried, *Rush: Revolution, Madness & the Visionary Doctor Who Became a Founding Father* (New York: Crown, 2018), 6.

25. "Beecher, Lyman," in: Ernest H. Cherrington, ed., *Standard Encyclopedia of the Alcohol Problem*, 6 vols., vol. 1 (Westerville, OH: American Issue Press, 1924), 296.

26. Lyman Beecher, *Six Sermons on the Nature, Occasions, Signs, Evils, and Remedy of Intemperance* (New York: American Tract Society, 1827), 7–8.

27. Rorabaugh, *The Alcoholic Republic*, 8–9, 30. Rorabaugh, "Estimated U.S. Alcoholic Beverage Consumption, 1790–1860." See also: Harry G. Levine and Craig Reinarman, *Alcohol Prohibition and Drug Prohibition: Lessons from Alcohol Policy for Drug Policy* (Amsterdam: Centrum voor Drugsonderzoek, 2004).

28. "Beecher, Lyman," in: Cherrington, ed., *Standard Encyclopedia of the Alcohol Problem*, vol. 1, 294. Jessica Warner, "Temperance, Alcohol, and the American Evangelical: A Reassessment," *Addiction* 104, no. 7 (2009): 1078.

29. See: Beecher, *Six Sermons on Intemperance*, 60, 75–77, 86.

30. Ibid., 63–68. On the passion of his speeches: James C. White, *Personal Reminiscences of Lyman Beecher* (New York: Funk & Wagnalls, 1882), 36.

31. Yacovone, "Black Temperance Movement," 285.

32. Beecher, *Six Sermons on Intemperance*, 73.

33. Morone, *Hellfire Nation*, 126. Henry Mayer, *All on Fire: William Lloyd Garrison and the Abolition of Slavery* (New York: St. Martin's Press, 1998), 48.

34. White, *Personal Reminiscences of Lyman Beecher*, 9. The YMCA traces its genesis to London in 1844. C. Howard Hopkins, *History of the Y.M.C.A. in North America* (New York: Association Press, 1951), 4.

35. White, *Personal Reminiscences of Lyman Beecher*, 37.

36. Beecher, *Six Sermons on Intemperance*, 90.

37. Jack Blocker Jr., *American Temperance Movements: Cycles of Reform* (Boston: Twayne Publishers, 1989), 11–14.

38. Harry G. Levine and Craig Reinarman, "From Prohibition to Regulation: Lessons from Alcohol Policy for Drug Policy," *Milbank Quarterly* 69, no. 3 (1991): 468. Rorabaugh, *The Alcoholic Republic*, 233.

39. Levine, *Martin Delany, Frederick Douglass*, 104.

40. Brian Danoff, "Introduction," in *Alexis de Tocqueville and the Art of Democratic Statesmanship*, ed. Brian Danoff and L. Joseph Hebert Jr. (New York: Lexington Books, 2011), 1.

41. Alexis de Tocqueville, *Democracy in America*, ed. Richard D. Heffner, abridged ed. (New York: Mentor Books, 1956), 201 (emphasis mine).

42. American Temperance Society, *Permanent Temperance Documents of the American Temperance Society*, vol. 1 (Boston: Seth Bliss, 1835), 52–53, 492. Also: Ian Tyrrell, *Woman's World, Woman's Empire: The Woman's Christian Temperance Union in International Perspective, 1880–1930* (Chapel Hill: University of North Carolina Press, 1991), 12, 16. Douglas Charles

Strange, *British Unitarians against American Slavery, 1833–65* (Rutherford, NJ: Fairleigh Dickinson University Press, 1984), 61.

43. John Allen Krout, *Origins of Prohibition* (New York: Alfred A. Knopf, 1925), 125. Henry M. Baird, *The Life of the Rev. Robert Baird, D.D.* (New York: A. D. F. Randolph, 1866), 111–24. Robert Baird, *Visit to Northern Europe*, 2 vols., vol. II (New York: John S. Taylor & Co., 1841), 196–347.

44. Eighth Report of the American Temperance Society, 1835, 35, in: American Temperance Society, *Permanent Temperance Documents of the American Temperance Society*, 489 (emphasis in original).

45. Mayer, *All on Fire*, 49. John Jay Chapman, *William Lloyd Garrison* (Boston: Atlantic Monthly Press, 1913), 41–42. *One Hundred Years of Temperance: A Memorial Volume of the Centennial Temperance Conference Held in Philadelphia, Pa., September, 1885* (New York: National Temperance Society and Publication House, 1886), 38.

46. William's elder brother, James Holley Garrison, was an alcoholic sailor. In 1841, the year before James's death, Garrison wrote, "So long as you have any appetite for ardent spirit—so long as you are not sure that you can resist its sorcery power—take the advice of a brother who loves you as he does himself, and remain where you will be the least exposed to be tempted and overcome. Liquor has been your worst foe. It has made you die a thousand deaths—robbed you of your hard earnings—subjected you to a vast amount of suffering—and made shipwreck of your moral nature. You ought to hate, fear, avoid it, at all times and under all circumstances, as you would the bite of a rattlesnake, or the infection of the plague." William Lloyd Garrison, "To James H. Garrison, January 4, 1841," in: Merrill, ed., *Letters of William Lloyd Garrison, III*, 4.

47. Mayer, *All on Fire*, 50. "Garrison, William Lloyd," in: Ernest H. Cherrington, ed., *Standard Encyclopedia of the Alcohol Problem*, 6 vols., vol. 3 (Westerville, OH: American Issue Press, 1926), 1072.

48. *One Hundred Years of Temperance*, 317. Theodore Weld's abolitionist activism similarly began in temperance work: David Brion Davis, *Inhuman Bondage: The Rise and Fall of Slavery in the New World* (New York: Oxford University Press, 2006), 252.

49. Ian Tyrrell, *Sobering Up: From Temperance to Prohibition in Antebellum America, 1800–1860* (Westport, CT: Greenwood Press, 1979), 164–67. Tyrrell, *Woman's World, Woman's Empire*, 12. Blocker, *American Temperance Movements*, 12. Richard S. Newman, *Abolitionism: A Very Short Introduction* (New York: Oxford University Press, 2018), 51. Morone, *Hellfire Nation*, 142.

50. Goldwin Smith, *The Moral Crusader William Lloyd Garrison* (New York: Funk & Wagnalls, 1892), 111–12. See also: Vladimir Tchertkoff and F. Holah, *A Short Biography of William Lloyd Garrison, with an Introductory Appreciation of His Life and Work by Leo Tolstoy* (London: Free Press, 1904), 108–10.

51. William Lloyd Garrison, "To the Editor of the *Christian Witness*, December 4, 1846," in: Merrill, ed., *Letters of William Lloyd Garrison, III*, 459.

52. Smith, *Moral Crusader*, 109.

53. Tchertkoff and Holah, *Short Biography of Garrison*, v, vii.

54. Ibid., xi–xii.

55. William Lloyd Garrison, "To the Editor of the Newburyport *Herald*, June 1, 1830," in: Walter M. Merrill, ed., *The Letters of William Lloyd Garrison, Volume I (1822–1835)* (Cambridge, MA: Belknap Press, 1971), 100. Also: Tchertkoff and Holah, *Short Biography of Garrison*, 33–34.

56. Chapman, *William Lloyd Garrison*, 80–81.

57. Smith, *Moral Crusader*, 113.

58. Morone, *Hellfire Nation*, 144. Mayer, *All on Fire*, 121. Davis, *Inhuman Bondage*, 263.

59. Mayer, *All on Fire*, 127. Owen M. Muelder, *Theodore Dwight Weld and the American Anti-Slavery Society* (London: McFarland & Company, 2011), 14.

60. *Constitution of the New-England Anti-Slavery Society: With an Address to the Public* (Boston: Garrison and Knapp, 1832), 8.

61. *The Boston Mob of "Gentlemen of Property and Standing": Proceedings of the Anti-Slavery Meeting Held in Stacy Hall, Boston, on the Twentieth Anniversary of the Mob of October 21, 1835* (Boston: R. F. Wallcut, 1855), 26–42.

62. Avery Craven, *The Coming of the Civil War* (Chicago: University of Chicago Press, 1957), 138.

63. Theodore Dwight Weld, *American Slavery as It Is: Testimony of a Thousand Witnesses* (New York: American Anti-Slavery Society, 1839), 115.

64. Levine, *Martin Delany, Frederick Douglass*, 102–103. Muelder, *Theodore Dwight Weld*, 13–14. Stephanie E. Jones-Rogers, *They Were Her Property: White Women as Slave Owners in the American South* (New Haven, CT: Yale University Press, 2019), 64.

65. Stowe, *Uncle Tom's Cabin*, 178, 418.

66. Frederick Douglass, *Narrative of the Life of Frederick Douglass: An American Slave [1845]* (New York: Cambridge University Press, 2011), 74–76.

67. Frederick Douglass, "Temperance and Anti-Slavery: An Address Delivered in Paisley, Scotland on March 30, 1846," in *The Frederick Douglass Papers. Series One: Speeches, Debates and Interviews*. Volume 1: *1841–1846*, ed. John W. Blassingame (New Haven, CT: Yale University Press, 1979), 205.

68. Levine, *Martin Delany, Frederick Douglass*, 117, 25.

69. Douglass, "Temperance and Anti-Slavery," 205. John R. McKivigan, Julie Husband, and Heather L. Kaufman, eds., *The Speeches of Frederick Douglass: A Critical Edition* (New Haven, CT: Yale University Press, 2018), 15.

70. Yacovone, "Black Temperance Movement," 282–83, 95.

71. Levine, *Martin Delany, Frederick Douglass*, 103–108.

72. Benjamin Quarles, *Black Abolitionists* (New York: Oxford University Press, 1969), 93–101. Denise Herd, "The Paradox of Temperance: Blacks and the Alcohol Question in Nineteenth-Century America," in *Drinking: Behavior and Belief in Modern History*, ed. Susanna Barrows and Robin Room (Berkeley: University of California Press, 1991), 360.

73. Jim Baumohl, "Washingtonians," in *Alcohol and Temperance in Modern History*, ed. Jack Blocker Jr., David Fahey, and Ian Tyrrell (Santa Barbara, CA: ABC-CLIO, 2003). Krout, *Origins of Prohibition*, 182–222. Klaus Mäkelä et al., *Alcoholics Anonymous as a Mutual-Help Movement* (Madison: University of Wisconsin Press, 1996), 14–15. Tyrrell, *Sobering Up*, 164–67.

74. Blocker, *American Temperance Movements*, 45.

75. Levine, *Martin Delany, Frederick Douglass*, 101–107. "Douglass, Frederick," in: Cherrington, ed., *Standard Encyclopedia of the Alcohol Problem*, 838–39. Rorabaugh, *The Alcoholic Republic*, 37.

76. Douglass, "Temperance and Anti-Slavery," 205. See extended discussion in Chapter 5.

77. Douglass, *Correspondence between Samuel H. Cox*, 5–6.

78. Jeffrey R. Kerr-Ritchie, *Rites of August First: Emancipation Day in the Black Atlantic World* (Baton Rouge: Louisiana State University Press, 2007).

79. Douglass, *Selected Speeches and Writings*, 46. Levine, *Martin Delany, Frederick Douglass*, 105.

80. Douglass, "Temperance and Anti-Slavery," 205. See also: Daniel R. Biddle and Murray Dubin, *Tasting Freedom: Octavius Catto and the Battle for Equality in Civil War America* (Philadelphia: Temple University Press, 2010), 100, 21.

81. Douglass, "Temperance and Anti-Slavery," 205.

82. Levine, *Martin Delany, Frederick Douglass*, 108–10.

83. Quoted in: Chaffin, *Giant's Causeway*, 163.

84. Quoted in: Ibid., 163–67. Levine, *Martin Delany, Frederick Douglass*, 109–10.

85. Eric Ortega, "Beer and Brewing," in *The World of the American West*, ed. Gordon Morris Bakken (Santa Barbara, CA: Greenwood, 2017), 338.

86. Neal Dow, *Reminiscences of Neal Dow: Recollections of Eighty Years* (Portland, ME: Evening Express Publishing Company, 1898), 145.

87. Elizabeth Putnam Gordon, *Women Torch-Bearers: The Story of the Woman's Christian Temperance Union* (Evanston, IL: National Woman's Christian Temperance Union Publishing House, 1924), 47.

88. Dow, *Reminiscences of Neal Dow*, 278–79, 345. Daniel Okrent, *Last Call: The Rise and Fall of Prohibition* (New York: Scribner, 2010), 11–12.

89. Dow, *Reminiscences of Neal Dow*, 339. "Dow, Neal," in Ernest H. Cherrington, ed., *Standard Encyclopedia of the Alcohol Problem*, 6 vols., vol. 2 (Westerville, OH: American Issue Press, 1924), 843.

90. Blight, *Frederick Douglass*, 213–17. Newman, *Abolitionism*, 88–98.

91. "Rev. Dr. Cheever on Temperance," *Frederick Douglass' Paper*, November 27, 1851.

92. "Petition. To the Legislature of the State of New York," *Frederick Douglass' Paper*, December 10, 1852. See also: "Prohibition in New York," *Frederick Douglass' Paper*, December 14, 1855; "Triumph in Vermont: The Decisive Triumph of the Maine Law," *Frederick Douglass' Paper*, February 25, 1853; "Maine Law in Connecticut," *Frederick Douglass' Paper*, May 13, 1852.

93. "Uncle William's Pulpit; Or, Life among the Lofty," *Frederick Douglass' Paper*, December 17, 1852.

94. "Temperance. The Maine Law in New York," *Frederick Doulgass' Paper*, May 11, 1855. For the following months, the *Paper* maintained a regular section updating readers on the enforcement of the prohibition law, before its eventual repeal. Levine, *Martin Delany, Frederick Douglass*, 111.

95. Randall C. Jimerson, "The Temperance and Prohibition Movement in America, 1830–1933," in *Guide to the Microfilm Edition of Temperance and Prohibition Papers*, ed. Randall C. Jimerson, Francis X. Blouin, and Charles A. Isetts (Ann Arbor: University of Michigan Publications, 1977), 5.

96. Nicholas Buccola, *The Political Thought of Frederick Douglass: In Pursuit of American Liberty* (New York: New York University Press, 2012), 50. "Frederick Douglass on Prohibition," letter to the editor of *The Issue*, republished in the *Washington Bee*, April 24, 1886, Frederick Douglass Papers Project, Indiana University–Purdue University Indianapolis.

97. "Frederick Douglass on Prohibition," *San Marcos (TX) Free Press*, May 19, 1887, 1, https://texashistory.unt.edu/ark:/67531/metapth295657/m1/1/?q=frederick%20douglass (accessed January 27, 2019). See also: Frederick Douglass, "Temperance" (n/d), Frederick Douglass Papers, Library of Congress Manuscripts Division, Washington, DC, https://www.loc.gov/item/mfd.32022/ (accessed October 12, 2018).

98. Charles T. White, *Lincoln and Prohibition* (New York: Abingdon Press, 1921), 10.

99. Ibid., 27, 31.

100. "First Debate with Stephen Douglas, Ottawa, Illinois, August 21, 1858," in: Abraham Lincoln, *Collected Works of Abraham Lincoln* (New Brunswick, NJ: Rutgers University Press, 1953), vol. 3, 6.

101. Ibid., vol. 3, 5, 16. See also: "Appendix II," in: ibid., vol. 8, 431, listing "forgeries and spurious or dubious items attributed to Lincoln." Also: Samuel Wilson, *Abraham Lincoln: An Apostle of Temperance and Prohibition* (Westerville, OH: American Issue Publishing Company, 1910), 2. White, *Lincoln and Prohibition*, 34–36.

102. White, *Lincoln and Prohibition*, 42–43. Only a brief excerpt of the speech is provided in: Abraham Lincoln, "Address before the Washingtonian Temperance Society. Springfield, Illinois. February 22, 1842," in *Speeches & Letters of Abraham Lincoln, 1832–1865*, ed. Merwin Roe (New York: E. P. Dutton & Co., 1907), 13–16.

103. White, *Lincoln and Prohibition*, 49, 54.

104. Richard Hamm, "The Prohibitionists' Lincolns," *Illinois Historical Journal* 86, no. 2 (1993): 93–99.

105. "Lincoln, Abraham," in: Ernest H. Cherrington, ed., *Standard Encyclopedia of the Alcohol Problem*, 6 vols., vol. 4 (Westerville, OH: American Issue Press, 1928), 1556.

106. White, *Lincoln and Prohibition*, 66–82. White's work contains the most detailed investigation into Lincoln's role in the Illinois Maine Law push.

107. Merrill D. Peterson, *Lincoln in American Memory* (New York: Oxford University Press, 1994), 249–50.

108. Ervin Chapman, *Latest Light on Abraham Lincoln and War-Time Memories* (New York: Fleming H. Revell Company, 1917), 160. Chapman was superintendent of the California Anti-Saloon League. "Lincoln, Abraham," in: Cherrington, ed., *Standard Encyclopedia of the Alcohol Problem*, vol. 4, 1556. White, *Lincoln and Prohibition*, 13.

109. Wilson, *Lincoln: Apostle of Temperance*, 11. See also: "Letter to James Smith, January 24, 1853," in: Abraham Lincoln, *Collected Works of Abraham Lincoln* (New Brunswick, NJ: Rutgers University Press, 1953), vol. 2, 188. "Letter to Henry C. Whitney, June 7, 1855," in: Ibid., 313. Anti-Saloon League founder Howard Hyde Russell undertook extensive correspondence with Merwin concerning his relationship with Lincoln. See: James B. Merwin Correspondence and Other Papers, 1909, 1915, Concerning Merwin's Association with Abraham Lincoln, Folder 41a, Reel 6; and Interviews, Undated, with James B. Merwin Concerning His Association with Abraham Lincoln, Folder 41b, Reel 6, Howard Hyde Russell Series, Temperance and Prohibition Papers, Ohio Historical Society, Columbus.

110. The sole "saloon" reference in the *Collected Works of Abraham Lincoln* relates a particular Philadelphia establishment—the Union Volunteer Refreshment Saloon—that provided food and hospital care for the wounded during the Civil War. See: "Letter to Henry Wilson, May 15, 1862," in: Lincoln, *Collected Works of Abraham Lincoln*, vol. 5, 218. Merwin's extended "saloon"-filled reminiscences of Lincoln can be found at: Chapman, *Latest Light on Abraham Lincoln*, 161–62. On losing documents to the fire, see: Merrill D. Peterson, Lincoln in American Memory, 249–50. Lincoln's use of the word "prohibition" is used almost exclusively in the context of prohibiting slavery.

111. "Lincoln, Abraham," in: Cherrington, ed., *Standard Encyclopedia of the Alcohol Problem*, vol. 4, 1555. Chapman, *Latest Light on Abraham Lincoln*, 162–63.

112. Chapman, *Latest Light on Abraham Lincoln*, 144.

113. Ibid., 169–74. White, *Lincoln and Prohibition*, 101–102.

114. "Reply to Sons of Temperance, September 29, 1863," in: Lincoln, *Collected Works of Abraham Lincoln*, vol. 6, 487–88. Lincoln's words were, "While [liquor] is, perhaps, rather a bad source to derive comfort from, nevertheless, in a hard struggle . . . it is some consolation to be aware that there is some intemperance on the other side, too, and that they have no right to beat us in physical combat on that ground." The *Collected Works* are full of letters concerning Union soldiers punished for drunken insubordination. Perhaps the most interesting is the case of Private Patrick McLaughlin of the Twenty-Ninth Pennsylvania Volunteers who was sentenced to be shot for drunkenness on duty and insubordination. Lincoln personally commuted his sentence to one year of hard labor. "Letter to Joseph Holt, June 26, 1863," in: Ibid., vol. 6, 297.

115. Peterson, *Lincoln in American Memory*, 250. Wilson, *Lincoln: Apostle of Temperance*, 8. Chapman, *Latest Light on Abraham Lincoln*, 174–75. It should be noted that anti-prohibitionists also concocted Lincoln tales. The most widespread one was the following quote, which was admitted to being a forgery by the mayor of Atlanta, John B. Goodwin, to oppose an 1887 local-option measure in the state: "Prohibition will work great injury to the cause of temperance. It is a species of intemperance within itself for it goes beyond the bounds of reason, in that it attempts to control a man's appetite by legislation, and in making comes out of things that are not crimes. A prohibitory law strikes a blow at the very principles on which our government was founded. I have always been found laboring to protect the weaker classes from the stronger and I can never give my consent to such a law as you propose to enact. Until my tongue be silenced in death, I will continue to fight for the rights of man." "Lincoln, Abraham," in: Cherrington, ed., *Standard Encyclopedia of the Alcohol Problem*, vol. 4, 1559.

Chapter 12

1. Peter Adams, *The Bowery Boys: Street Corner Radicals and the Politics of Rebellion* (Westport, CT: Praeger, 2005), xviii.
2. Tyler Anbinder, "'We Will Dirk Every Mother's Son of You': Five Points and the Irish Conquest of New York Politics," *Éire-Ireland* 36, nos. 1&2 (2001): 32.
3. Thomas Low Nichols, *Forty Years of American Life*, 2 vols., vol. 2 (London: John Maxwell and Company, 1864), 152–53. Nichols was a New Hampshire hydrotherapist, health educator, and writer, who patronized the utopian socialism of Charles Fourier, women's rights, and the free-love movement, as well as vegetarianism and temperance. Jean Silver-Isenstadt, "Nichols, Thomas Low (1815–1901)," in *American National Biography* (New York: Oxford University Press, 1999), https://doi.org/10.1093/anb/9780198606697.article.1200664 (accessed April 23, 2019).
4. J. Frank Kernan, *Reminiscences of the Old Fire Laddies and Volunteer Fire Departments of New York and Brooklyn* (New York: M. Crane, 1885), 12.
5. Frank Moss, *The American Metropolis: From Knickerbocker Days to the Present Time*, 3 vols., vol. 2 (New York: Peter Fenelon Collier, 1897), 377–79. T. J. English, *Paddy Whacked: The Untold Story of the Irish American Gangster* (New York: HarperCollins, 2005), 26–27. Herbert Asbury, *The Gangs of New York: An Informal History of the Underworld (1928)* (New York: Random House, 2008), 39. Anbinder, "'We Will Dirk Every Mother's Son of You,'" 40.
6. Sherlock Bristol, *The Pioneer Preacher: An Autobiography* (New York: Fleming H. Revell, 1887), 128–29.
7. Timothy J. Gilfoyle, "Scorsese's *Gangs of New York*: Why Myth Matters," *Journal of Urban History* 29, no. 5 (2003): 620–21.
8. Nichols, *Forty Years of American Life*, 159.
9. Adams, *Bowery Boys*, 31.
10. Nichols, *Forty Years of American Life*, 160–61.
11. *New York Daily Herald*, February 10, 1848, 4. Tyler Anbinder, "Isaiah Rynders and the Ironies of Popular Democracy in Antebellum New York," in *Contested Democracy: Freedom, Race, and Power in American History*, ed. Manisha Sinha and Penny Von Eschen (New York: Columbia University Press, 2007), 34.
12. Isaiah Rynders, *Oration Delivered July 4th, 1851, before the Old Guard at Their Annual Festival* (New York: C. C. Childs, 1851), 3.
13. Tyler Anbinder, *Five Points: The 19th-Century New York Neighborhood That Invented Tap Dance, Stole Elections, and Became the World's Most Notorious Slum* (New York: Free Press, 2001), 35–38.
14. Rynders, *Oration*, 5–6.
15. "The Liquor Party: Demonstration against the Prohibitory Liquor Law," *New York Daily Times*, April 28, 1855, 1.
16. Ian R. Tyrrell, "Women and Temperance in Antebellum America, 1830–1860," *Civil War History* 28, no. 2 (1982): 130.
17. *Fifth Report of the American Temperance Society, Presented at the Meeting in Boston, May, 1832* (Boston: Aaron Russell, 1832), Appendix, 11.
18. Tyrrell, "Women and Temperance," 133, 42.
19. Ibid., 133. Jed Dannenbaum, "The Origins of Temperance Activism and Militancy among American Women," *Journal of Social History* 15, no. 2 (1981): 237. *The Boston Mob of "Gentlemen of Property and Standing": Proceedings of the Anti-Slavery Meeting Held in Stacy Hall, Boston, on the Twentieth Anniversary of the Mob of October 21, 1835* (Boston: R. F. Wallcut, 1855), 26–42.
20. Dannenbaum, "Origins of Temperance Activism," 238.
21. Ibid., 237. Jed Dannenbaum, *Drink and Disorder: Temperance Reform in Cincinnati from the Washingtonian Revival to the WCTU* (Chicago: University of Illinois Press, 1984), 11. See: *The Pearl: A Ladies' Weekly Literary Gazette, Devoted to the Advocacy of the Various Ladies' Total*

Abstinence Associations, October 3, 1846, 140. Also: June 13, 1846, 52; October 10, 1846, 148; and November 7, 1846, 180.

22. Elizabeth Cady Stanton, *Eighty Years and More (1815–1897)* (New York: European Publishing Company, 1898), 59.

23. Ibid., 81. Douglas H. Maynard, "The World's Anti-Slavery Convention of 1840," *Mississippi Valley Historical Review* 47, no. 3 (1960): 466.

24. See: "Lucretia Mott to Maria Weston Chapman, Dublin, 7 Mo. 29th. 1840," in: Beverly Wilson Palmer, ed., *Selected Letters of Lucretia Coffin Mott* (Chicago: University of Illinois Press, 2002), 78–81. Previous temperance record in: "Lucretia Mott to Phebe Post Willis, Philada 9 Mo. 2nd. 1835," in: Ibid., 33–35.

25. Judith Resnik, "Sisterhood, Slavery, and Sovereignty: Transnational Antislavery Work and Women's Rights Movements in the United States during the Twentieth Century," in *Women's Rights and Transatlantic Antislavery in the Era of Emancipation*, ed. Kathryn Kish Sklar and James Brewer Stewart (New Haven, CT: Yale University Press, 2007), 22. Maynard, "World's Anti-Slavery Convention," 452.

26. See: Elizabeth Cady Stanton to Elizabeth J. Neall, Nov. 26, 1841, in: Ann D. Gordon, ed., *The Selected Papers of Elizabeth Cady Stanton and Susan B. Anthony* (New Brunswick, NJ: Rutgers University Press, 1997), 25. Indeed, beginning in 1842, Stanton's first public speeches were not on women's rights but on temperance. Lois W. Banner, *Elizabeth Cady Stanton: A Radical for Woman's Rights* (Boston: Little, Brown and Company, 1980), 29.

27. Banner, *Elizabeth Cady Stanton*, 31–41. Judith Wellman, *The Road to Seneca Falls: Elizabeth Cady Stanton and the First Woman's Rights Convention* (Chicago: University of Illinois Press, 2004), 12.

28. Wellman, *Road to Seneca Falls*, 82–83.

29. D. C. Bloomer, *Life and Writings of Amelia Bloomer* (Boston: Arena Publishing Company, 1895), 16.

30. Quoted in: Philip S. Foner, ed., *Frederick Douglass on Women's Rights* (New York: Da Capo Press, 1992), ix.

31. Ibid., x. Lisa Tetrault, *The Myth of Seneca Falls: Memory and the Women's Suffrage Movement, 1848–1898* (Chapel Hill: University of North Carolina Press, 2014), 12–13.

32. Stanton, *Eighty Years and More*, 127, 467. Lori D. Ginzberg, *Elizabeth Cady Stanton: An American Life* (New York: Hill and Wang, 2009), 25.

33. Tyrrell, "Women and Temperance," 139.

34. Ginzberg, *Elizabeth Cady Stanton*, 58–59.

35. Elisabeth Griffith, *In Her Own Right: The Life of Elizabeth Cady Stanton* (New York: Oxford University Press, 1984), 57. Benjamin Quarles, "Frederick Douglass and the Woman's Rights Movement," *Journal of Negro History* 25, no. 1 (1940): 35.

36. Banner, *Elizabeth Cady Stanton*, 53–54. Already by 1850, popular sentiment was widespread enough to convene a national women's rights convention in Worcester, Massachusetts, with delegates from across the Northeast and Midwest. Tetrault, *Myth of Seneca Falls*, 14–15.

37. Banner, *Elizabeth Cady Stanton*, 53–54.

38. *The Lily*, January 1, 1849, 1. In: Ann Russo and Cheris Kramarae, eds., *The Radical Women's Press of the 1850s* (New York: Routledge, 1991), vol. 2, 17–18. See also: Amelia Bloomer, "Emancipation from Intemperance, Injustice, Prejudice and Bigotry," *The Lily*, December 1851, 93. In: Russo and Kramarae, eds., *Radical Women's Press of the 1850s*, vol. 2, 20.

39. Deborah Chambers, Linda Steiner, and Carole Fleming, *Women and Journalism* (New York: Routledge, 2004), 148–49.

40. Bloomer, *Life and Writings of Amelia Bloomer*, 96–98.

41. "The Woman's Temperance Convention," *Frederick Douglass' Paper*, April 22, 1851. Reprinted in: Foner, ed., *Frederick Douglass on Women's Rights*, 53.

42. Sue Davis, *The Political Thought of Elizabeth Cady Stanton: Women's Rights and the American Political Traditions* (New York: New York University Press, 2008), 85.

43. Foner, ed., *Frederick Douglass on Women's Rights*, 54. Holly Berkley Fletcher, *Gender and the American Temperance Movement of the Nineteenth Century* (New York: Routledge, 2008), 40.

44. Banner, *Elizabeth Cady Stanton*, 54.

45. "Susan B. Anthony's Letter, From the 'Carson League,' Buffalo, July 28, 1852," in: Elizabeth Cady Stanton, Susan B. Anthony, and Matilda Joslyn Gage, eds., *History of Woman Suffrage*, 2 vols., vol. 1 (New York: 1881), 488–89.

46. Susan B. Anthony's Appointment as Agent of the Woman's New York State Temperance Society, May 23, 1852, in: Miscellany, 1840–1946, Mss41210, Box 10, Reel 5, Elizabeth Cady Stanton Papers, Library of Congress, Washington, DC, http://www.loc.gov/item/mss412100161 (accessed January 20, 2021).

47. Davis, *Political Thought of Elizabeth Cady Stanton*, 86.

48. "Women's New York State Temperance Society," *Frederick Douglass' Paper*, June 10, 1853, in: Foner, ed., *Frederick Douglass on Women's Rights*, 17, 60–63. See also: Helen Theresa Shea, "The Woman's Rights Movement in New York State, 1848–1854" (MA thesis, Columbia University, 1940), 32–35. Ginzberg, *Elizabeth Cady Stanton*, 74, 99–100.

49. "Some Thoughts on Woman's Rights," *Frederick Douglass' Paper,* June 10, 1853, in: Foner, ed., *Frederick Douglass on Women's Rights*, 58.

50. Simeon B. Chase, "The Independent Order of Good Templars," in *Centennial Temperance Volume: A Memorial of the International Temperance Conference, Held in Philadelphia, June, 1876* (New York: National Temperance Society and Publication House, 1877), 602. Especially following the Civil War, the IOGT would become "the leading temperance organization in the world," boasting lodges and adherents across North America, Europe, and around the globe. IOGT, *The Leading Temperance Organisation in the World* (Birmingham: IOGT Grand Lodge of England, 1890[?]). Guy Hayler, Temperance Tracts, University of Wisconsin-Madison, Special Collections, Vol. XI, No. 78. Ingrid Nilsson, *I.O.G.T.—Från orden till förening* (Sollentuna, Sweden: Intellecta Docusys AB, 2004), 8. Oskar Petersson, *Goodtemplarordens i Sverige historia* (Stockholm: Svenska Nykterhetsförlaget, 1903), 5–9.

51. Nichols, *Forty Years of American Life*, 196.

52. Robert C. Williams, *Horace Greeley: Champion of American Freedom* (New York: New York University Press, 2006), 17–18, 120, 57–59. "Monthly Record of Current Events," *Harper's Magazine*, September 1853, 548. Edwin G. Burrows, *The Finest Building in America: The New York Crystal Palace, 1853–1858* (New York: Oxford University Press, 2018), 1–5. On temperance, see: Horace Greeley, *Alcoholic Liquors: Their Essential Nature and Necessary Effects on the Human Constitution* (New York: Brognard, 1849), 5.

53. Mark Lawrence Schrad, *The Political Power of Bad Ideas: Networks, Institutions, and the Global Prohibition Wave* (New York: Oxford University Press, 2010), 43–46.

54. Wendell Phillips Garrison and Francis Jackson Garrison, *William Lloyd Garrison, 1805–1879: The Story of His Life Told by His Children*, 4 vols., vol. III: *1841–1860* (Boston: Houghton, Mifflin and Company, 1894), 283–84.

55. Ibid., 285.

56. James C. Nicholson, *The Notorious John Morrissey: How a Bare-Knuckle Brawler Became a Congressman and Founded Saratoga Race Course* (Lexington: University Press of Kentucky, 2016).

57. Virgil W. Peterson, *The Mob: 200 Years of Organized Crime in New York* (Ottawa, IL: Green Hill Publishers, 1983), 11.

58. Nicholson, *Notorious John Morrissey*. "Isaiah Rynders, Captain of the Empire Club, New York City," *New York Herald,* February 2, 1845. Asbury, *Gangs of New York*, 83–84. See also: "John Brown to Frederick Douglass, January 9, 1854," in: Frederick Douglass, *The Frederick Douglass Papers, Series Three: Correspondence*, vol. 2: *1853–1865* (New Haven, CT: Yale University Press, 2018), 71. Letter, Isaiah Rynders to President James Buchanan, March 14, 1857, Isaiah Rynders Letters, 1855–1857, MS 2958.8522, New-York Historical Society, New York. Anbinder, *Five Points*, 142–43.

59. Robert Ernst, *Immigrant Life in New York City, 1825–1863* (Syracuse, NY: Syracuse University Press, 1994), 90. Jacquelyn Ruth Parkinson, "*Beyond Antebellum Sectionalism: New York City's Local Scene during the 1850s as Reflected in the New York Times*" (MA thesis, Washington State University, 2008), 110–11. "The Liquor Dealers Demonstration," *New York Times*, April 28, 1855, 4. Edwin G. Burrows and Mike Wallace, *Gotham: A History of New York City to 1898* (New York: Oxford University Press, 1999), 777.

60. Joseph Gusfield, *Symbolic Crusade: Status Politics and the American Temperance Movement* (Urbana: University of Illinois Press, 1963). Lisa McGirr, *The War on Alcohol: Prohibition and the Rise of the American State* (New York: W. W. Norton & Company, 2016).

61. As for Macready: "The excitement was intense for almost a week, and for several days a great crowd stood in front of the New York Hotel, where Macready had stopped, urging him to come forth and be hanged. But the actor boarded a train at New Rochelle within two hours after the rioting of May 10, and went to Boston. From there he sailed to England, and never again returned to this country." Asbury, *Gangs of New York*, 39–41.

62. Rynders, *Oration*, 5–6.

63. Garrison and Garrison, *William Lloyd Garrison*, 292. William Lloyd Garrison, *The Words of Garrison: A Centennial Selection (1805–1905) of Characteristic Sentiments from the Writings of William Lloyd Garrison* (Boston: Houghton, Mifflin and Company, 1905), 133. Anbinder, "Isaiah Rynders," 39.

64. Anbinder, "Isaiah Rynders," 40.

65. Garrison and Garrison, *William Lloyd Garrison*, 294–95.

66. Carol Faulkner, *Lucretia Mott's Heresy: Abolition and Women's Rights in Nineteenth-Century America* (Philadelphia: University of Pennsylvania Press, 2011), 154.

67. Garrison and Garrison, *William Lloyd Garrison*, 299.

68. Faulkner, *Lucretia Mott's Heresy*, 154–55. Fletcher, *Gender and the American Temperance Movement*, 55–56. *Proceedings of the Woman's Rights Convention, Held at the Broadway Tabernacle, in the City of New York, on Tuesday and Wednesday, Sept. 6th and 7th, 1853* (New York: Fowlers and Wells, 1853), 40.

69. *Whole World's Temperance Convention Held at Metropolitan Hall in the City of New York on Thursday and Friday, Sept. 1st and 2d, 1853* (New York: Fowlers and Wells, 1853), 8. Susan B. Anthony Papers, Library of Congress.

70. Quoted in: Fletcher, *Gender and the American Temperance Movement*, 55. Also: Speech by Rev. Antoinette Browne, in: *Proceedings of the Woman's Rights Convention*, 40–42. Susan B. Anthony Papers, Library of Congress.

71. "The Female Pests," *New York Daily Times*, September 8, 1853, 4.

72. Faulkner, *Lucretia Mott's Heresy*, 154–55.

73. *Whole World's Temperance Convention*, 13. Susan B. Anthony Papers, Library of Congress.

74. Burrows and Wallace, *Gotham*, 815.

75. *Whole World's Temperance Convention*, 30. See also: Daniel Okrent, *Last Call: The Rise and Fall of Prohibition* (New York: Scribner, 2010), 10.

76. *Whole World's Temperance Convention*, 32.

77. Faulkner, *Lucretia Mott's Heresy*, 154–55.

78. Bloomer, *Life and Writings of Amelia Bloomer*, 102–104. Greeley was himself in attendance as well. Burrows and Wallace, *Gotham*, 777.

79. Bloomer, *Life and Writings of Amelia Bloomer*, 108–10.

80. Garrison noted in conclusion, "I doubt if the Maine Law would do all you give it credit for. There are laws against profanity, yet there is none the less swearing. There is a law against lewdness, but is it lessened thereby? He thought too much confidence is placed in law; men are apt to shift off their moral responsibility, and rely upon Legislation. All political reforms are the fruits and not the parents of morality. It is obvious that men who need laws to govern them are not fit to be trusted." *Whole World's Temperance Convention*, 62. Susan B. Anthony Papers, Library of Congress.

81. *New York Tribune*, September 3, 1853. In: Stanton, Anthony, and Gage, eds., *History of Woman Suffrage*, 511.

82. Faulkner, *Lucretia Mott's Heresy*, 154.

83. *Proceedings of the Woman's Rights Convention*, 4–6.

84. Dorothy Sterling, *Lucretia Mott* (New York: Feminist Press at the City University of New York, 1964), 167.

85. *Proceedings of the Woman's Rights Convention*, 22–23.

86. Ibid., 41–42.

87. Ibid., 54–55.

88. Faulkner, *Lucretia Mott's Heresy*, 154–55.

89. *Proceedings of the Woman's Rights Convention*, 76–77.

90. Margaret Hope Bacon, "By Moral Force Alone: The Antislavery Women and Nonresistance," in *The Abolitionist Sisterhood: Women's Political Culture in Antebellum America*, ed. Jean Fagan Yellin and John C. Van Horne (Ithaca, NY: Cornell University Press, 1994), 294. Faulkner, *Lucretia Mott's Heresy*, 154–55. Sterling, *Lucretia Mott*, 167.

91. Bacon, "By Moral Force Alone," 294.

92. Sterling, *Lucretia Mott*, 166–68.

93. Frank L. Byrne, *Prophet of Prohibition: Neal Dow and His Crusade* (Madison: State Historical Society of Wisconsin, 1961), 57.

94. Parkinson, "Beyond Antebellum Sectionalism," 108–109.

95. "The Liquor Dealers' Demonstration," *New York Daily Times*, April 28, 1855, 4.

96. "Tammanny [*sic*] Canvassing for the Liquor Vote," *New York Daily Times*, May 22, 1855, 8.

97. "Anti-Prohibition. Great Meeting in the Park," *New York Daily Times*, July 3, 1855, 1.

98. Byrne, *Prophet of Prohibition*, 62–64.

99. Parkinson, "Beyond Antebellum Sectionalism," 110–12. "The Riot in Portland," *New York Daily Times*, June 5, 1855.

100. "Temperance Movement," *New York Times*, May 22, 1858, 4.

101. "Tammany Hall," in: Ernest H. Cherrington, ed., *Standard Encyclopedia of the Alcohol Problem*, 6 vols., vol. 6 (Westerville, OH: American Issue Press, 1930), 2595.

Chapter 13

1. Carol Faulkner, *Lucretia Mott's Heresy: Abolition and Women's Rights in Nineteenth-Century America* (Philadelphia: University of Pennsylvania Press, 2011), 181.

2. "Harper, Frances Ellen Watkins (1825–1911)," in: Mary Ellen Snodgrass, ed., *American Women Speak: An Encyclopedia and Document Collection of Women's Oratory* (Santa Barbara, CA: ABC-CLIO, 2017), 333.

3. Especially with reference to Rosa Parks: Lisa Tetrault, *The Myth of Seneca Falls: Memory and the Women's Suffrage Movement, 1848–1898* (Chapel Hill: University of North Carolina Press, 2014), 4.

4. H. M. Parkhurst, *Proceedings of the Eleventh National Woman's Rights Convention: Held at the Church of the Puritans, New York, May 10, 1866* (New York: Robert J. Johnston, 1866), 46–47. New York's public transit had only been desegregated in 1855, through similar acts of civil disobedience by Elizabeth Jennings. Sam Roberts, "Elizabeth Jennings, Who Desegregated New York's Trolleys," *New York Times*, January 31, 2019, https://www.nytimes.com/interactive/2019/obituaries/elizabeth-jennings-overlooked.html (accessed February 18, 2019).

5. Daniel R. Biddle and Murray Dubin, *Tasting Freedom: Octavius Catto and the Battle for Equality in Civil War America* (Philadelphia: Temple University Press, 2010), 207–208, 324–34. See also: John Hepp, "Streetcars," in: *The Encyclopedia of Greater Philadelphia*, https://philadelphiaencyclopedia.org/archive/streetcars (accessed February 5, 2019).

6. Frances Ellen Watkins Harper, "We Are All Bound Up Together: Address before the Eleventh National Women's Rights Convention, New York City, May 1866," in: Snodgrass, ed., *American*

Women Speak, 336. This was hardly an isolated instance. Harper recounted a similar incident years earlier, in the pages of William Lloyd Garrison's abolitionist paper *The Liberator*. In 1858 a conductor said his streetcar wouldn't budge until she moved to the driver's platform behind the horse. "Now was not that brave and noble?" Harper mused. "As a matter of course, I did not." *The Liberator*, April 23, 1858. Quoted in: Margaret Hope Bacon, "'One Great Bundle of Humanity': Frances Ellen Watkins Harper (1825–1911)," *Pennsylvania Magazine of History and Biography* 113, no. 1 (1989): 28.

7. Parkhurst, *Proceedings of the Eleventh National Woman's Rights Convention*, 48–49.

8. Jack S. Blocker Jr., "Separate Paths: Suffragists and the Women's Temperance Crusade," *Signs* 10, no. 3 (1985): 460–61. Sarah K. Bolton, "The Woman's Crusade," in: *Centennial Temperance Volume: A Memorial of the International Temperance Conference, Held in Philadelphia, June, 1876* (New York: National Temperance Society and Publication House, 1877).

9. Denise Herd, "The Paradox of Temperance: Blacks and the Alcohol Question in Nineteenth-Century America," in *Drinking: Behavior and Belief in Modern History*, ed. Susanna Barrows and Robin Room (Berkeley: University of California Press, 1991), 355. See also: John R. Larkins, *Alcohol and the Negro: Explosive Issues* (Zebulon, NC: Record Publishing, 1965), 6–11. Hanes Walton Jr. and James E. Taylor, "Blacks and the Southern Prohibition Movement," *Phylon* 32, no. 3 (1971): 250–59.

10. "Negro, the, and Alcohol," in: Ernest H. Cherrington, ed., *Standard Encyclopedia of the Alcohol Problem*, 6 vols., vol. 4 (Westerville, OH: American Issue Press, 1928), 1878.

11. Lee L. Willis, *Southern Prohibition: Race, Reform, and Public Life in Middle Florida, 1821–1920* (Athens: University of Georgia Press, 2011), 91–93.

12. United States Bureau of the Census, *Ninth Census, Volume II: The Vital Statistics of the United States* (Washington, DC: Government Printing Office, 1872), table VII, 307. The rate of deaths for alcohol poisoning per 1,000 deaths among whites was 1.50, while only 0.90 among blacks; deaths from liver cirrhosis were 0.45 per 1,000 among whites, but only 0.10 among blacks.

13. United States Bureau of the Census, *Tenth Census, Part II: Report on the Mortality and Vital Statistics of the United States* (Washington, DC: Government Printing Office, 1886), lxvii.

14. John Koren, *Economic Aspects of the Liquor Problem, an Investigation Made under the Direction of a Sub-Committee of the Committee of Fifty* (New York: Houghton Mifflin and Company, 1899), 171.

15. Walton and Taylor, "Blacks and the Southern Prohibition Movement," 251. Citing: James Benson Sellers, *The Prohibition Movement in Alabama: 1702–1943* (Chapel Hill: University of North Carolina Press, 1943), 75–77.

16. Walton and Taylor, "Blacks and the Southern Prohibition Movement," 259.

17. Frederick Douglass, "Temperance" (n/d), Frederick Douglass Papers, Library of Congress Manuscripts Division, Washington, DC. pp. 7–9 of the second temperance speech in the collection, https://www.loc.gov/item/mfd.32022/ (accessed October 12, 2018).

18. Carla L. Peterson, *Doers of the World: African American Women Speakers and Writers in the North, 1830–1880* (New Brunswick, NJ: Rutgers University Press, 1998), 10. Bacon, "'One Great Bundle of Humanity,'" 23. Carole Lynn Stewart, *Temperance and Cosmopolitanism: African American Reformers in the Atlantic World* (University Park: Pennsylvania State University Press, 2018).

19. See: Johanna Ortner, "Lost No More: Recovering Frances Ellen Watkins Harper's *Forest Leaves*," *Common-place.org* 15, no. 4 (2015), http://common-place.org/book/lost-no-more-recovering-frances-ellen-watkins-harpers-forest-leaves/ (accessed March 12, 2019). Young not only helped found the Sons of Temperance in the state of Maryland, he was also long-time editor of its *Temperance Banner*. Patricia Dockman Anderson, "'By Legal or Moral Suasion Let Us Put It Away': Temperance in Baltimore, 1829–1870" (PhD dissertation, University of Delaware, 2008), 95–116.

20. "The Drunkard's Child (1854)," in: Frances Smith Foster, ed., *A Brighter Coming Day: A Frances Ellen Watkins Harper Reader* (New York: Feminist Press at the City University of New York, 1990), 63. Melba Joyce Boyd, *Discarded Legacy: Politics and Poetics in the Life of Frances E. W. Harper, 1825–1911* (Detroit: Wayne State University Press, 1994), 75–76.

21. Bacon, "'One Great Bundle of Humanity,'" 32. Harper, "We Are All Bound Up Together," 336.

22. "Nothing and Something," in: Frances E. Watkins Harper, *Sketches of Southern Life* (Philadelphia: Ferguson Bros. & Co., 1891), 51. Also: Foster, ed., *A Brighter Coming Day*, 251–52.

23. "Signing the Pledge," in: Harper, *Sketches of Southern Life*, 56–58.

24. Patricia J. Sehulster, "Frances Harper's Religion of Responsibility in Sowing and Reaping," *Journal of Black Studies* 40, no. 6 (2010): 1140–41. Peterson, *Doers of the World*.

25. Peterson, *Doers of the World*, 209. Doveanna S. Fulton, "Sowing Seeds in an Untilled Field: Temperance and Race, Indeterminacy and Recovery in Frances E. W. Harper's *Sowing and Reaping*," *Legacy* 24, no. 2 (2007): 210.

26. Frances E. W. Harper, "Sowing and Reaping (1876–77)," in *Minnie's Sacrifice; Sowing and Reaping; Trial and Triumph: Three Rediscovered Novels*, ed. Frances Smith Foster (Boston: Beacon Press, 1994), 98.

27. Sehulster, "Frances Harper's Religion of Responsibility," 1140–41.

28. Harper, "Sowing and Reaping," 106.

29. Ibid., 103–11.

30. Ibid., 161.

31. Fulton, "Sowing Seeds in an Untilled Field," 210–11. Michael Stancliff, *Frances Ellen Watkins Harper: African American Reform Rhetoric and the Rise of a Modern Nation State* (New York: Routledge, 2011), 90–91.

32. Mary F. Eastman, *The Biography of Dio Lewis, A.M., M.D.* (New York: Fowler & Wells Co., 1891), 74–77.

33. Dio Lewis, *Prohibition a Failure: Or, the True Solution of the Temperance Question* (Boston: J. R. Osgood and Company, 1875), 5. Jack Blocker Jr., *"Give to the Winds Thy Fears": The Women's Temperance Crusade, 1873–1874* (Westport, CT: Greenwood, 1985), 7.

34. Eastman, *Biography of Dio Lewis*, 48–49.

35. Ruth Bordin, *Woman and Temperance: The Quest for Power and Liberty, 1873–1900* (Philadelphia: Temple University Press, 1981), 16.

36. Eliza Jane Trimble Thompson et al., *Hillsboro Crusade Sketches and Family Records* (Cincinnati: Jennings and Graham, 1906), 58–59. On Lewis's role: T. A. H. Brown, "A Full Description of the Origin and Progress of the New Plan of Labor by the Women up to the Present Time," in *Fifty Years History of the Temperance Cause*, ed. Jane E. Stebbins (Hartford, CT: L. Stebbins, 1874), 398–402.

37. Bordin, *Woman and Temperance*, 17. Mary J. Oates, "Catholic Female Academies on the Frontier," *U.S. Catholic Historian* 12, no. 4 (1994): 125–26. Louise Michele Newman, *White Women's Rights: The Racial Origins of Feminism in the United States* (New York: Oxford University Press, 1999), 76–77.

38. Thompson et al., *Hillsboro Crusade Sketches*, 59–60.

39. Ibid., 64–65.

40. Brown, "A Full Description," 365. Frances E. Willard, *Glimpses of Fifty Years: The Autobiography of an American Woman* (Chicago: H. J. Smith & Co., 1889), 339. On Ohio saloons of this time period, see: William C. Smith, "The Cincinnati Saloon. 1880–1890," *Bulletin of the Historical and Philosophical Society of Ohio* 19, no. 4 (1961): 280–87.

41. Bordin, *Woman and Temperance*, 20. Clipping, *Cleveland Herald*, November (n/d), 1874, Scrapbook 4, Woman's Christian Temperance Union Series, Reel 30. Blocker, *Give to the Winds Thy Fears*, 103.

42. Matilda Gilruth Carpenter, *The Crusade: Its Origin and Development at Washington Court House and Its Results* (Columbus, OH: W. G. Hubbard & Co., 1893), 43–44.

43. Ironically, Lewis was not a prohibitionist. In fact, he wrote an entire book about how prohibitionism impeded the true goals of temperance, which could only be achieved through brotherly love and moral suasion. "Lewis, Dio(cletian)," in: Ernest H. Cherrington, ed., *Standard Encyclopedia of the Alcohol Problem*, 6 vols., vol. 4 (Westerville, OH: American Issue Press, 1928), 1536. Lewis, *Prohibition a Failure*, 5–6.

44. "The New Temperance Crusade," *Christian Union*, February 11, 1874, 111. On Beecher's temperance and suffragism, see: Debby Applegate, *The Most Famous Man in America: The Biography of Henry Ward Beecher* (New York: Doubleday, 2006), 383–97.

45. Jack Blocker Jr., "Separate Paths: Suffragists and the Women's Temperance Crusade," *Signs* 10, no. 3 (1985): 466.

46. Ibid., 467. Ida Husted Harper, *The Life and Work of Susan B. Anthony*, 2 vols., vol. 1 (Indianapolis: Bowen-Merrill Company, 1899), 457. See also: Elizabeth Cady Stanton, Susan B. Anthony, and Matilda Joslyn Gage, *History of Woman Suffrage*, 6 vols., vol. 3 (Rochester, NY: Susan B. Anthony, 1885), 500.

47. Undated speech (ca. 1872), in: Miscellany, 1840–1946, Scrapbooks, #1, prepared by Susan B. Anthony, Mss41210, Box 9, Elizabeth Cady Stanton Papers, 1814–1946, Library of Congress, Washington, DC.

48. Blocker, "Separate Paths," 468.

49. "Stanton, Elizabeth Cady," in: Ernest H. Cherrington, ed., *Standard Encyclopedia of the Alcohol Problem*, 6 vols., vol. 6 (Westerville, OH: American Issue Press, 1930), 2520.

50. Sara Hunter Graham, *Woman Suffrage and the New Democracy* (New Haven, CT: Yale University Press, 1996), 69–72.

51. Elizabeth Putnam Gordon, *Women Torch-Bearers: The Story of the Woman's Christian Temperance Union* (Evanston, IL: National Woman's Christian Temperance Union Publishing House, 1924), 13–14.

52. Clipping, March (n/d) 1874, Scrapbook 2, Sarah E. Turner Papers, 1834–1939, Michigan Historical Collections of the Bentley Historical Library, University of Michigan, Ann Arbor. Turner was a temperance worker and WCTU member from Adrian, Michigan. Bordin, *Woman and Temperance*, 23.

53. Bordin, *Woman and Temperance*, 24–25. Sarah Bolton's Reminiscences, *Union Signal*, December 20, 1883, 7–8.

54. Thompson et al., *Hillsboro Crusade Sketches*, 102. Carpenter, *The Crusade*, 84–85. Bordin, *Woman and Temperance*, 24.

55. Harper, "Sowing and Reaping," 167. Stancliff, *Frances Ellen Watkins Harper*, 87.

56. Frances Ellen Watkins Harper, "The Woman's Christian Temperance Union and the Colored Woman," *African Methodist Episcopal Church Review* 4 (1888): 313–16. In: Foster, ed., *A Brighter Coming Day*, 28–82.

57. Holly Berkley Fletcher, *Gender and the American Temperance Movement of the Nineteenth Century* (New York: Routledge, 2008), 79–101.

58. Anna A. Gordon, *The Beautiful Life of Frances E. Willard* (Chicago: Woman's Temperance Publishing Association, 1898), 93.

59. Ruth Bordin, "'A Baptism of Power and Liberty': The Women's Crusade of 1873–1874," *Ohio History Journal* 87, no. 4 (1978): 396–98. Blocker, "Separate Paths," 462.

60. Bordin, *Woman and Temperance*, 21–22. Gordon, *Women Torch-Bearers*, 9.

61. Blocker, "Separate Paths," 461–62.

62. Frances E. Willard, "Everybody's War" [ca. 1874], Box 19, Folder 1, Frances Willard House Museum and Archives, Evansville, Illinois. Gordon, *Beautiful Life of Frances Willard*, 95.

63. Frederick Douglass et al., "The Position of the National Woman's Christian Temperance Union of the United States in Relation to the Colored People," Boston, Massachusetts, February 6, 1895, Frances Willard House Museum and Archives, Evansville, Illinois, https://scalar. usc.edu/works/willard-and-wells/1894-wctu-convention-the-aftermath?path=timeline (accessed January 20, 2021). Glenda Elizabeth Gilmore, *Gender and Jim Crow: Women and the*

Politics of White Supremacy in North Carolina, 1896–1920 (Chapel Hill: University of North Carolina Press, 1996), 49.

64. Gordon, *Beautiful Life of Frances Willard*, 31–32.

65. Ibid. Frances E. Willard, "Laws of Fort City," 1854, Box 1, Folder 28, Frances Willard House Museum and Archives, Evansville, Illinois.

66. Itinerary: Gordon, *Beautiful Life of Frances Willard*, 68.

67. Bordin, *Woman and Temperance*, 46. Frances E. Willard, *Woman and Temperance: Or the Work and Workers of the Woman's Christian Temperance Union*, 4th ed. (Hartford, CT: Park Publishing Co., 1884), 18–22.

68. Gordon, *Beautiful Life of Frances Willard*, 61–66, 93–94.

69. "Willard, Frances Elizabeth," in: Ernest H. Cherrington, ed., *Standard Encyclopedia of the Alcohol Problem*, 6 vols., vol. 6 (Westerville, OH: American Issue Press, 1930), 2849.

70. Bordin, *Woman and Temperance*, 36.

71. Gordon, *Women Torch-Bearers*, 14–15.

72. Women's Christian Temperance Union, *Constitution, by-Laws, and Order of Business of the Women's Christian Temperance Union* (Toronto: Guardian Office, 1876), 3.

73. Bordin, *Woman and Temperance*, 36–37.

74. Ibid., 39. "Wittenmyer, Annie (Turner)," in: Ernest H. Cherrington, ed., *Standard Encyclopedia of the Alcohol Problem*, 6 vols., vol. 6 (Westerville, OH: American Issue Press, 1930), 2888–89.

75. Letter, Frances E. Willard to Annie Wittenmyer, September 16, 1875, Woman's Christian Temperance Union Series, Reel 11. Also letters of October 25 and 27, 1875. Bordin, *Woman and Temperance*, 48–51.

76. "World's Temperance Conventions and Congresses," in: Ernest H. Cherrington, ed., *Standard Encyclopedia of the Alcohol Problem*, 6 vols., vol. 6 (Westerville, OH: American Issue Press, 1930), 2917. Tyrell notes that the sole Japanese delegate was an American missionary on furlough. Ian Tyrrell, *Woman's World, Woman's Empire: The Woman's Christian Temperance Union in International Perspective, 1880–1930* (Chapel Hill: University of North Carolina Press, 1991), 20. Another, larger international temperance convention was held two days later under the auspices of the National Temperance Society, with over four hundred delegates from the United States, the United Kingdom, Canada, Sweden, and New Zealand. *Centennial Temperance Volume: A Memorial of the International Temperance Conference, Held in Philadelphia, June, 1876*, 345.

77. Willard, *Glimpses of Fifty Years*, 351.

78. Bordin, *Woman and Temperance*, 57. "Frances E. Willard to Annie Wittenmyer," May 24, 1876, Woman's Christian Temperance Union Series, Reel 11.

79. Frances E. Willard, *Home Protection Manual: Containing an Argument for the Temperance Ballot for Woman, and How to Obtain It, as a Means of Home Protection* (New York: The Independent, 1879), Frances E. Willard Papers, 1841–1991, Box 20, Folder 12, Frances Willard House Museum and Archives, Evanston, Illinois.

80. "Woman's Christian Temperance Union," *Woman's Journal*, October 11, 1879, 324. Willard, *Glimpses of Fifty Years*, 351–52. Mary Earhart, *Frances Willard: From Prayers to Politics* (Chicago: University of Chicago Press, 1944), 152. Bordin, *Woman and Temperance*, 57–58. See also: Frances Willard, "Speech at Queen's Hall, London, June 9, 1894," *Citizen and Home Guard*, July 23, 1894, Reel 41, no. 27, Woman's Christian Temperance Union Series. Gordon, *Women Torch-Bearers*, 33.

81. Bordin, *Woman and Temperance*, 63–64.

82. Ruth Bordin, *Frances Willard: A Biography* (Chapel Hill: University of North Carolina Press, 1986), 129–30. Woman's Christian Temperance Union, *Minutes of the Woman's National Christian Temperance Union, at the Seventh Annual Meeting, Boston, 27–30 October, 1880* (New York: National Temperance Society and Publication House, 1880), 9–25. Woman's Christian Temperance Union, *Minutes of the Woman's National Christian Temperance Union, at*

the Eighth Annual Meeting, in Washington, D.C., 26–29 October, 1881 (New York: Union-Angus Steam Printing, 1881).

83. Frances E. Willard, *Do Everything: A Handbook for the World's White Ribboners* (Chicago: Woman's Temperance Publication Association, 1895), vii. See also: Gary Scott Smith, *The Search for Social Salvation: Social Christianity and America, 1880–1925* (Lanham, MD: Lexington Books, 2000), 202, n. 138.

84. Harper, *Life and Work of Susan B. Anthony*, 117. Lois W. Banner, *Elizabeth Cady Stanton: A Radical for Woman's Rights* (Boston: Little, Brown and Company, 1980), 116–17. Sue Davis, *The Political Thought of Elizabeth Cady Stanton: Women's Rights and the American Political Traditions* (New York: New York University Press, 2008), 187.

85. Bordin, *Woman and Temperance*, 98–116.

86. Ibid., 98. Woman's Christian Temperance Union, *Minutes of the National Woman's Christian Temperance Union, at the Seventeenth Annual Meeting, in Atlanta, Georgia, 14–18 November, 1890* (Chicago: Woman's Temperance Publication Association, 1890), 55–60.

87. Ronald C. White and C. Howard Hopkins, *The Social Gospel: Religion and Reform in Changing America* (Philadelphia: Temple University Press, 1976), 119.

88. Bordin, *Woman and Temperance*, 76. Nancy A. Hardesty, "'The Best Temperance Organization in the Land': Southern Methodists and the W.C.T.U. in Georgia," *Methodist History* 28, no. 3 (1990): 188.

89. Willard, *Glimpses of Fifty Years*, 328–29. She also noted that the immigrant population was smaller in the South than in the cities of the North.

90. Anna A. Gordon, *Frances Willard: A Memorial Volume* (Chicago: Woman's Temperance Publishing Association, 1898), 107–108. "Frances Elizabeth Willard," in *Rock County, Wisconsin: A New History of Its Cities, Villages, Towns, Citizens and Varied Interests, from the Earliest Times, up to Date*, ed. William Fiske Brown (Chicago: C. F. Cooper & Co., 1908), 1081.

91. Bordin, *Woman and Temperance*, 77–78. See also: "Frances Willard to Anna Gordon," April 11, 1881, Woman's Christian Temperance Union Series, Reel 12. H. Paul Thompson Jr., *A Most Stirring and Significant Episode: Religion and the Rise and Fall of Prohibition in Black Atlanta, 1865–1887* (DeKalb: Northern Illinois University Press, 2013).

92. Gilmore, *Gender and Jim Crow*, 46. *Wilmington Morning Star*, March 12, 1881; *News and Courier* (Charleston, SC), March 15, 1881, and *Our Union*, May 1881, 10. In: Frances Willard Scrapbooks, Box 1, Folder 42, Frances Willard House Museum and Archives, Evanston, Illinois.

93. Edward L. Ayers, *The Promise of the New South: Life after Reconstruction* (New York: Oxford University Press, 2007), 181. Bordin, *Woman and Temperance*, 78–82.

94. Gilmore, *Gender and Jim Crow*, 49. Frederick Douglass et al., "The Position of the National Woman's Christian Temperance Union of the United States in Relation to the Colored People," Boston, Massachusetts, February 6, 1895, Frances Willard House Museum and Archives, Evansville, Illinois, https://scalar.usc.edu/works/willard-and-wells/1894-wctu-convention-the-aftermath?path=timeline (accessed January 20, 2021).

95. "The WCTU and Native Americans," in: Woman's Christian Temperance Union, *Minutes of the Woman's National Christian Temperance Union, at the Sixth Annual Meeting, in Indianapolis, 29 October–3 November 1879* (Cleveland, OH: Fairbanks & Co., 1879), 60. Bordin, *Woman and Temperance*, 85–87.

96. Woman's Christian Temperance Union, *Minutes of the National Woman's Christian Temperance Union, at the Twelfth Annual Meeting, in Philadelphia, PA, October 30th, 31st and November 2nd and 3d* (Brooklyn: Martin & Niper, Steam Printers, 1885), 5, National Headquarters, Minutes of the National Convention: 1885, Roll 2, Woman's Christian Temperance Union Series, Temperance and Prohibition Papers.

97. Bordin, *Woman and Temperance*, 88. See: "Annual Meeting Minutes, October 30, 1885, Philadelphia," 12, 62–67, Woman's Christian Temperance Union Series, Reel 2, WCTU National Headquarters, Evanston, Illinois. Also: "World's W.C.T.U. including Missionary

Work of Mary Clement Leavitt and Polyglot Petition, 1883–1894," Scrapbook 20, Reel 34, Woman's Christian Temperance Union Series. "Annual Meeting Minutes, October 19, 1886, Minneapolis, MN," lxxxvi–xc, Reel 2, Woman's Christian Temperance Union Series. World's Woman's Christian Temperance Union, *Report of the Convention of the World's Woman's Christian Temperance Union, Boston Massachusetts, U.S.A. October 17–23, 1906* (Chicago: White Ribbon Company, 1906), 2. Jane A. Stewart, "The Launching of the World's WCTU," *Union Signal*, October 2, 1913, 5. Ian Tyrrell, "Women and Temperance in International Perspective: The World's W.C.T.U., 1880s–1920s," in *Drinking: Behavior and Belief in Modern History*, ed. Susanna Barrows and Robin Room (Berkeley: University of California Press, 1991), 217–18. Tyrrell, *Woman's World, Woman's Empire*, 22.

98. Frances Willard, "The White Ribbon Movement," in: *Bericht über den V. Internationalen Kongress zur Bekämpfung des Missbrauchs geistiger Getränke zu Basel, 20–22 August 1895* (Basel: Schriftstelle des Alkoholgegnerbundes, 1896), 484–506. She'd also spoken at the International Temperance Convention commemorating the American centennial in Philadelphia in 1876. Frances W. Willard, "The Woman's National Christian Temperance Union," in: *Centennial Temperance Volume: A Memorial of the International Temperance Conference, Held in Philadelphia, June, 1876*, 686–704. See also: Tyrrell, *Woman's World, Woman's Empire*, 18. Dorothy Staunton, *Our Goodly Heritage: A Historical Review of the World's Woman's Christian Temperance Union, 1883–1956* (London: Walthamstow Press, 1956). On the racial divisions fracturing the IOGT in the American South, see: David M. Fahey, *Temperance and Racism: John Bull, Johnny Reb, and the Good Templars* (Lexington: University Press of Kentucky, 1996). *The Negro Question in the I.O.G.T.* (Birmingham: 1876). Guy Hayler Temperance Tracts, University of Wisconsin Special Collections, Vol. X, No. 20.

99. Frederick Douglass, *Selected Speeches and Writings* (Chicago: Lawrence Hill Books, 1999), 46. Robert S. Levine, *Martin Delany, Frederick Douglass and the Politics of Representative Identity* (Chapel Hill: University of North Carolina Press, 1997), 105.

100. Harper, "WCTU and the Colored Woman," in: Foster, ed., *A Brighter Coming Day*, 281–82. Reporting her activism began in 1875: Frances E. Willard, "Fifteenth Presidential Address (1894)," in *Let Something Good Be Said: Speeches and Writings of Frances E. Willard*, ed. Carolyn De Swarte Gifford and Amy R. Slagell (Urbana: University of Illinois Press, 2007), 206, n. 10. James William Clark Jr., "Frances Ellen Watkins Harper, 1825–1911: A Literary Biography" (MA thesis, Duke University, 1967), 107.

101. Sally G. McMillen, *Seneca Falls and the Origins of the Women's Rights Movement* (New York: Oxford University Press, 2008), 53.

102. Gilmore, *Gender and Jim Crow*, 48–49.

103. Here, I draw largely from: Alison M. Parker, "Frances Watkins Harper and the Search for Women's Interracial Alliances," in *Susan B. Anthony and the Struggle for Equal Rights*, ed. Christine L. Ridarsky and Mary M. Huth (Rochester, NY: University of Rochester Press, 2012), 152.

104. Harper, "We Are All Bound Up Together," 335.

105. Christine Stansell, "Missed Connections: Abolitionist Feminism in the Nineteenth Century," in *Elizabeth Cady Stanton, Feminist as Thinker: A Reader in Documents and Essays*, ed. Ellen Carol DuBois and Richard Cándida Smith (New York: New York University Press, 2007), 44–45. Michele Mitchell, " 'Lower Orders,' Racial Hierarchies, and Rights Rhetoric: Evolutionary Echoes in Elizabeth Cady Stanton's Thought during the Late 1860s," in *Elizabeth Cady Stanton, Feminist as Thinker: A Reader in Documents and Essays*, ed. Ellen Carol DuBois and Richard Cándida Smith (New York: New York University Press, 2007), 141–42.

106. Parker, "Frances Watkins Harper and the Search," 149. Bacon, " 'One Great Bundle of Humanity,' " 39. Still, *The Underground Rail Road*, 769. Shirley J. Yee, *Black Women Abolitionists: A Study in Activism, 1828–1860* (Knoxville: University of Tennessee Press, 1992), 149.

107. Gilmore, *Gender and Jim Crow*, 90.

108. This being the much-debated but never passed Blair Education Bill. Allen J. Going, "The South and the Blair Education Bill," *Mississippi Valley Historical Review* 44, no. 2 (1957): 257.

109. "Report of the NWCTU Annual Convention," *Union Signal*, November 8, 1883, 12. Bettye Collier-Thomas, "Frances Ellen Watkins Harper: Abolitionist and Feminist Reformer, 1825–1911," in *African American Women and the Vote, 1837–1965*, ed. Ann D. Gordon and Bettye Collier-Thomas (Amherst: University of Massachusetts Press, 1997), 58.

110. Frances E. Willard, "Work among the Colored People of the North," *Union Signal*, June 5, 1884. More generally: Alison M. Parker, *Articulating Rights: Nineteenth-Century American Women on Race, Reform, and the State* (DeKalb: Northern Illinois University Press, 2010).

111. Harper, "WCTU and the Colored Woman," 284. Thompson, *Most Stirring and Significant Episode*.

112. Bordin, *Woman and Temperance*, 83–84.

113. Frances E. Willard and Caroline B. Buell, "Letter from the National W.C.T.U. to the Colored People of the United States," *Union Signal*, January 12, 1888, 12. Parker, "Frances Watkins Harper and the Search," 158.

114. "Third Section Meeting, Report of Annual NWCTU Convention of 1886," *Union Signal*, November 11, 1886, 16.

115. Harper, "WCTU and the Colored Woman," 283. More generally, see: Parker, "Frances Watkins Harper and the Search," 154–55.

116. Frances Harper, "Work among the Colored People," in: Woman's Christian Temperance Union, *Minutes, 1885*, cxiv.

117. Willard, "President's Annual Address," in: Woman's Christian Temperance Union, *Minutes, 1885*, 68.

118. Frances Harper, "Department of Work for Colored People," *Union Signal*, October 7, 1886, 18. Parker, "Frances Watkins Harper and the Search," 156.

119. "Report of the Annual Meeting of the N.W.C.T.U.," *Union Signal*, November 21, 1887, 3–4.

120. Harper, "WCTU and the Colored Woman," 284.

121. Frances Harper, "Work among the Colored People," in: Woman's Christian Temperance Union, *Minutes, 1890*, 213–21.

122. Collier-Thomas, "Frances Ellen Watkins Harper," 57–58. Parker, "Frances Watkins Harper and the Search," 151.

123. Frances Watkins Harper, "Temperance," *African Methodist Episcopal Church Review*, 7 (1891): 372–75.

124. Carole Lynn Stewart, "Iola's War on Alcohol, Lynching, and the Rise of the Carceral State," *Canadian Review of American Studies* 49, no. 2 (2019): 187–93.

125. Frances E. W. Harper, *Iola Leroy, or Shadows Uplifted*, 2nd ed. (Philadelphia: Garrigues Brothers, 1893), 233–34.

126. For example, in taking to task a racist Reverend Cantor, a Dr. Latimer says, "Obedience to law is the gauge by which a nation's strength or weakness is tried. We have had two evils by which our obedience to law has been tested—slavery and the liquor traffic," and has been found wanting in regard to both. And while slavery had been abolished, "The liquor traffic still sends its floods of ruin and shame to the habitations of men, and no political party has been found with enough moral power and numerical strength to stay the tide of death." Ibid., 249–50.

127. P. Gabrielle Foreman, "'Reading Aright': White Slavery, Black Referents, and the Strategy of Histotextuality in *Iola Leroy*," *Yale Journal of Criticism* 10, no. 2 (1997): 339.

128. Harper, *Iola Leroy*, 158–59.

129. Ibid., 185–86.

130. Foreman, "'Reading Aright,'" 331–32.

131. I. Garland Penn, *The Afro-American Press, and Its Editors* (Springfield, MA: Willey & Co., 1891), 408.

132. Ida B. Wells, *Crusade for Justice: The Autobiography of Ida B. Wells*, ed. Alfreda M. Duster (Chicago: University of Chicago Press, 1970), 58. Boyd, *Discarded Legacy*, 220–21.

133. Ida B. Wells, *Southern Horrors: Lynch-Law in All Its Phases* (New York: New York Age, 1892), 14.

134. Census, *Tenth Census, Part II: Report on the Mortality and Vital Statistics of the United States*, lxvii.

135. *Free Speech*, May 21, 1892. Ida B. Wells, "Lynch Law in All Its Phases: Address at Tremont Temple in Boston, Feb. 13, 1893," *Our Day* 11, no. 65 (1893): 338.

136. Paula J. Giddings, *Ida: A Sword among Lions* (New York: Amistad, 2008), 1.

137. Caroline Bressey, *Empire, Race, and the Politics of Anti-Caste* (London: Bloomsbury Academic, 2015). David M. Fahey, "Catherine Impey," in *Oxford Dictionary of National Biography*, ed. H. C. G. Matthew and Brian Harrison (New York: Oxford University Press, 2004), 213. Fahey, *Temperance and Racism*, 139–46.

138. Wells, *Crusade for Justice*, 109–12.

139. Ibid., 202.

140. Frances E. Willard, "The Race Problem: Miss Willard on the Political Puzzle of the South," *New York Voice*, October 23, 1890, Frances Willard House Museum and Archives, Evanston, Illinois. The Center for Women's History and Leadership has put together a fabulous on-line resource chronicling the Willard-Wells dispute: "Truth-Telling: Frances Willard and Ida B. Wells," https://scalar.usc.edu/works/willard-and-wells/index (accessed March 8, 2020).

141. Willard, "The Race Problem."

142. Wells, *Crusade for Justice*, 112.

143. Ida B. Wells, "Temperance," *AME Church Review* (n/d), 1891. Cited in: "Ida B. Wells, Temperance, and Race Progress," in: Frances Willard House Museum and Archives, Evanston, Illinois, https://scalar.usc.edu/works/willard-and-wells/ida-b-wells-temperance (accessed January 20, 2021).

144. "Ida B. Wells Abroad," *Fraternity*, May 6, 1894, Frances Willard House Museum and Archives, Evanston, Illinois, https://scalar.usc.edu/works/willard-and-wells/ida-b-wells-abroad.27 (accessed March 8, 2020).

145. Frances E. Willard and Lady Henry Somerset, "An Unwise Advocate," *Union Signal*, June 21, 1894, Frances Willard House Museum and Archives, Evanston, Illinois, https://scalar.usc.edu/works/willard-and-wells/an-unwise-advocateinterview-with-willard-and-somerset-published-by-westminster-gazette?path=timeline (accessed January 20, 2021). Ida B. Wells, "Letter to the Editor," *Westminster Gazette*, May 22, 1894, 2, https://documents-alexanderstreet-com.libproxy.mit.edu/d/1000687405 (accessed March 20, 2020). Akiko Ochiai, "Ida B. Wells and Her Crusade for Justice: An African American Woman's Testimonial Autobiography," *Soundings: An Interdisciplinary Journal* 75, no. 2/3 (1992): 375.

146. Collier-Thomas, "Frances Ellen Watkins Harper," 59–60.

147. Stewart, "Iola's War," 195.

148. Frances E. Willard, "Presidential Address," in: Woman's Christian Temperance Union, *Minutes of the National Woman's Christian Temperance Union, at the Twenty-First Annual Meeting, Held in Cleveland, Ohio, 16–21 November, 1894* (Chicago: Woman's Temperance Publication Association, 1984), 129–31.

149. Ida B. Wells, "Miss Wells Lectures," *Cleveland Gazette*, November 24, 1894, 1–2. In: "The African-American Experience in Ohio, 1850–1920," The Ohio Historical Society, http://dbs.ohiohistory.org/africanam/html/pagea07e-2.html?ID=18231 (accessed March 20, 2020). See also: "About Southern Lynchings," *Baltimore Herald*, October 20, 1895, Scrapbook 70, No. 153, Woman's Christian Temperance Union Series, Reel 42.

150. See, for instance: Daniel Okrent, *Last Call: The Rise and Fall of Prohibition* (New York: Scribner, 2010), 42–43. Lisa McGirr, *The War on Alcohol: Prohibition and the Rise of the American State* (New York: W. W. Norton & Company, 2016), 17. On Willard's continued work, see: Diary Entry, February 11, 1896 (Jacksonville), in: Carolyn De Swarte Gifford, ed., *Writing Out My Heart: Selections from the Journal of Frances E. Willard, 1855–96* (Urbana: University of Illinois Press, 1995), 396.

151. Frederick Douglass, et al., "The Position of the National Woman's Christian Temperance Union of the United States in Relation to the Colored People," Boston, Massachusetts, February 6, 1895, Frances Willard House Museum and Archives, Evansville, Illinois, https://scalar. usc.edu/works/willard-and-wells/1894-wctu-convention-the-aftermath?path=timeline (accessed January 20, 2021). Also: Scrapbook 13, No. 213, Woman's Christian Temperance Union Series, Reel 32. Bordin, *Woman and Temperance*, 84–85. Of course, Douglass was a life-long defender of women's rights as well. "The Woman's Suffrage Movement: Address before Woman Suffrage Association, April 1888," *Woman's Journal,* April 14, 1888, in: Philip S. Foner, ed., *Frederick Douglass on Women's Rights* (New York: Da Capo Press, 1992), 111–13. "It was a great thing for the friends of peace to organize in opposition to war; it was a great thing for the friends of temperance to organize against intemperance; it was a great thing for humane people to organize in opposition to slavery; but it was a much greater thing, in view of all the circumstances, for woman to organize herself in opposition to her exclusion from participation in government." "Woman Suffrage Movement: Address before Bethel Literary Society," undated manuscript, Frederick Douglass Papers, Library of Congress, Manuscripts Division, Washington, DC. In: Foner, ed., *Frederick Douglass on Women's Rights*, 126–27. "Woman Suffrage," undated speech, Frederick Douglass Papers, Library of Congress, Manuscripts Division, Washington, DC. In: Foner, *Frederick Douglass on Women's Rights*, 137.

152. "An Appeal to My Countrywomen," in: Frances E. W. Harper, *Poems* (Philadelphia: 1006 Bainbridge Street, 1896), 74.

153. Ayers, *Promise of the New South*, 181. Similarly: Hardesty, "'Best Temperance Organization,'" 189.

154. Ayers, *Promise of the New South*, 180–81. See also: Janette Thomas Greenwood, "*New South Middle Class: The Black and the White Middle Class in Charlotte, 1850–1900*" (PhD dissertation, University of Virginia, 1991).

155. Wells, *Crusade for Justice*, 202.

156. Suzanne M. Marilley, "Frances Willard and the Feminism of Fear," *Feminist Studies* 19, no. 1 (1993): 123. Bordin, *Frances Willard*, 112.

157. Lisa M. F. Andersen, *The Politics of Prohibition: American Governance and the Prohibition Party, 1869–1933* (New York: Cambridge University Press, 2013), 62–64, 99, 283. See also: Roger C. Storms, *Partisan Prophets: A History of the Prohibition Party, 1854–1972* (Denver, CO: National Prohibition Foundation, 1972)..

158. Bordin, *Woman and Temperance*, 131–32. Similarly, see: "Richard T. Ely to Frances Willard," June 25 and August 2, 1889, Folder 56, Roll 15, Woman's Christian Temperance Union Series, Temperance & Prohibition Papers.

159. Bordin, *Woman and Temperance*, 151–52.

160. Frances E. Willard, *The "Do-Everything Policy": Address before the Second Biennial Convention of the World's Woman's Christian Temperance Union, and the Twentieth Annual Convention of the National Women's Christian Temperance Union, World's Columbian Exposition, Chicago, Illinois, USA, October 16th to 21st, 1893* (London: White Ribbon Publishing Co. , 1893), 2, HV5015 .Z9, Box 2, No. 9, National American Woman Suffrage Association (NAWSA) Collection, Library of Congress, Washington, DC, https://www.loc.gov/resource/rbnawsa.n8352/ (accessed January 20, 2021).

161. Ibid., 52–53. I took some liberties with punctuation to make her points clearer and more distinct.

162. Ibid., 54–57. Again, I have altered some punctuation for clarity.

163. Lori D. Ginzberg, *Elizabeth Cady Stanton: An American Life* (New York: Hill and Wang, 2009), 180.

164. Gordon, *Beautiful Life of Frances Willard*, 286–87.

Chapter 14

1. Graham Taylor, quoted in: Dores Robinson Sharpe, *Walter Rauschenbusch* (New York: Macmillan, 1942), 440. See also: Donovan E. Smucker, *The Origins of Walter Rauschenbusch's Social Ethics* (Montreal: McGill-Queen's University Press, 1994), 145–46. William M. Ramsay, *Four Modern Prophets: Walter Rauschenbusch, Martin Luther King Jr., Gustavo Gutiérrez, Rosemary Radford Ruether* (Atlanta: John Knox Press, 1986), 3–4.

2. Sharpe, *Walter Rauschenbusch*, 414.

3. Ibid., 394.

4. Ibid., 442, 446.

5. Christopher H. Evans, *The Kingdom Is Always but Coming: A Life of Walter Rauschenbusch* (Grand Rapids, MI: William B. Eerdmans, 2004), 94, 103, 178–79. John Lee Eighmy, "Religious Liberalism in the South during the Progressive Era," *Church History* 38, no. 3 (1969): 359.

6. Evans, *Kingdom Is Always but Coming*, 151–52, 68–69. Walter Rauschenbusch, "The New Evangelism," *Independent*, May 12, 1904, 6, Box 40, Rauschenbusch Family Manuscript Collection, American Baptist–Samuel Colgate Historical Library, Colgate Rochester Crozer Divinity School, Rochester, New York.

7. "Oh, These Temperance Fanatics / The Best We Can Say for the Saloon," n/d, Box 12, Folder 24, Speech Notes, Walter Rauschenbusch Papers, American Baptist Historical Society, Mercer University, Atlanta, Georgia. See also: Paul M. Minus, *Walter Rauschenbusch: American Reformer* (New York: Macmillan, 1988), 125.

8. Walter Rauschenbusch, *Christianity and the Social Crisis* (New York: Harper & Row, 1907), 133. 185, 408. Evans, *Kingdom Is Always but Coming*, 180–85.

9. Evans, *Kingdom Is Always but Coming*, 189–91. Sales figures: Sharpe, *Walter Rauschenbusch*, 418.

10. Sharpe, *Walter Rauschenbusch*, 393.

11. Ibid., 456.

12. Walter Rauschenbusch to Dores Robinson Sharpe, April 20, 1918, reprinted in: Ibid., 449–50.

13. Sharpe, *Walter Rauschenbusch*, 356, 379. On his sober self-restraint against nationalist hysterics in Americans' dealing with Germany, see: Walter Rauschenbusch, "Be Fair to Germany: A Plea for Open-Mindedness," *The Congregationalist*, October 15, 1914, Box 19, Dores Robinson Sharpe, Walter Rauschenbusch Collection, Colgate Rochester Divinity School, Rochester, New York. More generally, see: Warren L. Vinz, *Pulpit Politics: Faces of American Protestant Nationalism in the Twentieth Century* (Albany: State University of New York Press, 1997), 40.

14. Rauschenbusch, *Christianity and the Social Crisis*, 350.

15. Sharpe, *Walter Rauschenbusch*, 384.

16. Letter, Walter Rauschenbusch to Dr. Cornelius Woelfkin, May 1, 1918, Box 54, Folder 1, Walter Rauschenbusch Papers, American Baptist Historical Society, Mercer University, Atlanta, Georgia. See also: Letter, Winifred Rauschenbusch to Dores Robinson Sharpe, reprinted in: Sharpe, *Walter Rauschenbusch*, 391–92.

17. Letter, Walter Rauschenbusch to Dores Robinson Sharpe, May 19, 1918, Box 98, Folder 2, Walter Rauschenbusch Papers, American Baptist Historical Society, Mercer University, Atlanta, Georgia. Reprinted in: Sharpe, *Walter Rauschenbusch*, 450–51.

18. Letter, Pauline Rauschenbusch to Dores Robinson Sharpe, July 25, 1918, Box 155, Rauschenbusch Family Manuscript Collection, American Baptist–Samuel Colgate Historical Library, Colgate Rochester Crozer Divinity School, Rochester, New York. Also: Box 53, Folder 7, Telegrams (WR's Death), Walter Rauschenbusch Papers, American Baptist Historical Society, Mercer University, Atlanta, Georgia. Evans, *Kingdom Is Always but Coming*, 315.

19. Sharpe, *Walter Rauschenbusch*, 420–21.

20. James Timberlake, *Prohibition and the Progressive Movement, 1900–1920* (Cambridge, MA: Harvard University Press, 1963), 18.

21. Ibid., 18–34. Joshua David Hawley, *Theodore Roosevelt: Preacher of Righteousness* (New Haven, CT: Yale University Press, 2008), 125–28. William Hamilton Anderson, *The Church in Action*

against the Saloon: Being an Authoritative Statement of the Movement Known as the Anti-Saloon League (Westerville, OH: American Issue Publishing Co., 1910).

22. Timberlake, *Prohibition and the Progressive Movement*, 16 (emphasis mine).

23. Richard Hofstadter, *The Age of Reform: From Bryan to F.D.R.* (New York: Random House, 1955), 233–34. For an extension, see: Robert D. Johnston, *The Radical Middle Class: Populist Democracy and the Question of Capitalism in Progressive Era Portland, Oregon* (Princeton, NJ: Princeton University Press, 2003), 10–11.

24. Jed Dannenbaum, "The Origins of Temperance Activism and Militancy among American Women," *Journal of Social History* 15, no. 2 (1981): 3. Sally G. McMillen, *Seneca Falls and the Origins of the Women's Rights Movement* (New York: Oxford University Press, 2008), 52. See also: Chapter 1, n. 47.

25. Timberlake, *Prohibition and the Progressive Movement*, 12.

26. See: Lyman Beecher, *Six Sermons on the Nature, Occasions, Signs, Evils, and Remedy of Intemperance* (New York: American Tract Society, 1827), 60, 75, 76, 86.

27. Evans, *Kingdom Is Always but Coming*, xviii–xix, 50–53.

28. Ibid., 61–62. Walter Rauschenbusch, "The Kingdom of God," Box 26, Folder 14, Walter Rauschenbusch Papers, American Baptist Historical Society, Mercer University, Atlanta, Georgia.

29. Arthur Nichols Young, *The Single-Tax Movement in the United States* (Princeton, NJ: Princeton University Press, 1916), 100. Martin Adams, "Henry George: The Prophet of San Francisco," *Progress.org*, November 14, 2014, https://www.progress.org/articles/henry-george-the-prophet-of-san-francisco-part-1 (accessed September 13, 2019). George also had a mutual affinity with Leo Tolstoy. "In thirty years private property in land will be as much a thing of the past as now is serfdom. England, America, and Russia will be the first to solve the problem," Tolstoy said in an interview, adding, "Henry George had formulated the next article in the programme of the progressist Liberals of the world" [*sic*]. See: Henry George Jr., *The Life of Henry George (1900)* (New York: Doubleday, Doran & Company, 1930), 614.

30. Henry George, *Progress & Poverty: An Inquiry into the Cause of Industrial Depressions, and of Increas of Want with Increase of Wealth. The Remedy* (London: William Reeves, 1884), 412. Also: George Soule, *Ideas of the Great Economists* (New York: Mentor, 1955), 81.

31. Henry George, "To Destroy the 'Rum Power,'" *Arena* 1, no. 2 (1893): 196, 207, Harvard University Library, https://iiif.lib.harvard.edu/manifests/view/drs:15587300$15i (accessed October 13, 2019). Counterintuitively, George argues that government regulation only exacerbates both corruption and drunkenness. Therefore, to reduce both, one would need to abolish government regulation itself.

32. Quoted in: Young, *Single Tax Movement*, 54.

33. George, "To Destroy the 'Rum Power,'" 200.

34. Walter Rauschenbusch, *Christianizing the Social Order* (New York: Macmillan, 1912), 394. Evans, *Kingdom Is Always but Coming*, 63–64.

35. Smucker, *Origins of Rauschenbusch's Social Ethics*, 48, 113. Rauschenbusch, *Christianity and the Social Crisis*, 314–15.

36. Evans, *Kingdom Is Always but Coming*, 78–79.

37. Walter Rauschenbusch, "The Ideals of Social Reformers," *American Journal of Sociology* 2, no. 2 (1896): 210.

38. Walter Rauschenbusch, "The Stake of the Church in the Social Movement," *American Journal of Sociology* 3, no. 1 (1897): 27.

39. Evans, *Kingdom Is Always but Coming*, 177. Likewise, see: Walter Rauschenbusch, Lecture, "The Fundamental Purpose of Jesus: The Kingdom of God, Christianity, and the Social Crisis," Box 14, Folder 8, Walter Rauschenbusch Papers, American Baptist Historical Society, Mercer University, Atlanta, Georgia.

40. Rauschenbusch, *Christianity and the Social Crisis*, 237–39, 242.

41. Ibid., 269–71.

42. Ibid., 350–51.
43. Ibid., 312–14.
44. Between 1886 and 1902 Rockefeller funneled some twenty-two hundred dollars to Rauschenbusch. Box 6, Folder 1075, Series F: Financial Materials, Subseries V14, John D. Rockefeller Papers, 1855–1942, Rockefeller Archive Center, Sleepy Hollow, New York. See also: Rockefeller Correspondence, 1900–1915, Box 37, Folder 1, Walter Rauschenbusch Papers, American Baptist Historical Society, Mercer University, Atlanta, Georgia.
45. Evans, *Kingdom Is Always but Coming*, 80–81, 143.
46. Walter Rauschenbusch, "Notes on Alcoholismus (in Germany)," 1904, Box 10, Folder 14; "German Text of Lecture on Alcoholism in USA," 1910, Box 14, Folder 2; "Lecture Notes: Alcohol Question, Berlin," 1910, Box 12, Folder 16, Walter Rauschenbusch Papers, American Baptist Historical Society, Mercer University, Atlanta, Georgia. Rauschenbusch seemed to have no other connection to the biennial temperance conventions in Europe.
47. Rauschenbusch, *Christianity and the Social Crisis*, 355–57, 375–76.
48. Timberlake, *Prohibition and the Progressive Movement*, 40.
49. Ibid., 41–46. Some of these studies prompted an overlap between alcohol science and the emerging field of eugenics. Largely associated with (and discredited by) Nazi German politics of racial purity, the early transnational eugenics movement seized upon alcohol studies and the focus of alcohol as a "racial poison," targeting alcoholics in particular as a drag on their efforts to improve the genetic quality of the human population.
50. Ibid., 48–51. Ernest H. Cherrington, *The Evolution of Prohibition in the United States of America: A Chronological History of the Liquor Problem and the Temperance Reform in the United States from the Earliest Settlements to the Consummation of National Prohibition* (Westerville, OH: American Issue Press, 1920), 175. See also: On her tussles with the Committee of Fifty, see Mary Hunt's correspondences with committee members Dr. H. P. Bowditch, W. O. Atwater and Dr. J. S. Billings, Box 3, Folder 18, Reel 10, Scientific Temperance Federation Series, Temperance and Prohibition Papers, Ohio Historical Society. Judith B. Erickson, "Making King Alcohol Tremble: The Juvenile Work of the Woman's Christian Temperance Union, 1874–1900," *Journal of Drug Education* 18, no. 4 (1988): 333. Jonathan Zimmerman, "'The Queen of the Lobby': Mary Hunt, Scientific Temperance, and the Dilemma of Democratic Education in America, 1879–1906," *History of Education Quarterly* 32, no. 1 (1992): 1–3.
51. Timberlake, *Prohibition and the Progressive Movement*, 56.
52. Sarah A. McClees, *The Army Canteen: A History of the Pioneer Work of Women with Regard to the Canteen in the Military Service of the United States of America* (Oakland, CA: 1905), 74–76.
53. Timberlake, *Prohibition and the Progressive Movement*, 54–55.
54. Ibid., 67–72.
55. *New State Ice Co. v. Liebmann*, 285 US 262, 311 (1932) (Brandeis, J., dissenting).
56. See, for instance: Larry Engelmann, *Intemperance: The Lost War against Liquor* (New York: Free Press, 1979). John Kobler, *Ardent Spirits: The Rise and Fall of Prohibition* (Greenwich, CT: Fawcett Books, 1973). Henry Lee, *How Dry We Were: Prohibition Revisited* (Englewood Cliffs, NJ: Prentice-Hall, 1963). Thomas Pegram, *Battling Demon Rum: The Struggle for a Dry America, 1800–1933* (Chicago: Ivan R. Dee Publishers, 1998).
57. See: Mark Lawrence Schrad, "Policy Effectiveness in Historical Context: Pre-Prohibition Liquor-Control Studies Revisited," *World Medical and Health Policy* 6, no. 3 (2014): 190.
58. H. J. Boström, *Rusdryckslagstiftningen i Nordamerikas Förenta Stater* (Stockholm: Centraltryckeriet, 1908), 7–8.
59. Gerard Halfred von Koch, *Rusdrycksförbud: Studier av amerikansk nykterhetsrörelse och rusdryckslagstiftning* (Stockholm: A. B. Svenska nykterhetsförlaget, 1910), 130–90.
60. Eyvind Andersen, *Förbudskomedien i Sydstaterna* (Stockholm: Centraltryckeriet, 1909).
61. Richard Hamm, *Shaping the Eighteenth Amendment: Temperance Reform, Legal Culture, and the Polity, 1880–1920* (Chapel Hill: University of North Carolina Press, 1995), 128. See also: Robert Pitman, *Alcohol and the State: A Discussion of the Problem of Law as Applied to*

the Liquor Traffic (New York: National Temperance Society and Publishing House, 1878). Edwin A. Pratt, *Disinterested Management in Norway* (London: P. S. King & Son, 1907). John Larsson, *Review of the Working of the Gothenburg Public-House Licensing Co. (Göteborgs Utskänknings Aktiebolag) with Statistics of the Malt, Liquor and Wine Traffic, Not under the Control of the Company, Represented by Compendium, Tables and Explanations Compiled for the Alcohol Congress at Kristiania, 1890*, trans. John Duff (Göteborg: Göteborgs Handelstidnings Aktiebolags Tryckeri, 1890). A. Th. Kiaer, "The Norwegian System of Regulating the Drink Traffic," *Economic Journal* 9, no. 33 (1899). Joseph Rowntree and Arthur Sherwell, *British "Gothenburg" Experiments and Public-House Trusts* (London: Hodder & Stoughton, 1901).

62. Daniel C. Roper, "The Dispensary System—Results of Its Operation in the State of South Carolina," Box 6, Folder 25, Roll 12, Anti-Saloon League of America Series, Temperance and Prohibition Papers, Ohio Historical Society. Charles E. Ebersol, *"Types of Public Control of the Liquor Traffic: In Sweden; in Norway; in South Carolina; and in Athens, Georgia"* (MA thesis, Chicago Theological Seminary, 1904), 45–60. See also: Paul Aaron and David Musto, "Temperance and Prohibition in America: A Historical Overview," in *Alcohol and Public Policy: Beyond the Shadow of Prohibition—Panel on Alternative Policies Affecting the Prevention of Alcohol Abuse and Alcoholism*, ed. Mark Moore and Dean Gerstein (Washington, DC: National Academies Press, 1981), 148.

63. "South Carolina Dispensary System," *The Outlook*, December 16, 1893. A. M. Lee, *The South Carolina Dispensary Law and "Original Package" Decisions* (Charleston, SC: Lucas & Richardson Co., 1897). John Evans Eubanks, *Ben Tillman's Baby: The Dispensary System of South Carolina, 1892–1915* (Augusta, GA: n.p., 1950). Likewise note investigation of the "socialistic" "scheme" by the United States Brewers' Association: Gallus Thomann, *The South Carolina Dispensary: A Brief History of the Famous Experiment in State Control of the Liquor Traffic* (New York: United States Brewers' Association, 1905), 4–5.

64. E. R. L. Gould, *The Gothenburg System of Liquor Traffic* (Washington, DC: Government Printing Office, 1893). The Commission to Investigate the Gothenburg and Norwegian Systems of Licensing the Sale of Intoxicating Liquors, "Report to the General Court, No. 192" (Massachusetts General Court, 1894). Previous studies include: Oskar Carlheim-Gyllensköld, *A Memorandum Concerning the Use of Intoxicating Liquors in Sweden, the Amount of Crime Produced by Them, and Their Effects on the Health and Prosperity of the People: In Reply to Inquiries Made on Behalf of the State Board of Health of Massachusetts, Delivered to the Minister Resident of the United States of America* (Stockholm: P. A. Norstedt & Söner, 1872).

65. Minutes of the Committee of Fifty for the Investigation of the Drink Problem; Cambridge, Massachusetts, March 27, 1897—Francis Peabody, Secretary, John Crerar Library at the University of Chicago. Also: Dr. Frederick Howard Wines Microfilm Collection on Social Problems, University of Illinois at Urbana-Champaign. See also: Harry G. Levine, "The Committee of Fifty and the Origins of Alcohol Control," *Journal of Drug Issues*, Special Issue on the Political Economy of Alcohol (1983). John J. Rumbarger, "Social Origins and Function of the Political Temperance Movement in the Reconstruction of American Society, 1825–1917" (PhD dissertation, University of Pennsylvania, 1968), 188.

66. Timberlake, *Prohibition and the Progressive Movement*, 48–49.

67. John S. Billings, ed., *Physiological Aspects of the Liquor Problem: An Investigation Made for the Committee of Fifty*, 2 vols. (New York: Houghton Mifflin and Company, 1903). John S. Billings et al., *The Liquor Problem: A Summary of Investigations Conducted by the Committee of Fifty, 1893–1903* (New York: Houghton Mifflin and Company, 1905). Raymond Calkins, *Substitutes for the Saloon*, 2nd ed. (New York: Houghton Mifflin and Company, 1919), John Koren, *Economic Aspects of the Liquor Problem, an Investigation Made under the Direction of a Sub-Committee of the Committee of Fifty* (New York: Houghton Mifflin and Company, 1899). Frederic H. Wines and John Koren, *The Liquor Problem in Its Legislative Aspects: An Investigation Made under the Direction of the Committee of Fifty* (New York: Houghton Mifflin and Company, 1897).

68. Report of the Special Subcommittee on Substitutes for the Saloon, E. R. L. Gould, chairman pro-tempore, Minutes of the Committee of Fifty for the Investigation of the Drink Problem, New Haven, Connecticut, November 5, 1898—Henry Farnam, acting secretary. See also: John Koren, "Liquor Traffic without Private Profits," *Arena*, April 1894. John Koren, "Gothenburg System Not a Failure," *Catholic World* 59 (1894).

69. Mark Lawrence Schrad, *The Political Power of Bad Ideas: Networks, Institutions, and the Global Prohibition Wave* (New York: Oxford University Press, 2010), 151.

70. Quoted in: George M. Hammell, *The Passing of the Saloon: An Authentic and Official Presentation of the Anti-Liquor Crusade in America* (Cincinnati, OH: Tower Press, 1908), 6.

71. "William E. Johnson to Howard H. Russell," June 14, 1932, 1–2, Folder 42, Roll 6, Howard Hyde Russell Series, Temperance and Prohibition Papers, Ohio Historical Society, Columbus.

72. William E. Johnson, "Confessions of 'Pussyfoot' Johnson" (Cooperstown, NY: Fenimore Art Museum Library, n/d), V, 2–10. See also: William E. Johnson, *The South Carolina Liquor Dispensary* (Westerville, OH: American Issue Publishing Company, n/d), 3, Roll 12, Folder 8, Office of General Counsel and Legislative Superintendent, Anti-Saloon League of America, Temperance and Prohibition Papers, Ohio Historical Society, Columbus, Ohio. Ebersol, "Types of Public Control of the Liquor Traffic," 52.

73. Fred A. McKenzie, *"Pussyfoot" Johnson: Crusader, Reformer, a Man among Men* (London: Hodder and Stoughton, 1920), 39. William Johnson, *The Gothenburg System of Liquor Selling* (Chicago: New Voice Company, 1908). Similarly, see: Guy Hayler, *The "Disinterested" Liquor Monopoly Scheme: A Seathing Exposure* (n.p.: n.p., 1911). Guy Hayler Temperance Tracts, Vol. XIV, No. 34. Guy Hayler, *The Gothenburg System* (Birmingham: I.O.G.T. Grand Lodge of England, 1912). Guy Hayler Temperance Tracts, Vol. XIV, No. 26. *The Origin of the Gothenburg System, and Its Failure* (n.p.: n.p., 1912).

74. Letter, William E. Johnson to Howard Hyde Russell, June 21, 1932, "Notes on the Liquor Monopoly in Russia," 2, Folder 42, Roll 6, Howard Hyde Russell Series, Temperance and Prohibition Papers, Ohio Historical Society, Columbus.

75. Johnson, "Confessions," V, 11.

76. "Johnson, William Eugene 'Pussyfoot,'" in: Ernest H. Cherrington, ed., *Standard Encyclopedia of the Alcohol Problem*, 6 vols., vol. 3 (Westerville, OH: American Issue Press, 1926), 1410. William E. Johnson to Howard Hyde Russell, May 22, 1932, Howard Hyde Russell Series, Folder 42, Roll 6. "Pro-alcohol pedants": Ernest Gordon, *The Anti-Alcohol Movement in Europe* (New York: Fleming H. Revel Company, 1913), 29.

77. "I never went into a saloon, and in the little hotels I kept out of the bar-room unless, as some-times happened, the bar-room was the only room on the lower floor except the dining room." Theodore Roosevelt, *Theodore Roosevelt: An Autobiography* (New York: Charles Scribner's Sons, 1921), 120. See also: Mark Will-Weber, *Mint Juleps with Teddy Roosevelt: The Complete History of Presidential Drinking* (Washington, DC: Regnery History, 2014).

78. Twenty-five-year-old Alice died from kidney disease masked by her pregnancy, the same day and in the same house that Theodore's mother died of typhoid fever. She was forty-eight. In his diary for February 14, he scrawled a giant X, adding only, "The light has gone out of my life." Theodore Roosevelt, pocket diary entry, February 14, 1884, Manuscript Division, Library of Congress, American Treasures of the Library of Congress Exhibit, Memory Gallery C. http://www.loc.gov/exhibits/treasures/images/at0054.2s.jpg (accessed October 13, 2019). On the New York machines: Edward P. Kohn, *Heir to the Empire City: New York and the Making of Theodore Roosevelt* (New York: Basic Books, 2014).

79. Doris Kearns Goodwin, *The Bully Pulpit: Theodore Roosevelt, William Howard Taft, and the Golden Age of Journalism* (New York: Simon & Schuster, 2013), 67.

80. Roosevelt, *Autobiography*, 60.

81. George, "To Destroy the 'Rum Power,'" 200.

82. The *New York Herald* summarized the rival positions: "that Mr. Hewitt is a cruel and heartless despot and oppressor of labor, that Mr. George will be the savior or the destroyer of our social

system, or that Mr. Roosevelt is a young man of incomparable ability." Quoted in: Young, *Single Tax Movement*, 101–102.

83. Theodore Roosevelt, "Machine Politics in New York City," *The Century: A Popular Quarterly*, November 1, 1886: 74–83. In: Theodore Roosevelt, *Essays on Practical Politics* (New York: G. P. Putnam's Sons, 1888), 63–65.

84. Goodwin, *Bully Pulpit*, 209.

85. Theodore Roosevelt, "Closing the New York Saloons on Sunday," *McClure's Magazine* V, no. 5 (1895): 475. Roosevelt's position was actually president of the (unelected) New York City Board of Police Commissioners, which was soon reorganized.

86. Ibid.

87. Roosevelt, *Autobiography*, 190.

88. Roosevelt, "Closing the New York Saloons," 475. Similarly, see: Roosevelt, *Autobiography*. 189–90. "Letter from Theodore Roosevelt to Anna Roosevelt," June 30, 1895, Theodore Roosevelt Collection, MS Am 1834 (459), Harvard College Library, https://www.theodorerooseveltcenter.org/Research/Digital-Library/Record?libID=o283611 (accessed October 15, 2019).

89. Goodwin, *Bully Pulpit*, 210. Similarly, see: Letter from Henry Cabot Lodge to Theodore Roosevelt, August 11, 1895, Theodore Roosevelt Papers, Library of Congress Manuscript Division, https://www.theodorerooseveltcenter.org/Research/Digital-Library/Record?libID=o25648 (accessed April 27, 2020). Accessed via Theodore Roosevelt Digital Library. Dickinson State University.

90. "Letter from Theodore Roosevelt to Anna Roosevelt," September 29, 1895, Theodore Roosevelt Collection, MS Am 1834 (473), Harvard College Library, https://www.theodorerooseveltcenter.org/Research/Digital-Library/Record?libID=o283625 (accessed October 13, 2019).

91. Goodwin, *Bully Pulpit*, 210–11.

92. Roosevelt, *Autobiography*, 192.

93. This according to Lincoln Steffens's "Tweed Days in St. Louis," *McClure's*, October 1902. Included in: Lincoln Steffens, *The Shame of the Cities* (New York: McClure, Phillips & Co., 1904), 34.

94. Rauschenbusch, *Christianity and the Social Crisis*, 419.

95. Harry Emerson Fosdick, "Introduction," in *A Rauschenbusch Reader*, ed. Benson Y. Landis (New York: Harper & Brothers, 1957), xxi, 38. See also: Ronald C. White and C. Howard Hopkins, *The Social Gospel: Religion and Reform in Changing America* (Philadelphia: Temple University Press, 1976), 46–47. Or in Rauschenbusch's own words: "The only way to beat the socialists is to beat them to it." Rauschenbusch, *Christianizing the Social Order*, 395.

96. Roosevelt, "Closing the New York Saloons," 475. Quoted in: Hammell, *Passing of the Saloon*, 7, 16.

Chapter 15

1. Pyotr Sergieenko, *Tolstoi i ego sovremenniki* (Moscow: Tipografiya V. M. Sablina, 1911), 245.

2. Paxton Hibben, *The Peerless Leader: William Jennings Bryan* (New York: Farrar and Rinehart, 1929), 244–45. His consideration of the Gothenburg system likely came on his second trip to Europe in 1905–1906. William Jennings Bryan, *The Old World and Its Ways* (St. Louis: Thompson Publishing Company, 1907), 424. On his second trip: Daniel Scroop, "William Jennings Bryan's 1905–1906 World Tour," *Historical Journal* 56, no. 2 (2013), 459–86.

3. Bryan congratulated Tsar Nicholas II on establishing the International Court of Arbitration in The Hague, meant to substitute "the reign of reason for the rule of brute force"—though the tsar thought Bryan's ardent championing of free speech "a bit quaint." Hibben, *Peerless Leader*, 244–45. William Jennings Bryan and Mary Baird Bryan, *The Memoirs of William Jennings Bryan*

(New York: Haskell House Publishers, 1925), 317. Sergieenko, *Tolstoi i ego sovremenniki*, 244–45. William Jennings Bryan, "Russia and Her Czar," *The Commoner*, February 5, 1904, 3.

4. "William Jennings Bryan and the Social Gospel," 1966, in Box 3, Folder 5, Series 7, Speeches and Manuscripts, RG3198.AM, William Jennings Bryan Papers, Nebraska State Historical Society.

5. Leo Tolstoi, "Pis'mo gruppe shvedskoi intelligentsii, 7–9 yanvarya, 1899 g.," in *Polnoe sobranie sochinenii, tom 72: Pis'ma, 1899–1900*, ed. Vladimir G. Chertkov (Moscow: Gosudarstvennoe izdatel'stvo khudozhestvennoi literatury, 1933), 12–13. Kenneth C. Wenzer, "Tolstoy and Bryan," *Nebraska History* 77 (1996): 147, n. 13. Bryan and Rauschenbusch: Paolo E. Coletta, *William Jennings Bryan: Political Evangelist, 1860–1908* (Lincoln: University of Nebraska Press, 1964), 294.

6. "Tolstoi on Imperialism," *The Commoner*, January 23, 1901, 6.

7. Sergieenko, *Tolstoi i ego sovremenniki*, 245. Valentin Bulgakov, *O Tolstom: Vospominaniya i rasskazy* (Tula: Priokskoe knizhnoe izdatel'stvo, 1964), 129.

8. Sergieenko, *Tolstoi i ego sovremenniki*, 243–49.

9. Ibid., 251. Leo Tolstoi, "Predislovie k angliiskoi biografii Garrisona, sostavlennoi V.G. Chertkovym i F. Khola (1904)," in *Polnoe sobranie sochinenii, tom 36: Proizvedeniya, 1904-1906 gg.*, ed. Vladimir G. Chertkov (Moscow: Gosudarstvennoe izdatel'stvo "khudozhestvennaya literatura", 1936), 95–99. Leo Tolstoy, "Introduction to a Short Biography of William Lloyd Garrison (1904)," in *The Kingdom of God and Peace Essays* (London: Oxford University Press, 1936), 579.

10. Tolstoi, "Pis'mo gruppe shvedskoi intelligentsii," 12–13. Sergieenko, *Tolstoi i ego sovremenniki*, 251.

11. Sergieenko, *Tolstoi i ego sovremenniki*, 251. Stephen Bonsul, "Tolstoy Prophesies the Fall of America," in *Americans in Conversation with Tolstoy: Selected Accounts, 1887–1923*, ed. Peter Sekirin (Jefferson, NC: McFarland & Company, 2006), 137.

12. Leo Tolstoi, "Pis'mo Vil'yamu Braianu, 2 fevralya, 1904 g.," in *Polnoe sobranie sochinenii, tom 75: Pis'ma, 1904–1905* (Moscow: Gosudarstvennoe izdatel'stvo khudozhestvennoi literatury, 1956), 17–18.

13. Wenzer, "Tolstoy and Bryan," 140–41. Charlotte Alston, *Tolstoy and His Disciples: The History of a Radical International Movement* (London: I. B. Tauris, 2014), 106. Michael Kazin, *A Godly Hero: The Life of William Jennings Bryan* (New York: Anchor Books, 2006), 126.

14. Kazin, *Godly Hero*, 126.

15. William Jennings Bryan, "Tolstoi's Noble Appeal," *The Commoner*, May 3, 1901, 1. William Jennings Bryan, *The Prince of Peace* (New York: Funk & Wagnalls Company, 1914), 7–8.

16. Wenzer, "Tolstoy and Bryan," 141. Bulgakov, *O Tolstom*, 174.

17. Leo Tolstoi, "Pis'mo Raiersonu Dzhenningsu, 28 sentyabrya, 1908 g.," in *Polnoe sobranie sochinenii, tom 78: Pis'ma, 1908* (Moscow: Gosudarstvennoe izdatel'stvo khudozhestvennoi literatury, 1956), 231. Henry George was one of Tolstoy's last visitors before his death in 1910. "Amerikanskie sovremenniki o L.N. Tolstom," *Literaturnoe nasledie* (n/d), http://litena.ru/books/item/f00/s00/z0000031/st011.shtml (accessed November 15, 2019).

18. Kazin, *Godly Hero*, 151.

19. Ibid., 105.

20. Robert W. Cherny, *A Righteous Cause: The Life of William Jennings Bryan* (Norman: University of Oklahoma Press, 1994), 121. Bryan and Bryan, *Memoirs*, 290–91.

21. Bradley J. Longfield, *The Presbyterian Controversy: Fundamentalists, Modernists, and Moderates* (New York: Oxford University Press, 1991), 67. Willard H. Smith, "William Jennings Bryan and the Social Gospel," *Journal of American History* 53, no. 1 (1966): 53. "Christian Citizenship," *The Commoner*, January 16, 1903, 1–2.

22. William Jennings Bryan, "Roosevelt and Tolstoy," *The Commoner*, June 18, 1909, 5–6. Article reprinted from the *Detroit Times*.

23. William Jennings Bryan, "Tolstoy," *The Commoner*, December 2, 1910, 2. Wenzer, "Tolstoy and Bryan," 143.

24. James A. Field, "American Imperialism: The Worst Chapter in Almost Any Book," *American Historical Review* 83, no. 3 (1978): 644.

25. James A. Field, "Reply to Comments: American Imperialism: The Worst Chapter in Almost Any Book," *American Historical Review* 83, no. 3 (1978): 683.

26. Niall Ferguson, *Colossus: The Rise and Fall of the American Empire* (New York: Penguin, 2004), 3–26. Daniel Immerwahr, *How to Hide an Empire: A History of the Greater United States* (New York: Farrar, Straus and Giroux, 2019), 14. Ian Tyrrell and Jay Sexton, "Introduction," in *Empire's Twin: U.S. Anti-Imperialism from the Founding Era to the Age of Terrorism*, ed. Ian Tyrrell and Jay Sexton (Ithaca, NY: Cornell University Press, 2015), 1–8.

27. Vladimir I. Lenin, *Imperializm, kak vyschaya stadiya kapitalizma* (Petrograd: Zhizn' i znanie, 1917). See also: Ferguson, *Colossus*, 13. Wolfgang J. Mommsen, *Theories of Imperialism*, trans. P. S. Falla (New York: Random House, 1980), 46–52.

28. Frances Ellen Watkins Harper, "We Are All Bound Up Together: Address before the Eleventh National Women's Rights Convention, New York City, May 1866," in: Mary Ellen Snodgrass, ed., *American Women Speak: An Encyclopedia and Document Collection of Women's Oratory* (Santa Barbara, CA: ABC-CLIO, 2017), 336.

29. Immerwahr, *How to Hide an Empire*, 68–72.

30. Colin D. Moore, *American Imperialism and the State, 1893–1921* (New York: Cambridge University Press, 2017), 12–14. Tony Smith, *The Pattern of Imperialism: The United States, Great Britain, and the Late-Industrializing World since 1815* (New York: Cambridge University Press, 1981), 3–4.

31. William S. Bryan, ed., *Our Islands and Their People*, 2 vols. (New York: N. D. Thompson Publishing Co., 1899). Also see William Jennings Bryan's explicit discussion of "Citizen or Subject?" in: William Jennings Bryan, *Bryan on Imperialism* (New York: Arno Press, 1970), 78.

32. Eight of the nine justices were the same in hearing both cases. Michael Patrick Cullinane, *Liberty and American Anti-Imperialism, 1898–1909* (New York: Palgrave Macmillan, 2012), 93–114. Frederick Merk, *Manifest Destiny and Mission in American History: A Reinterpretation* (Cambridge, MA: Harvard University Press, 1995), 250–52. Immerwahr, *How to Hide an Empire*, 84–86.

33. Letter, Lemuel Quigg to Theodore Roosevelt, May 16, 1913. Footnote to letter to Henry Cabot Lodge, January 23, 1899, in: Elting E. Morison, ed., *The Letters of Theodore Roosevelt, Volume II: The Years of Preparation, 1898–1900* (Cambridge, MA: Harvard University Press, 1951), 920–21. The two-dollar reference was a staple of anti-imperialist rhetoric, even when the racial slurs were not. See: William Jennings Bryan to Andrew Carnegie, January 30, 1899, William Jennings Bryan Papers, Box 22, Correspondence, January 1899, Library of Congress, Washington, DC.

34. Charles S. Olcott, *William McKinley*, 2 vols., vol. 2 (Boston: Houghton Mifflin Company, 1916), 110–11. Merk, *Manifest Destiny*, 253. Nell Irvin Painter, *Standing at Armageddon: The United States, 1877–1919* (New York: W. W. Norton & Company, 1987), 147. Stuart Creighton Miller, *"Benevolent Assimilation": The American Conquest of the Philippines, 1899–1903* (New Haven, CT: Yale University Press, 1982).

35. Don Emilio Aguinaldo, *True Version of the Philippine Revolution* (Tarlac, Philippines: n.p., 1899), 10–12.

36. Immerwahr, *How to Hide an Empire*, 89.

37. William E. Johnson, "Confessions of 'Pussyfoot' Johnson" (Cooperstown, NY: Fenimore Art Museum Library, n/d), V, 15.

38. See: John D. Blanco, *Frontier Constitutions: Christianity and Colonial Empire in the Nineteenth-Century Philippines* (Berkeley: University of California Press, 2009), 14, 20, 185–87. Bonifacio S. Salamanca, *The Filipino Reaction to American Rule, 1901–1913* (Hamden, CT: Shoe String Press, 1968), 11–14.

39. "'Benevolent Assimilation' in the Philippines," S.I, 1899?, 5, Pamphlet DS P.I.16, Special Collections, Cornell University Library. My hunch is that this is a collection of commentaries written by William E. "Pussyfoot" Johnson under the nom de plume of "Nemesis" as managing editor of the *Manila Freedom* newspaper. He admits as much in the "Philippine Islands" entry in the *Standard Encyclopedia of the Alcohol Problem*, which he himself edited: Ernest H. Cherrington, ed., *Standard Encyclopedia of the Alcohol Problem*, 6 vols., vol. 4 (Westerville, OH: American Issue Press, 1928), 2153.

40. "'Benevolent Assimilation' in the Philippines."

41. By the founding president of Stanford University: David Starr Jordan, *Imperial Democracy: A Study of the Relation of Government by the People, Equality before the Law, and Other Tenets of Democracy, to the Demands of a Vigorous Foreign Policy and Other Demands of Imperial Dominion* (New York: D. Appleton and Company, 1899), 96.

42. See: Statement of Mary H. Hunt, in: *Sale of Intoxicating Liquors at the Army Canteens: Hearings before the Committee on Military Affairs of the United States Senate, December 7, 8, 11, 12, 13, and 14* (Washington, DC: Government Printing Office, 1900), 9, 21.

43. This is but one of many such reports in Van Meter, *Truth about the Philippines*, 430.

44. See statements by the Honorable Ogden E. Edwards and John Foreman in the testimony of Wilbur Crafts, in: *Sale of Intoxicating Liquors at the Army Canteens*, 20–21. On initial attempts at reconciliation, see: Salamanca, *Filipino Reaction*, 28–32.

45. *Proceedings of the Twelfth International Congress on Alcoholism* (London: National Temperance League, 1909), 228.

46. Cited in the testimony of Wilbur Crafts, in: *Sale of Intoxicating Liquors at the Army Canteens*, 25. As head of the International Reform Bureau, the Presbyterian Wilbur Crafts believed that missionary work among the "child races" of Africa and Asia were consistently being undercut by unscrupulous European liquor traffickers. Now American imperialists were doing the exact same thing. "We are trying to raise saints in hell," Crafts lamented. Wilbur F. Crafts et al., *Intoxicating Drinks & Drugs in All Lands and Times* (Washington, DC: International Reform Bureau, 1909), 14–15.

47. Mommsen, *Theories of Imperialism*, 36–39. Michael W. Doyle, *Empires* (Ithaca, NY: Cornell University Press, 1986), 30–46. According to prewar sources, a combined 916,501 liters of wines, malt liquors, distilled liquors, and other intoxicants were imported into the Philippines in 1893. In 1894, that number rose to 978,082. By contrast, during the first ten months of American occupation (August 22, 1898–July 1, 1899), that number was already 3,564,132. *Sale of Intoxicating Liquors at the Army Canteens*, 26.

48. William E. Johnson, *The New Voice*, August 16, 1900. In: Van Meter, *Truth about the Philippines*, 83.

49. Alice Stone Blackwell, "A National Disgrace," *The Woman's Column*, November 17, 1900, 1–3. William E. Johnson, *The New Voice*, August 23, 1900, in: Van Meter, *Truth about the Philippines*, 83–84. Ian Tyrrell, *Reforming the World: The Creation of America's Moral Empire* (Princeton, NJ: Princeton University Press, 2010), 139.

50. See the testimony of US Army Inspector General, Brigadier General Joseph C. Breckinridge, calling the arrangement "useful" and "beneficial" for college-age soldiers; Fourth Artillery Colonel Francis L. Guenther on reducing courts-martial, as well as Secretary of War Elihu Root, on "increasing the morality and health and discipline of the soldiers, but it is the one thing that makes it possible to make the camp, the military post, an agreeable place for the soldiers." in: *Sale of Intoxicating Liquors at the Army Canteens*, 62–64, 78.

51. Johnson, *The New Voice*, August 23, 1900, in: Van Meter, *Truth about the Philippines*, 83.

52. William P. F. Ferguson, *The Canteen in the United States Army: A Study of Uncle Sam as Grog-Shop Keeper* (Chicago: New Voice Press, 1900), 157–59.

53. Affidavit of Lieutenant Colonel Guy L. Edie, May 14, 1924, and Major Ira C. Brown, May 19, 1924 in: "Claim No. 38—J. Parsons," ed. American and British Claims Arbitration (Washington, DC: Government Printing Office, 1924), 6, 8.

54. And the only reason that we have any of this information today is that the British proprietor sued the United States for damages through a bilateral claims arbitration twenty-four years later, prompting sworn affidavits by Dr. Brown and other witnesses. Ibid., 6–7.

55. Johnson, "Confessions," V, 15–16.

56. Miller, *"Benevolent Assimilation,"* 61.

57. Interview in San Francisco on August 5, 1899. Ora Williams, *Oriental America: Official and Authentic Records of the Dealings of the United States with the Natives of Luzon and Their Former Rulers* (Chicago: Oriental America Pub. Co., 1899), 79.

58. Miller, *"Benevolent Assimilation,"* 61–62.

59. Ibid., 63. Immerwahr, *How to Hide an Empire*, 91–92.

60. Immerwahr, *How to Hide an Empire*, 9–107. Brian McAllister Linn, *The U.S. Army and Counterinsurgency in the Philippine War, 1899–1902* (Chapel Hill: University of North Carolina Press, 1989), 3.

61. Van Meter, *Truth about the Philippines*, 81.

62. Perhaps with the exception of one-time payments for conducting a census and relief for the 1903 rinderpest plague. Moore, *American Imperialism and the State*, 120.

63. On labor shortages, "reconcentration," and famine, see: Reynaldo C. Ileto, *Filipinos and Their Revolution: Event, Discourse, and Historiography* (Manila: Ateneo de Manila University Press, 1998), 110–12. On the "water cure": Richard E. Welch, "American Atrocities in the Philippines: The Indictment and Response," *Pacific Historical Review* 43, no. 2 (1974): 237. Edmund Block to Hon. H. L. Wilfrey, July 18, 1902, Records of the Bureau of Insular Affairs (Record Group 350), Series 2760, National Archives, Washington, DC; "Letter from General Malvar," July 4, 1901, Philippine Insurgent Records, Selected Documents 1132.8. On torture more generally: Major John G. Ballance to Commanding Officer, Bangued, November 2, 1900, Records of U.S. Army Overseas Operations and Commands, 1898–1942 (Record Group 395), Series 2150, Vol. 3, Letters Sent 2562; Major John G. Ballance to Commanding Officer, Bangued, November 12, 1900, Records of U.S. Army Overseas Operations and Commands, 1898–1942 (Record Group 395), Series 5583, Letters Received 3640. "Report of the Provincial Governor of Abra," December 16, 1901, Records of the Bureau of Insular Affairs (Record Group 350), Series 3599, "Abra File." All National Archives, Washington, DC. On reports and American public reaction, see: Cullinane, *Liberty and American Anti-Imperialism*, 118–19. Richard E. Welch, *Response to Imperialism: The United States and the Philippine-American War, 1899–1902* (Chapel Hill: University of North Carolina Press, 1979), 133–39.

64. William Cameron Forbes, "Diary Entry, August 22, 1904," Box 1, Vol. 1, W. Cameron Forbes Papers (1904–1946), Manuscript Division, Library of Congress. Immerwahr, *How to Hide an Empire*, 97.

65. Welch, *Response to Imperialism*, 138–41.

66. Miller, *"Benevolent Assimilation,"* 219–20.

67. David L. Fritz, "Before the 'Howling Wilderness': The Military Career of Jacob Hurd Smith, 1862–1902," *Military Affairs* 43, no. 4 (1979): 186. Brian McAllister Linn, *The Philippine War: 1899–1902* (Lawrence: University Press of Kansas, 2000), 221–24.

68. United States Bureau of the Census, *Census of the Philippine Islands: Taken under the Direction of the Philippine Commission in the Year 1903*, 4 vols., vol. 2 (Washington, DC: Government Printing Office, 1905), 17–24, 127. Marco Hewett, "Philippine-American War," in *The Encyclopedia of the Spanish-American and Philippine-American Wars: A Political, Social, and Military History*, ed. Spencer C. Tucker (Santa Barbara, CA: ABC-CLIO, 2009), 476–78.

69. Ferguson, *Canteen in the United States Army*, 8. Quite shockingly, the Philippine War isn't even mentioned in Michael McGerr, *A Fierce Discontent: The Rise and Fall of the Progressive Movement in America* (New York: Oxford University Press, 2003).

70. See: "Army Canteen," in: Ernest H. Cherrington, ed., *Standard Encyclopedia of the Alcohol Problem*, 6 vols., vol. 1 (Westerville, OH: American Issue Press, 1925), 207.

71. Testimony of Brigadier General Henry C. Corbin, in: *Sale of Intoxicating Liquors at the Army Canteens*, 51. See also: Ferguson, *Canteen in the United States Army*, 23–27. On the British canteen: John Fortescue, *A Short Account of Canteens in the British Army* (Cambridge: Cambridge University Press, 1928).

72. Bobby A. Wintermute, *Public Health and the U.S. Military: A History of the Army Medical Department, 1818–1917* (New York: Routledge, 2011), 190.

73. Sarah A. McClees, *The Army Canteen: A History of the Pioneer Work of Women with Regard to the Canteen in the Military Service of the United States of America* (Oakland, CA: n.p., 1905), 26. On "scientific" and life insurance arguments, see: McClees, *Army Canteen*, 15–17, 29.

74. Testimony of Lieutenant General Nelson A. Miles, who originally recommended the 1881 prohibition to the War Department, in: *Sale of Intoxicating Liquors at the Army Canteens*, 44. Also: "Army Canteen," in: Cherrington, ed., *Standard Encyclopedia of the Alcohol Problem*, 207.

75. *Department of Defense: Selected Manpower Statistics*, (Washington, DC: US Government Printing Office, 1997), 49. McClees, *Army Canteen*, 10.

76. James B. Dunn, *Anarchism, or, Shall Law Be Nullified? The Canteen Suppressed by Congress: Re-Opened by the Secretary of War* (New York: National Temperance Society and Publication House, 1900), 4.

77. Ibid., 6–8. Letter, William E. Johnson to James B. Dunn, secretary, National Temperance Society. Report on army camps to the National Temperance Congress, 1898, MssCol 1577, Manuscripts and Archives Division, New York Public Library, New York. Also: Ferguson, *Canteen in the United States Army*, 81–86.

78. Ferguson, *Canteen in the United States Army*, 89.

79. Dunn, *Anarchism, or, Shall Law Be Nullified?*, 8–9. Also: Wintermute, *Public Health and the U.S. Military*, 194.

80. Ferguson, *Canteen in the United States Army*, 89–90.

81. Ibid., 150. General Wood was cofounder and commander of the Rough Riders, with Theodore Roosevelt as his second in command.

82. *Military Notes on Cuba*, ed. Adjutant General War Department, vol. XXI (Washington, DC: Government Printing Office, 1898), 11–12.

83. Vincent J. Cirillo, *Bullets and Bacilli: The Spanish-American War and Military Medicine* (New Brunswick, NJ: Rutgers University Press, 2004), 94–95. Clay Risen, *The Crowded Hour: Theodore Roosevelt, the Rough Riders, and the Dawn of the American Century* (New York: Scribner, 2019), 244–45.

84. Quoted in: Ferguson, *Canteen in the United States Army*, 154–55.

85. Ibid., 152–53.

86. Quoted in: Wintermute, *Public Health and the U.S. Military*, 196.

87. Quoted in: Jordan, *Imperial Democracy*, 96–97.

88. Dunn, *Anarchism, or, Shall Law Be Nullified?*, 15–16.

89. See: Ibid., 21. Ferguson, *Canteen in the United States Army*, 119–49.

90. "High Government License in Manila," *New York Evening Post*. Reprinted in: *The National Advocate* XXXV, no. 3 (1900): 42. President McKinley, it seems, was well-informed of the canteen problem. See: "Liquor Traffic and Moral Conditions in the Philippines (1901)," Box 14, Folder 5, William McKinley Papers, 1847–1935, Manuscript Division, Library of Congress. Washington, DC.

91. Testimony of Elihu Root, in: *Sale of Intoxicating Liquors at the Army Canteens*, 78.

92. Ibid., 46, 62–63.

93. Testimony of Mrs. Mary H. Hunt, in: Ibid., 7–10.

94. According to prewar sources, a combined 916,501 liters combined of wines, malt liquors, distilled liquors, and other intoxicants were imported into the Philippines in 1893. In 1894, that number rose to 978,082. By contrast, during the first ten months of American occupation (August 22, 1898–July 1, 1899), the volume was already 3,564,132 liters. Ibid., 26. Van Meter, *Truth about the Philippines*, 82.

95. Testimony of Mrs. Margaret Dye Ellis, in: *Sale of Intoxicating Liquors at the Army Canteens,* 10–15, 25.

96. Wilbur F. Crafts, in: Ibid., 22.

97. Ibid., 19. Other reports of brothels in US Army canteens: Wintermute, *Public Health and the U.S. Military,* 193.

98. Testimony of Edwin Dinwiddie, in: *Sale of Intoxicating Liquors at the Army Canteens,* 26–29.

99. Ernest H. Cherrington, *History of the Anti-Saloon League* (Westerville, OH: American Issue Publishing Company, 1913), 59–60.

100. Michael Kazin, "The Forgotten Forerunner," *Wilson Quarterly* 23, no. 4 (1999): 26.

101. Bryan and Bryan, *Memoirs,* 187. On his oratorical upbringing, see: Kazin, *Godly Hero,* 10–11.

102. Hibben, *Peerless Leader,* 290. Matthew Harry Gore, *A History of the Cumberland Presbyterian Church in Kentucky to 1988* (Memphis, TN: Joint Heritage Committee of Covenant and Cumberland Presbyteries, 2000). Kazin, *Godly Hero,* 7–8.

103. Bryan and Bryan, *Memoirs,* 64.

104. Johnson, "Confessions," III, 11–12.

105. Lawrence Goodwyn, *The Populist Movement: A Short History of the Agrarian Revolt in America* (New York: Oxford University Press, 1978), xvii.

106. Kazin, *Godly Hero,* 21–27.

107. Paolo E. Coletta, "The Morning Star of the Reformation: William Jennings Bryan's First Congressional Campaign," *Nebraska History* 37 (1956): 115.

108. Lawrence H. Larsen and Barbara J. Cottrell, *The Gate City: A History of Omaha* (Lincoln: University of Nebraska Press, 1997), 97. Cherny, *Righteous Cause,* 119–20.

109. Coletta, "Morning Star of the Reformation," 115.

110. Hibben, *Peerless Leader,* 125.

111. Ibid. See also: Letter, William E. Johnson to William Jennings Bryan, October 16, 1890, Box 1, Folder 2, Series 1, Correspondence, RG3198.AM, William Jennings Bryan Papers, Nebraska State Historical Society, Lincoln. Jesse E. Boell, "*William Jennings Bryan before 1896*" (MA thesis, University of Nebraska, 1929), 51–52. M. R. Werner, *Bryan* (New York: Harcourt, Brace, 1929), 25–26.

112. Hibben, *Peerless Leader,* 290.

113. Coletta, "Morning Star of the Reformation," 116–17. Hibben, *Peerless Leader,* 124–25.

114. Douglas Steeples and David O. Whitten, *Democracy in Desperation: The Depression of 1893* (Westport, CT: Greenwood Press, 1998), 50.

115. Coletta, *William Jennings Bryan,* 294. Kazin, *Godly Hero,* 38–41. Smith, "William Jennings Bryan and the Social Gospel," 46.

116. Speech before Democratic National Convention ("Cross of Gold" speech), July 9, 1896, Box 2, Folder 5, Series 6, Speeches and Manuscripts, RG3198.AM, William Jennings Bryan Papers, Nebraska State Historical Society.

117. Kazin, *Godly Hero,* 61.

118. Harvey E. Newbranch, *William Jennings Bryan: A Concise but Complete Story of His Life and Services* (Lincoln, NE: University Publishing Co., 1900), 71.

119. "Liquor Selling in the United States Army: Speech of Hon. M. N. Johnson of North Dakota in the House of Representatives, Monday, Jan. 30, 1889," in: *Northwestern Christian Advocate,* February 22, 1899, 21. Also: Dunn, *Anarchism, or, Shall Law Be Nullified?,* 5.

120. Wintermute, *Public Health and the U.S. Military,* 195–96. On Bryan in Florida, see: C. F. Beck, "Bryan as a Soldier," *The Arena* XXIV, no. 4 (1900): 393–95. "Colonel Bryan's Bug-Bear," Box 3, Folder 1. RG3198.AM, William Jennings Bryan Papers, Nebraska State Historical Society.

121. Victor Vifquain, "Effects of the Canteen," *Army and Navy Journal,* February 2, 1901, 547.

122. Kazin, *Godly Hero,* 89, 102.

123. William Jennings Bryan, "What's Next?," *New York Journal,* February 12, 1899. In: Bryan, *Bryan on Imperialism,* 57–58. "The Filipinos," 1900, and "Bryan's Attitude towards the Philippines,"

1900, in: Box 3, Folder 2, Series 7, Speeches and Manuscripts, RG3198.AM, William Jennings Bryan Papers, Nebraska State Historical Society.

124. Warren L. Vinz, *Pulpit Politics: Faces of American Protestant Nationalism in the Twentieth Century* (Albany: State University of New York Press, 1997), 41. Stephen Howe, *Empire: A Very Short Introduction* (New York: Oxford University Press, 2002), 57. Robert L. Beisner, *Twelve against Empire: The Anti-Imperialists, 1898–1900* (New York: McGraw-Hill, 1968), 165–85.

125. Kazin, *Godly Hero*, 93. Cullinane, *Liberty and American Anti-Imperialism*, 54–73. See also: Bryan, "The Filipinos, 1900," and "Bryan's Attitude towards the Philippines, 1900."

126. Bryan, *Old World*, 199.

127. Smith, "William Jennings Bryan and the Social Gospel," 48.

128. William Jennings Bryan, "Why I Am for Prohibition," *The Independent*, July 17, 1916, 87.

129. Ibid., 88 (emphasis in original).

Chapter 16

1. William E. Johnson, "Confessions of 'Pussyfoot' Johnson," (Cooperstown, NY: Fenimore Art Museum Library, n/d), VII, 1–3. Paul Nesbit, "Haskell Tells of Two Conventions," *Chronicles of Oklahoma* 14, no. 2 (1936): 193.

2. "Francis E. Leupp Dies," *New York Times*, November 20, 1918, 15. See also Leupp's letter following Johnson's dismissal. Letter, Francis E. Leupp to William E. Johnson, October 15, 1911, Box 1, Folder 1, William E. "Pussyfoot" Johnson Papers, Fenimore Art Museum Library, Cooperstown, NY.

3. Letter, William E. Johnson to Howard H. Russell, June 21, 1932, 2, Folder 42, Roll 6, Howard Hyde Russell Series, Temperance and Prohibition Papers, Ohio Historical Society, Columbus.

4. James E. Klein, *Grappling with Demon Rum: The Cultural Struggle over Liquor in Early Oklahoma* (Norman: University of Oklahoma Press, 2008), 26–43.

5. Johnson, "Confessions," VII, 1–3. On Sweet's correspondence with Roosevelt, see: Family Correspondence, Series 1, Box 1, Evander McIver (E. M.) Sweet Jr. Papers, MSS 303, University of the Pacific, Stockton, California.

6. "A Personal Statement from 'Pussyfoot' Johnson," 1928, 1–2, Box 1, Folder 8, William E. "Pussyfoot" Johnson Papers, Fenimore Art Museum Library, Cooperstown, NY.

7. Ibid., XI, 15. William E. Johnson, Statement of Resignation from Indian Service, 1911, Box 1, Folder 1, William E. "Pussyfoot" Johnson Papers, Fenimore Art Museum Library, Cooperstown, NY.

8. Ibid., VII, 6.

9. Ibid., VII, 10. Diana Rice, "Valorous Pussyfoot," *New York Times*, August 13, 1922. If it sounds like something out of a Hollywood movie, the 1969 Robert Redford/Robert Blake western *Tell Them Willie Boy Is Here* is based on Pussyfoot and his deputies, though they're never explicitly mentioned. Theatrical trailer: https://www.youtube.com/watch?v=AhkH1FE1mZA (accessed January 20, 2021). See also: Clara True, "The Willie Boy Case and Attendant Circumstances," *Journal of California Anthropology* 5, no. 1 (1978).

10. Johnson, "Confessions," VII, 6–7. Kim Burdick, "Pussyfoot Johnson" (master's thesis, State University of New York College at Oneonta, 1976), 76.

11. Johnson, "Confessions," VII, 25–26.

12. "The Tiger Claws of 'Pussyfoot' Johnson," *Literary Digest*, May 1, 1926, 38. Fred Lockley, "'Pussyfoot' Johnson," *Overland Monthly and Out West Magazine* 90, no. 2 (1932): 49.

13. "Agent Cheerful over Plot to Kill Him. Government Agent Reports in an Unconcerned Way of Plans to Remove Him," *Philadelphia Inquirer*, July 28, 1907, 9. "Keeping Rum from Indians. Outlaws Put Price on Head of United States Special Officer," *Philadelphia Inquirer, December 12*, 1907, 2. Joseph Heighton, "'Pussy-Foot of Oklahoma': The Experiences of an 'Outlaw-Smasher,'" *Wide World Magazine*, June, 1914, 229–37.

14. Johnson, "Confessions," VIII, 5. Fred A. McKenzie, *"Pussyfoot" Johnson: Crusader, Reformer, a Man among Men* (London: Hodder and Stoughton, 1920), 53.

15. Walter Rauschenbusch, *Christianizing the Social Order* (New York: Macmillan, 1912), 395.

16. Paolo E. Coletta, "Will the Real Progressive Stand Up? William Jennings Bryan and Theodore Roosevelt to 1909," *Nebraska History* 65 (1984).

17. Ronald C. White and C. Howard Hopkins, *The Social Gospel: Religion and Reform in Changing America* (Philadelphia: Temple University Press, 1976), 179. William M. Ramsay, *Four Modern Prophets: Walter Rauschenbusch, Martin Luther King Jr., Gustavo Gutiérrez, Rosemary Radford Ruether* (Atlanta: John Knox Press, 1986), 17. Rauschenbusch's theology "was custom-made to appeal to Theodore Roosevelt, a salvation of struggle and effort. What he had already resolved to do personally—earn his hope, his purpose, in the here and now—the social gospel urged as a prescription for social regeneration." Joshua David Hawley, *Theodore Roosevelt: Preacher of Righteousness* (New Haven, CT: Yale University Press, 2008), 128.

18. Nathan Miller, *Theodore Roosevelt: A Life* (New York: William Morrow and Company, 1994), 365.

19. William Jennings Bryan, "'Let the People Rule,' Mr. Bryan's Speech at Banquet Given by People's Lobby at Newark, New Jersey, May 1, 1907," in *The Commoner, Condensed* (Chicago: Henneberry Company, 1908), 143. Michael Kazin, *A Godly Hero: The Life of William Jennings Bryan* (New York: Anchor Books, 2006), 151.

20. Hawley, *Theodore Roosevelt*, 110–11. Many thanks to Clay Risen for this reference. Letter from Frank Harper to S. Janette Reynolds, October 2, 1912, Theodore Roosevelt Papers, Library of Congress Manuscript Division, https://www.theodorerooseveltcenter.org/Research/Digital-Library/Record?libID=o230652 (accessed January 20, 2021), Theodore Roosevelt Digital Library, Dickinson State University.

21. Theodore Roosevelt, *Essays on Practical Politics* (New York: G. P. Putnam's Sons, 1888), 3.

22. James Timberlake, *Prohibition and the Progressive Movement, 1900–1920* (Cambridge, MA: Harvard University Press, 1963), 102.

23. Richard White, *Railroaded: The Transcontinentals and the Making of Modern America* (New York: W. W. Norton, 2011), 230.

24. John H. Garber, "Alcoholic Liquors," in *Twelfth Census of the United States, Taken in the Year 1900. Volume IX: Manufactures, Part III*, ed. Bureau of the Census (Washington, DC: United States Census Office, 1902), 597. Bureau of the Census, *Census of Manufactures, 1914: Volume II* (Washington, DC: Government Printing Office, 1919), 982–85.

25. George Kibbe Turner, "Beer and the City Liquor Problem," *McClure's Magazine*, September 1909, 534. August F. Fehlandt, *A Century of Drink Reform in the United States* (New York: Eaton and Mains, 1904), 210. Timberlake, *Prohibition and the Progressive Movement*, 102–103. William E. Johnson, *The Problem of the Hour* (Laurel, MD: s.n., 1906), 3, YA Pamphlet Collection, YA 21818, Special Collections, Library of Congress.

26. Turner, "Beer and the City Liquor Problem," 538. Garber, "Alcoholic Liquors," 597–99. Bureau of the Census, *Census of Manufactures, 1914: Volume II*, 982. Martin Stack, "Local and Regional Breweries in America's Brewing Industry, 1865 to 1920," *Business History Review* 74, no. 3 (2000): 435–36.

27. "Testimony of Mr. Edson Bradley, President of American Spirits Manufacturing Company and Vice-President of the Distilling Company of America," October 20, 1899, in: Industrial Commission, *Preliminary Report on Trusts and Industrial Combinations*, 2 vols., vol. 1 (Washington, DC: Government Printing Office, 1900), 814. Victor S. Clark, *History of Manufactures in the United States, Volume II: 1860–1893* (Washington, DC: Carnegie Institution, 1929), 505, in: M. H. Ross Papers, Box 74, Folder 6, "Manuscript and Research Files, 1893–1979," Special Collections, Georgia State University Special Collections and Archives, Atlanta.

28. K. Austin Kerr, "The American Brewing Industry, 1865–1920," in *The Dynamics of the International Brewing Industry since 1800*, ed. R. G. Wilson and T. R. Gourvish (London: Routledge, 1998), 180. Stack, "Local and Regional Breweries," 437–48.

29. Timberlake, *Prohibition and the Progressive Movement*, 104. Clark, *History of the Manufactures*, Vol. II, 175. On the history of American (and international) brewing consortia, see: *Documentary History of the United States Brewers' Association* (New York: United States Brewers' Association, 1896), Part I, 92–116.

30. Arthur Huntington Gleason, "The Saloon in New York, Part I: The Brewer's Man: The Saloonkeeper," *Collier's*, April 25, 1908, 16. On Tammany ties, see: *A Souvenir of New York's Liquor Interests* (New York: American Publishing and Engraving Co., 1893), 55, 128–33, 159–64.

31. Gleason, "Saloon, Part I," 16–17. Turner, "Beer and the City Liquor Problem," 535–37. Will Irwin, "The American Saloon V: The Texas 'Clean-Up' from Within," *Collier's Weekly*, May 9, 1908, 9–10. Timberlake, *Prohibition and the Progressive Movement*, 104–105. Kerr, "American Brewing Industry," 185–87.

32. Turner, "Beer and the City Liquor Problem," 536.

33. Arthur Huntington Gleason, "The Saloon in New York, Part II: Distributing the Burden," *Collier's*, May 2, 1908, 12. See also: Madelon Powers, *Faces along the Bar: Lore and Order in the Workingman's Saloon, 1870–1920* (Chicago: University of Chicago Press, 1998), 67, 108.

34. Peter H. Odegard, *Pressure Politics: The Story of the Anti-Saloon League* (New York: Columbia University Press, 1928), 41.

35. "Editorial Bulletin," *Collier's*, May 2, 1908, 6. More generally: Timberlake, *Prohibition and the Progressive Movement*, 156. Multipart investigations by Will Irwin and Arthur Gleason filled *Collier's* for months.

36. Emma Brush, "A Year of No-License; and What the Women Said," *Collier's*, June 27, 1908, 9.

37. Turner, "Beer and the City Liquor Problem," 541–43.

38. Ibid., 543.

39. George M. Hammell, *The Passing of the Saloon: An Authentic and Official Presentation of the Anti-Liquor Crusade in America* (Cincinnati, OH: Tower Press, 1908), 17.

40. Michael A. Lerner, *Dry Manhattan: Prohibition in New York* (Cambridge, MA: Harvard University Press, 2007), 23.

41. Gleason, "Saloon, Part II," 12.

42. Ibid. Gleason, "Saloon, Part I," 17. Lincoln Steffens, *The Autobiography of Lincoln Steffens* (New York: Heyday Books, 1931), Vol. 1, 231–65. John P. Peters, "Suppression of the 'Raines Law Hotels,'" *Annals of the American Academy of Political and Social Science* 32 (1908): 559–61.

43. Gleason, "Saloon, Part II," 12.

44. "Rum and Politics," *The Nation*, December 29, 1904, 516.

45. Will Irwin, "The American Saloon VI: The Model License League," *Collier's Weekly*, May 16, 1908, 9–10. Timberlake, *Prohibition and the Progressive Movement*, 113.

46. The brewers even tried concocting low-alcohol beers to circumvent the dry statutes, and complained vehemently when they were still labeled as alcoholic beverages. See: Deborah Blum, *The Poison Squad: One Chemist's Single-Minded Crusade for Food Safety at the Turn of the Twentieth Century* (New York: Penguin Press, 2018), 74–75.

47. Johnson, "Confessions," VII, 24.

48. A. J. Barton, "Brewery Control in Texas Politics," in *Proceedings: Seventeenth National Convention of the Anti-Saloon League of America. Indianapolis, Indiana, June 26–29, 1916* (Westerville, OH: American Issue Publishing Company, 1916), 186. Timberlake, *Prohibition and the Progressive Movement*, 109–10.

49. Thomas C. Cochran, *The Pabst Brewing Company: The History of an American Business* (New York: New York University Press, 1948), 312.

50. "The Facts about Temperance," *Utah Independent*, January 21, 1909, 1.

51. Busch letter reprinted in: Barton, "Brewery Control in Texas Politics," 180. On the Hepburn Act: Lindsay Rogers, "Interstate Commerce in Intoxicating Liquors before the Webb-Kenyon Act," *Virginia Law Review* 4, no. 5 (1917): 365–66.

52. Daniel Okrent, *Last Call: The Rise and Fall of Prohibition* (New York: Scribner, 2010), 36.

53. Ibid., 53, 57, 59. James A. Morone, *Hellfire Nation: The Politics of Sin in American History* (New Haven, CT: Yale University Press, 2003), 290.

54. Ernest H. Cherrington, *History of the Anti-Saloon League* (Westerville, OH: American Issue Publishing Company, 1913), 7–8.

55. Ibid., 10–11.

56. Howard Hyde Russell, "College vs. Seminary," May 22, 1885, Roll 3, Folder 30, Howard Hyde Russell Series, Temperance and Prohibition Papers, Ohio Historical Society, Columbus. Harry Malcolm Chalfant, *These Agitators and Their Idea* (Nashville: Cokesbury Press, 1931), 156–61. K. Austin Kerr, *Organized for Prohibition: A New History of the Anti-Saloon League* (New Haven, CT: Yale University Press, 1985), 77. Corning, Iowa, is more famously known as the birthplace of Johnny Carson. Even at its apex in the 1880s and 1890s—securing only 2 percent of the nationwide vote—the Prohibition Party had few resources for activism and was operating on a shoestring budget. "Minutes of the National Executive Committee," June 23, 1888, and "Minutes of the Prohibition National Committee," November 20, 1907, in: Book 1, Roll 1, Prohibition Party Series, Temperance and Prohibition Papers, University of Michigan, Bentley Historical Library, Ann Arbor.

57. Kerr, *Organized for Prohibition*, 78. Letter, Howard Hyde Russell to James Monroe, March 1, 1888, Series 1, Box 14. James Monroe Papers, 1819–1898, RG 30/022, Oberlin College Archives, Oberlin, Ohio. Monroe was a prominent Oberlin abolitionist turned US congressman, who maintained a keen legislative interest in both civil rights and temperance. See also: Series 3, Box 20, Files Relating to US Congress Dealing with Temperance and the Liquor Traffic, James Monroe Papers.

58. Records, 1874–1908, vol. 2, 21, Box 1, Oberlin Temperance Alliance Records, 1870–1917, RG 31/032, Oberlin College Archives, Oberlin, Ohio. Letter, G. W. Shurtleff to I. W. Metcalf, May 31, 1893, Series 5, Subseries 1, Box 5, Irving W. Metcalf Papers, 1877–1937, RG 30/009, Oberlin College Archives, Oberlin, Ohio. Howard Hyde Russell, "Founding of the Anti-Saloon League Movement," Autobiographical and Biographical Material, Folder 51, Reel 8, Howard Hyde Russell Series, Temperance and Prohibition Papers.

59. Kerr, *Organized for Prohibition*, 2.

60. The board of trustees began as the organization's "executive committee." Cherrington, *History of the Anti-Saloon League*, 44–46. Kerr, *Organized for Prohibition*, 80–82. Howard Hyde Russell, "A State Anti-Saloon Syndicate," *The Congregationalist*, October 17, 1895, 557–58. Howard Hyde Russell, "The Methods of Work of a Live Local League: The Churches Executing Their Resolutions," 1895, Reel 8, Folder 61, Howard Hyde Russell Papers, Temperance and Prohibition Papers, Ohio Historical Society, Columbus.

61. Randall C. Jimerson, "The Temperance and Prohibition Movement in America, 1830–1933," in *Guide to the Microfilm Edition of Temperance and Prohibition Papers*, ed. Randall C. Jimerson, Francis X. Blouin, and Charles A. Isetts (Ann Arbor: University of Michigan Publications, 1977), 340. On the Russell-Rockefeller friendship, see warm correspondence in: Fund for Dr. Russell, 1937–1943, Box 43, Folder 474, Series P: Welfare Interests, Office of the Messrs. Rockefeller Records, John D. Rockefeller Papers, 1855–1942, Rockefeller Archive Center, Sleepy Hollow, New York. John D. Rockefeller to Howard Hyde Russell, September 4 and September 9, 1920, Reel 5, Correspondence, Folder 37k (Also Reel 1, Folder 7), Howard Hyde Russell Series, Temperance and Prohibition Papers. Cherrington, *History of the Anti-Saloon League*, 49–54.

62. Rockefeller donated $24,500 to just the Ohio ASL between 1894 and 1903, with additional donations to other state and national leagues, as well as the Ohio WCTU. See: Series F: Financial Materials: Subseries V14: Charities Index Cards: Box 1, Folder 76; Box 6, Folders

924, 965, 994; Box 8, Folders 1470–72, John D. Rockefeller Papers, 1855–1942, Rockefeller Archive Center, Sleepy Hollow, New York. See also: Prohibition and Alcoholism, Ohio Anti-Saloon League, Box 44, Folders 475–76, Series P: Welfare Interests, Office of the Messrs. Rockefeller Records, Rockefeller Archive Center.

63. Lisa M. F. Andersen, *The Politics of Prohibition: American Governance and the Prohibition Party, 1869–1933* (New York: Cambridge University Press, 2013), 232–33. Jack Blocker Jr., *Retreat from Reform: The Prohibition Movement in the United States, 1890–1913* (Westport, CT: Greenwood Press, 1976), 185.

64. Kerr, *Organized for Prohibition*, 87. "Second Annual Report of the State Superintendent," June 30, 1895, Folder 19b, Reel 4, Ohio Anti-Saloon League Series, Temperance and Prohibition Papers. Howard Hyde Russell, "A New Kind of Politics," Autobiographical and Biographical Material, Folder 54, Roll 8, Howard Hyde Russell Series, Temperance and Prohibition Papers.

65. Howard H. Russell, "Mobilizing Public Sentiment for World Prohibition," in: *World-Wide Prohibition Program: Plans Inaugurated by the Conference of the Anti-Saloon League of America, Held in Columbus, Ohio, November 19–22, 1918* (Westerville, OH: American Issue Publishing Company, 1918), 35–36. Ernest H. Cherrington, *The Evolution of Prohibition in the United States of America: A Chronological History of the Liquor Problem and the Temperance Reform in the United States from the Earliest Settlements to the Consummation of National Prohibition* (Westerville, OH: American Issue Press, 1920), 253–54.

66. *American Issue*, April 9, 1900, 6–7, 10. Quoted in: Kerr, *Organized for Prohibition*, 103–104.

67. Cherrington, *History of the Anti-Saloon League*, 80–85.

68. See: Letters, Wayne Wheeler to Warren G. Harding, January 4, 16, and February 17, 1905, Roll 230, File 535, Warren G. Harding Papers, Ohio Historical Society, Columbus. Francis Russell, *The Shadow of Blooming Grove: Warren G. Harding in His Times* (New York: McGraw-Hill Book Company, 1968), 173.

69. Ernest H. Cherrington, "The Local Option Address," 1905, and "Status and Record of the Ohio Anti-Saloon League," 1905, in: Box 1, Folder 1, Roll 1, Ernest H. Cherrington Series, Temperance and Prohibition Papers, Ohio Historical Society, Columbus. Letter, John D. Rockefeller to Frederick T. Gates, February 17, 1905, Box 11, Volume 351, Letterbooks, Series L (FA431), John D. Rockefeller Papers, 1855–1942, Rockefeller Archive Center, Sleepy Hollow, New York. Kerr, *Organized for Prohibition*, 108–10.

70. Kerr, *Organized for Prohibition*, 110–14. William Cullen, *A History of Brewers in Portsmouth, Ohio* (Bloomington, IN: Xlibris, 2017).

71. Howard Hyde Russell, "The Methods of Work of a Live Local League: The Churches Executing Their Resolutions," 1895, Folder 61, Roll 8, Howard Hyde Russell Papers, Temperance and Prohibition Papers. H. Paul Thompson, "Myth: Temperance Advocates and Prohibitionists Shared the Same Goals and Tactics," in *Prohibition's Greatest Myths: The Distilled Truth about America's Anti-Alcohol Crusade*, ed. Michael Lewis and Richard F. Hamm (Baton Rouge: Louisiana State University Press, 2020), 15.

72. Kerr, *Organized for Prohibition*, 95.

73. Timberlake, *Prohibition and the Progressive Movement*, 140–41. Odegard, *Pressure Politics*, 87–88. Ernest H. Cherrington, ed., *Proceedings of the Eighth National Anti-Saloon Convention: Washington, D.C., December 9–11, 1903* (Westerville, OH: American Issue Publishing Company, 1904), 10–11.

74. Margaret Keck and Kathryn Sikkink, *Activists beyond Borders: Advocacy Networks in International Politics* (Ithaca, NY: Cornell University Press, 1998), 24–25. Daniel C. Thomas, *The Helsinki Effect: International Norms, Human Rights, and the Demise of Communism* (Princeton, NJ: Princeton University Press, 2001). Jonathan Fox, "The Uncertain Relationship between Transparency and Accountability," *Development in Practice* 17, no. 4–5 (2007): 663–64. Odegard, *Pressure Politics*. Freedom of Information Act: *McGehee v. CIA*, 697 F.2d 1095 (United States Court of Appeals, District of Columbia Circuit, January 4, 1983), 1109.

75. Theodore Roosevelt, *Theodore Roosevelt: An Autobiography* (New York: Charles Scribner's Sons, 1921), 391.

76. Michael McGerr, *A Fierce Discontent: The Rise and Fall of the Progressive Movement in America* (New York: Oxford University Press, 2003), 161–63. On drinking in the immigrant slums of Packingtown and the Union Stockyards, see: Perry Duis, *The Saloon: Public Drinking in Chicago and Boston, 1880–1920* (Urbana: University of Illinois Press, 1983), 103–104, 150.

77. Upton Sinclair, *The Jungle* (New York: Grosset & Dunlap, 1906), 17–18.

78. Ibid., 96. Powers, *Faces along the Bar*, 222. On saloon check-cashing: Duis, *The Saloon*, 182.

79. Sinclair, *The Jungle*, 110–11. See also: Duis, *The Saloon*, 116.

80. Kazin, *Godly Hero*, 174. See: correspondence with Upton Sinclair, Box 21, Folder 2, Roll 64, Ernest Hurst Cherrington Series, Temperance and Prohibition Papers, Ohio Historical Society.

81. Roosevelt, *Autobiography*, 63, 168–69.

82. Lincoln Steffens, *The Shame of the Cities* (New York: McClure, Phillips & Co., 1904), 34. Steffens, *Autobiography of Lincoln Steffens*, Vol. 1, 231–65.

83. Johnson, "Confessions," III, 7. Timberlake, *Prohibition and the Progressive Movement*, 108–109. We could add London journalist George R. Sims to the prohibitionist muckrakers. David W. Gutzke, *Pubs & Progressives: Reinventing the Public House in England* (DeKalb: Northern Illinois University Press, 2006), 3–4.

84. "A Mystery Unraveled: Startling Tales in Which Liquor, Prohibition, and Journalism Play Leading Rôles," *Collier's*, September 7, 1912, 11.

85. Johnson, "Confessions," XII, 4–5. Herbert Asbury, *The Great Illusion: An Informal History of Prohibition* (Garden City, NY: Doubleday & Company, 1950), 123.

86. Johnson, "Confessions," XII, 6.

87. Letter, William E. Johnson to Howard Hyde Russell, June 15, 1932, 3, Folder 42, Roll 6, Howard Hyde Russell Series, Temperance and Prohibition Papers, Ohio Historical Society, Columbus.

88. Lawrence Stone, "The Revival of Narrative: Reflections on a New Old History," *Past & Present* 85 (1979): 3.

89. Gerard Halfred von Koch, *Rusdrycksförbud: Studier av amerikansk nykterhetsrörelse och rusdryckslagstiftning* (Stockholm: A. B. Svenska nykterhetsförlaget, 1910), 130–90. H. J. Boström, *Rusdryckslagstiftningen i Nordamerikas Förenta Stater* (Stockholm: Centraltryckeriet, 1908), 7–8. Eyvind Andersen, *Förbudskomedien i sydstaterna* (Stockholm: Centraltryckeriet, 1909). See also: Cherrington, *History of the Anti-Saloon League*, 8–9.

90. See in particular the Policy Agendas Project, https://www.comparativeagendas.net/ (accessed April 20, 2020). Mark Lawrence Schrad, "Constitutional Blemishes: Understanding American Alcohol Prohibition and Repeal as Policy Punctuation," *Policy Studies Journal* 35, no. 3 (2007): 440–42. More generally: Frank R. Baumgartner and Bryan D. Jones, *Agendas and Instability in American Politics* (Chicago: University of Chicago Press, 1993). Bryan D. Jones, *Reconceiving Decision-Making in Democratic Politics: Attention, Choice and Public Policy* (Chicago: University of Chicago Press, 1994). Bryan D. Jones and Frank R. Baumgartner, *The Politics of Attention: How Government Prioritizes Problems* (Chicago: University of Chicago Press, 2005).

91. See, for instance, Harry Pratt Judson, *The Growth of the American Nation* (New York: Chautauqua-Century Press, 1895), 352–53. Ann-Marie Szymanski, *Pathways to Prohibition: Radicals, Moderates, and Social Movement Outcomes* (Durham, NC: Duke University Press, 2003), 144–48. Jack Blocker Jr., *American Temperance Movements: Cycles of Reform* (Boston: Twayne Publishers, 1989), 108.

92. William E. Unrau, *White Man's Wicked Water: The Alcohol Trade and Prohibition in Indian Country, 1802–1892* (Lawrence: University Press of Kansas, 1996), 37.

93. Charles J. Kappler, comp., *Indian Affairs, Laws and Treaties*, II, 311, 442–43, 758, in Maxwell, 1–2.

94. William E. Johnson, *Ten Years of Prohibition in Oklahoma* (Westerville, OH: American Issue Publishing Company, n/d), 4.

95. Amos DeZell Maxwell, "The Sequoyah Constitutional Convention" (master's thesis, Oklahoma Agricultural and Mechanical College, 1950), 12. Bill No. 15, October 23, 1903, Choctaw Nation of Oklahoma, *Acts and Resolutions of the General Council of the Choctaw Nation, Passed at Its Regular Session, 1903* (Hugo, Indian Territory: Hugo Husonian, 1903), 15.

96. Bill No. 18, October 23, 1903. In: Choctaw Nation of Oklahoma, *Acts and Resolutions,* 21–26.

97. Bill No. 15, October 23, 1903, in: Ibid., 15–17.

98. J. L. Franklin, "The Fight for Prohibition in Oklahoma Territory," *Social Science Quarterly* 49, no. 4 (1969): 883. US House of Representatives, *Hearing on Prohibition in the Proposed State of Oklahoma before the Committee on the Territories* (Washington, DC: Government Printing Office, 1905), 10–11.

99. Abbie B. Hillerman, *History of the Woman's Christian Temperance Union of Indian Territory, Oklahoma Territory, State of Oklahoma* (Sapulpa, OK: Jennings Printing & Stationery Co., 1925), 23.

100. US House of Representatives, *Oklahoma Prohibition Hearing,* 10. Franklin, "Fight for Prohibition in Oklahoma," 878–79, 883.

101. Maxwell, "Sequoyah Constitutional Convention," 85. E. M. Sweet, *Muskogee Phoenix,* October 29, 1905, 9. Indian Territory (Oklahoma) Church Federation for Prohibition Statehood, 1904–1905, Series 3, Box 1, Evander McIver (E. M.) Sweet Jr. Papers, MSS 303, University of the Pacific, Stockton, California.

102. Fran Grace, *Carry A. Nation: Retelling the Life* (Bloomington: Indiana University Press, 2001), 241. Carry A. Nation, *The Use and Need of the Life of Carry A. Nation* (Topeka, KS: F. M. Steves & Sons, 1908), 319.

103. Nesbit, "Haskell Tells of Two Conventions," 195–96.

104. Timberlake, *Prohibition and the Progressive Movement,* 122.

105. *Constitution of the State of Sequoyah* (Muskogee, Indian Territory: Phoenix Printing Co., 1905), 61–62. Grant Foreman, *Sequoyah* (Norman: University of Oklahoma Press, 1938). "The State of 'Sequoyah,'" *New York Times,* October 5, 1905.

106. James E. Klein, "A Social History of Prohibition in Oklahoma, 1900–1920" (PhD dissertation, Oklahoma State University, 2003), 54.

107. "Why Indian Territory Is Fighting Joint Statehood," *St. Louis Post-Dispatch,* July 30, 1905, 7. Oscar Presley Fowler, *The Haskell Regime: The Intimate Life of Charles Nathaniel Haskell* (Oklahoma City, OK: Harlow, 1933), 57.

108. Fowler, *Haskell Regime,* 49. Maxwell, "Sequoyah Constitutional Convention," 36. Nesbit, "Haskell Tells of Two Conventions," 198.

109. Nesbit, "Haskell Tells of Two Conventions," 203. Maxwell, "Sequoyah Constitutional Convention," 88.

110. "Statement of Rev. Edwin C. Dinwiddie," in: United States House of Representatives, *Oklahoma Prohibition Hearing,* 8–10. Klein, *Grappling with Demon Rum,* 17.

111. Luther B. Hill, *A History of the State of Oklahoma,* vol. 1 (Chicago: Lewis Publishing Company, 1909), 352–53. Letter from John M. Taylor to Theodore Roosevelt, December 22, 1906, Theodore Roosevelt Papers, Library of Congress Manuscript Division, https://www.theodorerooseveltcenter.org/Research/Digital-Library/Record?libID=o55062, Theodore Roosevelt Digital Library, Dickinson State University. "Acts, Bills, and Resolutions of the Choctaw Nation, 1903," January 24, 1903, Box 39, Folder 5, Western History Collections, University of Oklahoma, https://digital.libraries.ou.edu/cdm/singleitem/collection/choctawnat/id/7094/rec/36 (accessed April 18, 2020).

112. H.R. 12707, "An Act to Enable the People of Oklahoma and of the Indian Territory to Form a Constitution and State Government and Be Admitted into the Union on an Equal Footing with the Original States," June 16, 1906, 59th Congress, Session I, *United States Statutes at Large* 34, 269.

113. Kerr, *Organized for Prohibition*, 128–29.

114. Norbert R. Mahnken, "William Jennings Bryan in Oklahoma," *Nebraska History* 31 (1950): 262–63.

115. Ibid., 265–66.

116. Article II, Sections 31–32. U.S. Senate, *Constitution of the State of Oklahoma* (Washington, DC: Government Printing Office, 1908), 60th Congress, 1st Session, 12.

117. Nesbit, "Haskell Tells of Two Conventions," 212–13.

118. Ibid., 214–15. https://oac.cdlib.org/findaid/ark:/13030/kt3b69q92j/ (accessed January 20, 2021), E. M. Sweet Papers. Hill, *A History of the State of Oklahoma*, 376. Hillerman, *History of the WCTU of Oklahoma*, 50–61.

119. Ernest H. Cherrington, ed., *Standard Encyclopedia of the Alcohol Problem*, 6 vols., vol. 5 (Westerville, OH: American Issue Press, 1929), 2057–58.

120. Arrell Morgan Gibson, *Oklahoma: A History of Five Centuries*, 2nd ed. (Norman: University of Oklahoma Press, 1981), 189.

121. David R. Morgan, Robert E. England, and George G. Humphreys, *Oklahoma Politics and Policies: Governing the Sooner State* (Lincoln: University of Nebraska Press, 1991), 75–76. Mahnken, "William Jennings Bryan in Oklahoma," 264.

122. Johnson, "Confessions," VIII, 5. McKenzie, *"Pussyfoot" Johnson*, 53. The constitution was approved 180,333 in favor, only 73,059 against, though the prohibition clause was much closer: 130,361 in favor versus 112,258 against. Johnson, *Ten Years of Prohibition in Oklahoma*, 3. See also: White House Letter to William E. Johnson, March 12, 1908, Box 1, Folder 1, William E. "Pussyfoot" Johnson Papers, Fenimore Art Museum Library, Cooperstown, NY.

123. Rhode Island had a short-lived prohibition from 1886 to 1889, and North Dakota and South Dakota adopted prohibition in 1889, with South Dakota repealing its prohibition in 1896.

124. Johnson, "Confessions," VIII, 20.

125. Cherrington, *History of the Anti-Saloon League*, 112.

126. Kerr, *Organized for Prohibition*, 124–25. See also: Paul E. Isaac, *Prohibition and Politics; Turbulent Decades in Tennessee, 1885–1920* (Knoxville: University of Tennessee Press, 1965). James Benson Sellers, *The Prohibition Movement in Alabama: 1702–1943* (Chapel Hill: University of North Carolina Press, 1943).

127. See, for instance: Lisa McGirr, "How Prohibition Fueled the Klan," *New York Times*, January 16, 2019. https://www.nytimes.com/2019/01/16/opinion/prohibition-immigration-klan.html (accessed April 20, 2020). Morone, *Hellfire Nation*, 292–300. Okrent, *Last Call*, 42, 86.

128. Cherrington, *History of the Anti-Saloon League*, 99–100.

129. Ibid., 100–10. Similarly, see: John Lee Eighmy, "Religious Liberalism in the South during the Progressive Era," *Church History* 38, no. 3 (1969): 363–64. On Cannon, see: Robert A. Hohner, *Prohibition and Politics: The Life of Bishop James Cannon, Jr.* (Columbia: University of South Carolina Press, 1999), 179–87.

130. Cherrington, *History of the Anti-Saloon League*, 111.

131. Quoted in "The Liquor Press on Prohibition in Georgia," *Literary Digest*, August 24, 1907, 252. See also: Irwin, "The American Saloon V," 9–12. Irwin, "Model License League," 9–11. Cochran, *Pabst Brewing Company*, 312. Timberlake, *Prohibition and the Progressive Movement*, 157–58. Frank Foxcroft, "Prohibition in the South," *Atlantic Monthly* 101, no. 5 (1908): 630.

132. Foxcroft, "Prohibition in the South," 632.

133. Booker T. Washington, "Prohibition and the Negro," *Outlook* 88, no. 11 (1908): 587. Daniel J. Whitener, *Prohibition in North Carolina, 1715–1945* (Chapel Hill: University of North Carolina Press, 1946), 72–73, 134.

134. Booker T. Washington Papers, Special Correspondence, Boxes 523–530, Library of Congress, Washington, DC.

135. Letter from Elizabeth L. Bullard of the Massachusetts Indian Association, February 15, 1891, reprinted in: Louis R. Harlan, ed., *The Booker T. Washington Papers: Volume 3, 1889–95*

(Urbana: University of Illinois Press, 1974), 131–32. Original in Booker T. Washington Papers, Tuskegee University, Tuskegee, Alabama.

136. Letter from George V. Clark, October 12, 1895, in: Louis R. Harlan, ed., *The Booker T. Washington Papers: Volume 4, 1895–98* (Urbana: University of Illinois Press, 1975), 53–54. See also: R. T. Pollard to Booker T. Washington, October 14, 1895, Box 120, Part I: General Correspondence, Booker T. Washington Papers, Library of Congress, Washington, DC. Also: Isaiah T. Montgomery to Booker T. Washington, October 14, 1895, Box 113; W. H. Crogman to Booker T. Washington, October 19, 1895, Box 110.

137. Booker T. Washington to Charles Woodroph Hare, May 15, 1907, Box 36, Special Correspondence, Booker T. Washington Papers, Library of Congress, Washington DC. Such worries about state complicity in a corrupting traffic were a widespread critique of dispensary systems, as prohibitionists sought to undermine the image of their operations, even as they operated in Sweden: Ernest Gordon, *Breakdown of the Gothenburg System* (New York: National Temperance Society and Publication House, 1911). A. Symonds Ohlin, "Crown Prince of Sweden Favors Prohibition Measures," *Union Signal,* May 18, 1916. A. Symonds Ohlin, "Sweden's Progress on the Road to Prohibition," *Union Signal*, March 15, 1916.

138. Booker T. Washington, "A Town Owned by Negroes: Mound Bayou, Miss., an Example of Thrift and Self Government: An Article in *World's Work*, July 1907," in *The Booker T. Washington Papers, Volume 9: 1906–8*, ed. Louis R. Harlan and Raymond W. Smock (Urbana: University of Illinois Press, 1980), 315–16.

139. W. E. B. Du Bois, "Forward Backward," *The Crisis* 2, no. 6 (1911): 244.

140. Washington, "Prohibition and the Negro," 587. See also: Hanes Walton Jr. and James E. Taylor, "Blacks and the Southern Prohibition Movement," *Phylon* 32, no. 3 (1971): 247. "The Liquor Traffic a National Problem," *Union Signal*, January 15, 1914, 3.

141. Washington generally concluded that African Americans were no more prone to intoxication than other races, and that surveys of southern law enforcement, prosecutors, and judges offered at best a mixed picture of African Americans and the liquor question; but by reducing crimes committed by blacks, prohibition was largely a good thing. Booker T. Washington, "Negro Crime and Strong Drink: An Article in the *Journal of the American Institute of Criminal Law and Criminology*, September 1912," in *The Booker T. Washington Papers, Volume 12: 1912–14*, ed. Louis R. Harlan and Raymond W. Smock (Urbana: University of Illinois Press, 1982), 21.

142. Washington, "Prohibition and the Negro," 589.

143. See: Letter, Charles J. Liebmann to Hugh F. Fox, March 11, 1909, exhibit 846, in: Subcommittee on the Judiciary, United States Senate, *Brewing and Liquor Interests and German and Bolshevik Propaganda: Reports and Hearings*, 66th Congress, 1st Session, no. 62 (Washington, DC: Government Printing Office, 1919), vol. 1, 1091. By my count, Skarzynski was official delegate to the International Congresses Against Alcoholism in 1901, 1903, 1905, 1907, 1909, and 1913, where he frequently presented research on the advance of temperance in Russia and globally. Mark Lawrence Schrad, "The Prohibition Option: Transnational Temperance and National Decisionmaking in Russia, Sweden and the United States" (PhD dissertation, University of Wisconsin–Madison, 2007), Appendix A, 472–79. He was appointed by the Russian Imperial Ministry of Foreign Affairs to support the transnational temperance conference with a yearly stipend of six thousand to twelve thousand rubles per year. Ministry of Finance of the Provisional Government, f. 6996, op. 1, d. 307, ll. 1–5, 9–11, State Archives of the Russian Federation (GARF), Moscow, Russia. Also: *Bericht über den VIII. Internationalen Congress gegen den Alkoholismus, abgehalten in Wien, 9–14 April 1901* (Leipzig: F. Deuticke, 1902), 556.

144. Letter, Booker T. Washington to Louis Bronislavovich Skarzynski, March 11, 1909, Box 398, General Correspondence, Booker T. Washington Papers, Library of Congress, Washington, DC. Also reprinted in: Louis R. Harlan and Raymond W. Smock, eds., *The Booker T. Washington Papers: Volume 10, 1909–11* (Urbana: University of Illinois Press, 1981), 70–71.

145. Foxcroft, "Prohibition in the South," 632–33.

Chapter 17

1. Roger A. Fischer, "Pinback Put-Downs: The Campaign Button as Political Satire," *Journal of Popular Culture* 13, no. 4 (1980): 646.

2. "Address of Hon. William Warner, of Missouri, Notifying William Howard Taft of His Nomination for President, at Cincinnati, Ohio, July 28, 1908," in *Official Report of the Proceedings of the Fourteenth Republican National Convention Held in Chicago, Illinois. June 16, 17, 18, and 19, 1908*, ed. Milton W. Blumenberg (Columbus, OH: F. J. Heer, 1908), 211.

3. William Jennings Bryan, "Shall the People Rule? Accepting the Democratic Nomination, August 12, 1908," in *Speeches of William Jennings Bryan* (New York: Funk & Wagnalls Company, 1913), 102.

4. Lawrence W. Levine, *Defender of the Faith: William Jennings Bryan: The Last Decade, 1915–1925* (New York: Oxford University Press, 1965), 109. Robert W. Cherny, *A Righteous Cause: The Life of William Jennings Bryan* (Norman: University of Oklahoma Press, 1994), 119–20. Michael Kazin, *A Godly Hero: The Life of William Jennings Bryan* (New York: Anchor Books, 2006), 170–72.

5. Bradley J. Longfield, *The Presbyterian Controversy: Fundamentalists, Modernists, and Moderates* (New York: Oxford University Press, 1991), 67. Willard H. Smith, "William Jennings Bryan and the Social Gospel," *Journal of American History* 53, no. 1 (1966): 52–53. "Christian Citizenship," *The Commoner*, January 16, 1903, 1–2. Bryan's position was very much in line with progressive economist Richard T. Ely. See: Letters, William Jennings Bryan to Richard T. Ely, October 11, 1901, October 29, 1901, and May 25, 1903, Reel 21 / Box 20, Micro 924 / Wis Mss MK; and Letter, William Jennings Bryan to Richard T. Ely, May 25, 1903, Reel 26 / Box 24, Micro 924 / Wis Mss MK, Wisconsin Historical Society, Madison. William Jennings Bryan, "Individualism versus Socialism," *Century Magazine* LXXI (April 1906): 856–59. Coming full circle, Ely was a member of the Committee of Fifty; his copy of the organization's minutes are those now preserved as part of the Dr. Frederick Howard Wines Microfilm Collection on Social Problems, University of Illinois at Urbana-Champaign.

6. William Jennings Bryan, "World Missionary Conference," *The Commoner*, August 5, 1910, 15. Kazin, *Godly Hero*, 177. "William Jennings Bryan to Charles W. Bryan," December 12, 1912, File 13/14, William Jennings Bryan Collection, Occidental College Special Collections and College Archives, Los Angeles, California.

7. Kazin, *Godly Hero*, 176–77.

8. Elizabeth Putnam Gordon, *Women Torch-Bearers: The Story of the Woman's Christian Temperance Union* (Evanston, IL: National Woman's Christian Temperance Union Publishing House, 1924), 54.

9. William Jennings Bryan, "Why I Am for Prohibition," *The Independent*, July 17, 1916, 88.

10. C. M. Harger, "William J. Bryan on the Political Situation," *The Outlook*, January 6, 1912, 23. Notably, Theodore Roosevelt was at this time contributing editor to *The Outlook*. "Statement of I. J. Dunn Regarding 1912 Democratic National Convention," 1945, Box 3, Folder 5, Series 7, No. 464, William Jennings Bryan Papers, Nebraska State Historical Society, Lincoln. Letter, William Jennings Bryan to Charles W. Bryan, n/d, File 5, William Jennings Bryan Collection, Occidental College Special Collections and College Archives, Los Angeles, California.

11. K. Austin Kerr, *Organized for Prohibition: A New History of the Anti-Saloon League* (New Haven, CT: Yale University Press, 1985), 129–30.

12. Richard Hamm, *Shaping the Eighteenth Amendment: Temperance Reform, Legal Culture, and the Polity, 1880–1920* (Chapel Hill: University of North Carolina Press, 1995), 176–80.

13. Ibid., 180–81. Martin Stack, "Local and Regional Breweries in America's Brewing Industry, 1865 to 1920," *Business History Review* 74, no. 3 (2000): 448–56.

14. Hamm, *Shaping the Eighteenth Amendment*, 209–10. Kerr, *Organized for Prohibition*, 133.

15. Kerr, *Organized for Prohibition*, 136. *Bericht über den XIII. Internationalen Kongress gegen den Alkoholismus: Abgehalten im Haag (Scheveningen) vom 11.–16. September 1911* (Utrecht: J. van Boekhoven, 1912), 507–82.

16. Hamm, *Shaping the Eighteenth Amendment*, 212–13. Kerr, *Organized for Prohibition*, 137.

17. Wilbur F. Crafts et al., *Intoxicating Drinks & Drugs in All Lands and Times* (Washington, DC: International Reform Bureau, 1909), 50–51, 222–25. Janet L. Polasky, *The Democratic Socialism of Emile Vandervelde: Between Reform and Revolution* (Oxford: Berg Publishers, 1995), 67, 116.

18. James Chance, *1912: Wilson, Roosevelt, Taft & Debs—The Election That Changed the Country* (New York: Simon & Schuster, 2004), 13–14.

19. Kazin, *Godly Hero*, 179.

20. Henry Beach Needham, "Why Roosevelt Opposes Taft: An Interview with the Colonel Reviewing the President's Acts," *Saturday Evening Post*, May 4, 1912, 4.

21. Jack High and Clayton A. Coppin, "Wiley and the Whiskey Industry: Strategic Behavior in the Passage of the Pure Food Act," *Business History Review* 62, no. 2 (1988): 300. Deborah Blum, *The Poison Squad: One Chemist's Single-Minded Crusade for Food Safety at the Turn of the Twentieth Century* (New York: Penguin Press, 2018), 105, 122–23. Clay Risen, *American Whiskey, Bourbon & Rye: A Guide to the Nation's Favorite Spirit* (New York: Sterling Epicure, 2013), 39–40.

22. High and Coppin, "Wiley and the Whiskey Industry," 304–305. H. Parker Willis, "What Whiskey Is," *McClure's Magazine*, April 1910, 694.

23. Willis, "What Whiskey Is," 698.

24. Needham, "Why Roosevelt Opposes Taft," 44. Roosevelt's concern for the future of the act was quite widespread. Willis, "What Whiskey Is," 697–700. Blum, *Poison Squad*, 209. John C. Skipper, *Roosevelt's Revolt: The 1912 Republican Convention and the Launch of the Bull Moose Party* (Jefferson, NC: McFarland & Company, 2018), 66.

25. Jason Roberts, "Presidential Election of 1912," in *Encyclopedia of U.S. Campaigns, Elections, and Electoral Behavior*, ed. Kenneth F. Warren (Thousand Oaks, CA: Sage Publishing, 2008), 612.

26. Kazin, *Godly Hero*, 185.

27. William Menkel, "The Progressives at Chicago," *American Review of Reviews*, September 1912, 310.

28. Doris Kearns Goodwin, *The Bully Pulpit: Theodore Roosevelt, William Howard Taft, and the Golden Age of Journalism* (New York: Simon & Schuster, 2013), 718–19.

29. Menkel, "The Progressives at Chicago," 311.

30. Progressive Party Platform, 1912, Library of Congress Prints and Photographs Division, Theodore Roosevelt Digital Library, Dickinson State University, https://www.the odorerooseveltcenter.org/Research/Digital-Library/Record/ImageViewer?libID= o282587 (accessed May 12, 2020).

31. Wayne Wheeler, "The Inside Story of Prohibition's Adoption: Article V—Ratification of the Amendment," *New York Times*, April 1, 1926, 27.

32. Kazin, *Godly Hero*, 184.

33. "Source of Clark Funds: Liquor Interests Believed to Be Helping Finance His Campaign," *New York Times*, May 1, 1912, 1. "Liquor Men's Opposition to Wilson," *Current Literature*, June 1912, 611–12.

34. James Timberlake, *Prohibition and the Progressive Movement, 1900–1920* (Cambridge, MA: Harvard University Press, 1963), 168. Ray Stannard Baker, *Woodrow Wilson, Life and Letters, 8 vols., Volume 3: Governor, 1910–1913* (Garden City, NY: Doubleday, 1931), 62–64, 92, 151–52. Chance, *1912*, 137.

35. Letter, William Jennings Bryan to Henry Watterson, May 13, 1910. In: Henry Watterson Papers, 1863–1946, Mss. C B, Special Collections, Filson Historical Society, Louisville, Kentucky. Kazin, *Godly Hero*, 184–90.

36. Kazin, *Godly Hero*, 191.

37. Oliver E. Remey, Henry F. Cochems, and Wheeler P. Bloodgood, *The Attempted Assassination of Ex-President Theodore Roosevelt* (Milwaukee, WI: Progressive Publishing Company, 1912),

105–32. In his trial, Schrank claimed no allegiance to Tammany Hall and the Democratic machine of New York City.

38. Ibid., 15–24.

39. Kazin, *Godly Hero*, 191. Martha M. Allen, "Mr. Bryan in Harmony with Science in Discarding Wine," *New York Times*, May 5, 1913; reprinted in *Union Signal*, May 15, 1913, 11. "Woodrow Wilson," in: Ernest H. Cherrington, ed., *Standard Encyclopedia of the Alcohol Problem*, 6 vols., vol. 6 (Westerville, OH: American Issue Press, 1930), 2865.

40. Kerr, *Organized for Prohibition*, 137–38.

41. Andrew Sinclair, *Prohibition: The Era of Excess* (Boston: Little, Brown & Co., 1962), 154. Lillian M. N. Stevens, "Proclamation for National Constitutional Prohibition, Issued September 10, 1911," *Union Signal*, July 30, 1914, 12. Ernest H. Cherrington, *The Evolution of Prohibition in the United States of America: A Chronological History of the Liquor Problem and the Temperance Reform in the United States from the Earliest Settlements to the Consummation of National Prohibition* (Westerville, OH: American Issue Press, 1920), 317–23.

42. Lemuel D. Lilly, *The Saloon before the Courts* (Columbus, OH: Ohio Anti-Saloon League, 1912), 7–27. Such cases included: Samuel Freeman Miller and Supreme Court of the United States, *U.S. Reports, Bartemeyer v. Iowa, 85 U.S. 18 Wall. 129*, 1873; Joseph P. Bradley and Supreme Court of the United States. *U.S. Reports: Beer Co. v. Massachusetts, 97 U.S. 25*, 1877; Morrison Remick Waite and Supreme Court of the United States. *U.S. Reports: Stone v. Mississippi, 101 U.S. 814*, 1879; John Marshall Harlan and Supreme Court of the United States, *U.S. Reports: Mugler v. Kansas, 123 U.S. 623*, 1887; Stephen Johnson Field and Supreme Court of the United States, *U.S. Reports: Crowley v. Christensen, 137 U.S. 86*, 1890, Law Library of Congress.

43. Sinclair, *Prohibition: The Era of Excess*, 154.

44. This most damning vilification originated with an unauthorized hit piece that was published just a year after Wheeler's death in 1927. Justin Steuart, *Wayne Wheeler, Dry Boss: An Uncensored Biography of Wayne B. Wheeler* (New York: Fleming H. Revell Co., 1928), 11. Indeed, as debates over repealing prohibition escalated in Congress in 1930, both wet activists like Dr. Fred Buck and the infamous Senator Reed (of Reed "Bone Dry" fame) delighted in reading the anti-Wheeler broadsides into the record at congressional hearings. See: "Dr. F. W. Buck," in: *Hearings before the Committee on the Judiciary, House of Representatives, Seventy-First Congress, Second Session, on H.J. Res. 11, 38, 99, 114, 219, and 246; Serial 5, April 23 and 24, 1930, Part 3* (Washington, DC: Government Printing Office, 1930), 1264–65. Edward Behr, *Prohibition: Thirteen Years That Changed America* (New York: Arcade Publishing, 1996), 52. On Flanders: Daniel Okrent, *Last Call: The Rise and Fall of Prohibition* (New York: Scribner, 2010), 38.

45. Purley A. Baker, "The Next and Final Step," *American Issue*, June 1913, 2.

46. Margaret B. Platt, "Alcohol Beverages a Necessity? Oh, Yes, the Revenue," *Union Signal*, May 11, 1916, 9. On the history of American federal alcohol revenues, see: Mark Lawrence Schrad, "The First Social Policy: Alcohol Control and Modernity in Policy Studies," *Journal of Policy History* 19, no. 4 (2007): 440–41. Tun Yuan Hu, *The Liquor Tax in the United States* (New York: Columbia University Graduate School of Business, 1950), 50.

47. Wayne Wheeler, "The Inside Story of Prohibition's Adoption: Article I—Laying the Foundation for National Prohibition," *New York Times*, March 28, 1926, E1.

48. Kerr, *Organized for Prohibition*, 141–43. On taking a generation: Letter, Ernest H. Cherrington to James Cannon, March 26, 1915, 1, Box 25, Folder 1, Reel 76, Executive Committee File, Ernest Cherrington Series, Temperance and Prohibition Papers. William E. Johnson, "Columbus Convention, 1913," typescript, July 19, 1932, Folder 42, Reel 6, Howard Hyde Russell Series, Temperance and Prohibition Papers, Ohio Historical Society, Columbus. Bryan: Ralph A. Rossum, *Federalism, the Supreme Court, and the Seventeenth Amendment: The Irony of Constitutional Democracy* (Lanham, MD: Lexington Books, 2001), 191.

49. Kerr, *Organized for Prohibition*, 176–83.

50. Adam Hochschild, *To End All Wars: A Story of Loyalty and Rebellion, 1914–1918* (Boston: Houghton Mifflin Harcourt, 2011), 347. Lance Janda, "Casualties, Combatant and Noncombatant," in *The Encyclopedia of World War I*, ed. Spencer C. Tucker (Santa Barbara, CA: ABC-CLIO, 2005), 273–74.

51. Groucho Marx, "'One Morning I Shot an Elephant in My Pajamas': Dialogue from Animal Crackers," in *The Essential Groucho: Writings by, for, and about Groucho Marx*, ed. Stefan Kanfer (New York: Vintage Books, 2000), 27. Claims that "prohibition never had majority support in the United States, but it succeeded through brilliant organization and ruthless politics" are ubiquitous in the secondary literature. Reid Mitenbuler, *Bourbon Empire: The Past and Future of America's Whiskey* (New York: Viking Press, 2015), 171.

52. William Jennings Bryan and Mary Baird Bryan, *The Memoirs of William Jennings Bryan* (New York: Haskell House Publishers, 1925), 291.

53. Mark Lawrence Schrad, "Why Do We Blame Women for Prohibition?" *Politico Magazine*, January 13, 2019. https://www.politico.com/magazine/story/2019/01/13/prohibition-women-blame-history-223972 (accessed April 20, 2020). "Hon. Jeannette Rankin, First Woman Elected to United States Congress, in Her Addresses, Makes Frequent Reference to Her Attitude on Prohibition Question," *Union Signal*, March 29, 1917, 2.

54. Willis Rowland Skillman, *The A.E.F.: Who They Were, What They Did, How They Did It* (Philadelphia: George W. Jacobs & Company, 1920), 37.

55. "Afterthoughts on Prohibition and Woman Suffrage," *The Villager*, May 7, 1921, 202–203. Walter I. Clark, "Administering a Mission of the Master," *The Continent*, December 8, 1921, 1140.

56. Arthur Newsholme, "Some International Aspects of Alcoholism with Special Reference to Prohibition in America," *British Journal of Inebriety* XIX, no. 3 (1922): 99. See also: Edith Smith Davis, "What Other Lands Teach Our Own," *Union Signal*, July 30, 1914, 12.

57. Skillman, *The A.E.F.*, 23–24.

58. "Suffrage—A World Wave," *Union Signal*, August 19, 1915, 7. Richmond P. Hobson, "Raise the Struggle Against the Liquor Traffic to the International Plane," *Union Signal*, December 21, 1916, 4.

59. A. C. Archibald, "Explaining the World-Wide Prohibition Phenomena," *Union Signal*, December 30, 1915, 6. Congressman Richmond P. Hobson likewise recognized increased European enthusiasm on account of the war. "Richmond P. Hobson to Anna Gordon," September 2, 1915, Box 13, Folder 6, Richmond Pearson Hobson Papers, Library of Congress. See also: John A. Nicholls, "Ratification Will Hasten World Prohibition," *Union Signal*, December 19, 1918, 7.

60. "Kaiser Wilhelm Seeks to Curb Drink Evil," *Union Signal*, September 25, 1913, 2. "Kaiser Wilhelm's Influence Causes Decrease in Drink in Germany," *Union Signal*, February 19, 1914, 5. Ernest Gordon, *The Anti-Alcohol Movement in Europe* (New York: Fleming H. Revel Company, 1913), 325–26. Irving Fisher, "Changing Attitude of the World toward Alcohol," *Union Signal*, June 14, 1917, 4.

61. Marr Murray, *Drink and the War from the Patriotic Point of View* (London: Chapman and Hall, 1915). "Intoxicants Barred from the Navy," *Union Signal*, April 9, 1914, 2. A. W. Harris, "A Compensation of the War," *Union Signal*, June 8, 1916, 5. Guy Hayler, *Prohibition Advance in All Lands; a Study of the World-Wide Character of the Drink Question*, 2nd ed. (London: International Prohibition Confederation, 1914), 96.

62. L. Mervin Maus, "Total Abstinence a Natural Result of the War, Says Colonel Maus," *Union Signal*, May 20, 1915. Also: Harris, "A Compensation of the War," 5.

63. See: "Russia Sees in Drunkenness a National Menace," *Union Signal*, April 2, 1914, 5. "Russian Statesman Denounces Liquor," *Union Signal*, February 19, 1914, 5. "The Czar's Public Houses," *Temperance*, March 1913, 10. "The Drink Scourge in Russia," *Temperance*, November 1913, 15. "The Russian 'Drunken Budget,'" *Temperance*, September 1913, 12. Joseph Malins, *The Horrors of Russian Liquor Nationalisation: "An Object Lesson" For Britain* (Birmingham: Templar

Printing Works, 1916[?]). Guy Hayler—Temperance Tracts, Vol. XXI, No. 8, University of Wisconsin–Madison.

64. Vladimir A. Rebrikov, "O vliyanii zakonodatel'stva na potreblenie alkogolya v Rossii," in *Alkogol' i zdorov'e naseleniya Rossii: 1900–2000*, ed. Andrei K. Demin (Moscow: Rossiiskaya assotsiatsiya obshchestvennogo zdorov'ya, 1998), 144.

65. See: "The Truth Concerning Russia: Red Cross Nurses Recount What They Have Seen of the Effects of Prohibition in Russia," *Union Signal*, May 18, 1916, 7. Stephen Graham, "How the Russian Soldier Feels about Prohibition," *Union Signal*, October 5, 1916, 2. Also: Letter, William E. Johnson to Howard Hyde Russell, June 14, 1932, "Notes on the Liquor Monopoly in Russia," 2, Reel 6, Folder 42, Howard Hyde Russell Series, Temperance and Prohibition Papers.

66. "From a 'Budget of Drunkenness' to a 'Budget of Sobriety,'" *Union Signal*, October 29, 1914, 3. Walt Mason, "Prohibition in Russia," *Union Signal*, February 18, 1915, 5.

67. "The Miracle-Working Law of Russia," *Union Signal*, October 19, 1916, 2. "Russia Transformed: Passing of Vodka Brings Prosperity," *Union Signal*, January 1, 1915, 5. Christine I. Tinling, "The Story of a Russian Peasant," *Union Signal*, January 28, 1915, 14.

68. "Russia's Financial Stability and Prohibition," *Union Signal*, March 4, 1915, 7. Nicholas Iserguine, "Russian Bank Inspector Says Russia Is 'Bone Dry,'" *Union Signal*, March 8, 1917, 4. "Census in Russia Shows Popularity of Prohibition," *Union Signal*, July 1, 1915, 3. John Foster Fraser, "Teetotal Russia," *Union Signal*, November 23, 1916, 5. "Popular Sentiment Favors Prohibition in Russia," *Union Signal*, April 8, 1915, 4.

69. "Can a Nation Prosper without Liquor Revenue?" *Union Signal*, March 23, 1916, 9. "Russia's Wealth-Conserving Experiment: What the United States Can Learn from It," *Union Signal*, May 17, 1917, 13. "Russia Experiences Phenomenal Prosperity," *Union Signal*, August 17, 1916, 6. "Sale of Vodka to Be Prohibited Forever in Russia," *Chicago Tribune*, June 21, 1916. "Russian Budget under Prohibition Interesting Reading," *Union Signal*, December 21, 1916, 11. "How Russia Has Gone Dry," *Review of Reviews* 51 (1915): 97.

70. Ernest Barron Gordon, *Russian Prohibition* (Westerville, OH: American Issue Pub. Co., 1916), 56–57. Ernest Gordon, "Prohibition in Russia Proves Law Itself Schoolmaster," *Union Signal*, March 15, 1917, 5.

71. Peter L. Bark, "Memoirs," Sir Peter Bark Papers, Leeds Russian Archive, Special Collections, Leeds University Library (n/d), IX, 21.

72. "An Alcohol-Less, Therefore an Almost Bloodless Revolution," *Union Signal*, November 9, 1917, 5. John A. Nicholls, "Study of Conflicting Statements of Liquor Journals," *Union Signal*, September 20, 1917, 6. "Prohibition a Liberalizing Agency in Russia," *Union Signal*, April 12, 1917, 3.

73. Mark Lawrence Schrad, *The Political Power of Bad Ideas: Networks, Institutions, and the Global Prohibition Wave* (New York: Oxford University Press, 2010), 157.

74. Will Rogers, *The Cowboy Philosopher on Prohibition* (Stillwater: Oklahoma State University Press, 1975), xvi, 38–39.

75. "Prohibition Is Beaten in House: Hobson Resolution Fails of Two-Thirds, but Gets a Majority," *New York Times*, December 23, 1914, 7.

76. "The Hobson Prohibition Amendment." *Congressional Record*, Vol. 52, Part 1: 63rd Congress, 3rd Session (December 22, 1914), 496–97.

77. "Prohibition Is Beaten in the House," 1.

78. "The Resignation of William Jennings Bryan as Secretary of State and the Documents That Present the Issue," 1915, Box 3, Folder 13, Series 6, Speeches and Manuscripts, RG3198.AM, William Jennings Bryan Papers, Nebraska State Historical Society.

79. This is the argument he presented in some sixty speeches across Ohio in 1915. William Jennings Bryan, "Prohibition," *The Commoner*, January 16, 1916, 13–14. See also: "William J. Bryan Addresses Convention," *Union Signal*, November 30, 1916, 7, 14–15.

80. Kazin, *Godly Hero*, 247–52.

81. Wayne Wheeler, "The Inside Story of Prohibition's Adoption: Article III—Lining up Congress for Prohibition," *New York Times*, March 30, 1926, 27. When asked, both Wilson and Hughes pointed to the lack of a prohibition plank in their respective parties' platforms. Kerr suggests that this was in part due to the influence of the ASL's Purley Baker conferring with William Jennings Bryan not to make a political issue of it, while nevertheless posting delegations to each party's convention to ensure that the pro-liquor provisions were not inserted into the platforms. Kerr, *Organized for Prohibition*, 192.

82. Wheeler, "Inside Story, II," 21.

83. Wheeler, "Inside Story, III," 27.

84. William E. Johnson, "Confessions of 'Pussyfoot' Johnson" (Cooperstown, NY: Fenimore Art Museum Library, n/d), XII, 6–8. Wayne Wheeler liked to point out that it was a union shop, as opposed to most wet publishing houses, which were strongly nonunion. Wheeler, "Inside Story, II," 21. Howard Hyde Russell had actually offered Pussyfoot the position of business manager of the *American Issue* back in 1900, when Johnson was in Hong Kong and the Philippines. Letter, Howard Hyde Russell to William E. Johnson, March 28, 1900, Box 1, Folder 1, William E. "Pussyfoot" Johnson Papers, Fenimore Art Museum Library, Cooperstown, NY. Cherrington was the chief editor of the massive, six-volume *Standard Encyclopedia of the Alcohol Problem*, with Johnson as his associate editor. "Advanced Publicity," Box 1, Folder 1, Roll 1, Standard Encyclopedia of the Alcohol Problem Series, Temperance and Prohibition Papers.

85. See: P. J. Valekeapää to William E. Johnson, August 26 / September 8, 1913, Box 1, Folder 1; and Russian Minister of War Alexei Andreevich Polivanov to William E. Johnson, September 26/13, 1915, Box 1, Folder 2, William E. "Pussyfoot" Johnson Papers, Fenimore Art Museum Library, Cooperstown, NY. William E. Johnson to Howard H. Russell, June 14, 1932, 2, Folder 42, Roll 6, Howard Hyde Russell Series, Temperance and Prohibition Papers, Ohio Historical Society, Columbus.

86. Johnson, "Confessions," XII, 10. William E. Johnson, "Activity and Methods of American Liquor Organizations Against Temperance," in: *Compte-rendu du XIV Congrès international contre l'alcoolisme, Milan 22–28 Septembre 1913* (Milan: A. Bari, 1921), 127–31. Ernest H. Cherrington, ed., *Proceedings of the Fifteenth International Congress Against Alcoholism, Held at Washington, D.C., U.S.A. September 21–26, 1920* (Westerville, OH: American Issue Press, 1921), 351–52.

87. Letter, A. G. Wolfenbarger to William E. Johnson, December 14, 1916, Box 1, Folder 2, William E. "Pussyfoot" Johnson Papers, Fenimore Art Museum Library, Cooperstown, NY.

88. "Regenerated Russia," *Union Signal*, June 22, 1916, 15. See also: Francis B. Reeves, *Russia Then and Now: 1892–1917* (New York: G. P. Putnam's Sons, 1917), 113. "The Truth Concerning Russia," *Union Signal*, May 18, 1916, 7. "Russia's Wealth-Conserving Experiment," *Union Signal*, May 25, 1916, 4. "Russia Experiences Phenomenal Prosperity," *Union Signal*, August 17, 1916, 6. Stephen Graham, "How the Russian Soldier Feels about Prohibition," *Union Signal*, October 5, 1916, 2. John Foster Fraser, "Teetotal Russia," *Union Signal*, November 23, 1916, 5. "The Miracle-Working Law of Russia," *Union Signal*, October 19, 1916, 2.

89. Henry W. Miller, "Sees Russia Regenerated," *New York Times*, December 27, 1914, C7. See also: "How Prohibition Came to Russia," *New York Times*, November 19, 1914, 4. "How Russia Has Gone Dry," *Review of Reviews and World's Work* 51 (1915): 96–97. "Sale of Vodka to Be Prohibited Forever in Russia," *Chicago Tribune,* June 21, 1916. Note also: "Hearst Papers Declare for Full Prohibition," *Union Signal*, May 17, 1917, 3.

90. Wheeler, "Inside Story, III," 27.

91. Peter H. Odegard, *Pressure Politics: The Story of the Anti-Saloon League* (New York: Columbia University Press, 1928), 163, 267–69.

92. Wheeler, "Inside Story, III," 27. Skillman, *The A.E.F.*, 23–24.

93. Reed famously proclaimed that only white men should be allowed to emigrate to the United States, before espousing a racial hierarchy. "Regulation of Immigration," *Congressional Record,* Vol. 54, Part 1: 64th Congress, 2nd Session (December 12, 1917), 209.

94. Odegard, *Pressure Politics,* 161–62. Kerr, *Organized for Prohibition,* 196–97. Hamm, *Shaping the Eighteenth Amendment,* 238–39.

95. Randall C. Jimerson, Francis X. Blouin, and Charles A. Isetts, eds., *Guide to the Microfilm Edition of Temperance and Prohibition Papers* (Ann Arbor: University of Michigan Publications, 1977), 17.

96. Thomas C. Cochran, *The Pabst Brewing Company: The History of an American Business* (New York: New York University Press, 1948), 320.

97. Kazin, *Godly Hero,* 255. See also: Rev. Duncan C. Milner, "Kaiser William as a Prophet?" *Chicago Daily News,* reprinted in: *Union Signal,* August 1-8-15, 1918, 5.

98. Charles Thomas Johnson, "The National German-American Alliance, 1901–1918: Cultural Politics and Ethnicity in Peace and War" (PhD dissertation, Western Michigan University, 1997), 254–55. Wheeler kept Roosevelt informed of investigations into the NGAA, but "our correspondence terminated with a ringing editorial from the Roosevelt pen," which he admitted was of marginal help to the dry cause. K. Austin Kerr, "The American Brewing Industry, 1865–1920," in *The Dynamics of the International Brewing Industry since 1800,* ed. R. G. Wilson and T. R. Gourvish (London: Routledge, 1998), 189.

99. "Lever Bill before Senate," *New York Times,* June 17, 1917, 3. Timberlake, *Prohibition and the Progressive Movement,* 174.

100. See, for instance, "The Brewers to the Public," *Montgomery Advertiser,* November 27, 1917. Reprinted in: "State v. Advertiser Co.," *Southern Reporter* 77 (St. Paul: West Publishing Co., 1918), 759. Also, *Hearings before the Subcommittee of the Committee on the Judiciary, United States Senate. Sixty-Sixth Congress, First Session, on the Bills to Prohibit the Liquor Traffic and to Provide for the Enforcement of Such Prohibition and the War Prohibition Act* (Washington, DC: Government Printing Office, 1919), 325–26.

101. Letter, William Jennings Bryan to Edwin Y. Webb, July 27, 1917, Box 17, Edwin Yates Webb Papers, #3482, Southern Historical Collections, University of North Carolina, Chapel Hill. Kerr, *Organized for Prohibition,* 202. See also: Letters, William P. Halenkamp to Woodrow Wilson, August 3, 1917, and Joseph P. Tumulty to Woodrow Wilson, September 5, 1917, Series 4, No. 144, Reel 228, Woodrow Wilson Papers, Library of Congress.

102. Roosevelt agreed to do so, but it turned out not to be necessary. Wheeler, "Inside Story, V," 27.

103. Wayne Wheeler, "The Inside Story of Prohibition's Adoption: Article IV—Submitting the Amendment," *New York Times,* March 31, 1926, 25. Kerr, *Organized for Prohibition,* 203. As a prohibition president, Harding's occasional social drinking—and the small, private stock of whiskey he legally kept for his own use in the White House—was frequently a source of concern for Wheeler. Wayne Wheeler, "The Inside Story of Prohibition's Adoption: Article VI—Harding and the Volstead Act," *New York Times,* April 2, 1926, 21.

104. Kerr, *Organized for Prohibition,* 205. Wheeler, "Inside Story, IV," 25. Hamm, *Shaping the Eighteenth Amendment,* 247.

105. "Proposed Amendment to the Constitution," Joint Resolution, December 19, 1917, *United States Statutes at Large,* Volume 40, 1050. https://govtrackus.s3.amazonaws.com/legislink/pdf/stat/40/STATUTE-40-Pg1050.pdf

106. Hamm, *Shaping the Eighteenth Amendment,* 243.

107. Wheeler, "Inside Story, IV," 25.

108. "Mississippi First State to Ratify Federal Prohibition Amendment," *Union Signal,* January 17, 1918, 3.

109. Wheeler, "Inside Story, V," 27.

110. John M. Barry, *The Great Influenza: The Story of the Deadliest Pandemic in History* (New York: Penguin Books, 2005), 328, 59. President Wilson caught the flu while in Paris, with some suggestion it changed the tenor of deliberations there. Steve Coll, "Woodrow

Wilson's Case of the Flu, and How Pandemics Change History," *New Yorker*, April 17, 2020, https://www.newyorker.com/news/daily-comment/woodrow-wilsons-case-of-the-flu-and-how-pandemics-change-history (accessed May 10, 2020).

111. Fred Minnick, *Bourbon: The Rise, Fall, and Rebirth of an American Whiskey* (Minneapolis: Voyageur Press, 2016), 87–88.

112. "Whisky Banned as Medicine," *Temperance Cause*, April 1920, 26.

113. Joseph P. Tumulty, *Woodrow Wilson as I Know Him* (Garden City, NY: Doubleday, Page & Company, 1921), 413–14. Cherrington, *The Evolution of Prohibition in the United States*, 329, 354–55.

114. Ernest H. Cherrington, "A Survey of the World Problem, With Proposed Program for Universal Prohibition," in: *World-Wide Prohibition Program: Plans Inaugurated by the Conference of the Anti-Saloon League of America, Held in Columbus, Ohio, November 19–22, 1918* (Westerville, OH: American Issue Publishing Company, 1918), 22. Likewise: "Why a Prohibition War Measure?" *Union Signal*, April 19, 1917, 8. John A. Nicholls, "Life-Sustaining Food vs. Life-Destroying Drink: Save the Grain to Feed the Nation and the Allies," *Union Signal*, May 17, 1917, 5. William Harding Carter, "Modern War and Prohibition," *Union Signal*, May 31, 1917, 5. Jane Stewart, "Prohibition as a War Measure Advocated by Convention of National Organization of Nurses," *Union Signal*, May 31, 1917, 7. "A Great Business Asset," *Union Signal*, January 16, 1919, 6.

115. William J. Bryan, "Saving at the Spigot and Wasting at the Bunghole," *Union Signal*, May 31, 1917, 5. "Food Conservation," 1917, Box 3, Folder 13, Series 6, Speeches and Manuscripts, RG3198.AM, William Jennings Bryan Papers, Nebraska State Historical Society. International Reform Bureau, *Conservation of Food and Other Resources by War Prohibition: Facts and Figures* (Washington, DC: 1917), 13.

116. Timberlake, *Prohibition and the Progressive Movement*, 179–80.

117. William Jennings Bryan, "Who Will Assume the Responsibility?" *The Commoner*, September 1, 1919, 3, reprinted in: *Union Signal*, October 2, 1919, 7.

118. Wheeler, "Inside Story, V," 27. Michael A. Lerner, *Dry Manhattan: Prohibition in New York* (Cambridge, MA: Harvard University Press, 2007), 12–13.

119. Cherrington, ed., *Fifteenth International Congress against Alcoholism*, 343.

120. Richard M. Boeckel, "The States and the Prohibition Amendment," *CQ Researcher* (1931). Schrad, *Political Power of Bad Ideas*, 195–97. Mark Lawrence Schrad, "Myth: Prohibition Was Uniquely American," in *Prohibition's Greatest Myths: The Distilled Truth about America's Anti-Alcohol Crusade*, ed. Michael Lewis and Richard F. Hamm (Baton Rouge: Louisiana State University Press, 2020), 106–30.

121. Letter, Joseph P. Tumulty to Woodrow Wilson, May 9, 1919, Series 5B, No. 156, Reel 405, Woodrow Wilson Papers, Library of Congress. Tumulty, *Woodrow Wilson as I Know Him*, 415–17.

122. Wheeler, "Inside Story, VI," 26.

123. Johnson, "Confessions," VIII, 20.

124. Kerr, *Organized for Prohibition*, 223.

125. Tumulty, *Woodrow Wilson as I Know Him*, 420. Woodrow Wilson, "Statement on Prohibition Bill," October 27, 1919. Series 7B, Reel 480, Woodrow Wilson Papers, Library of Congress.

126. Timberlake, *Prohibition and the Progressive Movement*, 181.

127. Tumulty, *Woodrow Wilson as I Know Him*, 421.

128. "World League Against Alcoholism," in: Cherrington, ed., *Standard Encyclopedia of the Alcohol Problem*, 2910–11. Susan Mary Brook, "The World League Against Alcoholism: The Attempt to Export an American Experience" (MA thesis, University of Western Ontario, 1972).

129. Johnson, "Confessions," XII, 40. Letter, William E. Johnson to Ernest Cherrington, June 28, 1925, Box 1, Folder 5, William E. "Pussyfoot" Johnson Papers, Fenimore Art Museum Library, Cooperstown, NY.

130. Johnson, "Confessions," XIII, 10. Entry of November 11, 1918, William E. Johnson, *Diary*. Box 2, William E. "Pussyfoot" Johnson Papers, Fenimore Art Museum Library, Cooperstown, NY.

131. Letter, Johnson to Cherrington, June 28, 1925. Johnson lists 140 speeches given in Scotland, 25 in Wales, 35 to 40 in Ireland, 125 in England, 20 in France, 7 in Switzerland, 15 in Denmark, 10 in Finland, 10 in Bulgaria, 10 to 12 in Yugoslavia, 5 in Austria, "several" in Hungary, 5 in Czechoslovakia, 25 in Egypt, "several" in Zanzibar, 25 in Ceylon, 30 in India, 30 in Australia, 120 in New Zealand, 65 in South Africa, and visits to conferences and activist networking in Norway, Sweden, Romania, and Turkey without giving speeches or addresses. On his temperance activism in the Balkans, see: Nikolay Kamenov, *Global Temperance and the Balkans: American Missionaries, Swiss Scientists, and Bulgarian Socialists* (New York: Palgrave Macmillan, 2020).

132. Johnson, "Confessions," XIII, 15–16. Francis Scott McBride, "The Eyes of the World," WLAA Convention, Winona Lake, Indiana, July 18, 1924, 2, Roll 6, Box 2, Folder 42, F. Scott McBride Papers, Temperance and Prohibition Papers, Ohio Historical Society, Columbus.

133. Johnson, "Confessions," XIII, 15–16. See also: Letter, Johnson to Cherrington, June 28, 1925, 4–5. Ernest H. Cherrington, "Report of the General Secretary to the Executive Committee and Council," in: Ernest H. Cherrington, ed., *Report of the Activities of the World League Against Alcoholism, 1919–1927* (Westerville, OH: World League Against Alcoholism, 1927), 8. Robert Hercod, "The Alcohol Question before the League of Nations," *British Journal of Inebriety* 26, no. 3 (1929): 143–47. Charles F. Harford, "The Great Powers and the Liquor Traffic among the Native Races," in: Robert Hercod, ed., *Proceedings of the International Conference against Alcoholism at Geneva, 1st–3rd September 1925* (Lausanne: International Bureau against Alcoholism, 1925), 15–25.

134. Ian Tyrrell, *Reforming the World: The Creation of America's Moral Empire* (Princeton, NJ: Princeton University Press, 2010), 35, 86. Ian Tyrrell, "Prohibition, American Cultural Expansion, and the New Hegemony in the 1920s: An Interpretation," *Histoire sociale / Social History* 27, no. 54 (1994), 413–45. Greg Marquis, "'Brewers and Distillers Paradise': American Views of Canadian Alcohol Policies, 1919 to 1935," *Canadian Review of American Studies* 34, no. 2 (2004), 135–66.

135. Letter, Guy Hayler to Francis Smith, February 11, 1896, Guy Hayler Temperance Tracts, Vol. XIV, no. 23, University of Wisconsin–Madison. Matthew K. McKean, "World Prohibition Federation," in *Alcohol and Temperance in Modern History: An International Encyclopedia*, ed. Jack Blocker Jr., David Fahey, and Ian Tyrrell (Santa Barbara, CA: ABC-CLIO, 2003), 693. "The catholicity of the Temperance movement is remarkable. It links together in a fraternal bond of union, people of every nation, irrespective of colour, education, politics or religion, and through the agency of these bodies, the peoples of the earth are being linked together not only to drive the means of intoxication from the commerce of the world, but to secure peace and goodwill among nations." Hayler, *Prohibition Advance in All Lands*, 11.

136. E. J. Moore, "Financing the World-Wide Prohibition Movement," in: *World-Wide Prohibition Program*, 41–42.

137. Letter, William E. Johnson to Karl von Langi, January 21, 1928, in: Box 14, Folder 7, Roll 41, Ernest H. Cherrington Series, Temperance and Prohibition Papers, Ohio Historical Society. On the financial challenges of even maintaining a London office, see: Letter, Ernest H. Cherrington to William E. Johnson, October 3, 1930, Box 14, Folder 10, Roll 41, Ernest H. Cherrington Series, Temperance and Prohibition Papers, Ohio Historical Society.

138. Letter, William E. Johnson to Viscount Astor, February 27, 1928, in: Box 14, Folder 7, Roll 41, Ernest H. Cherrington Series, Temperance and Prohibition Papers, Ohio Historical Society. On Johnson's unfulfilled Gandhi plans: Letter, William E. Johnson to Ernest Cherrington, September 30, 1931: Box 14, Folder 10, Roll 41, Ernest H. Cherrington Series, Temperance and Prohibition Papers, Ohio Historical Society. The idea of promoting international prohibition to safeguard it at home was not new either. "World Prohibition Needed to Protect Prohibition in America," *Union Signal*, April 21, 1921, 8.

139. "Our 'Pussyfoot,' England's Hero and Pest," *Literary Digest* (1919): 47–56. ASLA Executive Committee File, 1914–1934, Box 27, Folder 9, Ernest H. Cherrington Papers, Temperance and Prohibition Papers, Ohio Historical Society; Cherrington-Johnson correspondence, Office File, 1928–1933, Box 14, Folders 7–10, Ernest H. Cherrington Papers. "'Pussyfoot' Johnson's Loss Proves Prohibition's Gain," *Union Signal*, December 18, 1919, 9.

140. Ernest Cherrington, "Report on Behalf of the American Committee on International Relations, to the Executive Committee and the Board of Directors of the Anti-Saloon League of America, in Session at the Raleigh Hotel, Washington, D.C.," January 12, 1924, 17, in: Box 5, Folder 1, Reel 8, Anti-Saloon League of America Series, Temperance and Prohibition Papers, Ohio Historical Society, Columbus, OH.

141. "World League Against Alcoholism: Officers," Box 2, Volumes 12–15, Roll 13, World League Against Alcoholism Papers, Temperance and Prohibition Papers. Brook, "World League Against Alcoholism," 136. The International Prohibition Association was formed in 1892, but only formally became affiliated with the WLAA in 1924. See: "Announcing the Response of the Intercollegiate Prohibition Association to the World-Wide Call," n/d, in: Box 1, Folder 60, Roll 4, and "IPA Constitution," n/d, Box 1, Folder 62, Roll 4, in: Intercollegiate Prohibition Association Series, Temperance and Prohibition Papers, Ohio Historical Society, Columbus. On Hercod and the "native races" question, see: Francesco Spöring, *Mission und Sozialhygiene: Schweizer Anti-Alkohol-Aktivismus im Kontext von Internationalismus und Kolonialismus, 1886–1939* (Göttingen: Wallstein Verlag, 2018), 74–75.

142. Cherrington, "Report of the General Secretary," in: Cherrington, ed., *Report of the Activities of the WLAA*, 6–7.

143. Maureen Ogle, *Ambitious Brew: The Story of American Beer* (New York: Harcourt, 2006), 184–210.

144. Timberlake, *Prohibition and the Progressive Movement*, 183. See also: *New York Times*, January 16, 1920, 1.

145. Longfield, *Presbyterian Controversy*, 67. "Complete List of Persons in Attendance at the Conference on World-Wide Prohibition, Columbus, Ohio, November 19–22, 1918," Box 2, Volumes 12–15, Roll 13, World League Against Alcoholism Papers, Temperance and Prohibition Papers.

146. Cherrington, ed., *Fifteenth International Congress against Alcoholism*, 351–52. *Compte-rendu du XIV Congrès international contre l'alcoolisme, Milan 22–28 Septembre 1913*. Letter, T. E. Burton to Wayne Wheeler, June 28, 1913, Box 32, Folder 22, Roll 99, Ernest Cherrington Series, Temperance and Prohibition Papers. Bryan did engage in temperance outreach even as secretary of state. Letter, William Jennings Bryan to William Harra, April 1, 1915, William Jennings Bryan Collection, G. E. Densmore Collection, William L. Clements Library, the University of Michigan. "Fourteenth International Congress Against Alcoholism," *Union Signal*, October 23, 1913, 7. On Bryan and the WCTU, see: Lenna Lowe Yost, "Our Washington Letter," *Union Signal*, February 6, 1919, 2.

147. Cherrington, ed., *Fifteenth International Congress against Alcoholism*, 342.

148. Ibid., 346–56.

Chapter 18

1. Letters, William E. Johnson to Henry Sowers, June 3, 1935, and April 2, 1937, Box 3, Folder 16, Roll 9; Letter, Mrs. W. E. Johnson to Boyd Doty, May 8, 1932, and Letter, Mrs. W. E. Johnson to Henry Sowers, November 16, 1932, Box 3, Folder 14, Roll 9, American Issue Publishing Company Archives, Temperance and Prohibition Papers, Ohio Historical Society.

2. Wayne Wheeler, "The Inside Story of Prohibition's Adoption: Article VI—Harding and the Volstead Act," *New York Times*, April 2, 1926, 21.

3. Robert Talley, "Depression Hits Anti-Saloon League; Donations Now Fail to Meet Payroll," *Pittsburgh Press*, March 14, 1932, 19. Letter, Henry B. Sowers to William E. Johnson, June [n/

d] 1932, Box 3, Folder 14, Roll 9, American Issue Publishing Company Archives, Temperance and Prohibition Papers, Ohio Historical Society.

4. Committee on Indian Affairs, *Indian Appropriation Bill: Hearings before a Subcommittee of the Committee on Indian Affairs of the House of Representatives, 1913* (Washington, DC: Government Printing Office, 1914), 272–73.

5. May's adult son Arnold had gifted Pussyfoot a new 1935 Underwood four-bank portable typewriter. Letter, Mrs. Johnson to Henry B. Sowers, February 27, 1935, Box 3, Folder 16, Reel 9, American Issue Publishing Company Archives, Temperance and Prohibition Papers, Ohio Historical Society, Columbus.

6. Letter, Mrs. Johnson to Henry B. Sowers, October 28, 1933, Box 3, Folder 15, Reel 9, American Issue Publishing Company Archives, Temperance and Prohibition Papers, Ohio Historical Society, Columbus.

7. "'Pussyfoot' with His Family, Plans Life Fight on Rum," *Los Angeles Evening Herald*, January 13, 1923. in: Scrapbook 2, William E. "Pussyfoot" Johnson Papers, Fenimore Art Museum Library, Cooperstown, NY.

8. Letter, Mrs. Johnson to Henry B. Sowers, February 27, 1935, Box 3, Folder 16, Reel 9, American Issue Publishing Company Archives, Temperance and Prohibition Papers, Ohio Historical Society, Columbus.

9. "'Dry Crusader' Buried. Less Than 50 Brave Weather for 'Pussyfoot' Johnson Rites," *New York Times*, February 5, 1945, 15.

10. William E. Johnson, "Confessions of 'Pussyfoot' Johnson," (Cooperstown: Fenimore Art Museum Library, n/d), XX, 13–14. This is similar to his argument before the 18th International Congress Against Alcoholism: *Bericht über den XVIII. internationalen Kongress gegen den Alkoholismus: Tartu (Dorpat) vom 21. bis zum 29 Juli 1926* (Tartu: C. Mattiesen, 1927), 303–304.

11. Winston Churchill, "What I Saw in America of Prohibition," *London Daily Telegraph*, December 2, 1929. Winston Churchill, "The Shattered Cause of Temperance," *Collier's Magazine*, August 13, 1932, Box 3, Churchill File, Association Against the Prohibition Amendment Records, Manuscripts Division, Library of Congress, Washington, DC. Also: "Has Prohibition Failed? Pussyfoot's Reply to Mr. Churchill," Unpublished manuscript, January 15, 1930, Box 5, Folder 3, Roll 8, Anti-Saloon League of America Series, Temperance and Prohibition Papers, Ohio Historical Society, Columbus.

12. Johnson, "Confessions," XX, 13–14. Pussyfoot's rebuke to Churchill concludes, "Any law telling the people what to drink and what not to drink would be overwhelmingly defeated in America. I would fight against such a law myself. What a man eats or drinks is an individual act, so long as nobody is affected thereby. But when a man engages in the business of selling what causes such a vast amount of trouble, society becomes directly and acutely affected, and it has the right and the duty of protecting itself against unsocial acts. Our laws against selling liquor rest upon exactly the same basis as our laws prohibiting the selling of rotten meat, impure milk or dangerous drugs." "Has Prohibition Failed? 'Pussyfoot's' Reply to Mr. Churchill," January 15, 1930 (Unpublished manuscript), Box 5, Folder 3, Reel 8, Anti-Saloon League of America Series, Temperance and Prohibition Papers, Ohio Historical Society, Columbus.

13. Lisa McGirr, *The War on Alcohol: Prohibition and the Rise of the American State* (New York: W. W. Norton & Company, 2016), 22–23.

14. See: Timothy Messer-Kruse, "The 'Undue Weight' of Truth on Wikipedia," *Chronicle of Higher Education*, February 12, 2012, https://www.chronicle.com/article/The-Undue-Weight-of-Truth-on/130704/ (accessed June 19, 2019).

15. "Eighteenth Amendment to the United States Constitution," *Wikipedia*, https://en.wikipedia.org/wiki/Eighteenth_Amendment_to_the_United_States_Constitution (accessed June 21, 2019; emphasis mine). I've retained PDFs and screenshots of the original from that date, in case it has subsequently been altered.

16. Alan Brinkley, "Richard Hofstadter's *The Age of Reform*: A Reconsideration," *Reviews in American History* 13, no. 3 (1985): 462.

17. David S. Brown, *Richard Hofstadter: An Intellectual Biography* (Chicago: University of Chicago Press, 2006), xiv, 115–18.

18. Ibid., 144.

19. Richard Hofstadter, *The Age of Reform: From Bryan to F.D.R.* (New York: Random House, 1955), 289–90, 293.

20. Ibid., 292.

21. Joseph R. Gusfield, "Social Structure and Moral Reform: A Study of the Woman's Christian Temperance Union," *American Journal of Sociology* 61, no. 3 (1955). On Gusfield more generally, see: "My Life and Soft Times," Box 1, Folder 4, Joseph Gusfield Papers, Special Collections and Archives, University of California at San Diego.

22. Joseph Gusfield, *Symbolic Crusade: Status Politics and the American Temperance Movement* (Urbana: University of Illinois Press, 1963), 1–2.

23. Ibid., 3, 10–11.

24. Ibid., 3, 10–11, 14–27.

25. Jessica Warner, "Temperance, Alcohol, and the American Evangelical: A Reassessment," *Addiction* 104, no. 7 (2009).

26. Scholars of nationalism, identity, and cultural pluralism will warn you of the theoretical and empirical minefield that comes with constructing such "primordialist"—often borderline racist—cultural typologies. Jack David Eller and Reed M. Couglan, "The Poverty of Primordialism: The Demystification of Ethnic Attachments," *Ethnic and Racial Studies* 16, no. 2 (1993). Anthony W. Marx, "Race-Making and the Nation-State," *World Politics* 48, no. 2 (1996), 180-208. Rogers Brubaker and Frederick Cooper, "Beyond 'Identity,'" *Theory and Society* 29, no. 1 (2000), 1-47. Ernst B. Haas, "Nationalism: An Instrumental Social Construction," *Millennium: Journal of International Studies* 22, no. 3 (1993), 505-545. Tellingly, such primordial, external, "objective" characterizations provided the foundation for Stalin's writings on nations and nationalism. Joseph Stalin, "Marxism and the National Question (1913)," in *Marxism and the National and Colonial Question* (New York: International Publishers, 1934), 8. This also tracks closely with the scholarly disdain for Samuel Huntington's reified "civilizations" as a basis for geopolitical culture clash. Samuel P. Huntington, *The Clash of Civilizations and the Remaking of the Modern World* (New York: Simon and Schuster, 1996).

27. Marni Davis, *Jews and Booze: Becoming American in the Age of Prohibition* (New York: New York University Press, 2012), 2, 5, 49–54.

28. Gusfield, *Symbolic Crusade*, 7.

29. Joseph Gusfield, "Benevolent Repression: Popular Culture, Social Structure and the Control of Drinking," in *Drinking: Behavior and Belief in Modern History*, ed. Susanna Barrows and Robin Room (Berkeley: University of California Press, 1991).

30. For example, Roberts falsely claims that "Control, both of self and others, was the underlying theme" of temperance activism. James S. Roberts, *Drink, Temperance, and the Working Class in Nineteenth-Century Germany* (Boston: George Allen & Unwin, 1984), 5. Gaines M. Foster, *Moral Reconstruction: Christian Lobbyists and the Federal Legislation of Morality, 1865–1920* (Chapel Hill: University of North Carolina Press, 2002), 1, 224.

31. McGirr, *War on Alcohol*, xviii. James A. Morone, "Bootleg Politics: *The War on Alcohol*, by Lisa McGirr," *New York Times*, January 3, 2016, http://www.nytimes.com/2016/01/03/books/review/the-war-on-alcohol-by-lisa-mcgirr.html (accessed March 10, 2016). More generally: Roberts, *Drink, Temperance, and the Working Class in Nineteenth-Century Germany*, 9.

32. Sally G. McMillen, *Seneca Falls and the Origins of the Women's Rights Movement* (New York: Oxford University Press, 2008), 52. James A. Morone, *Hellfire Nation: The Politics of Sin in American History* (New Haven, CT: Yale University Press, 2003), 281. John C. Burnham, "New Perspectives on the Prohibition 'Experiment' of the 1920s," *Journal of Social History* 2, no. 1 (1968): 51–68.

33. Reid Mitenbuler, *Bourbon Empire: The Past and Future of America's Whiskey* (New York: Viking Press, 2015), 176, 171. Daniel Okrent, *Last Call: The Rise and Fall of Prohibition* (New York: Scribner, 2010), 3. Also: Morone, "Bootleg Politics."

34. Michael McGerr, *A Fierce Discontent: The Rise and Fall of the Progressive Movement in America* (New York: Oxford University Press, 2003), 84, 88. For a review of historical saloon literature, see: David M. Fahey, "Old-Time Breweries: Academic and Breweriana Historians," *Ohio History* 116 (2009): 106–108.

35. Fran Grace, *Carry A. Nation: Retelling the Life* (Bloomington: Indiana University Press, 2001), 12–13. Similarly, see: Elaine Frantz Parsons, *Manhood Lost: Fallen Drunkards and Redeeming Women in the Nineteenth-Century United States* (Baltimore: Johns Hopkins University Press, 2009).

36. McGerr, *Fierce Discontent*, 20.

37. Burnham, "New Perspectives," 53. On post-repeal American alcohol policy, see: Pamela E. Pennock and K. Austin Kerr, "In the Shadow of Prohibition: Domestic American Alcohol Policy since 1933," *Business History* 47, no. 3 (2005). Leonard Harrison and Elizabeth Laine, *After Repeal: A Study of Liquor Control Administration* (New York: Harper & Brothers, 1936).

38. Frances E. Willard, *The "Do-Everything Policy": Address before the Second Biennial Convention of the World's Woman's Christian Temperance Union, and the Twentieth Annual Convention of the National Women's Christian Temperance Union. World's Columbian Exposition, Chicago, Illinois, USA, October 16th to 21st, 1893* (London: White Ribbon Publishing Co., 1893), 5, HV5015 .Z9, Box 2, No. 9, National American Woman Suffrage Association (NAWSA) Collection, Library of Congress, Washington DC, https://www.loc.gov/resource/rbnawsa.n8352/ (accessed January 21, 2021).

39. George M. Hammell, *The Passing of the Saloon: An Authentic and Official Presentation of the Anti-Liquor Crusade in America* (Cincinnati, OH: Tower Press, 1908), 397–98.

40. Quoted in: "Phillips, Wendell," in: Ernest H. Cherrington, ed., *Standard Encyclopedia of the Alcohol Problem*, 6 vols., vol. 5 (Westerville, OH: American Issue Press, 1929), 2157.

41. *Prohibition: A Film by Ken Burns & Lynn Novick, PBS*, http://www.pbs.org/kenburns/prohibition/people/ (accessed July 3, 2020). McGirr, *War on Alcohol*, 22–23. A similar accusation is made in Daniel Okrent's *Last Call*, a source for the Burns/Novick documentary. "How did a freedom-loving people decide to give up a private right that had been freely exercised by millions upon millions?" Okrent at least notes that, with the Eighteenth Amendment, "Now there were two exceptions: you couldn't own slaves, and you couldn't buy alcohol." (Actually, you couldn't *sell* alcohol.) Okrent, *Last Call*, 3.

42. Harry S. Warner, *Prohibition: An Adventure in Freedom* (Westerville, OH: American Issue Press, 1928). Emmett D. Nichols, *The Second Declaration of Independence, or a Suggested Emancipation Proclamation from the Liquor Traffic* (Boise, ID: Emmett D. Nichols, 1913).

43. Quoted in: "Our 'Pussyfoot,' England's Hero and Pest," *Literary Digest* (1919): 48–51 (emphasis mine).

44. "The Tiger Claws of 'Pussyfoot' Johnson," *Literary Digest*, May 1, 1926, 36. Kim Burdick, "Pussyfoot Johnson" (Master's thesis, State University of New York College at Oneonta, 1976), 5.

45. See: Peter Hall, "Conclusion: The Politics of Keynesian Ideas," in *The Political Power of Economic Ideas: Keynesianism across Nations*, ed. Peter Hall (Princeton, NJ: Princeton University Press, 1989). Daniel Yergin and Joseph Stanislaw, *The Commanding Heights: The Battle between Government and the Marketplace That Is Remaking the Modern World* (New York: Simon & Schuster, 1998), 141–49.

46. Anu-Hanna Anttila and Pekka Sulkunen, "The Inflammable Alcohol Issue: Alcohol Policy Argumentation in the Programs of Political Parties in Finland, Norway and Sweden from the 1960s to the 1990s," *Contemporary Drug Problems* 28, no. 1 (2001): 66.

47. John Marshall Harlan and Supreme Court of the United States, *U.S. Reports: Mugler v. Kansas, 123 U.S. 623,* 1887. Lemuel D. Lilly, *The Saloon before the Courts* (Columbus, OH: Ohio Anti-Saloon League, 1912), 18.

48. Lilly, *The Saloon before the Courts,* 11. Stephen Johnson Field and Supreme Court of the United States, *U.S. Reports: Crowley v. Christensen, 137 U.S. 86,* 1890. Law Library of Congress.

49. Warner, *Prohibition: An Adventure in Freedom,* 23–24.

50. Kathryn Schulz, *Being Wrong: Adventures in the Margin of Error* (New York: HarperCollins, 2010), 108–109. Moreover, see: Emily Pronin et al., "You Don't Know Me, but I Know You: The Illusion of Asymmetric Insight," *Journal of Personality and Social Psychology* 81, no. 4 (2001): 639–41. Emily Pronin, Daniel Y. Lin, and Lee Ross, "The Bias Blind Spot: Perceptions of Bias in Self versus Other," *Personality and Social Psychology Bulletin* 28, no. 3 (2002): 379. Emily Pronin, Thomas Gilovich, and Lee Ross, "Objectivity in the Eye of the Beholder: Divergent Perceptions of Bias in Self versus Other," *Psychological Review* 111, no. 3 (2004): 782–84. Joyce Ehrlinger, Thomas Gilovich, and Lee Ross, "Peering into the Bias Blind Spot: People's Assessments of Bias in Themselves and Others," *Personality and Social Psychology Bulletin* 31, no. 5 (2005): 681.

51. *Topeka Daily Capital,* February 8, 1901. *Chicago Tribune,* February 8, 1901. Mary K. Haman, "Wild Women of the Progressive Era: Rhetoric, Gender, and Agitation in the Age of Reform" (PhD dissertation, Pennsylvania State University, 2009), 89.

52. McGirr, *War on Alcohol,* 11–12 (emphasis mine).

53. Robert Wuthnow, "United States: Bridging the Privileged and the Marginalized?," in *Democracies in Flux: The Evolution of Social Capital in Contemporary Society,* ed. Robert D. Putnam (New York: Oxford University Press, 2002), 69–73.

54. Jean-Baptiste Michel et al., "Quantitative Analysis of Culture Using Millions of Digitized Books," *Science* 331, no. 6014 (2011): 176.

55. Frederic Richard Lees, *An Argument for the Legislative Prohibition of the Liquor Traffic* (Manchester: United Kingdom Alliance, 1857). Robert Pitman, *Alcohol and the State: A Discussion of the Problem of Law as Applied to the Liquor Traffic* (New York: National Temperance Society and Publishing House, 1878). E. R. L. Gould, *Popular Control of the Liquor Traffic* (Baltimore: Friedenwalt Company, 1895). William Johnson, *The Federal Government and the Liquor Traffic* (Westerville, OH: American Issue Publishing Co., 1911). Alexander Dunbar, *A Defense of the Liquor Traffic* (Washington, DC: n.p., 1887).

56. Claire Galofaro and Frances D'Emilio, "Purdue Foreign Arm Caught Up in Opioid Probe in Europe," *Associated Press,* May 29, 2019, https://apnews.com/d384c975e039474e8b93e11b9ace18e0 (accessed May 30, 2019). Paybarah, Azi, "El Chapo's $14 Billion Empire on Trial," *New York Times,* November 20, 2018, https://www.nytimes.com/2018/11/20/nyregion/newyorktoday/new-york-news-el-chapo-elections.html (accessed May 28, 2019).

57. Johnson, "Confessions," XX, 13–14. Lilian Lewis Shiman, *Crusade against Drink in Victorian England* (New York: St. Martin's Press, 1988), 76–77.

58. Carry A. Nation, *The Use and Need of the Life of Carry A. Nation* (Topeka, KS: F. M. Steves & Sons, 1908), 258–59.

59. Okrent, *Last Call,* 41, 76, 92, 107, 153, 159–60, 165–66, 284, 308, 344, 439, 473. W. J. Rorabaugh, *Prohibition: A Concise History* (New York: Oxford University Press, 2018), 48, 52, 56–57, 73, 86–87, 107. Morone, *Hellfire Nation,* 265. Traffic related to liquor: 289–90, 301–302, 307. Related to the "white slave traffic": 2, 261, 263, 265, 266, 269, 278. Mitenbuler, *Bourbon Empire,* 176.

60. Hofstadter, *Age of Reform,* 204. Gusfield, *Symbolic Crusade,* 123.

61. Adam Gopnik, "How the South Won the Civil War," *New Yorker,* April 1, 2019, https://www.newyorker.com/magazine/2019/04/08/how-the-south-won-the-civil-war (accessed May 28, 2019).

62. David W. Blight, *Frederick Douglass: Prophet of Freedom* (New York: Simon & Schuster, 2018), 142–43, 153, 175.

63. Nicholas Buccola, *The Political Thought of Frederick Douglass: In Pursuit of American Liberty* (New York: New York University Press, 2012), 51.

64. Andrew Mango, *Atatürk* (London: John Murray, 1999), 47, 292.

65. Victor Sebestyen, *Lenin: The Man, the Dictator, and the Master* (New York: Pantheon Books, 2017), 259. Robert Service, *Lenin: A Biography* (Cambridge, MA: Belknap Press, 2000).

66. Howard Zinn, *A People's History of the United States: 1492–Present* (New York: HarperCollins, 2003), 120.

67. McMillen, *Seneca Falls*, 52.

68. Beyond the scope of historical studies, regulatory economists have developed a conceptualization of the demand for market regulation called "Bootleggers and Baptists." While it may explain strange bedfellows in other areas of market regulation, its title is based on an unfortunate strawman mischaracterization of the fundamental causes and motivations for temperance and prohibition. See: Bruce Yandle, "Bootleggers and Baptists—The Education of a Regulatory Economist," *Regulation* 7, no. 3 (1983), 12–16. Bruce Yandle, "Bootleggers and Baptists in Retrospect," *Regulation* 22, no. 3 (1999), 5–7. Adam Smith and Bruce Yandle, *Bootleggers and Baptists: How Economic Forces and Moral Persuasion Interact to Shape Regulatory Politics* (Washington, DC: Cato Institute Press, 2014).

69. McGerr, *Fierce Discontent*, xiv, 68.

70. On the Bolsheviks' attempts to configure the "New Soviet Man" based on modesty, honesty, sobriety, education, and thrift, see: Mark Lawrence Schrad, *Vodka Politics: Alcohol, Autocracy, and the Secret History of the Russian State* (New York: Oxford University Press, 2014), 212.

71. McGerr, *Fierce Discontent*, 83–84. See also: Grace, *Carry A. Nation*, 9. Nation, *Use and Need of the Life*, 134.

72. McGerr, *Fierce Discontent*, 79.

73. Nation, *Use and Need of the Life*, 131. Grace, *Carry A. Nation*, 185.

74. Morone, *Hellfire Nation*, 10–11.

75. Ibid., 282–285.

76. Ibid., 289.

77. *Prohibition: A Film by Ken Burns and Lynn Novick*, October 2, 2011, https://www.pbs.org/kenburns/prohibition/photos/ (accessed June 20, 2020). This is not to say that the documentary is universally white. African American historian Freddie Johnson does appear occasionally to discuss the impact of prohibition in Kentucky. Some people of color also appear as jazz musicians and swing dancers in Prohibition Era speakeasies, as Wynton Marsalis's soundtrack plays over top. See: "Extended Look: The Jazz Age," https://www.wliw.org/programs/kenburns-prohibition/prohibition-preview-jazz-age/ (accessed January 21, 2021).

78. Ian Tyrrell, *Reforming the World: The Creation of America's Moral Empire* (Princeton, NJ: Princeton University Press, 2010), 4–5. Stephen Howe, *Empire: A Very Short Introduction* (New York: Oxford University Press, 2002), 9–10.

79. Tyrrell, *Reforming the World*, 52, 124.

80. Ibid., 35, 86. Ian Tyrrell, "Prohibition, American Cultural Expansion, and the New Hegemony in the 1920s: An Interpretation," *Histoire sociale / Social History* 27, no. 54 (1994), 413–45. Similarly: Greg Marquis, "'Brewers and Distillers Paradise': American Views of Canadian Alcohol Policies, 1919 to 1935," *Canadian Review of American Studies* 34, no. 2 (2004), 135–66.

81. Tyrrell, *Reforming the World*, 216. Johnson, "Confessions," XV, 1.

82. William E. Johnson, "Babylon and Way Stations" (Cooperstown: Fenimore Art Museum Library, 1930), VIII, 13.

83. Ramachandra Guha, *Gandhi before India* (New York: Random House, 2014), 48.

84. Tyrrell, *Reforming the World*, 216–17.

85. "India," in: Ernest H. Cherrington, ed., *Standard Encyclopedia of the Alcohol Problem*, 6 vols., vol. 3 (Westerville, OH: American Issue Press, 1926), 1298.

86. F. W. Farrar, "Africa and the Drink Trade," *Contemporary Review* 52 (July 1887): 45. In: Robert Elliott Speer (1867–1947) Manuscript Collection, Series VII: Clippings and Mimeographed Material, Subject File, Box 122, File 122:4, Princeton Theological Seminary Library, Princeton, NJ.

87. Quoted in: Wilfrid Lawson, *The Opium Traffic between India and China. The Debate in the House of Commons on Sir Wilfrid Lawson's Motion, Tuesday, May 10, 1870* (London: Aborigines Protection Society, 1870), 10.

88. David Starr Jordan, *Imperial Democracy: A Study of the Relation of Government by the People, Equality before the Law, and Other Tenets of Democracy, to the Demands of a Vigorous Foreign Policy and Other Demands of Imperial Dominion* (New York: D. Appleton and Company, 1899), 86.

89. Johnson, "Babylon and Way Stations," VI, 6. See also: "Khama," in: Ernest H. Cherrington, ed., *Standard Encyclopedia of the Alcohol Problem*, 6 vols., vol. 4 (Westerville, OH: American Issue Press, 1928), 1460–64.

90. "Baltimore Yearly Meeting Indian Committee Minutes," 1795–1815, 50, RG2/By/6, Friends Historical Library of Swarthmore College.

91. Johnson, "Babylon and Way Stations," II, 19.

92. William E. Johnson, "Activities of William E. ('Pussyfoot') Johnson, Special International Representative," in: Ernest H. Cherrington, ed., *Report of the Activities of the World League against Alcoholism, 1919–1927* (Westerville, OH: World League Against Alcoholism, 1927), 24.

93. Martha Finnemore, *The Purpose of Intervention: Changing Beliefs about the Use of Force* (Ithaca, NY: Cornell University Press, 2003), 20. This might be more akin to a more macro-level "supernorm," as elaborated by Sakiko Fukuda-Parr and David Hulme, "International Norm Dynamics and the 'End of Poverty': Understanding the Millennium Development Goals," *Global Governance* 17, no. 1 (2011), 20.

94. C. Rajagopalachari, "The War Against Drink, *Young India*, November 12, 1931," in *Selected Works of C. Rajagopalachari: Vol. V, 1931–35*, ed. Shakti Sinha, Ravi K. Mishra, and Narendra Shukla (Hyderabad: Orient BlackSwan, 2019), 207.

95. Howe, *Empire*, 9.

96. Finnemore, *The Purpose of Intervention*, 24–38.

97. Ibid., 4.

98. These human rights–based movements are largely valued on their own merits, immutable and inherent, unlike historians' preoccupation with charting alcohol-consumption rates to determine—centuries after the fact—whether alcohol was *really* such an important social problem in the first place. On the "justice cascade" of evolving transnational human-rights norms, see: Kathryn Sikkink, *The Justice Cascade: How Human Rights Prosecutions Are Changing World Politics* (New York: W. W. Norton & Company, 2011), 11–24. Ellen L. Lutz and Kathryn Sikkink, "The Justice Cascade: The Evolution and Impact of Foreign Human Rights Trials in Latin America," *Chicago Journal of International Law* 2, no. 1 (2001). Gary J. Bass, *Stay the Hand of Vengeance: The Politics of War Crimes Tribunals* (Princeton, NJ: Princeton University Press, 2000), 7. Gary J. Bass, *Freedom's Battle: The Origins of Humanitarian Intervention* (New York: Alfred A. Knopf, 2008), 7–8. Daniel C. Thomas, *The Helsinki Effect: International Norms, Human Rights, and the Demise of Communism* (Princeton, NJ: Princeton University Press, 2001). Emilie Hafner-Burton, *Forced to Be Good: Why Trade Agreements Boost Human Rights* (Ithaca, NY: Cornell University Press, 2009). David A. Lake and Wendy H. Wong, "The Politics of Networks: Interests, Power, and Human Rights Norms," in *Networked Politics: Agency, Power, and Governance*, ed. Miles Kahler (Ithaca, NY: Cornell University Press, 2009).

99. Finnemore, *Purpose of Intervention*, 144. Audie Klotz, "Transnational Activism and Global Transformations: The Anti-Apartheid and Abolitionist Experiences," *European Journal of International Relations* 8, no. 1 (2002): 63. On transnational activism, see: Margaret Keck

and Kathryn Sikkink, *Activists beyond Borders: Advocacy Networks in International Politics* (Ithaca, NY: Cornell University Press, 1998). Margaret Keck and Kathryn Sikkink, "Historical Precursors to Modern Transnational Social Movements and Networks," in *Globalization and Social Movements: Culture, Power, and the Transnational Public Sphere*, ed. John Guidry, Michael Kennedy, and Mayer Zald (Ann Arbor: University of Michigan Press, 2000), Thomas Risse-Kappen, ed., *Bringing Transnational Relations Back In: Non-State Actors, Domestic Structures, and International Institutions* (New York: Cambridge University Press, 1995). Matthew Evangelista, *Unarmed Forces: The Transnational Movement to End the Cold War* (Ithaca, NY: Cornell University Press, 1999). Sanjeev Khagram, James V. Riker, and Kathryn Sikkink, eds., *Restructuring World Politics: Transnational Social Movements, Networks, and Norms* (Minneapolis: University of Minnesota Press, 2002). Richard Price, "Transnational Civil Society and Advocacy in World Politics," *World Politics* 55 (2003). Sidney Tarrow, *The New Transnational Activism* (New York: Cambridge University Press, 2005). Kathryn Sikkink, "Patterns of Dynamic Multilevel Governance and the Insider-Outsider Coalition," in *Transnational Protest and Global Activism*, ed. Donatella della Porta and Sidney Tarrow (New York: Rowman & Littlefield, 2005). Donatella della Porta and Sidney Tarrow, eds., *Transnational Protest and Global Activism* (New York: Rowman & Littlefield, 2005). Akira Iriye, *Global and Transnational History: The Past, Present, and Future* (New York: Palgrave Macmillan, 2013). Charli Carpenter, *"Lost" Causes: Agenda Vetting in Global Issue Networks and the Shaping of Human Security* (Ithaca, NY: Cornell University Press, 2014). Celeste Montoya, *From Global to Grassroots: The European Union, Transnational Advocacy, and Combatting Violence against Women* (New York: Oxford University Press, 2013). Peter Evans and César Rodrguez-Garavito, eds., *Transnational Advocacy Networks: Twenty Years of Evolving Theory and Practice* (Bogotá: Dejusticia, 2018).

100. Vice historian David Courtwright suggests as much: in "one of history's great about-faces," by the late nineteenth century, the same stratum of Western political and economic elites who had long driven the unregulated global trade in alcohol and drugs acceded to restrictions and prohibitions, often at significant financial loss. Why? Courtwright's explanation focuses primarily on the material interest of elites: that industrialization created powerful entrepreneurs whose business interests were harmed by drunkenness, who balanced out those elites for whom the liquor trade was still profitable. While this logic holds merit, it is incomplete: it overlooks the broad-based, transnational prohibition movement that drove the normative shift about the inappropriateness of the state profiting from the misery of society. David T. Courtwright, *Forces of Habit: Drugs and the Making of the Modern World* (Cambridge, MA: Harvard University Press, 2002), 167, 78.

101. Hammell, *Passing of the Saloon*, 397–98.

102. See: Richmond P. Hobson, *The Truth about Alcohol* (Washington, DC: Government Publishing Office, 1914), 22.

103. This borrows the phrase often used to describe American agrarian populists, like Carrie Nation. Jim Bissett, *Agrarian Socialism in America: Marx, Jefferson, and Jesus in the Oklahoma Countryside, 1904–1920* (Norman: University of Oklahoma Press, 1999).

104. Nikolai I. Bukharin and Yevgenii A. Preobrazhenskii, *Azbuka kommunizma: Populyarnoe ob'yasnenie programmy Rossiiskoi Kommunisticheskoi Partii Bol'shevikov* (St. Petersburg: Gosudarstvennoe izdatel'stvo, 1920), 20. See also report delivered by the Soviet ambassador to Great Britain, Ivan M. Maisky, in: Thomas Murray, "Alcoholism in the USSR and the Measures Designed to Combat It," in: *The Twentieth International Congress on Alcoholism, July 30th–August 3rd, 1934: Volume of Proceedings* (London: Sainsbury Printers Ltd., 1934), 289.

105. Gunnar Jahn, "Award Ceremony Speech," Nobel Peace Prize Ceremony, December 10, 1947, https://www.nobelprize.org/prizes/peace/1947/ceremony-speech/ (accessed August 16, 2019).

106. Mike King, *Quakernomics: An Ethical Capitalism* (London: Anthem Press, 2014), 75–77, 117, 127. On the Quaker origins of the Society for the Suppression of the Opium Trade, see: Bruce D. Johnson, "Righteousness before Revenue: The Forgotten Moral Crusade against the Indo-Chinese Opium Trade," *Journal of Drug Issues* 5, no. 4 (1975): 304–306. On the actions of the Anti-Opium Committee of the Society of Friends, see: C. Rajagopalachari, "Editor's Notes, *Young India*, December 14, 1922," in *Selected Works of C. Rajagopalachari: Vol. II, 1921–22*, ed. Mahesh Rangarajan, N. Balakrishnan, and Deepa Bhatnagar (New Delhi: Orient BlackSwan, 2014), 407–408.

107. Aldon Morris, *The Origins of the Civil Rights Movement: Black Communities Organizing for Change* (New York: Free Press, 1984), 4–12.

108. See: Cecilia Autrique Escobar, "'To Save the Mexican Race from Degeneration': The Influence of American Protestant Groups on Temperance and Prohibition in Mexico, 1916–1933," in *Prohibitions and Psychoactive Substances in History, Culture and Theory*, ed. Susannah Wilson (New York: Routledge, 2019), 71. Letter, Homer C. Stunts to Ernest Cherrington, August 24, 1920, Box 15, Folder 12, Roll 24, World League Against Alcoholism Records, Temperance and Prohibition Papers, Ohio Historical Society.

109. Rogelio Luna Zamora, *La Historia del Tequila, de sus Regiones y sus Hombres* (Mexico City: Conaculta, 1991), 43. Sarah Bowen, *Divided Spirits: Tequila, Mezcal, and the Politics of Production* (Oakland: University of California Press, 2015), 31.

110. Gretchen Pierce, "*Pulqueros, Cerveceros*, and *Mezcaleros*: Small Alcohol Producers and Popular Resistance to Mexico's Anti-Alcohol Campaigns, 1910–1940," in *Alcohol in Latin America: A Social and Cultural History*, ed. Gretchen Pierce and Áurea Toxqui (Tucson: University of Arizona Press, 2014), 161–63. See also: "W.C.T.U. of Mexico Appeals to President Carranza to Prevent Invasion by American Brewers," *Union Signal*, January 2, 1919, 6. "Government Leaders of Mexico Favor Prohibition," *Union Signal*, October 21, 1920, 7. "Mexico" in: Cherrington, ed., *Standard Encyclopedia of the Alcohol Problem*, vol. 4, 1759.

111. "Mexico" in: Cherrington, ed., *Standard Encyclopedia of the Alcohol Problem*, vol. 4, 1758.

112. Pierce, "*Pulqueros, Cerveceros*, and *Mezcaleros*," 163–64.

113. Ibid., 164.

114. Cecilia Autrique Escobar, "La Prohibición del alcohol en Estados Unidos y sus efectos en México, 1920–1933" (PhD dissertation, Universidad Nacional Autónoma de México, 2016). Escobar, "'To Save the Mexican Race,'" 81–82.

115. Pierce, "*Pulqueros, Cerveceros*, and *Mezcaleros*," 165. Stephanie Mitchell, "Comité Nacional de Lucha contra el Alcoholismo," in: Jack Blocker Jr., David Fahey, and Ian Tyrrell, eds., *Alcohol and Temperance in Modern History: An International Encyclopedia*, 2 vols., vol. 1 (Santa Barbara, CA: ABC-CLIO, 2003), 168–69.

116. James Baldwin, "'I Picked the Cotton and I Carried It to Market and I Built the Railroads under Someone Else's Whip,' Debate v. William F. Buckley, 1965," *Speakola*, https://speakola.com/ideas/james-baldwin-v-william-f-buckley-1965 (accessed January 6, 2019). *James Baldwin Debates William F. Buckley* (1965), https://www.youtube.com/watch?v=oFeoS41xe7w (accessed January 6, 2019). In similar fashion, see: Daniel Immerwahr, *How to Hide an Empire: A History of the Greater United States* (New York: Farrar, Straus and Giroux, 2019), 15.

117. Claire Galofaro and Frances D'Emilio, "Purdue Foreign Arm Caught Up in Opioid Probe in Europe," *Associated Press*, May 29, 2019, https://apnews.com/d384c975e039474e8b93e11b 9ace18e0 (accessed May 30, 2019).

118. "In 1972, the psychologist Irving Janis defined groupthink as 'a mode of thinking that people engage in when they are deeply involved in a cohesive in-group, when the members' strivings for unanimity override their motivation to realistically appraise alternative courses of action.' Groupthink most commonly affects homogenous, close-knit communities that are overly insulated from internal and external criticism, and that perceive themselves as different from or under attack by outsiders. Its symptoms include censorship of dissent, rejection or

rationalization of criticisms, the conviction of moral superiority, and the demonization of those who hold opposing beliefs." Schulz, *Being Wrong*, 152.

119. Mark Lawrence Schrad, *The Political Power of Bad Ideas: Networks, Institutions, and the Global Prohibition Wave* (New York: Oxford University Press, 2010), 3.

120. Ibid., 216. Here quoting: Susanna Barrows and Robin Room, "Introduction," in *Drinking: Behavior and Belief in Modern History*, ed. Susanna Barrows and Robin Room (Berkeley: University of California Press, 1991), 3. See also: Robin Room, "Alcohol and Ethnography: A Case of Problem Deflation?," *Current Anthropology* 25 (1984), 169-191.

121. See: Thomas S. Kuhn, *The Structure of Scientific Revolutions* (Chicago: University of Chicago Press, 1970). Hans Reichenbach, *From Copernicus to Einstein* (New York: Philosophical Library, 1942).

INDEX

For the benefit of digital users, indexed terms that span two pages (e.g., 52–53) may, on occasion, appear on only one of those pages.